MICROECONOMICS

THEORY / APPLICATIONS

ELEVENTH EDITION

EDWIN MANSFIELD
and
GARY YOHE

MICROECONOMICS

T H E O R Y / A P P L I C A T I O N S

ELEVENTH EDITION

W • W • NORTON & COMPANY

NEW YORK • LONDON

W. W. Norton & Company has been independent since its founding in 1923, when William Warder Norton and Mary D. Herter Norton first published lectures delivered at the People's Institute, the adult education division of New York City's Cooper Union. The Nortons soon expanded their program beyond the Institute, publishing books by celebrated academics from America and abroad. By mid-century, the two major pillars of Norton's publishing program—trade books and college texts—were firmly established. In the 1950s, the Norton family transferred control of the company to its employees, and today—with a staff of four hundred and a comparable number of trade, college, and professional titles published each year—W. W. Norton & Company stands as the largest and oldest publishing house owned wholly by its employees.

The text of this book is composed in ITC Galliard with the display set in Myriad.
Composition by The GTS Companies/York, PA Campus.
Manufacturing by R. R. Donnelley, Crawfordsville.
Book design by Jack Meserole.
Cover design: Joan Greenfield.
Production manager: Ben Reynolds.
Project editor: Christopher Granville.

ISBN: 0–393–97918–0

W. W. Norton & Company, Inc., 500 Fifth Avenue, New York, N.Y. 10110
www.wwnorton.com

W. W. Norton & Company Ltd., Castle House, 75/76 Wells Street, London W1T 3QT

1 2 3 4 5 6 7 8 9 0

for LINDA, MARIELLE, and COURTNEY

Contents

CHAPTER 3 Consumer Behavior and Individual Demand 72

CHAPTER 4 Derivation of the Market Demand Curve 117

PART FIVE

Markets for Inputs

CHAPTER 15   Investment Decisions   **541**

About the Authors

GARY YOHE is the John E. Andrus Professor of Economics at Wesleyan University and a collaborator at the Center for Integrated Study of the Human Dimensions of Global Change at Carnegie Mellon University. A Phi Beta Kappa graduate of the University of Pennsylvania, he received his M.S. in mathematics from the State University of New York at Stony Brook and his Ph.D. in economics from Yale University. Professor Yohe is the author of more than ninety-five articles. In his research he applies the first principles of microeconomic analysis to decision making under uncertainty and explores the trade-off between mitigating climate change and abating its potential damage. Professor Yohe has served as chair of the economics department at Wesleyan, Director of Research and Sponsored Programs, and Director of the John E. Andrus Center for Public Affairs. His research has been supported by a variety of domestic and international organizations, including the National Science Foundation, the Department of Energy, the Socio-Economic Data Archive Center funded by NASA, the United States Climate Research Program, the International Human Dimensions Program, the United Nations Environment Program, the World Meterological Program, the World Climate Research Program, the Intergovernmental Panel on Climate Change, and the Millennium Ecosystem Assessment.

EDWIN MANSFIELD graduated from Dartmouth College, and received his M.A. and Ph.D. degrees from Duke University. Before coming to the University of Pennsylvania, where he served on the economics faculty for many years, Professor Mansfield taught at Carnegie-Mellon, Yale, Harvard, and California Institute of Technology. The author of over two hundred articles and thirty books, Professor Mansfield's textbooks in economics, microeconomics, managerial economics, and statistics have been adopted at more than 1,000 colleges and universities around the world.

Preface

The landscape of microeconomics has changed dramatically since the first edition of this book appeared. At the time that the First Edition was published, many of the mainstream ideas that are covered in the Eleventh Edition were just beginning to take hold. Ideas like the roles of risk and uncertainty, strategic behavior, auction design, and asymmetric information were just beginning to take their now significant places on the research frontier. Reflecting an evolving contemporary approach, the Eleventh Edition devotes an expanding number of pages to these and other topics. In addition, modern microeconomics sheds new light on applied topics that were unknown to previous generations of students. You will, as you work through the Eleventh Edition, come to grips with computing the value of information and the costs of inequity and discrimination. You will explore the role of insurance in a modern economy and come to grips with power of moral hazard and adverse selection. You will see the power of market-based incentives in the design of policy, and you will catch a glimpse of their limitations. You will understand how difficult it is to discount distant and/or uncertain futures. And you will see how basic microeconomic fundamentals can help explain how one might try to deal with the geographically and temporally distributed ramifications of global externalities like climate change.

My Personal goal in coauthoring *Microeconomics: Theory and Applications* was to bring a fine textbook that I had always admired to a new generation of students who inhabit new world with new problems. To do that, I have adhered to Edwin Mansfield's primary goal: to explain microeconomic theory in the clearest and most interesting way possible while offering a wide range of applications. I have, though, also brought my own objective to the table: to do all of that while clearly emphasizing the few fundamental economic concepts upon which the theory has been constructed. The Eleventh Edition therefore offers a reorganized treatment of strategic market behavior. It expands the previous discussions of asymmetric information. It includes and introductory treatment of auctions, their alternative designs, and their anticipated outcomes.

The Eleventh Edition also includes many more examples. Some are small and self-contained; they are presented as small interruptions scattered throughout the text. Others are built on broader foundations, though; and they are presented as applied perspectives that appear at the ends of major sections of the text. Some of the examples are drawn from the media coverage of current events. They are designed to demonstrate how the theory provides insight into what is going on in the world; i.e., to help you during those dark times when you wonder why anyone would ever worry about any of this stuff. Other examples are, however, drawn more directly from the current literature. These are designed to show how fundamental theoretical constructions can be manipulated in all their maddening abstraction to contribute to a more complete understanding of what is going on in the world outside. They will help you see how new theories are created, evaluated, and finally applied.

Finally, the Eleventh Edition is punctuated by "microlinks"—small essays that tell the reader when various topics should be reminiscent of previous material. Some of these links highlight how some apparently new constructions are really perfectly analogous to previously documented theories; only the names will have changed (indifference curves look for all the world like isoquants, for example). Others make it clear that how the same concept can be sustained across a wide range of applications (an equilibrium is an equilibrium is an equilibrium in the sense that nobody has an incentive to change behavior once it has been achieved, for example). In short, microlinks should give the reader the opportunity to make connections with previous material and thereby either improve his or her understanding of the previous material or make the new material easier to grasp.

As with previous editions, a workbook and study guide are available to accompany the text. *Microeconomic Problems: Case Studies and Exercises for Review*, Eleventh Edition, revised by James Peoples of University of Wisconsin at Milwaukee, guides students toward an understanding of the theories comprising and underlying microeconomics. Problems and questions are provided that test students' skills in applying microeconomic theory to real-world situations. *Microeconomic Problems* now contains about 1,100 questions and problems, together with their solutions. This book also contains numerous case studies.

An *Instructor's Manual and Test-Item File* is available to qualified instructors. In addition to teaching suggestions for each chapter, it includes a test bank of multiple-choice questions and problem sets that not only reflects the decision-making emphasis of the text, but also develops theory as a set of principles that yields insights into everyday problems. Kathryn Nantz has revised this volume for the Eleventh Edition, creating a fresh and varied menu of teaching materials, and this is the place to record my thanks to her.

Many instructors and reviewers have contributed in important ways to this and the previous editions. For previous editions this includes: Charles A. Berry, University of Cincinnati; Byron Brown, Michigan State University; Eleanor Brown, Pomona College; Neil Bruce, University of Washington; Donald Cell, Cornell College; Yongmin Chen, University of Colorado; Alvin Cohen, Lehigh University; Marshall Colberg, Florida

State University; Michael A. Crew, Rutgers University at Newark; James Dana, Northwestern University; Avinash Dixit, Princeton University; Robert Dorfman, Harvard University; Catherine Eckel, Virginia Polytechnic Institute; Allan Feldman, Brown University; Alan Fisher, California State University at Fullerton; J. Fred Giertz, University of Illinois; William Gunther, University of Alabama; Richard Harmstone, Pennsylvania State University; William Holohan, University of Wisconsin at Milwaukee; David R. Kamerschen, University of Georgia; Theodore E. Keeler, University of California, Berkeley; Elizabeth Sawyer Kelley, University of Wisconsin at Madison; Jonathan Kesselman, University of British Columbia; Thomas Kniesner, Indiana University; Charles Knoeber, North Carolina State University; John Laitner, University of Michigan; Richard Levin, Yale University; C. Richard Long, Georgia State University; Mark Machina, University of California San Diego; Paul Malatesta, University of Washington; Lawrence Martin, Michigan State University; M. R. Metzger, University of Central Oklahoma; Hajime Miyazaki, Ohio State University; David Molina, North Texas State University; Kathryn Nantz, Fairfield University; John Neufeld, University of North Carolina; Mancur Olson, University of Maryland; John Palmer, University of Western Ontario; C. Barry Pfitzner, Randolph-Macon College; Robert Pollak, University of Washington; Richard Porter, University of Michigan; Charles Ratliff, Davidson College; David J. Ravenscraft, University of North Carolina, Chapel Hill; Robert E. Rosenman, Washington State University; Anthony Rufolo, Portland State University; Sol S. Shalit, University of Wisconsin at Milwaukee; Barry Siegel, University of Oregon; N. J. Simler, Macalester College; A. Michael Spence, Stanford University; Daniel Sullivan, Northwestern University; Richard Sylla, New York University; W. James Truitt, Baylor University; Gordon Tullock, University of Arizona; David Vrooman, St. Lawrence University; A. R. Whitaker, U.S. Naval Academy; and Richard Zeckhauser, Harvard University.

In revising the Tenth Edition, I benefited from the insights of James Dearden, Lehigh University; Hadi Dowlatabadi, Carnegie Mellon University; Maxim Engers, University of Virginia; Richard Miller, Wesleyan University; James Peoples, University of Wisconsin at Milwankee; Farahmand Rezvaria, Montclair State University; Gilbert Skillman, Wesleyan University; Kenneth Strzepek, University of Colorado; Jeffrey Sundberg, Lake Forest College; and Kealoha Widdows, Wabash College.

Thanks also to Ed Parsons, the editor at Norton for the Tenth Edition and for the beginning of the revision process for the Eleventh Edition. He has moved on (to a rival publisher, but with expanded responsibilities). Before he left, however, he spent an enormous amount of time helping to frame the revision, helping to elucidate the list of new examples and applied perspectives, helping to identify places where the author really needed some help, and helping construct a feasible time-schedule. He was always there to pull me back (politely) whenever I was heading up a path that he could see would not be productive. He was also always there to encourage me (enthusiastically) to head up paths that he could see would be productive even if they were not necessarily in synch with what everyone else was doing. He understood monopolistic competition, in short; but he also understood non-pecuniary incentives. In short, this revision is far better for his efforts; and I wish him well in his new position.

Ed's departure did not leave me without skilled and strong support, though. The revision is also better for the efforts of Jack Repcheck, who stepped into Ed's position. Julia Hines worked tirelessly to keep me and the revision on track; and her colleagues Marian Johnson, Christopher Granville, and Ben Reynolds did an outstanding job on manuscript preparation. I thank them all.

G.Y.

Middletown, CT, 2003

Introduction

C H A P T E R 1

Microeconomics

INTRODUCTION

Jack Welch retired as chief executive officer of General Electric during the summer of 2001 after more than 20 relatively turbulent years. GE was extraordinarily successful during his tenure. Its total market value in 2001 was larger than that of any other company on the planet, and *Fortune* magazine voted GE the most respected corporation in America for each of Mr. Welch's last four years. To achieve such accolades for himself and his company, Mr. Welch made countless decisions over the years that depended on an understanding of economics.[1] This is not surprising. Economics helps us understand the nature and organization of our society, the arguments underlying many of the great issues of the day, and the operation of businesses and other economic organizations.

Microeconomics

Precisely what is economics? One standard definition describes economics as the study of how scarce resources are allocated among alternative uses. It is customary to divide economics into two parts. **Microeconomics** is the study of the economic behavior of individual units and decision-makers: consumers, firms, and the owners of resources, to name a few. Macroeconomics deals with the behavior of economic aggregates like gross domestic product and the level of employment. Since this book is concerned with microeconomics, we begin this chapter with a brief introduction to the tasks that any economic system must confront if it is to cope with resource scarcity. We will, however, turn quickly to an initial discussion about how the price system of a decentralized economy might work.

TASKS PERFORMED BY AN ECONOMIC SYSTEM

Economics deals with the functioning of economic systems just as, for example, biology deals with the functioning of natural systems. Perhaps the

---

[1]Interested readers can find out more about Welch from his autobiography, *Jack: Straight from the Gut*, published by Warner Books in the fall of 2001. Excerpts from that book plus an interview with David Margolis were published in the October 2001 issue of *Vanity Fair*.

best way of defining an economic system is to describe exactly what it does. It allocates scarce resources across competing uses, combining and processing these resources to produce goods and services. It determines what and how much to produce. It arranges for the distribution of goods and services across society. And it provides for future growth. Expressed as a series of short sentences, these tasks do not seem too daunting, but they are. To do justice, we offer a little more elaboration.

First of all, an economic system allocates resources so that the desired level and composition of output can be produced. Why is this a problem? Economic processes are enormously diverse. An industrial plant could, for example, employ several different combinations of machinery, material, and labor services to manufacture its product. It has a wide range of choices for delivering its product to its customers, and there are many different ways to inform potential customers of product availability. How should it choose among these options? How does the desired mix of products depend on these choices? And how can we be sure that these best choices will actually be made?

All of the following questions must be answered even before fundamental allocation issues can be successfully confronted. How many and what types of resources should be allocated to maintaining a strong military? To what extent should resources be devoted to building medical laboratories? To producing cotton and wool cloth? To producing computers or CDs and DVDs? In short, what is the proper combination of goods—weapons, laboratories, computers, cloth, CDs, DVDs, and so on—that should be produced? Addressing this question is the second task of an economic system. The enormous complexity of this question, as well as its importance, should be obvious. If you feel a bit overwhelmed, then you got the point.

| Example 1.1 | **Sugar and the Great Candy Squeeze** |

It is difficult to underestimate the power of prices in allocating resources—determining who produces what and where. ABC News reported in March 2002 that nearly all of the candy manufacturers who used to employ thousands of people across the upper tier of the United States had closed their doors and opened new production facilities across the border in Canada. Why? Not because the American plants were old or inefficient, and not because American workers were demanding wages that were dramatically higher than their counterparts got north of the border. The reason was the price of sugar. Sugar is, of course, a fundamental ingredient in candy, and it seems that the United States has had a long-standing policy of using an import tariff to protect domestic sugar producers from foreign competition. The price of sugar was, as a result, significantly higher in the United States than it was in Canada, and Canada has become a major producer of candy even though it does not grow much sugar.

Distribution is the third task of an economic system. Who should get how much of what? This question has generated an enormous amount of debate and controversy over the years, and the heat is still on. Some people having relatively egalitarian values would favor societies in which the amount received by one family would not be very different from the amount received by another of the same size. Others are less enamored of arguments for equity because they fear that more productive members of society might be less inclined to work hard if they were not rewarded for their efforts.

Finally, economic growth becomes a concern as soon as we recognize the passage of time. There is strong pressure in developed and developing countries, alike, for discovering new technologies, for adopting superior techniques, for increasing the stock of resources, for expanding and improving education, and so on. These are popular, in part, because they are viewed as the engines of growth—sources for increasing per capita income and associated access to wider collections of goods and services. Sounds like a plan? To be sure, until we realize that devoting current resources to functions that can expand economic activity in the future typically means sustaining less consumption today.

Example 1.2	The Explosion of New Products

We have all come to accept waves of new products that fundamentally change how we live and how we work. Technological advances are the engines of economic growth, and systems that have provided effectively for their introduction and dissemination have done so at a dramatically accelerating pace over the past century. Jonathan Lash, president of the World Resources Institute, has emphasized this point by documenting the length of time that was required for a few of the major inventions of the twentieth century to reach 25 percent of the American population. Mr. Lash reports, for example, that it took 50 years for 25 percent of all Americans to have electricity in their homes. The same degree of penetration took 25 years for private phones and 16 years for personal computers. And it took only 7 years for 25 percent of the population to gain personal access to the Internet.

BUILDING AND USING ECONOMIC MODELS

Model

How do economists come to grips with these issues as they try to understand how a mixed capitalistic system actually works? Much like scholars in other scientific disciplines, economists build and exercise models. A **model** is composed of a number of assumptions from which conclusions can logically be deduced. These conclusions sometimes sustain predictions of how people or firms might respond to changes in their economic environments. In other cases, they highlight precisely which economic circumstances might be most important. In short, models are designed to identify the sort of information that firms and individuals might need, and they elaborate the economic value of that information.

The value of modeling, itself, can perhaps best be understood in the context of a specific example drawn from outside the boundaries of the economic discipline. Suppose, for a moment, that we want to contemplate how the solar system works so that we can explain phenomena like solar eclipses on earth. The solar system is big and complicated, but its essential elements can be expressed simply in the form of an abstraction—an elementary model of the dynamics of a collection of bodies that rotate around a central anchor. We might represent each of the planets by a point in space, and we might make the assumption that each would change position according to certain mathematical equations—equations derived from physics that describe rotation. On the basis of this model, we might be able to explain how an eclipse might occur and perhaps even predict when it would occur.

To be useful, a model must be simple. Thus it must be an abstraction from the real situation that it is trying to describe. The assumptions that accomplish the abstraction must bear some relationship to reality, but they need not be exact replicas of reality. Nor are they confined to things that can be measured directly. In the solar system example, the fact that planets are in fact not points makes little difference. Nor does relying on assumed gravitational forces that cannot directly be measured. It may even make little difference if the equations representing their movements were somewhat in error. Despite all of these difficulties, the model may predict the cause of an eclipse well enough to be useful in conveying understanding; regardless of how it got there, an eclipse is caused by one celestial body blocking another from the rays of the sun. In both the natural and social sciences, models based on simplified and idealized circumstances have found many, many uses. Their usefulness depends on whether or not they result in models that are powerful and accurate.

There are a number of important reasons why economists, like other scientists, use models. One is that the real world is so complex that it is necessary to simplify and abstract if any progress is to be made. Another is that a simple model may be the cheapest way of obtaining *necessary* information. This does not mean, of course, that all models are good or useful. A model may be so oversimplified or so distorted that it is utterly useless. The trick is to construct a model in such a way that irrelevant and unimportant considerations and variables are neglected while the crucial factors—those that have an important effect on the phenomena the model is designed to predict—are included.

EVALUATING A MODEL

Accuracy of prediction

The purpose of a model is to make predictions concerning phenomena in the real world. In many respects, therefore, the proof is in the pudding. The most important test of a model is how well it predicts these phenomena, but judging the **accuracy of prediction** depends upon circumstance. A model that predicts the price of hamburger within plus or minus 1 cent a pound is better than a model that predicts the price of hamburger within plus or minus 10 cents a pound, but how much is this extra precision worth? We don't need enormous precision all of the time. For some purposes, like predicting routine weather, it is sufficient that a model be accurate on a county or regional scale.

For other purposes, like predicting where a tornado might touch down, a model's predictions must be accurate to within a mile or so. For others, like predicting the effectiveness of a designer drug to interrupt the replication of the AIDS virus, a model's predictions must hold at the atomic level.

Logical consistency

Modelers apply logic to their underlying assumptions to derive and to support their predictions. In the solar system example described above, the modeler might try to predict when an eclipse would occur by making computations based on the model's assumptions and employing the rules of logic. It follows from this observation that models can be evaluated on the accuracy of their underlying logic. Do the model's predictions really flow logically from the model's assumptions, or have errors crept into the analysis or the computation? Are the underlying assumptions logically consistent with one another, or do some contradict others? Are the assumptions compatible, or do some actually preclude the others?

Range of applicability

The range of phenomena to which a model will be applied should also be considered in evaluating a model. There is, in any science, a great and understandable desire to formulate models that are as general as possible. A model that can predict the behavior of any consumer in the economy is more valuable than one that can predict only the behavior of Mary Smith. The economist is therefore much more interested in a model that is relevant to many consumers in the economy than in one that is relevant to only one consumer. The more general a model is meant to be, though, the more difficult it is to attain a given degree of accuracy. It is relatively easy to construct empirically valid models with little or no generality. For example, if you wanted to go to the trouble of studying one particular person's eating habits, it is likely that you could formulate a model that would predict his or her choice of breakfast cereals pretty well. But it would be much more difficult to find a model that would be equally accurate in predicting the choice of any type of food by any consumer in the economy. If a theory is to be general, it must ignore many details (and sometimes even variables that are considerably more important than details). The result of this simplification is that its predictions are likely to fall short—perhaps considerably short—of a high degree of accuracy.

Use the best available

If you are interested in predicting the outcome of a particular event, then you will be forced to use the model that predicts best, even if this model still does not predict very well. The choice is not between a model and no model; it is between one type of model and another. When economists make simplifying assumptions and derive conclusions that are only approximately true, therefore, it is somewhat beside the point to complain that the assumptions are simpler than reality or that the predictions are not always accurate. All this may be true, but a model will be used if it does the best job in predicting—at least until something better comes along. A model that can predict the price of hamburger to within plus or minus 10 cents a pound will be used even if those interested in predicting the price of hamburger bewail the model's limitations and wish its accuracy could be improved to, say, a penny a pound.

At this point, a final word should be added concerning the microeconomic models discussed in subsequent chapters. No claim is made that these models are sufficiently accurate or powerful to solve all—or even most—of the problems that confront consumers, firms, governments, or others. Some of these models have been used to predict reasonably well; others have not been nearly as successful. Still others have not really been tested, and thus no one knows how well they would predict. Moreover, no claim is made that the models discussed in subsequent chapters are the last word on the subject. They will all be improved over time as modelers try to adhere to Robert Solow's succinct advice: "Keep it simple. Get it right. Make it credible." All that we claim in January 2003 is that a consensus of economists thinks that they are the best models available at the present moment.

POSITIVE ANALYSIS VERSUS NORMATIVE ANALYSIS

Positive analysis

Normative analysis

Economists generally take great care to distinguish between **positive analyses** designed to describe what would happen in a particular system if this or that were to change and **normative analyses** designed to uncover what should be done in response to such change. Arguments can erupt over a positive description of any given economic structure, but they generally focus on how the something was modeled or how the empirical estimations were conducted. These sorts of arguments can greet normative analyses, as well; but analyses that lead to conclusions of what should and should not be done can breed even deeper disagreements over the very norms and criteria from which judgments are drawn.

One could, for example, envision positive analyses that described how pharmaceutical companies price their products and how those decisions might change as economic conditions change. The results of these studies could then be compared with normative analyses of how the companies *should* price their products to maximize the revenue that they could devote to the research and development of new drugs. Perhaps the answers would be roughly the same, but perhaps not; and if not, perhaps a role for enhanced government support of pure research might be uncovered. Alternatively, the results of the positive analyses could be compared with normative analyses of how pharmaceuticals should be priced to promote equity, or at least to reduce the burden of necessary medical treatment felt by those who can least afford high prices. It is less likely that these results would match, of course; but striking differences would highlight an efficiency-equity trade-off of critical importance to millions of Americans and tens of millions of people living in other countries.

Example 1.3	Drug Prices at Home and across the Border

The debate over the prices that American consumers pay for their prescription needs has raged for years, especially since it has become clear that prices are dramatically lower just across the borders in Canada and Mexico. Table 1.1 records, for example, prices for a few prescription drugs that

Table 1.1	Drug	Description	Price
DRUG PRICES IN MEXICO	Retin-A	Anti-wrinkle and anti-acne cream (30 g)	$4.49
	Amoxicillin	Antibiotic (500 mg—50 capsules)	$8.99
	Ventolin or Proventil	Asthma and bronchial spasms (3 bottles)	$17.99
	Claritin	Antihistamine for allergies (10 mg—20 pills)	$8.99

were listed in an advertisement placed in the Brownsville, Texas, *Herald* in 1999 by Garcia's—a drugstore located just across a new bridge to Matamoros, Mexico. From the bridge, Garcia's is a 5-minute walk, and the prices listed in the ad were 50 to 70 percent lower than they were in Brownsville and comparably lower than any that could be found on the Internet. All four drugs listed in Table 1.1 can be found today in your local drugstore; how much do they cost now? Much more, I would bet. How could that be? You probably don't live in Brownsville.

There are many factors that weigh on companies when they set their prices. In this case, many American consumers subscribe to insurance plans that cover the cost of drugs after a $10 or $15 co-payment. In addition, U.S. import policies motivated by safety and regulatory concerns try to limit consumers' abilities to take advantage of the price differentials across international borders. Are the drug companies using these circumstances to charge efficient prices on both sides of the border so that they can maximize profits and sustain significant research programs? Or are they simply underwriting enormously expensive advertising campaigns in the United States? It really doesn't matter from an equity perspective. The burden on Americans who do not have access to adequate health insurance that covers prescription drug costs has been a lightning rod of debate in both economic and social policy arenas. You can find articles from the medical literature about the debate on-line at www.pdr.net.

MODELING THE PRICE SYSTEM—DEMAND, SUPPLY, AND EQUILIBRIUM

Price system We now turn to describing the workings of a decentralized **price system** in which individuals' decisions are guided by the information contained in the prices of various goods, services, and factors of production. We will now construct a simple model from which we can glean our first insights into how such a system might actually function. We begin by focusing attention on markets; and so we must start with a definition. What, exactly, do economists mean when they speak of markets or try to model their operation? These questions are not quite as straightforward as they may seem, at first glance, because markets are not well defined in a geographical or physical sense. The New York Stock Exchange is, for example, a market, but it is an atypical market in the sense that it is located principally in one particular building. NASDAQ is also atypical because it is also housed in one place—a bank of computers in Stamford, Connecticut. Contrast these markets with the market for computers, in which prospective buyers can be found on almost every street and confirmed suppliers can be found on six different continents. At the other extreme, markets for local produce materialize each summer; they draw buyers from the immediate surroundings and suppliers from the nearby gardens.

Market   So, what is a **market?** To an economist, a market is a group of firms and individuals who are in touch with one another for the purpose of buying or selling some good. Not every person in a market has to be in contact with every other person in the market, of course. Indeed, any person or firm is part of a market even if he, she, or it is in contact with at least a subset of the other participants. It follows, then, that markets vary enormously in size, structure, and procedure. Any description of how markets operate must therefore be able to accommodate an enormous amount of diversity.

◻ The Demand Side of the Market

The market for every good has a demand side and a supply side. The demand *Market demand* side can be represented by a **market demand schedule**—a table that shows *schedule* the quantity of the good that would be purchased at each possible price. The price of the good is, of course, the amount of money that must be paid to make a purchase of one unit. Suppose, for example, that the market demand schedule for crude oil in a typical winter month in the United States were given by the data recorded in Table 1.2. We would then know that a total of 730 million barrels of crude oil would be demanded in a typical winter month if its price were $18 per barrel; 710 barrels would be demanded if the price were $19 per barrel, and so on.[2]

Table 1.2	Price per barrel (dollars)	Quantity demanded (millions of barrels per month)
MARKET DEMAND SCHEDULE FOR OIL, WINTER 2003		
	18	730
	19	710
	20	700
	21	690
	22	680
	23	670
	24	665

[2]These figures are hypothetical, but they are adequate for present purposes. In subsequent chapters, we will provide data describing the actual relationship between the price and quantity demanded of various goods. At this point, the emphasis is on the concept of a market demand schedule, not on the detailed accuracy of these figures.

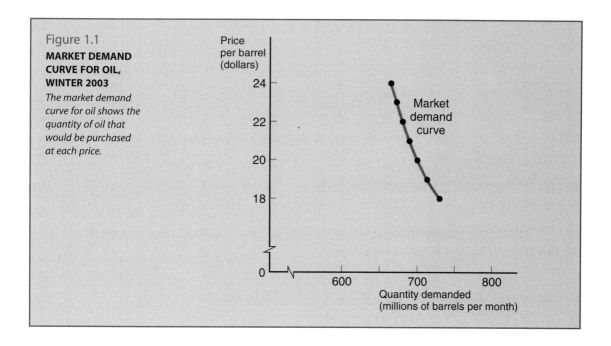

Figure 1.1

MARKET DEMAND CURVE FOR OIL, WINTER 2003

The market demand curve for oil shows the quantity of oil that would be purchased at each price.

Market demand curve

The data in Table 1.2 could be presented equally well by a **market demand curve**—a graphical plot of the market demand data. The vertical axis of the graph measures the price per unit of the good (dollars per barrel), and the horizontal axis measures the quantity of the good demanded per unit of time. Figure 1.1 shows the market demand curve for crude oil based on the figures in Table 1.2.

You should note two important features of Figure 1.1. First of all, the market demand curve for oil slopes downward from left to right. In other words, the quantity of oil demanded increases as the price falls. This is true of the demand curve for most goods. Demand curves almost always slope downward to the right. We will learn why this may not always be the case in subsequent chapters, but these reasons need not concern us at present. Second,

Time period

the market demand curve in Figure 1.1 pertains to a particular period of time: a typical month during the winter of 2003. It is important to recognize that any demand curve pertains to some period of time and that its shape and position depend on the length and other characteristics of that period. If we were to estimate the market demand curve for oil for the first week of 2003, for example, then it would be a different curve from the one portrayed in Figure 1.1. The total quantity demanded over an entire month should, of course, be much larger than the quantity demanded in one week. But that is not the only reason. Consumers should be able to adapt their purchases more fully to changes in the price of oil over the course of a month or a year, and so the quantity demanded should be more responsive to such changes.

Consumers' tastes

What other factors determine the position and shape of the market demand curve for a good? One important factor is the tastes of consumers. If consumers were to show an increasing preference for a product, then the demand curve would shift to the right. Why? Because consumers would want to buy more than before *at each and every price*. On the other hand, if consumers displayed a decreasing preference for a product, then the demand curve would shift to the left. At each price, in this case, consumers would want to buy less than before. So, if people became more energy-conscious and began to take more pride in cutting back on the unnecessary use of energy, then the demand curve for oil might shift to the left, as shown in Figure 1.2. The greater the shift in preferences, the larger the shift in the demand curve.

Consumers' incomes

Consumers' incomes can also influence the shape and position of a market demand curve. For most products, the demand curve would shift up and to the right if per capita income were to rise. For a few types of commodities, though, higher incomes might cause the demand curve to shift to the left. We will analyze why some goods fall into one category or the other in subsequent chapters. All that matters at this point is that changes in income can affect the demand curve. In the case of crude oil, we should expect that an increase in per capita income would shift the curve to the right. Why? Because people with higher incomes could easily want warmer houses, or they might not be as careful about taking shorter showers or driving smaller cars.

Other prices

The prices of other goods can influence demand, as well. Continuing our crude oil example, recall that natural gas can substitute for oil in many instances. As a result, the quantity of oil demanded at any price should depend on the price of natural gas. If the price of natural gas were high, then more oil would be demanded at any price than if the price of gas were low. People and firms would substitute gas for relatively high-priced oil, and they would substitute oil for relatively high-priced gas. Higher gas prices should therefore shift the market demand curve for oil to the right, just as depicted

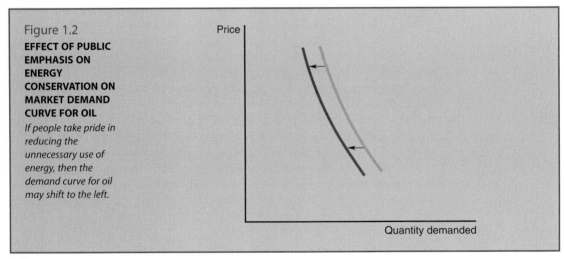

Figure 1.2
EFFECT OF PUBLIC EMPHASIS ON ENERGY CONSERVATION ON MARKET DEMAND CURVE FOR OIL

If people take pride in reducing the unnecessary use of energy, then the demand curve for oil may shift to the left.

Price

Quantity demanded

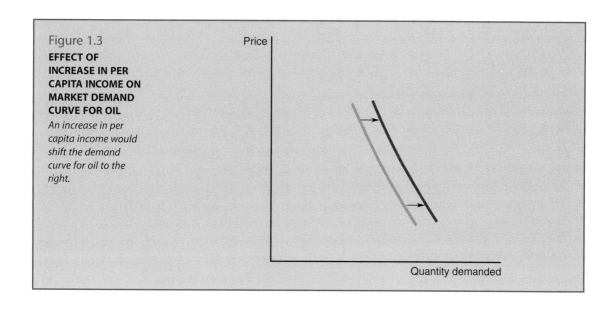

Figure 1.3

EFFECT OF INCREASE IN PER CAPITA INCOME ON MARKET DEMAND CURVE FOR OIL

An increase in per capita income would shift the demand curve for oil to the right.

Price

Quantity demanded

in Figure 1.3. But lower prices for natural gas should have the opposite effect—shifting the demand for oil to the left as in Figure 1.2.

▣ The Supply Side of the Market

Market supply schedule

Each market also has a supply side. It can usually be represented by a **market supply schedule**—a table that shows the quantity of a good that would be supplied at various prices. Suppose, for example, that the market supply schedule were as displayed in Table 1.3. We would then know that 600 million barrels of crude oil would be supplied in a typical month if its price were $18 per barrel, 650 million barrels would be supplied if the price were $19 per barrel, and so on. The **market supply curve** can also depict the same data graphically by using the vertical axis to reflect the price per unit and the horizontal axis to indicate the quantity supplied. Figure 1.4 follows

Market supply curve

Table 1.3	Price per barrel (dollars)	Quantity supplied (millions of barrels per month)
MARKET SUPPLY SCHEDULE FOR OIL, WINTER 2003	18	600
	19	650
	20	700
	21	750
	22	775
	23	800
	24	825

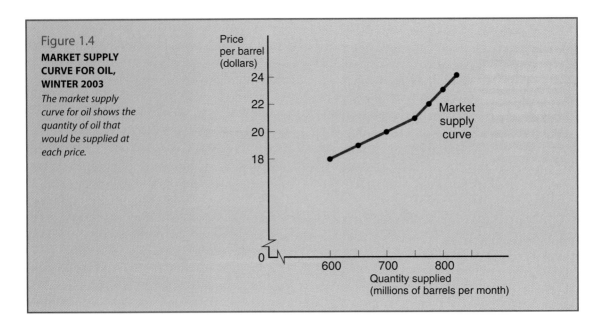

Figure 1.4

MARKET SUPPLY CURVE FOR OIL, WINTER 2003

The market supply curve for oil shows the quantity of oil that would be supplied at each price.

this convention in its depiction of the supply relationship reported in Table 1.3.

Two important features about Figure 1.4 must be emphasized. First, the market supply curve for oil slopes upward and to the right. In other words, the quantity of oil supplied increases as the price increases. This is because increases in its price give oil producers a greater incentive to refine it and to offer it for sale. Empirical studies indicate that the market supply curves for a great many commodities share this characteristic of sloping upward and to the right. In subsequent chapters, we will analyze in detail the factors responsible for the shape of a particular good's market supply curve.

Second, the market supply curve in Figure 1.4 pertains to a particular period of time: again, a winter month in 2003. Any supply curve pertains to some period of time, and its shape and position depend on the length and other characteristics of this period. For example, if we were to estimate the market supply curve for oil for the first week in 2003, it would be different from the one in Figure 1.4. The difference would arise, in part, because oil producers can adapt their output rate more fully to changes in oil's price over the course of a month than they can in just one short week.

What other factors determine the position and shape of the market sup-

Technology   ply curve for a good? **Technology** and the pace of technological change must surely play a role. As technology progresses, it generally becomes possible to produce a commodity more cheaply. As a result, firms become more willing to supply that commodity to the market at a lower price. Indeed, competition with other suppliers might force them to do so. Technological change therefore often causes the supply curve to shift to

14

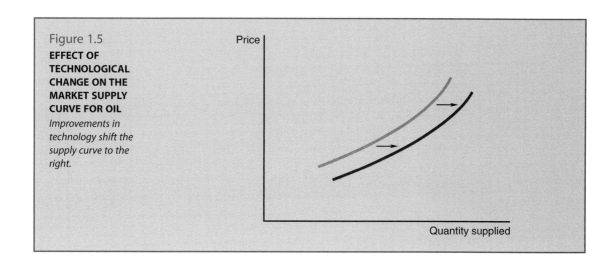

Figure 1.5

EFFECT OF TECHNOLOGICAL CHANGE ON THE MARKET SUPPLY CURVE FOR OIL

Improvements in technology shift the supply curve to the right.

Price

Quantity supplied

the right. Such a shift is portrayed for our oil example in Figure 1.5. It portrays, at least qualitatively, many of the important technological advances that have repeatedly affected the supply side of the oil market over the past 50 years.

Input prices   **Input prices** also influence supply—prices of resources like labor, capital, land, energy, and so on that are used in production. Reductions in the prices of these inputs make it possible for firms to produce their outputs more cheaply. As a result, falling input prices can also cause the supply curve to shift to the right and down. On the other hand, though, higher input prices may cause the supply curve to shift up and to the left. For example, if the wages paid to petroleum workers rose, then the supply curve for oil would probable shift up and to the left as shown in Figure 1.6.

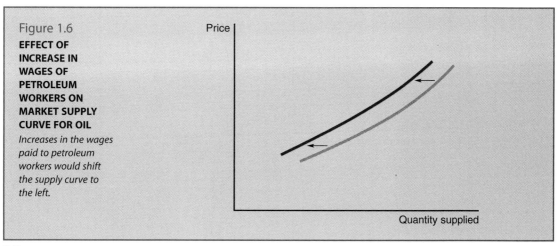

Figure 1.6

EFFECT OF INCREASE IN WAGES OF PETROLEUM WORKERS ON MARKET SUPPLY CURVE FOR OIL

Increases in the wages paid to petroleum workers would shift the supply curve to the left.

Price

Quantity supplied

◻ Market Equilibrium

Prices in a market-based capitalistic economy are important determinants of what is produced, how it is produced, for whom it is produced, and how rapidly per capita income grows. If it is to be of any value, therefore, our model of how a market works must provide some insight into how prices are determined. As a first step toward describing this process, we must define the equilibrium price of a good. You will encounter the concept of an equilibrium at many points in this text. It is an important concept in eco-

Equilibrium nomics, just as it is in many other scientific fields. An **equilibrium** is a situation from which there is no tendency to change. It is, in other words, a

Equilibrium price situation that can persist indefinitely. An **equilibrium price** is therefore a price that can be maintained over a long period of time. Why is that a special condition? Because there are basic forces at work in a market that will stimulate a change in a price unless they are somehow balanced.

The best way to understand what we mean by an equilibrium price is to take a particular case, such as the market for oil. Let's put both the demand curve for oil (from Figure 1.1) and the supply curve for oil (from Figure 1.4) together in the same diagram. The result is shown in Figure 1.7. It will help us determine the equilibrium price of oil.

We begin by seeing what would happen if various prices were established in the market. For example, if the price were $22 a barrel, then the demand curve indicates that 680 million barrels of oil would be demanded. The supply curve meanwhile indicates that 775 million barrels would be supplied. It is clear, therefore, that there would be a mismatch between the quantity supplied and the quantity demanded per month. Indeed, Figure 1.7 shows

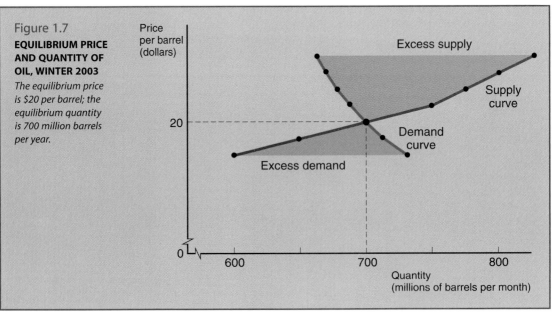

Figure 1.7

EQUILIBRIUM PRICE AND QUANTITY OF OIL, WINTER 2003

The equilibrium price is $20 per barrel; the equilibrium quantity is 700 million barrels per year.

that the rate at which oil would be supplied would exceed the rate at which it would be demanded by 95 million barrels. Said differently, there would be an excess supply of 95 million barrels at the $22 price. Under these circumstances, some of the oil supplied by producers could not be sold. Inventories of oil would build up. Supply depots would fill up. And eventually, suppliers would try to reduce their unwanted inventories by cutting their prices. So, a price of $22 per barrel would not be sustained; $22 per barrel cannot be an equilibrium price.

If the price were $18 per barrel, on the other hand, then the demand curve indicates that 730 million barrels of oil would be demanded while the supply curve indicates that only 600 million barrels would be supplied. We again find a mismatch between the quantity supplied and the quantity demanded per month. This time, though, the rate at which oil would be supplied would be less than the rate at which it would be demanded. Specifically, as shown in Figure 1.7, there would be an excess demand of 130 million barrels. Under these circumstances, some of the consumers who want oil at this price would have to be turned away empty-handed. There would be a shortage. Perhaps supplies would be rationed. In any case, suppliers would find it profitable to increase the price, and competition among buyers would bid the price up. A price of $18 per barrel would be no more sustainable than a price of $22, $18 per barrel cannot be an equilibrium price, either.

The equilibrium price must be the price where the quantity demanded equals the quantity supplied. Obviously, this is the only price at which there is no mismatch, and so it is the only price that can be sustained over a long period of time. In Figure 1.7, the price at which the quantity supplied equals the quantity demanded is $20 per barrel. It is the price where the demand curve intersects the supply curve. And it is the equilibrium price of oil under the circumstances visualized in Figure 1.7. How much would be demanded at $20? Exactly 700 million barrels per month. How much would be supplied? Again, 700 million barrels per month. This **equilibrium quantity** is also indicated by the intersection of the demand and supply curves.[3]

Equilibrium quantity

◻ Actual Price

If you have been paying close attention, you might be a little puzzled at this point. We set out to model the actual price of oil because the actual price is all that is observed in the real world. But we just described the equilibrium price. How are the two related? Good question. Models of markets generally assume that the actual price will approximate the equilibrium price. This seems to be reasonable enough, since the basic forces just described do tend to push the actual price toward the equilibrium price. And so, if the demand and supply curves remain fairly stable for a reasonable period of time, then the actual price should move toward and eventually approximate the equilibrium price.

[3]If $P = D(Q)$ is the demand curve and $P = S(Q)$ is the supply curve, we have two equations in two unknowns—price (P) and quantity (Q). To determine the equilibrium price, we can solve these equations simultaneously for P and Q.

To see how this might be the case, consider the market for oil depicted in Figure 1.7. What if the actual price were somehow set at $22 per barrel? There would then be real downward pressure on the price of oil for the reasons just described. Suppose now that the actual price, responding to the pressure of excess supply, were to fall to $21. The quantity demanded would still fall short of the quantity supplied, and we should expect to see that downward pressure on price continue. The actual price, responding to this pressure, might fall to $20.50. To $20.25. To $20.10. But the downward pressure would persist as long as the quantity supplied exceeded the quantity demanded. That is, the downward pressure would persist as long as the actual price were higher than the equilibrium price.

Conversely, upward pressure would be exerted on price as long as the actual price were lower than the equilibrium price. Tell yourself the story that makes it clear why this would be so; it is the exact analog of the preceding parable. Combining the two, then, it should now be clear that the *actual price should tend to move toward the equilibrium price as long as the actual price is not equal to the equilibrium value.* At what pace? It cannot be assumed that this movement must always be rapid. It can sometimes take a long time for the actual price to get close to the equilibrium price. The actual price may never even get to the equilibrium price, in fact, if the equilibrium price changed in the meantime. All that safely can be said is that the actual price will move toward the equilibrium price. But this information is of great value, both theoretically and practically. For many purposes, all that is required of a model is to predict whether the price will move up or down.

| Example 1.4 | New Year's Eve at the Rainbow Room |

The Rainbow Room, located high above Rockefeller Center, has long been famous for its New Year's Eve party—at least among the well-heeled residents of and visitors to New York City. The cost of attending the festivities has risen steadily over the years, and it reached $2,000 per person on December 30, 2000. The economics of supply and demand can influence even the most elevated markets, though. Recession, diminished tourism, and changes in individual preferences in favor of quieter and less opulent celebrations all combined to cause demand to collapse at the end of 2001. As a result, spaces at the party went empty while the price plummeted to a mere $600 per person—a reduction of 70 percent from the year before.

◙ The Effects on Price of Shifts in the Demand Curve

We have already seen that demand curves shift in response to changes in tastes, income, and prices of other products. Any supply-and-demand diagram is essentially a snapshot of the situation during a particular period of time. The results in Figure 1.7 are limited to a particular period because the demand and supply curves in the figure pertain only to that period. What would happen to the equilibrium price of a product (which we shall call good *X*) if its demand curve were to change from one period to the next?

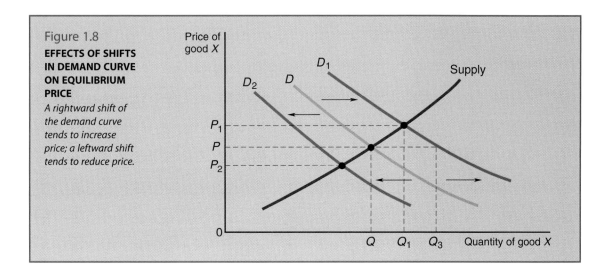

Figure 1.8

EFFECTS OF SHIFTS IN DEMAND CURVE ON EQUILIBRIUM PRICE

A rightward shift of the demand curve tends to increase price; a leftward shift tends to reduce price.

Suppose that consumer tastes changed in favor of good X so that the demand curve for good X shifted to the right. This state of affairs is shown in Figure 1.8, where D represents the original demand curve and D_1 portrays the new one. It is not hard to see the effect on the equilibrium price of good X. When D was the demand curve, the equilibrium price was P and the equilibrium quantity was Q. But if the demand curve shifted to D_1, then a shortage of $(Q_3 - Q)$ units would develop at this price. Suppliers would respond by raising their prices, and consumers would compete with each other to make their desired purchases at these new higher prices. After some testing of market reactions and trial-and-error adjustments, the price would tend to settle at P_1, the new equilibrium price, and quantity would tend to settle at Q_1.

Suppose now that consumer demand for good X fell, instead. Why? Perhaps because of a great drop in the price of a product that is an effective substitute for good X. The cause really does not matter. All that matters in determining the effect on the price of X is that the demand for good X would now shift to the left—say, from D to D_2 in Figure 1.8. What would happen to the equilibrium price of good X? Clearly, the new equilibrium price would be at a lower level, designated P_2, where the new demand curve intersects the supply curve.

Leftward shifts in a demand curve generally produce lower equilibrium prices; shifts to the right generally produce higher equilibrium prices. This is the lesson of Figure 1.8—a lesson that holds as long as the applicable supply curves slope upward to the right.

| **Example 1.5** | **Weather Patterns and the Price of Heating Oil** |

Consider the market for home heating oil, for a moment. The winter of 2001–2002 was unusually mild in the northeastern part of the United States and across most of the other parts of the country. In New England, for example, this winter was 25 percent warmer than normal in terms of "degree-days"—an index reported by meteorologists that is directly correlated with the amount of energy required to maintain a constant indoor temperature in most buildings. Perhaps it was the effect of a change in some regional atmospheric circulation pattern like El Niño. Perhaps not. It really doesn't matter. The mild weather caused the demand curve for heating oil to shift to the left. And what happened to the price of heating oil? In accord with the model, it fell significantly to approximately $1 per gallon. This average price was about 40 percent lower than the prices that cleared the market during the more normal winter of 1999–2000.

The winter of 2000–2001 showed the opposite effect. That winter was marked by colder than normal temperatures over long periods of time, as opposed to the more usual patterns of short episodes of severe cold followed by moderation. Snow that had fallen in early December was still on the ground in late March, and the demand for heating oil shifted to the right. The price effect again conformed to the model by climbing to levels in excess of $1.75 per gallon.

▣ The Effects on Price of Shifts in the Supply Curve

Supply curves, like demand curves, shift over time as circumstances change. What would happen to the equilibrium price of a good if its supply curve were to shift? Suppose that, because of technological advances, producers of good X were willing and able to supply more of good X at a given price than they used to. Specifically, suppose that the supply curve were to shift from S to S_1 in Figure 1.9. What would be the effect on the equilibrium price? Clearly, it would fall from P (where the S supply curve intersects the demand curve) to P_3 (where the S_1 supply curve intersects the demand curve).

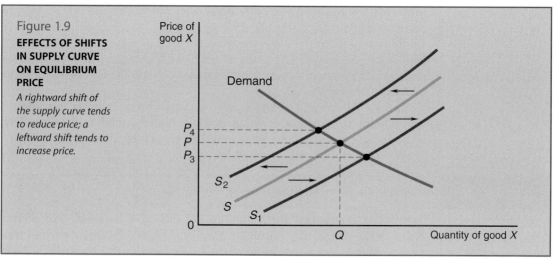

Figure 1.9

EFFECTS OF SHIFTS IN SUPPLY CURVE ON EQUILIBRIUM PRICE

A rightward shift of the supply curve tends to reduce price; a leftward shift tends to increase price.

By way of contrast, suppose instead that input prices rose. The supply curve would then shift from S to S_2 in Figure 1.9, so that the equilibrium price would increase from P to P_4 (where the S_2 supply curve intersects the demand curve).

In general, the equilibrium price falls when the supply curve shifts to the right and it increases when the supply curve shifts to the left. This conclusion depends, of course, on the assumption that the demand curve slopes downward from left to right, but downward-sloping demand is the rule and not the exception.

| Example 1.6 | The Copper Crunch That Never Came |

As late as the 1970s, most telecommunication in the developed world still flowed along copper wires, and this source of demand competed with the manufacturers of refrigerators, motors, all sorts of light and heavy machinery, piping, and pennies for increasingly scarce and expensive global supplies. Technology provided some substitutes for many of these uses (most were derived from aluminum), and large-scale recycling efforts were initiated. There was, though, growing concern that fixed copper resources might be a significant limiting factor on economic activity. Figure 1.10 displays how this predicament was projected to emerge in the price signal starting in 1970 for baseline estimates of demand and supply through the year 2050 published in *Toward a New Iron Age?* by Robert Gordon, Tjalling Koopmans, William Nordhaus, and Brian Skinner.

Scientists were, in the 1970s, just beginning to understand how light could carry information and how fiber-optic cable could carry light long distances and around corners. Inspired in large measure by the prospect of increasingly expensive copper, new technology emerged from this new

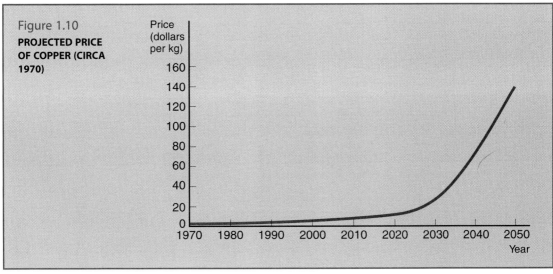

Figure 1.10
PROJECTED PRICE OF COPPER (CIRCA 1970)

knowledge in the form of fiber-optic cables that were installed to carry telecommunications under the streets of many densely populated areas like New York City. The technology worked wonderfully, increasing the capacity of a cable of any diameter to carry information and causing the demand for copper to plummet. In addition, crews that replaced thousands of miles of refined copper wire with fiber-optic cables quickly turned most of the major urban areas of the developed world into incredibly productive copper mines; they simply rolled the wire onto enormous spools and hauled them off to warehouses. It should be no surprise that the price of copper continued to plummet. Indeed, actual prices have tracked well below the projections displayed in Figure 1.10.

◻ The Effects on Price and Quantity of Simultaneous Shifts in Supply and Demand

Notwithstanding the power of even our simple model, it is not always possible to determine even the direction of a change in equilibrium price or quantity. The two panels of Table 1.4 illustrate this point for simultaneous shifts in supply and demand. Panel A, for example, indicates with minus $(-)$ or plus $(+)$ signs, respectively, that equilibrium prices would rise or fall, but it indicates two circumstances when it would be impossible to tell without careful analysis which net change would result. Panel B, meanwhile, indicates the corresponding information for equilibrium quantity.

Figure 1.11 provides some insight into how these conclusions can be drawn from a demand-and-supply model of a market. It depicts a simultaneous increase in demand from curve D to D' and contraction in supply from curve S to S'. Equilibrium therefore moves from point E to point E'. Notice immediately that the equilibrium price would be higher after these changes. Indeed, the increase in price would be much higher than it would be if only demand had increased or if only supply had diminished. As drawn, equilibrium quantity at E' is larger than at E, but that is an artifact of demand's having increased more than supply contracted. It would, indeed,

Table 1.4 **A. EFFECTS OF SIMULTANEOUS CHANGES IN SUPPLY AND DEMAND ON EQUILIBRIUM PRICE**

	Increased demand	Reduced demand
Increased supply	?	$(-)$
Reduced supply	$(+)$	?

B. EFFECTS OF SIMULTANEOUS CHANGES IN SUPPLY AND DEMAND ON EQUILIBRIUM QUANTITY

	Increased demand	Reduced demand
Increased supply	$(+)$	?
Reduced supply	?	$(-)$

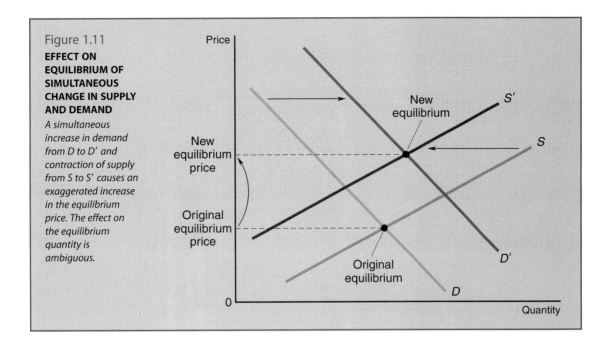

Figure 1.11

EFFECT ON EQUILIBRIUM OF SIMULTANEOUS CHANGE IN SUPPLY AND DEMAND

A simultaneous increase in demand from D to D' and contraction of supply from S to S' causes an exaggerated increase in the equilibrium price. The effect on the equilibrium quantity is ambiguous.

Price

New equilibrium

S'

S

New equilibrium price

Original equilibrium price

Original equilibrium

D'

D

0

Quantity

be easy to draw a smaller shift in the demand curve to produce a comparable price increase associated with a smaller equilibrium quantity. Similar graphs can validate the other parts of Table 1.4, and you are asked to construct them in Question 15 of the chapter ending exercises.

| Example 1.7 | **Stock Prices and the Terrorist Attack of 9/11/01** |

Remember that the New York Stock Exchange was offered earlier as our first example of a market. Its daily operations are enormously complex, to be sure. But the basic model of supply and demand can explain most of its fluctuation—be it observed from minute to minute, day to day, month to month, or over longer time periods. For example, the horrific events of September 11, 2001, produced immediate impacts on the world's financial markets driven in large measure by uncertainty about the stability of economic systems. People who owned stock suddenly wanted to sell, so the supply side of nearly every financial market expanded dramatically within hours of the attack. Potential investors also became reluctant to make new stock purchases, so the demand side contracted at the same time. The result, as predicted by the model, was a sharp drop in stock prices.

Figure 1.12 reflects this result, in both direction and magnitude, by tracking price indexes for major markets for the 30 hours running from just before the attack (around 8:30 A.M. in New York on September 11, 2001) through 1:00 P.M. the next day. Figure 1.12 also shows that the price shock eventually waned so prices could gradually begin to recover. Our model suggests that this was the result of increased demand. Perhaps investors

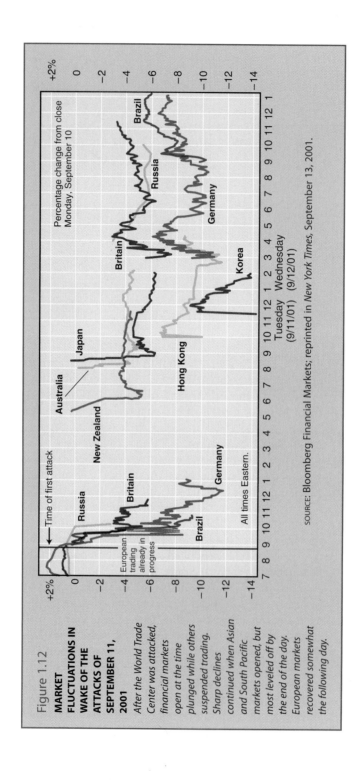

Figure 1.12

MARKET FLUCTUATIONS IN WAKE OF THE ATTACKS OF SEPTEMBER 11, 2001

After the World Trade Center was attacked, financial markets open at the time plunged while others suspended trading. Sharp declines continued when Asian and South Pacific markets opened, but most leveled off by the end of the day. European markets recovered somewhat the following day.

SOURCE: Bloomberg Financial Markets; reprinted in *New York Times*, September 13, 2001.

became less nervous about continued violence. Nonetheless, the New York Stock Exchange lost almost $1.4 trillion in value during the week of September 17—the first week that it opened after the attack.

SUMMARY

1. Economics deals with the way in which resources are allocated among alternative uses. Economic resources are scarce and have a nonzero price.

2. Economic theory is divided into two parts: microeconomics and macroeconomics. Microeconomics is concerned with the economic behavior of individual economic units like consumers, firms, and resource owners.

3. Any economic system must accomplish four tasks: it must allocate resources; it must determine the composition of output; it must distribute the product; and it must provide for growth. Much of microeconomics is devoted to explaining how prices and markets can accomplish these tasks.

4. Economists use models to explore the workings of economic forces. Their methodology is much the same as that used by scientists in other disciplines. Models are evaluated by considering their ability to support accurate predictions, the internal consistency of their simplifying assumptions, and the range of their applicability. They are not expected to answer all of the problems that face firms, consumers, governments, and others, but they are expected to offer any and all prospective clients some insight into the workings of the economy that they would otherwise have missed.

5. The market demand curve for a good almost always slopes downward from left to right. That is, the quantity demanded generally increases as the price falls. The position and shape of the market demand curve for a good depend on the tastes of consumers, the levels of consumer income, the prices of other goods, and the length of the time period to which the demand curve pertains.

6. The market supply curve for a good generally slopes upward from left to right. That is, the quantity supplied generally increases as the price rises. The position and shape of the market supply curve for a good depend on the state of technology, input prices, and the length of the time interval to which the market supply curve pertains.

7. An equilibrium price is one that can be maintained over a long period of time if conditions do not change. In a competitive market, it is the price where the quantity demanded equals the quantity supplied—i.e., it is the price where the demand curve intersects the supply curve. If the actual price exceeds the equilibrium price, then the resulting excess supply of the good will tend to force a reduction in the actual price. If the actual price is less than the equilibrium price, then the resulting excess demand will push the actual price up.

8. In general, a shift to the right in the demand curve will cause the equilibrium price to rise, whereas a shift to the left in the demand curve will cause it to fall. In general, a shift to the right in the supply curve will cause the equilibrium price to fall, but a shift to the left in the supply curve will cause it to rise.

QUESTIONS/ PROBLEMS

1. Medicare is a compulsory hospitalization-insurance plan plus a voluntary insurance plan covering doctors' fees for Americans aged 65 years and older. The hospitalization insurance pays for practically all the hospital costs of the first 90 days of each spell of illness, as well as some additional costs. Medicaid is a subsidy for medical care received by the poor. In the first few years

after the enactment of Medicare and Medicaid, the price of medical care rose about 9 percentage points more than consumer prices generally. Suppose that you are an adviser to the secretary of Health and Human Services, who is interested in why this price increase occurred. In particular, the secretary asks you whether the enactment of Medicare and Medicaid could have been responsible for it. What sort of model might you construct to help answer this question? Would you expect Medicare and Medicaid to have increased the amount of medical care demanded by the public? Would this have tended to push up the price?

2. In 1995, Russians increased their purchase of furs considerably. According to Jay Mechutan, a New York fur importer, "They used to send us anything they could. Now they are buying even the most expensive of their own products."[4] What factors may have been responsible for this? What sort of model might you construct to explain this phenomenon? The Russian economy virtually collapsed in 1998, and the value of their currency fell by more than 50 percent. Would you expect that Russian demand for furs has been sustained? Explain how your model might be used to support your answer.

3. Cigarette bootleggers take cigarettes from states with low cigarette taxes and sell them in states with high cigarette taxes. Such smuggling results in a loss in tax revenue to the high-tax states. The Advisory Commission on Intergovernmental Relations estimated that this loss in 1975 and 1979 was as follows:

	Loss from cigarette-tax evasion (millions of dollars)	
	1975	1979
All states	337	280
Florida	36	43

(a) If you had to construct a model to predict the amount of cigarettes bootlegged, what factors would you include? (b) On the basis of the above figures, do you think that Florida's cigarette-tax rate was lower than that of neighboring states? Why or why not? (c) Between 1975 and 1979, Florida changed its tax on a pack of cigarettes by 3 cents per pack. Do you think that it increased or decreased the tax? Why? (d) Could the change in the total loss from tax evasion have been due in part to the large increase in the price of gasoline in the late 1970s? Why or why not? New York City made all of this inconsequential in 2002 by adding over $1 to its tax; Connecticut added 61 cents. Would you expect cigarette sales in Massachusetts and New Jersey to change?

4. Economists disagree on most questions of policy. The economic advisers of Republican presidents have tended to have views somewhat different from those of the economic advisers of Democratic presidents. Does this prove that economics is not a science? Discuss the potential sources of disagreement. Are uncertain estimates of quantitative relationships the only source? Or do value judgments and decision criteria matter?

5. The median salary offered by colleges and universities to new assistant professors in economics and computer science is generally higher than the median salaries offered to historians and sociologists. What factors would you include in a model that tried to explain why?

[4] *New York Times,* October 22, 1995, p. A1.

6. It has been argued that a certain proposition must hold true for the whole system if it holds true for a part of that system. For example, suppose that a farmer will benefit from producing a larger crop. Does it follow that all farmers will benefit from producing larger crops? Explain.

7. In evaluating the accuracy of their statements, should you distinguish between (1) economists' descriptive statements, propositions, and predictions about the world and (2) their statements about what policies should be adopted? Explain your answer.

8. Suppose that you were given the task of constructing a model to predict Microsoft's total sales next year. How would you go about it? What variables would you include? Microsoft frequently seems to be under investigation for illegal restraint of trade. Could the way you build the model influence your opinion about whether or not Microsoft has been justly charged? Conversely, could your view of its guilt or innocence bias the model that you might construct?

9. Severe floods occurred in California's Salinas and Pajaro Valleys in March of 1995, causing extensive damage to the area's lettuce, strawberry, broccoli, celery, and artichoke crops. The Salinas Valley produces half the country's lettuce. At the Philadelphia Wholesale Market, lettuce prices (for cartons of 24 heads) were as follows on March 1, 1995, and April 4, 1995:[5]

Type of lettuce	March 1	April 4
Iceberg	$7.50–$9.00	$45–$55
Green leaf	$7.50–$8.00	$25–$28
Romaine	$10	$30–$35

(a) Were the price changes due to changes in the demand curve or the supply curve for lettuce? (b) Restaurants subsequently began to replace lettuce-based salads with ones containing pasta. Why? (c) Were lettuce producers outside the Salinas and Pajaro Valleys helped or hurt by these floods? Why?

10. Let demand and supply for some good Y be described by the tables below. Identify the equilibrium price. Suppose that the actual price were $70. Would you expect the price to rise or fall? If so, by how much? Why? What if the price were initially $90?

Demand schedule		Supply schedule	
Price	Quantity	Price	Quantity
50	25	50	0.0
55	22.5	55	1.7
60	20	60	3.3
65	17.5	65	5.0
70	15	70	6.7
75	12.5	75	8.3
80	10	80	10.0
85	7.5	85	11.7
90	5	90	13.3
95	2.5	95	15.0
100	0	100	16.7

[5] *Philadelphia Inquirer,* April 6, 1995.

11. The demand curve for a product is $P = 100 - 2Q_D$, where P is the product's price (in dollars per pound) and Q_D is the quantity demanded (in millions of pounds per year). The actual price of the product is $70 per pound. If the supply curve for the product is $P = 50 + 3Q_S$, where Q_S is quantity supplied (in millions of pounds per year), would you expect the price to rise or fall? If so, by how much? Why?

12. Suppose that the demand curve for cantaloupes is $P = 120 - 3Q_D$, where P is the price per pound (in cents) of cantaloupe and Q_D is the quantity demanded per year (in millions of pounds). Suppose that the supply curve for cantaloupes is $P = 5Q_S$, where Q_S is the quantity supplied per year (in millions of pounds). What is the equilibrium price per pound of cantaloupe? What is the equilibrium quantity of cantaloupes produced? Suppose that the government imposed a price floor of 80 cents per pound for cantaloupes. How much would then be supplied? Calculate the resulting surplus. What could the government do to eliminate the surplus and still maintain the price floor? Would the demand curve shift to the left, to the right, or stay in place if (a) a report by the U.S. Surgeon General suggested that eating cantaloupes causes cancer? (b) the price of honeydew melons rose by 10 percent? (c) per capita incomes rose by 20 percent? (d) the wages of workers employed in supplying cantaloupes to the market increased by 25 percent?

13. The United States has, from time to time, suffered energy shortages. Draw a graph of supply and demand in which a sudden reduction in supply demonstrates why the price might climb and the quantity demanded might fall. Explain why time can work to diminish upward pressure on price by increasing the quantity response to rising prices. Display your answer on your graph.

14. Draw graphs to illustrate the four cases of Table 1.4.

15. Sotheby's auctioned a copy of the Declaration of Independence in the spring of 2000. Printed by John Dunlop of Philadelphia on July 4 or 5, 1776, this edition was the first and most official of several versions printed that July. There were 25 known copies as of 1989; all were in private hands or owned by museums. This copy was found behind a torn painting by a man who was attracted to its old frame at a flea market in Bucks County, Pennsylvania. He paid $4 for the frame. It turns out that the frame was unsalvageable, but the backing of the painting was not. Assuming that all other copies of the Declaration were not for sale at any price, describe the supply curve for this "market." This copy was sold for $2.1 million in 1991 and for more than $6 million in 2000. Explain how that might have happened. (Source: www.sothebys.com.)

Consumer Behavior and Market Demand

Consumer Tastes and Preferences

Cable companies began in 1998 to offer direct Internet service that eliminated the need for telephone connections to services like America Online and Prodigy. By skipping the telephone link, customers could free themselves of their modems and gain almost instantaneous access to all sorts of services. But if it was such a great idea, why has it taken so long for broadband Internet service to catch on? One issue was, and continues to be, cost. Broadband access was several times more expensive than phone connections from the start, and it still is. Even at the same price, though, demand for services that could be supported only by broadband access was diluted by difficulties with its installation and possible congestion issues. Moreover, few consumers saw a fundamental need for more speed for the services that they were then demanding. Things may be changing, though. Major companies have become convinced that movies on demand, instant music downloads, and the next generation of broadband software and interactive television will begin to increase consumer demand for nanosecond communication. Indeed, Comcast, Inc., of Pennsylvania used backing from Microsoft to win a bidding war with AOL Time Warner for AT&T Broadband in December 2001. The combined bid of $72 billion speaks volumes about what these companies see as the future—a future that must be driven by consumer demand.

Brian Roberts, president of Comcast and CEO-designate of the proposed AT&T Comcast, based his considerable optimism and substantial wager (his $72 billion bid to purchase AT&T Broadband) on a number of factors. First was the advantage of enormous size. With over 22.1 million customers clustered in 17 of the nation's 20 top markets, AT&T Comcast would have a strong base from which to grow. Moreover, Comcast had already sold 10 percent of its nearly 10 million subscribers on broadband access. Many more had purchased digital cable—the service necessary for movies on demand, interactive television, and hundreds of movie and music channels—so demand for the products that broadband might deliver was there. The bugs had been worked out on the early subscribers, and Roberts hoped that consumer preferences would be influenced by the improving experiences of thousands of neighbors in growing markets. And then there was the Microsoft factor. Microsoft has long seen renting software by the minute over the Internet as the future of personal computing. Its involvement with and commitment to developing these software products held the promise of delivering an entirely new group of consumers who wanted broadband connections for entirely different reasons. Did the gamble pay off? You probably know by now. The key was to live up to a pledge to open broadband up to as many entrepreneurs as possible and thereby generate a demand for the service.[1]

Economists, as well as business types, have spent a considerable amount of time, effort, and money studying consumer preferences and behavior. Why? For one thing, U.S. consumers spend trillions of dollars each year to purchase more than 65 percent of the final goods and services produced in the United States (the other 35 percent is sold to businesses, to the government, and to foreign customers through export markets). And this is not simply an American phenomenon. Comparable percentages for a few of the world's developed and developing economies make one point clear: consumers wield enormous economic power.

This chapter presents a simple model that has been designed to represent consumers' tastes and preferences and to predict how much they will buy. We will introduce indifference curves, the marginal rate of substitution, the notion of utility, and the budget line. The model is interesting for its own sake, but it is also a first step toward consistently analyzing the forces that determine the shapes and positions of market demand curves.

Example 2.1	Consumption around the World

We have seen that consumers wield a lot of power in the United States, at least. A quick tour around the globe can, however, confirm that consumer power is ubiquitous; and a quick trip back in time will show that it is, for the most part, growing. Table 2.1 records data on household

Table 2.1 HOUSEHOLD CONSUMPTION AS A PERCENTAGE OF TOTAL PRODUCTION OF GOODS AND SERVICES	Country	1995	2000
	Australia	57.6	61.9
	Bangladesh	67.6	67.3
	Brazil	59.9	61.9
	Canada	57.4	56.7
	Egypt	72.6	74.2
	Germany	56.8	57.8
	Japan	60.1	62.4
	Thailand	54.4	56.1
	United Kingdom	63.7	65.8
	United States	67.1	67.8

[1]J. Roberts, "Cable's A-Team," *Newsweek*, December 31, 2001, pp. 35–36. See, as well, J. Hausman, J. G. Sidak, and H. Singer, "Cable Modems and DSL: Broadband Internet Access for Residential Customers," *American Economic Review*, vol. 91, no. 2, May 2001, pp. 302–307.

consumption, expressed as a percentage of the total value of goods and services, for 10 different nations in 1995 and 2000. This short list is hardly comprehensive, but it does include developed and developing countries from six different continents. The percentages in 1995 for all but one country lie above 55 percent. In the year 2000, 7 of 10 entries exceed 60 percent. And the percentage of GDP devoted to meeting consumer demand grew in 8 of 10 countries over the intervening 5 years. Clearly, consumers play critical roles across the globe in deciding how nations allocate their economic resources.

CONSUMER PREFERENCES

The simple model of consumer behavior presented here will enable us to predict how much of a particular commodity—hot dogs, paint, housing—a consumer will buy during a particular period of time. We begin to construct this model by looking at consumers' preferences. Some consumers like John Steinbeck novels while others like comic books; some like Puccini and others like John Lennon, Dave Matthews, or Madonna. And so it is obvious that differences in tastes should cause consumers to want to buy different commodities. Economists have responded to all of this complication and variety by making several basic assumptions about consumer tastes.

Complete

To begin with, suppose that a consumer is confronted with any two market "baskets," each containing various quantities of different commodities. One market basket might contain one ticket to a University of Connecticut basketball game and three chocolate bars. The other might contain four bottles of soda and one bus ticket. Economists begin by assuming that preferences are **complete** in the sense that all consumers would be able to decide whether they preferred the first market basket to the second, whether they preferred the second to the first, or whether they are indifferent between them. This certainly seems to be a plausible assumption.

Transitive

Second, economists assume that the consumer's preferences are **transitive**—that is, if he or she prefers Pepsi to Coke and Coke to Dr. Pepper, then he or she would prefer Pepsi to Dr. Pepper. If that were not true, then his or her preferences would not be transitive. They would, instead, be contradictory and mutually inconsistent. Tastes may be judged to be shallow or deep, lofty or mean, selfish or generous: this makes no difference to the theory. But preferences must be transitive. Some argue that not all consumers exhibit transitive preferences all of the time, but this assumption is certainly a plausible basis for a model of consumer behavior.

Nonsatiation

Third, economists generally make a **nonsatiation** assumption so that consumers always prefer more of a commodity to less. Suppose that one market basket contains 10 computer disks and 2 cups of coffee and a second contains 10 computer disks and 1 cup of coffee. We assume that the first market basket, which unambiguously contains more commodities, would be preferred. But there is more to it than that. Implicit in the "more is better" assumption is the notion that we can make the second basket equally desirable in the eyes of the consumer by adding more computer disks even if we hold the coffee allocation fixed at 1 cup. That is, we assume that we can make the consumer **indifferent** between the two alternatives. These assumptions, like the previous two, seem quite plausible.

Indifferent

DETERMINANTS OF CONSUMER TASTES AND PREFERENCES

Experience

Consumers' tastes can surely be changed by **experience.** The child whose widest grins of satisfaction are reserved for candy and other sweets may grow into an adult who declines a sweet drink in favor of dry white wine. The kid who regards the ballet as "lame" could grow to be the adult who pays $100 for a ticket to the Royal Ballet. Age has a great influence on a person's tastes, but so does education. Indeed, one of the benefits of education is that it allows individuals to appreciate and enjoy various forms of experience more keenly than they otherwise would.

Demonstration effects

Observations of what other consumers have also influence tastes. These effects are sometimes called **demonstration effects.** For example, if the Joneses have an Audi A6, their neighbors may feel that they should have one, too. Or if the Joneses' daughter can buy expensive clothes, then the neighbors might feel that their daughter should have them, too. Whether their daughter feels this way is another matter. It is sometimes critical to identify precisely *who* is making the consumption decision. Sometimes an opposite kind of effect is at work. Some people may *not* want something if too many other people already own one. Yogi Berra once observed, "Nobody goes there anymore. It's too crowded."

Advertising

Advertising and promotional money spent by manufacturers and sellers of various goods and services can also play a role in shaping consumer tastes. There can be no doubt that advertising influences the behavior of consumers, although the extent of its influence varies greatly from one product to another and from one consumer to another. For goods whose quality is hard for the consumer to measure and for which the relative advantages of the particular good or brand are not very great, advertising may play a very important role. Of course, advertising also plays a significant role merely by informing the consumer of the existence and characteristics of new products. Much more will be said about the effects of advertising in subsequent chapters.

Conspicuous consumption

Finally, a consumer's tastes are thought to be independent of the structure of prices. This rules out cases of **conspicuous consumption,** in which goods are consumed because they are expensive, and other cases in which quality is judged by price. This assumption of price-independence is a reasonable first approximation for most cases, but is obviously not for all cases. It is possible to extend our model to allow for violations of this assumption, but a discussion of such extensions properly belongs in a more advanced text.

Example 2.2 | **The Demand for Corporate Jets**

Consumers' preferences can change overnight, and the consequences can be quite sudden and pronounced. The sharp decline in commercial air travel that followed in the wake of the terrorist attacks of September 11, 2001, provides a dramatic example. Private jet aircraft were once the province of the rich and famous, but all of that changed when the risk associated with commercial aviation was inflated. Business travelers had already grown tired of long delays and changing planes at the hub airports of the major carriers like United and Delta, but mid-September saw them deserting commercial flights in droves. And how did they still make their appointed rounds? In privately owned Learjet 45s and Gulfstreams. Air Charter Guide, a national clearinghouse for information on private jet travel that also operates its own booking service, surveyed 100 charter companies on September 25 and 26. More than 80 percent of those surveyed reported increased demand, and the increase averaged over 100 percent across the 100 firms.

The supply side of a market can also respond swiftly to changing preferences. UAL Corporation, the parent company of United Airlines, had already seen the handwriting on the wall. It was investing heavily in a subsidiary that was to fly and maintain a fleet of business jets for corporate and private clients, and the sudden change only quickened the pace of that investment. Meanwhile, Eclipse Aviation of New Mexico announced on September 17 that it had just received a $1 billion order for 1,000 Eclipse 500 jets—a new, six-seat competitor for Learjet and Gulfstream that would operate as an air-taxi between small cities in South and North America. In addition, the commercial industry is turning its attention to procuring 50-seat "regional jets" like those produced by Canadair—jets that can service medium-sized destinations like Bradley Field in Hartford, Connecticut, or Tweed–New Haven in southern Connecticut.

SOURCE: R. Buck, "Business Fliers: Demand for Corporate Jets Soars," *Hartford Courant,* October 3, 2001.

INDIFFERENCE CURVES

Indifference curve

It turns out that we can represent any consumer's tastes or preferences by a set of "indifference curves" if the assumptions outlined in the preceding section hold true. What is an **indifference curve?** It is a curve, plotted in terms of units of alternative goods, that shows those market baskets (combinations of goods) among which the consumer is indifferent. Suppose, for example, we confine our attention to the 10 market baskets described in Table 2.2. The first market basket highlighted there contains 1 pound of meat and 4 pounds of potatoes, the second contains 1 pound of meat and 6 pounds of potatoes, and so on. Suppose that a consumer were asked to choose between various pairs of these market baskets and that he or she claimed indifference between some of them. The consumer may not care

Table 2.2	Market basket	Meat (pounds per unit of time)	Potatoes (pounds per unit of time)
ALTERNATIVE MARKET BASKETS	1	1	4
	2	1	6
	3	2	3
	4	2	4
	5	3	2
	6	3	3
	7	4	1
	8	4	2
	9	5	0
	10	5	1

whether he or she consumes 4 pounds of meat plus 2 pounds of potatoes or 2 pounds of meat plus 3 pounds of potatoes, for example. Baskets 3 and 8 would therefore lie on the same indifference curve.

Now suppose that we enlarge the number of market baskets (containing various quantities of meat and potatoes) under consideration. We now include all market baskets in which the meat allocation can run from 0 to 8 pounds *and* the potato allocation can run from 1 to 9 pounds. We could then plot all of the possible market baskets on a diagram like that in Figure 2.1; a curve like *A* could represent market baskets among which the consumer is indifferent. As drawn, in fact, curve *A* includes all the market baskets that the consumer regards as being equivalent (in terms of his or her satisfaction) to 4 pounds of meat plus 2 pounds of potatoes *and* to 2 pounds of meat combined with 3 pounds of potatoes.

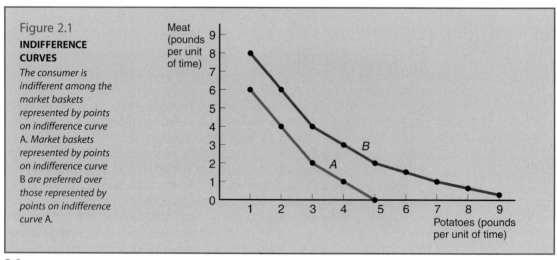

Figure 2.1

INDIFFERENCE CURVES

The consumer is indifferent among the market baskets represented by points on indifference curve A. Market baskets represented by points on indifference curve B are preferred over those represented by points on indifference curve A.

Curve *A* is an indifference curve. There are, of course, many such indifference curves possible for any one consumer, and each curve pertains to
a different level of satisfaction. Indifference curve *B* in Figure 2.1 is one such
alternative. It represents a higher level of satisfaction than indifference curve
A. Why? Because it includes market baskets with more of both meat and
potatoes than the market baskets represented by indifference curve *A*. It is
not difficult to visualize a series of indifference curves, then. One would
show all of the market baskets that are equivalent (in the eyes of the consumer) to 1 pound of potatoes and 2 pounds of meat. Another would show
all of the baskets that are equivalent to 2 pounds of potatoes and 2 pounds
of meat, and so on. The resulting series of indifference curves is called an
Indifference map **indifference map.**

A consumer's indifference map lies at the heart of the theory of con-
sumer behavior because it provides a representation of the consumer's tastes.
To see how, consider the various indifference maps in Figure 2.2. Consumer
A's indifference curves are relatively steep whereas consumer *B*'s indiffer-
ence curves are relatively flat. What does this mean? Apparently consumer
A needs several extra units of good *Y* to compensate for the loss of a single

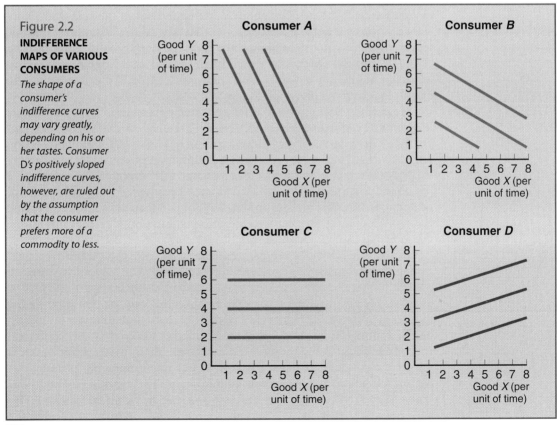

Figure 2.2

**INDIFFERENCE
MAPS OF VARIOUS
CONSUMERS**

*The shape of a
consumer's
indifference curves
may vary greatly,
depending on his or
her tastes. Consumer
D's positively sloped
indifference curves,
however, are ruled out
by the assumption
that the consumer
prefers more of a
commodity to less.*

unit of good X, whereas consumer B would trade several units of X for a single unit of Y. In this sense, good Y is less important (relative to good X) to consumer A than to consumer B.

What can we say about consumers C and D in Figure 2.2? Consumer C apparently regards good X as useless, since he does not care whether he has more or less of it. Consumer D, meanwhile, regards good X as a nuisance, since she is willing to reduce the amount of good Y she consumes in order to get rid of some of good X. Situations of this sort have been ruled out by the assumption that consumers prefer more of a commodity to less, but that does not mean that some things are not a nuisance or that other things are useless. It means only that we would define a commodity as the *lack* of good X for consumer D. Using this simple, legitimate trick, we no longer violate our assumption, since more of all commodities would now be preferred to less. And what about the uselessness of good X for consumer C? We preclude this case not because it cannot happen, but because it is not very interesting in a world of scarce resources.

All indifference curves have certain characteristics that should be noted. First, the fact that every commodity is defined so that more of it is preferred to less means that indifference curves must have a negative slope. This should be obvious. If more of both commodities is desirable and if one market basket has more of good Y, then it *must* have less of good X than another market basket if the two baskets are to be equivalent in the eyes of the consumer. Look at it another way: suppose that two market baskets are deemed to be equivalent, notwithstanding the fact that one contains more of both X and Y than the other. This would be the case if an indifference curve had a positive slope, but it would mean that either X or Y was not defined to ensure that more is preferred to less.

Second, the assumption that more is preferred to less means that higher indifference curves on graphs like Figure 2.1 connect market bundles that produce higher levels of consumer satisfaction. Curve B, for example, is preferred to curve A; i.e., it represents a higher level of consumer satisfaction. Why? Notice that curve B includes a basket with 4 pounds of meat and 3 pounds of potatoes while curve A associates 2 pounds of meat with 3 pounds of potatoes. Satisfaction must be higher along B than A as a result, because the extra 2 pounds of meat are worth something positive—they add to the consumer's satisfaction.

Third, transitivity in preferences combines with the "more is better" assumption to guarantee that indifference curves can never intersect. To prove this statement, let's show that a contradiction arises if two indifference curves are assumed to intersect. Take the case of two intersecting indifference curves in Figure 2.3. Market basket 1 is equivalent to market basket 2 along curve A. But notice that market basket 1 is also equivalent to market basket 3 along curve B. It follows, then, that market basket 2 must be equivalent to market basket 3. But this cannot be, since market basket 3 contains more of both commodities than market basket 2, and "more is better" means that basket 3 *must be preferred* to basket 2. We have our contradiction, and its only source is the intersection of curves A and B.

Figure 2.3 **INTERSECTING INDIFFERENCE CURVES: A CONTRADICTION OF THE ASSUMPTIONS**
If indifference curves A *and* B *were to intersect, then the consumer would be indifferent between market baskets 2 and 3. This is impossible since market basket 3 contains more of both commodities than market basket 2.*

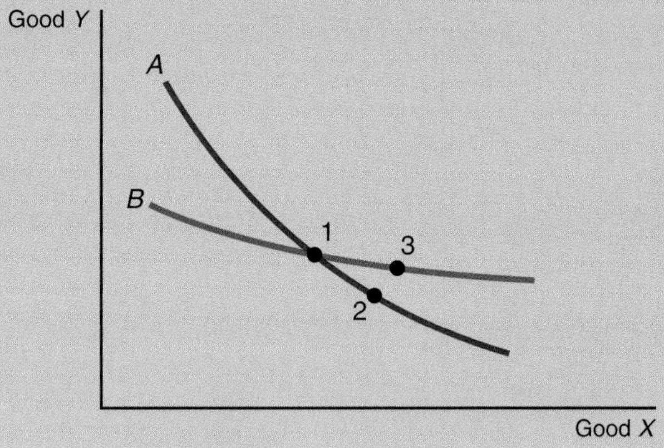

THE CONCEPT OF UTILITY

Utility

We stressed in the preceding section that the consumer's indifference map is a representation of his or her tastes. This certainly is true, since the consumer's indifference map can show each and every one of his or her indifference curves. This observation allows us to take the theory one step further. We can, in particular, use the indifference map of a particular consumer to attach a number, called a **utility,** to each of the market baskets that might confront our consumer. This utility indicates numerically the level of enjoyment or preference attached by this consumer to this market basket. And since all market baskets on a given indifference curve yield the same amount of satisfaction, they would all be assigned the same utility. Moreover, market baskets on higher indifference curves would have higher utilities than market baskets on lower indifference curves.

Attaching these utilities to market baskets allows us to tell at a glance which market baskets the consumer would prefer over other market baskets. If the utility attached to one market basket were higher than that attached to another, then the consumer would prefer the first over the second market basket. If the utility attached to the first market basket were lower than that of the second, then he or she would prefer the second over the first. If the utility attached to the first market basket were equal to that of the second, then he or she would be indifferent between the two market baskets.

How should we choose these utilities? Any way will do, as long as market baskets on the same indifference curve receive the same utility and market baskets on higher indifference curves receive higher utilities. Suppose that the consumer preferred market basket 1 to market basket 2 and market basket 2 to market basket 3, for example. Then the utility of market basket 1 must simply be higher than the utility of market basket 2 and the utility of market basket 2 must be higher than the utility of market basket 3. Do the numbers matter? No. Any set of numbers that preserves the ranking by conforming to these requirements would be an adequate measure of utility. The utility of market baskets 1, 2, and 3 could be 50, 40, and 30, or 10, 9, and 8. Either would be an adequate utility measure, since all that counts is that the utility of market basket 1 be higher than that of market basket 2, which in turn should be higher than that of market basket 3.

THE MARGINAL RATE OF SUBSTITUTION

Marginal rate of
substitution

Consumers can differ in the importance that they attach to an extra unit of a particular good. This is hardly news, of course, but the theory must accommodate this diversity. Economists have devised a measure called the **marginal rate of substitution** to do just that. The marginal rate of substitution is defined as the (maximum) number of units of good Y that the consumer would willingly sacrifice in return for an extra unit of good X while still keeping his or her level of satisfaction unchanged. Figure 2.4, for example, shows that the consumer would relinquish $(Y_2 - Y_1)$ units of good Y to receive $(X_2 - X_1)$ more units of good X, and this trade would leave him or her no better and no worse off. How do we know? Because both allocations lie on the same indifference curve. The marginal rate of substitution of good X for good Y in this case, then, is $(Y_2 - Y_1)/(X_2 - X_1)$. This is the number of units of good Y that must be given up per unit of good X received to maintain a constant level of satisfaction.

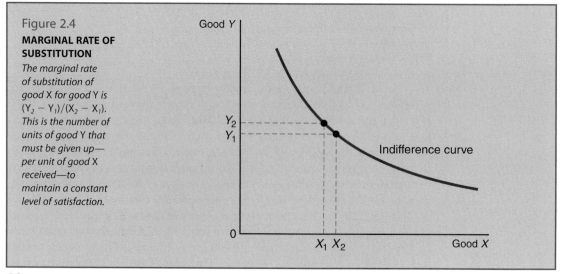

Figure 2.4

MARGINAL RATE OF SUBSTITUTION

The marginal rate of substitution of good X for good Y is $(Y_2 - Y_1)/(X_2 - X_1)$. This is the number of units of good Y that must be given up— per unit of good X received—to maintain a constant level of satisfaction.

More precisely, the marginal rate of substitution is equal to the absolute value of the slope of the indifference curve. Does this slope tell us anything about the relative importance of goods X and Y? Return to Figure 2.2 for a moment. Note there that the marginal rate of substitution of good X for good Y is higher for consumer A than it is for consumer B (because A's indifference curves are steeper than B's). We concluded earlier that X was more important to consumer A than to consumer B; this insight is confirmed now as we note that the marginal rate of substitution of good X for good Y is higher for consumer A than for consumer B.

Figure 2.2 is a bit misleading, though. The marginal rate of substitution will, in general, vary from point to point along a given indifference curve, since the slope of most indifference curves will vary from point to point. Indifference curves A and B in Figure 2.1 are more typical; they show that the marginal rate of substitution of potatoes for meat gets smaller as the consumer has more potatoes and less meat.

DECIPHERING THE SHAPES OF INDIFFERENCE CURVES

Figure 2.5 displays four different sets of indifference curves. Each portrays a set of preferences that can be differentiated by thinking in terms of the degree to which the consumption of good X influences the consumer's

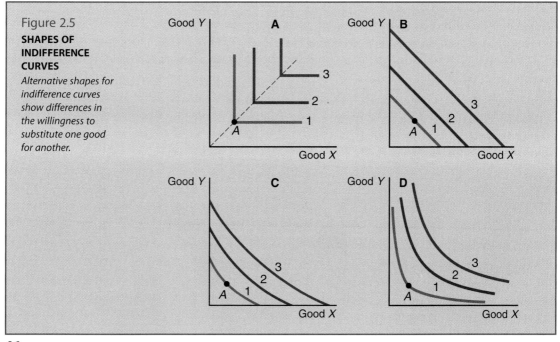

Figure 2.5

SHAPES OF INDIFFERENCE CURVES

Alternative shapes for indifference curves show differences in the willingness to substitute one good for another.

preference for good Y, and vice versa. Panel B displays perfect substitutes. The consumer would always be willing to trade one unit of Y for a fixed and constant number of units of X, regardless of how many units of Y were left and how many units of X were in hand. The marginal rate of substitution of X for Y is constant. Panel A displays the perfect complements case. Increasing the consumption of good X from the corner of any indifference curve *without increasing the consumption of* Y would have no effect on satisfaction or utility. Increasing the consumption of good Y without changing X would be equally futile. The marginal rate of substitution of X for Y is zero to the right of a corner and undefined at the corner. The exact proportion of joint consumption is a matter of preference. Panel C shows that goods X and Y can be substituted effectively to maintain any level of utility. Indeed, any level can be sustained by consuming only X or only Y. The marginal rate of substitution in panel C declines slowly as you move along an indifference curve to the right. (Panel B shows similar ability to sustain utility with only X or Y, but not intermediate substitution.) Panel D shows more limited substitution potential. The marginal rate of substitution declines quickly along any indifference curve. The indifference curves do not intersect the axes, so no level of satisfaction can be sustained by consuming good X without some Y or good Y without at least a little of good X.

Economists generally assume that indifference curves have the sort of shape exhibited by the curves in panels C and D of Figure 2.5. More specifically, the model of consumer behavior is built on an assumption that the marginal rate of substitution of one good (say, X) for any other good (say, Y) will fall as the consumption of good X increases. Put somewhat crudely, this amounts to assuming that a particular good becomes less important as it becomes more plentiful. In mathematical terms, this assumption means that indifference curves are convex. In other words, an indifference curve lies above its tangent, as illustrated in panel A of Figure 2.6. This contrasts with the case presented in panel B of Figure 2.6,

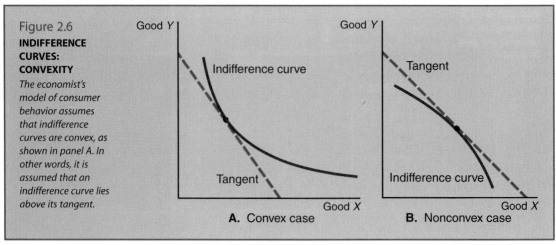

Figure 2.6
INDIFFERENCE CURVES: CONVEXITY
The economist's model of consumer behavior assumes that indifference curves are convex, as shown in panel A. In other words, it is assumed that an indifference curve lies above its tangent.

A. Convex case

B. Nonconvex case

where the indifference curve is concave. More will be made of this distinction later.[2]

| Example 2.3 | **Drug Advertising and Drug Prices** |

The importance of consumers' preferences in generating demand for products is, perhaps, seen most clearly in the amount of money that firms pay to manipulate those preferences. Consider the case of drug advertising by pharmaceutical companies. The Canadian government, in 1987, set drug prices equal to the average of prices in seven Western countries, and it has allowed those prices to increase at the rate of inflation ever since. As you might expect, Americans in the 1990s paid about 15 percent more for drugs than their Canadian counterparts—at least until 1998, when U.S. prices spiked. What happened? Advertising! Particularly for drugs for the same ailment for which there are close substitutes.

The U.S. Food and Drug Administration removed most controls on "direct-to-consumer" advertising in 1998, and pharmaceutical companies started to spend millions of dollars to influence consumers. Table 2.3 records promotional spending on 10 drugs in 1997 and 1998—the top 10 in 1998. The difference from 1997 to 1998 is dramatic. If you have watched television at all over the past few years, you have seen these advertisements; and you probably cannot even tell from the ads what condition goes with what drug. Notice that 3 of the top 10 are potential substitutes for allergy sufferers and 2 others (for whom advertising expenditures grew most quickly) compete directly with one another for the attention of people working to reduce their cholesterol levels. Why have the pharmaceutical companies spent so much money? Because influencing consumer preferences can pay off!

Table 2.3 PROMOTIONAL SPENDING (IN MILLIONS OF DOLLARS)	Drug	Targeted condition	1997	1998	Difference	% change
	Claritin	Allergies	185	267	82	44
	Propecia	Hair loss	92	111	19	21
	Zyrtec	Allergies	76	130	54	71
	Zyban	Smoking	64	85	21	33
	Pravachol	High cholesterol	60	111	51	85
	Allegra	Allergies	52	113	61	117
	Prilosec	Heartburn	50	102	52	104
	Zocor	High cholesterol	45	91	46	102
	Evista	Osteoporosis	42	93	51	121
	Prozac	Depression	41	101	60	146

SOURCE: K. Newman, "Drugs North of the Border," ABC News, May 2, 2001.

---

[2]The assumption of convexity may not always hold, but a discussion of cases where it fails belongs in a more advanced book.

THE BUDGET LINE

Economists also assume that the consumer is rational, given his or her tastes and preferences, in the sense that he or she tries to get on the highest possible indifference curve. In other words, we assume that the consumer tries to **maximize utility.** To do so, though, the consumer must consider factors other than his or her own tastes. He or she must consider the prices of various commodities and the level of his or her income, since both of these factors work to limit or to constrain the nature and size of the market basket that he or she can buy.

The consumer's money income is the amount of money that he or she can spend per unit of time.[3] If you had an infinite money income, then you would not have to worry about certain market baskets' being too expensive. You could simply buy whatever market basket you liked best—the market basket on your highest indifference curve. But no one has an unlimited money income. Even Bill Gates cannot achieve his highest indifference curve. And for us poorer folk, the problem is much more difficult, since our incomes are much smaller. What we can buy is much more severely constrained by our incomes.

Besides his or her money income, the consumer must also take into account the prices of all relevant commodities. The price of a commodity is the amount of money that the consumer must pay for a unit of that commodity. The higher prices are, the fewer units of a commodity can be bought with a given money income. For example, an income of $50,000 went a lot further when movies were 50 cents and sodas were 5 cents a bottle than it does now when movies are often $7 and sodas are $1 a can.

Let's see exactly how the consumer's money income and the level of commodity prices influence the nature and size of the market baskets available to the consumer. We assume, to make things simple but without distorting the essentials of choosing among a variety of goods, that the consumer can buy only two goods—good X and good Y. We assume, as well, that the consumer must spend all his or her money income on one or the other of these two commodities *and* that the consumer takes the prices of X and Y to be fixed. Clearly, then,

$$Q_x P_x + Q_y P_y = I, \qquad\qquad [2.1]$$

where Q_x is the amount the consumer buys of good X, Q_y is the amount the consumer buys of good Y, P_x is the price of good X, P_y is the price of good Y, and I is the consumer's money income.[4] If the price of good X were $1 a unit and the price of good Y were $2 a unit and the consumer's income were $100, for example, then $Q_x + 2Q_y = 100$.

---

[3]The amount that a consumer can borrow may, for some purposes, also be included as income. It would serve to increase the amount that the consumer could spend during the period.
[4]The consumer could also save some of his or her income. This model can handle savings by viewing future consumption as a commodity like any other.

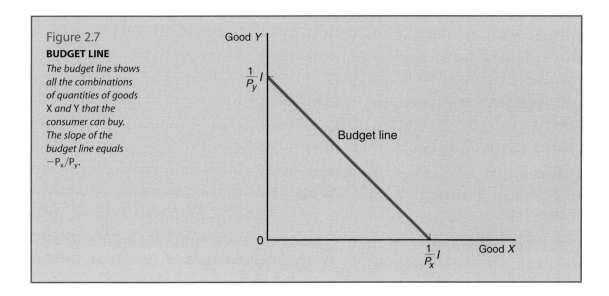

Figure 2.7

BUDGET LINE

The budget line shows all the combinations of quantities of goods X and Y that the consumer can buy. The slope of the budget line equals $-P_x/P_y$.

Good Y

$\frac{1}{P_y}I$

Budget line

0

$\frac{1}{P_x}I$ Good X

It is possible to plot the combinations of quantities of goods X and Y that the consumer can buy on the same graph as the indifference map. Solving Equation 2.1 for Q_y, we have

$$Q_y = \frac{I}{P_y} - \frac{P_x}{P_y}Q_x. \qquad [2.2]$$

Equation 2.2, which is a straight line, is plotted in Figure 2.7. The first term on the right-hand side of Equation 2.2 is the intercept of the line on the vertical axis. It is the amount of good Y that could be bought by the consumer if he or she spent all his or her income on good Y. The slope of the line is equal to the negative of the price ratio P_x/P_y.

Budget line   The straight line in Equation 2.2 is called the **budget line.** It shows all the combinations of quantities of good X and good Y that the consumer can buy with income I given prices P_x and P_y. In subsequent sections of this chapter, we will be interested in the effects of changes in product prices and money income on consumer behavior. These changes are reflected by changes in the budget line. Equation 2.2 shows that increases in money income increase the intercept of the budget line, but leave the slope of the budget line unaffected. Figure 2.8 shows the effect of an increase in income, with C representing the original budget line and D the budget line with the higher income. Conversely, reductions in income lower the intercept of the budget line. In Figure 2.8, E represents a budget line that might apply if income fell.

Equation 2.2 also shows what happens to the budget line if the price of good X changes. Increases in P_x increase the absolute value of the slope of the budget line; decreases in P_x decrease the absolute value of the slope. The vertical intercept of the line is unaffected by either change. Why? Because the amount of Y that the consumer can afford to buy if he or she devotes all of his or her income to Y is not at all dependent upon the price of good

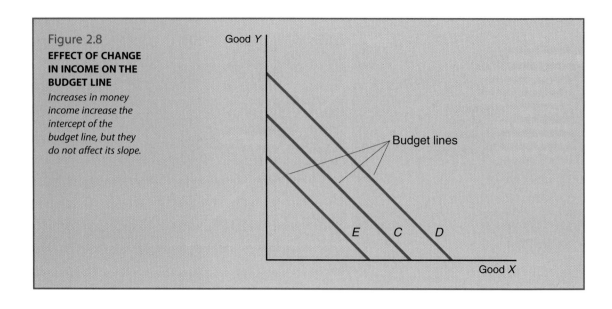

Figure 2.8

EFFECT OF CHANGE IN INCOME ON THE BUDGET LINE

Increases in money income increase the intercept of the budget line, but they do not affect its slope.

Good Y

Budget lines

E   C   D

Good X

X. Figure 2.9 shows the effect of changes in P_x on the budget line. Suppose that the original budget line is *F*. If P_x increased, then the budget line would rotate down to become *G*. If P_x were to fall, then the budget line would rotate up to something like *H*. It is easy to see why an increase in the price of good *X* results in the budget line's cutting the *x*-axis at a point closer to the origin. The point where the budget line cuts the *x*-axis equals the maximum number of units of good *X* that the consumer can buy with his or her fixed money income, and this number obviously is inversely related to the price of good *X*.

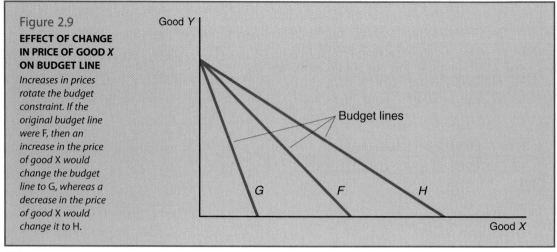

Figure 2.9

EFFECT OF CHANGE IN PRICE OF GOOD X ON BUDGET LINE

Increases in prices rotate the budget constraint. If the original budget line were F, then an increase in the price of good X would change the budget line to G, whereas a decrease in the price of good X would change it to H.

Good Y

Budget lines

G   F   H

Good X

Example 2.4

A wide variety of phone companies have begun to compete aggressively for customers by offering differentiated and sometimes very confusing rate schedules. Some, like MCI and Sprint, offer fixed long-distance rates per minute after receiving a subscription charge. Others, notably the newer digital cellular companies, offer free calls up to a certain threshold for a (typically higher) fixed fee. Ignoring time of day and geographical restrictions that confuse the issue even further, can we use budget constraints to explore circumstances under which a consumer might prefer one approach to the other? The answer is yes, and a few examples can show how.

Assume, to that end, that you have $50 per month to spend on phone calls and other forms of entertainment. What would your budget constraint look like if you were to sign up for a company (call it Spinx) that charges $20 to subscribe and then 10 cents per minute? Panel A of Figure 2.10 shows that you could afford $50 in entertainment with no calls with this plan. You could subscribe, make no calls, and have $30 for entertainment. Or you could afford any combination along line *AB* up to 300 minutes of calling time; then, of course, you would be shut out of other forms of entertainment.

Panel B repeats the construction for an alternative plan (from a company called Digit) that charges $30 per month for up to 200 minutes of free calling and 10 cents per minute thereafter. Line *CDE* is the applicable budget constraint in this case. Why? Because you could call for up to 200 minutes and enjoy $20 in other entertainment (segment *CD*) and add up to 200 additional minutes if you were willing to reduce your entertainment at the rate of 10 cents per minute of calling (segment *DE*).

Panel C puts the two constraints on the same graph. Segment *CDE* represents combinations of calling time and entertainment that could be achieved by contracting only with Digit; and segment *AB* represents combinations that could only be achieved by contracting with Spinx. So, it would appear that Spinx might be more attractive for customers who anticipate making fewer calls while Digit would appeal to people who like to talk on the phone. Could Digit do anything to make inroads into Spinx's "market"? Yes. You should be able to draw a new budget constraint to show that reducing its fee (to something like $25) for a reduced number of free minutes (to something like 150 minutes) would work. It would expand the area in which the budget constraint derived from its plan would lie outside and above the one associated with the Spinx plan.

EQUILIBRIUM OF THE CONSUMER

Given that the consumer is constrained to purchase one of the market baskets that lie on the budget line, which one will he or she choose? To answer this question, we assume, as noted in the previous section, that the

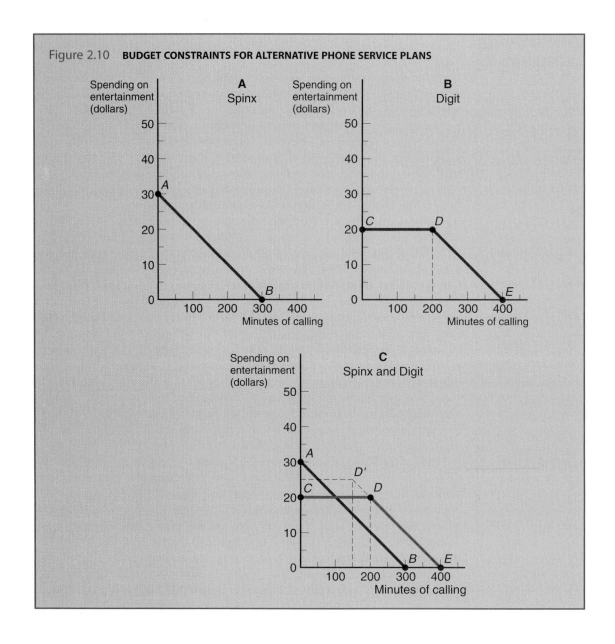

Figure 2.10 **BUDGET CONSTRAINTS FOR ALTERNATIVE PHONE SERVICE PLANS**

consumer tries to maximize utility. This assumption is so general and so reasonable that most people would accept it as a good approximation of reality. Although this is not to deny that some acts are irrational, by and large, people's deliberate actions seem to promote, not frustrate, the achievement of their goals. Even the ascetic, although his or her actions may seem irrational at first glance, can be regarded as attempting to maximize utility, if we recognize the peculiar nature of his or her tastes.

Going a step further, we note that the consumer may not succeed in maximizing utility, because of miscalculation or imperfect information. Indeed,

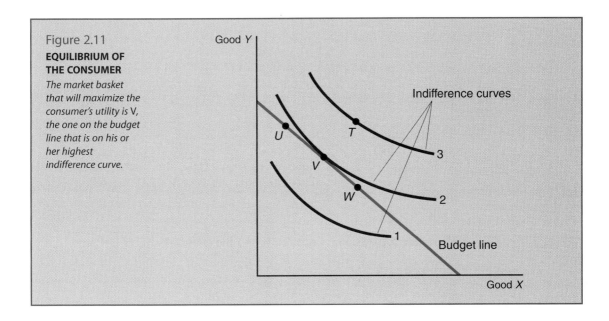

Figure 2.11

EQUILIBRIUM OF THE CONSUMER

The market basket that will maximize the consumer's utility is V, the one on the budget line that is on his or her highest indifference curve.

Good Y

Indifference curves

U

T

V

3

W

2

1

Budget line

Good X

the problem of maximizing utility may not be as simple as it looks. How many people, for example, know how much their cars really cost them? It is not that they do not know how to do the arithmetic, although even the brightest people have been known to have lapses in this regard. Rather, the calculation of that cost is very complicated. What should or should not be included in such a calculation? The answer is not always straightforward, and more will be said on this score in subsequent chapters. For the moment, simply note that consumers may not be able to achieve the maximization of utility—at least not right away.

What if the consumer were allowed some time to adapt and to learn? Perhaps he or she would eventually find the market basket that maximizes his or her utility. Let us define consumer equilibrium as a course of action that a consumer would not want to change as long as his or her money income and tastes remained the same and prices were constant. Equilibrium behavior would then lead our consumer to try as hard as possible to choose the market basket that maximizes his or her utility.

So, what market basket would maximize the consumer's utility? Figure 2.11 brings the consumer's indifference map together with his or her budget line. All the relevant information needed to answer this question is contained in Figure 2.11. The indifference map shows what the consumer's preferences are. Any market basket on indifference curve 3 would be preferred to any on indifference curve 2, and any market basket on indifference curve 2 would be preferred to any on indifference curve 1. The consumer would like to choose a market basket that lies on the highest possible indifference curve. This is the way to maximize his or her utility.

But not all market baskets are within reach. The budget line shows what the consumer could do with his or her money. He or she could choose any market basket such as *U*, *V*, or *W* on the budget line, but he or she could not obtain a market basket like *T*, which lies above the budget line. The consumer could also buy any market basket below the budget line, of course, but any such market basket would be on a lower indifference curve than at least one market basket that lies on the budget line, and so would not be chosen. Since this is the case, the market basket that would maximize the consumer's utility is one that simultaneously lies on the budget line *and* on his or her highest feasible indifference curve. This is point *V* in Figure 2.11. It can readily be seen that this market basket is characterized by the tangency of the budget line to the highest possible indifference curve. The rational consumer would, according to our model, strive for market basket *V*, and *V* would be predicted to be an equilibrium.

Microlink 2.1   Budget Constraints and the Determinants of Demand

Chapter 1 highlighted several determinants of demand for any good *X*. They included consumer tastes, consumer income, the price of *X*, and the prices of other goods. It is important to notice that the structure of consumer theory described here incorporates all of these. Tastes are reflected in preferences and thus utility functions. If tastes change (for any good, not just *X*), then the utility function changes and the demand for *X* can change. Meanwhile, prices and income enter directly through the budget constraint. More or less income moves the budget constraint out or in relative to the origin of graphs like Figure 2.11, and the demand for *X* can change. Higher or lower prices rotate the budget constraint, and the demand for *X* can change, again.

| Example 2.5 | **Budget Allocation by New York State** |

Just like consumers, government agencies have to allocate their scarce resources under budget constraints. In doing so, they make decisions that we can analyze with the consumer theory developed in this chapter. Consider a real case from New York State. The government in Albany received about $3 billion from federal transportation grants and a state gasoline tax in 1993. These funds were supposed to be spent on highways or mass transit (subways, buses, and urban rail lines). Either category of investment could contribute to meeting the transportation needs of the state's population. How should New York allocate this sum?

To answer this question, view New York State as a consumer, and regard highways and mass transit as two goods that the state government can buy. Each has a price, and the total amount that can be spent on them both is fixed. Assume that the state government is interested in maximizing the effectiveness of the state's transportation system, and draw indifference curves across combinations of extra miles of highway and extra miles of mass transit. The bigger the expected addition to either capability, the higher the indifference curve. As a result, the point on the budget line (which can be derived from the price of a mile of highway, the price

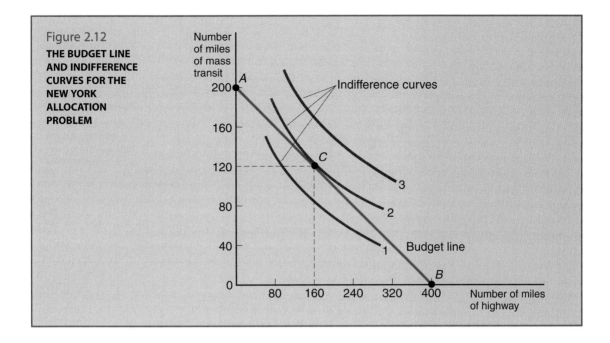

Figure 2.12

THE BUDGET LINE AND INDIFFERENCE CURVES FOR THE NEW YORK ALLOCATION PROBLEM

of a mile of mass transit, and the total budget to be allocated) that lies on the highest indifference curve will indicate the optimal allocation of the budget.

To attack the problem in this way, of course, the first step is to determine various "indifference curves" for the state government. Figure 2.12 shows what they might look like. As in Figure 2.1, each indifference curve slopes downward, since highways can be substituted for mass transit, and vice versa. Moreover, they are likely to be convex. What exactly does each indifference curve mean? Consider indifference curve 1. Each point on this indifference curve represents a combination of highways and mass transit that results in the same addition to transportation capability. That is to say, each point offers the same expected addition to the state's ability to transport people quickly and safely. The objective of state government in this context can now be viewed as maximizing the state's transportation capability. In other words, transportation capability (measured in this way) is a measure of this consumer's "utility." The consumer is indifferent among all the points on curve 1. And the consumer clearly prefers indifference curve 2 to indifference curve 1, because points on indifference curve 2 result in more transportation capability than those on indifference curve 1.

Having constructed the indifference curves, the next step is to construct the appropriate budget line. The state of New York had $3 billion to spend. Let's say each mile of mass transit costs $15 million and each mile of highway costs $7.5 million. The resulting budget line is *AB*. Given this budget line and the indifference map, the problem boils down to finding the point on the budget line that lies on the highest indifference curve. A point like

C, where state government funds the construction of 120 miles of mass transit and 160 miles of highways, seems to fit the bill.

Economic analysis of this kind has played an important role in policy-making in many government agencies in recent years. In practice, of course, the measurement of "transportation capability" or "social worth" often presents an extremely difficult problem. It is, in all honesty, not always possible to draw curves like 1, 2, and 3 with great accuracy. This does not mean that this type of analysis is not useful, though. On the contrary, it has proved very useful, since it provides a correct way of thinking about the problem. It focuses attention on the relevant factors and puts them in their proper places.

This example also illustrates the fact that most aspects of microeconomics are concerned with means to achieve specified ends and not with the choice of ends. Economists were interested in maximizing the transportation capacity to be obtained from a given budget in this case, but they took as given the hypothesis that it was a good thing to increase transportation capacity. In other words, they took as given the fact that the "utility" of the "consumer" should be increased. This hypothesis could be wrong in some circumstances. For example, suppose that the relevant decision-makers in the state government wanted to maximize their power and influence among voters rather than the state's transportation capacity. The same techniques could be used to look for their best strategy. All that would be required is a reinterpretation of the indifference curves.

SOURCE: *New York Times*, May 25, 1992.

CORNER SOLUTIONS

Although we have just stated that the consumer will choose the market basket for which the budget line is tangent to an indifference curve (market basket *V* in Figure 2.11), there are exceptions. The consumer may, in particular, consume none of some goods because even tiny amounts of them (or the minimum amount of them that can be bought) are worth less to the consumer than they cost. Although your money income may permit you to buy some Dom Perignon champagne (which you would presumably enjoy), you may not purchase any because even one swallow would be worth less to you than it would cost to purchase.

Figure 2.13 shows this situation graphically. We suppose, again for simplicity, that there are only two goods: Dom Perignon champagne and good *Y*. Given the position of the consumer's indifference curves, he or she will maximize utility by choosing market basket *M*, which contains all good *Y* and no Dom Perignon champagne at all. This market basket maximizes the consumer's utility because it is on a higher indifference curve than any other market basket on the budget line. It is a **corner solution,** in which the budget line reaches the highest achievable indifference curve along an axis (in this case, the vertical axis).

Corner solution

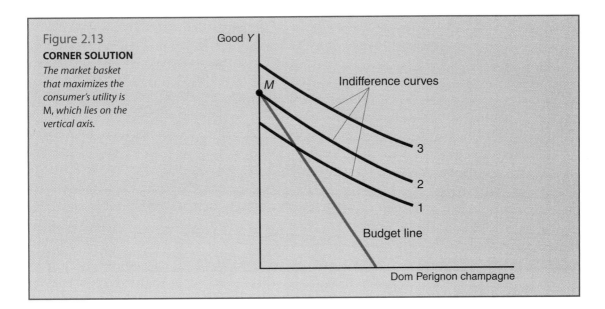

Figure 2.13

CORNER SOLUTION

The market basket that maximizes the consumer's utility is M, which lies on the vertical axis.

Good Y

M

Indifference curves

3

2

1

Budget line

Dom Perignon champagne

Example 2.6   **The Food Stamp Program**

The United States food stamp program included about 20 million individuals in 1990. This example explores one issue raised by the structure of the program—to what extent did the creation of an "interior corner" designed to guarantee a minimum level of food consumption restrict choice and actually reduce welfare? To that end, suppose that an eligible family receives food stamps that can be exchanged for $70 worth of food per week. Assume, as well, that this family also receives a weekly income of $250 from other sources.

This family's budget constraint is line *CD* in Panel A of Figure 2.14 without food stamps. *C* is the quantity of nonfood items that the family can buy with its entire income ($250) and *D* is the quantity of food that $250 will buy. The family's budget line with food stamps is *CEF* in panel A. *C* remains the quantity of nonfood items the family could buy. At point *E* the family uses all of its food stamps for food and spends all of its money income on nonfood items. At point *F* the family uses all of its food stamps and spends all of its money income on food. Indifference curve 1 indicates equilibrium at the interior corner, point *E*, so that the food stamps cover the entire food budget. Different preferences could put the equilibrium along segment *EF*.

Now suppose that the family were given $70 in cash and not food stamps. Its budget line would then be *GF* in panel B. The budget line would be higher because the family would have received an extra $70, but it would be parallel to the old budget line *CD* because the relative prices of food and other stuff would not change. With this budget line, the family could reach point *H* on indifference curve 2. Along budget line *CEF*, though, the best

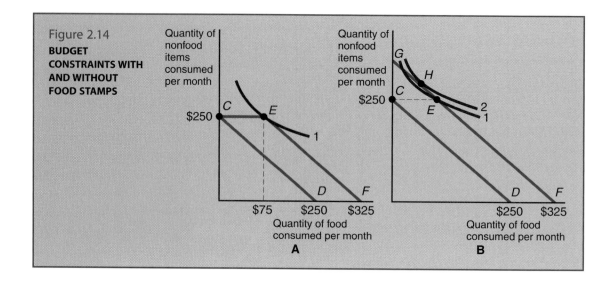

Figure 2.14
BUDGET CONSTRAINTS WITH AND WITHOUT FOOD STAMPS

it could do would be to reach point *E* on indifference curve 1. The family would achieve a higher level of satisfaction if it received the cash rather than the food because curve 2 is higher than curve 1. Not all families have indifference curves of this sort, though. Some have indifference curves for which the level of satisfaction with the food would be the same as it would be with the cash (with indifference curves tangent to the budget line along segment *EF* of either budget line).[5]

CORNER SOLUTIONS AND DIMINISHING MARGINAL RATES OF SUBSTITUTION

The theory can suggest another reason why a corner solution might appear, but it is less satisfying when applied to the real world. You will recall that we are assuming that the marginal rate of substitution of, for example, *X* for *Y* declines along any indifference curve as the level of consumption of *X* increases. It was this assumption that allowed us to draw convex indifference curves. We now ask a logical question: What would happen if this were not the case? Suppose that the marginal rate of substitution actually *rose* as we moved along an indifference curve? More to the point, why is it necessary to make any assumption about the way in which the marginal rate of substitution changes as a consumer moves along an indifference curve?

The first effect of an increasing marginal rate of substitution is benign enough. It would simply mean that indifference curves would be nonconvex,

[5]For further discussion, see K. Clarkson, "Welfare Benefits of the Food Stamp Program," *Southern Economic Journal*, July 1976; and M. MacDonald, *Food, Stamps, and Income Maintenance* (New York: Academic Press, 1977).

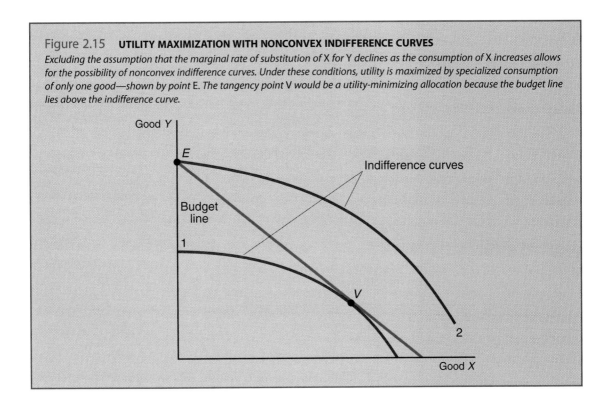

Figure 2.15 UTILITY MAXIMIZATION WITH NONCONVEX INDIFFERENCE CURVES

Excluding the assumption that the marginal rate of substitution of X for Y declines as the consumption of X increases allows for the possibility of nonconvex indifference curves. Under these conditions, utility is maximized by specialized consumption of only one good—shown by point E. The tangency point V would be a utility-minimizing allocation because the budget line lies above the indifference curve.

as will be seen in Figure 2.16 later in this chapter. Figure 2.15 shows the implications of this alternative shape on the solution to the consumer's utility maximization problem. It shows, more specifically, a market basket *V* characterized by the tangency of indifference curve 1 with the budget line, but this point now corresponds to the *minimum* level of utility that could be achieved with the prescribed budget. Indeed, moving to a point like *E* (on the vertical axis) would achieve the highest utility in this case.

In fact, nonconvex indifference curves always result in the maximum utility being along one of the axes. In other words, a nonconvex indifference curve always leads to an equilibrium in which the consumer spends all of his or her money on *a single good*. A theory based on this shape would therefore predict that the world should be populated with individuals who each consume only one good. They might not all choose the same good, but we would never see rational people spreading their money around.

Do we observe a world like that? Hardly! The empirical evidence certainly contradicts this conclusion, and so we must dismiss the theory that led us to that conclusion. Is it mathematically possible that the marginal rate of substitution not decline along an indifference curve? Sure. But we get results that describe reality only if we preclude that case—and so we assume that the marginal rate of substitution does indeed decline along the indifference curve.

Microlink 2.2   Evaluating Models

Chapter 1 included accurate predictions of behavior among the fundamental criteria against which models are evaluated. Much will be made later about the accuracy of estimates of demand based on consumer theory, but one possible model of consumer preferences can be dismissed on the basis of the predictions that it would support. We noted here that concave indifference curves with increasing marginal rates of substitution would predict that all consumers would try to consume only one good. This is a terrible prediction of consumer behavior, and so it can be dismissed out of hand. And it follows that the marginal rate of substitution must fall for most pairs of goods as we move along any indifference curve.

ORDINAL AND CARDINAL UTILITY

We have seen that economists assume that the amount of satisfaction a consumer gets from a particular market basket can be measured by its utility. Following the lead of E. Slutsky, Vilfredo Pareto, John Hicks, and others, economists generally assume that utility is measurable in an ordinal sense, which means that a consumer can only rank market baskets with regard to the satisfaction they give him or her.[6] For example, you may be able to say with assurance that you prefer two tickets to Final Four over two tickets to the San Francisco Opera, but you may not be able to say *how much* more satisfaction you get from the former than from the latter. For an ordinal measurement of utility, this is adequate, since all that is needed is a ranking.

Ordinal utility

Readers used to thinking of numbers with units attached may find this notion unsettling. The idea, though, is simple. Whereas architects might want to know the precise length and width of two tables so that they can determine which would fit most functionally into a particular space, economists would be satisfied with simply knowing which is larger. So, the architect would insist on knowing that table *A* was, say, 30 inches wide by 60 inches long while table *B* was 28 inches by 50 inches (or 0.75 meters by 1.50 meters versus 0.70 meters by 1.25 meters), but the economist interested in only the ordinal size ranking would not care if the tables were measured in inches, meters, or lengths of asparagus.

For several great nineteenth-century economists such as William Stanley Jevons of England, Karl Menger of Austria, and Leon Walras of France, though, utility was measurable in a cardinal sense. That meant that the difference between two measurements was itself numerically significant, and units would matter. If I weigh 140 pounds and you weigh 155 pounds, then the difference between these measurements has numerical significance. It says that I weigh 15 pounds less than you do, and that is a different circumstance

---

[6]For example, see J. Hicks, *Value and Capital* (New York: Oxford University Press, 1946); H. Hotelling, "Demand Functions with Limited Budgets," *Econometrica* 3 (January 1935); and P. Samuelson, *Foundations of Economic Analysis* (Cambridge, Mass.: Harvard University Press, 1947).

than if I weighed 20 pounds less, or 10 pounds less. Moreover, if the difference between Arnold Schwarzenegger's weight and Whoopi Goldberg's weight is 70 pounds, then it follows that the difference between my weight and yours is less than the difference between Arnold Schwarzenegger's weight and Whoopi Goldberg's. According to most nineteenth-century economists, utility was measurable in the same cardinal sense.

Our discussion in this chapter was based on the modern assumption that utility is ordinally measurable, which is less restrictive than the older assumption that utility is cardinally measurable. That is, we need not assume that a consumer can answer questions like, How much extra satisfaction will you get from a second helping of mashed potatoes? However, if one is willing to assume that the consumer can characterize his or her preferences by attaching a cardinal utility to each market basket, then it is possible to obtain some additional results. A few of these results are presented in this part of the chapter.

To make things simple so that we can focus on the important factors at work here, let's assume that there are only two goods, food and medicine. Consider a consumer making choices concerning how much of each good to buy. In contrast to our earlier discussion in this chapter, suppose that it is possible to measure the amount of satisfaction that the consumer gets from each market basket by its cardinal utility. For example, the utility attached to the market basket containing 2 pounds of food and 1 ounce of medicine may be 13 utils, and the utility attached to the market basket containing 1 pound *Util* of food and 1 ounce of medicine may be 8 utils. (A **util** is the traditional unit in which utility is expressed.)

MARGINAL UTILITY

Total utility
Marginal utility
It is important to distinguish between **total utility** and **marginal utility.** The total utility of a market basket is the number described in the previous paragraph, whereas the marginal utility measures the additional satisfaction derived from an additional unit of a commodity (when the levels of consumption of all other commodities are held constant). To see how marginal utility is obtained, let's take a close look at Table 2.4. The total utility that the consumer derives from the consumption of various amounts of food is given in the middle column of this table. For simplicity, we assume for the moment that only food is consumed (or that the amount of medicine consumed is fixed at some arbitrary level). The marginal utility, shown in the right-hand column, is the extra utility derived from each amount of food over and above the utility derived from 1 pound less of food. It equals the difference between the total utility of a certain amount of food and the total utility of 1 pound less of food.[7]

---

[7]Marginal utility is, more precisely, the ratio of the change in utility caused by a change in consumption of one good under the assumption that the consumption of all other goods is fixed. Expressed more mathematically, it is the partial derivative of the utility function with respect to any one of its consumption arguments.

Table 2.4	Pounds of food	Total utility (utils)	Marginal utility (utils)[a]
CONSUMER'S TOTAL AND MARGINAL UTILITIES FROM CONSUMING VARIOUS AMOUNTS OF FOOD PER DAY	0	0	—
	1	4	4 (= 4 − 0)
	2	9	5 (= 9 − 4)
	3	13	4 (= 13 − 9)
	4	16	3 (= 16 − 13)
	5	18	2 (= 18 − 16)

[a]These figures pertain to the interval between the indicated number of pounds of food and 1 pound less than the indicated number. This table assumes that no medicine is consumed.

For example, Table 2.4 indicates that the total utility of 3 pounds of food is 13 utils. This is to be interpreted as a measure of the total amount of satisfaction that the consumer gets from this much food. In contrast, the marginal utility of 3 pounds of food is the extra utility obtained from the third pound of food. It is, in other words, the 13 utils of total utility derived from 3 pounds of food less the 9 utils of total utility derived from 2 pounds of food. Specifically, it is 4 utils. Similarly, the total utility of 2 pounds of food is 9 utils while the marginal utility of the second pound of food is 5 utils (9 utils in total utility from 2 pounds of food less the 4 utils in total utility from 1 pound of food).

It seems reasonable to believe that the extra satisfaction derived from the last unit of the commodity consumed should decline as a person consumes more and more of a particular commodity (at least eventually). If a person consumed 2 pounds of food in a particular period of time, for example, then he or she might be well satisfied. If he or she consumed 3 pounds of food in the same period of time, though, the third pound of food is likely to yield less satisfaction than the second. And if he or she consumed a fourth pound of food in the same period of time, then this additional consumption is likely to yield less satisfaction than preceding pounds. And so on.

Law of diminishing marginal utility

This assumption or hypothesis is often called the **law of diminishing marginal utility.** This law states that, as a person consumes more and more of a given commodity (the consumption of other commodities being held constant), the marginal utility of the commodity eventually will tend to decline. In other words, it states that the relationship between the marginal utility of a commodity and the amount consumed will be like that shown in Table 2.4. Beyond some point (2 pounds of food in Table 2.4), the marginal utility declines as the amount consumed increases.

BUDGET ALLOCATION RULE

Budget allocation rule for cardinal utility

If the law of diminishing marginal utility holds true, *then the utility-maximizing consumer will allocate his or her expenditures among commodities so that, for every commodity purchased, the marginal utility of the commodity*

Table 2.5	Amount of each commodity consumed (in dollars)	Marginal utility of food (utils)	Marginal utility of medicine (utils)
CONSUMER'S MARGINAL UTILITY FROM CONSUMING VARIOUS AMOUNTS OF FOOD AND MEDICINE PER DAY	1	9	4
	2	7	3
	3	4	2
	4	3	1
	5	2	0

is proportional to its price. In the case of the consumer whose choices are limited to food and medicine, the optimal market basket is the one where

$$\frac{MU_F}{P_F} = \frac{MU_M}{P_M}, \qquad [2.3]$$

where MU_F is the marginal utility of food, MU_M is the marginal utility of medicine, P_F is the price of a pound of food, and P_M is the price of an ounce of medicine. This is a famous result. The rest of this chapter is devoted to an explanation of why it is true.

It is convenient to begin the explanation by pointing out that MU_F/P_F is the marginal utility of the last dollar's worth of food and that MU_M/P_M is the marginal utility of the last dollar's worth of medicine. Why? First consider the case of food. Since MU_F is the extra utility of the last pound of food bought, and since P_F is the price of this last pound, the extra utility of the last dollar's worth of food must be MU_F/P_F. For example, if the last pound of food resulted in an extra utility of 4 utils and this pound cost \$2, then the extra utility from the last dollar's worth of food would be

$$\frac{4 \text{ utils in additional utility for one unit additional consumption}}{\$2 \text{ per unit of consumption}} = 2 \text{ utils.}$$

In other words, the marginal utility of the last dollar's worth of food is 2 utils.

Since MU_F/P_F is the marginal utility of the last dollar's worth of food and MU_M/P_M is the marginal utility of the last dollar's worth of medicine, Equation 2.3 really means that the rational consumer will choose a market basket for which the marginal utility of the last dollar spent on all commodities purchased is the same. To see why this must be so, consider the numerical example described in Table 2.5, it shows the marginal utility that the consumer derives from various amounts of food and medicine. Rather than measuring food and medicine in physical units, we measure them in Table 2.5 in terms of the amount of money spent on them.

Given the information in Table 2.5, how much of each commodity should the consumer buy if his or her money income is only \$4? Clearly, the first dollar the consumer spends should be on food, since it would yield a marginal utility of 9. The second dollar should also be spent on food since a second dollar's worth of food has a marginal utility of 7 whereas the first dollar's worth of medicine has a marginal utility of only 4. The total (maximum) utility derived from the $2 of expenditure would thus be $9 + 7 = 16$.[8] The marginal utility of the third dollar would be 4 if it were spent on more food, but it would also be 4 if it were spent on medicine. Suppose that the consumer chose more food. The total utility derived from the $3 of expenditure would then be $9 + 7 + 4 = 20$. What about the final dollar? Its marginal utility would be 3 if it were spent on more food and 4 if it were spent on medicine. The consumer should therefore spend it on medicine, and so the total utility derived from all $4 of expenditure would be $9 + 7 + 4 + 4 = 24$.

Clearly, the consumer, if rational, would allocate $3 of his or her income to food and $1 to medicine. This is the equilibrium market basket—the market basket that maximizes the consumer's satisfaction. The important thing to note is that this market basket conforms to the budget allocation rule in Equation 2.3. The marginal utility derived from the last dollar spent on food would equal the marginal utility derived from the last dollar spent on medicine. Both would be 4. And so this market basket would satisfy Equation 2.3. The marginal utility of the last dollar spent on all commodities purchased is the same.

ORDINAL UTILITY REVISITED

Budget allocation rule for ordinal utility The budget allocation rule in Equation 2.3 can be derived from more general conditions. Since this rule provides valuable insight into rational decision-making, it should be understood. Its direct applicability is apparently limited by the fact that utility ordinarily is not cardinally measurable, but its more general applicability is not. To see why, we note that the ratio of marginal utilities equaled the marginal rate of substitution. Denoting the marginal rate of substitution of food for medicine by MRS_{FM}, for example, then

$$MRS_{FM} = \frac{MU_F}{MU_M}. \qquad [2.4]$$

But Equation 2.3 can easily be rewritten as

$$\frac{MU_F}{MU_M} = \frac{P_F}{P_M}. \qquad [2.5]$$

Equations 2.3 and 2.5 both represent equivalent characterizations of the condition that must be achieved by a rational consumer if his or her cardinal utility is to be maximized subject to a budget constraint. Combining Equations 2.5 and 2.4, though, we see that

$$MRS_{FM} = \frac{MU_F}{MU_M} = \frac{P_F}{P_M}. \qquad [2.6]$$

[8]Since the marginal utility is the extra utility obtained from each dollar spent, the total utility from the total expenditure must be the sum of the marginal utilities of the individual dollars of expenditure.

We see in Equation 2.6 that the characterization of consumer equilibrium reflected in Equation 2.3 can easily be manipulated to a form that is equivalent to the condition that must be achieved if consumers armed only with ordinal utility reflections of their preferences are to maximize their satisfaction subject to the same budget constraint. How? Recall from our earlier discussion in this chapter that consumer equilibrium in this context requires that the highest possible indifference curve be tangent with the budget constraint at the equilibrium point (call it E). But the tangency of the indifference curve and the budget constraint at point E would mean that the slopes of both lines were equal at E; i.e., the slope of the indifference curve ($= -MRS = -MU_F/MU_M$) in equilibrium must equal the slope of the budget constraint ($= -P_F/P_M$). And that is exactly the condition imposed on equilibrium by Equation 2.5.

REVEALED PREFERENCE

We have assumed, thus far, that the consumer's indifference curves were measured by asking him or her to choose between various market baskets. After thinking about this procedure for a short while, though, you might object that people cannot or will not provide trustworthy answers to direct questions about their preferences. The man who surreptitiously visits an erotic stage show may claim that such shows are sinful and repugnant to him. Is there any way to measure a person's indifference curves other than by asking direct questions concerning the person's tastes? Is there any way to deduce a consumer's indifference curves from his or her actual behavior rather than from his or her professed preferences?

Revealed preference   The theory of **revealed preference** is an attempt to do just that. We assume that we can vary the consumer's money income and the prices he or she faces. Then, assuming that the consumer's tastes remain fixed during the course of the experiment, we see how he or she reacts to the various levels of money income and prices. The basic idea behind the formulation and interpretation of the experiments is as follows. The consumer may choose one market basket over a second market basket either because he or she prefers the first to the second or because the first is cheaper than the second. Thus, if we vary prices so that the first market basket is not cheaper than the second and if the first is still chosen over the second, then we can be sure that the first market basket is preferred over the second.

To see how the process might work, consider the case of two commodities, good X and good Y. Let point A in Figure 2.16 represent the market basket (amount a of good X and a' of good Y) that the consumer purchases when his or her budget line is QQ'. It follows that every other point (each representing a market basket) on or below QQ' is revealed to be inferior to A in the eyes of this consumer. Why? Because all of these points were available to the consumer when he or she chose A. In addition, every point in the darkened area above and to the right of A is

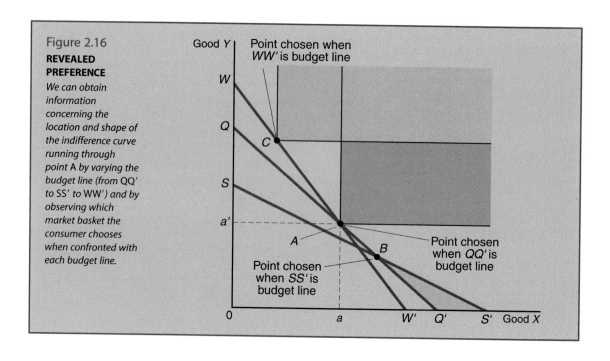

Figure 2.16

REVEALED PREFERENCE

We can obtain information concerning the location and shape of the indifference curve running through point A by varying the budget line (from QQ' to SS' to WW') and by observing which market basket the consumer chooses when confronted with each budget line.

preferred to *A*. Why? Because they all represent market baskets with at least as much of both commodities as *A*. The indifference curve running through point *A* must therefore lie between the budget line and the darkened area.

To get a better idea of the location and shape of this indifference curve, consider any other point on *QQ'*. The market basket represented by point *B*, for example, is inferior to *A*. There is, though, some budget line that will make the consumer purchase *B*. Suppose that this budget line is *SS'*. We can now deduce that the shaded triangle under *SS'* and above *QQ'* also contains points that are inferior to *A* in the eyes of the consumer. How do we know that? Every point there is inferior to *B*, and *B* is inferior to *A*. This procedure can be used to narrow the zone of ignorance below and to the right of *A* where we are unsure whether points are inferior or superior to *A*. To narrow the corresponding zone of ignorance above and to the left of *A*, we adopt the following procedure. We establish a new budget line, *WW'*, that includes point *A* and a new set of prices. Let *C* be the market basket that the consumer would choose against this budget line. Since *C* is no more expensive than *A* under these conditions, *C* must be preferred to *A*. All points above and to the right of *C* must also be preferred to *A* because they are preferred to *C*, and *C* is preferred to *A*.

We could eventually derive an indifference curve if these procedures were repeated over and over again, but this would be a long and laborious process. The theory of revealed preference is more important as a means of demonstrating that indifference curves can, in principle, be derived in this way than it is as a means of actually deriving them.

Microlink 2.3 Equilibrium in Different Contexts

The notion of market equilibrium developed in Chapter 1 and the concept of consumer equilibrium described here may seem quite different, but they are based on a common idea. An economic situation is in equilibrium if none of the economic actors involved have any incentive to change their behavior. Markets are in equilibrium at a specific price when the quantity willingly supplied equals the quantity willingly demanded. Consumer equilibrium is similarly sustained when individuals achieve as much utility as possible given the constraints of their budgets so that they cannot find any affordable substitutions that would improve their well-being. The concept of equilibrium is central to microeconomics, and it will crop up in other contexts as you work through the book.

SUMMARY

1. We assume that, when confronted with two market baskets, a consumer can say which one is preferred, or whether he or she is indifferent between them. We also assume that the consumer's tastes are transitive and that a commodity is defined in such a way that more is preferred to less.

2. An indifference curve is the locus of points representing market baskets among which the consumer is indifferent. A consumer's tastes can be represented by a set of indifference curves, or an indifference map. An indifference curve must have a negative slope, and two indifference curves cannot intersect. Market baskets on higher indifference curves provide more satisfaction than those on lower indifference curves.

3. Utility is a number that indexes the level of satisfaction derived from a particular market basket. Market baskets with higher utilities are preferred over market baskets with lower utilities. The consumer is assumed to be rational in the sense that he or she tries to maximize utility.

4. The slope of an indifference curve multiplied by -1 gives the marginal rate of substitution. The marginal rate of substitution shows approximately how many units of one good must be given up if the consumer, after receiving an extra unit of another good, is to maintain a constant level of satisfaction. We assume that the marginal rate of substitution declines as consumers move along an indifference curve.

5. The budget line indicates all the combinations of goods that the consumer can buy given his or her money income and the level of each price. In equilibrium, we would expect the consumer to attain the highest level of satisfaction that is compatible with the budget line. This means that the consumer will choose the market basket on the budget line that is on the highest indifference curve. This market basket is at a point where the budget line is tangent to an indifference curve (unless there is a corner solution).

6. The model of consumer behavior presented in this chapter has been used to solve problems of budget allocation by government agencies. To illustrate its use, we took up a case study involving a state's expenditures on transportation.

QUESTIONS/ PROBLEMS

1. In the figure on the next page, we show one of Ellen White's indifference curves and her budget line. If the price of good *A* is $50, what is Ms. White's income? What is the equation for her budget line? What is the slope of the budget line? What is the price of good *B*? What is her marginal rate of substitution in equilibrium?

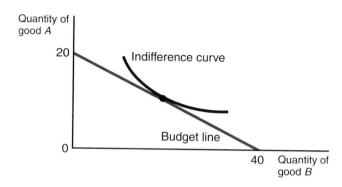

2. "A survey shows that most people would prefer to drive a Lexus than a Honda." What exactly does this mean? If this is true, why do more people drive Hondas than Lexuses?

3. One of Patricia Jones's indifference curves includes the market baskets shown in the table below. Each of these market baskets gives her equal satisfaction.

Market basket	Meat (pounds)	Potatoes (pounds)
1	2	8
2	3	7
3	4	6
4	5	5
5	6	4
6	7	3
7	8	2
8	9	1

What is the marginal rate of substitution of potatoes for meat in this case? How does the marginal rate of substitution vary as Ms. Jones consumes more meat and less potatoes? Is this realistic? If all of her indifference curves were shaped like the one portrayed here, how much meat would Ms. Jones purchase if the price of meat were twice the price of potatoes? 50 percent higher? 50 percent lower?

4. Martin Cole purchases 100 loaves of bread per year when the price is $1 per loaf. The price increases to $1.50. To offset the harm to Martin, his father gives him $50 a year. Will Martin be better or worse off after the price increase plus the gift than he was before? Will his consumption of bread increase or decrease? Draw the appropriate indifference curve graphs to show that your answer depends on the degree to which bread substitutes for other goods.

5. "Is utility some kind of glow or warmth, or is it just happiness? The answer is irrelevant; all that counts is that we can assign numbers to entities or conditions which a person can strive to realize." Comment on this argument. Do you agree with it? Why or why not? Do the numbers have to be precise, or do they simply have to reflect preferences in the sense that preferred bundles of goods are always assigned higher numbers?

6. Suppose that consumers in San Francisco pay twice as much for apples as they do for pears, while consumers in Los Angeles pay only 50 percent more for apples than they do for pears. If consumers in both cities maximize utility,

will the marginal rate of substitution of pears for apples be the same in San Francisco as in Los Angeles? If not, in which city will it be higher? Does your answer depend on the relative incomes of people living in L.A. or San Francisco? Why or why not? Offer some thoughts about why prices in the same state might be so different.

7. A consumer is willing to trade 2 pounds of steak for 3 pounds of hamburger. He currently is purchasing as much steak as hamburger per month. The price of steak is twice that of hamburger. Should he increase his consumption of hamburger and reduce his consumption of steak? Or should he reduce his consumption of hamburger and increase his consumption of steak? How would your answer change if the price of steak were 50 percent higher than hamburger?

8. Suppose that James Gray spends his entire income on goods X and Y. The marginal utility of each good is independent of the amount consumed of the other good; values are recorded in the table below. The price of X is $100 and the price of Y is $500.

Number of units	Mr. Gray's marginal utility (utils)	
of good consumed	Good X	Good Y
1	20	50
2	18	45
3	16	40
4	13	35
5	10	30
6	6	25
7	4	20
8	2	15

If Mr. Gray has an income of $1,000 per month, how many units of each good should he purchase? What if his income were $2,000 per month? Would his consumption of both goods change proportionately? Why or why not?

9. Steve Walcott spends a total of $4,000 per month on goods A and B. The price of A is $200 per unit, and the price of B is $800 per unit. Draw Mr. Walcott's budget line. At what point does it intersect the axis along which the quantity of A is measured? At what point does it intersect the axis along which the quantity of B is measured? What is its slope? Now let the price of A increase to $400 per unit. Answer each question again. What would happen if both prices fell by 50 percent from their original positions? What if the prices of both increased by 50 percent but Mr. Walcott's income increased by 50 percent, as well?

10. Eligible participants had to buy food stamps at a subsidized rate up until 1979. Redo the analysis of Example 2.6 under the assumption that an eligible participant would have to spend $35 to receive $70 in food stamps. Show, in particular, the possibility that an eligible citizen might choose *not* to participate in the program because his or her utility would be higher along the original budget constraint than along the one that included the opportunity to buy $70 worth of food for $35.

11. Consider a consumer's choice between Coca-Cola and Pepsi-Cola. Most people prefer one to the other, but only up to a point. Assume, for the sake of argument, that you would buy Pepsi over Coke if both cost $1.29 for a 2-liter bottle. Assume as well that you would switch to Coke if it were on sale for 79 cents. Use a revealed preference argument to see how they might be perfect substitutes, from a utility perspective, if there were no intermediate price for which you might buy a little of each.

12. Suppose, in Example 2.5, that government decision-makers want to maximize voter satisfaction. Suppose, as well, that upstate voters would support 1 additional mile of mass transit if and only if 6 additional miles of highway were constructed. Finally, assume that there are more upstate voters than downstaters who want no more roads. Maximizing voter satisfaction would then mean matching upstate preferences. Draw some indifference curves for the state decision-makers. What combination of mass transit and highways will accomplish the task?

Calculus Appendix

DEFINITION OF MARGINAL UTILITY

The marginal utility of any good X reflects the rate at which utility changes with the consumption of good X under the assumption that the consumption of *all other goods* is constant. If utility depends on two goods, X and Y, so that utility can be written functionally as

$$U = U(X, Y),$$

then marginal utility has a straightforward analog in the calculus. Specifically, the marginal utility of any good X is the partial derivative of $U(X, Y)$ with respect to X. Why? Because the partial derivative of $U(X, Y)$ with respect to X is defined simply as the derivative of $U(X, Y)$ with respect to X under the assumption that Y is a constant. Notationally, the marginal utility of X (denoted MU_X) is simply

$$MU_X \equiv \frac{\partial U}{\partial X}.$$

Similarly, the marginal utility of Y is

$$MU_Y \equiv \frac{\partial U}{\partial Y}.$$

And if utility depends on the consumption of n goods indexed X_1 through X_n, then the marginal utility of any good X_i is

$$MU_{X_i} \equiv \frac{\partial U}{\partial X_i}.$$

MARGINAL RATES OF SUBSTITUTION AND THE SLOPES OF INDIFFERENCE CURVES

We have seen that the marginal rate of substitution (MRS) between any two goods can be defined for any bundle of consumption goods by the absolute value of the slope of an indifference curve at whatever point represents the bundle in question. We also have a result that states that the MRS is equal to the ratio of the pertinent marginal utilities. To see why, totally differentiate $U = U(X, Y)$:

$$dU = \frac{\partial U}{\partial X} dX + \frac{\partial U}{\partial Y} dY.$$

But $dU = 0$, by definition, along any indifference curve (indifference curves plot combinations of X and Y for which utility does not change). As a result, collecting terms shows that the slope of the indifference curve must be

$$\left. \frac{dY}{dX} \right|_{dU=0} = -\frac{\partial U/\partial X}{\partial U/\partial Y} = -\frac{MU_X}{MU_Y}.$$

The notation $dY/dX|_{dU=0}$ simply indicates computing a slope dY/dX along an indifference curve along which utility does not change ($dU = 0$). Taking absolute values, therefore,

$$MRS = \frac{\partial U/\partial X}{\partial U/\partial Y} = \frac{MU_X}{MU_Y}.$$

AN ILLUSTRATIVE UTILITY FUNCTION: THE COBB DOUGLAS CASE

Utility functions can assume many forms. One of the most common, dubbed the Cobb-Douglas form in honor of its co-inventors, holds that

$$U(X, Y) = X^\alpha Y^\beta.$$

In this case, the marginal utility of X is easily calculated from the multiplication rule for derivatives:

$$\begin{aligned}
MU_X = \frac{\partial U}{\partial X} &= X^\alpha (\beta Y^{\beta-1}) \frac{dY}{dX} + Y^\beta (\alpha X^{\alpha-1}) \frac{dX}{dX} \\
&= X^\alpha (\beta Y^{\beta-1})(0) + Y^\beta (\alpha X^{\alpha-1})(1) \\
&= \alpha X^{\alpha-1} Y^\beta
\end{aligned}$$

because $dY/dX = 0$ when taking the partial derivative with respect to X (recall that Y is taken to be a constant in this calculation) and because

$dX/dX = 1$. Similarly, taking the partial derivative with respect to Y produces the comparable result that

$$MU_Y = \frac{\partial U}{\partial Y} = X^\alpha(\beta Y^{\beta-1})\frac{dY}{dY} + Y^\beta(\alpha X^{\alpha-1})\frac{dX}{dY}$$
$$= X^\alpha(\beta Y^{\beta-1})(1) + Y^\beta(\alpha X^{\alpha-1})(0)$$
$$= \beta X^\alpha Y^{\beta-1}.$$

In addition, we know that the marginal rate of substitution at any point along any indifference curve must be given by

$$MRS = \frac{\partial U/\partial X}{\partial U/\partial Y} = \frac{\alpha X^{\alpha-1}Y^\beta}{\beta X^\alpha Y^{\beta-1}} = \frac{\alpha}{\beta}\frac{Y}{X}.$$

We can, however, confirm this directly by using the notion that the MRS should be the absolute value of the slope of an indifference curve. To this end, note that an indifference curve in this case can be expressed as

$$Y = \frac{(U_{\text{fixed}})^{1/\beta}}{X^{\alpha/\beta}} = (U_{\text{fixed}})^{1/\beta} X^{-\alpha/\beta}.$$

How do we know that? By rearranging terms so that Y appears alone on the left-hand side of the equation and raising both sides to the $1/\beta$ power. It follows that

$$\frac{dY}{dX} = -\frac{\alpha}{\beta}(U_{\text{fixed}})^{1/\beta} X^{-[(\alpha/\beta)-1]} = -\frac{\alpha}{\beta}\frac{Y}{X}$$

along any indifference curve because $(U_{\text{fixed}})^{1/\beta}X^{-\alpha/\beta} = Y$, and so we see that $MRS = (\alpha/\beta)(Y/X)$.

Finally, it is interesting to note that α must be positive if the marginal utility of X is to be positive. Why? Recall that

$$MU_X = \alpha X^{\alpha-1}Y^\beta.$$

This expression will be positive only if $\alpha > 0$. Similar reasoning shows that $\beta > 0$, as well.

CONSTRAINED MAXIMIZATION: UTILITY MAXIMIZATION SUBJECT TO A BUDGET CONSTRAINT

The problem to be explored here is one of maximizing utility subject to a budget constraint. Let utility be given by

$$U = U(X, Y),$$

and let the budget constraint be defined by

$$I = P_X X + P_Y Y.$$

The Lagrangian technique requires an objective function (utility in this case) and a constraint written as (some expression) equals zero. The budget constraint must therefore be expressed as:

$$I - P_X X - P_Y Y = 0.$$

The appropriate Lagrangian, in this case, is

$$\Gamma(X, Y, \lambda) = U(X, Y) + \lambda(I - P_X X - P_Y Y),$$

where λ represents the *Lagrange multiplier* for the constraint. Maximization requires solving three first-order conditions for X, for Y, and for λ; i.e., taking partial derivatives of $\Gamma(X, Y, \lambda)$ with respect to these three variables and setting them equal to zero. As a result, the solution in this case is characterized by three equations:

First-order condition for X: $\quad \dfrac{\partial \Gamma}{\partial X} = \dfrac{\partial U}{\partial X} - \lambda P_X = 0$; i.e., $\dfrac{\partial U}{\partial X} = \lambda P_X$

First-order condition for Y: $\quad \dfrac{\partial \Gamma}{\partial Y} = \dfrac{\partial U}{\partial Y} - \lambda P_Y = 0$; i.e., $\dfrac{\partial U}{\partial Y} = \lambda P_Y$

First-order condition for λ: $\quad I - P_X X - P_Y Y = 0$; i.e., $I = P_X X + P_Y Y$

The first-order condition for λ simply replicates the budget constraint. The two conditions for X and Y combine to reveal that

$$\frac{\partial U/\partial X}{\partial U/\partial Y} = \frac{P_X}{P_Y}; \text{ i.e., } MRS = \frac{P_X}{P_Y}.$$

This last statement comes from an observation that

$$MRS = \frac{\partial U/\partial X}{\partial U/\partial Y},$$

but it is the same condition that emerged from the geometry.

Two caveats should be mentioned in passing. First, there are second-order conditions that must be satisfied to guarantee that this solution is indeed a maximum rather than a minimum. You can tell from our discussion of consumer behavior that these conditions must guarantee the convexity of the indifference curves. It should also be noted that these conditions characterize "interior" solutions; i.e., corner solutions do not necessarily involve tangency between the budget constraint and the highest indifference curve, so the $MRS = P_X/P_Y$ representation of the first two conditions need not hold.

AN ALTERNATIVE REPRESENTATION OF CONSUMER EQUILIBRIUM

For the case in which $U = U(X, Y)$, consumer equilibrium is the solution of two equations:

$$I = P_X X + P_Y Y$$

and

$$MRS = \frac{\partial U/\partial X}{\partial U/\partial Y} = \frac{P_X}{P_Y}.$$

Notice that the first equation is simply the budget constraint. The second, of course, is the combination of the first-order conditions for X and Y. It holds that the MRS must be equal to the price ratio, but it can be rearranged to show that solutions can also be characterized by equality across the ratios of marginal utility and price; i.e.,

$$\frac{\partial U/\partial X}{P_X} = \frac{\partial U/\partial Y}{P_Y} \quad \text{or} \quad \frac{MU_X}{P_X} = \frac{MU_Y}{P_Y}.$$

This alternative representation of the solution gives a second interpretation to consumer equilibrium: the marginal utility of the last dollar spent should be the same for all goods. How so? The ratio $1/P_X$ indicates, for example, how many units of good X could be purchased for \$1; and multiplying that number times $\partial U/\partial X$ gives an indication of the resulting increase in utility.

This alternative provides a simple representation of the solution when there are more than two goods with more than two prices. Indeed, if there are n goods in the utility function, denoted X_i, and if those goods are available for purchase at prices P_i, then utility will be maximized subject to a budget constraint if

$$\frac{MU_{X_i}}{P_i} = \frac{MU_{X_j}}{P_j}$$

for all goods X_i and X_j. Of course, in this case, the budget constraint would look like

$$I = X_1 P_1 + X_2 P_2 + \ldots + X_n P_n.$$

Finally, refer to the first-order conditions for utility maximization subject to a budget constraint. For good X, for example, we have shown that

$$M_{U_X} = \frac{\partial U}{\partial X} = \lambda P_X.$$

It follows that

$$\frac{MU_X}{P_X} = \lambda.$$

As a result, the multiplier λ can be interpreted as the marginal utility of income—the common utility value of the last dollar spent (regardless of where that dollar is spent).

A SPECIFIC EXAMPLE OF CONSUMER EQUILIBRIUM WITH COBB-DOUGLAS UTILITY

Let utility for some individual with \$100 to spend on two goods, X and Y, be given by

$$U(X, Y) = X^{1/2} Y^{1/2}.$$

Assume that the price of X is \$5 and the price of Y is \$2. The appropriate Lagrangian for utility maximization subject to the budget constraint in this case is then

$$\Gamma(X, Y, \lambda) = X^{1/2}Y^{1/2} + \lambda(100 - 5X - 2Y).$$

The corresponding first-order conditions are:

$$X: \frac{\partial \Gamma}{\partial X} = \tfrac{1}{2}X^{-1/2}Y^{1/2} - \lambda 5 = 0 \qquad [1a]$$

$$Y: \frac{\partial \Gamma}{\partial Y} = \tfrac{1}{2}X^{1/2}Y^{-1/2} - \lambda 2 = 0 \qquad [1b]$$

$$\lambda: \frac{\partial \Gamma}{\partial \lambda} = 100 - 5X - 2Y = 0 \qquad [1c]$$

The first two (Equations 1a and 1b) combine to set the marginal rate of substitution equal to the price ratio; i.e.,

$$\frac{\tfrac{1}{2}X^{-1/2}Y^{1/2}}{5} = \lambda \quad \text{and} \quad \frac{\tfrac{1}{2}X^{1/2}Y^{-1/2}}{2} = \lambda$$

so that

$$\frac{\tfrac{1}{2}X^{-1/2}Y^{1/2}}{\tfrac{1}{2}X^{1/2}Y^{-1/2}} = \frac{5}{2}. \qquad [2]$$

Equation 2 therefore characterizes all of the combinations of X and Y for which $MRS = 5/2$. It can be rewritten as

$$\frac{Y}{X} = \frac{5}{2} \quad \text{or} \quad Y = \frac{5}{2}X. \qquad [3]$$

Meanwhile, the third first-order condition (the one for λ) imposes the budget constraint; substitution can therefore reveal that

$$100 - 5X - 2Y = 100 - 5X - 2(\tfrac{5}{2})X = 100 - 10X = 0.$$

At a result, the utility-maximizing consumption of X is 10 units; and from Equation 3, the corresponding utility-maximizing consumption of Y is 25 units.

CHAPTER 3

Consumer Behavior and Individual Demand

INTRODUCTION

In this chapter, we proceed with the further development of a model of consumer behavior. Building on the results of the preceding chapter, we show how the consumer responds to changes in his or her money income and to changes in the prices of various commodities. In addition, we present some illustrations of how this theory has been applied to help solve important problems of public policy and personal self-interest. We offer, in particular, some initial insight into how economists calibrate the economic loss or gain associated with a change in economic circumstance, and we apply that insight to a preliminary analysis of the economic cost that would be associated with an increase in the price of energy. Finally, we apply the theory to the cost-of-living indexes used to measure changes in economic well-being.

It is useful to begin with a brief review of the conditions under which a consumer is considered to be in equilibrium. Rather than parroting what has already been said, though, we will take a slightly different tack. The preceding chapter indicated that a rational consumer's equilibrium market basket is the point on the budget line where his or her utility is maximized. Graphically, this maximum was highlighted by the tangency of the highest feasible indifference curve with the budget line.[1] Since the slope of the indifference curve is always equal to -1 times the marginal rate of substitution of good X for good Y (see page 41), and since the slope of the budget line is always $-P_x/P_y$ (see page 45), it follows that the rational consumer will choose in equilibrium to allocate available income between goods X and Y so that the marginal rate of substitution of X for Y equals P_x/P_y.

This is a famous result; it describes succinctly what can be called "necessary conditions" for maximizing utility by consuming positive quantities of both X and Y. This condition is very useful, and it should be understood fully before we proceed. It is easier to agree that it is true, though, than it

---

[1]For simplicity, we will assume throughout this chapter that the optimal market basket is not a corner solution. Consult pages 52–56 to review exactly what this assumption means.

is to see exactly what it means and precisely why it is true. Perhaps the best approach to a complete understanding starts with the definition of the **marginal rate of substitution:** the rate at which a consumer is *willing* to substitute good X for good Y just so that his or her total level of satisfaction is constant. If the marginal rate of substitution were 3, for example, then the consumer would be *willing* to trade at most 3 units of good Y in order to receive 1 additional unit of good X.

Marginal rate of substitution

Price ratio

The **price ratio,** P_x/P_y, meanwhile, reflects the rate at which the consumer *could actually* "substitute" good X for good Y in the market. Suppose that the price of X were 3 times the price of Y (i.e., let $P_x = \$6$ and $P_y = \$2$). In this case, the consumer would have to "sell" 3 units of Y to generate the funds necessary to "purchase" an additional unit of X. In other words, the consumer would find the market willing to trade $P_x/P_y = \$6/\$2 = 3$ units of Y for 1 unit of X. The famous result, therefore, means simply that the rate at which the consumer is *willing* to substitute good X for good Y (because satisfaction would be unchanged) *must equal* the rate at which he or she is *able* to substitute X for Y. Otherwise, it would always be possible to trade to another market basket that would increase the consumer's satisfaction—and so the initial market basket could not be the equilibrium one that maximizes consumer satisfaction.

What would happen in such a situation? Suppose that $P_x = \$4$ and $P_y = \$2$ so that $P_x/P_y = \$4/\$2 = 2$ (instead of 3, as in the preceding example). In this case, the consumer would be able to go to the market and "trade" 2 units of Y for 1 unit of X (or, conversely, selling 1 unit of X would produce enough money to buy 2 units of Y). But if his or her marginal rate of substitution were still equal to 3, then the consumer would have been willing to substitute 3 units of Y for 1 unit of X. Giving up 2 units of Y in the market for 1 unit of X would therefore yield a "surplus" of 1 unit of Y. How can this be so? The additional unit of X would be "worth" 3 units of Y, but only 2 units of Y would have actually been traded away. So as long as the "surplus" unit of Y has any value, the consumer's satisfaction *must* have increased.

If the marginal rate of substitution were less than the price ratio, of course, then the trading would have to go the other way—sacrificing X for more units of Y. Trades that improve welfare, therefore, can always be found, except when the marginal rate of substitution precisely equals the price ratio; only then does the consumer's market basket maximize his or her utility. This chapter builds on this insight to show how utility-maximizing behavior can be summarized by individual demand curves.

EFFECTS OF CHANGES IN CONSUMER MONEY INCOME

With this review in mind, let us begin to move in that direction by considering the effect of changes in money income on the amounts of goods X and Y purchased by the rational, welfare-maximizing consumer. For example, suppose that the consumer is a student whose income (from work and

Figure 3.1 EFFECTS OF CHANGES IN MONEY INCOME ON CONSUMER EQUILIBRIUM

The income-consumption curve connects points representing equilibrium market baskets corresponding to different levels of money income assuming that the prices of goods are fixed. The curve shown in panel A highlights points U, V, and W. Quantities corresponding to a, c, and k units of good X are demanded for incomes equal to (P_x times e units of X), (P_x times g units of X), and (P_x times i units of X), respectively. In panel B, the price of X is lower (equal to P_x') and the price of Y is now higher (equal to P_y'). The income-consumption curve for the same indifference curves would highlight points U', V', and W'. Quantities a', c', and k' units of good X would be demanded for incomes equal to (P_x' times e' units of X), (P_x' times g' units of X), and (P_x' times i' units of X), respectively.

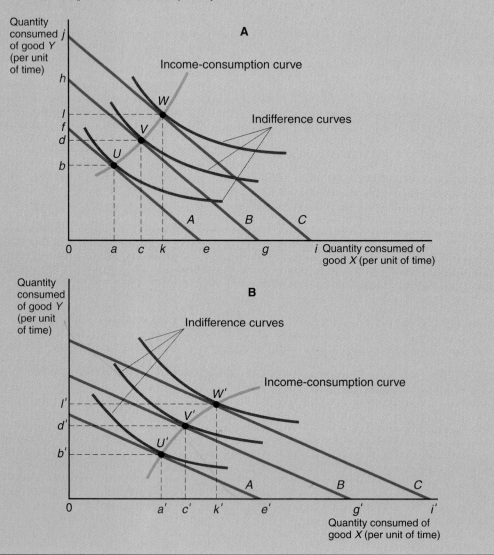

home) increased from $7,000 to $10,000 per year. What effect would this have on her purchases? How much of her extra money would be spent on books? Entertainment? Clothing? Food?

We saw in the preceding chapter that an increase in money income would result in an increase in the intercept of the budget line. The slope of the line would stay the same, though, as long as the prices of the various commodities remained unchanged. Similarly, a reduction in income would reduce the intercept. To determine what happens to consumption, we simply compare the equilibrium positions on the new budget lines with the original equilibrium position on the original budget line.

Suppose, to continue the example, that the budget for our student's initial $7,000 in income were portrayed by budget line *A* in panel A of Figure 3.1. Given the student's indifference map drawn there, the market basket that maximizes utility would be made up of *a* units of good *X* and *b* units of good *Y*. Now, suppose her income rises to $10,000, and assume that budget line *B* represents her new consumption possibilities. The market basket that maximizes her utility would now include *c* units of good *X* and *d* units of good *Y*.

The way in which an increase in money income influences a consumer's purchases clearly depends on his or her tastes. In other words, the nature of the market basket chosen at the old income, the nature of the basket chosen at any new income, and thus the nature of the difference between these two allocations is influenced by the shapes of the consumer's indifference curves and, in a very real way, by the price ratio (P_x/P_y). This price ratio was, of course, held constant when our consumer's money income changed, but the level at which those prices were fixed can dramatically influence the results. If, for example, the price of good *X* were lower and the price of *Y* were higher, then the budget lines drawn in panel A of Figure 3.1 would be much flatter. The *Y* intercept would be lower and the *X* intercept would be higher for each. Something like panel B would therefore apply. Notice that the consumer equilibria at any level of income would then involve more of good *X* and less of good *Y*.

Example 3.1   **Responding to Changes in Income and Prices**

How sensitive is consumption to changes in income and price? Table 3.1 records sensitivity estimates for a variety of goods consumed in the United States—long-term estimates expressed in terms of the percentage change that would result from either a 1 percent increase in income or a 1 percent increase in the price. The first column provides some idea of the relative importance of each good. The second column indicates that some goods, mostly durable goods, purchased meals, and airline travel, are relatively sensitive to income. They might be termed "luxury goods"—goods that people want to purchase, but only after their incomes had reached a level where they think that they can afford to do so. Others, like "off-premises" food (home cooking), telephone service, and alcoholic beverages are not particularly sensitive to income. These goods are actual necessities (or somewhat addictive), so changes in income cause little change after certain thresholds of consumption have been achieved.

The third column reports analogous sensitivities to price. Again, some (like audiovisual equipment, furniture and appliances, and alcoholic beverages) are relatively sensitive; but that is to be expected for long-term estimates. It is surprising, therefore, that a few goods display sensitivities as low as −0.25. For these goods, a 1 percent increase in price causes consumption to fall by 1/4 percent of 1 percent so that actual spending would climb.

▣ Income-Consumption Curves and Engel Curves

Holding commodity prices constant, we find that each level of money income corresponds to a different equilibrium market basket for our rational consumer. For example, the equilibrium market baskets corresponding to the three different income levels represented in Figure 3.1, panel A, are represented by three distinct points: *U*, *V*, and *W*. If we connect these points, along with the other equilibrium market basket allocations that are associated with all possible levels of money income, then we plot what is called the **income-consumption curve.** Figure 3.1 displays such a curve. Note that the quantities demanded of both X and Y increase with income, but in panel A the demand for Y seems to be more responsive to higher income, and in panel B the demand for X seems to be more responsive.

Income-consumption curves of this sort can be used to derive **Engel curves**—a second, more widely used representation of the sensitivity of consumption to changes in money income. An Engel curve represents the relationship between the equilibrium quantity purchased of a single good and the level of income.[2] Ernst Engel was a nineteenth-century German statistician who did the basic work related to these curves; economists have acknowledged his contribution to their discipline by attaching his name to any correspondence between consumption and income. It is easy to see how an Engel curve can be derived from the income-consumption curve. Figure 3.1 can serve as a point of departure. When money income equals P_x times e (or P_y times f, since they are equal), the income-consumption curve depicted there shows that the consumer buys a units of good X.[3] When money income equals P_x times g (or P_y times h), the income-consumption curve shows that the consumer buys c units of good X. And when money income equals P_x times i (or P_y times j), the income-consumption curve shows that the consumer buys k units of good X. These three points are the "X-axis" values associated with points U, V, and W on the income-consumption curve, respectively. Each is an equilibrium amount of X for a different level of money income, and so each should be represented on an Engel curve that traces equilibrium consumption of X against income. The result is displayed in Figure 3.2. Note that income is measured along the vertical axis and consumption is measured along the horizontal axis.

The key to keeping track of the difference between an income-consumption curve and an Engel curve can be found on the axes of their respective graphs. Income-consumption curves are drawn where indifference curves live, since they pick out points of tangency between indifference curves and a collection of budget lines with different incomes. They are, therefore, drawn in graphs where quantities of goods consumed are reflected by the scales of both axes—goods X and Y in Figure 3.1. Engel curves, meanwhile, plot income levels against consumption levels for a specific good that are read from an associated income-consumption curve. So, as shown in Figure 3.2, for example, the quantity of good X consumed for various budget lines is plotted horizontally against the levels of income that supports those budgets, and these income levels are measured against the scale recorded

---

[2]An Engel curve is often defined to be the relationship between a consumer's expenditure on a commodity and his or her money income. Since commodity prices are held constant in its construction, though, a consumer's expenditure on the commodity is strictly proportional to the number of units actually consumed. It makes no real difference, therefore, whether we use expenditure or quantity as the relevant variable.

[3]The expression P_x times e (or P_y times f) represents money income because it corresponds to the point where the consumption of good Y (or good X) is equal to zero. As a result, all income is being devoted to buying as much of good X (good Y) as possible, and so total income must equal total expenditure on good X (good Y).

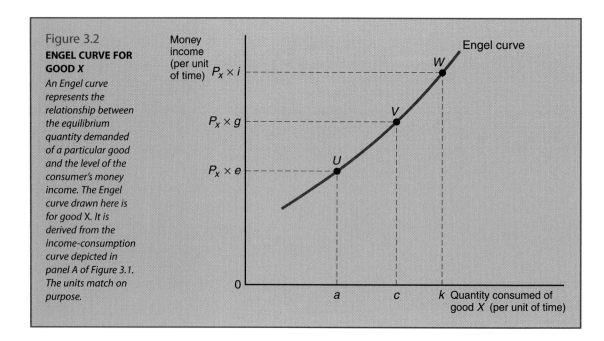

Figure 3.2

ENGEL CURVE FOR GOOD X

An Engel curve represents the relationship between the equilibrium quantity demanded of a particular good and the level of the consumer's money income. The Engel curve drawn here is for good X. It is derived from the income-consumption curve depicted in panel A of Figure 3.1. The units match on purpose.

along the vertical axis. We could have just as easily derived an Engel curve for good Y from the income-consumption curve.

| Example 3.2 | Using Engel Curves to Depict Sensitivity to Income |

Table 3.1 reported estimates of the degree to which consumption of selected major categories of goods and services would change with income. A list of numbers can be informative, to be sure; but we can sometimes convey their content more effectively by crafting illustrative graphics. We could, for example, display the range of sensitivities reported in the second column by hypothesizing Engel curves indexed to an initial position of 100. That is, we could assume that current income and consumption were assigned values of 100. A 10 percent increase in income would then be associated with an index value equal to 110, and the associated change in consumption of any good would be equal to 100 plus the reported sensitivity estimate (for a 1 percent increase) multiplied by 10. Figure 3.3 depicts these curves for most of the goods and services listed in Table 3.1, and it clearly reflects differences across goods that may be difficult to discern from the table. The steepest two lines make it clear, in particular, that demand for audio and video equipment and airline service is dramatically more responsive to changes in income than is the demand for alcoholic beverages and telephone service—the goods associated with the flattest two lines. Meanwhile, energy sources can be found in an intermediate cluster that is bounded by clothing and shoes on the high side and medical service on the low side.

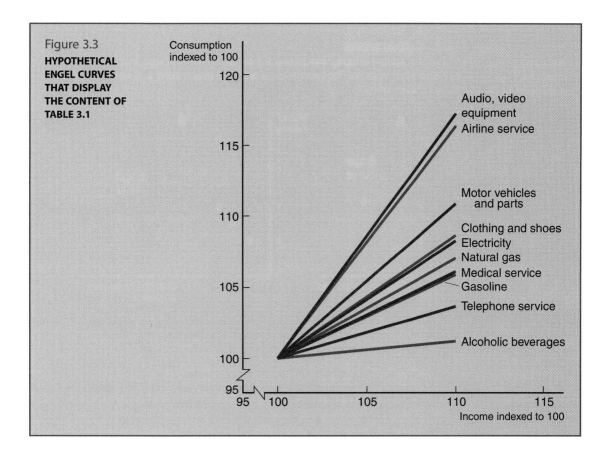

Figure 3.3

HYPOTHETICAL ENGEL CURVES THAT DISPLAY THE CONTENT OF TABLE 3.1

◻ Deriving Insight from the Shape of an Engel Curve

Shape of the Engel curve

Moving now to a more general context, the shape of a consumer's Engel curve for a particular good will depend on the nature of that good, the nature of the consumer's preferences and tastes, and the level at which prices are fixed. Figure 3.4 shows Engel curves for two goods—one in panel A and the other in panel B. They have quite different shapes. According to the Engel curve in panel A, the quantity consumed increases with income, but at a *decreasing rate.* It is similar in shape to the Engel curve drawn for good *X* in Figure 3.2 from the utility map portrayed in panel A of Figure 3.1. In panel B, by comparison, the quantity consumed increases with income at an *increasing rate.* (To test your understanding of the relationship between income-consumption curves and Engel curves, draw an Engel curve for good *Y* based on the structure of the utility map in panel A of Figure 3.1; note that its shape conforms to the shape of panel B in Figure 3.4.) A comparison of panels A and B shows that changes in income do not have as great an effect on the quantity consumed of the good in panel B as they do on the quantity consumed in panel A.

One would expect that Engel curves for goods such as salt and shoelaces would show that the consumption of these commodities is not very responsive

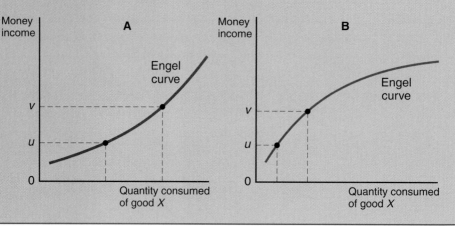

Figure 3.4 **ENGEL CURVES: VARIOUS SHAPES**

The quantity consumed of the good in panel A increases with income at a decreasing rate; the Engel curve drawn there mimics the shape of the curve depicted in Figure 3.2. The quantity consumed of the good in panel B increases with income at an increasing rate, so its shape is quite different.

to changes in income. It would be unusual to find a person who responded to an increase in income by buying massive quantities of salt or shoelaces. On the other hand, goods like designer clothes or imported sports cars might have Engel curves showing that their consumption increases significantly with increased income (at least after income has passed a given threshold). These are general statements, of course, and they are fraught with all of the usual problems associated with painting the behavior of many individuals with a single broad brush. The Engel curve for a consumer with a strong preference for American cars or safe sedans would not, for example, fit the above hypothesis.

Engel curves can nonetheless be used to provide quick and revealing portraits of consumer behavior. Example 3.3 shows how you might create a few Engel curves drawn from some aggregate data for a few broad commodity categories in the United States, and shows that consumption can decline for some goods even as income rises.

| Example 3.3 | **Aggregate Engel Curves** |

We have shown how Engel curves can be derived for a specific individual from a utility-maximization model of consumer equilibrium, but their first incarnation had nothing to do with that model. Ernst Engel was simply trying to devise a way to reflect diversity in the way consumers allocated their different incomes across a variety of goods; it simply turned out that more modern theory could explain why his approach was appropriate. We can, however, illustrate the power of his approach with more recent data for five major categories of goods in the United States.

Table 3.2 **CONSUMPTION PATTERNS FOR DIFFERENT INCOME CLASSES**

| Commodity | Income group | | | | |
	Less than $10,000	$10,000 to $29,000	$30,000 to $49,000	$50,000 to $69,000	Above $70,000
Owned dwellings	$ 854	$1,746	$3,882	$5,616	$9,736
Rented dwellings	$1,642	$2,053	$1,843	$1,514	$ 748
Health care	$1,034	$1,690	$1,947	$2,054	$2,703
Food	$2,461	$3,585	$5,118	$6,273	$8,137
Clothing	$ 867	$1,081	$1,997	$2,316	$3,668

SOURCE: Inferred from *The Consumer Expenditure Survey: 1992–93* (Washington, D.C.: U.S. Department of Labor, Bureau of Labor Statistics, 1994).

Table 3.2 records average expenditures on five commodities across five major income classes. Once again, the data are informative, but the graphical representation of the corresponding Engel relationships in Figure 3.5 can be more revealing. Notice, for example, that rental housing "turns back" on itself—people with higher income spend, on average, less on rent. Because they spend more on owner-occupied dwellings? Yes. Spending in that category increases at an increasing rate for households with more than $50,000 in income. Notice, as well, that food expenditures climb consistently

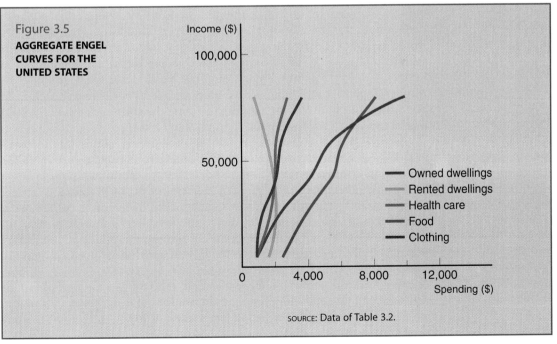

Figure 3.5
AGGREGATE ENGEL CURVES FOR THE UNITED STATES

SOURCE: Data of Table 3.2.

with income (the Engel curve is relatively straight) and more quickly than spending on clothing and health care (the Engel curve for food is flatter than the curves for clothing and health care).

EFFECTS OF CHANGES IN COMMODITY PRICES

The preceding section covered topics related to the effect of changes in money income on equilibrium market baskets assuming that the prices of all of the relevant commodities were held fixed. This condition raises an important question: What would be the effect of a change in the price of a commodity if income were held at the same level instead? For example, take the case of the college student mentioned above. Assume that her income has not risen, so that she has the original $7,000 in money income to spend however she pleases. Assume, as well, that only the price of food changes. We can now explore how the quantity of food she consumes (per unit of time) varies in response to changes in its price. What sort of relationship exists between the price of food and the equilibrium quantity of food?

This question is unnecessarily specific. To pose the question more generally, suppose that there are only two commodities, again denoted X and Y. Let the price of good Y and money income be held constant. What would happen if the price of X were to change? Let the budget line associated with the original price of good X be budget line B in Figure 3.6; point S identifies the equilibrium market basket with r units of X (and s units of Y) being consumed. If the price of X were to climb, then the new budget line would be C, along which the new equilibrium market basket would be point T. (In the preceding chapter, we saw that an increase in the price of good X would increase the absolute value of the slope of the budget line [P_x/P_y] but would leave the vertical intercept [money income/P_y] unchanged.) The increase in price would result in a reduction in the consumption of X from r units to u units; the consumption of Y would increase from s units to v units.

An equilibrium market basket can be determined in this way for each price of X. The curve that connects all of these equilibrium points is called the **price-consumption curve.** Figure 3.6 shows a price-consumption curve for our hypothetical consumer, given the level of his or her money income and the price of Y. Why should we be interested in the price-consumption curve? Because it can be used to derive this consumer's individual demand curve for X—the commodity in question because the price of X is changing. The individual demand curve shows how much of a given commodity the consumer would purchase (per unit of time) at various prices of that commodity. It is clear from the construction, though, that the prices of other commodities, money income, and the consumer's preferences *are all assumed to be unchanged.* The individual demand curve is a central concept in consumer theory, and its reliance on assuming "everything else is held constant" is fundamental.

Price-consumption curve

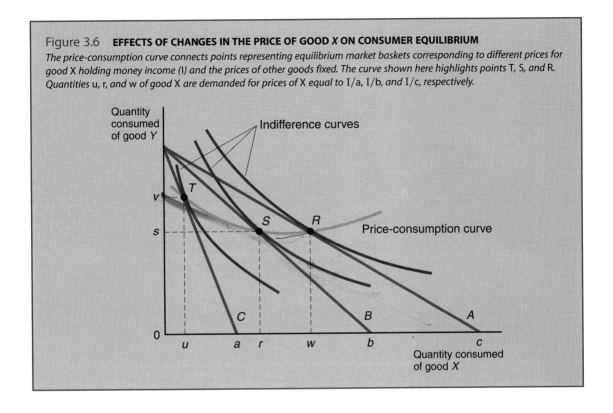

Figure 3.6 **EFFECTS OF CHANGES IN THE PRICE OF GOOD X ON CONSUMER EQUILIBRIUM**
The price-consumption curve connects points representing equilibrium market baskets corresponding to different prices for good X holding money income (I) and the prices of other goods fixed. The curve shown here highlights points T, S, and R. Quantities u, r, and w of good X are demanded for prices of X equal to I/a, I/b, and I/c, respectively.

How can the individual demand curve be derived from a price-consumption curve? To illustrate the procedure, refer to Figure 3.6. When the price of good X is I/a (where I denotes the constant money income of the consumer), then the price-consumption curve indicates that consuming u units of good X maximizes satisfaction.[4] If the price were I/b, though, then budget line B would apply and the price-consumption curve shows that the consumer would buy r units of good X. And if the price of X were I/c, then budget line A would apply and the consumer would buy w units of X. These three combinations of price and quantity demanded must lie on the individual demand curve. And we can produce an entire individual demand curve by plotting the full set of similar combinations of price and equilibrium consumption levels. The result is curve D in Figure 3.7.

The location and shape of an individual demand curve will depend on the level of money income, the prices of other goods, the nature of the commodity in question, and consumer tastes. Take, for example, the demand curve for good X just constructed from the underlying structure of Figure 3.6 and displayed in Figure 3.7. If the consumer's income were higher than I, then a different demand curve would result—perhaps curve E rather than curve D. A different demand curve would emerge if the price of good Y were higher (or

---

[4]We know from Figure 3.6 that the price of good X must be I/a when the budget line is C. Why? Because the consumer could afford to purchase a units of good X if she were to devote all of her income to the consumption of good X.

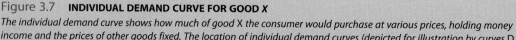

Figure 3.7 **INDIVIDUAL DEMAND CURVE FOR GOOD X**

The individual demand curve shows how much of good X the consumer would purchase at various prices, holding money income and the prices of other goods fixed. The location of individual demand curves (depicted for illustration by curves D, E, and F) depends on the variables that are held fixed in their construction: the consumer's money income and the prices of other goods.

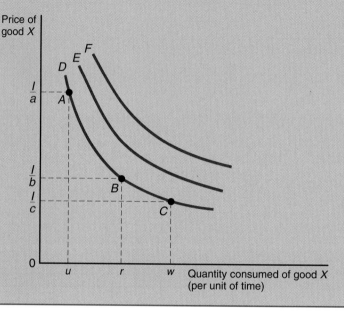

lower, for that matter) than assumed in Figure 3.6—perhaps curve F would have been drawn. It is essential to remember that each individual demand curve is drawn with specific assumptions about the level of money income, other prices, and tastes. Each is, in general, a valid representation of a consumer's responsiveness to changes in price only if those assumptions are satisfied.

It is equally important to distinguish between shifts in a consumer's demand curve for a particular commodity and changes in the amount of that commodity that he or she wants to consume. As we have just seen, a consumer's demand curve may shift because of changes in his or her income, or tastes, of the prices of other goods. These shifts are likely to result in changes in the quantity that he or she chooses to consume, but only because the entire curve moves. In addition, changes in the price of the good in question can cause the quantity demanded to change; it is these changes, when they occur alone, that are reflected by movement along a fixed demand curve. So, movement from point A to point B along curve D in Figure 3.7 would be an example of the latter—a change in the quantity of good X demanded *in response to a reduced price for good X, assuming that income, other prices, and tastes do not change.* A shift in the entire curve from D to E would be an example of the former—a shift resulting from a change in income, prices of *other* goods, or tastes that would mean that the quantity of good X demanded would now be higher *for any and all specified prices of X.*

Microlink 3.1   Tracking the Determinants of Demand

Chapter 1 identified several determinants of demand: consumers' tastes, consumers' incomes, and the prices of goods. This chapter developed tools for analyzing the effects of changes in some of these determinants, and together they reconfirm our original claims that income and prices play critical roles in consumer demand. Engel curves, income-consumption curves, and price-consumption curves all track changes in the quantity demanded as one of the determinants changes under the assumption that all of the other determinants are fixed. Engel curves and income-consumption curves, for example, track changes in the quantity demanded as incomes change for constant tastes and prices. And price-consumption curves track changes in quantity demanded as the price of one good changes for constant tastes, income, and prices of all other goods.

SUBSTITUTION AND INCOME EFFECTS

Consumers are affected in two ways when prices change. First, they are likely to substitute the now relatively cheaper goods for the more expensive ones, and second, they attain a different level of satisfaction irrespective of the degree to which the substitution is possible.[5] This section will explore the implications of both. The total effect of a change in the price of one good is illustrated in Figure 3.8. The original price ratio is given by the slope of budget line A. Given this price ratio, the consumer's equilibrium market bundle is point U on indifference curve 1. Notice that x_1 units of X are consumed. Now suppose that the price of good X increases so that budget line B applies. A new price ratio results; it is reflected by the steeper slope of line B. Given this new budget line, the consumer would choose to consume at point V on indifference curve 2. He or she would, at that point, consume x_2 units of X. The total effect of the price change on the quantity demanded is therefore a reduction in the quantity of good X demanded equal to $x_1 - x_2$ units.

As suggested above, the total effect of this (and, in fact, any price change) *Substitution effect* can be divided conceptually into two parts: a **substitution effect** and an *Income effect* **income effect.** We consider the substitution effect first. The increase in the price of good X depicted in Figure 3.8 clearly resulted in a reduction in the consumer's level of satisfaction: he or she wound up on indifference curve 2 rather than indifference curve 1. In defining the substitution effect, we will take careful notice of this change in welfare, and ask that you try the following thought exercise. Suppose that we could increase the consumer's income as the price rose by an amount exactly sufficient to maintain his or her old level of satisfaction. That is to say, suppose we could compensate the consumer for the price increase in such a way that he or she could remain on indifference curve 1. If this compensation were possible,

[5]The obvious exception is the case of changing the price of a perfect substitute. That would, however, result in a corner solution, and we have excluded those cases for present purposes.

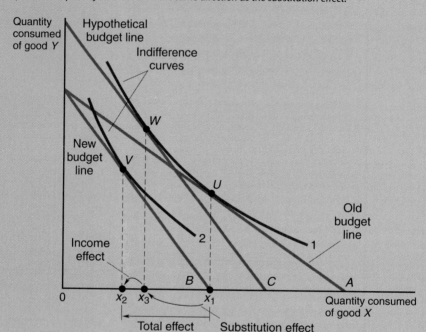

Figure 3.8 **SUBSTITUTION AND INCOME EFFECTS**

If the price of good X increases, the budget line rotates from budget line A to budget line B. The effect of the price change on the quantity demanded is a reduction from x_1 to x_2. The equilibrium market basket shifts from point U to point V. The total effect can be divided into two parts: the substitution effect from x_1 to x_3 (a reduction in quantity assuming sufficient compensation to maintain the same satisfaction level indicated by indifference curve 1) and an income effect from x_3 to x_2 (a further reduction in the quantity consumed caused by the reduction in real income). Good X is normal in this case; the income effect pushes the quantity demanded in the same direction as the substitution effect.

then we would be able to create an artificial, higher budget line that would have to be drawn parallel to *B* (reflecting the new price of good *X*) *and* tangent to indifference curve 1 (reflecting an unchanged level of satisfaction). This hypothetical budget line is drawn in Figure 3.8 as budget line *C*. The substitution effect can now be defined as the movement along the original indifference curve (curve 1) from the original equilibrium point *U* to an imaginary equilibrium point *W* that would be chosen if the hypothetical budget line were actually to apply. More precisely, the substitution effect reflects a reduction in the quantity of good *X* demanded from x_1 units to x_3 units. Put differently, it measures the change in the quantity of *X* demanded that would occur as the price changed if the level of satisfaction were somehow held constant.

We can now turn to the income effect. It is defined as movement from the hypothetical equilibrium point *W* to the actual new equilibrium point *V*. This movement does not involve any change in price because the price ratio is the same along hypothetical budget line *C* as it is along actual budget line *B*. It is, instead, a direct reflection of a change in total satisfaction (or utility).

The income effect is the change in the quantity demanded of good X due solely to a change in real income, all prices being held constant. In Figure 3.8, it is the reduction from x_3 units of X to x_2 units of X.

The total effect of the price increase depicted in Figure 3.8 is simply the sum of the substitution and income effects. The substitution effect reduced the quantity demanded from x_1 units of X to x_3 units of X. The income effect drove consumption down from x_3 units of X to x_2. The sum of the two, a cumulative reduction from x_1 units to x_2 units, matches the total effect exactly.[6]

The substitution effect is always negative. That is to say, if the price of some good X were to increase and real income (satisfaction) were held constant, then consumption of good X would always decline. Conversely, if the price of X were to fall, then the consumption of good X would climb, even with a fixed level of satisfaction. Perfect negative correlation of this sort follows from the fact that indifference curves are convex from the origin (see Chapter 2).

▣ Normal Goods

Normal goods

By way of contrast, the direction of the income effect cannot be predicted from the theory alone. One would expect that consumption of a specific good would rise or fall, respectively, with a rise or fall in real income; and that is true in most cases. Goods with this sort of positive correlation between changes in income and changes in consumption are called **normal goods.** Figure 3.8 depicts good X as a normal good because the income effect associated with a *reduction* in real income shows a *reduction* in the quantity of X demanded. Notice, as well, that both the income and substitution effects depicted in Figure 3.8 push the quantity of X demanded in the same direction (down). This observation holds for all price changes associated with any normal good. For normal goods, in other words, the income effect on the quantity demanded amplifies the substitution effect—making it larger and more pronounced. You may want to draw your own rendition of Figure 3.8 for the case in which the price of X falls to make sure that you understand this point; both the substitution and the income effects would, in that case, push the quantity of good X demanded up.

▣ Inferior Goods

Inferior goods

Not all goods are normal, however, recall the Engel curve for rental housing in Example 3.3; its slope turned negative for incomes greater than about $50,000. Goods like these are called **inferior goods** because they display a negative correlation between changes in consumption and changes in real income. Panel A of Figure 3.9 depicts the income effect for an inferior good for the same reduction in real income associated with the price increase that was portrayed in Figure 3.8. As income falls from the compensated level supporting budget line C to the actual level sustaining budget line B, consumption of good X actually climbs from x_3 units to x_2 units.

[6]For an explanation of the substitution and income effects in elementary mathematical terms, see the coverage of income effects, substitution effects, and the Slutsky equation in H. Varian, *Microeconomic Analysis,* 3d ed. (New York: Norton, 1992).

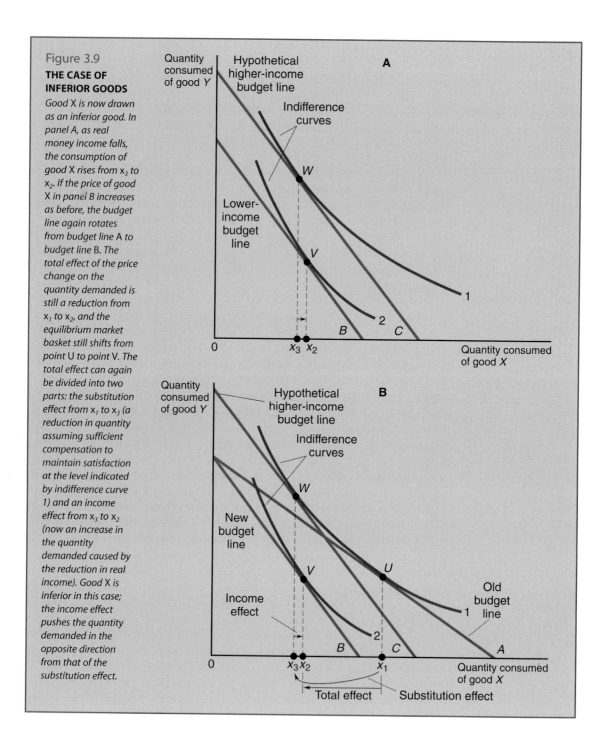

Figure 3.9

THE CASE OF INFERIOR GOODS

Good X is now drawn as an inferior good. In panel A, as real money income falls, the consumption of good X rises from x_3 to x_2. If the price of good X in panel B increases as before, the budget line again rotates from budget line A to budget line B. The total effect of the price change on the quantity demanded is still a reduction from x_1 to x_2, and the equilibrium market basket still shifts from point U to point V. The total effect can again be divided into two parts: the substitution effect from x_1 to x_3 (a reduction in quantity assuming sufficient compensation to maintain satisfaction at the level indicated by indifference curve 1) and an income effect from x_3 to x_2 (now an increase in the quantity demanded caused by the reduction in real income). Good X is inferior in this case; the income effect pushes the quantity demanded in the opposite direction from that of the substitution effect.

Quantity consumed of good Y

Hypothetical higher-income budget line

A

Indifference curves

W

Lower-income budget line

V

1

2

B   C

0   x_3 x_2 Quantity consumed of good X

Quantity consumed of good Y

Hypothetical higher-income budget line

B

Indifference curves

W

New budget line

V   U

Income effect

Old budget line

1

2

B   C   A

0   x_3 x_2 x_1 Quantity consumed of good X

Total effect   Substitution effect

Panel B of Figure 3.9 places this change in the context of the total effect of increasing the price of good X. The substitution effect still reduces consumption from x_1 units of X to x_3 units of X, but now the income effect actually *increases* consumption from x_3 units to x_2 units. As real income falls with the higher price, more specifically, the consumption of good X actually climbs in exactly the same way as depicted in panel A. The income effect therefore pushes consumption in the *opposite* direction from the substitution effect—a generally true observation for all inferior goods.

The total effect portrayed in Figure 3.9 is still negative—the increase in the price of X still produces an overall reduction in the quantity demanded (x_2 is still less than x_1). There is, however, no reason to believe that this correlation must hold for the total effect. It is possible for an inferior good paradoxically to have an income effect so great that it more than offsets the substitution effect. As a result, the quantity demanded could actually be directly (positively) related to the price, at least over some range of variation *Giffen good* in the price. A good of this sort is know as a **Giffen good.**

Since the income effect must push against the substitution effect if a good is to be a Giffen good, all such goods must be inferior. But not all inferior goods exhibit the paradox because it is surely possible, as depicted in Figure 3.9, for the substitution effect to dominate. Goods that display the positively sloped demand curves associated with Giffen's paradoxical behavior even over a limited range of prices are extremely rare. As a result, we will assume henceforth that all goods have individual demand curves with the usual negative slope.

Microlink 3.2 Normal Goods, Inferior Goods, and the Comparative Statics of a Shift in Supply

The income effect of a price change for a normal good pushes the quantity demanded up or down in the same direction as the substitution effect, but the income effect for an inferior good pushes in the opposite direction. It follows that we should expect that the quantity demanded of a normal good would, all other things being equal, be more responsive to a change in its price than an inferior good. Placing this observation into the context of the simple analysis of Chapter 1, we should therefore expect that a shift in supply for whatever reason would produce larger price effects for inferior goods and larger quantity effects for normal goods.

| **Example 3.4** | **The Energy Tax and Rebate Proposal** |

The 1970s were marked by sudden and potentially catastrophic interruptions in the supply of oil and natural gas to the United States from OPEC, the Organization of Petroleum Exporting Countries. The OPEC nations' idea was to increase international oil prices and thus their export revenue, but the transition to higher prices was far from smooth. Gas lines of 100 or more cars appeared almost overnight because higher prices could not bring demand down to match supply. Shortages were commonplace, and schemes that allowed people to buy fuel only every other day did little to reduce congestion. College students made money by offering to stand in line for harried adults, but their gain was hardly worth the fuss. Higher prices produced enormous economic damage and transferred enormous sums of money to OPEC.

Government officials were, of course, in a quandary. What should they do to facilitate the transition to higher prices and to minimize its welfare and distributional implications? The Carter administration responded by proposing a tax rebate scheme designed to mimic, to the extent possible, the hypothetical compensation mechanism by which economists define the substitution effect. Their proposal had two parts. An additional tax would be added at the pump for each gallon of gasoline purchased. But every April, every dollar paid in extra tax would be returned via a credit against personal income tax liabilities. Weird? Certainly, but the idea did have its roots in sound economic theory.

Gasoline is a normal good, so the tax would depress demand and alleviate some of the shortfall in supply. The rebate, however, would compensate consumers, so that welfare would not fall excessively. It would, to be sure, work against the tax, but consumption was still expected to fall. In other words, the substitution effect would dominate.

Two distinct income-consumption curves are drawn on Figure 3.10. The first corresponds to the pretax environment and highlights point U as the initial market equilibrium basket for a representative consumer; indifference curve

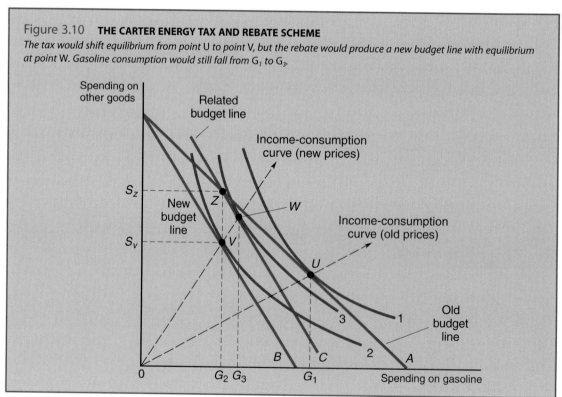

Figure 3.10 **THE CARTER ENERGY TAX AND REBATE SCHEME**

The tax would shift equilibrium from point U to point V, but the rebate would produce a new budget line with equilibrium at point W. Gasoline consumption would still fall from G_1 to G_3.

1 is thereby attained along budget line *A*. The second corresponds to the after-tax environment. It plots equilibrium combinations of gasoline and other goods given the new higher price of gasoline, and it highlights point *V* as the after-tax equilibrium along the steeper budget line *B*. Indifference curve 2 reflects welfare after the tax *but before the rebate*.

The two income-consumption curves show that (1) an uncompensated gasoline tax would lower gasoline consumption, (2) an income rebate equal to total gasoline tax payments would push consumption back up, (3) the combined effect of the tax and the rebate would nonetheless leave consumption lower than before, and (4) welfare would decline (but not by as much as it would without the rebate).

To see how, notice that the graph indicates that an uncompensated tax would shift the market equilibrium from point *U* to point *V*; gasoline consumption would fall from G_1 gallons to G_2 gallons. The distance *VZ* represents total tax payments at equilibrium point *V*. Why? Point *V* corresponds to consuming S_v dollars worth of other goods, but the consumer would be able to afford S_z dollars worth if no tax were collected. It follows that the consumer must be paying $(S_z - S_v)$ in tax. Line *C* on the figure drawn through point *Z* and parallel to budget line *B* must therefore represent the after-tax *and after-rebate* budget line. (It must go through point *V* because the rebate makes point *V* exactly affordable, and it must be parallel to line *B* because it incorporates the after-tax price of gasoline). Point *W* is the market equilibrium along budget line *C*. It picks G_3 gallons (with $G_2 < G_3 < G_1$). The rebate therefore works to increase gasoline consumption. The combined effect is, however, clearly negative, since point *W* lies to the left of point *U*. Point *W* also supports indifference curve 3; it lies above indifference curve 2 and below curve 1.

CONSUMER SURPLUS

We have presented a model of how consumers respond to changes in money income and price, but we have thus far only hinted at how this model can be used to solve practical problems. The balance of this chapter will be devoted to applications of the model.

Let's begin with a very simple case in which a consumer who actually consumes exactly 5 gallons of gasoline per week is given a coupon for 5 free gallons of gasoline. How much would these free gallons be worth? As trivial as this question might appear, its answer will lay the foundation for much of what economists have to say about a wide range of public-policy issues. Understanding how the notion of consumer surplus answers the value question is a productive start toward confronting such issues.

The proper economic question to ask in determining the value of the 5 free gallons of gasoline is simply put: How much would the consumer willingly have paid for the free gasoline—one unit at a time? The consumer's individual demand curve provides the answer. Suppose that this demand

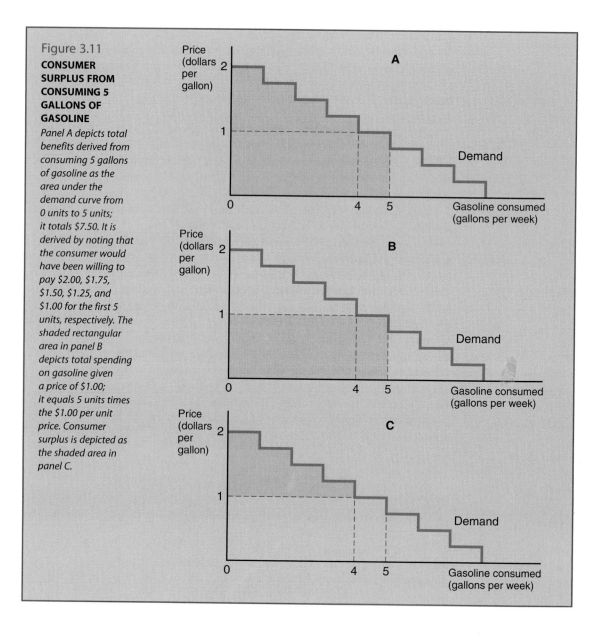

Figure 3.11

CONSUMER SURPLUS FROM CONSUMING 5 GALLONS OF GASOLINE

Panel A depicts total benefits derived from consuming 5 gallons of gasoline as the area under the demand curve from 0 units to 5 units; it totals $7.50. It is derived by noting that the consumer would have been willing to pay $2.00, $1.75, $1.50, $1.25, and $1.00 for the first 5 units, respectively. The shaded rectangular area in panel B depicts total spending on gasoline given a price of $1.00; it equals 5 units times the $1.00 per unit price. Consumer surplus is depicted as the shaded area in panel C.

curve were as portrayed in panel A of Figure 3.11. For simplicity, assume that the price of gasoline is $1.00 per gallon, and that gas can be purchased only in whole gallons. Notice from the demand curve that the consumer would indeed purchase 5 gallons of gasoline each week at the $1.00 per gallon price. Finally, assume that the consumer would use the coupon instead of cash to purchase this week's gasoline.

So, how much would the free gas be worth? It is tempting to respond "$5.00" (= 5 free gallons × $1.00 per gallon), because that is how much the consumer would save in actual expense. But $5.00 is wrong, because the demand curve indicates that she would have been willing to spend more for those five gallons of gasoline; $1.00 is only the price she was willing to pay for the *fifth* gallon of gas. Indeed, the consumer whose demand curve is depicted in Figure 3.11 would have been *willing* to spend $2.00 for the first gallon alone. If the price were then lowered to $1.75, our consumer would have been willing to buy a second gallon. At $1.50, she would have willingly purchased a third; at $1.25, a fourth. So, how much would the consumer have been willing to pay for the 5 gallons that have been offered free? The sum of $2.00 for the first gallon, $1.75 for the second, $1.50 for the third, $1.25 for the fourth, and $1.00 for the fifth—a grand total of $7.50.

It is important to note in passing that this total, the maximum value that the consumer would attach to 5 gallons of gasoline per week, equals the area under the demand curve from 0 gallons per week to 5 gallons per week. In other words, it is equal to the shaded area depicted in panel A of Figure 3.11. Why? That area is the sum of five rectangles, each with a width of one unit (gallon) and a height equal to the price that the consumer would willingly pay for that unit.

It is now time to compare the value of the 5 gallons of gasoline with the amount that the consumer would have had to pay if the free gas had not been offered. We have already noted that she would then have spent a total of $5.00—a sum equal to the area of the shaded rectangle in panel B of Figure 3.11 (the height of the rectangle [the $1.00 price] multiplied by the width [the 5 units consumed]).

So, the consumer would pay only $5.00 for the 5 gallons of gasoline even though their total value summed to $7.50. The difference between what the consumer would be willing to pay and what the consumer actu-

ally has to pay is called **consumer surplus.** In this case, consumer surplus equals $2.50; it is geometrically represented by the shaded area in panel C of Figure 3.11. To see why, notice that we simply deduct actual spending (the shaded rectangular area of panel B) from total value (the shaded area of panel A) to compute consumer surplus (the shaded area in panel C).

Finally, we can relax the assumption that gasoline can be purchased only in units of one gallon. Fractions of a gallon can certainly be purchased, and so the demand curve could be a smooth line of the sort drawn in Figure 3.12 rather than the series of steps drawn in Figure 3.11. Regardless of whether or not the demand curve is smooth or a series of steps, though, the maximum amount that the consumer would pay for 5 gallons of gasoline is the area under the demand curve from 0 to 5 gallons. Figure 3.12 portrays the more general case. The maximum amount that a consumer would pay for C units of some good X is area $0ABC$. Since the price of good X is represented by P, the amount that the consumer would pay for C units is area $0PBC$. Since consumer surplus equals the maximum amount that the consumer would pay (area $0ABC$) minus the amount actually paid (area $0PBC$), the shaded triangular area above the price line and below the demand curve (area PAB) is the consumer surplus.

Consumer surplus and its relationship to measures of economic benefit are of enormous practical importance. To illustrate how the concept of consumer surplus is used, let us examine briefly the widely held view (at least in Europe) that energy is significantly underpriced in the United States.

Figure 3.12 **DEMAND AND CONSUMER SURPLUS WITH FRACTIONAL UNITS**

Consumer surplus derived from consuming C units at a price of P is given by the area of triangle PAB. The trapezoidal area 0ABC represents the total benefit derived from consuming C units. The rectangular area 0PBC is total expenditure (= price, P, × quantity, C). The marginal benefit of consuming the last unit is read from the demand curve.

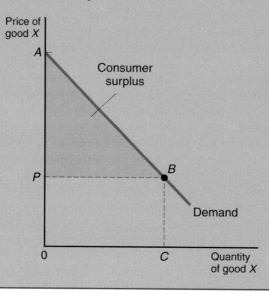

Trade negotiators make this claim when they talk about the sources of the relative competitiveness of U.S. businesses. Environmental negotiators make the same claim when they point to the high levels of energy consumption by U.S. households. Is the claim true? That is a matter of opinion. Without offering a judgment on whether U.S. prices are too low or European prices are too high, Table 3.3 offers some comparative data from the end of 1998

Table 3.3 **RETAIL PETROLEUM ENERGY PRICES IN THE UNITED STATES AND EUROPE**

Energy type	Price (in dollars per unit; European prices converted to dollars)[a]				
	United States	**Germany**	**United Kingdom**	**Spain**	**France**
Gasoline ($/liter)	$0.283	$0.901	$1.210	$0.794	$1.087
Heating oil ($/1,000 liters)	$221.4	$235.3	$189.4	$280.3	$333.9
Heavy fuel oil ($/metric ton)	n/a	$103.7	$126.3	$124.3	$104.7
Automotive diesel ($/liter)	$0.268	$0.572	$0.948	$0.521	$0.598

[a]Prices are converted into dollars including taxes for the middle of September 1998. Heavy fuel oil is used for industry in Europe; it is high-sulfur in the U.K., Spain, and France but low-sulfur in Germany. The gasoline price is for premium leaded gasoline for the U.K., Spain, and France; it is for regular unleaded in the U.S. and Germany.
SOURCE: International Energy Association Web site, www.iea.org/stat.htm, accessed September 1998. The data are updated monthly.

that confirm the impression that energy does indeed cost less in the United States than it does in Europe. To what end? How much additional value do American consumers gain by enjoying lower prices? Alternatively, what would be the harm of raising energy prices in the United States to a level that would be more in line with prices in Europe?

These are difficult questions to answer, but the theory of consumer surplus can help. Panel A of Figure 3.13 offers a representation of household demand for energy in the United States. The household would, given an initial price of P_0, choose to demand Q_0 units of energy per year. The total annual cost of energy to the household would therefore be $P_0 \times Q_0$—an amount equal to area $0P_0E_0Q_0$. We know, however, that this annual level of spending on energy underestimates what the energy is worth to the household. As stressed above, the household would enjoy total benefits equal to the area $0AE_0Q_0$ and consumer surplus is equal to the shaded area (area P_0AE_0) in panel A.

Now suppose that the U.S. government tried to bring energy prices up to European levels by, say, adding another layer of taxation to the price. In particular, let the price climb to P_1 as shown in panel B; the tax, then, is simply the difference between the original price, P_0, and the new price, P_1. In response to the higher price, the household would purchase somewhat less energy. Let that new, lower quantity be Q_1 units per year (with $Q_0 > Q_1$). The annual cost of energy to the household may go up or down in response to this change, but it is clear that total benefit (area $0AE_1Q_1$) and consumer surplus (area P_1AE_1) have both declined. The reduction in consumer surplus is shown by the shaded area in panel C. It is, by construction, the shaded

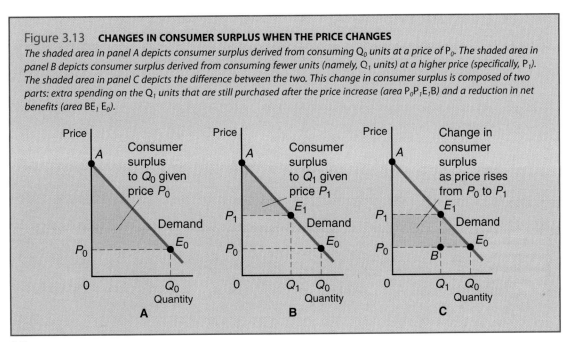

Figure 3.13   **CHANGES IN CONSUMER SURPLUS WHEN THE PRICE CHANGES**
The shaded area in panel A depicts consumer surplus derived from consuming Q_0 units at a price of P_0. The shaded area in panel B depicts consumer surplus derived from consuming fewer units (namely, Q_1 units) at a higher price (specifically, P_1). The shaded area in panel C depicts the difference between the two. This change in consumer surplus is composed of two parts: extra spending on the Q_1 units that are still purchased after the price increase (area $P_0P_1E_1B$) and a reduction in net benefits (area BE_1E_0).

consumer surplus area of panel A minus the shaded consumer surplus area of panel B. The loss in consumer surplus is, in other words, the area under the demand curve between the original price and the higher price.

To understand why the geometry makes sense, note that the shaded area in panel C can be divided into two parts: rectangle $P_0 P_1 E_1 B$ and triangle $BE_1 E_0$. The first part, rectangle $P_0 P_1 E_1 B$, is easily understood. It is the extra amount that the household must pay for the Q_1 units of energy that it still buys each year. Indeed, rectangle $P_0 P_1 E_1 B$ represents exactly the extra tax revenue collected by the government (the tax $[P_1 - P_0] \times$ the Q_1 units still consumed). The second part, triangle $BE_1 E_0$, is deadweight loss—lost consumer surplus that would not be transferred to the government through its augmented tax collections.

Example 3.5	Household Responses to Higher Energy Prices and Their Associated Losses in Consumer Surplus

The previous discussion outlined how to calculate changes in consumer surplus to estimate the welfare loss of higher energy prices. Changes in tax policy of the sort posed there set the stage for fierce political debate, of course. The Clinton Btu tax proposal of the mid-1990s was dead on arrival on Capitol Hill despite strong support from leading Democrats like Bill Bradley, then senator from New Jersey and soon to become a candidate for president. How can we make sense of the debate? From an economic standpoint, the first step in evaluating a tax change is to get a handle on the associated costs and benefits. The benefit side of an energy tax will be confronted later on; for the moment, suffice it to say that reduced reliance on foreign sources of energy, reduced pollution, and taking concrete steps toward an economic structure that might be more sustainable over the long run have all been advanced to support raising energy taxes. But what about the cost? Can we put real numbers into Figure 3.13 to get some idea of the magnitude of the economic damage that would be caused by, say, a 10 percent energy tax?

Table 3.4 records quantity and price data for household consumption of gasoline, natural gas, and electricity for the United States in the mid-1990s. The table also reports the percentage change in consumption that would be associated with a 1 percent increase in price. These data are

Table 3.4 HOUSEHOLD CONSUMPTION DATA FOR THE UNITED STATES IN 1992	Energy type	Quantity (10^{12} Btu)	Price (per 10^6 Btu)	Quantity sensitivity to a 1% increase in price
	Gasoline	28.80	$9.50	−0.39
	Natural gas	20.20	$6.01	−0.30
	Electricity	9.30	$23.70	−0.42

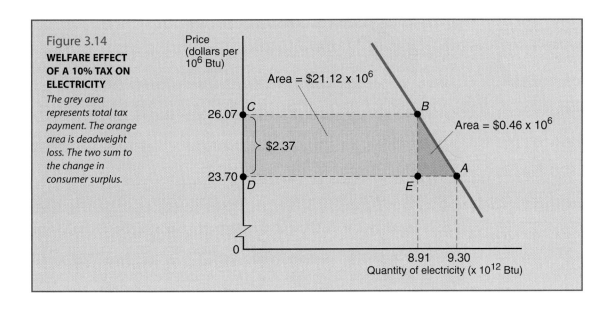

Figure 3.14

WELFARE EFFECT OF A 10% TAX ON ELECTRICITY

The grey area represents total tax payment. The orange area is deadweight loss. The two sum to the change in consumer surplus.

Price (dollars per 10^6 Btu)

Area = $21.12 x 10^6

Area = $0.46 x 10^6

26.07 — C — B

$2.37

23.70 — D — E — A

0

8.91   9.30

Quantity of electricity (x 10^{12} Btu)

sufficient for us to be able to compute total tax payments by households in the face of a 10 percent tax from then-current prices and the associated loss in net benefits—lost consumer surplus that is not transferred to the government. To see how, consult Figure 3.14; it illustrates an analysis for electricity. The demand curve is drawn through the initial data (point *A*) with a slope that associates a 10 percent increase in price ($26.07 per million Btu) with a 4.2 percent reduction (down to 8.91 trillion Btu) in quantity demanded (point *B*). Total lost consumer surplus is equal to the area of trapezoid *ABCD*; it equals $21.58 million. It is the sum of total tax payments (the area of rectangle *EBCD* = $21.12 million) and deadweight loss (the area of triangle *EAB* = $0.46 million). Notice, though, that this is a small fraction of the $232 million that households would actually be spending on electricity after the tax—an amount that is $12 million higher than the before-tax level. Table 3.5 reports the results of conducting the same calculations for gasoline and natural gas; you might find it instructive to construct your own graphs.

Table 3.5   AFTER-TAX PRICES, QUANTITIES, AND LOST CONSUMER SURPLUS FOR THE 10% TAX

Energy type	Quantity (10^{12} Btu)	Price (per 10^6 Btu)	Lost consumer surplus (millions)	Total tax payments (millions)	Deadweight loss (millions)
Gasoline	27.68	$10.45	$26.83	$26.30	$0.53
Natural gas	19.59	$6.61	$11.93	$11.75	$0.18

◻ Demand, Benefit, and Marginal Benefit

The concept of consumer surplus offers us a first glimpse into how economists measure the benefit derived from the consumption of an economic good or service. The story in Chapter 2 about weighing the value of the Spinx/Digit phone company deals against the unspecified burden of "strings" that came attached gave us a glimpse, but we can be more explicit. We just saw how consumer surplus is drawn directly from the idea that the price that a consumer would willingly pay for one more unit of consumption is a reasonable measure of the value that such a consumer places on the next unit of consumption. Stated in terms of our model, the entire construction of consumer surplus relied on the expectation that an individual demand curve for some good X relates the prices that the individual would pay for each and every unit (taken one at a time from the first to the last).

Marginal benefit   Prices read from an individual demand curve for some good X can therefore be interpreted as a measure of the **marginal benefit** of the next unit of consumption—the value, denominated in a currency like dollars, that an individual places on consuming one more unit of X. Why? Because that is exactly what the consumer would be willing to *pay* for one more unit. Indeed, this interpretation is required by the underlying mathematics (given a collection of technical assumptions) if the total area shaded in panel A of Figure 3.11 is to be considered a measure of the total value or total benefit of consuming 5 gallons of gasoline. In calculating consumer surplus, we are taking the total amount that the consumer would have been willing to
Total benefit   pay for those 5 gallons of gasoline to be a measure of the **total benefit** generated by his consuming those 5 gallons.[7]

Cast in the more general context of Figure 3.12, the total benefit of consuming C units of good X can be represented by area $0ABC$—the area under the demand curve from 0 to C units. It is denominated in dollars.[8] The marginal benefit of consuming the last of the C units is read from the demand curve—the distance BC (which also equals P). It is also denominated in dollars. We will frequently return to this observation as we interpret

---

[7]One further point needs to be made concerning the joint concepts of consumer surplus and associated measures of economic benefit. When we use either, we are implicitly making an assumption that is most easily explained in the context of indifference curves drawn with units of some good X on the horizontal axis and the amount of money spent on all other goods on the vertical axis. We assume, specifically, that all such indifference curves are vertically parallel for any value of X. This is a very restrictive assumption. Most economists agree, however, that it does little "violence to reality" if consumers devote only a small portion of their income to good X. It is therefore judged to be "good enough" in most practical applications. See R. Willig, "Consumer Surplus without Apology," *American Economic Review*, September 1976. When it is not, though, tools are available to aid the analyst in judging the size and direction of the error.

[8]Note carefully that benefits measured in currency are a cardinal measure of welfare—specific numbers are attached to specific levels of consumption. Consumer theory, itself, builds from an assumption that indifference curves reflect only an ordinal measure of well-being. The underlying preferences are required to do nothing more than sustain rankings of alternative bundles of goods. That is, individuals must be able to say only, for any two bundles A and B of goods, that A is preferred to bundle B, that B is preferred to A, or that they are indifferent between bundles A and B.

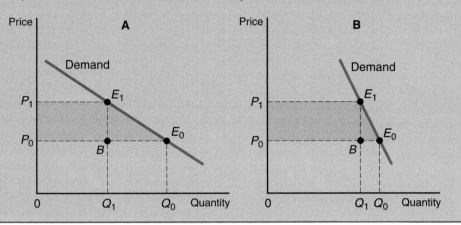

Figure 3.15 **COMPARING LOSSES IN CONSUMER SURPLUS FOR IDENTICAL INCREASES IN PRICE**

The shaded area in panel A depicts the loss in consumer surplus for a price increase from P_0 to P_1 given a demand curve that is very responsive to changes in price (i.e., very elastic at point E_0). The shaded area depicts the same in panel B for a demand curve in which the quantity demanded is relatively insensitive to changes in price (i.e., more inelastic at point E_0). Consumer surplus falls more under insensitive demand even though the net loss in benefits is smaller.

demand curves as marginal benefit curves and areas under demand curves as reflections of total benefit.

A simple illustration on two can, even now, demonstrate the analytical power of this interpretation. Consider, to that end, Figure 3.15. It displays the effect of identical increases in the prices of two goods whose only difference is the degree to which their quantities demanded respond to a change in their prices. Note that both panels show Q_0 units being demanded at an initial price of P_0, and Q_1 units being demanded at a higher price, P_1. The demand drawn in panel A is clearly more responsive to the price increase than the demand portrayed in panel B. As a result, the quantity demanded falls further for the case in panel A. Notice that the loss in consumer surplus associated with the higher price is nonetheless smaller in panel A (i.e., the area $P_0P_1E_1E_0$ is smaller in panel A than in panel B) and that a smaller portion of that loss is absorbed by the rectangle that reflects the extra amount that the household must pay (area $P_0P_1E_1B$) for Q_1 units. Nonetheless, the triangle representing the net benefit lost is relatively larger in panel A (area BE_1E_0).

Figure 3.16 turns the question around. It examines the welfare implications of price increases designed to reduce the quantity demanded by the same amount in the two demand configurations portrayed in Figure 3.15. Notice, now, that the more responsive demand of panel A means that a smaller price increase can accomplish the requisite demand reduction. As a result, the loss in consumer surplus is smaller in panel A than in panel B—this time because the spending rectangle and the net welfare-loss triangle are *both* smaller.

What does this mean for the energy markets described in Example 3.5? It is frequently observed that demand becomes more responsive to changes

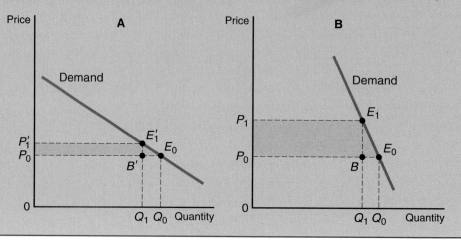

Figure 3.16   COMPARING LOSSES IN CONSUMER SURPLUS FOR IDENTICAL REDUCTIONS IN QUANTITY
The shaded area in panel A depicts the loss in consumer surplus when a higher price forces the quantity demanded to fall from Q_0 to Q_1 along a demand curve that is very responsive to changes in price (i.e., very elastic at point E_0). The shaded area does the same in panel B for a demand curve for which the quantity demanded is relatively insensitive to changes in price (i.e., highly inelastic at point E_0). A larger increase in price is required in panel B to effect the same reduction in the quantity demanded, so consumer surplus falls more under insensitive demand, and the net loss in benefits is larger.

in price as the time horizon expands. Households can do much more to conserve energy in response to higher prices if they have more time. They can install more energy-efficient windows. They can adjust their travel patterns. They can purchase a more fuel-efficient furnace. All of these responses take time, and so can be included only in a demand curve that includes "long-term" adaptation. With less time, households can turn off some lights and perhaps take fewer trips, but their ability to respond is much more limited. Qualitatively, then, the demand curves drawn in the panels labeled "A" in Figures 3.15 and 3.16 can be thought to reflect long-term demand responsiveness, and the ones drawn in the panels labeled "B," more restrictive, short-run options. It follows that the welfare implications of higher energy prices can be expected to change over time as the left-hand panels become more applicable.

INDEXES OF THE COST OF LIVING

The theory described in the previous sections has also been useful in constructing index numbers that reflect the *cost of living*, that is, the economic cost of maintaining a constant level of satisfaction or welfare. Cost-of-living indexes have always been closely associated with the notion of inflation. Indeed, the rate of inflation in the United States is frequently reported in terms of changes in the Consumer Price Index (CPI). The CPI is perhaps the most famous cost-of-living index. It has been calculated by the government's Bureau of Labor Statistics for more than 50 years. Labor unions that want to know whether or not wages are keeping pace with the cost of living keep track of the CPI. Automatic adjustments in wages based on changes in the CPI are incorporated into all Social Security payments made by the government to retirees and other beneficiaries.

In the following sections, we describe briefly how the CPI is constructed and point out why it is not an ideal price or cost-of-living index. Ideally, a cost-of-living index should be constructed so that we could be sure that a family would be worse off if its money income rose more slowly than the index and better off if its money income rose more quickly. If, for example, the ideal price index were 15 percent higher in 2002 than it was in 1999, then any family whose income rose by less than 15 percent over the same period of time would be worse off in 2002 than it was in 1999. Conversely, of course, any family whose income increased by more than 15 percent would be better off in 2002. This perfect correlation is the ideal. As you might expect, however, ideal price indexes are not very easy to come by in the real world, where the relative prices of various goods change, where tastes change over time, and where new products enter the marketplace while other products fade from our collective consciousness.

▣ The Consumer Price Index

We begin by showing how the Bureau of Labor Statistics calculates the CPI and how others use it to chart the course of inflation. Suppose, for simplicity, that there are only two goods in the economy, hamburger and coffee, and that the typical household bought 500 units of hamburger and 400 units of coffee per month in 1999. Assume, as well, that hamburger cost $3.00 per unit and coffee cost $1.25 per unit in 1999. The total amount that the typical household spent in 1996 on this market basket of goods was therefore $(500 \times \$3.00) + (400 \times \$1.25) = \$2,000$ per month. The "cost of living" in 1996 was, applying the methodology of the Bureau of Labor Statistics to this simple example, $2,000 per month.

Now suppose that the price of hamburger had risen to $4.00 per unit by 2002 while the price of coffee climbed to $2.00. The price of hamburger was thus 33.3 percent higher in 2002 than it was in 1999; the price of coffee, a whopping 60 percent higher. The CPI attempts to summarize or to describe these price increases in a single number. The first step that the Bureau of Labor Statistics would take in calculating this index is to determine how much the 1999 market basket of goods—500 units of hamburger and 400 units of coffee per month—would cost in 2002. Since the 2002 price of hamburger is $4.00 per unit, total expenditure on hamburger would be $2,000 in 2002. And since the 2002 price of coffee is $2.00, total expenditure on coffee would be $800. The 1999 market basket would therefore cost $2,800 ($2000 + $800) in 2002.

The next step in the calculation is to express the 2002 expenditure level as a multiple of the 1999 level. To do this, divide the 2002 cost ($2,800) by the 1999 cost ($2,000); the result is 1.40. This means that the "cost of living" rose by 40 percent ($1.40 is 40 percent larger than $1.00), because the total cost of sustaining an unaltered consumption bundle rose from $2,000 per month to $2,800 per month. As a result, the index value for the CPI would read 140 for 2002 if it had been normalized to read 100 in 1999. Notice that the 40 percent increase in the CPI is greater than the 33.3 percent increase in the price of hamburger but significantly less than the 60 percent increase in the price of coffee. The increase in the CPI is, in more technical terms, a "weighted average" of the increases in the two component prices.

More generally, suppose that the typical household bought H_1 units of hamburger and C_1 units of coffee in year 1. Let the price of hamburger be P_1^H per unit and the price of coffee be P_1^C per unit in year 1. The money income (I) required to purchase this market basket is then

$$I = (P_1^H)H_1 + (P_1^C)C_1. \quad [3.1]$$

In year 2 (subsequent to year 1), the money income I' required to buy the same market basket would be

$$I' = (P_2^H)H_1 + (P_2^C)C_1, \quad [3.2]$$

where P_2^H is the price (per unit) of hamburger and P_2^C is the price (per unit) of coffee in year 2. If the price index (the cost of purchasing the designated market basket) were set equal to 100 in year 1, then its value in year 2 would equal

$$p^* = 100\frac{I'}{I} = 100\frac{P_2^H H_1 + P_2^C C_1}{P_1^H H_1 + P_1^C C_1}. \quad [3.3]$$

The numerator of Equation 3.3 is simply the cost of maintaining the year 1 consumption bundle in year 2. The denominator, of course, is the cost of the same consumption bundle in year 1; their ratio is the foundation of the desired price index.

◻ Graphical Representation of the Price Index

To relate our discussion of the CPI to the material on consumer behavior presented earlier in this chapter, consider three distinct budget lines for the average household. *The first budget line describes this household's situation in year 1.* Because the household had a money income of I in year 1 and because the price of hamburger was P_1^H and the price of coffee was P_1^C in year 1, the equation of this budget line is

$$H = \frac{I}{P_1^H} - \frac{P_1^C}{P_1^H}C,$$

which we obtain by solving Equation 3.1 for H. This line is labeled "Year 1 budget line" in Figure 3.17.

The second budget line describes the household's situation in year 2, assuming that its money income in year 2 was the same as it was in year 1. Recalling that the prices of hamburger and coffee in year 2 were denoted P_2^H and P_2^C,

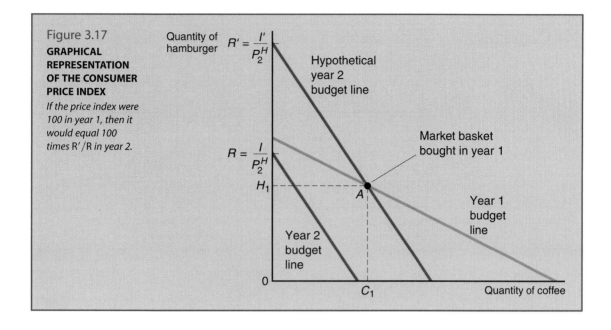

Figure 3.17

GRAPHICAL REPRESENTATION OF THE CONSUMER PRICE INDEX

If the price index were 100 in year 1, then it would equal 100 times R'/R in year 2.

Quantity of hamburger

$R' = \dfrac{I'}{P_2^H}$

Hypothetical year 2 budget line

Market basket bought in year 1

$R = \dfrac{I}{P_2^H}$

H_1

A

Year 1 budget line

Year 2 budget line

0

C_1

Quantity of coffee

respectively, it should be clear from Equation 3.2 that the equation for this budget line is

$$H = \frac{I}{P_2^H} - \frac{P_2^C}{P_2^H}C.$$

This budget line is labeled "Year 2 budget line" in Figure 3.17.

The third budget line to be considered is the hypothetical one that would de-scribe this household's situation in year 2 if it had just enough money (no more and no less) to buy the same market basket that it did in year 1. How is this line drawn? Recall that the household purchased H_1 units of hamburger and C_1 units of coffee in year 1; this combination is represented by point A in Figure 3.17. Since the hypothetical budget line assumes that the household can still afford to consume at point A, it must pass through point A. More-over, the line must have the same slope as the budget line for year 2 be-cause it has to reflect year 2 prices. It must, therefore, be drawn parallel to the "Year 2 budget line" *and* it must include point A. This line is labeled "Hypothetical year 2 budget line" in Figure 3.17.

Assuming for the sake of simplicity that the price index for year 1 equals 100, it is now easy to calculate the price index in year 2. The first step is to divide the vertical intercept (R') of the hypothetical year 2 budget line by the vertical intercept (R) of the actual year 2 budget line. Why? Because Equation 3.3 tells us that the new price index should be I'/I times 100 (where I' represents the income implicit in the hypothetical budget line). From Equations 3.1 and 3.2 we know that at these intercepts, where $C = 0$, $R' = I'/P_2^H$ and $R = I/P_2^H$, as shown in Figure 3.17. It follows, then, that $R'/R = I'/I$. The second step is simply to multiply R'/R by 100; the result is the price index in year 2.

103

Example 3.6 | **Calculating a Cost-of-Living Index**

Accocrding to the Bureau of Labor Statistics, the price of food in the United States was 1.1 percent higher in 2001 than it was in 2000 and the price of clothing was 1.7 percent higher (see Table B-58 in the *2001 Economic Report of the President,* U.S. Government Printing Office, Washington, D.C.). Assume that a family spent 50 percent of its 2000 money income on food and 50 percent on clothing in 2000. For this family, we can calculate the price index for 2001 given an index value of 100 for the year 2000, and we can see if this calculation could be indicative of the nation as a whole.

To see how, recall from Equation 3.3 that the value of the index in 2001 should be

$$100 \frac{F_1 P_2{}^F + C_1 P_2{}^C}{F_1 P_1{}^F + C_1 P_1{}^C},$$

where $P_1{}^F$ is the price of food in 2000, $P_1{}^C$ is the price of clothing in 2000, C_1 is the number of units of clothing purchased in 2000, and F_1 is the number of units of food purchased in 2000. The subscript 2 indicates prices in 2001. We can rewrite this formula as follows:

$$100 \frac{F_1 P_1{}^F (P_2{}^F/P_1{}^F) + C_1 P_1{}^C (P_2{}^C/P_1{}^C)}{F_1 P_1{}^F + C_1 P_1{}^C}$$

$$= 100 \frac{F_1 P_1{}^F}{F_1 P_1{}^F + C_1 P_1{}^C} \frac{P_2{}^F}{P_1{}^F} + 100 \frac{C_1 P_1{}^C}{F_1 P_1{}^F + C_1 P_1{}^C} \frac{P_2{}^C}{P_1{}^C}.$$

Since $F_1 P_1{}^F + C_1 P_1{}^C$ equals the family's 2000 income, the term $100 \times [F_1 P_1{}^F/(F_1 P_1{}^F + C_1 P_1{}^C)]$ is the proportion of its 2000 income that it devoted to food. According to our original assumption, it is 0.5. Similarly, the term $100[C_1 P_1{}^C/(F_1 P_1{}^F + C_1 P_1{}^C)]$ is the proportion devoted to clothing in 2000; it, too, is equal to 0.5. Since the Bureau of Labor Statistics has told us that $P_2{}^F/P_1{}^F = 1.011$ and $P_2{}^C/P_1{}^C = 1.017$, it follows that

$$(100)(0.5)(1.011) + (100)(0.5)(1.017) = 101.4$$

is the value of the price index for 2001.

If this family were typical, then we could conclude that prices rose by 1.4 percent across the country. Such an interpretation would require, however, that we verify the underlying assumption that the prices paid by this family rose at the same rate as the nation as a whole. If they increased more rapidly, then an index tailored more carefully to the family's location would be higher. The index could overestimate inflation for all of the reasons cited in the text. Note, however, that the impact could be small for this family. It might be difficult for the family to engineer much in the way of substitution between clothing and food even in the face of relatively higher food prices.

▣ Problems with the Consumer Price Index

Recall that an ideal price index would tell us the extent to which a family's money income would have to increase (or decrease) in a certain time period to offset exactly any changes in prices; the intent of such an index is to monitor what would be required to maintain the family's well-being. In practice, though, cost-of-living indexes are not ideal. In fact, a household that bought H_1 units of hamburger and C_1 units of coffee in year 1 would be *better off* if its income kept pace exactly with the Consumer Price Index.

To see why this is true, consult Figure 3.18. Notice immediately that Figure 3.18 reproduces the "Year 1 budget line" and the "Hypothetical year 2 budget line" from Figure 3.17. In addition, two of the household's indifference curves are drawn. Indifference curve 1 is the highest curve that the household could achieve in year 1. Its tangency with the year 1 budget line at point A is the market equilibrium point for year 1. As we know from the preceding section, the CPI rose from 100 in year 1 to $I'/I \times 100$ in year 2. If the household's money income rose by the same percentage, then it would actually have I' in money income in year 2 *and* the hypothetical year 2 budget line would actually apply. Would the household then stay at

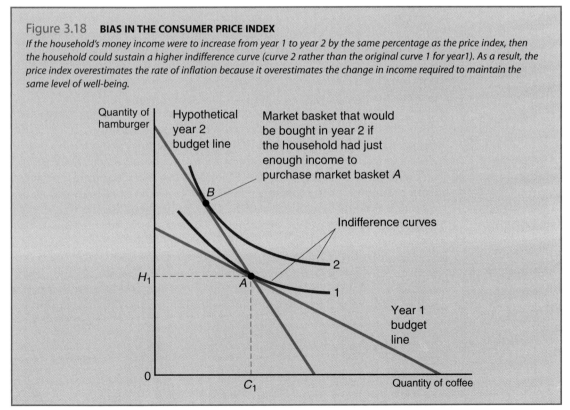

Figure 3.18 BIAS IN THE CONSUMER PRICE INDEX

If the household's money income were to increase from year 1 to year 2 by the same percentage as the price index, then the household could sustain a higher indifference curve (curve 2 rather than the original curve 1 for year1). As a result, the price index overestimates the rate of inflation because it overestimates the change in income required to maintain the same level of well-being.

Quantity of hamburger

Hypothetical year 2 budget line

Market basket that would be bought in year 2 if the household had just enough income to purchase market basket A

B

Indifference curves

2

H_1

A

1

Year 1 budget line

0

C_1

Quantity of coffee

point *A* and remain on indifference curve 1? No! The household would now choose point *B* on indifference curve 2. But indifference curve 2 is higher than curve 1. And so, welfare must have increased.

Changes in the overestimate inflation

Put another way, the CPI overestimates the rate of inflation. To understand why, it is important to understand that the CPI takes no account of the fact that households adjust their purchases from year to year as relative prices change. If the price of coffee goes up faster than the price of hamburger, for example, then a household that consumes both to begin with will try to cut back on its consumption of coffee and eat more hamburger. The CPI simply misses changes in households' market baskets because it compares the cost of purchasing a *fixed* market basket year after year.[9]

Substitution bias

As reported in the 1997 *Economic Report of the President,* this sort of **substitution bias** takes place in the computation of the CPI at two levels. At the "upper level," substitution occurs between the 207 categories of goods and services that make up the market basket actually surveyed by the Bureau of Labor Statistics (bananas are substituted for apples, for example). Each category, however, comprises a wide variety of individual commodities (like Macintosh, Granny Smith, Red Delicious, and other types of apples), and "lower-level" substitution certainly occurs within categories (so cheaper Red Delicious apples may be substituted for more expensive Macintoshes).

Quality changes

Computing the CPI is fraught with other problems, as well. The quality of a product often changes over time, for example, and it is difficult to know exactly how to adjust a price index to account for such a change. Suppose, for example, that the price of automobiles increased by 10 percent over a period in which new cars incorporated a number of quality improvements like air bags and antilock brakes. How much of the 10 percent increase in the price should be offset by an increase in quality in the CPI calculation?

New products

New products are equally troubling: when do they enter the designated market bundle? And how much of the price reduction that usually accompanies the maturing of a new product in the marketplace should be captured by changes in the CPI?

Shopping patterns

Finally, consumers' **shopping patterns** matter. Suppose that consumers shift their loyalties from high-priced department stores to low-priced outlets. Current methods assume that all such differences in price can be attributed to differences in quality. But is that really true?

The Advisory Commission to Study the Consumer Price Index has worked on these and other problems.[10] It issued a report to the Senate Finance Committee in 1998 that estimated that the sum of these sources of bias could overstate the current rate of inflation in the United States by 1.1

---

[9]A price index of this sort is often called a *Laspeyres price index.* If year 2 consumption levels were substituted for year 1 levels in the calculation, then we would be computing a *Paasche price index.*

[10]A brief accounting of the advisory commission's report can be found in the *Economic Report of the President* for the years 1997 and 1998 (Washington, D.C.: U.S. Government Printing Office, 1997 and 1998). The *Journal of Economic Perspectives* published an accessible symposium of papers on measuring the CPI in its winter 1998 issue (vol. 12, no. 1).

percentage points. Of that total, 0.15 percentage points were attributed to upper-level (between-category) substitution. Another 0.25 percentage points of bias were found in lower-level (within-category) substitution. New-product problems added 0.60 points, and shopping patterns accounted for 0.10 points. The commission's estimates were, as usual, uncertain, but it embedded its "best guess" within a plausible range from 0.8 percentage points to 1.6 percentage points.

The commission also offered some suggestions for improving the CPI. Most were technical, suggesting increased surveying and more responsive definitions of what actually constitutes the appropriate market basket. The Bureau of Labor Statistics had already begun to respond to such biases, though. It now allows generic drugs to be included when patents expire on proprietary brands. It adopted a procedure by which new stores are added to the underlying survey more quickly. It now includes actual transaction costs for hospital stays rather than scheduled prices. It changed the weighting procedures in anticipation of the commission's report. And it rotates goods into the basket more frequently in categories with histories of product innovations. These and other reforms will take several years to enact. The point of including them here is not to bog you down with details. It is, rather, to impress upon you that the devil *is* in the details, even for statistics with which we have all become comfortable.

Example 3.7	**Quality Change and the Cost of Light**

The text made it clear that significant changes in quality are problematic for price indexes because commodity prices reflect the cost of things that consumers buy and not the cost of attaining a given level of economic well-being or utility. Utility cannot be measured directly, of course, but William Nordhaus and others have suggested it might be useful to try to measure the prices of the fundamental characteristics of goods. He has argued that it would make sense, more specifically, to measure the cost of transportation rather than the price of automobiles. Or the cost of having a baby rather than the number of days spent in a hospital before bringing a baby home. Or the cost of lighting rather than the price of electricity.

Measuring the prices of these sorts of fundamental services would be difficult, to be sure, and so it is important to see if it would make much difference. Figure 3.19 suggests that it could. Three lines are plotted there. The first, identified as the "CPI," tracks overall consumer prices from series constructed back until 1800; it is provided for reference. The second, identified as a "Traditional light index," tracks a series derived from consumer or wholesale price indexes either for lighting fixtures or for the fuels that went into providing light (candles, town gas, kerosene, and electricity). It does not deviate significantly from the CPI series until the 1940s. Finally, the "True light index" was derived from studies of the efficiency of lighting devices, time series of energy price, and a fundamental measure of the quality of output—lumen-hours. Notice that the conventional price of light rose by a factor of 1,000 relative to the true price from 1800 through 1992.

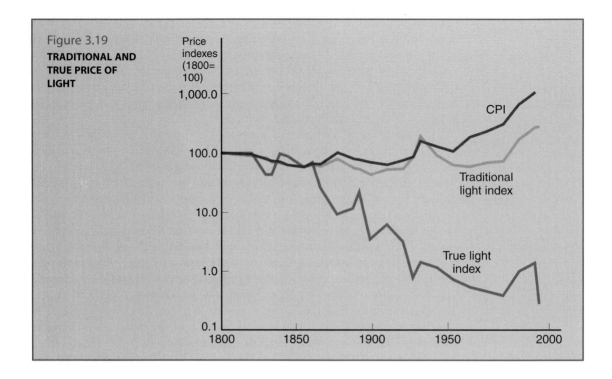

Figure 3.19

TRADITIONAL AND TRUE PRICE OF LIGHT

Lighting may be the only case in which we can compare characteristic service prices over such long periods of time, but the news is a bit unsettling. If similar differences over time are found elsewhere, then significant upward biases in price indexes have been experienced.

SOURCE: W. Nordhaus, "Quality Change in Price Indices," *Journal of Economic Perspectives,* Winter 1998, pp. 59–68.

SUMMARY

1. The rational consumer will maximize utility by allocating all of his or her income between any two goods X and Y so that the marginal rate of substitution of good X for good Y is exactly equal to the ratio of the price of good X to the price of good Y. Having achieved this condition, the consumer would find it impossible to find another affordable combination of X and Y for which his or her utility would be higher.

2. If we hold commodity prices constant, each different level of money income results in a different equilibrium market basket of goods for a consumer. The curve that connects the points identified by these equilibria is called the income-consumption curve. The income-consumption curve can be used to derive the Engel curve for each good purchased by a consumer, which plots the relationship between the equilibrium quantities purchased by a consumer and the level of his or her money income. Engel curves provide visual portraits of consumption patterns and income changes.

3. Holding the consumer's money income as well as the prices of all other goods and tastes (preferences) constant, we can determine the relationship between the price of a good and the quantity of that good that the consumer will purchase. This relationship is the consumer's individual demand curve

for the good in question. One of the central concepts in the theory of consumer behavior, the individual demand curve for any good X, can be derived from the price-consumption curve—the locus of equilibrium market baskets that the utility-maximizing consumer chooses as the price of X changes, holding income and other prices fixed.

4. The location and shape of an individual demand curve will depend upon the level of money income and the levels of the prices of other goods that are held constant in its construction. Both location and shape also depend upon consumer preferences. It is important to distinguish between shifts in a consumer's demand curve for any good X (caused by changes in income, the prices of goods other than X, or tastes) and movement along a demand curve (caused by changes in the price of X).

5. The total effect of a change in the price of some good X can be divided into two parts: the substitution effect and the income effect. The substitution effect is the change in the quantity of X demanded resulting from a price change when the level of satisfaction (utility) is held constant. The income effect shows the change in the quantity of X demanded resulting from the change in real income caused by the change in the price. The substitution effect is always negative; higher prices always reduce the quantity demanded and vice versa. The direction of the income effect cannot be predicted from theory alone. It pushes the quantity demanded in the same direction as the substitution effect for normal goods (goods for which the quantity demanded increases or decreases with income), but pushes in the opposite direction for inferior goods (goods for which the quantity demanded increases as income falls, and vice versa).

6. The area under a demand curve for some good X from 0 to a given quantity is a cardinal measure of the benefit derived from consuming that quantity of X. The value read from the demand curve itself is an analogous measure of the marginal benefit of the last unit of X (i.e., the amount that the consumer was willing to pay for the last unit purchased). The area under the demand curve but above a line indicating the price of some good X is a measure of the consumer surplus that the consumer enjoys. Consumer surplus is the difference between total benefit measured in dollars and actual expenditure.

7. The model of consumer behavior has been used to examine solutions to practical problems. It is a basis for evaluating the total benefits derived from a change in economic circumstance. Here we used it to examine the cost of increasing the price or restricting the quantity supplied of energy.

8. The model of consumer behavior has also been used to construct indexes of the cost of living and to examine the sources of their limitations. The inability of these indexes to handle adequately the notion of consumer substitution in the wake of changes in relative prices is particularly noteworthy.

QUESTIONS/ PROBLEMS

1. Lewis and Clark Lake is a large reservoir in South Dakota. It was created on the Missouri River by the Gavins Point Dam, and is located in an area where there are very few bodies of water of any size. Thus it has become very popular. Suppose that there are 10,000 families of potential users of the lake for recreational purposes and that each family's demand curve for recreational trips to the lake is represented by the step-schedule portrayed in the figure. (a) If an ordinance were passed that limited each family to no more than five

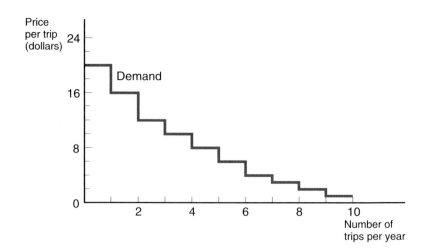

trips per year, how much economic benefit would be lost by each family?
(b) If an alternative ordinance were passed that allowed each family unlimited use of the lake for recreational purposes if it purchased a permit for $75
per year, would it be worthwhile for each family to buy the permit? (c) Suppose that we drew indifference curves on a graph with trips to the lake on
the horizontal axis and money spent on everything else on the vertical axis.
What would those indifference curves have to look like to guarantee the accuracy of the answers you gave to parts (a) and (b)? (d) How much consumer surplus would be enjoyed by each family if there were an $8 per visit
charge for each recreational trip to the lake? A $4 per visit charge?

2. Figure 3.11 displays an individual demand curve for gasoline. Construct indifference curves on a graph with gasoline on the horizontal axis and all
other goods on the vertical axis so that they support a price-consumption
curve consistent with the demand curve of Figure 3.11. That is, draw indifference curves and budget lines for a fixed income and constant prices
for other goods such that 1 gallon would maximize utility with a price of
$2, 2 gallons would maximize utility with a price of $1.75, and so on.

3. Suppose that all consumers pay 25 cents for a telephone call and 50 cents
for a newspaper. Assume that all consumers make some calls and buy at least
one newspaper. (a) If all consumers are maximizing utility, is it possible to
determine each consumer's marginal rate of substitution between telephone
calls and newspapers? (b) Is it possible that the marginal rates of substitution between telephone calls and newspapers are the same for all consumers?
(c) Pick two representative, but different, consumers. Draw budget lines
and indifference curves so that they maximize their utilities consuming different combinations of telephone calls and newspapers. Estimate the marginal rate of substitution between telephone calls and newspapers for each
consumer. Does your answer depend on whether the consumers' equilibrium bundles were different because their incomes, tastes, and preferences
were different? Why or why not?

4. A representative of the Texas Cattlemen's Association asserts that the proportion of income spent on food rises in the United States as income rises.
(a) Draw an Engel curve that would reflect his position. (b) Do the estimates recorded in Table 3.1 support his position?

5. Draw some Engel curves for a few of the goods and services listed in Table 3.1. Use the following protocol. Begin each with income and consumption both indexed to 100 (i.e., start each curve at income = 100 and consumption = 100). Plot the consumption points for a 10 percent increase in income (i.e., income = 110); for a 100 percent increase in income (income = 200); for a 300 percent increase in income (income = 400). (a) For which goods or services are the Engel curves that you drew closest to being straight lines? (b) Interpret what it would mean if an Engel curve were a straight line. (c) How much would consumption have to change for each 1 percent increase in income for an Engel curve to be a straight line? Now refer to Example 3.2 to check your work.

6. Some observers claim that the typical Irish family in the nineteenth-century potato famine was so poor that it spent almost all of its income on potatoes. When the price of potatoes fell, families could get the same amount of nutrition for a smaller expenditure, and so some of their incomes were diverted to vegetables and meat. Both provided extra nutrition, and soon even the consumption of potatoes declined. Assuming that this hypothesis is true, (a) were potatoes a normal good for Irish families? (b) Were they an inferior good? (c) Did they exhibit Giffen's paradox?

7. Suppose that families begin to devote sizable portions of their incomes to electronic games, appliances, and programs for their computers. Assume that many of these commodities are new products developed by the wizards at Microsoft and Hewlett-Packard. What problems do new products like these, which produce demand for new or substitute services, cause for the Bureau of Labor Statistics as it computes the Consumer Price Index?

8. Calculate a cost-of-living index for a family that consumes the following amounts of bread and clothing (and nothing else) in 1999 and 2002. Express your answer as an average *annual* rate of change over the three-year period.

	1999	2002
Units of bread purchased	100	140
Units of clothing purchased	120	130
Price of bread ($ per unit)	$0.30	$0.50
Price of clothing ($ per unit)	$30.00	$40.00

9. Example 3.4 presented an analysis of the Carter administration's plan to tax gasoline and then rebate the tax proceeds through the personal income tax. (a) If the tax alone had been enacted, would it have changed the slope of the consumer's budget line? (b) If the tax alone had been enacted, would it have changed the individual consumer's demand curve? If so, how? If not, why not? (c) If the tax had been enacted in concert with the rebate scheme, would both, working together, have changed the individual consumer's demand curve? In answering this question, take the price of gasoline at the pump *plus the tax* to be the price of gasoline actually paid by the consumer and assume that the price at the pump is unchanged. (d) Check your answer to part (c) by using Figure 3.10 to construct both a pretax and a post-tax-and-rebate demand curves.

10. It is frequently useful to explore the underlying geometry of microeconomic analysis. To that end, refer to panel A of the accompanying figure, which

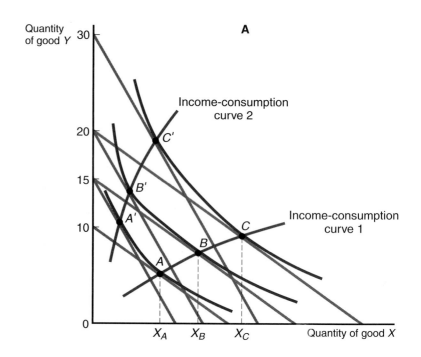

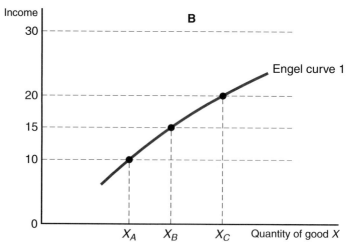

shows three indifference curves for goods X and Y that are relatively close substitutes for one another—i.e., the indifference curves are smooth and display a gradual convex curvature. Parallel budget lines are also drawn there so that each is tangent to one of the indifference curves. Assume that the price of good Y is $1 so that the vertical intercept of each budget line represents the income required to sustain consumption at the designated equilibria—points A, B, and C along the income-consumption curve 1. Use the information provided to see that the Engel curve 1 for good X drawn in panel B is correct. Now assume that the price of X doubles. Convince yourself that income-consumption curve 2 would now apply, and carefully draw a new Engel curve for X by using the coordinates of points A', B', and C'; to do so, you will have to be careful to read the required income from the vertical axis. Explain why the resulting Engel curve is steeper and higher than Engel curve 1. Repeat the process with your own graphs for the case where goods X and Y are more complementary so that the underlying indifference curves curve more sharply around points A, B, and C. Would the new Engel curve be higher or lower than Engel curve A? Would it be higher or lower than the second Engel curve drawn for the original case? Explain.

Calculus Appendix

CONSUMER EQUILIBRIUM WITH A MORE GENERAL COBB-DOUGLAS UTILITY FUNCTION

The Cobb-Douglas formulation of a utility function holds that

$$U(X, Y) = X^\alpha Y^\beta$$

with $0 < \alpha < 1$ and $0 < \beta < 1$. The appropriate Lagrangian for utility maximization subject to the budget constraint in this case is then

$$\Gamma(X, Y, \lambda) = X^\alpha Y^\beta + \lambda(I - P_X X - P_Y Y).$$

The corresponding first-order conditions are

$$X: \frac{\partial \Gamma}{\partial X} = \alpha X^{\alpha - 1} Y^\beta - \lambda P_X = 0; \qquad [1a]$$

$$Y: \frac{\partial \Gamma}{\partial Y} = \beta X^\alpha Y^{\beta - 1} - \lambda P_Y = 0; \qquad [1b]$$

$$\lambda: \frac{\partial \Gamma}{\partial \lambda} = I - P_X X - P_Y Y = 0. \qquad [1c]$$

The first two (Equations 1a and 1b) combine to set

$$\frac{\alpha X^{\alpha - 1} Y^\beta}{P_X} = \frac{\beta X^\alpha Y^{\beta - 1}}{P_Y} = \lambda. \qquad [2]$$

Equation 2 expresses the marginal utility of income in terms of ratios of the marginal utilities and prices of goods X and Y. Why? As shown before, the multiplier λ represents the increase in the maximum value of the objective function (utility in this case) that would result from loosening the constraint by 1 unit (by \$1 in this case). Rearranging,

$$\frac{\alpha X^{\alpha - 1} Y^\beta}{\beta X^\alpha Y^{\beta - 1}} = \frac{P_X}{P_Y}. \qquad [3]$$

Equation 3 characterizes all of the combinations of X and Y for which $MRS = P_X/P_Y$. It can be rewritten as

$$\frac{\alpha X^{\alpha-1} Y^{\beta}}{\beta X^{\alpha} Y^{\beta-1}} = \frac{\alpha X^{\alpha} Y^{\beta}/X}{\beta X^{\alpha} Y^{\beta}/Y} = \frac{\alpha Y}{\beta X} = \frac{P_X}{P_Y}.$$

Note in passing that we could have simply written this down if we had remembered, from earlier work, that $MRS = (\alpha/\beta),(Y/X)$. In either case, we would know that equilibrium would satisfy the condition that

$$\frac{Y}{X} = \frac{\beta}{\alpha}\frac{P_X}{P_Y};$$

i.e.,

$$Y = \frac{\beta}{\alpha}\frac{P_X}{P_Y}X. \qquad [4]$$

This is the income-consumption curve for our Cobb-Douglas utility function. Notice that it is a straight line from the origin with slope $(\beta/\alpha)(P_X/P_Y)$. The combination of X and Y that maximizes utility can now be seen to be the unique ordered pair (X^*, Y^*) that solves Equations 4 and the budget constraint—Equation 1c. That is, consumer equilibrium occurs at the intersection of the income-consumption curve and the budget constraint.

INDIVIDUAL DEMAND CURVES WITH COBB-DOUGLAS UTILITY

We have just seen that the intersection of an income-consumption curve with a budget constraint indicates the solution to the problem. More precisely, substituting the income-consumption curve displayed in Equation 4 into the replication of the budget constraint imposed by the first-order condition of Equation 1c, we see that

$$I - P_X X - P_Y Y = I - P_X X - P_Y\left(\frac{\beta}{\alpha}\frac{P_X}{P_Y}X\right) = 0.$$

As a result, we know that

$$I - \frac{\alpha + \beta}{\alpha} P_X X = 0,$$

and that

$$X = \frac{\alpha I}{(\alpha + \beta)P_X}. \qquad [5a]$$

Substituting Equation 5a back into the budget constraint (Equation 1c), meanwhile, produces

$$Y = \frac{\beta I}{(\alpha + \beta)P_Y}. \qquad [5b]$$

Equations 5a and 5b give solutions for utility parameters α and β, specific prices, and a fixed income. They will turn out to be individual demand curves for general Cobb-Douglas utility functions.

We can offer precise interpretations of the parameters α and β if we assume that $\alpha + \beta = 1$. This assumption would mean that Equations 5a and 5b can be rewritten as

$$X = \frac{\alpha I}{P_X} \quad \text{and} \quad Y = \frac{\beta I}{P_Y}.$$

Alternatively,

$$XP_X = \alpha I \quad \text{and} \quad YP_Y = \beta I.$$

We see, therefore, that α represents the proportion of income devoted to the spending on X, because

$$\text{total spending on } X = P_X X = \alpha I.$$

Meanwhile, $(1 - \alpha)$ is the proportion devoted to Y, because

$$\text{total spending on } Y = P_Y Y = (1 - \alpha)I.$$

THE COBB-DOUGLAS CASE WHERE THE EXPONENTS DO NOT SUM TO 1

It is equally important to understand that imposing the condition that $\alpha + \beta = 1$ does nothing to the solution of the utility-maximization problem or the individual demand curves. To see why, suppose that $V(X, Y) = X^a Y^b$ were a different utility function and let $(a + b) \neq 1$. Equation 4 would then read:

$$Y = \frac{b}{a} \frac{P_X}{P_Y} X. \qquad [4']$$

But if α in the original utility function had really been $a/(a + b)$ and β had really been $b/(a + b)$ in the original formulation, then Equation 4 would have immediately implied that

$$Y = \frac{\beta}{\alpha} \frac{P_X}{P_Y} X = \frac{b/(a + b)}{a/(a + b)} \frac{P_X}{P_Y} X = \frac{b}{a} \frac{P_X}{P_Y} X;$$

i.e.,

$$Y = \frac{b}{a} \frac{P_X}{P_Y} X. \qquad [4'']$$

These two structures would have produced the same equations in the end, and so their solutions would also have been the same. And since we could transform $V(X, Y)$ into $U(X, Y)$ with a positive monotonic transformation of the form

$$U(X, Y) = [V(X, Y)]^{1/(a + b)},$$

we see that any Cobb-Douglas utility function can be transformed into one for which the exponent assigned to any good must indicate the share of income devoted to its consumption. Just make the exponents sum to 1, and you are done.

APPLYING DEMAND CURVES

Recall the problem of maximizing utility for some individual with $100 to spend on two goods, X and Y, given by

$$U(X, Y) = X^{1/2}Y^{1/2},$$

when the price of X is $5 and the price of Y is $2. Straightforward application of the Lagrangian technique can do the trick; we showed this before.

The problem could be solved equally well by using the demand curves derived for the Cobb-Douglas case where the exponents sum to 1 (as they do in this case). For example, the demand curve for X tells us that 50 percent of income would be devoted to the consumption of X, so that

$$X = \frac{\alpha I}{P_X} = \frac{(\frac{1}{2})100}{5} = \frac{50}{5} = 10$$

in this case. Similarly, the other 50 percent of income would be devoted to the consumption of Y, so

$$Y = \frac{\beta I}{P_Y} = \frac{(\frac{1}{2})100}{2} = \frac{50}{2} = 25.$$

We also know that any monotonic transformation of this utility function would give the same answer. If, for example, utility were given by

$$V(X, Y) = X^5 Y^5,$$

then the answers would be the same, because $U(X, Y) = [V(X, Y)]^{1/10} = X^{1/2}Y^{1/2}$.

CHAPTER 4

Derivation of the Market Demand Curve

INTRODUCTION

We showed in Chapter 3 how an individual demand curve can be derived from a consumer's indifference map by using a price-consumption curve. The resulting demand curve displays the relationship between the quantity of the good demanded by the consumer (per unit of time) and the good's price. It is defined at every point in time *for a specific level of money income and a fixed set of prices for other goods.* The shape and level of the individual's demand curve obviously depend on the consumer's tastes, as reflected in his or her indifference map, but they also depend on the level of his or her money income and the relative prices of other goods.

Market demand curve

The **market demand curve** for any commodity is simply the horizontal summation of the individual demand curves of all the consumers in the market. Put differently, we add up the individual quantities demanded at each price to find the market quantity demanded at that price. Table 4.1, for example, shows the individual demand schedules for four consumers.[1] If these four consumers make up the entire market, then the market demand schedule is given in the last column of Table 4.1. Figure 4.1 shows the individual demand curves based on these same data. The resulting market demand curve appears as the curve lying farthest to the right. Be sure that you understand this construction. Take any price, like $2. Table 4.1 shows that individuals A through D would demand 40, 30, 25, and 19 units of the commodity, respectively. These values appear in the table and are highlighted by the dashed line in Figure 4.1. They total to 114 units; likewise, the highlighted point on the market demand curve shows 114 units in total quantity demanded at a price of $2. Because individual demand curves most often slope downward and to the right, market demand curves generally do the same.

Why spend so much effort explaining Figure 4.1 and its relationship with Table 4.1? Because the market demand curve for a commodity is one

---

[1]Recall from Chapter 1 that a demand schedule is a table showing the quantity demanded at various prices.

Table 4.1

**INDIVIDUAL AND
MARKET DEMAND
SCHEDULES**

Price (dollars per unit of the commodity)	Quantity demanded (units of commodity per unit of time)				Quantity demanded in market (units of commodity per unit of time)
	Individual A	Individual B	Individual C	Individual D	
1	50	40	30	20	140
2	40	30	25	19	114
3	30	20	18	18	86
4	25	15	13	17	70
5	20	14	13	16	63
6	15	13	11	15	54
7	10	12	9	14	45
8	8	11	7	13	39
9	6	10	5	12	33
10	5	9	3	11	28

of the most important concepts in microeconomics. The market demand curve shows how much of a commodity will be purchased (per unit of time) by all of the consumers in the market taken together, at each possible price. But since the market demand curve is derived directly from individual demand curves, its very construction assumes that the money incomes of

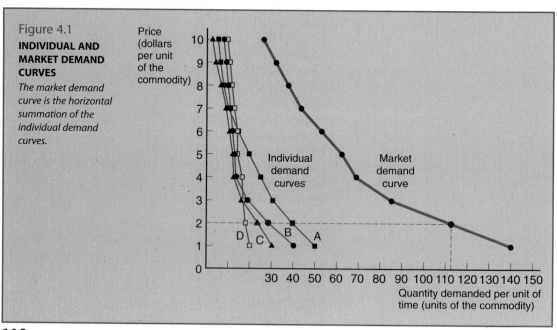

Figure 4.1

**INDIVIDUAL AND
MARKET DEMAND
CURVES**

*The market demand
curve is the horizontal
summation of the
individual demand
curves.*

the consumers and the prices of all other commodities are fixed and constant. Information regarding the market demand curve is nonetheless critically important to producers of the commodity. They need to know how much they can sell at various prices, and they need to know the sensitivity of those quantities to changes in the economic circumstances that influence their customers—their incomes and the prices of other goods. Economists are equally interested in market demand curves because, as explained in Chapter 1, they are critical in determining the prices of all sorts of commodities.

Example 4.1	Residential Demand for Water

Water is fundamental for people's existence no matter where they live. This does not mean, however, that residual demand for water is the same from one region to another. Researchers have, for example, estimated demand curves for water in six regions of the United States: New England and the North Atlantic region, the Midwest, the Southeast, the Plains and Rocky Mountain region, the Southwest, and the Pacific Northwest. Figure 4.2 displays the results.

Why are they different? And why are they so insensitive to price below a certain quantity? Because there are few good substitutes. Because it is difficult to conserve below a certain level. And because there is a certain "subsistence" level of demand for every person in the region. That explains

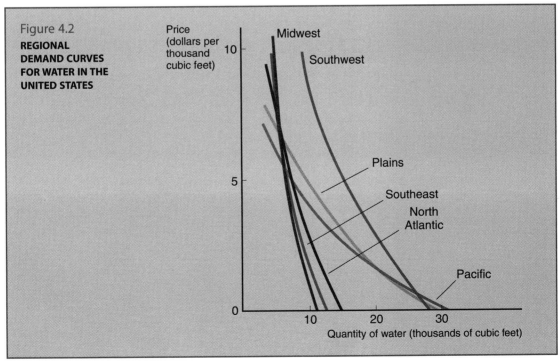

Figure 4.2

REGIONAL DEMAND CURVES FOR WATER IN THE UNITED STATES

why all of the curves, but one, turn nearly vertical below 7,000 cubic feet. The exception is the Southwest, where demand is highest except for the lowest prices. Even there, demand turns vertical around 12,000 cubic feet. Notice, though, that demand is most sensitive in regions where you might expect outdoor use is high. Why? For the opposite reason. Outdoor uses are less essential, so the quantity demanded can be more sensitive to changes in price.

Finally, would it make sense to add these demand curves horizontally to produce a market demand curve for the country as a whole? Not at all, unless it were possible to transport water from one region to another. Horizontal addition only makes sense if you can tell a story about an integrated market where demanders have access to multiple, if not all, suppliers.

For further discussion, see D. Gibbons, *The Economic Value of Water* (Washington, D.C.: Resources for the Future, 1986).

THE PRICE ELASTICITY OF DEMAND

*Price elasticity
of demand*

The **price elasticity of demand** at each point on the market demand curve is defined as the percentage change in the quantity demanded resulting from a 1 percent change in price. As such, the price elasticity of demand gauges the sensitivity of the quantity demanded to changes in price at a particular point on the demand curve.

*Role of close
substitutes*

The price elasticity of demand for a commodity depends first and perhaps foremost on the number and closeness of the substitutes that are available. If a commodity has many close substitutes, then its demand is likely to be price-elastic. A large proportion of its buyers would respond to an increase in its price by turning to the close substitutes that are available, and so the quantity demanded of the original commodity could fall dramatically. On the other hand, though, a great many buyers of substitutes could easily switch to this product if its price fell, and so the quantity demanded could rise just as dramatically in response to a price reduction.

The extent to which a commodity has close substitutes depends on how narrowly it is defined, of course. You should expect that a product would have more close substitutes and therefore its demand would be more price-elastic if its definition were narrower and more specific. The demand for a particular brand of shirts is likely to be more price-elastic than the overall demand for shirts. And the demand for shirts is likely to be more price-elastic than the demand for clothing products as a whole. Indeed, if a commodity is defined so that it has at least one perfect substitute, then its price elasticity of demand would be infinite. The cotton grown by one farmer, for example, is exactly the same as the cotton grown by other farmers in the same region. If a farmer were to increase his or her price even slightly above the price charged by the others, then his or her sales would likely collapse to zero. Why? Not because the demand for cotton was incredibly sensitive to changes in the price charged by one farmer, but because the demand for *the cotton raised by a single farmer* is determined by the prices charged by other farmers who grow *perfectly substitutable cotton.*

Budgetary importance

Second, it is sometimes asserted that the price elasticity of demand for a commodity is likely to depend on the importance of the commodity in consumers' budgets. The demand for commodities like paper clips, garlic, and pepper may be quite inelastic, because the typical consumer spends only a very small fraction of his or her income on such goods. On the other hand, the elasticity of demand may be higher for commodities that loom larger in the typical consumer's budget, like major appliances. Why? Consumers may be more conscious of changes in the prices of goods that require larger outlays, and so their demand might be more sensitive to those changes. Sounds reasonable, right? Notwithstanding the tendency of most consumers to notice when the prices of expensive items change, there is no guarantee that they do. The link between a commodity's price elasticity of demand and its importance in consumers' budgets seems to be much weaker than you might think. It frequently pays to actually examine the data and not rely exclusively on intuition; this is one of those cases.

Time period

Finally, the price elasticity of demand for a commodity is likely to depend on the length of the period to which the demand curve pertains. Every market demand curve pertains to a specific time interval, just like the individual demand curves from which they are derived. In many cases, demand is likely to be more elastic (or at least less inelastic) over a long period of time than over a shorter period of time. The longer the **time period,** the easier it is for consumers and business firms to substitute one good for another. If the price of natural gas should decline relative to other fuels, for example, then the consumption of natural gas over the course of the next year would probably increase very little. It takes some effort to switch to a natural-gas supplier for energy. Over a period of several years, though, people would have an opportunity to take account of the price decline in choosing the type of fuel to be used in new houses or to contemplate switching from oil or electricity in existing houses. You should expect, therefore, that the price reduction would have a greater effect on the consumption of natural gas over the longer term than it would over the shorter period of one year.[2]

Microlink 4.1   The Determinants of the Price Elasticity of Demand

It should be no surprise that the list of factors that determine the price elasticity of demand includes many of the determinants of demand listed in Chapter 1. Indeed, only budgetary importance has been added to a list that includes time period and the proximity of close substitutes. It is important to recognize, however, that the factors listed here are present because they

---

[2]For durable goods such as cars, the price elasticity of demand may be lower in the long run than in the short run. If the price of cars increases, the quantity demanded in the short term is likely to go down considerably, because many potential buyers will put off purchasing a new car. However, with the passage of time, the quantity of cars demanded will tend to go up, as old cars wear out.

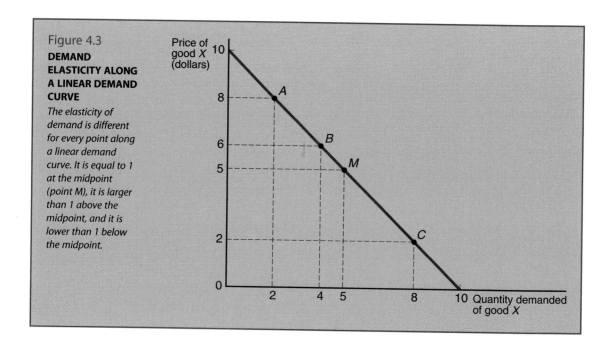

Figure 4.3

DEMAND ELASTICITY ALONG A LINEAR DEMAND CURVE

The elasticity of demand is different for every point along a linear demand curve. It is equal to 1 at the midpoint (point M), it is larger than 1 above the midpoint, and it is lower than 1 below the midpoint.

play a new role. They influence not only the position of a demand curve for some good, but also the sensitivity of the quantity demanded to changes in its own price.

◻ Price Elasticity and Linear Demand Curves

Figure 4.3 displays a linear demand curve for some good X—a straight line indicating an intercept of $10 and a slope equal to -1. We will use this curve to compute some elasticities, but we should stop for a moment to observe that the curve conveys an enormous amount of information all by itself. The intercept, as just noted, is $10; this means that nobody would consider buying even one unit of X if the price were $10 or higher. We noted that the slope was -1, too; this means that every $1 reduction in price would inspire somebody in the market to purchase one more unit of X.

But what of the price elasticity of demand? We can begin by noting that

$$\eta_D = -\frac{\%\ \text{change in quantity demanded}}{\%\ \text{change in price}}$$

$$= -\frac{(\Delta Q_D/Q_D) \times 100\%}{(\Delta P/P) \times 100\%}$$

$$= -\frac{\Delta Q_D}{\Delta P}\bigg/\frac{Q_D}{P}. \qquad [4.1]$$

In our simple example, though, $-\Delta Q_D/\Delta P = 1$. So what is the elasticity at, say, point A on Figure 4.3, where price is $8 and 2 units are demanded? Applying the revised formula, $\eta_D(A) = 1/(2/8) = 4$. And at point B,

122

where price is $6 and 4 units are demanded? Clearly, $\eta_D(B) = 1/(4/6) = 1.5$. And at the midpoint M, where the price is $5 and 5 units are demanded? $\eta_D(M) = 1/(5/5) = 1$. Finally, at a point below the midpoint such as C, where the price is $2 and 8 units are demanded, $\eta_D(C) = 1/(8/2) = 0.25$.

We could continue, but there is little point. This exercise has revealed that each point along the linear demand curve drawn in Figure 4.3 has its own distinct price elasticity. This is a result that turns out to be generally true for all linear demand curves. Indeed, the elasticity of demand is greater than 1 (exceeds unity) above the midpoint of a linear demand curve, it equals 1 at the midpoint, and it is less than 1 (falls short of unity) below the midpoint.

| **Example 4.2** | **Price Elasticities for Snack Foods** |

Did you ever think about your consumption decisions at the point of purchase? You go to a vending machine, for example, and you see a variety of choices. Should you buy some healthy food? Should you buy some less expensive Doritos? Not that Doritos are not healthy. It is just that they have a lot of salt and you may be a little worried about your blood pressure (with exams coming and paper deadlines looming). But how much would you be willing to pay for a healthier snack? And what about a choice between Doritos and pretzels? Would you pick one over the other on the basis of price?

It is unlikely that you have had this sort of conversation with yourself, but people in charge of marketing and pricing worry about these issues all the time. Market trials for new or different goods have long been used to produce preliminary but nonetheless workable estimates of their price elasticity of demand. One such trial, in fact, explored the sensitivity of the demand for low-fat snack foods from vending machines. New low-fat alternatives were introduced into the snack machines that serve high school and college students to see if they would be attractive alternatives. They were not. The same trials also changed the prices of more traditional snacks, and here the results showed some sensitivity. Indeed, 10 percent reductions in price increased the quantity demanded by an average of 9 percent; 25 percent reductions in price increased demand by 39 percent; and 50 percent price reductions produced 93 percent increases in units sold. Starting with initial price and quantity indexes of 100, Figure 4.4 displays a demand curve calibrated to these observations.

The price elasticity for the initial 10 percent price reduction from point A to point B was nearly unity. We can see that by computing arc-elasticity estimates according to

$$\eta_D \approx \frac{\Delta Q/[(Q_A + Q_B)/2]}{\Delta P/[(P_A + P_B)/2]},$$

where Q_A and P_A indicate the quantity and price at point A while Q_B and P_B represent the quantity and price at point B. This formula does nothing more than express the elasticity definition of Equation 4.1 in terms of proportions

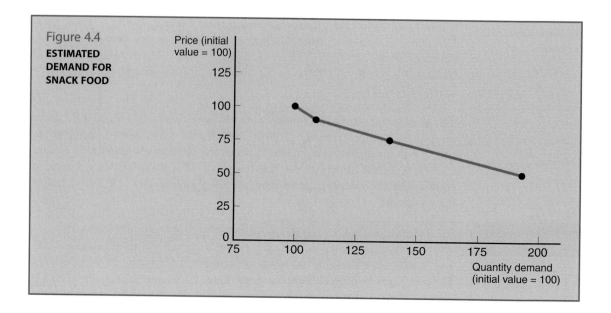

Figure 4.4
ESTIMATED DEMAND FOR SNACK FOOD

of the average prices and quantities at points A and B, respectively. Using this convention, then, an arc estimate of elasticity between points A and B is

$$\frac{9/[(100 + 109)/2]}{10/[(100 + 90)/2]} = \frac{0.086}{0.105} = 0.82.$$

Using the strict definition of Equation 4.1 would have given an estimate of 0.90; arc elasticities are only approximations.

Adding another 15-point reduction in price from an index of 90 at point B produced a 30-point increase in quantity between points B and C. The arc price elasticity in this region is therefore

$$\frac{30/[(109 + 139)/2]}{15/[(90 + 75)/2]} = \frac{0.242}{0.181} = 1.33.$$

And the final reduction added another 25-point reduction in price from point C to produce a 54-point increase in quantity at point D. The arc price elasticity in this region was nearly identical:

$$\frac{54/[(139 + 193)/2]}{15/[(75 + 50)/2]} = \frac{0.325}{0.240} = 1.35.$$

None of these estimates is too far from unity. You will not be surprised, after reading the next section, that average revenue per vending machine was relatively stable throughout the trial.

SOURCE: S. Boodman, "Prices Affect Choices," *Washington Post*, January 29, 2001.

☐ Price Elasticity and Total Expenditure

Price-elastic The demand for a commodity is said to be **price-elastic** if the elasticity of
Price-inelastic demand exceeds 1. The demand for a commodity is said to be **price-inelastic**

Table 4.2		Original price (dollars)	Original quantity demanded	New price (dollars)	New quantity demanded
ALTERNATE RESPONSES TO A PRICE INCREASE	Case A	$2.00	10,000	$2.02	9,900
	Case B	$2.00	10,000	$2.02	9,500
	Case C	$2.00	10,000	$2.02	9,950

Unitary elasticity

if the elasticity of demand is less than 1. And the demand for a commodity is said to be of **unitary elasticity** if the price elasticity of demand is equal to 1. Many important decisions hinge on the price elasticity of demand for a commodity. Why? One reason is because the price elasticity of demand determines whether a given change in price will increase or decrease the amount of money spent on a commodity. You can imagine that this is often a matter of basic importance to firms and government agencies.

To illustrate, we begin by noting explicitly that the amount spent on a commodity is simply equal to the price multiplied by the quantity demanded. If 10,000 units of some good X were demanded at a price of $2, then total spending would equal $20,000. If 9,900 units of X were demanded at a price of $2.02, then spending would again roughly equal $20,000. This is case A in Table 4.2. But if 9,500 units of X were demanded at the $2.02 price, then spending would fall to $19,190; this is case B. And if 9,950 units of X were demanded, then spending would rise to $20,099; this is case C.

Now suppose that the demand for a commodity is elastic; that is, assume that the price elasticity of demand exceeds 1. If the price were to rise in this case, then the percentage reduction in the quantity consumed would be greater than the percentage increase in the price. How do we know? Because that is what the definition of the price elasticity of demand tells us. Mathematically, having an elasticity exceed 1 means that

$$\frac{\% \text{ change in quantity demanded}}{\% \text{ change in price}} > 1$$

so that

$$\% \text{ change in quantity demanded} > \% \text{ change in price.}$$

As a result, the price increase must lead to a reduction in spending on the product—because one factor falls faster than the other rises. This possibility is reflected in case B of Table 4.2. Spending on X would fall by $810 in that case because quantity would fall to 9,500 units—a 5 percent reduction in quantity (from 10,000 units to 9,500 units) that would exceed the 1 percent increase in price (from $2.00 per unit to $2.02 per unit). Conversely, a price reduction would lead to an increase in spending on X because the price would fall more slowly than the quantity would rise.

Now suppose that the demand for a commodity were inelastic, so that the price elasticity of demand were less than 1. If the price rose in this situation, then the percentage reduction in the quantity consumed would be smaller than the percentage increase in price. This again follows directly from the definition of price elasticity. In the numerical example, case C of Table 4.2 would now apply. Quantity falling there from 10,000 units to 9,950 units (a 0.5 percent reduction in quantity) would be associated with the same 1 percent increase in price (from $2.00 to $2.02). A higher price would therefore cause spending on X to rise (from $20,000 to $20,099). Of course, a reduction in price would cause spending on X to fall.

Finally, if the demand for a product were of unitary elasticity, then price increases or decreases would not affect the expenditure on the product. Why? Because any percentage change in price would be matched by an equal percentage change in quantity *that moved in the opposite direction*. Case A of Table 4.2 would apply here. The 1 percent price increase (again, from $2.00 to $2.02) would cause quantity demanded to fall by a like 1 percent (from 10,000 units to 9,900 units) so that spending would hold constant at $20,000.

We can, finally, combine these results with the observations recorded earlier about elasticity values assumed along a linear demand curve. We noted there that the demand elasticity exceeds unity above the midpoint of a linear demand curve, it equals 1 at the midpoint, and it falls short of unity below the midpoint. We can now restate this result with a bit more technicality. Demand is elastic above the midpoint of a linear demand curve. It is inelastic below the midpoint. And demand displays unitary elasticity at the midpoint.

Example 4.3	The New York City Cigarette Tax

Mayor Michael Bloomberg of New York City proposed increasing the city tax on cigarettes from 8 cents per pack to $1.50 per pack in the winter of 2002. "The numbers are clear," said the mayor. "You raise cigarette taxes, the kids smoke less." City students were skeptical, though. "I doubt it," said Adam, an 18-year-old student who disputed the mayor's theory. "If kids can afford $5 a pack, another couple of bucks won't make much of a difference. Instead of spending a dollar on soda, I'll spend it on cigarettes." Other students planned to share cabs to save for cigarettes. So, who was right?

Empirical estimates of price elasticity can help. The various panels of Figure 4.5 provide graphic portraits of the cigarette market in the United States over the past 60 years. Overall consumption has been declining for some time, and increases in the real price of cigarettes can explain part of this trend. Indeed, Gary Becker, Michael Grossman, and Kevin Murphy provided estimates of long-run and short-run price elasticities in 1994; their estimates ran between 0.73 and 0.79 for the long run and between 0.36 and 0.44 for the short run. While many factors were considered in making these estimates, we can use the data depicted in Figure 4.5 to confirm that they are "in the right ballpark."

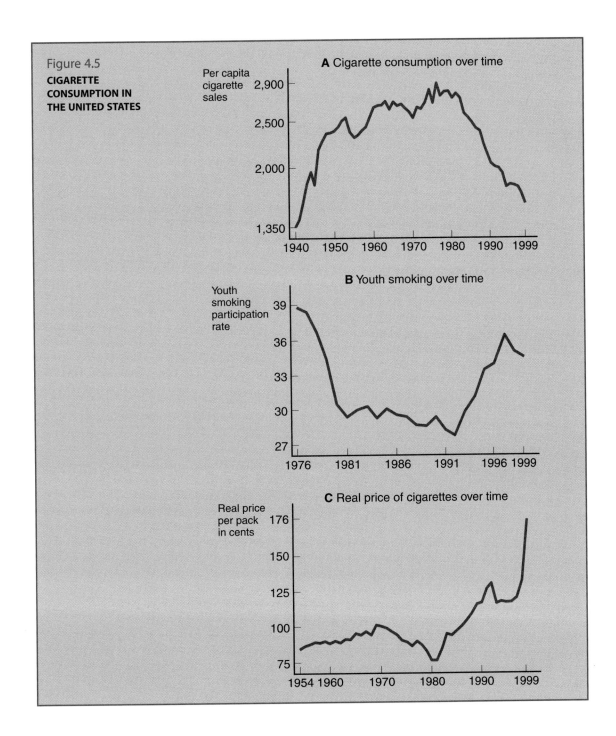

Figure 4.5

CIGARETTE CONSUMPTION IN THE UNITED STATES

A Cigarette consumption over time

Per capita cigarette sales

B Youth smoking over time

Youth smoking participation rate

C Real price of cigarettes over time

Real price per pack in cents

Notice, for example, that per capita consumption fell from roughly 2,700 to roughly 1,200 from 1980 through 1999 while the real price per pack rose from around 75 cents to about $1.75. Using a formula for the arc elasticity (an approach that anchors the calculation between any two points on a demand curve at their average in terms of price and quantity), an estimate of the long-term elasticity would be

$$\eta_D \approx \frac{(2{,}700 - 1{,}500)/[(2{,}700 + 1{,}500)/2]}{(175 - 75)/[(175 + 75)/2]} = \frac{0.57}{0.80} = 0.72.$$

It comes close to the results of Becker and co-authors.

It is equally important to note, for the New York example in particular, that youth smoking (measured by the proportion of high school students who have smoked) stopped following the national trend in the early 1990s. This is a source of concern even though youth combined demand is small (2–3 percent of overall demand), because surveys have found that three-quarters of American smokers began before their 19th birthday. Note in particular that participation rates for youth began to rise in 1992—just when a price war with discount brands broke out. Statistical analyses explain this with estimates of a short-run price elasticity for youth equal to 0.65. So, would higher taxes, added to dramatic increases in the price of cigarettes which began with the court settlement in the late 1990s and which are expected to continue over the next 10 years, turn the trend around? An elasticity of 0.65 suggests some reduction in quantity demanded, but nonetheless an increase in spending on cigarettes.

SOURCES: Denny Lee, "Buzz: New Cigarette Tax? Young Smokers Just Shrug," *New York Times,* February 24, 2002; Gary Becker, Michael Grossman, and Kevin Murphy, "An Empirical Analysis of Cigarette Addiction," *American Economic Review,* June 1994, pp. 396–418; and Jonathan Gruber, "Tobacco at the Crossroads: The Past and Future of Smoking Regulation in the United States," *Journal of Economic Perspectives,* Spring, 2001, pp. 193–212.

THE INCOME ELASTICITY OF DEMAND

We have, up to this point, been concerned solely with the effect of *price* on the quantity of a commodity demanded in the market. But price is not the only factor that influences market demand. The level and distribution of money income among the consumers in the market also play a critical role. If consumers had plenty of money to spend, for example, then the quantity demanded of a commodity like CDs would probably be greater than if the same consumers were poverty-stricken. Or if incomes in a particular community were high, then the quantity demanded of recreational equipment would likely be larger than if incomes in that community were low. Or if the incomes of vegetarians were larger than the incomes of nonvegetarians, then the quantity of beef demanded at local restaurants would be lower.

We saw in Chapter 3 that the relationship for individuals between money income (per period of time) and the amount consumed of a particular commodity (per period of time) can be represented by an Engel curve. Recall that this curve is based on the condition that the prices of all commodities remain constant. We can characterize the sensitivity of the amount consumed to changes in the consumer's money income *at any point* on an Engel curve

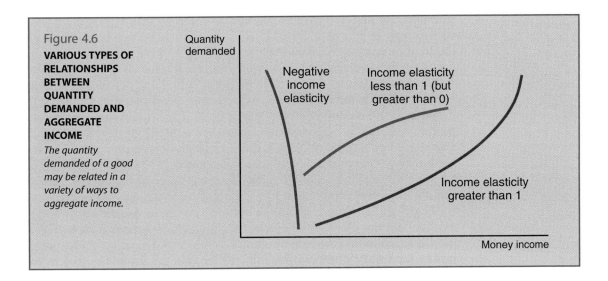

Figure 4.6

VARIOUS TYPES OF RELATIONSHIPS BETWEEN QUANTITY DEMANDED AND AGGREGATE INCOME

The quantity demanded of a good may be related in a variety of ways to aggregate income.

Income elasticity of demand

by defining the **income elasticity of demand:**

$$\eta_I = \frac{\Delta Q/Q}{\Delta I/I},$$

[4.2]

where ΔQ is the change in quantity consumed that results from a small change in the consumer's money income (denoted by ΔI), Q is the original quantity consumed, and I is the original money income of the consumer.

Some goods have positive income elasticities, indicating that increases in the consumer's money income result in increases in the quantity of the good consumed. We might generally expect, for example, that steak and single-malt scotch have positive income elasticities. Other goods have negative income elasticities, indicating that increases in the consumer's money income result in reductions in the quantity of the good consumed. Margarine, poor grades of vegetables, and other types of commodities might come to mind in this case.[3] Be careful, though: the income elasticity of demand for a good is likely to vary considerably at different levels of the consumer's money income. In some ranges of incomes, the income elasticity may be positive; in other ranges of income, it may be negative.

The concept of income elasticity of demand can be applied to an entire market as well as to a single consumer. We would simply have to interpret Q in Equation 4.2 as the total quantity demanded in the market, I as the aggregate money income of all consumers in the market, and ΔQ and ΔI as changes in total quantity demanded and in aggregate money income, respectively. Just as in the case of the individual consumer, computing this market elasticity assumes that the prices of all commodities are held constant.

Figure 4.6 shows a variety of possible relationships between the total quantity demanded in the market and the aggregate money income of the

[3]The similarity between goods with a negative income elasticity and inferior goods should be obvious.

consumers. In one case, the income elasticity is greater than 1, so that a 1 percent increase in money income results in more than a 1 percent increase in the total quantity demanded; the line slopes up as income increases, and it does so at an increasing rate. In another case, the income elasticity is less than 1 (but greater than 0), so that a 1 percent increase in money income results in less than a 1 percent increase in the total quantity demanded; the line still slopes up as income increases, but it now does so at a decreasing rate. In still another case, the income elasticity is negative, so that increases in aggregate money income actually result in reductions in the total quantity demanded; the line slopes down in this final case as income rises.[4] Notice, too, that the income elasticity changes as we move along any curve in Figure 4.6. This is true for every Engel curve that is not a straight line through the origin.

Luxuries and necessities

There are, of course, enormous differences among goods with respect to their income elasticities of demand. No refined statistical surveys are needed to tell us that the income elasticities of demand for luxuries like high-quality food and clothes are generally higher than the income elasticities of demand for necessities like salt and Kleenex. Indeed, one way to define luxuries and necessities is to say that "luxuries" are goods with high income elasticities of demand (when income is high) whereas "necessities" are goods with low income elasticities of demand.

Engel's Law

This definition finds its roots in an empirical relationship first observed by Ernst Engel in the nineteenth century. When he examined the budgets and expenditures of a large number of families, Engel found that the income elasticity of demand for food was quite low. He concluded from this result that the proportion of its income a country (or a family) spends on food is a good index of its welfare. Countries that were better off spent a smaller proportion of their incomes on food than did poorer ones. This generalization, dubbed **Engel's law,** is crude, but it is serviceable within limits even today.[5]

Table 3.1 recorded what can now be labeled income elasticities for a variety of commodities in its second column. All of the estimates listed there are positive, but only a few are greater than 1: motor vehicles, furniture and appliances, audio and video equipment, other durable goods, purchased meals, and airline service. The rest were less than 1. The elasticities for gasoline, natural gas, and medical service were less than 0.75; the elasticity for telephone service was less than 0.50; and the elasticity for alcoholic beverages claimed the lowest income elasticity, at 0.12. The economic definition of a necessity seems to conform with these estimates if you include addictive dependence on alcohol as a source of "necessity."

Microlink 4.2   Income Elasticities and the Income Effect

The income elasticity of demand measures the sensitivity of the quantity demanded to changes in income. Thus, it reflects the size of the income effect defined in Chapter 3. We therefore know that income elasticities can

---

[4]The quantity demanded may be influenced by the distribution of money income among consumers as well as the aggregate money income. We assume here that the income distribution is held constant.

[5]A number of economists, including Howard Houthakker, have made excellent empirical studies of Engel's law and its validity.

be negative for inferior goods and positive for normal goods. It follows that normal goods with high income elasticities should display large income effects whenever their prices change so that their price elasticities of demand should also be relatively large. Conversely, inferior goods with large negative income elasticities should display relatively small price elasticities.

THE CROSS-PRICE ELASTICITY OF DEMAND

We have thus far discussed the effects of two factors—the price of the commodity and the level of aggregate money income—on the quantity of a commodity demanded in the market. These factors do not exhaust the list of the important determinants of demand, however. The prices of other commodities can also play a critical role. Suppose we considered the implications of changes in the prices of other goods on the quantity demanded of some specific good while holding its own price and the level of money incomes fixed. We could then classify pairs of commodities as substitutes or complements, and measure the power of that relationship.

Cross-price elasticity of demand

To be more explicit, consider two commodities, good X and good Y. What would be the effect of an increase in the price of Y on the quantity of good X that was demanded (per unit of time)? The **cross-price elasticity of demand** is defined to calibrate the answer to that question. It is defined as

$$\eta_{XY} = \frac{\Delta Q_X / Q_X}{\Delta P_Y / P_Y}, \qquad [4.3]$$

where ΔP_Y is the change in the price of good Y, P_Y is the original price of good Y, ΔQ_X is the resulting change in the quantity demanded of good X, and Q_X is the original quantity demanded of good X. The cross-price elasticity of demand is thus the relative change in the quantity of good X resulting from a 1 percent change in the price of good Y.

The cross-price elasticity of demand plays a critical role in determining whether goods X and Y are classified as substitutes or complements. For example, suppose that an increase in the price of lamb tends to increase the quantity of pork demanded even when the price of pork remains constant. The cross-price elasticity would then be positive, and lamb and pork would

Gross complements and substitutes

be classified as **"gross" substitutes.** If, on the other hand, an increase in the price of fishing licenses caused a decline in the demand for fishing poles even when the price of fishing poles remained constant, then the cross-price elasticity would be negative. As a result, fishing licenses and fishing poles would be classified as **"gross" complements.**[6]

There is a technical reason why the preceding paragraph has inserted the adjective "gross" into the functional determination of whether goods X and

---

[6]For a single individual, goods can be classified as substitutes or complements more accurately on the basis of his or her utility function. Good Y is a substitute (complement) for good X if the marginal rate of substitution of good Y for money is reduced (increased) when good X is substituted for money in such a way as to leave the consumer no better or worse off than he or she was before.

Y are substitutes or complements. We can judge the relationship of two goods in two different directions. We can, for example, look at the relative change in the quantity demanded of good X caused by the relative change in the price of good Y. That is, we could measure η_{XY}. We could, however, just as easily look at the relative change in the quantity demanded of good Y caused by the relative change in the price of good X. This would give us an estimate of η_{YX}. We cannot, however, expect that these two elasticities will have the same numerical value. Goods X and Y may be substitutes, but the consumption of good X may be more sensitive to changes in the price of good Y than the consumption of good Y is to changes in the price of good X. It is only when consumers are compensated for any price increase so that their utility level is maintained that this troubling asymmetry can be avoided. More to the point, the two elasticities would be identical if their measurement somehow incorporated this compensation; if this were the case, depending on the sign of their common value, goods X and Y would be **"net" complements** (for a negative sign) or **"net" substitutes** (for a positive sign). The term "gross," then, used to describe complements or substitutes, indicates that the specific cross-price elasticities of demand do not incorporate such compensation.

THE MEASUREMENT OF DEMAND CURVES

Market demand curves play a very important role in microeconomics. Literally hundreds of published studies—and many more unpublished ones—have attempted to measure the market demand curves for particular commodities. This section briefly describes various ways in which such empirical studies have been conducted.

   Direct market experiments are sometimes used to estimate market demand curves. The idea in such experiments is to vary the price of the product while attempting to keep other market conditions fairly stable (or to take changes in other market conditions into account). The Parker Pen Company, for instance, once conducted an experiment to determine the price elasticity of demand for its ink product Quink. Parker raised the price from 15 cents to 25 cents in four cities and found that demand was quite inelastic. In some stores, the old package selling at 15 cents was put next to a package marked "New Quink, 25 cents"; the heavy sales of "New Quink" also indicated that demand was quite inelastic. The company attempted to estimate the cross-price elasticity of demand with other brands as well.

   Researchers sometimes interview consumers and administer questionnaires concerning their buying habits, motives, and intentions, but the direct approach of simply asking people how much they would buy of a particular commodity at particular prices does not seem to work very well in most cases. The snap judgments of consumers in response to such hypothetical questions do not seem to be very accurate. More subtle approaches have had some value, though. For example, interviews carried out by the Campbell Soup Company led it to introduce a new line of low-sodium soups. Interviews carried out by a maker of baby food indicated that most buyers of its

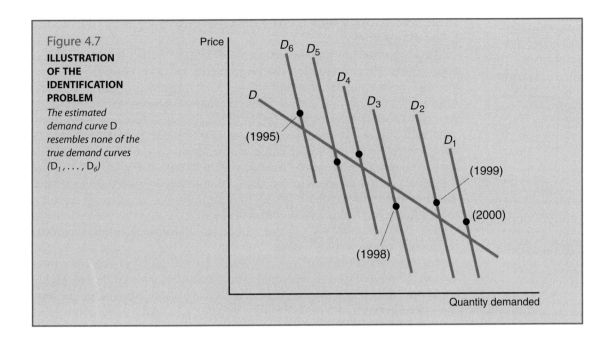

Figure 4.7

ILLUSTRATION OF THE IDENTIFICATION PROBLEM

The estimated demand curve D resembles none of the true demand curves ($D_1, \ldots, D_6$)

Statistical methods

product selected it on their doctor's recommendation and that most of them knew very little about prices or substitutes. This information, together with other data, led the manufacturer to the conclusion that the price elasticity of demand for its baby food was quite low.

Statistical methods have also been employed to extract information from historical data regarding sales, prices, incomes, and other variables. These techniques generally involve comparisons of various points in time or various sectors of the market. The idea is to see what effect observed variations in price, income, and other relevant variables have had on the quantity demanded. One might, for example, plot the quantity demanded in 2001 versus the 2001 price, the quantity demanded in 2000 versus the 2000 price, and so on, to estimate the price elasticity of demand. If the results were as shown by the points in Figure 4.7, one might presume that the demand curve resembled the curve D in Figure 4.7.

This presumption could be quite wrong, however, because it makes the naive assumption that the demand curve remained constant over the period examined. Suppose, instead, that the 2000 demand curve were D_1, that the 1999 demand curve were D_2, and so on; these curves also fit the points identified as measurements of demand. The estimated demand curve D would then resemble none of the true demand curves. Sophisticated *Econometric techniques* **econometric techniques** have been developed for dealing with this so-called identification problem. Econometric techniques have also been devised to measure at the same time the effect of money income and the prices of other commodities on the quantity demanded. Estimates can then be made of the relationship between a commodity's price and the quantity demanded, when these other factors are held constant. However, even an elementary description of these econometric techniques lies outside the scope of this book.[7]

Each approach to the measurement of demand curves has its disadvantages. Direct experimentation can be expensive or risky; customers may be lost and profits cut by the experiment. Such experiments can seldom be sufficiently controlled. They are often of relatively brief duration. And they generally produce only a small number of observations. Interviews and questionnaires also suffer from a great many disadvantages; some have already been noted. So do consumer clinics where consumers are placed in simulated market conditions and changes in their behavior are observed as the conditions of the experiment are changed. Consumer clinics are expensive and they cannot avoid the distortion arising from the consumers' realizing that they are in an experimental situation.

The difficulties involved in the application of statistical and econometric techniques are also considerable. Unreliable and biased results can be obtained if important variables are unwittingly (or wittingly) omitted from the analysis. If some of the variables influencing the quantity demanded are highly correlated, then it may not be possible to obtain reliable estimates of the separate effects of each of them. Demand functions are likely to be only one of a number of equations that connect the relevant variables, and it may be difficult to unscramble these equations adequately from the available statistics.

Example 4.4	**Estimates of Demand Elasticities**

There are no easy remedies for the problems that researchers confront when they try to examine demand relationships, but they are not always insolvable. Many important studies have produced estimates of demand curves for particular commodities; and many of these have focused attention on the price elasticity, the income elasticity, and cross-price elasticities with other goods. Indeed, it is possible to represent demand for some good X as

$$X = AP_X^\alpha I^\beta (P_1^{\delta_1} P_2^{\delta_2} \ldots P_N^{\delta_N})$$

where A is some calibrating constant, α is the price elasticity of demand for X, β is the income elasticity of demand, and the δ_k are the cross-price elasticities with other goods indexed from 1 to N.

The three panels of Table 4.3 present a sample of these results. They should make sense to you if you keep track of the intuition behind each reported elasticity. All of the cross-price elasticities are, for example, positive. Are all of the pairs of goods substitutes in your mind? Reversing the paired commodities never produces the same estimates—remember the distinction between gross and net substitutes? The price elasticities of grains are all relatively small, but the elasticity for wheat is the smallest. Does that make sense to you? The income elasticities for margarine and flour are negative. The income elasticities of some goods exceed unity; they fall below unity in other cases. Can you explain why (do the goods tend to be necessities or

[7]For a description of these techniques, see J. Johnston, *Econometric Methods*, 3d ed. (New York: McGraw-Hill, 1984); J. Kmenta, *Elements of Econometrics*, 2d ed. (New York: Macmillan, 1986); or E. Berndt, *The Practice of Econometrics* (Reading, Mass.: Addison-Wesley, 1991).

Table 4.3

ELASTICITY
ESTIMATES

A   ESTIMATED PRICE ELASTICITY 0F DEMAND FOR SELECTED COMMODITIES

Commodity	Price elasticity	Commodity	Price elasticity
Electricity	1.20	Potatoes	0.31
Beef	0.92	Oats	0.56
Women's hats	3.00	Barley	0.39
Sugar	0.31	Buckwheat	0.99
Corn	0.49	Haddock	2.20
Cotton	0.12	Tires	1.20
Wheat	0.08	Movies	3.70

B   ESTIMATED CROSS-PRICE ELASTICITY OF DEMAND FOR SELECTED COMMODITIES

Commodity	Cross-price elasticity with respect to price of:	Cross-price elasticity
Beef	Pork	+0.28
Butter	Margarine	+0.67
Margarine	Butter	+0.81
Pork	Beef	+0.14
Electricity	Natural gas	+0.20
Natural gas	Fuel oil	+0.44

C   ESTIMATED INCOME ELASTICITY OF DEMAND FOR SELECTED COMMODITIES

Commodity	Income elasticity	Commodity	Income elasticity
Butter	0.42	Meat	0.35
Cheese	0.34	Milk	0.07
Cream	0.56	Restaurant	
Eggs	0.37	consumption	1.48
Fruits and berries	0.70	Tobacco	1.02
Flour	−0.36	Haddock	0.46
Electricity	0.20	Dental services	1.41
Liquor	1.00	Furniture	1.48
Margarine	−0.20	Books	1.44

luxuries)? These are not idle questions. Good economic research ends with explanations of why the results make sense and not with mere equations or numerical citations.

SHIFTING DEMAND CURVES

Economists have adopted the practice of portraying individual or market demand curves for some good X on graphs that measure the price of X along the vertical axis and the quantity demanded along the horizontal axis. Figure 4.1 is just such a portrait. The preceding sections have provided in

Figure 4.8 **DEMAND SHIFTS IN RESPONSE TO CHANGES IN INCOME AND THE PRICES OF OTHER GOODS**
The demand curve shifts for every price in response to a change in income by an amount that is approximated by the percentage change in the income multiplied by the income elasticity of demand and the original quantity demanded. The demand curve shifts in response to a change in the price of another good by an amount that is approximated by the percentage change in the price of the other good multiplied by the cross-price elasticity of demand and the original quantity demanded.

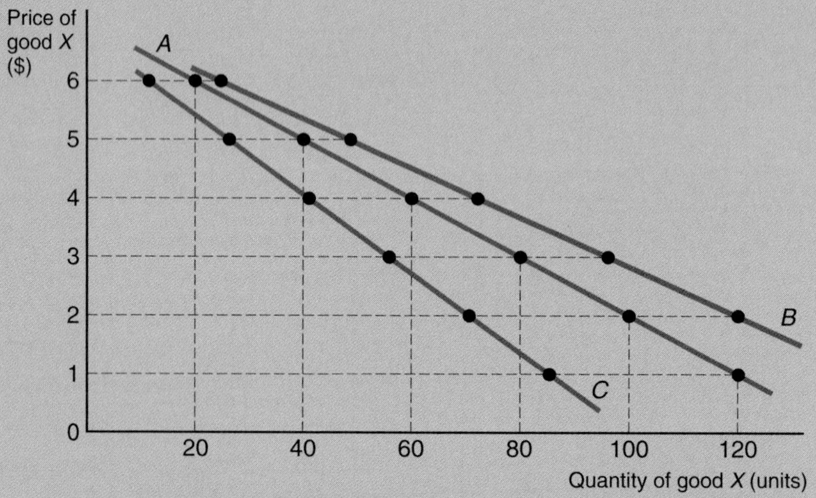

sight into how economists measure the sensitivity of the quantity demanded to changes in economic variables that are not reflected directly in these graphs—changes in income and changes in the prices of other goods. How are the changes reflected in the standard graphical context? We know from Chapter 3 that these changes shift the entire curve to the left or to the right. But by how much? Approximate answers lie in the estimates of the income and cross-price elasticities of demand.

Curve *A* in Figure 4.8 depicts a representative demand curve for good *X for a specific aggregate level of money income and for a specific set of prices for all other goods.* Now let aggregate income increase by 10 percent and assume that the income elasticity of demand for *X* is 2. Assuming that changes in the price of *X* have a negligible effect on the real income of all consumers, the demand curve would then shift to the right by 20 percent *for each price* (this income elasticity of demand tells us that the quantity demanded will increase 2 percent for every 1 percent increase in income; thus a 10 percent increase in income pushes demand up 20 percent). Curve *B* would now apply. At a price of $6, therefore, 24 units of *X* would be demanded; 24 is the original 20 units plus an additional 4 units representing the 20 percent increase in demand driven by the 10 percent increase in income. At $5, 48 units would then be demanded, and so on. What if the price of some complement were to rise by 20 percent and the cross-price elasticity of demand were equal to −1.5? Starting with the original demand curve of *A*, curve *C* would now apply, so that 14 units would be demanded at a price of $6

(14 is the original 20 units minus 6 units representing the 30 percent reduction in demand driven by the 20 percent increase in the price of a complement and a cross-price elasticity of −1.5). At $5, 28 units would be demanded, and so on.

This seems simple enough. Why did the first paragraph of this section emphasize that these answers would be approximate? Why did the last paragraph include the condition that changes in real income would be negligible? Because elasticities of all kinds are defined for specific points on the demand curve, and so even income and cross-price elasticities might be different at different points. A careful analysis would involve taking this possibility into account, but the approach just described can provide estimates that are, in most cases, close enough.

Example 4.5	Demand and Income Distribution—Working a Problem

We constructed market demand curves under the assumptions that the prices of other goods, total income, and the distribution of income were all fixed. We have since focused attention on how changes in total income might shift the demand curve to the right or to the left. The role of the distribution of income has, however, been ignored; i.e., when we have spoken of changes in total income, we have assumed implicitly that everyone's income has changed proportionately. But what would happen if this were not the case?

To explore what might happen, assume that there are 100 people in a market for some good X. Let half of them be relatively well off (RWO)—panel A in Figure 4.9 displays their individual demand curves—and assume that their income elasticity is equal to 1. Let the other half be less well off (LWO, with 50 percent of the income of the RWO folks and income elasticities equal to 2); and let panel B reflect their demand curves.

Schedule A in panel C depicts market demand for these 100 people. Neither type would demand anything unless the price were less than $10. The 50 RWOs contribute a portion of market demand that extends to 500 units when the price falls to $0; and the 50 LWOs contribute a smaller portion that adds another 250 units at the minimum price. Market demand, therefore, could go as high as 750 units (if they were giving the stuff away).

Now assume 10 percent of the income of the RWOs were redistributed to the LWOs. Demand from the RWOs would fall by 10 percent at every price, as a result; and their contribution would reach only 500 − 50 = 450 units when the price reached $0. Meanwhile, demand from the LWOs would increase by 40 percent at every price. How so? Ten percent of the income of an RWO would be 20 percent of the income of an LWO, and a 20 percent increase in income would increase demand by 2 × 20% = 40%. As a result, their contribution to market demand would reach 250 + (0.4)(250) = 350 units in the extreme case of a zero price. Market demand would then connect the zero demand point at a price of $10 with a total quantity of 350 + 450 = 800 units for a zero price. Moreover, total demand would now be schedule B in panel C—higher for every price less than $10 *even though total income had not changed.*

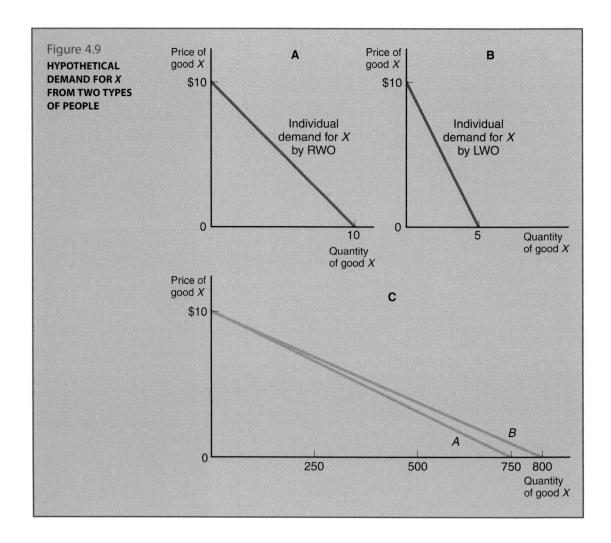

Figure 4.9
HYPOTHETICAL DEMAND FOR X FROM TWO TYPES OF PEOPLE

THE SELLER'S SIDE OF THE MARKET AND MARGINAL REVENUE

We have thus far looked at demand chiefly from the point of view of consumers. As we have already noted, though, spending by consumers translates directly into revenue for sellers. The next three sections are devoted to looking at demand from the other side of the market—the seller's side. We begin by defining marginal revenue. We then show how marginal revenue can be estimated from the demand curve. We discuss the differences between the demand curve for the industry and the demand curve for the firm. And finally, we discuss the relationship between marginal revenue and the price elasticity of demand. Our discussion here will serve as a bridge to our treatment in Part Three of the theory of the firm.

Table 4.4 QUANTITY DEMANDED, TOTAL REVENUE, AND MARGINAL REVENUE	Price ($ per unit of the commodity)	Quantity demanded (units of the commodity)	Total revenue ($)	Marginal revenue ($ per unit of the commodity)
	13	0	0	12
	12	1	12	10
	11	2	22	8
	10	3	30	6
	9	4	36	4
	8	5	40	2
	7	6	42	0
	6	7	42	−2
	5	8	40	−4
	4	9	36	−6
	3	10	30	

Total revenue

The sellers of a commodity are interested, of course, in the total amount of money spent by consumers on the commodity. Economists call this **total revenue.** The total revenue of the sellers at each price is, by definition, price times the quantity demanded. In Table 4.4, then, total revenue would be $36 if the price were $9 because 4 units would be demanded at that price. It would be $30 if the price were $3. And so on. The value of total revenue at various prices is shown in the third column of Table 4.4.

Marginal revenue

Economists and firms are also concerned with **marginal revenue**— additional revenue that can be attributed to the sale of one additional unit of a commodity. More specifically, let $R(q)$ be total revenue when q units are sold and $R(q - 1)$ be total revenue when one fewer units are sold. The marginal revenue between q units and $(q - 1)$ units is $R(q) - R(q - 1)$. Table 4.4 displays this calculation for various quantities in its rightmost column. It would, for example, be possible to charge a price of $12 for one unit, and total revenue would be $12. The marginal revenue between 1 unit of output and 0 units of output would therefore be ($12 − $0) = $12. Two units would sell at $11, so total revenue would then be $22. The marginal revenue between 2 units of output and 1 unit of output would therefore be ($22 − $12) = $10. Why is it not $11? The second unit is, after all, sold for $11. Because the first unit must now be sold for $11, as well—1 dollar less than before.

Table 4.4 makes it clear that total revenue from n units of output is equal to the sum of the marginal revenue of each unit from 0 to n. That is, $R(q)$ must equal the marginal revenue between 0 and 1 units of output, *plus* the marginal revenue between 1 and 2 units of output, *and so on* until the marginal revenue between $(n - 1)$ and n units of output is included. Total revenue for 2 units of output is $22, for example; $22 is the sum of marginal revenue between 0 and 1 units of output ($12) and marginal revenue between 1 and 2 units of output ($10). It is easy to prove that this will always be true: by the definition of marginal revenue, the sum of the marginal

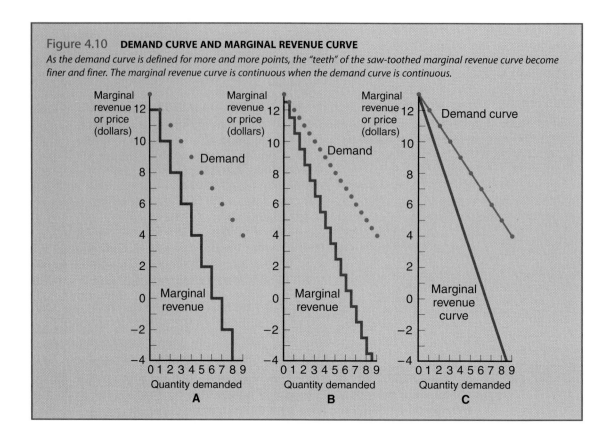

Figure 4.10 **DEMAND CURVE AND MARGINAL REVENUE CURVE**

As the demand curve is defined for more and more points, the "teeth" of the saw-toothed marginal revenue curve become finer and finer. The marginal revenue curve is continuous when the demand curve is continuous.

revenues between 0 and 1 units of output, 1 and 2 units of output, and so on up to $(n - 1)$ and n units of output is simply

$$[R(1) - R(0)] + [R(2) - R(1)] + [R(3) - R(2)]$$
$$+ \ldots + [R(n) - R(n - 1)].$$

Notice that $R(1)$, $R(2)$, . . . , $R(n - 1)$ must all cancel in this equation because they all appear in this equation with both positive and negative signs. Meanwhile, $R(0) = 0$. And so, this sum must equal $R(n)$.

The marginal revenue curve shows marginal revenue at various levels of output of a commodity. Panel A of Figure 4.10 shows the marginal revenue curve for the situation in Table 4.4. Note that the marginal revenue curve lies above 0 when total revenue is increasing, that it lies below 0 when total revenue is decreasing, and that it equals 0 when total revenue achieves its maximum. Panel A shows, for example, that the marginal revenue curve crosses 0 between 6 and 7 units of output, and inspection of Table 4.4 confirms that these are the output levels for which total revenue is maximized. Marginal revenue is positive for output levels of less than 6 units and negative for output levels of greater than 7 units; a quick review of Table 4.4 confirms that total revenue is increasing up to 6 units of output and is decreasing beyond 7 units of output.

The Seller's Side of
the Market and
Marginal Revenue

The marginal revenue curve consists of a number of "steps" when the demand curve is defined for only a relatively few points. This is clearly the case in panel A of Figure 4.10. If the demand curve were defined for more points, however, then the "teeth" of the saw-toothed marginal revenue curve would be finer. This is demonstrated in panel B. And marginal revenue is continuous when the demand curve is continuous; this is shown in panel C. Indeed, the marginal revenue curve for a linear demand curve can be shown to have the same intercept as demand and twice the slope.[8]

Example 4.6	**Fur Sales Take a Hit**

Retail sales of fur garments in the United States were $1.2 billion in 1995—not much higher than they were in the early 1980s. Sales had risen from 1972 through 1986 from about $400 million to about $1.8 billion, and they held in that vicinity through the rest of the decade. In 1990, though, they dropped by 40 percent, and they dropped another 20 percent in 1991. Figure 4.11 displays the time series but begs the question, What happened?

Bill Outlaw, a spokesman for the Fur Information Council of America, blamed the sales decline in 1990 and 1991 on a recession, saying "We're

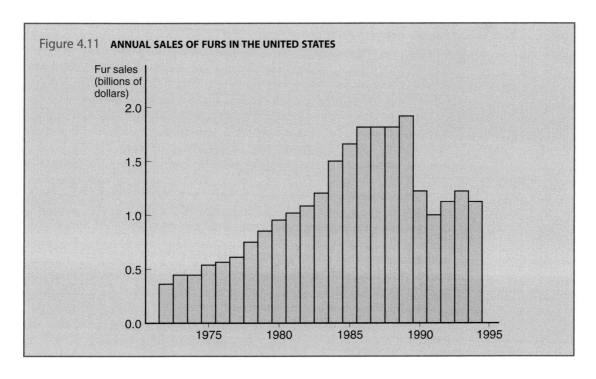

Figure 4.11   **ANNUAL SALES OF FURS IN THE UNITED STATES**

---

[8]To see this let $P = a - bQ$ be demand so that total revenue is $TR(Q) = P \cdot Q = aQ - bQ^2$. Marginal revenue is then

$$MR(Q) = \frac{TR(Q + \Delta Q) - TR(Q)}{\Delta Q} = \frac{(a - 2bQ - b\Delta Q)\Delta Q}{\Delta Q}$$

after a little algebra. In the limit as $\Delta Q \to 0$, therefore, $MR(Q) = a - 2bQ$.

facing the same problem as other luxury industries." But there are other possible explanations. The federal government imposed a 10 percent tax on expensive furs in 1990. Movement *along the demand curve* would be consistent with a decline in sales, but a price elasticity of 4 would be required for this to be the only explanation. Animal-rights activists have also claimed responsibility for all if not some of the decline. Their efforts made consumers less interested in buying furs and wearing them in public. Finally, the early 1990s were marked by mild winters in the northeastern corner of the United States, and furriers placed the blame there.

For further discussion, see the *Philadelphia Inquirer,* June 17, 1992; and the *New York Times,* May 1, 1994. Recent sales data were obtained from the Fur Information Council.

INDUSTRY AND FIRM DEMAND CURVES

We have been concerned throughout this chapter with the market demand curve for a commodity. It is important, however, to distinguish between the market demand curve for a specific commodity and the market demand curve for the output of a single firm producing that commodity. These are the same thing, of course, if only one (monopoly) firm produces the commodity. But the demand curve for the output of each firm will, in general, be quite different from the demand curve for the commodity when more than one firm serves the same market. The demand curve facing any single firm will, in fact, generally be more price-elastic than that facing the industry as a whole, since other firms produce goods that are close substitutes.

To make this point as clear as possible, suppose that there were a great many sellers of the product in question. Assume, to be concrete, that there were 50,000 sellers of the same size, so that the industry was perfectly competitive. Perfect competition will be the focus of an enormous amount of attention in subsequent chapters. For present purposes, though, it is sufficient to assume it means that a large number of firms offer homogeneous products to consumers with full knowledge of the market. In our specific case, for example, total industry output would increase by only 0.004 percent if, say, any single firm tripled its output and its sales. Even large adjustments in the output of any single firm would be too small to have any noticeable effect on the price of the commodity. This means that each seller could act as if variations in its own output would have no real effect on market price.

Put differently, it would appear to each firm that it could sell all it wants—within the range of its capabilities—without influencing the price. The "effective" demand curve facing the individual firm in perfect competition could therefore be viewed as a horizontal line drawn to reflect the market price. Its demand curve would, in other words, be infinitely elastic. Figure 4.12 shows such a demand curve. A very small decrease in price would result in an indefinitely large increase in the quantity that it could sell, but a very small increase in price would result in its selling nothing. Moreover, since price would not change in response to anything the firm did, each additional unit sold would increase total revenue by the amount equal to the given and

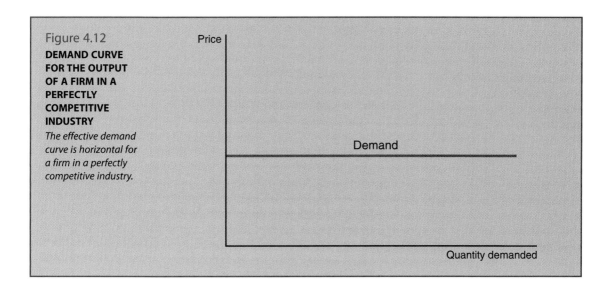

Figure 4.12

DEMAND CURVE FOR THE OUTPUT OF A FIRM IN A PERFECTLY COMPETITIVE INDUSTRY

The effective demand curve is horizontal for a firm in a perfectly competitive industry.

constant price. Price and marginal revenue would thus be identical, and the demand curve facing any single firm and the marginal revenue curve facing that firm would be one and the same.

What about the case in which the industry is not perfectly competitive? The demand curve for the output of a particular firm would not be horizontal, in that case. Marginal revenue would not equal price. It would, instead, be less than price. Why? Because demand would be less than infinitely elastic.

It is important to note that marginal revenue at a certain output level is related in the following way to price and the price elasticity of demand at that output level:

$$MR = P\left(1 - \frac{1}{\eta}\right),$$ [4.4]

where MR is marginal revenue, P is price, and η is the price elasticity of demand.[9] If the price of a good were \$10 and if its price elasticity of demand were 2, then marginal revenue would equal \$10$(1 - 1/2)$ = \$5.

[9]Marginal revenue can also be expressed as

$$MR(Q) = \frac{(P + \Delta P)(Q + \Delta Q) - PQ}{\Delta Q} = \frac{P\Delta Q + Q\Delta P + \Delta P\Delta Q}{\Delta Q}$$

where ΔP is the change in price associated along a demand curve for some change in quantity ΔQ. Again, in the limit for a small change, it follows that

$$MR(Q) = P + \frac{Q\Delta P}{\Delta Q} = P\left(1 + \frac{Q\Delta P}{P\Delta Q}\right) = P\left(1 + \frac{1}{\frac{\Delta Q/Q}{\Delta P/P}}\right).$$

And since the price elasticity of demand, η, is defined by

$$\eta = -\frac{\Delta Q/Q}{\Delta P/P},$$

143   Equation 4.4 is confirmed.

Example 4.7 | **Attracting Quality Students with Partial Scholarships**

Colleges all over the country try to attract students any way they can, and scholarships are an important tool. The issue is simple. How can a college or university maximize the value of its scholarship budget in terms of the number of highly qualified applicants who accept admission? Tulane University, for example, exhausted its entire merit-based scholarship budget for first-year students in 1995 on 111 full-tuition scholarships offered to its highest-priority applicants; each scholarship cost the university roughly $20,000 at a total cost of $2,220,000. As pleased as he was with the students who were thereby attracted to his campus, the dean of admissions was uncomfortable with his yield from a second set of 600 other high-priority applicants. Very few of this high-priority group chose to attend Tulane when they were faced with the prospect of receiving no financial aid at all. The dean responded in 1996 by offering only 50 full-tuition scholarships to a smaller highest-priority pool; he planned to use the rest of his budget to offer 50 percent scholarships to each member of the next year's cohort of 600 high-priority candidates. He was pleased to see more than 300 prospective high-priority first-year students accept his offer to attend Tulane.

We can use this experience to explore how the dean might have adjusted his offers in 1997 if the administration asserted that holding to the original $2,220,000 scholarship budget was supposed to be binding. Assume, for the sake of simplicity, that tuition held at $20,000 in 1997 (a bad assumption, to be sure, but a simple one). Assume, as well, that 10 and 310 of the 600 high-priority candidates chose Tulane in 1995 and 1996, respectively. The dean would have been in trouble in 1996 when his spending totaled $4,100,000, i.e., $1,000,000 ($= 50 \times $20,000$) for the highest-priority cohort and $3,100,000 ($= 310 \times $10,000$) for the high-priority students. One alternative would be to try to admit only 122 high-priority students by making partial scholarship offers to 236 students and expecting a yield of $52\% = (310/600) \times 100\%$.

But what if the dean changed the scholarship offer? Could more high-priority students be attracted for the same total cost of $1,220,000? To answer this question, we can use the arc elasticity formula described in Example 4.3 to compute the price elasticity of demand:

$$\frac{310 - 10}{(310 + 10)/2} \div \frac{\$20,000 - \$10,000}{(\$20,000 + \$10,000)/2} = 2.81.$$

This estimate suggests that every 1 percent increase in net tuition would cause the number of candidates who accepted a place in the entering class at Tulane to fall by 2.81 percent. Figure 4.13 tracks this relationship against the total cost of paying scholarships for these students. The schedule plotted there crosses the $1,220,000 threshold at about $8,200—an 18 percent increase in net tuition that would reduce demand by slightly more than 50 percent so that 150 high-priority students could still be expected to accept the offer. These numbers do not work exactly, because arc elasticities are approximations; but 150 students is more than the 122 that holding firm at a $10,000 scholarship would require.

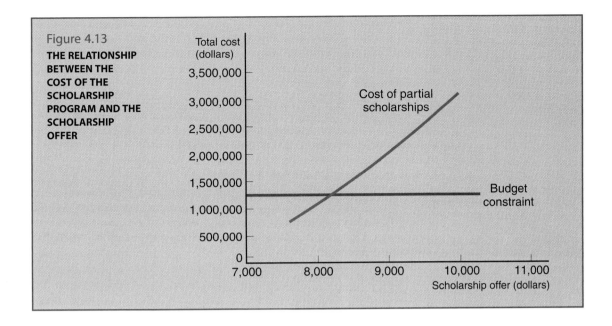

Figure 4.13

THE RELATIONSHIP BETWEEN THE COST OF THE SCHOLARSHIP PROGRAM AND THE SCHOLARSHIP OFFER

If competing schools offered similar packages in 1997, then it would also be useful to estimate the cross-price elasticity of demand to see the sensitivity of demand for admission to Tulane to those offers. Tulane's yield among the high-priority group should have been expected to fall if the competing schools offered an education and an educational experience that could substitute for the Tulane experience; it is reasonable to expect that the degree of substitution might be quite high, since they are termed "competing schools." Indeed, admissions officers at most schools track the number of accepted students lost to other universities very carefully.

SUMMARY

1. The market demand curve for a commodity is simply the horizontal summation of the individual demand curves of all the consumers in the market. Since individual demand curves almost always slope downward and to the right, it follows that market demand curves will do so, too.
2. The price elasticity of demand for a commodity depends on the number and closeness of substitutes that are available. If a commodity has many close substitutes, then its demand is likely to be elastic. The extent to which a commodity has close substitutes depends on how narrowly it is defined. More narrowly defined goods have more substitutes.
3. The income elasticity of demand is the percentage change in quantity demanded resulting from a 1 percent change in money income. Commodities differ greatly in their income elasticities. Goods that people regard as luxuries are generally assumed to have high income elasticities of demand. Indeed, one way to define luxuries and necessities is to say that luxuries are goods with high income elasticities of demand and necessities are goods with low income elasticities of demand.
4. The cross-price elasticity of demand is the relative change in the quantity demanded of good X divided by the relative change in the price of good Y.

Whether commodities are classified as gross substitutes or complements depends on whether the cross-price elasticity is positive or negative.

5. Marginal revenue is the additional revenue attributable to the addition of the last unit sold. Total revenue from n units of output is equal to the sum of the marginal revenues between 0 and 1 unit of output, 1 and 2 units of output, and so on up to $(n - 1)$ and n units of output.

6. It is important to distinguish between the market demand curve for a commodity and the market demand curve for the output of a single firm producing the commodity. In a perfectly competitive industry, the firm's demand curve will be horizontal. If the industry contains more than one firm but is not perfectly competitive, then the firm's demand curve will not be horizontal. It is still likely to be more elastic than the demand curve for the commodity.

7. Direct market experimentation can be employed to estimate market demand curves. Researchers sometimes interview consumers and administer questionnaires to explore consumers' habits, motives, and intentions. Statistical and econometric methods can also be used to extract information from historical data regarding sales, prices, incomes, and other variables. Each of these approaches has its disadvantages, and there is no easy remedy to the estimation problem. Nevertheless, the difficulties generally are not insurmountable. Many interesting and important estimates have been made of the demand curve for various goods.

QUESTIONS/ PROBLEMS

1. The three panels of Table 4.3 tell us that the long-run price elasticity of demand for electricity by all residential consumers is estimated to be 1.20, that the income elasticity of demand for electricity by such consumers is estimated at 0.20, and that the cross-price elasticity of demand for electricity with respect to the price of natural gas is estimated to be 0.20. (a) If the price of electricity were expected to rise by 1 percent in the long run, by how much would the price of natural gas have to change to offset the effect of this increase in electricity's price on the quantity of electricity consumed? (b) Among residential consumers in a Chicago suburb, holding other factors constant, the following relationship was identified between their aggregate money income and the amount of electricity they consumed:

Aggregate income (millions of dollars)	Quantity of electricity consumed
100	300
110	303
121	306

Is this evidence consistent with the results presented in Example 4.4? If not, what factors might account for the discrepancy? (c) Would you expect the income elasticity of demand and the cross-price elasticity of demand to be higher or lower in the short run than in the long run? Why?

2. A business analyst says that the demand curve for videocassette recorders (VCRs) has shifted to the right at the same time that the price elasticity of demand for VCRs has increased from 3 to 4. Is this possible? Can the new demand curve be entirely above and to the right of the old demand curve if the new price elasticity is 4 instead of 3?

3. The steel industry has long maintained that the demand for steel is price-inelastic. According to a well-known study by T. Yntema, the price elasticity of demand for steel is no more than 0.4. (a) Are there any major substitutes for steel? If so, what are some of them? (b) Some years ago the chief executive officer of Bethlehem Steel testified before a Senate committee that the price elasticity of demand for steel was much less than 1. If so, can we deduce that the demand for Bethlehem's steel is price-inelastic? (c) If the demand for Bethlehem's steel is inelastic at the price it is charging, is it maximizing its profits? (d) Is the cross-price elasticity of demand between Bethlehem's steel and imported Japanese steel positive or negative? Why?

4. The cross-price elasticity of demand can be used to determine which products belong to the same market. For example, in a famous antitrust case, the U.S. Department of Justice brought suit against the Du Pont chemical company for having monopolized the sale of cellophane. In its defense, Du Pont claimed that cellophane had many close substitutes, such as aluminum foil, waxed paper, and polyethylene. Can you guess how Du Pont used cross-price elasticities of demand in this case? (Incidentally, the Supreme Court accepted Du Pont's argument in a landmark decision handed down in 1953.)

5. Suppose that a consumer considers Doritos of such supreme importance that he spends all his income on Doritos. To this consumer, what is the price elasticity of demand for Doritos? What is the income elasticity of demand for Doritos? What is the cross-price elasticity of demand between Doritos and any other good? Suppose that a different consumer holds Doritos in similarly high esteem, but still wants to consume some Pepsi. Assume that this consumer always spends 50 percent of her income on Doritos. What is the price elasticity of demand for Doritos for this second consumer? What is the income elasticity of her demand for Doritos? What is the cross-price elasticity of demand between Doritos and any other good?

6. Could the demand curve for the output of each firm in the aluminum industry be horizontal? Why or why not? Is it less elastic than the demand curve for aluminum as a whole? Why or why not? Is the price of aluminum less than, equal to, or greater than marginal revenue?

7. Which of the following are likely to have a positive cross-price elasticity of demand: (a) automobiles and oil, (b) graphite tennis rackets and aluminum tennis rackets, (c) gin and tonic, (d) coffee and sugar, (e) a Harvard education and a Yale education?

8. The demand for refined sugar in the United States has declined greatly since 1975, due in part to reports that it causes tooth decay, reduces the nutritional value of the diet, and leads to obesity. Given that per capita consumption of refined sugar has declined, can we be sure that the price elasticity of demand for refined sugar is (a) less than 1, (b) greater than 1, or (c) greater than 0?

9. Suppose that the mayor of Boston asked you to advise him concerning the proper fare that should be charged by the Boston T (its rail mass transit system). In what way might information concerning the price elasticity of demand be useful? Would the information that you provide have any bearing on the mayor's view of the value of the new highway-construction project that will move to below ground the Interstates that pass through the city?

10. According to the Senate Subcommittee on Antitrust and Monopoly, the income elasticity of demand for automobiles in the United States is between

2.5 and 3.9. What does this mean? If incomes rose by 5 percent, what effect would this have on the quantity of autos demanded? How might this fact be used by General Motors?

11. Suppose you are a trustee of a major university. At a meeting of the board of trustees, one university official argues that the demand for places in the student body at this university is completely inelastic. As evidence, he cites the fact that, although the university has doubled its tuition in the last decade, there has been no appreciable decrease in the number of students enrolled. Do you agree? Comment on his argument.

12. According to W. Baumol, "Some mail-order houses have employed systematic programs in which a few experimental pages were bound inconspicuously into the catalogues distributed to customers within restricted geographical regions, thus permitting observation of the effects of price, product, or even catalogue display variations." Comment on the accuracy of this technique. What might be some of the problems in estimating a product's price elasticity of demand in this way? What techniques might be better than this one?

13. Show that, if the Engel curve for a good is a straight line through the origin, the income elasticity of demand for the good will be equal to 1 at all levels of income.

14. Many pharmaceutical companies patented extraordinarily popular drugs during the research boom of the 1970s and 1980s. They are now faced with the prospect of those patents expiring over the next few years. Patents last for 20 years, but the patent application process must be initiated so quickly after the development of a new drug that actual market insulation from generic competition usually lasts only about 12 years. Merck & Co, for example, will lose the exclusive right to produce and sell heart drugs like Vasotec and Mevacor; these and two other drugs combined accounted for more than half of the company's $6.18 billion in sales in 1998. Schering-Plough Corporation stands to lose exclusivity on the allergy drug Claritin and others that contributed 57 percent of its $2.61 billion in prescription sales. Bristol-Myers Squibb manufactured a heart drug called Capoten under a patent that expired in 1997. It sold the drug for 57 cents per pill under the patent. Faced with competition from a generic substitute that cost 3 cents a pill as soon as the patent expired, Capoten's sales fell 83 percent, from $146 million to $25 million per year. Use the concept of market demand to explain this phenomenon under the assumption that generic drugs are close but not necessarily perfect substitutes for their name-brand "equivalents." Do the sales data suggest that doctors might have responded to the competition by increasing the rate at which they prescribed Capoten or its generic substitute? Do they suggest that the price of the name-brand drug fell when the patent expired? And if so, would the price necessarily fall to the level of the generic competition? Would you expect similar effects for other drugs manufactured by other companies when their patents expire?

15. Would it make sense in Example 4.1 to sum regional demand curves for water to produce a national curve? Alternatively, could the price of water be different in different regions? If so, could that be efficient?

16. The price-consumption curve shown in the figure for good X is upward-sloping. (a) Prove that the consumer's demand curve for good X is price-inelastic. (b) Show that the consumer's demand curve for good X would be price-elastic if the price-consumption curve were downward-sloping.

(c) Show that the consumer's demand curve would display unitary price elasticity everywhere if the price-consumption curve were horizontal.

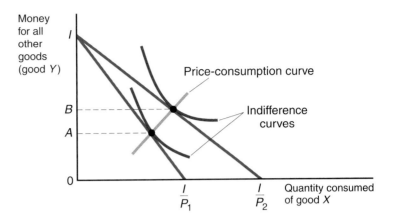

17. When the Democratic National Convention was held in New York City in 1992, Tim Zagat, publisher of a well-known restaurant guide, helped to organize an unusual treat for the convention delegates and others: about 100 of New York's leading restaurants offered a three-course lunch for $19.92. Although this was hardly a cheap meal, the price was well below that ordinarily charged by such restaurants. The result was a considerable increase in their business, and most maintained the $19.92 price after the end of the convention. (a) A French restaurant on East 52nd Street ordinarily served lunch for about 40 people each day before the price reduction; afterward, it served about 150 people per day. Its preconvention price for a lunch was $29. What was the price elasticity of demand for a lunch at this restaurant? (b) Did the daily total expenditure on lunches increase due to the price reduction? Is this consistent with your answer to (a)? (c) If another restaurant's preconvention price were $5 less than the first restaurant's but the price elasticity of demand were the same, could we be sure that the percentage increase in the number of lunches at this second restaurant would be smaller? (d) Is it possible that this price reduction could reduce a restaurant's profits? How could this occur?

18. The air route between Los Angeles and New York City is one of the most frequently traveled in the country. Assume that the price elasticity of demand for air travel between Los Angeles and New York City is about 0.67. (a) Suppose that an economic consultant says that the demand curve for air travel between Los Angeles and New York City is as shown in the figure. Is this graph in accord with the assumption about the price elasticity of demand? Why or why not? (b) Suppose that the airlines doubled the price of a ticket between Los Angeles and New York City. Would this price increase affect the demand curve for air travel between these two cities? If so, in what way? (c) Suppose that a severe recession occurred. Would this affect the demand curve for air travel between these two cities? If so, in what way? (d) Now suppose that an increase in the price of jet fuel (and other things) has raised appreciably the cost of providing air transportation between Los Angeles and New York City in recent decades. Does such a change in costs affect the demand curve for air travel between these two cities? If so, in what way?

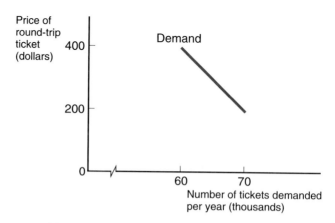

19. Draw a general linear demand curve for some good X with an intercept on the price axis of a and a slope of $-b$. Compute the elasticity of demand when the price is $(3a/4)$, when the price is $(a/2)$, and when the price is $(a/4)$. Also compute the elasticity when the price is zero. Now graph the total expenditures that correspond to this demand. They will be zero when the quantity of $X = 0$ and again when price equals zero. Show that total expenditures will reach a maximum at the midpoint of the demand curve. Explain why they are rising to the left of the midpoint in terms of demand elasticities that exceed unity to the left of the midpoint. Also explain why they are falling to the right of the midpoint in terms of demand elasticities that fall short of unity to the right of the midpoint. Finally, explain the maximum in terms of unitary elasticity at the midpoint.

Calculus Appendix

ELASTICITIES OF DEMAND

The calculus allows for relatively simple definitions of price, income, and cross-price elasticities of demand. Suppose, for example, that demand for some good X were given as a function of the price of X, the prices of other goods, and income; i.e., let

$$X_D = f_D(P_X, P_Y, I)$$

where P_X represents the price of X, P_Y represents the price of some other good Y, and I represents income. Note in passing that there may be many other goods, in which case we could be speaking of goods Y_1 through Y_n that are available at prices P_{Y_1} through P_{Y_n}, respectively. In any case, the price elasticity of demand can be expressed as

$$\eta_D = -\frac{\partial X_D/\partial P_X}{X_D/P_X}$$

and the income elasticity of demand as

$$\eta_I = \frac{\partial X_D/\partial I}{X_D/I}.$$

Additionally, we can define the cross-price elasticity of demand for X (with respect to the price of Y) as

$$\eta_{XY} = \frac{\partial X_D/\partial P_Y}{X_D/P_Y}.$$

The partial derivative notation has been employed here to indicate that the demand curve depends on more than one price as well as income. Since demand curves are frequently drawn under the assumption that these prices and income are fixed, however, it can be appropriate to use standard univariate notation:

$$\eta_D = -\frac{dX_D/dP_X}{X_D/P_X}.$$

PRICE ELASTICITIES FOR LINEAR DEMAND

Suppose for the moment that the demand for X is linear in the price of X; i.e., let

$$P_X = a - bX$$

with $a > 0$ and $b > 0$. This is, of course, a straight line on a graph with price measured up the vertical axis and quantity measured out the horizontal axis; the intercept is a and the slope is $-b$. For purposes of computing the elasticity, though, it is convenient to express quantity as a function of price; to that end, a little algebra shows that

$$X = \frac{a}{b} - \frac{1}{b}P_X.$$

Applying the definition, then,

$$\eta_D = -\frac{dX_D/dP_X}{X_D/P_X} = -\frac{-1/b}{X_D/P_X}.$$

Clearly, therefore, the price elasticity is different at every point along the demand curve. At the midpoint, though, where $P_X = a/2$ and $X = a/2b$,

$$\eta_D(\text{midpoint}) = -\frac{-1/b}{(a/2b)/(a/2)} = -\frac{-1/b}{1/b} = 1.$$

In addition, for points above the midpoint, $P_X > a/2$ and $X < a/2b$, so the denominator shrinks and $\eta_D > 1$; i.e., demand is elastic. For points below the midpoint where $P_X < a/2$ and $X > a/2b$, the denominator expands and $\eta_D < 1$; as a result, demand is inelastic.

MARGINAL REVENUE AND THE PRICE ELASTICITY OF DEMAND

Suppose, for the sake of clarity, that the demand for X depends only on the price of X. We can express this case simply by writing

$$P_X = f(X).$$

It follows immediately that total revenue from the sale of X is

$$TR(X) = Xf(X).$$

Marginal revenue, the derivative of total revenue with respect to X, can now be computed by applying the product rule of differentiation:

$$MR(X) = \frac{dTR}{dX} = f(X)\frac{dX}{dX} + X\frac{df(X)}{dX}$$

$$= f(X) + X\frac{df(X)}{dX}.$$

Since $P_X = f(X)$, though, substitution and factoring reveals that

$$MR(X) = P_X\left(1 + \frac{X}{P_X}\frac{df(X)}{dX}\right)$$

$$= P_X\left(1 + \frac{-1}{\eta_D}\right).$$

As a result, $MR(X) > 0$ only if demand is elastic so that $\eta_D > 1$. Similarly, if demand is inelastic (i.e., if we know that $\eta_D < 1$), then $MR(X) < 0$. And, of course, $MR(X) = 0$ when $\eta_D = 1$. For a linear demand curve, therefore, marginal revenue is positive above the midpoint, negative below the midpoint, and equal to zero at the midpoint.

MARGINAL REVENUE FOR LINEAR DEMAND

Return again to the linear case where $P_X = a - bX$ with $a > 0$ and $b > 0$. Total revenue and marginal revenue are then

$$TR(X) = XP_X = aX - bX^2$$

and

$$MR(X) = \frac{dTR}{dX} = a - 2bX.$$

Notice immediately that the marginal revenue curve for linear demand has the same intercept as the demand curve and twice the slope.

CHAPTER 5

Choices Involving Risk

The consequences of uncertainty are facts of life for every person on the planet, even people who don't invest their money in the stock market or buy lottery tickets. We must, in nearly everything we do, take account of the risks associated with not being able to control every part of our lives—not being able to tell exactly what will happen. For example, we assume the risk of having an accident every time we drive our cars. We assume the risk of fire or natural disaster every time we buy some property. We assume the risk of theft or loss nearly every time we make a purchase. Even when we are sure that the item or service that we purchase will not be stolen, lost, or turned into smoke, we assume the risk of being dissatisfied with its performance. The list of risks associated with living can be extended almost indefinitely. The point of starting it, for our purposes, is to emphasize that nearly every plan of action may produce intended or unintended consequences depending on both its inherent quality and the environment in which it is implemented.

Economists are not blind to this point. They see risk in every situation in which the outcome of an action is not certain, and they have devised theories with which to analyze how rational economic agents should make decisions under uncertainty. To be fair, we must emphasize from the start that economists are most comfortable with their theories when at least the probability of every possible outcome can be estimated. We therefore begin this discussion of the fundamental constructions upon which their theories have been built with the definition of what economists mean when they speak of "probabilities." After that, we take up expected monetary value, the expected value of information, and von Neumann–Morgenstern utility functions. Finally, we analyze the problem of how much insurance a person should buy, and we compare the results of maximizing expected utility with outcomes that emerge when the "precautionary principle" is used in making decisions.

PROBABILITY

Consider a situation in which one of a number of possible outcomes can take place. A probability is a number that is attached to each possible outcome that indicates the likelihood that it will occur. If you were to throw a single die, for example, then 1, 2, 3, 4, 5, or 6 could come up. If the die were fair, then each of the six possible numbers would be equally likely, so that each would have a one-sixth (approximately 0.167) chance of appearing. In this case, and in general, the probability that each outcome would come up can be viewed as the fraction of times that it would occur over the long run if the situation were repeated over and over again. The probability that 1 would come up from the roll of the die can thus be viewed as the proportion of times that 1 would appear if you threw the die many times. How many times is many? Probably thousands of times, depending upon the need for accuracy. Enough times, though, so that the proportion of times that 1 (and all of the other numbers, for that matter) appears is not significantly affected by successive sets of multiple throws of the die.

How about the probability that an American male who just turned 45 will die before his 46th birthday? That can be estimated by calculating the proportion of 45-year-old men that die before they turn 46. Detailed statistics are available concerning the proportion of people in a particular age group that die each year. You can calculate the proportion of 45-year-old American males that die, and this is a perfectly good estimate of the probability in question. You could even explore the data further to see how this probability changes with behavior. Is the probability of death among 45-year-old men who smoke higher than among those who don't? This can be interpreted as asking whether the proportion of 45-year-old men who die is higher for the subset who smoke than it is for the subset who don't.

In general, if outcome U occurs m out of a possible M times, then the probability of U, denoted here by $P(U)$, is simply

$$P(U) = \frac{m}{M}. \qquad [5.1]$$

So, the probability of a die's coming up a 1 must be 1/6 if the die is "true" (meaning that each of its sides is equally likely to come up when the die is rolled). Why? Because 1 would appear one-sixth of the time if the die were rolled many times. Notice, though, that this definition could be applied even if the die were not true; indeed, this definition could be employed to test whether or not the die were true. With each side equally likely, theory and common sense suggests that each side should appear one-sixth of the time. Suppose that someone had injected some loaded dice into a crap game and that one of the more suspicious players asks to examine one of them. Imagine his rolling this die again and again. Suppose, in fact, that 1 appeared an average of 195 times for each 1,000 rolls. The proportion of times that 1 appeared would be 0.195. This would be the probability that 1 would appear. And 0.195 is larger than 0.167. The suspicious player could thus conclude that his suspicions were well founded.

We have thus far offered only the **frequency definition** of probability. This concept of probability may be difficult to apply in some situations because they cannot be repeated over and over again. Consider, for example, the probability that any given student will pass all of his or her college courses. If he or she decided to attend the University of California at Los Angeles

(UCLA) in 2001, then this would define an "experiment" that could not be repeated over and over again under essentially the same set of circumstances. If he or she decided to attend UCLA in 2003, instead, then his or her knowledge and attitude, the identity of the professors, and a host of other relevant factors would likely be quite different.

Economists and statisticians sometimes deal with situations like this by using a *subjective* or personal definition of probability. According to this definition, the probability of an event is the degree of confidence or belief on the part of the decision-maker that the event will occur. If the decision-maker believed that outcome *A* were more likely to occur than outcome *B*, then he or she would assign a higher probability to *A* than to *B*. And if the decision-maker believed that it were equally likely that a particular outcome would or would not occur, then the probability attached to each outcome would be 0.50. The important factor in this alternative concept of probability is quantifying what the decision-maker believes.

| Example 5.1 | **Comparisons of Actual and Perceived Risk** |

Computing the probabilities required to undertake an expected-value calculation is not always a simple matter. It may not, for example, be possible to conduct repeated trials. Nor is it always possible to do some mathematics to produce theoretically based estimates of relative likelihood. Indeed, most interesting cases involve individuals' creating subjective views of probabilities from experience and/or careful reviews of scientific literature. Nonetheless, the output of an expected-value calculation will be only as good as its underlying data—estimates of outcomes in various states of nature and associated estimates of their relative probabilities. But how good are people at judging the critical outcomes and probabilities?

Paul Slovic, Baruch Fischoff, and Sarah Lichtenstein authored an early investigation of this question that still carries a lot of weight in the risk-assessment literature. Panels A and B in Figure 5.1 replicate two of their more informative figures. Panel A, more specifically, tracks expert judgments of the risk of death associated with a variety of activities. Actual deaths are measured along the horizontal axis, and estimated deaths are measured up the vertical axis. If the experts were correct in their assessments, then ordered pairs would lie along the heavy line "estimated = actual," but few of the plotted points come very close to the mark. Indeed, it would appear that experts systematically overestimate the chance of death associated with low-risk activities like skiing and vaccination and that they similarly underestimate the chance of death associated with high-risk activities like using handguns and smoking. Panel B plots pairs for the same sets of activities for judgments offered by laypeople. Notice that the same systematic tendencies toward under- and overestimation are visible. Indeed, the errors made by laypeople are actually more pronounced.

Finally, you should not be deceived into thinking that scientific estimates are devoid of uncertainty. Indeed, scientific understanding evolves over time, and so do techniques. As a result, estimates change and take their error bands with them. Panel C makes this point by displaying a time series of estimates

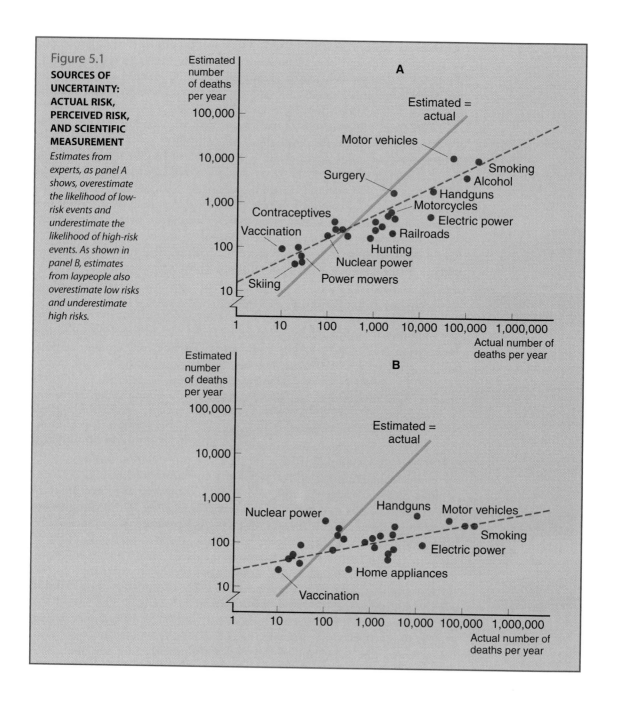

Figure 5.1

SOURCES OF UNCERTAINTY: ACTUAL RISK, PERCEIVED RISK, AND SCIENTIFIC MEASUREMENT

Estimates from experts, as panel A shows, overestimate the likelihood of low-risk events and underestimate the likelihood of high-risk events. As shown in panel B, estimates from laypeople also overestimate low risks and underestimate high risks.

A

Estimated number of deaths per year

100,000

Estimated = actual

10,000 — Motor vehicles

Surgery — Smoking — Alcohol — Handguns

1,000 — Motorcycles — Electric power

Contraceptives — Railroads

Vaccination

100 — Hunting — Nuclear power

Skiing — Power mowers

10

1   10   100   1,000   10,000   100,000   1,000,000

Actual number of deaths per year

B

Estimated number of deaths per year

100,000

10,000

Estimated = actual

1,000 — Handguns — Motor vehicles

Nuclear power — Smoking

100 — Electric power

Home appliances

10 — Vaccination

1   10   100   1,000   10,000   100,000   1,000,000

Actual number of deaths per year

of the speed of light—a physical constant that everybody learns early in their schooling. It was not always so well known, and its value was not always so well accepted.

SOURCE: P. Slovic, B. Fischoff, and S. Lichtenstein, "Rating the Risks," *Environment*, vol. 21, no. 3, April 1979, pp. 14–39.

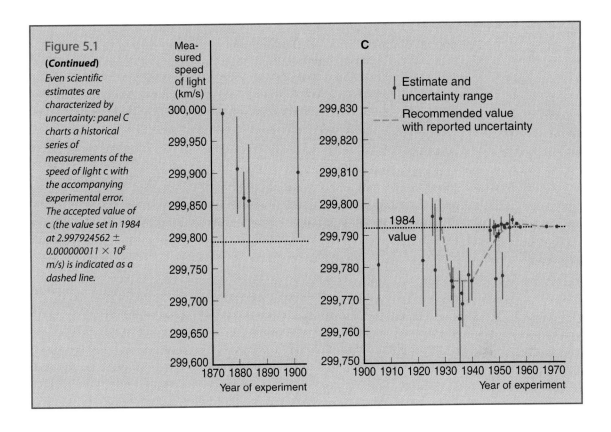

Figure 5.1
(Continued)
Even scientific estimates are characterized by uncertainty: panel C charts a historical series of measurements of the speed of light c with the accompanying experimental error. The accepted value of c (the value set in 1984 at 2.997924562 ± 0.000000011 × 10⁸ m/s) is indicated as a dashed line.

Expected Monetary Value

Stuart Shlien, the owner of a furniture store, is thinking of buying some stock in Pfizer, a big drug-manufacturing firm. Based on his estimates, he will gain $20,000 from the stock purchase if Pfizer gets approval from the Food and Drug Administration (FDA) to market a new drug that it has developed. He remembers fondly Pfizer's experience with Viagra, and doesn't want to miss the boat again. He estimates, though, that he will lose $4,000 if Pfizer does not get the required federal approval to move forward. In his judgment, there is a 0.5 probability that Pfizer will get approval and a 0.5 probability that the application will be denied. His is a common situation. A variety of outcomes can occur. He will make some money if one outcome occurs, but he will lose some money if another occurs. And he has some idea of the probabilities that can be assigned to each outcome.

It frequently is useful, in situations like this, to calculate the expected monetary value of the investment. The **expected monetary value** is the sum of the amount of money gained (or lost) if each outcome occurs multiplied by the probability that each outcome will materialize. In the case of Mr. Shlien, the expected monetary value of his prospective investment in Pfizer is ($20,000)(0.5) + (−$4,000)(0.5) = $8,000. To see why this is the expected monetary value, recall that there are only two possible

Expected monetary value

157

outcomes: (1) Pfizer gets approval to market its new drug, or (2) it does not get approval to do so. Multiply the amount of money that would be gained if the first outcome occurred by its probability of occurrence; the result is ($20,000)(0.5) = $10,000. Multiply the amount of money that would be lost if the second outcome occurred by its probability of occurrence; the result is (−$4,000)(0.5) = −$2,000. Sum these two results, and you see that $8,000 is the expected monetary value if he buys this stock.

The expected monetary value is important because it is the mean (i.e., the average) amount that a decision-maker would gain (or lose) if he or she were to accept a gamble over and over again. If Mr. Shlien were to buy Pfizer stock (under the above circumstances) repeatedly, the FDA would grant approval sometimes, but it would say no sometimes. Assuming that Mr. Shlien has the probabilities right, Pfizer would gain approval in exactly half of the cases. This would mean that it would not get approval in the other half of the cases, and the mean amount that he would make (per purchase) would be $8,000.

What would be the expected monetary value if Mr. Shlien did not buy this stock? If he were certain that he would experience neither a gain nor a loss if he did not buy it, then the expected monetary value of the decision not to buy would be $0—the amount of money gained or lost ($0) times its probability of this outcome (1). That is, the mean amount that he would make (per decision not to buy) would be 0. It can be considered rational to choose the action or gamble that has the largest expected monetary value. If these conditions hold, then Stuart Shlien will buy the Pfizer stock because the expected monetary value of the purchase is $8,000—a value that is larger than the $0 expected monetary value of not making the purchase. We will discuss when it is rational to maximize expected monetary value later in the chapter.

| Example 5.2 | **Minimizing Expected Cost: Evaluating Membership Offers from Weight Watchers** |

Weight Watchers International, Inc., offers dieters around the world a wide range of membership programs designed to attract them to weekly meetings and stimulate demand for proprietary food products. The program is enormously popular, and attending weekly meetings seems to be relatively effective in supporting dieters' attempts to reach and to sustain specific weight targets. Participants are weighed at the meetings, where they are offered a variety of incentives that reward progress toward individual goals. Perhaps more important, weekly meetings educate participants about a process that assigns "points" to a wide variety of foods. Staying on the diet is therefore reduced to maintaining daily food consumption within a balanced diet so that daily point totals fall below specific thresholds—a great improvement over trying to count calories and keep track of fat and other food contents.

Weight Watchers charges for the program, of course, and it offers at least three different payment schemes. Which one is best? That is, which one has the smallest expected cost? The answer depends on a participant's subjective

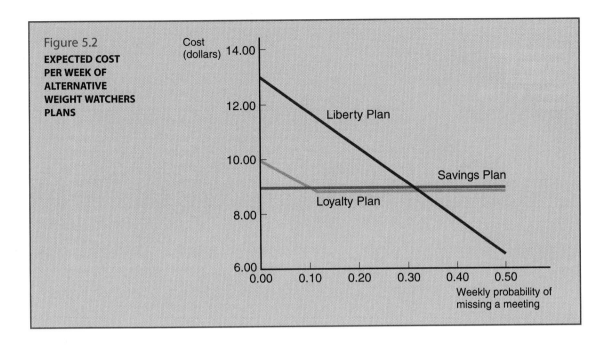

Figure 5.2
EXPECTED COST PER WEEK OF ALTERNATIVE WEIGHT WATCHERS PLANS

view of the likelihood that he or she will attend meetings regularly. As of the end of 2001 in Connecticut, for example, participants could choose a "Liberty Plan"—$13 for each weekly meeting attended. A "Ten-Week Savings Plan" was also available—$89.50 for 10 weeks (regardless of whether or not the participant actually attended any of the meetings). Finally, a "Loyalty Plan" was also available in which participants commit to a 26-week membership for $9.95 per week with three free "passes." Miss more than three meetings in 26 weeks, though, and they have to pay $9.95 for each of the missed meetings to keep the Loyalty Plan current.

Figure 5.2 plots the expected average cost per meeting over a 26-week period as a function of the likelihood that you would attend a meeting in any given week; Table 5.1 provides the details. The expected average cost for the Liberty Plan is, for example, simply

$$(1 - \text{prob})(\$13) + (\text{prob})(\$0),$$

where (prob) represents the probability of missing a meeting. It runs from $13.00 with (prob) = 0.00 down to $6.50 with (prob) = 0.50. The expected average cost for a series under the Ten-Week Savings Plan is simply $8.95, because you pay even if you miss. And the expected average cost of the Loyalty Plan is $9.95 if (prob) = 0. It is

$$\tfrac{25}{26}(\$9.95) + \tfrac{1}{26}(\$0) = \$9.57$$

if (prob) = 1/26, and it falls to a minimum of

$$\tfrac{23}{26}(\$9.95) + \tfrac{3}{26}(\$0) = \$8.80$$

159   if (prob) ≥ 3/26.

Table 5.1	Likelihood of missing a meeting	Expected weekly cost		
EXPECTED COST PER WEEK OF ALTERNATIVE WEIGHT WATCHERS PLANS		**Liberty Plan**	**Savings Plan**	**Loyalty Plan**
	0.00	$13.00	$8.95	$9.95
	0.04	$12.50	$8.95	$9.57
	0.08	$12.00	$8.95	$9.18
	0.12	$11.50	$8.95	$8.80
	0.15	$11.00	$8.95	$8.80
	0.19	$10.50	$8.95	$8.80
	0.23	$10.00	$8.95	$8.80
	0.27	$9.50	$8.95	$8.80
	0.31	$9.00	$8.95	$8.80
	0.35	$8.50	$8.95	$8.80
	0.38	$8.00	$8.95	$8.80
	0.42	$7.50	$8.95	$8.80
	0.46	$7.00	$8.95	$8.80
	0.50	$6.50	$8.95	$8.80

Assuming that the likelihood of attendance in any week is independent of attendance in any other week, the Savings Plan has the lowest expected average cost if the chance of missing a meeting is less than or equal to 3/26. The Loyalty Plan has a smaller cost between 4/26 and 9/26; and the Liberty Plan is best if the chance of missing a meeting in any week is greater than 10/26.

INVESTING IN AN OIL VENTURE: A CASE STUDY

We now turn to a second example to illustrate further the concept of expected monetary value. Suppose that a company must decide whether or not to drill an oil well in a particular location. It has information concerning the cost of drilling and the price of oil, as well as geologists' reports concerning the likelihood of striking oil. Analysts in the company believe, on the basis of the geologists' reports, that there is a 0.75 probability of finding something other than oil (i.e., something of no value, like really dirty water). Regardless of whether or not what they find is oil, the geologists' reports also indicate that there is a 0.60 chance of finding 100,000 barrels of something and a 0.40 probability of finding 1 million barrels of whatever is there. This means that there is a 0.15 probability of finding 100,000 barrels of oil, a 0.10 probability of finding 1 million barrels of oil, a 0.45 probability of finding 100,000 barrels of something other than oil, and finally a 0.30 probability of finding 1 million barrels of something other than oil. Notice that these probabilities add up to 1.00—they therefore exhaust all of the possibilities because the probability that one of these outcomes will occur is 1.00.

How do we know the probabilities of each of the four possible outcomes? Think of drilling the well 100 times. The company would then find nothing of value 75 times. It would find oil 25 times. It would find 100,000 barrels of oil 15 of those times (because $15/25 = 0.60$); and it would find 1 million barrels of oil 10 times (because $10/25 = 0.40$).

The company cannot, on the basis of these probabilities alone, decide whether or not to invest in drilling the well. Information concerning the gains or losses that would result in each outcome must be provided. Suppose, to that end, that the analysts also believe that it will cost $500,000 to drill the well and that the company can sell rights to the oil (if found) at $10 a barrel. They therefore see the possibility of selling rights to the well for $1,000,000 if 100,000 barrels are found and for $10,000,000 if 1 million barrels are found. And the other stuff that might be found? Assume for simplicity that it would be essentially worthless. On the basis of this information, should the company invest in drilling the well?

Assume that the company wants to maximize the expected monetary value of its decision. It thinks that it will lose $500,000 with a probability of 0.75 because that is the probability that no oil will be found. It thinks that it will make $500,000 with a probability of 0.15 because that is the probability of finding $1,000,000 in oil at a cost of $500,000. And it thinks that it will make $9,500,000 with a probability of 0.10 because that is the probability of finding $10,000,000 in oil at a cost of $500,000. The expected monetary value of the investment is therefore $0.75(-\$500,000) + 0.15(+\$500,000) + 0.10(+\$9,500,000) = -\$375,000 + \$1,025,000 = \$650,000$. The expected monetary value of not investing is $0, because it is certain that the company will gain nothing (nothing ventured, nothing gained). So the company should go ahead and drill the well.

THE EXPECTED VALUE OF PERFECT INFORMATION

Decision-makers can frequently obtain information that will dispel (at least some of) the relevant risk. Taken to its extreme, this possibility raises an interesting question: how much would perfect information be worth to the decision-maker? To answer this question, we define the **expected value of perfect information** as the increase in expected monetary value that would result from the decision-maker's obtaining completely accurate information concerning the outcome of the relevant situation. Why is it defined in terms of expected value? Because the decision-maker does not yet know what this information will be; he or she just knows that it will be perfect when it arrives.

Expected value of perfect information

The idea is perhaps best described in an example. Recall the case of Stuart Shlien; he was the potential investor who was thinking about buying some Pfizer stock earlier in this chapter. The expected value of perfect information for him would be the increase in expected monetary value that he could realize if he could obtain perfectly accurate information about whether or not the Food and Drug Administration will approve the marketing of Pfizer's new drug.

Only two steps are required to compute the expected value of this perfect information. We first evaluate the expected monetary value of the information under the assumption that nothing else has changed; then we calculate the extent to which this expected monetary value exceeds the expected monetary value of the investment option, based on the information that is currently available.

Step 1: Mr. Shlien would be able to make the correct decision if he had the correct information, regardless of whether the FDA approves the marketing of Pfizer's new drug. If the FDA said "yes," then he would know that he should buy the stock (assuming that he gets to the market before word of the decision has gotten out), and he would do so. If the FDA says "no," then he would know that he should not buy the stock and would walk away. Given access to perfect information, therefore, the expected monetary value of making the correct decision is 0.5($20,000) + 0.5(0) = $10,000. Notice that this calculation assumes that Mr. Shlien will have access to the information before he has to decide what to do, but it does not presume that he (or we, for that matter) *knows what that information will be* before he (or we) make the calculation. All that we assume in making this calculation is that Mr. Shlien will act rationally when the information becomes available. From our perspective, there is still a 0.5 probability that this information will show that the FDA will grant approval, and we assume simply that he would buy the stock in that case so that the gain would be $20,000. There is, as well, still a 0.5 probability that the information will show that the FDA will not grant approval, and we assume that he would not buy the stock in this case, so that the gain would be $0. And so, the expected monetary value of access to perfect information (that is not yet revealed) is $10,000.

Step 2: We have already computed the expected monetary value of the investment decision based on existing information; it is $8,000. The difference between these two figures—$10,000 − $8,000 = $2,000—is the expected value of perfect information to Mr. Shlien. This figure shows the amount by which the expected monetary value increases as a consequence of Mr. Shlien's having access to perfect information. And how much should he pay for that information? Not a penny more than its expected monetary value.

It is very important in many situations that a person know how much perfect information would be worth. People and businesses are continually being offered information by testing services, research organizations, news bureaus, and a variety of other organizations. Unless they know how much particular types of information are worth, they will not be able to tell whether the information's worth exceeds its cost, and so they find it difficult to decide rationally whether various types of information should be bought. The sort of analysis presented in this section is a useful guide in making these sorts of decisions.[1]

---

[1] We have dealt, in this section, only with the relatively simple case in which information is perfect. If the only available information is less than perfect (that is, if it still contains errors), can we determine whether its expected worth exceeds its cost? Under many circumstances, the answer is yes. We will tend to some of these details shortly.

▣ The Expected Value of Partial Information

There is nothing in the calculation of the expected value of perfect informa-tion that depends critically on the usual definition of the term "perfect." The real difference between the uncertain case and the perfect-information case was one of timing. Decision-makers facing uncertainty typically have to de-cide what they will do before they know what will happen. Armed with the knowledge that they will not have to decide until after they know exactly what will happen, these same people can make contingency plans. They can do the analysis and decide, "If X happens, then I will do A; if Y happens, then I will do B; and so on." The expected value of perfect information is therefore the expected value of decision-makers' abilities to act on those contingency plans.

Expected value of partial information

Having made that point, we do not have to confine our attention to the extreme of complete and perfect information. We can use the same tech-nique to examine the **expected value of partial information.** We can see if learning a little more about what will happen would be worth a lot or a little. We can see if some types of information would be worth more than other types of information. We can explore answers to questions like "What would it be worth to the company to find out this or that before it had to decide what to do?"

Let's return to the oil-well investment decision to see how these questions might be resolved. Recall that the expected monetary value of the project was $650,000. Assume that a consulting firm (Firm A) has told the company that its techniques could be used to determine whether there were 100,000 barrels or 1 million barrels of "something" under the ground. Firm A cannot, how-ever, honestly claim that its techniques could be used to determine whether or not the "something" would be oil, so the probability of finding oil would re-main 0.25. What would Firm A's information be worth? Step 1 instructs us to compute the expected monetary value of the new information. To do this, we must keep careful track of what the company would do with the information in each contingency. We must compute the value of making those decisions, and we must look at the probability that each contingency will actually occur.

Armed with the knowledge from Firm A that there were 100,000 bar-rels of "something" under the ground, for example, the company would compute an expected monetary value of investing in the well that would equal $0.75(-\$500,000) + 0.25(\$500,000) = -\$250,000$. Why? Firm A's information would tell the company that there is a 0.25 chance of finding 100,000 barrels of oil, and a 0.75 chance of finding 100,000 barrels of some-thing else. The company would lose $500,000 if there were no oil, but it will earn $500,000 if oil were found. The expected monetary value of not investing would be $0; so the company would not invest *if the consulting firm declared that only 100,000 barrels of "something" might be found.*

What about the case in which Firm A assured the company that there were 1 million barrels of "something" there? The expected monetary value of in-vesting in the well would then be $0.75(-\$500,000) + 0.25(\$9,500,000) = \$2,000,000$. The company would surely invest in this case—a case defined by the *contingency that the consulting firm declares that 1 million barrels of "something" might be found.*

We can now compute the expected monetary value of being able to act on this partial information. To do so, we need to be clear about exactly what the company now knows. It knows that there is a 0.60 probability that Firm A will tell it that there are 100,000 barrels of something to be found. It knows, as well, that it will not invest in that case; and its return would then be $0. The company also knows that there is a 0.40 probability that Firm A will tell it that there are 1 million barrels of something to be found. And it knows it would invest in the well in that case with an expected monetary return of $2,000,000. So, the expected monetary value of the investment *given the company's efficient use of the consultants' information* is 0.6($0) + 0.4($2,000,000) = $800,000.

What is the expected value of this information? Step 2 tells us to compare this value with the value of the investment in the absence of the information; that value was $650,000. Information that could distinguish a lot of potential oil from a little potential oil would therefore be worth $800,000 − $650,000 = $150,000. The company would be interested in hiring Firm A as consultants for this potential investment project, but only if its fee were no larger than $150,000.

Now consider consulting Firm B. Assume that its techniques could assure the company that there was oil to be found, but firm B cannot provide any insight into how much. What would this type of information be worth? The company would surely not invest if Firm B told it that there was no oil to be found. The company would walk away with a $0 return in this case. If firm B said that there was oil to be found, though, the company would again believe that there was a 0.60 probability of finding 100,000 barrels and a 0.40 probability of finding 1 million barrels. The expected value of the investment *contingent on Firm B's assurance that there is oil to find* would therefore be 0.60($500,000) + 0.40($9,500,000) = $4,100,000. What is the expected monetary value of the company's having access to this information? There is a 0.75 chance that Firm B will report that there is no oil to find, and a 0.25 chance that Firm B will report encouraging news. The expected monetary value of the investment with access to Firm B's information is therefore 0.75($0) + 0.25($4,100,000) = $1,025,000. And the expected monetary value of the information offered by Firm B? It is $1,025,000 − $650,000 = $375,000. The company would be interested in hiring Firm B, but only if its fees were no greater than $375,000. And now we know that the information offered by Firm B would be worth more than the information offered by Firm A.

| Example 5.3 | The Value of Weather Forecasts to Raisin Producers |

To illustrate how the expected value of perfect information can be employed, consider the California raisin industry. Raisins are produced by drying grapes in the sun in the early autumn. A farmer can suffer a considerable loss if it rains after he or she chooses to produce raisins. Why? Because the grapes would no longer dry in the sun, nor would they be of much use to a winery. If rain is expected, therefore, grapes are likely to be crushed to make wine, even though this may not be as profitable as using them to produce raisins (if weather permitted). Clearly, weather forecasting is very important to the California raisin industry, not to mention many other sectors of agriculture, as well as to the managers of summer and winter resorts, the organizers of outdoor concerts, and decision-makers in other weather-dependent industries.

L. Lave has calculated the expected value of perfect information concerning the likelihood of rain over a 3-week period to California raisin producers.[2] His results indicated that perfect 3-week weather forecasts would raise the raisin producers' profits by about $90 per acre. Summing over all of the land that produces grapes that could become raisins, the value of such forecasts to the California raisin industry would have been more than $20 million per year. This is a substantial amount, particularly since the raisin industry is relatively small. Results of this sort have played an important role in quantifying the economic benefits from improved weather-forecasting techniques.

SHOULD A PERSON MAXIMIZE EXPECTED MONETARY VALUE?

We suggested earlier that a rational individual may not want to maximize the expected monetary value of his or her options. How can that be? To see how, suppose that you were given a choice between (1) receiving $1,000,000 for certain and (2) entering into a gamble in which you would win $2,100,000 if a fair coin came up heads on a single toss but you would lose $50,000 if it came up tails. The expected monetary value for the gamble is $(0.5)($2,100,000) + (0.5)(-$50,000) = +$1,025,000$. If you made your decision on the basis of expected monetary value, you would therefore choose the gamble over the certainty of $1,000,000. But you may feel a little uncomfortable about the chance of actually losing $50,000. In fact, you probably feel that many people would prefer the certainty of $1,000,000. After all, $50,000 is a substantial sum, and the gamble would give you and them a 50 percent chance of having to come up with the money. In addition, many people would probably feel that the extra $1,100,000 that they would receive if they won the gamble would not be worth the risk of losing $50,000, even if they had $50,000 to lose.

We clearly need a theory that takes these feelings into account—one that recognizes that your reaction to the choice just described should depend on your attitude toward risk. A person of modest means would probably be overwhelmed at the thought of taking a 50 percent chance of losing $50,000. A wealthy speculator might not be the least bit unsettled by the prospect of losing $50,000 if the game held an equal chance of winning $2.1 million. And a person who enjoyed danger and risk might actually prefer the gamble even though a $50,000 loss would wipe him out completely.

---

[2]See L. Lave, "The Value of Better Weather Information to the Raisin Industry," *Econometrica*, January 1963. A more extended discussion can be found in R. Katz and A. Murphy, eds., *Economic Value of Weather and Climate Forecasts* (Cambridge, UK: Cambridge University Press, 1997), pp. 222.

Fortunately, there is no need to build a theory of decision-making under uncertainty entirely on the assumption that people want to maximize the expected monetary value of a risky situation. We can, instead, construct a von Neumann–Morgenstern utility function for the decision-maker that directly incorporates his or her attitude toward risk.[3] From this, we can then go on to find the alternative that is best for the decision-maker, given his or her attitude toward risk. The von Neumann-Morgenstern utility function was named after John von Neumann, a famous mathematician at the Institute for Advanced Study in Princeton, New Jersey, and Oskar Morgenstern, an economist at Princeton University. You should not confuse utility functions of this sort with the utility functions discussed in Chapter 2. As we shall see, they are quite different.

MAXIMIZING EXPECTED UTILITY

According to the theory put forth by von Neumann and Morgenstern, a rational decision-maker will maximize expected utility when confronted with risky situations. Their construction instructs the decision-maker to choose *Expected utility* the course of action with the highest **expected utility.** But what is utility in this context? It is a number that is attached to each and every possible outcome of a decision; these values will reflect the decision-maker's preferences with respect to risk. And what is expected utility? It is the sum of the utility that would be achieved in each outcome multiplied by the probability that *von Neumann–* that outcome will actually occur. This is the **von Neumann–Morgenstern** *Morgenstern utility* **utility function.** Suppose, for example, that a risky situation had two possible *function* outcomes. Assume that the first, outcome *A*, would yield a utility value of 5 if it occurred and that the second, outcome *B*, would yield a utility value of 10. If the probability of each outcome were 0.5, then the expected utility of this situation would be $0.5(5) + 0.5(10) = 7.5$.

To take a more complicated and realistic case, what would be the expected utility of the managers of the company in the oil-well example (absent any additional information)? It would be $0.75[U(-\$500,000)] + 0.15[U(\$500,000)] + 0.10[U(\$9,500,000)]$, where $U(-\$500,000)$ is the utility that the managers would assign to a monetary loss of $500,000, $U(\$500,000)$ is the utility that they would assign a gain of $500,000, and $U(\$9,500,000)$ is the utility that they would assign to the best news—a gain of $9,500,000. This is "expected" utility, since the probabilities of the $500,000 loss, the $500,000 gain, and the $9,500,000 gain are 0.75, 0.15, and 0.10, respectively. What is the expected utility of not investing in the oil well? It is $1 \times U(\$0)$, where $U(\$0)$ is the utility they attach to a $0 gain. Why? Because 1 reflects the certain probability that the gain or loss will be $0.

[3] J. von Neumann and O. Morgenstern, *Theory of Games and Economic Behavior* (Princeton, N.J.: Princeton University Press, 1944). For alternative approaches, see M. Machina, "Dynamic Consistency and Non-Expected Utility Models of Choice under Uncertainty," *Journal of Economic Literature,* December 1989.

The point of attaching a utility to each monetary value is that many people do not regard each and every dollar as being of equal weight and importance to them. You may feel that losing $10,000 would hurt more than a $10,000 gain would help. You might think that an extra $10 means a lot on your student's budget. But what would it be worth if you had a weekly income of $10,000? Probably a lot less. We can recognize these feelings by attaching utilities to each monetary value, and we can use those utilities to indicate how you should choose among various risky alternatives.

SHOULD THE COMPANY REALLY INVEST IN THE OIL VENTURE?

Decision-makers can frequently determine the utility values that they would attach to each possible outcome of a risky situation by responding to a series of questions that are designed to elicit information about their preferences with regard to risk. Other applications simply assume that the underlying utility functions are of one particular shape or another. (We will say more about this later.) Regardless of its source, though, the utility function itself can then be used to indicate whether the decision-maker should accept or reject a particular gamble, accept or reject the opportunity to invest in a risky project, accept or reject the opportunity to buy some insurance, and so on.

To illustrate all of this, we return once again to the oil-well example. Suppose that company managers approached the decision of whether or not to invest in drilling with the utility function displayed in Figure 5.3.

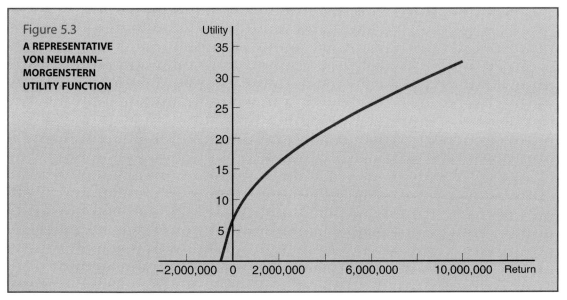

Figure 5.3

A REPRESENTATIVE VON NEUMANN– MORGENSTERN UTILITY FUNCTION

Assume, as well, that the company must make that decision with only the
original information: a 0.75 chance of not finding oil, a 0.15 chance of
finding 100,000 barrels, and a 0.10 chance of finding 1 million barrels.
According to the theory put forth by von Neumann and Morgenstern, the
decision should be made by comparing expected utility with and without
the investment. The company should invest in drilling the well if the expected utility that would result from making the investment exceeds the
expected utility of holding back. The expected utility of making the investment is

$$0.75\,U(-\$500{,}000) + 0.15\,U(\$500{,}000) + 0.10\,U(\$9{,}500{,}000).$$

According to Figure 5.3,

$$U(-\$500{,}000) = 0,$$
$$U(\$500{,}000) = 10,$$
and
$$U(\$9{,}500{,}000) = 31.6.$$

So, if the investment were made, expected utility would equal

$$0.75(0) + 0.15(10) + 0.10(31.6) = 4.66$$

If the investment were not made, though, expected utility would be
$U(0) = 7.1$, according to Figure 5.3. What should the company do? It
should not invest in drilling the well. Why? Because the expected utility of
making that investment is 4.66—a value that falls short of the expected utility
of walking away (7.1).

Besides being useful in indicating the sorts of decisions that people *should*
make, utility functions can also be useful in predicting the decisions that
they *actually will* make. To the extent that they conform to the theory put
forth by von Neumann and Morgenstern, decision-makers will choose the
course of action that maximizes expected utility. If we had a decision-maker's
utility function, therefore, we could predict which course of action he or she
would choose by duplicating his or her thought process—i.e., by comparing the expected utilities of the different courses of action. For example,
suppose that our firm managers were confronted with a choice between (1)
a certain venture with a guaranteed gain of $500,000 and (2) a risky ven-
ture in which there was a 0.25 probability that they would gain $5,000,000
coupled with a 0.75 probability that they would lose $500,000. Which would
they choose?

We can readily determine the utility attached to −$500,000, $500,000,
and $5,000,000 using the utility function displayed in Figure 5.3. These
utilities are 0, 10, and 23.5, respectively. The expected utility from the certain
venture therefore equals 10, and the expected utility from the risky venture
equals $0.75(0) + 0.25(23.5) = 5.9$. And so we should expect that the company would stick with the certain venture since its expected utility exceeds
that from the risky one. If the risky venture had different probabilities,
though, then the answer could be different. A 0.55-0.45 split in the
probabilities of loss or gain would, for example, yield an expected utility of
$0.55(0) + 0.45(23.5) = 10.6$, and so it would be preferred.

Example 5.4

Hospitals and the Health Insurance Bind

Medical-insurance companies frequently offer what is termed "point-of-service" coverage for individuals who subscribe to their insurance plans. This means that the insurance company will, subject to rules about co-payments and coverage limits, reimburse any hospital for the cost of the health services that it provides according to a fixed schedule of fees. Hospitals meanwhile agree to treat subscribers according to rules that are negotiated with the insurance company. Recently, a new wrinkle has been introduced into negotiations between hospitals and insurance companies. Insurance companies now typically negotiate what are termed "capitation rates" with hospitals that participate directly with the insurance company. These rates indicate the total amount of money that the insurance company will pay to the hospitals over the course of a year for the health-care services that they provide to its subscribers. Hospitals agree to provide all of the necessary health-care services over that time for all of these members. The insurance company agrees that hospitals get to keep a portion of any surplus revenue that might accrue if the fees incurred by the subscribers sum to an amount that falls short of the negotiated capitation rate; the insurance company keeps the rest of this excess profit. But the hospitals must also agree to cover a portion of any losses that might occur if the fees sum to an amount that is greater than the negotiated capitation rate. Moreover, payments to other hospitals for services offered to the company's subscribers are always made in full according to the predetermined schedule.

Capitation rates clearly bring uncertainty into any hospital's calculation of its expected income. Hospitals prefer less risk to more if they are risk-averse, and so they would like to see a smaller percentage difference between the capitation rate and the actual expenses charged to their accounts. And they want to avoid subscribers going to other hospitals. Why? Because other hospitals do not share in the risk that the capitation rate will fall short of actual total fees. As a result, both expected income and uncertainty (expressed as a percentage of expected income) depend on the number of times that subscribers seek medical care at a different hospital.

To see why and how, consider two illustrative cases of equal likelihood. Let the total capitation rate be $10 million, presume that the hospital and the insurance company share losses or gains on a 50-50 basis, and assume that the hospital hitting the capitation exactly would earn it a 10 percent profit. If subscribers went to another hospital 25 percent of the time, the hospital would expect income after fees to be derived from capitation revenues equal to $7.5 million, and so would expect $750,000 in profit. Suppose, in the first instance, that the capitation fee falls $1 million short, so that the hospital's net income would be $500,000 lower than expected (their 50 percent share of the $1 million loss); their profits would then be $250,000. Suppose, in the second, that the capitation fee exceeds total fees by $1 million, so that the hospital's net income would be $500,000 higher and their profits would be $1,250,000. Now assume that subscribers go to a different hospital 50 percent of the time. This would mean that expected capitation revenues would be $5 million and expected profit would be $500,000. The variation in revenue would still be plus or minus $500,000, though, because none of the variability would be passed on to the other hospitals. The hospital's profit picture would therefore vary between $0 and $1 million. Expected profit would therefore fall (as the number of patients seeking service elsewhere increased)—not good news.

PREFERENCES REGARDING RISK

Not all utility functions look like the one drawn in Figure 5.3. Although one can expect that utility should increase with the decision-maker's income, the shape of the utility function can vary greatly depending on the person's attitude toward risk. Figure 5.4 shows three general types of utility functions. Each will be discussed in turn.

Risk averters

Risk averters. The utility function in the top panel of Figure 5.4 is like that in Figure 5.3 in the sense that utility increases with the person's income at a decreasing rate. In other words, an increase in income of $1 is associated with smaller and smaller increases in utility as the person's income increases in size.[4] People with utility functions of this sort are "risk averters." When confronted with uncertain situations with equal expected monetary values, they prefer situations in which the outcome is more certain.

Suppose, for example, that the top panel of Figure 5.4 pertained to a recent college graduate who must choose between two job offers that are basically the same except for income. If she chose the first job, then her income would be certain; she would receive $40,000 a year to start. If she chose the second job, though, her income would depend on a variety of uncertain factors. Assume that there would be a 0.5 probability that it would be $20,000 a year and a 0.5 probability that it would be $60,000 a year. The second job therefore matches the first in the sense that it offers an expected income of $40,000. According to the top panel of Figure 5.4, the utilities that she would assign to incomes of $20,000, $40,000, and $60,000 are 20, 28, and 30, respectively. The expected utility that she would assign to the certainty of a $40,000 income would be 28, but the expected utility that she would assign to what amounts to a 50-50 gamble of earning $20,000 or $60,000 would be $0.5(20) + 0.5(30) = 25$. This means that she would choose the first job over the second since its expected utility would be higher. It will always be the case that a risk averter will choose a situation with a more certain outcome over one with a less certain outcome *if the expected monetary values of the situations are the same.*

Risk lovers

Risk lovers. The utility function in the middle panel of Figure 5.4 shows utility increasing at an increasing rate with income. In other words, an increase in income of $1 is associated with larger and larger increases in utility as income increases in size. People with utility functions of this sort are "risk lovers." When confronted with uncertain situations with equal expected monetary values, they prefer situations in which the outcome is *less* certain.

[4]Using the concepts described in the final sections of Chapter 2 (pp. 31–71), this amounts to saying that the marginal utility of income falls as income increases. That is, the additional (or marginal) utility resulting from an extra dollar of income declines as income goes up.

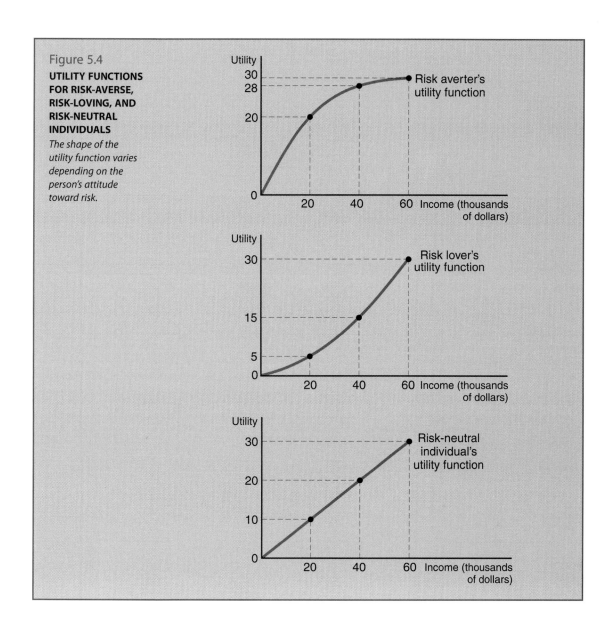

Figure 5.4

UTILITY FUNCTIONS FOR RISK-AVERSE, RISK-LOVING, AND RISK-NEUTRAL INDIVIDUALS

The shape of the utility function varies depending on the person's attitude toward risk.

To see that this is true, suppose that the middle panel of Figure 5.4 pertains to a second recent graduate who faces the same choice of jobs as the first. In her case, though, the utilities assigned to incomes of $20,000, $40,000, and $60,000 are 5, 15, and 30, respectively. She therefore assigns an expected utility of 15 to the job with the certain $40,000 income and an expected utility of 0.5(5) + 0.5(30) = 17.5 to the job with the uncertain income. This graduate will therefore choose the second job because she feels that it would produce a higher level of expected utility. It will always be the case that a risk lover will choose a situation with a less certain outcome over one with a more certain outcome *if the expected monetary values of the situations are the same.*

Risk-neutral people. The utility function in the bottom panel of Figure 5.4 shows utility increasing with income at a constant rate. In other words, an increase in income of $1 is always associated with a constant increase in utility as income grows larger and larger. Put still another way, there is a linear relationship between income and utility. People with utility functions of this sort are risk-neutral, and they always act to maximize expected monetary value regardless of the risk. We noted above that there were some circumstances under which it would be rational to choose the action or gamble that has the largest expected monetary value—i.e., to make decisions on the basis of expected monetary value and not expected utility. Now we know what these circumstances are. The decision-maker must be risk-neutral, because maximizing expected monetary value is then exactly equivalent to maximizing expected utility.

To illustrate this point, suppose that the bottom panel of Figure 5.4 pertains to one last recent graduate who faces the same choice of jobs as the other two. The utilities of $20,000, $40,000, and $60,000 are now 10, 20, and 30, respectively. This graduate therefore assigns a utility value of 20 to the job with the certain $40,000 income and an expected utility value of $0.5(10) + 0.5(30) = 20$ to the second. In contrast to either of the previous cases, this graduate is entirely indifferent between the two jobs since the expected utility attached to both is 20. No risk-neutral individual will ever be influenced by the fact that one situation is less certain than another as long as they have the same expected outcome. Risk simply does not matter to these people.[5]

| **Example 5.5** | **Two Consultants or One? Working a Problem** |

The text offered the oil-well company the advice of two different consulting firms. Recall that consulting company A could tell the company if there were 100,000 or 1 million barrels of "something" under the ground, while consulting company B could tell the company whether or not it could expect to find oil. The oil-well company could therefore collect perfect information by hiring both firms, because it could confirm any of the four possible outcomes (100,000 barrels of oil, 1 million barrels of oil, 100,000 barrels of something else, or 1 million barrels of something else). (1) Assume that the company is risk-neutral. How much would it be worth to the company to employ both consulting firms to obtain perfect information? (2) Would it be worthwhile to hire both consultants? (3) Now assume that the company's managers are risk averse; in fact, assume that their utility function is displayed in Figure 5.3. How much would it now be worth to the company to employ both firms to obtain perfect information?

SOLUTION (1) The company would not invest if it came to understand that there was no chance that it would find oil; it expects that this would happen with a probability of 0.75. The company would invest otherwise. It

---

[5]It is important to recognize that a person can be a risk averter under some circumstances, a risk lover under other circumstances, and risk-neutral under still other circumstances. The utility functions in Figure 5.4 are "pure" cases where the person is always only one of these types, at least in the range covered by the graphs.

would make $500,000 if it found 100,000 barrels (an event with a probability of 0.15) and $9,500,000 if it found 1 million barrels. The expected monetary value of the investment with this information would be $1,025,000. Since the investment would have an expected monetary value of $650,000 without any extra information, perfect information would be worth $375,000. (2) The expected monetary value of the investment with perfect information is identical to the expected monetary value of the investment with only the information provided by consulting company B. It would not pay, therefore, to engage consulting company A. (3) Figure 5.3 shows that utility values of 7.1, 10, and 31.6 would be assigned to $0, $500,000, and $9,500,000, respectively. The expected utility of the investment that would be associated with perfect information (or the information provided by consulting company B, only) would therefore be $0.75(7.1) + 0.15(10) + 0.10(31.6) = 10$. The certainty-equivalent income of the investment is therefore the income level to which a utility value of 10 is assigned; Figure 5.3 shows that this is $500,000—a value that is less than the expected monetary value of the investment just computed assuming perfect information for the risk-neutral case ($1,025,000). Figure 5.3 also shows that utility values of 0, 10, and 31.6 would be assigned to −$500,000, $500,000, and $9,500,000, respectively. The expected utility of the investment that would be associated with no further information would therefore be $0.75(0) + 0.15(10) + 0.10(31.6) = 4.7$. The certainty equivalent income of the investment would therefore be the income level to which a utility value of 4.7 is assigned; i.e., it would be roughly −$200,000. This is also a value that is smaller than the expected monetary value that would be relevant if the firm were risk neutral ($650,000). So, perfect information would be worth $500,000 − (−$200,000) = $700,000$. Note that this is larger than the value computed under the assumption of risk neutrality. Risk, to a company that is risk-averse, depresses the value of an investment, but it can increase the value of information about that investment.

WHY PEOPLE BUY INSURANCE

A great many consumers are unquestionably risk-averse. They try hard to reduce risk, even if it is not costless. This is, in fact, why people buy insurance; they pay a price for "coverage" that serves to reduce the risk that they face. We will now devote some attention to analyzing insurance markets to which they turn for this coverage—markets that play significant roles in the economies of the United States, Canada, and other developed market-based countries.

We begin by investigating exactly why a risk-averse individual would be willing to buy insurance. Suppose a young family moves into an area where driving is dangerous. Their utility function is displayed in Figure 5.5. They believe that there is a 0.5 probability that their car will be "totaled" in an accident over the next year. Assume that the car would cost $20,000 to replace—a substantial sum when compared with their $40,000 income. There is, therefore, a 0.5 probability that their net income after having to

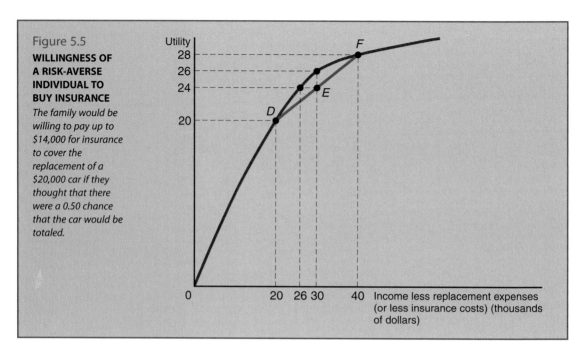

Figure 5.5

WILLINGNESS OF A RISK-AVERSE INDIVIDUAL TO BUY INSURANCE

The family would be willing to pay up to $14,000 for insurance to cover the replacement of a $20,000 car if they thought that there were a 0.50 chance that the car would be totaled.

replace the car will be $20,000, and a 0.5 probability that it will be $40,000 (because they will escape an accident over the entire year). The family would assign a utility of 20 to an income of $20,000 and a utility of 28 to an income of $40,000. Their expected utility therefore equals 0.5(20) + 0.5(28) = 24.[6]

Suppose now that an insurance company offered to sell the family a policy that would replace the car in the event of an accident for $10,000. The family could then be sure that its net income after the cost of the insurance would be $40,000 − $10,000 = $30,000. As shown in Figure 5.5, the family would assign a utility of 26 to a $30,000 net income—a value that exceeds the expected utility (24) without insurance. The family would therefore be quite willing to buy the insurance. Indeed, they would be willing to pay up to $14,000 for insurance of this kind. How do we know that? Because the family would assign a utility of 24 to a certain income of $26,000; economists call this the "certainty-equivalent income" to the risky situation. And so they would be willing to sacrifice the difference between their gross income and this certainty-equivalent income to guarantee that they would not face the financial risk of having an accident and losing $20,000. Their gross income is $40,000, and the certainty-equivalent income is $26,000. So they would be willing to pay $40,000 − $26,000 = $14,000 for the

[6]Expected utility can be determined geometrically by (a) drawing the chord between point *D* and point *F* in Figure 5.5 and (b) finding the midpoint of that chord. The midpoint is point *E*; we care about the midpoint because the probability of either outcome is 0.5. The vertical coordinate of point *E* is clearly the family's expected utility since it equals 0.5 times the utility of $20,000 plus 0.5 times the utility of $40,000. As shown in Figure 5.5, the vertical coordinate of this point is 24—a value that agrees with the algebraic result in the text equation just given.

insurance that would remove all risk. This amount is termed the "risk premium" by economists; it is the amount that the family would pay to avoid the risk completely.

Example 5.6	The Financial Health of Insurance Companies

Individuals think about buying insurance with complete confidence that their carriers will be able to compensate them for their losses in the event that a "bad state of nature" occurs—an accident, a fire, a theft, and so on. But is this confidence well founded? Some insurance companies have filed for bankruptcy from time to time, particularly after natural disasters caused enormous damage at specific locations where they had written multiple policies. Indeed, a particularly effective salesperson in a specific location can create significant exposure for companies who try to spread risk on the basis of expected monetary value calculations. The reinsurance industry—a secondary market populated by companies that sell insurance to insurance companies—has emerged over the past few decades as a major player in protecting the primary industry from this sort of exaggerated risk; but is it enough? Can private companies handle claims from catastrophic events?

This is a difficult question. Senator Dodd of Connecticut was concerned that the answer could be no, and so he introduced legislation that would provide public backstop support in the event of repeated disasters in the fall of 2001. Just how vulnerable were private companies at that time? Total claims from the World Trade Center attacks will certainly exceed $30 billion, and they may reach $50 billion. Compare these totals with the figures recorded in Table 5.2, and the picture becomes a bit clearer. Those figures summarize the financial health of the U.S. insurance industry prior to the attack. The first line includes $153.9 billion in premiums, $129.6 billion in incurred losses, and $43.2 billion in expenses. The loss of nearly $20 billion is more than covered by investment income and capital gains, but net after-tax income of $2.5 billion pales in comparison with anticipated claims from September. Nonetheless, the combined surplus of the industry was $298.20 billion as of June 30, 2001—a total that was 6 to 10 times larger than these anticipated claims. So it would appear that the industry will be able to weather the September storm, but not from an annual income stream. Multiple events would be extremely threatening over the long term.

Table 5.2		
FINANCIAL RESULTS FOR THE INSURANCE INDUSTRY IN THE UNITED STATES FOR THE FIRST HALF OF 2001	Net underwriting losses	−$19.6 billion
	Investment and other income	$18.4 billion
	Realized capital gain	$5.5 billion
	Taxes	−$1.1 billion
	Net after-tax income	$2.5 billion

SOURCE: The Insurance Information Institute at www.iii.org/media/financials, and the National Association of Independent Insurers. These data were reported in August of 2001.

☐ How Much Insurance Should an Individual Buy?

Now let's analyze the problem of how much insurance a person should buy. Suppose that somebody named Tiffany Rock owns a diamond worth $10,000, and that she wants to determine how much insurance she should purchase against the theft of the diamond. She can buy theft insurance at a cost of 2 percent of the face value of the insurance. That is, she must pay $200 for $10,000 worth of insurance; she must pay $100 for $5,000 worth of insurance, and so on. We can use Tiffany's von Neumann–Morgenstern expected utility function to determine how much insurance she should buy.

To see how, we must recognize that there are only two relevant possibilities facing Tiffany: (1) the diamond is stolen, or (2) the diamond is not stolen. The more insurance she buys, the greater the value of her assets if the diamond were stolen, but the smaller the value of her assets if the diamond were not stolen. If she bought $5,000 worth of insurance, for example, she would have $4,900 if it were stolen (a $5,000 payment from the insurance company less the $100 cost of the insurance coverage), and she would have $9,900 if it were not stolen (the $10,000 value of the diamond less the $100 cost of the insurance coverage). But if she bought $10,000 worth of insurance, then she would have $9,800 in either case: the $10,000 payment from the insurance company less the $200 cost of coverage if it were stolen would equal the $10,000 value of the diamond less the $200 cost of unused coverage if it were not stolen.

Table 5.3 shows the value of her assets if the diamond is stolen or not stolen for various levels of coverage. The value of her assets if it were to be stolen (which we designate along the vertical axis as W_s) is plotted against their value if it were not stolen (which we designate along the horizontal

Table 5.3 OUTCOMES FOR TIFFANY ROCK IF HER DIAMOND IS OR IS NOT STOLEN RELATED TO THE PURCHASE OF VARIOUS AMOUNTS OF INSURANCE			Value of Tiffany's assets if the diamond:	
Amount of insurance	Cost of insurance		Is stolen	Is not stolen
0	0		0	10,000
1,000	20		980	9,980
2,000	40		1,960	9,960
3,000	60		2,940	9,940
4,000	80		3,920	9,920
5,000	100		4,900	9,900
6,000	120		5,880	9,880
7,000	140		6,860	9,860
8,000	160		7,840	9,840
9,000	180		8,820	9,820
10,000	200		9,800	9,800

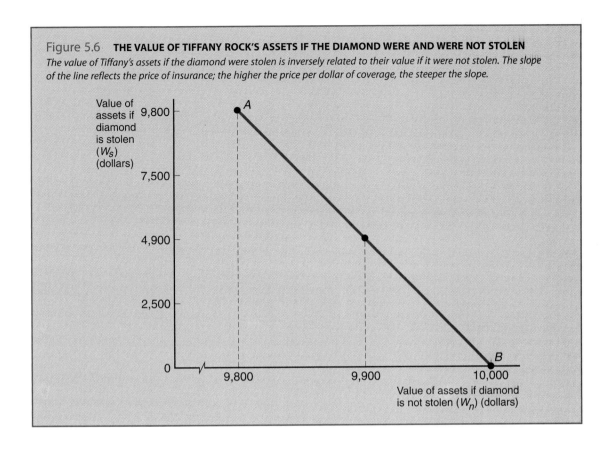

Figure 5.6 **THE VALUE OF TIFFANY ROCK'S ASSETS IF THE DIAMOND WERE AND WERE NOT STOLEN**
The value of Tiffany's assets if the diamond were stolen is inversely related to their value if it were not stolen. The slope of the line reflects the price of insurance; the higher the price per dollar of coverage, the steeper the slope.

axis as W_n) in Figure 5.6. As you can see, the relationship between these two values is a straight line, *AB*.

It is obvious by now that some account should be taken of her attitude toward risk if we are to determine correctly the amount of insurance that Tiffany should buy. If P represents the likelihood of theft, then her expected utility is $PU(W_s) + (1 - P)U(W_n)$, where $U(W_s)$ represents the utility that she would assign to having assets equal in value to W_s and $U(W_n)$ is the utility that she would assign to having assets equal in value to W_n. Tiffany wants to choose values of W_s and W_n so that her expected utility is as large as possible. Each curve in Figure 5.5 shows combinations of W_s and W_n that result in the same expected utility. Since increases in either W_s or W_n result in increases in expected utility, each of the curves in Figure 5.7 slopes downward and to the right.[7] Why? Because W_s must fall as W_n climbs, if Tiffany's expected utility is to remain constant (and vice

[7]Expected utility would be expected to increase with increases in the value of the assets involved. $U(W_s)$ should therefore increase as W_s increases, and $U(W_n)$ should increase as W_n increases. Since both P and $(1 - P)$ are positive, increases in either $U(W_s)$ or $U(W_n)$ should result in higher expected utility.

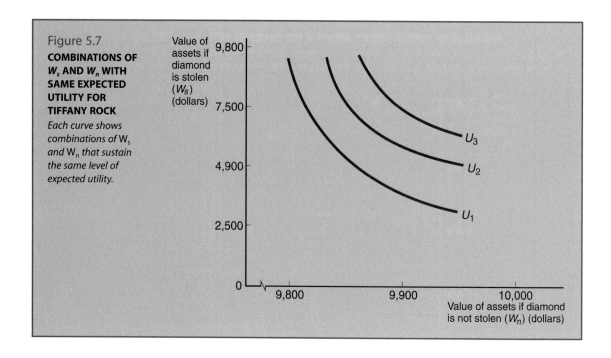

Figure 5.7

COMBINATIONS OF W_s AND W_n WITH SAME EXPECTED UTILITY FOR TIFFANY ROCK

Each curve shows combinations of W_s and W_n that sustain the same level of expected utility.

versa). Higher curves like U_3 represent higher levels of expected utility than lower ones like U_1. And since Tiffany would like to maximize expected utility, she would prefer points on higher curves like U_3 over points on lower curves like U_1.

We must now add line AB from Figure 5.6 to Figure 5.7 if we are to represent the solution to Tiffany's insurance problem. Figure 5.8 does just that. Recall that line AB contains all the possible combinations of the value of her assets if the diamond is stolen or is not stolen *for a given price of coverage* ($2 per each $100 in coverage). In other words, line AB shows the combinations of W_s and W_n that Tiffany can achieve given the existing insurance rates. It is a budget line, of sorts, and Tiffany must choose which point is best. Clearly, she should choose the point that is on the highest attainable curve shown in Figure 5.8 because each of these curves contains combinations of W_s and W_n that result in the same value of expected utility. Notice that the highest such curve attainable is U_2 and that she can afford to reach this curve only if she chooses point A, where $W_s = \$9,800$ and $W_n = \$9,800$.

How do we know that? We learned in Chapter 2 that consumer equilibrium is characterized by the tangency of the highest feasible indifference curve to the budget line. As a result, equilibrium occurs where the slope of the indifference curve (-1 times the marginal rate of substitution) is equal to the slope of the budget constraint (which is also negative). And so equilibrium satisfies the condition that the marginal rate of substitution equals -1 times the slope of the budget constraint. What is the slope of the budget constraint in this case? If the price of $1 in coverage is denoted by PR (for

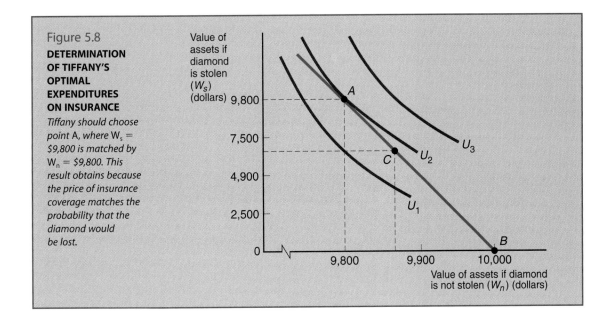

Figure 5.8

DETERMINATION OF TIFFANY'S OPTIMAL EXPENDITURES ON INSURANCE

Tiffany should choose point A, where $W_s = $9,800$ is matched by $W_n = $9,800$. This result obtains because the price of insurance coverage matches the probability that the diamond would be lost.

Value of assets if diamond is stolen (W_s) (dollars)

9,800 — — — — — — — A

7,500 — — — — — — — — — — — C

U_3
U_2
U_1

4,900

2,500

0

9,800   9,900   10,000   B

Value of assets if diamond is not stolen (W_n) (dollars)

premium), then every dollar of coverage reduces W_n by PR but increases W_s by ($1 − PR). The slope is therefore

$$\frac{\Delta W_s}{\Delta W_n} = -\frac{1 - PR}{PR}. \qquad [5.2]$$

And the marginal rate of substitution? Any expected utility indifference curve is defined in this case by

$$\text{fixed expected utility level} = P \times U(W_s) + (1 - P) \times U(W_n), \qquad [5.3]$$

where $U(W_s)$ represents the utility that Tiffany would assign to having assets equal in value to W_s, $U(W_n)$ is the utility that she would assign to having assets equal in value to W_n, and P is the probability of theft. It follows that the marginal rate of substitution is

$$\frac{(1 - P) \times MU(W_n)}{P \times MU(W_s)}, \qquad [5.4]$$

where $MU(W_s)$ and $MU(W_n)$ represent marginal utility when the diamond is and is not stolen, respectively. Equilibrium will therefore occur when

Equilibrium purchase of insurance

$$\frac{1 - PR}{PR} = \frac{(1 - P) \times MU(W_n)}{P \times MU(W_s)}. \qquad [5.5]$$

But if the probability of theft (P) matches the cost of insurance (PR), this equality can hold only if $MU(W_s) = MU(W_n)$; this, in turn, can happen only if $W_s = W_n$.

To reach point A, Tiffany must buy $10,000 worth of insurance. Why? Because only then will the value of her assets be equal to $9,800 regardless of whether or not the diamond is stolen. She will have fully insured herself against the loss and eliminated all risk. It turns out that individuals will fully

Actuarially fair insurance   insure if insurance companies are **"actuarially fair,"** in the sense that prices that they charge match the likelihood of paying out on a loss. In other words, the budget line drawn in Figure 5.8 is based on a 2 percent premium for insurance coverage ($2 for every $100 in coverage), and the expected utility curves drawn there are based on the assumption that there is a 2 percent chance (a 0.02 probability) that the ring would be stolen.

Example 5.7	Overinsuring against a Loss—Working a Problem

The text noted that individuals who maximize expected utility would choose to overinsure if the probability of a loss were larger than the premium charged for each dollar of coverage. This example will explore this possibility in two parts. We begin as in the text with the case when the premium matches the probability of loss. Panel A of Figure 5.9 depicts outcomes for an individual who is initially endowed with a $9,000 asset and faces an insurance company that is willing to sell each $1.00 of coverage against a loss for $0.33. According to Equation 5.2, the slope of the budget constraint is

$$-\frac{1 - PR}{PR} = -\frac{1 - 0.33}{0.33} = -2.$$

Panel A also depicts the case in which the probability of a loss is 33 percent, so the expected utility-maximizing position is point A, where the marginal rate of substitution is equal to 2 and the individual is fully insured. Equation 5.5 now tells us that

$$2 = MRS = \frac{(1 - 0.33) \times MU(W_n)}{0.33 \times MU(W_s)} = 2\left[\frac{MU(W_n)}{MU(W_s)}\right]$$

at point A. Since we can cancel 2 from both sides of this equation, we know in general that $MU(W_n) = MU(W_s)$, so that $W_n = W_s$; i.e., the expected utility-maximizing point lies along line 0A—the 45° line where $W_n = W_s$ and the individual is fully insured. Indeed, we know more specifically in panel A that $W_n = W_s = \$6,000$.

Now suppose that the probability of a loss is higher than 0.33. Let it be 50 percent. How could that be? Perhaps the insurance company has made an error in computing its premium. Or perhaps our individual becomes more careless when he is insured. Panel B depicts this case under the assumption that the premium is still $0.33 per $1.00 of coverage. Can point A still be the equilibrium point? No. The slope of the budget line is still equal to -2, but the marginal rate of substitution at point A is now

$$MRS = \frac{(1 - 0.50) \times MU(W_n)}{0.50 \times MU(W_s)} = \frac{MU(W_n)}{MU(W_s)} = 1$$

because $W_n = W_s = \$6,000$ and $MU(W_n) = MU(W_s)$ at point A. Notice, in fact, that the expected utility indifference curve is tangent to line BC at

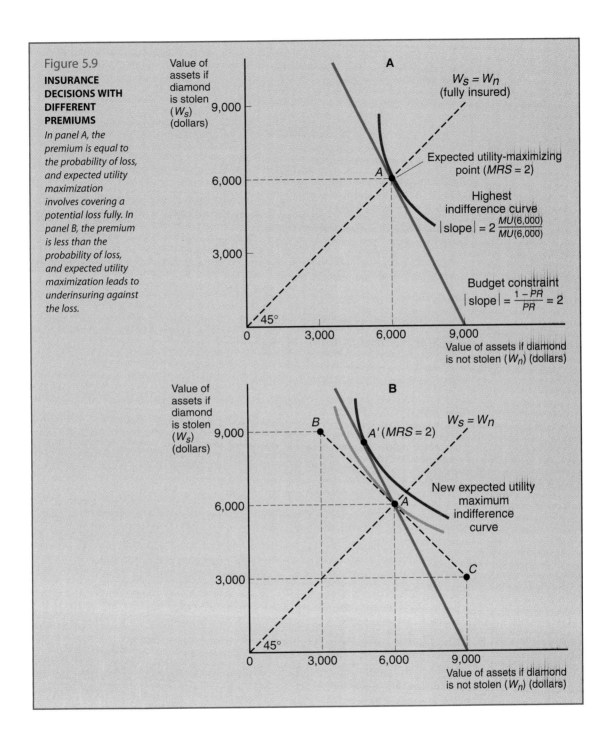

Figure 5.9

INSURANCE DECISIONS WITH DIFFERENT PREMIUMS

In panel A, the premium is equal to the probability of loss, and expected utility maximization involves covering a potential loss fully. In panel B, the premium is less than the probability of loss, and expected utility maximization leads to underinsuring against the loss.

A

Value of assets if diamond is stolen (W_s) (dollars)

$W_s = W_n$ (fully insured)

Expected utility-maximizing point ($MRS = 2$)

Highest indifference curve
$$|\text{slope}| = 2\frac{MU(6,000)}{MU(6,000)}$$

Budget constraint
$$|\text{slope}| = \frac{1 - PR}{PR} = 2$$

45°

Value of assets if diamond is not stolen (W_n) (dollars)

B

Value of assets if diamond is stolen (W_s) (dollars)

$W_s = W_n$

A' ($MRS = 2$)

New expected utility maximum indifference curve

45°

Value of assets if diamond is not stolen (W_n) (dollars)

181

point *A*—a line with a slope equal to −1. It follows that the requisite tangency with the budget constraint must now reside somewhere up the budget constraint at a point like *A′*, where the marginal rate of substitution is equal to 2. But if

$$MRS = \frac{MU(W_n)}{MU(W_s)} = 2,$$

then $MU(W_n) = 2MU(W_s)$. We now know that this individual would overinsure in this case. How? Because diminishing marginal utility in *W* means that $W_n < W_s$. And how do we know that equilibrium at point *A′* involves overinsurance? The outcome given a loss ($W_s > \$6,000$) is larger than the outcome without a loss ($W_n < \$6,000$).

Question 10 at the end of this chapter asks you to reconstruct this argument for a probability of loss that is smaller than the premium to convince yourself that underinsurance is also a possibility.

REVISITING THE VALUE OF INFORMATION WHEN PEOPLE ARE AVERSE TO RISK

We argued earlier in this chapter that people who are averse to risk always prefer less risk to more. It follows that they would place value on information that allowed them to see that the risk that they faced is, indeed, smaller than they had originally thought *even if the expected monetary outcome were the same*. Indeed, risk-averse people would be willing to pay for information that would serve to reduce their risk (or at least their perception of risk). But how much would they be willing to pay? How can we assess the value of information like this? Our earlier discussion expressed the value of information in terms of expected monetary value, but we are now asking questions that lie beyond the scope of that approach. Risk can be increased or decreased without making any change in the expected outcome of an uncertain situation, and so risk can change without making any change in the expected monetary value of that situation.

To see why, consider the individual whose utility is displayed in Figure 5.10. Suppose that she works in sales, so that at least part of her monthly income is generated from commissions. Assume, to be very specific, that she expects that her weekly income would equal either $800 with a probability of 0.50 or $1,200 with a probability of 0.50. The expected monetary outcome of this situation is clearly $1,000 per week. Figure 5.10 shows that she would assign utility values of 16 and 72.5 to the two income possibilities. She would assign a utility value of 62 to a certain income of $1,000 per week if that were possible, but it is not. Her expected utility given the uncertain income that she faces instead is 0.5(16) + 0.5(72.5) = 44.25. Notice that this same utility value of 44.25 could be sustained by a constant income of $890 per week: this is the certainty-equivalent income associated with her uncertain prospects.

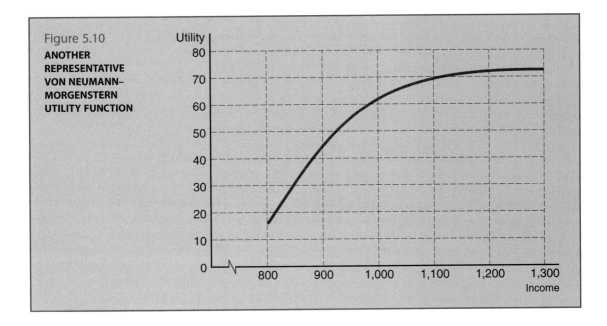

Figure 5.10
**ANOTHER
REPRESENTATIVE
VON NEUMANN–
MORGENSTERN
UTILITY FUNCTION**

Armed with the notion of certainty-equivalent income, we can now judge the damage caused by the uncertainty that she faces in her prospective income stream. The expected monetary value of her prospects is $1,000; it is therefore $110 larger than the corresponding certainty-equivalent income of $890. It follows that we can measure the damage caused by uncertainty as the difference between the expected monetary value of income and the corresponding certainty-equivalent income. In this case, the damage would be $1,000 − $890 = $110. Why is this an appropriate measure of damage? Because our subject would be willing to pay up to $110 for "income insurance" that would allow her to avoid the uncertainty by guaranteeing a constant income (of at least $890 per month). It is the applicable

Risk premium **risk premium**—the amount that she would pay to avoid the uncertainty completely.

Now consider an alternative situation in which new information has reduced the projected variability in sales so that she can expect her income to be more consistent. Assume, in particular, that the new information leads her to believe that her weekly income will be $900 with a probability of 0.50 and $1,100 with a probability of 0.50. The expected monetary outcome is still $1,000 per week, but she is better off. She would now assign utility values of 45 and 70 to the two income possibilities, and so her expected utility would now be 0.5(45) + 0.5(70) = 57.5, instead of the 44.25 value that we computed earlier. But how much is this increase in expected utility worth in dollars?

To answer this question, we return to the joint concepts of the certainty-equivalent income and its associated risk premium. Figure 5.10 suggests that our subject would assign a utility value of 57.5 to certain income of $967.

Recall that the expected monetary value of her situation is still $1,000. So, she would, in this case, pay a risk premium of no more than $33 for the guarantee that income would always be certain and equal to at least $967. And how much would this new information be worth to her? The difference between the risk premiums with and without the new information—that is, the difference between $110 and $33. The new information would, in other words, be worth $77.

BEHAVIOR IN THE FACE OF RISK

Everything that we have done thus far has assumed, at least implicitly, that individuals facing uncertainty are powerless to change their circumstances. Nothing could be further from the truth in many cases. Individuals can typically take actions that can change their sensitivity to risk or alter the dimension of that risk. But they can do so only at some cost. The question is, therefore, would any of these strategies be worth the effort? This section offers a brief introduction into how economists might answer this question by judging the value of giving any such strategy a try.

The preceding section offered some insight into the value of reducing variation around a fixed mean income. It was described in terms of improved information, but it could equally well describe efforts that could be undertaken to reduce risk. Suppose, for the sake of illustration, that we changed the context of the last few paragraphs of the last section. Suppose, in particular, that our subject could actually reduce her risk from a situation where income would be $1,000 plus or minus $200 to a situation where income would be $1,000 plus or minus $100. We know from the previous section that she could reduce the damage associated with uncertainty from $110 per month to $33, and so this reduction in uncertainty would be worth $77 to her. How might it be accomplished? Perhaps our subject has negotiated a contract that is less dependent on sales. And how much would she be willing to sacrifice per month in mean income to reduce her risk? She would accept an average income of no less than $923 (the previously assured expected income of $1,000 minus the $77 value of reduced uncertainty).

What role might sensitivity to risk play? Figure 5.10 displayed the utility function of a particular individual assuming a particular aversion to risk. Figure 5.11 displays a different perspective—one that reflects a diminished aversion to risk. How might our subject achieve this reduction? Perhaps she has located a friendly relative who will lend her a little money in bad times. Perhaps she has a roommate who can cover part of the rent in months when her income is limited. Perhaps she is simply less concerned about the value of income. It matters little. All that matters is that her aversion to risk has been diminished.

To what end? Faced with the original range of uncertain income, our risk-averse subject would now assign a utility value of 55 to a weekly income of $800, and a utility of 63.5 to an income of $1,200. The expected

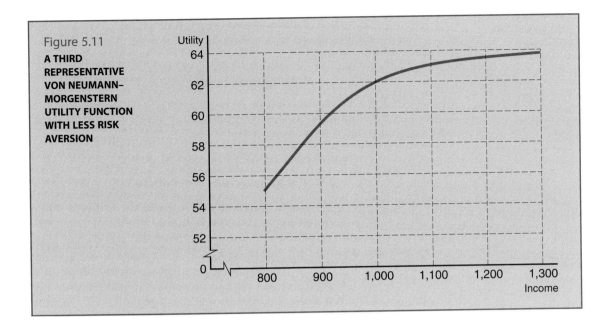

Figure 5.11

A THIRD REPRESENTATIVE VON NEUMANN– MORGENSTERN UTILITY FUNCTION WITH LESS RISK AVERSION

monetary outcome is still $1,000, but the expected utility of the original uncertainty would now be 59.25. And the certainty-equivalent income would now be $910. So how much damage would uncertainty do now? The risk premium would now be the difference between the expected monetary income of $1,000 and the new certainty-equivalent income of $910: it would amount to $90. Compared with the original risk premium of $110, it is now clear that reduced sensitivity to risk would save $20— the difference between the original damage estimate of $110 and the new estimate of $90. And it should also be clear that reduced sensitivity to risk would lower demand for insurance coverage *and/or* diminish risk-reducing behaviors.

Microlink 5.1   Expected Utility Maximization and Utility Maximization

The parallels between the utility-maximization framework of Chapters 2 and 3 and the expected utility-maximization framework presented here should be obvious, but it is useful to make the comparison explicit. Utility maximization for two goods (denoted X and Y) is, for example, based on a general utility function of the form $U = U(X, Y)$ and a budget constraint determined by income and the prices of X and Y. The marginal rate of substitution is then simply the ratio of the marginal utilities of X and Y, and the utility-maximizing combination of X and Y is characterized by

$$MRS \equiv \frac{MU_X}{MU_Y} = \frac{P_X}{P_Y}$$

185   and the budget constraint $I = P_X X + P_Y Y$.

Expected utility maximization across two states of nature (good and bad) is, by way of contrast, based on a specific utility function of the form

$$U(W_{good}, W_{bad}) \equiv \text{(probability of the good state)} \times U(W_{good}) \\ + \text{(probability of the bad state)} \times U(W_{bad})$$

where $U(W)$ is a utility function in income, wealth, or consumption now denoted by W. The marginal rate of substitution in this context incorporates the probabilities according to

$$MRS \equiv \frac{\text{(probability of the good state)} \times MU(W_{good})}{\text{(probability of the bad state)} \times MU(W_{bad})},$$

but it conveys the same content. The numerator is still the marginal utility of the first argument of the utility function (income, wealth, or consumption in the good state of nature). And the denominator is still the marginal utility of the second argument. Meanwhile, the expected utility-maximizing combination is characterized by matching this MRS with the slope of a budget constraint that represents the opportunity cost of providing one more unit of value in the bad state of nature by sacrificing some income, wealth, or consumption in the good state. How so? You buy \$1 of coverage by paying a premium of PR regardless of which state of nature appears. In the good state, you lose PR; in the bad state, you pay PR but receive \$1 for a net gain of $\$1 - PR$.

THE PRECAUTIONARY PRINCIPLE

The von Neumann-Morgenstern concept of expected utility is a powerful tool that economists have used to their advantage in exploring how to make decisions under uncertainty. It cannot, however, be applied to everyone's satisfaction in all situations. Applying the expected utility construction to risky situations that include the possibility of what are termed "high consequence–low probability" events can be particularly troublesome. These are cases where very large (nearly infinite) losses in utility might occur with very small (nearly infinitesimal) probability. The calculation of expected utility would then involve multiplying very large numbers by very small ones, and many observers question whether the results have any meaning.

Precautionary Decision-makers have responded to situations like this by constructing
principle an alternative decision criterion that has been dubbed the **precautionary principle.** In its strongest form, the precautionary principle holds that action should be taken in some circumstances to avoid unacceptably large risks at virtually any cost. In its weaker form, it holds that action should be taken to lower the probability of an unacceptably costly outcome below a specified number. Many of the exposure limits set in the U.S. economy by the Occupational Safety and Health Administration (OSHA) and the Environ-

mental Protection Agency (EPA) are, for example, the result of applying this principle to the workplace or the general environment. Indeed, most of the rules set by OSHA and the EPA limit the probability of developing cancer in response to exposure to a wide range of materials and chemicals (from benzene to formaldehyde) to 1 in 100,000 lifetimes. And since both agencies use 70 years to define a lifetime, their rules effectively limit the probability of developing cancer from exposure to less than 1 in 1 million. The FDA applies similar standards when it decides whether or not a new drug can be tested on humans.

Applying the precautionary principle to business decisions results in a very conservative investment philosophy. Researchers from a very large international oil company (that will remain nameless) once reported to the International Energy Workshop, for example, that its directors would not invest in any new well unless they could be assured that the well would pay off *in every conceivable future scenario*. It seems that the company had been burned by the failure of a large number of exploratory drillings, and so the directors wanted to make sure that this sort of "high-consequence" event would never have a probability other than 0. A rule like this can have dramatic consequences in limiting the options that might be undertaken.

To see how, recall our own oil-well example from earlier sections. The initial information there held that there was a 0.75 probability of losing $500,000 because no oil would be found. The large oil company of the previous paragraph would never decide to invest in drilling in this case, despite the fact that the expected monetary value of the well was $650,000. Why? Because there is a chance of losing money. And would the company be at all interested in the information that could be provided by consulting Firm A (the consultants who could tell the company whether the well would yield 100,000 or 1 million barrels of something that might be oil)? Absolutely not, despite the fact that their information would increase the expected monetary value of investing in the well to $800,000. Why? Because there would still be a 0.75 probability of not finding oil and losing $500,000. Would the company be interested in the information that could be provided by consulting Firm B (the consultants who could tell the company that the well would or would not find oil—just not how much oil they would find)? This is a bit trickier. The expected monetary value of the investment would then be $1,025,000, and the company would invest only after determining that there was oil to be found. So it would be interested in the information. And what would the company pay for this information? Perhaps nothing at all. Why? Because there is a 0.75 chance that the consultants would say that there was no oil and the company would have paid the fee in return for nothing of value.

Our little example makes it quite clear that applying a strict version of the precautionary principle to business decisions can be quite debilitating. As one current television commercial puts it, "The biggest risk may come from not acting." Indeed, our nameless big oil company almost went belly-up several years after adopting its precautionary drilling strategy. Why? Because it was running out of stuff to sell.

Table 5.4

THE COST OF RISK-LIMITING REGULATIONS

Regulated substance	Regulating agency	Initial annual risk	Annual lives saved	Cost per life saved
Passive restraints (air bags)	NHTSA	9.1 in 100,000	1850	$300,000
Airplane seat cushion flammability	FAA	1.6 in 10 million	37	$600,000
Benzene emissions	EPA	2.1 in 100,000	0.31	$2.8 million
Benzene in manufacturing	OSHA	8.8 in 10,000	3.8	$17.1 million
Asbestos	EPA	2.9 in 100,000	10	$104.2 million
Formaldehyde	OSHA	6.8 in 10 million	0.01	$72 billion

Example 5.8

The Cost of Exposure Limits That Have Been Set by Applying the Precautionary Principle

Kip Viscusi has recently published estimates of the cost of using the precautionary principle to justify limiting human exposure to various hazards.[8] He used the EPA target that the chance of a death over a 70-year lifetime from such exposure should be no larger than 1 chance in 100,000. A selection of his estimates, expressed in terms of millions of dollars spent to save one life, is displayed in Table 5.4.

The cost estimates are expressed as averages. They will be low if the cost of achieving the exposure limit is small or if the number of people removed from harm's way is high. Passive restraint (air bag) limitations imposed by the National Highway Traffic Safety Administration (NHTSA) apply to many people with relatively little additional expense; average cost is low for both reasons. Airline seat flammability restrictions imposed by the Federal Aviation Administration (FAA) apply to many people; average cost is low because the denominator is high. On the other extreme, average cost will be high if the cost is high or the number of people removed from danger is small. The formaldehyde restrictions imposed by OSHA seem to be high for both reasons.

Should these estimates be compared with the statistical value of a human life? This is a very contentious issue. Some argue that estimates of the value of human life have been used in court for years, and so it is appropriate to apply them to legal restrictions. Others argue that the idea is preposterous and sets one boundary on the ability of economics to value anything and everything.

[8]W. K. Viscusi, *Fatal Tradeoffs: Public and Private Responsibilities for Risk* (New York: Oxford University Press, 1992); or "Economic Foundations of the Current Regulatory Reform Efforts." *Journal of Economic Perspectives,* vol. 10, no. 3, Summer 1996.

1. The probability that a particular outcome will occur in an uncertain situation is the proportion of times that this outcome would occur over the long run if this situation were to occur over and over again. The expected monetary value of uncertain income is the sum of the amount of money gained (or lost) in each possible outcome multiplied by the probability of that outcome. Expected monetary value is the average amount that the decision-maker would gain (or lose) if he or she were to accept the underlying uncertainty over and over.

2. The expected value of perfect information is the difference between (a) the expected monetary value that the decision-maker could achieve if he or she had completely accurate information about which an uncertain set of possible outcomes will actually occur and (b) the expected monetary value of the same set of outcomes in the absence of any additional information. It is computed with the understanding that the uncertainty will be resolved before the decision-maker has to decide what to do. It is the maximum amount that the decision-maker would be willing to pay to obtain such information. The same techniques can be used to calculate the expected value of partial or imperfect information.

3. A decision-maker may or may not want to maximize expected monetary value. This decision depends on his or her attitude toward risk—an attitude that can be measured by a von Neumann–Morgenstern (expected) utility function. The von Neumann–Morgenstern utility function is useful in indicating the courses of action that the decision-maker should choose, and so it can also be used in predicting the decisions that a rational decision-maker will actually make.

4. Assuming a constant expected monetary value, people who are risk-averse prefer less uncertainty and risk to more uncertainty and risk. The reverse is true for risk lovers. People who are risk-neutral maximize expected monetary value; in their eyes, risk doesn't matter.

5. The concepts of expected monetary value and risk aversion can be applied to decisions about the purchase of insurance. The relationship between the amount of money available after an insured loss and the amount of money available without a loss can be represented by a straight line. The optimal amount of insurance can be determined by finding the point on this line that maximizes expected utility. Risk-averse people will fully insure against a loss if the cost per dollar of coverage equals the probability that the loss will occur.

6. The value of information can be redefined to accommodate risk aversion. The value of information that reduces risk is equal to the difference in the amount of money that individuals would be willing to pay to avoid the risk in the two situations. They would, in any risky situation, be willing to pay the difference between the expected monetary value and the certainty-equivalent income, for which utility exactly matches the level of expected utility. This is the risk premium that they would pay to avoid the risk completely, and the value of information that reduces risk is equal to the difference between the risk premiums with and without the information.

7. Individuals can respond to risky situations by changing their sensitivity to risk or reducing the dimension of that risk. Both actions can be expensive, but their value can be estimated by applying the procedure that produces estimates of the value of improved information when people are risk-averse.

8. Decision-makers sometimes employ the precautionary principle when confronted with high consequence–low probability outcomes. These decisions are very conservative, and can lead to the dismissal of many circumstances for which the expected monetary value is decidedly positive.

1. Professional golf and tennis have become big business around the world. In tournaments, there is typically a large disparity between the prize for the winner and that for the runner-up. One of the most glaring examples of this is the head-to-head match for $1 million arranged in the summer of 1999 between David Duval and Tiger Woods (the golfers then ranked numbers 1 and 2 in the world, respectively). Some have argued that it would make sense for competitors to have secret deals before the match to divide the prize money. They might, for example, agree that both the winner and the loser would get $500,000 and simply play for "bragging rights." (a) Should a risk-loving player who believes that he has a 0.5 probability of winning be willing to split the prize money? (b) Suppose that a player facing the Duval-Woods setup had the utility function portrayed in the figure. Would this player be willing to split if he thought his chances of winning were 50 percent? (c) What if the world rankings were right and the top player had a better chance of winning? Given the utility function shown in the figure, how large would his subjective probability that he would win have to be for him to decline the offer of a $500,000 split of the purse?

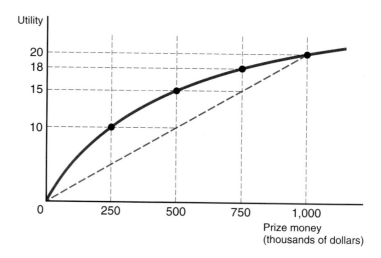

2. According to R. A. Fisher, a famous British statistician, advocates of subjective probability "seem forced to regard mathematical probability not as an objective quantity measured by observed frequencies but as measuring psychological tendencies, theorems respecting which are useless for scientific purposes." Do you think that subjective probabilities are useless in solving microeconomic problems?

3. The owner of the New York Yankees had to decide, before the 2002 season, whether or not to rehire David Wells—a 39-year-old pitcher who had just spent most of the previous season recovering from back surgery. Wells had been a very popular Yankee, though, and the owner thought that there was a 0.8 probability that profits would increase by $10 million if he signed him and the Yankees again became World Series champions. Even if the Yankees did not win the series, the owner felt that Wells's pitching would increase profits by $5 million. If he reinjured his back, though, Wells would

not pitch and the owner felt that he would certainly lose $3 million regardless of how the Yankees fared in the playoffs above and beyond the $1 million signing bonus and a $2 million salary in the first year (the boss had traded Tino Martinez, and so he needed a popular player on the field to keep the fans in the stadium). The owner, who is risk-neutral but very demanding, signed Wells to the contract. What probability did the owner attach to the likelihood that Wells's back would remain healthy for the entire season?

4. You work for a small company and must decide whether to go forward with an investment project. The company will gain $5 million if the project is successful, but it will lose $1 million if it is not successful. You believe that the probability of success is 0.2 and that the likelihood of failure is 0.8. What would be the expected value of perfect information to the company, assuming that it is risk-neutral? What would be the expected value of perfect information to you, assuming that you would receive a bonus of $250,000 if the project succeeds? Your utility function is displayed in the figure for Problem 1.

5. Mary Modem is considering the purchase of stock in an Internet services firm. She feels that there is a 50-50 chance, if she buys the stock, that she can make $6,000 or lose $12,000. What is the expected monetary value of buying the stock? If she maximizes expected monetary value, should she purchase the stock? If she is risk-averse, should she buy the stock? Now suppose that Ms. Modem assigns a utility of -20 to a $12,000 loss, a utility of 0 to a $0 gain, and a utility of 5 to a $6,000 gain. What is the expected utility of buying the stock? Should she purchase the stock? Why or why not? What is the expected value of perfect information in this case?

6. Return to our discussion of insurance purchases. Suppose that insurance rates go up so that theft insurance now costs 3 percent of the face value of the insurance. Will line AB in Figure 5.6 shift? If so, draw its new position in a graph.

7. Tyler Spaulding's von Neumann–Morgenstern utility function can be represented by $U(M) = 10 + 2M$, where U is utility and M is monetary gain. He has the opportunity to invest $25,000 in Coach's Bar and Grill in downtown Hartford. He thinks the world of Coach Calhoun and is thrilled that his team has just won the NCAA basketball tournament, but is very concerned that the Patriots have just pulled out of their deal to move to Hartford. He therefore thinks that there is a 0.5 probability that he will gain $32,000 because the basketball team will be successful next year (and patrons love to watch the games at Coach's), but there is a 0.5 chance that he will lose everything because no Patriots fans will show up on Sunday (there aren't any more Patriots fans in Connecticut). (a) Calculate his expected utility in making the investment. (b) Would making the investment increase expected utility? (c) What would be the value of perfect information about the profitability of Coach's to this investor?

8. Research and development decisions are frequently made incrementally. Suppose, for example, that a company were reviewing two research projects that would each cost $5 million to complete. The first, project A, would allow the company to bring a product to market and earn $10 million with a 0.5 probability, but it would fail completely with a 0.5 probability. The second,

project B, could earn $8 million with a 0.75 probability, but it, too, could
fail with a 0.25 probability. (a) Would either project be worth the expense
in terms of expected monetary value? (b) Would either be worth the expense if the company were risk-averse? (c) Now suppose that the company
could gain some improved information about the likelihood of success of
either project by undertaking partial development projects costing $1 mil-
lion. For either project, this partial investment would mean that the company would see a 0.5 probability of finding out the chance of success would
be 0.9 if the remaining $4 million were invested and a 0.5 probability of
finding out that it would certainly fail. Calculate the value of this information for both projects in terms of expected monetary value. (d) Why would
this information be more valuable for project A than for project B?

9. M. Friedman and L. J. Savage hypothesized that a person's von Neumann–
Morgenstern utility function for income might typically have the shape indicated in the figure. (a) Would the typical individual prefer the certainty
of an income of B to a gamble in which there is a 0.5 probability that his
income is A and a 0.5 probability that his income is C? (Note that B is the
average of A and C.) (b) Would he prefer the certainty of an income of D
to a gamble where there is a 0.5 probability that his income is C and a 0.5
probability that his income is E? (Note that D is the average of C and E.)
(c) Would the value of information be different in case (a) than in case (b)?
Why or why not?

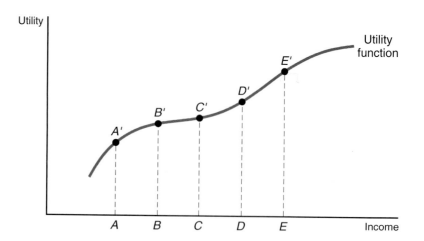

10. Return to panel A of Figure 5.9, where an individual faces the potential loss
of $9,000. If an insurance company *correctly* judges the probability of this
loss at 33 percent, then it would charge $33 for every $100 of coverage
and the individual would fully insure at point A. Panel B, meanwhile, shows
that this individual would overinsure if the actual probability of the loss
were higher than 33 percent. Use similar logic to show that she would underinsure if the probability of the loss were lower than 33 percent.

11. Explain the popularity of virus-scanning software and Electronic "firewalls"
for personal computers in terms of insurance. Does the expected utility
model explain this demand, or is the precautionary principle more
applicable?

Calculus Appendix

THE MARGINAL RATE OF SUBSTITUTION FOR EXPECTED UTILITY

Let utility be given by $U = U(W)$, and suppose that there are two possible states of nature. The bad state of nature where a loss occurs has a probability P and yields W_s, while the good state of nature with no loss occurs with probability $1 - P$ and yields W_n. Expected utility could then be represented by

$$EU = PU(W_s) + (1 - P)U(W_n).$$

To compute the marginal rate of substitution in expected utility, we need to totally differentiate this defining equation under the assumption that $d(EU) = 0$; i.e., we need to guarantee that expected utility is constant. Accordingly,

$$d(EU) = 0 = PU'(W_s)\, dW_s + (1 - P)U'(W_n)\, dW_n$$

where $U'(W_n)$ and $U'(W_s)$ represent marginal utility dU/dW evaluated at W_n and W_s, respectively. Collecting terms, therefore,

$$MRS = \left.\frac{dW_s}{dW_n}\right|_{d(EU)=0} = \frac{(1 - P)U'(W_n)}{PU'(W_s)}.$$

THE INSURANCE BUDGET CONSTRAINT

Let the price of insurance coverage be given by PR, the premium for $1 worth of coverage. So, for a price of PR to be paid in any state of nature, the insurance company would promise to pay $1 in the event of a covered loss. It follows, therefore, that an individual with initial wealth W_0 could have

$$W_n = W_0 - C \times PR$$

in the event that C in coverage were purchased and no loss was incurred and

$$W_s = W_0 - C \times PR + C = W_0 + C(1 - PR)$$

in the event of a loss. Collecting terms, then,

$$C = \frac{W_0 - W_n}{PR}$$

in the good state of nature and

$$C = \frac{W_s - W_0}{1 - PR}$$

in the bad state. Setting these equal to one another (they are the same C) and cross-multiplying, therefore,

$$(W_0 - W_n) \times (1 - PR) = (W_s - W_0) \times PR$$

and so

$$W_s = \frac{W_0}{PR} - \frac{1 - PR}{PR \times W_n}$$

is the budget constraint. Its slope is equal to

$$\frac{dW_s}{dW_n} = -\frac{1 - PR}{PR}.$$

CONSUMER EQUILIBRIUM

We now know that

$$MRS = \left.\frac{dW_n}{dW_s}\right|_{d(EU)=0} = \frac{(1 - P)U'(W_s)}{PU'(W_n)}$$

and that the slope of the budget constraint is

$$\frac{dW_s}{dW_n} = -\frac{1 - PR}{PR}.$$

Equilibrium sets the absolute value of the slope of the budget constraint equal to the MRS, so

$$\frac{1 - PR}{PR} = \frac{1 - P}{P} \times \frac{U'(W_s)}{U'(W_n)}.$$

If $PR = P$, therefore (i.e., if the premium is equal to the probability of a bad state of nature), then

$$\frac{U'(W_s)}{U'(W_n)} = 1,$$

i.e.,

$$U'(W_s) = U'(W_n)$$

so that

$$W_s = W_n$$

and equilibrium sustains full insurance.

A FULL INSURANCE RESULT FOR A RISK-AVERSE INDIVIDUAL WITH ACTUARILY FAIR INSURANCE

We begin by setting up a simple model that captures the essential characteristics of basing insurance decisions on maximizing expected utility. To that end, let P represent the probability of sustaining some loss L against initial wealth denoted by W. Let PR be the price per dollar of insurance coverage, and let C denote amount of coverage actually purchased. Finally, suppose that utility is given by some function $U = U(\text{net wealth})$, and assume that it is concave in its argument.

The problem is to maximize expected utility,

$$PU(W - L - C \cdot PR + C) + (1 - P)U(W - C \cdot PR),$$

with respect to C. The appropriate first-order condition is

$$P(1 - PR)U'(\text{bad}) - (1 - P)(PR)U'(\text{good}) = 0$$

where

$U'(\text{bad})$ simply denotes the derivative of U with respect to its argument evaluated in the bad state of nature $W - L - C^*(PR) + C^*$, with C^* representing the selected coverage, and

$U'(\text{good})$ similarly denotes dU/dw evaluated in the good state of nature $W - C^*(PR)$, with C^* still representing the selected coverage.

It follows that C^* solves

$$\frac{U'(\text{bad})}{U'(\text{good})} = \frac{(1 - P) \cdot PR}{P(1 - PR)}.$$

Meanwhile, actuarily fair insurance guarantees that the expected value of income in the good state of nature for the (risk-neutral) insurance company equals the expected value of outflow in the bad state of nature:

$$(1 - P)(PR)C = P(C - C \cdot PR) = PC(1 - PR).$$

After some algebra, therefore,

$$\frac{(1 - P)(PR)}{P(1 - PR)} = 1,$$

so that

$$U'(\text{bad}) = U'(\text{good}).$$

It must be true, as a result, that the outcome in the good state of nature matches the outcome in the bad state of nature. Mathematically, then,

$$W - L - C^*(PR) + C^* = W - C^*(PR).$$

But this could only happen if $C^* = L$, i.e., we see that the individual is fully insured because the coverage purchased (C) equals the potential loss (L).

The Demand for Airline Travel

Airline travel is big business, and it is expected to grow even larger over the foreseeable future. Figure 1, for example, displays growth forecasts through 2004 that were published early in 2000 for U.S. carriers by the International Air Transport Association. They all clearly show that each market is anticipated to grow significantly and steadily. Demand plummeted in the fourth quarter of 2001, of course, but forecasts of strong growth still hold significant weight. Airport managers and air traffic controllers on both sides of the Atlantic are expecting twice as many transatlantic flights in 2015 as there were in the year 2000. Notwithstanding these expectations for future growth in the industry, recent events clearly show that single participants in the industry are not invulnerable to economic downturns and external events. As a result, airlines compete vigorously for market share in many ways. Some are familiar to most of us; others are a bit more obscure. This Applied Perspective will review a few of them.

Alliances between carriers are perhaps the most obvious way that airlines try to increase their visibility if not their market shares. There were, in fact, almost 600 alliances among 220 different airlines in 2001. Some alliances involve simple code sharing—a sort of cross-listing procedure by which two or more airlines sell tickets for the same flight. The next level involves airlines' blocking a certain number of seats on each other's flights. Other arrangements include joint marketing and sharing frequent flyer programs. On occasion, two airlines, like KLM and Northwest, for example, actually agree to integrate their business operations, but this is the last bilateral step before a merger. Finally, large numbers of airlines have sometimes agreed to put some or all of their operations under a single umbrella. Star Alliance is the largest of these megacooperatives. It brings United Air Lines, SAS, Lufthansa, and Singapore Airlines together with nine smaller partners to account for 20 percent of world air traffic. Sky Team, meanwhile, joins Air France, Delta, Alitalia, Aeromexico, CSA, and Korean Air as primary partners who share flights, connections, frequent flyer programs, and airport lounges; and more than 20 other airlines participate to a varying degree.

Widespread traveler access to the Internet has also opened an important and growing opportunity. Five billion dollars worth of tickets were sold online in 2000, and that total is expected to grow sharply. Why? First of all, the 2000 figure represented only 4 percent of sales in North America and less than 1 percent of sales in Europe. Surely those percentages can only climb as comfort with the Internet expands across the population. Investors think so, at the very least. Four companies have been created recently to facilitate the process, and two (Hotwire and Orbitz) are actually owned by the airlines. Second, consumers have come to expect that Internet tickets are less expensive, and they are generally right. Airlines save money in operations by skipping travel agent commissions, so they can pass some of the savings on. More important, though, all of the successful new companies are programmed to help consumers find a selection of the lowest (albeit restricted) fares from one place to another.

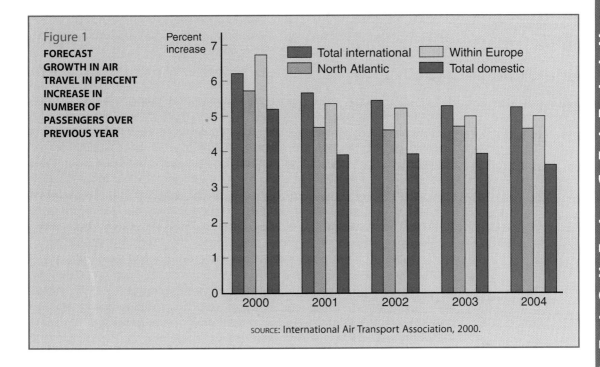

Figure 1

FORECAST GROWTH IN AIR TRAVEL IN PERCENT INCREASE IN NUMBER OF PASSENGERS OVER PREVIOUS YEAR

SOURCE: International Air Transport Association, 2000.

Mention of fares brings us to the most important competitive arena—pricing. Here, airlines have adopted what has been termed "yield management": the system by which they efficiently fill the maximum number of seats on any particular flight. The system allows an airline to determine more accurately the number of seats it needs to allocate to different types of travelers (leisure, business, or first class) on any particular flight. It estimates the number of seats that should be held for last-minute business travelers who will pay top dollar (sometimes 15 times what a discount-fare traveler might be paying to sit three rows back). Conversely, it estimates how many seats it should offer at a discount (because getting some money for seat 16A is better than flying from point A to point B with the seat empty).

This may seem like a set of simple problems in an age of information management, but it is severely complicated by the fact that most travelers of any sort must make connections at hub airports around the world. United Air Lines knows, for example, that 60 percent of the seats on any given flight leaving O'Hare Airport in Chicago will be filled by passengers who made connections from other locations. Yield-management systems need to be sensitive to surges and shortfalls in these connecting flights if they are to accommodate proper handling of different types of passengers. The airline would probably be more interested in making sure that the high-priced business traveler from Frankfurt can make her connection to Denver than it would in assuring that a domestic vacationer from Charlotte, North Carolina, got to San Francisco on time. United has been able to track more than 350,000 passengers a day over 3,000 separate flights and thereby generate an extra $50 to $100 million in revenue each year since 1997. These are big numbers for a company that made $500 million in profit in 1997 against $16.4 billion in gross revenue.

To exploit the advantages of yield management most thoroughly, however, airlines must have some idea of how different types of travelers respond to different prices. In the transatlantic market, for example, about 46 percent of the total number of tickets sold each year go to vacationers; and most of these are sold during the summer. Another 34 percent of travelers between North America and Europe are visiting friends or family, and the remaining 20 percent are businesspeople. Demand estimates have put the price elasticity of demand on these routes significantly below unity for business travelers and significantly above 1 for the others. While we postpone proof of this proposition until Chapter 10, you may not be surprised to know that this explains why airlines charge business travelers so much more for their tickets.

But how do airlines tell one type from another when they call a travel agent or tee up an Internet site? Business travelers, at least, certainly have no vested self-interest in identifying themselves if they are going to get socked with higher prices. There are, however, important differentiating signals. Business travelers sometimes need to get from point A to point B sometime within the next 24 hours. And even when they do not, they recognize that their travel plans can change almost instantly. Knowing this, airlines place restrictions on their cheaper fares that make canceling tickets or changing flights expensive if not impossible. Vacation travelers accept these restrictions because their plans are made well in advance, but business travelers do not.

Finally, it is important to recognize that the demand curve for transatlantic travel in general is not the demand curve facing any specific airline or alliance. Given a high degree of substitution, in fact, their demand curves are likely to be far more elastic. As a result, airlines compete right down to the quality of service, the diversity of their audio and video entertainment, the space between one row of seats and the next, the convenience of their departure times, and so on. Large alliances may dampen this competition, but not completely.

SOURCES: S. Borenstein and M. Zimmerman, "Market Incentives for Safe Commercial Airline Operations," *American Economic Review,* December 1988; N. Rose, "Fear of Flying? Economic Analysis of Airline Safety," *Journal of Economic Perspectives,* Spring 1992; and various issues of *The Economist.*

QUESTIONS

1. What information would you need to be sure that higher fares would increase revenue from business travelers and reduce revenue from vacation travelers? Has the text provided that information? Are you convinced that the statement is true?

2. Suppose that the demand for travel between two locations were given by $P = 10 - T$ for vacation flyers and $P = 30 - 5X$ for business travelers; P denotes the price in hundreds of dollars and T indicates the quantity demanded in hundreds of passengers per day. Note, for reference, that a $500 fare would produce 500 business travelers and 500 vacation travelers, and compute the price elasticity of demand at both points. Now compute the fares that would

maximize revenue from each type of traveler and compute the resulting demand for travel, and compute the price elasticity of demand at these locations. Explain how this information could save on the cost side even as it increased revenue.

3. Why do airlines allow standby passengers? Why do they not auction open seats to the highest bidder when standby demand is greater than the number of open seats?

4. Why do airlines put themselves at risk of overbooking flights; i.e., why do they sometimes sell more tickets than they have seats? When that happens, the airlines sometimes offer coupons for free travel up to $600 over one year to a passenger with a confirmed ticket in exchange for relinquishing his or her seat. How could this be good business? Approach this question from the perspective of making decisions under uncertainty. Would your answers change if the management of the airline were risk-averse in revenue? Risk-averse in maintaining the perception that they care about their customers?

5. The summer of 2002 saw the number of flights between Europe and North America fall as vacation demand fell. The result was extraordinarily full airplanes. Would increasing the density of co-share agreements make this more or less likely?

6. Should the demand for air travel between Europe and the United States depend on hotel prices in Europe? On the strength of the Euro vis-à-vis the dollar? On the cross-price elasticity of demand for domestic ground transportation in Europe and/or the United States?

7. Do you think that the long-run price elasticity for business travel is much higher than the short-run? Would it be as sensitive to the time period as the price elasticity for leisure travel?

The Firm: Its Technology and Costs

THREE

CHAPTER 6

The Firm and Its Technology

Sumner Redstone is the Chairman and Chief Executive Officer of a firm—Viacom, Inc. Bill Gates is Chairman and (now) Chief Software Architect at Microsoft. Rupert Murdoch is Chairman and Chief Executive at News Corporation. These three, plus 47 of their CEO colleagues, were featured in the 2002 version of "The New Establishment" article that appears every September in *Vanity Fair*. Each year, this article chronicles, and actually ranks, the accomplishments of 50 leaders of the information age. The high-profile firms that they head are some of the most closely watched in American business. But what exactly is a firm? And why should we be so interested in firms and their managers?

A firm, most fundamentally, is an economic unit that produces a good or service for sale. Firms typically try to make a profit, in direct contrast to not-for-profit institutions like the Ford Foundation, Amnesty International, or Choate Rosemary Hall. There are literally millions of firms in the United States. Some are proprietorships (owned by a single person). Others are partnerships (owned by two or more people). Still more are corporations—i.e., fictitious "legal persons" created under the purview of long-standing federal legislation. Corporations are typically owned by thousands of stockholders. About 86 percent of the goods and services produced in the United States are produced by firms; the rest are provided by government and not-for-profit institutions. It is obvious that a developed economy like the United States revolves around the activities of its firms.

Economists generally assume, in a first approximation, that firms attempt to maximize profits. Be warned, though: an economist's definition of profits does not coincide with an accountant's. Economists do not assume that firms attempt to maximize only the current, short-run profits measured by the accountant. Economists assume, instead, that firms try to maximize profits over a long period of time and that these profits are properly discounted to bring their value into the present. In addition, economists measure profit after taking account of the capital and labor provided by the owners. More will be said on this score in the next chapter.

Assuming that firms maximize profit serves as a reasonable first approximation of their underlying motives, but it has some obvious limitations.

For one thing, making profits generally requires the expenditure of time and energy. If the owners of a firm are its managers, then they may decide that it is preferable to sacrifice some profit for some additional leisure time with their families or on the golf course. It may be more accurate in cases like this to assume that the owner-manager, like the consumer, will allocate his or her time by maximizing *utility*—a measure of welfare represented best in this case as a function of his or her profits and the amount of leisure that he or she enjoys. We can use the sort of analysis presented in Chapter 2 to determine how much money the owner-manager will give up for leisure.

It should also be noted that the concept of maximum profits might not be clearly defined in an uncertain world. Any particular course of action will not necessarily result in a unique and certain level of profit in such a world. An action might, instead, produce a variety of possible levels of profit, and each might have a well-defined probability of occurrence. It would make no sense to speak about maximizing profit in such a case, but it could be meaningful to assume that a firm attempts to maximize *expected* profits. Chapter 5 has already suggested the complications that would arise if the analysis were extended in this way.[1] For simplicity, therefore, we shall assume in the following pages that the firm has full knowledge of the relevant variables and that there is no uncertainty in its understanding of how its actions will influence its profits.

Observers of modern corporations also sometimes argue that profits are not the sole objective that drives their actions. Industry spokespersons often claim that firms are also interested in achieving better social conditions in their communities, increasing (or at least maintaining) their market shares, creating an image as a good employer and a useful part of the community, and so forth. Oil firms often stress their concern for the environment, for example. They sometimes even express their concern that consumers waste too much fuel. Can we trust these claims? That depends. But how distinct are goals like these from the goal of maximizing profit? To the extent that many of these goals are simply means to sustain profits over the long run, there may be less inaccuracy in the profit-maximization assumption than might appear at first glance.[2]

Finally, economists are interested in the theory of the profit-maximizing firm because it provides rules of behavior for firms that do want to maximize profits. The theory of the profit-maximizing firm suggests how a firm should operate if it wants to make as much money as possible. The theory can therefore be useful even if a firm does not want to maximize profit. It can show how much the firm is losing by taking certain courses of action, and it can help the firm assess the cost of pursuing other objectives.

---

[1] Expected profit is the sum of the various possible levels of profit multiplied by the probability of their occurrence. Chapter 5 instructs us that the firm may be interested in the riskiness as well as the expected value of profits if it tries to maximize expected utility.

[2] Alcoa, for example, is trumpeting the merits of a long-term business plan which, if achieved, would make the corporation's net use of natural resources virtually zero by 2010. They see it as prudent economic policy as well as socially responsible.

TECHNOLOGY AND INPUTS

Technology is one of the fundamental determinants of any firm's behavior. Technology sets limits on what a firm can accomplish. It can be defined as the state of the industrial and agricultural arts. This is an accurate definition, but it is not very useful in explaining how we can represent the state of technology in a model of the firm. Offering such an explanation is the purpose of the rest of this chapter.

Input

We begin with a few definitions. An **input** is defined as anything that a firm uses in its production process. Most firms require a wide variety of inputs. The list of inputs for a major steel firm would include iron ore, coal, oxygen, skilled labor, the services of blast furnaces, open hearths, electric furnaces, and rolling mills, as well as the services of the people managing the companies. Computer manufacturers need skilled labor, silicon chips, electronic devices, high-quality wiring, plastic and lightweight metal, the innovative services of designers and managers, and so on.

We will assume that all inputs can be divided into two categories: fixed inputs and variable inputs. An input is considered fixed if its quantity *cannot* be changed during the period of time under consideration. An input is considered variable if its quantity *can* be changed during the same period of time. Time is clearly critical in these definitions; the length of time chosen will vary from problem to problem and question to question. The number of workers hired for a construction job, for example, can often be increased or decreased on short notice. The amount of water used at a car wash can be varied within limits simply by turning the relevant knobs. Most inputs can be varied to some extent, no matter how brief the time interval. For some, though, the cost of a quick adjustment is so large that making any change is simply impractical and uneconomical. Plant and equipment come to mind immediately when lists of these types of inputs are compiled. These are the inputs that economists typically regard as fixed.

THE SHORT RUN AND THE LONG RUN

Whether an input is regarded as variable or fixed depends on the length of time being considered. The longer the period, the more inputs that can be classified as variable. Notwithstanding the diversity that this flexibility allows, economists have found it useful to focus special attention on two time periods: the

Short run

short run and the long run. The **short run** is defined to be the period of time in which at least some of a firm's inputs are fixed. And since plant and equipment are among the most difficult inputs to change quickly, the short run is generally understood to mean the length of time during which plant and equip-

Long run

ment cannot be practically or economically adjusted. The **long run,** on the other hand, refers to a period of time in which all inputs are variable. Firms can change just about anything in their environments in the long run.

Assuming that some inputs like plant and equipment are fixed in the short run does not mean that firms cannot vary the proportions of other inputs that

205

are used in production. This is the point of contemplating the long run. Input proportions can be varied considerably if manufacturers are given enough time. Modern automobile manufacturers can, for example, choose to create parts using conventional machine tools (more labor and less expensive equipment), or computerized machine tools (less labor and more expensive equipment). Similarly, McDonnell-Douglas can make parts for the international space station by hand labor or by creating fancy equipment that needs only to be turned on. Many opportunities for changing input proportions exist even in the short run. Most firms can, for example, adjust the proportion of labor to capital by adding another shift. Indeed, production processes in which input proportions are fixed will be only one special case in the explorations that follow.

THE PRODUCTION FUNCTION

The production function for any good or service is simply the relationship between the quantities of various inputs employed in a given period of time and the *maximum* quantity of the commodity that can thereby be produced over that same period of time. Production functions can be described in a table, they can be displayed on a graph, and they can be summarized by an equation. In every case, their representation shows the *maximum* output that can be produced from any specified combination of inputs. Furthermore, production functions summarize the characteristics of existing technology at a given point in time, and so they define the technological constraints with which a firm must cope.

We begin with the simplest case—one in which there is one fixed input and one variable input. Suppose that the fixed input is the service of 10 acres of land, that the variable input is labor (in units per year), and that the output is corn (in bushels harvested per year). We will think about an analytically inclined farmer who has decided to find out what would happen if he applied more or less labor to the land. We will, more specifically, assume that he has come to understand that Table 6.1 summarizes the relationship between output

Table 6.1 OUTPUT OF CORN WHEN VARIOUS AMOUNTS OF LABOR ARE APPLIED TO 10 ACRES OF LAND	Amount of labor (units per year)	Output of corn (bushels per year)
	0	0
	1	60
	2	135
	3	210
	4	280
	5	340
	6	380
	7	380
	8	370

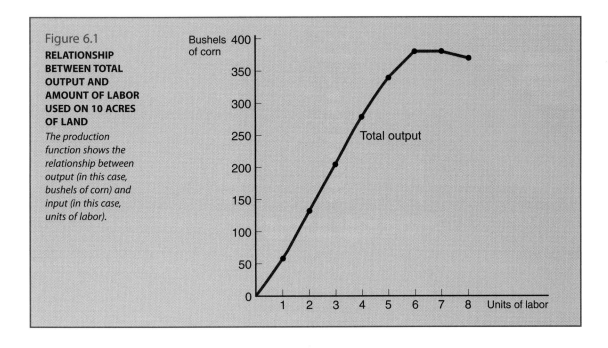

Figure 6.1

RELATIONSHIP BETWEEN TOTAL OUTPUT AND AMOUNT OF LABOR USED ON 10 ACRES OF LAND

The production function shows the relationship between output (in this case, bushels of corn) and input (in this case, units of labor).

and employment. Table 6.1 is, in other words, a tabular representation of his production function; Figure 6.1 displays the same information graphically.

Drawing useful information from the data embodied in any representation of a production function is the next step in analyzing any firm's technology. Two more concepts, the average and marginal products of any given input, will play important roles in this analysis. The **average product** of an input is total product (that is, total output) divided by the amount of the input used to produce this amount of output. The **marginal product** of an input is the addition to total output that can be attributed to the addition of the last unit of the input under the assumption that the levels of all of the other inputs were fixed.

Average product

Marginal product

We can return to the production function displayed in Table 6.1 to illustrate these concepts. We can compute the average product and the marginal product of labor directly from the data recorded there. Both the average product and the marginal product of labor vary with the level of employment. If $Q(L)$ represents total output when L units of labor are employed, then the average product of labor when L units of labor are employed is

$$AP_L = \frac{Q(L)}{L}.$$

The marginal product of labor between the situations when L and $(L-1)$ units of labor are employed is

$$MP_L = Q(L) - Q(L-1).$$

From Table 6.1, then, the average product of labor would be $60/1 = 60$ bushels of corn per unit of labor if 1 unit of labor were employed; the marginal product of this first unit of labor would be $60 - 0 = 60$ bushels of

Table 6.2	Amount of labor	Total output	Average product of labor	Marginal product of labor[a]
AVERAGE AND MARGINAL PRODUCTS OF LABOR	0	0	—	—
	1	60	60.0	60
	2	135	67.5	75
	3	210	70.0	75
	4	280	70.0	70
	5	340	68.0	60
	6	380	63.3	40
	7	380	54.3	0
	8	370	46.2	−10

[a]These figures pertain to the interval between the indicated amount of labor and 1 unit less than the indicated amount of labor.

corn. The average product of labor would be 135/2 = 67.5 bushels of corn per unit of labor if 2 units of labor were employed; the marginal product of the second unit of labor would be 135 − 60 = 75 bushels of corn. These results and those for other levels of employment are shown in Table 6.2.

Panel A of Figure 6.2 shows the average-product curve for labor. The numbers plotted here are taken from Table 6.2. It is typical for the average product of labor (the only variable input in this case) to rise, reach a maximum, and then fall. Panel B of Figure 6.2 shows the marginal-product curve for labor. These numbers also are taken from Table 6.2; the marginal values for each additional unit of labor are plotted at the midpoint between old

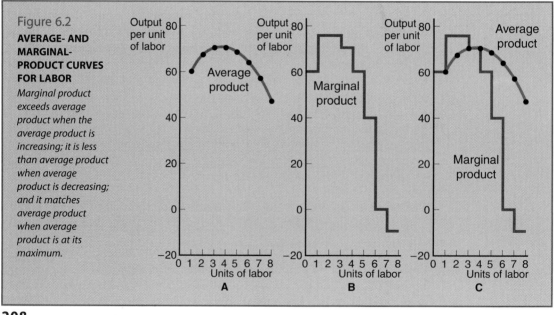

Figure 6.2

AVERAGE- AND MARGINAL-PRODUCT CURVES FOR LABOR

Marginal product exceeds average product when the average product is increasing; it is less than average product when average product is decreasing; and it matches average product when average product is at its maximum.

and new levels: the marginal product of the second unit of labor is 75; thus it is plotted at 1.5 units of labor. It is also typical for the marginal product of labor to rise, reach a (different) maximum, and then fall.

Panel C of Figure 6.2 shows both the average-product curve and the marginal product curve for labor on the same graph. As is *always* the case, the marginal product of labor (any input) exceeds its average product when average product is rising, it equals its average product when average product reaches a maximum, and it is less than its average product when average product is falling. Why is this always the case? It is simply a matter of arithmetic. An average will always increase if you add a bigger number to the total (your batting average will go up if you have a better-than-average day— 4 for 5 when you had been batting 0.250). It will always stay the same if you add an equal number (your batting average will not change if you have an average day—1 for 3 when you had been batting 0.333). And it will always fall if you add a smaller number (your batting average will fall if you have a bad day—0 for 5 when you had been batting only 0.150).

Tables 6.1 and 6.2 were constructed on the assumption that land, the fixed input, is held fixed at 10 acres. What would happen if the farmer doubled the size of his cornfield? What effect would this have on total output? On the average product of labor? On the marginal product of labor? Over the relevant range of production, an increase in the fixed input will generally cause all of them to rise. Figure 6.3 offers an illustrative portrait. And

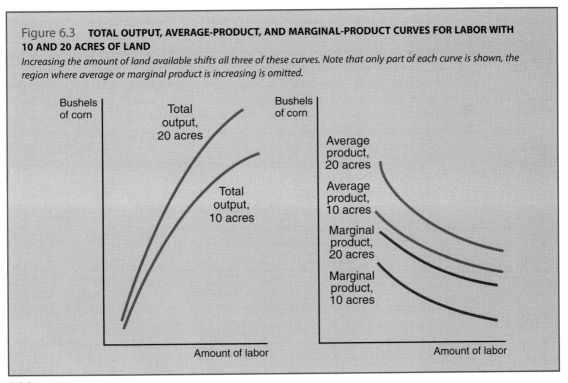

Figure 6.3   **TOTAL OUTPUT, AVERAGE-PRODUCT, AND MARGINAL-PRODUCT CURVES FOR LABOR WITH 10 AND 20 ACRES OF LAND**
Increasing the amount of land available shifts all three of these curves. Note that only part of each curve is shown, the region where average or marginal product is increasing is omitted.

what would happen if the farmer adopted modern "smart-farming" practices that increased the yield potential of each acre without adjusting the size of the field? Roughly the same thing—at least qualitatively. Technological change can be expected to increase the output associated with any combination of inputs. And so it, too, should shift the production function up.

THE LAW OF DIMINISHING MARGINAL RETURNS AND THE GEOMETRY OF AVERAGE- AND MARGINAL-PRODUCT CURVES

*Law of diminishing
marginal returns*

The preceding section defined the production function and the average and marginal products of an input. We are now in a position to discuss one of the most famous laws of microeconomics—the **law of diminishing marginal returns.** The law of diminishing marginal returns is often quoted and frequently misinterpreted. It states that *the marginal product of any input will (eventually) fall as the employment of that input climbs.* Recalling the definition of marginal product, therefore, the law of diminishing marginal returns holds that output will eventually climb by smaller and smaller amounts as the level of employment of one input increases one unit at a time. Pretty simple, to be sure; but beware. The law speaks of marginal products, so it speaks only to cases in which the employment of one input is being adjusted while the employment of *all other inputs is held fixed.* And it also speaks only to cases where the technology, as embodied in the underlying production function, is fixed. Table 6.2 offers an illustration of this law; the marginal product of labor begins to fall when employment climbs past 3 units of labor.

You should make certain that you are clear on several points before proceeding. First, the law of diminishing marginal returns is an empirical generalization; it is not a deduction drawn from physical or biological laws. Economists' belief in the law stems entirely from the fact that it seems to hold for most production functions in the real world. Second, it is worth repeating that the law assumes that technology remains fixed. The law of diminishing marginal returns cannot predict the effect of an additional unit of input when technology is allowed to change. Third, never forget that the law assumes that there is at least one input whose quantity is being held constant. The law of diminishing marginal returns does not apply to cases in which there is a proportional increase in all inputs.

The production function T in Figure 6.4 displays a typical relationship between total output and the amount of the variable input employed under three assumptions: (1) there is at least one fixed input, (2) there is exactly one variable input, and (3) output can vary continuously with continuous adjustments in the variable input (so that the production function T can be drawn as a smooth curve). Given such a graph, how can we determine the average product and the marginal product of the variable input? Consider, first, the average product of the variable input. Since average product equals total output divided by the amount of variable input, the average product of employing amount A of variable input equals C divided by A. But from

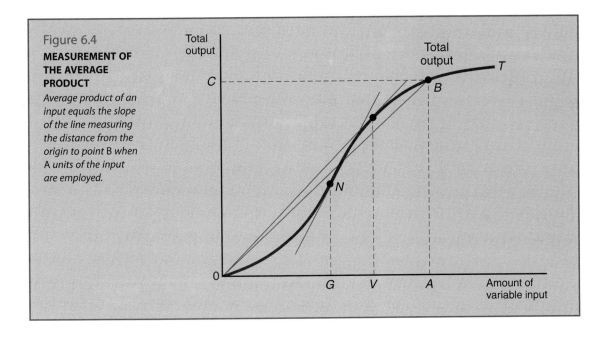

Figure 6.4

MEASUREMENT OF THE AVERAGE PRODUCT

Average product of an input equals the slope of the line measuring the distance from the origin to point B when A units of the input are employed.

a geometrical standpoint, we know that the distance from the origin to C equals the distance from A to B, and that by dividing the distance AB by the distance from the origin to A we get the slope of the line $0B$—a line that joins the origin with point B on the production function curve that corresponds to employing A units of the variable input. And so the slope of the line joining the origin and the relevant point on the total output curve is equal to the average product of the variable input.

Now turn to Figure 6.5 to consider the marginal product of the variable input. The production function drawn in Figure 6.5 is the same as the one drawn in Figure 6.4. How can we determine the marginal product of the variable input from the underlying geometry? We start by observing that total output would increase from H to I if the amount of variable input employed were to increase from E to F. The ratio $(I - H)/(F - E) = HI/EF$ would not be a bad guess at the marginal product of $F - E$ units of the variable input (for employment levels between E and F). But what would happen if we made the employment increment E to F smaller? The extra output divided by the extra variable input, that is, the ratio HI/EF, would approach the slope of the production function curve at point S. Using the slope of the production function as an approximation of marginal product would not be that far off even if the increment were EF. The slope of the total output curve would be $KL/SK = KL/EF$, and this ratio would be fairly close to HI/EF. Thus, since the slope of a curve at any point equals the slope of its tangent at that point, we can determine the marginal product of any amount of variable input by drawing the tangent to the total output curve at that amount of variable input and measuring its slope. The slope of SL is, therefore, the marginal product of variable input when E units of variable input are employed.

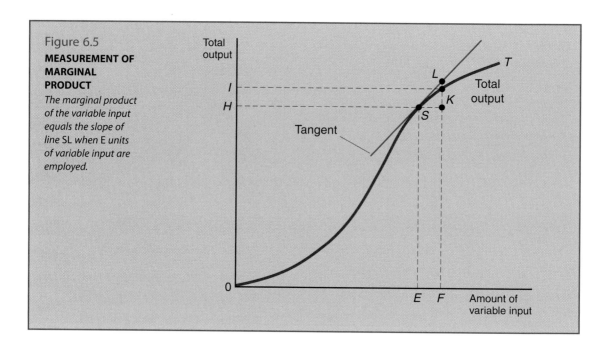

Figure 6.5

MEASUREMENT OF MARGINAL PRODUCT

The marginal product of the variable input equals the slope of line SL when E units of variable input are employed.

We now close this section by using the geometry of marginal and average products to prove a number of interesting results. Since the line joining the origin and a point on the total output curve in Figure 6.4 will have the same slope when the line is tangent to the production function curve, it follows that the average product must reach its maximum if *V* units of variable input are employed. Moreover, the tangent to the total output curve is exactly the same as the line joining the origin and the total output curve when *V* units of the variable input are used. As a result, the slope of the tangent must equal the slope of this line; and so marginal product must equal average product when *V* units are employed. More generally, therefore, marginal product must equal average product at the maximum of the average-product curve. Finally, where along production function curve *T* is marginal product the greatest? At some point like *N*, where the production function is steepest (and *G* units of variable input are employed). Note that employment level *G* is smaller than *V*; it follows that the maximum marginal product occurs at a lower level of employment than the maximum average product.

THE PRODUCTION FUNCTION: MORE THAN ONE VARIABLE INPUT

We have thus far concerned ourselves with the case in which there is only one variable input. We now take up the more general case in which there are two variable inputs. These variable inputs might be working with one or more fixed inputs in a short-run situation, or they might be the only two inputs of a production process working in a long-run situation. In either case, it is

Table 6.3		Units of labor employed					
HYPOTHETICAL PRODUCTION FUNCTION FOR WHEAT (IN BUSHELS) WITH TWO VARIABLE INPUTS[a]	**Acres of land**	**1**	**2**	**3**	**4**	**5**	**6**
	10	1,258	1,349	1,405	1,446	1,478	1,505
	20	1,349	1,446	1,505	1,549	1,584	1,614
	30	1,405	1,505	1,568	1,614	1,650	1,680
	40	1,446	1,549	1,614	1,661	1,698	1,729
	50	1,478	1,584	1,650	1,698	1,736	1,768
	60	1,505	1,614	1,680	1,729	1,768	1,801

[a]These data are derived from the production function described in Example 6.4 under the assumption that only A (area planted in acres) and L (labor employed) can vary. All of the rest of the variables are assumed to be fixed, so that production is summarized by $Q = 1,000(AL)^{0.1}$.

easy to extend the results for two variable inputs to as many inputs as one likes. We begin in this section by focusing on the production function.

The production function becomes slightly more complicated when we increase the number of variable inputs from one to two, but it still summarizes the relationship between various combinations of inputs and the maximum amount of output that can be obtained from their employment. The only change, really, is that output must be represented as a function of two variables rather than one. Suppose, for example, that we allowed both land and labor to vary in a different agricultural example. The results might be given in tabular form by the data recorded in Table 6.3. Note that we can compute the marginal product of each input by holding the other input constant. For example, the marginal product of labor would be $(1,661 - 1,614)/(4 - 3) = 47$ bushels if 40 acres of land were farmed and labor employment were increased from 3 units to 4 units. Similarly, the average product of either land or labor can be computed simply by dividing the total output recorded in the table by the amount of either land or labor that is employed.

Example 6.1	**Energy Intensity across the World—Sample Production Functions**

What form do production functions take? Cobb-Douglas representations of aggregate production have been employed by many researchers involved to explore the equity, sustainability, and efficiency implications of globalization. William Nordhaus and Joseph Boyer have, for example, calibrated functions of the form

$$GDP = AK^{\alpha}L^{1-\alpha-\beta}(ES)^{\beta}$$

when they investigated the critical role played by energy consumption across eight different regions of the world. In writing their function, GDP represents the total value of goods and services produced in a region, K represents the relevant capital stock, L reflects labor participation, and ES denotes

Table 6.4	Region	Capital exponent (α)	Energy services exponent (β)
CALIBRATING COBB-DOUGLAS PRODUCTION FUNCTIONS ACROSS THE WORLD	United States	0.3	0.091
	Europe	0.3	0.057
	Other high income	0.3	0.059
	China	0.3	0.096
	Eastern Europe	0.3	0.08
	Middle income	0.3	0.087
	Lower middle income	0.3	0.087
	Lower income	0.3	0.074

SOURCE: W. Nordhaus and J. Boyer, *Warming the World—Economic Models of Global Warming* (Cambridge, Mass.: MIT Press, 2000).

energy services; and the exponents reflect the relative importance of each input in the production of goods and services. Notice, to begin with, that the exponents sum to 1. Why? Because the analytical techniques that they employed to run their models 100 years into the future required constant returns to scale, because they presumed competitive global markets in capital and energy over that time span, and because historically based estimates of aggregate production have displayed constant returns.

Table 6.4 records their regional calibrations for energy services across the eight regions. Even though α was set consistently at 0.3 for all regions, striking differences in reliance on energy services across the regions are perfectly clear. The energy exponent for the United States ranks second only to China, where coal supplies are abundant. This should not be a surprise; the United States economy is highly dependent upon energy. Other high-income countries like Japan, Australia, and Canada are different. They join the European countries with the smallest energy exponents. We can use these estimates to conclude that the United States and China are 50 percent more energy-intensive in their overall economic activity than Japan, Australia, Canada, and Western Europe.

ISOQUANTS

Isoquant An **isoquant** reflects various combinations of inputs that can produce the same level of output. When production depends on two variable inputs, for example, isoquants are curves that show all of the possible (efficient) combinations of inputs that are capable of producing a certain quantity of output. Several isoquants, each pertaining to a different output rate, are shown in Figure 6.6. Each has been drawn from the data recorded in Table 6.3. The two axes measure the quantities of two inputs that might be employed. The lowest line, for example, shows combinations of land and labor that could be employed to produce 1,446 bushels of wheat. Three of the combinations

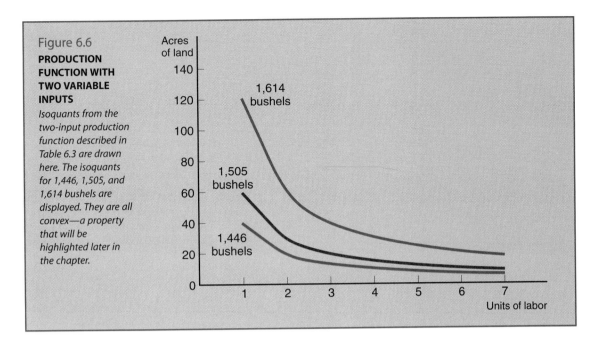

Figure 6.6

PRODUCTION FUNCTION WITH TWO VARIABLE INPUTS

Isoquants from the two-input production function described in Table 6.3 are drawn here. The isoquants for 1,446, 1,505, and 1,614 bushels are displayed. They are all convex—a property that will be highlighted later in the chapter.

(1 unit of labor working 40 acres of land; 2 units of labor working 20 acres of land; 4 units of labor working 10 acres of land) are recorded explicitly in Table 6.3. Other combinations, like using 3.5 units of labor to work 11.3 acres, might also work, even though they are not recorded in the table.

Figure 6.7 displays a second set of isoquants. We assume in drawing Figure 6.7 that labor and capital—not labor and land—are the relevant inputs

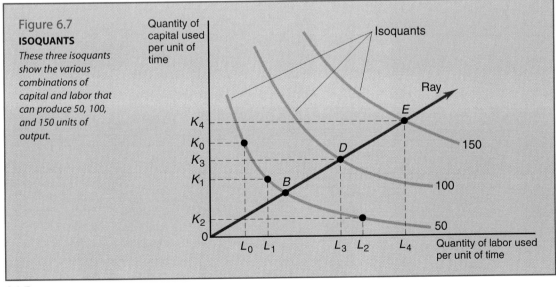

Figure 6.7

ISOQUANTS

These three isoquants show the various combinations of capital and labor that can produce 50, 100, and 150 units of output.

in this case. The curves show the various combinations of inputs that can produce 50, 100, and 150 units of output. According to the lowest one, it would be possible to produce 50 units if L_0 units of labor and K_0 units of capital are employed. But 50 units could also be produced by employing L_1 units of labor and K_1 units of capital, or L_2 units of labor and K_2 units of capital, or any other combination highlighted by the curve.

A ray is a line that starts from some point and goes off into space. A ray from the origin, such as $0BDE$ in Figure 6.7, describes all input combinations where the capital-labor ratio is constant. How do we know? Because the slope of the ray is constant and equal to the ratio of capital to labor at every point. At points D and E, for example, 100 and 150 units of output are produced with a capital-labor ratio of $K_3/L_3 = K_4/L_4$. We can therefore see that various outputs can be produced by various combinations of inputs that preserve the ratio of one input to another. So, isoquants highlight combinations of inputs that can all produce the same level of output; rays highlight combinations of inputs of fixed proportion that can produce different levels of output.

Isoquants play much the same kind of role in production theory that indifference curves play in demand theory. Indifference curves show the various combinations of two commodities that provide a constant level of satisfaction to the consumer; isoquants show the various combinations of two inputs that can be used to produce a constant output for the firm. It should be obvious that isoquants, like indifference curves, can never intersect.

Microlink 6.1   Utility Functions and Production Functions

There is a direct analogy between the construction of the theory of demand from utility functions and the theory of cost from production functions. The graphs of isoquants and isocost lines drawn in this chapter should look very familiar; they mimic the graphs of indifference curves and budget lines from Chapters 2 and 3. There is, however, one fundamental difference. Consumer theory depended on ordinal representations of preferences by utility functions. Actual units and numbers did not matter as long as higher numbers were assigned to preferred bundles of goods. Production theory is, by way of contrast, decidedly cardinal. Numbers matter because output is measured in specific units. Marginal and average products have exact interpretations that depend on size. And returns to scale are measured by looking to see exactly how much bigger or smaller one output is than another.

Example 6.2   **Representative Cobb-Douglas Production Functions for Selected Industries**

Many worthwhile estimates of production functions for specific industries have been based on a more general formulation of the Cobb-Douglas structure in which

$$Q = AL^{\alpha_1} K^{\alpha_2} M^{\alpha_3},$$

where Q is the output rate, L is the quantity of labor, K is the quantity of capital, M is the quantity of raw materials, and A, α_1, α_2, and α_3 are

Table 6.5	Industry	Country	α_1	α_2	α_3	$\alpha_1 + \alpha_2 + \alpha_3$
ESTIMATES OF α_1, α_2, AND α_3 FOR SELECTED INDUSTRIES	Gas	France	.83	.10	—	0.93
	Railroads	United States	.89	.12	.28	1.29
	Coal	United Kingdom	.79	.29	—	1.08
	Food	United States	.72	.35	—	1.07
	Metals and machinery	United States	.71	.26	—	0.97
	Cotton	India	.92	.12	—	1.04
	Jute	India	.84	.14	—	0.98
	Sugar	India	.59	.33	—	0.92
	Coal	India	.71	.44	—	1.15
	Paper	India	.64	.45	—	1.09
	Chemicals	India	.80	.37	—	1.17
	Electricity	India	.20	.67	—	0.87
	Paper[a]	United States	.62	.37	—	0.99
	Telephone	Canada	.70	.41	—	1.11
	Chemicals[b]	United States	.54	.38	.11	1.03
	Aircraft[b]	United States	.79	.18	.04	1.01

[a]The figure for α_1 is the sum of the figures given for production workers and nonproduction workers.
[b]In these cases, M is cumulated past expenditure on research and development, not the quantity of raw materials, and K is the quantity of capital services.
SOURCES: A. A. Walters, "Production and Cost Functions," *Econometrica,* January 1963; J. Moroney, "Cobb-Douglas Production Functions and Returns to Scale in U.S. Manufacturing," *Western Economic Journal,* March 1967; A. Dobell, L. Taylor, L. Waverman, T. Liu, and M. Copeland, "Communications in Canada," *Bell Journal of Economics and Management Science,* Spring 1972; and Z. Griliches, "Returns to Research and Development Expenditures in the Private Sector," in J. Kendrick and B. Vaccara, *New Developments in Productivity Measurement and Analysis* (Chicago: National Bureau of Economic Research, 1980).

parameters that vary from case to case. It is ordinarily assumed that the value of each of the α_j parameters is less than 1. This ensures that the marginal product of each input decreases as its employment climbs.

Table 6.5 shows estimates for α_1, α_2, and α_3 for a number of industries in the United States and abroad. The data are relatively old, and more recent studies have assumed functional forms that are more complicated than Cobb-Douglas; indeed, Example 6.3 will show you some. In the meantime, though, these studies still provide interesting information about production relationships. How so, if they are more than 25 years old? Some industries have not experienced enough change over the intervening decades to alter the estimates significantly. In other cases, the technology employed in developed economies in the 1970s might be anticipated in developing countries today. Exploring the ramifications of these technologies based on a quantitative understanding of the past might help emerging economies avoid the mistakes of earlier development strategies. An example in Chapter 7 will, in fact, suggest that more modern

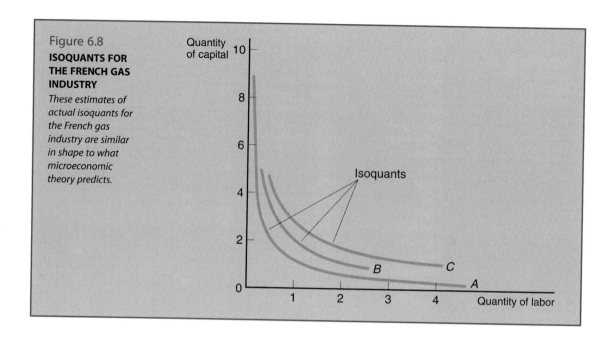

Figure 6.8

ISOQUANTS FOR THE FRENCH GAS INDUSTRY

These estimates of actual isoquants for the French gas industry are similar in shape to what microeconomic theory predicts.

technologies that are appropriate for developed economies can be entirely inappropriate in other regions of the world, where economic conditions can be dramatically different.

To see the implications of the estimates recorded in Table 6.5 more clearly, note that α_1 is the percentage increase in output resulting from a 1 percent increase in labor, holding the quantities of the other inputs constant. It is estimated, therefore, that a 1 percent increase in labor in the Indian paper industry would have resulted in a 0.64 percent increase in output; in the United States, the same 1 percent increase in labor would produce an estimated 0.62 percent increase. Similarly, α_2 is the percentage increase in output resulting from a 1 percent increase in capital, holding the quantities of other inputs constant; and so on, with α_3 corresponding to raw materials.

Figure 6.8, meanwhile, displays some isoquants for the French gas industry. They have a shape similar to the hypothetical curves drawn in Figures 6.6 and 6.7.

Microlink 6.2 Isoquants and Indifference Curves

Isoquants depict combinations of inputs that produce the same level of output. Recall that indifference curves, described in Chapter 2, depict combinations of goods that sustain the same level of utility. Isoquants and indifference curves are therefore analogous constructions that display many of the same properties in decidedly different contexts. The slope of an indifference curve is, for example, the marginal rate of substitution (*MRS,* in the notation of Chapter 2); it is the rate at which a consumer would willingly trade one good for another while maintaining a constant level of satisfaction. The slope of an isoquant is, analogously, the marginal rate of technical substitution (the *MRTS*); it is the rate at which a firm could substitute one input for another while maintaining a constant level of output. We will soon show that

$$MRTS_{LK} = \frac{MP_L}{MP_K}.$$

This result is entirely consistent with the content of Equation 2.4, in which

$$MRS_{FM} = \frac{MU_F}{MU_M}$$

when utility was determined by the consumption of food (F) and medicine (M).

SUBSTITUTION AMONG INPUTS

It is important, from both a practical and a theoretical point of view, to study the rate at which one input must be substituted for another to maintain a constant output rate. Isoquants will clearly play a central role here. Consider the isoquant Z in Figure 6.9, for example. It shows that a given level of output can be sustained with L_0 units of labor and K_0 units of capital. If the amount of labor employed were to increase to L_1, though, then the same output rate could be sustained with less capital: K_1 units rather than K_0. Starting at point A on isoquant Z, therefore, $L_1 - L_0$ units of labor could be substituted

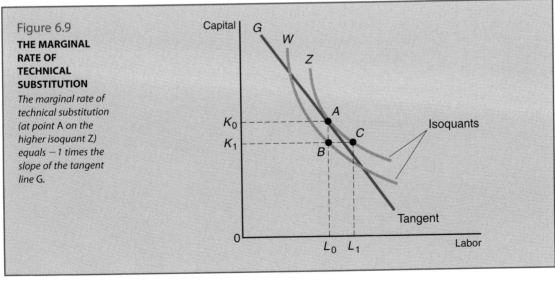

Figure 6.9

THE MARGINAL RATE OF TECHNICAL SUBSTITUTION

The marginal rate of technical substitution (at point A on the higher isoquant Z) equals −1 times the slope of the tangent line G.

for $K_0 - K_1$ units of capital. The rate at which labor can substitute for capital at this point on this isoquant is therefore $-(K_0 - K_1)/(L_0 - L_1) = BA/BC$. The minus sign is added to make the result a positive number. If we consider a very small increase in labor (L_1 being very close to L_0), BA/BC equals -1 times the slope of the line that is tangent to the isoquant at point A; this is line G in Figure 6.9. This number (including the minus sign) is called the **marginal rate of technical substitution.** It measures, for small changes in labor, the change in capital required per unit change in labor to sustain output at a constant level. Note that, as its name indicates, the marginal rate of technical substitution is analogous to the marginal rate of substitution in demand theory.

Marginal rate of technical substitution

It is easy to use Figure 6.9 to demonstrate that the marginal rate of technical substitution of labor for capital is equal to the ratio of the marginal product of labor to the marginal product of capital. Suppose that labor input were held at L_0 while capital increased from K_1 to K_0. Output would increase from the original level (say, Q_1) corresponding to isoquant W to a new level (say, Q_0) corresponding to isoquant Z. The marginal product of capital for this change in employment (i.e., with L_0 units of labor employed throughout and capital starting at K_1 units) would then be $(Q_0 - Q_1)/(K_0 - K_1) = (Q_0 - Q_1)/BA$. Now suppose that capital were held constant at K_1 while labor is increased from L_0 to L_1. The marginal product of labor in this instance would be $(Q_0 - Q_1)/(L_1 - L_0) = (Q_0 - Q_1)/BC$. So, the ratio of the marginal product of labor to the marginal product of capital equals

$$\frac{(Q_0 - Q_1)/BC}{(Q_0 - Q_1)/BA} = \frac{BA}{BC};$$

this is the same ratio identified above as representing the marginal rate of technical substitution.

It is also easy to show that the marginal rate of technical substitution of labor for capital tends to decrease as an increasing amount of labor is substituted for capital. To see this, we begin by showing that the marginal product of labor tends to fall as labor is substituted for capital. This is true for two reasons. First of all, increases in labor, holding capital *constant,* result in a reduction in the marginal product of labor. Second, the marginal product of labor declines even more as the amount of capital employed declines, because less capital generally produces a downward shift in the marginal-product curve for labor (recall Figure 6.3, in which changes in the amount of land cultivated produced entirely new marginal product schedules). Put these effects together, and the claim is demonstrated. The same reasoning can also be used to demonstrate that the marginal product of capital rises as more labor is substituted for capital. How? Just run the previous arguments in reverse. And since the marginal rate of technical substitution equals the ratio of the marginal product of labor (which is falling) with the marginal product of capital (which is rising), the marginal rate of technical substitution must fall as labor is substituted for capital.

It follows from this observation that isoquants, like indifference curves must be convex (see page 42). The marginal rate of technical substitution equals -1 times the slope of the isoquant. The marginal rate of technical substitution falls as we move to the right along an isoquant, and so the absolute value of the slope of the isoquant must be getting smaller. But if the absolute value of the slope is getting smaller as we move to the right, then the isoquant must be convex.

| Example 6.3 | **Alternative Production Functions That Reflect Different Abilities to Substitute between Inputs** |

Cobb-Douglas production functions have been widely applied in theoretical and empirical work, but they are simply a special case of a more general functional form that is far more versatile in accommodating variety in the ability to substitute one input for another. If we consider a simple case in which the production of some good X depends on capital (K) and labor (L), this more general "constant elasticity of substitution" (CES) form is

$$X = A[aK^{\rho} + (1 - a)L^{\rho}]^{1/\rho},$$

where the a parameters lie between 0 and 1 and the ρ parameter can assume any value from 1 down to negative infinity. This clearly a more complicated function, but it has several advantages.

First of all, as promised, we can report that the Cobb-Douglas representation

$$X = AK^a L^{1-a}$$

can be viewed as the limit of the more general CES form when $\rho \to 0$; but that is a technicality. More to the point, but also a technicality, the "elasticity of substitution" reflects the sensitivity of the marginal rate of substitution to changes in the capital-labor ratio. To a mathematician, it is the curvature of an isoquant for any combination of capital and labor; and it turns out to equal $1/(1 - \rho)$ for the CES functional form. For our purposes, though, it simply allows more versatility in our representations of production. Notice, for example, that

$$X = aK + (1 - a)L$$

when $\rho = 1$; this is the case in which capital and labor are perfect substitutes and the elasticity of substitution is equal to infinity. In the other extreme, capital and labor must always be employed in the same proportion if ρ approaches negative infinity and the elasticity of substitution is 0. And for the Cobb-Douglas case? The elasticity is equal to 1.

Figure 6.10 displays representative isoquants for two extreme cases just mentioned plus three intermediate cases with values of ρ equaling $-1.5, 0$ (the Cobb-Douglas case), and 0.5. As drawn, all five isoquants correspond to parameterizations where $a = 0.5$ and $A = 10$; as a result, the isoquants correspond to 10 units of output, and all five isoquants pass through the point where $K = L = 1$ unit. Notice that $\rho < 0$ implies less curvature in the isoquant than the Cobb-Douglas case and necessitates the employment of both capital and labor to sustain production. In the extreme case where the elasticity of substitution is zero, capital and labor are perfect complements. This means that one

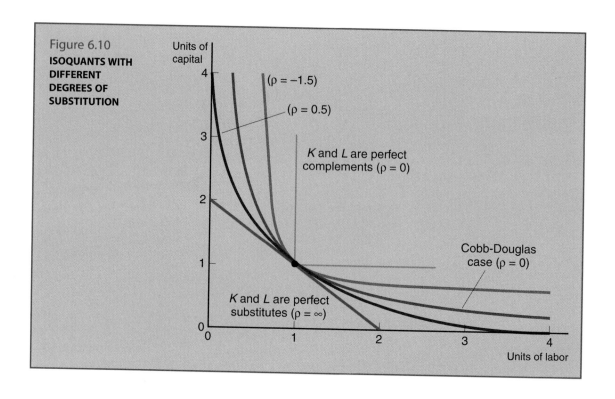

Figure 6.10

ISOQUANTS WITH DIFFERENT DEGREES OF SUBSTITUTION

Units of capital

4

($\rho = -1.5$)

($\rho = 0.5$)

3

K and L are perfect complements ($\rho = 0$)

2

1

Cobb-Douglas case ($\rho = 0$)

K and L are perfect substitutes ($\rho = \infty$)

0

0   1   2   3   4

Units of labor

unit of labor must always be employed to operate one unit of capital for our specific parameterization. The Cobb-Douglas case is, however, the limiting case for which that is true. In other cases where $\rho > 0$, diminished curvature means increased ability to substitute to the point where the isoquants actually intersect both axes. In the extreme where the elasticity of substitution is infinite, capital and labor are perfect substitutes. This means that one unit of capital can always substitute for one unit of labor for our illustration.

Empirical estimates of CES functions have provided valuable insight in our understanding of production and the potential for firms to adapt to changing input prices by substituting one input for another. Works authored by Alan Manne and Richard Richels, and by Dale Jorgenson and Peter Wilcoxen, are cases in point. They both considered production functions that related aggregate output (GDP) to the employment of energy resources (R) and other inputs (I) of the form

$$\text{GDP} = A[aR^\rho + (1 - a)I^\rho]^{1/\rho}.$$

Manne and Richels have published short-run estimates of $\rho \approx -1.5$ for developed, high-income countries and $\rho \approx -2.33$ for developing countries. These estimates translate into elasticities of substitution equal to 0.4 and 0.3, respectively; and they indicate that high-income countries could respond more robustly to changes in the relative price of energy resources caused, say, by global climate policy or efforts to improve environmental sustainability. Jorgenson and Wilcoxen, meanwhile, produced similar estimates for the short run in the United States; but their estimates for the long run suggested that $\rho \approx -0.33$ for an elasticity of 0.75. This is more evidence, in a different context, of a common theme: longer time periods expand the set of options for adapting to changes in relative prices, and so they thereby allow economic actors to be more responsive.

SOURCES: A. Manne and R. Richels, *Buying Greenhouse Insurance: The Economic Cost of CO$_2$ Emission Limits,* (Cambridge, Mass.: MIT Press, 1992); and D. Jorgenson and P. Wilcoxen, "Reducing U.S. Carbon Dioxide Emissions: The Cost of Different Goals," in J. R. Moroney, ed., *Energy, Growth and the Environment* (Greenwich, Conn.: JAI Press, 1991), pp. 125–128.

THE LONG RUN AND RETURNS TO SCALE

The preceding sections of this chapter have shown how a firm's technology can be represented by a production function. They have also described properties of production functions and their related concepts (like marginal and average product) that seem to hold in general for production processes. We have, however, failed so far to describe how output responds in the long run to changes in the scale of the firm. We have not, in other words, considered a long-run situation in which *all* inputs are variable. We now correct this omission and suppose that the firm might want to increase its employment of all inputs by the same proportion. What would happen to output? This is an important question. It will turn out that its answer helps economists determine whether firms of certain sizes can survive in an industry. More about that in later chapters.

Staying on point, what would happen to output if the employment of all inputs were increased in the same proportion? There are three possibilities. Output could increase faster than employment—i.e., it could climb by a larger proportion. Doubling the employment of all inputs would, in this case, cause output to more than double. This is the case of **increasing returns to scale.** Output could just as easily increase more slowly than employment—i.e., it could climb by a smaller proportion. Doubling the employment of all inputs would, in this alternative case, cause output to fall short of doubling. This is the case of **decreasing returns to scale.** Finally, output could increase at the same rate as employment—i.e., it could climb by exactly the same proportion. Doubling the employment of all inputs in this case would lead to an exact doubling of output. This final case describes **constant returns to scale.**

It may appear at first glance that all production functions that describe the real world must exhibit constant returns to scale. After all, two identical factories built with the same equipment and employing the same types of workers should produce twice as much output as one. It is not as simple as that, though. A firm that doubles its scale may be able to use techniques that were not feasible at a smaller scale. Doubling a firm's size by simply building an additional and identical factory would then be inefficient. Why? Because one large factory may be more efficient than two smaller factories of the same total capacity; it may simply be large enough to use certain techniques that fall beyond the capabilities of the smaller factories.

Increasing returns to scale

Decreasing returns to scale

Constant returns to scale

Increasing returns to scale can also be the result of certain geometrical relations. The volume of a box that is 4 m by 4 m by 4 m is 64 times as great as the volume of a box that is 1 m by 1 m by 1 m. But the area of the six sides of the 4-m by 4-m by 4-m box is 96 square meters (6 times the 16-m² area of each 4-m by 4-m side), whereas the area of the six sides of the 1-m by 1-m by 1-m box is 6 m². The larger box requires only 16 times as much material to make as the smaller, but it holds 64 times as much.

Increased specialization also can result in increasing returns to scale. Increasing the employment of labor and machines allows managers to subdivide tasks so that various inputs can be specialized and efficiency improved. Increasing returns can also arise because of probabilistic considerations. The aggregate behavior of a larger number of customers tends to be more stable, and so a firm's inventory may not have to increase in proportion to its sales.

Decreasing returns to scale can also occur. Coordination is the most frequently cited reason. It can be difficult even in a small firm to obtain the information required to make important decisions; these sorts of difficulties can be magnified in a larger firm. The advantages of large organizations capture the public fancy from time to time. They were even displayed throughout the 1990s by a series of record-setting corporate mergers. But there are often great disadvantages to being large. For example, in certain kinds of research and development, there is evidence that large engineering teams tend to be less effective than smaller ones and that large firms tend to be less effective than small ones.

Figure 6.11 can be used to analyze and to describe the returns-to-scale potential of a particular firm. Panel A displays the case of constant returns to scale. The isoquants for outputs of 50, 100, and 150 units intersect any ray from the origin, like 0A, at equal distances. So, $0D = DC = CB$. In other

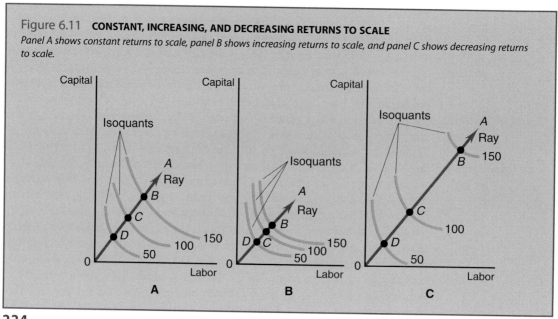

Figure 6.11 CONSTANT, INCREASING, AND DECREASING RETURNS TO SCALE

Panel A shows constant returns to scale, panel B shows increasing returns to scale, and panel C shows decreasing returns to scale.

words, this firm needs to employ twice as much of both inputs if it wants to produce 100 units of output instead of 50, and three times as much of both inputs if it wants to produce 150 units. Panel B illustrates increasing returns to scale. Successive isoquants come closer and closer together as you move out a ray from the origin, so that, for example, $0D > DC > CB$. This firm would need to employ less than twice as much of both inputs if it wanted to produce 100 units of output instead of 50; indeed, doubling employment would increase production by nearly 200 percent, to something close to 150 units. Finally, panel C portrays the case of decreasing returns to scale. Successive isoquants move farther and farther apart as you move out a ray from the origin, so that $0D < DC < CB$. Employment would have to more than double if this firm wanted to increase output from 50 units to 100.

Deciding whether or not a firm displays constant, increasing, or decreasing returns to scale in a particular situation is an empirical question that must be settled case by case. There is no simple, all-encompassing answer. Indeed, all three cases can be consistent with the law of diminishing returns, and all three can sustain convex isoquants. The available evidence in some industries sometimes indicates increasing returns to scale over a certain range of output. In other industries, though, decreasing or constant returns to scale seem to dominate. We turn our attention briefly to a discussion of empirical studies in the last section of this chapter.

Example 6.4

Should Two Kansas Wheat Farms Merge?

Agricultural economists have estimated the production function for many types of farms, here and abroad. Suppose that a study came up with the following result for a particular type of Kansas wheat farm:

$$Q = KA^{0.1}L^{0.1}E^{0.1}S^{0.7}R^{0.1},$$

where Q is output per period, A is the amount of land used, L is the amount of labor used, E is the amount of equipment used, S is the amount of fertilizer and chemicals used, R is the amount of other resources used, and K is a constant.

The owner of a Kansas wheat farm of this type is concerned that his farm may be too small to compete effectively with larger wheat farms. His farm is of below-average size, and he is troubled by the possibility that larger farms may be more efficient than his. He is considering the merger of his farm with a neighboring farm that is essentially the same (in size and other characteristics) as his own, and he hires you to advise him on this score. What's the answer?

According to the estimate of the production function given above, there are increasing returns to scale in wheat farming of this type. To see that this is true, if the amount of every input is doubled, the production function states that output will equal Q', where

$$\begin{aligned} Q' &= K(2A)^{0.1}(2L)^{0.1}(2E)^{0.1}(2S)^{0.7}(2R)^{0.1} \\ &= 2^{(0.1+0.1+0.1+0.7+0.1)}(K)(A^{0.1}L^{0.1}E^{0.1}S^{0.7}R^{0.1}) \\ &= 2^{1.1}Q \\ &= 2.14Q. \end{aligned}$$

Consequently, a 100 percent increase in all inputs leads to a 114 percent increase in output.

If this production function were a reliable representation of the technology of Kansas wheat farms of this type, then it would appear that the proposed merger would increase productivity (since doubling all inputs would more than double output). Before making a final decision, though, the farmer should make sure that the production function is based on accurate data that really do pertain to farms like his own. If the data pertained entirely to farms that are much smaller than his, for example, then these results could be quite misleading. In addition, there are other factors to consider besides the effects on productivity. For example, would the merger expose the farmer to additional financial risk? All that can be said on the basis of the evidence presented here is that the proposed merger might well increase productivity.

▣ Technological Change

Economists have long recognized that technologies are not static. Firms learn from doing, and so the same combinations of inputs can produce more and more output (up to a point, of course). They become more productive by reorganizing production processes, changing their organizational structures, reducing lost time and material, improving maintenance procedures, and so on. Notwithstanding a diverse set of possible sources, it is easy to represent mathematically the net effect of technological change. Suppose, for the sake of argument, that a production function for some good X that depended upon capital K and labor L at some point in time t were represented by

$$X_t = A \times F(K_t, L_t).$$

The subscripts on X, K, and L simply identify the time period, and the parameter A simply calibrates the value derived from $F(K, L)$ into units of output. Now suppose that technological change could be expected to augment the output that could be expected from any combination of capital and labor by $g \times 100\%$ per year. It would then be convenient to express this potential by

$$X_t = [A(1 + g)^t]F(K_t, L_t).$$

It follows that technological change renumbers isoquants that would otherwise be stationary. And even though the marginal rate of substitution for any specific combination of inputs would therefore be unaffected, the marginal and average productivities of all inputs would increase by $g \times 100\%$ per year.

Figure 6.12 illustrates this point. It shows the same isoquants drawn in Figure 6.6 in terms of land and labor, but they are associated with higher levels of output to reflect 2 percent technological change over 5 years for a total of about 10.41 percent growth in output. How is that? Annual technological change of 2 percent would mean that $g = 0.02$ and

$$(1 + 0.02)^5 = (1.02)^5 \approx 1.1041 = (1 + 0.1041).$$

Expressing 0.1041 as a percentage produces the promised 10.41 percent.

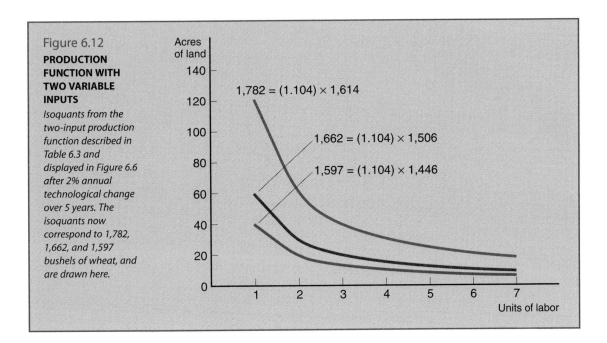

Figure 6.12

PRODUCTION FUNCTION WITH TWO VARIABLE INPUTS

Isoquants from the two-input production function described in Table 6.3 and displayed in Figure 6.6 after 2% annual technological change over 5 years. The isoquants now correspond to 1,782, 1,662, and 1,597 bushels of wheat, and are drawn here.

Acres of land

$1,782 = (1.104) \times 1,614$

$1,662 = (1.104) \times 1,506$

$1,597 = (1.104) \times 1,446$

Units of labor

Example 6.5

Technological Change That Augments the Productivity of Selected Inputs

The brief discussion of technological change focused on neutral technological change that augmented the output of combinations of inputs. It is, of course, possible that advances in technology or organization work to make one or a few inputs more productive. Suppose, for the sake of argument, that these advances only increased the productivity of labor at some annual rate g_L. In that case, the appropriate representation of the production function over time would be

$$X_t = AF(K_t, [(1 + g_L)^t L_t])$$

so that the employment of "effective" labor would grow even if the number of people employed did not. You might expect that this asymmetry would distort the marginal rate of substitution between capital and labor because it would affect only the marginal and average products of labor directly, and you would be right for some complicated production functions. For the simpler Cobb-Douglas forms described in Examples 6.1 and 6.2, however, the only effect would be to dilute the effect of technological change on output. To see why, write the production function as

$$X_t = AF(K_t, [(1 + g_L)^t L_t]) = A\{K_t^{\alpha_k}[(1 + g_L)^t L_t]^{\alpha_L}\}$$

and note that simple algebra collapses this form into

$$X_t = [A(1 + g_L)^{\alpha_L t}](K_t^{\alpha_k} L_t^{\alpha_L}) = [A(1 + g_L)^{\alpha_L t}]F(K_t, L_t).$$

As a result, labor augmenting technological change at 2 percent per year would look like neutral technological change at $g \times 100\%$ per year where g solves

$$1 + g = (1 + 0.02)^{\alpha_L}$$

If $\alpha_L = 0.5$, therefore, $g \approx 0.01$. If $\alpha_L = 0.25$, $g \approx 0.005$. And if $\alpha_L = 0.75$, $g \approx 0.015$.

THE MEASUREMENT OF PRODUCTION FUNCTIONS

Statistical analysis of time series

Economists and statisticians have devoted a great deal of time and effort to the measurement of production functions. Three distinct methods have proven to be most useful. The first is based on the statistical analysis of historical time-series data that track the employment and output levels of inputs and products over time. You might, for example, be able to collect data that record the amount of labor, the amount of capital, and the amount of various raw materials used in the aluminum industry during each year from 1961 to 2001. If you could find similar data and information on the annual output of aluminum from 1961 through 2001, you might then be able to estimate a relationship between these employment levels and the resulting series of production output.

Statistical analysis of cross-sectional data

Other statistical analyses rely on cross-sectional data that collect employment and output records for various firms or sectors of an industry at a given point in time. To adopt this approach, you would need data on the amount of labor, the amount of capital, and the amount of raw materials used in various firms in the aluminum industry in the year 2001. You might then be able to estimate a comparable relationship between employment and output on the basis of data drawn from a single year.

Technical information

The third method relies on technical information supplied by engineers, scientists, and sometimes managers. Information can be collected by experiment or from experience with the day-to-day workings of a technical process. This is generally viewed by students to be the most logical approach to the estimation problem. It is direct. The range of applicability of the data is easily understood. And, more technically, the estimation procedure is not limited to a potentially narrow range of observed data; experiments can be designed to accommodate a wide range of circumstances, whereas time-series and cross-sectional data are produced only from events that have actually happened. But it turns out that each approach is plagued by its own set of weaknesses.

All three approaches are, for example, handicapped by the fact that the data may not always represent technically efficient combinations of inputs and output. Errors in judgment or constraints imposed on the aluminum industry in 2001, for example, may have caused the industry to employ more inputs than were absolutely necessary. But the production function should, at least theoretically, include only efficient input combinations. Inefficiencies that may have characterized 2001 should, in other words, be excluded if the measurement of the production function is to be believed.

And then there is the issue of how to measure the capital input. The principal difficulty here stems from the fact that the stock of capital is composed of various types and ages of machines, buildings, and inventories. Combining them into a single measure—or a few measures—is a formidable problem.

Errors can arise in both of the statistically based techniques because the data are assumed to reflect the same production function when, in fact, they are evidence drawn from several production relationships. Identification problems of this sort are not confined to the demand curve context described in Chapter 4. Errors can arise in the engineering method because it is difficult to combine information about specific processes into an overall production function for an entire plant or firm (an entity that is, in reality, a collection of production processes). Engineering data generally pertain to only a part of the firm's activities, and so combining them into a vision of the "big picture" is often a very hard job. In addition, engineering data tell us little or nothing about the firms' marketing or financial activities, but these can be just as important in specifying the production function relationship as the detailed portraits of the nuts and bolts and silicon of fabrication.

| Example 6.6 | **Telecommunications and Economic Development** |

Many observers of modern life have argued that developed economies around the world rely heavily on telecommunications and its underlying infrastructure to support their vitality and sustain their growth. Indeed, Figure 6.13 supports their view by offering strong evidence of a significant correlation between the number of mainline connections to communications infrastructures per household and real per capita GDP across a collection of major developed economies. This sort of casual correlation cannot, however, support a claim of causality.

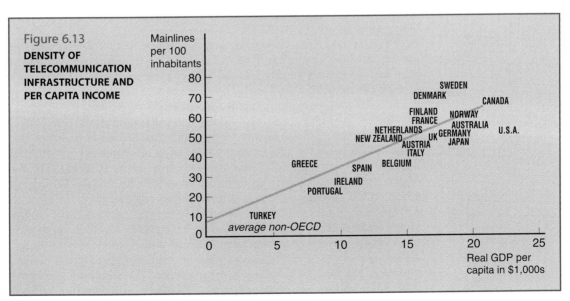

Figure 6.13
DENSITY OF TELECOMMUNICATION INFRASTRUCTURE AND PER CAPITA INCOME

Lars-Hendrik Roller and Leonard Waverman have used the microeconomic fundamentals of production theory and Cobb-Douglas production functions to investigate this correlation more completely. The simplest model simply related aggregate economic activity (GDP) with three distinct variables: the overall capital stock (K), total labor force participation (TLF), and telecommunication penetration (PEN, measured as the number of telecommunication mainlines per capita). In other words, they estimated a function of the form

$$GDP = AK^{\alpha_K}\text{TLF}^{\alpha_{\text{TLF}}}\text{PEN}^{\alpha_{\text{PEN}}}.$$

Interestingly, their estimates for this simple model across a collection of developed countries showed increasing returns to scale with $\alpha_K = 0.411$, $\alpha_{\text{TLF}} = 0.627$, and $\alpha_{\text{PEN}} = 0.154$. They did, though, also note a threshold effect. They were able to discern, in applying similar models to less developed countries, that the ability of telecommunications to promote economic activity was greatly diminished if penetration lay below a critical mass that was quite close to providing universal access to service.

SOURCE: L.-H. Roller and L. Waverman, "Telecommunications Infrastructure and Economic Development: A Simultaneous Approach," *American Economic Review*, vol. 91, no. 4, September 2001, pp. 909–923.

SUMMARY

1. Economists generally assume, as a first approximation, that firms attempt to maximize profits. This is the standard assumption because it is close enough to the objectives that drive firm decisions for many important purposes and because it provides rules of behavior for firms that do want to make as much money as possible.

2. The production function is used by economists to represent the technology available to the firm. For any commodity, the production function is the relationship between the quantities of various inputs employed in a given period of time and the maximum quantity of the commodity produced over the same period of time.

3. In analyzing production processes, we generally assume that all inputs can be divided into two categories: fixed and variable. In the short run, the firm's plant and equipment are fixed; in the long run, all inputs are variable. Both in the short run and in the long run, a firm's production processes ordinarily permit substantial variation in input proportions.

4. The law of diminishing marginal returns states that output will (eventually) increase at a decreasing rate when a firm increases the employment of one input while it holds the level of employment of all other inputs constant. The marginal product of any input measures these increments in output. The law of diminishing marginal returns therefore holds that the marginal product of any input will (eventually) diminish as its employment rises.

5. An input's marginal product must equal its average product when the average product reaches its maximum value. An input's marginal product reaches its maximum at a lower level of employment, where its average product is still rising.

6. An isoquant is a curve that shows all possible combinations of inputs that are capable of producing a certain quantity of output. The absolute value of the slope of an isoquant drawn to reflect a production function relating (for example) the employment of capital and labor (with capital measured along the

vertical axis) is the marginal rate of technical substitution of labor for capital. It is equal to the ratio of the marginal product of labor to the marginal product of capital. The marginal rate of technical substitution declines along an isoquant as the employment of labor climbs.

7. Production can display increasing, constant, or decreasing returns to scale if increasing all inputs by the same proportion causes output to increase by a greater, equal, or smaller proportion, respectively. Whether there are constant, increasing, or decreasing returns to scale is an empirical question that must be settled case by case.

8. Economists and statisticians have devoted a great deal of time and effort to measuring production functions. Three methods have been used in most of these studies: statistical analysis of historical time series of inputs and output, statistical analysis based on cross-sectional data on inputs and output, and careful analysis of engineering data. Estimation is difficult regardless of which technique is applied, but worthwhile estimates of production functions have been published.

QUESTIONS/ PROBLEMS

1. (a) Fill in the blanks in the following table:

Number of units of variable input	Total output (number of units)	Marginal product of variable input[a]	Average product of variable input
3	—	Unknown	30
4	—	20	—
5	125	—	—
6	—	5	—
7	—	—	19

[a]These figures pertain to the interval between the indicated amount of the variable input and 1 unit less than the indicated amount of the variable input.

(b) Does the production function displayed in the table exhibit diminishing marginal returns? If so, at what number of units of variable input do diminishing marginal returns begin to set in? Can you tell on the basis of the table?

2. Explain why the point where marginal product begins to decline is encountered before the point where average product begins to decline (as the employment of an input increases). Explain, too, why the point where average product begins to decline is encountered before the point where total output begins to decline.

3. Suppose that a good is produced with two inputs: labor, denoted by L, and capital, denoted by K. Let the production function be given by $Q = 10 \times (K^{1/2})(L^{1/2})$, where Q is the quantity of output. Does this production function exhibit increasing returns to scale? Decreasing returns to scale? Constant returns to scale? Explain. How would your answers change if the exponents on K and L summed to 0.9? to 1.1?

4. Econometric studies of the cotton industry in India indicate that the Cobb-Douglas production function can be applied and that the exponent of labor is 0.92 and the exponent of capital is 0.12. Suppose that both capital and labor were increased by 1 percent. By what percentage would output increase? Does this industry display constant, increasing, or decreasing returns to scale?

5. Suppose that you were assured by the owner of an aircraft factory that his firm displayed constant returns to scale with regard to its two inputs: labor

and capital. The owner also claims that output per worker is a function of capital per worker only. Is he right?

6. Use the data recorded in Table 6.3 to show how the marginal product of labor (unit by unit) depends on the (fixed) employment of other inputs. Pick a production function specification from the parameters listed in Example 6.2. Show that the marginal product of labor would increase if the employment of capital were enlarged.

7. Assume that 3 units of labor can always take the place of 2 units of capital in the production of some good X. What is the marginal rate of technical substitution between capital and labor when 6 units of labor and 4 units of capital are being employed? when 6 units of labor and 2 units of capital are being employed? when 2 units of labor and 6 units of capital are being employed? Draw a few isoquants for this production process.

8. Assume that some good Y can be produced by a process (process I) for which 2 units of capital must always be employed in association with 3 units of labor for each unit of output. (a) Draw a few isoquants for output equal to 1, 2, and 3 units. (b) Assume that a second process (process II), which *always* requires 1 unit of capital and 5 units of labor for each unit of output, is also possible. Draw some isoquants for this second process. (c) Draw an isoquant for 10 units of output that indicates the possibility of running process I exclusively, process II exclusively, or running both processes simultaneously. Note, in particular, the combination of capital and labor that would be required if each process were employed to produce 5 units.

9. A manufacturer of lasers reports that the marginal product of labor is 10 units of output per hour of labor and that the marginal rate of technical substitution of labor for capital is 5. What is the marginal product of capital?

Calculus Appendix

PRODUCTION FUNCTIONS—DEFINITIONS AND RESULTS

Let the production of some good Y be summarized functionally by

$$Y = F(K, L)$$

where K represents the capital stock and L reflects the quantity of labor employed. We can then define the marginal products of labor and capital (denoted MP_L and MP_K, respectively) as partial derivatives:

$$MP_L \equiv \frac{\partial Y}{\partial L} = \frac{\partial F(K, L)}{\partial L} = F_L(K, L)$$

and

$$MP_K \equiv \frac{\partial Y}{\partial K} = \frac{\partial F(K, L)}{\partial K} = F_K(K, L).$$

The last terms in these definitions reflect convenient notation; notice that they clearly indicate that both marginal products depend on the levels of employment of both inputs. Meanwhile, the average products of labor and capital (denoted AP_L and AP_K, respectively) are:

$$AP_L \equiv \frac{Y}{L} = \frac{F(K, L)}{L}$$

and

$$AP_K \equiv \frac{Y}{K} = \frac{F(K, L)}{K}.$$

The relationship between average and marginal products can now be explored. Consider, for example, the sensitivity of the average product of labor to changes in labor; i.e., consider

$$\frac{\partial AP_L}{\partial L} = \frac{\partial [F(K, L)/L]}{\partial L}.$$

Applying the quotient rule for derivatives, then,

$$\frac{\partial AP_L}{\partial L} = \frac{\partial [F(K, L)/L]}{\partial L}$$

$$= \frac{L[\partial F(K, L)/\partial L] - F(K, L)(\partial L/\partial L)}{L^2}$$

$$= \frac{\partial F(K, L)/\partial L - F(K, L)/L}{L}.$$

The average product of labor reaches its maximum when $\partial AP_L/\partial L = 0$. We now see that this condition holds whenever $\partial F(K, L)/\partial L = F(K, L)/L$, i.e., whenever $MP_L = AP_L$. The same result, of course, holds for the marginal and average products of capital.

An isoquant represents combinations of inputs that sustain the same levels of output. Any isoquant can therefore be defined implicitly by

$$Y_{\text{fixed}} = F(K, L).$$

It follows immediately that

$$d Y_{\text{fixed}} = \frac{\partial F(K, L)}{\partial K} dK + \frac{\partial F(K, L)}{\partial L} dL = (MP_K) \, dK + (MP_L) \, dL$$

so that the marginal rate of technical substitution is

$$MRTS = \left| \left(\frac{dK}{dL} \right)_{Y_{\text{fixed}}} \right| = \frac{MP_L}{MP_K}.$$

This result can be demonstrated, just as in the case of the marginal rate of substitution in a utility context, by observing simply that

$$d Y_{\text{fixed}} = 0$$

by definition along any isoquant.

233

CHAPTER 7

Optimal Input Combination and Cost Functions

We were concerned in the preceding chapter with the motivation of the firm and the way in which its available technology can be represented. We decided to assume, as a first approximation, that firms attempt to maximize profit. We also decided to represent the technology available to the firm with production functions that conform to certain rules, like the law of diminishing marginal returns. These decisions take us partway—but only partway—toward a model of the firm. The next step is to determine how a profit maximizing firm will combine inputs to produce a given quantity of output given technology and *given input prices*. That is the purpose of this chapter.

To be specific, suppose that Toyota anticipates selling 100,000 of its new "hybrid cars" in the United States next year. Suppose, in accord with the conclusions of the preceding chapter, that Toyota is an out-and-out profit maximizer. Assume, as well, that its production function, derived largely through engineering studies and statistical analyses, is well established. On the basis of this information, can we predict what combination of inputs Toyota will use to produce these cars next year and how much it will cost to produce them? If we were offering consulting advice to Toyota, to put the question in a different context, how would we decide what combination of inputs to recommend? And how would we estimate the cost of production?

We begin this chapter by determining which combination of inputs a firm will choose if it minimizes the cost of producing a given amount of output. This would be the first step in our work for Toyota. We will then discuss costs—what is meant by a cost and how various concepts of cost differ from one another. This would prepare us to have meaningful conversations with the accountants at Toyota. We then proceed by showing how the short-run and long-run cost functions of the firm can be derived theoretically, and finally we will use those constructions in a brief discussion of how these cost functions can be measured—the heart of our consulting work over the long term.

234

OPTIMAL COMBINATION OF INPUTS

Let's, for the sake of generality, consider a firm of any sort—not just Toyota. If the firm maximizes profit, it will either minimize the cost of producing a given output or maximize the output derived from a given level of cost.[1] This seems obvious, but not everything that seems obvious is necessarily true. To see why this *is* true, suppose that the firm is a perfect competitor in the input markets; this means that it takes input prices as given. (The case in which the firm can influence input prices will be taken up in Chapter 14.) Suppose as well that two inputs, capital and labor, are variable in the relevant time period. What combination of capital and labor should the firm choose if it wants to maximize the quantity of its output at a given level of cost?

As a first step toward answering this question, let's determine the various combinations of inputs that the firm can obtain for a given expenditure. For example, if the price of labor is P_L per unit and the price of capital is P_K per unit, then the input combinations that can be obtained for a total outlay of R must satisfy a cost equation of the form

$$P_L L + P_K K = R,$$

where L is the amount of the labor employed and K is the amount of the capital employed. Given P_L, P_K, and R, it follows from a little algebra that

$$K = \frac{R}{P_K} - \frac{P_L}{P_K} L.$$

Isocost curve

The various combinations of capital and labor that can be purchased, given P_L, P_K, and R, can therefore be represented by a straight line like that shown in Figure 7.1. Capital is plotted there on the vertical axis; labor is plotted on the horizontal axis. This line, called an **isocost curve** because it displays all of the combinations of K and L that cost the same, has an intercept on the vertical axis equal to R/P_K and a slope equal to $-P_L/P_K$.

Maximizing output given costs

We can readily determine graphically which combination of inputs will maximize the output for the given expenditure if we superimpose the relevant isocost curve on the firm's isoquant map. The firm should obviously pick the point on the isocost curve that also lies on the highest isoquant. This would be point P in Figure 7.2, for example. Notice that the isocost curve is exactly tangent to the isoquant at point P. This is a general result, and it means that the minimum cost combination of inputs must occur where the slope of the isocost curve is exactly equal to the slope of the isoquant. The slope of the isoquant is $-P_L/P_K$, which is equal to -1 times the marginal rate of technical substitution. The optimal combination of

---

[1]The conditions for minimizing the cost of producing a given output are the same as the conditions for maximizing the output that can be sustained at a given cost; maximizing output subject to a cost constraint is the "dual" problem to minimizing cost subject to an output constraint. This is the point of the present section; we can view the firm's problem from either perspective.

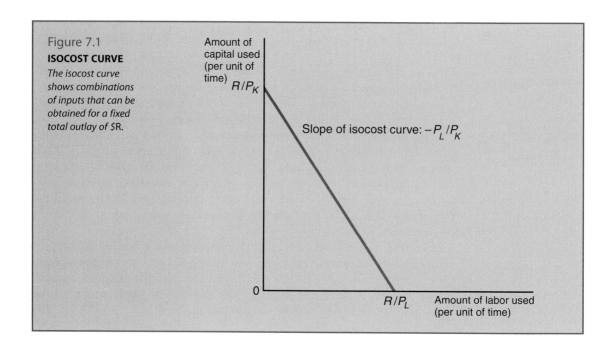

Figure 7.1

ISOCOST CURVE

The isocost curve shows combinations of inputs that can be obtained for a fixed total outlay of $R.

Amount of capital used (per unit of time)

R/P_K

Slope of isocost curve: $-P_L/P_K$

0

R/P_L

Amount of labor used (per unit of time)

inputs must therefore satisfy the condition that the ratio of input prices, P_L/P_K, equals the marginal rate of technical substitution at the tangency point. And since the marginal rate of technical substitution of labor for capital equals the ratio of marginal products MP_L/MP_K, it follows that the

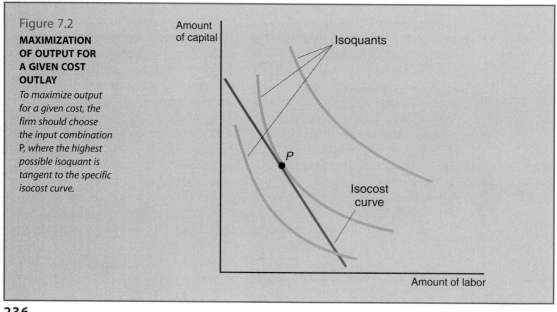

Figure 7.2

MAXIMIZATION OF OUTPUT FOR A GIVEN COST OUTLAY

To maximize output for a given cost, the firm should choose the input combination P, where the highest possible isoquant is tangent to the specific isocost curve.

Amount of capital

Isoquants

P

Isocost curve

Amount of labor

optimal combination of inputs also satisfies the condition that

$$\frac{MP_L}{MP_K} = \frac{P_L}{P_K} \quad \text{or (equivalently)} \quad \frac{MP_L}{P_L} = \frac{MP_K}{P_K}. \qquad [7.1]$$

In general, firms maximize output by distributing their expenditures among various inputs so that the marginal product of a dollar's worth of any one input is equal to the marginal product of a dollar's worth of any other input used. The firm will therefore choose an input combination such that

$$\frac{MP_a}{P_a} = \frac{MP_b}{P_b} = \ldots = \frac{MP_m}{P_m}, \qquad [7.2]$$

where MP_a, MP_b, ..., MP_m are the marginal products of inputs a, b, ..., m, and P_a, P_b, ..., P_m are the prices of inputs a, b, ..., m, respectively. Notice that this is the equivalent of the second representation of Equation 7.1 when there are $m > 2$ inputs.

Returning to the case in which labor and capital are the only two inputs, suppose that a firm decides to spend $200 on these inputs and that the price of labor is $10 per unit and the price of capital is $20 per unit. Table 7.1 shows the marginal product of each input when various combinations of inputs lying along the $200 isocost curve are used. What combination is best? According to Equation 7.2, the marginal product of capital should be set at twice the marginal product of labor, since the price of a unit of capital is twice the price of a unit of labor. This condition can be satisfied by employing 14 units of labor and 3 units of capital; this is the optimal combination.

The following mind exercise can help make it clear that this allocation of cost ($140 to labor and $60 to capital) is optimal. Suppose, for the sake of argument, that $20 were shifted from labor to capital so that only $120 were devoted to employing labor and $80 were devoted to employing capital. Augmenting the capital budget by $20 would increase capital by one

Table 7.1	Amount of input		Marginal product[a]	
MARGINAL PRODUCTS OF CAPITAL AND LABOR	**Labor**	**Capital**	**Labor**	**Capital**
	2	9	20	4
	4	8	18	6
	6	7	16	8
	8	6	14	10
	10	5	12	12
	12	4	10	14
	14	3	8	16
	16	2	6	18
	18	1	4	20

[a]The marginal products are defined for the interval between the indicated amount of labor or capital and 1 unit (capital) or 2 units (labor) less than this amount.

unit; the marginal product of this extra unit of capital equals 14 units of output, so output would climb by 14 units. Reducing the labor budget by $20, however, would cost 2 units of labor. The marginal product of each of these units can be taken to equal 8 units of output; so output would fall by a total of 16 units. In total, then, output would fall by $(16 - 14)$ units. Similarly, the transfer of $20 from capital to labor would also reduce output; take a minute to convince yourself.

Minimizing the cost of a given output

Now let's turn the question around. Suppose that the firm had a particular level of output in mind and wanted to choose the combination of inputs that would (1) generate the desired level of output and (2) do so at least cost. A graph similar to the one drawn in Figure 7.2 can be used to answer this question. The firm's targeted level of output specifies a targeted isoquant along which the firm wants to produce. Moving along this isoquant, we must now find the point that lies on the lowest isocost curve. Point W in Figure 7.3 does the trick, for example. Input combinations on isocost curves like C_0 that lie below W are cheaper than W, but they cannot produce the desired output. Input combinations on isocost curves like C_2 that lie above W will produce the desired output, but at a higher cost than W. It is obvious that the optimal point W is a point where the isocost curve is tangent to the isoquant. And so, the firm must find where the marginal rate of technical substitution is equal to the ratio of input prices if it is to either minimize the cost of producing a given output or to maximize the output from a given cost outlay. And, of course, the condition portrayed in Equation 7.2 must hold in either case.

We have finally made some progress toward solving the problem posed at the beginning of the chapter—the problem of suggesting to Toyota how it

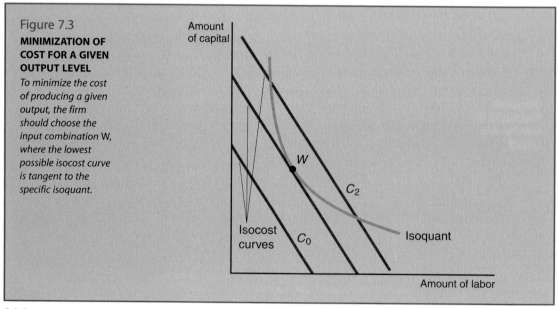

Figure 7.3

MINIMIZATION OF COST FOR A GIVEN OUTPUT LEVEL

To minimize the cost of producing a given output, the firm should choose the input combination W, where the lowest possible isocost curve is tangent to the specific isoquant.

Amount of capital

W

C_2

Isocost curves

C_0

Isoquant

Amount of labor

might want to configure production to deliver 100,000 cars to U.S. markets
at least cost. All that we need to do is to estimate the isoquant that pertains
to an output of 100,000 cars. If we are given Toyota's production function,
this is simple enough. If we have to estimate the function ourselves, then
we have a lot of work to do. We can then draw isocost curves, like the ones
in Figure 7.3, and determine the point like W where the isoquant is tangent
to an isocost curve. This point would represent the optimal combination of
inputs. Or, in the case that the production of the hybrid car involves more
than 2 inputs (say, m inputs), we can combine the $(m - 1)$ equations represented in Equation 7.2 with the production function to solve for optimal,
cost-minimizing levels for each of the m inputs.

To show how this construction can be applied to improve decision-
making, we return in this example to the Kansas farm that was highlighted
in Chapter 6. The idea this time is to help the farm decide how many acres
to plant and how many people to hire for the summer planting season. These
are decisions that must be made early in the spring after decisions about fertilizer and equipment have been taken. The Cobb-Douglas form presented
in Example 6.4 therefore reduces to

$$Q = (\text{constant})A^{0.1}L^{0.1}$$

where Q represents output, A represents the number of acres of land to be
cultivated in wheat, and L represents the amount of labor to be contracted
for summer employment. Several isoquants for this production function were
displayed in Figure 6.6; they reappear in Figure 7.4.

What is the optimal combination of land and labor? This is an important question, both to farm managers and to the general public. Wheat is a

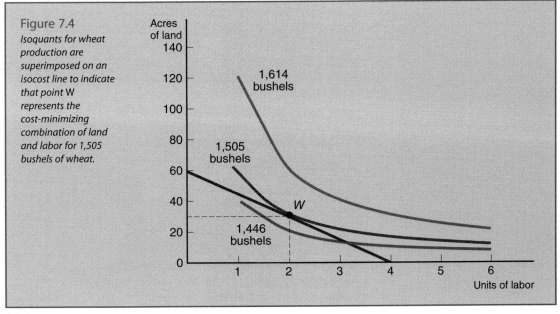

Figure 7.4

Isoquants for wheat production are superimposed on an isocost line to indicate that point W represents the cost-minimizing combination of land and labor for 1,505 bushels of wheat.

very valuable crop, and it is important that it be produced as economically as possible. Suppose that the farmer were thinking of harvesting 1,505 bushels of wheat. (Why the peculiar output target? Because we have a convenient isoquant for that quantity.) Assume that it would cost him $200 per acre to plant the wheat (designated P_A) and $3,000 to hire one worker for the summer (designated P_L). The slope of the relevant isocost curves would therefore be equal to $-P_L/P_A = -\$3,000/\$200 = -15$. Draw a few on Figure 7.4. Spending $6,000 would allow 30 acres of land and no labor, or 2 laborers with no land to work on, or any other combination on the line

$$A = 30 - 15L.$$

The isocost line with $12,000 in total expenditure is the first to hit the 1,505 isoquant; it is tangent at 2 units of labor and 30 acres. The optimal combination would therefore allocate equal proportions of cost to land and labor. At that point, the marginal product of labor is 75, the marginal product of land is 5, and the ratio of marginal products matches the ratio of input prices $(= \$3,000/\$200 = 75/5 = 15)$.

Microlink 7.1   Utility Maximization and Output Maximization

We have just argued that output can be maximized for a given total expenditure on two inputs if their employment is determined by setting the marginal rate of technical substitution equal to the ratio of their prices. This is the dual problem to minimizing the cost of producing a specific level of output. In either case, this condition is equivalent to determining employment levels of two inputs by setting the ratio of their marginal products equal to the ratio of their prices since the marginal rate of technical substitution is equal to the ratio of the marginal products of two inputs. For a production function in capital K and labor L, then, output would be maximized for a specified level of expenditure or costs minimized for a specific level of output if

$$MRTS = \frac{MP_L}{MP_K} = \frac{P_L}{P_K}.$$

Notice that this condition mimics consumer equilibrium. Equation 2.6 recorded, in particular, that utility that depended on the consumption of medicine (M) and food (F) would be maximized by setting the ratio of the marginal utilities of food and medicine equal to the corresponding ratio of the prices of food and medicine; i.e.,

$$MRS = \frac{MU_F}{MU_M} = \frac{P_F}{P_M}.$$

Example 7.1   **Milling Rice in Indonesia**

The isocost-isoquant structure can provide valuable insights into many technology transfer issues involved in trying to stimulate sustainable development in developing countries. Planners in Indonesia were, for example, interested in determining how best to mill its rice crop in the 1970s. There were several options available, and it took some work to demonstrate that

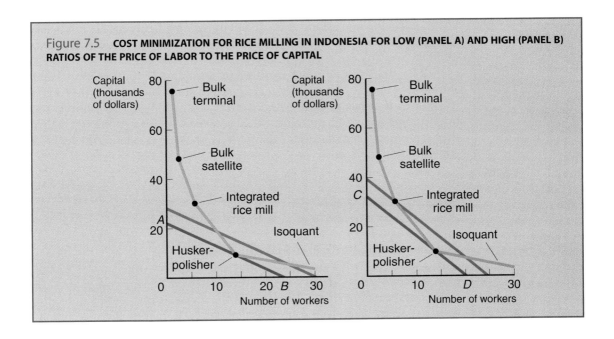

Figure 7.5 **COST MINIMIZATION FOR RICE MILLING IN INDONESIA FOR LOW (PANEL A) AND HIGH (PANEL B) RATIOS OF THE PRICE OF LABOR TO THE PRICE OF CAPITAL**

the economically correct choice was not necessarily the most advanced and modern technologies that were available in developed economies like the United States and Europe. Labor, capital, and other inputs can be more or less plentiful in different countries with decidedly different economic structures, so it was necessary to examine all of the options.

Peter Timmer, a Harvard economist, responded to their inquiries by constructing an isoquant for rice milling that reflected each technological option; both panels of Figure 7.5 depict the product of his work. Planners could adopt any combination of technologies, and their decision depended on the relative prices of capital and labor. If, for example, the applicable isocost curves were all parallel to line *AB* in panel A, then the husker-polisher approach would be the most cost-effective choice. If the isocost curves were parallel to the steeper line *CD* in panel B (so that labor was relatively more expensive than in panel A), the husker-polisher would still be preferred. It turns out that Timmer was uncertain about the ratio of the price of labor to the price of capital, but he thought that lines *AB* and *CD* spanned the range of plausibility; and it also turned out that the best choice of technologies did not change across that range.

Engineers did not necessarily agree with his analysis, however. They had suggested using bulk terminals and bulk satellites—new technologies that were necessary to "modernize" the Indonesian rice industry. The idea, though, was to minimize cost and thereby select technologies that are most appropriate for the specific region. It is by no means assured that the most modern technologies that have been developed where, for example, labor is scarce and commands a high price are appropriate in developing economies where labor is plentiful and labor prices are lower. An isocost

line that has the same slope as the segment running between the bulk satellite and bulk terminal points would be required for them to tie as the cost-
minimizing choices. It would have a slope roughly equal to $(77 - 44)/(4 - 2) = 16.5$ (a value approximated by assigning 77 units of capital and
2 units of labor to the bulk terminal and 44 units of capital with 4 units
of labor to the bulk satellite). And so the ratio of the price of labor to the
price of capital would have to be roughly equal to 16.5—significantly higher
than Timmer's estimated ratio range of 1 (the slope of line AB) to 1.75
(the slope of line CD).

COSTS

The costs incurred by a firm are often thought to include only the money
outlays that the firm must make to buy the resources that it wants to employ. A firm's money outlays are, however, only part of the cost picture. In
many cases, economists are interested in the social costs of production—the
costs to society when its resources are employed to make a given commodity. Economic resources are, by definition, limited, and they can generally
be employed only once. Once some energy is expended in making a car, for
example, it cannot be used to produce a computer. So, allocating resources
determines output, and reallocating resources from one product to another
means less of the one and more of another.

The economist's definition of cost tries to take this allocation problem
to heart. To an economist, the cost of producing a certain product is the
value of other products that could have been produced if the resources had
been allocated differently. The cost of producing airplanes, for example, is
the value of the goods and services that could be obtained from the labor,
equipment, and materials currently employed in aircraft production. So, the
cost of employing a particular input is the value of that input if it were employed in its most valuable alternative use. It is these costs that can be combined with a firm's production function to determine the cost of producing
Alternative cost or   the product; to use these costs is to adopt what has been termed the **alter-**
opportunity cost   **native cost or opportunity cost** doctrine.

It is important to note that the opportunity cost of an input may not
equal its historical cost—i.e., the amount the firm actually paid for it. If
somebody buys the Brooklyn Bridge for $1,000, this does not mean that
the bridge is worth $1,000, either to the buyer or to society. Similarly, if a
firm invests $1 million in a piece of equipment that is quickly outmoded
and is too inefficient relative to new equipment to be worth operating, then
its value is clearly not $1 million. Conventional accounting rules place great
emphasis on historical costs, but the economist—as well as the sophisticated
accountant and the manager—stresses that historical costs should not necessarily be accepted uncritically.

The opportunity cost of an input depends, of course, on the use for
which the cost is being determined. Is the cost of a pound of aluminum
used in the transportation sector equal to the amount that the aluminum

would be worth if it were used in the nontransportation sectors of the economy? Is the cost of a pound of aluminum to the aircraft industry equal to the amount that the aluminum would be worth if it were employed in other transportation industries as well as in the nontransportation sectors? Is the cost of a pound of aluminum to Boeing equal to the amount that the aluminum would be worth to other aircraft manufacturers as well as in all nonaircraft sectors? The opportunity cost doctrine would say yes! to each question under some conditions. Suppose that aluminum were homogenous, so that a pound is a pound is a pound. All of these opportunity costs should then be the same because aluminum could be transferred from low-value uses to high-value uses until its value in all uses were the same. If, however, aluminum were not homogeneous, then these alternative costs would not necessarily be equal.

The alternative uses of a resource will often be different in the long run than in the short run. In the short run, a plumber generally cannot enter fields requiring specialized skills unrelated to plumbing, but given time, he or she can acquire other skills and become a programmer or a machinist. In the long run, alternatives tend to be greater and more varied than in the short run. Frequently, the alternative cost of an input is underestimated because people look only at its alternative uses in the short run.

SOCIAL COSTS VERSUS PRIVATE COSTS

The social cost of producing a given commodity need not always equal the private cost—the cost incurred by the individual producer. A steel plant may, for example, discharge waste products into a river located near the plant. To the plant, the private cost of disposing of the wastes is simply the cost of the pumping operation. If the river becomes polluted, though, then its recreational uses could be destroyed and the water could become unfit for drinking. Additional costs would then be incurred by other people. Differences of this sort between private and social costs occur frequently. They are explored briefly in Example 7.2 and more extensively in Part Six.

| Example 7.2 | An Economic Perspective on Controlling Pollution |

Economists frequently confront the difference between private and social costs when they are asked to estimate, for example, the economically efficient level of pollution control. The question, simply put, is, How much of a firm's pollution should be eliminated from its discharges into the environment? Your first reaction may be, All of it, but that need not be the case—at least from a cost-minimizing perspective.

Figure 7.6 displays several cost curves. In panel A, notice that one labeled "Costs from pollution" is representative of relationships that come first to people's minds. It falls at a decreasing rate as the percentage of pollution removed from a polluter's discharge climbs from zero (the status quo) to 100 percent (a total elimination of pollution from the discharge).

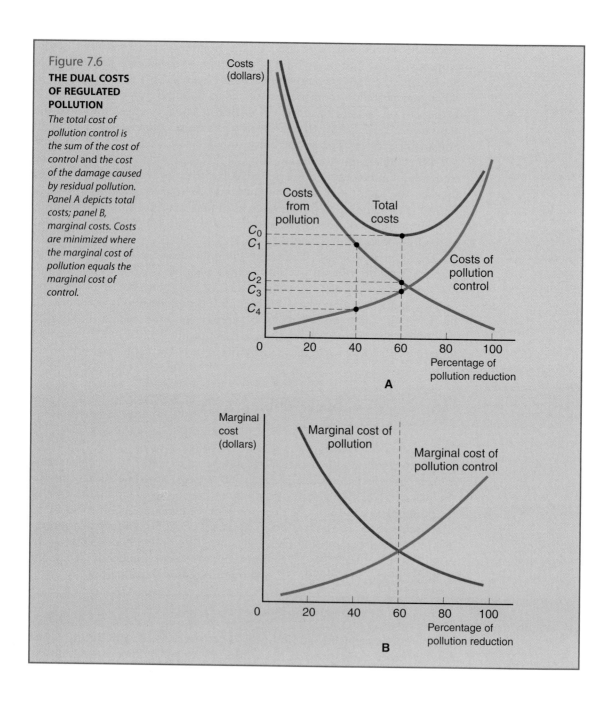

Figure 7.6

THE DUAL COSTS OF REGULATED POLLUTION

The total cost of pollution control is the sum of the cost of control and the cost of the damage caused by residual pollution. Panel A depicts total costs; panel B, marginal costs. Costs are minimized where the marginal cost of pollution equals the marginal cost of control.

This curve captures the economic value of the potential health effects from exposure to polluters' hazardous emissions. It captures the economic losses that might be caused by the pollutants' accelerating decay or erosion of personal and public property. It reflects the economic damage caused to environmental resources like fisheries and forests. You can add to the list. You can even wonder how things like ecosystem damage might be included, but the answer to this question is beyond the scope of our present focus.

The second cost curve drawn in panel A picks up the cost to the polluter of reducing the discharge of hazardous effluent. It is labeled "Costs of pollution control." It starts at zero and climbs at an increasing rate; and it captures expenditures that the firm would have to make to reduce its emissions. These are expenditures that secure the employment of resources that could otherwise be employed somewhere else in the economy if it were not for their application to reducing this firm's pollution. They are, therefore, appropriate components of the cost of controlling pollution, and they are not simply private costs borne by the polluter. They are, in a very real sense, social costs borne by the economy at large.

Where is the cost-minimizing level of pollution control? The third cost curve drawn in panel A is the sum of the first two. It represents the total social cost of reducing pollution by x percent. And total costs include both the costs derived from the damage caused by the $(100 - x)$ percent of the pollution that is still allowed *and* the costs derived from diverting resources to the elimination of the first x percent of the pollution. Panel A shows that total costs are minimized at 60 percent, but this is clearly a function of the underlying curves.

And panel B? What does that show? It reconfirms cost minimization at roughly 60 percent reduction because that is where the marginal cost of the pollution that remains equals the marginal cost of pollution control designed to remove 60 percent of the contamination. But we are a bit ahead of ourselves.

EXPLICIT COSTS VERSUS IMPLICIT COSTS

Explicit costs

Implicit costs

Turning to the private costs of production, it is important to recognize that there are two types of costs. Both are important, and they are both quite different. The first type, labeled **explicit costs,** reflects ordinary expenses that accountants include as the firm's expenses. They include the firm's payroll, payments for raw materials, and so on. The second type, labeled **implicit costs,** includes the costs of the resources owned and used by the firm's owner. Implicit costs are often omitted in accounting for the costs of the firm.

Implicit costs arise because the alternative cost doctrine must be applied to the firm as well as to society as a whole. Consider the proprietor of a firm who invests her own labor and capital in the business. These inputs should be valued at the amounts she would have received if she had used them in another way. For example, perhaps she could have received a salary if she worked for someone else, or she could have received dividends if she had invested her money in someone else's firm. She should value her labor and her capital at rates determined by the salary that she could have earned and the returns she could have enjoyed. It is important that implicit costs be included in a firm's total costs. Their exclusion can result in serious errors.

PROPER COMPARISON OF ALTERNATIVES

It is also important to note that costs incurred in the past often are irrelevant when decisions are to be made in the present or the future. Suppose that you were going to make a trip and that you wanted to determine whether it would be cheaper to drive your car or to go by plane. What costs should be included if you drive your car? Since the only extra costs that would be incurred would be the gas and oil (and a certain amount of wear and tear on tires, engine, etc.), they would be the only costs that should be included. Costs incurred in the past, such as the original price of the car, should not be included. Nor should costs that would be the same regardless of whether or not you make the trip by car be included. But if you are indeed thinking about *buying* a car to make this and many other trips, then at least a fraction of these costs should be included.

As an illustration, consider the case of a major airline that deliberately runs extra flights that do no more than return a little more than their out-of-pocket costs. Suppose that the airline is faced with the decision whether to run an extra flight between city X and city Y. Suppose that the fully allocated costs—the out-of-pocket costs plus a certain percentage of overhead, depreciation, insurance, and other such costs—are $45,000 for the flight. Suppose that the out-of-pocket costs—the actual sum that the airline has to disburse to run the flight—are $20,000 and the expected revenue from the flight is $31,000. In a case of this sort, the airline will run the flight. This is the correct decision, since the flight will add $11,000 to profit. It will increase revenue by $31,000 and costs by $20,000. Overhead, depreciation, and insurance would be the same whether the flight were run or not. In this decision, the correct concept of cost is out-of-pocket, not fully allocated costs. Fully allocated costs are irrelevant and misleading here, and the importance of looking carefully at context before costs are computed cannot be overemphasized.

COST FUNCTIONS IN THE SHORT RUN

We began this chapter by showing how the profit-maximizing firm will choose the cost-minimizing combination of inputs to produce any given level of output. Given this optimal input combination, it is a simple matter to determine the profit-maximizing firm's cost of producing any level of output; it is simply the sum of the amount of each input employed by the firm multiplied by the price of the input. And we use this information to define the firm's cost functions—functions that play a very important role in the theory of the firm. Cost functions show various relationships between the cost of production and the level of output over the short or long run. This section focuses on short-run cost functions; we will then consider long-run cost functions.

The short run is a time period so brief that the firm cannot change the quantity of some of its inputs. More and more inputs become variable as the length of the time period increases, of course, and there are time periods that

Table 7.2 FIXED, VARIABLE, AND TOTAL COSTS	Units of output	Total fixed cost (dollars)	Total variable cost (dollars)	Total cost (dollars)
	0	1,000	0	1,000
	1	1,000	50	1,050
	2	1,000	90	1,090
	3	1,000	140	1,140
	4	1,000	196	1,196
	5	1,000	255	1,255
	6	1,000	325	1,325
	7	1,000	400	1,400
	8	1,000	480	1,480
	9	1,000	570	1,570
	10	1,000	670	1,670
	11	1,000	780	1,780
	12	1,000	1,080	2,080

are so short that it is impossible to adjust the employment of any inputs. Any time interval between one in which no input is variable and one in which all inputs are variable can serve as a reasonable definition of the short run. We will, however, use a more specific definition. Following the convention adopted in Chapter 6, we will say that the short run is the time period so brief that the firm cannot vary its capital configuration of plant and equipment. These are the firm's fixed inputs, and they determine the firm's scale of plant. There will, however, be time to vary inputs like labor; these are the firm's variable inputs over the **short run.** The actual amount of time corresponding to the short run will be longer in some industries than in others. The short run can be very short, indeed, in industries where fixed inputs are small and relatively easily changed. But the short run can last for years in other industries where fixed inputs are large, complicated, and difficult to modify.

Short run

Three concepts of total cost are important in the short run: total fixed cost, total variable cost, and total cost. **Total fixed costs** are the total obligations per period of time incurred by the firm for fixed inputs. Since the quantity of the fixed inputs is fixed (by definition), total fixed cost will be the same regardless of the firm's output—be it 0 units or 1 million units or whatever. What constitutes a fixed cost? Depreciation of buildings and equipment. Property taxes on plant, equipment, and property. Rent on property that is not owned. Table 7.2 displays a hypothetical example in which the total fixed costs are assumed to be $1,000; the firm's total fixed cost function is shown graphically in Figure 7.7.

Total fixed cost

Total variable costs sum the costs incurred by the firm for *employing the cost-minimizing combination of variable inputs associated with any level of output.* Total variable costs increase as the firm's output rate increases because firms must employ more variable inputs if they are to sustain larger outputs. The hypothetical example of Table 7.2 also records variable cost, and Figure 7.7

Total variable costs

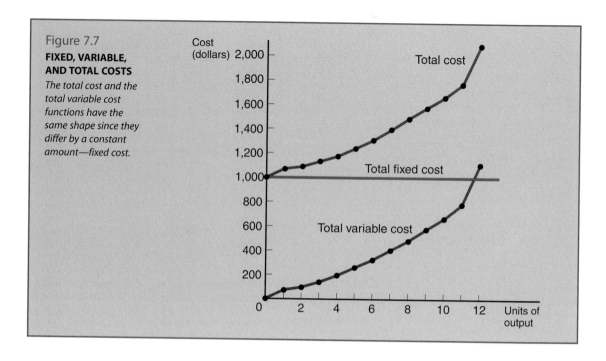

Figure 7.7

FIXED, VARIABLE, AND TOTAL COSTS

The total cost and the total variable cost functions have the same shape since they differ by a constant amount—fixed cost.

shows the corresponding total variable cost function. Total variable costs increase at a decreasing rate up to a certain output rate (in our example, 2 units of output); beyond that output, total variable costs increase at an increasing rate. This latter characteristic of the total variable cost function follows from the law of diminishing marginal returns. At small levels of output, increases in the employment of variable inputs may result in increases in their productivity, so that total variable costs increase with output at a decreasing rate. Once diminishing returns set in, though, variable costs increase with output at an increasing rate. More will be said on this score in the next section.

Total costs Finally, **total costs** are the sum of total fixed costs and total variable costs. So, simply add total fixed cost and total variable cost at each output to derive the last column in Table 7.2. The corresponding total-cost function is shown in Figure 7.7. Notice that the total-cost function has the same shape as the total variable cost function. Why? Because they differ by only a constant amount—the level of total fixed cost.

▢ Average and Marginal Cost

Average- and marginal-cost functions sometimes offer more insight into the behavior of costs. There are three average-cost functions—one each for the three different total cost functions. **Average fixed cost** is total fixed cost divided by output. Table 7.3 and Figure 7.8 show the average fixed cost function for the hypothetical example portrayed in Table 7.2. Average fixed cost declines with increases in output; mathematically, the average fixed cost function is a rectangular hyperbola.

Average fixed cost

248

Table 7.3 **AVERAGE AND MARGINAL COSTS**

Units of output	Average fixed cost (dollars)	Average variable cost (dollars)	Average total cost (dollars)	Marginal cost[a] (dollars)
1	1,000.00 (= 1,000 ÷ 1)	50.00 (= 50 ÷ 1)	1,050.00 (= 1,050 ÷ 1)	50 (= 1,050 − 1,000)
2	500.00 (= 1,000 ÷ 2)	45.00 (= 90 ÷ 2)	545.00 (= 1,090 ÷ 2)	40 (= 1,090 − 1,050)
3	333.33 (= 1,000 ÷ 3)	46.67 (= 140 ÷ 3)	380.00 (= 1,140 ÷ 3)	50 (= 1,140 − 1,090)
4	250.00 (= 1,000 ÷ 4)	49.00 (= 196 ÷ 4)	299.00 (= 1,196 ÷ 4)	56 (= 1,196 − 1,140)
5	200.00 (= 1,000 ÷ 5)	51.00 (= 255 ÷ 5)	251.00 (= 1,255 ÷ 5)	59 (= 1,255 − 1,196)
6	166.67 (= 1,000 ÷ 6)	54.17 (= 325 ÷ 6)	220.83 (= 1,325 ÷ 6)	70 (= 1,325 − 1,255)
7	142.86 (= 1,000 ÷ 7)	57.14 (= 400 ÷ 7)	200.00 (= 1,400 ÷ 7)	75 (= 1,400 − 1,325)
8	125.00 (= 1,000 ÷ 8)	60.00 (= 480 ÷ 8)	185.00 (= 1,480 ÷ 8)	80 (= 1,480 − 1,400)
9	111.11 (= 1,000 ÷ 9)	63.33 (= 570 ÷ 9)	174.44 (= 1,570 ÷ 9)	90 (= 1,570 − 1,480)
10	100.00 (= 1,000 ÷ 10)	67.00 (= 670 ÷ 10)	167.00 (= 1,670 ÷ 10)	100 (= 1,670 − 1,570)
11	90.91 (= 1,000 ÷ 11)	70.91 (= 780 ÷ 11)	161.82 (= 1,780 ÷ 11)	110 (= 1,780 − 1,670)
12	83.33 (= 1,000 ÷ 12)	90.00 (= 1,080 ÷ 12)	173.33 (= 2,080 ÷ 12)	300 (= 2,080 − 1,780)

[a]Note that marginal cost pertains to the interval between the indicated output level and 1 unit less than this output level.

Average variable cost **Average variable cost** is total variable cost divided by output. The average variable cost function for Table 7.2 example is shown in Table 7.3 and Figure 7.9. Notice that increases in output cause average variable cost to fall for a while, but there is an output above which average variable cost climbs with output. The results of the theory of production in Chapter 6 lead us to expect this

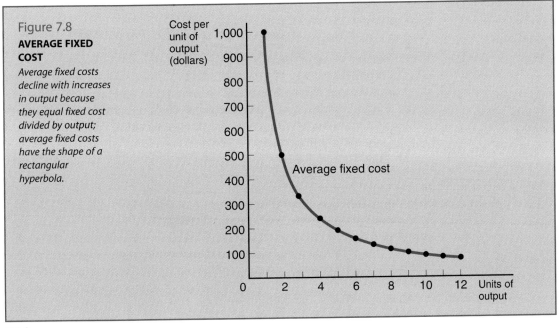

Figure 7.8

AVERAGE FIXED COST

Average fixed costs decline with increases in output because they equal fixed cost divided by output; average fixed costs have the shape of a rectangular hyperbola.

Average fixed cost

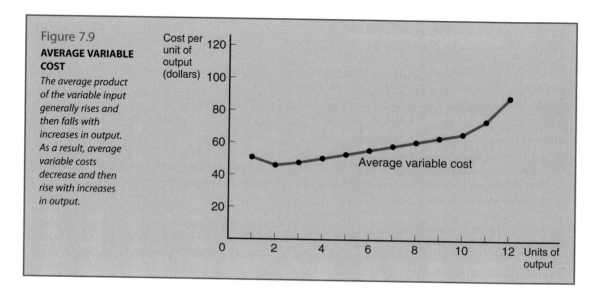

Figure 7.9

AVERAGE VARIABLE COST

The average product of the variable input generally rises and then falls with increases in output. As a result, average variable costs decrease and then rise with increases in output.

curvature of the average variable cost function. If $AVC(Q)$ and $TVC(Q)$ are the average variable cost and total variable cost of producing a quantity Q of output, respectively, $V(Q)$ is the cost-minimizing quantity of the variable input associated with Q, and W is the price of the variable input, it is obvious that

$$AVC(Q) = \frac{TVC(Q)}{Q} = \frac{WV(Q)}{Q}.$$

And since $Q/V(Q)$ is the average product of the variable input (denoted here as $AVP[V(Q)]$),

$$AVC(Q) = W\frac{1}{AVP[V(Q)]}.$$

Recall that the average product of a variable input generally rises and then falls as output climbs (see Figure 6.2). $AVC(Q)$ must therefore decrease and then rise as output climbs because W is assumed to be constant. The shape of the average variable cost curve thereby follows directly from the characteristics of the production function; this is an important insight that should be fully understood before you proceed.

Average total cost — **Average total cost** is total cost divided by output. The average total cost function derived from Table 7.2 is shown in Table 7.3 and Figure 7.10. Average total cost equals the sum of average fixed cost and average variable cost; this connection helps to explain its shape. Average total costs must fall with output for those levels where both average fixed cost and average variable cost decline. Average total cost achieves a minimum, though. This minimum occurs at a higher level of output than the minimum of average variable cost because increases in average variable cost are, for some time, more than offset in the definition of average total cost by decreases in average fixed cost.

Marginal cost — **Marginal cost** is the addition to total cost resulting from the addition of the last unit of output to the mix. That is, if $C(Q)$ represents the total

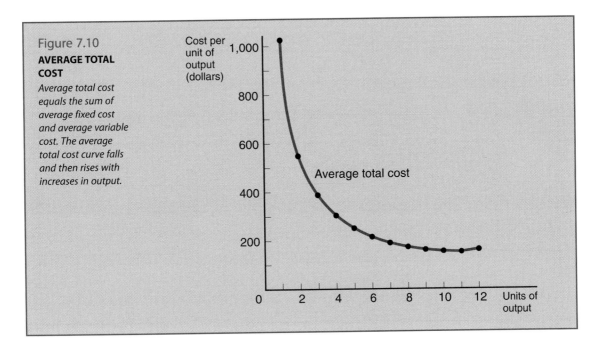

Figure 7.10

AVERAGE TOTAL COST

Average total cost equals the sum of average fixed cost and average variable cost. The average total cost curve falls and then rises with increases in output.

cost of producing Q units of output, then the marginal cost between Q and $(Q - 1)$ units of output is $C(Q) - C(Q - 1)$. The marginal-cost function for the data in Table 7.2 is shown in Table 7.3 and Figure 7.11. Marginal cost may fall through low output levels (as it does in Figure 7.11), but it increases as output climbs once it passes its minimum. The reason for this behavior is also found in the law of diminishing marginal returns. If $\Delta TVC(Q)$ represents the change in total variable costs resulting from a change in output from a level Q to a level $(Q + \Delta Q)$, and if $\Delta TFC(Q)$ is the change in total fixed costs resulting from the same ΔQ change in output, then marginal cost at output Q can be defined by

$$MC(Q) = \frac{\Delta TVC(Q) + \Delta TFC}{\Delta Q} = \frac{\Delta TVC(Q)}{\Delta Q}$$

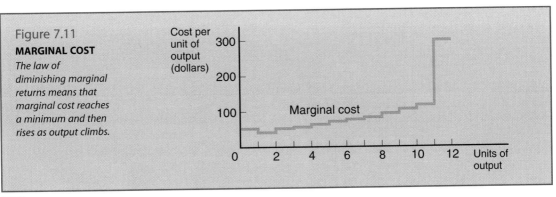

Figure 7.11

MARGINAL COST

The law of diminishing marginal returns means that marginal cost reaches a minimum and then rises as output climbs.

because $\Delta TFC(Q)$ is zero by definition. Now let the price of the variable input again be fixed at W so that

$$\Delta TVC(Q) = W(\Delta V(Q)),$$

where $\Delta V(Q)$ is the change in the quantity of the variable input required to increase output from Q to $(Q + \Delta Q)$. Marginal cost must therefore equal

$$MC(Q) = W\frac{\Delta V(Q)}{\Delta Q} = W\frac{1}{MP[V(Q)]},$$

where $MP[V(Q)]$ is the marginal product of the variable input at the cost-minimizing level required to produce output Q. Since marginal products generally increase, attain a maximum, and then decline as output climbs (again see Figure 6.2), marginal-cost functions normally decrease, attain a minimum, and then increase. The fact that the shape of the marginal-cost function also depends so critically on the law of diminishing marginal returns is also important and should be fully understood.

Figure 7.12 provides an overview of this entire cost construction by superimposing graphs of average total cost, average variable cost, average fixed

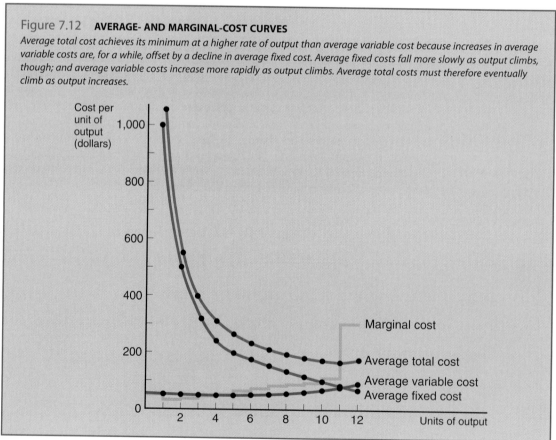

Figure 7.12   **AVERAGE- AND MARGINAL-COST CURVES**
Average total cost achieves its minimum at a higher rate of output than average variable cost because increases in average variable costs are, for a while, offset by a decline in average fixed cost. Average fixed costs fall more slowly as output climbs, though; and average variable costs increase more rapidly as output climbs. Average total costs must therefore eventually climb as output increases.

cost, and marginal cost. Their shape and position are typical of cost curves in general. The next section describes why.

| **Example 7.3** | **Perhaps the First Average-Cost Curve** |

Economists began to work on the concept of average cost sometime in the early 1900s, but a German music company more than a century earlier calculated and used output-dependent estimates of average cost for two different methods of printing sheet music. It seems that Gottfried Härtel purchased a Leipzig book and music publishing house for 106,000 German reichsthalers. There were, at the time, two different processes for printing sheet music: engraving (a labor-intensive technique that took 6 to 8 hours per page) and movable type (much less labor-intensive per page and a bit more efficient to run). Härtel, upon completion of the purchase, set out to explore how to set prices and allocate effort, and he produced the average-cost estimates displayed in Figure 7.13.

Härtel is reported to have drawn several conclusions from his analysis. First, an anticipated price of 15 to 18 pfennigs per (clean) sheet for works net of agents' margins, shipping costs, and inventory losses would support a tolerable profit. This led him to decide that he could pay an honorarium of 3 to 4 pfennigs per sheet to the composer if sales were expected to exceed 300 copies. Evidence of this second conclusion can apparently be documented in his negotiations with Ludwig von Beethoven. Härtel also concluded that he needed to improve quality and reduce the number of defective copies printed to be solvent. Did he succeed? His business is

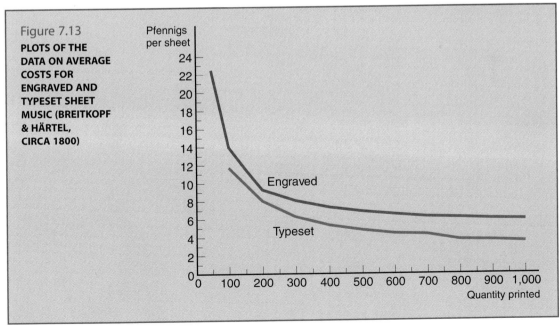

Figure 7.13

PLOTS OF THE DATA ON AVERAGE COSTS FOR ENGRAVED AND TYPESET SHEET MUSIC (BREITKOPF & HÄRTEL, CIRCA 1800)

still in existence, so it would appear so. And finally, he invested in lithography, a new technology invented in the 1790s, because he thought that it would quickly supplant engraving for high-quality publications. Why? Because the average cost was always lower and the quality was always comparable.

SOURCE: F. Scherer, "An Early Application of the Average Total Cost Concept," *Journal of Economic Literature,* vol. 39, no. 3, September 2001, pp. 897–901.

▣ The Geometry of Average- and Marginal-Cost Functions

We will frequently want to derive the average- and marginal-cost functions from total-cost functions. Unless specified to the contrary, average cost will henceforth signify average total cost. The purpose of this section is to show how this can be done graphically. The procedures are quite similar to those used in Chapter 6 to derive average- and marginal-product curves. Figure 7.14 shows how the average-cost function can be derived from a typical total-cost function—a function depicted by line TT' in panel A. The average cost at any output level is given by the slope of the ray from the origin to the relevant point on the total-cost function. The average cost at an output Q_0 is, for example, the slope of ray $0R$. We plot this slope, which equals Z, against Q_0 in panel B. We can, of course, plot the slope of any ray from the origin to the relevant point on the total-cost function against the output; the result is curve AA', and it depicts the average-cost function. Beginning

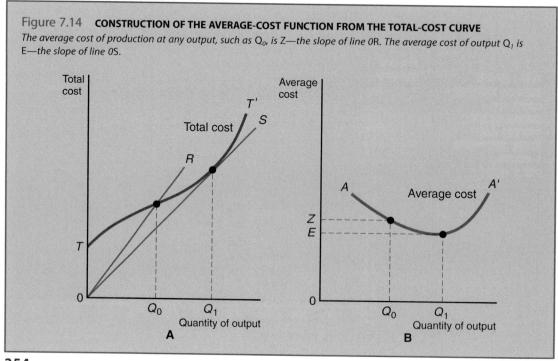

Figure 7.14 **CONSTRUCTION OF THE AVERAGE-COST FUNCTION FROM THE TOTAL-COST CURVE**
The average cost of production at any output, such as Q_0, is Z—the slope of line $0R$. The average cost of output Q_1 is E—the slope of line $0S$.

with a very small output, it is clear from Figure 7.14 that average cost initially falls as output increases because the slopes of appropriate rays decline as output climbs. It is also clear, however, that average cost reaches a minimum at Q_1. Why? Because the slopes of the rays increase as output climbs beyond Q_1.

Figure 7.15 illustrates the analogous derivation of the marginal-cost function. As output increases from Q_2 to Q_3, total cost read from the same TT' curve drawn again in panel A increases from C_2 to C_3. The extra cost per unit of output is therefore equal to

$$\frac{C_3 - C_2}{Q_3 - Q_2} = \frac{BA}{CB}.$$

And if we shrink the distance between Q_2 and Q_3 until it is extremely small, then the slope of the tangent UU' at A becomes a very good estimate of BA/CB. In the limit, in fact, the slope of the tangent to the total-cost function at Q_3 is exactly equal to marginal cost when output equals Q_3. Line MM' in panel B shows the slope of the tangent to the total-cost curve at each output, and so line MM' is the marginal-cost function. It is evident from Figure 7.15 that marginal cost decreases as output climbs through small levels, since the slope of the tangent to the total-cost function decreases in that region. Marginal cost reaches a minimum, V, at Q_4, though, and increases thereafter because the slope of the tangent to the total cost function reaches a minimum at Q_4.

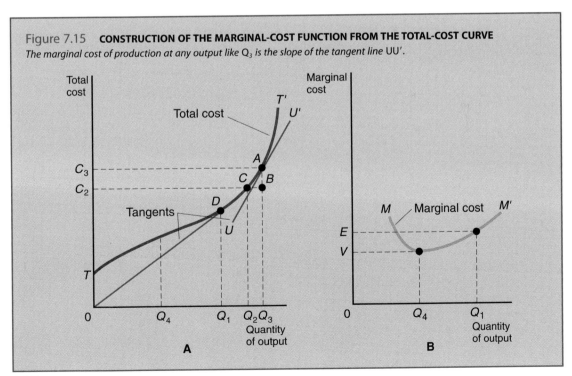

Figure 7.15 **CONSTRUCTION OF THE MARGINAL-COST FUNCTION FROM THE TOTAL-COST CURVE**
The marginal cost of production at any output like Q_3 is the slope of the tangent line UU'.

Figure 7.16 **MARGINAL COST EQUALS AVERAGE COST AT THE MINIMUM OF THE AVERAGE-COST CURVE**

Marginal cost equals average cost at the minimum of the average-cost curve—output Q_1 for which average cost equals E. Average cost for output Q_1 is the slope of line 0D; it equals C_1/Q_1, = E in the right panel. Marginal cost for output Q_1 is the slope of the same line because line 0D is tangent to the total-cost curve at point D.

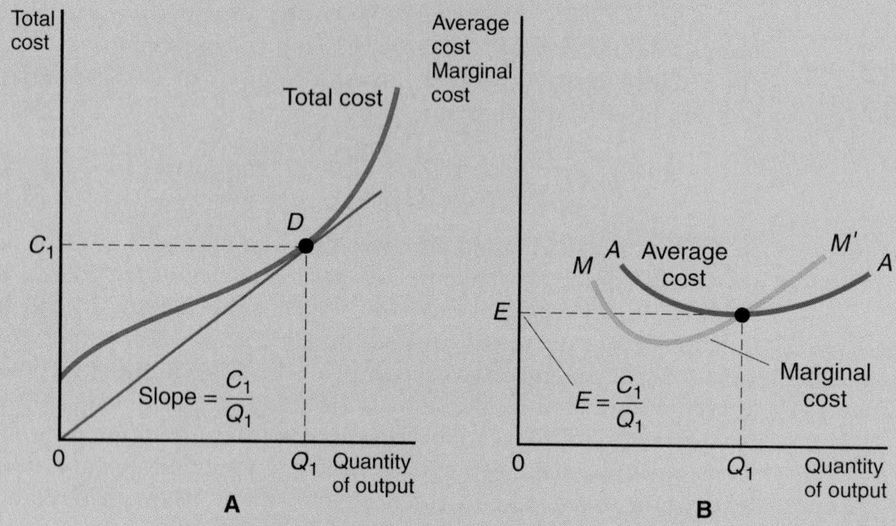

Notice, finally, that average cost reaches its minimum (at output Q_1) where the slope of the ray $0D$ equals the slope of the tangent to the total-cost function. This result holds simply because line $0D$ is, indeed, tangent to the total-cost function at point D. Average cost equals the slope of the ray $0D$, of course, and marginal cost equals the slope of the tangent to the total-cost function. It follows immediately that average cost must equal marginal cost at the output level where average cost is a minimum. This is confirmed in Figures 7.14 and 7.15 because marginal cost and average cost both equal E when output is Q_1. It is also displayed in Figure 7.16, where marginal cost and average cost are drawn on the same graph.

Example 7.4 **Falling Lakes and the Cost of Shipping Cargo**

Rainfall has been below long-term averages in the regions that feed the Great Lakes of North America for nearly two decades. Water levels in Lake Superior and Lake Michigan have, as a result, declined over time to the point where the cost of transporting merchandise and raw materials on giant cargo ships has been affected. Indeed, recent estimates suggest that every one-inch reduction in the level of either lake means that these ships must reduce their loads by 100 tons. We can use this simple observation and the fundamentals of cost curves to see how costs might change as a result.

Suppose, for the sake of illustration, that a round trip for a cargo ship between Windsor, Ontario, and Chicago, Illinois, would cost a shipping company $100,000 for any size load (plus fixed cost, but we will ignore

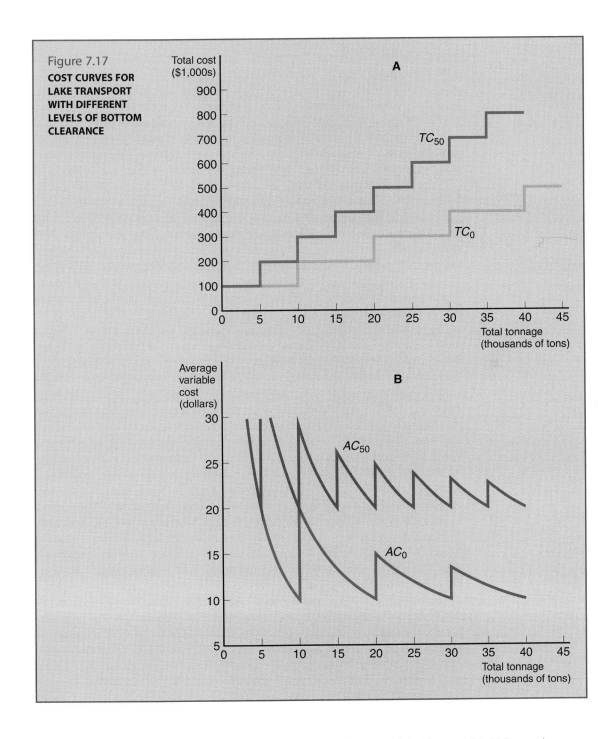

Figure 7.17

COST CURVES FOR LAKE TRANSPORT WITH DIFFERENT LEVELS OF BOTTOM CLEARANCE

that). Assume, as well, that the ship could hold up to 10,000 tons in cargo absent any constraints imposed by lower lake levels. Lines TC_0 and AC_0 in panels A and B of Figure 7.17 depict the resulting total and average cost curves as a function of total monthly tonnage carried between Windsor and

Chicago. Both are drawn under the final assumption that our company fills all but the last ship required to service demand over the month. Notice that total costs climb in steps and average cost projects a saw-toothed shape. This is because variable costs increase only by the trip and because average variable costs would be minimized at $10 per ton only if the shipping company could always operate full ships (i.e., if the last ship of the month were full just like the others). The extra cost of the last load's being partially empty does, however, become smaller, on average, as the company arranges to complete more and more round trips during the month.

Now assume that the levels of Lakes Michigan and Superior fall by 50 inches. (This is a lot, but it makes the graphs easier to work with.) Each ship could, as a result, accommodate only 5,000 tons of cargo. Lines TC_{50} and AC_{50} in panels A and B of the figure depict the resulting cost curves. Notice that the steps are steeper for total costs and that the saw-tooth pattern for average variable costs repeats itself more rapidly. Moreover, total and average costs are higher after the lake level falls for every monthly total in excess of one shipload, or 5,000 tons. Indeed, the minimum of average costs is 100 percent higher.

COST FUNCTIONS IN THE LONG RUN

Long run Firms can build any scale or type of plant in the **long run**—the time period in which all inputs are variable and there are no fixed costs. It is sometimes instructive to look at the long run as a planning horizon. While operating in the short run, firms must continually plan ahead to decide their strategies for the long haul. Their decisions about the long run determine the sort of short-run positions they will occupy in the future. A firm might, for example, consider adding a new type of product to its line; such a firm is "planning" in its long-run decision mode, during which time it can choose among a wide variety of types and sizes of equipment to produce the new product. Once the investment has been made, though, the firm will be confronted with a short-run situation; the type and the size of equipment will have, to a considerable extent, been frozen.

To understand these points more thoroughly, consider a firm that has the wherewithal to construct only one of three alternative scales of plant. Let the short-run average-cost function for each scale of plant be represented in Figure 7.18 by curves S_1S_1', S_2S_2', and S_3S_3', respectively. In the long run, of course, the firm could decide to build any one of these plants, but which scale would be most profitable? If the firm wants to produce where average cost is smallest, the answer obviously depends on how much the firm wants to produce in the long run. If the firm anticipates producing output Q, then the firm should choose the smallest plant since it could then produce Q units of output per period of time at a cost per unit of C. This average cost is smaller than the minimum that could be sustained in producing Q units with either the medium-sized plant or the large plant. How can we tell? The graph shows that the cost per unit in using the medium plant to produce Q units

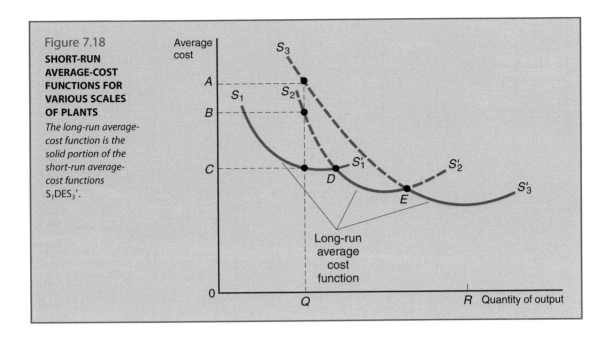

Figure 7.18

SHORT-RUN AVERAGE-COST FUNCTIONS FOR VARIOUS SCALES OF PLANTS

The long-run average-cost function is the solid portion of the short-run average-cost functions S_1DES_3'.

Long-run average-cost function

could never be less than $B > C$, and the cost per unit in using the large plant to produce Q units could never be less than $A > B > C$. If the anticipated output rate were R, though, then the firm should choose the largest plant. And if its plans were somewhere in between, then region DE on curve S_2S_2' highlights a region where the medium-sized plant would be best.

The **long-run average-cost function** shows the minimum cost per unit of producing each output level when any desired scale of plant can be built. The long-run average-cost function in Figure 7.18 is the solid portion of the short-run average-cost functions that is carved out by "hybrid curve" S_1DES_3'. The broken-line segments of the short-run functions are not included because they do not designate the lowest average costs for the corresponding output.

What would happen to this analysis if there were more than three alternative scales of plant? What if, in fact, there were a great many alternative scales? Firms would then be confronted with a host of short-run average-cost functions, and their combined portrait would look something like Figure 7.19. The minimum cost per unit of producing each output level is given in Figure 7.19 by the long-run average-cost function, LL'. This long-run average-cost function is tangent to each of the short-run average-cost functions at the output where the plant corresponding to the short-run average-cost function is optimal (i.e., where average costs are minimized). Mathematically, the long-run average-cost function is the envelope of the short-run functions. Note, however, that the long-run average-cost function (LL') is not tangent to the short-run functions at their minimum points unless the LL' curve is horizontal. When the LL' curve is decreasing, for example, it is tangent to the short-run functions to the left of their minimum points.

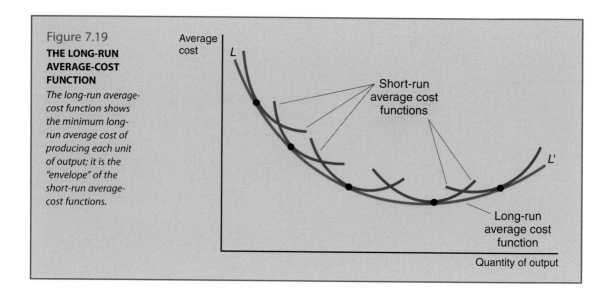

Figure 7.19

THE LONG-RUN AVERAGE-COST FUNCTION

The long-run average-cost function shows the minimum long-run average cost of producing each unit of output; it is the "envelope" of the short-run average-cost functions.

Average cost

L

Short-run average cost functions

Long-run average cost function

L'

Quantity of output

When the LL' curve is increasing, it is tangent to the short-run functions to the right of their minimum points.

Long-run average-cost functions indicate the smallest cost per unit output for any level of output. They are constructed under the assumption that all inputs are variable. So, any point on a long-run average-cost curve implies that inputs have been allocated so that the marginal product of a dollar's worth of one input equals the marginal product of a dollar's worth of any other input. In other words, firms can achieve a point on the long-run average-cost curve only if they use the least-cost combination of all inputs to produce each level of output.

It is easy to derive the long-run total cost of the output from the long-run average-cost curve. Total costs in the long run are always equal to long-run average cost multiplied by output. Figure 7.20 shows a typical (but not universal) relationship between long-run total cost and output; this relationship is called the long-run total-cost function. And it is easy to derive the long-run marginal-cost function from the long-run total-cost function. Long-run marginal-cost curves show the relationship between output and the minimum additional cost that was incurred by producing the last unit of output. Since long-run marginal costs are derived from long-run total costs, though, their calculation implicitly assumes that the firm has plenty of time to make the optimal changes in the quantities of all of the inputs that it employs. Long-run marginal cost must be less than long-run average cost when average costs are decreasing with output, equal to long-run average cost when average costs have achieved a long-run minimum, and greater than long-run average cost when average costs are rising. It can also be shown that long-run marginal cost and short-run marginal cost will be equal when firms are operating plants of exactly the correct (cost-minimizing) scale for their intended outputs.

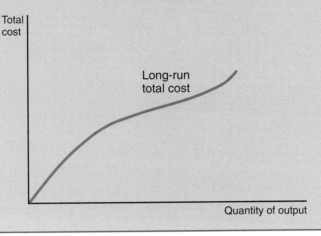

Figure 7.20 **THE TYPICAL SHAPE OF LONG-RUN TOTAL-COST FUNCTIONS**
The long-run total-cost function identifies the minimum cost of producing any output level; it is equal to the long-run average cost of production multiplied by total output. The shape displayed here is derived from the long-run average-cost function portrayed in Figure 7.19. It is typical of many long-run functions.

| Example 7.5 | **The Sensitivity of Production Costs to Input Prices** |

We now understand that cost curves are themselves the solutions to constrained minimization problems under the assumption that technologies and input prices are fixed. By construction, therefore, cost curves submerge their sensitivity to changes in those prices. It turns out that the degree to which production costs would change as the price of some input (call it input A) changes depends on several factors. The proportion of total cost attributed to input A plays a critical role, as does the ability of the firm to substitute into or out of input A within the given technology. How do we know that? By computing general cost curves from general production functions of the sort described in Example 6.3.

Other production functions support other cost functions, but how much of a difference can underlying productive structure make in any case? Table 7.4 offers some evidence derived from estimates of the degree to which production costs would climb (as a percentage of current costs) if energy prices were to rise by 20 percent in response to a tax on the carbon content of fossil fuel. Estimates are reported there for four energy-intensive industries in nine developed economies. Notice that they vary widely from country to country for each sector and from sector to sector within most countries. It follows that producers of comparable products in different countries do not use identical or even similar processes in terms of their energy intensities or their ability to conserve. Moreover, it is equally clear that the technologies for different products are systematically different in their reliance on energy.

Table 7.4	Country	Iron and steel	Nonferrous metals	Chemical products	Pulp and paper
THE SENSITIVITY OF PRODUCTION COSTS TO ENERGY PRICES	United States	1.7	1.6	1.4	1.6
	Canada	3.6	1.9	2.1	2.5
	Japan	2.0	0.7	1.0	0.6
	Australia	5.8	11.4	1.7	2.6
	France	2.4	1.4	1.3	0.6
	Germany	2.6	1.2	1.4	1.0
	United Kingdom	3.6	1.9	1.2	1.2
	Italy	2.0	1.1	1.3	0.7
	Belgium	7.3	0.8	1.6	0.6

SOURCE: Estimates derived from R. Baron and ECON-Energy (*Economic/Fiscal Instruments: Competitiveness Issues Related to Carbon/Energy Taxation,* Policies and Measures for Common Action Working Paper 14, Organization of Economic Cooperation and Development and the International Energy Agency, Paris, 1997) under the assumption that the tax would increase energy prices by 20% in North America and by 10% elsewhere. Estimates are expressed as percentage increase in average cost.

◻ The Expansion Path and Long-Run Total Costs

It is worthwhile at this point to stop for a moment to show how a firm's long-run total-cost function can be derived from its isoquants. Figure 7.21 shows a firm's isoquants corresponding to output levels of 50, 100, and

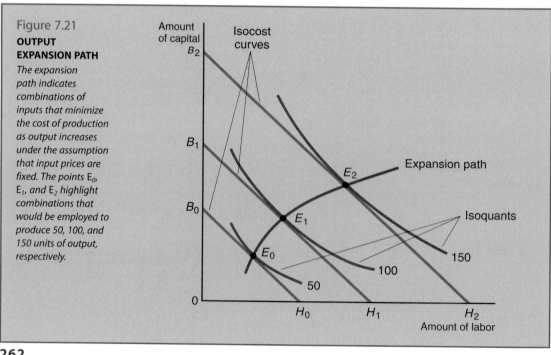

Figure 7.21

OUTPUT EXPANSION PATH

The expansion path indicates combinations of inputs that minimize the cost of production as output increases under the assumption that input prices are fixed. The points E_0, E_1, and E_2 highlight combinations that would be employed to produce 50, 100, and 150 units of output, respectively.

Expansion path

150. The least-cost combination of inputs to produce 50 units of output is represented by point E_0, where the isoquant is tangent to the relevant isocost curve. Similarly, the least-cost combination of inputs to produce 100 units of output is represented by point E_1, and the least-cost combination of inputs to produce 150 units of output is represented by point E_2. These tangency points (E_0, E_1, E_2), as well as those representing the least-cost combinations of inputs to produce other quantities of output, lie along a curve known as the **expansion path.** The expansion path for our firm's isoquants is shown in Figure 7.21. The expansion path indicates how the employment of each input changes as output changes *under the assumption that input prices are fixed.*

It is a simple matter to derive the long-run total-cost function from the expansion path if capital and labor are the only inputs. Each point on the expansion path represents the least-cost combination of inputs to produce a certain output in the long run (since neither input is fixed). Consider point E_0. It corresponds to an output of 50 units. The total cost of the combination of inputs represented by E_0 is H_0 times P_L, the price of a unit of labor. Why? Because point E_0 is on isocost curve B_0H_0, so that the input combination at point E_0 costs the same as that at point H_0. And the cost of the input combination at point H_0 equals H_0 times P_L.

To obtain one point on the long-run total-cost function, then, we simply plot H_0 times P_L against 50 units of output. This is shown as point E_0 in Figure 7.22. To obtain a second such point, consider point E_1 on the

Figure 7.22 **DERIVATION OF THE LONG-RUN TOTAL-COST FUNCTION FROM THE EXPANSION PATH OF FIGURE 7.21**

The total cost of the input combinations designated by points E_0, E_1, and E_2 in Figure 7.21 are $H_0 \times P_L$, $H_1 \times P_L$, and $H_2 \times P_L$, respectively (where P_L is the price of labor per unit). The minimum cost of producing 50 units of output is therefore $H_0 \times P_L$; the minimum cost of producing 100 units of output is $H_1 \times P_L$; and the minimum cost of producing 150 units is $H_2 \times P_L$. All of these points appear on the total-cost curve above their respective outputs.

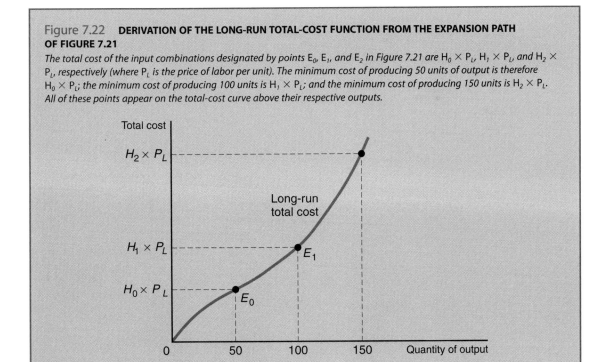

expansion path. It corresponds to an output of 100 units, and the total cost of the combination of inputs represented by E_1 is H_1 times P_L. The minimum cost of producing 100 units of output in the long run is therefore H_1 times P_L, so point E_1 on the long-run total-cost function corresponding to an output of 100 units is H_1 times P_L. Consequently, H_1 times P_L is plotted against 100 units of output in Figure 7.22. By repeating this procedure for each of a number of different output levels, we obtain the long-run total-cost function shown in Figure 7.22.

◻ The Shape of the Long-Run Average-Cost Function

The long-run average-cost function in Figure 7.19 had much the same shape as the short-run average-cost function. Both decrease with output up to a certain point, reach a minimum, and then increase. The factors responsible for this shape are not the same in the two cases, however. The theory of diminishing marginal returns operates behind the scenes in the construction of the short-run average-cost curve. The short-run average-cost function turns upward because reductions in average fixed costs are eventually counterbalanced by increases in average variable costs that are themselves derived from reductions in the average product of the variable input. The law of diminishing marginal returns, however, is not responsible for the shape of the long-run average cost function. How could it be? There are no fixed inputs in the long run.

The shape of the long-run average-cost function is determined in part by economies of scale, and in part by diseconomies of scale. Chapter 6 suggested that increases in scale can often produce important economies, at least up to a point. Larger scale can permit the introduction of different kinds of techniques because larger productive units are more efficient and because larger plants permit greater specialization and division of labor. To the extent that these efficiencies exist and can be exploited, the long-run average-cost function declines as output climbs. The range of output over which the average-cost function declines varies from industry to industry, and it can change from time to time in response to the advent of new technology.

So there we have half of the story—but why does the long-run average-cost function turn upward? The answer that is generally given is that increases in scale beyond some threshold result in inefficiencies in management. More and more responsibility and power must be given to lower-level employees. Coordination becomes more difficult. Red tape increases. Flexibility can be reduced. It is not easy to determine just when these diseconomies of scale begin to offset the economies of scale already cited. Empirical studies seem to indicate that long-run average cost can be constant over a considerable range of output; Figure 7.23 offers a representative portrait. Economists generally expect, however, that the long-run average-cost function will eventually begin to rise.

It is important to note that the shape of the long-run average-cost function is of great significance from the viewpoint of public policy. If the long-run average cost function in a particular industry decreases markedly up to

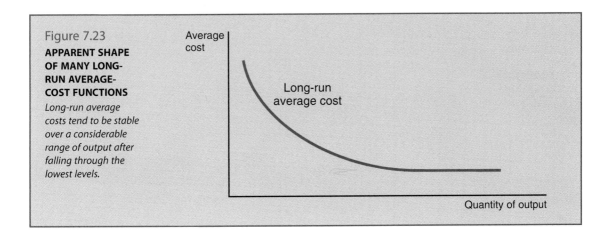

Figure 7.23

APPARENT SHAPE OF MANY LONG-RUN AVERAGE-COST FUNCTIONS

Long-run average costs tend to be stable over a considerable range of output after falling through the lowest levels.

Average cost

Long-run average cost

Quantity of output

a level of output that corresponds to all, or practically all, that the market demands of the commodity, then it makes little sense to force competition in this industry. To do so would increase costs, since output would be divided among a number of firms that could not then produce at the long-run minimum scale. In this case, the industry is a natural monopoly, and government agencies like the Federal Energy Regulatory Commission and the Federal Communications Commission, rather than competition, often are relied on to regulate the industry's performance. This topic will be discussed further in Chapter 10.

Example 7.6 **The Shape of Cost Curves**

Richard Miller has recently applied first principles to explain why short-run marginal- and average-cost curves could be horizontal for large ranges of output before they turn up—the opposite shape of the long-run average-cost curve portrayed in Figure 7.23 and not at all consistent with the shapes drawn in earlier figures. We will see in Example 7.7, however, that this is a common shape; and so the theory does indeed "have some explaining to do"!

Miller's notion is that long-run decisions fix the stock of capital but that they do not mandate that a firm must employ its full capacity all of the time. Panel A of Figure 7.24 displays his structure. A firm with a production process characterized by constant returns to scale has, by virtue of long-run cost minimization, decided to invest in K_1 units of capital. The planned efficient level of output would therefore be Q_1, and L_1 units of labor would be employed. We know this because the long-run isoquant for Q_1 units is tangent to an isocost line at point H. Miller then observes that short-run decisions involved in producing less than Q_1 units could be best described by employing labor and capital services in fixed proportions along expansion path $0H$; short-run technological options are depicted along that path by the L-shaped isoquants for outputs Q_2 and Q_3. Output levels in excess of Q_1 cannot be achieved because "stretching" the available capital stock

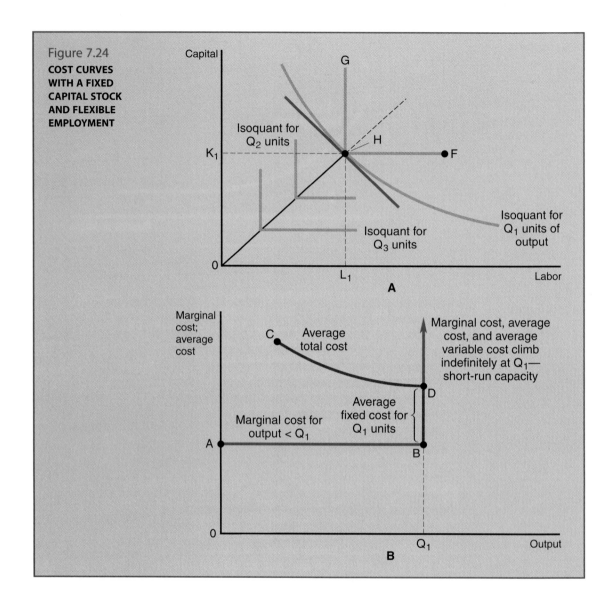

Figure 7.24
COST CURVES WITH A FIXED CAPITAL STOCK AND FLEXIBLE EMPLOYMENT

Capital

G

Isoquant for Q_2 units

K_1

H

F

Isoquant for Q_3 units

Isoquant for Q_1 units of output

0

L_1

Labor

A

Marginal cost; average cost

C

Average total cost

Marginal cost, average cost, and average variable cost climb indefinitely at Q_1—short-run capacity

D

Average fixed cost for Q_1 units

Marginal cost for output < Q_1

A

B

0

Q_1

Output

B

and suffering the consequences of diminishing marginal productivity of labor (by moving along an expansion path given by ray *HF*) is disallowed by the L-shaped isoquant *GHF*.

Assuming, as usual, that the prices of both capital and labor are fixed, we can now draw short-run marginal- and average-cost curves up to output Q_1; and we can explore what would happen if the firm were to try to produce more than Q_1. Output from 0 to Q_1 can be produced by employing capital services and labor in fixed proportions. The firm has already paid a fixed cost for the capital stock, and so it gets the capital services "for free" on the margin. The marginal cost of production must therefore be constant, assuming constant returns to scale, and it must match average variable cost along line *AB* in panel B of Figure 7.24. Short-run average total costs fall along curve *CD*, though, because average fixed costs fall; short-run average costs are minimized at point *D*, where output equals Q_1. Trying to push output in the short run beyond Q_1 brings the firm squarely against a capacity constraint. Marginal cost jumps from point *B*, average costs climb abruptly, and average variable costs follow suit.

SOURCE: R. Miller, "Ten Cheaper Spades: Production Theory and Cost Curves in the Short Run," *Journal of Economic Education*, vol. 31, no. 1, Winter 2000, pp. 119–130; and "Firms' Cost Functions," *Review of Industrial Organization*, vol. 18, no. 1, Winter 2001, pp. 183–200.

ECONOMIES OF SCOPE

Discussions of cost functions generally focus attention on the costs of producing a single product without reference to whatever other products the firm might be making at the same time. Some firms, like Du Pont or Exxon or any one of the newly merger-created conglomerates, turn out hundreds of different products. And firms that produce more than one product may

Economies of scope   experience economies or diseconomies of scope. **Economies of scope** exist when a single firm can jointly produce two or more products more cheaply than separate firms. Diseconomies of scope occur when the opposite condition occurs—when the production of one good seems to interfere with the production of another.

The degree of economies of scope can be measured. One statistic is

$$\frac{TC(Q_1) + TC(Q_2) - TC(Q_1 + Q_2)}{TC(Q_1 + Q_2)},$$

where $TC(Q_1)$ is the total cost of producing Q_1 units of the first good only, $TC(Q_2)$ is the total cost of producing Q_2 units of the second good only, and $TC(Q_1 + Q_2)$ is the total cost of jointly producing Q_1 units of the first good and Q_2 units of the second good. There are diseconomies of scope if this measure is negative, because the cost of producing the goods jointly is then greater than if they are produced separately. There are economies of scope if this measure is positive, because the cost of producing the goods jointly is then lower than if they are produced separately.

Economies of scope often occur because the production of various products uses common production facilities or other inputs. The production of cars and trucks may use the same sheet metal or engine-assembly facilities, for example. In other cases, economies of scope occur because the production of one product produces by-products that the producer can also sell or use. For example, a cattle producer may sell for leather the hides of its cattle that are raised for beef. Regardless of the reason for their existence, it is important to recognize that economies of scope can be significant.[2]

[2]For further discussion, see E. Bailey and A. Friedlander, "Market Structure and Multiproduct Industries: A Review Article," *Journal of Economic Literature*, September 1982.

TECHNOLOGICAL CHANGE, PRODUCTION, AND COSTS

An earlier section of this chapter examined cost-minimizing decisions for a wheat farmer who was equipped with a production function of the form

$$Q = (\text{constant}) A^{0.1} L^{0.1},$$

where A represented land and L represented labor. Figure 6.12 in the previous chapter also showed that neutral technological change would simply renumber the isoquants of this or any production function. Recall, for example, that 2 percent per year growth over 5 years would increase output by 10.41 percent, so that combinations of land and labor that used to produce 1,505 bushels of wheat would now sustain an output of 1,662 bushels. We can now combine the two examples to explore the implications of this sort of neutral technological change on costs.

We begin by examining whether or not neutral technological change would alter the cost-minimizing combinations of inputs. We noted earlier that $12,000 would be the minimum cost of producing 1,505 bushels of wheat with 2 units of labor and 30 acres of land if $P_A = $200 per acre and $P_L = $3,000 per summer. This was accomplished at point W in Figure 7.4. If neutral technological change at 2 percent per year increased output by 10.41 percent over the course of 5 years, however, then the marginal product of land would increase by the same 10.41 percent from 5 at point W to 5.52. But the marginal product of labor would also increase at point W by the same 10.41 percent from 75 to 82.81. As a result, the marginal rate of substitution at point W, now associated with 1,662 units of output, would still equal 15; i.e.,

$$MRS\,(\text{at } W) = \frac{82.81}{5.52} = 15.$$

Clearly, therefore, 2 units of labor and 30 acres of land would still minimize the cost of producing at point W; the only difference would be that output would be 10.41 percent higher.

We now know that a maximum of 1,662 bushels of wheat could be expected from an outlay of $12,000 after 5 years of technological change. Average cost would fall, as a result, by roughly 9.4 percent from $12,000/1,505 = $7.97 per bushel to $12,000/1,662 = $7.22.

THE MEASUREMENT OF COST FUNCTIONS

Economists have made a great many studies to estimate cost functions in particular firms and industries. These studies have typically been based on the statistical analysis of historical data regarding cost and output. Some studies have relied primarily on time-series data in which the output level of

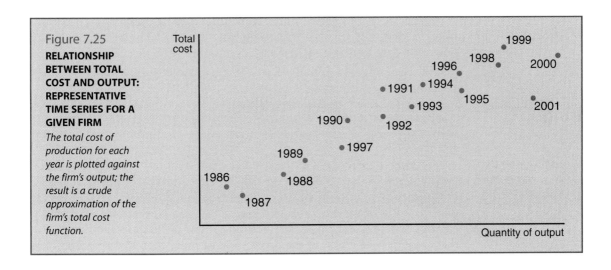

Figure 7.25

RELATIONSHIP BETWEEN TOTAL COST AND OUTPUT: REPRESENTATIVE TIME SERIES FOR A GIVEN FIRM

The total cost of production for each year is plotted against the firm's output; the result is a crude approximation of the firm's total cost function.

a firm is related to its costs. Figure 7.25, for example, plots the output level of a hypothetical firm against its costs in various years in the past. Other studies have relied primarily on cross-sectional data in which the output levels of various firms at a given point in time are related to their costs. Figure 7.26 illustrates these data by plotting the 2001 output of eight firms in a given hypothetical industry against their 2001 costs. Using data of this sort, as well as engineering data, economists have attempted to estimate the relationship between cost and output.

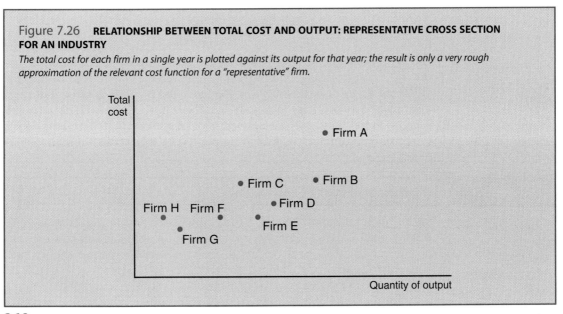

Figure 7.26   **RELATIONSHIP BETWEEN TOTAL COST AND OUTPUT: REPRESENTATIVE CROSS SECTION FOR AN INDUSTRY**

The total cost for each firm in a single year is plotted against its output for that year; the result is only a very rough approximation of the relevant cost function for a "representative" firm.

There are a number of important difficulties in estimating cost functions in this way. First of all, accounting data (which are generally the only cost data available) suffer from a number of deficiencies when used for this purpose. The time period used for accounting purposes generally is longer than the economist's short run. The depreciation of an asset over a period of time is determined largely by the tax laws, not by applying economic criteria. Many inputs are valued at historical, rather than alternative, cost. And accountants often use arbitrary allocations of overhead and joint costs.

Second, engineering data also suffer from important limitations. Engineering data, like cost accounting data, relate to processes within the firm. One difficulty in using them to estimate cost functions for an entire firm is that the costs of various processes may affect one another and may not be additive. There is also the inevitable arbitrariness involved in allocating costs that are jointly attached to the production of more than one commodity in multiproduct firms.

Third, cross-sectional studies are frequently thought to be contaminated by the so-called **regression fallacy.** What is that? It is often argued that the output produced and sold by the firm is only partly under the control of the firm, and that actual and expected output will differ. When firms are classified by actual output, firms with very high output levels are likely to be producing at unusually high levels, and, of course, firms with very low output levels are likely to be producing at unusually low levels. Since firms producing at unusually high levels of output are likely to be producing at lower unit costs than firms producing at unusually low levels of output, cross-sectional studies are likely to be biased. The argument holds, in short, that the observed cost of producing various output levels will be different from the minimum cost of producing those output levels.

Estimates of cost functions have nonetheless proven to be extremely useful, both to economists interested in promoting better managerial decisions and to economists interested in testing and extending economic theory. From the latter point of view, one of the most interesting conclusions of the empirical studies is that the long-run average-cost functions in most industries seem to be L-shaped (as in Figure 7.23) and not U-shaped. That is, there is no evidence that they turn upward as output expands. They seem, rather, to remain horizontal even at high output levels (that lie within the range of observation).

Example 7.7	**Empirical Estimates of Cost Curves**

As shown in Tables 7.5 and 7.6, empirical studies seem to indicate that marginal cost in the short run tends to be constant in the relevant output range. This result seems to be at variance with the theory presented here—a theory which holds that marginal-cost curves should be U-shaped. Critics have asserted that the empirical studies are biased toward constant marginal cost by the nature of accounting data and the statistical

Table 7.5   **RESULTS OF STUDIES OF COST FUNCTIONS: GENERAL INDUSTRY**

Author	Industry	Type	Period	Result
Johnson	Multiple product	TS	S	"Direct" cost is linearly related to output. MC is constant.
Dean	Leather belts	TS	S	Significantly increasing MC rejected by Dean.
Dean	Hosiery	TS	S	MC constant. SRAC "failed to rise."
Dean and James	Shoe stores	CS	L	LRAC is U-shaped (interpreted as not due to diseconomies of scale).
Holton	Retailing (Puerto Rico)	E	L	LRAC is L-shaped. But Holton argues that inputs of management may be undervalued at high outputs.
Ezekiel and Wylie	Steel	TS	S	MC declining, but large sampling errors.
Yntema	Steel	TS	S	MC constant.
Ehrke	Cement	TS	S	Ehrke interprets as constant MC. Apel argues that MC is increasing.
Nordin	Light plant	TS	S	MC is increasing.
Gupta	29 manufacturing industries (India)	CS	L	LRAC is L-shaped in 18 industries, U-shaped in 5, and linear in the rest.
Jansson and Schneerson	Shipping	CS	L	Economies of scale in hauling, but not in handling.
Norman	Cement	CS, E	L	Substantial economies of scale
Zagouris, Caouris, and Kantsos	Solar desalinization	E	L	Economies of scale
Daugherty and Nelson	Trucking	CS, TS	S	Effects of regulation
Allen and Liu	Motor carrier	CS	S	Estimates of scale economies

Note: MC = marginal cost, SRAC = short-run average cost, LRAC = long-run average cost, S = short run, L = long run, E = engineering data, CS = cross section, and TS = time series.
SOURCES: A. A. Walters, "Production and Cost Functions," *Econometrica,* January 1963; V. Gupta, "Cost Functions, Concentration, and Barriers to Entry in 29 Manufacturing Industries in India," *Journal of Industrial Economics,* 1968; J. Jansson and D. Schneerson, "Economies of Scale of General Cargo Ships," *Review of Economics and Statistics,* May 1978; G. Norman, "Economies of Scale in the Cement Industry," *Journal of Industrial Economics,* June 1979; N. Zagouris, Y. Caouris, and E. Kantsos, "Production and Cost Functions of Water Low-Temperature Solar Desalinization," *Applied Economics,* September 1989; A. Daugherty and F. Nelson, "An Econometric Analysis of the Trucking Industry," *Review of Economics and Statistics,* February 1988; and W. B. Allen and D. Liu, "Service Quality and Motor Carrier Costs," *Review of Economics and Statistics,* August 1995.

methods used. Others have argued that the data used in these studies often do not cover periods when the firm was operating at the peak of its capacity. Although marginal costs may well be relatively constant over a wide range, it is inconceivable that they do not eventually increase with increases in output. Example 7.6 reported on some recent theoretical work by Richard Miller that reconciled the fundamental theory with these empirical results.

Table 7.6 RESULTS OF STUDIES OF COST FUNCTIONS: PUBLIC UTILITIES

Author	Industries	Type	Result
Nerlove	Electricity (U.S.A.)	CS	LRAC excluding transmission costs declines, then shows signs of increasing.
Johnston	Coal (UK)	CS	Wide dispersion of costs per ton
Johnston	Road passenger transport (UK)	CS	LRAC either falling or constant.
Johnston	Life assurance	CS	LRAC declines.
McNulty	Electricity (U.S.A.)	CS	Average costs of administration are constant.
Dhrymes and Kurz	Electricity (U.S.A.)	CS, TS	Substantial economies of scale
Eads, Nerlove, and Raduchel	Airlines (U.S.A.)	CS, TS	No evidence of substantial economies of scale
Knapp	Sewage purification (UK)	CS	Significant economies of scale up to 10 million gallons daily
Stevens	Refuse collection (U.S.A.)	CS	Considerable economies of scale in cities up to 20,000 population
Borts	Railways (U.S.A.)	CS	LRAC increasing in East, decreasing in South and West.
Broster	Railways (UK)	TS	Operating cost per unit of output falls.
Mansfield and Wein	Railways (U.S.A.)	TS	MC is constant.
Griliches	Railways (U.S.A.)	CS	No significant economies of scale to an indiscriminate expansion of traffic
Caves, Christensen, and Swanson	Railways (U.S.A.)	CS	Economies of scale
Friedlander and Spady	Railways (U.S.A.)	CS	Economies of scale
Harmatuck	Railways (U.S.A.)	CS	Economies of scale
Harris	Railways (U.S.A.)	CS	Economies of scale
Keeler	Railways (U.S.A.)	CS	Economies of scale
Sidhu, Charney, and Due	Railways (U.S.A.)	CS	Economies of scale

Note: CS = cross section, TS = time series, LRAC = long-run average cost, MC = marginal cost.
SOURCES: A. A. Walters, "Production and Cost Functions," *Econometrica,* January 1963; P. Dhrymes and M. Kurz, "Technology and Scale in Electricity Generation," *Econometrica,* July 1964; G. Eads, M. Nerlove, and W. Raduchel, "A Long-Run Cost Function for the Local Service Airline Industry," *Review of Economics and Statistics,* August 1969; Z. Griliches, "Railroad Cost Analysis," *Bell Journal of Economics and Management Science,* 1972; M. Knapp, "Economies of Scale in Sewage Purification and Disposal," *Journal of Industrial Economics,* December 1978; B. Stevens, "Scale, Market Structure, and the Cost of Refuse Collection," *Review of Economics and Statistics,* August 1978; D. Caves, L. Christensen, and J. Swanson, "Productivity Growth, Scale Economies and Capacity Utilization in U.S. Railroads, 1955–74," *American Economic Review,* December 1981; A. Friedlander and R. Spady, *Freight Transport Regulation* (Cambridge, Mass.: MIT Press, 1981); D. Harmatuck, "A Policy-Sensitive Railway Cost Function," *Logistics and Transportation Review,* May 1979; R. Harris, "Rationalizing the Rail Freight Industry," University of California, Berkeley, 1977; T. Keeler, "Railroad Costs, Returns to Scale, and Excess Capacity," *Review of Economics and Statistics,* May 1974; N. Sidhu, A. Charney, and J. Due, "Cost Functions of Class II Railroads and the Viability of Light Traffic Density Railway Lines," *Quarterly Review of Economics and Business,* Autumn 1977; R. Braeutigam, A. Daughety, and M. Turnquist, "The Estimation of a Hybrid Cost Function for a Railroad Firm," *Review of Economics and Statistics,* August 1982; S. Jara-Diaz and C. Winston, "Multiproduct Transportation Cost Functions: Scale and Scope in Railroad Operations," Massachusetts Institute of Technology, 1981; and T. Keeler, *Railroads, Freight, and Public Policy* (Washington, D.C.: Brookings Institution, 1983).

1. To minimize the cost of producing a given level of output, a firm must combine inputs so that the marginal product of a dollar's worth of any one input is equal to the marginal product of a dollar's worth of any other input employed. The optimal combination of inputs can be determined graphically by superimposing the relevant isocost curves on the firm's isoquant map. The cost-minimizing combination is defined by the point at which the relevant isoquant touches the lowest isocost curve; it is a point of tangency.

2. The cost of producing a certain product is the value of the other products that the resources used in its production could have produced instead. This is the alternative cost or opportunity cost doctrine. The opportunity cost of an input may not be equal to its historical cost, and it is likely to be smaller in the short run than in the long run.

3. The social costs of producing a given commodity do not always equal the private costs. In making decisions, costs incurred in the past and costs that are the same for all alternative courses of action may be irrelevant.

4. A cost function is a relation between a firm's costs and its output rate. The firm's production function and the prices it pays for inputs determine a firm's cost function; it reflects the minimum cost that must be incurred to sustain production at a designated level.

5. Seven concepts of cost are important in the short run: total fixed costs, total variable costs, total costs, average fixed costs, average variable costs, average costs, and marginal costs.

6. The short-run average-cost function decreases at first, but eventually it turns up because of the law of diminishing marginal returns. Similarly, the marginal-cost curve eventually turns up for the same reason. The short-run marginal-cost curve intersects the short-run average-cost curve at the minimum of the average-cost curve.

7. The long run is perhaps best viewed as a planning horizon. Economies and diseconomies of scale affect the shape of the long-run average-cost function. The long-run average-cost curve is likely to decrease up to some point because of economies of scale. As output becomes greater and greater, though, it is often stated that diseconomies of scale will eventually appear; if that happens, the long-run average-cost curve will turn upward. The shape of the long-run average-cost curve in a particular industry is of great importance from the viewpoint of public policy.

8. Many studies have estimated the cost functions of particular firms and industries. These studies have typically been based on historical data regarding cost and output. Accounting data, which are generally the only cost data available, suffer from a number of deficiencies when used for this purpose.

9. One of the most interesting conclusions of these studies is that the long-run average-cost curve seems to be L-shaped. However, the evidence is limited. Another interesting conclusion is that the short-run marginal-cost function often seems to be horizontal, not U-shaped.

1. The National Academy of Engineering has reported that the long-run average total cost of producing an aircraft would increase by about 35 percent if 350 units were produced instead of the originally targeted run of 700. From the end of World War II to the 1990s, the number of prime manufacturers of large commercial aircraft decreased from 22 to a few. Are these

two facts related? If so, how? Sales agreements concluded at the 1999 Paris Airshow seem to signal an increase in demand for commercial aircraft. Might this portend a reversal in this downward trend in the number of independent manufacturers? What effect would increased uncertainty about travel demand have on your answer?

2. Fill in the blanks in the table. Assume that the resulting data were derived from cost minimization given a production function of the form $X = K^a L^b$, where K and L represent capital and labor, respectively. Each of the inputs is available at a constant price. Fixed cost is determined by capital only.

Output of X	Total cost (dollars)	Total fixed cost (dollars)	Total variable cost (dollars)	Average fixed cost (dollars)	Average variable cost (dollars)
0	50	—	—	—	—
1	70	—	—	—	—
2	100	—	—	—	—
3	120	—	—	—	—
4	135	—	—	—	—
5	150	—	—	—	—
6	160	—	—	—	—
7	165	—	—	—	—

Suppose that the price of one or more important input(s) increased so much that each of the total cost figures rose by 50 percent. What effect would this have on the value of marginal cost? Would this effect necessarily mean that the price of K must have increased? Would it necessarily mean that the price of L must have also increased? If so, was the increase in L at the same rate as the increase in the price of K?

3. According to the U.S. Department of Agriculture, 8,500 pounds of milk can be produced by a cow fed the following combinations of hay and grain:

Quantity of hay (pounds)	Quantity of grain (pounds)
5,000	6,154
5,500	5,454
6,000	4,892
6,500	4,423
7,000	4,029
7,500	3,694

(a) If the price of a pound of hay equals one-half the price of a pound of grain (which equals P), what is the cost of each combination? What is the minimum-cost combination (of those shown in the table)? (b) Plot the isocost curves and the isoquant. Use this graph to determine the minimum-cost combination. Compare your results with those obtained in part (a).

4. The economist T. Yntema estimated the short-run total cost function of the United States Steel Corporation (now USX Corporation) in the 1930s to be $C = 182.1 + 55.73Q$, where C is total annual cost (in millions of dollars) and Q is millions of tons of steel produced. (a) What was U.S. Steel's fixed cost? (b) If U.S. Steel produced 10 million tons of steel, what

was its average variable cost? (c) What was U.S. Steel's marginal cost? (d) Do you think that this equation provided a faithful representation of U.S. Steel's short-run total-cost function, regardless of the value of Q? (e) If you needed to estimate this firm's marginal cost in 2002, would you use this equation?

5. The accompanying graph shows the average total cost of producing a ton of ammonia using the partial oxidation process and the steam re-forming process, with plants of various sizes (as measured by daily capacities). Curve C pertains, in particular, to the partial oxidation process when naphtha is used as a raw material. Curve D, meanwhile, pertains to the steam re-forming process when naphtha is used as a raw material, and curve E pertains to the steam re-forming process when natural gas is used as a raw material. (a) Can the short-run cost function for ammonia be derived from this graph? (b) This graph assumes that naphtha costs $0.008 per pound and natural gas costs $0.20 per cubic foot; if this assumption is true, which process should be used? (c) Does this graph suggest that there are economies of scale in ammonia production? (d) The graph pertains to conditions in the early 1960s. In the late 1960s, a new process for producing ammonia was introduced. Using this new process, a plant with a capacity of 1,400 tons per day had an average cost of about $16 per ton. Did the long-run cost function for the production of ammonia shift between the early and late 1960s?

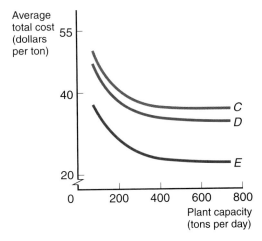

6. A plant producing a component for commercial buses can produce any number of these components (up to 100 per week) at a total cost of $100, but it cannot produce more than 100 per week, regardless of how much its costs are. Graph its marginal-cost curve. Suggest why few (if any) plants in the real world have a marginal-cost curve of this sort.

7. Suppose that a semiconductor plant's production function is $Q = 5LK$, where Q is its output rate, L is the amount of labor it uses per period of time, and K is the amount of capital it uses per period of time. Suppose that the price of labor is $1 a unit and the price of capital is $2 a unit. The firm's vice president for manufacturing hires you to figure out what combination of inputs the plant should use to produce 40 units of output per period. What advice would you give?

8. Show that the long-run total-cost curve is a straight line from the origin if production displays constant returns to scale. Interpret the constant slope of such a line. What would the long-run cost curve look like if production displayed decreasing returns to scale? Increasing returns to scale?

9. Manufacturers frequently produce intermediate parts that are integrated eventually into their final products. They set up intermediate production processes every time they need to replenish their inventories of these parts. Japanese manufacturers discovered a trade-off between the cost of setting up production processes and the cost of maintaining inventories in the 1950s. The accompanying figure below reflects their insight. The annual cost of setup declines with the number of parts produced with each setup—the "lot size." This relationship is displayed by the downward-sloping "setup cost" curve. The cost of maintaining inventories that are eventually depleted is proportional to the number of parts included in each lot. This relationship is reflected by the upward-sloping "cost of carrying inventory" curve. Total cost, the sum of these two components, is therefore U-shaped. The figure shows that total costs are minimized when the lot size of each run is set at 70,711 units. (a) Use the figure to show that the cost-minimizing lot size would climb if setup costs rose. (b) Use the figure to show that the cost-minimizing lot size would also climb if the cost of carrying inventories fell. (c) Suppose that the manufacturer of a digital camera incurred a setup cost of $100,000 each time that it began to produce a particular part. Compute setup costs if 50,000 parts are required each year and the manufacturer chose a lot size of 10,000. (d) Compute the average level of inventory held by this manufacturer over the course of the entire year. (e) Let the cost of carrying inventory be $2 per part. What is the sum of annual setup cost and annual inventory-carrying cost? (f) Is 10,000 the cost-minimizing lot size? If so, why? If not, what is?

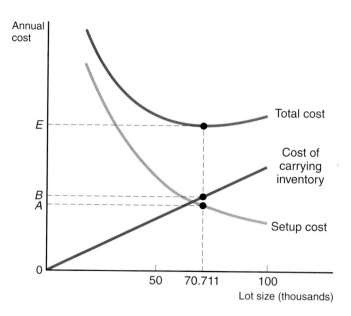

10. Suppose that production in the short run with 5 units of capital were represented by this table:

Output	Capital input	Labor input
0	5	0
8	5	1
15	5	2
21	5	3
26	5	4
30	5	5
32	5	6
33	5	7

Assume that the price of capital is $15 per unit and that labor is paid $6 per unit. (a) Compute and plot short-run marginal- and average-cost curves. (b) What would happen to both curves if only the price of labor doubled? Graph the new curves in a different color. (c) What would happen to both curves if only the price of capital doubled? Graph the new curves in yet a different color. (d) Now assume that overall productivity increases by 50 percent for every input combination. What would happen to both curves then, assuming the original prices for capital and labor?

Calculus Appendix

COST FUNCTIONS—DEFINITIONS AND RESULTS

Let the cost of producing some good X be the sum of fixed costs F and variable costs $V(X)$ so that we can summarize total costs as

$$C(X) = F + V(X).$$

Average cost, denoted $AC(X)$, is then

$$AC(X) = \frac{C(X)}{X} = \frac{F}{X} + \frac{V(X)}{X}.$$

In other words, average cost is the sum of average fixed cost F/X and average variable cost $V(X)/X$. This identity can be represented notationally as

$$AC(X) = AF(X) + AV(X).$$

Note in passing that average fixed cost depends on output even though fixed cost does not. Also remember that fixed costs are zero in the long run because all costs are then variable.

The marginal cost of producing any amount of X, denoted $MC(X)$, is simply the derivative of total costs with respect to output. Since fixed costs are constant, however,

$$MC(X) \equiv \frac{dC(X)}{dX} = \frac{dVC(X)}{dX}.$$

Moreover, application of the quotient rule shows that

$$\frac{dAC(X)}{dX} = \frac{X[dC(X)/dX] - C(X)(dX/dX)}{X^2}$$

$$= \frac{MC(X) - C(X)/X}{X}$$

$$= \frac{MC(X) - AC(X)}{X}.$$

As a result, average cost reaches a minimum where $MC(X) = AC(X)$, so that $dAC(X)/dX = 0$. The very same logic implies that average variable cost reaches its minimum where $MC(X) = AVC(X)$.

DERIVING COST FUNCTIONS FROM PRODUCTION FUNCTIONS

Cost functions reflect the *minimum* cost of producing any level of output given a production technology and given specific input prices. Suppose, for example, that the production function for some good X is given by $X = F(K, L)$, where K and L are capital and labor, respectively. The appropriate Lagrangian for minimizing the cost of producing an arbitrary output X_0 is then

$$\Gamma(K, L, \lambda) = rK + wL + \lambda[X_0 - F(K, L)]$$

where r and w are the unit costs of capital and labor. The corresponding first-order conditions are

$$K: \quad \frac{\partial \Gamma}{\partial K} = r - \lambda F_K(K, L) = 0; \text{ i.e., } r = \lambda MP_K \qquad [1a]$$

$$L: \quad \frac{\partial \Gamma}{\partial L} = w - \lambda F_L(K, L) = 0; \text{ i.e., } w = \lambda MP_L \qquad [1b]$$

$$\lambda: \quad \frac{\partial \Gamma}{\partial \lambda} = X_0 - F(K, L) = 0. \qquad [1c]$$

The first two (Equations 1a and 1b) combine to set

$$\frac{r}{MP_K} = \frac{w}{MP_L} = \lambda. \qquad [2]$$

Equation 2 expresses the marginal cost of income in terms of ratios of input prices and their marginal products. Rearranging,

$$\frac{MP_L}{MP_K} = \frac{w}{r}. \qquad [3]$$

Equation 3 again characterizes all combinations of K and L for which $MRTS = r/w$, i.e., all of the combinations of K and L for which the ratio of the marginal products equals the corresponding ratio of input prices.

One might also approach the problem as one of maximizing output for a specific expenditure C_0. The appropriate Lagrangian would then be

$$\Gamma(K, L, \lambda) = F(K, L) + \lambda(C_0 - rK - wL).$$

First-order conditions would then require that

$$K: \quad \frac{\partial \Gamma}{\partial K} = F_K(K, L) - \lambda r = 0; \text{ i.e., } r = \lambda MP_K \qquad [4a]$$

$$L: \quad \frac{\partial \Gamma}{\partial L} = F_L(K, L) - \lambda w = 0; \text{ i.e., } w = \lambda MP_L \qquad [4b]$$

$$\lambda: \quad \frac{\partial \Gamma}{\partial \lambda} = C_0 - rK - wL = 0. \qquad [4c]$$

Notice that Equations 4a and 4b duplicate equations 1a and 1b. Both sets reduce to the same condition—that the $MRTS$ must be set equal to the input price ratio, i.e., that

$$MRTS = \frac{MP_L}{MP_K} = \frac{w}{r}.$$

If the output level is the same, therefore, the employment levels of K and L that would maximize output subject to a cost constraint would be the same as the employment levels of K and L that would minimize the cost of producing that output.

COST FUNCTIONS WITH COBB-DOUGLAS PRODUCTION—AN ILLUSTRATION

A Cobb-Douglas Production function with constant returns to scale sets $X = F(K, L) = K^\alpha L^{1-\alpha}$. The appropriate Lagrangian for cost minimization subject to an arbitrary output constraint X_0 is then

$$\Gamma(K, L, \lambda) = rK + wL + \lambda(X_0 - K^\alpha L^{1-\alpha})$$

The corresponding first-order conditions are

$$K: \quad \frac{\partial \Gamma}{\partial K} = r - \lambda \alpha K^{\alpha-1} L^{1-\alpha} = 0; \text{ i.e., } r = \lambda MP_K \qquad [1a']$$

$$L: \quad \frac{\partial \Gamma}{\partial L} = w - \lambda(1 - \alpha)K^\alpha L^{-\alpha} = 0; \; w = \lambda MP_L \qquad [1b']$$

$$\lambda: \quad \frac{\partial \Gamma}{\partial \lambda} = X_0 - K^\alpha L^{1-\alpha} = 0. \qquad [1c']$$

The first two (Equations 1a' and 1b') combine to set

$$\frac{r}{MP_K} = \frac{r}{\alpha K^{\alpha-1}L^{1-\alpha}} = \frac{w}{MP_L} = \frac{w}{(1-\alpha)K^{\alpha}L^{-\alpha}} = \lambda. \qquad [2']$$

Equation 2' expresses the marginal cost of income in terms of ratios of input prices and their marginal products. Rearranging,

$$\frac{MP_L}{MP_K} = \frac{(1-\alpha)K^{\alpha}L^{-\alpha}}{\alpha K^{\alpha-1}L^{1-\alpha}} = \frac{w}{r}. \qquad [3']$$

Equation 3' again characterizes all combinations of K and L for which $MRTS = w/r$. It can be rewritten as

$$\frac{K}{L} = \frac{\alpha}{1-\alpha}\frac{w}{r} \qquad [4]$$

so that

$$K = \frac{\alpha}{1-\alpha}\frac{w}{r}L. \qquad [5]$$

Equation 5 describes a straight line from the origin with slope $[\alpha/(1-\alpha)]$ (w/r); it is called the *output expansion path*. Its intersection with the isoquant for the output constraint indicates the solution to the problem. More precisely, substituting Equation 5 into the replication of the production function constraint imposed by first-order condition 1c',

$$X = \left(\frac{\alpha}{1-\alpha}\frac{w}{r}L\right)^{\alpha}L^{1-\alpha} = \left(\frac{\alpha}{1-\alpha}\frac{w}{r}\right)^{\alpha}L$$

so that the derived demand for labor as a function of X is

$$L(r, w; X) = X\left(\frac{1-\alpha}{\alpha}\frac{r}{w}\right)^{\alpha}. \qquad [6a]$$

It follows from Equation 4' that

$$K(r, w; X) = \frac{\alpha}{1-\alpha}\frac{w}{r}L(r, w; X) = X\left(\frac{1-\alpha}{\alpha}\frac{r}{w}\right)^{\alpha-1}. \qquad [6b]$$

APPLICATION: THE LONG-RUN COST FUNCTION IN A COBB-DOUGLAS CASE

Economists define the long-run cost of producing any output X as the minimum expenditure required to sustain that output. It relates this minimum expenditure required to produce this output for different input prices under the long-run assumption that all inputs are variable:

$$C_{LR}(X; r, w) = rK(r, w; X) + wL(r, w; X)$$

where $K(r, w; X)$ and $L(r, w; X)$ simply indicate notationally that the cost-minimizing levels of employment for both capital and labor in the long run depend on input prices r and w for any level of output X.

Illustration. Let $X = K^{1/2}L^{1/2}$ so that Equations 6a and 6b indicate that

$$L(r, w; X) = X\left(\frac{1 - \frac{1}{2}}{\frac{1}{2}}\frac{r}{w}\right)^{1/2} = X\left(\frac{r}{w}\right)^{1/2}$$

and

$$K(r, w; X) = X\left(\frac{1 - \frac{1}{2}}{\frac{1}{2}}\frac{w}{r}\right)^{1/2} = X\left(\frac{w}{r}\right)^{1/2}.$$

As a result, the long-run cost function is

$$C_{LR}(X; r, w) = rX\left(\frac{w}{r}\right)^{1/2} + wX\left(\frac{r}{w}\right)^{1/2} = 2X(wr)^{1/2}.$$

Note that fixed costs are zero and that total costs match variable costs. Also note that

$$MC(X) = AC(X) = AVC(X) = 2(wr)^{1/2}.$$

The first equation holds generally in the long run; that it collapses to

$$C_{LR}(X; r, w) = 2(wr)^{1/2}X$$

is a specific result for the given production function.

APPLICATION: THE SHORT-RUN COST FUNCTION IN A COBB-DOUGLAS CASE

Economists define the short-run cost of producing any output X as the minimum expenditure required to sustain that output, given that the employment of at least one input is fixed. It relates the minimum expenditure required to produce this output for different input prices under the short-run assumption that fixed costs exist. For the two-input case and a fixed amount of capital K_0,

$$X = F(K_0, L(X; K_0))$$

implicitly defines $L(X; K_0)$ that satisfies the output condition. As a result, short-run costs are

$$C_{SR}(X; r, w) = rK_0 + wL(X; K_0).$$

Illustration continued. For $X = K^{1/2}L^{1/2}$,

$$X = K_0^{1/2}L^{1/2} \Rightarrow X^2 = K_0L \quad \text{so that} \quad L(X; K_0) = \frac{X^2}{K_0}$$

and

$$C_{SR}(X; r, w) = rK_0 + w\frac{X^2}{K_0}.$$

In the short run, therefore,

- Fixed cost is $FC = rK_0$.
- Average fixed cost is $AFC(X) = r(K_0/X)$.
- Variable cost is $VC(X) = w(X^2/K_0)$.
- Average variable cost is $AVC(X) = w(X/K_0)$.
- Average (total) cost is $AC(X) = AFVC(X) + AVC(X) = r(K_0/X) + w(X/K_0)$.
- Marginal cost is $MC(X) = \partial C_{SR}(X; r, w)/\partial X = 2w(X/K_0)$.

Convince yourself that the minimum of this short-run average cost is, in this specific case, equal to

$$C_{LR}(X; r, w) = 2(wr)^{1/2}.$$

Technological Advances

We have spent the last two chapters describing how production functions reflect technology, how they support the creation of equally instructive cost curves, and how the representation of either can capture dynamic technological change. In short, we have seen that production functions are the foundation of the supply side of any market. But can they offer us more than that? Can the intuition that underlies the relationship between technology and cost provide any insight into what the future might hold, especially if the extraordinary pace of innovation that we have experienced over the last few decades continues? We close Part Three by focusing attention on one specific illustration for which the answer to this question is decidedly affirmative. We will, in particular, show that the falling cost of storing information on disk drives could pose extraordinary legal and economic questions for future societies even if expanding demand may not keep pace with expanding capacity.

SOME HISTORICAL BACKGROUND

IBM built the first disk drive in 1956 as part of a business machine named RAMAC (Random Access Method for Accounting and Control). It took up about as much space as a refrigerator, and it was powered by a motor that could have run a small cement mixer. Fifty aluminum disks that could turn at a speed of 1,200 revolutions per minute served as its core, and the entire unit had a capacity of about 5 megabytes—just about enough for a few MP3 recordings in today's world.

You might not be very impressed. Disk drives of the early 1990s held about 120 megabytes, but the ones that you can buy on-line today hold 1,000 times that amount for half the price. Don't be too quick to judge, however. The latest disk drives work much like the first one—reading and writing heads hover over the surface of spinning platters to read or record digital (zero-one) signals. Indeed, it is said that an engineer from the original RAMAC project would have little problem understanding how the new drives work. The only difference seems to be scale. Your brand-new disk drive has three 3.5-inch platters—meaning that the surface area of the core has contracted by a factor of 800—but their information capacity has increased by 24,000 times. Putting these figures together, the number of bytes held per square inch in your disk drive is nearly 20 million times higher than the RAMAC prototype ($800 \times 24,000 = 19,200,000$).

ECONOMIC IMPLICATIONS

How did they do it? Much of the progress can be attributed to scale effects—everything now is *much* smaller. Additionally, your new drive has two heads. Old-style electromagnetic heads are still used for writing, but the reading mode now uses a "magnetoresistive" head that was introduced by IBM in 1991 and significantly improved in 1997. Both of these innovations can be detected by changes in the slope of the line drawn in Figure 1—a portrait of the growth in memory density over time. Density increased at a compound rate of about 25 percent per year through the 1970s and 1980s (doubling every three years), but it increased to 60 percent per year between

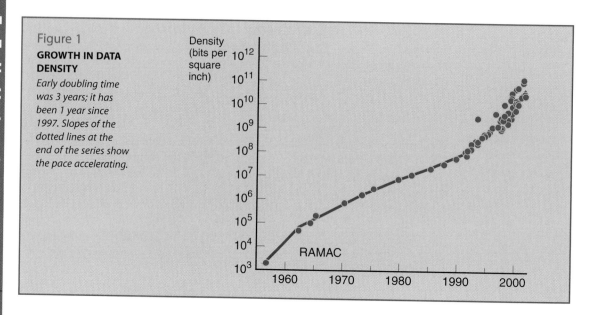

Figure 1

GROWTH IN DATA DENSITY

Early doubling time was 3 years; it has been 1 year since 1997. Slopes of the dotted lines at the end of the series show the pace accelerating.

Density (bits per square inch)

RAMAC

1991 and 1997. The pace quickened even more after 1997 to 100 percent per year; i.e., capacity has doubled in each of the last five years. Had the original pace persisted, we would now have 1 gigabyte of memory in every square inch of disk. Instead, we enjoy the services of 100 gigabytes over the same area.

Figure 2 reflects this history in terms of cost. A megabyte of memory in the original RAMAC configuration cost about $10,000. That cost fell to around $100 in the 1980s and to roughly $10 in the mid 1990s and to less than a penny by the year 2000. Indeed, the cost of storing information on disk is now less than the cost of using paper or film for the same function.

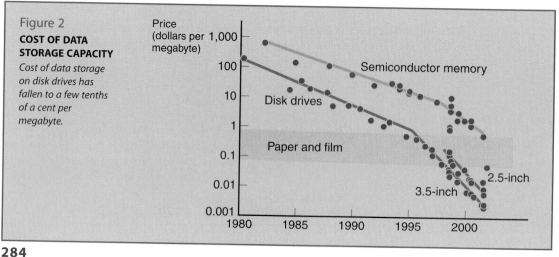

Figure 2

COST OF DATA STORAGE CAPACITY

Cost of data storage on disk drives has fallen to a few tenths of a cent per megabyte.

Price (dollars per megabyte)

Semiconductor memory

Disk drives

Paper and film

3.5-inch

2.5-inch

Will the trend continue at the same pace? Two new technologies hold some significant promise. One, using the element ruthenium, is already in use. Commercially available drives now offer 34 gigabytes per square inch, and laboratory versions have surpassed 100 gigabytes. The green dots on Figure 1 show the commercial options, and the red dots record laboratory prototypes; widespread use of the latter will produce yet another kink in the curve. When, as expected, the conventional disk-platter technology does reach its limit, though, perpendicular recording that works at an atomic level should become available. Small demonstration projects already exist, and it is expected that disks capable of holding 120 terabytes of information per square inch will be available by 2012 or so.

What is the point? Will this progress continue to be driven by demand? Probably not, because you would have a lot of trouble using that much memory. You could read and save a book a day for 80 years and use less than 1 percent of a disk with a capacity of 120 terabytes. You could take 100 high-resolution pictures a day for 80 years with a digital camera and use only 25 percent to save the entire set. You could copy MP3s all day every day for 80 years and use only 33 percent. The entire contents of the Library of Congress would occupy less than 25 percent. Video recording is the only current use that might hit the capacity constraint—all day, every day recording would use all 120 terabytes in a little more than 7 years.

FUTURE CONSEQUENCES

Absent a new source of demand, like automatic video recording of your life as it unfolds by cameras in your glasses, demand will not drive further development in memory technology. But this does not mean that it will not happen; and it certainly does not mean that there will not be consequences. Forget, for a moment, about the absurdity of trying to use 120 terabytes over a lifetime. Think instead about trying to buy enough stuff to fill even a small fraction of that capacity. When you do, you will realize that providing capacity of this magnitude will put enormous downward pressure on the prices of books, music, film, and other forms of intellectual and artistic property. Expressed in the jargon of economics, pricing products far above the medium by which they are distributed may not be a sustainable equilibrium.

We have already seen how such an equilibrium might begin to dissolve on a small scale. Remember the trouble that Napster caused by offering MP3s over the Internet for free. That experience taught us that it is quite possible that the prices of these sorts of properties could fall as fast as the cost of memory toward a "not inconceivable" limit of zero. What's wrong with that, you might ask. The music industry sued to stop Napster from offering free recordings to protect its royalties and its profitability, to be sure; but it argued its case on the basis of economic incentives. Why should people work to produce good music (or literature, or ideas) if they will not be rewarded for their efforts? In short, if the marginal cost of producing artistic and/or intellectual property is higher than the reward, then it will be underprovided.

Here, then, lies a challenge for society. How can we augment our economic system so that we can take advantage of technological innovation without undercutting the incentive to advance our knowledge? It will be an enormous challenge driven by falling prices for some critical components of our technological environment. Will the price of disk memory fall close to zero? Perhaps, but perhaps not. Be warned that the last time people spoke of technological change producing something for free, they were speaking from the Eisenhower administration about electricity produced from nuclear power plants.

SOURCE: Brian Hayes, "Terabyte Territory," *American Scientist*, vol. 90, no. 4, May–June 2002, pp. 212–216.

QUESTIONS

1. Rapid technological advances of the sort described here drastically reduce cost. Do they also reduce marginal cost?

2. Consider a production process that uses information intensively. We now know that the productivity of this input has risen significantly over time. Suppose that there has been no corresponding technological change in the productivity of other inputs. Draw some old and new isoquants for several different cases—at least one where data storage needs are directly proportional to the employment of other inputs and another where there is some possible substitution between the two. We have also tracked the cost of information-storage technology; it has fallen dramatically. Does that mean necessarily that the new cost-minimizing combination would use more data storage in proportion with other inputs?

3. Discuss more fully the problems associated with a precipitous decline in value of intellectual and artistic property rights. Construct at least a heuristic model to explain why intellectual and artistic property might or might not become underprovided if these values were to fall even a little. Be precise in defining the benchmark against which you are measuring "underprovision."

4. Can you think of reasons why technological change has been so rapid in data storage and other digital contexts and so slow (relatively) in energy conservation and environmental preservation techniques?

Market Structure, Price, and Output

Perfect Competition

INTRODUCTION

The United States produced about 2,527 million bushels of wheat in 1998. The price was about $2.90 per bushel, although it varied from week to week. Why did the United States produce this much? Why was this generally the price? To answer these questions, you must understand how markets work. Some preliminary answers to these questions were provided in Chapter 1, but Chapters 8 to 12 will cover this topic in much greater detail. We will distinguish between various types of markets. Economists have found it useful to classify markets into four general types: perfect competition, monopoly, monopolistic competition, and oligopoly. This classification is based largely on the number of firms in the industry that supplies the product and on the ability of consumers to distinguish between the products of the few or many firms that supply a market. There are many sellers in perfect competition and monopolistic competition; each firm produces only a small portion of the industry's output in these cases. At the other extreme, the industry consists of only a single, monopoly firm. Oligopoly is an intermediate case in which there are a few sellers.

This chapter is devoted to an investigation of how price and output are determined in perfectly competitive markets. Monopoly, monopolistic competition, and oligopoly are taken up in subsequent chapters. The analysis in this chapter builds on a synthesis of the topics discussed in previous chapters. We emphasized the important role played by the market demand and market supply curves in Chapter 1. In Chapter 4, we used the tools of Chapters 2 and 3 to show how a product's market demand curve can be derived. We will now use the tools introduced in Chapters 6 and 7 to show how a product's market supply curve can be derived. Armed with these constructions, we will be able to discuss in detail the way in which the demand and supply sides of the market interact to determine the equilibrium price and output of the firm and the industry in both the short run and the long run.

PERFECT COMPETITION

What does an economist mean by perfect competition? Students sometimes find it difficult to grasp at first because the economist's view is quite different from the concept of competition used by their relatives and friends in the business world. When business executives speak of a highly competitive market, they generally mean a market where each firm is keenly aware of its rivalry with a few others and where advertising, packaging, styling, and other competitive weapons are used to attract business. The basic feature of the economist's definition of perfect competition is, in stark contrast, its impersonality. No firm views another as a competitor in the economist's view because there are so many suppliers in the industry. One small wheat farmer hardly ever views another small wheat farmer as a competitor.

Perfect competition

Perfect competition is, more specifically, defined by four conditions. First, perfect competition requires that the *product of any one seller be the same as the product of any other seller.* This is an important condition because it makes sure that buyers do not care whether they purchase the product from one seller or another as long as the price is the same.

Second, perfect competition requires that *each participant in the market, whether a buyer or a seller, be so small in relation to the entire market that he or she cannot affect the product's price.* No buyer can be large enough to wrangle a better price from the sellers, and no seller can be large enough to influence the price by altering his or her output rate. All producers acting together to change output will certainly affect price, but any producer acting alone cannot do so. Recall from Chapter 4 that this means that the firm's demand curve is horizontal.

Perfect competition also requires that *all resources be completely mobile.* Each resource must, in other words, be able to enter or leave the market with ease and to switch from one use to another without fuss or bother.[1] So, labor must be able to move from region to region and from job to job. Raw materials cannot be monopolized. New firms can enter an industry at will, and existing firms can leave an industry without serious consequence. Needless to say, this condition is not often fulfilled in a world where considerable retraining is required to allow a worker to move from one job to another and where patents, large investment requirements, and economies of scale make the entry of new firms difficult.

Finally, perfect competition requires that consumers, firms, and resource owners have *perfect knowledge of the relevant economic and technological data.* Consumers must be aware of all prices. Laborers and owners of capital must be aware of how much their resources will bring in all possible uses. Firms must know the prices of all inputs and the characteristics of all relevant technologies. And in its purest sense, perfect competition requires that all of

---

[1]This does not mean that these sorts of resource reallocations do not take time. In the short run, many resources cannot be transferred from one use to another.

these economic decision-making units have an accurate knowledge of the past, the present, *and the future*.

It should be obvious that no industry is perfectly competitive, but this does not mean that the study of the behavior of perfectly competitive markets is useless. Recall from Chapter 1 that a model may be quite useful even though some of its assumptions are unrealistic. The conclusions derived from the model of perfect competition have proven to be very useful in explaining and predicting behavior in the real world, and they have permitted a reasonably accurate view of resource allocation in important segments of our economy.

Example 8.1 **Experimenting with Competitive Markets**

Vernon Smith and others have conducted a variety of simple experiments designed to explore how competitive markets work. The subjects (often college students) trade a commodity with no intrinsic value. Buyers earn economic profit by making purchases from other subjects and reselling their "take" to the experimenter. Sellers earn economic profit by buying units from the experimenter and selling them to the buyers. The terms of trade with the experimenter are known, and they work to determine supply and demand curves.

In one of Smith's experiments, an auction was held in which public bids and offers were articulated. There were five trading periods, and each participant was free to accept or reject whatever terms he or she chose. Figure 8.1 displays the supply and demand curves in the left panel, and the right panel plots the price of every sale in order. The competitive price was clearly

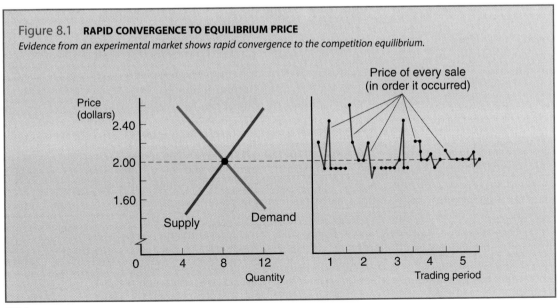

Figure 8.1 **RAPID CONVERGENCE TO EQUILIBRIUM PRICE**
Evidence from an experimental market shows rapid convergence to the competition equilibrium.

$2, and the actual price converged relatively quickly—always within 10 percent of the equilibrium from the fourth trading period.

Was this a competitive market? Not really, because there were only a few participants. Results from other experiments varied with the number of participants and with how the market was organized, but the "not bad" criterion of Chapter 1 seems to be met more often than not.[2] In particular, the competitive equilibrium is generally a reasonable approximation to the eventual outcome even though the number of buyers and sellers was not very large.

PRICE DETERMINATION IN THE SHORT RUN

▣ Output of the Firm

We begin our exploration of the rarified environment of perfect competition by exploring the output decisions of an economic profit-maximizing competitive firm in the short run. The firm can expand or contract its output rate in the short run by increasing or decreasing the rate at which it employs its variable inputs. Since the market is perfectly competitive, the firm cannot affect the price of its product, but any competitive firm can sell any amount of its product that it wants at the prevailing price. Table 8.1 offers a simple illustration of a typical situation for a competitive firm. The market price is $10 per unit, and the firm can produce as much as it chooses.

Table 8.1   **COST AND REVENUE OF A FIRM: PRICES TAKEN AS GIVEN BY THE FIRM**

Output per period (units)	Price (dollars)	Total revenue (dollars)	Total fixed cost (dollars)	Total variable cost (dollars)	Total cost (dollars)	Total economic profit (dollars)
0	10	0	12	0	12	−12
1	10	10	12	2	14	−4
2	10	20	12	3	15	5
3	10	30	12	5	17	13
4	10	40	12	8	20	20
5	10	50	12	13	25	25
6	10	60	12	23	35	25
7	10	70	12	38	50	20
8	10	80	12	69	81	−1

[2]For further discussion, see C. Plott, "Theories of Industrial Organization as Explanations of Experimental Market Behavior," in S. C. Salop, ed., *Strategy, Predation, and Antitrust Analysis* (Washington, D.C.: Federal Trade Commission, 1981); V. Smith, A. Williams, W. K. Bratton, and M. Vannoni, "Competitive Market Institutions: Double Auctions vs. Sealed Bid-Offer Auctions," *American Economic Review*, March 1982; and J. Kagel and A. Roth. *The Handbook of Experimental Economics* (Princeton, N.J.: Princeton University Press, 1995).

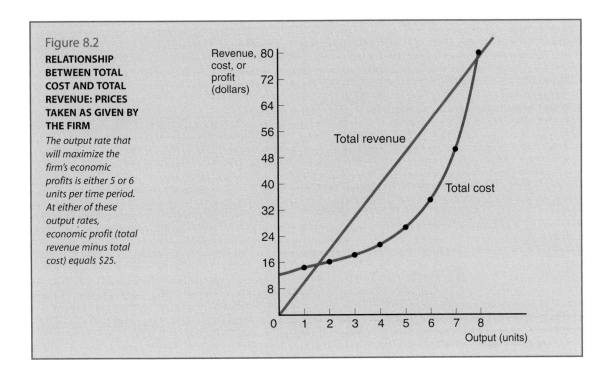

Figure 8.2

RELATIONSHIP BETWEEN TOTAL COST AND TOTAL REVENUE: PRICES TAKEN AS GIVEN BY THE FIRM

The output rate that will maximize the firm's economic profits is either 5 or 6 units per time period. At either of these output rates, economic profit (total revenue minus total cost) equals $25.

The firm's total revenue at various output rates is given in column 3 of Table 8.1. The firm's total fixed cost, total variable cost, and total cost are given in columns 4, 5, and 6. The last column shows the firm's total economic profit—the difference between total revenue and total cost, at various output rates.

Figure 8.2 provides a graphical portrait of Table 8.1; it displays the relationship between total revenue and total cost, on the one hand, and output, on the other. The total-revenue curve is a straight line through the origin because the firm can sell either large or small volumes of output at the same price per unit. How so? Because the firm is taking the price as given. The total-cost curve has a shape that we would expect, on the basis of Chapter 7, for a short-run total-cost curve. The vertical distance between the total-revenue curve and the total-cost curve corresponds to the economic profit that could be earned at each output. This distance is negative below 2 units and above 7 units of output, and it is positive between 2 and 7 units of output. Economic profits are maximized (the positive distance between revenue and cost is greatest) at either 5 or 6 units.

It will be convenient for many purposes to present marginal-revenue and marginal-cost curves in addition to their associated total-revenue and total-cost curves. Table 8.2 shows marginal revenue and marginal cost at each output rate. These figures were derived from the data recorded in Table 8.1 in the way shown in Chapters 4 and 7. Figure 8.3 shows the resulting marginal-revenue and marginal-cost curves. Marginal revenue equals price because the firm takes the price as fixed (the change in total

Table 8.2	Output per period (units)	Marginal revenue (dollars)	Marginal cost[a] (dollars)
MARGINAL REVENUE AND MARGINAL COST: PRICES TAKEN AS GIVEN BY THE FIRM	1	10	2
	2	10	1
	3	10	2
	4	10	3
	5	10	5
	6	10	10
	7	10	15
	8	10	31

[a]This is the marginal cost between the indicated output level and 1 unit less than this output level.

revenue resulting from a 1-unit change in sales must therefore necessarily equal the price).

It is important to note that the maximum economic profit is achieved at the output rate where price (= marginal revenue) equals marginal cost. Both the figures in Table 8.2 and the curves in Figure 8.3 indicate that price equals marginal cost at an output rate between 5 and 6 units, and we know from Table 8.1 and Figure 8.2 that the economic **profit-maximizing output**

Profit-maximizing output

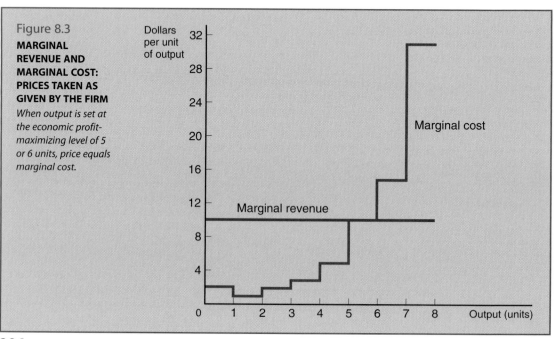

Figure 8.3

MARGINAL REVENUE AND MARGINAL COST: PRICES TAKEN AS GIVEN BY THE FIRM

When output is set at the economic profit-maximizing level of 5 or 6 units, price equals marginal cost.

lies in this region. It turns out that this is *not* a chance occurrence. The economic profit-maximizing output will almost always be characterized by the equality of marginal cost and marginal revenue, and marginal revenue *for a perfectly competitive firm* will always be equal to the price that it takes as given.

▢ Price Equals Marginal Cost Where Economic Profits Are Maximized

How can we be sure that the optimal output rate will be determined by the equality of price and marginal cost as long as the firm is a "price taker"? To see how, consider Figure 8.4. It displays a typical short-run marginal-cost curve. Suppose that the price were P_0. Price exceeds marginal cost at any output less than X (not counting an irrelevant range in which marginal cost is falling). Any increase in output from such a level would necessarily increase economic profit because it would add more to total revenues than to total costs. Price falls short of marginal cost at any output rate above X, though, so any reduction in output from such a level will increase economic profits. Why? Because it would reduce total cost more quickly than it would diminish total revenue. So, increasing output to X would increase economic profit, but going past X would cause economic profit to fall. It follows, then, that X must be the economic profit-maximizing output.

Is the firm earning a positive economic profit? Maybe, but maybe not. If the price were P_2 in Figure 8.4, for example, short-run average costs would exceed the price at all possible outputs. The short run is too short to allow the firm to alter the scale of its plant. There is simply not enough time for it to liquidate its plant. The firm would, in fact, have only two options: produce

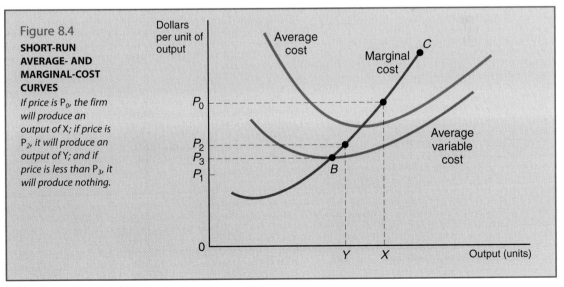

Figure 8.4

SHORT-RUN AVERAGE- AND MARGINAL-COST CURVES

If price is P_0, the firm will produce an output of X; if price is P_2, it will produce an output of Y; and if price is less than P_3, it will produce nothing.

at a loss or discontinue production altogether. The firm's decision would depend on whether the price of the product would cover average variable costs. If there were an output rate where price exceeded average variable costs, then it would pay the firm to produce even though price would not cover average total costs. But if price falls short of average variable costs at every output, then the firm would be better off to produce nothing at all. For the average variable-cost curve shown in Figure 8.4, then, the firm would produce if the price were P_2, but not if it were P_1.

The reasoning behind this conclusion is easily explained. A firm must always pay its fixed costs even if it is producing nothing at all. This means that fixed costs represent the maximum loss that a firm should accept. If the loss resulting from production were smaller than its fixed costs, then it would be more economically profitable (in the sense that losses would be smaller) to produce something rather than shut down. On a per-unit basis, this means that it would be better to produce than to discontinue production as long as the loss per unit of production were less than average fixed costs. Adopting some familiar notation, it would be better to produce something if $ATC - P < AFC$, where ATC is average total costs, P is price, and AFC is average fixed cost. But this would be so if $ATC < AFC + P$, since P has merely been added to both sides of the inequality. Subtracting AFC from both sides, then, this would be so only if $ATC - AFC < P$. Recall that $ATC - AFC$ is average variable costs and we have proven what we set out to prove: that it is better to produce than to discontinue production if price exceeds average variable costs.

Discontinuing production in the short run

If a price-taking competitive firm maximizes economic profit or minimizes losses, therefore, it sets its output rate so that short-run marginal cost equals price. But this rule, like most others, has an exception. If the market price is too low to cover the firm's average variable costs at any conceivable output rate, then the firm will minimize losses by discontinuing production.

It is now a simple matter to derive the firm's short-run supply curve. Suppose that the firm's short-run cost curves were as given in Figure 8.4. If the price of the product were below P_3, then the firm would produce nothing, because there would be no output level for which price exceeded average variable cost. If the price were higher than P_3, though, then the firm would set its output rate at the point at which price equals marginal cost and economic profits would be maximized. So, if the price were P_0, then the firm would produce X units of output. If the price were P_2, the firm would produce Y, and so forth. The resulting supply curve is shown in

Short-run supply curve for a firm

Figure 8.5 as $0P_3BC$. *The short-run supply curve is, by construction, exactly the same as the firm's short-run marginal-cost curve for prices above* P_3, *but the supply curve coincides with the price axis at or below* P_3.

▣ The Short-Run Supply Curve of the Industry

The analysis of the previous section took the price of the industry's product as given. Where did it come from? How was it determined? It was, to be sure, influenced both by the consumers that demanded the good and the

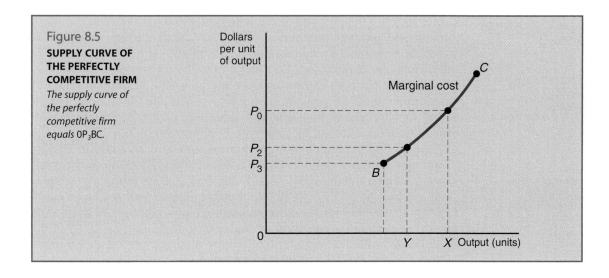

Figure 8.5

SUPPLY CURVE OF THE PERFECTLY COMPETITIVE FIRM

The supply curve of the perfectly competitive firm equals $0P_3BC$.

firms that supplied it. The determinants of the industry demand curve (that is, the market demand curve) were discussed in previous chapters (particularly in Chapter 4). In this section, we discuss the determinants of the short-run industry supply curve (that is, the short-run market supply curve); in the next section we will combine the demand and supply curves to determine the industry's price and output in the short run.

As a rough approximation, the industry's short-run supply curve can be regarded as the horizontal summation of the short-run supply curves of all the firms in the industry (see Figure 8.6). Suppose, for example, that there were three firms in the industry. Let their supply curves be represented by

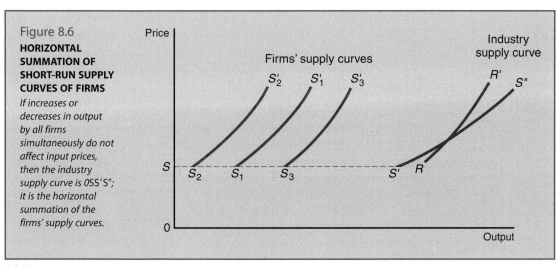

Figure 8.6

HORIZONTAL SUMMATION OF SHORT-RUN SUPPLY CURVES OF FIRMS

If increases or decreases in output by all firms simultaneously do not affect input prices, then the industry supply curve is $0SS'S''$; it is the horizontal summation of the firms' supply curves.

*Short-run supply
curve for the
industry*

curves $0SS_1S_1'$, $0SS_2S_2'$, and $0SS_3S_3'$ in Figure 8.6. The industry's supply curve would be then be $0SS'S''$, since $0SS'S''$ shows the quantities that all the firms would supply together at various prices—the sum of their individual supplies. If there were only three firms, of course, then the industry would not be perfectly competitive, but we can ignore this inconsistency for the time being. The point of Figure 8.6 is to illustrate the fact that the industry supply curve is the horizontal summation of the firm supply curves, at least under one important assumption.

The assumption underlying this construction of the short-run industry supply curve is that supplies of inputs to the industry as a whole are perfectly elastic. In other words, it is assumed that simultaneous changes in outputs of all of the firms do not affect input prices. This is a strong assumption. Changes in the output of one firm alone often leave input prices unaffected, but the simultaneous expansion or contraction of the outputs of all of the firms could easily alter input prices. The cost curves of individual firms—and thus the supply curves of the individual firms—would then shift. For example, an expansion by the industry as a whole may well bid up the price of certain inputs, and the cost curves of every firm in the industry would thereby be pushed upward.

If, contrary to the assumption underlying Figure 8.6, input prices were influenced in this way by expansion of the industry, what would be the effect on the short-run industry supply curve? It would make the short-run industry supply curve less elastic than $0SS'S''$. In the relevant price range, the curve might be more like RR'. To see this, note that expansion of the industry would cause the short-run average-cost curve and the short-run marginal-cost curve to move upward by virtue of the accompanying increase in input prices. But if the marginal-cost curve moved upward, then price would equal marginal cost at a lower output for every firm.

In summary, then, the shape of the short-run supply curve is determined by (1) the number of firms in the industry, (2) the size of the plants and other factors determining the shape of the marginal-cost curves of each firm in the industry, and (3) the effect of changes in industry output on the prices of its inputs.

▣ The Price Elasticity of Supply

Market supply curves vary in shape just like market demand curves. They vary, in particular, with respect to the sensitivity of quantity supplied to price. For some goods, a small change in price causes a large change in quantity supplied; for other goods, a large change in price produces only a small change in quantity supplied. To gauge the sensitivity of the quantity supplied to changes in price, economists use a measure called the **price elasticity of supply.** This elasticity is defined to be the percentage change in quantity supplied resulting from a 1 percent change in price. If a 1 percent increase in the price of natural gas resulted in a 0.5 percent increase in the quantity supplied, for example, then the price elasticity of supply of natural gas would be 0.5.

The price elasticity of supply is clearly analogous to the price elasticity of demand. Like the latter, it is expressed in terms of relative, not absolute, changes in price and quantity, and so it, too, should not be confused with the slope of the supply curve. Its value is likely to vary from one point to another on a supply curve. For example, the price elasticity of the supply of natural gas may be higher when the price is low than it is when it is high. In general, the price elasticity of supply would be expected to increase with the length of the period to which the supply curve pertains. Why? Because manufacturers of the good will be able to adapt their output rates more fully to changes in its price if the period is long rather than short.

If we have a market supply schedule showing the quantity of a commodity supplied at various prices, we can readily estimate the price elasticity of supply. Let ΔP be the change in the price of the good and ΔQ_S be the resulting change in its quantity supplied. If ΔP is very small, we can compute the *Point elasticity of supply* **point elasticity of supply:**

$$\eta_S = \frac{\Delta Q_S}{Q_S} \bigg/ \frac{\Delta P}{P}. \qquad [8.1]$$

Arc elasticity of supply If ΔP is not so small, we can compute the **arc elasticity of supply** by using the average value of Q_S and P in Equation 8.1. The calculations are similar to (but not exactly the same as) those required to compute the price elasticity of demand.

$$\eta_S = \frac{\Delta Q_S}{(Q_{S1} + Q_{S2})/2} \bigg/ \frac{\Delta P}{(P_1 + P_2)/2}$$

▣ Short-Run Equilibrium Price and Output for the Industry

We know from Chapter 1 that the short-run equilibrium price is the one at which the quantity demanded equals the quantity supplied in the short run. If the demand curve were D and the supply curve were S as shown in Figure 8.7, then the equilibrium would occur at the intersection of curves D and S. Equilibrium industry output would be Q, and the equilibrium price would be P. Once enough time had elapsed for firms to adjust their utilization of the variable inputs, the price would tend to equal this equilibrium level. If the price were above this equilibrium level, the quantity supplied would tend to exceed the quantity demanded and so the price would tend to fall. If the price were below this equilibrium level, then the quantity demanded would tend to exceed the quantity supplied and the price would tend to rise. There is no tendency for the price to move in one direction or the other if and only if it is at the equilibrium level.

That is kind of old news, but we now know more about equilibrium. We now know that the equilibrium price would equal the marginal cost of production for all of the firms who chose to produce something (i.e., chose not to shut down their plants). And we know that the equilibrium price could be above or below average total cost in the short run; this observation will be critical when we turn to consider the long run. In the meantime, though, we can still be certain that an increase in demand would increase equilibrium

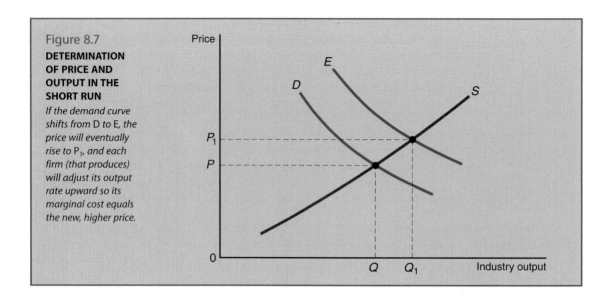

Figure 8.7

DETERMINATION OF PRICE AND OUTPUT IN THE SHORT RUN

If the demand curve shifts from D to E, the price will eventually rise to P_1, and each firm (that produces) will adjust its output rate upward so its marginal cost equals the new, higher price.

price and output in the short run. The demand curve's shifting from D to E in Figure 8.7 would, for example, cause excess demand at the old price, P. The price would therefore eventually be pushed up to P_1. At the same time, each firm would adjust its output rate upward so that its marginal cost would be equal to the higher price, and industry output from the existing firms would grow to Q_1.

Example 8.2 | **The Market for Sulfur Emissions Permits**

Title IV of the 1990 Clean Air Act Amendments in the United States established the first large-scale, long-term environmental program designed to rely on marketable permits to control pollution. The program was intended to cut acid rain by reducing sulfur dioxide emissions from electric-power generating plants to about 50 percent of 1980 levels starting in 1995. The program itself was complicated, but the underlying notion was quite simple. The idea was that a power plant needed a permit to release any sulfur into the air. Each source was given a certain allocation of permits, and the sum of these allocations came close to the targeted level of total pollution to be allowed. The government held a small number of permits back to accommodate firms that needed more or new firms that needed some. In any case, sources would then judge whether or not they could "live" at or below their allocation. If they could, then they could actually sell any surplus permits to other firms. If they could not, then they could purchase permits from other firms. And, of course, they could invest in new technology that would reduce their sulfur emissions—and thus their need for permits. These investments would bring their demand for permits closer to their allocations, or could even support a new revenue source for firms that had surplus permits to sell.

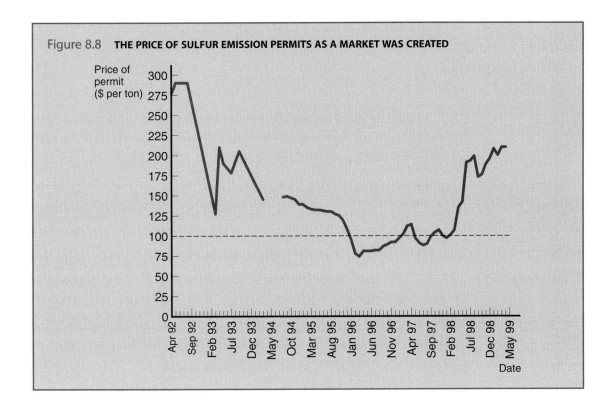

Figure 8.8 **THE PRICE OF SULFUR EMISSION PERMITS AS A MARKET WAS CREATED**

Figure 8.8 tracks the price of permits over the first seven years of the market. Was short-run equilibrium achieved, and how long did it take? The data reveal high prices late in 1992 and almost no market activity for over a year. Then they show declining prices through the middle of 1996 followed by gradually rising prices after 1998. A case can be made that the short-run equilibrium price was around $100 per ton. Why? Because the early high prices were derived from modeling exercises that tried to anticipate how utilities would respond to their new environment; i.e., they were not actual prices derived from market activity. Creating the market was a new experience, and the models missed something important—the fact that low-sulfur coal from the western part of the United States had became economically and technically viable for eastern power plants early in the 1990s. Additionally, market activity was sparse for the first few years as utilities became comfortable with its operation. Utilities were, initially, reluctant to sell permits when there was a chance that they would have to buy some later on. But eventually, things settled down and the price stabilized for a time at a price that could be interpreted as equilibrium. And why did it begin to climb late in 1997? Because more utilities were regulated and the supply of permits was contracted—deviations that disturbed the short-term equilibrium.

SOURCE: See R. Schmalensee, P. L. Joskow, A. D. Ellerman, J. P. Montero, and E. M. Bailey, "An Interim Evaluation of Sulfur Dioxide Emissions Trading," *Journal of Economic Perspectives,* Summer 1998. Figure 8.8 is derived from their Figure 3.

▣ The Long-Run Adjustment Process

Firms can change everything in the long run. Firms can change their size by investing in more capital or shutting down one or more plants. This means that established firms can, if they so choose, leave an industry entirely if they are earning below-average economic profits. It also means that new firms can enter an industry if they see firms in that industry earning above-average economic profits. The next two sections are concerned with the long-run equilibrium of a perfectly competitive industry. This section tells a story of industrywide adjustment over time. Not every competitive industry will experience every episode in the story, but the story will cover the dynamics of adjustment across the widest range of possibilities.

Long-run profit-maximizing output
  Suppose, to begin our story, that a firm operated a plant with the short-run average- and marginal-cost curves identified as A_0A_0' and M_0M_0' in Figure 8.9. Suppose as well that the price of the product were P. The firm would then be making a small economic profit on each unit of output with its existing plant—setting marginal cost equal to P and producing Q. Our firm would, of course, not be limited to this plant in the long run. It could build a plant corresponding to any of the short-run cost curves in Figure 8.9. It could build a medium-sized plant corresponding to the short-run

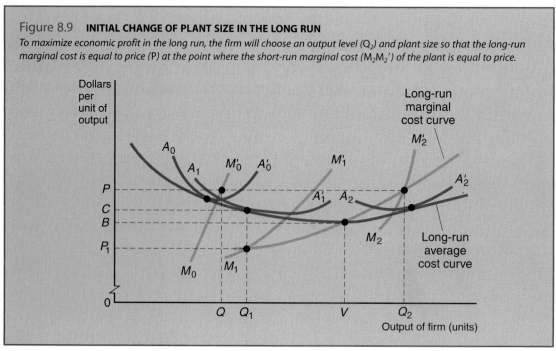

Figure 8.9   **INITIAL CHANGE OF PLANT SIZE IN THE LONG RUN**
To maximize economic profit in the long run, the firm will choose an output level (Q_2) and plant size so that the long-run marginal cost is equal to price (P) at the point where the short-run marginal cost (M_2M_2') of the plant is equal to price.

cost curves of A_1A_1' and M_1M_1', or it could build an even larger plant corresponding to the short-run cost curves of A_2A_2' and M_2M_2'. In fact, it could build any size plant, and it would know that the long-run average-cost and long-run marginal-cost curves summarized the cost potentials of each and every option.

So, what should our firm do? It wants to maximize economic profit, so it should choose to build the plant corresponding to the short-run cost curves of A_2A_2' and M_2M_2'. The maximum attainable economic profit given the three options displayed in Figure 8.9 (and given the price P) would clearly be earned using this plant to produce Q_2 units of output per period of time. It turns out that building this plant would be best even if the firm considered the innumerable plant-size options captured along its long-run cost curves. Indeed, the only solid requirement for this plant to be the best of them all is that the price of output be P.

The geometry of Figure 8.9 illustrates the general result that maximum economic profit will be earned in the long run by producing at an output rate where the long-run marginal cost of production is set equal to the price. But identifying the economic profit-maximizing output in this way also identifies the economic profit-maximizing plant size—the best plant size is the one that supports a short-run marginal-cost curve that equals both the price and the long-run marginal cost at the desired long-run output. Note in Figure 8.9, in particular, that price, short-run marginal cost, and long-run marginal cost are all equal at an output of Q_2 units, and so we know that the plant corresponding to short-run cost curves A_2A_2' and M_2M_2' would be best if the price were P.

If all of the firms in the industry but one (the one whose situation is illustrated in Figure 8.9) were already operating plants of optimal size, then the expansion of our single and laggardly firm would have no significant influence on price. Price P would be greater than the average cost of producing Q_2 units at every firm, and so all firms would be earning a positive economic profit. Recall from Chapter 7 that economists embrace the opportunity cost (alternative cost) doctrine of cost accounting. The cost curves drawn in this chapter therefore include the returns that could have been earned from the most lucrative alternative use of the firms' resources. Earning positive economic profit therefore means that the owners of our firm would be making more than they could if they devoted their resources to producing something else. More to the point, their investments in capital would be earning a return that is higher than it would be if they were invested elsewhere—in other companies, in other markets, in government bonds, wherever. The above-average economic profits depicted in Figure 8.9 would be the sign of very happy entrepreneurs, but their happiness (or, more accurately, the above-average economic profits that would be making them so happy) would also attract new entrants to the industry. And the adjustment process would continue when these new firms arrived.

The arrival of new entrants would shift the industry supply curve to the right. That is, more would be supplied at a given price than before. If, for

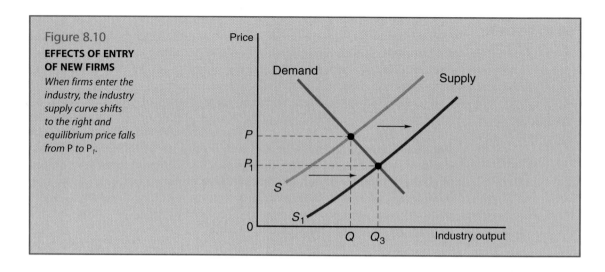

Figure 8.10

EFFECTS OF ENTRY OF NEW FIRMS

When firms enter the industry, the industry supply curve shifts to the right and equilibrium price falls from P to P_1.

example, the industry supply curve shifted from S to S_1 in Figure 8.10, then the price would drop from P to P_1 and industry output would increase from Q to Q_3. Total output would climb (because of the new entrants), but the output of each of the firms would be smaller. Given that the price would now equal P_1, the optimal output of each firm would be Q_1 rather than Q_2 on Figure 8.9. And the optimal plant size there would now correspond to the short-run cost curves A_1A_1' and M_1M_1'. Firms with plants corresponding to the short-run cost curves A_2A_2' and M_2M_2' would lose a great deal of money. So, too, would firms with plants corresponding to the short-run cost curves A_0A_0' and M_0M_0'. But even firms that had plants of optimal size (corresponding to the short-run curves A_1A_1' and M_1M_1') would lose $C - P_1$ dollars per unit.

This would not mean that these firms were not maximizing economic profits. On the contrary, it is evident from Figure 8.9 that long-run marginal cost equals short-run marginal cost equals the price at P_1 where firms produce Q_1 units of output with the plant corresponding to the short-run cost curves A_1A_1' and M_1M_1'. *This is the economic profit-maximizing solution.* The trouble is that firms cannot make an economic profit even though they are doing their best. Firms are instead suffering economic losses, and so they will leave the industry. The returns that could be obtained from the firms' resources would be greater in other industries, and so entrepreneurs would transfer resources to those other industries. And what happens in this industry? The adjustment process continues because firms' exiting would shift the industry's supply curve to the left.

We lost track of our firm in all of the confusion of below-average economic profits. If our firm stayed with its original plant size, its owners would be experiencing lower than expected returns on their investments when the price fell to P_1. They would now be losing money. And if they had invested in the large plant size that was optimal for price P? Things would be even worse. Our owners would be looking longingly at alternative investments even if they had anticipated the price reduction and opted for the middle-sized

304

alternative in Figure 8.9. We are now back to where we started. Nothing has been resolved, really. *What should the owners of our firm have done to anticipate where the industry would go in the long run?* To answer this question, we need to understand how the long-run adjustment would play itself out into an equilibrium.

Example 8.3   **Agricultural Prices and Output**

Agriculture is perhaps the sector of the U.S. economy that comes the closest to being perfectly competitive, even though far fewer people are engaged in it than ever before. Why? Farming has become very capital-intensive, and large farms dominate the landscape. Farming has become increasingly efficient, though. Agricultural prices have generally fallen relative to other prices over time, but they are extremely variable. Farm incomes therefore vary significantly between good times and bad to a much greater extent than nonfarm incomes, even though farm output tends to be more stable than industrial output.

Why have agricultural prices fallen over time? Panel A of Figure 8.11 displays some representative demand and supply curves for farm products at various points in time. The demand for food does not grow very rapidly in this country, but we would nonetheless expect the demand curve to shift relatively slowly to the right—from D in the first period to D_1 in the second period to D_2 in the third period. On the other hand, great technological improvements in agriculture have been instrumental in shifting the supply curve relatively rapidly to the right—from S in the first period to S_1 in the second period to S_2 in the third period. To what end? Our theory of competitive markets suggests that agricultural prices should have fallen (relative to other prices) from P to P_1 to P_2.

It is also easy to see why farm incomes are so unstable. The demand curve for basic farm products is relatively inelastic and the supply curve for basic farm products is relatively inelastic in the short run. Since both the demand curve and the supply curve are inelastic, a small shift (to the right or left) in either curve can produce large changes in price. Panels B and C of Figure 8.11 makes this point clear. Panel B depicts demand and supply curves that are much less elastic than the ones drawn in panel C. Small but equal shifts in the demand curve result in a much bigger change in price in panel B than in panel C.

Although agricultural prices have generally fallen (relative to industrial prices) over the past 60 years, the trend was reversed sharply in 1973 and 1974 when farm prices rose at an astonishing rate. Why? Harvests were very poor in other countries, so there was increased demand for U.S. farm products. The dollar had suffered severe devaluation in the wake of rapidly rising oil prices, so U.S. products were cheaper abroad than they had been. And opening trade with the then–Soviet Union created a whole new market for U.S. products. Each of these effects pushed the demand curve for U.S. farm products up and to the right. And, as would be predicted by our theory, farm prices rose rapidly—sometimes by more than 150 percent over the course of one year. Anyone who witnessed the proceedings would have been quick to agree that farm prices behaved in accord with our model.

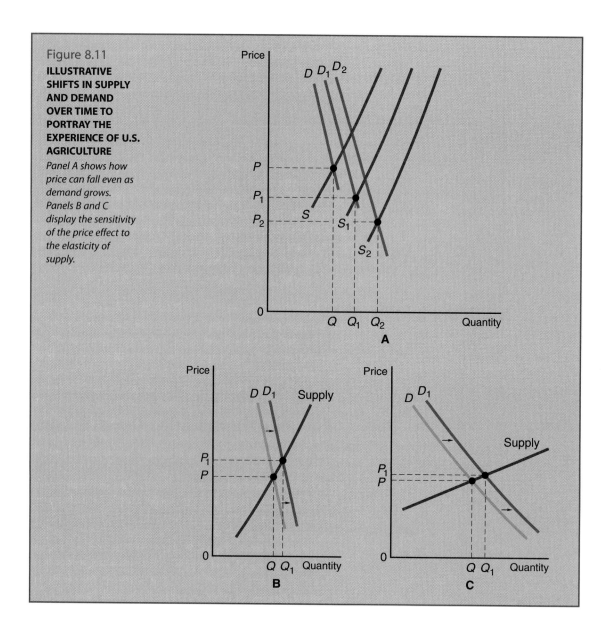

Figure 8.11

ILLUSTRATIVE SHIFTS IN SUPPLY AND DEMAND OVER TIME TO PORTRAY THE EXPERIENCE OF U.S. AGRICULTURE

Panel A shows how price can fall even as demand grows. Panels B and C display the sensitivity of the price effect to the elasticity of supply.

▣ Long-Run Equilibrium of the Firm

To be more specific, when and where would this adjustment process end? Enough firms would have to leave the industry that economic losses (below-average returns) would be eliminated. Firms would then be satisfied with their lots—no longer looking with envy at alternative investments and to diversity in the use of their resources. But economic profits (above-average returns) would also have to be eliminated, so that no other firms would look longingly at this industry. The remaining firms would then be in equilibrium. The long-run equilibrium of the industry would put each firm in the position where price equals long-run average total costs. If price were higher than average total costs for any firm, then positive economic profits would be earned and new firms would enter the industry. And if price fell short of average total costs for any firms, then those firms would eventually leave the industry.

Going a step further, we can argue that price must be equal to the lowest value of long-run average total costs. In other words, firms in **long-run equilibrium** must produce at the minimum of their long-run average-cost curves. How so? *Firms set price equal to long-run marginal cost to maximize their economic profits. But long-run equilibrium in the market can be sustained only if price equals long-run average cost so that economic profits are equal to 0 and returns to employed resources are normal. And both of these conditions are satisfied* only *where long-run marginal cost equals long-run average cost at the minimum of the long-run average cost curve.*

Long-run equilibrium

This equilibrium position for any firm is illustrated in Figure 8.12. Price equals *B* after all long-run adjustments are made. The (effective) demand curve is horizontal at *B*. The marginal-revenue curve is the same as the demand curve. Indeed, both are represented by *BB'*. The equilibrium output of the firm is *V*, and its plant corresponds to short-run average- and marginal-cost curves *AA'* and *MM'*. Long-run marginal cost equals short-run marginal cost equals price at output *V*. This condition ensures that the firm is maximizing economic profit. But long-run average cost equals short-run average cost equals price at *V*, as well. This ensures that economic profits are 0. And the equilibrium point occurs at the bottom of the long-run average-cost

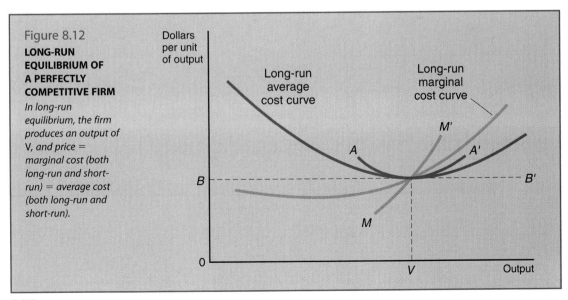

Figure 8.12

LONG-RUN EQUILIBRIUM OF A PERFECTLY COMPETITIVE FIRM

In long-run equilibrium, the firm produces an output of V, and price = marginal cost (both long-run and short-run) = average cost (both long-run and short-run).

curve because the long-run marginal cost and the long-run average cost must be equal.

The equilibrium price must be the same for all firms in the industry. So, the minimum of the long-run average-cost curve must be the same for all firms. Can this really be? It is not as unrealistic as it might appear at first glance. Firms that appear to have lower costs than others in the industry often have unusually good resources or particularly able managers. The owners of superior resources (including management ability) could obtain a higher price if they were put to alternative uses than could more ordinary resources. Consequently, the alternative (or implicit) costs of using superior resources are higher than those of using ordinary resources. If this is taken into account and if these superior resources are costed properly, then the vision of firms with apparently lower costs is a mirage.

Finally, let's finish the story of the firm whose initial position was depicted in Figure 8.9. How does the story of long-run equilibrium help it to decide what to do with its plant-size decision? Assume that the owners of our firm know their industry and the technology of supplying product to its markets—i.e., assume that the cost curves drawn in Figure 8.9 are the state of the art in technological understanding so that our owners are not misinformed. We now understand that the long-run equilibrium price will be B. It is obvious, then, that our firm should look to build the plant whose *Long-run plant size* size sustains the minimum average cost of production. It would then pro-*decision* duce along the corresponding short-run marginal-cost curve as the market adjusts toward equilibrium, but it would be in the right place over the long haul, expecting to produce V units of output.

| **Example 8.4** | **The Highest Price of Cotton since the Civil War** |

According to the National Cotton Council, cotton clothing was becoming more popular in the 1990s so that cotton's share of the fibers used in U.S. manufactured goods had been rising (from 42 percent in 1985 to 65 percent in 1993). Meanwhile, other major producers had very poor crops in 1995; the U.S. crop of 20 million bales was the world's largest, but it was not nearly enough to maintain prices. As a result, the price rose from $0.66 to $1.10 per pound between October of 1994 and March of 1995—the highest price since the Civil War.

How can this sudden increase be explained? By shifting demand? Perhaps, to some degree; but sudden shifts in demand are seldom large enough to cause a 67 percent increase in price. By a reduction in the price elasticity of demand caused by increased reliance on cotton to supply fiber to the clothing manufacturers? Probably. And certainly poor crops in India and Pakistan were primary culprits, as well. U.S. growers had determined their capacities under the expectation that these two nations would offer the largest supplies to the world market. And when that did not happen, they were unable to expand production. Figure 8.13 displays the result. Contracting supply shifted the supply curve up, and growing reliance on cotton made demand more inelastic. The supply-driven increase in

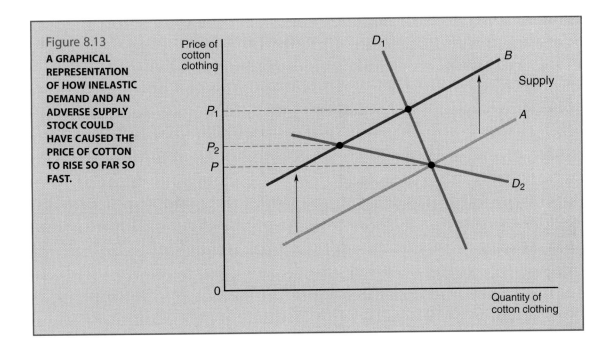

Figure 8.13

A GRAPHICAL REPRESENTATION OF HOW INELASTIC DEMAND AND AN ADVERSE SUPPLY STOCK COULD HAVE CAUSED THE PRICE OF COTTON TO RISE SO FAR SO FAST.

price (that would have been from P to P_2 along a more elastic demand curve) would have thereby been exaggerated so that the new price would be $P_1 >>> P_2$.[3]

◻ Constant-Cost Industries

We have assumed implicitly, in the preceding sections, that the industry exhibited constant costs so that expansion did not cause input prices to rise. Figure 8.14 reprises long-run equilibrium under conditions of constant cost. Panel A shows the short- and long-run cost curves of a typical firm in the industry. Panel B shows the demand and supply curves in the market as a whole; D is the original demand curve and S is the original short-run supply curve. We know that the industry is in long-run equilibrium because the price line at P is tangent to the long-run and short-run average-cost curves at their minimum points.

Assume, now, that the demand curve in panel B shifts to D_1. In the short run, with the number of firms fixed, the price of the product would rise from P to P_1. Each firm would expand output from Q to Q_1, and each firm would be making positive economic profits (and earning above-average returns) since P_1 would exceed the short-run average costs of producing Q_1. Firms would be attracted to the industry by the positive economic profits. Their entry would shift the supply curve to the right, and the price would settle back down to P. What would happen to the costs of

[3]For further discussion, see *Business Week*, March 13, 1995, and the *Philadelphia Inquirer,* March 11, 1995.

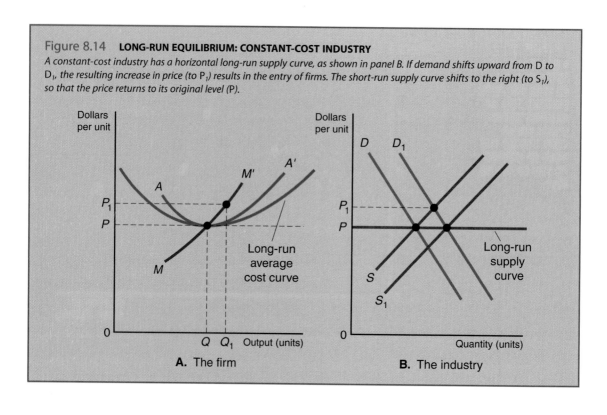

Figure 8.14 **LONG-RUN EQUILIBRIUM: CONSTANT-COST INDUSTRY**

A constant-cost industry has a horizontal long-run supply curve, as shown in panel B. If demand shifts upward from D to D_1, the resulting increase in price (to P_1) results in the entry of firms. The short-run supply curve shifts to the right (to S_1), so that the price returns to its original level (P).

A. The firm

B. The industry

production? The entrance of new firms would not affect the costs of existing firms if this were a constant-cost industry. How could this be? The inputs employed in this industry might be employed in many other industries so the appearance of the new firms in this industry could have a very small impact on the inputs' total demand. If that were the case, then input prices would not climb and the production costs of existing firms would not change.

Long-run supply with constant costs

We can now summarize an important observation: constant-cost industries have horizontal long-run supply curves. Output can be expanded by increasing the number of firms, all of which would produce Q units at an average cost of P, so the long-run supply curve is horizontal at P—the minimum of the long-run average-cost curve of each optimally sized plant. And industry output can be expanded or contracted, in accord with demand conditions, without altering this long-run equilibrium price.

◻ Increasing- and Decreasing-Cost Industries

Figure 8.15 displays an increasing-cost industry. The original conditions are the same as in Figure 8.14. Curve D is the original demand curve, S is the original supply curve, P is the initial equilibrium price, and the long-run and short-run average-cost curves of each firm are shown in panel A by LL' and AA'. The original position is one of long-run equilibrium; the price line is tangent to the average-cost curves at their minima.

310

Figure 8.15 **LONG-RUN EQUILIBRIUM: INCREASING-COST INDUSTRY**

An increasing-cost industry has a positively sloped long-run supply curve, as shown in panel B. After long-run equilibrium is achieved, increases in output require increases in the price of the product.

A. The firm

B. The industry

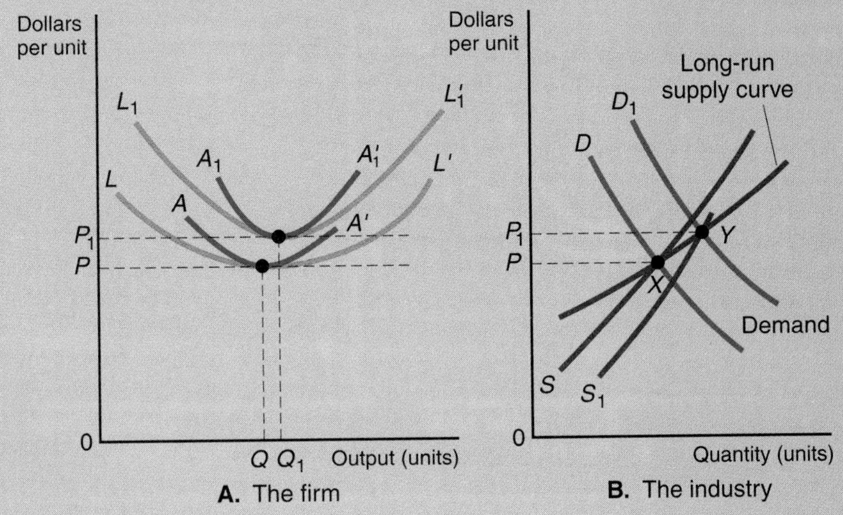

Now suppose that the demand curve shifts to D_1, so that the price of the product would climb and firms would earn positive economic profits (again, higher than average returns). New entrants would thereby be attracted to the industry. In an increasing-cost industry, though, the prices of inputs climb as more are demanded by the industry. Costs would therefore increase for established firms as well as for the new entrants, so that the average-cost curves would be pushed up to L_1L_1' and A_1A_1'.

If the marginal-cost curve of each firm were shifted to the left by the increase in input prices, then the industry supply curve would tend to shift to the left. This tendency would, however, be more than counterbalanced by the effects of the increase in the number of firms, which would work to shift the industry supply curve to the right. The latter effect must more than offset the former because there would otherwise be no expansion in total industry output. (No new resources would have been attracted to the industry, and there would have been no reason for input prices to climb.) The process of adjustment would continue in this case until a new point of long-run equilibrium were reached. In Figure 8.15, this point is depicted as the point where the price of the product is P_1 and each firm produces Q_1 units;[4] the new short-run supply curve is S_1.

An increasing-cost industry has a positively sloped long-run supply curve. That is, after long-run equilibrium is achieved, increases in output require increases in the price of the product. Points X and Y in Figure 8.15 are, for

Long-run supply with increasing costs

[4]We cannot be sure that Q_1 exceeds Q, as shown in Figure 8.15. It is possible for Q_1 to be less than or equal to Q.

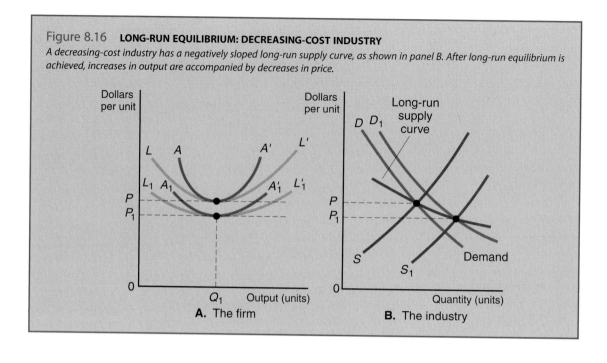

Figure 8.16 **LONG-RUN EQUILIBRIUM: DECREASING-COST INDUSTRY**
A decreasing-cost industry has a negatively sloped long-run supply curve, as shown in panel B. After long-run equilibrium is achieved, increases in output are accompanied by decreases in price.

A. The firm

B. The industry

example, both on the long-run supply curve for the industry. The difference between constant-cost and increasing-cost industries is now clear: new firms enter constant-cost industries in response to an increase in demand until price returns to its original level; new firms enter increasing-cost industries until the minimum point on the long-run average-cost curve has increased to the point where it equals the new price.[5]

A decreasing-cost industry is shown in Figure 8.16. Once again, we begin with an industry in long-run equilibrium. The original demand curve is D, the short-run supply curve is S, price is P, and the long-run and short-run average-cost curves of each firm are LL' and AA', respectively. We postulate, as before, an increase in demand to D_1. Positive economic profits appear for established firms; new firms again enter. In this case, though, the industry expansion causes costs to fall. The new long-run equilibrium occurs at a price like P_1; the equilibrium output of each firm is then Q_1, and the new long-run and short-run average-cost curves are L_1L_1' and A_1A_1', respectively.

Decreasing-cost industries have negatively sloped long-run supply curves. After long-run equilibrium is reached, increases in output are accompanied by decreases in price. External economies, which are cost reductions that occur when the industry expands, may be responsible for the existence of

[5]This is only one way in which equilibrium can be achieved in increasing-cost industries. It is also possible that the increase in input prices (due to the expansion of industry output) raises average cost more than the increase in demand raises average revenue. Thus some firms may experience losses, some firms may leave the industry, and the remaining firms may produce at a larger scale.

decreasing-cost industries. Transportation networking might, for example, improve with the expansion of an industry so that the costs facing each firm in the industry could fall. External economies can be quite powerful, but beware: external economies are quite different from economies of scale.

Many economists believe that increasing-cost industries are encountered most frequently. Decreasing-cost industries are most unusual, except perhaps among collections of young industries whose production technologies and input markets have not yet matured.

| Example 8.5 | **Explaining the Domestic Prices of Computers and Peripherals** |

Panel A of Figure 8.17 tracks the recent experience of domestic purchases of computers and computer peripherals against a price index. Real prices for computing services and computer characteristics have clearly fallen and real expenditures have clearly risen over the past 30 or more years. Is there a supply-and-demand interpretation of these data, and can this interpretation explain why the trend line appears to be growing steeper? Yes. It turns out that these data support a strong case that technological advances have produced outward shifts of the supply curve at rates that have dramatically outpaced the increase in demand for computer services.

Panel B depicts this story. Suppose that technological change caused the supply curve for computational services to shift from S_1 to S_2 over some period of time. The supply curves are drawn horizontally because there is no evidence of rising marginal cost in producing additional computer speed, memory, or other characteristics with a given technology. If demand were fixed at D_1 over the same time period, then the equilibrium quantity of computer characteristics would have climbed from C_1 to C_2 and expenditures on computers would have risen from $P_1 \times C_1$ to $P_2 \times C_2$. If, on the other hand, demand had shifted to something like D_2, then quantity would have climbed to C_3 and expenditures would have risen to $P_2 \times C_3 > P_2 \times C_2$. If the case in which demand shifted were more descriptive of reality, therefore, the trend line depicted in panel A should be flattening out over time. The rates of declines in price and increases in expenditures have grown over the most recent five years (the dots are farther apart), but the trend line is getting steeper rather than flatter. So, if demand has shifted, it has not shifted by very much.

SOURCE: R. Gordon, "Does the 'New Economy' Measure Up to the Great Inventions of the Past?" *Journal of Economic Perspectives*, vol. 14, no. 4, Fall 2000, pp. 49–74.

☐ Resource Allocation

At this point, it is instructive to describe the process by which a perfectly competitive economy—an economy composed of perfectly competitive industries—would allocate resources. We noted in Chapter 1 that the

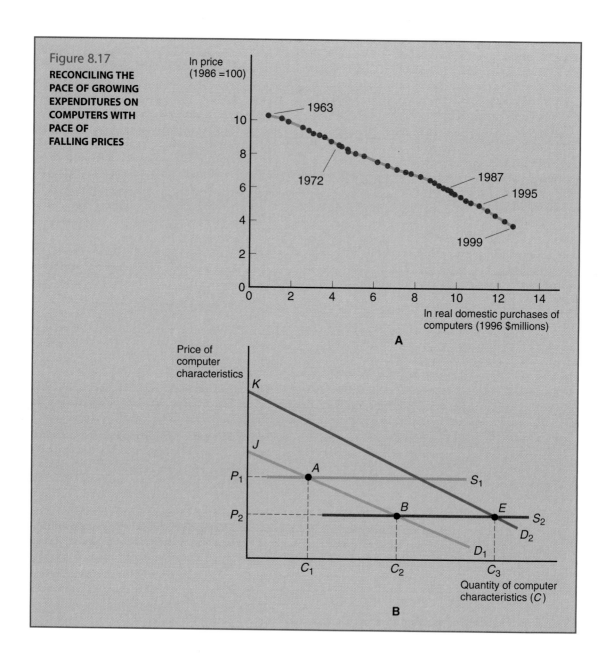

Figure 8.17

RECONCILING THE PACE OF GROWING EXPENDITURES ON COMPUTERS WITH PACE OF FALLING PRICES

In price (1986 =100)

1963

1972

1987

1995

1999

In real domestic purchases of computers (1996 $millions)

A

Price of computer characteristics

K

J

P_1

P_2

A

B

E

S_1

S_2

D_2

D_1

C_1

C_2

C_3

Quantity of computer characteristics (C)

B

allocation of resources among alternative uses is one of the major functions of an economic system. Equipped with the concepts of this and previous chapters, we can now go much further than we could in Chapter 1 in describing how a perfectly competitive economy goes about shifting resources in accord with changes in consumer demand.

To be specific, suppose that tastes changed so that consumers were more favorably disposed toward blue jeans and less favorably disposed toward khakis than they had been in the past.[6] What would happen in the short run? The demand for jeans would increase (the demand curve would shift to the right) and drive their price higher. The output of jeans would, to some degree, increase as manufacturers moved up along their marginal-cost curves and the market moved up along the short-run supply curve. The production of jeans could not increase very substantially, however, because the capacity of a fixed number of producers could not be expanded in the short run. Similarly, the demand for khakis would decline (the demand curve would shift to the left). The price of khakis would fall (or at least inventories would climb and The Gap would run a sale) so that the output of khakis would also fall. The output of khakis would not be curtailed greatly, though, because producers would continue to deliver product to their wholesalers as long as they could cover variable costs.

The change in the relative prices of jeans and khakis would tell producers that a reallocation of resources would be appropriate over the longer term. How would this information be conveyed? Higher prices for jeans would mean that their manufacturers would be earning positive economic profits (higher than normal returns to their investments of resources and time), but lower khaki prices would mean that their producers were showing economic losses (lower than normal returns to their investments of resources and time). This would trigger a redeployment of resources. If some variable inputs that were employed in producing khakis (some machinery, labor, stitching material, etc.) could be used as effectively in producing jeans, then these variable inputs could be withdrawn from khakis and switched to jeans. Adjustment could even occur in various interrelated industries. The key, though, is that producing jeans would attract other resources at the expense (ultimately) of khaki production.

Short-run equilibrium might be attained in both markets prior to the reallocation of resources. In fact, it is conceivable that time would limit the ability of producers to add new capacity for producing jeans or to liquidate old capacity for producing khakis. But neither industry would then necessarily be operating at minimum average cost. Jeans manufacturers could easily be producing in the short run at levels that were higher than the output associated with minimum average cost; khaki manufacturers could be producing in the short run at levels that were smaller than the output associated with minimum average cost.

So what would happen in the long run? The shift in consumer demand from khakis to jeans would result in greater adjustments in production and smaller adjustments in price than in the short run. In the long run, existing khaki manufacturers might abandon some khaki production while they, and

---

[6]This example stretches the definition of perfect competition because consumers can surely distinguish between different manufacturers of jeans and, to a lesser extent, different manufacturers of khaki pants. This discussion, for the sake of argument, assumes that any type of jeans is a perfect substitute for any other kind, and that any brand of khaki pants is a perfect substitute for any other. If this does violence to your sense of fashion, then you will enjoy the future discussion of monopolistic competition.

perhaps others, entered the jeans market. Short-run economic losses in producing khakis would mean that some orders for non-denim fabric would be canceled. Related equipment specific to the styles associated with khakis would be allowed to run down. And some khaki producers might be liquidated (at least some khaki production facilities would be closed). The supply curve for khakis would therefore shift to the left, the price would rebound, and the transfer of resources out of khaki production would stop when the price had increased and costs had decreased back to a point where economic losses had been eliminated.

Jeans production would, of course, be adding to the resources that it was employing. Short-run economic profits in selling jeans would attract new firms. The increased demand for inputs might raise input prices (e.g., denim might become more expensive) and the cost curves associated with jeans production, but the price of jeans would ultimately be depressed somewhat by the supply curve's shifting to the right (because of the entry of new firms). Entry would finally cease when positive economic profits were no longer being earned. At that point, long-run equilibrium would be re-achieved with more firms supplying more jeans to the expanded market and employing more resources of all types.

Long-run equilibrium would thereby be reestablished in both industries, and the reallocation of resources would be complete. It is important to note, though, that this reallocation could affect industries other than jeans and khakis. The full repercussions can be analyzed by general equilibrium analysis—a topic that is broached in Chapter 16.

Microlink 8.1 Competitive Equilibrium, Efficiency, and Costs

We have seen that a competitive equilibrium can be sustained only if all of the firms supplying product to the market earn zero pure economic profit, and we have seen that each firm will produce at the minimum of its average-cost curve. These two conditions combine to give competitive equilibria the cache of maximum efficiency, but this property depends on the proposition that all sources of cost are reflected in the firms' calculations of their economic costs. We have emphasized, more specifically, that zero pure economic profit means that capital is earning a normal return because paying for capital is part of economic cost. We now emphasize that zero pure economic profit also means that all sources of implicit costs described in Chapter 7 are similarly included in the calculations. Otherwise, costs are underestimated and prices are too low (just as they are if all social costs are not included).

SUMMARY

1. Perfect competition is defined by four conditions: (1) no participant in the market can influence price, (2) output must be homogeneous, (3) resources must be mobile, and (4) all participants must have access to perfect knowledge about all of the relevant characteristics of the market.
2. A price-taking firm maximizes economic profits (or minimizes losses) in the short run by producing the output for which marginal cost equals price unless the price is lower than the minimum of its average variable-cost curve.

In that case, the market price is lower than the average variable cost of producing any and all levels of output, so the firm will minimize losses by discontinuing production. The firm's short-run supply curve is the same as its marginal-cost curve as long as price exceeds average variable cost.

3. The short-run price of a product is determined by the interaction between the demand and supply sides of the market. As a rough approximation, the industry's short-run supply curve can be regarded as the horizontal summation of the short-run supply curves of the individual firms. This summation does not work if input prices are not constant for any relevant level of employment.

4. The price elasticity of supply, defined as the percentage change in the quantity supplied resulting from a 1 percent change in price, is a measure of the responsiveness of supply to changes in price. The price elasticity of supply will generally vary from one point to another on a supply curve. Arc elasticities are sometimes used to approximate point elasticities of supply between two distinct points on a supply curve.

5. The short-run equilibrium price level is the price at which the quantity demanded and the quantity supplied are equal in the short run. In equilibrium, price will equal marginal cost for all firms that choose to produce (rather than shut down their plants).

6. Firms can change their plant size, leave the industry, or enter the industry in the long run. Long-run equilibrium puts the firm at the point where its long-run average costs equal price. The point corresponds with the minimum point on the long-run average-cost curve, and so price equals long-run marginal cost, as well.

7. Industries can be divided into three types: constant cost, increasing cost, and decreasing cost. Constant-cost industries have horizontal long-run supply curves. Increasing-cost industries have positively sloped long-run supply curves. Decreasing-cost industries have negatively sloped long-run supply curves. Increasing-cost industries are most frequently observed.

QUESTIONS/ PROBLEMS

1. Tom Kelly's dairy farm in Tyrone, Pennsylvania, has 81 cows and 350 acres. Mr. Kelly has owned this farm for 20 years and operates it with the help of 3 hired workers (2 part-time) in the summer or 2 hired workers (1 part-time) in the winter. His teenage son sometimes helps with the farm work. In November 2001, Mr. Kelly received a price of 13.3 cents per gallon for his milk. (a) If his farm can be regarded as perfectly competitive, describe the demand curve for milk facing Mr. Kelly in November 2001. Was it downward-sloping to the right? Why or why not? (b) What was Mr. Kelly's marginal revenue from an extra gallon of milk sold in November 2001? Can you answer this question without knowing how much milk his farm produced then? Why or why not? (c) According to the U.S. Department of Agriculture, the price elasticity of demand for fluid milk is about 0.26. Does this mean that Mr. Kelly, if he reduces the price of his milk by 10 percent, will experience a 2.6 percent increase in the quantity of his milk that is demanded? Why or why not? (d) The income elasticity of demand for fluid milk has been estimated to be less than 0.1. Does this mean that future increases in consumer incomes will have little or no effect on the price that Mr. Kelly can get for his milk?

2. The price of coffee fell in August 1992 to its lowest level in 17 years—about 51 cents per pound. According to one analyst, "At these prices, or close to them, it doesn't pay to sell. The price will not cover the costs of harvest and transportation." (a) Does this mean that 51 cents per pound is below average variable cost? (b) If price were below average variable cost in one coffee-producing country but above it in another coffee-producing country, would the supply of coffee cease? Why or why not?

3. If the textile industry were a constant-cost industry and if the demand curve for textiles shifted upward, what would be the steps by which a competitive market would ensure that quantities would increase sufficiently to clear the market? What would happen if the government would not allow textile prices to rise?

4. An economist estimates that, in the short run, the quantity of men's socks supplied at each price is as follows:

Price (dollars per pair)	Quantity supplied per year (millions of pairs)
1	5
2	6
3	7
4	8

Calculate the arc elasticity of supply when the price is between $3 and $4 per pair.

5. According to D. Suits and S. Koizumi, the supply function for onions in the United States is

$$\log q = 0.134 + 0.0123t + 0.324 \log P - 0.512 \log c,$$

where q is the quantity supplied in a particular year, t is the year (less 1924), P is the price last season, and c is the cost index last season. Suppose that price is estimated by one forecaster to be 10 cents this season but that another expert says that it will be 11 cents. Holding other factors constant, how much difference would this make in forecasting the quantity supplied next season?

6. Explain how it is possible for a constant-cost industry to be composed of firms for which marginal costs are increasing.

7. The cotton textile industry was sometimes described as being closer to perfect competition than any other manufacturing industry in the United States during the years between the First and Second World Wars. Considerable excess capacity existed in the cotton textile industry from about 1924 to 1936. Evidence of this overcapacity is presented in the accompanying table, where the economic profit rate in cotton textiles is shown to have been considerably below that in other manufacturing. For example, during 1924–1928 and 1933–1936, textile economic profits averaged less than 4 percent of the value of the firms' capital stock, while economic profits in all other manufacturing averaged 8 percent. It was noted, as well, that economic profit rates in cotton textiles were higher in the South than they were in the North because the prices of many inputs—like labor and raw cotton—were lower in the South.

	Economic profits as a percentage of capital stock value	
Period	Cotton textiles	All manufacturing
1919–1923	15.3	11.0
1924–1928	4.7	11.0
1933–1936	2.4	4.3

(a) Was the industry in long-run equilibrium between 1919 and 1923? between 1924 and 1928? (b) What sorts of changes were required to make the industry approach long-run equilibrium between 1919 and 1923? between 1933 and 1936?

8. Richard Webster is a Nebraska farmer who produces corn on 1,000 acres of land, 500 of which are rented and 500 of which are owned. In an interview reported in the *New York Times,* he estimated that his costs per acre for corn produced on his rented land were as shown in the following list:

Fertilizer	$ 41.84
Herbicides	2.76
Insecticides	5.50
Fuel	18.00
Seed	16.50
Electricity	15.00
Cost of services of plant and equipment	85.46
Labor	15.00
Insurance	10.00
Land rent	110.00
Total	$320.06

(a) Do the data suggest that the average cost of producing corn was $320.06? Why or why not? (b) Mr. Webster does not have to pay a rent of $110 on each acre of land that he owns. Does this mean that the cost of using his own land is less than that of using rented land? (c) If each acre of land yielded 120 bushels of corn and if the price of a bushel of corn were expected to be 80 cents, should Mr. Webster produce any corn? (d) If the price were expected to be $1.50, should he produce any corn?

9. According to a study by N. Ericsson and P. Morgan, the supply curve for shale oil was as shown in the figure. Producers of shale oil have to dispose of the spent shale and cope with any air pollution that might be created. (a) If the disposal of spent shale costs $10 per ton, would you expect the quantity supplied to be more or less than 16 million barrels per day if the price of oil is $40 per barrel? (b) Colorado air pollution standards are stricter than federal standards. If the Colorado standards are applied, would you expect the quantity supplied to be more or less than 16 million barrels per day if the price of oil is $40 per barrel? (c) Since no commercial-scale shale oil plants had been built, the supply curve below was based on engineering estimates. Do you think that this supply curve is very accurate? Why or why not? (d) A shale oil plant is estimated to

cost over $1 billion. Would an investment in such a plant be risky? Why or why not? Would this influence the position and shape of the supply curve?

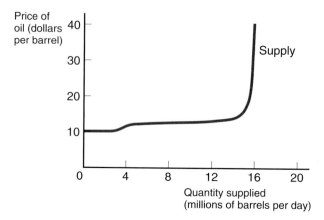

10. A perfectly competitive profit-maximizing firm has the following total-cost function:

Total output (units)	Total cost (dollars)
0	200
5	240
10	300
20	420
30	550
40	690
50	840
60	1,000
70	1,170
80	1,350
90	1,550

(a) How much would the firm produce in the short run if the price of its product were $6? $13? $17? (b) How would your answers to part (a) change if fixed cost increased by $50? (c) Suppose that the firm had enough time to exit the market but that other firms did not have enough time to enter. How much would the firm produce if the price of its product were $6? $13? $17?

11. Approximate the long-run equilibrium price for a market for which the firm portrayed in Question 10 is entirely representative of all potential firms that might supply its product. Suppose that there were 10 identical firms supplying the market. Construct their market supply curve and graph it. Draw a demand curve on the graph for which 10 firms would be the correct equilibrium number.

12. You have the following information about a profit-maximizing firm in a perfectly competitive market. Total revenue matches total cost at $6,000. Total

variable cost amounts to 75 percent of total cost. Average cost is at its minimum level, marginal cost is rising, and average variable cost is $0.75. Is the firm in the correct position, or should it make some sort of adjustment in price or quantity produced and sold? Why?

13. You have the following information about a profit-maximizing firm in a perfectly competitive market. Output is 3,000 units and total revenue equals $9,000. Average cost is $3.25 and marginal cost is rising at $3.00. Is the firm in the correct position, or should it make some sort of adjustment in price or quantity produced and sold? Why?

14. You have the following information about a profit-maximizing firm in a perfectly competitive market. Total revenue equals $20,000; it exceeds total cost by $2,000. Average cost is $3.60 and marginal cost is rising at $4.00. Is the firm in the correct position, or should it make some sort of adjustment in price or quantity produced and sold? Why?

15. In which of the cases described in Questions 12 through 14 is there enough information to determine the long-run equilibrium price? In the other two, can you identify an upper or lower limit on the equilibrium price from the information provided?

16. The market supply curve for good Y is a straight line through the origin. Does the price elasticity of supply vary with good Y's price? What is good Y's price elasticity of supply?

Calculus Appendix

PROFIT MAXIMIZATION FOR A PRICE TAKER

Let the cost of producing some good X be given by $C(X)$ and assume that a firm faces a constant price P. Total economic profit is then

$$\pi(X) = PX - C(X).$$

The first-order condition for the profit-maximizing output X^* is therefore

$$\frac{d\pi}{dX} = P - \frac{dC(X)}{dX} = 0$$

so that output X^* must satisfy the condition that

$$P = MC(X);$$

i.e., marginal cost must equal price. Meanwhile, the second-order condition for maximization requires that

$$\frac{d^2C}{dX^2} > 0.$$

In other words, marginal cost must be rising.

DEFINITION OF THE ELASTICITY OF SUPPLY

Let $X_S(P)$ represent a supply curve for some good X where P is the price of X. The price elasticity of supply is then simply

$$\eta_S = \frac{\% \text{ change in } X_S(P)}{\% \text{ change in } P}$$

$$= \frac{dX_S(P)/dP}{P/X_S(P)}.$$

The notation indicates that the elasticity can depend on the quantity, but that is not always the case. If supply is linear in price so that

$$X_S(P) = bP,$$

then

$$\eta_S = \frac{dX_S(P)/dP}{P/X_S(P)}$$

$$= \frac{b}{P/X_S(P)}$$

$$= \frac{b}{P/bP}$$

$$= 1.$$

In addition, if

$$X_S(P) = \alpha_S P^{\beta_S},$$

then

$$\eta_S = \frac{\alpha_S \beta_S P^{\beta_S - 1}}{P/\alpha_S P^{\beta_S}}$$

$$= \beta_S.$$

ELASTICITY AND THE SENSITIVITY OF EQUILIBRIUM PRICE TO CHANGES IN SUPPLY OR DEMAND

Let supply and demand for some good X be given by

$$X_S = \alpha_S P^{\beta_S} \quad \text{and} \quad X_D = \alpha_D P^{-\beta_D},$$

respectively. Convince yourself that the price elasticity of demand is β_D; you already know that the price elasticity of supply is β_S. Equilibrium price $P^\star$ will now set quantity demanded equal to quantity supplied, so

$$X_S = \alpha_S (P^\star)^{\beta_S} = X_D = \alpha_D (P^\star)^{-\beta_D}.$$

It follows, then, that the equilibrium price must satisfy

$$P^\star = \left(\frac{\alpha_D}{\alpha_S} \right)^{1/(\beta_D + \beta_S)}.$$

Taking a derivative and collecting terms,

$$\frac{\partial P^*}{\partial \alpha_D} = \frac{-1}{\beta_D + \beta_S}$$

and

$$\frac{\partial P^*}{\partial \alpha_S} = -\frac{-1}{\beta_D + \beta_S}.$$

As stated in the text, therefore, the relative change in P^* for a change in either α_D or α_S is large if the elasticities of supply and/or demand are small, and it is small if those elasticities are large. Note, as well, that P^* moves in opposite directions when α_D or α_S changes.

Applying the Competitive Model

INTRODUCTION

Economists and others often contend that perfectly competitive markets are socially optimal. Why? Because competitive markets can (under the right conditions) sustain an efficient distribution of resources in the sense that the aggregate economic welfare of consumers and producers is maximized. We begin our discussion of this result taking a first look at how perfectly competitive markets can promote this type of economic efficiency, and we will examine exactly what maximizing aggregate economic welfare means. We will return to this topic in greater detail in Chapters 16 through 18.

Notwithstanding the enormous amount of lip service that is paid to the virtues of competitive markets, the governments of all developed economies are continually feeling the temptation to intervene. Manhattan apartment dwellers put pressure on their city government to impose a ceiling on rents. Dairy farmers lobby the federal government to put floors under milk prices. Auto firms and their employees clamor for protection against foreign imports. Governments need revenue, and so they tax gasoline, tires, cigarettes, liquor, real estate transactions, and sales of all kinds. It is important for you to see how competitive markets respond to such governmental intervention and to be able to estimate, at least roughly, the gains and losses to consumers and producers that result. Will the gains or losses be large? Or small? How will they be distributed between producers and consumers? How will they be distributed among consumers? Among producers? The usual economist's answer to all of these questions is, It depends. This chapter provides the analytical tools with which you can build an understanding of the answer to the next question: On what?

PRODUCER SURPLUS AND TOTAL SURPLUS

We begin by discussing the efficiency of a competitive market. Many economists believe that a competitive market maximizes the aggregate economic

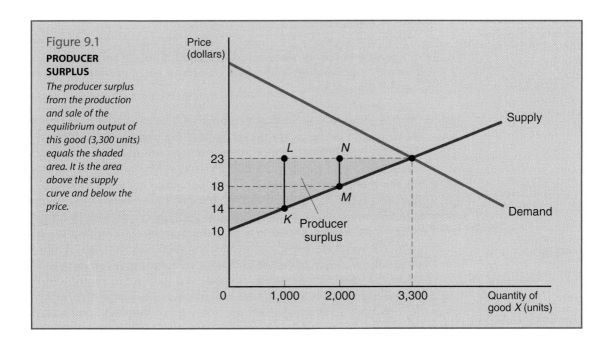

Figure 9.1

PRODUCER SURPLUS

The producer surplus from the production and sale of the equilibrium output of this good (3,300 units) equals the shaded area. It is the area above the supply curve and below the price.

welfare of consumers and producers. To understand their arguments, it is useful to begin by defining producer surplus. Producer surplus is analogous to consumer surplus, but it relates to producers. Recall that consumer surplus was defined in Chapter 3 as the net benefit that consumers receive above and beyond what they have to pay for a good. **Producer surplus** is the amount producers receive above and beyond the minimum prices that would have been required to get them to produce and sell their output.

Producer surplus

Figure 9.1 portrays how producer surplus can be calibrated on the basis of the demand and supply curves for some good X. The equilibrium price indicated in Figure 9.1 is $23. According to the supply curve, producers would be willing to supply the 1,000th unit of this good for $14, but they receive the equilibrium price of $23 when it is sold. So, producers receive a bonus or surplus of $23 − $14 = $9 from the production and sale of the 1,000th unit. Similarly, they receive a bonus or surplus of $23 − $18 = $5 from the sale of the 2,000th unit that they produce because they would have been willing to supply this unit for a price of $18. The bonus or surplus received by producers from the production and sale of a particular unit of output is the vertical distance from the horizontal line at the equilibrium price ($23) down to the supply curve at this output. The surplus is $KL = $9 from the 1,000th unit and $MN = $5 from the 2,000th unit. Adding up these vertical distances for each of 3,300 units of output produced and sold in equilibrium, we find that the producer surplus from all the 3,300 units is $21,450. It is a value that equals the area of the shaded region portrayed in Figure 9.1; i.e., *producer surplus is the area above the supply curve and below the price.* Given that this area is a triangle with a base of $23 − $10 = $13 and a height of 3,300, producer surplus is equal to $(1/2)(\$13)(3,300) = \$21,450$.

Producer surplus is the sum of

1. The aggregate profits of firms supplying good X to the market and
2. The excess compensation paid to the owners of the inputs employed in the production of X

And how is this excess compensation computed? The owners of each of the resources employed in the production of X have "minimum reservation payments" for that employment. That is, they can compute the smallest amount that they would accept in exchange for allowing their resources to be employed in the production of good X. And so, producer surplus measures the net benefit to producers (to firms and perhaps to the owners of the inputs that the firms employ) in just the same way as consumer surplus measures the net benefit to consumers. Consumers would like to increase consumer surplus; producers would like to increase producer surplus. The two can be added together because both are calibrated in dollars (or some other currency). The *Total surplus* result of this addition, dubbed **total surplus,** is a measure of the aggregate net benefit accruing to both consumers and suppliers—to consumers because they are purchasing some good at a given price and to suppliers because they are producing the same good and receiving the same price.

The shaded area in Figure 9.2 shows the total surplus if the perfectly competitive output of 3,300 units were produced and sold. The top shaded area

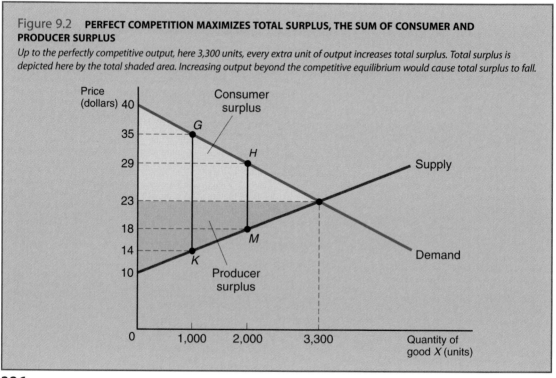

Figure 9.2 **PERFECT COMPETITION MAXIMIZES TOTAL SURPLUS, THE SUM OF CONSUMER AND PRODUCER SURPLUS**

Up to the perfectly competitive output, here 3,300 units, every extra unit of output increases total surplus. Total surplus is depicted here by the total shaded area. Increasing output beyond the competitive equilibrium would cause total surplus to fall.

shows the consumer surplus—the amount that consumers would have willingly paid for these 3,300 units (one unit at a time) above and beyond the $23 per unit that they had to pay (for each and every unit). The bottom shaded area shows the producer surplus—the amount that producers received above and beyond the minimum that would have been required to get them to produce and sell the same 3,300 units (again, one unit at a time). Since total surplus is defined as the sum of consumer and producer surplus, total surplus equals the sum of the top shaded area and the bottom shaded area in Figure 9.2.

Total surplus is a measure of the total net gain to consumers and producers from the production and sale of a particular number of units of the good. Consider, for example, the 1,000th unit. Figure 9.2 shows that consumers would be willing to pay up to $35 for this unit. Figure 9.2 also shows that producers would have taken $14 for producing and selling this unit. The total net gain to society from the production and sale of the 1,000th unit is simply the difference between the most that consumers would have paid and the least that suppliers would have accepted: $35 − $14 = $21. This difference, of course, is the vertical distance KG in Figure 9.2. Similarly, the total net gain from the production and sale of the 2,000th unit is $29 − $18 = $11—the vertical distance MH in Figure 9.2. If we add these vertical distances for all the 3,300 units produced and sold, then we get the total shaded area in Figure 9.2. It equals $49,500 (the area of the largest shaded triangle is $1/2 \times$ [$40 − $10] $\times$ 3,300 = $15 $\times$ 3,300 = $49,500). Consumer surplus equals the area of the lighter-shaded triangle; it equals $1/2 \times$ ($40 − $23) $\times$ 3,300 = $8.50 $\times$ 3,300 = $28,050. We already know that producer surplus equals $21,450. And so the sum equals $28,050 + $21,450 = $49,500. To check our calculations, note that total surplus must equal the area of a triangle with a height equal to $40 − $10 = $30 and a base equal to 3,300 units. The appropriate area, therefore, is equal to $1/2 \times$ $30 $\times$ 3,300 = $49,500. It checks!

Microlink 9.1   Producer Surplus and Consumer Surplus

Producer and consumer surplus are two sides of the same coin, and their derivations are quite similar. Recall that consumer surplus was derived by comparing the sum of the prices that consumers would be willing to pay for successive units of some good X with the total cost that they would in fact pay at some given price. Producer surplus is similarly derived by comparing the cost of producing successive units of some good like X with the revenue that producers would in fact receive by selling X at some given price.

PERFECT COMPETITION AND THE MAXIMIZATION OF TOTAL SURPLUS

Total surplus varies with how many units are produced. But if the maximum amount that consumers are willing to pay for an extra unit exceeds the minimum amount that producers would accept for producing and selling it, then the production and sale of this extra unit increases total surplus. In Figure 9.2, for example, every extra unit up to the perfectly competitive output of

3,300 units increases total surplus. Why? Because the demand curve (which shows the maximum amount that consumers would pay for an extra unit of the good) lies above the supply curve (which shows the minimum amount that producers would accept for producing and selling it). Beyond the perfectly competitive output of 3,300 units, though, every extra unit reduces total surplus because the demand lies below the supply. The value to society of every extra unit above 3,300 units (as reflected by what people would willingly pay for one more unit) is less than the cost to society of producing that unit (as reflected by what producers would require in compensation for its production). There is, of course, nothing magic about 3,300 units; it is simply the output in this case that would be achieved by a competitive market. Taking the argument to a more general level, then, it should be clear that total surplus rises as output increases up to the perfectly competitive level, but it would fall if output rose beyond that point. It follows, then, that *total surplus is maximized when output is at the perfectly competitive level.*

This result—that the perfectly competitive output maximizes the total net gain to consumers and producers—is important. It is a major reason why economists tend to prefer perfect competition to other market structures like monopoly. It is also the basis of using the competitive solution as a benchmark of aggregate economic efficiency. Economists measure the efficiency losses caused by all sorts of distortions and market failures in terms of the difference between the total surplus achieved under competitive conditions and the maximum total surplus that could be achieved under different circumstances. This benchmark role will become clear as we work through a collection of government interventions in a few examples, and it will continue to be exploited in later chapters as we contemplate the efficiency properties of alternative market structures, equilibria under conditions of imperfect information, and the like.

Before proceeding, though, you should recognize that the comparison of total surplus with value that could be achieved at the competitive equilibrium makes a number of implicit assumptions that will be discussed at length in subsequent chapters. For one thing, *using competitive equilibria as the benchmark of maximum efficiency assumes that private costs and benefits match social costs and benefits.* If this were not the case (and it might not be the case in many applied circumstances), then the competitive equilibrium would not maximize social welfare. There could then exist social advantages to the government's intervening in the market so that output would deviate from the competitive outcome. How so? One example should suffice as an answer. The social costs of polluting the air or water frequently exceed the corresponding private costs incurred by the firms who are doing the polluting. As a result, society may be better off if output, and hence pollution, were smaller than the competitive output. In such a situation, the price of the product would include reflections of both the marginal private costs of production *and* the extra marginal social costs that accompany that production, and so the price would be higher. In other words, the benchmark for maximum total surplus would occur at an output that fell short of the competitive equilibrium.

You should also be clear that *using total surplus as a measure of aggregate social welfare ignores distributional issues entirely.* The calculation of total surplus assumes, in particular, that a dollar in value that might be lost or gained should be given the same weight regardless of who feels the pain or enjoys the gain. It does not matter whether the affected individual is rich or poor, deserving or undeserving, consumer or producer. In short, every dollar counts the same. Suppose, as an illustrative example, that the price of a particular good were pushed below the equilibrium by some government policy so that consumer surplus rose by $1 million. Suppose, as well, that the same policy caused producer surplus to fall by $1 million. Total surplus would be unchanged, but the relative economic conditions of producers and consumers would be different. Consumers would gain and producers would lose, but the total surplus measure of social welfare would be unaffected.

THE EFFECT OF A PRICE CEILING

Government agencies often intervene to maintain a price that is below the competitive level. Why? Perhaps because the distributional consequences of the competitive price are intolerable. Or perhaps because consumers have an enormous amount of political power. The federal government has, for example, worked hard to hold the line on the escalating cost of health care because the prices for various procedures and treatments were too high for the poor or the elderly to pay. Perhaps the government even decided that the cost was too high for its own insurance programs. The reason doesn't matter. We are concerned here with the effect. We showed in Chapter 1 that a shortage is likely to be created if the price of a good falls below its equilibrium level. Figure 9.3 displays the reason. If the government established a price ceiling of P_1, then the quantity

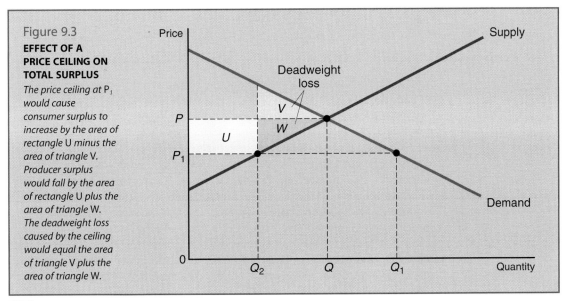

Figure 9.3

EFFECT OF A PRICE CEILING ON TOTAL SURPLUS

The price ceiling at P_1 would cause consumer surplus to increase by the area of rectangle U minus the area of triangle V. Producer surplus would fall by the area of rectangle U plus the area of triangle W. The deadweight loss caused by the ceiling would equal the area of triangle V plus the area of triangle W.

demanded would be Q_1, and the quantity supplied would be Q_2. The quantity demanded would therefore exceed the quantity supplied by $Q_1 - Q_2$. We can now extend this analysis, using the concepts of consumer and producer surplus, to evaluate who would gain, who would lose, and by how much. And we can use total surplus to evaluate whether aggregate social welfare would rise or fall.

Price ceiling

Consider consumers first. The **price ceiling** lowered the price from the equilibrium level, P, to P_1, and so the quantity supplied would fall from Q to Q_2. Some consumers who used to be able to buy the product would no longer find any on the shelves. The lucky ones who could still buy the product would, however, enjoy an increase in consumer surplus equal to the area of rectangle U because they would pay price P_1 rather than P. But those who were frustrated in their shopping experience would suffer a loss of consumer surplus equal to the area of triangle V. Thus, the net change in consumer surplus would be equal to the area of U minus the area of V. Notice that these changes in consumer surplus are drawn in Figure 9.3 so that $U > V$; thus social welfare (on the consumption side of the market) would be improved *despite the fact that some consumers were worse off*.

Turning now to producers, notice that the remaining suppliers would receive price P_1 for their product rather than P. They would therefore experience a loss in producer surplus equal to the area of rectangle U. In addition, output would fall from Q to Q_2 so that producer surplus would fall even more—by an amount equal to the area of triangle W. The total loss of producer surplus would be equal to the area of U plus the area of W.

Consumers in Figure 9.3 would gain from the price ceiling, and producers would lose. But would the consumers' gains exceed the producers' losses? It is easy to show that the answer is no. The ceiling would have caused

Deadweight loss

a reduction in total surplus by an amount that economists call the **deadweight loss**. How do we know that total surplus would fall? Recall that the (net) increase in consumer surplus would be area $U -$ area V and that the reduction in producer surplus would be area $U +$ area W. Total surplus would therefore change by

$$(U - V) - (U + W) = -(V + W) < 0.$$

And so the deadweight loss of the price ceiling would equal area $V +$ area W because this is a measure of lost total surplus.

Consumers gained from the price ceiling in Figure 9.3, but even this is not always the case. If the demand for the product were sufficiently price-inelastic, then a price ceiling could actually reduce consumer surplus as well as producer surplus. Figure 9.4 shows how. The key point to note is that triangle V—the measure of lost consumer surplus to those consumers who could no longer buy the good—is much bigger in Figure 9.4 than it was in Figure 9.3. It is bigger even than area U—the measure of increased consumer surplus enjoyed by consumers who could buy the good at a lower price. And so net consumer welfare would fall in this case *despite the fact that some consumers were better off*. Why? Inelastic demand of the sort portrayed in Figure 9.4 means that frustrated consumers would place a high value on each unit of forgone consumption, and so the contraction in supply would be more damaging to them than it was in Figure 9.3.

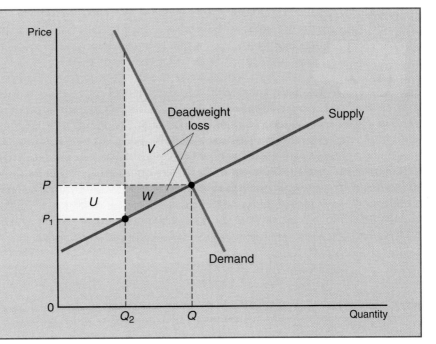

Figure 9.4

EFFECT OF A PRICE CEILING ON TOTAL SURPLUS (INELASTIC DEMAND)

Consumer surplus, as well as producer surplus, would fall if demand were sufficiently price-inelastic because the area of triangle V can exceed the area of rectangle U in that case.

| Example 9.1 | **A Price Ceiling for Gasoline?** |

The U.S. government tried to curb inflationary pressures and avoid unpopular increases in the price of gasoline during the 1970s by maintaining a price ceiling on gasoline. In accord with our theory, there was a shortage of gasoline; that is, the quantity demanded exceeded the quantity supplied. The rationing system that developed was based on how long people were willing to wait at gas pumps. Lines of cars would form at gas stations, and those people who were willing to wait eventually got the gasoline they wanted. Those who were unwilling to spend their time in this way did not get gasoline (or hired people to get it for them). We are now in a position to use market analysis to explore the implications of this approach.

Suppose, to that end, that the demand and supply for gasoline in the 1970s were as shown in Figure 9.5, and assume that the government targeted 75 cents as the ceiling price (these prices are low to your experience, but remember we are looking at the late 1970s when a price of 75 cents was more than 100 percent higher than the price that cleared the market in 1972). Consumer surplus would equal the area of triangle *GEA* at the market-clearing price of $1.00, and it would equal area *FDBA* with a price ceiling of 75 cents. The ceiling would therefore increase consumer surplus by

$$\text{area } FDCG - \text{area } CEB$$
$$= (\$1.00 - \$0.75) \times (90 \text{ billion}) - (1/2)(\$1.25 - \$1.00)$$
$$\times (100 \text{ billion} - 90 \text{ billion})$$
$$= \$21.25 \text{ billion}.$$

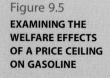

Figure 9.5

EXAMINING THE WELFARE EFFECTS OF A PRICE CEILING ON GASOLINE

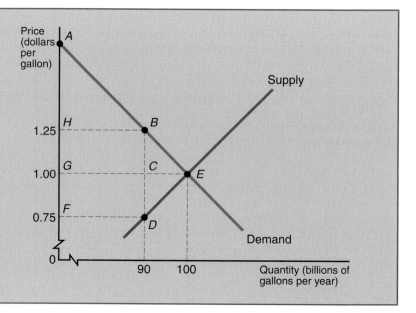

Producer surplus would meanwhile fall by

area *FDEG* = area *FDCG* + area *DEC*

= ($1.00 − $0.75) × (90 billion) + (1/2)($1.00 − $0.75) × (100 billion − 90 billion)

= $23.75 billion.

Notwithstanding benefits to consumers, deadweight loss in the amount of

$23.75 billion − $21.25 billion = $2.5 billion

would be felt.

THE EFFECT OF A PRICE FLOOR

Price floor

Governments frequently require that the price of a good be above, rather than below, the equilibrium price. That is, they often impose **price floors** rather than price ceilings. Suppose, for example, that lobbyists for the lumber industry succeeded in persuading the government to establish a price floor of P' in Figure 9.6. A price floor should cause the quantity demanded (Q_2) to fall short of the quantity supplied (Q_1). If producers cut back their output so it equaled the quantity demanded (Q_2), then consumer surplus would fall by the area of rectangle A because consumers would pay $P' − P$ dollars more for each of the Q_2 units of the good that they would buy. In addition, consumers would lose consumer surplus equal to the area of triangle B because they would consume Q_2 rather than Q units of the good.

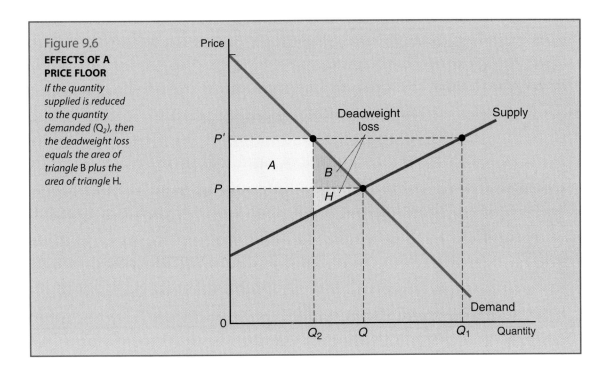

Figure 9.6

EFFECTS OF A PRICE FLOOR

If the quantity supplied is reduced to the quantity demanded (Q_2), then the deadweight loss equals the area of triangle B plus the area of triangle H.

Producers, on the other hand, would receive extra revenue equal to the area of rectangle A because they would receive a price that is $P' - P$ dollars higher for the Q_2 units that they would sell, given the price floor. But they would lose producer surplus equal to the area of triangle H because they would sell only Q_2 rather than Q units of the good. So, producers' net gain (or loss) would equal the area of rectangle A minus the area of triangle H. Consumers would lose an amount equal to the areas of rectangle A and triangle B. And so there would be a reduction in the aggregate welfare of consumers and producers equal to the change in total surplus:

$$(\text{area } A - \text{area } H) - (\text{area } A + \text{area } B) = -(\text{area } H + \text{area } B) < 0.$$

This loss in total surplus (the sum of the net change in producer surplus plus the loss in consumer surplus) would be the deadweight loss caused by the price floor.

| Example 9.2 | **Regulating Rents for New York Apartments** |

"▮ hate it," said Andrea Bochmann. She was trying to find an apartment in Manhattan. She, her husband, and her 9-year-old daughter were about to spend a year in New York. She was a journalist; he had a fellowship. And the housing market in New York City was quite different from anything that they had experienced. It was, in fact, different from what she might have expected anywhere else in the United States. Only about 30 percent of New Yorkers own their own homes—less than half the countrywide average of

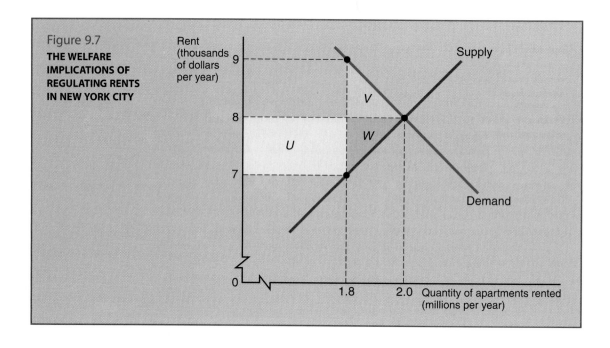

Figure 9.7

THE WELFARE IMPLICATIONS OF REGULATING RENTS IN NEW YORK CITY

over 60 percent. New York is a city of renters who often live in large apartment buildings. More to the point, though, the quantity of apartments demanded in New York has historically exceeded the quantity supplied—and so Mrs. Bochmann's frustration.

The bulk of New York City's apartments do not rent at the levels that would prevail in a free market. The rents paid for apartments that were constructed between 1947 and 1971 are, instead, regulated by the New York City Rent Guidelines Board. This board establishes how big rent increases can be, and it sets limits on vacancy allowances (increases in rent that are permitted when an apartment becomes vacant and is re-rented to another tenant).

Figure 9.7 provides a highly simplified but adequate representation of the demand and supply of apartments in New York City. There are about 1.8 million apartments in the city, and the average rent in 1995 was about $7,000 per year. In the absence of rent regulations, the equilibrium rent would be about $8,000 according to the figure. Following the techniques just described, we can calculate the gains and losses to renters and landlords due to the rent ceiling in New York City by computing the areas of rectangle U and triangles V and W in Figure 9.7:

$$U = 1.8 \text{ million} \times (\$8,000 - \$7,000) = \$1,800 \text{ million}$$
$$V = \tfrac{1}{2}(2.0 \text{ million} - 1.8 \text{ million}) \times (\$9,000 - \$8,000) = \$100 \text{ million}$$
$$W = \tfrac{1}{2}(2.0 \text{ million} - 1.8 \text{ million}) \times (\$8,000 - \$7,000) = \$100 \text{ million}$$

The gain in consumer surplus due to rent regulations is therefore

$$U - V = \$1,800 \text{ million} - \$100 \text{ million} = \$1,700 \text{ million per year.}$$

334

And the loss in producer surplus is

$$U + W = \$1,800 \text{ million} + \$100 \text{ million} = \$1,900 \text{ million per year.}$$

In other words, landlords lose $1,900 million per year—an amount that is $200 million more than what renters gain. As a result, there is an estimated deadweight loss of $200 million per year. This is a measure of the efficiency cost of rent control—the reduction in the aggregate welfare of landlords and renters.[1] And what about the distribution of gains and losses among renters and frustrated apartment shoppers? New Yorkers who can find apartments enjoy extra consumer surplus equal to area U ($1,800 million); frustrated apartment shoppers lose consumer surplus equal to area V ($100 million).

▣ Agricultural Price Supports—A Variation on a Theme

We assumed, in the preceding section, that producers would respond to a price floor by willingly reducing their output to a level that matched a lower quantity demanded (Q_2 in Figure 9.6). This is not always the case, however. Agricultural price supports are frequently arranged so that producers may grow as much as they please at the stated price level. What happens to the surplus? The government buys it. This situation is depicted in Figure 9.8. Suppose, to understand the figure, that the support price were set equal to P'. The quantity supplied would then equal Q_1; the quantity demanded would equal $Q_2 < Q_1$. And so the government would have to buy the difference—an amount equal to $Q_1 - Q_2$.

Do the producers of farm products gain more from such programs than the consumers of farm products lose? That is a good question. How much would consumers lose? Consumer surplus would equal the area of triangle PMK without the price support—the area under the demand curve and above the price, taken here to be P. With the price support, consumer surplus would equal the area of triangle $P'LK$—the area under the demand curve and above the support price P'. The price support would therefore cause consumer surplus to fall by an amount equal to the shaded areas A and B. How much would producers gain? Producer surplus without the price support would equal the area of triangle PMR—the area above the supply curve and below the price P. And producer surplus would equal the area of triangle $P'NR$ with the price support—the area above the supply curve and below P'. The price support would therefore cause producer surplus to grow by an amount equal to the shaded areas A, B, and C.

---

[1] It is important to recognize that this model is simplified in a variety of ways. For example, not all apartments in New York City are rent-controlled. Also, apartments are by no means homogeneous, and the demand and supply elasticities in Figure 9.7 are only illustrative. The present analysis is for instructive purposes. For much more detailed and sophisticated studies of this topic, see E. Roistacher, "Rent Regulation in New York City: Simulating Decontrol Options," *Journal of Housing Economics*, 1992; and H. Pollakowski, "The Effects of Partial Rent Deregulation in New York City," Joint Center for Housing Studies, Harvard University, Cambridge, Mass., 1992. See the *New York Times*, April 23, 1995, for the background data and a story about the plight of Mrs. Bochmann.

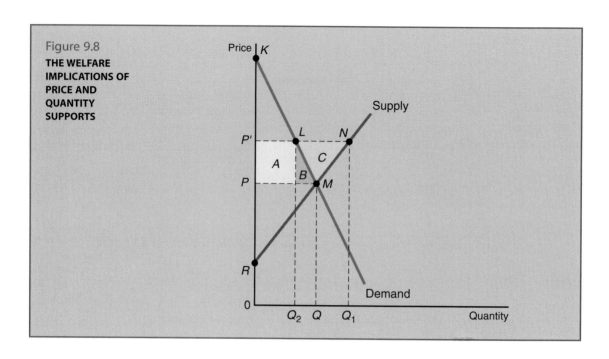

Figure 9.8

THE WELFARE IMPLICATIONS OF PRICE AND QUANTITY SUPPORTS

So, consumer surplus would fall by areas A and B and producer surplus would increase by areas A, B, and C. It would appear that producers would gain more than consumers would lose, but this is true only because we have ignored the cost to the government of buying $Q_1 - Q_2$ units of the product to support its price at P'. That cost would amount to $P' \times (Q_1 - Q_2)$ since the government would buy $(Q_1 - Q_2)$ units of the product at a price of P'. This cost, which equals area $Q_2 L N Q_1$, would be borne by the taxpayers and should be factored into the calculation. The total cost of the program would therefore equal area $Q_2 L N Q_1$ plus areas A and B; this total would greatly exceed the associated increase in producer surplus.

Many economists have suggested that it would be more efficient for consumers simply to transfer directly to producers an amount of money equal to areas A, B, and C and to eliminate the price support. Producers would be as well off if this suggestion were adopted as under the price support; they would gain areas A, B, and C in either case. Consumers and taxpayers would be better off because the cost to them (areas A, B, and C) would be much less than under the support system (area $Q_2 L N Q_1$ plus areas A and B).

One big reason why the cost is so great under price supports is that consumers, in the guise of taxpayers, finance the government's purchase of farm products that consumers do not want at the support price. To reduce the amount that the government has to purchase (and store or dispose of), production controls frequently are imposed. These controls often take the form of quotas on the acreage used to grow the product. They tend to lower the cost to consumers of farm price supports, but still consumers lose more than producers gain.

PROTECTING DOMESTIC PRODUCERS: TARIFFS AND QUOTAS

Governments also impose tariffs and quotas to protect domestic producers from foreign competition. Like the price ceilings and price floors discussed in previous sections, these tariffs and quotas are likely to reduce the efficiency of the economy. Consider the case of textiles. Suppose that the demand and supply curves in the United States for textiles are shown in Figure 9.9. With no international trade, the equilibrium price would be P and the equilibrium output would be Q. But now suppose that the world price for textiles is P_W, which is below P. If international trade were allowed, then the price of textiles in the United States would have to fall to the world level. The quantity of textiles supplied by U.S. producers would fall to Q_S. The quantity of textiles demanded by U.S. consumers would rise to Q_D. And the United States would import $Q_D - Q_S$ units from abroad.

Who would gain from the opening up of international trade? Clearly, consumer surplus would increase by the areas of trapezoid G plus triangle F plus triangle E. Why? Because the area under the demand curve and above the price would equal area PBC without international trade and area P_WAC with trade; the difference is the area of the trapezoid P_WPBA. Consumers would be happy; they could buy their textiles at a lower price. But U.S. producers would not be at all happy. Their producer surplus would fall by the area of trapezoid G with the opening of trade. The area above the supply curve and under the price would equal the area of triangle ZBP without international trade and it would equal the area of triangle ZHP_W with trade;

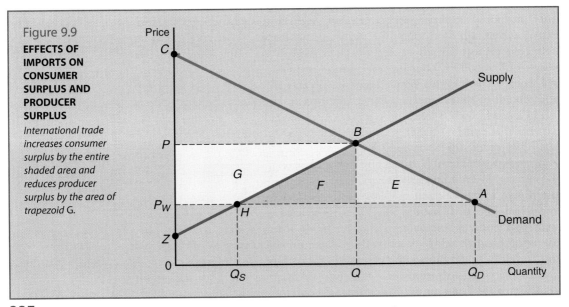

Figure 9.9

EFFECTS OF IMPORTS ON CONSUMER SURPLUS AND PRODUCER SURPLUS

International trade increases consumer surplus by the entire shaded area and reduces producer surplus by the area of trapezoid G.

the difference is the area of trapezoid $PBHP_W$, that is, trapezoid G. Their unhappiness would stem directly from the fact that they would produce less product for a lower price.

Example 9.3

Opening Trade—A Quick Look at the North American Free Trade Agreement

Analyses based on competitive models like the one depicted in Figure 9.9 predict lots of good things from opening trade—lower domestic prices, increased consumer surplus, the transfer of employment to more productive sectors of the economy (the people and resources who are laid off when domestic production falls), and higher demand for labor in sectors whose demand from abroad expands. Economists have long argued that these benefits outweigh the losses felt by other actors in the economy, but are the conclusions always true? What can go wrong? The adoption of the North American Free Trade Agreement (NAFTA) in the 1990s provides an interesting experiment with which to examine these questions.

Many consumers on both sides of the border between Mexico and the United States benefited from NAFTA, just as expected in Figure 9.9; but there have been losers, as well. One problem, of course, has been that "winners" (the consumers who pay lower prices) do not typically compensate losers (the people whose businesses contract) even when total surplus increases. We have already discussed the shortcomings of strictly applying producer and consumer surplus in this regard. Each market intervention, even if it increases total surplus as in Figure 9.9, redistributes welfare to some degree; and the only conclusion to be drawn when total welfare rises is that these benefits are large enough to allow winners to be better off even if they compensated losers. As usual, NAFTA does not explicitly include provisions for this sort of compensation.

Perhaps more fundamentally, though, the increase in demand for foreign products implied in Figure 9.9 as domestic prices fall to world levels (i.e., U.S. prices fall to reflect Mexican supply) was expected to increase the demand for labor in Mexico and thereby increase wages. Mexican workers would therefore be better off, but this has not happened. Why? Not because the demand in the U.S. for Mexican products has not increased. Rather, it is because Mexico suffered 35 percent unemployment in 1995. Upward pressure on wages was not felt, therefore, because employers could simply expand their workforces by hiring willing workers at existing wages. Employed workers are no better off than before, in general; but thousands of unemployed workers do now have jobs.

SOURCE: http://www.mexico-trade.com/nafta.html.

Faced with losses in producer surplus of the sort depicted in Figure 9.9, domestic producers (and their workers whose jobs would be in jeopardy as production fell) frequently press the government for protection from foreign competition. The government could provide this protection by imposing a tariff on imports. The government could, for example, charge a

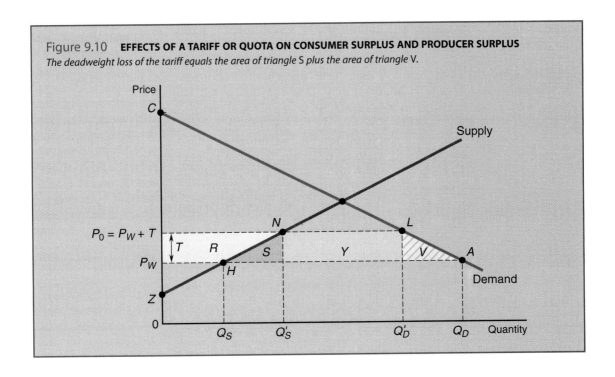

Figure 9.10 **EFFECTS OF A TARIFF OR QUOTA ON CONSUMER SURPLUS AND PRODUCER SURPLUS**
The deadweight loss of the tariff equals the area of triangle S plus the area of triangle V.

tariff (i.e., a tax) of T dollars per unit on all textiles imported into the United States. The result of such a policy is shown in Figure 9.10. The price charged by foreign producers would rise in the United States by T dollars per unit (that is, from P_W to P_0 where $P_0 = P_W + T$). The quantity demanded would therefore fall from Q_D to Q_D', but domestic output would rise from Q_S to Q_S'. And, of course, imports would fall from $Q_D - Q_S$ to $Q_D' - Q_S'$.

What effects would imposing this tariff have on consumer surplus and producer surplus? Consumer surplus would fall by an amount equal to the areas of trapezoid R + triangle S + rectangle Y + triangle V. Why? Because consumer surplus would equal area P_WAC under free trade and area P_0LC after the imposition of the tariff. Producer surplus would meanwhile climb by the area of trapezoid R because producer surplus would equal area ZHP_W under free trade and area ZNP_0 after the imposition of the tariff. Finally, the government would collect revenue equal to the amount of the tariff times the quantity of textiles imported—an amount equal to the area of rectangle Y. Adding things up, then, the gains to domestic producers and the government would be the sum of the areas of trapezoid R and rectangle Y. Comparing losses and gains, therefore, the difference between the reduction in consumer surplus and the gains received by producers and the government would be the areas of

$$(R + Y) - (R + S + Y + V) = -(S + V).$$

This is the deadweight loss of the tariff.

The government could, of course, choose to protect domestic producers by establishing an import quota instead of a tariff. Suppose that the U.S. government decided not to allow imports of textiles to exceed $Q_D' - Q_S'$ in Figure 9.10. Foreign producers would then charge a price of P_0 so that the market would clear. The quantity supplied by domestic producers would then be exactly $Q_D' - Q_S'$ units short of the total quantity demanded. Notice that $P_0 = P_W + T$. Consumers would, as a result, pay the same price as they would under the tariff considered in the preceding paragraphs, and domestic producers would receive the same price. The associated changes in consumer and producer surplus would therefore be the same as they would be under the tariff. Unlike a tariff, though, a quota would not necessarily provide the government with revenue. And so an amount equal to the area of rectangle Y could go to foreign producers in the form of higher profits unless the government sold the rights to sell Q_D' minus Q_S' units in the United States to the highest bidder.[2]

Example 9.4	**Gains and Losses from Steel Import Quotas—A Worked Example**

High unemployment levels in the United States and Europe placed pressure on free trade during the recessions of the 1980s. Bethlehem Steel Corporation, for example, lost about $1.5 billion in 1982. Faced with stiff price competition from Japanese and other foreign steelmakers, U.S. firms such as Bethlehem petitioned for limitations on steel imports. Their pleas were heard: quotas were established in 1984 that limited steel imports to 20 percent of the U.S. market by 1989.

The Federal Trade Commission (FTC) had conducted a review of the various issues concerning these sorts of restrictions in 1977. The microeconomic basis for their analysis is displayed in Figure 9.11. U.S. demand and supply curves for steel are shown there. So, too, is the supply curve for foreign-produced steel: the horizontal line drawn at $311 per ton: Curve *SGW* is the horizontal sum of U.S. and foreign supply; it represents the supply curve for all steel. Notice that it intersects demand at point. *A*. Initial equilibrium therefore occurred at a price of $311 per ton with 91.7 million tons demanded. Of that total, 78.1 million tons (designated by point *G*) was supplied by U.S. firms the remainder, 13.6 million tons, was imported.

What would be the effect of the U.S. government's imposing a quota that limited imports to 11 million tons? That is, what would be the resulting domestic price for steel? How much would be demanded at the new equilibrium? And how much would be produced by U.S. steelmakers? Demand would exceed domestic supply by exactly 11 million tons if the price of steel were to climb to $322 per ton. So the quota would increase the price to that level. The new equilibrium would occur at point *B*, where 90.8 million tons of steel would be demanded. Of this total, 79.8 million tons would be sold by domestic suppliers and 11 million tons would come in from abroad.

---

[2]If the government maintained a quota by selling rights to import a particular quantity of the good per year, it could obtain revenue equal to the area of rectangle Y. How so? Because this area represents the total value of such rights to the importers (and the tariff represents the market clearing price of the right to import 1 unit). Import rights are frequently given away, though, so the area of rectangle Y is transferred as a windfall to the recipients.

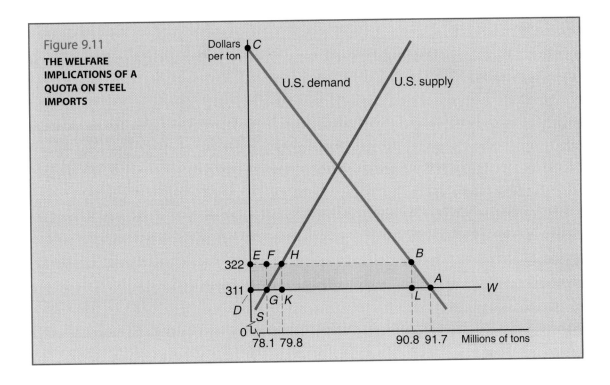

Figure 9.11

THE WELFARE IMPLICATIONS OF A QUOTA ON STEEL IMPORTS

We can also compute the size and distribution of resulting changes in producer and consumer surplus at home and abroad. Consumer surplus would equal the area of triangles *DCA* before the quota and *ECB* after the quota. Consumer surplus would therefore fall by the area of trapezoid *DEBA* (the shaded area). This area equals ($322 − $311) × 1/2 × (90.8 million + 91.7 million) = $1,003.75 million. U.S. steel producers would gain in two ways. First, they would sell the original 78.1 million tons of steel at $322 per ton instead of $311. The extra profit from these sales would be the area of rectangle *DEFG*: ($322 − $311) × 78.1 million = $859.1 million. They would also be able to sell an additional 1.7 million tons (= 79.8 million − 78.1 million). Their profit for these units would equal the area of triangle *GFH*: 1/2 × ($322 − $311) × (79.8 − 78.1) = $9.35 million. (This calculation assumes that their supply curve represents marginal cost so that this area picks up the additional revenue net of cost for each extra unit between 78.1 million and 79.8 million.) The imposition of the quota would meanwhile see foreign steel producers sell each of the 11 million units at a price that was $11 per unit higher. Their profit would therefore increase by the area of rectangle *KHBL*: ($322 − $311) × 11 million = $121 million. Since their supply curve is horizontal, there is no loss in profit from the reduction in the quantity exported to the United States.

The loss in consumer surplus net of the increase in profits earned by U.S. steelmakers represents the loss in welfare for the United States: $1,003.75 million − $859.1 million − $9.35 million = $135.3 million. Welfare would

climb by $121 million abroad, so the net global loss in welfare would be
$135.3 million − $121 million = $14.3 million.[3]

Lest you think that the issue of protecting the U.S. steel industry is
ancient history from the 1980s, you should recall that the Bush administration imposed new duties on steel imports from much of the world in
March 2001. Why? Because the U.S. steel industry had suffered 31 bank-
ruptcies over the previous 4 years. Lobbyists for the industry blamed
"dumping" by foreign producers (selling product at prices below marginal
cost) and had demanded that a 40 percent tariff be imposed. The administration responded to the demand by exempting only imports from Canada
and Mexico (partners in the North American Free Trade Agreement—
NAFTA) plus developing countries from a 30 percent tariff over the next
3 years. These provisions guaranteed that the tariff would apply to the four
major sources of imported steel: Korea, Japan, Russia, and Brazil.

EFFECTS ON PRICE OF AN EXCISE TAX

Governments also impose taxes on goods like cigarettes, beer, tires, gasoline,
and a variety of other goods. In this section, we discuss the effects of such a
tax on the price of a good; in the next section, we take up the tax's effects on
consumer and producer surpluses. Suppose that such a tax is imposed on a particular good, say cigarettes.[4] You might even see this analysis as germane to the
effect of the 1998 court settlement between a large number of states and the
tobacco industry. The tobacco industry agreed to pay the states amounts that
are measured in tens of billions of dollars, and tobacco producers agreed to
raise these sums by increasing the price of cigarettes by 45 cents per pack.[5]

Imposing an
excise tax

In either case, Figure 9.12 shows the relevant demand and supply curves,
D and *S*, for cigarettes before the imposition of the tax or the advent of the
court settlement. Obviously, the equilibrium price of a pack of cigarettes is
$3.20, and the equilibrium quantity is 50 million packs. If a tax of 40 cents
were imposed on each pack produced, what would be the effect on the price
of each pack? Or to see it from a smoker's perspective, how much of the tax
would be passed on to the consumer in the form of a higher price?

Since the tax would be collected from the sellers, the supply curve would
shift upward by the amount of the tax. In Figure 9.12, the after-tax supply
curve is S_T. If a pretax price of $2.80 a pack had been required to induce

[3]For further discussion, see D. Tarr, *A General Equilibrium Analysis of the Welfare and
Employment Effects of U.S. Quotas in Textiles, Autos and Steel* (Washington, D.C.: Federal Trade
Commission, 1989), and National Academy of Engineering, *The Competitive Status of the U.S.
Steel Industry* (Washington, D.C.: National Academy Press, 1985).
[4]For simplicity, we assume that the market for cigarettes is perfectly competitive. In later chapters, we present models that pertain to cases where there are relatively few producers. Recall
that Example 4.3 provided some insight into the demand side of the cigarette market.
[5]Estimates, as of January 2002, saw prices rising another 50 cents a pack through 2010 as states
tried to raise revenue. These increases were expected on top of price responses to the court
settlement; see J. Pope, "Cigarette Prices Could Jump 22 Cents," Associated Press, August
31, 1999.

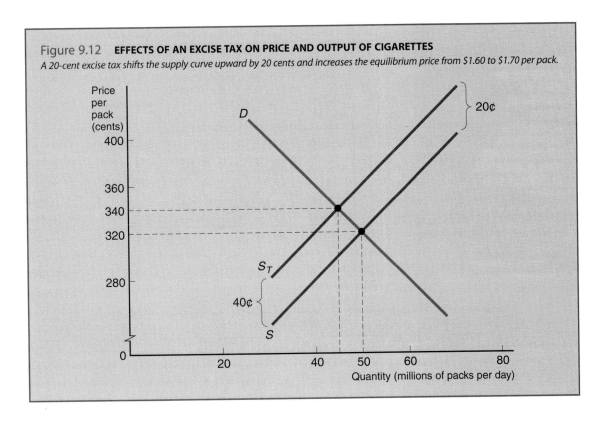

Figure 9.12 **EFFECTS OF AN EXCISE TAX ON PRICE AND OUTPUT OF CIGARETTES**
A 20-cent excise tax shifts the supply curve upward by 20 cents and increases the equilibrium price from $1.60 to $1.70 per pack.

sellers to supply 40 million packs of cigarettes, then the after-tax price would have to be 40 cents higher—or $3.20 a pack—to induce the same supply. Similarly, if the pretax price had to be $3.20 a pack to induce sellers to supply 50 million packs of cigarettes, then the after-tax price would have to be 40 cents higher—or $3.60 a pack—to induce the same supply. Why? Simply because suppliers have to pay 40 cents per pack directly to the government.

Distributing the burden of an excise tax

Figure 9.12 shows that the equilibrium price of cigarettes would be $3.40 after the tax is imposed. This would be an increase of 20 cents over the pretax price. In this case, then, half the tax would be passed on to consumers, who would pay 20 cents more for cigarettes. The other half of the tax would be swallowed by the sellers, who would receive (after they paid the tax) 20 cents less per pack. It is not always true that sellers pass half the tax on to consumers and absorb the rest themselves. On the contrary, in some cases, consumers may bear almost all of the tax while sellers bear practically none of it; in other cases, consumers may bear almost none of the tax because sellers are forced to bear practically all of it. The allocation of burden depends on how sensitive the quantity demanded and the quantity supplied are to changes in the price of the good; i.e., the allocation of burden depends on the price elasticities of supply and demand.

To explore this point, consider panel A of Figure 9.13. It shows the effect of a 40-cent-per-pack tax for two representations of the cigarette market. In the first, the quantity demanded (D_1) is much more sensitive to price than

343

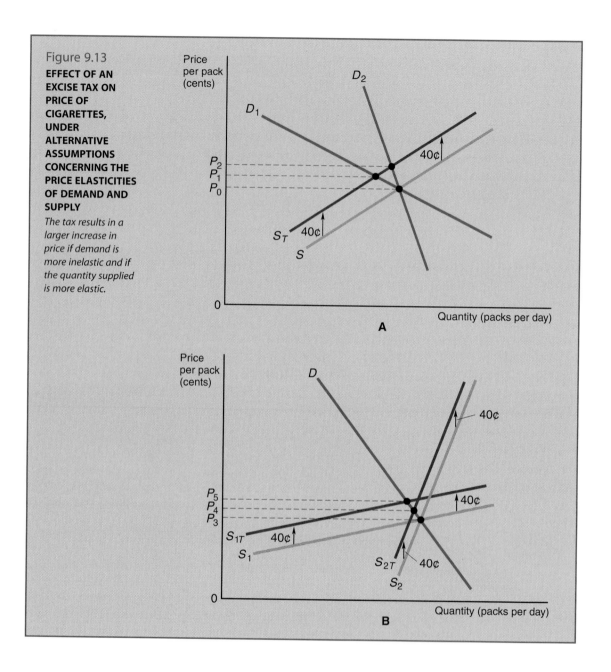

Figure 9.13

EFFECT OF AN EXCISE TAX ON PRICE OF CIGARETTES, UNDER ALTERNATIVE ASSUMPTIONS CONCERNING THE PRICE ELASTICITIES OF DEMAND AND SUPPLY

The tax results in a larger increase in price if demand is more inelastic and if the quantity supplied is more elastic.

in the other (D_2). Before the tax, the equilibrium price would be P_0 regardless of whether D_1 or D_2 represented the demand curve. After the tax, the equilibrium price would be P_1 if the demand curve were D_1, or P_2 if the demand curve were D_2. Clearly, the increase in the price to the consumer would be greater if the quantity demanded were less price-elastic (D_2) than if it were more price-elastic (D_1). Panel A therefore demonstrates a general result: larger portions of an excise tax are shifted to consumers, holding the supply curve constant, when demand is more inelastic.

Panel B demonstrates the analogous result for differences in supply. Larger portions of an excise tax are absorbed by suppliers when, holding the demand curve constant, the supply of the good subjected to the tax is more inelastic. Panel B, in particular, shows the effect of a 40-cent-per-pack tax on cigarettes for two different representations of the supply side of a market. The quantity supplied in the first (S_1) is much more sensitive to price than in the other (S_2). The equilibrium price is P_3 before the tax regardless of whether S_1 or S_2 is the pretax supply curve. The equilibrium price after the tax is P_4 if the (pretax) supply curve is S_2 or P_5 if the (pretax) supply curve is S_1. Clearly, the increase in the price to the consumer is greater if the quantity supplied is more price-elastic (S_1) than if it is less price-elastic (S_2).[6]

DEADWEIGHT LOSS FROM AN EXCISE TAX

Figure 9.14 can now be used to determine the effects of an excise tax on consumer and producer surpluses. The figure shows that the pretax price and output are P and Q, respectively. The after-tax output is Q_0. It would be supported by consumers' paying a price of P_b and sellers' receiving an

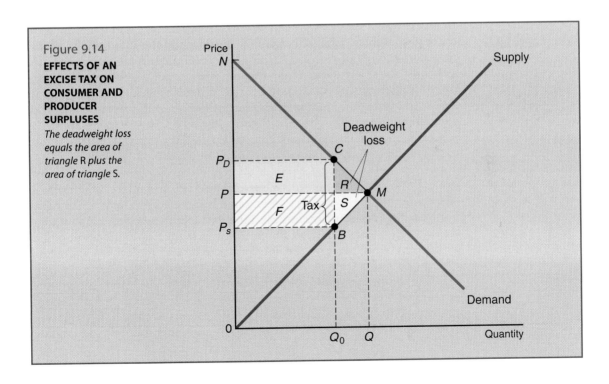

Figure 9.14

EFFECTS OF AN EXCISE TAX ON CONSUMER AND PRODUCER SURPLUSES

The deadweight loss equals the area of triangle R plus the area of triangle S.

[6]To summarize the results of this and the preceding paragraph, the proportion of a tax passed through to consumers equals $\eta_S/(\eta_S + \eta)$, where η_S is the price elasticity of supply and η is the price elasticity of demand.

after-tax price of P_s. The price paid by the buyer, P_b, would exceed the net price received by the seller, P_s, by the amount of the tax.

What would be the effect of the excise tax on consumers? Consumer surplus equals the area of triangle PMN before the tax; it would equal the area of triangle P_bCN after the tax. The tax would therefore reduce consumer surplus by an amount equal to the area of rectangle E plus the area of triangle R.

What would be the effect on producers? Producer surplus equals the area of triangle $0PM$ before the tax; it would equal the area of triangle $0P_sB$ after the tax. And so the tax would reduce producer surplus by an amount equal to the area of rectangle F plus the area of triangle S.

Finally, government tax revenue would equal the after-tax output, Q_0, multiplied by the amount of the tax. Revenue would thus equal the area of rectangle E plus the area of rectangle F. Part of the lost consumer surplus (the part designated by the area of rectangle E) would therefore go to the government in the form of tax payments. And part of the lost producer surplus (the part designated by the area of rectangle F) would also go to the government in the form of tax payments. Ultimately, then, the net change in social welfare caused by the tax would equal the change in consumer surplus plus the change in producer surplus net of the revenue collected by the government. The net change in social welfare would be equal to

$$(E + R) - (F + S) + (E + F) = -(R + S).$$

In other words, the tax would reduce total surplus by an amount equal to the lost consumer surplus that is not absorbed by the government in tax revenue (the area of triangle R) plus lost producer surplus that is not absorbed by the government in tax revenue (the area of triangle S). This sum is the deadweight loss caused by the tax. Notice explicitly that this loss is measured against the maximal efficiency of the original, pretax competitive equilibrium.[7]

| Example 9.5 | **Should the Gasoline Tax Be Raised?** |

The Clinton administration turned Example 9.1 around in 1993 by proposing that the federal tax on gasoline be raised. It was not a new idea. For example, presidential candidate John Anderson suggested such a tax increase as early as 1980. The Clinton idea was motivated in part by a desire to inspire energy conservation in its own right and in part by a growing concern that U.S. energy consumption was contributing to global warming. The idea was supported by then Senator Bill Bradley from New Jersey and future presidential candidate Al Gore from Tennessee, but it was opposed vehemently by the congressional delegations from the oil-producing states. Producers of gasoline were joined by consumer groups in advocating

[7]It is easy to extend this analysis to show the effects of a subsidy. Under a subsidy, the seller's price exceeds the price to the buyer; the difference between these two prices is equal to the subsidy. Put differently, a subsidy can be regarded as a negative tax. The benefit of a subsidy is divided between consumers and producers. If the price elasticity of demand is small and the price elasticity of supply is large, the benefit goes mostly to consumers; if the opposite is true, it goes mostly to producers.

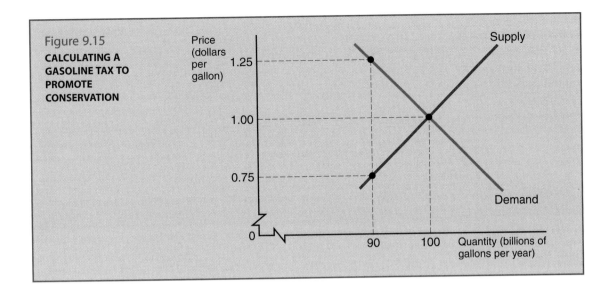

Figure 9.15

CALCULATING A GASOLINE TAX TO PROMOTE CONSERVATION

against the idea. The opponents defeated the bill that carried the idea to Congress.

To explore why, suppose that the market demand and supply curves for gasoline were as shown in Figure 9.15, and assume that the federal government wanted to increase prices by 25 percent from $1.00 to $1.25 per gallon. Notice, first of all, that a 50 cents per gallon tax would be required. Consumer surplus would have been reduced by ($1.25 − $1.00) × 90 billion + (1/2) × ($1.25 − $1.00) × (100 billion − 90 billion) = $23.75 billion. Consumers were right to have been concerned if they were thinking only of welfare derived over the short term from energy consumption, but there is not enough information to judge whether the long-term conservation and environmental benefits would have been larger. Producer surplus would have been reduced by ($1.00 − $0.75) × 90 billion + (1/2) × ($1.00 − $0.75) × (100 billion − 90 billion) = $23.75 billion. Producers concerned with short-term gains and losses were right to be opposed, as well, but they, too, were ignoring longer-term issues that might have turned their calculations around. The government would have received revenue of 50 cents times 90 billion = $45 billion, but the short-term deadweight loss would have been $23.75 billion + $23.75 billion − $45 billion = $2.5 billion per year.

POSTSCRIPT

Much of this chapter and its examples has been devoted to the study of government policies. We have seen that a perfectly competitive economy maximizes the total net gain of consumers and producers. We then showed in more detail how deadweight losses—reductions in economic efficiency—result if the government

347

imposes a price ceiling (which maintains the price below the competitive level), a price floor (which maintains the price above the competitive level), a tariff, a quota, or an excise tax. The general theme of these findings seems to be that the economy would be better off if the government quit meddling and let competitive markets alone. In many cases, this is sound advice, but not always. For one thing, policy makers and the public often are concerned about objectives other than economic efficiency (for example, equity and the distribution of welfare). For another thing, the government might be worried that private and social costs do not match. These and other relevant considerations are taken up in Chapters 16 through 18, where we will analyze the role of government and markets in much more detail.

| Example 9.6 | Going the Other Way—The Efficiency of Artificial Markets |

Economists have long held that market efficiencies can reduce the cost of achieving specific policy objectives. We can explore this view by considering how markets arose for permits to emit some sort of polluting compound like sulfur dioxide. Figure 9.16 provides a simple context for this work. Marginal-cost schedules for reducing SO_2 emissions are displayed there for two different firms; points E_{Imax} and E_{IImax} indicate maximum emissions for firms I and II, respectively, in the absence of any government intervention. Now suppose that the government wanted to reduce emissions by 50 percent so that a total of $(E_{\text{Imax}} + E_{\text{IImax}})/2$ is actually emitted. How could this target be achieved at least cost? The total cost of emissions reduction would be minimized if the marginal cost of the last unit removed from the effluent of firm I were equal to the marginal cost of the last unit removed from the effluent of firm II. How do we know that? Assume to the contrary that the marginal cost for firm II was higher than for firm I. Then total costs could

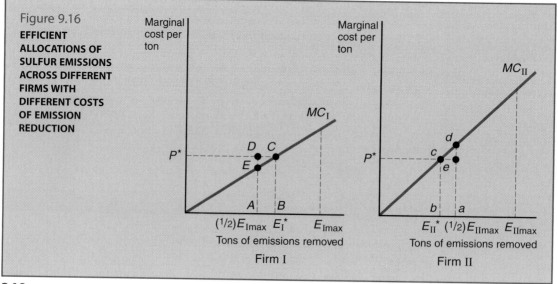

Figure 9.16

EFFICIENT ALLOCATIONS OF SULFUR EMISSIONS ACROSS DIFFERENT FIRMS WITH DIFFERENT COSTS OF EMISSION REDUCTION

be reduced if firm I lowered its emissions by one more unit while firm II were allowed to increase its emissions by a like amount. Total emissions would stay the same, but total cost would fall by the difference between the marginal cost at firm II (costs saved because they would no longer be incurred by firm II) and the marginal cost at firm I (costs incurred because firm I would have to do more). Adjustments like this would, indeed, always be possible unless the marginal costs of the two firms were identical; and this condition is achieved with firm I emitting E_I^* and firm II emitting E_{II}^*.

The government could, therefore, achieve its objective at least cost by setting strictly enforced emissions limits E_I^* and E_{II}^* for firms I and II, respectively. But it could do this only if it had enough information to be able to compute those targets. Absent this information, the government might set a standard for firm I that would permit it to emit $E_{Imax}/2$ units of SO_2 and a corresponding standard for firm II that would permit it to emit $E_{IImax}/2$. Or it might give an equal number of permits (i.e., $(E_{Imax} + E_{IImax})/4$ permits) to both firms. Or it could come up with a different allocation scheme. But it could not be assured of minimizing the cost of meeting its aggregate reduction objective without relying on incredible luck or adding an economic wrinkle to its control mechanism. What sort of wrinkle? A market-based one. If the government allowed the firms to buy or sell permits to emit, then the efficiency of the market could be expected to lead firms to the least-cost solution regardless of how the permits were distributed. With access to such a market, for example, firm I could use a permit to emit a unit of pollution or it could sell it to firm II; and it would consider such a sale only if firm II were willing to offer more for the permit than it was worth to firm I. How much is that? The marginal cost for firm I of reducing emissions by one more unit (because selling the permit would mean that that is exactly what firm I would have to do). It follows that transactions of this sort would occur as long as the marginal cost of emissions reduction for firm I did not equal the marginal cost of emissions reduction for firm II; that is, the transactions would continue until firms I and II were left with E_I^* and E_{II}^* permits, respectively.

What sort of efficiency gain might be expected from allowing this market to work? That depends on the degree to which the government misses E_I^* and E_{II}^* with its initial allocation. The figure shows cost reductions for equal initial allocations. Firm I would then sell up to $E_I^* - (1/2)E_{Imax}$ at a price of P^*. Total revenue for firm I would therefore climb by area $ABCD = P^* \times [E_I^* - (1/2)E_{Imax}]$ from the sale of permits, but its emissions reduction costs would climb by the area under the marginal cost curve from to $(1/2)E_{Imax}$ to E_I^* (i.e., area $BCEA$). Firm I would therefore see a net gain equal to area ECD. Firm II, on the other hand, would buy $(1/2)E_{IImax} - E_{II}^*$ at a price of P^*. These permits would cost area $abce = P^* \times [(1/2)E_{IImax} - E_{II}^*]$, but the cost of emissions reduction would fall by the area under firm II's marginal-cost curve from E_{II}^* to $(1/2)E_{IImax}$ (i.e., area $bcda$). Firm II would therefore also see a net gain equal this time to area ecd.

Markets of this sort were, in fact, created for sulfur dioxide in the United States in the mid-1990s. Actual gains in efficiency were not immediately observed, in part because initial allocations to polluting firms were proportional to historical experience; it takes time to make the capital adjustments that would be required to meet emissions standards after trading some permits away. Nonetheless, estimates of the potential gain from trade have run in excess of $200 million for 1995 and 1996—over 25 percent of the estimated cost of national compliance without trading—and there is every reason to believe that these cost savings have begun to kick in.

SOURCE: C. Carlson, D. Burtraw, M. Cropper, and K. Palmer, "Sulfur Dioxide Control by Electric Utilities: What Are the Gains from Trade?" *Resources for the Future*, April 2000.

Microlink 9.2   Market Equilibrium with and without Distortions

Chapter 8 displayed the same simple concept of equilibrium as Chapter 1—a quantity and price pair for which the quantity willingly demanded matches the quantity willingly supplied; it has been exploited vigorously, here, under a variety of different distortions. The key to these applications is simple. Equilibrium in a distorted market must recognize that participants on one side of the market or the other find it impossible to meet fully their individual objectives. Nonetheless, equilibrium still matches the quantity supplied with the quantity demanded where one or the other is subject to a binding constraint; that is, participants still do the best that they can for themselves given limitations imposed by the market or by other participants who have the upper hand. A binding price ceiling, for example, sets the quantity willingly supplied, and demanders buy all they can find at the specified price. A binding floor sets the quantity willingly demanded, and suppliers do all they can to find those willing customers.

SUMMARY

1. Producer surplus is the amount producers receive above and beyond the minimum price that would be required to get them to produce and sell a particular output. Total surplus is the sum of consumer and producer surpluses. It is a measure of the total net gain to consumers and producers from the production and sale of a particular number of units of a good. Total surplus is maximized in this model when output is at its perfectly competitive level. This result is important, but depends on a number of assumptions—not the least of which is an assumption that the private and social costs of production are identical.

2. Government policies that hold a good's price below the equilibrium level reduce producer surplus. Whether there is an increase or decrease in consumer surplus depends on the good's price elasticity of demand; in either case, consumers who can purchase the good at a lower price are better off while other consumers who are frustrated by the resulting shortage in supply are worse off. Even if there is an increase in consumer surplus, this increase is less than the reduction in producer surplus. A deadweight loss—a reduction in total surplus—results.

3. Government policies that hold a good's price above the equilibrium level reduce consumer surplus. If suppliers produce only what can be sold, there is also a fall in producer surplus. Here, too, there is a deadweight loss.

4. Agricultural price-support programs often call for the government to buy the surplus output produced at the support price. Economists have suggested that consumers would be better off if they could simply give producers a transfer equal to the gain in producer surplus that such programs would sustain.

5. Tariffs and quotas are imposed by governments to protect domestic producers. Protective measures of this sort, like agricultural support programs, result in deadweight losses.

6. Since an excise tax is collected from the sellers, the supply curve of the good on which the tax is imposed is shifted upward by the amount of the tax. The price increase paid by consumers will increase by an amount that depends on the price elasticity of demand and the price elasticity of supply of the good. The rest of the tax will be paid by producers, who see the net price of their product fall.

7. An excise tax reduces both consumer surplus and producer surplus. There is a deadweight loss because the total loss to consumers and producers exceeds the tax revenue collected by the government.

QUESTIONS/ PROBLEMS

1. Rent control exists in many cities, including New York. Suppose that the demand and supply curves for rental housing in a particular city were as shown in the figure and that rent control were instituted. In particular, landlords would no longer be allowed to charge rents exceeding $600 per month. For simplicity, assume that all the city's apartments are basically the same in size and desirability and that no landlord can evade the $600 price ceiling. (a) According to the graph, rent control would result in fewer apartments (100,000 rather than 130,000) offered for rent. What would be the effect of rent control on the consumer surplus of those people who get apartments? (b) What would be the effect on the consumer surplus of those who could no longer obtain apartments? (Assume that those who are willing to pay the most for apartments are the ones who get them.) (c) What would be the effect of rent control on producer surplus? (d) What would be the effect on total surplus, and why is this of significance in judging the social desirability of rent control? (e) Would there be any deadweight loss? If so, how big would it be? If not, why not?

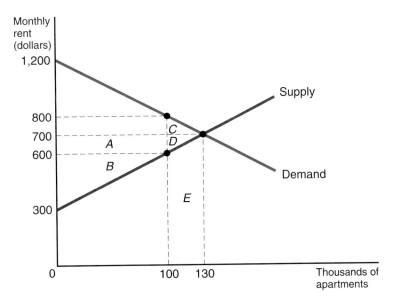

2. The demand and supply for cotton cloth are shown in the following figure. (a) If the price is $100 per ton, what is producer surplus? (b) If the price is $200 per ton, what is producer surplus? (c) If output is 1 million tons, what is total surplus? (d) If output is 2 million tons, what is total surplus?

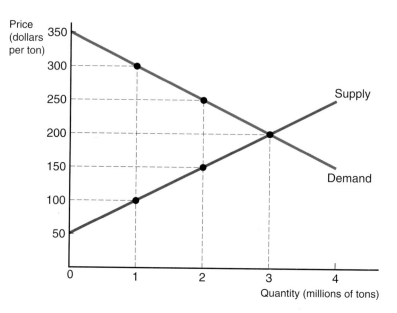

3. A researcher estimates the demand and supply curves for cucumbers. For this good, $Q_D = 10 - 2P$ and $Q_S = 3P$, where Q_D is the quantity demanded per year (in millions of tons), Q_S is the quantity supplied per year (in millions of tons), and P is the price (in dollars per ton). (a) If the price of this good is at its equilibrium level, how great is producer surplus? (b) How great is consumer surplus? (c) How great is total surplus? (d) Would total surplus increase if the price moved from the equilibrium?

4. Suppose, in Figure 9.6, that the support price (P') were $2 per ton, that the equilibrium price (P) were $1 per ton, that 100 million tons would be demanded if the price were $2, that 200 million tons would be supplied if the price were $2, and that the equilibrium quantity demanded and supplied were 150 millions tons. (a) In dollar terms, how great would be the loss to consumers due to the price support? (b) In dollar terms, how great would be the gain to producers? (c) What would be the effect on total surplus?

5. We assumed that markets existed in our discussion of their efficiency. This could be a faulty assumption if it were sufficiently costly to establish a market. Suppose that the following figure displays the demand and supply curves for some good. If the cost of establishing and maintaining a market for this good exceeded $1.05 billion per year, would it exist? Why or why not?

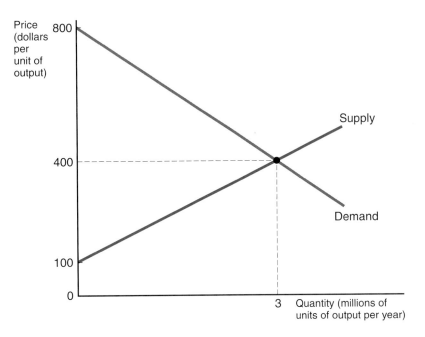

Price (dollars per unit of output)

800

Supply

400

Demand

100

0

3 Quantity (millions of units of output per year)

6. Charges designed to cover the cost of a court settlement caused the price of cigarettes in Connecticut to increase by roughly 40 cents per pack in December 2001. Comparable price increases were seen in 34 other states. (a) If, as some economists believe, the supply curve for cigarettes is horizontal, how much of this price increase was passed on to consumers? (b) According to a 1981 study, about 93 percent of any increase in a state's cigarette tax rate was quickly reflected in cigarette prices. How close is this estimate to your answer to (a)?

7. We have assumed in this chapter that suppliers collect an excise tax and send the revenue to the government. For example, the cigarette manufacturer in Figure 9.12 was assumed to collect the tax of 40 cents per pack from the consumer and to send this amount to the government. Suppose instead that the consumer had to send the 40 cents per pack to the government. Would the effect of the tax on price and output be any different from that shown in Figure 9.12? Why or why not?

8. In late 1992, the U.S. government announced that it would begin collecting within 30 days a substantial tax on all still white wine imported from Europe. This import tax (or tariff) was announced in an effort to get European governments to reduce the subsidies they paid their farmers. According to the U.S. government, these subsidies had unfairly reduced the demand for U.S. exports of agricultural goods. White wine was singled out because France, the staunchest opponent of compromise in this dispute with the United States, was Europe's chief exporter of white wine to the United States (1991 sales: $125 million). (a) According to Banfi Products Corporation, a large wine importer, the retail price of a typical bottle of French white wine was likely to rise from $9.50 to $28.25 if this import tax went into effect. Was this because of a rightward shift of the demand

curve for French white wine? Or was it because of a leftward shift of the supply curve for French white wine? (b) Harry F. Mariani, president of Banfi Products Corporation, said the price of French white wines that retailers acquired before the tax would probably rise after the imposition of the tax: "Whoever has some white wine left will probably raise the price at the end, even if they didn't pay the tax." Should such behavior be legal? Why should a consumer pay a retailer for a tax that the retailer did not pay? (c) If the demand for French white wine is price-elastic, would this tax reduce the amount spent by U.S. consumers on French white wine? (d) Would this tax affect the demand curve for California wine? If so, how? (e) A few weeks after the U.S. government announced this new tax on European white wine, a compromise was reached with European governments on how to reduce farm subsidies. The new tax proposal was dropped soon thereafter. French farmers marched in protest in Paris. Was this because they favored the tax?

9. The demand and supply curves for beer are $Q_D = 50 - 2P$ and $Q_S = 2P$, where Q_D is the quantity of beer demanded per year (in millions of cases), Q_S is the quantity of beer supplied per year (in millions of cases), and P is the price of beer (in dollars per case). If a tax of \$5 per case were imposed, how much deadweight loss would result?

10. Suppose that the demand and supply curves for autos in the United States were reflected in the following figure. (a) If the price of an auto in the world market were \$15,000 and if the government imposed an import quota of 2 million cars per year, what would be the price of a car in the United States? (b) What would be the effect of the quota on consumer surplus? (c) What would be the effect on producer surplus? (d) Would there be a deadweight loss? If so, how big would it be? If not, why not?

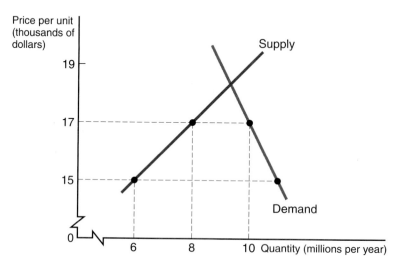

11. On July 22, 1995, the following editorial appeared in the New York Times:

New England Senators and Governors are pressuring Bob Dole, the Senate majority leader, to submit a pernicious bill to a hasty vote before it clears committee.

The bill creates a compact among Maine, Vermont, New Hampshire, Connecticut, Rhode Island, and Massachusetts to raise milk prices above Federal levels. By some estimates the cost of a gallon of milk would rise from about $2.50 to between $2.85 and $3. Overall, the price increase would pump perhaps $500 million a year into the bank accounts of New England dairy farmers. But it would needlessly pummel poor parents by forcing them to spend up to 20 percent more to buy milk. Besides discouraging milk drinking, the compact sets an ugly precedent. New England cannot enforce artificially high prices unless it keeps milk produced outside New England from flowing into the region. That is why the bill imposes what amounts to a protective tariff on "imported" milk.

(a) Would this bill increase consumer surplus? (b) Would it increase producer surplus? (c) Would it increase total surplus?

12. Use the analysis in Example 9.4 to track the transfer of consumer surplus to domestic and foreign steelmakers. How much surplus would go to each? Compute the residual deadweight loss of the quota directly from the graph in the example. Show that it is exactly the net change in global welfare computed in the last paragraph of the example.

13. Analyses of changes in consumer surplus look at how consumers and producers are affected as a whole. But these analyses ignore different effects on different consumers and producers. There are inevitably winners and losers in each group. Consider the analysis in Example 9.4 and try to sort out who wins and who loses. Do all consumers lose, or just some? Distinguish between consumers who lose because they pay more for steel and those who lose because they no longer buy any steel. Can you show where employment changes might be reflected in the analysis?

CHAPTER 10

Monopoly

INTRODUCTION

A. C. Nielsen's ratings of the size of the national audience for particular television shows are of great importance to the communications industry. Television ratings guide firms' decisions about where to advertise and how much to spend for a half minute of air time. All told, advertising on television runs well over $10 billion per year. And, of course, advertising revenues are used to help television networks determine which individual shows should live and which should die. Nielsen has sometimes been labeled a monopolist because it is the only firm engaged in the measurement of television audiences. A **monopoly** exists whenever there is a single source of supply. Nielsen fits the definition pretty well, but it is not alone. Whether you live in the United States or Canada or Australia or the United Kingdom or one of the countries that have emerged from the dissolution of the Soviet Union, you have probably encountered some firms that are monopolists, or close to it. Electric companies, telephone companies, water companies, and cable companies are all examples that come to mind quickly when we think about monopolies in the developed market economies of the West. Perhaps more surprising, though, many of the newly privatized firms in emerging market economies hold monopoly power because they were originally created by governments to supply planned markets that spanned entire countries.

Monopoly

Models of monopoly, like models of perfect competition, are extremely useful tools in microeconomic analysis. The conditions defining monopoly are easy to state. There must exist one, and only one, seller in a market. Unregulated monopoly, like perfect competition, does not often correspond more than approximately to conditions in real industries. As we have noted several times before, however, a model must be judged by its predictive ability and not by the "realism" of its assumptions, and the model of monopoly that we are about to discuss has done pretty well in that regard.

Monopoly and perfect competition are opposites in many ways. The firm in a perfectly competitive market has so many rivals that competition becomes impersonal in the extreme; a monopoly has no rivals at all. Under monopoly, one firm is the sole supplier, and there is no competition. A monopoly faces the entire market demand curve all by itself, so it can set both price and quantity. A competitive firm faces so little of the market demand that its effective demand curve is horizontal at whatever price the market will bear. A competitive firm can decide only the output that it would like to supply to the market given that price.

Having said all of this, it is important to add that monopolists must cope with certain indirect and potential forms of competition. A monopolist is not completely insulated from the effects of actions taken elsewhere in the economy. All commodities are rivals for the consumer's favor. This indirect rivalry occurs among different products just as easily as it does among the producers of a given commodity. Meat, for example, competes in a very real sense with butter, with eggs, and even with men's suits. Of course, the extent of the competition from other products depends on the extent to which other products are substitutes for the monopolist's product. But a firm that somehow obtained a monopoly on the supply of aluminum in a particular market would still face considerable competition from producers of lightweight steel, plastics, and other materials that are reasonably good substitutes for aluminum in many if not all of its uses.

In addition, the threat of potential competition can act as a brake on the ability of a monopolist to do what it pleases. The monopolist may be able to maintain its monopoly position only if it does not extract an excessive amount of short-run profit. Its economic profits might be so high that other firms may enter its market and try to break its monopoly power if it sets prices above a certain point. And if entry could occur, then a monopolist must take that possibility into account in every decision that it makes. Failure to do so could make it an "ex-monopolist."

▣ Reasons for Monopoly

Complete control of a basic input

Why do monopolies exist? There are many reasons, but four seem to be particularly important. First, a single firm may control the entire supply of a basic input that is required to manufacture a given product. The example that is cited most often to illustrate this possibility is the pre–World War II aluminum industry. Bauxite is an input used to produce aluminum, and for some time, practically every source of bauxite in the United States was controlled by the Aluminum Company of America (Alcoa). Alcoa simply got to the bauxite first and, as a result, sustained its position as the sole producer of aluminum in the United States for a very long time.

Second, a firm may become a monopolist because the average cost of producing the product reaches a minimum at an output that is big enough to satisfy the entire market at a price that is profitable. If there were more than one firm producing the product in a situation like this, then each would have to produce where the average cost of production was higher than necessary (i.e., higher than the long-term minimum). Each supplier would therefore be tempted to cut the price so that it could increase its output rate and reduce its average costs. The result would probably be economic warfare, and the single survivor would establish a monopolistic position. Cases in

Natural monopoly which costs are minimized at or close to market demand are called **natural monopolies;** the public often insists that the behavior of natural monopolies be regulated by the government.

Patents Third, a firm may acquire a monopoly over the production of a good by having **patents** on the product or on certain basic processes that are used in its production. The patent laws of the United States permit an inventor to get the exclusive right to make a certain product or to use a particular process for 20 years from the initial filing of a patent. Parents can be very important in keeping competitors out. For example, Alcoa held important patents on basic production processes used to make aluminum; these patents certainly helped Alcoa to sustain its monopoly power. Pharmaceutical companies offer another example. They typically hold patents on drugs for many years after their introduction into the market. These patents prohibit the introduction of competing generic substitutes. It is often possible, however, to "invent around" another company's patents. Although a firm cannot use a product or process on which another firm has a patent without the latter's permission, it may be able to develop a closely related product or process and to obtain a patent on that "variation on a theme."

Government-sanctioned franchises Fourth, a firm may become a monopolist by being awarded a market **franchise** by a government agency. Such a firm is granted the exclusive privilege to produce a given good or service in a particular area. In exchange for this right, the firm agrees to allow the government to regulate certain aspects of its behavior and operations. For example, as we shall see in a later section, the government may set limits on the firm's price or on the return to its investment in capital. Regardless of the form of regulation, the important point is that a monopoly of this sort will have been created by the government.

| Example 10.1 | **The Microsoft Finding and the Value of Start-Up Software Companies** |

On November 5, 1999, U.S. District Judge Thomas Penfield Jackson issued a finding of fact in the government's antitrust case against Microsoft. Judge Jackson concluded, "Microsoft has demonstrated that it will use its prodigious market power and immense profits to harm any firm that insists on pursuing initiatives that could intensify competition against one of Microsoft's core products." In light of that finding and other events, Microsoft lost the case and began to work the system for a settlement. It was successful with the Justice Department, but several states continued court cases to challenge the settlement. Meanwhile, software start-up companies did not back down from their claims that they are forced to decide between accepting a Microsoft buyout offer for their recent developments and seeing a close substitute distributed free on the next version of Windows. If such threats were made less credible by the court's decision and the states' persistence, what would it mean for the value of these start-ups?

The answer to this question depends on many things, but we can explore some of the fundamentals with a simple example. Suppose that a start-up company has one asset—a newly developed piece of software worth $1 million net of $200,000 in development costs if Microsoft leaves it alone and nothing (after covering development costs) if Microsoft responds to the competition by installing a close substitute on Windows. If there were a 50 percent chance that Microsoft would respond in this way, then the expected monetary value of the start-up would be $(0.5) \times (\$1 \text{ million}) + (0.5) \times (\$0) = \$500,000$; this is what Microsoft might offer as a buyout package. But if the court case reduced the likelihood of a Microsoft response by 50 percent (so that Microsoft would weaken pending cases and make future action less likely), then the expected monetary value would climb to $(0.75) \times (\$1 \text{ million}) + (0.25) \times (\$0) = \$750,000$, and the Microsoft offer would have to climb by 50 percent. And if the owners of the start-up were risk-averse (an unlikely assumption for people who create technology startups?), then application of the results of Chapter 5 would make it clear that the offered price in either situation would fall (assuming that Microsoft knew that the owners were risk-averse).

▣ A Monopolist's Demand Curve

A monopolist is the only firm producing a product. It is therefore obvious that the monopolist's demand curve is precisely the same as the market demand curve for the product. And so the factors determining the shape of the monopolist's demand curve are the same factors that determine the shape of the demand curve for the product. As we saw in Chapter 4, these factors include the prices of other related products (substitutes and complements), incomes, and tastes. Monopolists can sometimes affect the prices of related products, though, and they frequently believe that they can influence consumer tastes. Monopolists often make considerable expenditures on advertising with the intention of shifting the market demand curve up and to the right.

Since the monopolist's demand curve is negatively sloped (because the demand curve for almost all products is negatively sloped, save for a few cases of little significance), average and marginal revenue are not the same. This is quite different from the case of perfect competition, where average and marginal revenue were both equal to the market price. To illustrate the situation faced by a monopolist, consider the hypothetical case described in Table 10.1. The second column displays the price at which each quantity shown in the first column can be sold. Total revenue, the product of the first two columns, is shown in the third column. Average revenue is, in each case, the price that supports the sale of any specific quantity.

Marginal revenue is a bit more elusive. We already know from Chapter 4 that marginal revenue between q and $q - 1$ units of output is defined as $R(q) - R(q - 1)$, where $R(q)$ is the total revenue when the output and sales equal q and $R(q - 1)$ is total revenue when sales equal $(q - 1)$. But we cannot apply this definition directly to the data presented in Table 10.1. Those data are not recorded for each level of output; indeed, we have only data for $q = 3, 8, 15$, and so on. To cope with this problem, we assume that

Table 10.1 **REVENUE OF A** **MONOPOLIST**	**Quantity sold**	**Price** **(dollars)**	**Total revenue** **(dollars)**	**Marginal revenue** **(dollars)**
	3	100.00	300.00	
				68.00 (= 340/5)
	8	80.00	640.00	
				67.14 (= 470/7)
	15	74.00	1,110.00	
				60.00 (= 360/6)
	21	70.00	1,470.00	
				57.00 (= 285/5)
	26	67.50	1,755.00	
				52.50 (= 210/4)
	30	65.50	1,965.00	
				27.00 (= 81/3)
	33	62.00	2,046.00	
				27.00 (= 54/2)
	35	60.00	2,100.00	

revenue $R(q)$ is approximately linear in quantity between 3 and 8, between 8 and 15, between 15 and 21, and so on. This means that marginal revenue can be approximated by $(R[8] - R[3])/(8 - 3) = (\$640 - \$300)/5 = \$68.00$ for every output between 3 and 8 units; by $(R[15] - R[8])/(15 - 8) = (\$1,110 - \$640)/7 = \$67.14$ for every output between 8 and 15 units, and so forth. The results are shown in the last column of Table 10.1. This complication with the data has not been entered just to make your life difficult. Data seldom appear in the most convenient form, and economists and their students have to learn how to evaluate all forms of data.

◻ A Monopolist's Costs

A monopolist in the product market may be a perfect competitor in the market for inputs. It may, in particular, buy such a small proportion of the total supply of each input that it cannot affect input prices. If this were always the case, then there would be no need to dwell further on the monopolist's costs; the theory presented in Chapter 7 would apply without modification. In many cases, however, the monopolist is not a perfect competitor in the input markets because it buys a large proportion of certain specialized resources that have little use elsewhere in the economy. When this case applies, the price that the monopolist pays for this input depends on how much it intends to buy. The more the firm wants, the more it will generally have to pay. Cases of this sort are discussed at some length in Chapter 14. We ignore their complication in the present chapter by assuming that the monopolist is a perfect competitor in the market for inputs.

Table 10.2 COSTS OF A MONOPOLIST	Output	Total variable cost (dollars)	Fixed cost (dollars)	Total cost (dollars)	Marginal cost (dollars)
	0	0	500	500	
					36.67 (= 110/3)
	3	110	500	610	
					26.00 (= 130/5)
	8	240	500	740	
					21.43 (= 150/7)
	15	390	500	890	
					28.33 (= 170/6)
	21	560	500	1,060	
					38.00 (= 190/5)
	26	750	500	1,250	
					52.50 (= 210/4)
	30	960	500	1,460	
					76.67 (= 230/3)
	33	1,190	500	1,690	
					125.00 (= 250/2)
	35	1,440	500	1,940	

Table 10.2 shows the costs of our hypothetical monopolist. The first column highlights various output levels, the second shows the total variable cost for each output recorded in the first column, and the third column shows the firm's fixed costs. The fourth column shows the monopolist's total cost at each level of output, and the fifth column shows the firm's marginal costs.[1]

SHORT-RUN EQUILIBRIUM PRICE AND OUTPUT

A monopolist who is unregulated and free to maximize profits will, of course, choose the price and output at which the difference between total revenue and total cost is largest. Combining the data from Tables 10.1 and 10.2 into Table 10.3, we can see that our hypothetical monopolist will choose to produce something between 26 and 30 units and sell them for a price somewhere in the range between $65.50 and $67.50, where profit equals $505. Figure 10.1 shows the situation graphically.

Note that any output in this range is smaller than the output for which price would equal marginal cost. The profit-maximizing output under perfect

[1]The marginal-cost values reported in the fifth column were computed using the same procedure just outlined for marginal revenue; the implicit assumption here is that marginal cost is "piecewise linear" in output between the reported quantities.

Table 10.3	Output	Total revenue (dollars)	Total cost (dollars)	Total profit (dollars)
REVENUE, COST, AND PROFIT OF A MONOPOLIST	3	300	610	−310
	8	640	740	−100
	15	1,110	890	220
	21	1,470	1,060	410
	26	1,755	1,250	505
	30	1,965	1,460	505
	33	2,046	1,690	356
	35	2,100	1,940	160

competition would set price equal to marginal cost, of course, and maximum economic efficiency would be achieved where the price matches marginal cost. But Table 10.2 shows that the marginal cost of producing 26 to 30 units of output is approximately $52.50 (read, according to the convention of the table, between the sixth and seventh lines for outputs between 26 and 30 units), and $52.50 < $65.50. Indeed, it is obvious from Tables 10.1 and 10.2 that output would have to rise above 30 units for price to fall toward a rising marginal cost.

Marginal cost equals marginal revenue for maximum profits

So what conditions characterize profit maximization for a monopoly? Monopolies maximize profits by producing where marginal cost equals marginal

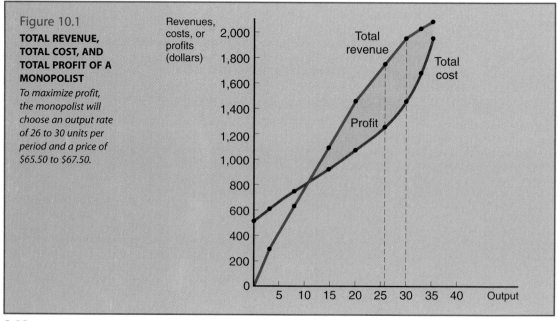

Figure 10.1

TOTAL REVENUE, TOTAL COST, AND TOTAL PROFIT OF A MONOPOLIST

To maximize profit, the monopolist will choose an output rate of 26 to 30 units per period and a price of $65.50 to $67.50.

	Output	Total profit (dollars)	Marginal cost (dollars)	Marginal revenue (dollars)
Table 10.4 **MARGINAL COST AND MARGINAL REVENUE OF A MONOPOLIST**	0	—		
			36.67	—
	3	−310		
			26.00	68.00
	8	−100		
			21.43	67.14
	15	220		
			28.33	60.00
	21	410		
			38.00	57.00
	26	505		
			52.50	52.50
	30	505		
			76.67	27.00
	33	356		
			125.00	27.00
	35	160		

revenue. Table 10.4 and Figure 10.2 show that this result rings true for our simple example. But it is easy to prove that it holds in general. Suppose that a monopolist were producing an output, q_1, for which marginal revenue, MR_1, was higher than marginal cost, MC_1. Profit could then be increased by producing one additional unit of output because the extra revenue generated by its sale (i.e., an amount approximated by MR_1) would exceed the extra cost involved in its production (i.e., an amount approximated by MC_1). Profit would increase, in fact, by roughly $MR_1 - MC_1 > \$0$. So, profit cannot be maximized by selling any output for which marginal revenue exceeds marginal cost. And what if a monopolist were producing an output q_2 for which marginal cost, MC_2, was higher than marginal revenue, MR_2? Profit could then be increased by producing one fewer unit of output because the revenue lost by forgoing its sale (i.e., an amount approximated by MR_2) would be smaller than the cost savings involved in stopping its production (i.e., an amount approximated by MC_2). Profit would now increase, in fact, by roughly $MC_2 - MR_2 > \$0$. So, profit cannot be maximized by selling any output for which marginal revenue falls short of marginal cost. It follows, then, that profit is maximized by selling exactly the output for which marginal cost equals marginal revenue (that's the only case we have left).

Microlink 10.1 Marginal Revenue under Monopoly and Perfect Competition

The marginal-revenue curves for monopolists and perfect competitors are both derived from the applicable effective demand curves. Recall that a

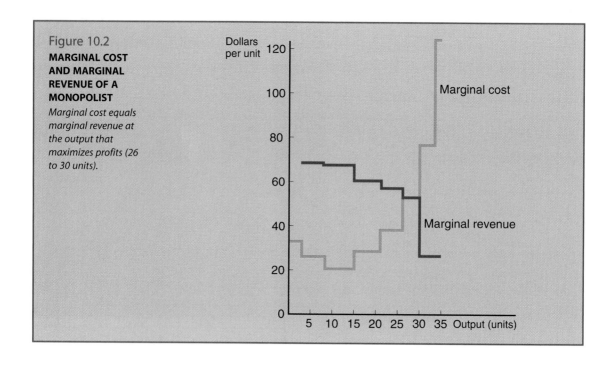

perfectly competitive firm faces a horizontal demand curve at the price "announced" by the market. The corresponding marginal-revenue curve is therefore also horizontal because a competitive firm is so small that it can always sell one more unit at that price. The monopolist, though, faces the downward-sloping market demand curve, so the marginal-revenue curve is always lower than price. Why? Because it must lower the price to sell one more unit (move along the demand curve) *and* it must sell all of its original output at that lower price, as well. For a linear demand curve like

$$P = a - bX,$$

for example, marginal revenue is given by

$$MR = a - 2bX;$$

that is, the marginal-revenue curve has the same intercept and twice the slope as the demand curve. In both cases, though, profits are maximized where marginal cost equals marginal revenue.

It is now a simple task to use this result to represent graphically the short-run equilibrium of the monopolist. Figure 10.3 shows the demand curve, the marginal-revenue curve, the marginal-cost curve, and the average total-cost curve faced by a typical monopolist. The profit-maximizing monopolist would find short-run equilibrium at output Q, where the marginal-cost curve intersects the marginal-revenue curve. And what price should the monopolist charge? The demand curve shows that the market would bear a

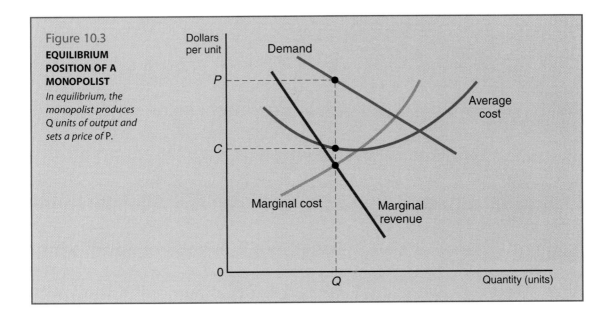

Figure 10.3

EQUILIBRIUM POSITION OF A MONOPOLIST

In equilibrium, the monopolist produces Q units of output and sets a price of P.

price of P if Q units of output were delivered to its customers, and so it should charge P per unit. Indeed, it must charge the price read from the demand curve because the marginal-revenue curve on which the output decision was based assumes that this would happen. In so doing, the monopolist would make $P - C$ in profit per unit of output because the average-cost curve indicates that average costs are C at an output of Q units. Total profits would therefore be $Q \times (P - C)$.

The monopolist would earn a profit in this case, but this need not always be so. It does not follow that a firm that holds a monopoly over the production of a particular product must make a profit. The demand curve for the product could be so low that average cost exceeds the price even at the profit-maximizing output where marginal revenue equals marginal cost. A monopoly on the sale of pearl-handled buggy whips might not be profitable, and holding monopoly power over the production of 5¼-inch floppy disks would not be worth much anymore, either. In the short run, then, a monopolist may not be able to cover its variable costs, and just like a competitive firm in such a situation, it would quickly discontinue production.

We have already shown that economists can define a unique relationship between the price of the product and the amount supplied for a competitive, price-taking firm. This is the firm's supply curve (at least the portion for which price would exceed the minimum average variable cost). We also demonstrated how to sum these individual supply curves horizontally to produce an industry's supply curve. It turns out that there is no such unique relationship between the product's price and the amount supplied for a monopolist. Put more succinctly, monopolists do not have supply curves. At first, this is likely to strike the reader as being extremely strange; indeed, one can be pardoned for questioning whether it really is so.

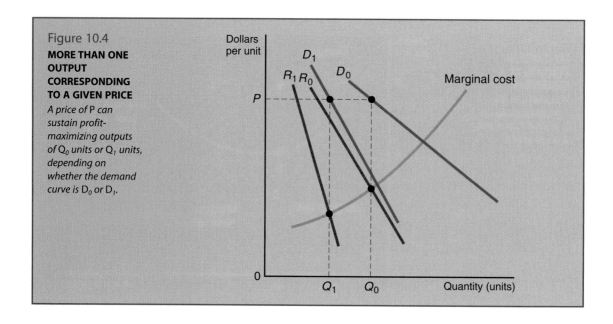

Figure 10.4

MORE THAN ONE OUTPUT CORRESPONDING TO A GIVEN PRICE

A price of P can sustain profit-maximizing outputs of Q_0 units or Q_1 units, depending on whether the demand curve is D_0 or D_1.

To see why, consider Figure 10.4, which shows the marginal-cost curve of a monopolist as well as two distinct demand curves labeled D_0 and D_1. If demand curve D_0 were operable, then the firm would produce Q_0 units (since the marginal-cost curve intersects the marginal-revenue curve, R_0, at Q_0) and the price would be P. If demand curve D_1 were in play, however, then the firm would produce Q_1 units (since the marginal-cost curve intersects the new marginal-revenue curve, R_1, at Q_1), but the price would still be P. This result shows that there is no unique relationship between price and quantity. A price of P could result in the monopolist's producing Q_0, or Q_1, or any other output for a different demand curve whose marginal-revenue curve intersected marginal cost someplace else. Any price can therefore sustain a wide variety of output levels in profit-maximizing equilibrium, depending on the shape and level of the demand curve.

Microlink 10.2 The Geometry of Profit Maximization

Figure 10.1 displayed total-revenue and total-cost curves for a monopolist. Profits are maximized where the revenue curve is exactly parallel to the cost curve—somewhere in the region between 26 and 30 units of output where marginal revenue (the slope of the revenue curve) is equal to marginal cost (the slope of the cost curve). There is a corresponding graph for a perfect competitor. It must show the same relationship between the revenue and cost curves for the profit-maximizing output, but it must also show the particular characteristics that mark the economic environment of a perfect competitor. More specifically, the revenue curve must be linear,

366

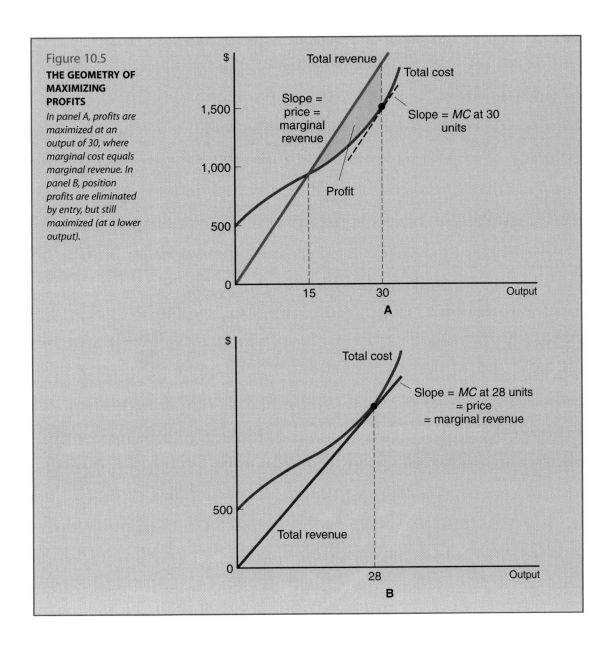

Figure 10.5

THE GEOMETRY OF MAXIMIZING PROFITS

In panel A, profits are maximized at an output of 30, where marginal cost equals marginal revenue. In panel B, position profits are eliminated by entry, but still maximized (at a lower output).

A

$

Total revenue

Total cost

Slope = price = marginal revenue

Slope = MC at 30 units

1,500

1,000

500

Profit

0

15   30   Output

B

$

Total cost

Slope = MC at 28 units = price = marginal revenue

500

Total revenue

0

28   Output

since the competitor faces a given price and that price defines marginal revenue. Panel A of Figure 10.5 displays the appropriate structure so that positive maximum profits occur in the same region as before. This is not, however, a long-run equilibrium for a competitor. Positive profits would attract firms to the market and lower the price until maximum profits are zero. Panel B identifies this point as a tangency between revenue and cost (so that price equals marginal revenue and now equals marginal cost) at a smaller output.

In contrast to perfect competition, the long-run equilibrium of a monopolistic industry is not marked by the absence of economic profits or losses. A monopolist who earns a positive economic profit in the short run will not necessarily be confronted in the long run with competitors. The entrance of additional firms into the industry would, of course, not be compatible with the existence of monopoly, and so there are issues of how to deter entrance. We will address these issues later. We assume, for the moment, that the long-run equilibrium of a monopoly may include its earning positive economic profits.

A monopolist could, however, incur short-run economic losses. It would then be forced to look for other, more profitable uses for its resources. Its existing plant might not be optimal, and so it might be possible for the monopolist to earn economic profits if it altered the scale and characteristics of its plant appropriately. If this were the case, then it would make these alterations in the long run and remain in the industry. If, however, it determined that economic losses would be unavoidable even if the scale of plant were adjusted, then it would ultimately leave the industry.

In the case in which the monopolist earns positive short-run profits, it must decide in the long run whether it can make even larger profits by altering its plant. To see how, assume that Figure 10.6 displays the monopo-

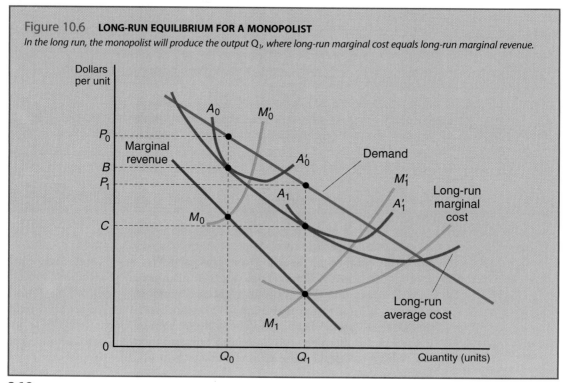

Figure 10.6   **LONG-RUN EQUILIBRIUM FOR A MONOPOLIST**
In the long run, the monopolist will produce the output Q_1, where long-run marginal cost equals long-run marginal revenue.

list's demand curve, marginal-revenue curve, short- and long-run average-cost curves, and short- and long-run marginal-cost curves. Suppose that the firm currently operated a plant corresponding to short-run average-cost curve $A_0 A_0'$ and short-run marginal-cost curve $M_0 M_0'$. In the short run, it would produce Q_0 units and set a price of P_0. And since short-run average cost would equal B, the firm's short-run profits would be $Q_0 \times (P_0 - B)$.

This firm could nonetheless adjust its plant in the long run so that profits would exceed $Q_0 \times (P_0 - B)$. Indeed, it is easy to show that the monopolist would maximize profit in the long run by producing the output for which long-run marginal cost equals long-run marginal revenue. The reasoning behind this rule is precisely the same as that given in the section before last. The firm would therefore plan to produce Q_1 units in the long run, since this is the point at which the long-run marginal-cost curve intersects the marginal-revenue curve. The long-run average cost would be C, the price would be P_1, and total profit would be $Q_1 \times (P_1 - C)$. The resulting plant would have short-run averages and marginal-cost curves of $A_1 A_1'$ and $M_1 M_1'$, respectively. Notice that the monopolist would not produce at the minimum of either the short-run or the long-run average-cost curve.

Example 10.2	De Beers—An Unregulated Monopoly

According to the *New York Times*, the Central Selling Organization controlled by De Beers Consolidated Mines Ltd. is "probably the world's most successful monopoly."[2] De Beers was founded in South Africa by Cecil Rhodes at the end of the nineteenth century. It controlled over 99 percent of world diamond production until about 1900. The firm presently mines only about 15 percent of the world's diamonds, but many claim that it still controls the sales of over 80 percent of gem-quality diamonds through its Central Selling Organization. The organization markets the output of other major diamond-producing countries like Zaire, Russia, Botswana, Namibia, and Australia, as well as its own production. De Beers disputes this claim, arguing that Russian sales outside of the Central Selling Organization amounted to $1 billion in 1995.[3] If true, this would mean that Russian sales probably exceeded 20 percent of the total for the entire organization.

Despite this bickering, nobody doubts that De Beers controls the price of diamonds. Diamond merchants are offered small boxes of assorted diamonds at a price set by De Beers on a "take it all or leave it" basis. Those who choose not to buy may have to wait some time before getting another opportunity. Why do they put up with this treatment? Because De Beers protects its investment by standing ready to buy diamonds to support the price if demand falls. Indeed, demand fell during the early 1980s, when inflation slowed and diamonds lost much of their sparkle as an investment; De Beers protected the price, but saw its stockpile of diamonds increase

[2] *New York Times*, September 7, 1986, p. F4.
[3] *Business Week*, October 16, 1995.

from $360 million to about $2 billion between 1979 and 1984. De Beers did the same thing in the first half of 1992, when its earnings fell by about 25 percent in response to a global recession that reduced the demand for diamonds.

Besides limiting the quantity supplied, De Beers also works hard and cleverly to push the demand curve for diamonds to the right. Its sales campaigns strive to link diamonds and romance: the slogan "A Diamond Is Forever" is theirs, and it is 60 years old. It both spurs demand for diamonds and works to keep "pre-owned" diamonds off the market—a good that is drenched with lasting sentiment is less likely to be sold when times get tough. De Beers' policies have paid off in very substantial profits, but consumers have probably paid higher prices than they would have if the diamond market were more competitive. Probably? Perhaps the price would have been higher if stable prices hadn't made diamond exploration and mining such an attractive investment. Remember the lessons of Chapter 5, where we uncovered the potentially debilitating effect that high risk has on investment. Less exploration could have meant smaller supplies and ultimately the same high prices people pay today for diamonds.

MULTIPLANT MONOPOLY

We assumed in previous sections that the monopolist operates only one plant. This, of course, is an unrealistic assumption in many industries. Even readers with the most superficial knowledge of the structure of various industries will recognize that many firms operate more than one plant and that cost conditions may vary among these plants. This section extends the analysis to cover the case where the monopolist operates more than one plant.

An illustrative case is shown in Table 10.5. It presumes that the monopolist operates two plants. Output is indicated in the first column; the marginal-cost curves for the two plants are shown in the second and third

| Table 10.5 | | Marginal cost[a] | | |
COSTS OF A MULTIPLANT MONOPOLY	Output	of plant *A* (dollars)	of plant *B* (dollars)	for firm (dollars)
	1	5	7	5
	2	6	9	6
	3	7	11	7
	4	10	13	7
	5	12	15	9

[a]These figures pertain to the interval between the indicated output and 1 unit less than the indicated output.

columns. We begin the story by asking which plant would be employed if the firm decided to produce only one unit of output. It would, judging from the figures in these columns, decide to use plant *A*. Why? Because the marginal cost of producing the first unit at plant *A* is $5—an amount that is smaller than the $7 that it would cost if plant *B* were chosen. For the firm as a whole, then, the marginal cost of the first unit of production would be $5, and plant *A* would be the location of choice.

What if the firm decided to produce two units of output? It would have to decide whether it would want to produce a second unit at plant *A* (for $6) or one unit at plant *B* (for $7). It would again select plant *A*, and the marginal cost of the second unit of production for the firm as a whole would be $6. And the third unit? It would cost $7 as either the third unit from plant *A* or the first unit from plant *B*, so the firm would not care. In either case, then, the overall marginal-cost curve would indicate that the cost of the third unit would be $7. And now we know that the fourth unit would also cost $7; it would be produced at whichever plant was not chosen for the third unit. Overall marginal cost would still be $7; plant *A* would produce 3 units and plant *B* would produce 1. Continuing in this fashion, we can derive the marginal-cost curve for the firm as a whole. It is shown in the fourth column of Table 10.5 for the plant-specific marginal-cost curves reflected in the second and third columns.

The underlying geometry of the marginal-cost curve for the firm as a whole is displayed in Figure 10.7. Panels A and B portray smooth marginal-cost curves for two separate plants, *A* and *B*. Panel C highlights the resulting marginal-cost curve for the firm as a whole. It is the horizontal

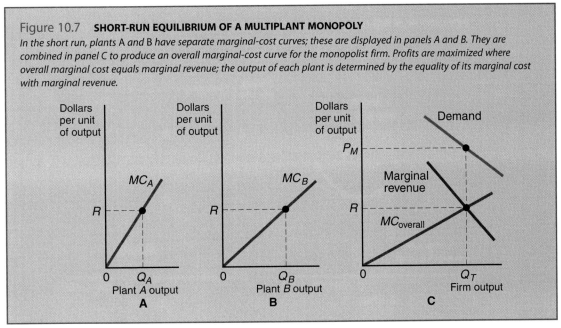

Figure 10.7   **SHORT-RUN EQUILIBRIUM OF A MULTIPLANT MONOPOLY**
In the short run, plants A and B have separate marginal-cost curves; these are displayed in panels A and B. They are combined in panel C to produce an overall marginal-cost curve for the monopolist firm. Profits are maximized where overall marginal cost equals marginal revenue; the output of each plant is determined by the equality of its marginal cost with marginal revenue.

sum of the marginal-cost curves of its two plants. Why? Because the multiplant monopolist will always minimize the costs by allocating total output so that the marginal cost of producing the last unit in one plant is equal to the marginal cost of producing the last unit in (all of) the other(s). And to maximize profit, the monopolist will choose an output for which marginal revenue equals marginal cost. In Figure 10.7, marginal revenue equals overall marginal cost at Q_T units of output—the output at which overall marginal cost intersects marginal revenue. What price would the monopolist charge? Whatever the market would bear—the price P_M read from the demand curve for Q_T units of output, as long as that price lies above the marginal revenue curve. And how much would be produced at each plant? Outputs Q_A and Q_B, such that the marginal cost in each plant equaled overall marginal cost and marginal revenue. Notice, finally, that total quantity supplied ($Q_T = Q_A + Q_B$) would equal total quantity demanded at price P_M.

The monopolist can, of course, vary the number and size of its plants in the long run. It would, therefore, operate only a plant of the optimal size. To see what this means, consult Figure 10.8. The preferred short-run average-cost curve (designated AA' in panel A of Figure 10.8) would equal the long-run average cost at the minimum point on the long-run average-cost curve. The curve CC' is the corresponding short-run marginal-cost curve. Each plant would produce q units of output at an average cost of u dollars per unit, and any expansion in total output would be accommodated by building more plants of the optimal size. The long-run marginal-cost curve would therefore be a horizontal line at u, as shown in panel B. And

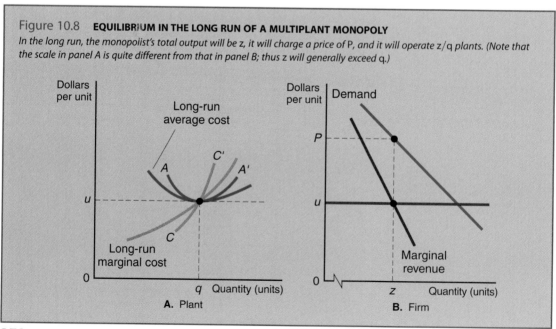

Figure 10.8 **EQUILIBRIUM IN THE LONG RUN OF A MULTIPLANT MONOPOLY**

In the long run, the monopolist's total output will be z, it will charge a price of P, and it will operate z/q plants. (Note that the scale in panel A is quite different from that in panel B; thus z will generally exceed q.)

since long-run marginal cost must equal marginal revenue in equilibrium, the firm's total output in the long run would be z. It would operate z/q plants, and it would charge a price of P.[4]

A COMPARISON OF MONOPOLY WITH PERFECT COMPETITION

It is important to note the differences between the long-run equilibrium of a monopoly and a perfectly competitive industry. Suppose that we could perform an experiment in which an industry first operated under conditions of perfect competition and then under conditions of monopoly. Assuming that the demand curve for the industry's product and the industry's cost curves would be the same in either case, what would be the difference in the long-run equilibrium?

The output of a perfectly competitive industry tends to be greater and price tends to be lower than under monopoly. The perfectly competitive firm operates at the point at which price equals marginal cost, but the monopolist operates at a point at which price exceeds marginal cost. Under various circumstances, price is a good indicator of the marginal social value of the good. Consequently, under these conditions, a monopoly produces at a point where the marginal social value of the good exceeds the good's marginal social cost. In a static sense, then, society would be better off if more resources were devoted to the production of the good and if the marginal social value of the product were set equal to the marginal social cost of the product—as it is in perfect competition.

To see why, it is sufficient for now to show that consumers lose more from monopoly than the monopolist gains. To see this, consider Figure 10.9, where the equilibrium price and output in monopoly are compared with the price and output in perfect competition. To maximize profit, the monopolist produces Q_M units of output, since this is where marginal cost equals marginal revenue; to sell this number of units, the monopolist must set a price of P_M. But price would equal marginal cost in a perfectly competitive market, so the output produced under perfect competition would be Q_C. This is the only output along the demand curve at which the price equals marginal cost—the long-run equilibrium for a competitive market. So, if the perfectly competitive industry produces Q_C units of output, the demand curve shows that the price must equal P_C.

If the perfectly competitive industry in Figure 10.9 were transformed into a monopoly, how much would consumers be hurt? In other words, how much consumer surplus would be lost? Consumer surplus would equal the area of triangle $P_C SA$ under perfect competition and the area of triangle

---

[4]We are ignoring the problem that z/q may not be an integer. Also, we are assuming that z will generally be bigger than q. Neither assumption is guaranteed, of course. The monopolist would choose to produce more or less than z so that profits are maximized by rounding z/q up or down. And the case where z is not larger than q would never sustain a multiplant monopolist to begin with.

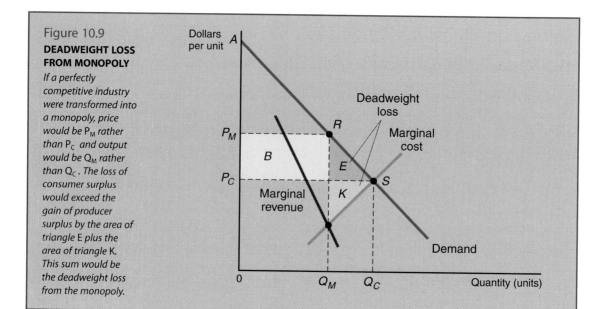

Figure 10.9

DEADWEIGHT LOSS FROM MONOPOLY

If a perfectly competitive industry were transformed into a monopoly, price would be P$_M$ rather than P$_C$ and output would be Q$_M$ rather than Q$_C$. The loss of consumer surplus would exceed the gain of producer surplus by the area of triangle E plus the area of triangle K. This sum would be the deadweight loss from the monopoly.

$P_M R A$ under a monopolist. The difference in consumer surplus must therefore be the sum of the area of rectangle B and the area of triangle E. And how much of this loss finds its way to the monopolist? The monopolist would gain the area of rectangle B by selling the product at a higher price (P_M rather than P_C), but it would lose the area of triangle K—the extra profit that it would have made by selling $Q_C - Q_M$ extra units of output at the competitive price. Thus, the increase in producer surplus due to monopoly is the area of rectangle B minus the area of triangle K.

Would the gains earned by the monopolist outweigh the losses suffered by consumers? The difference between the loss in consumer surplus (rectangle B plus triangle E) and the gain in producer surplus (rectangle B minus triangle K) equals the area of triangle E plus the area of triangle K. This total area, indicated in Figure 10.8, is often called the **deadweight loss from monopoly.** It equals the amount by which the consumers' losses would exceed the producer's gains, and so it is the loss in total surplus due to monopoly. There would be deadweight loss even if the monopolist's profits were turned back to consumers.[5]

Deadweight loss from monopoly

Microlink 10.3   Long-Run Equilibrium for a Multiplant Monopolist and Perfect Competition

Figure 10.8 depicts long-run equilibrium for a multiplant monopolist. It is highly reminiscent of the graph of long-run equilibrium in a perfectly competitive market. Indeed, there are only two differences, and only one

[5]A. C. Harberger, "Monopoly and Resource Allocation," *American Economic Review*, May 1954; and G. Tullock, "The Welfare Costs of Monopoly and Theft," *Western Economic Journal*, June 1967. Also see K. Cowling and D. Mueller, "The Social Costs of Monopoly Power," *Economic Journal*, December 1978; and F. Fisher, "The Social Costs of Monopoly and Regulation: Posner Reconsidered," *Journal of Political Economy*, April 1958.

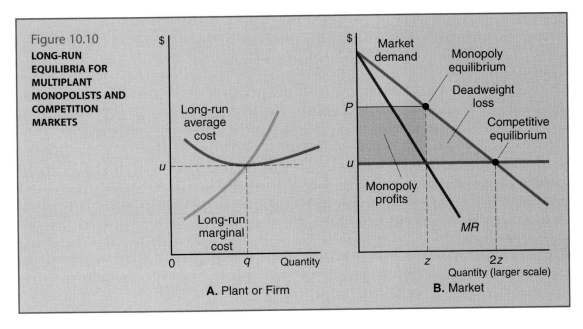

Figure 10.10

LONG-RUN EQUILIBRIA FOR MULTIPLANT MONOPOLISTS AND COMPETITION MARKETS

A. Plant or Firm

B. Market

will necessarily be clear from the graph. Different firms own all or most of the different plants in a competitive market, of course, but their representations on the left side of the graph could be identical. The only difference can be detected graphically by noting the equilibrium price. The equilibrium price for a monopolist is defined by the point on the market demand curve that lies directly above the intersection of marginal revenue and (constant) long-run marginal cost. Equilibrium is meanwhile defined for a competitive market by the point on the demand curve where it intersects marginal cost. As portrayed in Figure 10.10, this means that the deadweight loss for the monopoly captures only lost consumer surplus.

Even more can be gleaned from this comparison if demand were linear as depicted in Figure 10.10. Since the marginal-revenue curve facing a monopolist would then have the same intercept as the market demand curve and twice the slope, monopoly output would always be one-half of the competitive output in this case. Deadweight loss would then be the area of a triangle whose base matched the monopoly output and whose height equaled the slope of the demand curve multiplied by that quantity. It follows, then, that deadweight loss would always be one-half of monopoly profits; and it would be directly related to the magnitude of the slope of the demand curve.

MONOPOLY POWER

We noted early in the chapter that situations of pure monopoly—a single seller servicing an entire market—are relatively uncommon. There are many cases in which a few firms are the principal suppliers of a particular good or service. But cases in which only a single supplier exists are the exception and lie far from the rule. Nonetheless, a firm can have a certain amount of market power even if it is not the only supplier of a particular good—at least in the sense that it, unlike a perfectly competitive firm, might find it profitable to raise its price above marginal cost. Suppose, for example, that the company that produces the computer-based technology that can manufacture three-dimensional silicon chips charges $200,000 to install the mechanism even though the marginal cost of its production is $150,000. This firm clearly has some monopoly (or market) power. If it did not, it would have to set price equal to marginal cost like any perfectly competitive firm.

Lerner index   Economists often use the **Lerner index** (named after Michigan State University professor Abba Lerner) to measure monopoly or market power. The index is quite simple:

$$L = \frac{P - MC}{P},$$

where P is the firm's price and MC is its marginal cost. The index varies between 0 and 1 depending upon the monopoly power of the firm in question. Price equals marginal cost for a perfectly competitive firm (recall Chapter 8), so the Lerner index equals 0 in situations of perfect competition. But the higher, is L the higher is the degree of monopoly power. The Lerner index can also be expressed in terms of the reciprocal of the price elasticity of (effective) demand for the firm's product. How can we show this? Recall from Chapter 4 that

$$MR = P\left(1 - \frac{1}{\eta}\right),$$ [10.1]

where P is price, MR is marginal revenue, and η is the price elasticity of demand facing the firm. A profit-maximizing firm will, of course, set marginal cost equal to marginal revenue, so

$$MC = P\left(1 - \frac{1}{\eta}\right),$$ [10.2]

where MC represents marginal cost. Clearly, then,

$$\frac{MC}{P} = 1 - \frac{1}{\eta},$$

and so $$\frac{1}{\eta} = 1 - \frac{MC}{P} = \frac{P - MC}{P} = L.$$ [10.3]

Note that the elasticity, η, is not necessarily the same as the price elasticity of demand for the industry's product. It is, instead, the percentage increase in the quantity demanded of the *firm's* product if it cuts its price by 1 percent; that is, it is the price elasticity of the firm's effective demand curve. That demand curve is the market demand curve only when the firm is a pure monopolist.

What factors influence the price elasticity of demand for a firm's product? That is, what factors influence the firm's degree of monopoly power, as measured by the Lerner index? Notwithstanding the warning offered at the end of the preceding paragraph, the price elasticity of demand for any firm's product is likely to be higher if the price elasticity of demand for the industry's product is high. Second, the industry is more competitive if there are a large number of firms supplying the market. And so, the price elasticity of demand for any individual firm's product is likely to be large (and the degree of monopoly power small) if there are many competitors.

Example 10.3   **Some Economic Evidence from the Microsoft Case**

Economic analysis is sometimes introduced into court proceedings in an attempt to prove that one side or the other is or is not guilty of anti-competitive practices. This example describes "evidence" that was introduced by the defense to demonstrate that Microsoft must be operating in a competitive environment because the price that it was charging for its Windows operating system was so much lower than the price that would have maximized its profits if it could, indeed, exercise monopoly power. The supporting documentation began with the observation that the average price of a personal computer in 1997 (denoted P_c) was roughly \$2,000. At the same time, the average price paid by computer manufacturers for licensing Windows 98 (denoted P_0) was about \$50 per unit, and it was assumed that the marginal cost of licensing an additional copy of Windows 98 (denoted by MC) was zero. With perfect competition in the PC industry, the price of the other components of any computer was taken to be \$2,000 − \$50 = \$1,950. The price elasticity of demand for Windows (denoted η_0) could then be approximated by the price elasticity of demand for computers (denoted η_c) multiplied by the fraction of the cost of a PC that could be attributed to the operating system; that is,

$$\eta_0 = \frac{P_0 \eta_c}{P_c}.$$

And what is the price elasticity of demand for computers? Something in excess of 1 but less than 2 seemed reasonable. So, if Microsoft were pricing Windows according to the profit-maximizing condition reflected in Equation 10.3, then

$$\frac{P_0 - MC}{P_0} = \frac{1}{\eta_0} = \frac{1}{P_0 \eta_c / P_c}$$

where $MC = 0$, $P_c = \$1,950 + P_0$, and $1 < \eta_c < 2$. Setting $\eta_c = 2$, this condition means that Microsoft would have tried to charge \$1,950 for Windows 98 if it had monopoly power, and \$3,900 if $\eta_c = 1.5$.

The counterargument held that Microsoft charged so little because it would gain extra revenue (denoted by R) by selling programs that would run well only in the Windows environment. If that were the case, then the profit-maximizing pricing rule would solve

$$\frac{P_0 - MC + R}{P_0} = \frac{1}{\eta_0} = \frac{1}{P_0 \eta_c / P_c},$$

and a high estimate of extra revenues on the order of \$500 per unit would lower the monopoly price to only \$950 per unit with $\eta_c = 2$.

Price discrimination occurs when the same commodity is sold at more than one price. For example, a pen manufacturer might sell the same pen for $1.95 in the front of the stationery store, where people look for functional pens, and for $11.95 at the back of the store, where people look for inexpensive graduation gifts. Even if the commodities are not precisely the same, price discrimination is said to occur if very similar products are sold at prices that are in different ratios to marginal costs. The mere fact that differences in price exist among similar goods is not evidence of discrimination; discrimination occurs only if there is evidence that these differences do not reflect real cost differentials.

Under what conditions can a firm with monopoly power willingly engage in price discrimination? It is necessary that buyers fall into categories with considerable differences in the price elasticity of demand for the product. These different categories can, for all intents and purposes, be considered different and distinct markets. The monopolist must also be able to identify these markets and segregate them at moderate cost. And buyers must not be able to transfer the commodity easily from one market to another; if they could, then it would be possible for persons to make money by buying the commodity in the low-price market and selling it in the high-price market.

Where do the differences in elasticity come from? Different markets may be composed of buyers from different income levels. Their tastes may be different. And their perceptions of the availability of substitutes could vary widely. The price elasticity of demand for a certain good may be lower for the rich than it is for the poor. The elasticity of demand for functional pens may be different from the elasticity for graduation gifts. Mechanical pencils may serve as substitutes for functional pens, but not for gifts. It is not difficult to tell stories of how markets might be segregated.

Firms that practice discrimination of this sort must make two decisions. They must decide how much output should be allocated to each market, and they must decide what price to charge in each. To examine how these decisions might be made, consider a case where there are only two categories of markets; the analysis can handle more than two, but the story is more complicated to tell. Assume, also for simplicity at the start of this discussion, that the firm has already decided on its total output. The only real question at this stage is how this output should be allocated between the two markets. Each market can be represented by a demand curve showing the quantity demanded at various prices, and so there is a corresponding marginal-revenue curve for each market.

Profits maximized when marginal revenue is the same in both (all) markets

The monopoly will maximize its profit, given these marginal-revenue curves, by allocating the total output between the two markets so that the marginal revenue of the last unit sold in one market is equal to marginal revenue in the other. Indeed, if there were more than two markets, then profits would be maximized by an allocation that set the marginal revenue of the last unit sold in any market equal to the marginal revenue in every other market. The reason behind this result is clear. Suppose that the marginal revenue of the last unit sold in the first market were $5 while the marginal revenue of the last unit sold in the second were $3. Profits would then climb if the firm increased sales in the first market by one unit at the expense of reducing sales in the second by one unit. Revenue would rise by $5 in the first and fall by $3 in the second. Net revenue would climb by $2, costs would be unaffected, and so profits would climb. What made this possible? The fact that marginal revenue in the first market did not equal marginal revenue in the second. Conversely, it would be impossible to increase profit by reallocating sales if the marginal revenues in both markets were the same. And so, profits are maximized only when the marginal revenues are equal.

Notice, though, that the equality of marginal revenues does not imply that prices are equal. To explore this point more fully, recall Equation 10.1. If there were two markets and the marginal revenues in both were equal, then $MR_1 = MR_2$ would mean that

$$P_1\left(1 - \frac{1}{\eta_1}\right) = P_2\left(1 - \frac{1}{\eta_2}\right),$$

where P_1 is the price charged in the first market in which η_1 is the price elasticity of demand and P_2 is the price charged in the second market where the price elasticity of demand is η_2. As a result, the ratio of the price charged in the first category to the price charged in the second must equal

$$\frac{P_1}{P_2} = \frac{1 - 1/\eta_2}{1 - 1/\eta_1}.$$

It would therefore not pay for the monopolist to discriminate between two markets if their price elasticities were equal. And, in cases where discrimination would be profitable, the price would be lower in the market for which demand was more elastic.

Now let's consider the more realistic case in which the firm must also decide on its total output. The firm must now look at its costs as well as demand. The firm would choose the output where the marginal cost of the firm's entire output is equal to the common value of the marginal revenue in the two markets. To see this, consider Figure 10.11. Curves D_1 and R_1 in panel A portray demand and marginal revenue for the first market. Curves D_2 and R_2 in panel B portray different demand and marginal revenue in the second market. The firm would begin its determination of profit-maximizing total output by summing horizontally over the two marginal-revenue curves R_1 and R_2. The result is curve Z in panel C. This composite curve shows, for each level of marginal revenue, the total output that would be required if marginal revenue in both markets were to be maintained at this level. The **profit-maximizing output** Q is identified in panel C by the point where the composite marginal-revenue curve Z intersects the marginal-cost curve. Given this output, marginal cost equals the common value of marginal revenue in each market. If this were not the case, then profits could be increased by expanding output (if marginal cost were less than marginal revenue) or by contracting output (if marginal cost were greater than marginal revenue). How would these Q units be allocated between the two markets? The preceding paragraph tells us that the firm would sell Q_1 units in the first market and Q_2 units in

Profit-maximizing output

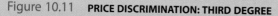

Figure 10.11 PRICE DISCRIMINATION: THIRD DEGREE

Panels A and B display demand and marginal-revenue curves for two markets; they are D_1, D_2, R_1, and R_2, respectively. Panel C shows overall marginal revenue (the horizontal sum of the marginal-revenue curves of the two markets) as curve Z. To maximize profit, the firm will produce a total output of Q units where overall marginal revenue equals marginal cost; i.e., where curve Z intersects marginal cost. The firm will then set a price of P_1 in market 1 and a price of P_2 in market 2 so that it can sell Q_1 units of output in market 1 and Q_2 units in market 2. Note that Q_1 and Q_2 sum to Q.

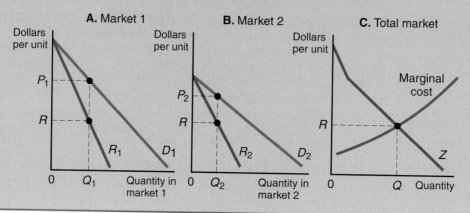

the second market, because these are the quantities for which $MR_1 = MR_2$ and $Q_1 + Q_2 = Q$. And what prices would be charged? Price P_1 would be the price in the first market and P_2 would be the price in the second.

| Example 10.4 | **Manipulating Prices for Information and Profit** |

A few companies have gotten themselves into hot water recently by trying to explore the sensitivity of demand to changes in price and by reacting to information about the sensitivity of consumer preferences to external conditions. Two illustrations are instructive in these regards. Amazon.com, one of the most potent competitors in e-commerce, has been caught charging different prices to different customers for the same item. Armed with detailed records of 23 million customers, Amazon tried to charge its regular customers higher prices for DVDs because it had already established their loyalty. Sometimes the difference was in the 3 to 5 percent range; other times it was slightly higher. The point was to try to see how much customers would pay for the convenience of turning to only one source for their shopping needs. Their plans hit a snag, however, when customers communicated with themselves on DVDTalk.com. It would seem that differential pricing, so common in "brick and mortar" retailing where distances are real, can be undermined by the same electronic efficiencies that created e-commerce to begin with. In any case, Amazon reported soon after word got out that it had dropped the practice.

Moving on to consumer preferences, reports also surfaced in 2000 that Coca-Cola tested a vending machine that would boost prices for soft drinks when it was hot, particularly at sporting events. Then CEO Douglas Ivester suggested in an interview that it was reasonable that summer heat would increase customers' cravings for soft drinks so that "it's fair that it should be more expensive." The new machine would simply make this dynamic pricing automatic. Reaction to the idea, once it was made public, was swift and brutal. Indeed, the resulting public relations fiasco may have contributed to Mr. Ivester's departure from Coke.

SOURCE: D. Streitfeld, "Amazon Pricing Test Angers Customers," *Washington Post,* September 28, 2000.

▣ Other Types of Price Discrimination

Third-degree price discrimination

First-degree price discrimination

Price discrimination can take a number of forms. The type we have just discussed is often called **third-degree price discrimination**—an expression that was coined by A. C. Pigou, an English economist.[6] As you might now suspect, Pigou also identified what he termed first-degree and second-degree price discrimination. **First-degree price discrimination** would be possible if the firm were aware of the maximum amount that each and every consumer would pay for each unit purchased. Assuming that the product could not be resold, the firm could then charge each consumer a different price. And so a profit-maximizing firm would be able to extract from each consumer the full value of his or her consumer surplus.

To illustrate this case, suppose first that each consumer buys only 1 unit of the commodity. In this very simple case, the firm would establish a price for each consumer that is so high that the consumer would be on the verge of refusing to buy the commodity. In the more complicated case in which each consumer might buy more than 1 unit of the commodity, then it is assumed that the firm would know each consumer's demand curve for the commodity and that it could adjust its offer accordingly. For example, suppose that the maximum amount that a particular consumer would pay for 20 units of the commodity were $50 and that 20 units were the profit-maximizing amount for the firm to sell to this consumer (i.e., that the cost of producing 20 units were less than $50). Then the firm would make an all-or-nothing offer of 20 units of the commodity for $50. And how would the consumer determine this $50 maximum price for 20 units? He or she would compute the area under his or her demand curve from 0 to 20 units. So, the monopolist would still be extracting all of the consumer surplus from the consumer.

Second-degree price discrimination

First-degree price discrimination is a limiting case that could occur only in the few cases in which a firm has a small number of buyers and is able to guess the maximum prices each would be willing to accept. Second-degree price discrimination is an intermediate case. In **second-degree price discrimination,** the firm takes only part of the buyers' consumer surplus. Consider the case of a gas company as an example. Suppose that each of its consumers has the demand curve shown in Figure 10.12. The company could charge a high price, designated P_0, if the consumer purchased fewer than X units of gas per month. But it could also charge a medium price, designated P_1, for each unit purchased above the threshold of X units per month. The company might charge an even lower price, designated P_2, for each unit purchased above a second threshold

[6]A. C. Pigou, *The Economics of Welfare,* 4th ed. (London: Macmillan & Co., 1950).

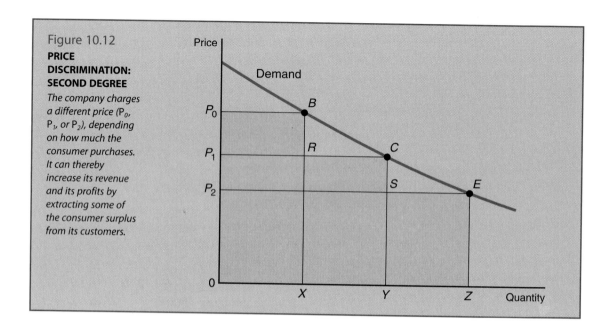

Figure 10.12

PRICE DISCRIMINATION: SECOND DEGREE

The company charges a different price (P₀, P₁, or P₂), depending on how much the consumer purchases. It can thereby increase its revenue and its profits by extracting some of the consumer surplus from its customers.

of Y units per month. The company's total revenues from a consumer purchasing Z units would therefore equal the shaded area of Figure 10.12, because consumers would purchase X units at a price of P_0, $(Y - X)$ units at a price of P_1, and $(Z - Y)$ units at a price of P_2.

It is obvious that the gas company, by charging different prices for various amounts of the commodity, can increase its revenue and profits considerably. After all, if it were permitted to charge only one price and it wanted to sell Z units, then it would have to charge a price of P_2. The firm's total revenue would then equal only the area of rectangle $0P_2EZ$—an amount that would be considerably less than the total shaded area in Figure 10.12 Charging different prices enables the firm to extract part of the consumer surplus. Some authorities see the schedules of rates charged by many public utilities—gas, water, electricity, and others—as a type of second-degree price discrimination.[7]

▣ Discrimination and the Existence of the Industry

Under some circumstances, a good or service cannot be produced without some degree of price discrimination. To see why, consider the case in Figure 10.13. Two types of consumers are depicted there by different demand curves: D_0D_0' and D_1D_1'. Adding the two curves together, we find that the total (market) demand curve for the commodity is the piecewise linear curve D_0UV. For the average total-cost curve drawn in Figure 10.13, though, there is no output for which price is greater than or equal to average total cost, at least not unless price discrimination were practiced. If, however, Q_0 units

---

[7]Ralph Davidson, *Price Determination is Selling Gas and Electricity* (Baltimore: Johns Hopkins University Press, 1975); and C. Cicchetti and J. Jurewitz, *Studies in Electric Utility Regulation* (Cambridge, Mass.: Ballinger, 1975).

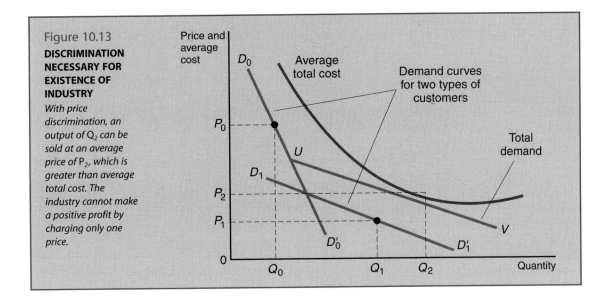

Figure 10.13

DISCRIMINATION NECESSARY FOR EXISTENCE OF INDUSTRY

With price discrimination, an output of Q_2 can be sold at an average price of P_2, which is greater than average total cost. The industry cannot make a positive profit by charging only one price.

could be sold at a price of P_0 to one type of consumer and Q_1 units could be sold at a price of P_1 to the second type of consumer, then total output (which equals Q_2) would bring an average price of P_2. As drawn, P_2 is greater than the average total cost of producing Q_2 units.[8] Should such discrimination be allowed? Yes, because consumer surplus would be positive, so welfare would improve over the case in which no output was forthcoming.

TWO-PART TARIFFS

Two-part tariff

Firms with monopoly power have other pricing tricks at their disposal. Some employ what is termed a **two-part tariff,** which requires the consumer to pay an initial fee for the right to buy the product as well as some sort of usage fee for each unit of the product that he or she buys. There are many examples of this technique in the real world. Telephone companies, for example, charge a basic monthly fee for telephone service plus an amount for each call (at least each long-distance call). Private golf clubs sometimes charge an annual membership fee plus a "greens fee" for each round of golf.

A firm that uses this pricing technique must determine how high the initial fee should be, and it must decide what to charge as a usage fee. The lower the initial fee, clearly, the greater the number of consumers that will purchase the right to buy the product. Lower initial fees are therefore likely to result in greater profits from the usage fees earned from sales of the product. But there is a trade-off. The firm also receives profits from the initial fees that it charges, and lower initial fees mean that these profits are smaller

[8]This section assumes that there are no government subsidies for the product in question. If such subsidies exist, it may be profitable to produce the product in Figure 10.13 without price discrimination.

383

than they might otherwise be. Consequently, the firm would be expected to choose the initial fee and usage fee so that its total profit—both from the sales of the product and from initial fees—is maximized.

Example 10.5	Two-Part Tariffs in the National Football League

We have argued that two-part tariffs can increase profits, but is that always true? And what other factors need to be considered in pricing policies? This example will explore these questions in the context of selling tickets to sporting events. Why? Because the *Wall Street Journal* reported on September 27, 1996, that it had observed a growing practice in the National Football League of selling, for four-figure sums, "personal seal licenses" that entitled the holder to the privilege of buying tickets. The important questions, therefore, focus attention on pricing licenses and tickets and the cost of administrating a system that sustains fan interest.

Figure 10.14 displays a hypothetical situation. It is an individual (family; ticket unit) demand curve for season tickets for the New England Patriots in their new stadium. Suppose that the Patriots charged $750 per ticket. They would generate 3 × $750 = $2,250 in revenue, but the ticket unit would have been willing to spend more. How much more? The consumer surplus area under the demand curve and above $750; that is, $250 extra for the first ticket plus $150 extra for the second. The license fee could therefore have been as high as $400. The Patriots could therefore generate $2,650 in total revenue—an average of $833 per ticket.

What combination would maximize the sum of the maximum license fee and ticket revenue? We need only compute the average return per ticket across

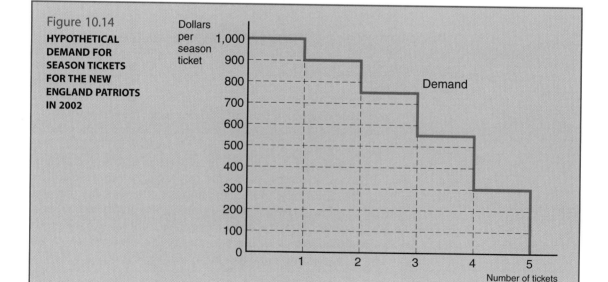

Figure 10.14

HYPOTHETICAL DEMAND FOR SEASON TICKETS FOR THE NEW ENGLAND PATRIOTS IN 2002

Table 10.6	Ticket price	Quantity demanded per purchasing unit	Maximum license fee	Total revenue	Average revenue
REVENUE FROM TICKET SALES AND LICENSES	$1,000	1	$0	$1,000	$1,000
	$900	2	$100	$1,900	$950
	$750	3	$400	$2,650	$883
	$550	4	$1,000	$3,200	$800
	$300	5	$2,000	$3,500	$700

all pricing combinations to see; Table 10.6 records the results. It is clear that the Patriots would maximize revenue by selling tickets one at a time with no license fee, but only if they could still sell out the stadium. Why would that be an issue? Fans would not be guaranteed the chance to actually sit together with their friends during the game on a one-for-one purchase basis unless an elaborate matching mechanism were installed and administered. Given the cost of such a system, it is not so puzzling that teams typically offer four-ticket blocks.

TYING

Tying

Firms that produce products that will function properly only if used in conjunction with other products may require their customers to buy the complete set of requisite products in one inseparable package. This pricing technique, called **tying,** has often been used in the office equipment and computer industries. Several decades ago, the Xerox Corporation insisted that firms or individuals that leased its copiers had to buy their copy paper from Xerox. The IBM Corporation insisted that those who leased its computers had to use paper computer cards that it made. Similarly, in the late 1990s, Microsoft insisted that its Internet browser be included in its market-dominating Windows operating system. Industry complaints attracted the attention of the Justice Department, which charged that Microsoft was trying to monopolize the browser market. And to return to the links, some golf courses require that players rent carts, even though half of the fun of a round of golf is taking a long, slow walk with three of your best friends.

Why do firms adopt this technique? It sometimes allows them to charge higher prices to customers that use their products intensively. Price discrimination of this sort often is difficult to accomplish because a firm frequently does not know how intensively each customer uses its product. But as we know from preceding sections, price discrimination of this sort can, under the proper conditions, increase a firm's profits.[9]

[9]Firms often argue that tying ensures that their products will be used with the proper kind of complementary products so that good performance will result. See B. Klein and L. Salt, "The Law and Economics of Tying Contracts," *Journal of Law and Economics,* May 1985.

Bundling

Bundling is yet another pricing technique that is sometimes used by firms with some market power. **Bundling** occurs when a firm requires customers to buy one of its products together with another of its products. This procedure can increase the firm's profits if customers have quite different tastes and if the firm cannot otherwise engage in price discrimination.

The strategy of bundling should be familiar to you. Many computer companies bundle software in packages with their computer, to enhance both your attraction to the computer and demand for the software. Other computer companies bundle years of service contracts for their computers or upgrade guarantees with the purchase of one type of computer or another. Or look at professional magazines and journals for bundles that are created for specific audiences. Various sports teams, including colleges, sell bundles of tickets for several games so that high demand for one game can be exploited to sell tickets for others. If, for example, you want to see the University of Connecticut Lady Huskies play the University of Tennessee, then you must buy a bundle of tickets that includes UConn games against teams with whom the rivalry is not nearly as intense and for which the national implications are not nearly as significant.

To see why bundling can be profitable, consider an example in which a software company wants to sell two types of programs: utility programs that can help maintain order on consumers' hard drives and virus-scanning programs that can help protect those hard drives from "disease." Call those programs "Utility" and "Antibug." Let there be, as well, equal numbers of two types of consumers. One type, call them "Disorganized," is interested in a utility program; the other type, call them "Cautious," is concerned about picking up a virus from imported files. Table 10.7 shows the amount that each would be willing to pay for each type of program.

If the programs were sold separately, then $24.95 is the most that could be charged for "Utility" if the company wanted to be able to sell to both types of consumers; $19.95 is the most that could be charged for "Antibug" if, again, the company wanted to be able to sell to both types. Why? Because the company could not reach both markets if it charged more than the smaller price that either type of consumer would pay. The most it could get for both programs would therefore be $24.95 + $19.95 = $44.90. But what if the company

Table 10.7		Type of consumer	
MAXIMUM PRICES FOR "UTILITY" AND "ANTIBUG" SOLD SEPARATELY OR AS A BUNDLE (CASE IN WHICH BUNDLING IS PROFITABLE)	Program	"Disorganized"	"Cautious"
	"Utility"	$29.95	$24.95
	"Antibug"	$19.95	$39.95
	Bundled together	$49.90	$64.90

insisted that consumers could not buy one program without the other? In this case, as shown in the last row of Table 10.7, the most "Disorganized" consumers would pay is $49.90 (= $29.95 + $19.95) and the most that "Cautious" consumers would pay is $64.90 (= $24.95 + $39.95). The software company could therefore charge $49.90 for a package of programs—$5.00 more than the $44.90 that it could obtain if it marketed the programs separately.

It turns out that the software company would find it profitable to sell programs in a bundle as long as the relationship between the amount one type of consumer would pay for the programs were inversely related to the amount that the other type would be willing to pay. Panel A of Figure 10.15 shows that the data in Table 10.7 do, in fact, display such an inverse relationship. If this relationship were direct, as in panel B, though, then there would be no advantage to bundling. Panel B shows the relationship embodied

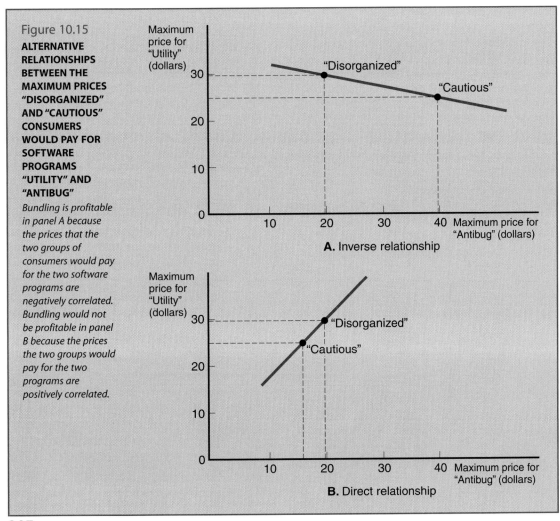

Figure 10.15

ALTERNATIVE RELATIONSHIPS BETWEEN THE MAXIMUM PRICES "DISORGANIZED" AND "CAUTIOUS" CONSUMERS WOULD PAY FOR SOFTWARE PROGRAMS "UTILITY" AND "ANTIBUG"

Bundling is profitable in panel A because the prices that the two groups of consumers would pay for the two software programs are negatively correlated. Bundling would not be profitable in panel B because the prices the two groups would pay for the two programs are positively correlated.

A. Inverse relationship

B. Direct relationship

Table 10.8

		Type of consumer	
Program		"Disorganized"	"Cautious"
"Utility"		$29.95	$24.95
"Antibug"		$19.95	$15.95
Bundled together		$49.90	$40.90

in Table 10.8. The program "Utility" could still be sold for $24.95, but "Antibug" can now earn at most $15.95 on its own. Sold separately, therefore, the two programs would generate total revenue equal to $40.90 (= $24.95 + $15.95); this is exactly the maximum price that could be charged if the programs were bundled.[10]

Example 10.6	Examples of Price Discrimination, Bundling, and Associated Issues

Examples of price discrimination are all around, but each approach brings a secondary set of questions to the fore. Here is a short list of discriminatory practices that you may have encountered; each is accompanied by an associated issue that is examined in a problem found at the end of the chapter.

1. Airlines frequently charge business flyers more than others, and they often market discount fares through special offers or Web site addresses. They hold a number of seats for each type of flyer, though, until a few days before the actual flight. How do they decide that allocation?
2. Cleaners sometimes charge more to clean and press women's blouses than they do men's shirts. They charge more to shorten women's slacks than men's pants; and more to press a woman's sport jacket than a man's suit. Price elasticities of demand tell you why, but is the practice illegal discrimination on the basis of gender?
3. Many manufacturers discriminate across the buying public by offering coupons in newspapers, magazines, and sometimes directly through their retailers. Why does this make sense?
4. Retailers can sometimes charge higher prices to customers who want a product immediately and lower prices to people who are more patient. What should determine those differences?
5. Utilities frequently charge different prices for their products during periods of peak demand than they do during slack times. Should peak prices be higher or lower? And should a utility determine its capacity on the basis of peak demand, slack demand, or something in between?

[10]For further discussion, see W. Adams and J. Yellen, "Commodity Bundling and the Burden of Monopoly," *Quarterly Journal of Economics,* August 1976; and R. Schmalensee, "Commodity Bundling by Single-Product Monopolies," *Journal of Law and Economics,* April 1982.

6. Businesses that sell tickets for a series of events, ranging from professional
baseball teams to regional theaters, often offer packages of tickets to multiple events at lower per unit cost to the customer. Packages that include
only a few events are therefore marketed alongside larger packages that
include more popular offerings; and both thereby compete for attention
with season tickets. How should these packages be priced, and what events
should they include as they try to inspire consumers to "trade up"?

The first four practices are really examples of third-degree price discrimination. Questions 8, 9, 15, and 18 at the end of this chapter focus attention
on the mechanics of profit maximization when firms have the requisite ability to differentiate and segregate two distinct markets. The fifth practice
describes a "peak-load" pricing problem, and Question 19 provides a specific
context within which the associated issues might be explored. The last practice speaks to issues of profitable bundling that are illustrated in Question 20.

PUBLIC REGULATION OF MONOPOLY

State regulatory commissions often have substantial influence over the prices
charged by public utilities like gas and electric companies. These public
utilities often are natural monopolies whose power has been created by the
government in recognition of the strong economies of scale in delivering
their services. To see how these commissions might decide what prices would
be allowed, consider the firm whose demand curve, marginal-revenue curve,
average-cost curve, and marginal-cost curve are as shown in Figure 10.16.

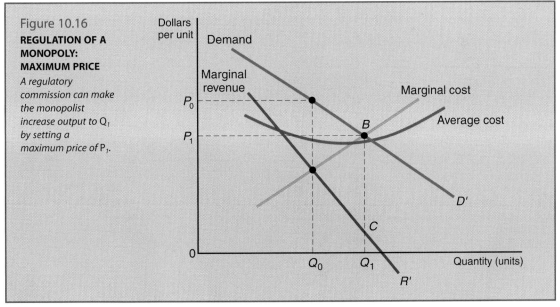

Figure 10.16

REGULATION OF A MONOPOLY: MAXIMUM PRICE

A regulatory commission can make the monopolist increase output to Q_1 by setting a maximum price of P_1.

The firm would charge a price of P_0 and it would produce Q_0 units of the commodity without regulation. The regulatory commission might set the price at P_1, however, so that the monopolist would increase output; this would bring the industry equilibrium closer to what it would sustain if it were organized competitively. How would this work? Imposing a maximum price of P_1 would mean that the firm's effective demand curve would be P_1BD'. The associated marginal-revenue curve would then be P_1BCR', and its profit-maximizing output would rise to Q_1 (where the new, effective marginal-revenue curve intersects marginal cost). What price would be charged? The targeted P_1 selected by the regulating commission. Establishing the maximum price would help consumers, who would be paying a lower price for more of the good, but it would also deprive the monopolist firm of much of its profits.

Regulatory commissions often set the price—or the maximum price—at the level at which it equals average total cost, including a "fair" rate of return on the company's investment. In Figure 10.17, for example, a commission following this rule would set the price at P_2, where the demand curve intersects the average total-cost curve. If the latter curve includes what the commission regards as a fair profit per unit of output, then the owners of the utility would be earning normal returns on their investments. But what would constitute a fair rate of return? And how much of the utility's investment should be included in the calculation of the fair return? These are contentious issues around which spirited debate has erupted more often than not when regulatory commissions hold their public meetings.

Regulatory commissions also govern the extent to which price discrimination can be employed by public utilities. Intricate systems of price

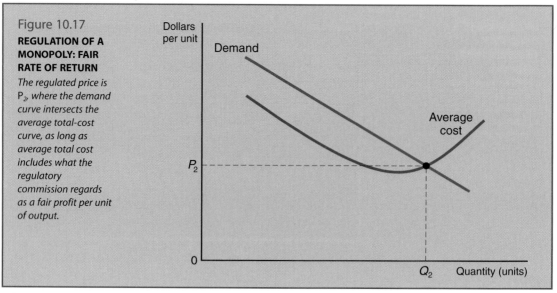

Figure 10.17

REGULATION OF A MONOPOLY: FAIR RATE OF RETURN

The regulated price is P_2, where the demand curve intersects the average total-cost curve, as long as average total cost includes what the regulatory commission regards as a fair profit per unit of output.

discrimination exist in the rate structures of electric and gas companies, telephone companies, and others. Some types of price discrimination are prohibited by law or by the rules set by the regulatory authorities, but other types can be practiced or are even encouraged if they are "reasonable." A utility may be permitted to charge a lower rate for service for which it must meet stiff competition. It may be permitted to charge higher rates during periods of peak demand. In every case, though, discussions about rate discrimination focus on important questions of equity, the redistribution of income, and economic efficiency.

Nothing in public-utility control is more conventional and more securely established in regulatory methods than the idea of a "reasonable return on the value of a firm's existing plant." It is this reasonable rate of return that the regulatory commissions have been interested in establishing over many decades of history and case law. Still, a host of questions remain. Some are obvious. Others are difficult even for trained engineers and accountants. What is "reasonable"? What is the "value of a firm's *existing* plant"? What should be done about new plants and equipment?

Many commissions insist that firms base their estimates of the value of any plant on its original or historical cost, but some now allow firms to base their estimates on replacement-cost valuations instead. Regulated firms often sought rates of return between 10 and 15 percent through the early 1980s, but commissions have more recently worked to assure approved rates of return between 6 and 10 percent.[11] Each case offers its own set of detailed and difficult questions, and each case offers profitable employment for a great many lawyers, accountants, engineers, and economists.

Considerable controversy has even centered on the regulatory process itself. Many observers feel that the regulatory commissions have been too lax, perhaps because they tend to be too intimately tied to the industries they are supposed to regulate. Even effective regulation can create unfortunate and unanticipated consequences. The Civil Aeronautics Board, for example, was established in 1938 to regulate the prices charged by the interstate scheduled airlines and to monitor entry into the airline industry. It was criticized severely during the 1970s for preventing price competition among airlines and for permitting very little new entry. Congress phased out the CAB's powers in the early 1980s.[12] The result has been more competition on popular routes, but less competition along less-traveled connections. Low-cost, no-frills airlines have entered some markets, but real questions of safety have been raised about them. The deregulation movement of the 1980s extended to a variety of other industries, but it did not end the debate.

[11]See W. Shepherd and C. Wilcox, *Public Policies toward Business*, 6th ed. (Homewood, Ill.: Irwin, 1979); and W. Shepherd, *Public Policies toward Business: Readings and Cases* (Homewood, Ill.: Irwin, 1979).

[12]For an appraisal of the airlines' performance and suggestions for improvement, see S. Morrison and C. Winston, "Enhancing the Performance of the Deregulated Air Transportation System," in M. Baily and C. Winston, eds., *Brookings Papers on Economic Activity*, 1989.

Example 10.7 **Shaking the Tree of Global Telecommunications Markets**

Table 10.9 clearly shows that Nippon Telegraph and Telephone Corporation (NTT) was the world's largest telecommunications group through 1998. On July 2, 1999, however, NTT was required to dissolve into a holding company that comprised two domestically focused companies and a new international unit. It should be no surprise that its breakup and its entry into the global marketplace in July 1999 sent shock waves across Japan and around the world. NTT entered a global market that was already undergoing structural upheavals triggered by deregulation and technological advances. The domestic reorganization, meanwhile, was the result of government intervention at home. It would seem that NTT was, in 1999, simultaneously playing two roles. On the one hand, it was the new entrant into a (global) market dominated by a few major players but threatened by a highly competitive fringe. One the other, it was a dominant firm trying to maintain (domestic) market power.

We tell the international story first. Unlike many other telecommunications carriers that started out as old-fashioned telephone companies, NTT chose to place priority on data transfer and supplemental services from the outset of its entry into international markets. "We are a latecomer in the global market. . . . We see no business incentive in doing the same thing as the others," said Tatsuo Kawasaki, NTT's vice president in charge of global strategy. Competitors believed that NTT's strength lay in its huge corporate

Table 10.9		Value of stock as of May 20, 1999[b]	Annual sales 1998[b]
TOP 10 COMMUNICATIONS CARRIERS WORLDWIDE	1 AT&T (U.S.)	197.0	53.2
	2 SBC/Ameritech (U.S.)[a]	176.5	46.0
	3 NTT (Japan)	164.4	81.1
	4 MCI WorldCom (U.S.)	159.9	30.4
	5 Bell Atlantic/GTE (U.S.)[a]	149.5	57.0
	6 NTT DoCoMo (Japan)	118.9	26.0
	7 Vodafone (Britain)/ AirTouch (U.S.)[a]	116.8	9.2
	8 British Telecommunications (Britain)	106.8	30.4
	9 Deutsche Telekom (Germany)	102.2	40.7
	10 BellSouth (U.S.)	90.3	23.1

[a]Merger incomplete as of July 1,1999.
[b]In billions of dollars.
SOURCE: *Japan Times,* July 1, 1999.

customer base; its sheer size allowed it to offer a comprehensive range of products, from fixed-line to mobile services. In addition, NTT's entry into the global market came at a time when traditional alliances designed to offer similar menus of services were at a turning point. Deregulation and rapid growth, particularly in the United States, was putting pressure on members of these informal alliances to break away and violate their implicit contracts.

More specifically, traditional alliances were assaulted by the results of worldwide deregulation that promoted competition in the markets of many countries. Moreover, multinational companies like NTT were better at providing the seamless services around the globe that customers were increasingly demanding. Traditional carriers within alliances had been friendly to one another because their geographic territories were well defined. As a result, they did not compete with one another on the same "turf." But, by 1999, carriers were forced to compete in each other's markets to service even their domestic customers. They were no longer friends. Indeed, one of the largest alliances, called World Partners, dissolved at the end of 1999 because one of its major members, AT&T, established a joint venture with British Telecommunications that directly challenged the profitability of the partnership.

Technological change also played a role in creating the turmoil in the global marketplace. Deregulation had spawned a new breed of telecommunications carriers like Level 3 Communications and Qwest Communications. Both were born in the United States and both had grown rapidly by using Internet-based technology to build lower-cost networking infrastructures. Level 3 had, in fact, reduced the cost of building a network to 1/27 of the cost of traditional carriers, and operating their networks required fewer employees. But because these carriers had weak customer bases and little experience, NTT saw an opportunity. NTT therefore entered the world depicted in Table 10.9 as one of a few large players who might adopt the new technologies (or subsume the smaller Internet-based companies) most efficiently.

To that end, NTT maintained a position that it would not enter exclusivity contracts with anyone. "We are not saying that we won't team up with anyone," Kawasaki said on the eve of the international venture. "[But if we do,] it would be on a project-by-project basis or a regional basis" and "we will not do the old type of exclusive alliance because we don't see the point of such tie-ups."

One final hurdle in the reorganization of NTT to include an international component was overcome on July 1, 1999, when the U.S. government prohibition on preferential treatment of foreign suppliers for components used in the U.S. market was replaced by an agreement to let NTT determine its own procurement procedures. U.S. regulators would simply monitor behavior to make certain that NTT treated all potential suppliers equally. In so doing, both sides accepted the argument advanced by Professor S. Daigo of the University of Tokyo—that competition would be the best regulator.

As it set its sights on overseas markets, though, NTT could not afford to rest on its laurels at home. Foreign carriers were entering Japanese markets, too. Darryl Green, president of AT&T Japan Ltd., observed that "there is a lot of room to compete with NTT domestically." The prospect of coping with this competition was made more difficult by the required breakup of NTT into separate, regionally defined companies. Contrary to expectations, though, NTT reached an agreement with Japanese regulators that allowed it to reorganize as a holding company under which both regional companies as well as its new international entity could operate.

The hope of domestic competitors had been that NTT would be completely divided, so that it would no longer hold a dominant position in the Japanese market. The creation of the large holding company was therefore a big disappointment to some. Rivals find it problematic, for example, that NTT Communications Corporation (the international and long-distance carrier) could award sales commissions to its two regional carriers—East-Nippon Telegraph and Telephone Corporation and West-Nippon Telegraph and Telephone Corporation. Rival carriers, who must rely on NTT's local networks, worried that the sister companies of NTT would not push the rivals' services with the same zeal as NTT's. Rivals noted, as well, that the holding company was allowed to begin operation before the details about regulation were hashed out; thus NTT was allowed to establish certain levels of procedural inertia that would be hard to overcome.

There was some good news for rivals, though, from those who pointed out that the working associations within the holding company would likely depreciate with time. At the very least, cross-subsidization among the components of NTT would stop, and this would diminish the ability of NTT to engage in price competition with existing firms.

SUMMARY

1. Monopoly exists when there is one, and only one, seller in a market. Monopolies arise because a single firm controls the entire supply of a basic input, because a firm has a patent on the product or on certain basic processes, because the average cost of producing the product reaches a minimum at an output rate that is large enough to satisfy an entire market at a price that is profitable, because the firm is awarded a franchise, or because of other reasons.

2. The demand curve facing the monopolist is the market demand for the product. The cost conditions facing a monopolist may be no different from those facing a perfectly competitive firm if the monopolist is a perfect competitor in the input markets.

3. A monopolist maximizes profit by setting its output at the point where marginal cost equals marginal revenue. It does not follow that a firm that holds a monopoly over the production of a particular product must make a profit. If the monopolist cannot cover its variable costs, it will shut down, even in the short run.

4. There is no unique relationship between the price charged by a monopolist and the quantity supplied. The long-run equilibrium of a monopoly is not necessarily marked by the absence of economic profits. If the monopolist has more than one plant, then it should allocate production among its

plants so that the marginal cost of production at any plant is equal to the marginal cost of production at every other plant. It should also set its overall output so that this common marginal cost equals marginal revenue.

5. There are a number of important differences between the long-run equilibrium of a monopoly and of a perfectly competitive industry. Under perfect competition, each firm operates at the point where both long-run and short-run average costs are at a minimum. A multiplant monopolist can sometimes achieve the same condition, but a single-plant monopolist can sometimes expand its long-run equilibrium for which average costs are not minimized. In either case, the output of a perfectly competitive industry tends to be greater and price tends to be lower than under monopoly. The perfectly competitive firm operates at the point where price equals marginal cost, whereas the monopolist operates at a point where price exceeds marginal cost (because price exceeds marginal revenue). The loss of consumer surplus due to monopoly exceeds the gain in producer surplus. Monopoly power can therefore create deadweight loss.

6. Price discrimination occurs either when the same commodity is sold at more than one price or when similar products are sold at prices that do not vary systematically with their marginal costs. A firm will be able and willing to practice price discrimination if various markets with different buyers displaying different elasticities of demand can be identified and if the commodity cannot be transferred easily from one market to another.

7. Firms with monopoly power sometimes use two-part tariffs that require the consumer to pay an initial fee for the right to buy the product in addition to a fee for each unit that he or she buys. Firms that produce goods that function properly only if they are used in conjunction with another product sometimes require their customers to buy both products at the same time. This practice is called tying. Still another pricing technique is bundling—a situation in which consumers are required to purchase groups of goods in inseparable packages.

8. Regulatory commissions frequently have the power to set the prices charged by public utilities like gas or electric companies. They often set prices at a level that matches estimates of average total cost that include a "fair" rate of return on the company's "existing" investment in plant and equipment. Controversy continues over what constitutes a "fair" rate of return and over what should be included in the company's "existing" investment.

QUESTIONS/ PROBLEMS

1. The U.S. Postal Service has been a government monopoly in the United States since 1845. Suppose that the short-run demand and cost curves of the Philadelphia post office are as portrayed in the figure. (a) Does the post office appear to be a natural monopoly? (b) If the post office is a natural monopoly, must it be operated under government ownership? (c) If the Philadelphia post office wanted to carry as many pieces of mail as it could without incurring a short-run deficit, how much mail should it carry per day? (d) The available evidence indicates that average revenue (per piece of mail) has exceeded average total cost and marginal cost for first-class mail, but not for third-class mail. Which type of mail is likely to attract private competitors? (e) What advantages might accrue if the post office were to

face increased private competition? Who might enjoy these benefits? What are the potential risks? Assess the effect of e-mail. Did the 37-cent stamp increase revenue?

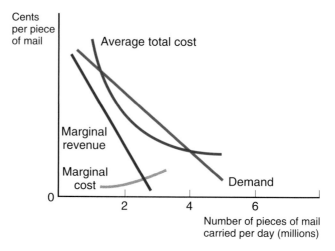

2. A monopolist has two plants with two different marginal cost functions:

$$MC_1 = 20 + 2Q_1$$

and

$$MC_2 = 10 + 5Q_2,$$

where MC_1 is marginal cost in the first plant, MC_2 is marginal cost in the second plant, Q_1 is output in the first plant, and Q_2 is output in the second plant. If the monopolist is minimizing its costs while producing 9 units of output at the first plant, how many units is it producing at the second plant? Suppose demand is given by $P = 57 - 1.5x$. What is the profit-maximizing output? What is marginal revenue? How much should be produced at each plant?

3. Prostatix, Inc., a hypothetical pharmaceutical manufacturer, is a monopolist. Its president says that its price at its profit-maximizing output is triple its marginal cost. What is the price elasticity of demand of its product?

4. A monopolist has the total cost function and demand curve reflected in the following table:

Price (dollars)	Output (units)	Total cost (dollars)
8	5	20
7	6	21
6	7	22
5	8	23
4	9	24
3	10	30

What price should it charge?

5. A. C. Harberger, in his study cited in footnote 5, found that the misallocation of resources due to monopoly was quite small. This conclusion stimulated considerable controversy. He assumed that the price elasticity of demand was unity everywhere. Would a rational monopolist operate at a point where the price elasticity of demand is unity? Assume demand is linear. Argue why a monopolist facing this demand curve with nonzero marginal cost would operate in the elastic region of demand. Would this make the estimate of deadweight loss, measured as a percentage of total surplus, larger or smaller than the Harberger estimate?

6. You own a metals-producing firm that is an unregulated monopoly. Your marginal-cost curve can be approximated by a straight line, $MC = 60 + 2Q$, where MC is marginal cost (in dollars) and Q is your output. Moreover, suppose that the demand curve for your product is $P = 100 - Q$, where P is the product price and Q is your output. If you want to maximize profit, what output should you choose? What price should you choose? What price would a regulator choose as a maximum if she wanted you to produce the largest output possible while still allowing your profits to be no less than zero?

7. Authors customarily receive a royalty that is a fixed percentage of the selling price of their books. For this reason, economists have pointed out that an author has an interest in a book's price being lower than the price that maximizes the publisher's profits. Prove that this is true.

8. Suppose that you are hired as a consultant to a firm producing ball bearings. This firm sells in two distinct markets, one of which is completely sealed off from the other. The demand curve for the firm's output in one market is given by $P_1 = 160 - 8Q_1$, where P_1 is the price of the product and Q_1 is the amount sold in the first market. Meanwhile, the demand curve for the firm's output in the second market is given by $P_2 = 80 - 2Q_2$, where P_2 is the price of the product and Q_2 is the amount sold in the second market. The firm's marginal-cost curve is $5 + Q$, where Q is the firm's entire output (destined for either market). The firm asks you to suggest what its pricing policy should be. (a) How many units of output should it sell in the second market? (b) How many units of output should it sell in the first market? (c) What prices should it charge? Check your answers by confirming that your price ratio between markets matches the appropriate ratio of price elasticities.

9. The Errata Book Company is a monopolist that sells in two markets. The marginal-revenue curve in the first market is $MR_1 = 20 - 2Q_1$, where MR_1 is the marginal-revenue in the first market and Q_1 is the number of books sold per day in the first market. The marginal-revenue curve in the second market is $MR_2 = 15 - 3Q_2$, where MR_2 is the marginal revenue in the second market and Q_2 is the number of books sold per day in the second market. If the marginal cost of a book is $6, how many books should the Errata Book Company sell in each market? What prices should it charge in each market? (Hint: Work backward from the marginal-revenue curves to solve for market demand curves.)

10. The Henreid Company produces a particular type of briefcase. It charges a price of $99 for each of its briefcases. Its marginal cost equals $61. What is the value of the Lerner index for this firm? What is the price elasticity of demand for this firm's product? If the Henreid Company were a perfectly competitive firm, what would be the value of the Lerner index for this firm? If it were a perfect monopolist?

11. For a particular good that is monopolized, $P = 12 - 2Q_D$, $MR = 12 - 4Q_D$, and $MC = 2Q$, where P is its price (in dollars per ton), Q_D is the quantity demanded per year (in millions of tons), MR is its marginal revenue (in dollars per ton), MC is its marginal cost (in dollars per ton), and Q is the quantity produced per year (in millions of tons). How great is the deadweight loss due to monopoly?

12. Federal and state officials have found evidence that executives at large national and regional dairy firms have rigged bids on milk products sold to schools and military bases. For example, consider the bidding for the contract to supply milk for the school districts in Pinellas County, Florida. Before the bidding, a vice president of Pet Milk, the general manager of Borden's Tampa plant, and the manager of Pet's largest distributor in the area met at a restaurant in Tampa, Florida. They agreed that Borden would bid too high, so that Pet would get the Pinellas contract; in return, Pet would cede to Borden part of the milk business in another county. A prosecutor said that as a result, the Pinellas schools paid about 14 percent more than they otherwise would have for milk.[13] (a) Did this result in a decrease in consumer surplus? (b) Did it result in an increase in producer surplus? (c) Did it result in an increase in total surplus?

13. In 1983, the Santa Fe and Southern Pacific railroads announced a plan to merge. The two railroads run parallel to one another; they provide the only rail service between southern California and Texas (and the Gulf of Mexico ports). Legislation passed by Congress in 1980 reduced the amount of regulation in this industry. Nonetheless, the Interstate Commerce Commission, which has regulated the railroad industry since 1887, had to approve the merger application, and in 1986 it refused to do so on a 4-to-1 vote of the commissioners. (a) According to analysts at the U.S. Department of Justice, the merger would have resulted in a substantial price increase by the railroads.[14] In the figure, the price would have increased from P to P'. (For the two firms combined, their demand curve and their marginal-cost curve are shown in the figure. For simplicity, marginal cost is assumed to be constant.) These analysts estimated that the area of rectangle C equaled about $404 million. Is this the shippers' loss due to having to pay a price of P' rather than P for the Q' units of railroad services they would buy after the merger? (b) With regard to rectangle C, do the railroads gain what the shippers lose? (c) These analysts estimated that the area of rectangle B equaled about $57 million. Is this the loss to the railroads from the reduction in their output (from Q to Q') that was earning more than marginal cost? (d) These analysts estimated that the area of triangle A was about $22 million. Is this the loss to shippers of the consumer surplus from the railroad services they bought when the price was P but would not buy when it is P'? (e) On balance, are shippers hurt by the merger, according to these estimates? Do the railroads benefit? (f) If the merger reduces the firms' cost considerably, should the savings be deducted from the social costs of the merger?

[13] *New York Times*, May 23, 1993.
[14] R. Pitman, "Railroad and Competition: Why the Santa Fe/Southern Merger Had to Die," U.S. Department of Justice, August 1988.

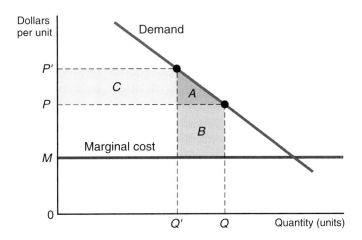

14. You operate a natural, unregulated monopoly and you select your output and price to maximize profit. You operate on the downward-sloping part of your long-run average-cost curve. Could you increase output and lower average cost in the short run if you were forced to lower the price to deter the entry of a potential competitor? And if you could, why wouldn't you do so even if there were no potential entrant in sight? Now suppose that you operate on the upward-sloping region of your long-run average-cost curve. Do your marginal costs exceed average cost? If so, why do you tolerate such a situation? Would increasing output to deter a potential competitor now be possible with lower average cost in the short run?

15. Suppose that a monopolist producing some good X with constant long- and short-run average costs equal to $2 faced a market made up of two types of customers. There are 50 of each type of customer. The first type of customers have demand curves represented by $P = 10 - 0.1X$; the second have demand curves represented by $P = 5 - 0.01X$. Compute the maximum-profit price and quantity if the monopolist must set a single price. Now compute a second-degree price-discrimination scheme that would increase profits. Specify two prices and a threshold quantity that distinguishes the two; i.e., designate a threshold so that one price holds for quantities up to that limit while the second holds for quantities greater than that threshold.

16. You have the following information about a profit-maximizing monopolist. Total revenue equals $8,000 with 4,000 units being sold. Average cost is $1.80; it is $0.20 lower than marginal cost. Is the firm in the correct position, or should it make some sort of adjustment in price or quantity produced and sold? Why?

17. You have the following information about a profit-maximizing monopolist. Price is $2.50 and the quantity demanded equals 10,000 units. Price exceeds marginal revenue by 20 percent. Fixed costs amount to $4,000, average cost is $3.00, and marginal cost is $2.00. Is the firm in the correct position, or should it make some sort of adjustment in price or quantity produced and sold? Why?

18. In the 1970s, the United Brands Company marketed its bananas in a variety of countries in Europe. The bananas were sold to wholesalers for distribution in individual national markets. They were all of the same type and entered Europe through either Bremerhaven or Rotterdam. Although the cost of unloading them was essentially the same at these two ports, the prices that United Brands charged distributors differed considerably from country to country. The average difference in price per 20-kilogram box was about 11 to 18 percent, but some differences were much greater. For example, the price charged to Denmark was about 2.4 times the price charged to Ireland.

Suppose that you are an adviser to the United Brands Company and that the company's president asks you whether its pricing policy resulted in maximum profit. After conversations with the company's marketing personnel, suppose that you find that their studies indicate that the price elasticity of demand for the firm's bananas was about 2 in Denmark, about 2.5 in Germany, and about 4 in Ireland. Other company executives state that the marginal cost of shipping bananas to each of these countries (and marketing them) did not differ from country to country. What's the answer to the president's question?

19. Assume that a monopolist can produce some good X at a constant marginal cost $c > 0$, but only up to a given capacity X_{cap}. Producing above this capacity is impossible, but the firm can determine this threshold. Assume, as well, that the monopolist faces two different demand curves for X at different times during the month and that it has the ability to charge different prices depending upon which demand curve is operating. The first demand curve, given by $P = a_1 - bX$, appears $\pi \cdot 100\%$ of the time with $a_1 > 0$, $b > 0$, and $1 > \pi > 0$. The second demand curve, given by $P = a_2 - bX$, appears the rest of the time, i.e., $(1 - \pi) \cdot 100\%$ of the month. Let demand in the second period be higher than in the first, so that $a_2 > a_1$.

a. Show that the capacity that maximizes expected profits is the weighted average of the capacities that would maximize profits if curve 1 or 2 were certain to be sustained for the whole month. Indeed, show that the probabilities π and $(1 - \pi)$ are the weights for the two "certainty capacities."

b. Show, by actually solving for the expected-profit maximizing prices, that the price charged when demand curve 2 is operating would always be higher than the price charged when demand curve 1 is operating.

c. Now assume that a regulator intervenes so that the firm must always supply at least as much as the quantity demanded *and* that it must always charge the *same price*. What single price for both periods of demand would maximize expected profits over the month?

d. Would expected social welfare be higher or lower under the regulation than it would be if the firm were left to its own devices? Would expected profits be higher or lower?

20. The University of Connecticut has taken to bundling tickets for the games that its men's basketball team plays at the Hartford Civic Center. The Civic Center holds more fans than Gampel Pavilion (the on-campus facility), so there are extra seats to sell for the games held in Hartford. Incidentally, the university does not bundle tickets for its women's program, which sells out even the Civic Center with season tickets. Assume that there are two types of basketball fan. One is a fan of the game; he or she will pay the same price to see a game regardless of whom UConn is playing. The other is a "Big East" fan who will pay a lot to see a league game or a game against a ranked opponent but who also has almost no interest in seeing UConn play somebody else. Use your understanding of the underlying theory of price discrimination to argue why the university offers ticket combinations that bundle tickets for games against Big East and ranked teams with tickets for games against other competition.

Calculus Appendix

PROFIT-MAXIMIZING CONDITIONS FOR A MONOPOLIST

Suppose that a market demand curve for some good q were given by $P = D(q)$, where P represents price. Let $C(q)$ represent the cost of production. A monopolist interested in maximizing profits would then choose the value $q^{\star}$ that maximized profits given by

$$\Pi(q) = q \times P - C(q) = q \times D(q) - C(q).$$

The appropriate first-order condition for this problem is easily recorded; the profit-maximizing output $q^{\star}$ would solve

$$\Pi'(q^{\star}) = 0,$$

where $\Pi'(q^{\star})$ represents the first derivative of the profit function evaluated at output $q^{\star}$. Adding some detail, therefore, we know that $q^{\star}$ would satisfy the condition that

$$q^{\star} D'(q^{\star}) + D(q^{\star}) - C'(q^{\star}) = 0, \qquad [1]$$

where $D'(q^{\star})$ represents the first derivative of the demand curve evaluated at quantity $q^{\star}$ and $C'(q^{\star})$ represents the first derivative of the cost curve evaluated at $q^{\star}$. Notice, of course, that Equation 1 can be rewritten as

$$q^{\star} D'(q^{\star}) + D(q^{\star}) = C'(q^{\star}).$$

In this form, it is easy to see that the first-order condition that characterizes the profit-maximizing output $q^{\star}$ requires that marginal revenue (the left-hand side) equal marginal cost (the right-hand side) precisely at $q^{\star}$. There are, of course, second-order conditions to ensure that $q^{\star}$ is at worst a local maximum and not a minimum.

The monopolist's problem could have, equally as well, been expressed directly in terms of a revenue function $R(q) = q \times D(q)$. In that case, profits would have been

$$\Pi(q) = R(q) - C(q)$$

and the first-order condition characterizing $q^{\star}$ would have been

$$R'(q^{\star}) = C'(q^{\star}).$$

Again, marginal revenue must equal marginal cost at $q^{\star}$.

PROFIT-MAXIMIZING CONDITIONS WHEN A MONOPOLIST FACES TWO DISTINCT MARKETS

Now suppose that our monopolist had monopoly power selling the same product in two distinct markets. Let $R_1(q_1)$ represent the revenue that could be generated by selling q_1 in market 1 and let $R_2(q_2)$ represent the revenue derived by selling q_2 in the second market. Total output would be $q_1 + q_2$, of course, so the cost of production must depend on both. Represent these costs by $C(q_1 + q_2)$ so that the profit function will be

$$\Pi(q_1 + q_2) = R_1(q_1) + R_2(q_2) - C(q_1 + q_2).$$

As a result, two first-order conditions would be required to characterize the profit-maximization pair $(q_1{}^*, q_2{}^*)$. The first, derived by setting the partial derivative of $\Pi(q_1 + q_2)$ with respect to q_1 equal to zero, would set

$$R_1'(q_1{}^*) - C'(q_1{}^* + q_2{}^*) = 0.$$

And rearranging,

$$R_1'(q_1{}^*) = C'(q_1{}^* + q_2{}^*); \qquad [2a]$$

i.e., the marginal revenue earned by selling the last unit in market 1 must equal the marginal cost of producing the last unit of total output.

Meanwhile, for market 2, an analogous condition would be derived by setting the partial derivative of $\Pi(q_1 + q_2)$ with respect to q_2 equal to zero. Accordingly,

$$R_2'(q_2{}^*) = C'(q_1{}^* + q_2{}^*). \qquad [2b]$$

Notice that Equations 2a and 2b represent two equations in two unknowns. Notice, as well, that they can be combined to show that profits would be maximized only if the marginal revenue of the last unit sold in market 1 were equal to the marginal revenue of the last unit sold in market 2 (and both would equal marginal cost).

PROFIT-MAXIMIZING CONDITIONS FOR A MULTIPLANT MONOPOLIST

Finally, suppose that the monopolist faced one market but produced its product at two different plants. Let $C_1(q_1)$ represent the cost of producing q_1 at plant 1 and let $C_2(q_2)$ represent the cost of producing q_2 at the second plant. Total output would still be $q_1 + q_2$, of course, but now it is revenue that would depend on both quantities. Representing this revenue function by $R(q_1 + q_2)$, profits would be

$$\Pi(q_1 + q_2) = R(q_1 + q_2) - C_1(q_1) - C_2(q_2).$$

Two different first-order conditions would then characterize the profit-maximization pair $(q_1{}^*, q_2{}^*)$. The first, derived by setting the partial derivative of $\Pi(q_1 + q_2)$ with respect to q_1 equal to zero, would set

$$R'(q_1{}^* + q_2{}^*) - C_1'(q_1{}^*) = 0.$$

Rearranging again,

$$C_1'(q_1{}^*) = R'(q_1{}^* + q_2{}^*); \qquad [3a]$$

i.e., the marginal cost of producing the last unit at plant 1 must equal the marginal revenue of selling the last unit regardless of where it was produced.

Meanwhile an analogous condition can be derived for plant 2 by setting the partial derivative of $\Pi(q_1 + q_2)$ with respect to q_2 equal to zero. Accordingly,

$$C_2'(q_2{}^*) = R'(q_1{}^* + q_2{}^*). \qquad [3b]$$

We again have two equations for two unknowns. Now, though, Equations 3a and 3b combine to show that profits would be maximized only if the marginal cost of the last unit produced at plant 1 were equal to the marginal cost of the last unit produced at plant 2 (and both would equal marginal revenue).

CHAPTER 11

Monopolistic Competition

INTRODUCTION

What do Ray Kroc (the founder of McDonald's Corporation), Estée Lauder (the founder of Estée Lauder Companies), and Sam Walton (the founder of Wal-Mart Stores, Inc.) have in common? They were all featured in the December 7, 1998, *Time* magazine special issue "Builders and Titans of the 20th Century." Why? Because they all made enormous fortunes without holding pure monopoly power in industries that were not perfectly competitive. This should not be surprising. Models of perfect competition and monopoly are useful tools for shedding light on how markets work, but both are polar cases. And both are extremely rare. In the next three chapters, we consider models that describe more realistically how many industries function. This chapter focuses attention on monopolistic competition; it will present a theoretical construction that applies well to many industries, such as retail trade, fast food, and cosmetics. The theory of oligopoly explored in Chapter 12 similarly pertains to industries such as electrical equipment, commercial aircraft manufacturers, and computers. Our discussion of oligopoly will employ game theory as a new analytical tool; and a few applications of this tool to other aspects of strategic decision-making will be examined in Chapter 13.

MONOPOLISTIC COMPETITION

Bergdorf Goodman has a monopoly on the sale of its dresses. Eddie Bauer and J. Crew have monopolies on the sale of their particular brands and styles of clothing. L. L. Bean has a monopoly on its own merchandise. Nonetheless, other firms such as Filene's and Nordstrom also sell dresses like those found in Bergdorf Goodman. The Gap sells clothing not all that different from what you could find at J. Crew. And Lands' End competes directly in the mail with L. L. Bean. Every firm in each of these examples has a monopoly over the sale of its own product, but they all face stiff competition

Product differentiation

from other firms that offer very close substitutes. These are cases of **product differentiation.** In other words, there is no single, homogeneous commodity called a dress, or a sweater, or a fuzzy vest. Sellers instead make their products different from others' by subtle nuances in style (or by flagrant display of their name). Cases like these are prevalent in the modern economy. Each difference offers each seller an amount of monopoly power, but it is usually small because the products of other firms are very similar. These sorts of sellers operate in markets that economists have labeled "monopolistically competitive."

Monopolistic competition

Monopolistic competition is a market structure in which just enough product differentiation exists to support elements of both monopoly and perfect competition. There are a large number of firms producing and selling goods that are close substitutes—goods that are not, in contrast to perfectly competitive situations, completely homogeneous from one seller to another. Retail trade is often cited as an industry with many of the characteristics of monopolistic competition, but there are other examples. Edward Chamberlin of Harvard University pioneered the development of the theory of monopolistic competition.[1] His work has been met with considerable criticism, but it was nonetheless a noteworthy attempt to take reality into account by developing a model to handle the important middle ground between perfect competition and monopoly.

| Example 11.1 | **Textbooks in Intermediate Microeconomic Theory** |

There may be no better example of monopolistic competition than the market for textbooks in intermediate microeconomic theory. There must be more than 20 different texts offered to today's academic community by a wide range of publishers. They all cover roughly the same material with varying degrees of reliance on graphs, algebra, and/or calculus, but significant product differentiation across the market is otherwise difficult to see. Publishers fiddle with size of pages, the number of colors allocated to all of the graphs, and the cover designs. Authors fiddle with style, order of presentation, and coverage on the margin. And both fiddle with ancillary material, like the microlinks and examples that have dotted this text so far. Indeed, many publishers have recently placed enormous emphasis on the number of examples reported in each chapter—snippets from the popular press that are designed to convince the reader that the theory is more than an academic exercise. The only problem is that examples grow less timely and become more artificial as the time between publication and reading expands. Some are so perfect, like the Carter energy tax idea matching with substitution and income effects, that they will always fit well; but others just become old news.

The examples presented thus far have nonetheless followed this format for the most part, but you will notice that their character will gradually

[1]E. Chamberlin, *The Theory of Monopolistic Competition* (Cambridge, Mass.: Harvard University Press, 1933). Another very important work of the same period was J. Robinson, *The Economics of Imperfect Competition* (New York: Macmillan, 1933).

change over the next eight chapters. They will move away from reporting evidence of how the basic theory might work to explain some simple observations and toward illustrating how the theory can be manipulated to produce models that can explain more complicated situations and answer more difficult questions. They will, as a result, begin to assume a character that is different from most of the competition. Part of the reason is product differentiation, to be sure. But be assured that the dominant rationale for the evolution is pedagogical. Chapter 1 described how models are used and evaluated, but you have not really seen how they are constructed to (1) capture the essence of an applied problem while (2) abstracting from unnecessary complication. Many of the examples that you will see in Chapters 12 through 18 will try to correct this omission. They will typically begin with an observation from reality, a question posed by economic behavior, or an independent verification that a researcher has made an important contribution to economic knowledge; and they will continue by presenting abstract constructions designed to get to the heart of the matter. The hope is that you will see how economists apply the insights drawn from fundamental theory to new situations to push our understanding of economic issues forward even if their models look, for all the world at first blush, as if they are the product of the purported "assume a can opener" approach.

We begin our coverage of Chamberlin's work by reviewing his notion of an economic structure that was neither perfectly competitive nor completely monopolistic. The firms included in a perfectly competitive industry are easy to identify because they all produce the same product. But if many firms produce goods that are all slightly different from one another, then defining the boundaries of an industry is considerably more problematic. Chamberlin nonetheless believed that it is useful to group firms that produce similar products together in what he termed a **product group.** We can, for example, formulate a product group called "dresses," or "sweaters," or "khaki pants." But the criteria by which we combine firms into designated product groups are bound to be somewhat arbitrary. There is no precise way to decide how close a pair of substitutes must be in order to be included in the same product group, and so we need to take care in interpreting results that are based on group designations about which there could be considerable disagreement.

Product group

How did Chamberlin's theory work with this idea of product groups? Chamberlin assumed, first of all, that the product that defined the group included a large number of firms whose specific offerings to the market could be distinguished by consumers. And he assumed that every firm offered goods that were fairly close substitutes for the offerings of the other firms in the group. Second, the number of firms in the product group was taken to be so large that each firm expected its actions to go unheeded by its rivals and to be unimpeded by any retaliatory measures on their part. Third, he assumed that every firm in the group faced the same demand curve with identical costs. This, of course, was a lightning rod for criticism: if the products offered by different firms were different, then why should their demand and cost curves be identical?

Defining the boundaries of a product group is not simply an academic problem for people who model monopolistically competitive industries. Setting those boundaries can play a critical role in the application of the antitrust laws of the United States. The Federal Trade Commission, for example, went to court in 1986 to prevent the acquisition of the Dr Pepper Company by the Coca-Cola Company. The FTC held that the acquisition would violate Section 7 of the Clayton Act, which prohibits an acquisition by one company of stock or assets of another that would substantially lessen competition. The FTC argued that carbonated soft drinks constituted the applicable product group so that the merger would increase Coke's market share by nearly 5 percentage points nationwide (and by 10 to 20 percentage points in some geographic markets where Coke's share already approached 50 percent). The legal team for Coca-Cola argued, unsuccessfully, that the more appropriate product group was all beverages; indeed, they wanted to include tap water as a potential competitor. The judge, Gerhard Gesell, noted that rival firms made their pricing, marketing, and even advertising decisions on the basis of comparisons with rival soft-drink manufacturers, and so he found that the FTC definition of the relevant product group made more sense. The merger never happened, nor did the proposed purchase of Seven Up by Pepsi-Cola.

EQUILIBRIUM PRICE AND OUTPUT IN THE SHORT AND LONG RUNS

It is now time to investigate the implications of the Chamberlin assumptions on equilibrium price and quantity. Each firm's product in a Chamberlin world is somewhat different from the products of its rivals, so the demand curve for its product is downward-sloping. Be aware, though, that the demand curve's position depends critically on the prices charged by the other firms in the product group. An increase in other firms' prices would cause it to shift up and to the right, but a reduction in those prices would cause it to shift down and to the left.

Short-run equilibrium

Figure 11.1 displays one such demand curve for a specified set of prices for other firms' products; it also illustrates the **short-run equilibrium.** The short-run equilibrium price and output for the firm depicted in Figure 11.1 would be P_1 and Q_1, respectively. Both are characterized by the intersection of the marginal-revenue curve (derived from the firm's *effective* demand curve) and the firm's marginal-cost curve. Having achieved this position, the firm would have no incentive to change its price from P_1. The equality of marginal revenue and marginal cost at output Q_1 means that the firm believes that it would maximize its profits by maintaining its price at P_1. The firm in Figure 11.1 would earn positive short-run profits equal to the shaded area, but this need not be the case. Firms could easily experience losses in a short-run equilibrium. As long as P_1 exceeded the firm's average variable costs of producing Q_1, though, the firm would continue to produce in the short run.

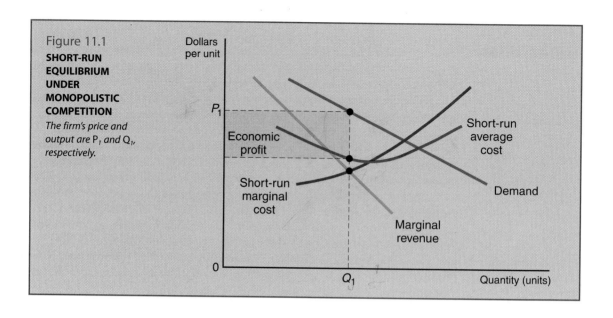

Figure 11.1

SHORT-RUN EQUILIBRIUM UNDER MONOPOLISTIC COMPETITION

The firm's price and output are P_1 and Q_1, respectively.

What about the long run? Monopolistically competitive firms are just like their perfectly competitive counterparts in the sense that they can make changes in the scales of their plants in the long run. They can decide to leave the industry if they are earning negative economic profit, and they could decide to enter an industry if they saw the prospect of earning positive economic profit. As a result, the **long-run equilibrium** price and output of the representative firm must satisfy conditions that are depicted in Figure 11.2. The equilibrium price for the firm depicted there would be P_2, and the equilibrium output would be Q_2. Why? Because free entry and exit in a monopolistically competitive industry means that long-run equilibrium can be sustained only when all firms in the industry (the product group) earn no more and no less than zero economic profits. This is similar to the long-run equilibrium in a perfectly competitive industry.

Long-run equilibrium

Take care to note that the cost curves portrayed in Figure 11.2 are long-run cost curves; they are not, to be more specific, the short-run cost curves shown in Figure 11.1. Long-run equilibrium occurs when the firm produces the output where the long-run average-cost curve is tangent to the demand curve. It is also characterized by the equality of the long-run marginal-cost curve and marginal revenue. The firm is maximizing profit because marginal revenue equals marginal cost (and because the tangency of the average-cost and demand curves means that average cost exceeds price for every output other than Q_2). Finally, economic profits equal 0 because average cost equals price at Q_2.

How is this long-run equilibrium position reached? The adjustments that take place can be described in terms of changes in the position of the demand curve facing the representative firm. The demand curve facing any single firm can shift in response to the entry of new firms and the exit of old firms. Increases in the number of firms in the product group shift the

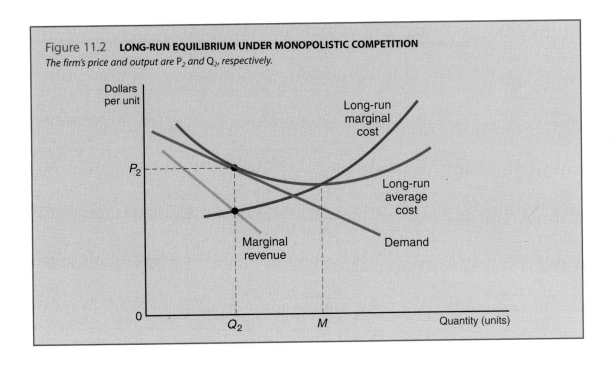

Figure 11.2 **LONG-RUN EQUILIBRIUM UNDER MONOPOLISTIC COMPETITION**
The firm's price and output are P_2 and Q_2, respectively.

demand curve facing the representative firm to the left, because the market (which is relatively fixed) must be divided among more firms. Reductions in the number of firms shift the demand curve facing the representative firm to the right, because the market must be divided among fewer firms. So, entry and exit push the demand curve facing any single firm toward the equilibrium position where it is tangent to the long-run average-cost curve.

You can now return to the short-run situation depicted in Figure 11.1 to add some detail to this story. The firm portrayed there is typical of others in the group; all would be making an economic profit given the current price of P_1. Positive economic profit would encourage new firms to enter the group, and so the demand curve facing the representative firm would shift to the left. And it would shift further to the left as long as entry continued. Indeed, long-run equilibrium would be established only when the situation portrayed in Figure 11.2 emerged. Then, and only then, the demand curve would be tangent to the long-run average-cost curve, economic profit would be maximized at zero, and all incentive to enter the product group would evaporate.

Example 11.3	**The Price Elasticity of Demand for a Monopolistic Competitor—Working a Problem**

Graphs of a monopolistic competitor's economic environment generally show shallowly sloped demand. The reasons for this are quite intuitive. Any firm that increases the price of its product when customers see a multitude of close substitutes risks losing market share notwithstanding loyalty of its customers to its particular brand. To illustrate this, suppose that 20

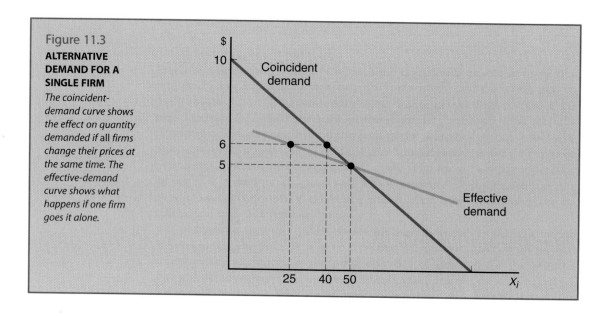

Figure 11.3

ALTERNATIVE DEMAND FOR A SINGLE FIRM

The coincident-demand curve shows the effect on quantity demanded if all firms change their prices at the same time. The effective-demand curve shows what happens if one firm goes it alone.

identical, monopolistically competitive firms (an arbitrary assumption, to be sure, but it makes the arithmetic easier without undermining the insight) faced a demand for some product group X given by

$$P = 10 - 0.005X.$$

Let the initial equilibrium price be $5. Then each firm would produce 50 units of its own variety of X for a total of 1,000 units. The price elasticity of demand at the market equilibrium would then be equal to 1 (this is the midpoint of a linear market demand curve). The price elasticity of the demand that each firm might face, if all firms moved their prices in concert, would also equal 1 because each would face a "coincident" demand curve given by

$$P_i = 10 - 0.01X.$$

But if any firm were to understand that it would lose, say, 50 percent of its original market share to other competitors for each $1 that it, acting alone, increased its price, then the price elasticity of its effective demand curve would be 50%/20% = 2.5 (because a $1 increase from $5 would represent a 20 percent increase in price). Figure 11.3 shows the difference.

Microlink 11.1 Equilibria in Monopolistic and Perfectly Competitive Markets

It is instructive to stop, at this point, to reflect on the differences in short-run and long-run equilibria in the three market structures discussed thus far. Figure 11.1 displays a short-run equilibrium for a single monopolistic competitor. It looks virtually the same as the portrait of short-run equilibrium for a monopolist depicted in Figure 10.3. Both figures show short-run conditions where maximum profits are positive, but either could also depict conditions where maximum profits were negative. Note, in particular, that profit-maximizing output is identified in both by the intersection of marginal cost and marginal revenue, that the price which supports profit maximization is read from the respective (downward-sloping) demand curve, and that profits are positive as drawn (because this price exceeds average cost). Figure 8.3 portrays the comparable situation under perfect competition. The firm depicted there faces a horizontal (effective) demand curve at a price that is determined by market conditions. This price is taken as fixed, and so it determines marginal revenue. Profits are still, therefore, maximized at the quantity where marginal cost equals marginal revenue, and profits can be positive at that price if price is again drawn in excess of average cost.

Figures 11.2 and 8.12 meanwhile depict the corresponding long-run equilibria under conditions of monopolistic and perfect competition, respectively. Both show long-run prices for which the economic profits of the participating firms are zero. Why? Because equilibrium in both situations is the result of firms' leaving or entering the market in response to negative or positive short-run profits, respectively. Long-run monopoly profits are, by way of contrast, positive in Figure 10.8. Notice, though, that the cost structure of a multiplant monopolist can mimic the competitive situation because each plant produces at the minimum of its long-run average-cost curve. The downward-sloping demand curve for a close substitute drawn from a product group combines in Figure 11.2 to guarantee that this condition is not met under monopolistic competition.

EXCESS CAPACITY AND PRODUCT DIVERSITY

The Chamberlin theory can be used to argue that a firm operating in a monopolistically competitive market will tend to operate with excess capacity. In other words, it is alleged that the firm will construct a plant smaller than the minimum-cost size of plant and operate it at less than the minimum-cost output. Why? Because, as shown in Figure 11.2, the negatively sloped demand curve must be tangent in long-run equilibrium to the long-run average-cost curve.

The details of the argument proceed in steps from this fundamental observation about the Chamberlin equilibrium. Since the demand curve is downward-sloping, the long-run average-cost curve must also be downward-sloping at the long-run equilibrium output. So, the firm's output must be less than M—the output at which long-run average cost would be minimized (the long-run average-cost curve slopes downward only for outputs that are smaller than M). Now refer to Figure 11.4. It depicts two short-run average- and marginal-cost curves for this plant. One set, labeled AC_M and MC_M, corresponds to the scale of plant required to produce output M at the minimum of long-run average costs. The other, labeled AC_C and MC_C, corresponds to the smaller scale of plant required to produce output Q_2 so that long-run equilibrium can be sustained. It is clear from these short-run cost curves that monopolistically competitive firms that behave in the Chamberlin way would build a smaller-than-minimum-cost plant so that they could operate at point E.

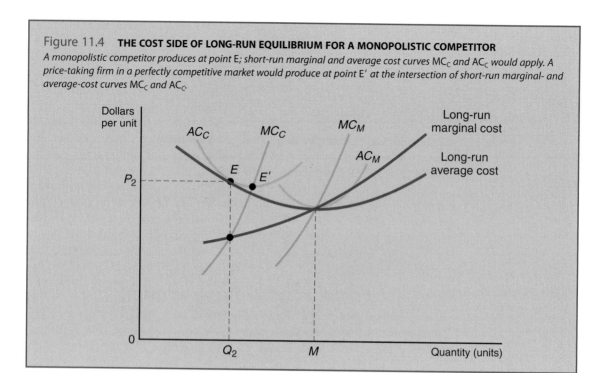

Figure 11.4   THE COST SIDE OF LONG-RUN EQUILIBRIUM FOR A MONOPOLISTIC COMPETITOR

A monopolistic competitor produces at point E; short-run marginal and average cost curves MC$_C$ and AC$_C$ would apply. A price-taking firm in a perfectly competitive market would produce at point E' at the intersection of short-run marginal- and average-cost curves MC$_C$ and AC$_C$.

It is also clear that the short-run average-cost curve AC_C is tangent to the long-run average-cost curve at point E. So, AC_C is also downward-sloping at point E, and the firm would not even be producing at the minimum of its short-run average-cost curve (point E'). Society's resources would therefore be wasted in producing any and all of the goods collected in this product group.

To summarize, then, Chamberlin-style monopolistic competitors tend to produce outputs that are smaller than their minimum-cost alternative outputs even in the short run. It follows that more firms can exist under these circumstances than if there were no excess capacity and that each firm is expending too many of society's resources to the production of its output. And so, it has been argued, there will be some inefficient "overcrowding" in monopolistically competitive industries. More recent research suggests that this argument may be somewhat myopic. Avinash Dixit, Michael Spence, Joseph Stiglitz, and others *Product diversity* have suggested that the **product diversity** offered to consumers by monopolistic competition supports an important benefit to society. Like most consumers, you probably value the ability to choose among a wide variety of clothes, restaurant meals, and other styles and types of products and services. Perhaps the social benefits from product diversity can be substantial; perhaps they might even exceed the social costs cited in the previous paragraphs.[2]

[2]See A. Dixit and J. Stiglitz, "Monopolistic Competition and Optimum Product Diversity," *American Economic Review,* June 1977; M. Spence, "Product Selection, Fixed Costs, and Monopolistic Competition," *Review of Economic Studies,* June 1976; K. Lancaster, "Socially Optimal Product Differentiation," *American Economic Review,* September 1975; and H. Leland, "Quality Choices and Competition," *American Economic Review,* March 1977.

Example 11.4

The question of how much product diversity to offer to the marketplace is not simply an issue of social value. Some large corporations face the same issue. General Motors, for example, divided its marketing into seven different divisions: Chevrolet, Cadillac, Buick, Oldsmobile, Pontiac, Saturn, and GMC. Each division presumably targets different types of car buyers, but each division also offers a wide range of different types of cars so that the boundaries are extraordinarily blurred for both customers and, it can be argued, corporate executives. Faced with increased competition from other manufacturers as well as across divisions within its own structure, General Motors announced in the fall of 2001 that it would close the Oldsmobile division after the 2004 model year. This followed the closing of the Plymouth division of DaimlerChrysler in November 1999. In addition, General Motors has also canceled production of a few of its specific offerings within its remaining lines even as it creates new products. The new Ecotec 2.2 environmentally friendly and fuel-efficient engine is evidence of the latter strategy. The cancellation of the Pontiac Firebird is an example of the former. Keep track of these changes on GM's website, www.gm.com, though; the Firebird, like the Ford Thunderbird and Michael Jordan, may "unretire" before the end of the decade.

MARKUP PRICING

Empirical studies suggest that many monopolistically competitive (and other) firms use markup or cost-plus pricing techniques. There are two basic steps in this approach to pricing. The firm must first estimate the cost per unit of output for the product in question. Since this cost will generally vary with output, firms generally base this computation on some assumed output level— a level that is usually taken to be between two-thirds and three-quarters of capacity. The firm then adds a markup (generally expressed in the form of a percentage) to the estimated average cost. This markup is meant to include certain costs that cannot be allocated to any specific product, and it is expected to provide a reasonable return on the firm's investment. The size of the markup therefore depends on the rate of profit that the firm believes it can earn. Some firms even set target rates of return (e.g., 20 percent) that they hope to earn and compute the markup from there.

There has been considerable controversy over the extent to which markup pricing is compatible with profit maximization. It might appear at first glance to some observers (and students) that it is unlikely that this form of pricing could result in maximum profits. Markup pricing seems naive because it takes no explicit account of the parameters that we now know can influence the profit-maximizing output—the price elasticity of demand, marginal and not average costs, and so on. Nevertheless, if marginal cost were really what was being "marked up" and if the price elasticity of demand were used to determine the size of the markup, then markup pricing could be a handy tool with which to maximize profit.

To see why, recall from Equation 4.4 that

$$MR = P\left(1 - \frac{1}{\eta}\right),$$

where MR is the firm's marginal revenue, P is its price, and η is the price elasticity of demand of the firm's product. Solving this equation for P and recognizing that marginal revenue will be equal to marginal cost (denoted MC) if the firm is maximizing profit, we get

$$P = MC\left(\frac{1}{1 - 1/\eta}\right) = MC + MC\left(\frac{1/\eta}{1 - 1/\eta}\right). \qquad [11.1]$$

If the markup were based on marginal cost and not average cost, therefore, the firm could maximize profits by setting the markup (in absolute terms) equal to $MC[1/\eta \div (1 - 1/\eta)]$.

Equation 11.1 can be a very useful result for the manager of a firm. Surprising as it may seem, this equation shows that a firm's managers need only to know their product's marginal cost and price elasticity of demand to determine the price that maximizes profits. The news is not all good, though. We saw in Chapters 4 and 7 that precise estimates of a product's marginal cost and price elasticity of demand may be hard to come by. How sensitive might the application of Equation 11.1 be to the quality of those estimates? If marginal cost equaled $10 and the price elasticity of demand were about 2, then a price of about $10[1 \div (1 - 1/2)] = $20 would maximize profit. If the estimate of the price elasticity were off by 50 percent (about 3 instead of 2), though, then a price of $15 = $10[1 \div (1 - 1/3)] would be more appropriate (i.e., a price that would be 25 percent lower than previously estimated). It would pay to investigate several alternatives, test profitability in each, and apply the fundamentals of decision-making under uncertainty that we discussed in Chapter 5. But at least Equation 11.1 simplifies the range of calculations that would be required. It is also worth noting that Equation 11.1 can be useful for monopolists, monopolistic competitors, and other firms that have some discretionary power over setting the price that they charge.

COMPARISONS WITH PERFECT COMPETITION AND MONOPOLY

Attempts are frequently made to compare the long-run equilibria that result from various market organizations. Recall the benchmark role of maximum efficiency attributed to perfectly competitive equilibria. This section will compare the long-run equilibrium of an industry that conforms to our definition of monopolistic competition with one that would result if the industry were either perfectly competitive or purely monopolistic. What difference would assuming a monopolistically competitive structure have on the long-run behavior of the industry? It is difficult to interpret this question in a meaningful way, let alone answer it. The output of the industry would be heterogeneous in one case and homogeneous in the other. And cost curves that are consistent with one industry structure are not necessarily consistent with the curves that might sustain another. Many economists nevertheless seem to believe that differences of the following kinds should be expected.

First, the firm under monopolistic competition would probably produce less and set a higher price than it would under perfectly competitive conditions. The demand curve confronting the monopolistic competitor would not be perfectly elastic, but in perfect competition the demand curve would be perfectly elastic (horizontal). Marginal revenue would therefore be lower than price in monopolistic competition but not in perfect competition. And so the monopolistically competitive firm would produce an amount that would be smaller than the efficient output for which price equals marginal cost. This larger efficient output would, of course, be the level that the firm would attain under perfectly competitive conditions where price equals marginal cost equals the minimum of average cost. Would the difference matter? Maybe, but maybe not. The demand curve facing a monopolistically competitive firm may be close to perfectly elastic if its product has lots of close substitutes.

How about a comparison with the monopoly output? Monopolistically competitive firms are likely to have lower profits, greater output, and lower prices. The firms in a product group might obtain and share monopoly economic profits if they were to collude and behave as a monopolist. Profits would rise and the producers would be better off. But consumers would be worse off because prices would be higher and fewer goods would be sold.

Finally, we noted above that monopolistically competitive firms are sometimes accused of being (somewhat) inefficient because they produce an output that is less than that which would minimize long-run average cost and short-run average cost. If the differences among their products were real and were clearly understood by consumers, though, the greater variety of alternatives available under monopolistic competition could be worth a great deal to consumers. Indeed, we have already noted that the social benefits from product diversity may outweigh these apparent inefficiencies.[3]

ADVERTISING EXPENDITURES: A SIMPLE MODEL

Industries with the characteristics of monopolistic competition spend very large amounts on advertising. Newspapers, which account for about 30 percent of total advertising expenditure in the United States, are full of advertisements

---

[3]Chamberlin's theory has often been criticized. George Stigler from the University of Chicago, for example, and others have argued that the definition of the group of firms included in the product group is extremely ambiguous. They contend that a group may contain only one firm, or it could include all of the firms in the economy. Moreover, in Stigler's view, the concept of the group is not salvaged by the assumption that each firm neglects the effects of its decisions on other firms in the group and that each firm has essentially the same demand and cost curves. Indeed, according to Stigler, the firms in the group must be selling homogeneous commodities if the assumption of similar demand and cost curves for all firms in the group is to be at all realistic. But if the commodities are homogeneous, then there is no reason why firms should have downward-sloping demand curves.

Table 11.1	Advertising expenditures (millions of dollars)	Quantity sold of product (millions of units)
RELATIONSHIP BETWEEN ADVERTISING EXPENDITURES AND THE QUANTITY SOLD OF THE FIRM'S PRODUCT	0.8	5.0
	0.9	7.0
	1.0	8.5
	1.1	9.5
	1.2	10.0

by food stores, clothing stores, and other retailers. Cosmetic firms advertise on television. Clothing manufacturers do the same thing. How much should a profit-maximizing firm spend on advertising? This is a very important question that has occupied the attention of many economists in the 70 years since Chamberlin's work. In this section, we derive a simple rule that helps to answer this question.

Suppose that the quantity that a particular firm sells is a function of the product's price and the level of the firm's advertising expenditure for the product. In particular, assume that there are diminishing marginal returns to advertising expenditures. This means that successive increments of spending on advertising beyond some point will yield smaller and smaller increases in sales. Table 11.1 offers an illustrative case. Successive increments of $100,000 in advertising there result in smaller and smaller increases in quantity sold. The quantity sold would increase by 2.0 million units if advertising expenditures rose from $800,000 to $900,000, for example, but sales would increase by only 1.5 million units if they rose from $900,000 to $1 million.

Now assume, for the sake of argument, that neither price nor the marginal cost of producing an extra unit of the product would change if advertising expenditures were slightly adjusted. Let P be the price of a unit of the product and let MC be the marginal cost of production; the firm would therefore receive a gross profit of $P - MC$ from each additional unit of the product that it made and sold. Why is this the *gross* profit of making and selling an additional unit of output? Because it takes no account of whatever additional advertising expenditures happened to be required to sell this extra unit of output. The firm must deduct these additional advertising outlays from the gross profit to get an estimate of *net* profit.

To maximize its total net profits, a firm must set its advertising expenditures at the level where an extra dollar of advertising results in an equal increase in gross profit. Why? Because the firm's total net profits could otherwise be increased by changing its advertising outlays. If an extra dollar of advertising resulted in more than a dollar increase in gross profit, then the extra dollar should be spent on advertising because it would raise total net profits. But if an extra dollar (or, more to the point, the last dollar) of advertising caused gross profit to increase by less than a dollar, then advertising outlays should be cut.[4]

[4]We assume for simplicity that the gross profit due to an extra dollar spent on advertising is essentially equal to the gross profit due to the last dollar spent on advertising. This is an innocuous assumption.

If ΔQ were the number of extra units of output sold due to an extra dollar of advertising, then this argument instructs us that the firm should set its advertising expenditures so that

$$\Delta Q(P - MC) = \$1. \qquad [11.2]$$

Only then would the right-hand side of this equation (the extra dollar of advertising cost) equal the extra gross profit generated by that dollar. Multiplying both sides of Equation 11.2 by $P/(P - MC)$, we obtain

$$P \Delta Q = \frac{P}{P - MC}. \qquad [11.3]$$

Now recall that the profit-maximizing firm should produce where marginal cost (MC) equals marginal revenue (MR). Substituting MR for MC in Equation 11.3, then, the firm should set its advertising expenditures so that

$$P \Delta Q = \frac{P}{P - MR}. \qquad [11.4]$$

Equation 10.3 can finally be used to show that the right-hand side of Equation 11.4 equals η, the price elasticity of demand for the firm's product.

Meanwhile, the left-hand side of Equation 11.4 is the marginal revenue from an extra dollar of advertising since it equals the price times the extra number of units sold due to an extra dollar of advertising. To maximize profit, therefore, the firm should set its advertising expenditures so that

marginal revenue from an extra dollar of advertising =
price elasticity of demand. [11.5]

This rule, derived by Robert Dorfman of Harvard University and Peter Steiner of the University of Michigan, is as interesting as it is useful.[5]

To illustrate its use, consider the Terratech Corporation. Assume that it knows that the price elasticity of demand for its product equals 1.5. If this firm maximizes profit, then the rule in Equation 11.5 says that it should set the marginal revenue from an extra dollar of advertising equal to 1.5. If Terratech's managers believed that an extra $100,000 of advertising would increase the firm's sales by $180,000, then they would believe that the marginal revenue from an extra dollar of advertising is approximately $180,000/$100,000 = 1.8. More important, they would believe that the marginal revenue from an extra dollar of advertising is larger than 1.5—the price elasticity of demand. Terratech should, under these conditions, expect to increase its profit by doing more advertising. But if the managers believed that the marginal revenue of an extra dollar of advertising were less than the price elasticity of demand for its product, then they should reduce their advertising budget. In short, Terratech would maximize profit by advertising only up to the point where the marginal revenue from an extra

[5]R. Dorfman and P. Steiner, "Optimal Advertising and Optimal Quality," *American Economic Review*, December 1954.

dollar of advertising fell to 1.5—the estimated value of the price elasticity of demand.[6]

Example 11.5 **Advertising by Firms with Market Power**

Ever wonder why firms with significant market power, like regulated cable companies and health-insurance carriers, advertise heavily on television and in the newspaper? To answer this question, recall from Chapter 10 that the Lerner index of market power (denoted there and here by *L*) can be written in two ways, one of which reads

$$L = \frac{P - MC}{P} = \frac{1}{\eta}$$

where *P* represents price charged for a product, *MC* represents the marginal cost (of producing the last unit of the product), and η is the price elasticity of demand. High values for η approximate perfect competition and produce low Lerner indexes. Indeed, perfect competition is the limiting case where $\eta = \infty$. A low price elasticity of demand would, on the other hand, reflect high market power and a correspondingly high Lerner index.

Meanwhile, the content of Equation 11.5 holds that the economic value of advertising for a firm can be maximized by setting the marginal revenue of the last dollar of advertising equal to η; that is, advertising expenditures should be determined by setting this marginal revenue equal to $1/L$. High market power (a high value for *L*) should therefore mean that advertising should continue until the marginal revenue of the last dollar of advertising equals a low number (i.e., equal to $1/L$ for large values of *L*). Assuming that the marginal revenue of the last dollar of advertising is positive but decreasing as advertising expenditure climbs, it follows that we should expect firms with significant market power to have large advertising budgets.

OPTIMAL ADVERTISING EXPENDITURES: A GRAPHICAL ANALYSIS

We can now go a step further to see how much a profit-maximizing firm should spend on advertising. A graph will help. Take the case of the Miller Electronics Company depicted in Figure 11.5. Suppose that curve *F* drawn there shows the relationship between the price elasticity of demand of Miller's product and the amount that it spends on advertising. With little or no advertising, consumers would regard Miller's product as similar to a host of other products. Its price elasticity of demand would therefore be very high (i.e., small changes in price would cause large substitution into or out of

---

[6]This analysis is highly simplified, and the rule in Equation 11.5 is by no means a full or adequate answer to the complex question of how much a firm should spend on advertising. It is, nonetheless, offered for the interest that it has drawn. You can find a discussion of the game-theoretic considerations involved in advertising decisions in Chapter 12.

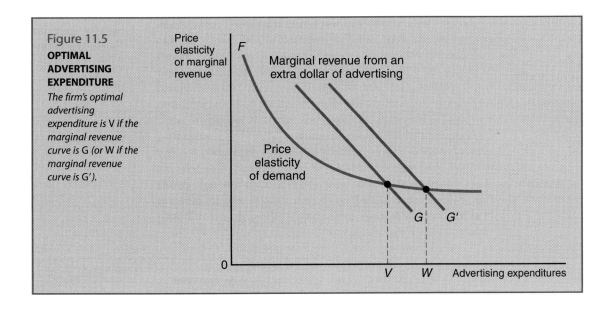

Figure 11.5

OPTIMAL ADVERTISING EXPENDITURE

The firm's optimal advertising expenditure is V if the marginal revenue curve is G (or W if the marginal revenue curve is G').

Miller's product). Appropriate advertising could, however, induce consumers to attach importance to the features that distinguish Miller's good from the rest of the product group and thereby reduce its price elasticity considerably. At each level of advertising expenditure, then, curve G might show the marginal revenue from an extra dollar of advertising. Notice that curve F intersects curve G when Miller's advertising expenditure is V dollars. On the basis of Equation 11.5, therefore, Miller's optimal level of advertising expenditure is V dollars.

A firm's optimal advertising expenditure clearly depends on the position and shape of curves G and F. If Miller's curve G were, for example, to shift right to G', then Miller's optimal level of advertising expenditure would climb to W dollars. Why might curve G shift? Perhaps its advertising agency has found ways to increase the effectiveness of its advertisements. We have all seen ads that catch our eye, and we have all seen ads that make us less inclined to go to the store (in which case curve G would shift to the left).

Example 11.6	Too Much Advertising?—Working a Problem

Advertising is, of course, designed to increase demand for a product, or at least market share for a monopolistic competitor; and the Dorfman-Steiner rule is designed to help companies decide when to stop. From an economic perspective, though, advertising can also be modeled as a component of fixed cost that does not affect the marginal cost of production. It is, in this context, easy to contrast situations in which advertising may or may not improve a company's profit picture, i.e., cases in which the marginal revenue of the last dollar of advertising may or may not even be positive.

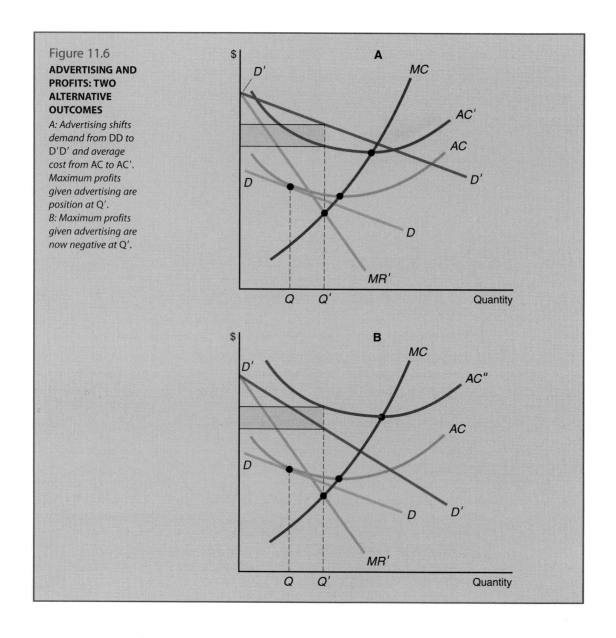

Figure 11.6

ADVERTISING AND PROFITS: TWO ALTERNATIVE OUTCOMES

A: Advertising shifts demand from DD to D'D' and average cost from AC to AC'. Maximum profits given advertising are position at Q'.
B: Maximum profits given advertising are now negative at Q'.

Panel A of Figure 11.6 displays the first case. Advertising shifts the demand curve out from DD to $D'D'$, but it also increases average cost from AC to AC'. Notice that the minima of both AC and AC' occur along a fixed marginal-cost curve MC. Maximum profits before advertising are zero at quantity Q, in accordance with long-run equilibrium in a monopolistically competitive industry; and positive at quantity Q' (the shaded area) afterward. This represents a case where advertising helps, and the Dorfman-Steiner rule can come into play.

Panel B of Figure 11.6 displays the opposite case. Advertising increases average costs to AC''—so much that profits (still the shaded area) turn negative. The same situation could arise if the demand response to advertising were small. In either case, the Dorfman-Steiner rule is almost irrelevant. If advertising can never generate a positive marginal revenue, then it can be dismissed without more detailed analysis.

THE SOCIAL VALUE OF ADVERTISING

We have thus far considered advertising from the point of view of the firm. But what about society as a whole? Certain kinds of advertising present obvious social disadvantages. To begin with, some advertising misleads consumers notwithstanding the efforts of private groups like the National Advertising Review Board and government agencies like the Federal Trade Commission to stamp out blatantly deceptive ad campaigns. Many consumers are properly skeptical about advertising claims, but some may be duped into making purchasing decisions that are far from optimal from their own point of view (but fine from the advertiser's perspective).

In addition, advertising may tend to augment the advertiser's monopoly power and may permit the advertiser more latitude to raise its price and profits. According to William Comanor and Thomas Wilson, the higher the ratio of advertising expenditures to sales in an industry, the higher the industry's profit rates.[7] If advertising makes customers recognize certain brands and if it encourages them to be loyal to these brands, then sellers may have more power to raise prices without losing sales to competitors. In many retail establishments, advertised brands are priced higher than lesser-known brands. Advertising encourages customers to think that advertised brands are better than other brands, even though they may be essentially the same.

On the other hand, consumers may benefit from advertising. Nobel laureate George Stigler has been joined by Phillip Nelson in pointing out that consumers frequently do not know the minimum price that they could pay for a commodity.[8] And it can be costly and time-consuming for consumers to shop around in order to obtain this information. It could, by way of example, cost a consumer $12 worth of time and travel expense to locate the store that offered a saving of $10 on the price of an item. If so, it would not be worthwhile for the consumer to try to locate this store. If, on the other hand, advertising that indicated prices at various stores enabled consumers to identify the lowest-price seller of this particular item at an additional cost of only $2, then identification of this lowest-price store would be worthwhile in the sense that advertising would make consumers better off.

Advertising can also work to enlarge the market for a firm's product. And if this product's average cost fell as its output rose, then the saving in production costs could more than offset the cost of advertising. Eyeglass retailing is a case in point. Example 11.7 offers evidence that significant

---

[7]W. Comanor and T. Wilson, *Advertising and Monopoly Power* (Cambridge, Mass.: Harvard University Press, 1974).
[8]See G. Stigler, "The Economics of Information," *Journal of Political Economy,* June 1961; or P. Nelson, "The Economic Consequences of Advertising," *Journal of Business,* April 1975.

economies of scale can be realized in eyeglass retailing. It can, however, be difficult to achieve the requisite volume if sellers are constrained by bans on advertising and other restrictive provisions sometimes found in, for example, optometrists' codes of ethics.

The view that advertising promotes monopoly power has also drawn some criticism. Both Stigler and Nelson conclude that advertising tends to increase the price elasticity of demand for products. According to their findings, the demand for goods that are not widely advertised tends to be price-inelastic. The greater the advertising effort, the more price-elastic the demand for a good becomes. And the market for a good tends to become more competitive as demand becomes more elastic. Frequently, therefore, advertising can lower the price charged to consumers because it fosters competition.

It should be clear by now that advertising has a variety of social effects. Some are positive; others are negative. To the extent that advertising provides trustworthy information to consumers about product quality and other matters, its effects may be positive. But its effects can be negative if it is grossly misleading. And, to the extent that advertising enables consumers to shop around for lower prices more efficiently and at lower cost, its effects tend to be positive. But its effects can still be negative if it is used to increase the advertiser's monopoly power. It is, in short, nearly impossible to generalize about whether or not advertising is socially beneficial. The answer depends on the nature of the advertising and the circumstances under which it takes place.

Advertising by retail stores, which informs consumers of the price and availability of goods, is more likely to be socially beneficial than radio commercials consisting of mindless ditties. Advertising aimed at professional purchasers of equipment is more likely to be socially beneficial than television commercials that feature lots of movie stars and sports heroes but few facts. So why is there so much advertising of all kinds if the jury on its social value is still out? Because firms find that it pays dividends to commission clever ditties as long as they catch consumers' ears. And they understand that it pays to hire movie stars and basketball players as long as they are held in high esteem. Nike's cancellation of contracts with basketball players during the National Basketball Association's lockout during the 1998–1999 season is clear evidence that this last connection can work in the opposite direction, too. Firms will adopt advertising strategies only if they work to increase net profits.

| Example 11.7 | Advertising for Eyeglasses—Good or Bad? |

The theory of monopolistic competition emphasizes the significance of selling expenses, including advertising. The market for eyeglasses in large cities is a classic example because it has many of the characteristics of monopolistic competition. There are typically a large number of sellers of eyeglasses, and each one's product is slightly different from the others. Some states have nonetheless banned advertising of prices by sellers of eyeglasses. Table 11.2 shows the average price of eyeglasses in these states as well as in the states with no advertising restrictions. The data are old, but they are still revealing and suggestive.

Table 11.2		Average price	
THE PRICE OF EYEGLASSES	**Nature of state law**	**Eyeglasses**	**Eyeglasses and eye examinations**
	Ban on advertising	$33.04	$40.96
	No ban on advertising	26.34	37.10

Since firms must pay for advertising, it is reasonable to see advertising costs reflected in the prices of their products. Studies of markets for eyeglasses do suggest that advertising has generally improved consumers' knowledge of prices and services and that the cost of collecting this information has been much higher in locations where it has been banned; this may explain why prices are lower in markets where advertising is allowed.

Microlink 11.2 Evaluating Models of Monopolistic Competition

Our very first chapter highlighted the roles that models play in supporting our understanding of how economic systems work, and it suggested several criteria for evaluating their utility. One important criterion focused our attention on the ability of models to produce results that accurately reflect reality even though they are simplified representations of enormously complicated sets of interactions, and so the assumptions that accomplish the necessary simplifications are always a source of concern. The Chamberlin model of monopolistic competition was, for example, built around an assumption that individual firms producing differentiated close substitutes faced identical demand curves with identical cost structures. Many subsequent researchers have criticized this assumption, and a few have explicitly set out to determine whether or not insights drawn from the Chamberlin model could survive modeling extensions that envisioned different cost structures, different demand schedules, or both. Specific results, like the precise representation of long-run equilibria with identical prices and equal outputs across firms, did not. They were clearly direct implications of Chamberlin's assumed symmetry within a product group; but they were also not the major message of the basic model presented here. More fundamental, qualitative insights about efficiency, the value of advertising, and the value of product diversity did survive these extensions because their robustness had nothing to do with firm symmetry.

SUMMARY

1. Under monopolistic competition, a large number of firms produce and sell goods that are all close substitutes. The products of monopolistic competitors are not completely homogeneous. Each seller tries to make its product a little different by altering its physical makeup, the services that it offers, and other related characteristics.
2. A monopolistically competitive firm is likely to produce less and set a higher price than it would under perfect competition. It is likely to operate with

excess capacity—a source of lost social welfare—but the greater variety of alternatives available under monopolistic competition may be worth a great deal (more) to consumers.

3. To maximize profit, a firm should set its advertising expenditures at the level where the marginal revenue from an extra dollar of advertising equals the price elasticity of demand for its product. If the marginal revenue of advertising is greater than the price elasticity, then the firm should increase its advertising expenditures; if the marginal revenue of advertising is less than the price elasticity, then it should decrease its advertising expenditures.

4. Advertising may or may not be socially beneficial. Its value depends on the nature of the advertising and the circumstances under which it takes place. From society's point of view, there are obvious disadvantages in advertising that misleads rather than informs and in advertising that augments an advertiser's monopoly power. On the other hand, advertising that enables sellers to take advantage of economies of scale in production or that allows consumers to shop around for lower prices more efficiently can be socially beneficial.

**QUESTIONS/
PROBLEMS**

1. Decide which is a more appropriate designation of a product group for each of the following, and think about how your answer might depend on what sort of question you might be asking: (a) bargain soft drinks or carbonated beverages; (b) fruit juice or decaffeinated beverages; (c) introductory economics textbooks or elementary economic theory texts; (d) whitening toothpaste or dental-care products; (e) college-logo sweatshirts or sports-logo apparel.

2. A monopolistic competitor faces a linear demand curve for its version of some good X given by $P(X) = 10 - 0.001X$ with a cost schedule given by $C(X) = 0.004X^2 + FC$, where FC represents fixed cost. Compute the long-run equilibrium price and quantity for this firm. Compute its fixed cost.

3. Explain in detail why you believe that each of the following industries can or cannot be represented by the theory of monopolistic competition: (a) copper; (b) toothpaste; (c) airlines; (d) airline service along a specific route; (e) pharmaceuticals.

4. Explain why monopolistic competitors might be prone to large advertising budgets. Would their advertising be more effective in the long run if they tried to increase "product-group market share" at the expense of other firms or if they tried to increase overall demand for the product group as a whole?

5. Pharmaceutical companies sometimes run TV ads for their drugs without telling the viewer what the drug does. Why might this be the case?

6. Explain what would happen to long-run equilibrium in a monopolistically competitive market if the fixed costs of one firm increased.

7. Is there any incentive for a monopolistic competitor to move down a long-run average-cost curve to take advantage of economies of scale? If so, what would happen to long-run equilibrium? If not, why not?

8. Describe the factors that would affect the deadweight loss associated with a monopolistically competitive industry. What would make it high? What would make it low? Be sure to think carefully about the competitive benchmark against which you would compute deadweight loss.

Calculus Appendix

LONG-RUN EQUILIBRIUM FOR A MONOPOLISTIC COMPETITOR

You may have been suspicious about the joint characterization of the long-run equilibrium for a monopolistic competitor. On the one hand, profits are being maximized, so marginal revenue must equal marginal cost. On the other, maximum profits are equal to zero, so average cost must be tangent to the demand curve even as price equals average cost. It turns out that these two conditions are equivalent. To see how and why, let effective demand for such a firm be given by $P = D(q)$, and let total cost be represented by $C = C(q)$. The slope of the demand curve at the equilibrium quantity $q^\star$ is $D'(q^\star)$. Average cost is, meanwhile,

$$AC(q) = \frac{C(q)}{q}$$

so that the slope of average cost at $q^\star$ is

$$\frac{q^\star C'(q^\star) - C(q^\star)}{(q^\star)^2} = \frac{C'(q^\star) - [C(q^\star)/q^\star]}{q^\star} = \frac{MC(q^\star) - AC(q^\star)}{q^\star}. \quad [1]$$

The last part of Equation 1 denotes marginal and average cost evaluated at $q^\star$ by $MC(q^\star)$ and $AC(q^\star)$, respectively. It follows from Equation 1, therefore, that the tangency condition for equilibrium sets

$$D'(q^\star) = \frac{MC(q^\star) - AC(q^\star)}{q^\star}$$

so that $$q^\star \times D'(q^\star) = MC(q^\star) - AC(q^\star). \quad [2]$$

In addition, the zero profit condition for equilibrium guarantees that equilibrium price $P^\star$ equals average cost. As a result,

$$P^\star = AC(q^\star);$$

i.e., $$D(q^\star) = AC(q^\star). \quad [3]$$

Substituting Equation 3 into Equation 2 and rearranging slightly, we find that

$$D(q^\star) + q^\star \times D'(q^\star) = MC(q^\star).$$

But the left-hand side of Equation 3 is marginal revenue evaluated at $q^\star$, and the right-hand side is marginal cost evaluated at $q^\star$. So we are done. We have shown that marginal revenue must equal marginal cost wherever demand is tangent to average cost. (Convince yourself that this is true for any market structure where equilibrium brings effective demand tangent to average cost—like the long-run equilibrium for a competitive firm).

Oligopoly and Game Theory

Oligopoly   We now move to another form of market structure—**oligopoly.** Unlike the case of monopolistic competition, the supply side of an oligopoly market is composed of a few firms. As a result, each oligopolist formulates its policies and strategies with an eye to their effects on its rivals. Since an oligopoly contains a small number of firms, any change in the firm's price or output influences the sales and profits of competitors. Each firm must therefore recognize that changes in its own policies are likely to elicit changes in the policies of its competitors as well.

Because of this interdependence, oligopolists face a situation in which the optimal decision of one firm depends on what other firms decide to do. And so there is opportunity for both conflict and cooperation. The U.S. beer industry is a good example. Only a handful of firms, led by Anheuser-Busch, account for the bulk of the industry's sales (notwithstanding the recent growth in microbreweries). Each of the major beer producers must take account of the reaction of the others when it formulates its price and output policy because its optimal strategy is likely to depend in part on how its competitors are likely to respond. When Miller and Coors cut the price of their beers by as much as 25 percent, for example, they had to anticipate how other firms, like Anheuser-Busch, would respond. In fact, Anheuser-Busch met their price reductions.

Oligopoly is a common market structure in the United States. The automobile industry, for example, contains relatively few major firms: General Motors, Ford, DaimlerChrysler, Toyota, Nissan, and Honda. Portions of the electrical equipment industry are dominated by General Electric and Westinghouse. The aerospace industry is dominated by Boeing, McDonnell-Douglas, and United Technologies. These are only some highly visible examples. Not all oligopolists are large firms. Two grocery stores that exist in an isolated community are oligopolists, too; the fact that they are small firms does not change this situation.

CHARACTERISTICS OF OLIGOPOLIES

There are many reasons for oligopoly. Economies of scale come to mind first. Low costs cannot be achieved in some industries unless a few firms are producing outputs that account for substantial percentages of the total available market. As a result, the number of firms will tend to be rather small. The number of firms can also be small if the market is small (the grocery store example just cited supports this claim). There may be economies of scale in sales promotion as well as in production, and this too may promote oligopoly. There may even be barriers that make it very difficult to enter the industry. Finally, of course, the number of firms in an industry may decrease over time because participating firms want to weaken competitive pressures. The popularity of mergers and acquisitions in the United States clearly illustrates this possibility.

Regardless of why oligopolies exist, their fundamental feature is that each firm must carefully take account of its rivals' reactions as it decides what it wants to do in terms of output and pricing. It follows that accurately portraying the interactions between firms across a wide range of possibilities is the critical task of any model of an oligopolistic market, and major advances in accomplishing this task can be attributed directly to the appearance and elaboration of the theory of games over the past several decades. The seminal work on game theory was published by John von Neumann and Oskar Morgenstern in 1944.[1] This is, of course, the same von Neumann who contributed so much to our understanding of decision-making under uncertainty in Chapter 5, but the significance of using game theory to describe economic situations is perhaps even more significant. Indeed, game theorists John Harsanyi, John Nash, and Reinhard Selten shared the Nobel Prize in economics in 1994. Taking a cue from the Nobel committee, this chapter will also present the basic objectives and concepts of game theory and will show how they can be applied to simple oligopolistic markets. Chapter 13 will continue the dual function of this chapter by using game theory to explore extensions of these simple models.

Example 12.1	Locating Wal-Mart Stores

Ever wonder how Wal-Mart grew from 153 stores to 1,009 stores over a 10-year period when many of its closest competitors across the United States were having trouble staying afloat? Remember Grant's and Woolworth's and Two Guys and Ames? They were discounting giants not 15 years ago, but all have disappeared into bankruptcy and beyond. Caldor and Kmart may be more familiar names; but they, too, are now having some trouble just staying one step ahead of the creditors.

Meanwhile, Wal-Mart is now the largest company in the world in large measure because it has generally followed a strategy of locating its stores in towns with populations of less than 100,000. Not too much less than 100,000, of course; but servicing a market of that size made it clear to competitors that investing in a nearby store would be foolish. There was

---

[1]Their work was entitled *Theory of Games and Economic Behavior* (Princeton, N.J.: Princeton University Press, 1944). More recent descriptions of note include J. Tirole, "Noncooperative Game Theory: A User's Manual," in Tirole, *The Theory of Industrial Organization* (Cambridge, Mass.: MIT Press, 1988); A. Dixit and S. Skeath, *Games of Strategy* (New York: W. W. Norton, 1999); R. Gibbons, "An Introduction to Applicable Game Theory," *Journal of Economic Perspectives,* Winter 1997; and R. Myerson, "Nash Equilibrium and the History of Economic Theory," *Journal of Economic Literature,* September 1999.

enough demand for one store, but not enough for two. And so the preemptive construction of a Wal-Mart store closed the door on the competition. They were left to slug it out with each other in places where the profitability threshold was less certain.

As we contemplate theories of alternative market structures, we need to be able to explain stories like this; and we must be able to draw more general insight from those explanations.

THE NASH EQUILIBRIUM

We determined the price and quantity that would exist in the market in equilibrium when we studied perfect competition, monopoly, and monopolistic competition. To do this for an oligopolistic market, we must recognize the interdependence among oligopolists stressed in the introduction to this chapter. Any change in an oligopolist's price or output is likely to influence the sales and profits of its rivals and thus induce changes in their price and output. Under these circumstances, it is difficult to determine the equilibrium price and output of each firm. Each firm's behavior depends on what its rivals do (and on what it expects them to do), and the rivals' behavior depends in turn on what this firm does (and on what they expect it to do).

To resolve this problem, economists often assume that each firm will simply try to do the best it can given what its rivals decide to do. This is, of course, consistent with our discussions of perfect competition, monopoly, and monopolistic competition. In every one of these cases, we assumed that each firm maximized its profits. In these cases, though, we spent no time being concerned about what rivals would do because each firm could regard the demand curve for its product as fixed in the short run and determined by impersonal and anonymous market forces. In oligopoly, on the other hand, each firm is forced to formulate its own price and output decisions on the basis of its assumptions about what its rivals will do, and it knows who those rivals are.

Nash equilibrium A **Nash equilibrium** is a situation in which each firm is doing the best it can given the behavior of its rivals. It was named after the Nobel laureate John Nash, a Princeton mathematician who did pioneering studies of this type of equilibrium. (Yes, this is the John Nash whose life was portrayed in the Ron Howard movie *A Beautiful Mind*.) Economists have made extensive use of the idea of a Nash equilibrium, and much more will be said on this topic in the next chapter, where we take up game theory and strategic behavior. The next section provides a more concrete and detailed discussion of the nature of a Nash equilibrium.

AN EXAMPLE OF A NASH EQUILIBRIUM: THE COURNOT MODEL OF OLIGOPOLY

The classic context within which to introduce and to illustrate the concept of a Nash equilibrium was in fact a theory of firm behavior put forth by

Augustin Cournot more than 150 years ago.[2] As you might expect, this theory is too simple to capture much of the richness of oligopolistic situations in a modern economy. Nonetheless, it has attracted considerable attention and is still cited. We will use it here in deference to that attention.

Cournot considered the case in which there were two sellers; that is, he worked on the case of **duopoly.** His model can easily be generalized to include the case of three or more sellers, but it is convenient to stick with his simple formulation. We will, accordingly, assume that only two firms, firm I and firm II, produce the same product. Call it good X. Both firms will have the same cost functions; marginal costs are in fact assumed to be constant, and so they match average cost. Both firms are also perfectly aware of the linear market demand curve for good X. Each firm will try to maximize its own profits. And each firm will assume that its rival will hold its output constant at the existing level regardless of what output it decides to produce. So, each firm takes the other firm's output level as given and chooses its own output level to maximize profit. The level of output that it chooses will, of course, depend on how much it thinks its rival will produce, and therein lies the rub.

To explore this interaction of perception and reality further, consider the situation in Figure 12.1. The three panels drawn there show effective (perceived) demand curves for firm I's product based on three alternative assumptions by firm I about how much X firm II will be delivering to the market. Each displays a constant marginal cost of production equal to $7.50, and together they face a market demand curve given by

$$P = 15 - 0.025X_T$$

where X_T is the total quantity of X demanded, P is the price of X, and a and b are positive constants. We will take each in sequence. Panel A portrays the case in which firm I thinks that firm II will produce and sell nothing. Firm I therefore thinks that its effective demand curve is the market demand curve because it thinks that it will be the sole producer of good X. Note that

$$MR = 15 - 0.05X_T$$

in this case, so that 150 units would maximize profits for a monopoly (or firm I thinking that it was a monopoly). Why? Because marginal revenue for $X_T = 150$ is

$$15 - 0.05(150) = 7.5,$$

and that matches marginal cost. This confirms panel A of Figure 12.1.

If firm II were producing 100 units, then the effective demand curve facing firm I would be

$$P = 15 - 0.025(X_I + 100) = 12.5 - 0.025X_I$$

and firm I would face an effective marginal revenue given by

$$MR = 12.5 - 0.05X_I.$$

[2]A. Cournot, *Recherches sur les Principes Mathématiques de la Théorie des Riches* (New York: Macmillan, 1897). He first published his model in 1838.

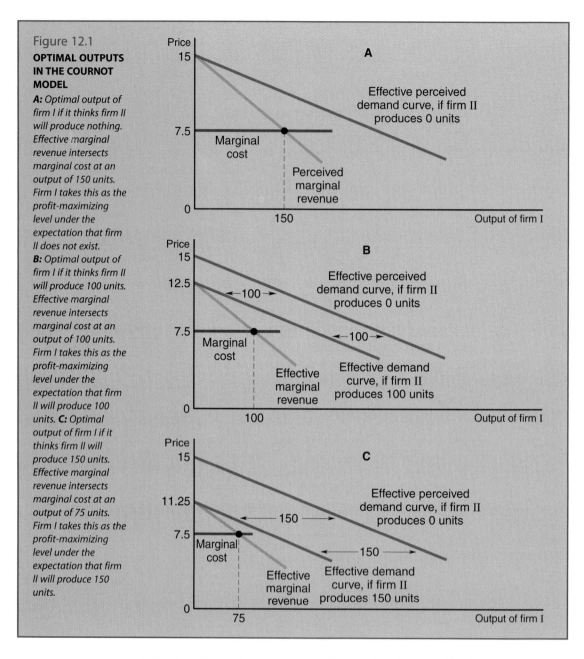

Figure 12.1

OPTIMAL OUTPUTS IN THE COURNOT MODEL

A: Optimal output of firm I if it thinks firm II will produce nothing. Effective marginal revenue intersects marginal cost at an output of 150 units. Firm I takes this as the profit-maximizing level under the expectation that firm II does not exist. **B:** Optimal output of firm I if it thinks firm II will produce 100 units. Effective marginal revenue intersects marginal cost at an output of 100 units. Firm I takes this as the profit-maximizing level under the expectation that firm II will produce 100 units. **C:** Optimal output of firm I if it thinks firm II will produce 150 units. Effective marginal revenue intersects marginal cost at an output of 75 units. Firm I takes this as the profit-maximizing level under the expectation that firm II will produce 150 units.

This situation is depicted in panel B by showing an effective demand curve for firm I that lies 100 units to the left of market demand. Why? Because firm I now expects to sell the total quantity demanded less the 100 units that firm II is expected to produce and sell. Firm I would then produce 100 units because marginal revenue for $X_T = 100$ would now equal

$$12.5 - 0.05(100) = 7.5.$$

This confirms panel B of Figure 12.1.

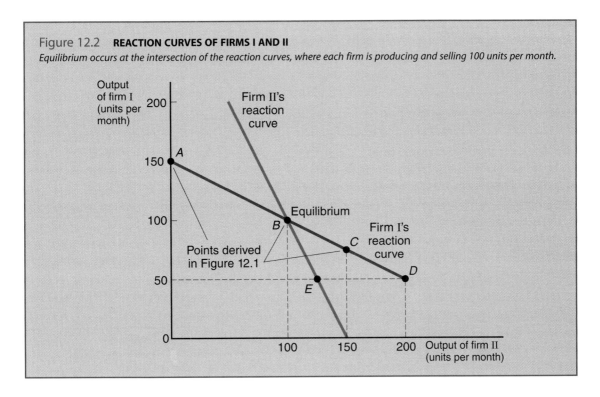

Figure 12.2 **REACTION CURVES OF FIRMS I AND II**

Equilibrium occurs at the intersection of the reaction curves, where each firm is producing and selling 100 units per month.

Panel C depicts the situation in which firm I thinks that firm II will produce and sell 150 units. The effective demand curve now lies 150 units to the left of the market demand. The effective demand curve is now

$$P = 15 - 0.025(X_I + 150) = 11.25 - 0.025X_I,$$

effective marginal revenue is

$$MR = 11.25 - 0.05X_I,$$

and firm I would maximize profits by producing only 75 units. Check for yourself that marginal revenue for 75 units now matches marginal cost of $7.50.

These results (and others) can be summarized by a curve that reflects how firm I's output depends on how much it thinks that firm II will produce and sell. The past three paragraphs derived three points on this curve. They are labeled *A*, *B*, and *C*, respectively, on Figure 12.2. Other points,

Reaction curve derived the same way, can be combined to produce firm I's **reaction curve**—a curve that shows how firm I will react in making its output decision to its perception of how much it thinks firm II will produce and sell.

Firm II also has a reaction curve. It, too, is portrayed in Figure 12.2 under the assumption that the two firms have identical costs. Firm II's reaction curve shows how much firm II will react in making its output decision to its perception of how much it thinks that firm I will produce and sell. It can be derived in precisely the same way that we derived firm I's reaction curve. You should, however, be comfortable with the symmetry of the two reaction curves drawn in Figure 12.2 on an intuitive level without doing all of that work. We have assumed in this discussion that firms I and II are identical. They have identical costs. They face the same market demand with the same Cournot perception of what the other firm will do as it changes its output (i.e., each firm thinks that the other firm will *not* change its output). Their reaction curves *should* look the same.

The Cournot model holds that a Nash equilibrium occurs at the point where the firms' reaction curves intersect. In Figure 12.2, therefore, we should be able to explain why a Nash equilibrium would occur at point *B*, where both firm I and firm II would produce and sell 100 units per month. At point *B*, each firm's expectation concerning the other's output would be correct and each firm would be maximizing its profit (given that its rival's output was what it was). How can we judge the firms' expectations? Notice that firm I would operate at point *B* only if it expected firm II to produce 100 units per month—and this in fact is what firm II would produce at point *B*. Similarly, firm II would operate at point *B* only if it expected firm I to produce 100 units per month—and this expectation would also be validated at point *B*. And so neither firm would be surprised by the other's output at point *B*. Equally important, there would be no incentive for either firm to alter the behavior predicted at point *B*. Both firms would be maximizing their profits by producing 100 units per month under the confirmed assumption that the other firm would produce and sell a like amount.

Notice in passing that *B* is the only Nash equilibrium displayed in Figure 12.2. To see why, think a little about a point like *D*. Firm I would maximize profit by producing 50 units at point *D* under the assumption that firm II would produce 200 units. But firm II's reaction function suggests that it would produce only 125 units (at point *E*) if it thought that firm I would deliver 50 units to the market. This cannot be an equilibrium, therefore, because firm I's expectation about firm II's output cannot be sustained by the output that firm I would select in its own efforts to maximize profit.

The Cournot model is useful in illustrating the concept of a Nash equilibrium, but it has some severe limitations. Perhaps most significantly, the Cournot model provides no satisfactory description or explanation of the way in which firms might move toward an equilibrium of the sort displayed in Figure 12.2. Cournot's own explanation was naive in many respects and is rejected by most economists today. We will shortly take up models that pay more attention to dynamic considerations; they will be far richer and, we hope, more interesting.

| Example 12.2 | A More General Cournot Case—Working a Problem |

Suppose that the market demand curve were given by the linear relationship

$$P = a - bX_T$$

where X_T represents total quantity supplied to the market by two duopolists and where $a > 0$ and $b > 0$. If firm I thought that firm II was producing X_{II}, then it would assume that it would move along an effective demand curve

$$P = a - b(X_I + X_{II}) = (a - bX_{II}) - bX_I.$$

It follows that the marginal revenue associated with this derivative demand curve for firm I can be written

$$MR = (a - bX_{II}) - 2bX_I,$$

because $a - bX_{II}$ represents the intercept and $-b$ is the slope of effective demand. Assume that the marginal cost of production in firm I is constant at c_I, and let firm I think that firm II will produce X_{II} units. Firm I profits would then be maximized where $MR = MC$, so that

$$MC = c_I = MR = (a - bX_{II}) - 2bX_I^*$$

so that
$$X_I^* = \frac{a - bX_{II} - c_I}{2b} = \frac{a - c_I}{2b} - \frac{1}{2}X_{II}. \qquad [12.1]$$

Note, in passing, that the reaction function for firm I drawn in Figure 12.2 is

$$X_I^* = \frac{7.5}{0.05} - 0.5X_{II} = 150 - 0.5X_{II} \qquad [12.2a]$$

because $a = 15$, $b = 0.025$, and $c_I = 7.5$. This is line AD in Figure 12.2.

Turning now to firm II, let its marginal cost be c_{II}. The same calculation would show that

$$X_{II}^* = \frac{a - bX_I - c_{II}}{2b} = \frac{a - c_{II}}{2b} - \frac{1}{2}X_I. \qquad [12.3]$$

So, the reaction function for firm II in Figure 12.2 is

$$X_{II}^* = \frac{7.5}{0.05} - 0.5X_I = 150 - 0.5X_I, \qquad [12.2b]$$

because $a = 15$, $b = 0.025$, and $c_{II} = 7.5$. The Cournot equilibrium would therefore solve Equations 12.1 and 12.3 simultaneously under the Nash equilibrium condition that $X_I = X_I^*$ and $X_{II} = X_{II}^*$.

Some algebra reveals, therefore, that

$$X_I^* = \frac{a - 2c_I + c_{II}}{3b}$$

and
$$X_{II}^* = \frac{a - 2c_{II} + c_I}{3b}.$$

In the symmetric case where $c_I = c_{II} = c$, output for both firms is one-third of the competitive output; i.e., $X_I^* = X_{II}^* = (a - c)/3b$. And in the specific case of Figure 12.2, $X_I^* = X_{II}^* = (15 - 7.5)/3(0.025) = 100$.

COLLUSION AND CARTELS

Conditions in oligopolistic industries tend to promote collusion, since the number of firms is small and the firms recognize their interdependence. The advantages to the firms of collusion seem obvious: increased profits, decreased uncertainty, and a better opportunity to prevent others' entry. Collusive arrangements, however, are often hard to maintain. Firms can generally increase their individual profits by cheating on any collusive agreement; these incentives make such agreements unstable. And, of course, collusive arrangements are illegal, at least in the United States.

Cartels   Open and formal collusive arrangements are called **cartels.** Cartels are common and legally acceptable in many countries in Europe. In the United States, though, most collusive agreements, whether secret or open cartels, were essentially declared illegal in 1890 by the Sherman Antitrust Act. This does not mean that such agreements do not exist, of course. There was widespread collusion among U.S. electrical equipment manufacturers during the 1950s.[3] Moreover, trade associations and professional organizations sometimes perform functions that are very similar to what a cartel would try to do; they need to skate very carefully along the boundaries of the law in deciding what they can and cannot do. And finally, some types of cartels have actually received official sanction from the U.S. government.

| Example 12.3 | **Avoiding the Watchful Eye of the Justice Department** |

The United States Department of Justice serves as a watchdog against mergers and acquisitions that might bring too much market power into the hands of a few competitors. Economists working there keep track of market concentration as a "proxy" for market power by computing the Herfindahl-Hirschman index (the HHI) for various industries. What is the HHI for an industry? It is the sum of the squared market shares of its participants. So, if an industry had n identical firms, then the index would be

$$\text{HHI} = \left(\frac{100}{n}\right)^2 + \ldots + \left(\frac{100}{n}\right)^2 = n\left(\frac{100}{n}\right)^2 = \frac{100^2}{n}.$$

Notice that this HHI would go to zero if n became very large, as it would for a perfectly competitive industry. A monopolist would, by way of contrast, have a 100 percent share, so its HHI would equal $(100)^2 = 10,000$. And an industry would see its HHI climb from 500 ($= 20 \times 5^2$) to 550 ($= 10^2 + 18 \times 5^2$) if 2 of its original 20 identical firms were to merge.

In theory, then, the HHI can run between 0 and 10,000. The eyes of the Department of Justice could be drawn to mergers and acquisitions in any industry with an HHI over 1,000, but only if the net effect were sufficiently

[3]The Department of Justice charged early in the 1960s that a large number of companies and individuals in the electrical equipment industry were guilty of fixing prices and dividing up the market for circuit breakers, switchgears, and other important products. Most of the defendants were found guilty. The companies, including General Electric and Westinghouse, were fined and some of the guilty executives were sent to prison. The price-fixing agreements were reached in various ways. Many of the meetings occurred at conventions of the National Electrical Manufacturers Association and other trade groups. Some agreements were made through telephone calls and written memoranda transmitted from one sales executive to another. Efforts were made to keep the meetings and agreements secret. For example, codes were used, and the participants at meetings sometimes disguised their records and did not use their companies' names when registering at hotels. The executives clearly recognized that their behavior and the resulting agreements were illegal.

large. In fact, it would consider getting involved if a merger created an HHI between 1,000 and 1,800 by adding more than 100 points to the index; and it would strongly consider intervening if the merger accounted for more than 50 points of a postmerger index greater than 1,800.

The Bureau of the Census reports estimates of the HHI for various manufacturing industries; you can find them under economic data at the bureau's Web site, www.census.gov. Meanwhile, the Department of Justice has published its *Horizontal Merger Guidelines* at www.usdoj.gov. As of 1997, none of the entries listed HHI over 3,000. Notable industries that fell between 1,000 and 2,000 include dog and cat food, cookies, underwear, roasted nuts, and office furniture. Others, between 2,000 and 3,000, included soybean products, breakfast cereal, chocolate, tobacco products, guided missiles, household appliances, pharmaceuticals, house slippers, and men's clothing. You can download the latest estimates yourself; see what catches your eye.

Suppose that a cartel were established irrespective of legal impediments. Suppose, as well, that it wanted to set a uniform price for a particular (homogeneous) commodity. How would it go about determining what price to charge? To begin with, the cartel must estimate the marginal-cost curve for the cartel as a whole. If input prices do not increase as the cartel expands, then this marginal-cost curve is the horizontal sum of the marginal-cost curves of the individual firms. Suppose that the resulting marginal-cost curve for the cartel were as depicted in Figure 12.3. If the demand curve for the industry's product and the relevant marginal-revenue curve were as shown there, then output Q_0 would maximize the total profit of the cartel. To

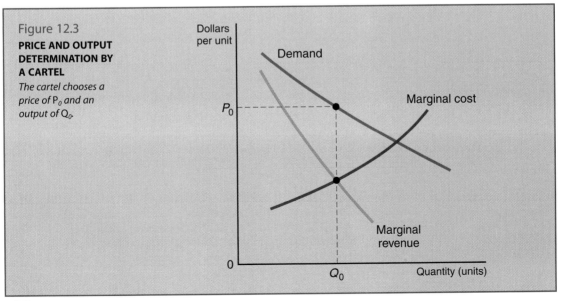

Figure 12.3

PRICE AND OUTPUT DETERMINATION BY A CARTEL

The cartel chooses a price of P_0 and an output of Q_0.

maximize cartel profits, the cartel would choose a price equal to P_0. This, of course, would match the monopoly price.

And how would the cartel distribute the industry's total sales among its member firms? If the aim of the cartel were to maximize cartel profits, then it would allocate sales so that the marginal costs of production for all members were equal. The cartel could otherwise lower costs by reallocating output among members so that the cartel's total profit for a fixed output would climb. If, for example, the marginal cost at firm I were higher than at firm II, then the cartel could increase its total profits by transferring some production from firm I to firm II; costs would fall and revenue would be unaffected.

Ideal allocation

This allocation of output—sometimes called the **ideal allocation** by economists—is unlikely to occur because the allocation of cartel output usually determines the allocation of cartel profits. For this reason, allocation decisions are the result of negotiation between firms with varying interests and varying capabilities. It is likely to be a political process in which various firms have different amounts of influence that may have nothing to do with the cost-efficiency of their production processes. Firms with the most influence and the shrewdest negotiators typically receive the largest sales quotas even though concentrating production there could increase total cartel costs. Moreover, high-cost firms could receive larger sales quotas than cost minimization would dictate because they would be unwilling to accept the small quotas dictated by cost minimization. Indeed, some evidence indicates that sales are often distributed in accord with firms' past sales levels or their productive capacity. Cartels sometimes even divide a market along geographic boundaries so that some firms are given certain regions or countries while other firms are given other regions or countries. Each of these noneconomic allocation rules can cost the cartel money (in terms of reduced profit), but they may be necessary to preserve the stability of what could otherwise be a very fragile arrangement.

Example 12.4	Pricing Tires

Many sellers sometimes service the same small, local retail market. In other towns, however, only one or two retail outlets can be found. An isolated community in the Northeast or the Southwest could, for example, have only one retailer offering tires for sale; this seller would have (local) monopoly power. Other local markets might be served by two, three, four, or perhaps five retailers; they would be (local) oligopolists. How might we tell if these (local) oligopolists were colluding to extract monopoly profits? Price data might help.

Table 12.1 reports average prices charged across a variety of local markets—markets that are distinguishable only by the number of retail outlets available to the consumer. Do they suggest that price exceeds the competitive level when there are fewer than six sellers? Absolutely. Do these price data conform to what might be expected from a Cournot model? Not really. The Cournot model would lead us to expect that the price would be lower for two sellers than for one. Why? Because the Cournot equilibrium

Table 12.1	Number of sellers	Average price per tire
PRICING TIRES	1	$54
	2	$55
	3	$53
	4	$51
	5	$50
	Many	$43

output is larger than the monopolist solution, and so the market clearing price must be lower. The data in Table 12.1 do not show a significant decline in price until four or five or more retailers service the market. Do duopolistic tire retailers act as if they were a monopolist, at least in terms of pricing their product? That is, do the data suggest that they collude? Since $54 is very close to both $55 and $53, it would appear so.

SOURCE: T. Bresnahan and P. Reiss, "Entry and Competition in Concentrated Markets," *Journal of Political Economy*, October 1991.

THE INSTABILITY OF CARTELS

Why are cartel agreements fragile? We have already suggested that members generally have an incentive to cheat on the agreement to earn higher-than-expected short-term profits at the expense of their partners. We now make that point explicitly. To see why member firms would be tempted to leave the cartel (or to grant secret price concessions to favored customers), consider the case of the firm portrayed in Figure 12.4. If this firm were to leave the cartel (or if it were to contemplate offering secret price concessions in violation of the cartel agreement), it would be faced with a demand curve of DD' as long as the other firms in the cartel maintained the agreed price of P_0. Its effective demand curve would be very elastic, and so the firm would be able to expand its sales considerably with even small reductions in price.

Cheating on a cartel agreement   Under these circumstances, the firm's maximum profit if it left the cartel or secretly lowered its price would be achieved by selling Q_1 units of output at a price equal to P_1. We know this because marginal cost equals (effective) marginal revenue at output Q_1. Note that line RR' is the firm's effective marginal-revenue curve, and note as well that $P_1 < P_0$. Profits would amount to $Q_1 \times BP_1$—an amount that would be higher than if the firm conformed to the price agreement dictated by the cartel. How do we know that for sure? Because the firm could have chosen price P_0, but it did not because profits were maximized elsewhere. So, a firm that breaks away from a cartel—or secretly cheats—could increase its profits as long as other firms do not do the same thing and as long as the cartel does not

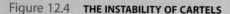

Figure 12.4 **THE INSTABILITY OF CARTELS**

If it left the cartel and charged the profit-maximizing price P_1 (to sustain sales of output Q_1, where marginal cost equals marginal revenue), then the firm's profit would equal $Q_1 \times BP_1$. This would be higher than if it adhered to the price and sales quota established by the cartel.

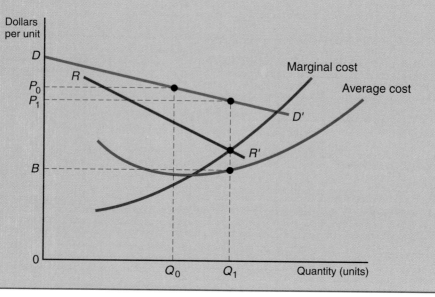

punish it in some way. But if all (or most) of the member firms lowered their prices, then the cartel would break down (and demand curve DD' would no longer apply).

The very existence of cartels that are not maintained by legal provisions is thereby threatened each and every time member firms make price and output decisions. Its members have an incentive to cheat. And once a few members cheat, others may follow. Price concessions made secretly by a few "chiselers" or openly by a few malcontents would cut into the sales of cooperative members of the cartel, who would be hard pressed not to match the renegades.

Example 12.5	**OPEC and the International Supply of Crude Oil**

The Organization of Petroleum Exporting Countries (OPEC) is a classic example of an open cartel. It first hit the headlines in 1973 when its members seemed to precipitate a crisis in the United States and other developed countries by announcing a cutback in its collective oil exports. What happened? As shown in Figure 12.5, the international price of crude oil increased from $2.50 per barrel in 1973 to roughly $10 per barrel in 1974. Again in 1979, in the wake of the Iranian revolution, OPEC supplies were restricted and the price of oil rose suddenly to over $30 per barrel. The price fell to around $15 by 1986, as the demand for oil fell (the result of extensive

438

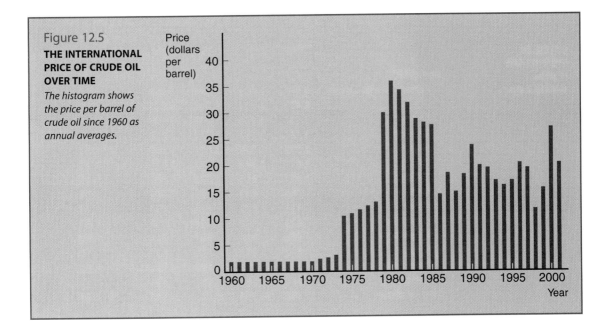

Figure 12.5

THE INTERNATIONAL PRICE OF CRUDE OIL OVER TIME

The histogram shows the price per barrel of crude oil since 1960 as annual averages.

conservation initiatives and profitable substitution out of oil as an energy source in the developed world); and it has hovered between $15 and $25 ever since (with the exception of 2000, when the price again approached $30 per barrel).

What is OPEC? OPEC now consists of 11 major oil-producing countries; they are listed in the bottom section of Table 12.2. They collectively support a secretariat in Vienna, Austria, where analysts keep careful track of international demand and the supply capacities of non-OPEC nations; and their ministers meet regularly to choose price targets and allocate supply contributions consistent with those targets. Table 12.2 displays some of the data that have recently supported their negotiations. It highlights, in particular, production levels (in thousands of barrels of crude oil per day) for countries that produced at least 50,000 barrels per day from 1996 through 1999. The OPEC cartel has controlled less than 50 percent of the world's oil production since 1990 (down from more than 60 percent in the 1970s), but its ministers still hold considerable sway over the world price. The time series depicted in Figure 12.5 offers some vivid evidence of this power. Notice, for example, that the price of crude was approximately $20 per barrel (on average) in both 1996 and 1997. Total global production increased during that time, suggesting that some OPEC members may have exceeded their quotas, but the price did not fall. Why not? Unexpectedly severe winters in Europe and the United States kept demand higher than anticipated. The international price of crude did fall in 1998, however, even though the pace of the increase in total production declined. Slack demand was blamed, and OPEC ministers expressed their concern by cutting production by nearly

Table 12.2		1996	1997	1998	1999	**Change between** **1998 and 1999**
CRUDE OIL **PRODUCTION** **(1,000s** **BARRELS/DAY)**	*Non-OPEC*					
	Former Soviet Union	6,921	7,003	7,094	7,194	100
	U.S.	6,472	6,452	6,244	5,938	(306)
	China	3,151	3,210	3,200	3,195	(5)
	Norway	3,101	3,151	3,015	3,018	3
	Mexico	2,856	3,026	3,071	2,940	(131)
	UK	2,617	2,543	2,633	2,725	92
	Canada	1,837	1,910	2,017	1,889	(128)
	Brazil	784	841	956	1,086	130
	Egypt	925	875	866	852	(14)
	Colombia	623	652	754	816	62
	Argentina	780	835	847	801	(46)
	Syria	613	563	553	537	(16)
	Denmark	208	230	238	300	62
	Congo	210	265	265	264	(1)
	Total of above	*31,098*	*31,556*	*31,753*	*31,555*	*(198)*
	OPEC (all countries)					
	Saudi Arabia	8,080	8,349	8,297	7,738	(559)
	Iran	3,670	3,636	3,608	3,511	(97)
	Venezuela	2,970	3,185	3,122	2,784	(338)
	UAE	2,293	2,254	2,282	2,060	(222)
	Nigeria	2,148	2,287	2,132	1,965	(167)
	Iraq	575	1,149	2,110	2,523	413
	Kuwait	2,049	2,103	2,075	1,868	(207)
	Libya	1,393	1,422	1,392	1,347	(45)
	Indonesia	1,393	1,364	1,300	1,277	(23)
	Algeria	818	853	824	757	(67)
	Qatar	485	625	661	633	(28)
	Total of above	*25,873*	*27,227*	*27,801*	*26,463*	*(1,338)*

SOURCE: Centre for Global Energy Studies and *Mining Annual Review*, 2000.

1,500 barrels per day in 1999. The result? Oil prices nearly doubled because the winter of 2000 was cold.

Exactly how does OPEC exert its control over the price? Member countries, having agreed to a target price and output allocations, impose excise taxes on their product for specified periods of time. These taxes are computed to bring the marginal cost of extraction (sometimes as low as 50 cents per barrel) in line with the target, and they are well publicized. More important, they are treated as a cost by international oil companies that operate within an OPEC member country. Therefore no company can afford to sell OPEC oil for less than its extraction cost plus the tax, and so these companies give OPEC the power to set the prevailing price around the world.

440

SOURCE: M. Takin, *Mining Annual Review,* 2001.

Game theory

Game theory is a tool that has been created to help us study decision-making in situations in which there is a mixture of conflict and cooperation. Oligopoly is thus a perfect context in which to display its power. A *game* is a competitive situation in which two or more players pursue their own interests and no player can dictate the outcome. Poker, for example, is a game, but so, too, is a situation in which two firms are engaged in a competitive advertising campaign. A game is described in terms of the players, the rules of the game, the payoffs of the game, and the information that players have about the details of the game. These elements are common to all conflict situations, and they constitute the fundamental characteristics of a game.

Turning now to the specifics of a game, the decision-making unit is called a *player* (which can be a single person, a firm, or an organization). Each player has a certain endowment of resources to devote to the game, and the rules of the game describe how these resources can be used. For example, the rules of poker indicate how bets can be made, which hands are better than others, and how winnings are distributed. A game is called **cooperative** if the players can negotiate binding contracts that allow them to implement and to enforce joint strategies. By contrast, in a **noncooperative game,** the negotiation or enforcement of a binding contract is not possible. This chapter will focus almost entirely on noncooperative games. A *strategy* is a complete specification of what actions a player will take under each contingency in the playing of a game. For example, a corporation president might tell her subordinates not only how she wants an advertising campaign to start, but also what should be done at subsequent points in time *in response to various actions of competing firms.*

Cooperative game

Noncooperative game

A game's outcome clearly depends on the strategies used by each player. A player's *payoff* varies from game to game. It is win, lose, or draw in checkers; it is various sums of money in poker. The relevant features of a two-player game can be shown by constructing a **payoff matrix.** To illustrate how, suppose that Coke and Pepsi were about to stage advertising campaigns and that each had a choice of emphasizing television or movie ads. A representative payoff matrix, expressed in terms of profits for each firm for each combination of strategies, is shown in Figure 12.6. For example, if Coke were to emphasize movies while Pepsi emphasized television, the lower-left payoff entry shows that Coke would make a profit of $300 million and Pepsi would earn $200 million. Notice that the matrix displays a comparative advantage in television advertising for Pepsi and a corresponding comparative advantage for Coke in movie advertising. Perhaps this is a reflection of Pepsi's popularity among people who watch the cable channels, but that is really beside the point. The important observation is that game theory offers a systematic method of uncovering the implications of that advantage.

Payoff matrix

Dominant strategy

Each player has a **dominant strategy** in the game described in Figure 12.6. That is to say, Coke would make more profit by emphasizing movies rather than television *regardless of whether Pepsi emphasized television or movies;* emphasizing movie advertising is therefore a dominant strategy for Coke. Similarly, regardless of whether Coke emphasizes movies or television, Pepsi

441

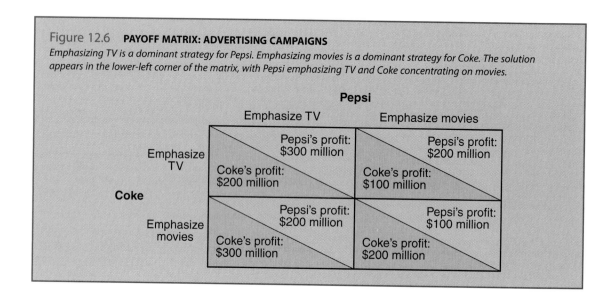

Figure 12.6 PAYOFF MATRIX: ADVERTISING CAMPAIGNS

Emphasizing TV is a dominant strategy for Pepsi. Emphasizing movies is a dominant strategy for Coke. The solution appears in the lower-left corner of the matrix, with Pepsi emphasizing TV and Coke concentrating on movies.

	Pepsi	
	Emphasize TV	Emphasize movies
Coke Emphasize TV	Pepsi's profit: $300 million / Coke's profit: $200 million	Pepsi's profit: $200 million / Coke's profit: $100 million
Emphasize movies	Pepsi's profit: $200 million / Coke's profit: $300 million	Pepsi's profit: $100 million / Coke's profit: $200 million

would make more profit if it emphasized television ads. Emphasizing television is therefore Pepsi's dominant strategy. The "solution" to this game is now easy to determine. Coke would emphasize movies while Pepsi concentrated its attention on television (the combination recorded in the lower-left portion of the payoff matrix). Coke would then make $300 million in profit, and Pepsi, $200 million. This would be the best that either player—that is, either firm—can do.

Simultaneous moves

One additional point should be noted regarding this particular game: it is an example of a game in which the players move *simultaneously*. Each player selects a strategy before observing any action or strategy chosen by the other player. Not all games are of this type. As we shall see, sometimes one player can go first; in such games, the order of play can make a big difference in the outcome. The best strategies in this simple example, though, are the same regardless of whether the players choose their strategies simultaneously or whether one or the other player goes first.

GAME TREES

Game trees

Game trees are, for some, the best way to investigate these sorts of issues. They certainly display graphically the difference between games that involve simultaneous moves and other games in which the order of play is specified. Figure 12.7 offers an alternative presentation of the game whose payoff matrix is recorded in Figure 12.6. It is drawn, however, to indicate that Coke must decide whether to emphasize movies or television ads *before* Pepsi must commit. The small square on the left-hand side represents Coke's decision. From this square, Coke could take one of two "branches." The upper branch corresponds to choosing to emphasize television ads; the lower branch corresponds to choosing movie ads.

442

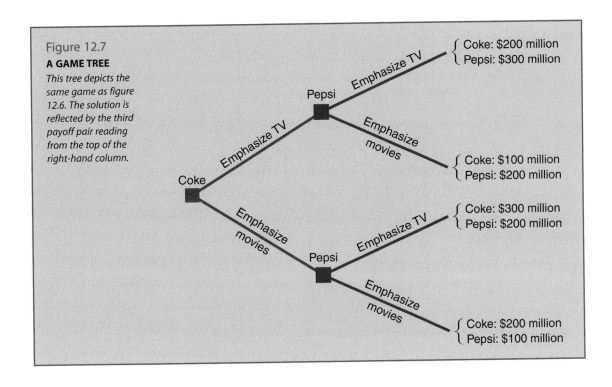

Figure 12.7

A GAME TREE

This tree depicts the same game as figure 12.6. The solution is reflected by the third payoff pair reading from the top of the right-hand column.

Coke: $200 million / Pepsi: $300 million

Emphasize TV

Pepsi

Emphasize movies

Coke: $100 million / Pepsi: $200 million

Emphasize TV

Coke

Coke: $300 million / Pepsi: $200 million

Emphasize TV

Emphasize movies

Pepsi

Emphasize movies

Coke: $200 million / Pepsi: $100 million

If Coke were to choose the upper branch by emphasizing television, then the next decision would be Pepsi's to make. This decision is represented by the small square with "Pepsi" printed above it. It connects with two branches that highlight Pepsi's two choices. If Pepsi were to choose the upper branch (emphasizing television), the outcome recorded on the right-hand edge of the game tree shows that Coke would receive $200 million in profit while Pepsi would garner $300 million. This is the outcome reported in the upper-left corner of the Figure 12.6 matrix. If Pepsi were to select the lower branch, though, Coke would see profits of only $100 million while Pepsi would see $200 million (the upper-right corner of the Figure 12.6 matrix). Similar descriptions hold for the lower branch that would be initiated by Coke's deciding to emphasize movies. The outcomes correspond to the lower entries of the payoff matrix; make sure that you understand why.

The game tree portrayed in Figure 12.7 enables us to determine each firm's optimal strategy. If Coke were to choose to emphasize television, then it is clear that Pepsi would choose TV because its profits would then be $300 million (along the upper branch) instead of $200 million (along the lower branch). If Coke were to select movies, though, Pepsi would inspect the outcomes of the lower branch to again choose television (seeing $200 million in profit instead of $100 million). As a result, Coke can see that it would earn $200 million in profit if it chose to concentrate on television in its advertising plans (because Pepsi would then select television, too); and it would earn $300 million if it selected a movie campaign (because Pepsi would still select television). The solution of the game, therefore, would correspond to the upper Pepsi branch along the lower Coke branch (the third set of outcomes). It is the same as the solution determined by the intersection of the two dominant strategies that were discovered in Figure 12.6. You should be able to convince yourself that the same solution would emerge from a game tree in which Pepsi went first. Later applications will explore some cases in which the order of play matters. Until then, we will focus on games for which a payoff matrix is the easier presentation.

THE PRISONERS' DILEMMA

Prisoners' dilemma

Having described the basic features of game theory, we now turn our attention to an important type of game known as the **prisoners' dilemma.** It has been the source of some of the insight with which we approach modern oligopoly theory as well as many other areas of economic, behavioral, and political science.

The dilemma is perhaps best understood in terms of a specific illustration that lies outside the strict purview of economics. In fact, it lies more squarely in the purview of *NYPD Blue*. Suppose, more specifically, that the detectives of the 15th Precinct arrest two people who they suspect have committed a crime; call them John and Schultzie. As is their custom, the detectives lock each prisoner in a separate room and offer each the following deal: "If you confess while your partner does not, then we can work with the D.A. to try to get you a 2-year sentence; and we are sure that your partner would get 12 years." Both suspects have been "around the block," though, so they know they would both get something like 5 years if they both confessed. And if neither confessed? The circumstantial evidence would be sufficient to convict them only of a lesser crime for which the sentence would be 3 years.

Both John and Schultzie would thus have two possible strategies—to confess or not to confess—and there are four possible outcomes depending upon which strategy each selects. The payoff matrix is displayed in Figure 12.8. What strategy would Schultzie choose? If John did not confess, the better strategy for Schultzie would be to confess. Schultzie would then serve less time (2 years) than if he did not confess (3 years). If John did confess, on the other hand, confessing would still be the better choice for Schultzie because he would still get a lighter sentence (5 years instead of 12). Schultzie should confess, therefore, regardless of what John does; confessing is a dominant strategy for Schultzie.

What would John do? The matrix is symmetric, so it should be obvious that confessing is also a dominant strategy for John. The noncooperative solution to the game would see both men confessing *even though both players would be better off if neither confessed*. The cooperative solution could be reached if they could trust each other not to confess. It could also emerge if the two suspects had the opportunity to communicate with one another so that they could get their stories straight and each could be sure that the other would not double-cross his accomplice. In that case, each would serve 3 years instead of 5.

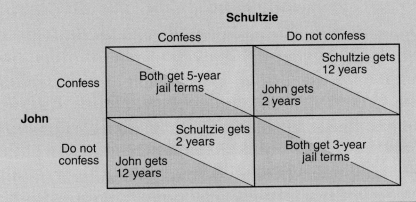

Figure 12.8 **PAYOFF MATRIX: THE PRISONERS' DILEMMA**
Confessing is a dominant strategy for both players. The solution appears in the upper-left corner of the matrix; it is a Nash equilibrium. The cooperative solution appears in the lower-right corner; it is not a Nash equilibrium.

Schultzie

Confess · Do not confess

John

Confess — Both get 5-year jail terms · Schultzie gets 12 years / John gets 2 years

Do not confess — Schultzie gets 2 years / John gets 12 years · Both get 3-year jail terms

---

Example 12.6

Cheating in a Cournot Context—Working a Problem

The prisoners' dilemma game is useful in analyzing oligopoly behavior. It can, for example, help to indicate the circumstances under which firms would be tempted to cheat on a cartel agreement by planning secretly to cut their prices and thereby garner a larger market share and maximum profits at the expense of other members of the cartel.

To explore this application in some detail, suppose that the two firms in the Cournot case depicted in Figures 12.1 and 12.2 were engaged in a collusive agreement in which they produced the monopoly output and shared monopoly profits. Recall that they were facing a linear demand curve,

$$P = 15 - 0.025 X_T.$$

We also assumed, for the sake of simplicity, that both firms could produce X at a constant marginal cost equal to $7.50. Under their collusive agreement, therefore, they would agree to produce a combined total output equal to $X_m = 150$ and to sell their product at a price equal to

$$P_m = 15 - (0.025)(150) = \$11.25.$$

Total profits would then be

$$(\$11.25 - \$7.50)(150) = \$562.50.$$

Each firm could expect to earn positive profits equal to $281.25 by producing 75 units at a unit cost of $7.50 and selling each for a price of $11.25. Is there an incentive for either firm to cheat on this agreement? And if so, by how much? Firm I, if it thought that firm II were producing one-half of the monopoly output per the colluding agreement, could maximize profits by producing the amount read from its reaction function. Why? Because reaction functions were constructed to provide precise answers to

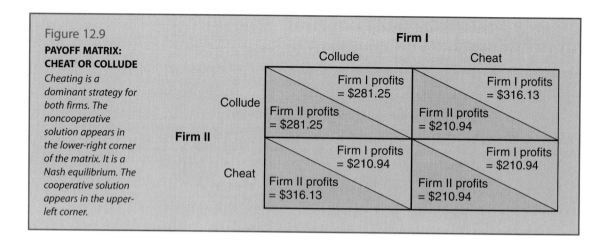

Figure 12.9

PAYOFF MATRIX: CHEAT OR COLLUDE

Cheating is a dominant strategy for both firms. The noncooperative solution appears in the lower-right corner of the matrix. It is a Nash equilibrium. The cooperative solution appears in the upper-left corner.

questions like "If firm I knew that firm II would produce X_{II} units of X, then how much should firm I produce to maximize its own profits?" We therefore use the reaction function in Equation 12.2 or 12.3 for a specific set of demand and cost parameters to explore the potential gains from cheating on a collusive agreement. Equation 12.2, for example, tells us that firm I could, for example, maximize profits by increasing output to $150 - (0.5)(75) = 112.5$ units under the assumption that firm II would continue to adhere to the collusive agreement. Total output would then equal $112.5 + 75 = 187.5$ and support a price of $10.31. Profits for firm I would climb to

$$(\$10.31 - \$7.50)(112.5) = \$316.13,$$

but profits for firm II would fall to

$$(\$10.31 - \$7.50)(75) = \$210.94.$$

And if firm II also increased output to 112.5 units according to Equation 12.3 under the (incorrect) assumption that firm I would hold to the collusive agreement? The price would fall to $9.38 and both firms would earn

$$(\$9.38 - \$7.50)(112.5) = 210.94.$$

Figure 12.9 portrays the payoff matrix for this game. Cheating is a dominant strategy for both firms, so the noncooperative Nash equilibrium solution appears in the lower-right corner of the matrix. The cooperative solution appears in the upper-left corner, but it can be sustained only if both firms maintain their commitments to collude and to share monopoly profits.

THE REPEATED PRISONERS' DILEMMA AND THE TIT-FOR-TAT STRATEGY

It is essential, at this point, to recognize a fundamental difference between the situation facing firms I and II, on the one hand, and circumstances confronting John and Schultzie, on the other. It may have been reasonable for

John and Schultzie to assume that they would play the game portrayed in Figure 12.8 just once. They might assume that they would never work together again (especially since they got caught), and so there would be no reason for *Repeated game*   either to think that the game would be repeated. For firms I and II, though, such an assumption would border on the absurd. Each of these firms must, at every point in time in a more realistic game, decide whether or not to cheat, and so each must consider the long-term consequences of its decision.

This turns out to be an important distinction, because its logical consequences can easily undermine the validity of the preceding analysis. Indeed, a cooperative solution can be sustained as an equilibrium over time, even when an inefficient noncooperative equilibrium exists for a "single-shot" version, if

1. The game will be repeated an infinite number of times,
2. The game will be repeated a finite but unknown number of times, or
3. Players are forced to act with incomplete information about how rivals will behave.[4]

To begin to see why, assume that both players understood that the game depicted in Figure 12.9 would be repeated an infinite number of times, and suppose that firm I decided that it would

1. Refuse to cheat the first time that it had to make a decision,
2. Continue to stick to the cartel agreement as long as its rival did the same, but
3. Revert to the safe policy of "cheating" if its rival failed even once to cooperate.

If firm II did the same, then both could expect to reap higher profits indefinitely. But if either cheated, then its profit would increase for one period and then fall permanently. As a result, it could easily be the case that *it would not be in the best interest of either firm to cheat for even a single period*. It is important to recognize that firms I and II could achieve this outcome even if they did not collude to do so or otherwise make any sort of binding agreement. If each simply presumed that the other would be smart enough to maintain the cooperative price, then its presumption would turn out to be correct. It would, therefore, be sustainable as a Nash equilibrium over the long term.

Tit-for-tat strategy   The strategy outlined above comes close to the **tit-for-tat strategy** identified by R. Axelrod. Axelrod simulated a variety of strategies on a computer for playing a repeated game. He concluded that players who committed themselves to doing in this round whatever the other player had done in the previous round would do very well over the long run.[5] In our case, firm I would abide by the agreement in the first round and every round thereafter as long as firm II complied. But if firm II ever cheated, then firm I should

---

[4]See P. Seabright, "Is Co-operation Habit-Forming?" in P. Dasgupta and K. Maler, eds., *The Environment and Emerging Development Issues* (Oxford: Clarendon Press, 1997).
[5]See R. Axelrod, *The Evolution of Cooperation* (New York: Basic Books, 1984).

cheat from then on. Meanwhile, firm II would do the same, and so the cooperative solution would be stable over the indefinite future.

In accord with Axelrod's findings, some cartels seem to have adopted tit-for-tat strategies in the past. The cartel that set the price of railroad freight in the United States in the 1880s (prior to the passage of the Sherman Antitrust Act), for example, retaliated against members who cut prices to increase their market shares.[6]

It is important to note, though, that this analysis assumed implicitly that the game would be repeated indefinitely. If it were repeated only a finite number of times and if the number of repetitions were known to the players, then the entire structure supporting the efficiency result could break down. To understand how that is possible, suppose that both firms I and II knew that the game would be repeated only N times. The number N can be quite large as long as it is finite. Firm I might then reason as follows: "We know that firm II will follow a tit-for-tat strategy. We cannot, therefore, cheat on the agreement until the last iteration of the game. Why? We would be punished in all subsequent periods if we cheated earlier than the last period, and the long-term losses would outweigh the short-term gain. But we cannot be punished after period N (the last period) because the game would be over, and so we would have nothing to lose by setting a low price in period N. Let's charge the high price until period N, and then let's cheat."

Firm II, of course, would discover the same logic. Firm II would therefore know that firm I will cheat in period N. Firm II would thereby be excused from worrying about the threat of retaliation in period N for cheating in period $N - 1$. Firm II would certainly cheat in period $N - 1$ as a result, because that would be its only chance of reaping the rewards of breaking the cooperative solution. Firm I has all of the data, though, and it would surely see right through firm II's strategy. It would, as a result, plan to cheat preemptively on firm II in period $N - 2$. But firm II would foresee this ploy, and so it would cheat in period $N - 3$. And so on. This cycle of **backward induction** finally leads to only one conclusion: the only rational outcome of repeating the prisoners' dilemma game defined by Figure 12.9 a *known* and *finite* number of times would see both firms cheating on the cooperative agreement by charging a low price *every period, beginning with the first.*

Now for some more complication. Two more glimpses of reality can undermine even this alternative path to the noncooperative solution. If one or both players doubted the ability of the other to complete the reasoning just described, then it would not be able to rely on its tangled logic of rational behavior. In other words, it would be possible that one firm would not carry the logic to its ultimate conclusion if it believed that there were a chance that the other firm would cooperate as long as it did. *Uncertainty about the behavior of other players* could therefore resurrect the logic of the infinite game. So, too, could uncertainty about the length of the game. If players did not know when the game would end, then they would have no benchmark on which to build the backward logic of undercutting from the last period. Simply put, neither player would know exactly when the game would

[6]See R. Porter, "Study of Cartel Stability," *Bell Journal of Economics,* Autumn 1983.

end, and so neither would have any basis for concluding that the other player would not be able to retaliate against cheating because the game was over.

On the other side of the coin, cooperation could break down or never begin, even in an infinitely repeated game, if the environment that defined the payoff matrix of the game were uncertain and thus open to the subjective interpretation of the various players. Uncertainties about demand or costs, for example, could make it extraordinarily difficult for a cooperative solution to persist. Suppose that firms I and II both decided that it would be rational to cooperate, but they had different perceptions of the marketplace. Firm I might think that setting the price equal to $8 per unit would be consistent with its contribution to the cooperative solution while firm II might think that $6 was the appropriate choice. Blind to the motivation that dictated firm II's decision to charge $6 and following the tit-for-tat strategy, firm I could easily conclude that firm II cheated and respond in the next period by cutting its price permanently.

Several of the problems at the end of this chapter will exercise your understanding of each of these points. Related applications will appear in subsequent chapters. One, for example, will build on the notion of discounting future earnings; it will modify the tit-for-tat strategy to allow for retaliation over a finite period of time. Another will explore the ramifications of asymmetric information. Each will carry content of its own, and they will all be designed to show how game theory has become a valuable analytic tool in areas that extend far beyond considerations of alternative market structures.

| Example 12.7 | Crisis in the Banking Sector—Bank Runs as an Equilibrium Condition |

Part of the power of game theory is derived from its ability to explain how social behavior that seems to be irrational can in fact be an equilibrium condition even when all actors are behaving rationally; and perhaps more important, it can highlight circumstances that can bring such an equilibrium to the fore. This example will illustrate this point by suggesting how a bank run could be a Nash equilibrium.

Why might this be important in a modern economy? The early 1990s were marked by the failure of a large number of savings and loans across the United States. S&Ls were banking institutions that accepted deposits and made loans outside the normal banking structure. Administrators of S&Ls were not restricted by many of the rules that limited the operations of more traditional banks, but the protection offered by the Federal Deposit Insurance Corporation was not automatically extended to their depositors. As a result, depositors earned higher rates of interest, but they would be exposed to considerable risk of losing everything if the savings and loan became insolvent. And how might a savings and loan become insolvent? Its investments could fail and/or its depositors could demand their money.

Consider, as an illustrative model, an S&L with two depositors—not much of a clientele, but enough to make the point. Both have made deposits of D, and the S&L has invested these deposits in some sort of long-term project (like a real estate investment). If the S&L were forced to liquidate the project early, a total of $2r$ would be recovered; assume that $D > r > D/2$.

If the project reached maturity, it would pay $2R$ with $R > D$. If both depositors withdrew their claims before maturity, therefore, both would receive r and the game would be over. If one investor made an early withdrawal, then he or she would get D and the other would be stuck with $(2r - D)$, and the game would end. If neither made an early withdrawal, then the project would mature. Both depositors could then withdraw R. If one made a withdrawal at that time, he or she could receive $(2R - D)$ while the other would get D; and if neither made a withdrawal, then the S&L would distribute R to both. Panels A and B of Figure 12.10 display these payoffs in two distinct matrices.

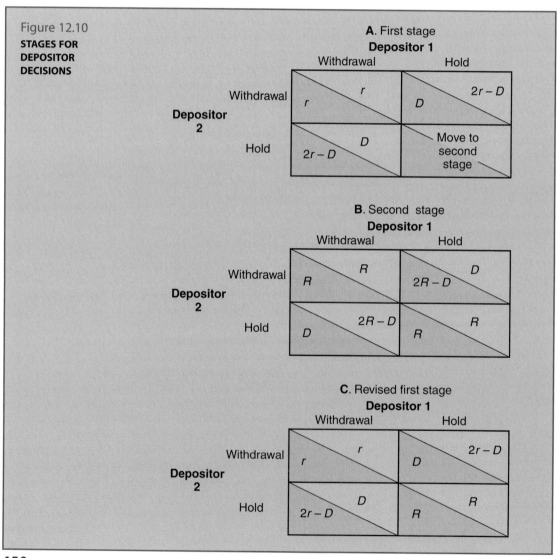

Figure 12.10
STAGES FOR DEPOSITOR DECISIONS

A. First stage

B. Second stage

C. Revised first stage

We now work backward, as we did in the "tit-for-tat" discussion. Notice first of all that withdrawal would be the dominant strategy for both in the second round, so we know that the payoff if neither player withdrew funds in the first round would be $R for both players. This observation allows us to produce panel C as the payoff matrix for the first-round decision. We can also now observe that there are two Nash equilibria in the first round. One would see both players making a withdrawal; the other would see neither at the withdrawal window. The first equilibrium is the bank-run scenario, but when will it emerge? This model does not predict when, but Chapter 5 can help us there. If other events (like a downturn in the real estate market or failure in other S&Ls) made the likely payoff after stage 2 fall so that the expected value of $R fell below $D, then withdrawal would become a dominant strategy for both investors and they would run to the bank.

SOURCE: R. Gibbons, *Game Theory for Applied Economists* Princeton, N.J.: Princeton University Press, 1992, Chap. 2.

NASH EQUILIBRIA: FURTHER DISCUSSION

Example 12.7 raised the possibility that some games may not display a unique equilibrium because dominant strategies may not exist for any or all players in every application. It is, though, important to note that this possibility does not negate the utility of the Nash formulation of equilibrium. If all players have dominant strategies, then their best choices are clear regardless of what the other players do. If they do not have dominant strategies, however, Nash equilibrium simply requires that each player adopt his or her best strategy *given what the other players do in equilibrium*. Equilibria supported by dominant strategies are therefore Nash equilibria; but not all Nash equilibria are supported by dominance across all of the strategies available to all of the players.

| Example 12.8 | Multiple Equilibria and the Wal-Mart Success Story |

Example 12.1 drew your attention to an expansion strategy that sustained Wal-Mart's incredible growth in the discount retail trade—open new stores in communities with slightly under 100,000 residents. A little game theory can show exactly how that works and make it clear that Wal-Mart needed more than a clear idea of the market size threshold. It needed to be able to exploit a preemptive strategy of building first to make the threshold work.

Suppose, for the sake of a numerical example, that Figure 12.11 were the relevant payoff matrix for Wal-Mart and a potential competitor like Kmart as they contemplated opening a new store in Berlin, Connecticut. Neither can find a dominant strategy, and there are two Nash equilibria. One equilibrium, in the upper-right corner, would see Wal-Mart moving to town without worrying about attracting any competition. The other, in the lower-left corner, would support a new Kmart at the exclusion of any other store. Which equilibrium should we expect? We cannot tell unless we know that Wal-Mart

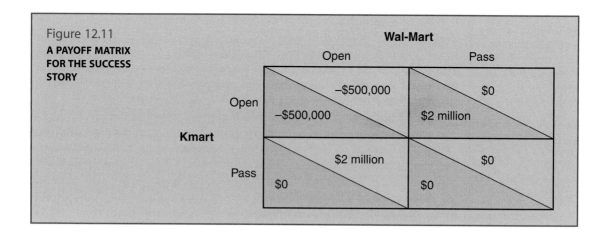

Figure 12.11

A PAYOFF MATRIX FOR THE SUCCESS STORY

reviews the demographics so quickly that it gets to decide first. If that were the case, Wal-Mart's planners would know that building a new store would pay off immediately because *it would be in the best interest of the Kmart people to pass on the option to build given that a Wal-Mart had already been established.*

Our discussion of Nash equilibria has, thus far, been based on the assumption that all of the players act rationally, that is, that every player chooses a strategy that maximizes his or her individual welfare, or profits or whatever. Perhaps more important, our discussion has assumed that all of the players in a game understand what motivates all of the other players. As a result, they can anticipate the decisions of others and act accordingly. But what if that were not the case? Or what if one player did not trust that the others would choose rationally? Such a player might then adopt a conservative approach and choose a strategy that would maximize his or her minimum outcome across the payoff matrix—the so called "maximin" approach. He or she would then be guaranteed of suffering the least harm—at the expense sometimes of missing out on the maximum gain.

| Example 12.9 | **British Petroleum, Maximin Strategies, and the Precautionary Principle** |

The late 1980s were bad times at British Petroleum. BP had suffered a series of losses from unlucky exploratory drillings for North Sea oil that essentially turned up nothing of value. Its management responded by adopting an extremely conservative investment strategy, one that would allow BP to move on a project only if it would earn a profit under any conceivable scenario of how the future might unfold. Thinking that these futures might be dominated by scientific uncertainty of where oil deposits might lie, we could use the precautionary principle introduced at the end of Chapter 5 to describe this behavior. Recall that the precautionary principle called for making decisions based on keeping the likelihood of a bad event below a certain threshold. It therefore represented a very conservative response to risk; and in the case of BP, the risk threshold for failure was zero.

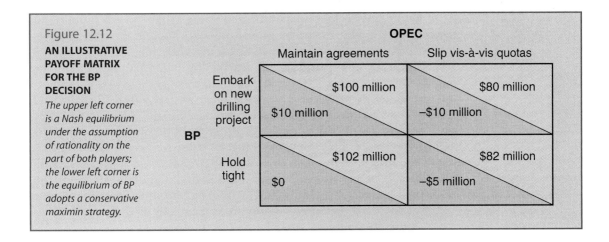

Figure 12.12

AN ILLUSTRATIVE PAYOFF MATRIX FOR THE BP DECISION

The upper left corner is a Nash equilibrium under the assumption of rationality on the part of both players; the lower left corner is the equilibrium of BP adopts a conservative maximin strategy.

		OPEC	
		Maintain agreements	Slip vis-à-vis quotas
BP	Embark on new drilling project	$10 million / $100 million	−$10 million / $80 million
	Hold tight	$0 / $102 million	−$5 million / $82 million

The maximin strategy just presented extends this theme so that it can be applied to circumstances where additional risk is created by socioeconomic conditions. To see how, return to our discussion of OPEC in Example 12.5. We noted there that OPEC's ability to maintain the international price of oil depended upon fluctuation in demand over the short run and member-by-member discipline in limiting production over the medium term. Now suppose that BP were contemplating the economic return of drilling in a specific field where it was certain that it could find oil. It is not very far-fetched to assume that this return could easily depend on OPEC's ability to meet its price targets.

We can make this story a little more concrete by attaching some numbers to the outcomes that could arise from four different combinations of OPEC behavior and BP investment decisions. Figure 12.12 displays an illustrative payoff matrix designed to do just that. Notice that maintaining discipline is a dominant strategy for OPEC, as a whole, regardless of whether BP adds new capacity by drilling a few new wells. Knowing this, BP would choose to add to its capacity *if it were certain that OPEC discipline would hold.* The upper left-hand corner is a perfectly good candidate for a Nash equilibrium *under the assumption that both "players" are rational and trying to maximize return (combined return in the case of OPEC).*

Cartels are fragile, of course, and this is certainly not news to BP. They might doubt that discipline would be maintained, and so their conservative decision rule could lead them to choose a strategy that maximized the minimum return. This maximin approach would lead them to withhold support for the drilling project. It would sustain a Nash equilibrium regardless of the behavior of OPEC or any of its member nations.

Microlink 12.1 Profit-Maximizing Conditions

All of the material presented since Chapter 8 has focused attention on profit-maximizing firms that chose their outputs by equating marginal cost to "effective" marginal revenue and read their price from their "effective" demand curve. For the competitive firms of Chapters 8 and 9, "effective" demand *and* marginal revenue were given by the market price. This price was taken to be constant by the individual firm even though it was determined by the interaction of market demand with market supply—in turn the horizontal sum of the marginal-cost curves of individual firms. For the monopolists of Chapter 10, "effective" marginal revenue was determined by the market demand curve, and the price was read from that demand. Monopolistic competitors behaved similarly against the more elastic "effective" demand for their own variant of the relevant product group. Oligopolists have even more trouble computing an "effective" demand curve, since it is determined both by market demand and by the actions of other suppliers. Nonetheless, the fundamental result of profit maximization holds. They, too, chose their outputs by equating marginal cost to "effective" marginal revenue, and they, too, read the operative price from their "effective" demand curves.

SUMMARY

1. Oligopoly is characterized by a small number of firms that operate within the same market with a great deal of actual and/or perceived interdependence.
2. A Nash equilibrium is a situation in which each firm is doing the best it can given the behavior of its rivals. The Cournot model is an early theory based on the supposition that each firm believes that the other firm will hold its output constant at the existing level.
3. Conditions that sustain oligopolistic industries also tend to promote collusion. The advantages of collusion are obvious: increased profits, decreased uncertainty, and a better opportunity to control the entry of new firms. But collusive arrangements are often hard to maintain because any member firm can increase its profits by "cheating" on the agreement (charging a lower price and increasing market share). Collusive arrangements are generally illegal in the United States, but that is not universal. The Organization of Petroleum Exporting Countries (OPEC) is a cartel; it has played an important role in determining the world price of oil.
4. Faced with the difficulties of forming an effective cartel, oligopolists may attempt to cooperate without making explicit agreements with one another.
5. A game is a competitive situation in which two or more players pursue their own interests and no player can dictate the outcome. Constructing a payoff matrix is one convenient way of displaying the relevant features of a two-player game. Game trees are another. In some games, each player has a dominant strategy—a strategy that is best regardless of what strategy the other players choose. A Nash equilibrium is sustained by a collection of strategies for which each player is best off given what the other players decide to do.
6. The prisoners' dilemma is a type of game that has proved very useful in analyzing oligopoly behavior. In particular, it helps to explain why firms have a tendency to cheat on cartel agreements. However, if this game is repeated indefinitely (or for a finite but unknown number of times), then firms may not cheat; they may, instead, adopt a tit-for-tat strategy. When games are repeated a fixed and known number of times, however, the cheating solution can return.

**QUESTIONS/
PROBLEMS**

1. Suppose that two firms produce spring water for commercial sale. Assume that the cost for both firms is zero. The marginal-revenue curve for their combined output is $MR = 10 - 2Q$, where MR is marginal revenue and

Q is the number of gallons per hour of spring water sold by both together. (a) What combined output would be forthcoming if the two producers colluded to maximize their total profits? Why? (b) Describe the corresponding Cournot equilibrium. (c) Construct a payoff matrix for both firms if they initially collude to restrict output to the monopoly level and agree to share profits.

2. Farmland Dairies, a New Jersey milk producer, began selling milk on Staten Island in 1986. (Staten Island is one of New York City's five boroughs.) Its low fixed price was 40 cents per gallon lower than the then-current price on Staten Island. New York State law dictated that each milk producer like Farmland must get a license to sell milk, borough by borough. Existing dairies in New York City argued that the entry of Farmland into other boroughs of the city would not benefit consumers because it costs a great deal to distribute milk there. Furthermore, they said that New York jobs should not go to New Jersey. In January 1987, a federal judge ruled in favor of Farmland, saying that a state decision barring its expansion of sales in New York was unconstitutional. Evaluate in detail the arguments offered by the (then) existing New York dairies in terms of changes in consumer surplus that Farmland's entry would create. Track the change in existing dairies' producer surplus assuming an upward-sloping supply curve. Where are employment concerns reflected in your analysis?

3. Verify the entries in the payoff matrix of Example 12.6 on page 445.

4. Suppose that a cartel were formed by three firms whose total-cost functions were summarized by these data:

	Total cost		
Units of output	Firm 1	Firm 2	Firm 3
0	20	25	15
1	25	35	22
2	35	50	32
3	50	80	47
4	80	120	77
5	120	160	117

If the cartel decided to produce 11 units of output, how should the output be distributed among the three firms if they wanted to minimize total cost? Compute marginal revenue under the assumption that 11 units maximizes total profits for the cartel. What can you say given this information about equilibrium price?

5. Firms A and B are the only producers of a homogeneous good. Firm A's marginal revenue (in dollars) equals $100 - 4Q_B - 8Q_A$ where Q_A is firm A's monthly output and Q_B is firm B's monthly output. (Both Q_A and Q_B are expressed in units of output per month.) (a) If firm A's marginal cost equals $4 per unit of output, derive the equation for firm A's reaction curve. (b) Assume that firms A and B are identical. Compute market equilibrium if both firms are Cournot duopolists. (c) Do all of the points on firm A's reaction curve represent a Nash equilibrium? Why or why not?

6. Two firms, C and D, exist in a particular market. Each has two strategies. The payoff matrix for the various combinations of strategies is given in the figure.

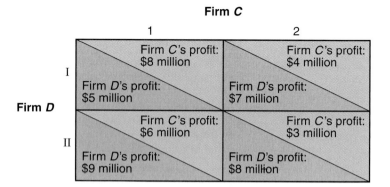

(a) Does firm *C* have a dominant strategy? If so, what is it? (b) Does firm *D* have a dominant strategy? If so, what is it? (c) What is the solution to this game? Is it a Nash equilibrium? (d) Does this particular game reflect the characteristics of a prisoners' dilemma?

7. The Ewe Company and the Zee Company are the only firms in a particular market. The payoff matrix for alternative strategies for both is recorded in the figure.

Zee

	Build plant on East Coast	Build plant on West Coast
Ewe — Build plant on East Coast	Zee's profit: −$60 million / Ewe's profit: −$50 million	Zee's profit: $30 million / Ewe's profit: $60 million
Ewe — Build plant on West Coast	Zee's profit: $70 million / Ewe's profit: $40 million	Zee's profit: −$40 million / Ewe's profit: −$30 million

(a) Are there one or more Nash equilibria? (b) If so, how many? Identify as many as you can. (c) Is this a prisoners' dilemma game? (d) Is there a first-mover advantage in this game? (e) What strategies might either company employ to try to predetermine the outcome of the game prior to committing to a strategy?

8. The Miller Company must decide whether or not to advertise its product. If its rival, the Morgan Corporation, decided to advertise its product, then Miller would make $4 million if it advertised and $2 million if it did not advertise. If Morgan chose not to advertise, Miller would make $5 million if it advertised and $3 million if it did not. (a) Is it possible to determine the payoff matrix from the information provided? Why or why not? (b) Can you tell whether Miller has a dominant strategy? If so, what is it?

9. The Morgan Corporation, introduced in Question 8, must decide whether to advertise its product. If its rival, the Miller Company, decided to advertise, Morgan would make $2.5 million if it advertised and $2 million if it did not advertise. If Miller chose not to advertise, Morgan would make $2 million if it advertised and $2.5 million if it did not. (a) On the basis of the

data in this and the previous question, is it possible to determine the pay-off matrix? If so, what is it? (b) Do both firms have dominant strategies? If so, what are they? (c) Is there a Nash equilibrium? If so, what is it? (d) Is this now a prisoners' dilemma game?

10. Ever notice that every town seems to have a "hamburger strip"—a street with a wide variety of fast-food stores located very close to one another? Game theory offers an explanation of why fast-food restaurants tend to cluster like this. To illustrate, suppose that there were a suburban road with 100 families distributed evenly over its length. Assume, for the sake of argument, that any restaurant located on that road could expect $20 per week in profit from each family for which it was the closest source of fast food. Assume, as well, that there are two fast-food restaurants, A and B, that have decided to open establishments somewhere along the road. (a) Suppose that restaurant A located at the midpoint of the road. How would the profits of B depend on the location that B chose? (b) Suppose that restaurant A located somewhere other than the midpoint of the road. How would the profits earned by B then depend on the location that B chose? (c) Use your answers to parts (a) and (b) to construct both a game tree and a payoff matrix that describes a game in which restaurants A and B have two strategies: locate at the midpoint of the road or someplace else. You have enough information to record precise levels of profits in some cases and to put upper or lower bounds on profits in other cases. (d) Demonstrate that the solution to this game would see both restaurants locating at the center of the road. (e) Argue why this is a Nash equilibrium. (f) Is there a first-mover advantage in this game?

11. It is instructive to draw a specific payoff matrix for the cartel model described in this chapter. To that end, assume that the demand for some good X is given by $P = 12 - 2X$. Let X be denominated in millions of units. Assume that two firms service the market and that each can produce X at a constant marginal and average cost of $4 per unit. (a) What is the marginal-revenue schedule for this demand curve? (b) Show that the cartel collusion solution would see both firms sharing $8 million in monopoly profits. Assume for the remainder of the problem that the cartel agreement would see firm A producing 500,000 units for a 25 percent share of total profit while B produces 1.5 million units to receive a 75 percent share. (c) Suppose that firm A considered "cheating" by adjusting its output under the Cournot assumption that firm B would continue to produce 1.5 million units. Compute the output for firm A, the total output that would then result, the price that would clear the market, and the profit that would be returned to both firms. (d) Now suppose that firm B considered "cheating" by adjusting its output under the Cournot assumption that firm A would continue to produce 500,000 units. Compute the output for firm B, the total output that would then result, the price that would clear the market, and the profit that would be returned to both firms. (e) Now suppose that both firms "cheated" by producing the outputs computed for each in parts (c) and (d). Compute the total output that would then result, the price that would clear the market, and the profit that would be returned to both. (f) Record the results of parts (b) through (e) in a payoff matrix in which each firm can choose one of two strategies: to "cheat" or not to "cheat" as described. (g) Does either firm have a dominant strategy? If so, identify it. Identify the game's solution. Is it a Nash equilibrium?

12. Redo Question 11 under the assumption that the colluding agreement would have the two firms share monopoly profits and output equally. Would the game display the characteristics of a prisoners' dilemma?

13. The Amherst Company must decide whether to buy all or part of its steel from the Duquesne Corporation. If Duquesne provides prompt delivery of the steel it sells, Amherst will make $2 million if it buys all its steel from Duquesne and $1 million if it buys only part from Duquesne. But if Duquesne does not provide prompt delivery, Amherst will lose $50 million if it buys all its steel from Duquesne and $1 million if it buys only part from Duquesne. If it receives an order for all of Amherst's steel requirements, Duquesne will make $3 million if it provides prompt delivery and $2 million if it does not do so. If it receives an order for part of Amherst's steel requirements, Duquesne will make $2 million if it provides prompt delivery and $1 million if it does not do so.

(a) Amherst must decide whether to buy all or part of its steel from Duquesne, and Duquesne must decide whether to provide prompt delivery. What is the payoff matrix for this game? (b) Does each player have a dominant strategy? If so, what is it? (c) Does this game have a Nash equilibrium? If so, what is it? (d) Suppose that Duquesne's managers are known to be inefficient and not much interested in how much money their firm makes. Do you think that Amherst will act in accord with the Nash equilibrium? Why or why not?

14. Consider a duopoly facing a linear demand curve of the form $P = a - bX_T$, where P is price and X_T is total output. Assume that both firms have constant marginal costs equal to c. Confirm that the matrix shown in the figure accurately describes the payoff matrix for firms I and II if they were to consider cheating on an agreement to share monopoly output and profits.

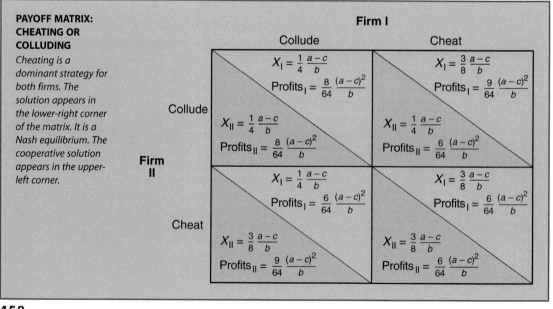

PAYOFF MATRIX: CHEATING OR COLLUDING

Cheating is a dominant strategy for both firms. The solution appears in the lower-right corner of the matrix. It is a Nash equilibrium. The cooperative solution appears in the upper-left corner.

Firm I

	Collude	Cheat
Collude	$X_I = \frac{1}{4}\frac{a-c}{b}$ Profits$_I = \frac{8}{64}\frac{(a-c)^2}{b}$ $X_{II} = \frac{1}{4}\frac{a-c}{b}$ Profits$_{II} = \frac{8}{64}\frac{(a-c)^2}{b}$	$X_I = \frac{3}{8}\frac{a-c}{b}$ Profits$_I = \frac{9}{64}\frac{(a-c)^2}{b}$ $X_{II} = \frac{1}{4}\frac{a-c}{b}$ Profits$_{II} = \frac{6}{64}\frac{(a-c)^2}{b}$
Cheat	$X_I = \frac{1}{4}\frac{a-c}{b}$ Profits$_I = \frac{6}{64}\frac{(a-c)^2}{b}$ $X_{II} = \frac{3}{8}\frac{a-c}{b}$ Profits$_{II} = \frac{9}{64}\frac{(a-c)^2}{b}$	$X_I = \frac{3}{8}\frac{a-c}{b}$ Profits$_I = \frac{6}{64}\frac{(a-c)^2}{b}$ $X_{II} = \frac{3}{8}\frac{a-c}{b}$ Profits$_{II} = \frac{6}{64}\frac{(a-c)^2}{b}$

Firm II

CHAPTER 13

Strategic Competition

The first principles of oligopoly theory were introduced in Chapter 12, and the potential utility of applying game theory in trying to understand their content was displayed. We turn, in this chapter, to extensions of the theory designed to explore the role of strategic behavior in oligopolistic models. The first part of the chapter will, in particular, review models that extend the behavior of the firm beyond the naive confines of the Cournot model that was introduced in the last chapter. Firm interdependence will still matter, and we will find value in understanding how rivals might respond to the price or output decisions of any given firm. We will also reaffirm the economic benefit in creating and maintaining market power. It will become abundantly clear that firms can exert discretionary power in their own best interest over more variables than just price and quantity.

THE STACKELBERG MODEL

The first stop in this discussion is a simple extension of the original Cournot model published in the 1930s by Heinrich von Stackelberg, a German economist. He thought about a two-firm duopoly in which firm I knew that firm II would behave as a Cournot duopolist—that is, that firm II would take firm I's output as fixed and given. Stackelberg's work highlighted the value of (extra) information and the potential value of being a market leader, in the sense of being able to act first in setting output. Both insights were derived by noting that the added information about how firm II would behave made firm I a "Stackelberg leader" that enjoyed a strategic advantage over firm II (the "Stackelberg follower"). The key to understanding how this advantage might pay dividends can be found in Example 12.2. More specifically, Equation 12.2b recorded the reaction function for firm II

$$X_{II} = 150 - 0.5X_I \qquad [13.1]$$

where X_{II} is the amount produced and sold by firm II and X_I is the amount produced and sold by firm I. So what? The Stackelberg assumption means that firm I would know as much about Equation 13.1 as you do *and could*

Figure 13.1   **OPTIMAL OUTPUT OF FIRM I IF IT THINKS FIRM II WILL BEHAVE AS A COURNOT DUOPOLIST**
Effective marginal revenue intersects marginal cost at an output of 150 units. Firm I takes this as the profit-maximizing level under the expectation that firm II will behave as a Cournot duopolist so that the reaction curve of Equation 13.1 applies.

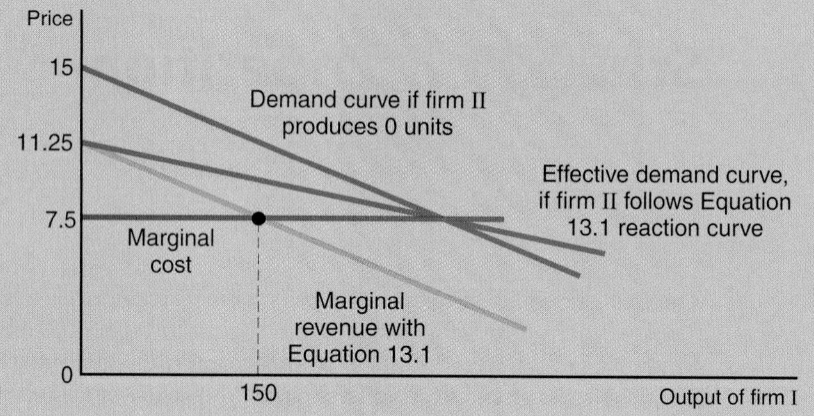

use that information in its own output determination. An equilibrium would no longer occur at the point where the two firms' reaction curves intersect because firm I would no longer take firm II's output as given. On the contrary, it would recognize that firm II's output would depend on its own in accord with Equation 13.1, and this recognition would allow it to raise its profits above the level sustained by a Cournot equilibrium. How? By picking the point along the reaction function (Equation 13.1) where its own profits would be maximized.

Figure 13.1 displays such an equilibrium for the circumstances depicted in Figure 12.2. The effective demand curve facing firm I is depicted there under the assumption that the market demand for good X is summarized by

$$P = 15 - 0.025X_T. \qquad [13.2]$$

For each price, it incorporates the reaction function explicitly. To see how, recall that $X_T = X_I + X_{II}$, so that, substituting the reaction function of Equation 13.1,

$$P = 15 - 0.025[X_I + (150 - 0.5X_I)]$$
$$= [15 - (0.025)(150)] - (0.025)(0.5)X_I$$
$$= 11.25 - 0.0125X_I. \qquad [13.3]$$

It follows immediately that the corresponding effective marginal-revenue curve for firm I is now

$$MR = 11.25 - 0.025X_I.$$

How do we know that? Marginal revenue for a linear demand curve of the sort displayed in Equation 13.3 has the same intercept and twice the slope.

To maximize profit in the Stackelberg case, firm I would therefore choose to produce where this effective marginal revenue exactly matched marginal cost. Assuming a constant marginal cost of $7.50, firm I would choose to produce 150 units because $11.25 - (0.025)(150) = 7.5$. And firm II? Equation 13.1 tells us that firm II would respond by producing $150 - (0.5)(150) = 75$ units. A total of 225 units would then be sold for a price, read from Equation 13.2, of $15 - (0.025)(225) = \$9.38$. Firm I would earn

$$(\$9.38 - \$7.50)(150) = \$282.25$$

while firm II would earn

$$(\$9.38 - \$7.50)(75) = \$141.13.$$

More generally, the Stackelberg leader would expand its output relative to the Cournot equilibrium at the expense of a reduction in the output of the follower. Would it be a Nash equilibrium? Certainly. Firm I would be maximizing profit given that firm II was behaving as a Cournot duopolist. It would therefore have no incentive to change anything. And firm II? Its expectations that firm I would be producing 150 units of output would be realized. And it would be maximizing profit given those expectations. How do we know that? Because the equilibrium would lie on firm II's reaction function. Firm II would therefore not have any incentive to change anything, either. And how do we know that firm I's profits would be higher—that is, how do we know that this information about firm II's reaction function had any value? Because firm I could have chosen the old Cournot equilibrium and did not. That can only mean that profits were higher elsewhere and that the information had some value.

Finally, we promised some insight into the value of being a market leader and being able to "move first." Suppose that firm I got to choose its output level first with a complete understanding of how firm II would respond. As shown in Figure 13.2, firm I could maximize its profit by choosing output $X_I' = 150$ units, which would be larger than the Cournot equilibrium value of $X_I = 100$ units. Going first would therefore give firm I a strategic advantage over firm II. It could establish its own output level and firm II would be left to react as best it could (maximizing its own profit by settling for the relatively low output level of $X_{II}' = 75$ units < 100 units). The advantage that firm I enjoyed in this short story by going first is often called the "first-mover advantage."

| Example 13.1 | First-Mover Advantage—Working a Problem |

The first-mover advantage can be depicted most clearly in a payoff matrix for a simple duopoly game. Figure 13.3 displays a payoff matrix for two firms that are contemplating Stackelberg strategies. The values recorded there are derived from our recurrent example, where market demand is given by

$$P = 15 - 0.025X_T.$$

Both firms face identical and constant marginal costs of $7.50 per unit. The Cournot output from Chapter 12 is recorded in the upper left-hand corner

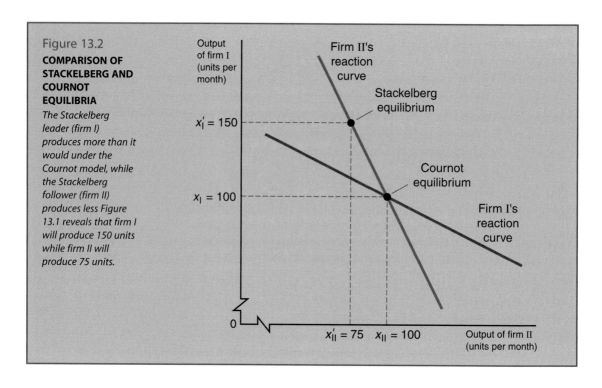

Figure 13.2

COMPARISON OF STACKELBERG AND COURNOT EQUILIBRIA

The Stackelberg leader (firm I) produces more than it would under the Cournot model, while the Stackelberg follower (firm II) produces less Figure 13.1 reveals that firm I will produce 150 units while firm II will produce 75 units.

Output of firm I (units per month)

Firm II's reaction curve

Stackelberg equilibrium

$x'_I = 150$

Cournot equilibrium

$x_I = 100$

Firm I's reaction curve

$x'_{II} = 75$ $x_{II} = 100$

Output of firm II (units per month)

of the matrix; both firms produce 100 units and earn $250 in profit by charging a price of $15 − 0.025(200) = $10. The two cases where one or the other firm chooses to play the Stackelberg strategy while the other does not are recorded in the upper-right and lower-left boxes. These are the numbers just computed in the text. But what if both firms played the Stackelberg strategy? Both would produce 150 units for a total of 300 units, the market clearing price would be $7.50, and pure economic profits would fall to $0. This is the lower right-hand box.

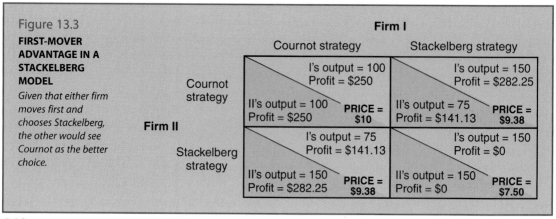

Figure 13.3

FIRST-MOVER ADVANTAGE IN A STACKELBERG MODEL

Given that either firm moves first and chooses Stackelberg, the other would see Cournot as the better choice.

Firm I

	Cournot strategy	Stackelberg strategy
Firm II Cournot strategy	I's output = 100 Profit = $250 II's output = 100 Profit = $250 **PRICE = $10**	I's output = 150 Profit = $282.25 II's output = 75 Profit = $141.13 **PRICE = $9.38**
Stackelberg strategy	I's output = 75 Profit = $141.13 II's output = 150 Profit = $282.25 **PRICE = $9.38**	I's output = 150 Profit = $0 II's output = 150 Profit = $0 **PRICE = $7.50**

462

Neither firm has a dominant strategy in this game, and there are two Nash equilibria: the upper-right box and the lower-left. And how do we know which one would materialize? By knowing which firm got to go first. If firm I went first, for example, then it would choose to play the Stackelberg strategy; and given that, firm II would remain Cournot. As a result, firm I would see higher profit associated with higher output despite charging a price that was lower than the Cournot equilibrium. *This* is the first-mover advantage.

THE BERTRAND MODEL

We have assumed thus far that oligopolistic firms focus on output and not price in making their decisions. We now change our perspective by assuming, instead, that firms simultaneously choose a price rather than an output. This is the situation studied by Joseph Bertrand, another nineteenth-century French economist. His work recognized explicitly that buyers will patronize only the firm that is charging the lower price. If firm I charged a lower price than firm II in a duopoly setting, for example, then firm I would have the entire market to itself and firm II's sales would be zero. If firms I and II set the same price, though, Bertrand assumed that each would sell the same amount. This was an arbitrary assumption, to be sure. But it was based on the presumption that buyers facing equal prices from two suppliers would not care where they went to make their purchases (and so there would be a 50-50 chance that any buyer would go to firm I or to firm II).

This model may seem to be quite similar to ones that we have already discussed, but it is really quite different. In contrast to the Cournot and Stackelberg models, it will turn out that the Nash equilibrium in the Bertrand model is the perfectly competitive outcome. Both firms will set price equal to marginal cost (and so both will also set price equal to average cost because of the constant-cost assumption). Both firms will earn a profit of zero, and together they will offer the competitive output to the marketplace. It should be clear that this outcome is entirely different from the equilibria predicted by the Cournot and Stackelberg models. There, recall, output fell short of the competitive solution, price was higher than marginal cost, and both firms earned a positive economic profit.

Why is the Nash equilibrium so different in the Bertrand world from what it was in the Cournot and Stackelberg models? Because each firm in the Bertrand model has an incentive to cut price as long as production remains profitable. If either firm cut its price, even slightly, it could expect to supply the entire market and thereby increase its profits. Consequently, each would set its price slightly below that of the other, until price was pushed down to the level of marginal cost (assumed to be the same for each firm). And at that price, economic profit would be zero (constant marginal cost means that marginal cost matches average cost).

To see that this is in fact the Nash equilibrium, notice that there would be no incentive for either firm to change its price once the price charged by both firms was set to equal marginal cost. If either lowered its price, then it would supply the entire market, but at a price that would fall short of marginal cost and the average cost. It would, therefore, be worse off than before because it would incur an economic loss. If either raised its price, on the other hand, then it would be no better off because it would sell nothing (because all buyers would patronize its rival).

Although the Bertrand model is of interest, it has plenty of shortcomings. For one thing, firms that produce exactly the same product seem to compete more by focusing on quantities than on prices, but at least now we know why. And even if they did focus on price, so that they set the same price in accord with the model, there is no real assurance that they would split the market equally. Notwithstanding these issues, though, the Bertrand model does drive home one major point: the firms' choice of strategic focus—price or output, in this case—can have a surprisingly major effect on the nature of equilibrium under oligopoly.

| Example 13.2 | **Pricing Coal from the Powder Ridge Basin** |

We now have a few models of duopoly behavior, and we have claimed that they are instructive in providing qualitative insight into the workings of oligopolistic markets. We have argued, for example, that these models suggest why and when it is important for firms to worry about each other as much as anything else. And we think that they have taught us that a limited number of suppliers can lead to economic inefficiency. But can we really believe them? The models are simple. But applying the Solow criteria from Chapter 1, do they "get it right," and are they credible?

It is generally difficult to answer these questions for duopoly because two firms seldom constitute the entire supply side of a market. Never say "never," though. Darius Gaskins discovered a "natural experiment" during his time in top management of the Burlington Northern Railroad—competition that developed in the late 1980s between Burlington Northern and CMW for shipping coal from the Powder Ridge Basin to Midwestern markets after the Staggers Act deregulated freight pricing. We will follow his lead in this example by using observed data from this "experiment" to explore whether or not any of our models seems to be descriptive of actual pricing behavior.

Just as Gaskins did before us, let's begin by hypothesizing a linear demand curve of the form

$$P = a - b(\text{coal shipped})$$

for shipping coal from the basin. Assuming constant marginal cost, denoted by c, he also observed that our theory thus far would produce the price and output combinations recorded in Table 13.1 for four different market structures. The prices reported in Table 13.1 are independent of the slope parameter from demand, though, so we only need estimates for the intercept and marginal cost to produce some idea of what price would have emerged if any of these structures had accurately described this market. Gaskins estimated that $a \approx 27$ mills per ton-mile and $c \approx 7$ mills per ton-mile. As a result, we can

| Table 13.1 | Market demand: $P = a - Bx$ | | | | |
| DUOPOLY EQUILIBRIA UNDER ALTERNATIVE MARKET STRUCTURES FOR LINEAR DEMAND AND CONSTANT MARGINAL COST | Constant marginal cost $= c$ | | | | |

Market demand: $P = a - Bx$
Constant marginal cost $= c$

Market structure	Firm I	Firm II	Total output	Price
Perfect competition	$(a - c)/2b$	$(a - c)/2b$	$(a - c)/b$	c
Bertrand competition	$(a - c)/2b$	$(a - c/2b$	$(a - c)/b$	c
Monopoly	$(a - c)/4b$	$(a - c)/4b$	$(a - c)/2b$	$(a + c)/2$
Cournot equilibrium	$(a - c)/3b$	$(a - c)/3b$	$2(a - c)/3b$	$(a + 2c)/3$
Stackelberg leader	$(a - c)/2b$	$(a - c)/4b$	$3(a - c)/4b$	$(a + 3c)/4$

(Table title: Table 13.1 — DUOPOLY EQUILIBRIA UNDER ALTERNATIVE MARKET STRUCTURES FOR LINEAR DEMAND AND CONSTANT MARGINAL COST. Column group header: Firm output over Firm I and Firm II.)

conclude that the price would have been 17 mills per ton-mile [i.e., from Table 13.1, $(1/2)(27 + 7)$ mills] if the two carriers were sharing monopoly profits. Not by colluding, mind you. That would have been illegal. This monopoly price would have been the Nash equilibrium of a series of repeating games of unknown duration, of the sort described in Example 12.7 with each player adopting a "tit-for-tat" strategy. If the two players had engaged in price competition in the Bertrand style, by way of contrast, then the price would have collapsed to the competitive level, 7 mills per ton-mile. If Burlington Northern and CMW had been Cournot players, then Table 13.1 tells us that 13.67 mills per ton-mile [i.e., $(1/3)(27 + 14)$ mills] would have been observed; and if one firm had been a Stackelberg leader, then roughly 12 mills per ton-mile [i.e., $(1/4)(27 + 21)$ mills] would have persisted over time.

What do the data show? Table 13.2 shows the time series. The price hovered between 15.2 mills and 16.7 mills per ton-mile in the early 1980s

Table 13.2	Year	Price (mills per ton-mile)
PRICE SERIES FOR SHIPPING COAL FROM THE POWDER RIDGE BASIN	1983	16.1
	1984	16.7
	1985	16.1
	1986	13.4
	1987	13.8
	1988	14.0
	1989	13.5
	1990	13.4
	1991	13.1
	1992	13.0
	1993	12.5
	1994	12.1
	1995	11.9
	1996	11.6
	1997	11.6

(Table title: Table 13.2 — PRICE SERIES FOR SHIPPING COAL FROM THE POWDER RIDGE BASIN.)

when only Burlington Northern carried the coal. These prices are, of course, very close to the estimated monopoly price of 17 mills per ton-mile. CMW entered the market in 1985, though, and the price started to fall in 1986. The decline continued until the end of the decade, when it seemed to converge to something close to 12 mills per ton-mile (actually flirting with 13 mills early in the 1990s before stabilizing within a range of 11.6 mills to 12.5 mills starting in 1992). It would appear, therefore, that the Stackelberg leader model was reasonably predictive; and in fact the management of Burlington Northern had followed a strategy of announcing hauling capacity well in advance of CMW and letting market bidding determine the price.

SOURCE: D. Gaskins, "A Naturally Occurring Duopoly Experiment," Wesleyan University Seminar, March 1999.

PRICE LEADERSHIP

Oligopolists who are faced with the difficulties of forming an effective cartel may attempt to collude implicitly. In other words, they may attempt to cooperate without actually making explicit agreements with one another. A useful model of this sort of oligopolistic behavior is based on the supposition that one of the firms in the industry is the **price leader.** This form of behavior seems to be quite common in oligopolistic industries where one firm (or a few firms) apparently sets the price and the rest follow its lead. Steel, nonferrous alloys, agricultural implements, and even commercial banking (where one bank tends to set the prime rate and other banks follow) come to mind as examples of industries that have been characterized by price leadership in one or more studies.

Price leader

To explore how such a market might operate, assume that there is a single large **dominant firm** in the industry and a number of small firms, called the "competitive fringe." Assume, as well, that the dominant firm sets the price for the industry knowing full well that firms in the "fringe" will take that price as given and sell as much as they want. That is why the "fringe" is "competitive"—each firm behaves as a price taker just as it would if it were operating in a competitive industry. To be more exact, each firm in the fringe produces an amount that is determined by setting marginal cost equal to the price announced by the leader. What can the leader sell in this environment? However much the market will bear at the announced price after the smaller firms have sold however much they choose to supply.

Dominant firm

The careful reader will wonder how we can speak of the price leader as a "dominant firm" when it will simply "mop up" demand after the fringe gets finished doing what it wants to do. The answer lies in the information that the dominant firm has. Just like the Stackelberg leader, this dominant firm *knows* how the fringe will respond to any price it might announce. And so it can take those reactions into account and mold the fringe's behavior

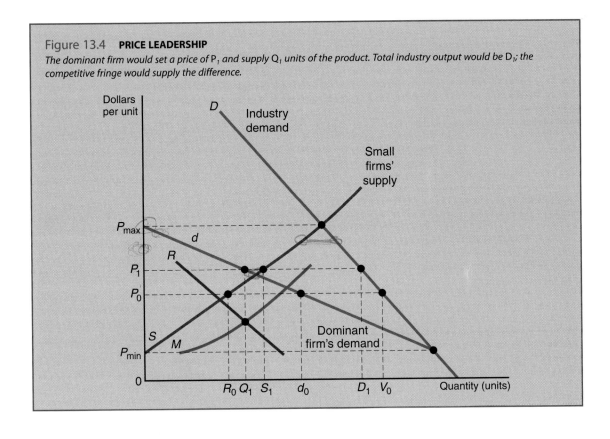

Figure 13.4 PRICE LEADERSHIP

The dominant firm would set a price of P₁ and supply Q₁ units of the product. Total industry output would be D₁; the competitive fringe would supply the difference.

to its own best interest. Remember, the leader is not a monopolist; it cannot simply assume the fringe away. It must instead cope with its existence, and an understanding of how the fringe will respond to its price decisions is a powerful tool in determining how to maximize profits.

Given the structure of this model, it is easy to derive the price that the dominant firm will set if it maximizes profits. Since each small firm takes the price as given, it produces the output at which price equals marginal cost. Thus a supply curve for all small firms combined can be drawn by summing horizontally the marginal-cost curves of the small firms. This supply curve is labeled S in Figure 13.4. The demand curve for the dominant firm can now be derived by subtracting the amount supplied by the small firms at each price from the total amount demanded at that price. Consequently, if curve D is the demand curve for the industry's product, then the effective demand curve for the output of the dominant firm, curve d, can be determined by finding the horizontal difference at each price between the demand curve D and the fringe's supply curve S.

To illustrate the derivation of demand curve d, suppose that the dominant firm set a price of P_{max}. The S curve shows that the small firms would then supply all that the market would demand so the leader would not be able to sell anything. Demand curve d therefore shows a 0 as the quantity for price P_{max}. What about price P_{min}? The supply curve S shows that the fringe would shut down at that price, so the leader could have the entire market to itself. Demand curve d therefore intersects the market demand curve D at price P_{min}. Now consider an intermediate price like P_0. The fringe would then supply R_0. The D curve shows that the total amount demanded would be V_0. And so the amount to be supplied by the dominant firm would be $V_0 - R_0$. This is the quantity shown on the effective demand curve d at price P_0. In other words, d_0 is set equal to $V_0 - R_0$. The process by which the other points on curve d are determined is exactly the same; this procedure can be repeated at various price levels.

Given the effective demand curve d for the dominant firm, it is a simple matter to derive the dominant firm's effective marginal-revenue curve R. It is equally simple to determine the output that will maximize the profits of the dominant firm: it is the quantity for which marginal cost reflected in curve M equals marginal revenue. And so output Q_1 highlighted in Figure 13.4 maximizes the leader's profit given price P_1 read from the effective demand curve d for output Q_1. Having announced that price, the leader will know that its profits would be maximized with total industry output equal to D_1; it follows that the small firms of the competitive fringe would supply $S_1 = D_1 - Q_1$ units of output. Is this a Nash equilibrium? Sure, as long as members of the fringe were not suffering economic losses. The leader would be maximizing profit, given the behavior of the other firms; it would have no incentive to change anything. And each member of the fringe would be equally happy because it would be maximizing profit given the behavior of the other members of the fringe and the dominant firm.

Example 13.3   OPEC as a Price Leader

If, as is often the case, a cartel controls only part of an industry, then perhaps the price leadership model can be used to analyze its behavior. The model has, for example, been applied successfully to describe why OPEC can play the role of a "dominant firm" in the international oil market. Example 12.5 suggested that OPEC tries, at least over the short to medium term, to maintain a stable price; but that behavior can be entirely consistent with maximizing profit as a price leader when the marginal cost of extraction is very small. It is estimated that the marginal cost of delivering a barrel of oil to market from Middle Eastern oil fields is 50 cents, so that condition certainly holds when the target price is in excess of $20 per barrel.

Can OPEC control price when it is so much larger than marginal cost? The extent to which a cartel can push the price around depends on the price elasticity of demand of curve d in Figure 13.4. The cartel could not, for example, push too hard if its effective demand were very price-elastic. And what could make effective demand elastic? Perhaps the supply offered by countries outside the cartel is elastic. In OPEC's case, however, this is not the case. The data reported for non-OPEC members in Table 12.2 have been quite stable over time, indicating that these countries consistently operate very close to their capacities; that is, their contribution to world supply is very inelastic, as a result.

Longer time periods make demand relatively price-elastic, of course, and this lesson has not been lost on the OPEC ministers. They have periodically worried about long-run demand rather than short-run demand in making their production and pricing decisions, but others have made this point in the academic literature. Martin Weitzman, for example, observed in the early days when OPEC began to flex its market muscles that ministers should be very wary of the long-run price elasticity of demand. High prices can inspire significant substitution out of oil and natural gas as well as significant energy conservation, more generally. Pushing too hard could therefore significantly erode the ability of a cartel like OPEC to exploit its leadership position in maximizing profits over the long run. Did they push too hard? Their market share has declined over time (from over 60 percent in the 1970s to around 50 percent at the turn of the century); so perhaps they have.

Has this newfound concern over long-run elasticity altered OPEC's behavior? It would appear so. Ministers have recently expressed as much concern about sudden reductions in even a portion of the supply delivered to the world market by their member nations as they have about overproduction. Why? Because they understand that sudden shortfalls can cause price spikes and price spikes can remind the world's importing countries that they need to pursue alternative supplies and vigorous conservation programs.

SOURCE: A. Shihab-Eldin, R. Lounnas, and G. Brennand, "Oil Outlook to 2020," *OPEC Review*, December 2001, pp. 291–314.

ENTRY AND CONTESTABLE MARKETS

We now turn our attention to the importance of the entry of new firms and the exit of old firms in modifying the structure of an oligopolistic industry. An oligopolistic industry may not be oligopolistic for long if every potential investor with a few extra dollars can enter. Whether or not the industry remains oligopolistic in the face of relatively easy entry depends on the size of the market for the product relative to the optimum size of the firm. If the market is small relative to the optimum size of the firm in this industry, then economies of scale will tend to keep the number of firms small enough to preserve the oligopoly.

There are a variety of other barriers to entry. Entry into some industries requires new firms to build and maintain large, complicated, and expensive plants. The scale of this sort of undertaking is likely to discourage many potential entrants. The existence of patents can also make entry difficult. And then there is the availability (or lack thereof) of raw materials. This factor is often cited in the case of industries for which nickel, sulfur, diamonds, or bauxite is a requisite input. Finally, the government itself is sometimes responsible for creating barriers to entry. Taxicabs and buses must often obtain governmentally issued franchises; local licensing laws may limit the number of plumbers, barbers, and so on.

It is not always the case, however, that entry into an oligopolistic industry is very difficult. Economists speak of **contestable markets** when they discuss

Contestable markets

markets for which "entry is absolutely free, and exit is absolutely costless."[1] The essence of contestable markets is that they are vulnerable to hit-and-run entry. "Even a very transient profit opportunity need not be neglected by a potential entrant, for he can go in, and before prices change, collect his gains and then depart without cost, should the climate grow hostile."[2]

Ease of entry means that a contestable market would perform much like a competitive market, even though it contains only a few firms (or perhaps only one firm). Economic profit would tend to be zero. If profit were positive, a new entrant could enter the market, produce the same output (at the same cost) as a firm already in the market, undercut the existing firm's price slightly, and make a profit. Entrants would do this if economic profit were positive, and the price would be pushed down to the point where economic profit was zero. In other words, entrants could "hit and run" if they wished; this possibility dictates what equilibrium will look like.

Equilibrium in a contestable market would mimic a competitive equilibrium because firms would produce where average costs are minimized. Why? Because firms would otherwise enter the industry, produce at lower costs than the existing firms, undercut the existing firms' price, and make a profit. Moreover, price could not exceed marginal cost in equilibrium. If existing firms were charging a price in excess of marginal cost, then it would again be profitable for an entrant to undercut the price of the existing firms.

To illustrate this sort of equilibrium for a contestable market, suppose that an industry contained three firms. Let Figure 13.5 display the marginal- and

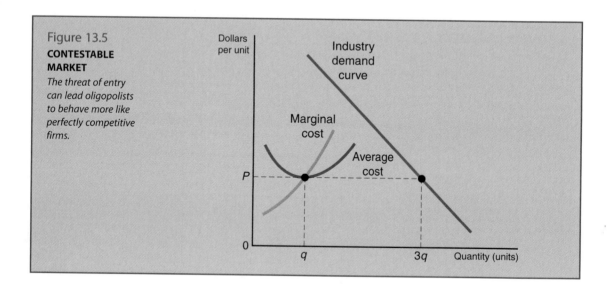

Figure 13.5

CONTESTABLE MARKET

The threat of entry can lead oligopolists to behave more like perfectly competitive firms.

[1]W. Baumol, "Contestable Markets: An Uprising in the Theory of Industry Structure," *American Economic Review*, March 1982, p. 3. Also see W. Baumol, J. Panzar, and R. Willig, *Contestable Markets and the Theory of Industry Structure* (San Diego: Harcourt Brace Jovanovich, 1982).
[2]Baumol, "Contestable Markets," p. 4. For criticism of this theory, see W. Shepherd, "Competition versus Contestability," *American Economic Review*, June 1984.

average-cost curves for each. If each firm produced q units of output and charged a price of P, then total output would be 3 times q and all three firms would earn zero economic profit. These firms could try to collude to push up the price, but they would be ill-advised to do so. They should understand that new firms could enter the market very quickly and undercut their price. So, given that entrants could sell the product at a price of P, each firm would indeed maximize its profit by producing q units of output and selling it at price P.

The theory of contestable markets is only about 20 years old, but it has already provoked considerable controversy. Its critics charge that it is based on extremely unrealistic assumptions concerning entry and exit. In reality, of course, entry is not free and exit is not costless. But is the model useful in the sense articulated in Chapter 1? It is too early to tell, at this point. Without question, though, this relatively new theory has had a noteworthy impact on the way many economists view oligopoly. It has certainly taught us all that assuming substantial barriers to entry could be extraordinarily misleading.

Example 13.4	WorldCom, AT&T, and the Fax Wars

AT&T controlled nearly two-thirds of the United States fax market at the end of 1997—a market whose annual revenues amounted to nearly $7 billion at that time. AT&T's position was relatively secure, except for the potential entry by WorldCom with a brand-new technology that would use Internet connections instead of phone lines.

Where did WorldCom come from? It began as a small long-distance phone company in Mississippi, but it quickly grew to the fourth largest long-distance provider in the nation by buying up its rivals. It gained access to local phone networks by acquiring MFS Communications in 1996. And it worked out a deal with CompuServe and America Online to expand ownership of UUNet into the largest Internet service provider in the world.

Why did AT&T have to worry? WorldCom worked from its position to introduce UUFax—a service that allows faxes to travel over the Internet instead of regular long-distance lines for about half the cost. As suggested by the contestable markets literature, AT&T was left with the choice of holding firm with its pricing structure and seeing market share fall or reducing its revenues directly by lowering its prices.

STRATEGIC MOVES

Assuming barriers to entry is one thing, but what about creating barriers to entry? Perhaps the most important lesson of the theory of contestable markets is that there may be considerable benefit to erecting structures that dissuade potential entrants and thereby preserve some degree of market power even if they are not costless. To evaluate those benefits, though, existing firms must understand how and why potential rivals might become discouraged; and so game-theoretic constructions can once again provide some productive insights. Following the lead of Thomas Schelling, a past president of the American Economic Association, the rest of the chapter will be devoted to expanding the application of game theory to frame the decisions of oligopolists in terms of strategic moves that, in Schelling's words, influence "the other person's choice in a manner favorable to one's self, by affecting the other person's expectations of how one's self will behave."[3] For example, managers of an existing firm with market power might react strategically to a rival's price cut by reducing their own price to a level that imposes losses on their upstart rival. Why? Because such a move could punish the rival; we will argue here that it might also influence how other firms *expect* them to behave. Responding with a lower price would, in this context, be a strategic move because it could influence how other firms would behave in the future.

Firms can engage in a variety of types of strategic moves. Some may not be threatening to a firm's rivals in any way. American Airlines might, for example, raise some of its fares in the hope that rival airlines might follow suit. The problem with such a move is that other airlines may not cooperate by increasing their fares. If such a move could be rescinded quickly and cheaply, then this problem might not be very important in the grand scheme of things. But if this sort of quick and inexpensive retreat were not possible, then such a move would be very risky.

Other types of moves are clearly threatening in nature. The American Hospital Supply Corporation once considered marketing a newly developed container for intravenous solutions. This move threatened Baxter Travenol Laboratories, which already sold products of this type. In weighing the pros and cons of making such a move, a firm must try to estimate how likely it is that there will be retaliation, judge its speed, and assess its potential effects. The American Hospital Supply Corporation determined that the pros outweighed the cons and proceeded with its marketing plans, and it met substantial retaliation from Baxter. Indeed, Baxter cut its prices considerably and tried as hard as possible to wrest business away from the American Hospital Supply Corporation.[4]

To prevent its rivals from carrying out threatening moves, a firm often tries to lead its rivals to believe that they can expect rapid and effective retaliation if they attempt any move that might be threatening. Firms often engage in vicious price-cutting, for example, to drive out a firm that enters their market. The idea is that this will (1) hurt the actual entrant and (2) teach other potential entrants that it does not pay to threaten or challenge them.

[3]See T. Schelling, *The Strategy of Conflict* (New York: Oxford University Press, 1960); as well as M. Porter, *Competitive Strategy* (New York: Free Press, 1980). Many of the concepts and results presented here are explored in more detail in these two early contributions to the game-theoretic literature.
[4]See Schelling, *The Strategy of Conflict,* for a full account of this episode.

Commitment is an important element of any firm's strategic planning. If a firm can convince its rivals that it is unequivocally committed to a particular move, then those rivals may back down without retaliating. They might conclude that they would lose more than they would gain from a protracted struggle. If a firm can convince its rivals that it is unequivocally committed to retaliate if a rival makes one particular move or another, then no rival may make such a move.

Commitments tend to be more persuasive, of course, if they seem binding and irreversible. Suppose that a firm decided to enter a particular market. If this firm bought a plant rather than leasing it, then it would be signaling a significant and potentially irreversible (at least in the short run) commitment to entering. If it signed a long-term contract for raw materials instead of a short-term deal, then other firms would get the same message. Or suppose that a firm committed itself to meeting any price reduction offered to the marketplace by any of its rivals. If this firm made written or spoken agreements with customers to meet any price cut, then it would make such a commitment irreversible and thus more persuasive. But if a firm's rivals felt that the firm could easily renounce or ignore a particular commitment, then they would not be terribly likely to pay much attention to any announced commitment.

To be credible, though, a firm's commitments must be backed up with the assets and expertise required to carry them out. If a firm committed itself to invading another firm's market if the latter firm invaded first, then it must have the financial power and technological skill needed to act on this commitment. Firms' commitments are thus more credible if they have long histories of staying true to their word. Here, as in other aspects of life, firms' and their managers' reputations count. Rivals of a firm with a well-deserved reputation for honoring its past commitments will likely pay careful attention to whatever new commitments it makes.

THREATS: EMPTY AND CREDIBLE

Firms frequently send signals to one another indicating their intentions, motives, and objectives. Some signals come in the form of threats. For example, suppose that the Smith Company learned that the Jones Corporation, its principal rival, intended to lower the price of its competing commodity. Smith could announce its intention of lowering its own price significantly, and thus signal to Jones that it would be willing to engage in a price war if Jones went ahead with its price reduction. Indeed, some of Smith's executives would likely make sure that this message got transmitted indirectly to some of Jones's executives.

Not all threats are credible, though. If, for example, the payoff matrix shown in Figure 13.6 were applicable, then Smith's threat would not be very credible. To see why, let's compare Smith's profits if it were to set a low price with its profits with a high price. (For simplicity, assume that price can be set at only one of these two levels.) If Jones set a high price, then Smith would make

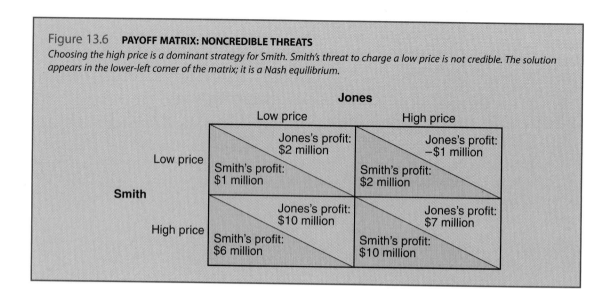

Figure 13.6 **PAYOFF MATRIX: NONCREDIBLE THREATS**

Choosing the high price is a dominant strategy for Smith. Smith's threat to charge a low price is not credible. The solution appears in the lower-left corner of the matrix; it is a Nash equilibrium.

$10 million if it set a high price and $2 million if it set a low price. If Jones set a low price, though, Smith would make $6 million if it set a high price and $1 million if it set a low price. Regardless of whether Jones set a high price or a low price, therefore, Smith would do better charging the higher price.

Given the outcomes depicted in Figure 13.6, then, it certainly seems unlikely that Smith would carry out its threat to cut its price to the lower level. After all, as we've just seen, Smith would earn higher profits by keeping its price high even if Jones cut its price. As a result, Jones could dismiss Smith's threat as no more than an empty gesture if it could be sure that Smith would take the course of action that maximized its profit.

Smith would nonetheless prefer that Jones not cut its price. If Smith could convince Jones that it would not choose to hold its price high and thereby maximize its profit, then it could make its threat credible. Specifically, if Smith could convince Jones that it would match Jones if Jones set the low price even though this response would lower Smith's own profits, then Jones might decide not to set the low price. After all, Jones's profits would be higher ($7 million versus $2 million) if it maintained a high price (and Smith did the same).

How could Smith convince Jones that it would lower its price, even though to do so would seem to be irrational? Smith's managers may develop a reputation for doing what they say, regardless of the costs. They may have a well-publicized taste for facing down opponents and for refusing to back down, regardless of how crazy their actions might appear to be. Faced with the "irrational" Smith Company, the Jones Corporation might then decide not to cut its price. But it Smith could not convince Jones of its irrationality, then Jones would rightly regard Smith's threat to lower its price as not credible, and Jones would opt for its preferred strategy (given the expectation that Smith will keep its price high)—cutting its price.

Firms, like nations and politicians, try to discourage entrants from invading their turf. We have seen repeatedly that the entry of new firms into a market can reduce the profits of existing firms. To illustrate the situation, consider the Mason Company, which faces the threat of entry by the Newton Company. Figure 13.7 shows the profits of each firm, depending on whether Newton enters the market and on whether Mason resists Newton's entry (for example, by cutting price and increasing output). Notice that there is no difference in Mason's profit figures if Newton does not enter the market; there is simply no difference in Mason's circumstances without the confusion caused by a new entrant.

In this game, the first move is up to Newton. It must decide whether or not to enter. If it enters, Mason must decide whether or not to resist. On the basis of the payoff matrix in Figure 13.7, Mason would not resist if it were rational, because its profits would be $1 million less (that is, $2 million rather than $3 million) if it resisted. Knowing this, Newton will enter, because its profits will be $3 million higher (that is, $11 million rather than $8 million). Mason might threaten to resist, of course, because it would prefer that Newton not enter. But the threat would not be credible given the nature of the payoff matrix in Figure 13.7 (and assuming that Mason would behave rationally). The game's solution would see Newton entering the market, and Mason would not resist; Newton would earn $11 million in profit while Mason would see profits of only $3 million.

What could Mason do to deter Newton's entry into the market? The difference in Mason's profits with and without Newton in the market is very large, so there could easily be some "wiggle room" within which Mason could alter the game. It could, to be more specific, alter the payoff matrix

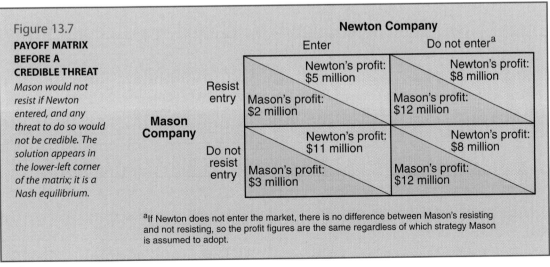

Figure 13.7

PAYOFF MATRIX BEFORE A CREDIBLE THREAT

Mason would not resist if Newton entered, and any threat to do so would not be credible. The solution appears in the lower-left corner of the matrix; it is a Nash equilibrium.

	Newton Company	
	Enter	Do not enter[a]
Mason Company Resist entry	Newton's profit: $5 million / Mason's profit: $2 million	Newton's profit: $8 million / Mason's profit: $12 million
Do not resist entry	Newton's profit: $11 million / Mason's profit: $3 million	Newton's profit: $8 million / Mason's profit: $12 million

[a]If Newton does not enter the market, there is no difference between Mason's resisting and not resisting, so the profit figures are the same regardless of which strategy Mason is assumed to adopt.

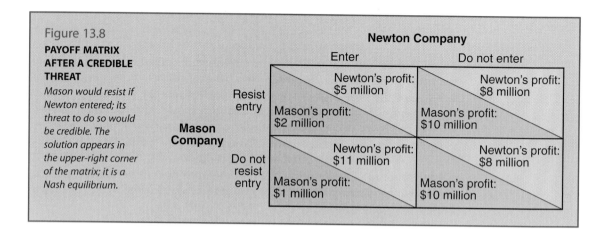

Figure 13.8

PAYOFF MATRIX AFTER A CREDIBLE THREAT

Mason would resist if Newton entered; its threat to do so would be credible. The solution appears in the upper-right corner of the matrix; it is a Nash equilibrium.

Newton Company

		Enter	Do not enter
Mason Company	Resist entry	Newton's profit: $5 million / Mason's profit: $2 million	Newton's profit: $8 million / Mason's profit: $10 million
	Do not resist entry	Newton's profit: $11 million / Mason's profit: $1 million	Newton's profit: $8 million / Mason's profit: $10 million

by building some excess productive capacity—capacity that would be unnecessary if Newton did not enter, but that could be used to increase output (and lower price) if Newton did choose to enter. It costs money to keep excess capacity on hand, of course, and so Mason's profits would be reduced by, say, $2 million if it did not resist entry or if Newton did not enter the market. Having excess capacity on hand could, though, allow Mason to maintain its profitability if Newton did enter and Mason chose to resist. How? Selling more product, even at a lower cost, could generate more revenue, while having more capacity could lower average cost.

It turns out, however, that this does not matter; Newton will no longer see any advantage to entering the market. Figure 13.8 displays a new payoff matrix. Notice that it shows no change in Mason's profit level if Newton entered and Mason chose to fight; that is, the $2 million in profit recorded in the upper left-hand box is the same as in Figure 13.7. Notice, more importantly, that Mason's profits would now be greater if it resisted Newton's entry than if it did not ($2 million versus $1 million in the left-hand column of the matrix). As a result, Mason's threat to resist has become credible and Newton will not enter (the top row shows $5 million in profit with entry that is less than the $8 million that Newton would otherwise earn given that Mason will resist).

As paradoxical as it may seem, Mason's building excess capacity would convince Newton not to enter even though it would reduce Mason's own profits if it did not resist entry. The strategy would work, though, because the excess capacity amounts to making an irrevocable commitment to fight. If Newton entered, Mason would be ready to fight (by increasing output and driving price down) *and* would have an incentive to fight (since its profits would be higher than if it did not fight). Indeed, the altered game's solution would see Newton resisting the temptation to enter so that its profit would stay at $8 million while Mason would enjoy $10 million. Comparing solutions, then, Mason's return to building capacity that it would not use would be an extra $7 million (this $10 million minus the $3 million that emerged from the solution to the earlier game).

| **Example 13.5** | **Airport Slots, Potential Competition, and Barriers to Entry** |

The European Union opened all of its airports to service by any European carrier on April 1, 1997. The hope was that the threat of entry would inspire state-owned airlines to become more efficient because they would suddenly face the threat of increased competition from airlines that could charge lower fares. Did analysts see much hope that lower fares would materialize? Not really, for two reasons.

The predatory behavior of existing state-owned airlines that were still being subsidized by their governments was the source of their first concern. Governments typically subsidize their national airlines, and this simple fact made their threat of resisting a new entrant by dramatically lowering prices extremely credible. If the resulting losses would be covered by increased subsidies, it should be little surprise that few airlines took up the challenge of entering a market that would bring along the ravages of a prolonged price war.

Second, many European airports had a shortage of landing slots. At Heathrow in the United Kingdom and at Frankfurt in Germany, this capacity constraint was real. All of the slots were claimed by one airline or another nearly all of the time. At other airports, though, the obstruction was political—national policies that dictated airport policy typically favored the domestic carrier even if there was excess capacity. In either case, the new rules persisted in the convention that airlines would lose slots only if they did not use them. It should be no surprise that airlines routinely invested in "excess capacity" by flying inefficient routes (sometimes at a loss) simply to make sure that they were using all of their allotted slots.

LIMIT PRICING

Limit price   A **limit price** is a price that discourages or prevents entry. Economists have often asserted that a firm can deter entry by keeping its price relatively low. Paul Milgrom has used game theory to suggest why this might be true. To see his logic, suppose that Moran Manufacturing was a very low-cost producer of hardware. If potential entrants knew how low, they would not be foolish enough to enter the industry. But they would have no reliable way of estimating Moran's costs. Surely Moran would like to exploit at least some of its monopoly power, so price would not be a guide. Nor would annual reports or accounting statements; most companies are so complex that public versions of these documents do not provide sufficient detail.

Moran could, however, signal potential entrants that it is a very low-cost producer by setting relatively low prices. Profits would be lower in the short run, to be sure; but profits over the long term could be much higher if Moran could lower the likelihood that it would have to share the market with a potential entrant. Simply announcing low costs would not work, especially if prices were markedly higher; we can expect that potential entrants would be smart enough to see through that sort of ruse.

Example 13.6 | **Playing a Game with Incomplete Knowledge**

We know, from previous discussions, that Nash equilibria are based on the twin assumptions of perfect, error-free decision-making and consistent behavior, but we have just seen that the limit-pricing model depends critically on how people respond to incomplete information. The idea is that an existing firm can discourage potential entrants from exploring a market by signaling, albeit imperfectly, that its production costs are low. Potential entrants will, of course, find out if the signal is accurate only by giving it a try. What can game theory, and its core concept of Nash equilibrium, teach us about this circumstance? Jacob Goeree and Charles Holt have recently published a paper in which they report the results of a variety of experiments that were designed to explore questions like this; and one of their examples seems to be close to the mark for considering the validity of a game-theoretic approach to limit pricing. They call this example the "one-shot traveler's dilemma game."

In this game, two players independently choose an integer between 180 and 300. Both players are paid the lower of the two numbers, but an amount R is transferred from the player with the higher number to the one with the lower number. For instance, if one person chooses 210 and the other chooses 250, then they receive $210 + R$ and $(210 - R)$, respectively. What is the Nash equilibrium? It would clearly be best for either player to undercut the other by 1, so 300 cannot be a good choice. But if both players recognize this, then 299 cannot be a good choice, either. Reasoning in the spirit of the Bertrand model, only the lower bound of 180 survives this iterated decision process and emerges as the Nash equilibrium; and this conclusion is independent of the size of R. How can this be made to look like a limit-pricing game? Look at the imperfectly informed world of a potential entrant. From that perspective, a low-cost incumbent firm could undercut a price so that it could claim at least some of any anticipated profit from the entrant as long as the entrant anticipated costs higher than the absolute minimum.

But do people routinely make such rational and consistent determinations? More generically, can the limit-pricing theory (or any theory, for that matter) rely completely on the power of rationality? Goeree and Holt offer a number of illustrations designed to explore this question. Their answer would probably be "with care." For example, they asked 50 subjects to play the traveler's dilemma game with $R = 5$ and then with $R = 180$. The results of their experiment are displayed in Figure 13.9. With $R = 180$, nearly 80 percent of the participants chose strategies that were very close to the Nash equilibrium. So far, so good. With $R = 5$, however, roughly 80 percent chose numbers that were very close to 300; indeed, the average bid was 280. Notwithstanding the theoretical result, behavior clearly depended on the potential payoff. As we view the limit-pricing model, therefore, perhaps we need to recognize that the signal would be most powerful and the theory most predictive if it included the credible threat that a low-cost producer has the capacity to respond quickly and

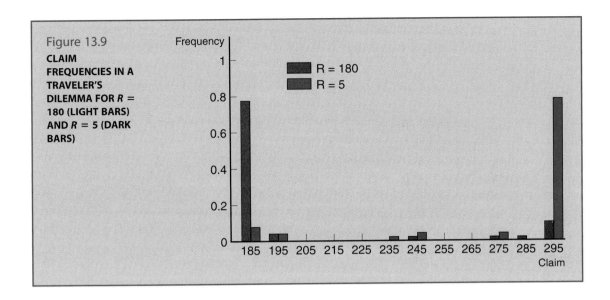

Figure 13.9

CLAIM FREQUENCIES IN A TRAVELER'S DILEMMA FOR R = 180 (LIGHT BARS) AND R = 5 (DARK BARS)

forcefully to maintain a large market share by cutting prices close to its cost; that is, the penalty to having the audacity to challenge would have to be severe.

SOURCE: J. Goeree and C. Holt, "Ten Little Treasures of Game Theory and Ten Intuitive Contradictions," *American Economic Review,* vol. 91, no. 5, December 2001, pp. 1402–1422.

CAPACITY EXPANSION AND PREEMPTION

The notion of preemptive strategies offers a context within which to expand our consideration of capacity decisions. The decision of whether and how much to expand production capacity is one of the most important strategic decisions made by a firm. Indeed, some firms can adopt a **preemptive strategy** that would involve trying to expand before their rivals and thereby discourage competitors from building extra capacity of their own. It can be an effective strategy in markets where the future growth of demand can be forecast with reasonable precision.

Preemptive strategy

To explore this point, suppose that two firms, the Monroe Company and the Madison Corporation, were the only producers and sellers of a particular kind of machine tool. Assume that the demand for this type of machine tool is growing substantially and that each firm is considering the construction of an additional plant. The payoff matrix is shown in Figure 13.10. If only one of the firms built an additional plant, then it would make $10 million, but if both firms built added capacity, then both would lose $5 million. Why? Because there would then be too much capacity. The status quo in which neither firm builds an additional plant is the competitive equilibrium in which both firms earn zero (pure economic) profit.

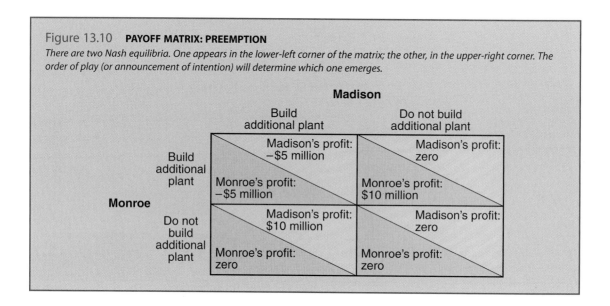

Figure 13.10 **PAYOFF MATRIX: PREEMPTION**

There are two Nash equilibria. One appears in the lower-left corner of the matrix; the other, in the upper-right corner. The order of play (or announcement of intention) will determine which one emerges.

Madison

	Build additional plant	Do not build additional plant
Monroe Build additional plant	Madison's profit: −$5 million / Monroe's profit: −$5 million	Madison's profit: zero / Monroe's profit: $10 million
Do not build additional plant	Madison's profit: $10 million / Monroe's profit: zero	Madison's profit: zero / Monroe's profit: zero

There are two Nash equilibria in this game (just as in the "first-mover" illustration given earlier). In the first, Madison alone would build an additional plant; in the other, Monroe would be alone with an additional plant. Which equilibrium emerges depends on which firm moves first. If Madison moved first, then it would choose to build an additional plant since it would know that Monroe's rational response would be to stand pat (otherwise, it would build the market's second additional plant and would lose $5 million). Similarly, if Monroe moved first, it would choose to build an additional plant because Madison's rational response would be to defer.

Preemptive strategies can be risky, though. If, for example, the demand for the product grew more slowly than expected (or not at all), then the firm that pursued this strategy could be stuck with a plant that would be an unprofitable "white elephant," perhaps for a long period of time. Moreover, assessing the value of undertaking a preemptive strategy relies heavily on a complete understanding of how rivals will respond. Suppose that its rival refused to yield to this preemptive strategy and built its own additional plant. Why would it do that? Either because it was irrational or because it had an overly optimistic forecast of growth in future demand. As predicted by the Bertrand model, the industry could then plunge into a price war that could do serious harm to both firms.

Example 13.7	**McDonald's Failure to Preemptively Expand Capacity**

McDonald's restaurants dominate many streets in many towns across the United States, so it is hard to think that there are too few golden arches dotting the American landscape. Nonetheless, a slowdown in the pace of expansion once apparently caused some trouble that perhaps could have been avoided. The fast-food market had always been competitive, but internal documents from the middle of the 1990s reveal that McDonald's had added the adjective "hostile" to the perception of it. Indeed, those documents suggest strongly that McDonald's had contributed to its significant competitive difficulties by not building very many new restaurants in the 1980s. Combined with prices that were a bit too high, the slowdown essentially opened an umbrella for people to come in underneath. And once there, these competitors reduced prices and expanded their own real estate development in new towns. The result: more competitors in more places than would otherwise have been the case, and price competition that threatened to erode the market power of the world's largest feeder.

SOURCE: R. Gibson, "Changes at McDonald's Suggest Trouble in McFamily," *Wall Street Journal*, September 27, 1995.

NONPRICE COMPETITION

Many firms operating in oligopolistic industries tend to use nonprice competition, such as advertising and variation in product characteristics, as a strategic weapon. They seem to view price-cutting as a dangerous tactic, since it can start a price war that may have grave long-term consequences. Advertising and product variation are viewed, in contrast, as less risky ways of wooing customers away from competitors.

When a firm advertises, it attempts to shift the demand curve for its product to the right. Recall from Chapter 11 that an effective advertising campaign can make it possible for a firm to sell more at the same price. How does this work? Firms can use advertising to differentiate their product from those of their competitors, and customers may be induced to stick with a particular brand name even though the products of all firms in the industry are much the same. For example, various brands of beer are quite similar, but they are not identical (at least they come in different bottles and cans). Watch sports programs on TV for an afternoon, and it will be clear that the beer industry spends tens of millions of dollars a year on advertising to impress its brand names, and whatever differences exist among brands, on the consumer.

Advertising expenditures sometimes only raise the costs of the entire industry, since one firm's advertising campaign causes other firms to increase their advertising. The total market for the industry's product may not increase in response to the increased advertising, and the effects on the sales of individual firms may actually cancel out. Once every firm has increased its advertising expenditures, though, no single firm can reduce them to their former size without losing sales. And so cost curves—including both production and selling costs—are pushed upward.

To see why an individual firm may spend a large amount on advertising even though its profits might have been higher with a smaller advertising budget, recall the prisoners' dilemma. If each firm believed that its profits would fall if its rival spent more on advertising, it might feel that a large advertising budget was in its own interest even though its profits would be larger if everyone agreed to spend less on advertising. This is the situation

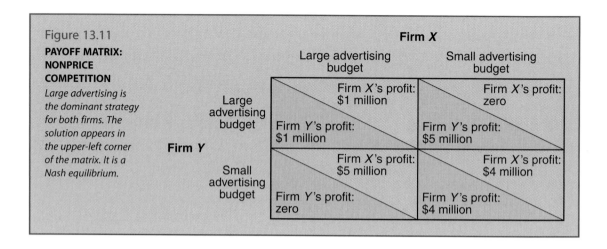

Figure 13.11

PAYOFF MATRIX: NONPRICE COMPETITION

Large advertising is the dominant strategy for both firms. The solution appears in the upper-left corner of the matrix. It is a Nash equilibrium.

Firm X

		Large advertising budget	Small advertising budget
Firm Y	Large advertising budget	Firm X's profit: $1 million / Firm Y's profit: $1 million	Firm X's profit: zero / Firm Y's profit: $5 million
	Small advertising budget	Firm X's profit: $5 million / Firm Y's profit: zero	Firm X's profit: $4 million / Firm Y's profit: $4 million

depicted in Figure 13.11. Both firms X and Y would be expected to adopt large advertising budgets (since this is the dominant strategy for each firm), even though both would enjoy higher profits ($4 million rather than $1 million) if they both adopted small advertising budgets.

Oligopolistic firms frequently vary the characteristics of their products even as they conduct advertising campaigns in order to differentiate their products from those of their competitors. They can, in this way, also manipulate the demand curves for their products. Changes in product, like other competitive tactics, often result in retaliatory moves by competitors, of course. Successful changes in design or quality tend to be imitated by competitors (who may lag behind to some degree), and they can be expensive. The automobile industry has been engaged in intense competition of this sort for many years, and the annual cost of model changes can be as high as $5 billion or more.

Example 13.8 | **Nonprice Competition with the Big Guns**

Never underestimate the power of nonprice competition; but don't expect that its benefits will last forever. These are the lessons of Corel Corporation and its short-lived success in competing with Microsoft in the market for software "suites"—bundles of office applications that businesses use. Microsoft Office has, of course, been the dominant product in this market for a long time. It controlled 90 percent of the suites market in the mid-1990s when Michael Cowpland crafted a strategy designed to link Word-Perfect (newly acquired at a bargain-basement price from Novell) with Corel's graphics program called Draw.

The strategy was a gamble, because WordPerfect had fallen out of favor (sales in 1994 were $407 million, down from $629 million in 1993) to the point where its host suite claimed only 3.6 percent of the market. It combined undercutting Microsoft by 50 percent in price with an aggressive plan to advertise widely, offer frequent updates to adopters through the Internet, and provide immediate on-line service for problems and custom designs. And it worked, at least for a while. Sales rose in June 1996 to 80,000 units— a 400 percent increase from the previous year to a total that exactly matched Office for the month. But immediate success did not guarantee long-term success. Customers were slow to upgrade to a Windows 95 version, and corporate adoptions lagged even in the middle of 1996. As a result, the promise of rapid emergence into an extremely dynamic market soon eroded. WordPerfect has not become a significant challenger to Word, and the Corel suite has not gained market share at the expense of Office.

THE EFFECTS OF OLIGOPOLY

Having completed our discussion of strategic moves, let's return to the general topic of oligopoly. We have considered some of economists' favorite oligopoly models over the past two chapters. Since there is no agreement that any of these models is an adequate general representation of oligopolistic behavior, it is difficult to estimate the effects of an oligopolistic market structure on price, output, and profits. Nevertheless, we can draw a few general conclusions.

First, the models we have discussed usually indicate that price will be higher under oligopoly than under perfect competition. The difference between the oligopoly price and the perfectly competitive price will depend, of course, on the number of firms in the industry and the case of entry. The larger the number of firms and the easier it is to enter the industry, the closer the oligopoly price will be to the perfectly competitive level.

Second, if the demand curve is the same under oligopoly as under perfect competition, then it also follows that output will be less under oligopoly than under perfect competition. It is not always reasonable, however, to assume that the demand curve is the same under oligopoly as under perfect competition. The large expenditures for advertising and product variation that characterize many oligopolistic markets may tend to shift the demand curve to the right. In some cases, therefore, both price and output may be higher under oligopoly than under perfect competition.

Third, the use of some resources for advertising and product variation can certainly be worthwhile, since advertising provides buyers with information and product differentiation allows greater freedom of choice. Whether oligopolies spend too much for these purposes is by no means obvious. It is sometimes claimed, nonetheless, that in some oligopolistic industries such expenditures have been expanded beyond the levels that are socially optimal.

Fourth, one would expect on the basis of most oligopoly models that the profits earned by oligopolists would be higher, on average, than the profits earned by perfectly competitive firms. A seminal study authored more than 50 years ago by J. Bain reported that firms in industries in which the largest firms had a high proportion of total sales tended to have higher rates

	Output			Profit			
Model	Firm I	Firm II	Total	Firm I	Firm II	Total	Price
Cournot	$(a - c)/3b$	$(a - c)/3b$	$2(a - c)/3b$	$(a - c)^2/9b$	$(a - c)^2/9b$	$2(a - c)^2/9b$	$(a + 2c)/3$
Stackelberg	$(a - c)/2b$	$(a - c)/4b$	$3(a - c)/4b$	$(a - c)^2/8b$	$(a - c)^2/16b$	$3(a - c)^2/16b$	$(a + 3c)/4$
Bertrand	$(a - c)/2b$	$(a - c)/2b$	$(a - c)/b$	0	0	0	c
Monopoly	$(a - c)/4b$	$(a - c)/4b$	$(a - c)/2b$	$(a - c)^2/8b$	$(a - c)^2/8b$	$(a - c)^2/4b$	$(a + 2c)/2$

of return than firms in industries in which the largest firms had a small proportion of total sales. At what cost? There has been considerable disagreement over the interpretation of this sort of evidence. Some point to an abuse of market power and assess large costs. Others argue that results such as these are due in large measure to the superior efficiency of the largest firms in oligopolistic industries.

Microlink 13.1 Market Equilibria for Linear Demand

Table 13.3 expands on Table 13.1 in its elaboration of the nature of market equilibria under alternative forms of market structure given linear demand of the form

$$P = a - bX_T$$

and given constant marginal cost c. The parameters a and b are both positive. Notice that the total quantity demanded is highest under the Bertrand assumption of price competition; indeed, it matches the competitive equilibrium of $(a - c)/b$ with a market clearing price that matches marginal cost. The monopoly output is smallest, and comes with the highest price [determined directly by substituting the profit-maximizing monopoly output $(a - c)/2b$ directly into the demand curve]. Colluding duopolists could achieve this as a cooperative solution to the game depicted in Example 12.6. The Stackelberg and Cournot solutions can both be achieved by manipulating the more general reaction curves of Example 12.2. Notice that the Cournot duopolists each produce one-third of the competitive output. Note, as well, that the output of the Stackelberg firm matches the monopoly output and that its Cournot market mate is consigned to 50 percent of that amount. Since they therefore combine for three-fourths of the competitive output, the price that they charge is lower than if both remained Cournot.

SUMMARY

1. Stackelberg and Bertrand models represent two early elaborations of how economists try to describe the behavior of oligopolistic firms.
2. The "price leader" model is based on the supposition that one of the firms in the industry is a price leader and that other firms operate as price takers.

3. The theory of contestable markets emerged in the 1980s. It assumes that entry is absolutely free and exit is absolutely costless. According to this theory, the threat of entry means that oligopolists should behave much like perfectly competitive firms. The theory remains controversial, but it has taught us that assumptions about the ease or difficulty of entry into a market are critical.

4. A firm can engage in a variety of types of strategic moves. Some are threatening to its rivals, but others are not. Commitment is an important element of a firm's strategic planning. A firm that can convince its rivals that it is unequivocally committed to a particular move can discourage those rivals from retaliating since they may be convinced that they would lose more than they would gain from a protracted struggle.

5. Although firms frequently threaten their rivals, not all threats are credible. One way for a firm to make its threats credible is to develop a reputation for doing what it says, regardless of the costs. In another, a firm can alter the payoff matrix to make its threat credible. Either strategy can be effective in deterring entry, for example.

6. The firm that makes the first move often has an advantage. Some firms therefore adopt preemptive strategies when it comes to investment decisions. They try, in practical terms, to expand before their rivals do (or at least send a credible signal that they intend to expand first).

7. The effects of oligopoly are difficult to predict, but most models suggest that price and profits will tend to be higher than under perfect competition. Since oligopolists frequently engage in nonprice competition, advertising and product differentiation can be very important.

QUESTIONS/ PROBLEMS

1. American Coach Lines of Maryland sold its Washington, D.C., bus terminal to Peter Pan, the country's largest privately owned bus company, on June 1, 1992. On July 24, 1992, Peter Pan cut its one-way fare on the Washington–New York route from $25 to $9.95. Greyhound, its only rival on this route, responded by cutting its one-way fare to $7. Peter Pan answered with $6.95. Greyhound went to $5, and Peter Pan matched it. It costs about $480 to operate a bus that can carry 47 passengers from New York to Washington. (a) Is this an example of a contestable market? Why or why not? Is this an example of Bertrand competition? (b) Is the $5 fare an equilibrium price? Why or why not?

2. A firm estimates that the average total cost of producing 10,000 units is $10 per unit. It thinks that 10,000 units is 80 percent of capacity. Its goal is to earn 20 percent on its total investment of $250,000. What price should it set to achieve this goal if it could be sure that it could sell all 10,000 units? Could it be sure of selling 10,000 units if it set this price?

3. The top four beer firms—Anheuser-Busch, Miller, Coors, and Stroh's— accounted for over three-quarters of all beer produced in the United States in 1992. Anheuser-Busch alone had 42 percent of the market. (a) Do you think that the market for beer is a contestable market? (b) In the 1960s, the long-run average cost of producing beer was at a minimum when a firm produced about 2 million barrels per year. In the late 1970s, it was at a minimum when a firm's output was about 18 million barrels per year. Can you guess why this change occurred? (c) Do you think that this change in the

long-run average-cost curve helped to cause the decrease shown in the accompanying table in the number of firms in the brewing industry?

Year	Number of firms	Year	Number of firms
1963	171	1972	108
1967	125	1976	49

(d) Can you offer an explanation for the recent growth in microbreweries in the United States? Would this alter your assessment of the applicability of the contestable market model?

4. Grain producers in the Midwest must deal with only a few rail carriers to get their product to market. The details of their markets are public knowledge. They can negotiate long-term hauling contracts in one of two ways. They can ask the carriers how much capacity will be available and compete with themselves over the price. Or they can ask carriers for a price and then specify the quantities that they want to transport. Which option should the producers prefer? Which option should the rail carriers prefer?

5. Suppose that you are on the board of directors of a firm that is the price leader in the industry. It lets all the other firms sell all they want at the prevailing market price. In other words, the other firms act as perfect competitors. Your firm, on the other hand, sets the price that all of the other firms accept. The demand curve for your industry's product is $P = 300 - Q$, where P is the product's price (in dollars per unit) and Q is the total quantity demanded. The total amount supplied by the other firms is equal to Q_r, where $Q_r = 49P$; this is the supply curve for the "competitive fringe." Your firm's marginal-cost curve is $2.96Q_b$, where Q_b is the output of your firm. What output would maximize your profit? What price should you charge? How much would the industry as a whole produce at this price? (Q, Q_b, and Q_r are expressed in millions of units.) Is your firm the dominant firm in the industry?

6. The industrial robot is one of the most important technological innovations of recent decades. In 1985, about 50 U.S. firms produced robots, but the following six firms then accounted for about 70 percent of total sales:

	Sales (millions of dollars)
GMF Robotics	180
Cincinnati Milacron	59
Westinghouse	45
ASEA	39
GCA	35
DeVilbiss	33

(a) Would you expect that nonprice competition was important in this industry? (b)From 1979 to 1982, the robotics industry experienced substantial losses even though its sales increased at a relatively rapid rate. Offer some reasons why firms stayed in this industry in the face of these losses. (c) Does the fact that they stayed in the industry mean that they were "irrational"? (d) General Motors sold its interest in GMF Robotics in 1992. Some other U.S. firms had already left the industry. Does it appear that robotics firms had been overly optimistic in the 1980s? If so, did this optimism cause them to estimate incorrectly some of the figures in their applicable payoff matrices (that is, the profits they would receive if they adopted particular strategies and their rivals adopted the same or other strategies)?

7. The Brooks Company's managers begin to sense that the Harris Corporation may attempt to enter their market. (a) What steps might they take to dissuade Harris from doing so? (b) What factors are likely to determine whether they will succeed? (c) What actions that they might have taken (or not taken) in the past could play an important role in influencing whether Harris tries to enter?

8. Some economists such as Paul Krugman have argued in recent years that governments may be able to raise national welfare at another country's expense by supporting their firms in international competition.[5] To explore this possibility, suppose that the United States and France are the only two countries capable of producing a fuel-efficient 250-seat passenger aircraft. Assume, as well, that only Boeing in the United States and Airbus in France have the productive capability to do so. Each firm has the choice of producing or not producing the aircraft, but assume that Boeing has a head start that would permit it to commit itself to produce the plane before Airbus's decision. In the absence of government intervention, let the payoff matrix be as shown in the figure, (a) Without government intervention, will each firm produce this aircraft? Why or why not? (b) Would the payoff matrix change if the French government committed itself in advance to pay a subsidy of $50 million to Airbus if it produced the plane? If so, how? (c) Would this French subsidy alter the behavior of Boeing and Airbus? If so, how? (d) Would the profits of Airbus increase by more than the amount of the subsidy? (e) Would France's adopting a strategic trade policy of this sort tend to provoke retaliation from the United States?

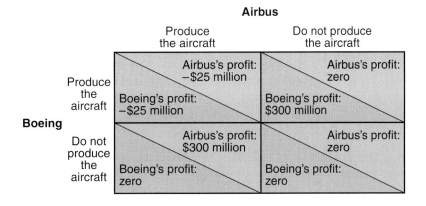

[5]See P. Krugman, "Is Free Trade Passé?" *Journal of Economic Perspectives*, Fall 1987; and J. Brander and B. Spencer, "International R&D Rivalry and Industrial Strategy," *Review of Economic Studies*, May 1983.

9. Suppose that the Intel Corporation and the Microsoft Corporation were considering a joint venture. Assume that each would have to invest $10 million in assets that were of no use or value outside this project. If both firms act in accord with their promises, then the annual economic profit to each firm would be $2.5 million; if one or both violated the agreement, then let annual economic profit to each be reflected in the accompanying payoff matrix. (a) If a contract could be formulated that would ensure that both firms would act in accord with their promises, would this contract be drawn up and signed by both firms (if the attorneys' fees were nominal)? Why or why not? (b) If such a contract could not be formulated, would either firm enter into the joint venture? Why or why not? (c) Why might it be very difficult to formulate an effective contract of this sort? (d) Is this an ordinary prisoners' dilemma game? If not, why not?

Microsoft

	Act in accord with the agreement	Do not hold to the agreement
Intel — Act in accord with the agreement	Intel's profit: $2.5 million / Microsoft's profit: $2.5 million	Intel's profit: −$1 million / Microsoft's profit: $5 million
Intel — Do not hold to the agreement	Intel's profit: $5 million / Microsoft's profit: −$1 million	Intel's profit: zero / Microsoft's profit: zero

When and How to Fight a Price War

You may be skeptical that price wars ever happen. When have you ever seen prices fall? If you think about it objectively, price wars are not as rare as you might think. You may have noticed, for example, that Sprint announced in July 1999 that it would charge 5 cents per minute for nighttime long-distance phone calls. MCI matched Sprint that August; and AT&T eventually responded to falling long-distance revenues by offering 7 cents per minute all day for a $5.95 per month fee. The result? Consumers were happy, if a bit confused by complicated rate structures (see Example 2.4), but stock prices for all three companies fell by as much as 4.7 percent. In the summer of 2002, moreover, the fallout continued when the parent company of MCI revealed that it had been grossly overestimating profits over this period.

Want another example? E-Trade and other electronic brokers changed the market for financial services with extraordinarily low fees per trade—down in 2002 to $8 per trade from $30 just a few years earlier. Will the recent wave of corporate wrongdoing and financial fraud affect this market? To be sure. Will it reverse the price spiral as consumers look for quality and trustworthy advice at a price? Perhaps. The point is that a price war was the first signal of trouble in this paradise.

How are price wars explained? Or, perhaps more important, how can we determine the building blocks of price stability in markets where positive economic profits offer one cooperating firm the potential of economic gain by seizing more market share with a lower price? And what has Part Four taught us about how to answer this question? We have covered many theories of market structure over the last few chapters. Each has had its own brand of equilibrium—especially with respect to price. We now know that perfect competition would lead to prices that match the minimum of average cost. We saw how a monopolist could exploit full market power and charge whatever the market would bear for the quantity where marginal cost equaled marginal revenue. Our discussion of monopolistic competition married these two ideas to show how market prices might match average costs for outputs that deviated from efficient minimization of average cost. Various models of oligopoly produced other outcomes. Cournot firms shared output at a price that was located somewhere between the competitive low and the monopolistic high. Stackelberg exploitation of differential information yielded some benefit to one firm at a lower price. The price leadership model offered some hope for price stability without really explaining how a firm might become a price leader. And Bertrand competition finally took us back to the competitive pricing floor.

It is now time to see what applying and, when necessary, expanding these models can teach us about pricing outcomes more generally. Under what (more realistic) conditions might we expect to see stable prices that are higher than the (noncooperative) competitive or Bertrand equilibrium? In other words, under what circumstances might it be more likely that a cooperative solution with relatively higher prices and positive economic prices might emerge even without illegal collusion? And conversely, under what circumstances might it be more likely for a price war to erupt from such an equilibrium—a war that could drive prices down to and below the competitive equilibrium where negative economic prices would result? Moreover, what could firms do to avoid such a price war under these conditions? Are there ways to compete vigorously and to punish firms that try to take unfair advantage while avoiding the perils of a downward price spiral?

It should be no surprise that the key to pricing decisions lies in judging the long-term value of noncooperative price behavior (price-cutting from an established equilibrium or not following a price increase in response to some outside shock to the market). As a result, it should also be no surprise that the key to preserving a cooperative solution lies in discouraging price-cutting. Unfortunately, traditional static models, of the sort described in Chapters 11 through 13, offer little help in this regard. Take the Cournot model described in Chapter 12, for example. The reaction functions portrayed in Figure 12.2 can certainly be used to tell an action-reaction story that converges to the traditional equilibrium for two identical firms. Firm I might start in period 1 with the monopoly output (producing one-half of the competitive output). Firm II would read that output, and so its reaction function tells us that it would choose to produce one-fourth of the competitive output in period 2. Firm I would then see that it is not a monopolist, and so we see from its reaction function that it would respond by reducing output to three-eighths of the competitive level in period 3. But then firm II would change its mind (since firm I was producing less than expected) and increase its output to five-sixteenths of the competitive output in period 4. This sequential process could continue, of course, until both firms end up producing one-third of the competitive output.

The problem with this convenient fantasy is that this is hardly a realistic model of firms that make a series of output (and pricing) decisions as time unfolds. Why? Because it presumes that each firm makes its output decision on the basis of what the other produced last period. Would not a smart firm in such a repeating game pick its output and thus its price on the basis of what it thinks the other will produce this period or the next? Clearly, in the Cournot story, last period's output of either firm is a bad predictor of next period's production (unless, of course, both firms are in equilibrium). And what about the stability of a Cournot equilibrium? The Stackelberg variant showed that either firm could improve its profit picture by exploiting an understanding that its competitor was a Cournot firm. Adjusting its output and cutting price would, in short, increase its profits—as long as the other firm did not do the same thing. Without much work, therefore, we produced the seeds of a price war even without forward-looking dynamics.

In an effort to construct a more descriptive model, consider a market that is supplied by n identical firms, where n is a relatively small number. Assume that each firm is initially making positive profits in a tacit cooperative equilibrium—a total of $\Pi_{cooperate}$, so that each firm receives $\Pi_{cooperate}/n$. Now, assume that something happens to trouble the waters. One firm, call it firm I, thinks (correctly) that it can expand its market share and increase its own profits to $\Pi_{defect} > \Pi_{cooperate}/n$ at the expense of the others by defecting from the cooperative solution with a lower price. What would happen?

Since prices are set for specific periods of time, the other firms could respond. Suppose, in fact, that the other firms had adopted and announced a "tit-for-tat" strategy that warned that they would always set their prices next period at the lowest price quoted by their competitors in the previous period. Such a strategy runs the risk of a price war, of course, but only if the first-period gains to firm I exceeded its valuation of the subsequent stream of losses (relative to the original cooperative solution). To analyze circumstances that would make the cooperative equilibrium more or less likely to persist, therefore, we need only keep track of one period's worth of gain from defecting and the associated downstream losses that it would produce. More precisely, we need only think about circumstances that would cause the gain, $\Pi_{\text{defect}} - (\Pi_{\text{cooperate}}/n)$, to grow or shrink and circumstances that would make the retaliation swift and precise.

Several generic factors have been discovered in the literature. Shorter and more frequent pricing periods would do the trick. If prices held for only one week instead of one month or one quarter, then the gains from defection would be much smaller. So, too, would the uncertainty about demand or supply conditions. Either would make it easier to detect when a price adjustment was a true defection worthy of punishment instead of some good-faith effort to respond to a change in economic environment. The existence of a price leader whose threat to retaliate would be most credible and who might use its own size and inventories to insulate the market from uncertainty could also promote price stability. Finally, Example 15.7 will show that a high degree of patience (i.e., a willingness to trade future gains or losses against the present at a low premium) could also work to promote price stability.

Are there comparable structural factors that influence price dynamics? Absolutely. High market concentration would mean that the number of major firms would be small so that $\Pi_{\text{cooperate}}/n$ would be larger (and closer to Π_{defect} by default). Higher market concentration would also make it easier to detect and to identify a defector; indeed, anything that makes it easier to detect the defecting actor can promote price stability. Multimarket contacts across firms would also help—they would allow the threat of retaliation to extend beyond one market so that the downstream penalties could be larger. All of the news is not good for the cooperating firms, however. Asymmetric firm size across the market could work to destabilize a pricing agreement, since small firms could see much larger gains from defection (if they could handle the increased demand). The prevalence of lumpy, long-term orders would also work against price stability, because they would expand the pricing period. Finally, high proportions of fixed cost would increase the likelihood of high gains to defection during times of slack demand because marginal cost would be steeper.

We cannot underestimate the destabilizing influence of these last three factors. Northwest Airlines started a disastrous, across-the-board price war in the U.S. airline industry in the spring of 1992. This price war deepened industrywide losses that had already set records in the wake of the 1990 crisis in the Persian Gulf. Northwest fired the opening volley in this war despite operating in a highly concentrated industry where fares were instantaneously published so that it was easy to detect who cut fares by how much. Why did they do it? Northwest was a small player with a high proportion of fixed cost playing in a concentrated industry. As a result, its potential gain from deviating from standard higher fares was drawn from significant asymmetry in market share; and the likelihood of its deviating from those norms was enhanced by the potential of moving down a relatively steep marginal-cost curve. Moreover, Northwest had a reputation of poor service, an inferior frequent flyer program, and unreliable scheduling. Other airlines could expect, therefore, that their customers would remain loyal even as they maintained high fares; but conversely, Northwest could expect to fly many near-empty planes if it persisted with those fares.

Under these conditions, Northwest determined that its best hope to stay alive was to move prices down to expand overall demand for air travel, especially during the summer months, when discretionary vacation travelers, who are more sensitive to price and less concerned about service, would enter the market. In addition, other airlines were already flying close to their capacities. Northwest would have been better off if other airlines had not responded by cutting fares, to be sure, but it was nonetheless reasonable for Northwest to expect that much of the increased demand would come its way in either case. Northwest may have been right—it was in its best interest to cut fares.

It must be emphasized, however, that an all-out price war was not the only possible response for the other airlines even if they were playing a tit-for-tat strategy. Akshay Rao, Mark Bergen, and Scott Davis have argued that the first step in fighting a price war should be a systematic analysis of the "battleground." Careful consideration should be given to (1) customer behavior and price sensitivity, (2) internal firm capability, (3) secondary competitor response, and (4) the reactions of other interested parties. It might have been possible, for example, for the other airlines to cut fares only for those routes where Northwest offered competitive flights. Matching the lower fares might not have been necessary even for those routes if customers were sensitive to superior flight schedules, superior reliability, better service, and other measures of higher quality. Northwest would have found these responses difficult to match (public perception being what it was); and they might have even found them irrelevant given that they were themselves targeting a segment of market demand that was indifferent to such things. In any case, it is widely known that the strategy of maintaining or improving quality was employed successfully by the Ritz-Carlton Hotel in Kuala Lumpur when political and economic instability caused the tourist trade to collapse in 1997. The Ritz maintained high demand and captured enormous market share when it improved the range of amenities offered to its guests in the wake of rate-cutting by competitor hotels. But would the other airlines have been content to allow Northwest to persist with its low fares beyond the summer months? Perhaps, if unionized employees were convinced that long-term fare reductions were not sustainable because they would require significant and unacceptable reductions in benefits and salaries.

The take-home measure from Rao, Bergen, and Davis is that there are many ways to fight a price war and that many of them do not involve cutting prices. Indeed, cooperative prices that exceed average cost and therefore generate positive economic profits can be sustained in many circumstances even while directly punishing a defecting collaborator by enacting nonprice measures. In many cases, in fact, there are a multitude of ways to undercut the long-term sustainability of a price-cutting defector without precipitating a Bertrand-type price spiral. So, maybe you were right; price wars are rare. Take a look around your experience and see.

SOURCES: "The Dynamics of Pricing Rivalry," Chap. 10 in D. Besanko, D. Dranove, and M. Shanley, *Economics of Strategy* (New York: J Wiley, 1996); and A. Rao, M. Bergen, and S. Davis, "How to Fight a Price War," *Harvard Business Review,* March–April, 2000. More detailed references to the literature for many points can be found in the footnotes of Besanko, Dranove, and Shanley.

QUESTIONS

1. Review and present the long-run price implications of cooperative equilibria for two identical firms that (a) collude to share monopoly profits, (b) operate under Cournot assumptions, (c) operate in a market where one firm correctly adopts a Stackelberg approach to output decisions, (d) operate in a market where both firms adopt a Stackelberg approach to output decisions, and (e) conduct Bertrand-style price competition.

2. Explain how special and sometimes secret pricing arrangements can influence price stability above the competitive solution.

3. Explain how the number of buyers can influence price stability above the competitive solution.

4. Why would summer demand for air travel in the Northern Hemisphere be more price-elastic than winter demand?

5. Argue and illustrate graphically why a higher proportion of fixed cost at the point where average cost is minimized makes marginal cost steeper.

6. Discuss how one might analyze the trade-off between the cost of production and product quality. Assume that improved quality increases cost but also increases demand. Explain why the trade-off focuses on the marginal buyer—the one who might be attracted by a marginal increase in quality.

7. Products can be priced at the loading dock (so that customers pay for shipping) or at the point of delivery (so that the supplier pays delivery cost). Explain how the former might make selective response to a competitor's price reduction more difficult.

8. Richard Miller's explanation of how short-run marginal cost might be horizontal up to capacity was highlighted in Chapter 7. Explain how his construction would make price stability more likely. Also explain why it did not apply to Northwest Airlines in 1992.

Markets for Inputs

Price and Employment of Inputs

INTRODUCTION

Why do major executives seem to earn wages in the neighborhood of $1,000 an hour ($2.5 million per year for 250 days at 10 hours a day)? Why do secretaries earn about $15 or $20 per hour? Why would the Texas Rangers agree to pay Alex Rodriguez more than $9 million a year to play shortstop for a team that does not play in the postseason? To answer these questions, you must understand the determinants of input prices. Wages paid to a worker (an executive, a secretary, or a shortstop) represent the price of a particular input from the viewpoint of the firm. The preceding six chapters were devoted to analyses of supply. How much of what goods and services will be produced under different circumstances? And how much will they cost to buy? We now turn our attention to exploring how employment decisions are made and how inputs are priced.

Several points should be noted at the outset. First of all, much of the theory presented in the preceding chapters can be applied to inputs as easily as it was to commodities. The prices of commodities *and* inputs are both determined by the interaction of supply and demand. The critical difference lies in the reversal of the roles played by firms and consumers. Firms supply commodities to the marketplace, but they demand inputs; consumers demand commodities from the marketplace, but they supply some very important inputs.

Second, it was customary in the nineteenth century for economists to classify inputs into three categories: land, labor, and capital. The theory of input pricing was therefore a theory of the distribution of income among landowners, wage earners, and capitalists—the three important economic and social classes of the time who earned rents, wages, and profits, respectively. Modern economies, however, are much more complex. The simple classification of inputs into three categories would now mean that each category would be forced to span an enormous amount of variation. Labor, for example, would include the services of a Nobel Prize–winning biochemist and the services of people who prepare her manuscripts for publication and the undergraduates who work in her lab. We will, therefore, seldom use the traditional tripartite classification. We will instead try to present results in general terms so that the user of the model can classify inputs to fit any particular problem.[1]

Finally, a note about presentation. The theory presented here has been widely applied. The examples offered here are, as usual, designed to give you some insight into the flavor of those applications. Some are theoretical; others are empirical. In each case, though, the fundamental theory offers us the ability to answer questions that would have otherwise been extraordinarily difficult to approach.

PROFIT MAXIMIZATION AND INPUT EMPLOYMENT

We do not have to start from scratch in constructing a model of input pricing and utilization under perfect competition. We learned a great deal of relevant and useful information in Chapters 7 and 8, where we analyzed the firm's decisions concerning input combinations and output level. With a moment's reflection you should be able to recall that we determined how much of each input the firm would demand under various sets of circumstances when we determined how much the firm would produce and what input combination it would use. This is an important beginning.

To review what we learned in Chapter 7, recall how a firm combines inputs so that it can minimize its costs. We showed there, in particular, that a firm should pick the combination of inputs for which the ratios of its marginal products to its prices are all equal. That is, a cost-minimizing firm should set

Cost-minimizing conditions

$$\frac{MP_x}{P_x} = \frac{MP_y}{P_y} = \cdots = \frac{MP_z}{P_z}, \qquad [14.1]$$

where MP_x is the marginal product of input x, P_x is the price if input x, MP_y is the marginal product of input y, P_y is the price of input y, and so on. If Equation 14.1 did not hold, a firm could always reduce its costs by changing the utilization of certain inputs. Suppose, for example, that the marginal product of one unit of input x were 2 units of output and that x's price were $1. Assume, as well, that the marginal product of one unit of input y were 6 units of output and that y's price were $2. The firm could then reduce its costs by using 1 fewer unit of input x (which would reduce output by 2 units and lower costs by $1) while simultaneously employing 1/3 of a unit more of input y (increasing output by 2 units and increasing costs by only $0.67). This substitution of input y for input x would have no effect on output, but it would reduce costs by $0.33.

[1]A fourth "factor of production" was recognized toward the end of the nineteenth century. Economic profits were then taken to be the return to the entrepreneur so that interest could be viewed as the return to the owner of capital.

Going a step further, it can also be shown that each of the ratios in Equation 14.1 for a cost-minimizing firm equals the reciprocal of the firm's marginal cost. In other words,

$$\frac{P_x}{MP_x} = \frac{P_y}{MP_y} = \ldots = \frac{P_z}{MP_z} = MC, \qquad [14.2]$$

where MC is its marginal cost. To prove this, consider input x. How much would it cost to produce an extra unit of output if this additional output were achieved by increasing *only* the utilization of input x? Since an extra unit of input x would yield MP_x extra units of output, $1/MP_x$ units of input x would be required to produce 1 extra unit of output. And since $1/MP_x$ units of input x would cost $P_x \times 1/MP_x$, it must be true that P_x/MP_x equals marginal cost. The same reasoning would apply to any input, of course, so Equation 14.2 holds in its entirety.

Suppose, as an illustration, that there were only two inputs in some production process. Call them input x and input y. Suppose that the marginal product of input x were 2 (units of output), that the price of input x were \$1 per unit, that the marginal product of a unit of input y were 4, and that the unit price of input y were \$2. The conditions of Equation 14.1 would therefore be satisfied. How much would it cost to produce an extra unit of output? It would cost \$0.50 if the extra production were achieved by increasing only the employment of input x. Why? Because the requisite 1/2 unit of input x would cost \$1 × 1/2 = \$0.50. Similarly, it would also cost \$0.50 if the extra production were achieved by increasing only the employment of input y. The requisite 1/4 unit of input y would cost \$2 × 1/4 = \$0.50. The ratio of the price of each input to its marginal product would therefore equal marginal cost (of producing one more unit of output); i.e., it would cost \$0.50 regardless of which input were employed in increasing output.

Going even a step further, we also know from Chapter 8 that the profit-maximizing firm must be operating at the output for which marginal cost equals marginal revenue. It follows, therefore, that

$$\frac{P_x}{MP_x} = \frac{P_y}{MP_y} = \ldots = \frac{P_z}{MP_z} = MC = MR, \qquad [14.3]$$

where MR is the firm's marginal revenue. Rearranging the terms in Equation 14.3, then,

$$MP_x \times MR = P_x, \qquad [14.4]$$
$$MP_y \times MR = P_y, \ldots$$
$$MP_z \times MR = P_z.$$

And so we conclude that the profit-maximizing firm should employ each input up to the point where its marginal product multiplied by the firm's marginal revenue equals the input's per unit price. We will shortly see that this result can provide the basis for defining the firm's demand curve for any input.

THE FIRM'S DEMAND CURVE:
THE CASE OF ONE VARIABLE INPUT

Our first step in analyzing the demand for an input is to consider the demand curve of an individual firm for some input (call it x) under the assumption that x is the only variable input in the firm's production process. In other words, we will assume, for the moment, that the quantities of all other inputs are fixed. This assumption will be relaxed shortly, but be aware that this really is a short-run assumption with some applicability. The demand curve of a firm for this input shows the quantity of input x that the firm would demand at each possible price. Assuming that the firm maximizes its profits, it will demand that amount of input x for which the value of the extra output produced by the employment of the last unit of x is equal to the price of that unit of x. This is the meaning of Equation 14.4.

To make this meaning more concrete, suppose that we knew the firm's production function, and suppose that we knew that the firm operated in a perfectly competitive market. Assume, as well, that we were able to deduce that the marginal product of input x at each level of employment were as given in Table 14.1. If we knew that the price of the product were $3, then we would know that its marginal revenue must also equal $3 (the firm operates in a perfectly competitive market, remember, so price equals marginal revenue). The value to the firm of the extra output that could be derived from increasing its employment of input x by one unit is shown in the last column of Table 14.1. Economists call this value the **marginal revenue product** of input x; it is equal to the marginal product of input x multiplied by the marginal revenue of increased sales. In this case, it equals $MP_x \times P$, where P is the price of the product. Since $P = MR$ in perfect competition, the value of the marginal product (i.e., the marginal revenue product of input x) is the left-hand side of Equation 14.4.

Marginal revenue product

Table 14.1	Quantity of x	Marginal product[a]	Value of marginal product[a] (dollars)
THE MARGINAL REVENUE PRODUCT OF INPUT x WITH A FIXED OUTPUT PRICE OF $3	3	8	24
	4	7	21
	5	6	18
	6	5	15
	7	4	12
	8	3	9
	9	2	6

[a]The figures pertain to the interval between the indicated quantity of input x and 1 unit less than the indicated quantity of input x.

How many units of input x should the profit-maximizing firm use if the price of input x is $12 a unit? A 1-unit increase in the utilization of input x would add the amount shown in the last column of Table 14.1 to the firm's revenue stream, and it would add $12 to its costs (under the additional assumption that the firm could not influence the price of any input). So, the firm should increase its employment of input x as long as the increase in revenue exceeds the associated increase in costs; in other words, as long as the figure in the last column of Table 14.1 exceeds $12. If the firm employed 4 units of input x, then adding one more unit would increase revenues by $18 while costs would climb by only $12; this would be a good deal. What about adding still another unit? If the firm were employing 5 units of input x, then one more unit would increase revenue by $15 and costs by $12—still a good deal. In fact, adding x to the employment mix until 7 units were employed would increase profits. Beyond that point, though, each extra unit of input x would increase costs more than revenues, and so their employment would not pay off. The firm in Table 14.1 should use 7 units of input x. Why? Because the marginal revenue product of the seventh unit would be $12—an exact match for its marginal cost.

We now know that the optimal employment of input x is characterized by the equality of the marginal revenue product of input x and its price. This is, of course, just another way of stating the result in Equation 14.4. If the firm demands the optimal amount of input x at each price of input x, then its demand schedule for input x must be the marginal revenue product recorded in the last column of Table 14.1. For example, if the price of input x were between $6 and $9, then the firm should demand 8 units of input x. If the price of input x were between $9 and $12, then the firm should demand 7 units of input x.[2] The firm's demand curve for input x is the marginal revenue product curve. It will generally slope downward and to the right, because it is proportional to the curve showing the input's marginal productivity (and because the price of the output is fixed).

THE FIRM'S DEMAND CURVE: THE CASE OF SEVERAL VARIABLE INPUTS

Firm's demand curve

Suppose now that input x were only one of several inputs that the firm could vary. The **firm's demand curve** for input x would no longer be its marginal revenue product curve. Why not? Because a change in the price of input x would cause the employment of other variable inputs to change; these changes would, in turn, affect the employment of input x. They would, at the very least, affect the marginal product of x.

---

[2]This assumes that the quantity of the input can be varied continuously. While this is often the case, Table 14.1 offers only discrete, one-unit steps in employment. As a result, this rule must be changed somewhat here. In this case, the optimal number of units of input x is the largest integer at which the value of the marginal product of input x is greater than or equal to the price of input x.

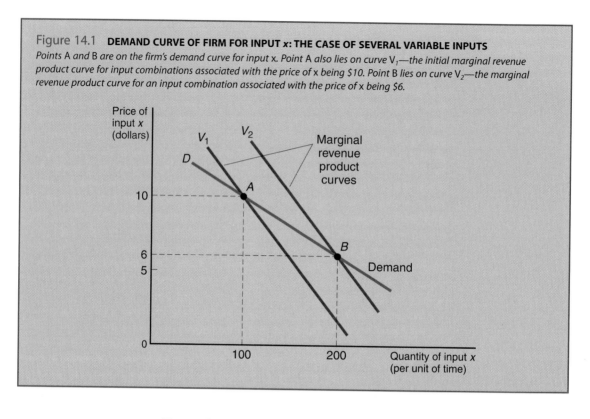

Figure 14.1 **DEMAND CURVE OF FIRM FOR INPUT x: THE CASE OF SEVERAL VARIABLE INPUTS**

Points A and B are on the firm's demand curve for input x. Point A also lies on curve V_1—the initial marginal revenue product curve for input combinations associated with the price of x being $10. Point B lies on curve V_2—the marginal revenue product curve for an input combination associated with the price of x being $6.

To see this point clearly, consider an example. Suppose that the price of input x were initially $10 and that 100 units were employed. This combination is represented by point A on curve V_1 in Figure 14.1. Curve V_1 is the marginal revenue product curve for x. Its very construction assumes that the employment of other inputs is fixed, and it would be the demand curve for x if none of the other inputs were variable. But what would happen if the price of input x fell to $6 and other inputs were variable? What would happen to the quantity of input x demanded by the firm? The marginal revenue product of input x would now exceed its new price, and so the firm would tend to expand its use. But increasing the employment of input x would shift the marginal revenue product curves of other inputs. If, for example, another variable input were complementary to input x, then its marginal revenue product curve would shift up and to the right. The marginal revenue product curve of a substitute input would shift down and to the left. And these shifts would mean that the employment of other variable inputs would change. But, more important for present purposes, it would also mean that the marginal revenue product curve of input x would change.

After all of these changes have worked their way through the firm's costminimizing decision system, the firm would be on a different marginal revenue product curve for input x—say, V_2 in Figure 14.1. And the employment of input x would be determined by the point where its new marginal revenue product curve intersects a new price line at $6. We have already noted that the firm would demand 100 units of input x given a price of \$10; this is indicated by point A on curve V_1. We now know that the firm would demand 200 units of input x given a price of \$6; this is indicated by point B on curve V_2. As a result, we can be sure that points A and B would *both* lie on the firm's demand curve for input x. Other points for other prices could be determined in a similar fashion. The result of their determination is the complete demand curve for input x. This demand curve is represented in Figure 14.1 by curve D; as would be expected, it can be shown that all demand curves of this type slope down and to the right.

Example 14.1	Implications of Internet Efficiency in Distinguishing Workers

Most of our discussions have assumed a homogeneous labor force—one in which all workers are essentially the same. This is hardly a reasonable assumption, of course, so our discussion of the derived demand when there is more than one variable input can apply directly to firm's decisions about how much of what type of labor to employ. This quick assertion begs one question, however. Exactly how can an employer distinguish one type of labor from another? How, more specifically, can an employer tell whether an applicant would be a highly productive employee? And would the employer want to install different technologies if he or she could answer that question with any degree of certainty?

It is widely expected that the Internet will help potential employers judge the qualifications of prospective employees more accurately. In the extreme, the Net offers employers the possibility of seeing and digesting more information about more people without restrictions that might otherwise be imposed by geographical boundaries and/or significant distances. Employers should therefore be able to do a better job matching the skills of prospective employees to the skills that they require. Will this improved ability make everyone better off? David Autor constructed a simple, abstract model to examine this question, and he showed that the answer is, as always, "It depends." We review his example here.

Autor assumed, in particular, that there were two types of prospective employees: high-productivity people and low-productivity people. He let the pool of potential employees be populated by two people—one was a high-productivity person with sophisticated technological skills, and the other was not. He assumed, as well, that there were three types of technology available to an employer. One embodied so much high-end technology (think advanced technological devices) that only a high-productivity worker could use it. A second, costing the same, embodied low-end technology that only a low-productivity worker could use productively (think preprogrammed devices that would bore a high-productivity worker). A third, costing twice as much as the others, adopted a more general technology (envision a more involved computer-driven gadget whose program could be preset or manipulated at will); operating this technology required one high-productivity person (to do the manipulating) and a companion low-productivity sidekick (to do the mindless repetitions). Finally, Autor assigned outputs that would

Table 14.2

A: HYPOTHETICAL OUTPUTS FOR DIFFERENT TYPES OF WORKERS WITH DIFFERENT TYPES OF CAPITAL

B: HYPOTHETICAL OUTPUTS FOR DIFFERENT TYPES OF WORKERS WITH DIFFERENT TYPES OF CAPITAL

A

Technology type	Worker type	
	High	Low
General	5	4
High-skill	8	0
Low-skill	0	6

B

Technology type	Worker type	
	High	Low
General	5	4
High-skill	8	0
Low-skill	0	3

SOURCE: D. Autor, "Wiring the Labor Market," *Journal of Economic Perspectives,* vol. 15, no. 1, Winter 2001, pp. 25–40; as well as D. Acemoglu, "Changes in Employment and Wage Inequality: An Alternative Theory and Some Evidence," *American Economic Review,* vol. 89, no. 5, December 1999, pp. 1259–1278.

result from matching either type of employee with each of the three possible technologies; they are recorded in panel A of Table 14.2.

Autor then assumed that the employer anticipated hiring both people. Absent the informational efficiencies that the Internet could bring to bear on her decision, there was a 50-50 chance she would not be able to match technologies to skills. How should she allocate her investment? Absent any screening information, her best bet would be to give the general technology a try. That would produce an expected return of $5 + 4 = 9$ from the two employees. But what if the employer could use information from the Internet to differentiate perfectly between the high-productivity and the low-productivity worker before making her investment and allocating her capital? She could then purchase different technologies and allocate the high-skilled version to the high-productivity worker and the low-skilled technology to the low-productivity worker. Total output would then be $8 + 6 = 14$. This would make everyone better off. The employer would see output rise. The high-productivity worker, paid her marginal product, would see higher compensation (i.e., $8 > 5$). And so would the low-productivity worker ($6 > 4$).

But what if complementary processes made the low-productivity worker more productive with the general technology so that panel B of Table 14.2 were more descriptive of reality? Then the differentiated investment would still benefit the employer (output would be $11 = 8 + 3 > 9$). The high-skilled worker would also benefit in comparison with an investment in the general technology (8 is still bigger than 5); but the low-skilled worker would see compensation fall (3 is less than 4). It follows that improving employers' abilities to differentiate prospective employees need not improve everyone's welfare.

The short run was defined, in earlier chapters, in terms of the ability to adjust the employment of a limited number of inputs. It was typically assumed that it would take longer to adjust the capital stock than it would to hire or fire labor, for example, so short-run cost schedules were constructed for fixed amounts of capital. Long-run cost curves assumed, by way of contrast, that firms had enough time to exercise discretion over the employment of all of their inputs. It follows that the demand curves that we produced in the one-variable case can be interpreted as short-run demand curves in the sense that there was enough time to adjust the employment of only one factor of production. Demand curves that were constructed later in the two-variable case can, correspondingly, be viewed as longer-run schedules. Notice, finally and consistent with the determinants of price elasticity, that the two-variable demand curve D depicted in Figure 14.1 is, indeed, more elastic at either point A or point B than the underlying single-value curves V_1 and V_2.

THE MARKET DEMAND CURVE

When we derived a market demand curve for a commodity in Chapter 4, we summed horizontally over the demand curves of individual consumers of the commodity. It may seem, at first glance, that we can derive the market demand curve for an input by simply summing horizontally over the demand curves of individual firms for the input. Although this would provide a first approximation, it would not yield the correct result because it would neglect the effect of changes in the input price on the product price.

Each firm's demand curve for an input is based on the supposition that any firm's decisions cannot affect the price of its output. In Table 14.1, for example, we assumed that the price of its product would be $3 regardless of how the firm changed its output or altered its employment of input x in response to changes in the price of input x. This is a perfectly reasonable assumption to make when we are working at the firm level, because one firm represents only a very small portion of the industry. But it is not a good assumption when we are trying to construct the demand curve for an entire market. The market demand curve shows the total amount of the input demanded at various possible prices of the input. It must therefore show the effect of changes in input price on employment of the input when all firms in the industry respond at the same time, and so it must reflect changes in the price of output that would likely accompany any change in an input price.

This is a complication that cannot be ignored. To see why, suppose that the price of input x decreased substantially. All of the firms that find input x useful would increase their employment of it, and so total output in all of the industries that employ input x would climb. Higher levels of production by any single firm cannot affect the price of an industry's product, but the combined expansion of output by all firms in an industry would generally cause the price of their product to fall. We should therefore expect that this reduction in the price of the product would shift each firm's marginal revenue product curve for input x to the left. And finally, we should also expect to see each firm's demand curve for input x shift slightly to the left—not by enough to make the employment of x fall from its original level, but at least by a little bit.

To see how to derive the market demand curve for input x out of all of this complication, suppose that its initial price were $8 and that each firm in the market were in equilibrium. Let the demand curve for input x be curve d drawn in panel A of Figure 14.2. Each firm would use q units of input x. Multiplying q by the number of firms in the market, we would get Q for the total quantity demanded at a price of $8. This is point A on the market demand curve (D) drawn in panel B of Figure 14.2.

Now suppose that the price of input x fell to $6. Each firm would increase its employment of input x and increase its output. The price of the firms' product(s) would fall and the individual firm demand curves for input x would shift down and to the left—toward curve e in panel A of Figure 14.2. Each firm would end up employing r units of input x. Note that r is smaller than the s units that each firm would have employed if it had remained on demand curve d; but also note that r is still larger than the q units that were

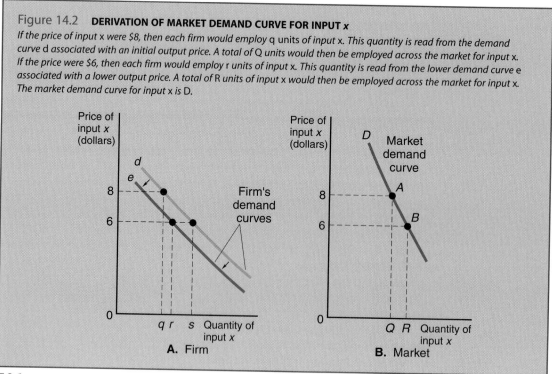

Figure 14.2 **DERIVATION OF MARKET DEMAND CURVE FOR INPUT x**

If the price of input x were $8, then each firm would employ q units of input x. This quantity is read from the demand curve d associated with an initial output price. A total of Q units would then be employed across the market for input x. If the price were $6, then each firm would employ r units of input x. This quantity is read from the lower demand curve e associated with a lower output price. A total of R units of input x would then be employed across the market for input x. The market demand curve for input x is D.

demanded originally. Multiplying r by the number of firms in the market, we would get R, the total quantity demanded at a price of $6. This is point B—another point on the **market demand curve.** Other points on the market demand curve can be obtained in similar fashion; the complete market demand curve for input x is curve D.

Market demand curve

Example 14.2	**Implications of Internet Efficiency in Distance Employment**

The Internet has also opened the possibility that employees need not actually work in a central location. It follows that labor markets that were once segregated by distance can now be integrated into a single market. Clearly, this would dramatically change the market demand for labor; and the result should, again, be improved efficiency. Will everyone necessarily benefit this time? Maybe they will, maybe they won't. To see why, David Autor constructed another simple but abstract model that captures the essence of distance employment, and we will review this model here, in two steps. We begin by describing equilibria in two labor markets that are segregated by distance. We then describe new equilibria under the assumption that the Internet allows distance employment so that the boundaries of that segregation evaporate.

Autor envisioned two cities, A and B. They were the same size, and so they offered the same number of people to the supply side of a labor market. The two panels of Figure 14.3 show this with perfectly inelastic supply at a fixed level I_0. To make the model interesting, though, Autor assumed that the citizens of city A were more productive than the citizens of city B (now you know why the cities do not have real names). Demand curves for labor in the two cities were also drawn in the two panels under an initial assumption that the two markets were segregated (i.e., nobody in city A could work in

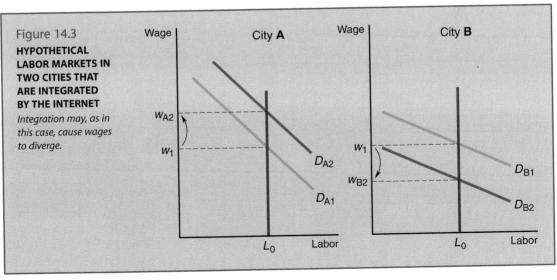

Figure 14.3
HYPOTHETICAL LABOR MARKETS IN TWO CITIES THAT ARE INTEGRATED BY THE INTERNET
Integration may, as in this case, cause wages to diverge.

city B, and vice versa); they are denoted D_{A1} and D_{B1}, respectively. Notice that they supported identical equilibrium wages denoted W_1. How could that be if people in city A were more productive? Remember that the demand for labor reflects the *marginal revenue product* of labor. Identical wages could therefore be sustained if city A produced a product whose price was lower than the price of the output produced in city B.

Autor then assumed that distance employment integrates the two labor markets. Demand curve D_{A2} indicates that demand for the high-productivity workers in city A would climb as employers in city B sought out employees who could now work for them. The equilibrium wage in city A would therefore climb to W_{A2}. At the same time, however, demand for low-productivity workers in city B would fall and bring the equilibrium wage in city B down to W_{B2}. It follows that integration might actually cause wages across the two cities to diverge—in direct contrast to the convergence that would be expected if the initial equilibrium had different wages in the two cities and integration were accomplished by allowing firms to move from one town to the other. It should be noted that this result is consistent with evidence provided by E. Brynjolfsson and M. Smith that Internet-based business-to-consumer commerce has, indeed, led to increased price dispersion in commodity markets.

SOURCE: D. Autor, "Wiring the Labor Market," *Journal of Economic Perspectives,* vol. 15, no. 15, Winter 2001, pp. 25–40; as well as E. Brynjolfsson and M. Smith, "Frictionless Commerce? A Comparison of Internet and Conventional Retailers," MIT Sloan School of Management, 1999.

DETERMINANTS OF THE PRICE ELASTICITY OF DEMAND FOR AN INPUT

We pointed out in Chapter 4 that the price elasticity of demand varies enormously from one commodity to another. The quantity demanded of some commodities can be very sensitive to changes in their prices, but the quantity demanded of other commodities can be quite insensitive to similar changes in price. The price elasticity of demand for inputs can be equally diverse. The quantity demanded of some inputs can be very sensitive to changes in their prices, whereas the quantity demanded of other inputs might not be at all sensitive to similar changes. Why is this the case? What determines whether the price elasticity of demand for a particular input will be high or low? Several factors are important in answering these questions:

1. The more easily other inputs can be substituted for a certain input—say, input x—the more price-elastic is the demand for input x. This certainly makes sense. If the technologies of the firms using input x allow these firms to substitute other inputs readily for input x, then a small increase in the price of input x should result in a substantial reduction in its use.

Determinants of the
Price Elasticity of
Demand for an Input

But if firms cannot substitute other inputs readily for input x, then even a large increase in the price of input x could result in only a small reduction in its employment.

2. The larger the price elasticity of demand for the commodity whose product relies on input x, the larger the price elasticity of demand for input x. This should make sense, as well. The demand for any input is derived from the demand for the final product. The greater the price elasticity of demand of that product, the more sensitive is the output of the product to changes in its price that occur in response to changes in the price of input x.

3. The greater the price elasticity of supply of other inputs, the larger is the price elasticity of demand for input x. The supply curve for any input is the relationship between the amount of the input that is supplied and the input's price. The price elasticity of input supply is the percentage increase in the quantity supplied of the input resulting from a 1 percent increase in the price of that input.[3] If small increases in price inspire large increases in the quantity of other inputs supplied, then the demand for input x should be more price-elastic. Why? Because firms would not be constrained by the availability of other inputs in responding to, say, a reduction in the price of input x. But if even large increases in prices of other inputs inspire only small increases in the quantity supplied of those inputs, then the demand for input x should be more price-inelastic. Why, again? Because limited supplies of other inputs at reasonable prices would inhibit the firms' abilities to respond to reductions in the price of input x.

4. The price elasticity of demand for any input is likely to be larger in the long run than in the short run. The reasoning here is similar to the reasoning that supported an analogous result for commodities in Chapter 4. The idea in both cases is that it takes time to adjust fully to a price change. Suppose, for example, that the price of skilled labor increased. It might not be possible for many firms to reduce significantly the quantity of skilled labor demanded in the short run because their plants were built to fairly rigid specifications about how many people were required to run the machines or operate the computers. In the long run, though, firms could design and build new plants and bring more sophisticated computers on-line that reduce the role of skilled labor in their production processes.[4]

Microlink 14.2   The Determinants of the Price Elasticities of Demand

Chapter 4 highlighted several determinants of the price elasticity of demand for a commodity: the availability of close substitutes, budgetary importance,

---

[3]More accurately, the price elasticity of supply is $(dQ/dP)/(Q/P)$, where Q is the quantity supplied of the input and P is its price.

[4]This proposition may not hold for durable inputs (see footnote 2 in Chapter 4). Another frequently advanced proposition is that the demand for an input will be less elastic if the payments to this input are a small, rather than a large, proportion of the total cost of the product. There may be a good deal of truth in this proposition, but it does not always hold.

and time frame were all noted. Each can be found in the list of the determinants of the price elasticity of demand for an input. Two (ease of substitution in the production process and the elasticity of supply of other inputs) play directly into the first category—the availability of close substitutes. The differentiation between the short and long run similarly mimics the role of time periods for commodity demand. Budgetary importance was not mentioned here; but surely inputs whose roles in production are quite small should have low price elasticities of derived demand. In fact, only the sensitivity of the price elasticity of demand for inputs to the elasticity of demand for the associated product is really new.

THE MARKET SUPPLY CURVE

Market supply curve

The supply of an input to an individual firm under perfect competition (in the input market) is generally thought to be infinitely elastic. In other words, a single firm should be able to buy all it wants without influencing the price. The story behind the **market supply curve** for an input, however, can be quite different. Remember that the supply curve should display the relationship between the price of the input and the total quantity of that input supplied to the entire market; there is no reason that this overall relationship should display an infinite elasticity. In many cases, in fact, the total quantity supplied to the entire market increases only when the price climbs. And it is alleged, in some cases, that the market supply curve is perfectly inelastic—that is, it is sometimes the case that the total quantity supplied to the entire market is fixed and completely unresponsive to the price.

There is, of course, no contradiction between the assertion that the supply of an input to an individual firm is perfectly elastic under perfect competition and the assertion that the market supply curve may not be perfectly elastic under perfect competition. Any amount of arable land, for example, may be available to any one farmer at a given price, yet the aggregate amount of arable land available to all farmers may increase only slightly as the price per acre climbs. We saw this same phenomenon in the sale of commodities. Chapter 8 showed how any single firm under perfect competition could believe that it could sell as much as it wanted at the existing price even though the total quantity demanded across the entire market usually rose or fell only if the price fell or rose.

There seems to be a tendency to underestimate the extent to which the market supply of an input will be increased in response to an increase in its price. Some argue, in fact, that a country is endowed with a certain amount of land and a fixed store of mineral resources. These people claim that there is no way to change these amounts, and so they assume that the market supply of these inputs is perfectly inelastic (that total supply is completely unresponsive to price). But this claim can be quite wrong. For present purposes, it is important to recognize that it is the amount of land

and mineral resources that are employed that counts. Employment can be constrained by physical limits, but only if employment has reached a capacity that is known and binding. Up until that point, large increases in the prices of natural resources and even land will generally increase their availability for employment. How so? Higher prices will usually inspire more exploration for resources, the reopening of high-cost mines, the resurrection of high-cost farms, the irrigation and upgrading of poorer land, and so on.

Example 14.3	The Supply of Engineers in the United States

Top government officials in the federal government, and in some state governments for that matter, have long been concerned that the supply of engineers in the United States was inadequate to meet the nation's needs. The 1960s and 1970s made this concern look unfounded when the nation's colleges and universities turned out an excess supply of engineers, but the situation turned around in the 1980s. Potential employers across the nation began to complain that they could not fill all of their openings. In addition, the National Science Board observed in 1988 that an anticipated 23 percent decline in the college-aged population through the year 1995 could exacerbate the problem.

Richard Freeman, a Harvard economist, thought that economic theory might be able to explain the troubling experience and to suggest what might be done to ameliorate the problem. He first collected detailed data on (1) the annual number of first-year students enrolling in engineering programs in U.S. colleges and universities, (2) the annual number of engineering graduates who tried to find work as engineers upon graduation, and (3) the annual starting salary of engineers with bachelor's degrees. He then conducted careful statistical analysis to produce two different components of the supply for engineers. In the first, he estimated the effect of starting salaries on the number of first-year students enrolling in engineering. Holding other factors constant, he found a significant relationship that is summarized in panel A of Figure 14.4; numerically, his estimate of the elasticity of first-year enrollments with respect to starting salaries was 2.9 (i.e., a 1 percent increase in salaries would, on average, increase first-year enrollment by 2.9 percent). In the second, portrayed in panel B, he found a similarly significant relationship between starting salaries and the number of students actually graduating with engineering degrees; here, the elasticity was 1.0 (so a 1 percent increase in salaries would, on average, increase the number of engineering graduates by 1 percent).

These results have some clear implications for national policy—the supply of new engineers is sensitive to salary, so pushing salaries up should increase supply. But they also carry some significance for us—"traditional" market forces of the sort described here can go a long way in explaining employment trends.

SOURCE: National Science Board, *Science and Engineering Indicators* (Washington, D.C.: U.S. Government Printing Office, 1988).

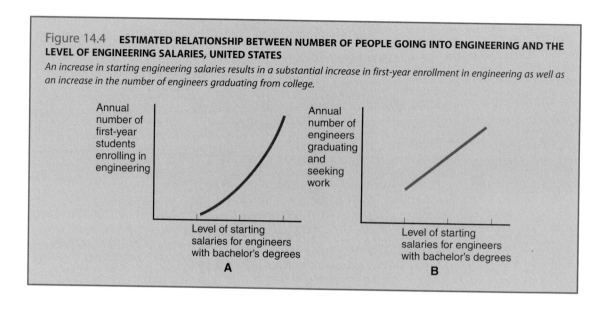

Figure 14.4 **ESTIMATED RELATIONSHIP BETWEEN NUMBER OF PEOPLE GOING INTO ENGINEERING AND THE LEVEL OF ENGINEERING SALARIES, UNITED STATES**

An increase in starting engineering salaries results in a substantial increase in first-year enrollment in engineering as well as an increase in the number of engineers graduating from college.

Most inputs are intermediate goods—that is, they are goods that are bought from other business firms. Coal, for example, is an important input for the electric power industry, and firms that operate coal-fired power plants buy their coal from firms in the coal industry. The supply curve for inputs of this kind has already been covered in Chapter 8 and throughout Part Four (it doesn't matter whether the demand side of those markets is composed of individual consumers who purchase final goods or individual firms that purchase intermediate goods). There is no need to discuss once again the determinants of the nature and shape of the market supply curve in those cases.

Some inputs are not supplied by business firms, however. *Individuals* provide labor, for example. In so doing, individuals are supplying something that they themselves can use, since the time that they do not work can be used for leisure activities. As sellers of labor, therefore, individuals want to keep some time for themselves. And, in general, the amount of inputs like labor that individuals supply to firms depends on the quantities of these inputs that they want to keep for themselves.

We saw in Chapter 8 that the market supply curve for inputs supplied by business firms will generally slope upward and to the right. In other words, higher prices are generally required to increase the quantity willingly supplied. The supply function for inputs supplied by individuals, by way of contrast, can actually bend backward, so that higher prices can actually *reduce* the quantity supplied. Supply curve *SS'* in Figure 14.5 displays this possibility.

Backward-bending supply curve

To see how this could occur, consider the labor time supplied by a single worker. She has 24 hours a day to allocate between work and leisure. She values leisure time, and its price (i.e., its opportunity cost) is the hourly wage rate that she could earn if she worked instead of played. The wage,

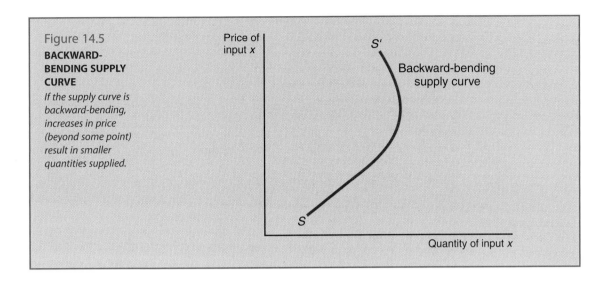

Figure 14.5

BACKWARD-BENDING SUPPLY CURVE

If the supply curve is backward-bending, increases in price (beyond some point) result in smaller quantities supplied.

in other words, is the amount of money that she would sacrifice to enjoy an hour of leisure time. What would be the effect of an increase in the wage rate on the amount of leisure time that she would demand? It should be clear that this is a standard problem of consumer choice. If you do not see why when it is expressed in terms of the quantity of labor supplied, then consider the same question expressed in terms of the quantity of leisure time demanded. "What would be the effect of an increase in the wage rate on the quantity of labor supplied?" is the mirror image of asking "What would be the effect of an increase in the price of leisure time (the opportunity cost of leisure) on the quantity of leisure time demanded?" The theoretical tools discussed in Chapter 4 can help us answer this second question.

We learned in Chapter 3 that we can divide the effect of the price increase into two parts: the substitution effect and the income effect. The **substitution effect** shows the effect of the increase in the cost of leisure relative to other commodities. Since other consumer goods would become relatively less expensive, the substitution effect would lead her to reduce her leisure time and increase her purchases of other consumer goods. In short, the substitution effect would push her toward increasing the amount of labor time that she would offer to her employer.

We must now consider the **income effect;** it is quite different in this context from what it was when we were contemplating changes in the purchase of consumer products. In the first place, the income effect here would work in the opposite direction, even if leisure were a normal good. Why? We saw in Chapter 3 that the income effect of a higher price would generally reduce consumption because the higher price would reduce the consumer's real purchasing power. In this case, though, an increase in the price of her leisure time (a higher wage) would make her more affluent and better able to afford the things that she wants—a list of valued things that would

Substitution effect

Income effect

include leisure time. The income effect of an increase in the price of leisure
would therefore work to increase the demand for leisure.

The income effect in this case differs from the income effect for most
consumer products in another important respect: it is likely to be much
stronger than for most consumer products. In general, the consumer spends
only a small percentage of his or her budget on the product in question, so
an increase in its price has only a small impact on his or her real income. In
the case of leisure, though, an increase in its price will almost certainly have
a great effect on the consumer's real income, especially for people whose
incomes are derived significantly from the "sale" of labor time. We should
therefore not be surprised to see that an increase in the price of leisure time
(the wage rate) would have a large effect on an individual's income and
consumption patterns.

Chapter 3 instructed us to add the income and substitution effects to
judge the overall effect of a change in a price. We now see that the income effect of a higher wage would push the labor-leisure allocation in
the opposite direction from the substitution effect. The substitution effect
would favor more labor; but the income effect would favor more leisure
(and thus less labor). The income effect could, in fact, be large enough
(for high wage rates) to offset the substitution effect so that an increase
in the wage rate could actually reduce the quantity of labor supplied (because it would increase the quantity of leisure time demanded). This is
the potential source of the backward bend in the supply curve displayed
in Figure 14.5.

Institutional constraints often prevent workers from choosing their own
working hours, of course. The 35-hour work week is common in many
industries. But the typical, or average, work week responds to the shape of
the supply curve for labor. And so, workers in the United States have negotiated shorter work weeks as they have become more affluent. The average
work week was almost 70 hours in 1850; it was 40 hours throughout most
of the middle of the twentieth century; now it is generally 35 hours.

Microlink 14.3   Income and Substitution Effects in the Supply of Labor

The fact that the relative strengths of income and substitution effects can
produce the backward bend in the supply curve for labor has a direct
connection to our earlier discussions. Figure 14.6 makes this link clear by
formalizing a model in which utility is given as a function of consumption
(denoted by C) and leisure (denoted by F, for free time); that is, $U = U(C, F)$.
We can assume that consumption is derived entirely from wage income so
that $C = wL$, where w is the wage rate and L is the quantity of labor supplied.
With a fixed amount of time (like 120 hours in a 5-day work week) to allocate between work and leisure, this "budget constraint" can be rewritten
as $C = w(120 - F)$. Figure 14.6 looks at utility-maximizing combinations
of C and F for three different wage rates, $w_0 < w_1 < w_2$. Panel A, in particular, shows how the quantity of free time might change as the wage climbs
from the lowest level, w_0, to an intermediate level, w_1. Free time falls in this
case as equilibrium moves from E_0 to E_1; notice that the substitution effect

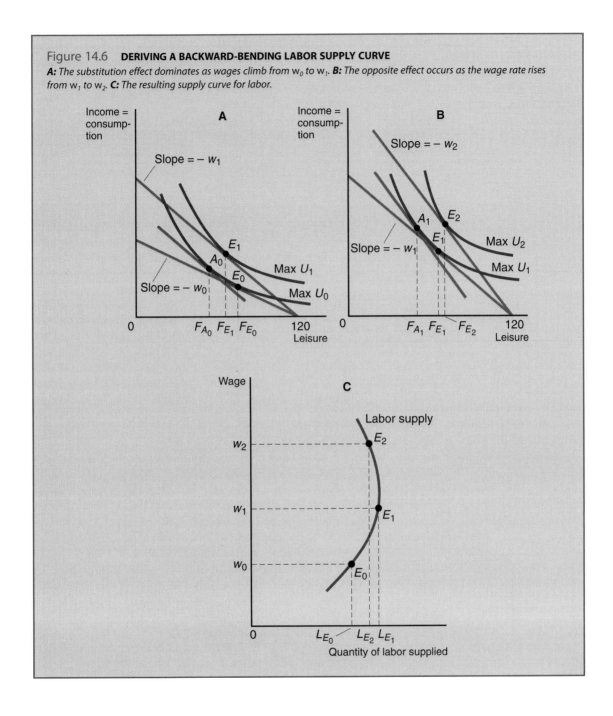

Figure 14.6 **DERIVING A BACKWARD-BENDING LABOR SUPPLY CURVE**

A: The substitution effect dominates as wages climb from w_0 to w_1. **B:** The opposite effect occurs as the wage rate rises from w_1 to w_2. **C:** The resulting supply curve for labor.

in response to a higher wage (the move from E_0 to A_0 along the Max U_0 indifference curve) is larger than the income effect (from A_0 to E_1). The result is an increase in the quantity of labor supplied, depicted in panel C by the move from E_0 to E_1 and the corresponding move from L_{E_0} to a higher L_{E_1}. Panel B repeats the process as the wage continues to climb from w_1 to a higher level, w_2. Free time climbs, this time, as equilibrium moves from E_1 to E_2 because the substitution effect (the move from E_1 to A_1 along the Max U_1 indifference curve) is now dominated by the enhanced income effect (from A_1 to E_2). The result is a reduction in the quantity of labor supplied, depicted in panel C by the move from E_1 to E_2 and the corresponding move from L_{E_1} to a lower L_{E_2}.

EQUILIBRIUM PRICE AND EMPLOYMENT OF AN INPUT

Equilibrium The market demand and supply curves for an input determine the input's equilibrium price. The price of the input will tend in equilibrium to settle to the level at which the quantity of the input demanded equals the quantity of the input supplied. In Figure 14.7, therefore, the **equilibrium price** of the input is P_0. If the price were higher than P_0, then the quantity supplied would exceed the quantity demanded and there would be downward pressure on the price. If the price were lower than P_0, then the quantity supplied would fall short of the quantity demanded and there would be upward pressure on the price.

The equilibrium quantity is also given by the intersection of the market demand and supply curves. In Figure 14.7, Q_0 units of the input would be employed in equilibrium. In equilibrium, the marginal revenue product of an input would equal the price of the input in each and every place of employment—and, of course, the prices paid by each and every employer would be identical under perfect competition.

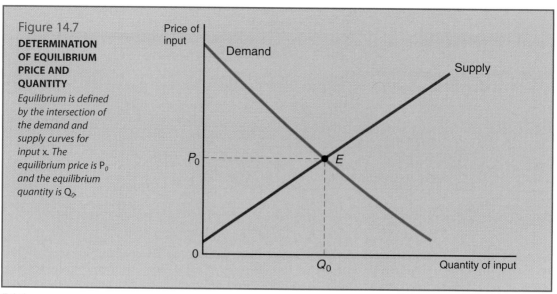

Figure 14.7
DETERMINATION OF EQUILIBRIUM PRICE AND QUANTITY
Equilibrium is defined by the intersection of the demand and supply curves for input x. The equilibrium price is P_0 and the equilibrium quantity is Q_0.

| Example 14.4 | **Does Immigration Benefit the United States?** |

The *New York Times* editorialized on June 11, 1995, that "immigration . . . promises to become an incendiary issue in the 1996 elections." That turned out not to be true, but many still believe that current levels of immigration into the United States (around 1 million people a year by legal means) are excessive and economically harmful. Although this is only partially an economic issue, the debate surrounding immigration certainly does have some economic content; and it turns out that exercising the market equilibrium concepts presented here can offer some insight into who (if anybody) wins and who (if there is anybody left) loses.

To see how, of course, we need an economic model that captures the salient features of the immigration issue without adding undue complication. To that end, suppose that the marginal revenue product curve for labor were as displayed in Figure 14.8. Let the domestic supply of labor in the United States be given by L_1; but suppose, as well, that immigration suddenly increased supply to L_2. The equilibrium wage would drop from W_1 to W_2, of course, but that is not the end of the story. Since nonimmigrant labor was given by L_1, we can immediately see that the total wage income of U.S. labor would drop by $(W_1 - W_2) \times L_1$, an amount equal to the area of rectangle $W_1 W_2 GC$. Total wage payments to both types of labor would, however, be equal to $W_2 \times L_2$. It follows that $W_1 \times L_1$ would be paid to U.S. labor and $W_2 \times (L_2 - L_1)$ would be paid to immigrants.

U.S. labor loses, therefore, and immigrant labor presumably wins. But what about the other agents in the U.S. economy? The American owners of capital and the domestic suppliers of other inputs would see their share of input climb from the area of triangle AW_1C to the area of triangle AW_2E. How do we know that? Because the marginal revenue product curve for labor

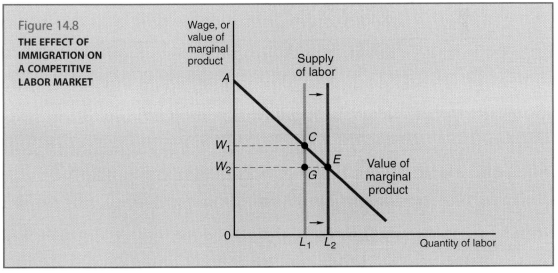

Figure 14.8

THE EFFECT OF IMMIGRATION ON A COMPETITIVE LABOR MARKET

indicates the marginal value of hiring each unit of labor. As a result, the area under the derived market demand curve for labor represents the total value of output, and the portion not paid to labor must go to everyone else. These other agents are clearly winners, too. How do we know? The reduction in wage payments to U.S. labor (rectangle $W_1 W_2 GC$) represents a transfer of income within the country—payments now directed to one group of Americans instead of another. In addition, an amount equal to the area of rectangle $L_1 L_2 EG$ would be paid to immigrant labor. It follows that American owners of capital and the suppliers of other inputs would also receive a supplement above the domestic transfer equal to the area of triangle GEC.

For other views on this controversial topic, see G. Borjas, "The Economic Benefits from Immigration"; R. Friedberg and J. Hunt, "The Impact of Immigrants on Host Country Wages, Employment, and Growth"; and K. Zimmermann, "Tackling the European Migration Problem"—all in *Journal of Economic Perspectives,* Spring 1995. See, as well, Council of Economic Advisers, *Economic Report of the President, 1999* (Washington, D.C.: U.S. Government Printing Office, 1999), pp. 110–112.

RENT

We stated earlier in this chapter that there is a tendency to underestimate the extent to which the market supply of an input will increase in response to an increase in its price. That point notwithstanding, there are some inputs, like certain types of land, whose supply may indeed be relatively fixed. To explore the ramifications of this condition, suppose that the supply of some input were completely fixed so that higher prices would not increase its supply and lower prices would not diminish its supply. Following the terminology of the classical economists of the nineteenth century, the price of such an input is called

Rent   a **rent.** Note immediately that the use of the word "rent" in this context is quite different from everyday usage. We are not discussing the price of using an apartment or car or some other object owned by someone else. We are, instead, talking about the price of something where supply is absolutely fixed.

If the supply of an input were fixed, then its supply curve would be a vertical line as shown in Figure 14.9. The price of such an input, its rent, would be determined entirely by the demand curve for the input. If the demand were given by curve D, then the rent would be P; if demand were given by curve D_0, then the rent would be P_0. The price of the input can be raised or lowered without influencing quantity supplied; this fact gives the term "rent" a more functional definition—it is a payment above and beyond the minimum level required to attract the designated amount of input.[5]

Economists in recent years have tended to extend the use of the word "rent" to encompass all payments to inputs that are above the minimum

[5]Note that the degree to which rent is a price-determined cost depends on whether we are looking at the matter from the point of view of a firm, a small industry, a large industry, or the whole economy. Payment to an input that is in fixed supply to the whole society or a large industry may be a rent from the point of view of the society or the industry, but it may appear to be a price-determining cost to an individual small firm or a small industry.

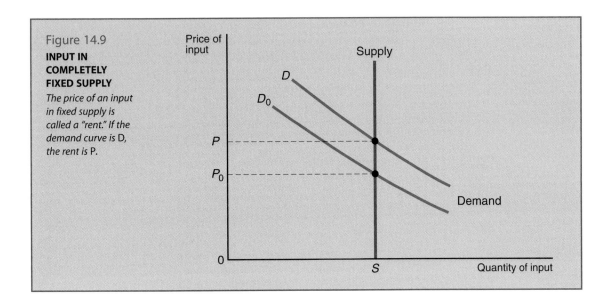

Figure 14.9

INPUT IN COMPLETELY FIXED SUPPLY

The price of an input in fixed supply is called a "rent." If the demand curve is D, the rent is P.

required to make these inputs available to the industry or to the economy. These payments are, to a great extent, costs to individual firms because they must make them to attract and keep these inputs that might otherwise be useful to other firms in the industry. But if the inputs have no use in other industries, then these payments are not costs to the industry as a whole or to the economy as a whole because the inputs would be available whether or not these payments were made.

Why is it important to know whether or not a certain payment for inputs is a rent? Because a reduction in payment will not influence the availability and use of the inputs if the payment is a rent, but a reduction in payment *is* likely to change the allocation of resources if the payment is not a rent. And so, if it wanted, a government could impose a tax on rents without affecting the supply of the resource to the economy.

Quasi-rent   The payment to any input in temporarily fixed supply is called a **quasi-rent.** We have seen in preceding chapters that many inputs are in fixed supply to a firm in the short run. A firm's plant cannot be changed appreciably in the short run. Indeed, fixed inputs of any kind cannot be withdrawn from their current use and transferred to another use where the returns would be higher in the short run. Nor can fixed inputs be supplemented with other similar inputs in the short run. Payments to the fixed inputs must therefore be determined differently from payments to the variable inputs. Inputs that are variable in quantity are free to move where the returns are highest, but fixed inputs are stuck where they are. So firms must pay the variable inputs as much as they can earn in alternative uses, but the fixed inputs receive whatever is left over.

The return earned by a fixed input is a quasi-rent; it is a residual. To understand its nature, it is useful to consider the short-run cost curves displayed in Figure 14.10. Suppose that the price were P_0. The firm would then produce Q_0 units and its total variable costs would be equal to area $0GBQ_0$ (since G equals its average variable cost). This area, $0GBQ_0$, represents the

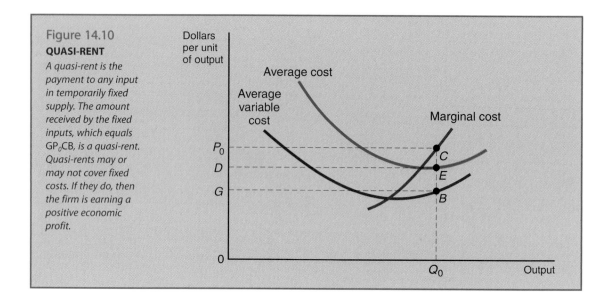

Figure 14.10

QUASI-RENT

A quasi-rent is the payment to any input in temporarily fixed supply. The amount received by the fixed inputs, which equals GP_0CB, is a quasi-rent. Quasi-rents may or may not cover fixed costs. If they do, then the firm is earning a positive economic profit.

amount that the firm must pay in order to attract and keep the variable in-puts required to produce an output of Q_0. It could not pay less than that and expect to keep them. The fixed inputs get paid the residual—area GP_0CB; this is their quasi-rent. Total fixed costs would equal area $GDEB$. And so this firm would be making positive economic profit equal to area DP_0CE. Total quasi-rents would therefore exceed fixed costs by the amount of these profits. Needless to say, quasi-rents need not be greater than total fixed costs. Firms with pure economic losses do not have quasi-rents that are large enough to cover total fixed costs.

| Example 14.5 | **The Implications of Restricting Child Labor** |

K. Basu has recently reviewed an expanding literature on international labor standards paying particular attention to restrictions on child la-bor. Is that still a problem at the turn of the twenty-first century? Table 14.3 suggests that it is in some parts of the world. A simple model can, perhaps, suggest why. Citizens who live in countries that unilaterally impose restric-tions on the participation of children in labor markets can suffer significant harm if nearby countries with similar economies do not follow suit.

To see why, consider a simple low-skill labor market across two identical countries of the sort proposed by Basu. The supply curve for labor in either country is depicted in the left panel of Figure 14.11. It is drawn to reflect the usual assumption that low-income households can determine a thresh-old wage W_{min} for adult laborers. If adult members of the household are paid more than W_{min}, then the children need not work. But if adults are paid less than W_{min}, then the household falls below a subsistence income and chil-dren must work to sustain the household. For wages greater than W_{min},

Table 14.3 **PARTICIPATION RATES FOR CHILDREN, 10–14 YEARS**

	1950	1960	1970	1980	1990	1995	2000[a]	2010[a]
World	27.57	24.81	22.30	19.91	14.65	13.02	11.32	8.44
Africa	38.42	35.88	33.05	30.97	27.87	26.23	24.92	22.52
Latin America and Caribbean	19.36	16.53	14.60	12.64	11.23	9.77	8.21	5.47
Asia	36.06	32.26	28.35	23.42	15.19	12.77	10.18	5.60
Europe	6.49	3.52	1.62	0.42	0.10	0.06	0.04	0.02
Ethiopia	52.95	50.75	48.51	46.32	43.47	42.30	41.10	38.79
Brazil	23.53	22.19	20.33	19.02	17.78	16.09	14.39	10.94
China	47.85	43.17	39.03	30.48	15.24	11.55	7.86	0.00
India	35.43	30.07	25.46	21.44	16.68	14.37	12.07	7.46
Italy	29.11	10.91	4.12	1.55	0.43	0.38	0.33	0.27

[a]Estimated.
SOURCE: Basu, "Child Labor," Table 2.

therefore, labor supply is given by the adult population of a country (denoted L_A); and for wages less than W_{min}, supply is given by the sum of the adult and child populations ($L_A + L_C$). This supply curve is given by line *aklm* for either country. The right-hand panel shows the total market supply for both countries—the horizontal sum of the two supply curves for the two countries. It is depicted by the corresponding line *AKLM*.

The demand for labor is given by D_i in either country (the left panel) and by D in the aggregate across both countries (the right panel). There are two possible equilibria—E_G without child labor, and E_B with. Absent any restrictions on employing children, however, employers prefer E_B, with an

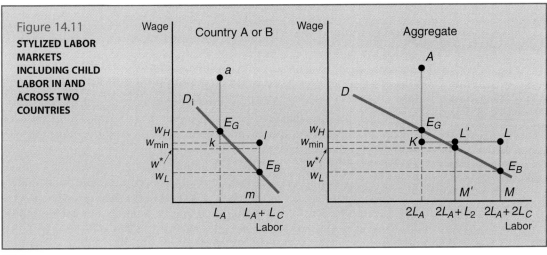

Figure 14.11
STYLIZED LABOR MARKETS INCLUDING CHILD LABOR IN AND ACROSS TWO COUNTRIES

equilibrium wage equal to W_L. What would happen if both countries banned child labor? That is easy to see. Both countries would see labor supply restricted to L_A. The equilibrium wage would be $W_H > W_{min}$. And no household would want its children to have to work.

Now, what would happen if only one country banned child labor? Call that country I. If firms could not move from one country to another, then W_H would again emerge in country I as an equilibrium wage and the wage in the other country (country II) would stay at W_L. This dispersion in wages could, however, provide sufficient incentive for firms to move low-paying employment opportunities to the country that still allowed child labor. The aggregate supply of labor would now miss only the contribution from the children from country I, and so it would be given by line $AKL'M'$, and a new equilibrium wage W^* would emerge in both countries. Notice that $W_L < W^* < W_H$. More important, though, note that $W^* < W_{min}$. If W_{min} were truly chosen on the basis of critical need for subsistence compensation, then poor families in country I would be much worse off than they were without the labor restraint.

SOURCE: K. Basu, "Child Labor: Cause, Consequence, and Cure, with Remarks on International Labor Standards," *Journal of Economic Literature,* vol. 37, no. 3, September 1999, pp. 1083–1119.

IMPERFECTLY COMPETITIVE OUTPUT MARKETS

We now return to our development of the theory of input markets. We have, thus far, focused on industries that were perfectly competitive. But what would the theory say about a case in which there was perfect competition in the market for the input but imperfect competition (that is, monopoly, oligopoly, or monopolistic competition) in the relevant product markets? In other words, what difference would it make if some of the firms that were potential buyers of an input had some degree of monopoly power in the sale of their products? What would then determine the price and employment of the input?

To answer these questions, we begin again by assuming that firms can vary only input x. A profit-maximizing firm would hire input x up to the point where the value of the extra output produced by an extra unit of input x equaled the unit price of input x. This was the content of Equation 14.4, but a specific example will help us sort out its meaning. To that end, suppose that the data recorded in the second column of Table 14.4 summarized the marginal product of input x at various levels of employment. Let the third column record the associated levels of total output. The fourth column provides evidence that the firm is, indeed, an imperfect competitor; note there that the price of its product varies with the amount that it sells. The total revenue generated by each level of total output is computed for the fifth column by multiplying the output in the third column by the price in the fourth column.

Finally, the sixth column of Table 14.4 shows how total revenue changes with the employment of each additional unit of input x. Employing a fifth unit of input x, for example, would increase the firm's total revenue by $131 (i.e., revenue would climb from $819 to $950 if employment of x increased from 4 units to 5 units). Similarly, employing the seventh unit of input x

| | | | Price of | Total | Marginal revenue |
| | Marginal | Total | good | revenue | product of x^a |
Quantity of x	product of x^a	output	(dollars)	(dollars)	(dollars)
3	10	33	20.00	660.00	—
4	9	42	19.50	819.00	159.00
5	8	50	19.00	950.00	131.00
6	7	57	18.50	1,054.50	104.50
7	6	63	18.00	1,134.00	79.50
8	5	68	17.50	1,190.00	56.00
9	4	72	17.00	1,224.00	34.00

Table 14.4

THE MARGINAL REVENUE PRODUCT OF INPUT x WHEN THE PRICE OF OUTPUT VARIES WITH QUANTITY

^{a}These figures pertain to the interval between the indicated amount of input x and 1 unit less than the indicated amount of input x.

would increase the firm's total revenue by $79.50. The heading of the sixth column claims that the increase in total revenue generated by the employment of each additional unit of input x is the marginal revenue product of input x. The marginal revenue product of input x is, of course, equal to the marginal physical product of input x multiplied by the firm's marginal revenue. That is what the left-hand side of Equation 14.4 claimed. Are these two claims mutually consistent? Sure. Notice, for example, that the marginal product of the fifth unit of x is 8. Marginal revenue between 42 and 50 units of output is meanwhile $\Delta TR/\Delta\text{output} = \$131/(50 - 42) = 16.375$, where TR equals total revenue. And so multiplying the marginal product of x by the applicable marginal revenue equals $131 in revenue—the change in revenue identified in the sixth column as the marginal revenue product.

So we now know that a profit-maximizing firm should set the marginal revenue product of input x equal to the price of input x even if it has market power in the product market. The firm's demand schedule for input x must therefore be its marginal revenue product schedule. For the data in Table 14.4, for example, Equation 14.4 would tell us that the firm should demand 8 units of input x if its price were $56, because that would set the marginal revenue product of input x equal to $56. And if the price of input x were $34? The firm should demand 9 units of input x because that would guarantee that the marginal revenue product of input x equaled $34. The curve that reflects all such points is drawn in Figure 14.12.

Figure 14.12 displays a curve that slopes downward and to the right. This general shape will apply to nearly every marginal revenue product curve for at least one of two reasons. First, the marginal product of any input should decline as its employment rises. And second, the marginal revenue of any imperfect competitor should decline as its output rises (recall that it would be constant and equal to the output price in the case of perfect competition). As the multiplicative product of declining marginal physical product and declining (or at best constant) marginal revenue, marginal revenue product cannot hope to do anything but fall as employment rises.

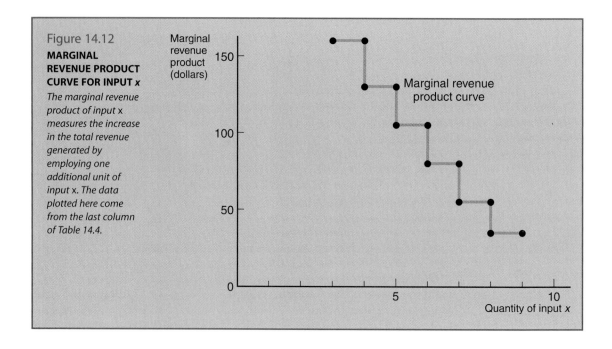

Figure 14.12

MARGINAL REVENUE PRODUCT CURVE FOR INPUT *x*

The marginal revenue product of input x measures the increase in the total revenue generated by employing one additional unit of input x. The data plotted here come from the last column of Table 14.4.

Marginal revenue product (dollars)

Marginal revenue product curve

Quantity of input *x*

To find the equilibrium price of input *x* when demanders are imperfect competitors, the demand curves of the individual firms in the input market must be combined into a single market demand curve for the input. The procedure described above still works. Both the equilibrium price of the input and its total level of employment will be determined by the intersection of this market demand curve with the input's market supply curve. The nature and determinants of an input's market supply curve, discussed earlier in this chapter, need not be altered by the existence of imperfect competition in the product market.

MONOPSONY

Monopsony

We now reverse the story to consider input markets in which the demanding firms have some market power. Indeed, we turn our attention to the case of **monopsony**—a situation in which there is a single buyer of a particular input. Does this ever happen? It is not difficult to tell a story that fits the bill. A group of small firms may be set up to provide tools, supplies, or materials for a single large manufacturing firm. This large firm might be the only one of its type in the area, and its requirements might be very specialized. In this case, it is reasonable to think that the large firm could easily be the only buyer for the product of the small firms. This would be a case of monopsony.

Note carefully the difference between monopsony and monopoly. Monopsony is a case of a single buyer of some product. Monopoly is a case of a single seller. We could also study oligopsony situations where there are a few buyers, or monopsonistically competitive situations where there are many buyers who can tell the difference between similar but heterogeneous inputs. You can imagine the complication in either case, and you may be relieved to know that we will not cover their details. It is sufficient for present purposes to limit our attention to monopsony.

Just how might a monopsony occur? There are many possible reasons that extend beyond the short story told above. In some cases, a particular type of input might simply be much more productive in one kind of use than it would be in others. Land that is rich in iron ore would presumably be much more profitable if it were devoted to iron mining than if it were devoted to some other use. A person with certain specialized skills would be much more profitably employed in jobs that require those skills than in a job where they would be irrelevant. Would you buy a car from Roger Clemens? Or George Steinbrenner? Add to either situation the condition that there is only one firm that rents such land or hires such labor, and the result is a monopsony.

The classic case of monopsony is the old company town in which a single firm is the sole buyer of labor services. Many mill towns and mining towns were dominated by a single firm. This firm would be a monopsonist as long as workers were unable or unwilling to move elsewhere to work. Increased labor mobility could break such a monopsony, at least partially. But the difficulties involved in increasing the mobility of labor should not be underestimated, even in today's world. Workers become emotionally attached to particular areas and to their friends and family who are located there. They can be unaware of employment opportunities located elsewhere, and they sometimes lack the money and skills required to move.

| Example 14.6 | **Labor Markets in Professional Sports as a Laboratory for Monopsony Theory** |

It is widely known and sometimes lamented that professional baseball players earn enormous salaries in North America, but that observation is not sufficient to prove that they would have been paid less if the market for their services were less competitive. Lawrence Kahn has, however, noted that the history of major professional sports has, from time to time, provided almost controlled experiments that can test the validity of such a claim. We are about to show that a monopsonist would, indeed, be able to offer a wage below the competitive equilibrium. It follows that his work in this economic laboratory should have a direct bearing on whether or not you should believe this result.

Kahn begins by noting the historical time series of average baseball salaries depicted in Figure 14.13. There is a clear upward trend in nominal and real terms from the 1870s through the 1920s, but that is not the news, here. Kahn noticed, instead, that definite peaks appear in the late 1890s, the early 1900s, and around 1915. It seems that the National League held monopoly power until 1882 when the American Association was formed and offered competition to existing teams for hiring players. Salaries climbed until the American Association collapsed in 1891. A new rival league, the American League, was founded in 1901—the beginning of a second peak in salaries. But the two leagues merged during the 1903 season and salaries fell again. Finally, the Federal League formed in 1913 and offered long-term contracts to players. The

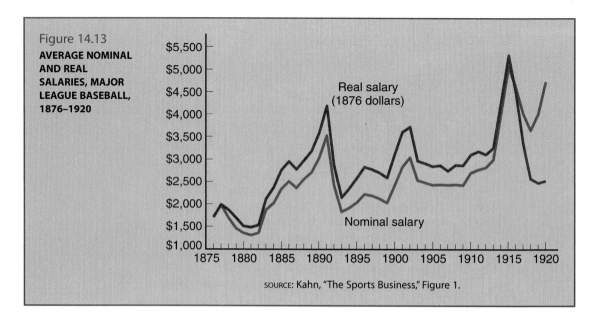

Figure 14.13

AVERAGE NOMINAL AND REAL SALARIES, MAJOR LEAGUE BASEBALL, 1876–1920

SOURCE: Kahn, "The Sports Business," Figure 1.

third peak materialized, but quickly evaporated, when many of the new league's owners were "bought out" by combined National and American Leagues.

This history is suggestive, but more recent experience in other professional sports leagues is even more telling. Table 14.5 reports contemporaneous average salaries for players in four sports. Credible rival leagues were formed in hockey and basketball during the late 1960s, and players in those sports outearned their counterparts in football and baseball through 1977 when, oddly enough, the rival leagues went out of business. And what of football? Why did salary growth for football players grow so fast in the late 1970s despite declines in attendance and television revenues for NFL teams? Because competition for the National Football League appeared in the form of the United States Football League.

SOURCE: L. Kahn, "The Sports Business as a Labor Market Laboratory," *Journal of Economic Perspectives,* vol. 14, no. 3, Summer 2000, pp. 75–94.

Table 14.5

AVERAGE PLAYER SALARIES, MAJOR LEAGUE TEAM SPORTS, SELECTED YEARS

	Major league baseball	National Basketball Association	National Hockey League	National Football League
1967	$ 19,000	$ 20,000	$ 19,133	$ 25,000
1970	$ 29,000	$ 40,000	$ 25,000	$ 34,600
1972	$ 34,092	$ 90,000	$ 44,109	$ 35,000
1977	$ 76,349	$143,000	$ 96,000	$ 55,288
1982	$241,497	$215,000	$120,000	$102,250

SOURCE: Kahn, "The Sports Business," Table 1.

▣ Input Supply Curves and Marginal Expenditure Curves

A monopsonist faces the market supply curve of the input in question. This is the key feature of monopsony (just as the key feature of monopoly is that the monopolist faces the market demand curve). The monopsonist is, quite simply, the sole buyer of the input in question. We also know now the market supply curve for most inputs is upward-sloping. As a result, a monopsonist must increase the price of the input if it wishes to increase its employment; but it can reduce the input's price if it chooses to employ less of it.

The contrast between monopsonistic and perfectly competitive input markets should not be missed. Each firm facing a perfectly competitive input market buys only a very small proportion of the total supply; each firm therefore faces a perfectly elastic supply curve. Each firm can, in other words, buy all it wants of an input without affecting its price.

By way of contrast, Table 14.6 illustrates the situation facing a monopsonist in the employment of input x. The market supply schedule for input x is shown in the first two columns. They show, for example, that 8 units of input x would be supplied if the price of input x were $10.00, 9 units of input x would be supplied if the price of input x were $10.50, and so forth. The third column shows the total cost to the firm of buying the quantities of input x recorded in the first column. The total cost of 8 units would be $80.00 and the total cost of 9 units would be $94.50; these amounts, of course, are simply the products of the figures in columns 1 and 2.

Marginal expenditure

The fourth column shows the additional cost to the firm of increasing its employment of input x by 1 unit. This is called the **marginal expenditure** for input x. The marginal expenditure for the ninth unit of input x, for example, would equal $14.50 (= $94.50 − $80.00), and the marginal expenditure for the tenth unit of input x would be $15.50. Note that the marginal expenditure numbers for each unit are higher than the corresponding prices. This is a general phenomenon when the market supply curve for the input is upward-sloping. The reason for this is simple. A monopsonist who wants to increase the employment of some input like x by one unit cannot

Table 14.6 MARGINAL EXPENDITURE FOR INPUT x	Quantity of x	Price of x (dollars)	Total cost of x (dollars)	Marginal expenditure for x[a] (dollars)
	8	10.00	80.00	—
	9	10.50	94.50	14.50
	10	11.00	110.00	15.50
	11	11.50	126.50	16.50
	12	12.00	144.00	17.50
	13	12.50	162.50	18.50
	14	13.00	182.00	19.50

[a]Each figure pertains to the interval between the indicated amount of input x and 1 unit less than the indicated amount of input x.

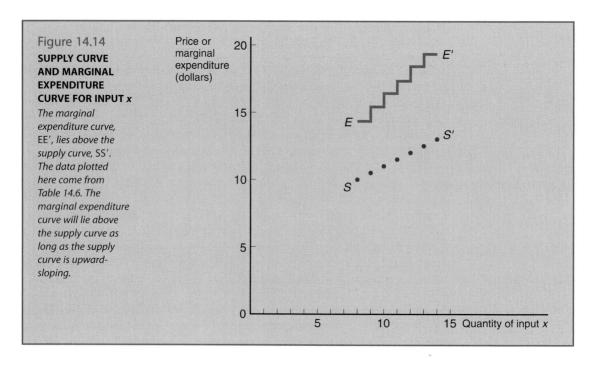

Figure 14.14

SUPPLY CURVE AND MARGINAL EXPENDITURE CURVE FOR INPUT x

The marginal expenditure curve, EE', lies above the supply curve, SS'. The data plotted here come from Table 14.6. The marginal expenditure curve will lie above the supply curve as long as the supply curve is upward-sloping.

just pay the higher price to the marginal unit; it must pay the higher price for each and every unit employed. The firm in Table 14.6 might, for example, want to increase its employment of input x from 8 to 9 units. It would have to pay for the ninth unit a price of $10.50, but it would also have to pay the other 8 units an extra 50 cents. Its cost would therefore increase by $10.50 + (8 \times \$0.50) = \$14.50$. This, of course, is the marginal expenditure figure recorded in the fourth column for the ninth unit of x.

Figure 14.14 shows the supply curve, SS', for input x of Table 14.6. If the input were bought by a single buyer, then the monopsonist's marginal expenditure curve would be EE'. This marginal expenditure curve lies above the supply curve because the supply curve is upward-sloping.

▣ Price and Employment: A Single Variable Input

What would all of this do to equilibrium in an input market? The answer to this question is most simply explored when there is only one variable input. A profit-maximizing monopsonist would employ increasing quantities of the input as long as the extra revenues derived from their addition were at least as large as the extra cost involved in their employment. The monopsonist would, of course, stop expanding employment when additional costs exceeded additional revenues.

Table 14.7 offers some specific context within which we can see what this would mean to equilibrium. The first two columns and the last replicate part of Table 14.6. The third column shows the marginal revenue product of the input—that is, it records the additional revenue derived from an additional unit of the input. The profit-maximizing monopsonist would expand

Table 14.7 OPTIMAL EMPLOYMENT OF INPUT x: MONOPSONY	Quantity of input x used by monopsonist	Price of x (dollars)	Marginal revenue product of x[a] (dollars)	Marginal expenditure for input x[a] (dollars)
	5	8.50	17.50	—
	6	9.00	16.90	11.50
	7	9.50	16.20	12.50
	8	10.00	15.40	13.50
	9	10.50	14.50	14.50
	10	11.00	13.50	15.50
	11	11.50	11.50	16.50
	12	12.00	8.50	17.50

[a]These figures pertain to the interval between the indicated amount of input x and 1 unit less than the indicated amount of input x.

Monopsony equilibrium

employment as long as the marginal expenditure figures recorded in the fourth column were no larger than the marginal revenue product values recorded in the third column. The monopsonist described in Table 14.7 would therefore choose to employ 9 units of input x. The same sort of outcome is displayed in Figure 14.15. There, the marginal revenue product curve is DD' and the marginal expenditure curve is EE'; the profit maximizing monopsonist would employ Q units of the input.

Note the difference between the condition for profit maximization under monopsony and the condition for profit maximization when there is perfect competition in the input market. Under perfect competition in the input market, we saw in Equation 14.4 that the firm must set

$$MP_x \times MR = P_x.$$

A monopsonistic firm would, by way of contrast, set

$$MP_x \times MR = ME_x, \qquad [14.5]$$

where ME_x is the marginal expenditure for input x.

The difference between Equations 14.4 and 14.5 lies in the quantities on the right-hand side: P_x in one case and ME_x in the other. Recall that ME_x is greater than P_x if the input's supply curve is upward-sloping. Recall as well that the marginal revenue product of input x decreases as more of input x is employed. It follows that less of input x would be used if Equation 14.5 were met than if Equation 14.4 were met. We should expect, therefore, that the monopsonist would employ less of the input than would be used if the input market were perfectly competitive.

And what about equilibrium price? The monopsonist would set the price at the level for which the quantity that it demanded would be matched by the quantity supplied. In Table 14.7, then, it would set a price of $10.50, because 9 units of x would be supplied and 9 units is the point where the marginal revenue product of x equals the monopsonist's marginal expenditure. And in Figure 14.15, the monopsonist would set a price of P. And what about under

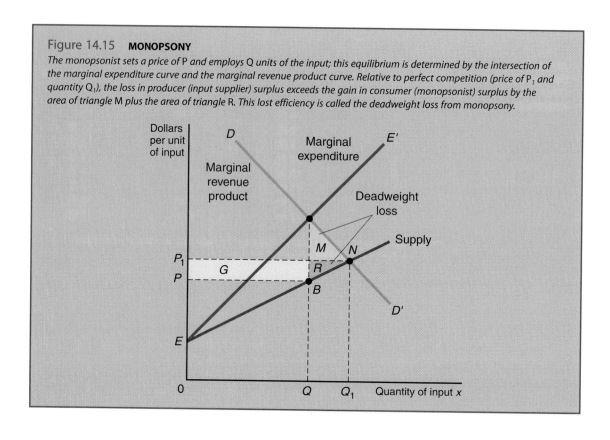

Figure 14.15 **MONOPSONY**

The monopsonist sets a price of P and employs Q units of the input; this equilibrium is determined by the intersection of the marginal expenditure curve and the marginal revenue product curve. Relative to perfect competition (price of P_1 and quantity Q_1), the loss in producer (input supplier) surplus exceeds the gain in consumer (monopsonist) surplus by the area of triangle M plus the area of triangle R. This lost efficiency is called the deadweight loss from monopsony.

perfect competition? Table 14.7 would support a competitive equilibrium at a price of $11.50 with 11 units employed. Why? Because the marginal revenue product of x would equal its price at 11 units. Note that the price set by the monopsonist would be lower than the price that would emerge from the workings of a competitive market for the input, but note, too, that the quantity employed by the monopsonist would be smaller. These are general results as long as supply is upward-sloping. Both are clearly displayed in Figure 14.15 as well. The competitive equilibrium there would be P_1 rather than the lower P if curve DD' were the demand curve for input x, and the equilibrium quantity employed would be Q_1 rather than the smaller Q.

Who would win and who would lose in a monopsonistic situation? Suppliers of the input would be hurt because the price of the input that they would deliver to the market would be lower under monopsony than under perfect competition. We can see how much harm they endure by using the concepts of producer and consumer surplus discussed in Chapters 9 and 10. In Figure 14.15, the suppliers of the input are the "producers." If the market were perfectly competitive, producer (input supplier) surplus would be the area of triangle EP_1N; under monopsony, it would equal only the area of triangle EPB. Recall that producer surplus is the area above the supply curve and below the price and that the price would be P_1 in the case of perfect competition and P in the case of monopsony. The loss in producer (input supplier) surplus due to monopsony would be equal to the area of rectangle G plus the area of triangle R.

| Example 14.7 | Does the Minimum Wage Cause Unemployment in the United States? |

The minimum wage was increased to $4.25 per hour in October 1996 and to $5.15 per hour in September 1997; and the summer of 2002 saw Congress considering raising it again by $1.50, from $5.15 to $6.65 per hour, in three installments over the next few years. The proposal guarantees that long-standing debate among economists and others about the employment effects of these increases will continue. In a competitive market, increasing a wage floor above the equilibrium would surely increase unemployment—the number of people who would be willing to work at the quoted minimum who cannot find jobs because the total quantity demanded falls short of the total quantity willingly supplied. But what if labor markets were monopsonistic? D. Card and Anne Krueger have argued that increasing the minimum wage under monopsonistic conditions might actually increase employment—but only to a point.

Figure 14.16 can be used to illustrate their argument. If the minimum wage were set at W_0, then the effective marginal expenditure curve facing the monopsonist would be W_0GHE and he would hire L_0 units of labor. Why? Becase this would be the point where the marginal expenditure curve would intersect the marginal revenue product curve. As a result, there would be no unemployment—but don't get excited. We start here to specify a benchmark against which to track the effect of raising the minimum wage. No sense confusing the issue and biasing the results by starting with some unemployment.

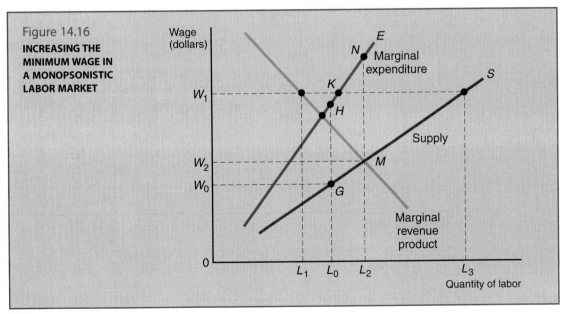

Figure 14.16

INCREASING THE MINIMUM WAGE IN A MONOPSONISTIC LABOR MARKET

Now suppose that the minimum wage were raised to W_1. The effective marginal expenditure curve would now be W_1KE, and L_1 units of labor would be employed. Since $L_3 > L_1$ units of labor would be supplied at this wage, unemployment would result. Moreover, $L_1 < L_0$, so total employment would have fallen as well, much as in the perfectly competitive case. But what if the minimum wage had been increased only to W_2? Then $L_2 > L_0$ units of labor would have been demanded and supplied because W_2MNE would become the effective marginal expenditure curve. There would still be no unemployment, but the overall level of employment would have increased. So, would an increase in the minimum wage reduce employment and increase unemployment? As always in economics, it depends.

For further discussion, see D. Card and A. Krueger, *Myth and Measurement* (Princeton, N.J.: Princeton University Press, 1995); D. Deere, K. Murphy, and F. Welch, "Employment and the 1990–1991 Minimum-Wage Hike," *American Economic Review,* May 1995; C. Brown, C. Gilroy, and A. Kohen, "The Effect of the Minimum Wage on Employment and Unemployment," *Journal of Economic Literature,* June 1982; and Council of Economic Advisers, *Economic Report of the President,* 1999, Box 3-2. For more recent news, consult http://www.chn.org/minimumwage/minwageissuebrief.html.

Meanwhile, the monopsonist plays the role of the "consumer" in Figure 14.15. After all, the monopsonist buys the input. The monopsonist would gain consumer surplus equal to the area of rectangle G because the price of the Q units that the monopsonist buys is P rather than P_1. The savings area of rectangle G is equal to $Q \times (P_1 - P)$. But the monopsonist would also lose the profit from the extra $Q_1 - Q$ units that it would have employed if the market had been competitive. This profit would have been equal to the area of triangle M. The monopsonist would therefore see its consumer surplus area climb by the area of rectangle G minus the area of triangle M.

Comparing the lost producer (input supplier) surplus (rectangle G plus triangle R) with the augmented consumer (monopsonist) surplus (rectangle G minus triangle M), we see that the loss would exceed the gain by an amount equal to the area of triangle R plus triangle M. This total area, indicated in *Deadweight loss* Figure 14.15, is often called the "**deadweight loss** from monopsony." It tells us how much the input suppliers' losses would exceed the monopsonist's gains. This deadweight loss would persist even if the monopsonist's gains were turned over to the input suppliers, because less of the input would still be used (in comparison with the perfectly competitive benchmark).

Microlink 14.4 Calculating Deadweight Loss in Input Markets

The calculation of the deadweight loss caused by exerting monopsony power was based on reasoning that parallels previous derivations that were applied to estimating the efficiency loss caused by monopoly power in Chapter 10 and other distortions in Chapter 9. All of these calculations use competitive equilibria as benchmarks of comparison. Figure 14.7 may be the easiest context within which to see the analogy. Equilibrium occurs there at point E, where the quantity supplied equals the quantity demanded (Q_0) at the market clearing price P_0. Why does this point also correspond to maximum net benefits?

Notice, first of all, that the area under the demand curve from 0 to Q_0 represents the total value of output produced by employing Q_0 units of the input; that is, it represents total benefits derived by consumers from consuming output supported by the employment of Q_0 units of input. How do we know that? Because each point on the demand curve reflects the marginal revenue product of employing successive units, one at a time, up to Q_0. The area under the supply curve, meanwhile, represents total cost because each point there reflects marginal cost in the usual sense; that is, each point on S indicates the amount that the suppliers must be compensated to offer successive units for employment, one at a time, up to Q_0. Net benefits are therefore maximized at E. Hiring more than Q_0 units would mean extending employment into the range where marginal cost exceeds marginal benefit so that net welfare would fall; and stopping before you get to Q_0 would mean forgoing the employment of units for which marginal benefits would exceed marginal cost.

EFFICIENCY WAGE THEORY

Finally, we turn to study the effects of asymmetric information on unemployment in the labor markets. On the basis of the simple competitive model, we can argue that substantial unemployment would not be expected if unemployed persons were willing to work for a lower wage than employed persons. Firms would simply find it profitable to lower wage rates and thereby increase employment.

Efficiency wage theory

Efficiency wage theory, a relatively recent development, makes a different assumption. It assumes that a worker's productivity (that is, his or her output per hour of labor) depends on the level of the wage rate. The preceding section argued that firms sometimes find it difficult to measure the effort being supplied by each worker. Under these circumstances, its workers could have an incentive to shirk if their firm paid the wage where the quantity of labor demanded equaled the quantity of labor supplied (W_0 in Figure 14.17). Why? Firm managers may not be able to detect the shirking. And even if they could and tried to fire the workers who are involved, these workers could readily obtain employment elsewhere at the same wage. There would, as a result, be little incentive for workers to work hard.

Firms can avoid this problem by paying a wage higher than W_0. Employees would not shirk under these circumstances because they would have to take a cut in pay if they were fired and had to work for some other firm at the perfectly competitive wage, W_0. They would not want to sacrifice the relatively high wage that they were earning, and so they would see a clear incentive to work hard. The wage rate where no shirking takes place is called

Efficiency wage

the **efficiency wage;** it is higher than the perfectly competitive wage.

All firms in the labor market would be in the same situation, though, and so they would all pay the efficiency wage rather than the perfectly competitive wage. This does not mean, however, that workers would be less motivated to work hard. The efficiency wage is higher than the perfectly competitive wage. Less labor would be demanded than supplied at the

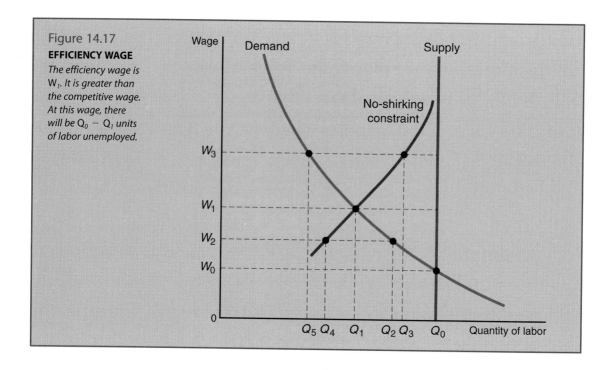

Figure 14.17

EFFICIENCY WAGE

The efficiency wage is W_1. It is greater than the competitive wage. At this wage, there will be $Q_0 - Q_1$ units of labor unemployed.

efficiency wage, and so there would be some unemployment. A worker who was fired for shirking would then take a place among the unemployed before finding another job at some other firm. The prospect of unemployment would, therefore, induce workers to work hard.

What factors determine the level of the efficiency wage? According to J. Yellen, J. Stiglitz, and others, the minimum wage rate that workers would have to earn in order not to shirk is inversely related to the level of unemployment.[6] For example, if the wage rate were W_2 in Figure 14.17, then $Q_0 - Q_4$ units of labor must be unemployed in order to induce workers not to shirk (otherwise there might be a job waiting for a fired worker). And if the wage rate were W_3, then $Q_0 - Q_3$ units of labor must be unemployed to keep workers from shirking. Economists sometimes draw the

No-shirking-constraint curve

so-called **no-shirking-constraint curve** to describe this situation; it is the curve showing the amount of unemployment (measured horizontally from Q_0 to the left) required at each wage rate to prevent shirking. The efficiency wage will tend to be at the point where this curve intersects the market demand curve for labor; it is W_1 in Figure 14.17.

Why is W_1 the equilibrium value of the efficiency wage? Because unemployment (the horizontal distance between the supply and demand curves) matches the level required to prevent shirking at this wage. Recall that the horizontal difference between the supply and no-shirking-constraint curves is this required "no-shirking" level. Suppose that the efficiency wage were

[6] J. Yellen, "Efficiency Wage Models of Unemployment," *American Economic Review,* May 1984; and J. Stiglitz, "The Causes and Consequences of the Dependence of Quality on Price" *Journal of Economic Literature,* March 1987.

W_2 (with $W_2 < W_1$). Unemployment would then equal $Q_0 - Q_2$ units of labor—a quantity that would be smaller than the $Q_0 - Q_4$ units of labor required to prevent shirking. The efficiency wage would tend to rise in this case. If the efficiency wage were W_3 (with $W_3 > W_1$), then unemployment would equal $Q_0 - Q_5$ units of labor—a quantity that would be greater than the $Q_0 - Q_3$ units of labor required to prevent shirking. The efficiency wage would tend to fall in this case.

This is clearly a highly simplified model, but it has been used to help explain a variety of phenomena. On January 12, 1914, for example, Henry Ford reduced the length of the working day at his automobile manufacturing company from 9 to 8 hours and raised the minimum daily pay from $2.34 to $5.00. It was a decision that received international attention. It was very unusual for a firm to announce that it would double the wage rate it pays. Yet Ford himself said it "was one of the finest cost-cutting moves we ever made."[7] Detailed analysis bears out the fact that the average cost of Ford's cars declined after this announcement because labor productivity rose so significantly. The higher wage resulted in fewer layoffs, firings, and resignations, and the workers seemed to exert more intensive and productive effort. The available evidence indicates that what Ford did was to pay an efficiency wage, enabling him to obtain better workers than his rivals.[8]

SUMMARY

1. If there is only one variable input, then the firm's demand curve for an input under perfect competition is the same as the marginal revenue product curve (the price or marginal revenue of the product multiplied by the marginal product of the input). The market demand curve for the input can be derived from the demand curves of the individual firms in the market, but it is not the simple horizontal sum of the individual demand curves. Lower input prices would cause all firms to expand their employment of that input and expand their output. The price of their product would fall, and so the marginal revenue product curves of all firms would shift down and to the left.

2. The supply of an input to an individual firm facing a competitive input market is infinitely elastic. The market supply curve for an input reflects the relationship between the price of the input and the total quantity supplied across the entire market. This need not be infinitely elastic.

3. Many inputs are supplied by business firms. Other inputs, like labor, are supplied by individuals. The supply curve for these inputs may be backward-bending, in the sense that increases in the input price can result in a reduction in the quantity supplied (at least over some range of variation of the input price); thus, a higher wage can reduce the quantity of labor supplied.

4. Given the market demand and supply curves for an input, the price of the input will tend in equilibrium to the level at which the quantity of the input demanded equals the quantity of the input supplied. The equilibrium

[7]H. Ford, *My Life and Work* (Garden City, N.Y.: Doubleday, Page, 1922), p. 147.
[8]For a detailed discussion, see D. Raff and L. Summers, "Did Henry Ford Pay Efficiency Wages?" *Journal of Labor Economics*, January 1987. See also T. Kniesner and A. Goldsmith, "A Survey of Alternative Models of the Aggregate U.S. Labor Market," *Journal of Economic Literature*, September 1987, for a useful survey of models of the aggregate labor market.

employment of an input can therefore be characterized by the intersection of the market demand and supply curves.

5. Payment to an input that is completely fixed in supply is called a rent; payment to an input that is temporarily in fixed supply is called a quasi-rent.

6. If there is imperfect competition in product markets, perfect competition in input markets, and only one variable input, then the firm's demand curve for the input is the same as the marginal revenue product curve (the marginal revenue of the product multiplied by the marginal product of the input).

7. Monopsony is a situation in which there is a single buyer. The supply curve of the input facing the monopsonist is the market supply curve. If the monopsonist maximizes profit, it will set the marginal expenditure for the input equal to its marginal revenue product.

8. A monopsonist will employ less of an input than would be used if the input market were perfectly competitive. A monopsonist will also set a lower price for the input than if the input market were perfectly competitive. A deadweight loss is evident when monopsony is compared with perfect competition. The deadweight loss reflects the degree to which losses incurred by input suppliers exceed the gains garnered by monopsonists.

QUESTIONS/ PROBLEMS

1. Many people have complained recently about a shortage of nurses. Suppose that you are an adviser to a U.S. senator who wants you to estimate how much of an effect a 1 percent increase in the wage paid to nurses would have on the shortage. The senator tells you that the quantity of nurses demanded currently exceeds the quantity supplied by 14 percent, that the price elasticity of demand for nurses is 0.3, and that the price elasticity of supply for nurses is 0.1. If these estimates are correct, what is the answer?

2. Studies by J. Landon and R. Baird indicate that, when other factors are held equal, the level of teachers' salaries in a school district depends on the number of other school districts in the district's county. (a) If there are a relatively large number of other districts in the country containing a particular school district, would you expect the salary level of teachers in this district to be relatively high or relatively low? Why? (b) Suppose that teachers could move costlessly to school districts outside the county. Would this influence your answer to part (a)? (c) There has been a tendency in recent years for large metropolitan school districts to decentralize into a number of autonomous districts, each of which makes its own hiring and firing decisions. What effect, if any, do you think that such decentralization will have on teachers' salaries? (d) What types of arguments would you expect from people who favor such decentralization?

3. A perfectly competitive firm can hire labor at $30 per day. The firm's production function is as follows:

Number of days of labor	Number of units of output
0	0
1	8
2	15
3	21
4	26
5	30

If each unit of output sells for $5, how many days of labor should the firm hire?

4. A firm sells its product for $10 per unit. It produces 100 units per month, and its average variable cost is $5. What is its quasi-rent? If its average fixed cost is $4, does its quasi-rent equal its economic profit?

5. A firm's demand curve for its product is given in the following table:

Output	Price of good (dollars)
23	5.00
32	4.00
40	3.50
47	3.00
53	2.00

The marginal product and total product of labor (the only variable input) are as given in this second table:

Amount of labor	Marginal product of labor	Total output
2	10	23
3	9	32
4	8	40
5	7	47
6	6	53

(Note that the figures regarding marginal product pertain to the interval between the indicated amount of labor and 1 unit less than the indicated amount of labor.) Given these data, how much labor should the firm employ if labor costs $12 a unit?

6. M. Feldstein estimated that physicians have a backward-bending supply curve for labor. He found that the price elasticity of supply of physicians' services was about −0.91. (a) Draw a graph where hours per week devoted to leisure are plotted along the horizontal axis, and income derived from working is plotted along the vertical axis. Letting leisure be one good and income derived from working be the other, construct an individual physician's budget line and indifference curves. (b) Using the graph constructed in (a), show how the physician's desired amount of leisure is influenced by a decrease in her wage rate if her supply curve for labor is backward-bending. (c) The American Medical Association has argued that any legislation that reduces the fees that physicians can charge will cut the supply of physicians' services. On the basis of Feldstein's results, does this appear to be true?[9]

7. The market for a particular input is a monopsony. For this input, $MRP = 8 - 2Q_D$, $P = 2Q_S$, and $ME = 4Q_S$, where MRP is this input's marginal revenue product, P is its price, ME is marginal expenditure for this input, Q_D is the quantity demanded of this input, and Q_S is the quantity supplied

[9]Note that Feldstein's study, while very influential, is only one of many; results vary from study to study.

of this input. *MRP*, *P*, and *ME* are expressed in dollars per unit of input; Q_D and Q_S are expressed in thousands of units per day. How large is the deadweight loss due to monopsony? Interpret your result.

8. Redo problem 7 under the assumption that the supply curve for the input is $P = 2 + 2Q_S$, so that the marginal expenditure function is $ME = 2 + 2Q_S$. Compare your answers with your results from Problem 7 to show that the deadweight loss due to monopsony is higher when the supply of the input is relatively inelastic (or lower when the supply is relatively elastic).

9. Economic models are like toys: you can play with them. Play with the model of monopsony to explore the ramifications of monopoly power in the product market. Assume, in particular, that the accompanying figure displays two demand curves for a monopolist. One, labeled $P \times MP$, reflects demand for input *x* if the monopolist sets price equal to marginal cost; the other, labeled $MR \times MP$, reflects demand for input *x* if the monopolist sets price to clear the market where marginal cost equals marginal revenue. The monopolist is also a monopsonist, facing supply curve *S* with an associated marginal expenditure curve *ME*. Compare the deadweight losses that would occur if the firm (a) exerted only its monopoly power in the product market, (b) exerted only its monopsony power in the input market, and (c) exerted both its monopoly and monopsony powers. Could their relative sizes change with different demand and supply conditions?

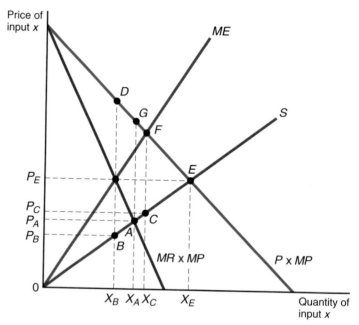

10. Consider the next figure. It displays a demand for union labor and an associated marginal revenue curve *RR'*. Assume that the union has M_1 members. (a) Suppose that the union wanted to keep its membership fully employed. What is the highest wage that would allow it to achieve its goal? (b) Now suppose that the union wanted to maximize the total income of its members. What wage would allow it to achieve this objective? (c) Suppose that it wanted to guarantee that its most senior members were

employed. If there were M_3 senior members whose employment mattered, what wage would pay them the most while still achieving the union's objective?

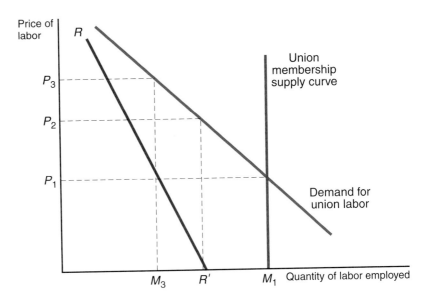

11. Suppose that the economy could be divided into a union sector and a nonunion sector. The accompanying figure could well offer a stylized version of what might happen. The demand curve for union labor there is D_u, the demand curve for nonunion labor is D_n, and the total demand for both sectors combined would be D_c if both sectors were paid the same wage. (a) Identify the equilibrium wage that would be obtained if there were no union. (b) If the advent of union power caused this union wage to jump to \$10, how many workers would be laid off in the unionized sector? (c) If all of these workers found jobs in the nonunion sector, what would happen to the nonunion wage? (d) Compute the efficiency loss associated with the migration of these workers form the union to the nonunion sector.

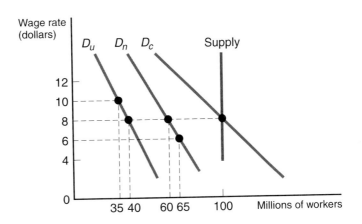

12. The next figure displays estimates of the marginal revenue product of irrigation water in growing cotton in Arizona under the assumptions that the price of cotton is 76 cents per pound or 51 cents per pound (of lint). (a) Which of the curves drawn must be the one for the higher price? (b) About how much water would be demanded if the price of water were $50 per acre-foot and the price of cotton were 76 cents? 51 cents? (c) Most studies indicate that the demand for irrigation water is relatively inelastic. Are the data embodied in these two demand curves consistent with that conclusion?

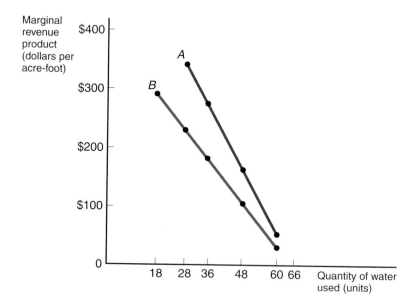

13. (Advanced) Suppose that a chemical firm's production function is $Q = L^{.8}K^{.2}$, where Q is output, L is the amount of labor used, and K is the amount of capital used. If the firm takes the product price and the input prices as given, show that total wages paid by the firm will always equal 80 percent of its revenues.

CHAPTER 15

Investment Decisions

INTRODUCTION

The preceding chapter offered some insight into the details of firms' employment decisions, and it reviewed the factors that work to govern input prices. It did not, however, provide a full treatment of a very important topic—firms' investment decisions. A firm like Microsoft increases its stock of capital when it invests; it adds to its supply of durable items like plant and equipment. We already know that capital of this sort is critical to most production processes. And we know that capital lasts a long time. Indeed, capital was one of the factors with which we distinguished the short run from the long run. A firm that is considering an investment in a particular factory or piece of equipment must therefore consider more than the present. It must account for costs and revenues that will be realized in both the present and the future.

This chapter looks at the processes of saving and investment. It will take some time to emphasize the determinants of the interest rate. It will present the central concept of present value (sometimes called present discounted value) and describe how to evaluate properly a stream of future payments. The present-value techniques presented here are as applicable to individuals' decisions as they are to the deliberations of firms.

INTERTEMPORAL CHOICE: CONSUMPTION AND SAVING

People generally try to maintain a balance between consumption in the present and consumption in the future (just as they try to maintain a balance among a wide variety of consumer goods). Older people who receive a lump-sum payment when they retire usually set much of it aside to cover anticipated expenses in subsequent years. People who are approaching retirement usually save some of their income to create or supplement a "nest egg." Younger people sometimes borrow against future income so that they can enjoy the benefits of owning a home or buying a new car before they actually have the cash on hand to cover the cost. Even younger people are sometimes forced by their parents to put birthday-present money from their relatives into the bank so that they will have access to it later, when they'll do "something responsible" with the money. In this section, we consider a model that economists have used to explain how people make the sorts of intertemporal decisions that determine their long-term consumption patterns.

The choice between the amount consumed this year and the amount consumed next year can be analyzed using the simple model of consumer behavior presented in Chapter 2. We need only assume that consumers have preferences between consumption this year and consumption next year just as they have preferences between meat and potatoes. The simplest version of the model considers only two periods: this year and next year. Preferences over two successive years can then be represented by an indifference map like the one shown in Figure 15.1; note its similarity with the indifference curves drawn in Figure 2.1. The consumer would, in addition, be confronted by a budget line. This time the budget line indicates the alternative combinations of present and future consumption that she could attain. For the sake of argument, suppose that our consumer knew that her income would be $30,000 this year and only $11,000 next year. This budget line is also

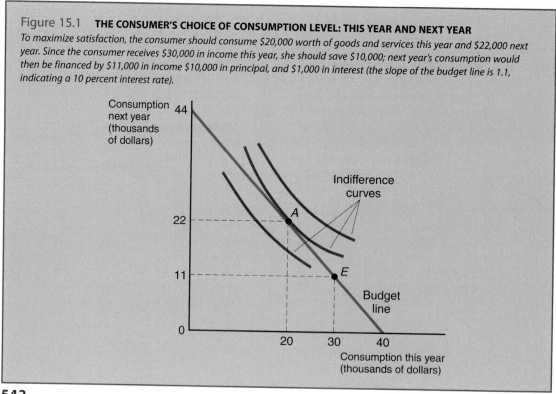

Figure 15.1 **THE CONSUMER'S CHOICE OF CONSUMPTION LEVEL: THIS YEAR AND NEXT YEAR**
To maximize satisfaction, the consumer should consume $20,000 worth of goods and services this year and $22,000 next year. Since the consumer receives $30,000 in income this year, she should save $10,000; next year's consumption would then be financed by $11,000 in income $10,000 in principal, and $1,000 in interest (the slope of the budget line is 1.1, indicating a 10 percent interest rate).

portrayed in Figure 15.1. We can now examine her intertemporal consumption decisions over two years. If she could borrow or lend at an annual rate of interest of 10 percent, how much would she consume this year? How much next year? How much would she have to borrow or save to achieve these levels of consumption?[1]

The optimal choice for the consumer modeled in this way is still represented by the point on the budget line that is on the highest indifference curve. Point A is the optimal point in Figure 15.1. Our consumer would, given the geometry of Figure 15.1, consume $20,000 worth of goods and services this year and $22,000 next year. How would she get to point A with a $30,000 income this year followed by an $11,000 income next year? That is, how would she get from **endowment point** E on the budget line to point A? She would save $10,000 of this year's income, and she would earn 10 percent on those savings ($1,000). As a result, $22,000 in consumption next year could be sustained by $11,000 in next year's income, $10,000 in savings from the present, and $1,000 in interest.

Endowment points

The slope of the budget line indicates the terms at which the consumer can borrow or lend. It is, more specifically, equal to -1 times the extra amount that could be consumed next year if the consumer lent somebody a dollar for a year. How is that? Lending somebody a dollar would mean that current consumption would fall by $1. But next year, the $1 would be paid back with interest. Notice that the rate of interest functions here like a premium that must be paid to an individual in return for her lending somebody $1 for one year. And so, the slope of the budget line in Figure 15.1 must equal $-(1 + r)$, where r is the **interest rate** expressed as a fraction (so that 10 percent interest would mean that $r = 0.1$, 5 percent interest would mean that $r = 0.05$, and so on). Saving $1 (moving to the left by $1 along the "consumption this year" axis) would return $1 in "principal" plus r in interest; in sum, then, saving $1 would allow the consumer to move up the "consumption next year" axis by $(1 + r)$. In Figure 15.1, more specifically, the slope equals -1.10 because the 10 percent interest rate is 0.1 when represented as a fraction. Notice, finally, that the interest rate plays a critical role in defining the price of present consumption. Indeed, $(1 + r)$ would be the price of a dollar today if it were expressed in terms of dollars paid one year from now. If, for example, the interest rate equaled 0.10 (i.e., 10 percent), then a dollar today would be worth $1.10 in one year's time.

Interest rate

The position of the consumer's budget line is determined by the consumer's endowment position, that is, by her income each year. As noted in passing above, the consumer's endowment position is represented in Figure 15.1 by point E, since her income would be $30,000 this year and

---

[1]We assume that the prices of goods and services next year are the same as they are this year—i.e., we assume that there is no systematic inflation. Note, too, that the consumer is assumed to have no reason to leave part of her receipts unspent at the end of the second year because there are only two years in the model. A more general model can have more than two years but is very hard to graph in two dimensions.

$11,000 next year. The critical idea here is that the consumer no longer has to consume her income every year. She could borrow or save and thereby move to other points on the budget line. We have already seen that moving up the budget line from point E would be accomplished by saving. It would result in consumption next year exceeding income because income this year exceeded consumption. Borrowing can be similarly represented by moving down the budget line to points below and to the right of point E. This would result in income next year exceeding consumption because consumption this year overran income. Part of next year's income would then have to be devoted to paying back the loan *and* the interest on the loan; moving $1 to the right from point E along the "consumption this year" axis would cause "consumption next year" to fall by $$(1 + r)$. Finally, the endowment point *must* be on the budget line; our individual can always choose to consume her income in both years by neither borrowing nor saving.

Example 15.1	A Theoretical Bias against Both Borrowing and Saving—Working a Problem

Panel A of Figure 15.2 portrays a situation in which an individual is endowed with the same income this year and next (endowment point E). Notice, as well, that it shows the more realistic circumstance in which the rate of interest that would be paid on a loan (denoted r_B) is larger than the interest that would be earned from saving (denoted r_S). You can see this by observing that the slope of the borrowing portion of the budget constraint is steeper than the slope of the saving portion. A higher rate on borrowing thereby produces a corner at the endowment point that makes it more likely that an individual would neither borrow nor save. Indeed, all circumstances in which

$$1 + r_B \geq MRS \,(\text{at endowment point } E) \geq 1 + r_S$$

would guarantee that neither borrowing nor saving would maximize utility.

While this condition would hold even if point E did not indicate the same income in both periods, symmetry in the endowment point provides a benchmark that economists have found useful. They implicitly define the *Pure rate of time preferences* pure rate of time preferences (typically denoted ρ) to reflect the marginal rate of substitution for points where consumption in period 1 equals consumption in period 2 by setting

$$1 + \rho \equiv MRS \,(\text{equal consumption in both periods}).$$

It follows that utility-maximizing individuals will neither borrow nor save, given a constant stream of income, as long as

$$r_B \geq \rho \geq +r_S.$$

If $\rho \geq r_B$, though, then these individuals will borrow to maximize intertemporal utility; and if $r_S \geq \rho$, then they will save.

What evidence do we have for estimating the value of ρ? Panel B of Figure 15.2 relates estimates of the corresponding discount factor [i.e.,

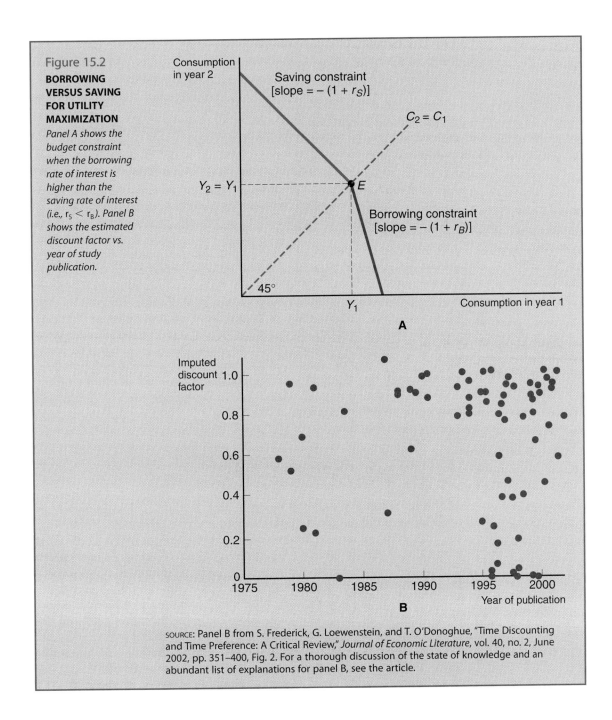

Figure 15.2

BORROWING VERSUS SAVING FOR UTILITY MAXIMIZATION

Panel A shows the budget constraint when the borrowing rate of interest is higher than the saving rate of interest (i.e., $r_S < r_B$). Panel B shows the estimated discount factor vs. year of study publication.

Consumption in year 2

Saving constraint
[slope $= -(1 + r_S)$]

$C_2 = C_1$

$Y_2 = Y_1$

E

Borrowing constraint
[slope $= -(1 + r_B)$]

45°

Y_1

Consumption in year 1

A

Imputed discount factor

1.0

0.8

0.6

0.4

0.2

0

1975   1980   1985   1990   1995   2000

Year of publication

B

SOURCE: Panel B from S. Frederick, G. Loewenstein, and T. O'Donoghue, "Time Discounting and Time Preference: A Critical Review," *Journal of Economic Literature*, vol. 40, no. 2, June 2002, pp. 351–400, Fig. 2. For a thorough discussion of the state of knowledge and an abundant list of explanations for panel B, see the article.

$1/(1 + \rho)]$ with the date of their publication. All were derived from statistical analyses of actual behavior or experimental results. Estimated values recorded there are mostly less than 1; this corresponds to a positive discount rate, and that is to be expected. Persistent variability across estimates, corresponding to estimates of ρ falling between 6 percent and well over 200 percent, is a surprise. Unlike the convergence over time in estimates of the speed of light (reported in Example 5.1), more sophisticated attempts to estimate personal discount rates have not produced much agreement. Researchers will continue to try to explain why. In the meantime, with interest on loans seldom running higher than 15 percent for car loans, 20 percent for credit card debt, and 8 percent for home mortgages, it is perhaps not difficult to see why so many people carry so much debt.

Microlink 15.1   The Budget Constraint Revisited—A Variation on a Theme

The paradigm of modeling individual behavior in terms of utility maximization subject to a budget constraint, applied here to borrowing and saving decisions, should be familiar from as far back as Chapter 2. It follows that interpreting the slope of the budget constraint as a reflection of opportunity cost must also carry over. When utility depended on two private goods, say, X and Y, then the equilibrium condition that the marginal rate of substitution between X and Y should equal the price ratio P_X/P_Y meant that the price ratio reflected the opportunity cost of consuming the last unit of X instead of $P_X X/P_Y$ units of Y. In the same way, utility-maximizing equilibria across time set the marginal rate of substitution between consumption today and consumption in the future (say, 1 year) equal to $1 + r$, where r is the rate of interest. That means that $1 + r$ is the opportunity cost of consuming 1 unit of something today instead of $1 + r$ in the future. And how do you get those units? Forgo consumption for one period, and then enjoy that "principal" plus a return of $r \times 100\%$ on that investment.

CHANGES IN THE INTEREST RATE

This simple consumer-choice model makes it clear that consumers' intertemporal decisions can be influenced by the rate of interest. To see that this is the case, suppose that the consumer in Figure 15.1 were confronted with a higher rate of interest. As shown in Figure 15.3, the increase in the interest rate would rotate the budget constraint around the endowment point. It would, specifically, be steeper than before. It would still pass through the endowment point E, though. Why? Because staying at E by neither saving nor borrowing would still be possible and must therefore still lie on the budget line. Notice that the higher rate of interest makes saving more attractive (points on segment BE that could not be attained with the lower rate of interest now lie on the budget line). Notice, as well, that the higher rate of interest makes borrowing less attractive (points on segment EF used to lie on the budget line but can no longer be attained with higher interest payments along segment EG). And what difference would all of this make? Figure 15.3 shows that our consumer would move from point A to point D if the interest rate were to climb. She would save an additional $1,000, so that consumption this year would fall (relative to the endowment) by more than before, and consumption next year would climb for two reasons— savings would be higher and each dollar saved would earn more interest.

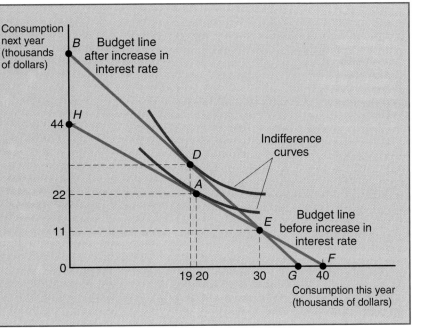

Figure 15.3

THE EFFECT OF HIGHER INTEREST RATES ON SAVING

With the higher interest rate indicated by the slope of budget line BG, the consumer saves $11,000; with the lower interest rate indicated by budget line HF, saving equals $10,000.

| Example 15.2 | **Income and Substitution Effects** |

The two panels of Figure 15.4 show that thinking of the rate of interest as the opportunity cost of future consumption can help break the effect of a change in the interest rate on either borrowing or saving into income and substitution effects. Panel A considers the case in which the individual under scrutiny is initially borrowing so that consumption in period 1 exceeds income. A higher interest rate rotates the budget constraint around the endowment point *E*. It produces a substitution effect from point *A* to point *B* along the original indifference curve that pushes down consumption in period 1 (borrowing falls). Notice, as well, that it also produces an income effect to point *C* (under the assumption that consumption in both periods is a normal good) that also pushes period 1 consumption down and further reduces borrowing.

Panel B, however, shows that the income effect pushes in the opposite direction for the saving decision. A higher interest rate still produces a substitution effect from point *A* to *B* that reduces period 1 consumption and thereby works to increase saving. But the higher interest rate tends to push real income up, in this case. As a result, the income effect pushes consumption in period 1 higher, from point *B* to point *C*; and the overall effect is ambiguous. It follows that higher interest rates can be expected to have a greater effect on borrowing than on saving. Indeed, higher interest rates could actually cause saving to fall.

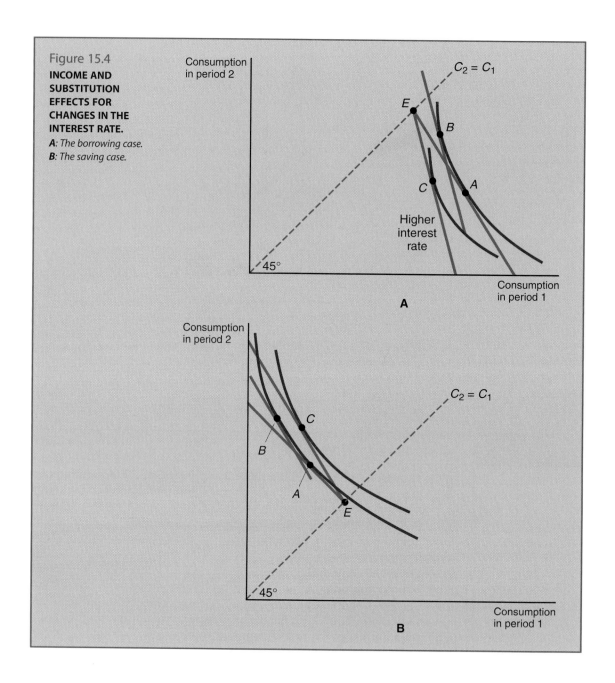

Figure 15.4

INCOME AND SUBSTITUTION EFFECTS FOR CHANGES IN THE INTEREST RATE.

A: The borrowing case.
B: The saving case.

INTEREST RATES AND INVESTMENT

Producers, like consumers, are influenced by rates of interest. They must decide whether or not to expand their productive capacity by investing in new buildings and factories. They must decide whether or not to buy new equipment that may embody new technology. They must decide whether to increase or decrease their inventories. All of these decisions have consequences that are felt sometimes in the future. And so we must take time into account as we think about how producers should make these types of decisions. The rule that should guide them is actually quite simple to state: producers should make an investment only if the rate of return that they would earn would exceed the interest rate they would have to pay if they had to borrow the requisite funds. And this rule would hold even if they did not have to borrow to make the investment. The interest rate always stands as the *opportunity cost* of using funds to underwrite an investment because the interest rate always represents the return that could be earned by putting the money to use elsewhere.

To see how this rule works, consider what would happen to a firm that borrowed money at a 9 percent interest rate to underwrite investing in a project with an 8 percent rate of return. It would clearly lose 1 percent on every dollar invested. And if the firm did not have to borrow money to finance the project? The firm could lend its money to others at the prevailing interest rate and thereby earn a greater return. It would still lose 1 percent on every dollar invested compared with the alternative. The reverse story, of course, would play out if the interest rate were, say, 7 percent. The investment would then pay an extra return of 1 percent if borrowing were required, and its return would exceed the opportunity cost if borrowing were not required.

Holding technology and the quantity of noncapital resources in the economy constant, the rate of return from an extra dollar of investment is likely to fall as investment climbs, for two reasons. First of all, this statement is true in large measure because of the law of diminishing marginal returns. If the stock of available capital were to increase (due to increased investment), then we should expect that the marginal product of capital would fall if technology and the employment of noncapital inputs remained constant. And a declining marginal product should mean that investment in an extra unit of capital would sustain smaller and smaller expansions in total output. It follows from the law of diminishing marginal productivity, therefore, that a larger capital stock should reduce the rate of return from an extra dollar of investment. In addition, higher levels of total investment across an economy could cause the price of capital goods to rise. An extra dollar of investment would then support the purchase of fewer capital goods, and this, too, would reduce the return from an extra dollar of investment.

Suppose that the relationship between the total amount of investment and the rate of return from an extra dollar of investment were shown by the curve in Figure 15.5. The curve slopes downward and to the right, so it displays the observations recorded in the preceding paragraph. For present purposes, it is important to note that this "investment demand curve" can tell us how much firms would like to invest at various interest rates. If the interest rate were 6 percent, for example, then they would like to invest $10 billion. Why? Because that is the level for which the rate of return from an extra dollar of investment would match the quoted 6 percent rate of interest. If they invested less than $10 billion, then the rate of return from an extra

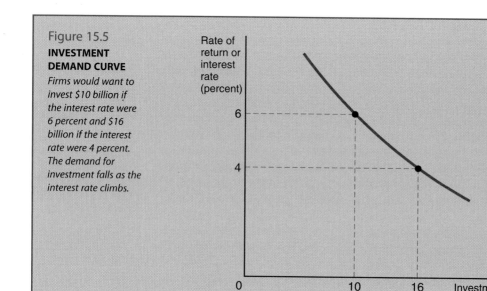

Figure 15.5

INVESTMENT DEMAND CURVE

Firms would want to invest $10 billion if the interest rate were 6 percent and $16 billion if the interest rate were 4 percent. The demand for investment falls as the interest rate climbs.

Rate of return or interest rate (percent)

Investment (billions of dollars)

dollar of investment would exceed the interest rate, and so producers could make more money by increasing investment even if they had to borrow to do so. To continue the example, if the rate of return from an extra dollar of investment were 8 percent while the interest rate were 6 percent, then firms could make 2 percent on the next increment of investment. How? By borrowing an extra dollar at 6 percent interest and investing it to obtain an 8 percent return. If, on the other hand, they invested more than $10 billion, then the rate of return from an extra dollar of investment would be less than the interest rate and they could make money by reducing investment. If the rate of return from an extra dollar of investment were 4 percent while the interest rate were 6 percent, firms could make money by reducing investment by a dollar and lending this dollar to somebody else at the prevailing 6 percent interest rate.

Given that the investment demand curve in Figure 15.5 slopes downward and to the right, it is clear that hikes in the interest rate tend to reduce investment and that cuts in the interest rate tend to raise investment. A reduction of the interest rate from 6 to 4 percent in Figure 15.5 would, for example, increase investment from $10 billion to $16 billion.

| Example 15.3 | **Neil Simon Goes Off-Broadway** |

Alarm bells went off all across the theater district in New York when Neil Simon, the hugely successful playwright, decided to open his new play *London Suite* in a smaller Off-Broadway theater. The producer, Emanuel Azenberg, cited pure economics for the decision to abandon Broadway. He had estimated that an investment of $1.3 million would have been required to open on Broadway and that it would have cost only $440,000 to open

Table 15.1		Broadway	Off-Broadway
COSTS AND EARNINGS ON BROADWAY AND OFF	Receipts	$13,000,000	$5,668,000
	Expenses		
	Rent and house crew	$ 2,340,000	$ 624,000
	Salaries	2,808,000	1,040,000
	Advertising	1,560,000	780,000
	Lights and sound rental	312,000	182,000
	Administration	1,664,000	572,000
	Royalties	1,222,000	728,000
	Other	832,000	338,000
	Profit	$ 2,262,000	$1,404,000

Off-Broadway. Table 15.1 records their anticipated expenses for a one-year run—expenses above and beyond the investment cost. For simplicity, assume that any profit would have been received at the end of the year but that expenses would have to be paid "up front." Assume, as well, that the playwright and producer would have to create an $800,000 contingency account from which additional and unanticipated expenses would be covered. Assuming a 10 percent interest rate, was either choice a good investment?

According to our derivation of the demand curve for investment, the relevant question is whether or not a guaranteed investment of either $1.24 or $2.1 million for one year would pay as much as investing in the play. Investing $2.1 million at 10 percent would do better than investing in a play on Broadway. It would produce $210,000 in return from elsewhere compared with $162,000 (= $2,262,000 − $1,300,000 − $800,000) for the Broadway production. Investing $1.24 million would meanwhile pay $124,000 elsewhere versus $164,000 for the Off-Broadway production. Clearly, investing Off-Broadway was the better choice (earning more than 10 percent on a smaller investment). If the appropriate opportunity cost for an alternative investment were 14 percent however, even the Off-Broadway option would have failed. Higher interest rates, as displayed in Figure 15.5, can reduce investment!

THE EQUILIBRIUM LEVEL OF INTEREST RATES

We have seen that the interest rate is really a price. It is the price that borrowers pay lenders to use their funds, and it is the opportunity cost of using funds to finance an investment. It should come as no surprise, therefore, that interest rates are determined by the supply and demand of loanable funds.

Figure 15.6 portrays a supply curve for loanable funds—the relationship between the quantity of loanable funds supplied and the interest rate. The supply of loanable funds comes from households and firms that find the

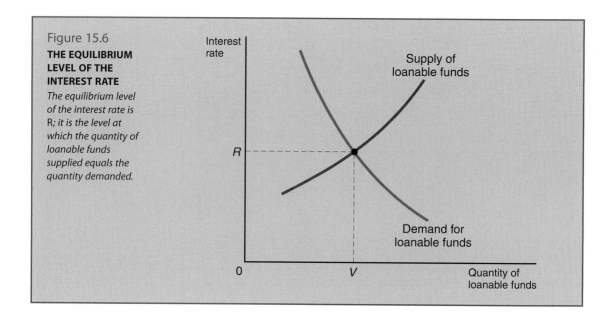

Figure 15.6

THE EQUILIBRIUM LEVEL OF THE INTEREST RATE

The equilibrium level of the interest rate is R; it is the level at which the quantity of loanable funds supplied equals the quantity demanded.

available rate of interest sufficiently attractive to induce them to save. Recall the consumer in Figure 15.1 who contributed $10,000 to the supply of loanable funds this year by saving. Since the incentive to save is generally thought to be greater when interest rates are higher, the supply curve usually slopes upward to the right, as shown in Figure 15.6.[2]

The demand curve for loanable funds, also shown in Figure 15.6, is the relationship between the quantity of loanable funds demanded and the interest rate. The preceding section suggested that a large portion of the demand for loanable funds stems from firms that want to borrow money to invest in capital goods like machine tools and buildings. Large portions of demand also stem from consumers who want to buy houses, cars, and other items and from governments that need to finance schools, highways, and many other types of public projects. The quantity of loanable funds demanded tends to decline as the rate of interest rises, and so the demand curve drawn in Figure 15.6 slopes downward to the right.

Equilibrium　　The **equilibrium** interest rate is the level for which the quantity of loanable funds demanded equals the quantity of loanable funds supplied. It is *R* in Figure 15.6.

Figure 15.6 seems to imply that there is only one interest rate in the economy, but nothing could be further from the truth. Loans vary greatly. Some last for 50 years; others last for 50 days. Some borrowers are extremely likely to repay the loan; others are not. Some borrowers are individuals, others are governments, and still others are corporations. There is a demand curve and supply curve of the sort shown in Figure 15.6 for each.

[2]The consumer-choice model of saving presented above allows for the possibility that the supply of loanable funds might bend backward for high rates of interest, just like the supply of labor. This potential has to do with income and substitution effects explored in Example 15.2.

And the equilibrium interest rate varies from one type of loan to another. In general, interest rates for riskier loans (for which there is a higher probability that the borrower will not pay in full or not pay on time) are relatively higher than those for less risky loans. Small, financially rickety firms usually have to pay higher interest rates than large, blue-chip firms, but even large, well-known firms have to pay higher interest rates than the federal government does.

PRESENT VALUE

Having looked briefly at the nature and determinants of interest rates, we must now indicate how interest rates enable firms and individuals to put amounts of money gained or lost at different points in time on a comparable footing. This is something firms and individuals must do in making investment decisions. Microsoft, for example, thinks that a dollar received today is worth more than a dollar received a year from today, and so should you. Why? Because you and Microsoft could always invest your available money now and earn interest on it. If the interest rate were 6 percent, for example, then a dollar received now would be equivalent to $1.06 received one year from now. All you would need to do is invest the dollar now and collect $1.06 in a year's time. Similarly, a dollar received now would be equivalent to $(1.06)^2$ dollars in 2 years' time. You could simply invest the dollar now and have 1.06 dollars in one year, and $(1.06)^2$ dollars at the end of the second year if you reinvested the first year's amount for a second year at 6 percent. And in 4 years' time? You could generate $(1.06)^4$ dollars if you could invest at 6 percent for the full 4 years.

We now turn this exercise around. We suppose, more generally, that you could invest at a compound rate of r percent per year, and you wanted to know the **present value** (the value today) of one dollar received in n years' time. This should be easy to determine given the earlier discussion. The present value, sometimes called "present discounted value," would be

Present value

$$\frac{\$1}{(1 + r)^n}.$$

Why? Because investing $\$1/(1 + r)^n$ today for n years at an interest rate of r would result in $\$1/(1 + r)^n \times (1 + r)^n = \$1$ in n years' time. If the interest rate were 0.10 and $n = 4$, for example, then we would be asking how much $1 received 4 years from now would be worth today. The answer—the present value of this dollar—would equal

$$\frac{1}{(1 + 0.1)^4} = \frac{1}{1.4641} = \$0.683.$$

To see that this answer is correct, think about what would happen if you invested 68.3 cents today. Table 15.2 shows that this investment would be worth 75.1 cents after 1 year, 82.6 cents after 2 years, 90.9 cents after 3 years, and $1 after 4 years. So, 68.3 cents must be the present value of a dollar

Table 15.2	Number of years in the future	Return received (cents)	Value of investment (cents)
VALUE OF 68.3 CENTS INVESTED AT 10 PERCENT INTEREST	1	68.3(0.10) = 6.830	68.3 + 6.830 = 75.13
	2	75.13(0.10) = 7.513	75.13 + 7.513 = 82.64
	3	82.643(0.10) = 8.264	82.643 + 8.264 = 90.91
	4	90.907(0.10) = 9.091	90.907 + 9.091 = 100.00

received in 4 years' time; if you invested the 68.3 cents today at 10 percent interest, then you would have exactly \$1 in 4 years.

Table 15.3 shows the value of $1/(1 + r)^n$ for various values of r and n. According to this table, then, the present value of a dollar received 10 years hence would be 46.3 cents if the interest rate were 0.08. The present value of \$1 in 25 years would be slightly more than one penny (\$0.01048) if the interest rate were 20 percent.

Table 15.3		Value of r								
PRESENT VALUE OF A DOLLAR RECEIVED IN n YEARS GIVEN AN INTEREST RATE OF r	n	0.01	0.02	0.03	0.04	0.06	0.08	0.10	0.15	0.20
	1	.99010	.98039	.97007	.96154	.94340	.92593	.90909	.86957	.83333
	2	.98030	.96117	.94260	.92456	.89000	.85734	.82645	.75614	.69444
	3	.97059	.94232	.91514	.88900	.83962	.79383	.75131	.65752	.57870
	4	.96098	.92385	.88849	.85480	.79209	.73503	.68301	.57175	.48225
	5	.95147	.90573	.86261	.82193	.74726	.68058	.62092	.49718	.40188
	6	.94204	.88797	.83748	.79031	.70496	.63017	.56447	.43233	.33490
	7	.93272	.87056	.81309	.75992	.66506	.58349	.51316	.37594	.27908
	8	.92348	.85349	.78941	.73069	.62741	.54027	.46651	.32690	.23257
	9	.91434	.83675	.76642	.70259	.59190	.50025	.42410	.28426	.19381
	10	.90529	.82035	.74409	.67556	.55839	.46319	.38554	.24718	.16151
	11	.89632	.80426	.72242	.64958	.52679	.42888	.35049	.21494	.13459
	12	.88745	.78849	.70138	.62460	.49697	.39711	.31683	.18691	.11216
	13	.87866	.77303	.68095	.60057	.46884	.36770	.28966	.16253	.09346
	14	.86996	.75787	.66112	.57747	.44230	.34046	.26333	.14133	.07789
	15	.86135	.74301	.64186	.55526	.41726	.31524	.23939	.12289	.06491
	16	.85282	.72845	.62317	.53391	.39365	.29189	.21763	.10686	.05409
	17	.84436	.71416	.60502	.51337	.37136	.27027	.19784	.09293	.04507
	18	.83602	.70016	.58739	.49363	.35034	.25025	.17986	.08080	.03756
	19	.82774	.68643	.57029	.47464	.33051	.23171	.16354	.07026	.03130
	20	.81954	.67297	.55367	.45639	.31180	.21455	.14864	.06110	.02608
	21	.81143	.65978	.53755	.44883	.29415	.19866	.13513	.05313	.02174
	22	.80340	.64684	.52189	.42195	.27750	.18394	.12285	.04620	.01811
	23	.79544	.63414	.50669	.40573	.26180	.17031	.11168	.04017	.01509
	24	.78757	.62172	.49193	.39012	.24698	.15770	.10153	.03493	.01258
	25	.77977	.60953	.47760	.37512	.23300	.14602	.09230	.03038	.01048

You can use Table 15.3 to determine the present value of receiving any amount of money in n years' time; i.e., you are not stuck thinking only about $1. If, in particular, you received x dollars in n years' time, then the present value of that x dollars would be

$$\frac{x}{(1 + r)^n}.$$

To determine the present value, therefore, simply multiply x by the value of $1/(1 + r)^n$ noted in Table 15.3.

To illustrate, a promise of receiving $10,000 in 10 years with an interest rate of 15 percent would be worth $10,000 \times 1/(1 + r)^n$ with $r = 0.15$ and $n = 10$. Table 15.3 shows that $1/(1.15)^{10} = 0.24718$, so the present value of the promised $10,000 would be $10,000 \times (0.24718) = \$2,471.80$.

VALUING A STREAM OF PAYMENTS

An individual or firm will frequently receive a stream of payments at various points in time. A firm that leases a warehouse to another firm might, for example, expect to receive $100,000 per year in payments for each of the next 5 years. What would be the present value of this stream of payments? To see how questions of this sort can be answered, it is convenient to begin by considering the simple case in which you would receive $1 per year for n years at an interest rate of r. You would, more specifically, expect to receive $1 in 1 year's time, another dollar in 2 years' time, and so on until you received your last dollar in n years' time. Applying what we learned in the preceding section, the present value of this stream of $1 receipts would be the sum of the present values of each receipt—i.e., it would equal

Present value of a stream of income

$$\frac{1}{(1 + r)} + \frac{1}{(1 + r)^2} + \ldots + \frac{1}{(1 + r)^n}.$$

The present value of being paid $1 at the end of each of the next 5 years with an interest rate of 10 percent, therefore, would be

$$\frac{1}{(1 + 0.1)} + \frac{1}{(1 + 0.1)^2} + \frac{1}{(1 + 0.1)^3} + \frac{1}{(1 + 0.1)^4} + \frac{1}{(1 + 0.1)^5}$$
$$= 0.90909 + 0.82645 + 0.75131 + 0.68301 + 0.62092$$
$$= \$3.79. \tag{15.1}$$

Table 15.3 provided the figures for Equation 15.1. How? Note that the final term on the right side of the second line of the equation is 0.62092. It is the present value of a dollar to be received after 5 years with an interest rate of 10 percent, and it is the fifth entry down in Table 15.3 when the value of r is 0.10.

Table 15.4, meanwhile, shows why $3.79 would indeed be the present value of receiving $1 at the end of each of the next 5 years if the interest

Table 15.4	Number of years in the future	Return received (dollars)	Amount withdrawn (dollars)	Net value of investment (dollars)
$3.79 INVESTED AT 10 PERCENT INTEREST WOULD PROVIDE EXACTLY $1 AT THE END OF EACH OF THE NEXT 5 YEARS	1	3.79(0.10) = .379	1	3.79 + .379 − 1.00 = 3.169
	2	3.169(0.10) = .3169	1	3.169 + .3169 − 1.00 = 2.486
	3	2.486(0.10) = .2486	1	2.486 + .2486 − 1.00 = 1.735
	4	1.735(0.10) = .1735	1	1.735 + .1735 − 1.00 = 0.909
	5	0.909(0.10) = .0909	1	0.909 + .0909 − 1.00 = 0

rate were 0.10. As you can see from the table, you would be able to withdraw $1 at the end of each year and end the fifth year with nothing left over if you invested $3.79 for 5 years at 10 percent interest. And how much would you pay today for a contract that promised to pay you $1 at the end of each of the next 5 years? If the interest rate were 10 percent, you would pay no more than $3.79. Why? Because Table 15.4 shows you how to generate that stream of income from an alternative investment of $3.79.

Annual payments from most contracts and investment projects, of course, will differ from $1. Suppose that you expect to receive payments at the end of each of the next n years and that the interest rate is r. Let the expected payment for the end of the first year be X_1, the expected payment for the end of the second year be X_2, and so on. The present value of this series of potentially unequal payments would then be

$$\frac{X_1}{(1 + r)} + \frac{X_2}{(1 + r)^2} + \ldots + \frac{X_n}{(1 + r)^n}.$$

You can also use Table 15.3 to help carry out this computation. For example, suppose that $r = 0.10$, that $n = 3$, and that you expect to receive $3,000, $2,000, and $1,000 at the ends of the first, second, and third years, respectively. Table 15.3 shows that $1/(1 + 0.10) = 0.90909$, $1/(1 + 0.10)^2 = 0.82645$, and $1/(1 + 0.10)^3 = 0.75131$. The present value of this stream of anticipated payments is therefore

$$\frac{\$3,000}{(1 + r)} + \frac{\$2,000}{(1 + r)^2} + \frac{\$1,000}{(1 + r)^3}$$
$$= \$3,000(0.90909) + \$2,000(0.82645) + \$1,000(0.75131)$$
$$= \$5,131.48.$$

Example 15.4	**Recovering Lifetime Earnings in the Face of a Loyalty Bias**

Anne Preston followed the work of Edward Lazear and Sherwin Rosen to offer a "loyalty bias" explanation for why women are compensated less than apparently equally qualified men—earning starting salaries that are roughly 75 percent of those offered to comparably skilled men and seeing those salaries increase only half as fast for a significant period of time early in their careers. Their argument revolves around the notion that employers require a "loyalty" signal from women. That is, employers want to make certain that women are committed to the workplace, more generally, and to their specific jobs, more specifically, before they are allowed to enter the "career track"—a track that, from the employer's perspective, involves potentially costly investments in training and educating new hires. The perceived problem is that women frequently interrupt their careers to begin families so that employers might never see benefits of these investments from a majority (or at least a significant proportion) of women. Preston, Lazear, and Rosen hypothesize that women must signal that this will not happen by remaining in the workforce for the first 5 to 10 years of their working lives. They are underpaid until the signal is recognized, and so progress up the compensation ladder is delayed.

Our discussion of present value has put us into a position from which we can examine how much this structure, if it is an accurate description of employer behavior, costs women over the course of their working lifetimes. Table 15.5 shows two sets of numbers for various discount rates and two different signaling periods. The second rows of either panel show, the present value of lifetime earnings for a woman (as a fraction of the comparable lifetime earnings of a man) under the assumption that a 25-year-old woman entering the labor force would (1) be paid a starting salary equal to 75 percent of a man's, (2) receive 2 percent raises per year for a signaling period of 5 years (instead of the 4 percent that a man would receive), and (3) receive the same 4 percent raises as a man over the next 30 years. Lifetime earnings for such a woman would be remarkably stable across different discount rates—equaling slightly more than two-thirds of her male counterpart.

The first rows indicate rates of compensation increase that would be required to bring a woman's lifetime earnings up to the same level as a

Table 15.5

LIFETIME EARNINGS FOR WOMEN WHO PAY A "LOYALTY PENALTY"
A: 5 YEARS UNTIL THE "LOYALTY SIGNAL" IS RECOGNIZED
B: 10 YEARS UNTIL THE "LOYALTY SIGNAL" IS RECOGNIZED

A

	Discount rate			
	1%	3%	5%	10%
Lifetime earnings (fraction of a man's)	0.683	0.684	0.686	0.692
Catch-up rate (versus 4% for a man)	5.68%	5.91%	6.23%	7.45%

B

	Discount rate			
	1%	3%	5%	10%
Lifetime earnings (fraction of a man's)	0.626	0.630	0.636	0.650
Catch-up rate (versus 4% for a man)	6.53%	6.90%	7.39%	9.36%

man's if the appropriate increases did not begin until after the signal was recognized. The interest rate plays a much larger role, here. Notice, in fact, that these increases would have to be nearly twice as large as a man's if a 10 percent discount rate were used for the calculations.

SOURCES: E. Lazear and S. Rosen, "Male-Female Differentials in Job Ladders," *Journal of Labor Economics*, vol. 8, no. 3, March 1990, pp. S106–S123; and A. Preston, "Sex, Kids and Commitment to the Workplace: Employers, Employees and the Mommy Track," discussion paper, Averell Harriman School for Management and Policy, State University of New York at Stony Brook, 1998.

THE NET-PRESENT-VALUE RULE FOR INVESTMENT DECISIONS

The calculation of present value plays a critical role in evaluating investment decisions. To see exactly how, suppose that manufacturing engineers at the Microsoft Corporation proposed building a new plant with new equipment. Why? Let's assume they think that the investment would reduce costs. Now assume, as well, that Microsoft's marketing executives have proposed investments in new warehouses and marketing facilities, and that Microsoft's research directors have proposed the purchase of additional instrumentation and the construction of new laboratories. Should Microsoft accept any of these proposals? All of them? Which one would be best if it could afford only one (after paying legal bills or something like that)?

The answer to these questions is simple. Accept an investment proposal if the present value of the expected future cash flows from the investment is greater than the investment's cost (even if you have to borrow because you have to pay the lawyers). For example, suppose that an investment costs $100 today and that it would sustain $60 in profits in each of the next two years. Assuming that the profit would materialize at the end of each year,

Net present value the **net present value** of the investment would be the present value of the future cash flows minus the initial cost of the investment. In this case, then, the net present value would equal

$$-\$100 + \frac{\$60}{(1 + r)} + \frac{\$60}{(1 + r)^2},$$

where r is the "discount rate." When an interest rate is used to calculate the

Discount rate net present value of an investment, it is called the **discount rate.**

In general, if an investment costs C dollars now and if it is expected to yield cash flows of X_1 dollars in one year's time, X_2 dollars in two years' time, . . . , and X_n dollars in n years' time, then the net present value of the investment equals

$$-C + \frac{X_1}{(1 + r)} + \frac{X_2}{(1 + r)^2} + \ldots + \frac{X_n}{(1 + r)^n}. \qquad [15.2]$$

The net present value is a measure of the benefits to be derived from an investment net of its cost. Clearly, a firm should accept an investment project only if its net present value is positive. This is the so-called *net-present-value rule*.

To evaluate the net present value, the firm must choose a value for r, the discount rate. What value should it choose? To answer this question, the firm must estimate the rate of return that it could obtain if it used the money it would spend on this investment in alternative ways. Any firm typically has a variety of investment projects that it could carry out. Our Microsoft example had Bill Gates pondering investments in new plant and equipment to reduce costs, in new warehouses to facilitate marketing, or in additional instrumentation and new laboratories to foster research. But Microsoft could also invest in stocks and bonds, for that matter. And so Microsoft, or any firm, should use a discount rate that matches its opportunity cost of capital—the rate of return that it could obtain if it invested its money in some other, comparable investment project.

But what do we mean by a "comparable" investment project? In general, investors require higher rates of return on riskier investments than they do on less risky ones. This, of course, is why interest rates tend to be higher on riskier loans than they are on safer ones. If lenders have doubts about getting their money back, they will charge a higher interest rate than if they are sure of being repaid. A "comparable" investment project is one that is as risky as the investment project under consideration. So, firms discount their investment options using the returns that they could obtain from other, equally risky investment projects.

Let's assume, for the moment and for simplicity only, that the investment under consideration is riskless. Let's assume, in other words, that the firm is certain that the expected future cash flows from the investment will materialize. Under these circumstances, the preceding discussion tells us that the appropriate discount rate is the rate of interest on government bonds. Why? Because the firm could purchase equally riskless government bonds with its funds if it did not accept the investment under consideration. Later in this chapter, we will discuss how to deal with the more typical and more complex case where the investment under consideration is risky.

| **Example 15.5** | **Present Value of a Perpetuity—Working A Problem** |

Perpetuities are financial assets, like a bond, that pay a fixed annual amount forever. In Britain, perpetuities that were issued about 500 years ago are still being traded. What is the present value of holding such an asset? That is, what is such an asset worth today? Suppose, for the sake of argument, that a perpetuity stipulated that it would pay its holder $100 per year forever. The present-value question of what such a promise would be worth is one of asking the value of Y you would have to invest to guarantee that it could pay $100 per year if the interest rate were given by r. Clearly, the value Y must solve

$$\$100 = r \times Y.$$

To find Y, simply divide both sides by r so that

$$Y = \frac{\$100}{r}.$$

If $r = 0.04$ (a 4 percent interest rate), then $Y = \$100/0.04 = \$2,500$. The perpetuity would be worth \$2,500 because it could, given a 4 percent return, pay \$100 in interest every year and still maintain its principal.

In general, a perpetuity paying $\$X$ per year would be worth

$$Y = \frac{X}{r}$$

because the present value of an indefinitely long stream of annual payments of X would be X/r. To see why, notice that

$$Y = \frac{X}{1 + r} + \frac{X}{(1 + r)^2} + \frac{X}{(1 + r)^3} + \dots$$

$$= X\left[\frac{1}{1 + r} + \frac{1}{(1 + r)^2} + \frac{1}{(1 + r)^3} + \dots\right].$$

Multiplying both sides of this equation by $(1 + r)$, we obtain

$$(1 + r)\,Y = X\left[1 + \frac{1}{1 + r} + \frac{1}{(1 + r)^2} + \frac{1}{(1 + r)^3} + \dots\right]$$

$$= X + X\left[\frac{1}{1 + r} + \frac{1}{(1 + r)^2} + \frac{1}{(1 + r)^3} + \dots\right]$$

$$= X + Y.$$

Subtracting Y from both sides of this equation,

$$rY = X$$

$$Y = \frac{X}{r}.$$

Microlink 15.2 Present Discounted Value and the Slope of the Demand for Investment

Figure 15.5 depicted a downward-sloping demand curve for investment. This is entirely consistent with results that can be derived by applying present-discounted-value calculations to investment decisions. To see why, refer to Equation 15.2 and contemplate investors facing an array of possible investment projects. For any specific interest rate, some might have positive present values and others might have negative present values. The demand for investment would simply be the sum of the initial costs that would be incurred if all of the projects with positive present values were undertaken. Now notice that all of the positive terms in Equation 15.2 appear in years where they are diminished by appropriate discounting by a presumed interest rate. A higher rate would therefore make it less likely that any single project would have a positive present value, and demand for investment would fall if the present value of even one project were to turn negative. To be more precise, think about a project whose present value was zero for some interest rate, like 5 percent. Recomputing its present value with a discount rate of 6 percent or 7 percent (actually, with any rate greater than 5 percent) would mean that its present value would turn negative and it would no longer be an attractive opportunity. It follows immediately that the demand for investment would fall because at least one project would no longer appear on the list of projects that support such demand.

THE INVESTMENT DECISION: AN EXAMPLE

The net-present-value rule has found widespread application, but using it requires a lot of knowledge and information. To illustrate its use, consider a firm that has to decide whether or not to purchase a machine that would reduce its labor requirements. Should the firm buy the machine? The net present value rule can help us answer this question, but what sort of information would we need? We would need to know how much the machine would cost; assume it would cost $25,000. We would need to know how long it would last; assume that it would last for 5 years. We need to know whether or not the machine would be worth anything after its productive lifetime had passed; assume that it would have no salvage value at the end of 5 years. We would need to know how much the firm would save in labor costs if it bought the machine; assume that Table 15.6 provides the data. We would need to know how confident the firm was that these data were accurate and would actually hold up over time; assume that the firm takes them as certain and guaranteed. And we need to know what discount rate to apply. The firm is certain of the cost and revenue data, so we need to know the riskless rate of interest on government bonds; assume that it is 10 percent.

Should the firm buy the machine? According to the net-present-value rule, the answer depends on whether the net present value of the investment is positive, and we have assumed enough information to apply the rule.

Table 15.6 EFFECTS OF MACHINE ON FIRM'S STREAM OF CASH INFLOW	Number of years in the future	Effect on cash inflow[a] (dollars)
	0	−25,000
	1	2,000
	2	6,000
	3	8,000
	4	14,000
	5	12,000

[a]Positive numbers indicate cash inflows; negative numbers indicate cash outflows.

Using Equation 15.2 and those assumptions, the net present value of this investment would equal

$$-\$25{,}000 + \frac{\$2{,}000}{(1 + 0.1)} + \frac{\$6{,}000}{(1 + 0.1)^2} + \frac{\$8{,}000}{(1 + 0.1)^3}$$

$$+ \frac{\$14{,}000}{(1 + 0.1)^4} + \frac{\$12{,}000}{(1 + 0.1)^5} = \$4{,}800,$$

given that $C = \$25{,}000$, $X_1 = \$2{,}000$, $X_2 = \$6{,}000$, $X_3 = \$8{,}000$, $X_4 = \$14{,}000$, $X_5 = \$12{,}000$, and $r = 0.10$. Since the net present value of the investment is positive, the firm should buy the machine (assuming that it got its numbers right and that the returns were, indeed, certain and guaranteed).

Note two things. First, the net present value of this investment depends on the value of the discount rate. In particular, the net present value equals

$$-\$25{,}000 + \frac{\$2{,}000}{(1 + r)} + \frac{\$6{,}000}{(1 + r)^2} + \frac{\$8{,}000}{(1 + r)^3} + \frac{\$14{,}000}{(1 + r)^4} + \frac{\$12{,}000}{(1 + r)^5},$$

where r is the discount rate. Figure 15.7 shows that the net present value decreases as the discount rate increases. This is true of many investments, not just this one. According to Figure 15.7, the net present value equals 0 when the discount rate equals about 15.5 percent (i.e., $r \approx 0.155$). This value of r (the value for which the net present value is 0) is called the internal rate of return; we will return to this point in a later section. For discount rates below about 0.155, the net present value is positive, and the firm should invest in this project. For discount rates above 0.155, the net present value is negative, and the firm should not invest in this project.

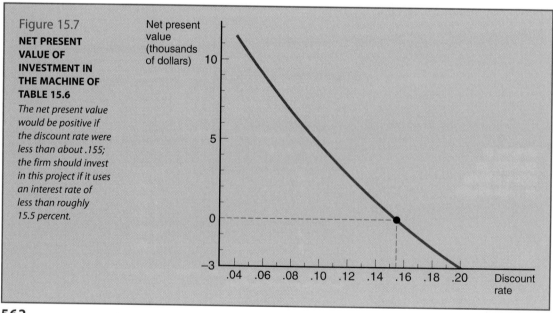

Figure 15.7

NET PRESENT VALUE OF INVESTMENT IN THE MACHINE OF TABLE 15.6

The net present value would be positive if the discount rate were less than about .155; the firm should invest in this project if it uses an interest rate of less than roughly 15.5 percent.

Second, there is no reason why all of the Xs in Equation 15.2 have to be positive. Recall that the Xs are the future cash flows. The firm could easily lose money in the first few years because of start-up costs and "teething" problems. In these cases, X_1—the cash flow during the year following the investment—could be negative. This causes no problem in calculating the net present value of the investment. Indeed, X_2, X_3, . . . , or even X_n could be positive or negative. The validity and usefulness of Equation 15.2 are unaffected by this complication, even though negative flows "downstream" diminish the likelihood that the net present value would be positive. Convince yourself, for example, that the net present value of the machine at a 10 percent interest rate would be $-\$654.54$ if the cash flow reported in Table 15.6 for one year from now were $-\$4,000$ instead of $+\$2,000$.

| Example 15.6 | Working Out the Best Deal for Leasing a Car |

Have you ever been confused by the range of financing options offered by new car dealerships, especially for leasing? Yes? Not yet? Just wait, you will. But being able to compute the present value of alternatives will help you out. For example, Table 15.7 reports some "raw data" taken from the newspaper in July 2002. A local Honda dealership was offering three different 39-month leasing arrangements on a selected stock of 2002 Accord LXs. Perhaps you would not be excited by an Accord, but assume for the moment that you are. Which option should you choose?

The first thing to sort out is the difference between "money down" and "amount due at lease inception." The former amounts to payments against the financing that the dealer will use to underwrite the lease; the latter includes things like dealer preparation charges, taxes, and registration fees that are added to the price of the car.

The next thing to do is try to sort out the difference between an annual rate of interest (quoted, for example, by banks for car loans) and the equivalent monthly rate of interest (to be used to compute the present value of 39 equal monthly payments). That is, if $x \cdot 100\%$ is the annual rate of interest,

Table 15.7		Deal A	Deal B	Deal C
ALTERNATIVE PAYMENT OPTIONS FOR LEASING A NEW HONDA	Term	39 months	39 months	39 months
	Money down	$0	$999	$1,999
	Amount due at lease inception	$595.08	$1,667.28	$2,672.02
	Security deposit	None	None	None
	Monthly payment	$259	$239	$219
	Obligation at the end of the lease	Surrender vehicle	Surrender vehicle	Surrender vehicle

Table 15.8	Annual interest rate				
THE PRESENT VALUE OF EACH OPTION FOR ALTERNATIVE INTEREST RATES	**1%**	**3%**	**5%**	**7%**	**9%**
Option A	$12,654.75	$11,740.75	$10,842.75	$10,105.75	$9,373.75
Option B	$12,959.75	$12,069.75	$11,245.75	$10,479.75	$9,766.75
Option C	$13,196.75	$12,332.75	$11,529.75	$10,785.75	$10,094.75

what is the equivalent rate assuming monthly compounding? The answer, $y \cdot 100\%$, implicitly solves the equation

$$(1 + y)^{12} = 1 + x$$

so that

$$y = (1 + x)^{-12} - 1.$$

Table 15.8 compiles the results of doing the appropriate present-value calculations; they are displayed graphically in Figure 15.8. For each option, in particular, the present value of total payments over 39 months is

$$\text{amount due at inception} + \frac{\text{monthly payment}}{1 + y} + \ldots + \frac{\text{monthly payment}}{(1 + y)^{39}},$$

where y is the equivalent monthly interest rate. Notice that the option with the lowest down payment has the lowest present discounted value regardless of the discount rate, and the option with the lowest monthly payments has the highest present value. Is this true in general? Probably not, so "Buyer beware!"

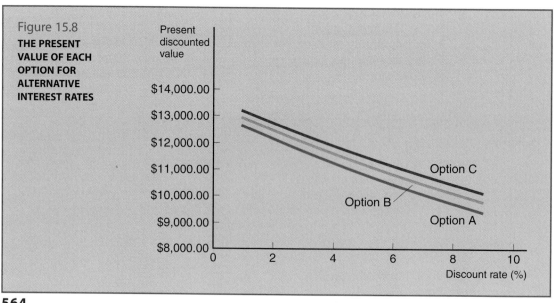

Figure 15.8

THE PRESENT VALUE OF EACH OPTION FOR ALTERNATIVE INTEREST RATES

REAL VERSUS NOMINAL INTEREST RATES

Real interest rate

Nominal interest rate

It is important, to avoid creating confusion, to distinguish between real and nominal interest rates. The **real interest rate** is the annual percentage increase in real purchasing power that the lender receives from the borrower in return for making the loan. The **nominal interest rate** is the annual percentage increase in money that the lender receives from the borrower in return for making the loan. The crucial difference between the real rate of interest and the nominal rate of interest is that the former is adjusted for inflation, whereas the latter is not. Expressed algebraically,

$$\text{real rate of interest} = \text{nominal rate of interest} - \text{inflation rate}. \quad [15.3]$$

To illustrate why this distinction is important, suppose that a firm borrowed $1,000 for a year at 12 percent interest, during which time the rate of inflation was 9 percent. The firm would repay the lender $1,120 at the end of the year, but this amount of money would be worth only $1,120/1.09, or about $1,030, when corrected for inflation. The real rate of interest on this loan would be 3 percent, then, not 12 percent (the nominal rate). Why? Because the lender would receive only $30 in constant (beginning-of-the-year) dollars in return for making the loan. Notice that this would be exactly 3 percent of the original $1,000 loan. This exact equality agrees with the content of Equation 15.3. Since the nominal rate of interest was 12 percent and the inflation rate was 9 percent, Equation 15.3 tells us that the real rate of interest should equal $12 - 9 = 3$ percent.

Why is this distinction between real and nominal interest rates important when we calculate the net present value of an investment? Because the numerators and denominators in Equation 15.2 must match. If the expected future cash flows (the Xs in Equation 15.2) are expressed in real terms (corrected for inflation), then the discount rate must also be expressed in real terms—that is, it must be a real rate of interest. But if the expected future cash flows are expressed in nominal terms (uncorrected for inflation), then the discount rate must also be expressed in nominal terms—that is, it must be a nominal rate of interest. The real rate of interest can depart substantially from the nominal rate of interest in periods of relatively high inflation. So using the wrong type of discount rate can produce incorrect results and lead to costly investment decisions.

INTERNAL RATES OF RETURN

Internal rate of return

The net present value of an investment project is not the only commonly used indicator of an investment project's profitability. The **internal rate of return,** which is defined as the discount rate that equates the present value of the net cash inflows from the project to the project's investment outlay, is sometimes used. In other words, the internal rate of return is the interest rate that the investor would really earn from his or her investment in the project. Holding the riskiness of a project constant, investors generally prefer projects with higher internal rates of return to ones with lower internal rates of return. Moreover, the investment rule that leads firms to invest only in projects with position present discounted values is equivalent to a rule that would allow investment only in projects whose internal rates of return exceed the applicable discount rate.

Computing the internal rate of return is not as easy at it might appear. To see this point, suppose that you invested $47,550 in a project that yielded cash inflows of $15,000 per year for each of the next 4 years. To determine the internal rate of return for this project, you must find the value of r^* that satisfies the following equation:

$$\$47,550 = \frac{\$15,000}{(1 + r^*)} + \frac{\$15,000}{(1 + r^*)^2} + \frac{\$15,000}{(1 + r^*)^3} + \frac{\$15,000}{(1 + r^*)^4}.$$

Why is r^* the interest rate that is earned on this investment? Because it is the discount rate that makes the present value of the net cash inflows from the project (the positive values on the right-hand side of this equation) equal to the investment outlay of $47,550. Simple computer programs or trial-and-error techniques in a spreadsheet can solve this equation for r^*. The solution in this example is $r^* = 0.10$; that is, the internal rate of return for this investment is 10 percent.[3]

| Example 15.7 | Defining "Impatience" in Terms of Discount Rates |

You will perhaps recall that the Applied Perspective for Part Four described a model of dynamic price decisions in which n identical firms supplied a market, where n is a relatively small number. We assumed that each firm was initially making positive profits in some sort of cooperative equilibrium—a total of $\Pi_{\text{cooperate}}$ so that each firm received $\Pi_{\text{cooperate}}/n$. We then contemplated what might happen when something disturbed this equilibrium. One firm, firm I, correctly deduced that it could expand its market share and increase its own profits to $\Pi_{\text{defect}} > \Pi_{\text{cooperate}}/n$ at the expense of the others by lowering its price. Since prices were set for specific periods of time, the other firms could respond to this defection. In fact, we envisioned an open "tit-for-tat" strategy through which each firm would always set its prices next period at the lowest price quoted by its competitors in the previous period. Such a strategy ran the risk of a price war, of course, but only the gains to firm I from defection, $\Pi_{\text{defect}} - (\Pi_{\text{cooperate}}/n)$, were higher than the downstream penalties.

[3]Hand-held calculators that compute rates of return are constructed to solve equations of this sort. For a description of trial-and-error methods, as well as a discussion of the relationship between the net-present-value rule and the internal rate of return, see E. Mansfield, *Managerial Economics*, 4th ed. (New York: W. W. Norton, 1999). One disadvantage of the internal rate of return is that it is not always unique. That is, more than one value of r^* will sometimes make the present value of the cash flows equal to the cost of the investment.

It turns out to be quite instructive to continue the example by specifying exactly what those penalties might be. To that end, note that the immediate return to firm I for its defection would be maximized if it captured a monopolist's share for one period. If the other firms followed its price lead in subsequent periods, however, it would have to share these profits with the others in the penalty phase. As a result, downstream profits to firm I would be $\Pi_{\text{defect}}/n < \Pi_{\text{cooperate}}/n$. We can now assert that firm I would cooperate in the first period only if the present value of a constant profit equal to $\Pi_{\text{cooperate}}/n$ were deemed to be larger than the present value of earning Π_{defect} in the first period and Π_{defect}/n thereafter. Applying the perpetuity result of Example 15.5, therefore, we now know that firm I would cooperate only if

$$\frac{\Pi_{\text{cooperate}}/n}{r} > \Pi_{\text{defect}} + \frac{(\Pi_{\text{defect}}/n)/r}{1+r}, \qquad [15.4]$$

where r is the interest rate used by firm I in its present-value calculations. The left-hand side of Equation 15.4 represents the present value of cooperating and earning a perpetual stream of profit equal to Π_{defect}/n. The right-hand side of Equation 15.4, meanwhile, represents the present value of defecting to earn Π_{defect} in the first period and a perpetual stream of profit equal to Π_{defect}/n beginning in period 2.

To see the import of Equation 15.4, multiply both sides by $1 + r$ and collect terms. One then finds that firm I will find it attractive to cooperate in period 1 only if

$$\frac{1}{n} \frac{\Pi_{\text{cooperate}} - \Pi_{\text{defect}}}{\Pi_{\text{defect}} - (\Pi_{\text{cooperate}}/n)} \geq r \qquad [15.5]$$

Interpreting Equation 15.5 can now allow us to put some significant economic content into the notion of "patience." Patience, in economic terms, means that people are more willing to delay income or consumption in the sense that these future earnings are not discounted very heavily. In other words, patient people or firms use low interest rates to discount the future because they do not need to be paid quite as much next period to be adequately compensated for postponing income or consumption. Equation 15.5 therefore instructs us directly that firm I would be less likely to defect if it were more patient (i.e., if it worked with a lower interest rate). Why? Because lowering the operational interest rate would make it easier for the left-hand side of Equation 15.5 to exceed the interest rate that sits alone on the right-hand side. In words, a lower interest rate would mean that downstream penalties would not be discounted as severely so that the gain in period 1 would not have to be as large to compensate.

Equation 15.5 can also provide direct support for some of the other claims in the Applied Perspective. We argued there, for example, that increased market concentration would make defection less likely. In terms of Equation 15.5, higher market concentration would mean a smaller number of firms (a smaller n); and reducing n would make the left-hand side of the equation grow so that it would be easier to satisfy the critical inequality for cooperation. We also argued in the Applied Perspective that shorter pricing periods would make cooperation more likely; and we also know from the calculation of monthly interest rates in Example 15.6 that shorter time periods mean lower interest rates. Clearly, therefore, shorter pricing periods would make the right-hand side of Equation 15.5 smaller; as before, meeting the criterion for cooperation would be easier.

PRICING EXHAUSTIBLE RESOURCES

Some resources, like oil and copper, could be used up some day. The earth contains only a finite stock of each, and so the more we use today, the less we have tomorrow. Developing an understanding of the pricing of these resources over time builds on the foundation laid by many of the concepts discussed in this chapter. The notion of present value, for example, is critical because an analysis of the pricing of exhaustible resources must focus our attention on more than one time period.

To see how such an analysis works, suppose that you owned an oil well, that you wanted to maximize profits, and that the current price of oil exceeded the marginal cost of extraction by $10 per barrel. In other words, you could earn $10 in profit for every barrel of oil that you produced and sold this year. Be clear about your position, though. You own one oil well, and so you own a fixed amount of oil. Indeed, every barrel that you produced and sold this year would be 1 less barrel that you could produce and sell in the future. There is, therefore, an opportunity cost of exploiting the oil today because it would not then be available at a later date. The amount of oil that you produced and sold this year should therefore depend not only on current profits of $10 per barrel, but also on the price (net of the marginal cost of extraction) that you could receive in the future.

Think about the details of this story for a minute. If you expected the price net of marginal extraction costs to rise at an annual rate that exceeded the rate of interest, then you should keep your oil in the ground so that you could sell it in the future. Why? Because the present value of the profit from a barrel of oil extracted and sold in the future would be greater than $10— the profit that you could make from its current extraction and sale. To see this, assume that r were the interest rate. The present value of the profit from a barrel of oil that you extracted and sold one year from now would therefore be

$$PV = \frac{G_{t+1}}{(1 + r)},$$ [15.6]

where G_{t+1} is the price net of marginal extraction costs one year from now. Clearly, this present value would exceed $10 if G_{t+1} exceeded $10 \times (1 + r)$, but this condition would certainly be met by your expectation that the net price would increase at an annual rate that exceeded the rate of interest.

If, on the other hand, you expected that the price net of marginal extraction costs would rise at an annual rate that fell short of the rate of interest, then you should extract as much oil as possible from your well and sell that oil now. Why? Because the present value of the profit from each barrel extracted and sold in the future would be less than $10. The present value of the profit from a barrel of oil extracted and sold a year from now would be given by Equation 15.6. This would surely be lower than $10 if the net price of your oil rose at an annual rate that was less than the rate of interest.

Turning from your oil well to the international petroleum market as a whole, it is clear that the price net of the marginal cost of extraction should increase over time at an annual rate equal to the interest rate. Why is this so? If the net price were to increase more slowly, then you and the other owners of oil wells would sell as much oil as possible as soon as possible, and the current price of oil would fall. And if the net price were to increase at a rate higher than the rate of interest, then you and your fellow owners would sell as little oil as possible so that the current price of oil would rise. In equilibrium, therefore, the price of oil net of the marginal cost of extraction should tend to increase at an annual rate equal to the rate of interest. As shown in Figure 15.9, then, the quantity demanded should fall over time. The price should, for example, increase from P_0 in 1998 to P_1 in 2018 and to P_2 in 2038 as the quantity demanded falls from Q_0 to Q_1 to Q_2. Figure 15.10 displays some forecasts of the international price of crude oil published in 1987 by many of the world's leading experts in the wake of a dramatic fall in real prices. Notice that the trajectories of their forecasts look a lot like the hypothetical curve drawn in Figure 15.9, but notice, too, the sensitivity of forecasts to current conditions.

Figure 15.9   **CHANGES OVER TIME IN PRICE AND QUANTITY DEMANDED OF AN EXHAUSTIBLE RESOURCE**
The price (less the marginal cost of extraction) increases at an annual rate equal to the interest rate. The price should increase from P_0 in 1998 to P_1 in 2018 and to P_2 in 2038. The quantity demanded should therefore fall from Q_0 in 1998 to Q_1 in 2018 to Q_2 in 2038.

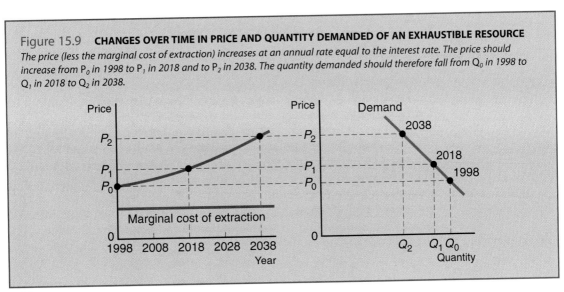

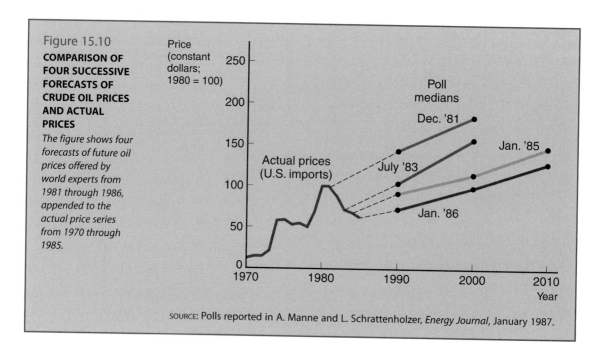

Figure 15.10

COMPARISON OF FOUR SUCCESSIVE FORECASTS OF CRUDE OIL PRICES AND ACTUAL PRICES

The figure shows four forecasts of future oil prices offered by world experts from 1981 through 1986, appended to the actual price series from 1970 through 1985.

Price (constant dollars; 1980 = 100)

Poll medians

Dec. '81

Jan. '85

Actual prices (U.S. imports)

July '83

Jan. '86

SOURCE: Polls reported in A. Manne and L. Schrattenholzer, *Energy Journal*, January 1987.

The model whose results are displayed in Figure 15.9 is very simple. It assumes perfect competition. And it ignores the many difficulties involved in forecasting prices, extraction costs, and interest rates. Figure 15.10 shows, however, that its rudiments have found application in many studies of the markets for oil, copper, and other resources.[4] One of the key lessons to be learned from this model is that the marginal cost of producing and selling an exhaustible resource may far exceed the marginal cost of extraction. The marginal cost of producing and selling a barrel of oil might be very substantial even if extraction costs were zero because of the opportunity cost incurred when a barrel of oil is actually consumed (and is no longer available). According to some estimates, opportunity costs of this type might amount to half the price of oil if it were sold in competitive markets.

The model also ignores technological change that might be induced by the rising price of a natural resource. Early studies saw the price of copper rising over the long term at an annual rate approximating the rate of interest—much like the trajectories displayed in Figures 15.9 and 15.10. As explained in Example 1.6, the price of copper plummeted in the late 1970s. Why? Because fiber-optic cables became economically feasible and turned every major urban area around the world into a copper mine. Copper electric and phone cables were rapidly replaced by fiber-optic cables, so that the old cables became an abundant source of pliable and preprocessed copper. And the price of oil fell in the 1980s as the effect of the OPEC oil shocks wore off.

[4]This model was first put forth in H. Hotelling, "The Economics of Exhaustible Resources," *Journal of Political Economy*, April 1931.

Increased supplies from non-OPEC sources and technology-supported reductions in demand were the keys.

Finally, market power can play an interesting role in the pricing of exhaustible resources. Consider, for a moment, what would happen if a monopolist owned an exhaustible resource. Recall that the price of the resource, net of its marginal cost of extraction, should increase at an annual pace that matches the rate of interest. This price trajectory would guarantee that the price exactly matched the sum of the marginal cost of extraction and the marginal opportunity cost of consumption early rather than late. Recall, as well, that the monopolist would maximize profit by setting marginal cost equal to marginal revenue, not price. It follows, therefore, that the monopolist would guarantee that the marginal revenue derived from selling its resource net of the marginal cost of extraction would increase at the same annual rate. But price exceeds marginal revenue for a monopolist. And so the price charged by the monopolist would increase at a pace that was slower than marginal revenue—that is, at an annual rate that fell short of the rate of interest.[5] Interestingly, therefore, the price of the resource would increase more slowly in a monopolistic market than it would in a competitive market; the quantity demanded would fall more slowly, as well.

Example 15.8	The Quality of Energy Price Forecasts

The ability to support accurate predictions was identified in Chapter 1 as one of the basic criteria used to evaluate the quality of an economic model. Figure 15.10 highlights the medians of forecasts for long-term future oil prices that were authored in the 1980s, and the text draws attention to both their sensitivity to then-current prices and their similarity to trajectories that would be supported by a depletion model for exhaustible resources. So, how did they do? Have actual oil prices moved along paths that coincide with any of the earlier forecasts?

Panel A of Figure 15.11 tracks the high and low forecasts depicted in Figure 15.10 and extends actual nominal prices through 2000. Notice that actual prices seem to be tracking just below the bottom of the forecast range and were, at least before the fall of 2001, moving into that range. This tendency is even more pronounced in panel B, where real oil prices are plotted; note that the bottom of the range and actual prices both display almost no trend since 1985. Having solidified a firm benchmark price in the mid 1980s, therefore, the theory does not do too badly in generating reasonable forecasts. It is also interesting to note that real oil prices at the end of 2002 were only 33 percent higher than they were in 1970 (when the price of a gallon of gasoline in the United States was about 25 cents).

---

[5]To see this, recall from Chapter 5 that $MR = P[1 - (1/\eta)]$, where MR is marginal revenue, P is price, and η is the price elasticity of demand. A profit-maximizing monopolist sets $MR =$ marginal cost, so $1 - (1/\eta)$ must be positive as long as marginal cost is positive. The rate of increase of MR, denoted g_{MR}, is therefore a linear function of the rate of increase in price, denoted g_P. In particular, $g_{MR} = g_P + K$, where $K = 1[1 - (1/\eta)]$ is a positive constant. Clearly, then, $g_{MR} > g_P$.

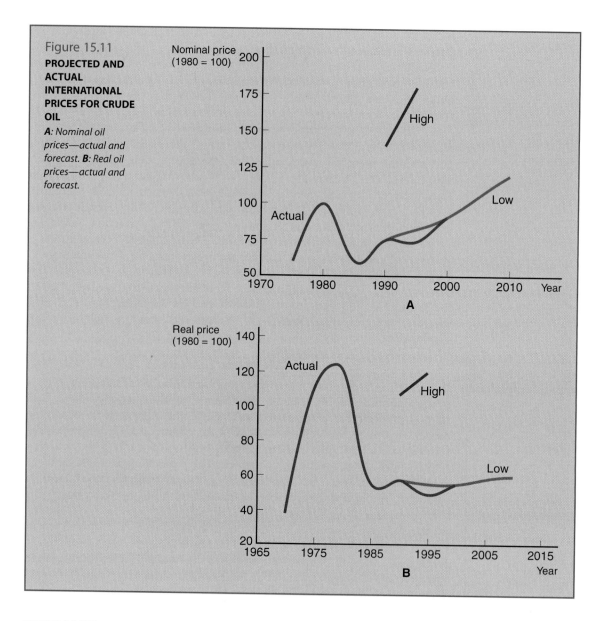

Figure 15.11

PROJECTED AND ACTUAL INTERNATIONAL PRICES FOR CRUDE OIL

A: Nominal oil prices—actual and forecast. B: Real oil prices—actual and forecast.

SUMMARY

1. Consumers have preferences between consumption this year and consumption next year. These preferences can be represented by sets of indifference curves. Consumers are confronted by budget lines that indicate the combinations of present and future consumption that they can attain. The slope of these budget lines is $-(1 + r)$, where r is the interest rate. The optimal choice between the amount consumed this year and the amount consumed next year is represented by the point on the budget line that lies on the highest indifference curve; tangency between the highest indifference curve and the budget line characterizes this optimal point.

2. Higher interest rates often lead to more saving. The investment demand curve shows that higher interest rates tend to reduce total investment by

firms. For equilibrium to occur, the quantity demanded of loanable funds must equal the quantity supplied. The equilibrium rate of interest is the level at which this equality occurs.

3. If you expected to receive X dollars n years from now, then the present value of this income would be $\$X/(1 + r)^n$, where r is the rate of interest. If you received X_1 dollars one year from now, X_2 dollars two years from now, . . . , and X_n dollars n years from now, then present value of this series of payments would be $\$X_1/(1 + r) + \$X_2/(1 + r)^2 + \ldots + \$X_n/(1 + r)^n$.

4. If an investment costs C dollars now and if it is expected to yield cash flows of X_1 dollars in 1 year's time, X_2 dollars in two years' time, . . . , and X_n dollars in n years' time, then the net present value of the investment would equal $-C + \$X_1/(1 + r) + \$X_2/(1 + r)^2 + \ldots + \$X_n/(1 + r)^n$, where r is the discount rate. The net present value is a measure of the benefits of an investment net of its cost. A firm should accept an investment project only if its net present value is positive.

5. In calculating the net present value of an investment project, a firm should use the rate of return that it can obtain from other, equally risky investment projects as the value of r, the discount rate. If expected future cash flows are expressed in real terms (corrected for inflation), then the discount rate must be expressed in real terms, as well (i.e., the real interest rate must be used). If the expected future cash flows are expressed in nominal terms (uncorrected for inflation), then the discount rate must be the nominal interest rate. The real interest rate equals the nominal interest rate minus the rate of inflation.

6. Another indicator (besides net present value) of the profitability of an investment project is the internal rate of return, which is defined as the interest rate that equates the present value of the net cash flows from the project to the project's investment outlay. Holding constant the riskiness of a project, investors generally prefer projects with high internal rates of return to projects with low internal rates of return.

7. The price of an exhaustible resource should reflect both the cost of extraction and the opportunity cost of consumption. The price, net of the marginal cost of extraction, should therefore increase over time at an annual rate that matches the rate of interest. The quantity demanded should fall over time as the price rises.

QUESTIONS/ PROBLEMS

1. A major oil company evaluated a proposed investment in improved vis-breakers, a particular type of petroleum-refining equipment. According to the company's analysts, these improvements would require an investment of $10 million and would result in savings of $2 million per year for the following 9 years. If the investment were made in 2003, the effect on the firm's cash flow would be given by the following table:

Year	Effect on cash flow (millions of dollars)	Year	Effect on cash flow (millions of dollars)
2003	−10	2008	2
2004	2	2009	2
2005	2	2010	2
2006	2	2011	2
2007	2	2012	2

(a) Calculate the net present value of this investment if the interest rate is 10 percent. (b) Calculate the net present value if cost overruns amounting to $3 million were anticipated. (c) Calculate the internal rate of return for the project with and without the overruns. (d) Calculate the probability of an overrun for which the expected net present value of the project would be exactly zero. (e) Would the company be wise to make the investment if it thought that the probability of overruns were greater than the value you calculated in part (d)? (f) Would the company make the investment if it were risk-averse and thought that the probability of overruns were exactly the value that you calculated in part (d)?

2. What important factors might cause the supply curve drawn in Figure 15.6 to shift to the right? What effect would such a shift in the supply curve have on the equilibrium level of the interest rate? What important factors might cause the demand curve in Figure 15.6 to shift to the right? What effect would such a shift in the demand curve have on the equilibrium level of the interest rate? What would happen to the equilibrium level of the interest rate if both curves shifted to the right?

3. An investment will have the following effect on a firm's annual cash inflow:

Year	Net effect
2003	−$5,000
2004	+$2,000
2005	+$2,000
2006	+$1,000
2007	+$1,000

(a) Should this firm make this investment if the interest rate is 10 percent? (b) Compute the internal rate of return.

4. A firm has developed a new product that lowers the costs of drilling oil wells by speeding up the drilling process. (This is an actual case.) The accompanying table displays the effect that investment in this product had on the firm's cash flow. (These figures, which were provided by the firm, have been rounded to make the computations simpler.)

Year	Effect on cash flow (millions of dollars)	Year	Effect on cash flow (millions of dollars)
1980	−100,000	1990	15,000
1981	−100,000	1991	200,000
1982	−100,000	1992	700,000
1983	−100,000	1993	700,000
1984	−100,000	1994	700,000
1985	−100,000	1995	700,000
1986	−100,000	1996	700,000
1987	15,000	1997	700,000
1988	15,000	1998	700,000
1989	15,000	1999	700,000

(a) Assuming a 10 percent interest rate, was the firm wise to make this investment? (b) Would the firm have been wise to make the investment if its effect on the firm's cash flow from 1987 through 1990 had been zero?

5. Suppose that a government bond pays $10 per year in perpetuity. That is, the government has promised to pay the bearer $10 a year forever. How much would you be willing to pay for the bond if the interest rate were 5 percent? 10 percent? 20 percent? Draw a curve that shows how this price varies with the interest rate. Is it linear? Why or why not?

6. Show that the income and substitution effects always push borrowing in the same direction. That is, show that higher interest rates tend to lower borrowing because both the income and substitution effects reduce current consumption.

7. The Carborundum Corporation had to decide whether to expand its production capacity for Ceramax, a ceramic material that it manufactured. Sales for this material had been growing rapidly, and its only manufacturing plant had reached capacity. The firm could expand its existing plant in Lockport, New York, or build a new plant in Birmingham, Alabama. Carborundum's staff calculated the net present value of the two options; they were $-\$163{,}000$ and $-\$153{,}000$ for expanding in New York or building a new plant in Alabama, respectively.[6] (a) Based on these results, does it appear that Carborundum should expand the Lockport plant? (b) Does it appear that it should build a new plant? (c) In calculating the net present value of the investment in the new plant, Carborundum's staff considered only the first 5 years after its construction. Does that seem to be the relevant period? (d) In calculating the net present values given above, Carborundum's staff used a discount rate of 15 percent, although the firm's return on comparable investments during the previous decade appeared to have averaged less than 10 percent. Does this figure of 15 percent seem too high? (e) If the discount rate that was used were too high, would this bias the net present values upward or downward? Why? Why might Carborundum think that 15 percent was an appropriate interest rate even if comparable investments had earned less than 10 percent?

8. Newspapers such as the *Wall Street Journal* frequently run articles discussing the effects of changes in the interest rate on the behavior of savers. They are particularly worried about the effect of taxation of the interest earned on savings. The accompanying figure shows the budget lines for a saver before and after an increase in the effective interest rate caused by a reduction in the tax rate applied to interest income. Point A indicates this individual's anticipated income for this year and next. (a) Which budget line pertains to the period before the tax treatment changed? (b) How much would this individual have saved before the change? How much after? (c) Compare your result with the results demonstrated in Figure 15.3. Does this comparison suggest a backward-bending relationship between the (after-tax) rate of interest and the quantity of saving? (d) Could a similar ambiguity appear if you applied this model to borrowers?

[6]For further discussion, see R. Hayes, S. Wheelwright, and K. Clark, *Dynamic Manufacturing* (New York: Free Press, 1988).

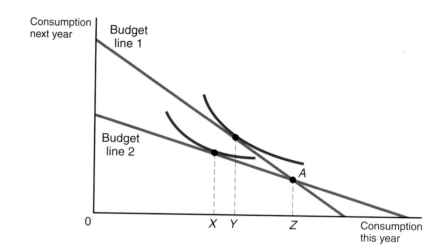

9. Property owners have long understood that real estate taxes have a direct effect on the value of their holdings. Suppose that Proposition 13 in California lowered the taxes owed on a particular piece of property in Sacramento by $1,000 per year. Assume that people looked at the political situation in California and felt that this reduction would be permanent. How much would the value of property owned in California increase if the rate of interest were 15 percent? 10 percent? 5 percent? Why should people's perception of the long-term interest rate have any effect on the value of property through the valuation of a tax reduction?

10. Assume that you own a natural-gas field that holds a fixed supply. In making your decision about whether or not to deliver any gas to your distributor for sale in any year, would you pay any attention to word from the Federal Reserve Board about whether or not they thought that they would raise or lower interest rates over the next 12 months? If you were paid immediately for any gas that you delivered to the marketplace, would you pay any attention to whether or not interest rates were likely to increase or decrease at the next meeting of the Board of Governors of the Fed? Would you find it informative to subscribe to professional journals in which near- and long-term forecasts of the price of energy were published? How would you feel about a global climate policy that would tax the carbon content of fuel, knowing that natural gas has the smallest carbon content of any fossil fuel?

11. The adjustments in forecasts over time depicted in Figure 15.10 show that current prices played a critical role in determining the anticipated trajectory of future prices. Research and analysis has asserted that these adjustments placed an inordinate amount of weight on current prices. Argue why both income and substitution effects should work to increase oil consumption over the near term as current prices fall. Argue why this increase in consumption should accelerate the depletion of oil reserves. Would you expect that this exaggerated early depletion would cause future prices to converge toward the highest forecast trajectory as the future unfolds?

12. Assume, as in Figure 15.1, that an individual's utility depends on consumption this year and next (years 1 and 2) according to $U = U(C_1, C_2)$. Let her endowment point E be defined by her income this year and next,

denoted Y_1 and Y_2. With a common interest rate r for both saving and borrowing, the appropriate budget constraint is a straight line through point E with a slope equal to $-(1 + r)$. (a) Suppose that she decides to save an amount $S = Y_1 - C_1$ in year 1. Show that

$$C_2 = Y_2 + S + rS$$

can be manipulated into the equation of her budget constraint in Figure 15.1 and thereby convey all possible combinations of consumption in years 1 and 2 associated with saving some amount S in year 1 and earning interest rS for that saving in year 2. (b) Suppose that she decides to borrow an amount $B = C_1 - Y_1$ in year 1. Show that

$$C_2 = Y_2 - B - rB$$

can be manipulated into the equation of her budget constraint and convey all combinations associated with borrowing some amount B in year 1 and paying interest plus principal in year 2. (c) Show that either budget constraint can be rearranged so that it makes clear that the present value of consumption in both periods must equal the present value of income in both periods regardless of whether she borrows or saves.

13. Chapter 13 made a point of emphasizing methods by which firms might make their threats credible in a game-theoretic situation. This problem will explore circumstances under which the cost of undertaking such an action would be profitable in the long run. The idea is that firms could incur short-term costs in return for long-term benefits, and so future benefits must be discounted if they are to be compared accurately with costs. We will return to a story from Chapter 12 to illustrate this point, but it is easy to envision circumstances in which these sorts of decisions must be made. Take, for example, airline behavior in Europe after April 1, 1997. The rules of the European Union (EU) changed that day to allow any European airline to operate from any airport within the EU. European airfares had always been very high in comparison with U.S. fares despite the subsidization of many state-owned airlines. Despite this apparent inefficiency, most airlines responded to the new rules by maintaining or expanding their use of existing slots in airports across Europe to prevent the entry of rivals.

Let's return to the case of the Mason Company facing the possibility that the Newton Company will enter its market that we used in Chapter 13. Assume that Figure 13.7 reflects annual profits. Notice that "do not resist entry" is a dominant strategy for Mason. As a result, Newton will enter the market, since it would earn an additional $3 million per year. The solution to the game appears in the lower-left corner of the payoff matrix; it is a Nash equilibrium. Mason would prefer to detect Newton's entry, but its threat to resist would not be credible.

Figure 13.7 portrayed the payoff matrix that would be operational if Mason invested in excess capacity that would not be used if it were successful in deterring Newton's entry. It would continue to be a deterrent only if it were maintained, of course, and maintaining capacity even if it is unused can be expensive. Figure 13.10 shows that Mason's profits would fall by $2 million per year if Newton entered and it did not resist *or* if Newton did not enter at all. Resisting entry would be a dominant strategy. The solution, a Nash equilibrium, appears in the upper-right corner of the matrix.

(a) Assume Mason's investment in excess capacity would deter Newton's entry into the market over the indefinite future. How much extra profit would Mason earn each year? How much would Mason be willing to invest in excess capacity if the interest rate were 10 percent? If it were 5 percent? If it were 15 percent? (b) Now assume that the investment in new capacity would have a finite lifetime of T years. Explore the trade-off between the rate of interest and the lifetime T required to make the investment worthwhile. Assume, in particular, that the investment would cost $50 million in the current year. Compute the number of years required to cover that cost if the interest rate were 2.5 percent, 5.0 percent, 7.5 percent, 10.0 percent, 12.5 percent, and 15.0 percent. Do the same for a $70 million cost; for a $30 million cost. Are there circumstances in which it would not be in Mason's best interest to use investment in excess capacity to deter Newton's entry?

14. Chapter 12 noted that the cooperative solution to a prisoners' dilemma game could be sustained in a repeated game if a tit-for-tat strategy were employed by players who understood that the game would be repeated an indefinite (or a finite but unknown) number of times. Think, perhaps, of the U.S. cellular phone industry, where two or more providers share similar technologies and costs. Given their parallel economic incentives, the challenge is to find and maintain prices that create the largest markets and then to compete largely on factors such as distribution and service quality. The threat always exists that companies would retaliate if one competitor undercut the going price, but the incentive to return to the stability of the original cooperative solution would always persist.

In this example, we look at this incentive by considering a case in which each player would play "trust" if its rival played "trust" in the last iteration, but it would punish the rival by "cheating" from then on if the rival "cheated" in the preceding round. We will see that the time horizon for punishment need not be infinite; a player could return to "trust" after a finite number of punishment rounds. We will also see that tit-for-tat might not even work in its infinite form. The key will be to compare the discounted future cost of being punished with the short-term gain from cheating.

The following payoff matrix describes a game within which we can make these points. It offers two firms, A and B, the choice between trusting their

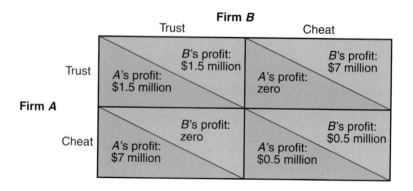

rival or cheating, in making one move each per year. Cheating is a dominant strategy for both firms, so the noncooperative solution to the game appears in the lower-right corner of the matrix below.

(a) If A were interested in deterring B's cheating, how long would A have to play cheat in response to B's violating its trust if the interest rate were 5 percent? 10 percent? 20 percent? (b) How does the length of time required for credible punishment vary with the size of the temptation to cheat (the difference between cheating on a trusting rival and sustaining that trust)?

Applied Perspective
[Part 5]

Explaining Wage Discrimination and Wage Differentials

"Equal pay for equal work" has been the mantra of social activists for decades, but it has been left up to economists to explain why it is not the economic law of the land. Why has it been necessary for Congress to pass laws like the Equal Pay Act of 1964 to prohibit discrimination? If there were only one employer of a particular type of labor, then it would be easy to understand how discrimination might occur. Even if men and women were equally productive, for example, a monopsonist could increase profits by separating labor supply into two groups according to gender. To see why, recall from Chapter 14 that a monopsonist maximizes profit by setting *each input's* marginal revenue product equal to its corresponding marginal expenditure. If the supply curve for women were less elastic than for men, as depicted in Figure 1 (because, for example, women had fewer job opportunities), then the marginal expenditure curves for men and women could be E_M and E_W, respectively. Even if the marginal revenue product for men and women were the same, at X, the wage paid to men would be P_M and the wage paid to women would be P_W. Clearly, in the case drawn in Figure 1, $P_M > P_W$.

Some researchers have argued that this model explains the content of Figure 2; it is drawn from the *1999 Economic Report of the President*. Figure 1 certainly got the sign right—men are paid more than women. Notice that women's earnings still tended to be lower than men's at the end of the series despite some movement toward equality after 1964 and despite a significant increase in labor for participation by women. In fact, the gap in average earnings between men and women in 2000 was about 15 percent for workers between the ages of 20 and 24; but it was nearly 40 percent among workers between the ages of 45 and 54. But are labor markets really monopsonistic? If they were

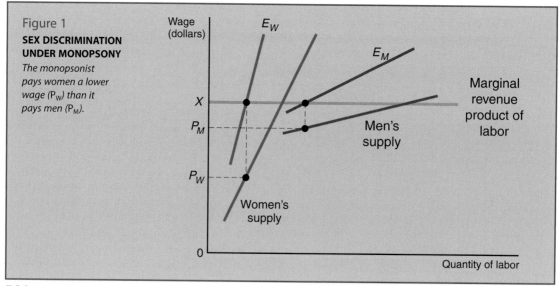

Figure 1

SEX DISCRIMINATION UNDER MONOPSONY

The monopsonist pays women a lower wage (P_W) than it pays men (P_M).

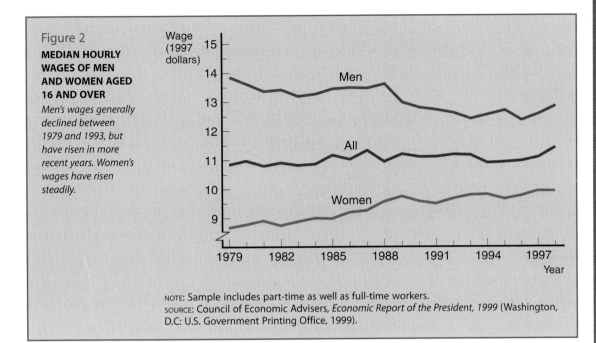

Figure 2

MEDIAN HOURLY WAGES OF MEN AND WOMEN AGED 16 AND OVER

Men's wages generally declined between 1979 and 1993, but have risen in more recent years. Women's wages have risen steadily.

NOTE: Sample includes part-time as well as full-time workers.
SOURCE: Council of Economic Advisers, *Economic Report of the President, 1999* (Washington, D.C: U.S. Government Printing Office, 1999).

competitive, by way of contrast, then there would surely be limitations in the degree to which employers could discriminate. If, for example, male lawyers earned $200,000 at a firm where equally talented and productive women lawyers were paid $160,000, then an employer could make $40,000 extra by hiring a woman. As more and more employers realized this, they would bid the price of female lawyers until the wage differential disappeared.

So what gives? One model predicts one thing and another predicts something else. Are there systemic reasons why comparable people are paid differently? The Council of Economic Advisers has suggested that "the average employed man has more experience, fewer interruptions in that work experience, and longer tenure with his current employer than does his female counterpart of comparable age."[1] Example 15.4 offers one explanation for how this might translate, efficiently, into wage differentials, and econometric evidence suggests that these factors explain some of the gap. It is, however, not always possible to tell the direction of causality. To some extent, low earnings may encourage interrupted work lives, since the opportunity cost of leaving work is low.

As if the puzzle of persistent wage differentials between men and women were not enough, recent analysis of the dispersion between the highest- and lowest-paid men and women adds more confusion to the picture. Figure 3, drawn from the work of Lawrence Katz, shows that the gap between the top and bottom has widened markedly since the 1970s. This is perhaps not

[1] *Economic Report of the President* (Washington, D.C.: U.S. Government Printing Office, 1987, p. 220). The point was reiterated in the 1999 *Economic Report of the President*.

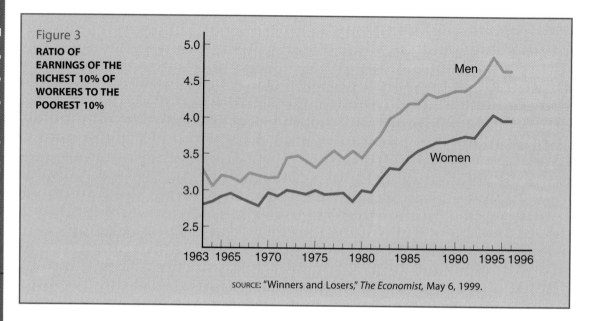

Figure 3

RATIO OF EARNINGS OF THE RICHEST 10% OF WORKERS TO THE POOREST 10%

SOURCE: "Winners and Losers," *The Economist*, May 6, 1999.

a surprise. What might be a surprise is that the gap is widening more quickly for men than it is for women. In 1979, the richest 10 percent of fully employed male Americans earned 3.6 times more than the poorest 10 percent; the ratio was 3 for women. In 1996, the richest men earned almost 5 times as much as their poorest counterparts, while the ratio was a laggardly 4 times for women. Nothing quite like this has been observed in other countries. In Europe, for example, where pay ratios have been relatively inflexible, unemployment has soared. Is it better to be paid less but be working than it is to be out of work?

How do we explain these new data in a way that is consistent with the old? Some researchers point an accusing finger at globalization. Rising foreign imports mean lower wages for Americans, especially the less skilled members of the U.S. labor force. But the U.S. economy is far less integrated into the global economy than Europe. Shouldn't we see a magnified effect like the one portrayed in Figure 3 in Europe? We don't. Others point to technology. The data show that people who use computers and have the skills to handle mountains of information are paid more than people who don't and can't. George Will has often pointed to the ability to process information as the next great source of inequality in the United States, and he may be right. Figure 4 provides some support for this perspective by showing that the return to spending a year in either high school or college has increased over the past 40 years at an increasing pace.

Perhaps the explanation of increased wage dispersion lies in the way American businesses conduct business. Companies seem to be moving away from large departments where workers perform uniform tasks in favor of smaller, customer-oriented teams where people need to work together, cover for each other, and perform multiple tasks. Talk about why graduates from

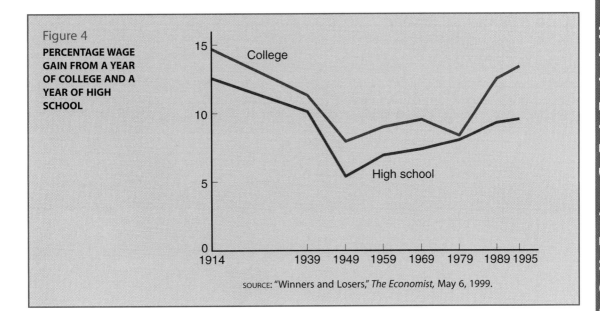

Figure 4

PERCENTAGE WAGE GAIN FROM A YEAR OF COLLEGE AND A YEAR OF HIGH SCHOOL

SOURCE: "Winners and Losers," *The Economist,* May 6, 1999.

liberal arts schools are in such high demand these days! Moreover, since some studies show that women are more adept at "multitasking" than men, perhaps we have a candidate for explaining why the gap depicted in Figure 2 has been declining. Companies are now rewarding workers who are flexible. Their best-paid employees have a wide range of skills that they bring to the table every day; and they adapt to new situations well. Gone, it would seem, are the days of Henry Ford when loyal workers with a single skill would be handsomely rewarded for longevity and uninterrupted service.

QUESTIONS

1. Draw a graph displaying equilibrium in which a perfectly inelastic supply of 100 people is allocated evenly across two completely segregated labor markets. Each person would be equally productive in both markets, but discrimination across some other characteristic means that the wage paid to one group of 50 workers is twice as high as the wage paid to the others. Confirm that there is a deadweight loss in this situation, and display it graphically. Describe the efficient equilibrium.

2. Suggest the structure of a model and construct an argument based on the model to explain why globalization could cause the wages paid to the most productive workers to climb faster over time than the wages paid to the least productive. Are there reasons why your argument might not hold in all cases?

3. If women are better at meeting the demands of the new, integrated workplace than men, then why should the wages of the most successful women be rising more slowly (relative to the least successful women) than the wages of the most successful men (relative to the least successful men)?

4. Suggest reasons why the employment careers of men are interrupted less frequently. Some may be economic, but some may not. Should they all matter in determining the starting salaries for equally qualified men and women?

Information, Efficiency, and Government

General Equilibrium Analysis and Resource Allocation

We said at the beginning of this book that microeconomics is concerned with the economic behavior of individual decision-making units like consumers, resource owners, and firms. At first glance, and even after working through 15 chapters of text, you might interpret this statement to mean that microeconomics views the behavior of such individual units and the workings of individual markets in isolation—each unit or market being considered separately. This impression could not be further from the truth. Microeconomics is concerned with these sorts of issues, to be sure, but microeconomics is also concerned in an important way with how these units and these markets fit together. Indeed, some of the intellectually most exciting and practically most significant aspects of microeconomics deal with the interrelations among individual units and among various markets.

We have thus far looked in detail at the behavior of individual decision-making units and the workings of individual markets. Now we must show how economists have attempted to form an integrated model of the economy as a whole. This clearly is an important task. Every schoolchild knows that it is important not to get so engrossed in the trees that one loses sight of the forest. It is equally important to know when looking at the trees rather than the forest is appropriate. Contemplating the workings of the economy as a whole takes a lot of work, and it is sometimes simply not worth the effort. But at other times it is essential to do so. And so we provide, in this chapter, a brief introduction to general equilibrium analysis—the branch of microeconomics that deals with the interrelations among various decision-making units and various markets. After defining general equilibrium analysis, we will explore the conditions under which we can be reasonably sure that a state of general equilibrium can exist in a perfectly competitive economy. Finally, we will build a simple general equilibrium model and take up some questions concerning the efficient allocation of resources.

PARTIAL EQUILIBRIUM ANALYSIS VERSUS GENERAL EQUILIBRIUM ANALYSIS

Previous chapters have, indeed, focused on a single market and sometimes single firms or consumers viewed in isolation. The models that we have used have taught us that the price and quantity in each such market are determined by supply and demand, and we have seen how the curves that represent supply and demand are drawn under the assumption that other prices are fixed and known. Each market has been regarded as an independent and self-contained unit, for all practical purposes. We have, in particular, assumed that changes in price in the one market under analysis do not have significant repercussions on the prices in other markets.

This assumption may, in reality, be seriously flawed. No market can adjust to changes in its condition without causing changes in other markets, and changes in the other markets can be substantial and significant. To see this point, suppose that the demand for pork shifts to the left. We assumed in previous chapters that the prices of other products would stay the same when the price and output of pork changed. But the market for pork is not isolated in any functional way from the markets for lamb, beef, and other meats.[1] Nor, for that matter, is it completely isolated from the markets for other food products or from the markets for other, less similar products, such as washing machines and automobiles. So, the market for pork cannot be expected to adjust without disturbing the equilibria of many other markets, and so it cannot adjust without creating feedbacks into the market for pork.

Partial equilibrium analyses
General equilibrium analyses

Analyses that assume that changes in price can occur without causing significant changes in prices in other markets are called **partial equilibrium analyses.** Analyses that take account of the interrelationships among the prices of a wide range if not all of the goods in an economy are called **general equilibrium analyses.** Both are very useful. Partial equilibrium analyses are perfectly adequate in cases in which the effect of a change in market conditions in one market has little or no effect on prices in other markets. Studying the effects of a small excise tax on the production of an insignificant commodity may work perfectly well under the assumption that the prices of all other commodities are fixed. Those prices might not change, and so it would not be worth the effort to model feedbacks and interactions that are not at all large; a partial equilibrium analysis of the sort presented earlier would then be appropriate. On the other hand, studying the effects of a large excise tax on a commodity whose purchase absorbs significant proportions of consumer income could be inappropriate if its repercussions on other prices were not considered. In these cases, a general equilibrium analysis could be required to make certain that the feedbacks and interactions did

---

[1]Quantitative evidence on this point was presented in Table 4.3, where the cross-elasticity of demand for beef with respect to the price of pork was reported to be +0.28.

not seriously undermine the validity of conclusions drawn from a partial equilibrium approach.

THE EXISTENCE OF GENERAL EQUILIBRIUM

General equilibrium analysis, like partial equilibrium analysis, can be used to solve problems of many kinds. It can, for example, be used to answer one of the most fundamental problems in economics. Suppose that we could somehow establish a perfectly competitive economy. Would it be possible for equilibrium to occur simultaneously in all markets? That is, does a set of prices exist such that all the markets would be in equilibrium simultaneously? If so, great. If not, then our theory would not be very useful, because we live in a world with many different goods and services and therefore many different markets.

General equilibrium

Approaching this problem somewhat differently, let us define **general equilibrium** to be a state of the economy in which the following conditions hold:

1. Every consumer chooses his or her preferred market basket subject to his or her budget line—an individual constraint that is determined by the prices of inputs and the prices of products.
2. Every consumer supplies whatever amount of inputs he or she chooses, given the input and product prices that prevail.
3. Every firm maximizes its profits subject to the constraints imposed by the available technology, the demand for its product, and the supply of inputs.
4. Long-run economic profits are zero for every firm.
5. The quantity demanded equals the quantity supplied at the prevailing prices in all product and input markets.

Given this definition of a general equilibrium, the problem is simply stated: Can we be sure that a general equilibrium can be achieved? It is evident from the definition that a great many conditions must be satisfied simultaneously if such an equilibrium is to be achieved. Can we be sure that all these conditions can all be satisfied at the same time? Or can they all be satisfied only under certain conditions? If so, what are these conditions? These are important questions, and they have received considerable attention from economic theorists.

Work by the Nobel laureates Kenneth Arrow, Gerard Debreu, and Herbert Scart and by others has established that a general equilibrium can be achieved in a perfectly competitive economy under a fairly wide set of conditions. As Robert Kuenne has put it, "Judged . . . against the characteristics of our abstract economic models [of consumption and production], the pragmatic assertion of a faith that our data would need to be constrained in wholly acceptable ways to guarantee a solution under all allowable conditions of their initial values seems to be well justified on the whole."[2] But are the prices and outputs that make up a general equilibrium unique? That is, is there only one set of prices and outputs for which the quantity supplied equals the quantity demanded in all markets? Clearly, the answer is no. Only relative prices affect the decisions of consumers, firms, and resource owners. If all markets were in equilibrium at one set of prices, then they would also be in equilibrium if all prices were increased or decreased in the same proportion. (Recall that consumers' incomes are determined by the price of the inputs that they supply, so their incomes would climb proportionately with all prices.) So it is more interesting to ask if there is more than one set of *relative* prices that can sustain a general equilibrium. This is a more difficult question. Its answer is, as usual, "It depends." On what, is a topic for advanced textbooks; it is beyond the scope of this one.

It is important to know that general equilibrium can be achieved under a wide set of conditions in a perfectly competitive economy. We shall see that economists have concluded that, under certain circumstances, a perfectly competitive economy has a variety of desirable characteristics. For this reason, a perfectly competitive economy continues to be held up as a benchmark for comparison. It would surely be embarrassing for those who hold this view to find out that this kind of economy was based on behavioral assumptions and market mechanisms that were so incompatible that a general equilibrium could not be achieved. Fortunately, no such embarrassment is necessary.

A SIMPLE MODEL OF GENERAL EQUILIBRIUM

This section is devoted to a presentation of some of the mathematical details of a simple general equilibrium model of a very simple economy. This model displays the nature of general equilibrium in a perfectly competitive economy more completely. The analysis will, however, require that the reader be familiar with the idea of and the notation for a set of equations. Readers who are uncomfortable with these notions can skip to the next major heading without losing the thread of the argument. Readers who are more than comfortable with these notions might want to view a more technical treatment of more complicated models in more advanced texts.[3]

---

[2]R. Kuenne, *The Theory of General Economic Equilibrium* (Princeton, N.J.: Princeton University Press, 1963), p. 566. Also see K. Arrow and G. Debreu, "Existence of an Equilibrium for a Competitive Economy," *Econometrica,* July 1954; G. Debreu, *Theory of Value* (New York: Wiley, 1959); L. McKenzie, "On the Existence of General Equilibrium for a Competitive Market," *Econometrica,* January 1959; J. Quirk and R. Saposnik, *Introduction to General Equilibrium Theory and Welfare Economics* (New York: McGraw-Hill, 1968); and K. Arrow and F. Hahn, *General Competitive Analysis* (San Francisco: Holden-Day, 1971). To be more specific, Arrow and Debreu showed that a general equilibrium exists if increasing returns to scale exist for no firm, at least one primary input is used to produce each commodity, the quantity of a primary input supplied by a consumer is not greater than his or her initial stock of the input, each consumer can supply all primary inputs, each consumer's ordinal utility function is continuous, his or her wants cannot be satiated, and his or her indifference curves are convex. These conditions are sufficient but not necessary.

[3]See, for example, H. Varian, *Microeconomic Analysis,* 3d ed. (New York: W. W. Norton, 1999).

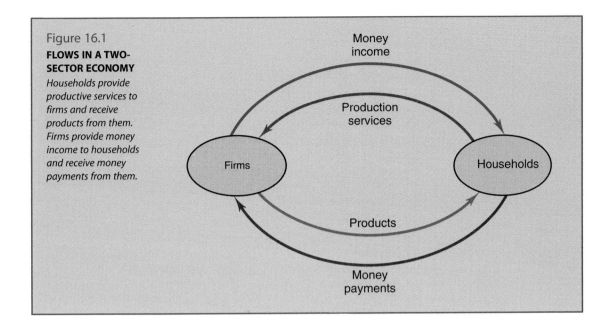

Figure 16.1

FLOWS IN A TWO-SECTOR ECONOMY

Households provide productive services to firms and receive products from them. Firms provide money income to households and receive money payments from them.

Money income

Production services

Firms

Households

Products

Money payments

Assume, for simplicity, that the economy is composed of two sectors. Let one be a business sector and the other be a consumer sector. Figure 16.1 displays a diagram that describes the flows of income, payments, products, and services in such an economy. Note that there is no government sector in this economy, and there is no foreign sector. These sectors, among others, could be added. But the essential features of general equilibrium can be described with only two sectors, and so we stop there. Now assume that firms (and not consumers) do all of the production and that consumers (and not firms) provide all of the inputs. This means that there are no intermediate goods. Assume, as well, that consumers obtain their incomes only from the sale of inputs to firms and that this income must be spent entirely on the products of these firms. And let the quantity of inputs supplied by each consumer be fixed and independent of the level of input prices. This assumption is made because it simplifies the analysis and not because of necessity or realism; it could easily be relaxed in more advanced treatments of this topic. Finally, assume that inputs must be used in fixed proportions to produce each commodity. This assumption, too, can easily be relaxed as long as production displays constant returns to scale.

When this simple two-sector model is in equilibrium, the total flow of money income from firms to households must equal the flow of payments from households to firms. We will be concerned with the characteristics of this simple economy in equilibrium and not with the path by which it might move from one equilibrium to another. Let the economy consist of A consumers, C consumer products, and D types of inputs; that is, if there are 2 million consumers, 500 consumer products, and 1,000 types of inputs, then A would equal 2 million, C would equal 500, and D would equal 1,000. Every market, whether it be a product market or an input market, is perfectly competitive.

□ Equations of the Model

There are three kinds of equations in this simple model of general equilibrium. First, there are equations representing the demand by consumers for commodities. Let r_{ca} be the amount of the cth commodity demanded by the ath consumer. We know from Chapter 3 that r_{ca} will depend on the prices of all commodities and on the tastes of the ath consumer. The quantity r_{ca} will also depend on the prices of all the inputs, because they (together with the amount of each input supplied by the consumer) determine the consumer's income. So, there are $A \times C$ equations of the form

$$r_{ca} = r_{ca}(p_1, \ldots, p_C, w_1, \ldots, w_D), \qquad \begin{array}{l}(c = 1, \ldots, C) \\ (a = 1, \ldots, A)\end{array} \quad [16.1]$$

where p_c is the price of the cth commodity and w_d is the price of the dth input. The consumer's tastes (and his or her supply of inputs) determine the functional form of each of these equations.

Letting R_c be the total quantity demanded by consumers of the cth commodity, it is obvious that

$$R_c = r_{c1} + r_{c2} + \ldots + r_{cA} \qquad (c = 1, \ldots, C).$$

It follows from the equations represented in 16.1 that

$$R_c = R_c(p_1, \ldots, p_C, w_1, \ldots, w_D) \qquad (c = 1, \ldots, C). \quad [16.2]$$

In other words, the total quantity demanded of each commodity depends on all commodity and input prices, and the form of the relationship will be different from commodity to commodity.

We now turn to analogous equations that ensure that the total amount of each input employed by firms is equal to the total amount of the input supplied by consumers. That is, firms cannot use more inputs than are supplied, and there is no unemployment of inputs. If u_{cd} is the amount of the dth type of input used to produce 1 unit of the cth consumer good, this means that

$$X_d = u_{1d}R_1 + u_{2d}R_2 + \ldots + u_{Cd}R_C \qquad (d = 1, \ldots, D), \quad [16.3]$$

where X_d is the total amount of the dth type of input supplied by consumers.

We also need equations that ensure that the long-run conditions of perfect competition are met—that is, we need to be sure that the production of each commodity results in neither economic profit nor economic loss. In other words, the price of each commodity must equal the average cost of its production. Since inputs must be used in fixed proportions, the average cost of producing the cth commodity is

$$AC_c = u_{c1}w_1 + u_{c2}w_2 + \ldots + u_{cD}w_D \qquad (c = 1, \ldots, C), \quad [16.4]$$

where w_1 is still the price of the first input, w_2 is the price of the second input, and so on. So, if the price of the cth commodity equals its average cost, then

$$p_c = u_{c1}w_1 + u_{c2}w_2 + \ldots + u_{cD}w_D \qquad (c = 1, \ldots, C). \quad [16.5]$$

Microlink 16.1   Budget Constraints for General Equilibrium

The budget constraints described in Chapters 2 and 3 were determined by a specified amount of income. If goods X and Y were available for sale at prices P_X and P_Y, for example, then an individual would maximize utility

$$U = U(X, Y)$$

subject to the constraint that

$$M \geq P_X X + P_Y Y,$$

where M now denotes income. Notice that this constraint can be written as

$$M - P_X X - P_Y Y \geq 0.$$

In the general equilibrium model, however, income is "endogenous"; that is, income for any specific individual is determined by the quantity of inputs that each offers to the marketplace and the prices of those inputs. Once that association has been made, however, then the notion of a budget constraint could be

$$w_1 I_1 + \ldots + w_D I_D \geq P_X X + P_Y Y$$

or, alternatively, that

$$w_1 I_1 + \ldots + w_D I_D - P_X X - P_Y Y \geq 0$$

for D different inputs (denoted by the I_j) whose prices are given by the w_j. The only difference, then, is that consumer utility must now reflect the disutility involved in providing inputs. In other words,

$$U = U(X, Y, I_1, \ldots, I_D)$$

where the marginal utility of the I_j is negative.

▣ Existence of a Solution

Equations 16.2, 16.3, and 16.5 form a simple general equilibrium model. The fact that we have written down all of these equations does not, however, ensure that a solution exists. In other words, we cannot be certain that at least one consistent and feasible set of numbers can be assigned to all the variables so that all these equations are satisfied. We can, though, compare the number of equations in the model with the number of variables to be determined. Table 16.1 shows the number of equations

Table 16.1	Equations		Variables	
NUMBER OF EQUATIONS VERSUS NUMBER OF VARIABLES	**Equation**	**Number**	**Variable**	**Number**
	16.2	C	R_c	C
	16.3	$D - 1$	W_d	D
	16.5	C	P_c	C

in the model and the number of variables to be determined. Note that the number of equations represented in 16.3 is given as $D - 1$, rather than D. This is because one of the equations in 16.3 is not independent. If all the other equations in the model hold, then it can be shown that this equation must hold, too. So, there are only $D - 1$ independent equations in 16.3.[4]

Table 16.1 shows that the number of equations is one less than the number of variables. This means that the model cannot determine values for each of the variables to be determined. The situation is similar to having one equation and two variables to be determined. Only certain pairs of numbers can be solutions in such a system, but there is no single solution. We might, however, obtain a solution if we took the price of one commodity or input as given; the number of equations would match the number of variables if we arbitrarily selected one commodity or input as *Numeraire* the **numeraire** and assigned it a price of 1. This is just like setting one variable equal to 1 and solving for the other variable in a case where there are two variables and one equation. In effect, the prices of all commodities and inputs are thereby expressed in relative terms with the numeraire serving as the basis of comparison. So, for example, if $p_3 = 3$ were part of the solution, then we would know that the price of the third commodity would have to be 3 times the price of the numeraire. For reasons that are too technical to concern us here, equality of the number of variables and the number of equations does not always guarantee that a solution exists. The existence of a solution, in fact, depends on the

---

[4]Suppose that each of the equations in 16.5 holds and that all but one of the equations in 16.3 hold. That is, assume that

$$p_c = \sum_d u_{cd} w_d, \quad \text{where } c = 1, \ldots, C,$$

and
$$X_d = \sum_c u_{cd} R_c, \quad \text{where } d = 1, \ldots, D - 1.$$

It is easy to show that the remaining equation in 16.3 must hold too. Since the total amount spent by consumers must equal their total income,

$$\sum_c R_c p_c = \sum_d X_d w_d.$$

And since $p_c = \sum_d u_{cd} w_d$, it follows that

$$\sum_d X_d w_d = \sum_c R_c \sum_d u_{cd} w_d.$$

Moreover, since $\sum_{d=1}^{D-1} X_d w_d = \sum_{d=1}^{D-1} \sum_c u_{cd} R_c w_d,$

$$X_D w_D = \sum_c R_c \sum_d u_{cd} w_d - \sum_{d=1}^{D-1} \sum_c u_{cd} R_c w_d$$

$$= \sum_c R_c \sum_d u_{cd} w_d - \sum_c R_c \sum_{d=1}^{D-1} u_{cd} w_d$$

$$= \sum_c R_c u_{cD} w_D.$$

Therefore, since $w_D > 0$, $X_D = \sum_c u_{cD} R_c$: this is what we set out to prove.

functional form of the equations, and whether the solution is economically meaningful depends on the solution's satisfying various nonnegativity constraints.[5]

RESOURCE ALLOCATION AND THE EDGEWORTH BOX DIAGRAM

We now turn our attention to a somewhat different, but related, topic. We have stated repeatedly that microeconomics is concerned with the way in which resources should be allocated. Consideration of more than a single market makes it possible to consider many interesting questions of resource allocation that could not otherwise be investigated. The rest of this chapter is devoted to a discussion of some of these questions.

Edgeworth box diagram

Simple models can make productive use of what economists have dubbed the "Edgeworth box diagram." An **Edgeworth box diagram** shows the interaction between two economic activities when the total quantities of commodities consumed or inputs are fixed. Figure 16.2 offers some insight into how an Edgeworth box diagram is constructed and how it should be interpreted. We assume that there are two goods, food and medicine, and two consumers, Tom and Harry. Tom and Harry must share a total of $O_H F$ units of food and $O_H M$ units of medicine.

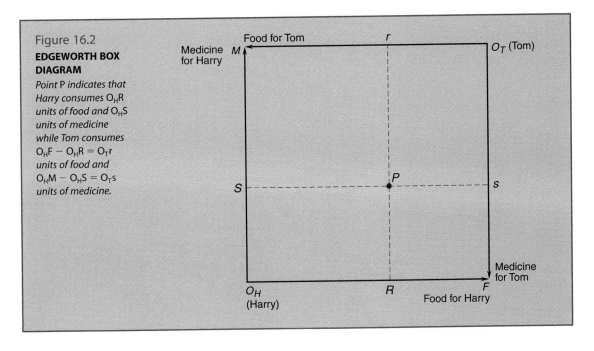

Figure 16.2

EDGEWORTH BOX DIAGRAM

Point P indicates that Harry consumes $O_H R$ units of food and $O_H S$ units of medicine while Tom consumes $O_H F - O_H R = O_T r$ units of food and $O_H M - O_H S = O_T s$ units of medicine.

---

[5]These nonnegativity constraints are not hard to understand; it makes no sense for some variables, like the production of corn, to be negative.

The quantity of food that Harry consumes is measured horizontally from the origin at O_H in the usual way, and the quantity of medicine Harry consumes is measured vertically from the same origin. Any point in the box diagram therefore indicates a certain allocation of food and medicine to Harry. Point P, for example, indicates that Harry consumes $O_H R$ units of food and $O_H S$ units of medicine. The quantity of food that Tom consumes is meanwhile measured by the horizontal distance to the left of a second origin—point O_T on the upper-right corner of the box diagram. And the vertical distance downward from the same origin measures the quantity of medicine that Tom consumes. Every point in the box therefore indicates a certain allocation of food to Tom. Point P, therefore, also indicates that Tom consumes $O_T r$ units of food and $O_T s$ units of medicine.

The dimensions of the box provide even more information. They define the total quantities of food and medicine available to both Harry and Tom— $O_H F$ units of food and $O_H M$ units of medicine. So, point P indicates that Tom consumes $O_T r = O_H F - O_H R$ units of food—that is, the total amount of food ($O_H F$) less that consumed by Harry ($O_H R$). As can be seen in the diagram $O_T r = RF = O_H F - O_H R$. Likewise, Tom consumes $O_T s = O_H M - O_H S = SM$ units of medicine. The length and width of an Edgeworth box diagram represent the total quantities of two commodities that are available to both consumers. And each point in an Edgeworth box represents an allocation between two consumers of the total quantities of the two goods supplied.

EXCHANGE

We can now use the Edgeworth box construction to anchor a discussion of the process of exchange. To that end, consider an economy of the simplest sort. There are still only two consumers, Tom and Harry, and only two commodities, food and medicine. There is no production. The only economic problem is the allocation of a given amount of food and medicine between the two consumers. If it helps, you may regard Tom and Harry as two shipwrecked sailors marooned on a desert island with a certain amount of food and medicine that they rescued from their ship. Not much of an economy, to be sure, but one with enough richness to assist in exploring the process of exchange.

We need first to establish individual endowments of food and medicine. Assume that Harry brought $O_H H$ units of food and $O_H I$ units of medicine from the crippled ship. This is indicated by point P in the Edgeworth box displayed in Figure 16.3. Tom, meanwhile, brought $O_H F - O_H H$ units of food and $O_H M - O_H I$ units of medicine from the ship. The total amount of food brought to the island by both men is $O_H F$, and the total amount of medicine brought to the island by both men is $O_H M$.

What sort of trading might take place (if the two men were free to trade with one another)? What can be said about the efficient allocation of the commodities between the two men? To find out, we must insert indifference curves for Tom and Harry into the Edgeworth box diagram in Figure 16.3. Three of Harry's indifference curves are drawn there: H_1, H_2, and H_3. Of

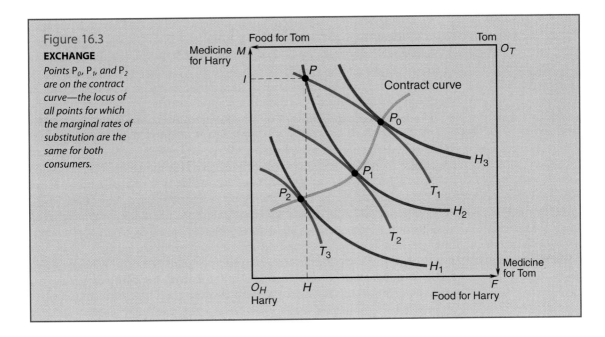

Figure 16.3

EXCHANGE

Points P$_0$, P$_1$, and P$_2$ are on the contract curve—the locus of all points for which the marginal rates of substitution are the same for both consumers.

the three, the highest indifference curve is H_3; the lowest is H_1. Three of Tom's indifference curves are also drawn there: T_1, T_2, and T_3. The highest indifference curve of the three is T_3; the lowest is T_1. Harry's satisfaction would generally improve if we moved his allocation from points close to his origin (point O_H) to points closer to the upper-right corner of the box. Conversely, Tom's satisfaction would generally improve if we moved his allocation from points close to the upper-right corner of the box to points closer to the origin O_H.

Given the initial allocation of food and medicine, we find that Harry is on indifference curve H_2 and Tom is on indifference curve T_1 at point P. At this point, Harry's marginal rate of substitution of food for medicine is much higher than Tom's. How do we know that? Figure 16.3 shows that the slope of H_2 at point P is larger than the slope of T_1. If both men were free to trade, therefore, Harry would be interested in trading some medicine to Tom in exchange for some food. The exact point to which they might move cannot be predicted. If Harry were the more astute bargainer, then he might get Tom to accept the allocation at point P_0 where Tom would be no better off than before (since he would still be on indifference curve T_1) but Harry would be better off (since he would have moved to indifference curve H_3). If, on the other hand, Tom were the better negotiator, then he might be able to get Harry to accept the allocation at point P_1. At that point, Harry would be no better off than before (since he would still be on indifference curve H_2) but Tom would be better off (since he would have moved to indifference curve T_2). If neither Tom nor Harry were so skilled in negotiating that he could extract all of the "surplus value" from the trade, then (as would be most likely), the ultimate point of equilibrium would lie somewhere between P_0 and P_1.

And what would characterize this equilibrium? The absence of any trades that (1) would be acceptable to both Tom and Harry and (2) would improve the welfare of one or both of them. That is to say, the marginal rates of substitution of food for medicine would have to be the same for both—i.e., their indifference curves would have to be tangent to one another at the point of equilibrium.

The notion of equilibrium can be extended. If the object were to make the men as well-off as possible (given their unfortunate circumstance to begin with), then an efficient allocation of the commodities would be one in which the marginal rate of substitution of food for medicine were the same for both men. As we just argued from the other side, if that were not the case, one man could be made better off without making the other worse off. Tangency of indifference curves is therefore the key to characterizing equilibrium, but it does not yield a unique solution to the trading question. Indeed, there is a locus of points at which the two men's indifference curves are tangent; this locus is called the **contract curve.** It is shown in Figure 16.3, and it includes all of the points, like P_0, P_1, and P_2, for which the marginal rates of substitution are equal for both consumers. The contract curve is a set of efficient points in a very special sense. Consumers like Tom and Harry who might be at a point that lies off the contract curve can always find a point on the contract curve that is preferable to both. Why? Because moving to such a point would not cost either any welfare even though it would guarantee that the welfare of at least one of them would improve.

Example 16.1   **Allocation of Fissionable Material**

The 1990s witnessed a noticeable reduction in international tension over nuclear weapons, but recent events have also shown that we are a long way from achieving global peace. We still have concerns over nuclear proliferation, and particular worries have erupted in the Indian subcontinent, where India and Pakistan have detonated their own nuclear devices. Back in the days of the Cold War, though, other issues were the hot topics of debate. The military establishment in those days was very concerned about how to allocate its resources between tactical and strategic forces. Tactical forces were given the task of preparing to fight a war anywhere in the world, but particularly in Europe. Strategic forces were, by way of contrast, given the task of making sure that such a war would not erupt, participating in a strategy of mutual deterrence with the then Soviet Union. And so the question of those days was how to efficiently allocate a fixed number of aircraft and fissionable material (read, nuclear bombs) between the two competing concerns.

Figure 16.4 illustrates the problem graphically. There were a fixed total number of aircraft ($O_S A$) and a fixed supply of fissionable materials ($O_S M$) in the short run. Every point in the Edgeworth box diagram shown in the figure indicates an allocation of fissionable material and airplanes to the tactical and strategic forces. For example, point P represents a case in which strategic forces would be allocated $O_S U$ units of aircraft and $O_S V$ units of fissionable material while tactical forces would have $O_S A - O_S U$ units of aircraft and $O_S M - O_S V$ units of fissionable material at their disposal. Within

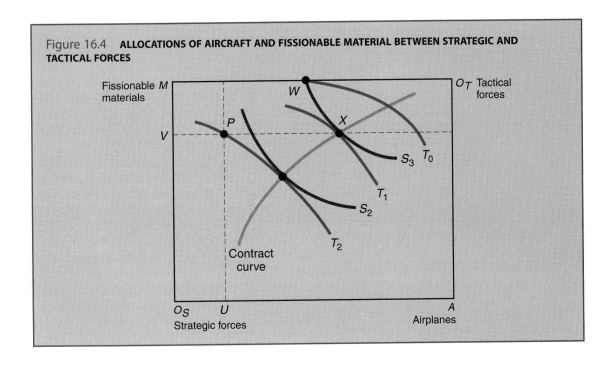

Figure 16.4 **ALLOCATIONS OF AIRCRAFT AND FISSIONABLE MATERIAL BETWEEN STRATEGIC AND TACTICAL FORCES**

limits, it was possible to substitute airplanes for fissionable material and vice versa. Fewer aircraft would be required to destroy a certain number of targets if nuclear weapons, rather than conventional weapons, were used. Curve T_1 contains combinations of aircraft and fissionable material that would be equally effective in the hands of the tactical forces. Curve T_0 also contains combinations that would result in equal effectiveness of the tactical forces, but at a lower level than curve T_1. Curve S_2 contains combinations of aircraft and fissionable material that would be equally effective in the hands of the strategic forces. Curve S_3 also contains combinations that would result in equal effectiveness of the strategic forces, but at a higher level than curve S_2. The allocation at that time was represented by point W. Was this an efficient choice?

No, because point W is not on the contract curve. The U.S. Defense Department could have increased the effectiveness of either the tactical or strategic forces without reducing the effectiveness of the other by moving to a point on the contract curve. Point X, for example, would produce the same effectiveness in strategic forces as point W, since both points lie along curve S_3. But point X would sustain greater effectiveness in tactical forces than point W. In fact, this simple kind of economic analysis was used to help solve this important policy problem (under the dubious assumption, perhaps, that defense planners try to maximize efficiency and do not, for example, try to maximize the share of their own particular service).[6]

[6]For further discussion, see S. Enke, "Using Costs to Select Weapons," *American Economic Review*, May 1965; and "Some Economic Aspects of Fissionable Materials," *Quarterly Journal of Economics*, May 1964.

PRODUCTION

The preceding section focused our attention on the case in which consumers exchange quantities of commodities in the absence of production. In this section and the next, we take up the equivalent simple case in which there is production but no consumption. Be assured, though, that we ultimately will combine the results and consider a case in which there is both consumption and production.

To that end, consider now a simple economy in which only two goods are being produced. One sector of the economy produces food and the other produces medicine. Suppose, for the sake of simplicity, that labor and capital are the only inputs. Let the total amount of labor to be allocated between the two sectors be O_FL and the total amount of capital to be allocated between the two sectors be O_FK. Finally, suppose that the initial allocation of labor and capital between the two sectors were represented by point Z in the Edgeworth box diagram portrayed in Figure 16.5. Notice that the food industry starts with O_FA units of labor and O_FB units of capital while the medicine sector comes to the table with $O_FL - O_FA$ units of labor and $O_FK - O_FB$ units of capital.

On the basis of the production functions for food and medicine, we can insert isoquants for both food production and medicine production in Figure 16.5. Three isoquants for food production are displayed there: F_1, F_2, and F_3. Of the three, the isoquant that reflects combinations of capital and labor

Figure 16.5   **PRODUCTION**

Points U and V are on the contract curve—the locus of all points for which the marginal rates of technical substitution between the inputs are the same for both industries.

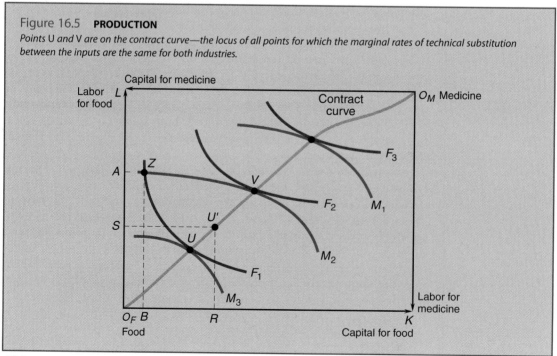

with the highest output of food is F_3, and the isoquant for the lowest output of food is F_1. Three isoquants for medicine production are also displayed: M_1, M_2, and M_3. Again, of the three, the isoquant that reflects combinations of capital and labor with the highest output of medicine is M_3, and the isoquant for the lowest output of medicine is M_1.

What would be an efficient allocation of inputs between the two industries? At the original allocation at point Z, the marginal rate of technical substitution of capital for labor in producing food is higher than it is in producing medicine. This observation is based on the fact that the slope of F_1 at point Z is greater than the slope of M_2. The fact that the marginal rates of technical substitution are unequal at point Z means that the inputs are not being allocated efficiently. To see why, suppose that the food industry operating at point Z could substitute 2 units of labor for 1 unit of capital without changing its output while the medicine industry would have to substitute 1 unit of labor for 2 units of capital to maintain its output. In this case (where the medicine industry uses more labor and less capital relative to the food industry), it would be possible for one industry to expand its output without any reduction in the other industry's output. Specifically, it would be possible to move to point U, where the output of food would be the same as at point Z even though the output of medicine would climb to the level corresponding to M_3. It would also be possible to move to point V, where the output of medicine would be the same as at point Z but the output of food would climb to the level corresponding to F_2. And, of course, it would be possible to move to a point between U and V for which the outputs of both sectors would expand relative to their levels at point Z.

Regardless of which point were chosen, the same idea described above should apply. Production should occur at a point at which the marginal rates of technical substitution between inputs are the same for all producers. Only then would the allocation of inputs be efficient in the sense that an increase in the output of one commodity could be achieved only by a reduction in the output of the other commodity. An efficient allocation of inputs must therefore lie somewhere along the locus of points where the marginal rates of technical substitution are equal, and so it must lie at a point where a food isoquant is tangent to a medicine isoquant. The locus of these points, like the analogous set in the preceding section, is also called the *contract curve;* it is shown in Figure 16.5. This curve represents an efficient set of points in a very special sense. Producers who find themselves at a point that lies off the contract curve can, if society is interested in producing as much as possible of each good, move to a point where the output of one industry can be increased without a reduction in the other industry's output.

THE PRODUCTION POSSIBILITIES CURVE

The contract curve in Figure 16.5 showed the various allocations of inputs that are efficient in the special sense described in the preceding section. There is, of course, a level of output for food and medicine corresponding to each

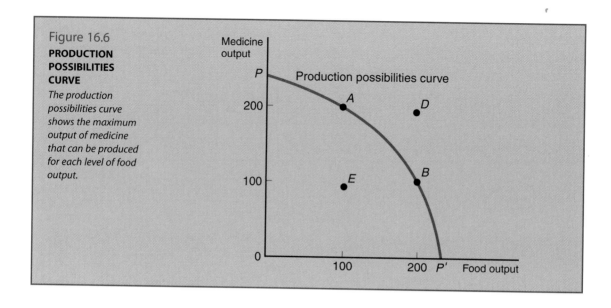

Figure 16.6

PRODUCTION POSSIBILITIES CURVE

The production possibilities curve shows the maximum output of medicine that can be produced for each level of food output.

point on the contract curve. Consider, for example, point U in Figure 16.5. If the level of output of food corresponding to isoquant F_1 were 100 and if the level of output of medicine corresponding to isoquant M_3 were 200, then an output of 100 units of food and 200 units of medicine would correspond to the point U. Similarly, if the level of output of food corresponding to isoquant F_2 were 200 and if the level of output of medicine corresponding to isoquant M_2 were 100, then an output of 200 units of food and 100 units of medicine would correspond to the point V.

Proceeding in this way, we can find the pair of outputs corresponding to each point on the contract curve. And we can then plot each such pair of points in a graph like that in Figure 16.6, where the amount of food produced is shown on the horizontal axis and the amount of medicine produced is shown on the vertical axis. For example, the pair of outputs corresponding to point U on the contract curve are plotted as point A in Figure 16.6, and the pair of outputs corresponding to point V on the contract curve are plotted as point B in Figure 16.6. The origin of Figure 16.5, where food production is zero because medicine employs all of the capital and labor, is portrayed by point P in Figure 16.6. And the opposite origin in Figure 16.5, where medicine production is zero because food employs all of the capital and labor, is portrayed by point P' in Figure 16.6. The curve PP' in Figure 16.6 is the result of plotting all these points—i.e., the output combinations associated with all of the points on the contract curve. It is called the *Production possibilities curve* **production possibilities curve;** you may remember this concept from your first lecture in introductory economics (but it was probably derived from a production function with only one input).

The production possibilities curve shows the various combinations of food output and medicine output that can be derived from the economy's input base. In our simple model, this base is $O_F L$ units of labor and $O_F K$ units of capital. More specifically, it shows the maximum output of one good that can be produced under the assumption that the output of the other good is held fixed. Given the economy's input base and existing technology, it is impossible to attain a point like D in Figure 16.6 that is outside the production possibilities curve. On the other hand, it is possible to attain a point like E that is inside the production possibilities curve, but it would be inefficient to do so. Indeed, a point like E would correspond to a point like Z in Figure 16.5—an allocation of inputs that does not lie along the contract curve. As long as production is efficient so that input allocations lie along the contract curve for which the marginal rates of technical substitution are equal for each sector, production occurs at some point along the production possibilities curve.

PRODUCTION AND EXCHANGE

We now, finally, consider a simple model that includes both production and exchange. Our simple economy contains two consumers (Tom and Harry), two commodities (food and medicine), and two inputs (labor and capital). As in the preceding two sections, this economy can use a total of $O_F L$ units of labor and $O_F K$ units of capital. The allocation question can now be cast in this combination world. Given the input base, the indifference maps of the consumers, and the production functions in the two industries, how should these inputs be allocated between industries? And how should the output of goods be allocated between the consumers?

☐ Allocating Consumption between Individuals

If the isoquant map in each industry displayed in Figure 16.5 were applicable, then we would know from the preceding section that the various combinations of food output and medicine output that could be derived from this input base were given by the production possibilities curve PP' in Figure 16.6. This curve PP' is reproduced in Figure 16.7. Suppose, for the moment, that we also knew the composition of output (i.e, the amount of food and medicine) that should be produced in the economy. We could then insert an Edgeworth box diagram similar to that in Figure 16.3 into Figure 16.7. The upper-right corner of the box would simply be the point on the production possibilities curve corresponding to this predetermined composition of output.

To be more specific, suppose that we knew that the composition of output in the economy should be represented by point A', where the quantity of food produced would equal Q and the quantity of medicine produced would be N. We could then draw an Edgeworth box diagram for consumption with Q as its width and N as its height. Since Q and N would be the total amount of food and medicine to be distributed to Tom and Harry, respectively, this box diagram could be used to see how much of the total output of each good would go to each consumer. Figure 16.7 shows indifference curves for each consumer (T_1', T_2', and T_3' for Tom and H_1', H_2',

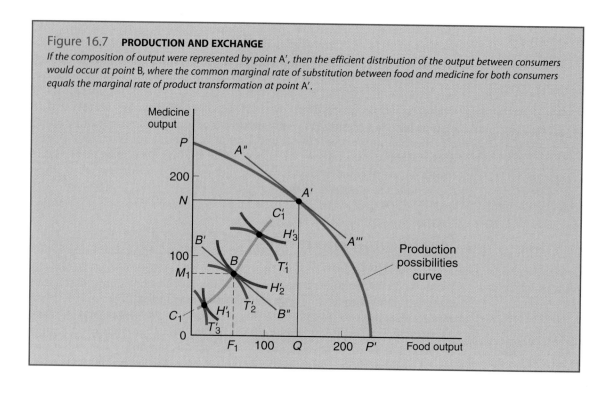

Figure 16.7 **PRODUCTION AND EXCHANGE**

If the composition of output were represented by point A', then the efficient distribution of the output between consumers would occur at point B, where the common marginal rate of substitution between food and medicine for both consumers equals the marginal rate of product transformation at point A'.

and H_3' for Harry) within the box defined by Q, A', N, and the origin. It also shows the contract curve, C_1C_1'. Recall that this is the locus of points where Tom's indifference curves are tangent to Harry's.

We know from before that the distribution of output between the two consumers should be such that they should lie on the contract curve C_1C_1'. But where? We show in the following section that, if the economy's output were allocated so that consumer satisfaction were maximized, then the **marginal rate of product transformation** (the magnitude of the slope of the production possibilities curve) should equal the marginal rate of substitution. If the economy's output were allocated to maximize consumer satisfaction, then the consumers should be at the point on the contract curve where the common slope of their indifference curves equals the slope of the production possibilities curve at A'.

Where on the contract curve would the common slope of their indifference curves equal the slope of the production possibilities curve at A'? An examination of Figure 16.7 shows that this condition would be fulfilled at point B on the contract curve, where Harry would receive F_1 units of food and M_1 units of medicine while Tom would receive $Q - F_1$ units of food and $N - M_1$ units of medicine. The slopes of the indifference curves at point B equal the slope of the production possibilities curve at point A'. How do we know? The tangent lines $B'B''$ and $A''A'''$ are parallel. So, given the amount to be produced of each commodity, we have devised a way to determine the amount of each commodity that should be allocated to Tom and Harry.

Marginal rate of product transformation

▣ Allocating Inputs between Commodities

There is more to the story. We can also find the amount of labor and capital that should be allocated to the production of each commodity by consulting the Edgeworth box diagram in Figure 16.5. Recall that the contract curve drawn there underlies the production possibilities curve drawn in Figure 16.7. Recall, as well, that each point on the production possibilities curve corresponds to a point on the contract curve in Figure 16.5, and that each point on the contract curve in Figure 16.5 corresponds to a particular allocation of labor and capital between the production of the two commodities. For example, assume that point A' on the production possibilities curve corresponds to point U' on the contract curve in Figure 16.5. So, if we knew that the composition of output in the economy should be given by point A', then we would know that $O_F S$ units of labor should be devoted to the production of food and $O_F L - O_F S$ units of labor should be devoted to the production of medicine. We would know that $O_F R$ units of capital should be devoted to the production of food, and that $O_F K - O_F R$ units of capital should be devoted to the production of medicine. Finally, we would know that this allocation of inputs would guarantee that the marginal rates of technical substitution between capital and labor would be equal in the production of both food and medicine. How so? Because point U' lies on the contract curve.

▣ The Marginal Rate of Product Transformation, Marginal Rate of Substitution, and Consumer Satisfaction

We asserted in the preceding section that consumer satisfaction would not be maximized unless the marginal rate of product transformation between two goods is equal to the marginal rate of substitution between the two goods. This section is devoted to proving this claim. For simplicity, suppose that firm A produces both food and medicine and that it supplies all of these commodities consumed by Tom. Suppose, as well, that Tom initially consumes M_T units of medicine and F_T units of food, and that his marginal rate of substitution of medicine for food is X. Finally, suppose that firm A produces M units of medicine and F units of food and that the marginal rate of product transformation between food and medicine is Y.

We first show that consumer satisfaction cannot be maximized if X is less than Y. Let X be less than Y and consider what would happen if we decreased both the amount of medicine produced by firm A and the amount of medicine consumed by Tom by 1 unit. To maintain Tom's level of satisfaction, he would have to be given X additional units of food to offset the loss of the 1 unit of medicine. This follows from the definition of the marginal rate of substitution given in Chapter 2. So, suppose that firm A were to give him the extra X units of food. How might it do that? It could decrease its production of medicine by 1 unit and make an additional Y units of food. This follows from the definition of the marginal rate of product transformation, which equals the extra number of units of one good that can be produced if 1 less unit of another good is produced. Firm A could now supply Harry with just as much medicine as before, since its total output of medicine and Tom's consumption of medicine were both reduced by 1 unit. And it could now supply Harry with an extra $Y - X$ units of food (the extra Y units it can produce less the X units it has given Tom). As a result, Harry's welfare could improve without hurting Tom. And what would make this possible? The condition that $Y > X$. So, consumer satisfaction cannot be maximized if $Y > X$.[7]

But what if X were greater than Y? If X were greater than Y, we could think about increasing the amount of medicine produced by firm A and the amount of medicine consumed by Tom by 1 unit. Tom would maintain the same level of satisfaction if he sacrificed X units of food. Suppose that he gave these X units to firm A, whose output of food was now Y units short. Firm A could therefore supply Harry with as much medicine as before and an extra $X - Y$ units of food (the X units Tom will have sacrificed minus the Y-unit reduction in total food production). Harry could thereby be made better off without hurting Tom if X were greater than Y. So, consumer satisfaction cannot be maximized if $X > Y$.

If consumer satisfaction cannot be maximized if X is less than Y, and if it cannot be maximized if X is greater than Y, then it follows that consumer satisfaction can be maximized only if X is equal to Y. This, of course, is what we set out to prove.

THREE CONDITIONS FOR ECONOMIC EFFICIENCY

The preceding sections have told a long story from which we can draw some general insight into the conditions that characterize an efficient allocation of resources—i.e., an allocation where it is impossible to improve somebody's welfare without causing harm to somebody else. Indeed, it turns out that there are three such conditions. If resources are to be allocated efficiently, then

1. The marginal rates of substitution between any two goods must be the same for all individuals (otherwise, at least two individuals can get together for a mutually beneficial trade and thereby increase the utility of one or both people).
2. The marginal rates of technical substitution between any two inputs must be the same in the production of all goods (otherwise, two producers can get together to trade inputs and thereby increase the output of one or both products).

[7]A numerical example may make this easier. If Tom's marginal rate of substitution of medicine for food were 1 and if the marginal rate of product transformation between food and medicine were 2, then firm A could reduce its output of medicine by 1 unit and provide Tom with 1 less unit of medicine. Firm A could thereby also increase its production of food by 2 units and give Tom 1 extra unit of food to compensate for his loss of medicine. There would be 1 unit of food left over. Giving this unit to Harry could make him better off without hurting Tom. Thus consumer satisfaction was not maximized at the outset.

3. The marginal rate of transformation between any two goods must equal the common marginal rate of substitution for all individuals (otherwise resources can be reallocated to increase the production of some goods at the expense of others to bring the product mix into line with consumer preferences).

ECONOMIC BENEFITS FROM FREE TRADE

Trade with other countries can be an enormous source of economic gain. We have demonstrated this result within the partial equilibrium context of Chapter 9; and we can underscore its strength by applying even simple general equilibrium tools. To understand what are termed "the gains from (foreign) trade" in a general equilibrium context, you must become comfortable with the concept of comparative advantage. Suppose that Germany could produce 2 computers or 6,000 pounds of textiles with 1 unit of resources while England could produce 1 computer or 4,000 pounds of textiles with 1 unit of resources. Under these circumstances, Germany would be a more productive and less costly supplier of both computers and textiles than England because it could produce more of each good from a unit of resources than England could. Germany would thereby have an **absolute advantage** over England in the production of both of these goods.

Absolute advantage

But comparative advantage is not the same as absolute advantage. One country has a **comparative advantage** over another in the production of a particular good if the cost of making this good, compared with the cost of making other goods, is lower in the first country than it is in the other. The simple example above would give Germany a comparative advantage over England in the production of computers. Why? Because the (opportunity) cost of a computer in Germany is 3,000 pounds of textiles (since both would require 1/2 unit of resources) while the cost of a computer in England is 4,000 pounds of textiles (since both require 1 unit of resources). As a result, computers would be cheaper to produce in Germany than in England relative to the cost of producing other goods (in this case, textiles).

Comparative advantage

If a country has a comparative advantage in the production of a particular commodity and if it can trade freely with other countries, then it is likely to find that it can improve its economic lot by specializing in the production of this commodity. It would, as a result, be able to export some of its production of its advantaged good to other countries while importing those commodities for which it does not have a comparative advantage. Consider the case of Germany outlined above. Figure 16.8 shows Germany's production possibilities curve. If Germany cannot trade with England, perhaps because of protectionist measures (tariffs, quotas, and the like) in both countries, consumer satisfaction in Germany would be maximized by choosing point *G*, where the marginal rate of substitution between the two commodities equals the marginal rate of product transformation between them. Point *G* is on indifference curve 1.

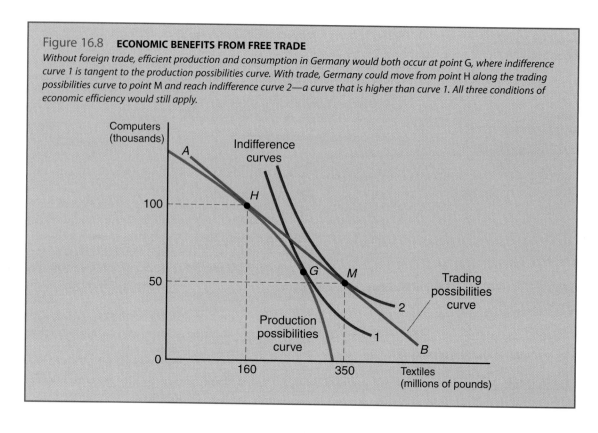

Figure 16.8 **ECONOMIC BENEFITS FROM FREE TRADE**

Without foreign trade, efficient production and consumption in Germany would both occur at point G, where indifference curve 1 is tangent to the production possibilities curve. With trade, Germany could move from point H along the trading possibilities curve to point M and reach indifference curve 2—a curve that is higher than curve 1. All three conditions of economic efficiency would still apply.

Now suppose that free trade were permitted, so that Germany could trade the commodity in which it has a comparative advantage (computers) for English textiles. Note that England has a comparative advantage in textile production.[8] The line *AB* in Figure 16.8, called Germany's "trading possibilities curve," shows the various amounts of computers and textiles that Germany could consume if it chose point *H* on its production possibilities curve. Moving to point *H* would involve producing 100,000 computers and 160 million pounds of textiles; trading along line *AB* would mean that Germany would not have to consume at point *H*. The slope of line *AB* equals (in absolute value) the number of computers Germany must "pay" for 1,000 pounds of English textiles.

Germany would clearly increase consumer satisfaction if it moved along line *AB* from point *H* to point *M*. Notice that indifference curve 2 is tangent to line *AB* at point *M*. In this way, Germany would reach a higher indifference curve than before. And how would it get there? At point *M*, Germany would be exporting 100,000 − 50,000 = 50,000 computers and importing

[8]The cost of 4,000 pounds of textiles in England is the same as the cost of 1 computer (since both require 1 unit of resources). In Germany 4,000 pounds of textiles costs 1.33 computers (since 1 unit of resources could produce 2 computers or 6,000 pounds of textiles, two-thirds of a unit of resources could produce (2/3) × 2 = 1.33 computers or (2/3) × 6,000 = 4,000 pounds of textiles). Relative to the cost of producing other goods (in this case, computers), therefore, textiles are cheaper to produce in England than in Germany.

350 million − 160 million = 190 million pounds of textiles. Since indifference curve 2 is considerably higher than indifference curve 1, Germany's consumers would be much better off than in the days when trade was not permitted.

At the same time, England would see an increase in consumer satisfaction if it specialized in the production of textiles (where it has a comparative advantage) and exported them to Germany. It would do so by cutting back its production of computers and importing them from Germany. So both countries would tend to specialize in the production of those goods for which they had a comparative advantage and export them to the other country.

Free trade of this sort would benefit many people in both countries, but it would not help everyone—that is, it would not be "Pareto-improving" (as explained in the next section). German textile producers (and textile workers) would probably be hurt considerably by the cut in textile output in Germany. And English computer manufacturers (and computer workers) would also incur losses because of the reduction in computer production in that country. It would not be surprising if these groups were to oppose free trade and press for protection from imports.

Finally, notice that the free trade equilibrium displayed in Figure 16.8 can be seen to satisfy the three conditions for economic efficiency in a general context. Domestic production occurs at point H on the production possibility frontier; it follows that the marginal rates of technical substitution between inputs employed in the production of textiles and computers must be equal. An Edgeworth box can be constructed between the origin and the consumption point (point M). Consumers could operate within that box so that their marginal rates of substitution would be equal to the world price ratio given by the slope of line AB. It follows that they would be on the contract curve with that box. Finally, the marginal rate of transformation between computers and textiles in domestic production is also equal to the slope of line AB at point H. As a result, the common marginal rates of substitution for all consumers would equal the marginal rate of transformation.

| Example 16.2 | Computable General Equilibrium and the Gains from Integration |

The Intergovernmental Panel on Climate Change (IPCC) recently published updated emissions scenarios that were designed to replace the earlier IS92 scenarios in a way that more accurately represents our understanding of the uncertainties of future economic development.[9] These "SRES" scenarios exclude "surprise" or "disaster" scenarios for climate change, but each is firmly rooted in one of four different "narrative story lines" that cover a wide range of demographic, economic, and technological futures. The A1 "Rich World" story line, for example, describes a future with very rapid economic growth supporting a global population that peaks mid-century. New and more efficient technologies are produced and introduced easily while significant capacity building across the globe results in significant reductions in regional differences in per capita income. The A2 "Divided World" story

[9]Intergovernmental Panel on Climate Change, *Special Report on Emissions Scenarios* (Cambridge: Cambridge University Press, 2000).

line, meanwhile, describes a world that continues to be extremely self-reliant and heterogeneous. Economic development is regionally oriented so that economic growth and technological change are more fragmented and slower. The B1 "Sustainable Development" story line mirrors A1 somewhat, but adds rapid changes in economic structure toward information and service economies. Material intensity declines with the introduction of clean and efficient technology driven in part by global solutions to economic, social, and environmental sustainability and equity. Finally, the B2 "Dynamics as Usual" story line brings the same orientation toward sustainability and social equity to a world that focuses its attention regionally much in the same way envisioned in A2.

While the scenarios were designed to support research into possible climate change, they can also display the types of insights that can be drawn only from general equilibrium analyses. Many research groups have, in particular, used the SRES story lines to calibrate computable general equilibrium models of economic activity across the globe. Panels A and B of Figure 16.9

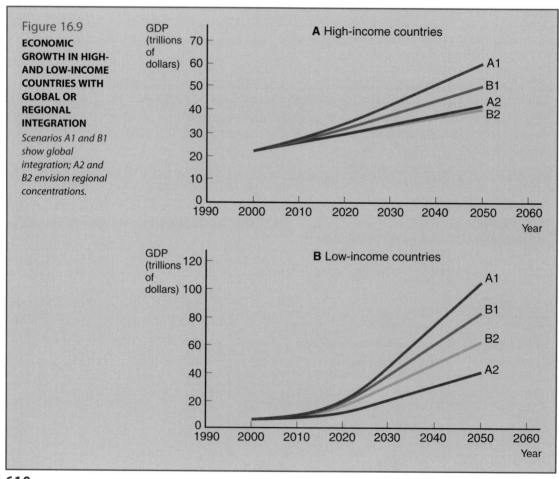

Figure 16.9

ECONOMIC GROWTH IN HIGH- AND LOW-INCOME COUNTRIES WITH GLOBAL OR REGIONAL INTEGRATION

Scenarios A1 and B1 show global integration; A2 and B2 envision regional concentrations.

plot typical results that were produced for the IPCC by the Pacific Battelle National Laboratory. They display possible future economic activity in high- and low-income countries, respectively, in terms of gross domestic product (GDP—the sum of the value of goods and services produced within a country or, in this case, a region). Notwithstanding the uncertainties involved in projecting economic activity 50 years into the future, the striking differences between the four story lines can be attributed directly to the ability of general equilibrium analyses to reflect different degrees of economic interaction between regions and different production possibilities. Notice, in particular, that the A1 and B1 trajectories run consistently higher than their A2 and B2 counterparts. Global integration would be beneficial to both high- and low-income countries because expanding the range of efficient transaction reduces costs and improves overall productivity; and a general equilibrium approach allows these benefits to shine through in ways that would be missed entirely by partial equilibrium analyses. Additionally, notice that transition to service and information sectors would shrink conventional economic activity as measured by GDP; but it would also reduce the sensitivity of future growth to assumptions about global integration. Why? Because service and information technologies move more automatically across national boundaries, so that the regional story line automatically includes some beneficial interaction.

A WORKING DEFINITION OF ECONOMIC EFFICIENCY

To understand how these three conditions support a working definition of economic efficiency, it is essential that we recognize an important limitation of microeconomics. It turns out that there is no scientifically meaningful way to compare the utility levels of various individuals. You may recall that we were not required to make these sorts of interpersonal comparisons in our discussions of utility and demand theory in Chapters 2 and 3. This was fortunate and, frankly, intentional. There is no way that one can state scientifically that a piece of Aunt Mary's apple pie would bring you more satisfaction than it would me. Nor can anyone prove that your headache is worse than mine. This is because there is no absolute and cardinal scale on which we can measure pleasure or pain to support any type of interpersonal comparison.

The implications of this observation are, to some degree, unsettling. We cannot make interpersonal comparisons of utility, so we cannot tell whether one distribution of income is better than another. You might receive twice as much income as someone else in your class. But economics cannot tell whether this is a better distribution of income than if she received twice as much income as you. Comparisons like this involve value judgments, and one person's values do not necessarily jibe with another's. This point notwithstanding, it must be said that most problems of public policy involve changes in the distribution of income. Even a decision to increase the production of digitally controlled machine tools and to reduce the production of conventional machine tools might mean that certain stockholders and workers gain while others lose. Why? Some machine tool firms specialize more heavily than others in the production of digital tools. They, and their workers, would benefit at the expense of others. So what? Difficulty in evaluating the effects of such a decision on the distribution of income means that there is corresponding difficulty in deciding whether such a decision is good or bad.

Faced with this problem, economists have adopted a number of approaches. Each of them has its own important difficulties, but each has its own advantages, as well. Some economists have simply paid no attention to the effects of proposed policies on the distribution of income. Their approach has the advantage of using currency as a unit of value, but they miss much of the richness of the political economy of most policy issues. Others have taken the existing income distribution as optimal, so that any deviation from it is bad. Their approach has the advantage of a well-established benchmark, but they spend much of their time defending its relevance. Still others have asserted that income distributions exhibiting less inequality of income are preferable to those exhibiting more inequality of income. Their approach has the advantage of a different standard of evaluation, but they spend much of their time justifying its value. Purists have argued that we cannot assert that a change represents an improvement unless somebody is made better off without hurting anybody else. These folks have endorsed the resource allocation efficiency criteria that were articulated above, but they have missed the boat entirely when it comes to the distribution of income.

Much of our earlier analysis has, quite frankly, been built on the assumption that a dollar gained or lost by any person should be given the same weight regardless of whether the person is a producer or a consumer, rich or poor, old or young, deserving or undeserving. You should recall that this approach was part of our examination of total surplus in earlier chapters. We noted there that this assumption, while it may be a useful first approximation, is too crude to support some types of analyses. If, for example, a change in economic circumstance resulted in Tom's gaining $50 and Harry's losing $50, then the $50 that Harry lost might mean more to him than the $50 that Tom gained. Indeed, different marginal valuation of income was the point of the expected utility analysis of Chapter 5. Nonetheless, an analysis that gave every dollar equal weight would say that Tom had gained exactly what Harry had lost so that aggregate welfare would not have changed.

Economists clearly have some difficulty when it comes to coping with these issues. For present purposes, it is enough to note that economics has adopted at least one criterion, attributed to Vilfredo Pareto. According to his view of the world, a change in economic circumstance that harms no one even as it improves the lot of at least one person must be an improvement.[10] It is called the **Pareto criterion.** Notice that it evades most of the interesting questions about the distribution of income. The criterion has nothing to say about a change that benefits one group of people and harms

Pareto criterion

[10]V. Pareto, *Manuele di Economie Politica* (1906).

another. The Pareto criterion has, nonetheless, received a lot of attention. Indeed, most economists agree that the adoption of changes that satisfy this criterion should be considered very seriously. In their view, society should at least look for changes that would harm no one while they improved the lot of some. If all such changes had been carried out so that there were no remaining opportunities to make "Pareto-improving" changes, then the situation would be deemed to have achieved **economic efficiency.** And how would we know if all Pareto-improving opportunities had been exhausted? If the three conditions for economic efficiency highlighted earlier in this chapter had been satisfied.

Example 16.3	Fairness, Equity, and Efficiency—Working a Problem

Economists have struggled long and hard with the trade-off between equity and efficiency. One of their more innovative approaches was to formalize the notion of fairness. Hal Varian, for example, suggested that an allocation of goods and services could be deemed "equitable" if no one prefers someone else's allocation to his or her own; moreover, an allocation could then be declared "fair" if it were both efficient and equitable.[11] Why impose efficiency on the definition of fairness? Because adding efficiency to the requirement guarantees that it is impossible to improve the welfare of everyone at the same time; it therefore provides a benchmark of utility and precludes reducing inequity by improving the lot of the least well off.

We can now work with this definition of fairness to see what it can teach us. Consider panel A of Figure 16.10. Point $E_{(1/2)}$ in the Edgeworth box indicates an equal allocation of X between Amanda and Danielle. Is it equitable? Is it fair? Surely it is equitable, but it is not fair because it is not efficient. Point $ME_{(1/2)}$ meanwhile indicates the market equilibrium that would emerge from an initial endowment designated by point $E_{(1/2)}$. Is it equitable? Is it fair? Yes to both. It is efficient, and neither Amanda nor Danielle would want to switch allocations. To see this, note that point $S_{(1/2)}$ represents the "swap point" where the allocations are reversed. Both Danielle and Amanda would be on lower indifference curves at $S_{(1/2)}$. In particular, $ME_{(1/2)}$ supports Danielle and Amanda at $U_{A(1/2)}^*$ and $U_{D(1/2)}^*$, respectively. Meanwhile, $S_{(1/2)}$ supports Danielle at $U_{DS(1/2)} < U_{D(1/2)}^*$ and Amanda at $U_{AS(1/2)} < U_{A(1/2)}^*$.

Now refer to panel B. Point $E_{(3/4)}$ indicates an initial allocation in which Amanda gets 75 percent of the available quantities of both X and Y. Is it fair? No, because it is neither equitable nor efficient. The swap point now is point E', and Danielle would surely prefer that. Point $ME_{(3/4)}$ would be the market equilibrium for an endowment set at $E_{(3/4)}$. It is efficient, but it is still not fair because its swap point is $S_{(3/4)}$, and Danielle would prefer to switch. Notice, though, that Danielle's utility would increase by less in moving from $ME_{(3/4)}$ to $S_{(3/4)}$ than it would in moving from $E_{(3/4)}$ to E'. Market efficiency has "improved" the "equitability" of Danielle's position relative to Amanda's, but not all the way to the point of being "fair."

[11]See H. Varian, "Equity, Envy, and Efficiency," *Journal of Economic Theory*, January 1974.

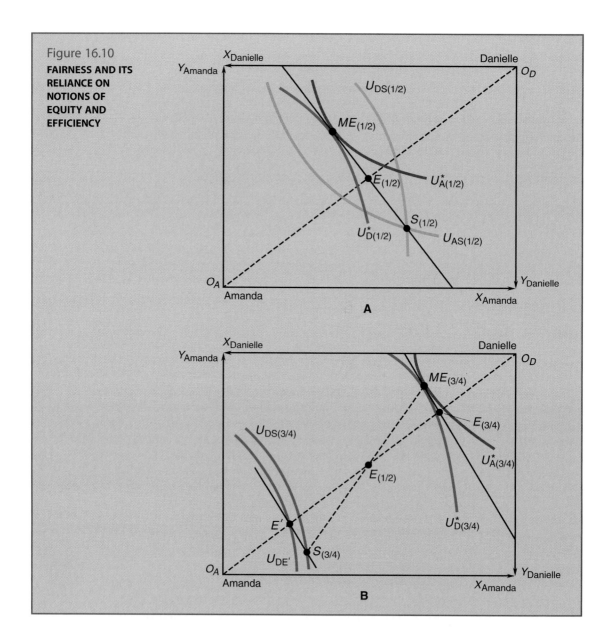

Figure 16.10

FAIRNESS AND ITS RELIANCE ON NOTIONS OF EQUITY AND EFFICIENCY

PERFECT COMPETITION AND ECONOMIC EFFICIENCY

First theorem of welfare economics

One of the most important and most fundamental findings of microeconomics is that a perfectly competitive economy in equilibrium satisfies the three conditions for economic efficiency. This result is frequently dubbed the **first theorem of welfare economics.** The argument for allowing competition to flourish can be made in various ways. Some people favor competition simply because it prevents the undue concentration of power and the exploitation of consumers. But to the economic theorist, the basic argument for a perfectly competitive economy is drawn from this theorem. We devote this section to a sketch of its proof.

The proof is really quite simple. We will demonstrate how a competitive economy satisfies each of the three conditions of economic efficiency. The first condition for economic efficiency, for example, mandates that the marginal rate of substitution between any pair of commodities must be the same for all consumers. To see that this condition is met under perfect competition, recall from Chapter 3 that consumers operating in competitive markets choose their purchases so that the marginal rate of substitution between any pair of commodities is equal to the ratio of their prices. But prices, and thus price ratios, are the same for all buyers under perfect competition. It follows, then, that the marginal rates of substitution between any pair of commodities must be the same for all consumers.

The second condition for economic efficiency mandates that the marginal rate of technical substitution between any pair of inputs must be the same for all producers. To see that this condition is met under perfect competition, recall from Chapter 7 that producers operating in competitive markets will choose to employ inputs so that the marginal rate of technical substitution between any pair of inputs is equal to the ratio of their prices. Input prices, and thus input price ratios, are also the same for all producers under perfect competition. It follows, then, that the marginal rate of technical substitution must be the same for all producers.

The third condition for economic efficiency mandates that the marginal rate of product transformation must equal the marginal rate of substitution for each pair of goods. The proof that this condition is met under perfect competition is somewhat lengthier. To begin with, we must note that the marginal rate of product transformation is the number of units of some good A that must be sacrificed by the economy as a whole to produce an additional unit of some other good B. The additional cost of producing the extra unit of good B is, of course, the marginal cost of good B. To see how many units of good A must be sacrificed to produce an extra unit of good B, we must divide the marginal cost of good B by the marginal cost of good A. This will tell us how many extra units of good A would cost as much to produce, on the margin, as one extra unit of good B. So, the marginal rate of product transformation under perfect competition equals the ratio of the marginal cost of good B to the marginal cost of good A.

Recall, now from Chapter 8, that price equals marginal cost under perfect competition. As a result, the ratio of the marginal cost of good B to the marginal cost of good A must equal the ratio of the price of good B to the price of good A under perfect competition. This means that the marginal rate of product transformation is equal to the ratio of the price of good B to the price of good A under perfect competition. We have, in addition, already noted in our discussion of the first condition of economic efficiency that the marginal rate of substitution for all consumers would equal the ratio of the price of good B to the price of good A under perfect competition. So, finally, it follows that the marginal rate of product transformation equals the marginal rate of substitution between any pair of products for any consumer under perfect competition.

| Example 16.4 | **General Equilibrium Effects of Taxation in Distorted Markets** |

General equilibrium effects that extend beyond the boundaries of a specific market can sometimes significantly change estimates of the economic cost of a preexisting market distortion. Figure 16.11 illustrates this point for a market (for some good X) in which a price ceiling had been imposed. The efficient equilibrium, in the absence of the ceiling, would have occurred at point E against the original demand curve; and so the appropriate deadweight loss attributable to the ceiling would be the area of triangle ABE.

Now suppose, for the sake of argument, that the government imposed a tax on the consumption of some other good Y, and assume that X and Y are substitutes for one another. The demand for X would increase for every price, as a result; and a new demand curve for X would then be in play. The deadweight loss attributable to the ceiling would expand to the area of triangle $AB'E'$, since the new market equilibrium would now appear at point E'. It follows that the economic cost of the tax on Y should include not only the deadweight loss created in the market for Y, but also the additional deadweight loss felt in the market for X—the area of trapezoid $BB'E'E$.

SOURCE: J. Hines, "Three Sides of Harberger Triangles," *Journal of Economic Perspectives,* vol. 13, no. 2, Spring 1999, pp. 167–188.

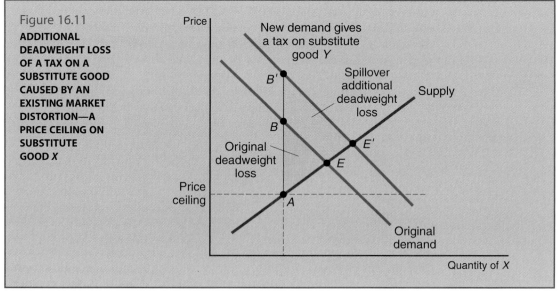

Figure 16.11

ADDITIONAL DEADWEIGHT LOSS OF A TAX ON A SUBSTITUTE GOOD CAUSED BY AN EXISTING MARKET DISTORTION—A PRICE CEILING ON SUBSTITUTE GOOD X

THE UTILITY POSSIBILITIES CURVE

Having stated the three necessary conditions for economic efficiency, we must now emphasize that they are incomplete guides to an optimal allocation of resources. Why? Because they say nothing about the distribution of income. To focus on this issue, it is convenient to return to the two-commodity, two-consumer, two-input case discussed earlier in this chapter. Recall that there were two consumers, Tom and Harry; two commodities, food and medicine; and two inputs, labor and capital. Scarcity was reflected in the model by limitations on the total availability of labor and capital. In particular, L units of labor and K units of capital were available.

The production functions were displayed in Figure 16.5; they were combined with the input limitations to produce the production possibilities curve portrayed in Figure 16.6. This curve is reproduced in Figure 16.12 by PP'. At any point on this curve, inputs are allocated so that the second condition for economic efficiency is satisfied—that is, the marginal rates of technical substitution of labor for capital are identical in both sectors for any point on PP'. We could, of course, construct an Edgeworth box within the boundary of PP' if we knew the amount of food and the amount of medicine that would be produced. If, for example, the total quantity of food produced were F, then the maximum amount of medicine that could be produced

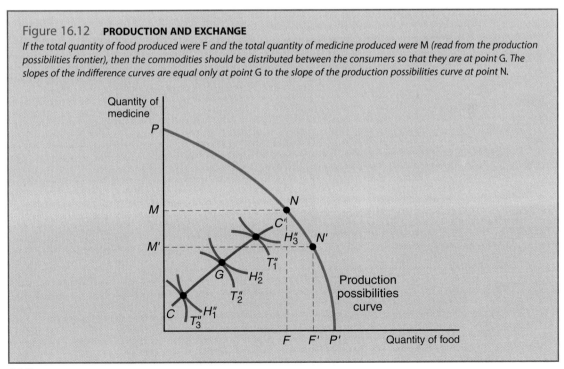

Figure 16.12 **PRODUCTION AND EXCHANGE**
If the total quantity of food produced were F and the total quantity of medicine produced were M (read from the production possibilities frontier), then the commodities should be distributed between the consumers so that they are at point G. The slopes of the indifference curves are equal only at point G to the slope of the production possibilities curve at point N.

would be M and the Edgeworth box diagram would have a width of F and a height of M; this, too, is displayed in Figure 16.12. Figure 16.12 also shows the three indifference curves for Tom and Harry (T_1'', T_2'', and T_3'' for Tom and H_1'', H_2'', and H_3'' for Harry) and the contract curve, CC'. Commodities are allocated at any point on this contract curve so that the first condition for economic efficiency is satisfied—that is, the marginal rates of substitution of food for medicine are the same for Harry and Tom for any point on CC'.

Assuming that F units of food and M units of medicine are produced, then the third condition for economic efficiency dictates that the commodities be distributed between the consumers so that they are at point G. Why? Because the third condition requires that the common marginal rates of substitution of food for medicine match the marginal rate of product transformation at the point selected on the production possibilities frontier. This condition is satisfied in Figure 16.12 only at point G. There, the common slopes of their indifference curves (the negative of the marginal rates of substitution) equal the slope of the production possibilities curve at point N (the negative of the marginal rate of product transformation). And finally, this distribution of commodities at point G between Tom and Harry means that Tom achieves a certain level of utility and Harry achieves a certain level of utility. Suppose that this pair of utility levels corresponds to point R in Figure 16.13.

Now suppose that we had taken a different point on the production possibilities curve in Figure 16.12, say, N'. We could then have drawn a new Edgeworth box diagram with width F' and height M'. Drawing Tom's and Harry's indifference curves in this new Edgeworth box diagram, we could have found a different contract curve. And so we could have found a different point on this new contract curve for which the common slopes of the

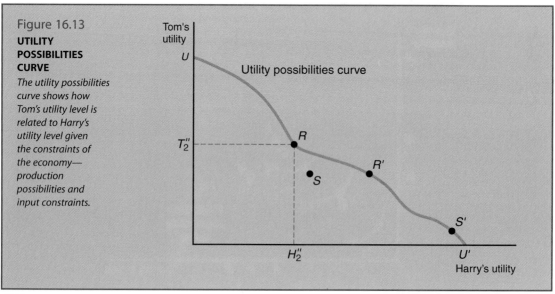

Figure 16.13

UTILITY POSSIBILITIES CURVE

The utility possibilities curve shows how Tom's utility level is related to Harry's utility level given the constraints of the economy— production possibilities and input constraints.

indifference curves would equal the slope of the production possibilities curve at point N'. The marginal rates of substitution for Tom and Harry would then equal a new and slightly higher marginal rate of product transformation. Let point R' in Figure 16.13 depict the utility levels for Tom and Harry that correspond to this point.

We could, indeed, repeat this fairly tedious process for all points on the production possibilities curve (some mathematics makes it easier). And if we did, we would create a locus of points like UU' in Figure 16.13 that shows the various possible pairs of utility levels of Tom and Harry *for which all three conditions for economic efficiency would be satisfied.* This locus of points is called the **utility possibilities curve.** As would be expected, UU' is negatively sloped. The greater the level of satisfaction achieved by Tom, the smaller the level of satisfaction achieved by Harry. This must be so because the three conditions of economic efficiency guarantee that Harry could not be made better off without hurting Tom and vice versa. The economy will, of course, come to a decision about which point on UU' would be chosen. Choosing this point is basically a choice about the distribution of income, and the problem of allocating resources would be solved in this case once this choice has been made.

*Utility possibilities
curve*

| Example 16.5 | **Utility Possibilities with Technology Transfer** |

Is it possible to use constructions like utility frontiers to explore what the future might look like in terms of equity? The story lines that underlie the SRES scenarios described in Example 16.2 can be used to show that the answer to this question can be yes. Figure 16.14 displays a frontier derived

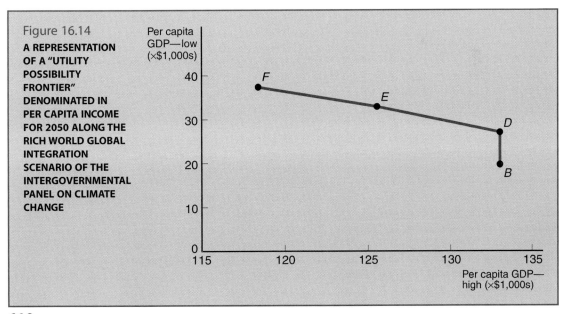

Figure 16.14

A REPRESENTATION OF A "UTILITY POSSIBILITY FRONTIER" DENOMINATED IN PER CAPITA INCOME FOR 2050 ALONG THE RICH WORLD GLOBAL INTEGRATION SCENARIO OF THE INTERGOVERNMENTAL PANEL ON CLIMATE CHANGE

from a general equilibrium model that was calibrated to the A1 "Rich World" future; it displays "not implausible" combinations for per capita income in high- and low-income countries for four different scenarios. A base case included relatively flexible production techniques in high-income countries operating along a not implausible future in which energy prices increase 1 percent per year without any policy intervention. Low-income countries operated within the same energy future with more population growth, less flexible technology, and a lower capital stock. The result of this scenario in the year 2050 is reflected by point *B*.

The second scenario allowed efficient investment by low-income countries in the technology available to high-income countries. They did not abandon any of their capital until its productive lifetime was over; but they replaced scrapped capital with new technology "imported" from high-income countries to the degree that was efficient given their relative abundance of labor. The outcome for this scenario is given by point *D*. High-income GDP was unaffected, but low-income countries saw increased economic activity.

Two other scenarios envisioned direct capital transfers to the low-income countries at the expense of investment in high-income countries. Point *E* shows the result of allocating 10 percent of high-income country investment to low-income countries; point *F*, the result of transferring 20 percent of this investment to low-income countries. Taking the contour *BDEF* as a reflection of a utility frontier for the year 2050, which point is optimal? Which point would reflect a vision of where we might want to see the globe at the middle of the century? That is impossible to tell without specifying an objective function. If we were trying to maximize the well-being (or at least the per capita income) of the world's poorest people, on average, then point *F* would be selected as the visioning target. But if we were trying to maximize average per capita income across the globe, then something like point *D* could be the target.

SOURCE: T. Malone and G. Yohe, "Knowledge Partnerships for a Sustainable, Equitable and Stable Civilization," *Journal of Knowledge Management,* vol. 6, no. 4, Fall 2002, pp. 368–378.

EQUITY CONSIDERATIONS

The selection of a point on the utility possibilities curve involves questions of equity. If point *R'* in Figure 16.13 were chosen instead of point *R*, then Tom's utility level would be lower and Harry's utility level would be higher. Harry would no doubt prefer point *R'* to point *R*, but Tom would surely prefer point *R* to point *R'*. Which point would be fairer? This is clearly a value judgment; the answer depends on one's concept of fairness. There is no scientifically valid way of making interpersonal comparisons of utility, but this does not mean that people cannot and should not have views about what constitutes an equitable distribution of income.

Some argue that each person should receive the same amount of goods and services (that is, the same income). This is the *egalitarian* view of equity. According to others, such as Harvard philosopher John Rawls, income inequality is justified only to the extent that it benefits the least advantaged. Still others believe that the most equitable allocation would be produced by the unfettered workings of competitive markets because, in their view, this rewards the ablest and most diligent people. Some beliefs regarding what constitutes an equitable distribution of income can be represented by a social welfare function that specifies the weights that are attached to each person's utility level. For example, one such function might specify that Tom's utility level and Harry's utility level should be weighted equally so that social welfare would simply be the sum of their utility functions. This is called

a **Benthamite welfare function,** but notice that its construction crosses the line of not making interpersonal comparisons of utility values (because it adds them up and says that one unit of utility for Tom would be equivalent to one unit of utility for Harry).

Efficient allocations of resources (in the Pareto sense that says that nobody could be made better off without hurting somebody else) may be regarded as less socially desirable than inefficient allocations if they result in a very inequitable distribution of income. At the extreme, an allocation that would give you all of the resources on the globe would be efficient, but it would hardly meet with much approval beyond your small (but certainly growing) circle of friends. The choice between points S and S' in Figure 16.13 illustrates the point with a little less precision. Point S portrays an inefficient allocation of resources. We know this because point S is below and to the left of the utility possibilities curve, so that either Tom or Harry could increase his utility without making the other worse off. Still, this allocation of resources may be regarded as socially preferable to the allocation of resources at point S', where the allocation of resources is efficient. Why? Because point S' means that Tom's utility level is very low.

Although economic efficiency is a reasonable goal, then, it need not be the only goal. The distribution of income is important, too, and economic efficiency does not guarantee an acceptable distribution of income. Recognizing this fact, economists do not claim that all changes that result in improved economic efficiency are worthwhile. Society has, for example, worked to achieve some of its equity objectives by establishing tax systems and government expenditure programs to help the poor even though devices of this sort tend to reduce economic efficiency. Taxes may dull incentives to work and to produce; income subsidies may do the same thing.

Example 16.6	John Rawls on Social Justice—Working a Problem

Example 16.5 focused our attention briefly on equity by presenting a rough utility frontier for the globe denominated in the very gross aggregate index of per capita income in poor and rich countries. In most modern democratic societies, of course, an equitable distribution of income is a major political objective; and there are many arguments for and against more equity in that distribution.

J. Rawls has put forth a theory of social justice in which he asserts that inequality is justified only to the extent that it benefits the least advantaged. Indeed, his theory would have society maximize the well-being of its least

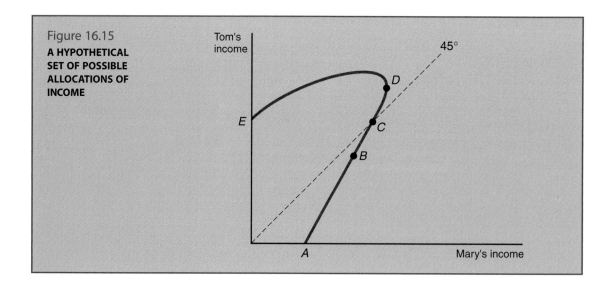

Figure 16.15

A HYPOTHETICAL SET OF POSSIBLE ALLOCATIONS OF INCOME

well-off citizens. This example explores his theory. Suppose that a society consists of two people, Tom and Mary, and that any combination of their incomes on curve *ABCDE* in Figure 16.15 is attainable.

Several questions can now be posed. If this society moved from point *B* to point *C*, for example, would it be reducing income inequality? Would this be an improvement according to Rawls? Would income inequality fall if society moved from point *C* to point *D*? Would Rawls approve of this move? Is it really possible to define what is a "just" distribution of income without considering how various people act (how much and what sort of work each does, what other contributions they make, and so on) and the process by which the distribution of income is determined?

First of all, Mary's income would exceed Tom's income at point *B* since point B lies below and to the right of the 45° line.[12] Mary's income would equal Tom's at point *C* since point *C* lies on the 45° line. This would be an improvement, according to Rawls. Mary's income would, however, be less than Tom's income at point *D* since point *D* lies above and to the left of the 45° line; their incomes would be equal at point *C*. Movement from point *C* to point *D* would not reduce income inequality. Rawls, however, would see this as an improvement because even the poorer person (Mary) would benefit in the move from *C* to *D*; her income at point *D* would exceed her income at point *C*. Many economists argue that justice occurs when a person's rewards (or lack of them) are related properly to his or her actions. One criticism of Rawls's theory is that it is concerned with the distribution of benefits without much regard for the actions of Mary and Tom.[13]

[12]The 45° line is the locus of points where the value measured along the horizontal axis (Mary's income) equals the value measured along the vertical axis (Tom's income). At points below and to the right of the 45° line, the former value exceeds the latter value; at points above and to the left of the 45° line, the reverse is true.

[13]For further discussion, see J. Rawls, *A Theory of Justice* (Cambridge, Mass.: Harvard University Press, 1971).

1. Previous chapters have been concerned with partial equilibrium analysis, in which it is assumed that changes in price can occur in one market without causing significant changes in prices in other markets. General equilibrium analyses account for the interrelationships among prices in various markets.

2. General equilibrium analysis has been used to help examine the conditions under which it is possible for equilibrium to occur simultaneously in all markets in a perfectly competitive economy. Modern work has established that a general equilibrium can be achieved in a perfectly competitive economy under a fairly wide set of conditions.

3. General equilibrium analysis provides a framework within which economists can study the relationships between prices and quantities for both commodities and inputs across the economy as a whole. Its purpose is to show what the equilibrium configuration of prices, outputs, and inputs will be in various markets given a certain set of consumer preferences, a set of production functions, and a set of input supply functions.

4. The simplest of general equilibrium models involves three kinds of equations—one for products, one for inputs, and one that guarantees that the conditions of perfect competition are satisfied. The simplest model of all assumes that the supply of inputs is given (and independent of prices) and that the coefficients of production are fixed. It nonetheless illustrates the nature of general equilibrium models.

5. Expanding the scope of analysis beyond a single market makes it possible to consider many interesting questions concerning the efficient allocation of resources across markets. The Edgeworth box diagram can be employed to examine efficient allocations of commodities between consumers. The contract curve summarizes those allocations. They are all characterized by equality in the marginal rates of substitution across all consumers.

6. The efficient allocation of inputs between industries also lies on a contract curve drawn in an Edgeworth box whose dimensions define the limits of input employment. This contract curve can be used to construct a production possibilities curve for an economy. Every point on the contract curve is characterized by equality of the marginal rates of technical substitution across all producers.

7. Even simple general equilibrium models can accommodate both production and exchange. Consumer satisfaction cannot be maximized unless the marginal rate of product transformation between (any) two goods is equal to the marginal rate of substitution between them for every consumer.

8. Perfectly competitive economies satisfy the three sets of conditions for economic efficiency. To the economic theorist, this is one of the basic arguments in favor of a perfectly competitive economy.

1. Gasohol is a blend of 10 percent ethanol and 90 percent regular gasoline. Ethanol can be made from corn. In late 1979, the cost of a gallon of ethanol made from corn was estimated to equal $1.20. The refinery price of regular gasoline was 85 cents per gallon. To encourage the production of gasohol, the federal government exempted gasohol from the federal gasoline tax. This was worth 40 cents per gallon on the 10 percent ethanol content of gasohol. Many states also exempted gasohol from their motor fuel taxes; this was worth another 40 cents to $1 per gallon of ethanol. (a) Does each

gallon of ethanol used in gasohol necessarily result in a 1-gallon reduction in the amount of regular gasoline (or other fuels) used in the United States? (b) Given these tax incentives, was it profitable to produce gasohol? If so, was it likely that gasohol would displace regular gasoline completely? (c) What are the effects of these tax exemptions on corn prices? On the value of corn-producing land? Partial equilibrium analysis is clearly incapable of answering these questions. Explain why.

2. John and Joan go to a Chinese restaurant together. They order lemon chicken and sweet-and-sour pork. When the food arrives, they divide each portion completely between themselves. Indicate how the Edgeworth box diagram might be used to analyze the way in which they divided the food, and how they should have divided the food. Is it reasonable to assume that Joan's satisfaction depends only on the amount of food she consumes and not on the amount John consumes too? And vice versa?

3. How would you go about predicting, on the basis of partial equilibrium analysis, the effect of a $1 per pound tax on the output of butter? If margarine were a close substitute for butter, what would be the advantages, if any, of using a general equilibrium analysis to answer this question?

4. Suppose that you have 6 bottles of beer and no potato chips and your roommate has 4 bags of potato chips and no beer. Your college has no policy prohibiting beer in the dorm (right?). It is late at night, and the stores are closed. You decide to swap some of your beer for some of her potato chips. The accompanying figure displays the relevant Edgeworth box diagram. Your indifference curves are labeled I and II; note that they favor beer. Hers are labeled 1 and 2; they favor chips, but beer is OK. Label the point on the diagram that represents your pretrade situation. Suppose that you decide to swap 3 bottles of your beer for 1 bag of your roommate's potato chips. Is this a rational offer? That is, would her acceptance of this offer make you better off? Explain. Suppose that you offer to swap 2 bottles of your beer for 1.5 bags of your roommate's potato chips. Would your roommate agree to this? Would this be a rational offer on your part?

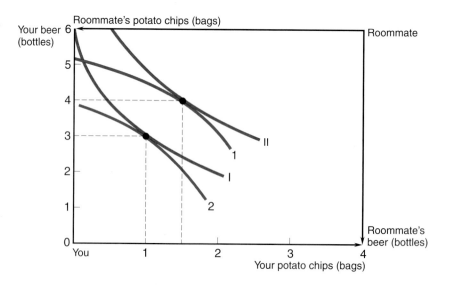

5. Suppose that the simple economy in Figure 16.5 were suddenly endowed with some additional labor (perhaps due to immigration). What would be the effect on the curves in Figure 16.5? What would be the effect on the production possibilities curve in Figure 16.6? Would the utility of everyone necessarily increase? Why or why not?

6. Suppose that the government ordered a 4 percent reduction in the price of a particular good for which market equilibrium had been achieved (say that it lowered its excise tax so that the price paid by consumers fell by 4 percent). (a) Based on a partial equilibrium analysis, would the output of this good be expected to fall? Would a shortage of this good be expected? (b) Besides ordering a 4 percent reduction in the price of this good, suppose that the government ordered a reduction in the prices of many other goods including substitutes for this good (maybe it lowered its general sales tax). On the basis of general equilibrium analysis, would you come to the same conclusions as in (a)? Why or why not?

7. Martin Cantine dies and leaves an estate consisting of 200 acres of land and 50 paintings. His will stipulates that his estate should be divided equally between his two children, Mary and John. So, each child should receive half the land and half the paintings. (a) Construct an Edgeworth box diagram showing the various ways in which the estate might be divided. (b) Show the point in this diagram that represents the division of the estate that is specified by the will. (c) Can we be sure that this point is on the contract curve?

8. Can moving from an initial allocation to a point of exchange efficiency on the contract curve for two consumers ever cause the utility of one person to fall?

9. If any move from an endowment of goods would reduce the utility levels of all individuals, what can be said about the location of the endowment relative to the contract curve?

10. The marginal rates of technical substitution between capital and labor are the same for two industries along a contract curve; capital and labor are the only inputs required. Cost minimization means that the marginal rates of technical substitution must match the ratios of input prices that the two industries effectively face. Does it follow that both industries face the same set of relative input prices? Suppose that the quantity of labor available to the two industries increased. Assume that society nonetheless wanted to keep the output of one industry fixed. Could the wage rate paid to labor ever climb relative to the price of capital? Why or why not?

11. Suppose that the marginal rate of substitution between the only two goods in an economy were equal to 2 for the only two individuals in the economy. Suppose, as well, that the marginal rate of transformation between the two goods were equal to 1. What should the people do to improve their utilities?

12. Suppose that two consumers, after swapping goods back and forth, have arrived at a point on the contract curve. In other words, neither can be made better off without making the other worse off; there are no "mutually beneficial trades" remaining. Does this mean that neither of them can find a point off the contract curve which is preferable to their point of equilibrium? If it does not mean this, why do economists claim that points on the contract curve are to be preferred?

13. According to Nicholas Kaldor, a change is an improvement if the people who gain attach a higher dollar figure to their gain than the dollar figure that the losers attach to their losses. For example, suppose that a proposed change benefited Jean and harmed Mary. Assume that Jean would be willing to pay up to $100 to see the change occur while Mary would pay up to $50 to avoid the change. Kaldor would say that the change would be an improvement even if Jean made no attempt to compensate Mary. What do you think of this view? It is the basis of cost-benefit analysis. Can you see any problems with this view? If so, what are they?

14. Suppose that the market for DVD players were in disequilibrium—that is, suppose that the actual price did not equal the equilibrium price. If all of the industries in the economy were perfectly competitive (including the market for DVD players), would the necessary conditions for economic efficiency be satisfied?

15. Refer to Figure 16.15 in Example 16.6. Find the point that Rawls would like the best. Find the point that would maximize the sum of the utilities of Tom and Mary.

16. Much has been made of the potential for global climate change to cause serious damage in the future. Many argue that policies designed to mitigate this damage should begin now. The idea, therefore, is that present generations should foot the bill for protecting future generations from the resulting damage. Assume that the global economy will grow over the intervening 50 or 75 years. Can you see any logic behind the claim offered by Robert Lind that applying the Rawlsian criterion to the climate-policy issue would imply that we should do nothing now because, in an intertemporal sense, we are the least well-off citizens who will inhabit the earth over the next 75 years?

Coping with Asymmetric Information

Information is vitally important to every actor in any economic arena: firms, consumers, the suppliers of inputs, and so on. With the exception of Chapter 5, however, we have generally examined the behavior of individuals and economic organizations that have been endowed with complete and perfect information about anything that might influence their economic choices. It would, of course, be more realistic to assume that these individuals and organizations are not perfectly informed. It would follow immediately that it would be important to examine circumstances in which some parties to any given transaction might actually be *better* informed than their counterparts. Chances are, for example, that a seller would know more than you about the strengths and defects of a motorcycle that you were about to buy. But you know more about your motivation to work hard this week than your employer; and you know more about the care that you take to protect your health or your valuable belongings than your insurance company. These and a multitude of other examples fall under the general rubric of **asymmetric information**—the topic of this chapter.

Asymmetric information

How does asymmetric information influence the decisions of buyers and sellers? How does it affect the operation of markets? The results that we will present here help to explain a wide variety of phenomena in the modern economy ranging from the disproportionate number of defective cars in the used car market to the pitfalls that must be avoided when governments or private firms design auctions. In addition, our results will show how even perfectly competitive markets might fail if participants come to the table with incomplete, imperfect, and different information. We will, in short, be examining the vulnerability of our benchmark of efficiency to another stress. How will it fare? Not well.

Indeed, the significance of these results cannot be underestimated, since asymmetric information may be the most pervasive source of inefficiency in developed market economies. The Nobel committee underscored their import by awarding the 2001 prize in economics to three pioneers in the field:

George Akerlof, Michael Spence, and Joseph Stiglitz. Samples of the work of these three Nobel laureates, displayed in its simplest and most accessible form, will populate the chapter; so, too, will a few examples that bring the abstraction of their models closer to the real world. In addition to advancing your understanding of microeconomic theory, these presentations and their associated examples have been designed to highlight models that clearly meet the criteria of Chapter 1 and illustrate how to fight through their exquisite abstraction to expand your understanding of the workings of your economic environment.

Example 17.1	**Asymmetric Information and the Value of Reputation**

Sellers' reputations count heavily in situations where buyers have less information, and we don't need fancy models to tell us that. A buyer of diamonds, for example, may go to Tiffany's because he or she feels that Tiffany's has a fine reputation. It follows that sellers work hard to earn and to *maintain* good reputations for high quality. In this way, they cope with the many problems of asymmetric information. Two examples follow.

1. Dawat is often cited in reviews as the best Indian restaurant in New York City. Dawat's owners could increase their profits on any given night by paying less for inferior quality rice and fish, but they do not. Why? Because long-term losses derived from bad reviews from anyone who happened by that night could easily exceed the present value of the short-term gain.
2. McDonald's has a reputation for uniform, standardized food. A Big Mac is a Big Mac is a Big Mac whether it is in New York, Hong Kong, or Colombo, Sri Lanka. This is important for hungry travelers who find themselves in unfamiliar territory (in Texas or China); and it may be very important for the children of those travelers who have grown up with Ronald. Travelers will come "home" from time to time because they know what they are getting—across town or on the other side of the world.

For further discussion, see P. Milgrom and J. Roberts, *Economics, Organization and Management* (Englewood Cliffs, N.J.: Prentice Hall, 1992).

USED CARS: THE CLASSIC EXAMPLE OF ASYMMETRIC INFORMATION

Who would imagine that an analysis of the used-car market would lead to a Nobel Prize? It did for George Akerlof, who, in 1970, helped open up the field of asymmetric information with his study of "lemons," that is, cars that are plagued with mechanical problems. Typically, the seller of a used car knows a lot more about its performance and deficiencies than any potential buyer, and this asymmetry of information will influence how the market for used cars might operate. To see how, George Akerlof devised a simple model that allowed him to examine the essential role played by accurate and/or inaccurate information.[1] Akerlof began by assuming that all new cars were either good or defective and that buyers would find out only after they made a purchase. Anyone who has bought a car knows that it is more complicated than that; but anyone who has bought a car also knows that this is the essence of the problem. How can I know, without driving this thing for 5,000 miles, whether or not it is any good? Akerlof also recognized that you would not be stuck forever with a "lemon" if things turned out poorly. Any owner of a new car could turn around and offer the car for sale for a variety of reasons. Maybe it is a lemon, but maybe the need for a car (or second car) has evaporated. The seller would know its quality, but a potential buyer would be in the dark—unable to determine (before buying the car) whether or not it was good or defective.

Under these circumstances, the equilibrium price of a used car would be less than the price of a new car. Why? Note first that good and bad used cars should both sell at the same price because potential buyers cannot tell the difference prior to the sale. But this common price must be less than the price of a new car because it would otherwise cost nothing to buy a new car, determine whether it is defective, and (if it proved to be defective) sell it and buy another new car. If the price of a used car were not less than the price of a new one, quite simply, there would be no demand for used cars.

Lemons would likely constitute a portion of the used cars offered for sale. Owners of good used cars could easily find that the equilibrium price of a used car was so low that they would not be motivated to offer many of their cars for sale. On the other hand, owners of defective used cars would not feel similarly restrained. And this insight would make potential buyers even more inclined to be wary of entering the market for used cars and to offer relatively low prices for used cars if they did.

The buyer of a used car would be willing to pay more than the equilibrium price if he or she were sure of getting a good one, and the seller of a good used car would be delighted to agree to such a transaction. But the asymmetry of information across the market and the fact that only the seller knows whether the used car is good or defective makes it difficult for these sorts of transactions to occur. Faced with this situation, sellers of used cars try in various ways to signal buyers that their cars are good. They cite relevant facts concerning their cars. They encourage the buyer to have his or her experts inspect the car before purchase. Maybe they even offer money-back guarantees (valid for short periods of time) or free service contracts.

A GRAPHICAL ANALYSIS OF THE MARKET FOR USED CARS

To analyze the forces at work in the used car market in more detail, let's continue to assume that all cars are either good or defective. But let's begin

---

[1]For a seminal article on this topic, see G. Akerlof, "The Market for Lemons," *Quarterly Journal of Economics,* August 1970. Old, you might say, but still very much on target!

this section by supposing that information is not asymmetric. Let's assume, in other words, that car buyers have complete information so that they can tell whether any car is good or defective before actually making a purchase. If this were the case, then panel A of Figure 17.1 would apply. The demand curve for defective cars (on the right-hand side of panel A) would be lower than the demand curve for good cars (on the left-hand side of panel A) because buyers would be willing to pay more for a good car than a bad one. The supply curve for defective cars (on the right-hand side of panel A)

Figure 17.1 **THE MARKET FOR USED CARS: COMPLETE AND ASYMMETRIC INFORMATION**

Panel A shows the situation with complete and perfect information. Panel B shows a different situation under incomplete and asymmetric information.

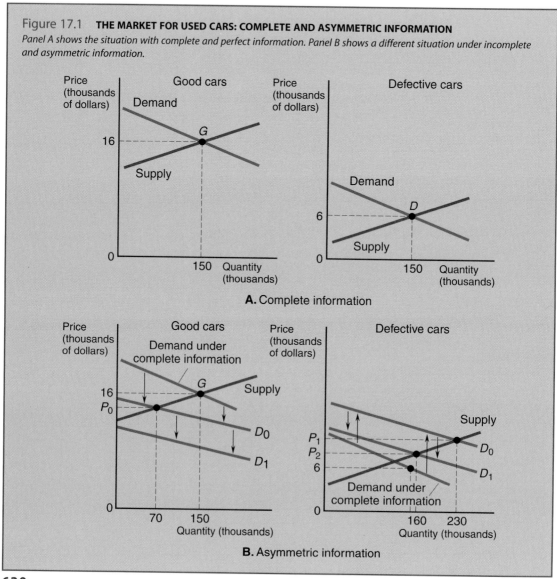

A. Complete information

B. Asymmetric information

would be lower than the supply curve for good cars (on the left-hand side of panel A) because owners of defective cars would be willing to take a lower price than owners of good cars. Both markets would clear with 150,000 units of each being sold. The price of a good car would equal $16,000 and the price of a defective used car would be $6,000. Points G and D in panel A highlight these equilibria.

Now let's see how the situation would change if we recognized that owners of used cars know much more about the condition and quality of their cars than potential buyers do. To be specific, suppose that we adopt the assumption of the preceding section that a buyer will learn whether a used car is good or defective only after buying it. Panel B of Figure 17.1 shows what would happen if this were the case. The supply curves for both good and defective cars would be the same as they were in panel A. After all, the number of cars (of either type) that owners would be willing to supply at a given price should not be affected by the buyers' knowledge about the quality of the cars.

By way of contrast, though, panel B shows that the demand curve for good cars would be altered considerably by the fact that potential buyers could not tell in advance of purchase whether a car was good or defective. Potential buyers would no longer be certain that a car sold in the "good car" market was really good. The demand curve for such cars would therefore initially shift down from its position under complete information (shown in panel A and reproduced in panel B) to D_0 in panel B. The price of a good car would initially fall to P_0, and 70,000 of them would be sold. At the same time, the demand curve for defective cars would initially shift up from its position under perfect information (shown in panel A and reproduced in panel B) to D_0 in panel B. Why? Because potential buyers could no longer be certain (before purchase) that a car sold in the "defective car" market was really defective. Even a small chance that it might be good would be enough incentive to shift demand. So, the price of a defective car would initially rise to P_1, and 230,000 of them would be sold.

But this would not be an overall equilibrium. The D_0 demand curve was drawn based on the assumption that about 50 percent of used cars would be good; recall that the market-clearing quantities in panel A were equal. But potential buyers would now learn that only 70,000/300,000 or 23 percent of used cars were good. The demand curve for used cars would therefore fall again—this time to D_1. Panel B shows the possibility that no good cars would be offered for sale. As shown, the price that potential buyers would be willing to pay given the high probability that the used car would be a lemon is too low to induce the owner of a good car to part with it.

Figure 17.1 portrays a highly simplified case, of course. Some good used cars could be offered and sold under other conditions (if curve D_1 were not so much lower than D_0). The important point is that the number of good cars offered and sold would be much smaller in panel B, where buyers struggle with imperfect information, than it would be in panel A, where they were perfectly informed.

Quality control has been a serious problem in many countries because poor quality can depress demand and lower prices. There have, for example, been many complaints in the United States about firms' producing more defective products than their Japanese rivals, and so consumers are sometimes willing to pay a premium for imported goods. We can use Akerlof's analytical structure to see why this might be the case.

Consider, to this end, the market for a metal fixture that does not depreciate with use when it is produced correctly and assume that consumers value these high-quality fixtures at $1,000 a piece. Suppose, though, that it is widely known that $\delta \times 100\%$ of these fixtures are defective when they are delivered to the marketplace. Maybe they don't work well. Maybe they wear out quickly. It doesn't really matter. All that is important is that the consuming public has a subjective view of that $\delta > 0$. Assume, as well, that there is a market for used fixtures. In either market, though, a potential buyer cannot tell whether or not any fixture is defective before actually installing it somewhere.

Can Figure 17.1 be used to portray equilibrium in the two markets? Certainly. The demand curve for good fixtures would be horizontal at $1,000 in the case of perfect certainty, but the risk that a new fixture might be defective would mean that the price for new fixtures would fall below $1,000. Moreover, it is possible that the price of new fixtures could fall so low that only defective fixtures would appear on the supply side of the used-fixture market.

What could we tell about δ if we knew that the equilibrium price in the used-fixture market was $600, that the equilibrium price in the new-fixture market was $880, and that consumers were risk-neutral? The parameter δ provides information about risk that should be reflected in the price of new fixtures. To see why, notice, first of all, that the expected monetary value of a new fixture would be

$$\delta \times \$600 + (1 - \delta) \times \$1,000.$$

Why? The first term is the value of a defective fixture weighted by the probability that it is, in fact, defective; and the second term is the value of a good fixture weighted by the probability that it is good. The indicated sum is thus the expected value of a new fixture. In equilibrium, then, this expected value should match the price if all consumers are risk-neutral (and so maximize expected monetary value). It follows, therefore, that

$$\delta \times \$600 + (1 - \delta) \times \$1,000 = \$880$$

so $\delta = 0.30$; that is, 30 percent of the fixtures are defective. Notice, finally, that the price of new fixtures would climb if quality were to improve (or at least the perception of quality were to increase so that δ would fall).

For further discussion, see David Kreps, *A Course on Microeconomic Theory* (Princeton, N.J.: Princeton University Press, 1990).

Sellers, and buyers for that matter, sometimes engage in an activity called "market signaling" to convey information about the quality of the products or services that they are offering. Why? Because they find it productive and profitable to combat the potentially detrimental effects of asymmetric information. Michael Spence was perhaps the first to describe how this might work even when the signal itself was only a "proxy" for quality.[2] We begin this section with a presentation of the simplest of a collection of increasingly realistic models of labor market behavior.

Recall from Chapter 14 that we have thus far assumed that a firm can readily determine the marginal productivity of a prospective employee. But this may not always be true. Take, for example, the plight of a personnel director of an electronics firm. She is interviewing several applicants for a particular job. She can obtain information concerning their previous experience and education, but it is nonetheless very difficult for her to predict how productive each applicant might be if he or she were hired. The key here is that the personnel office knows less about the productivity of the potential workers in her office than do the workers themselves.

To solve this problem, the firm could hire a number of workers provisionally and see which ones were actually most productive. They could then extend the contracts of the best new employees and let the rest go. This procedure can work, but it can also be very expensive. Firms must, in many cases, make large investments of time and money in on-the-job training for a new worker and then wait months (or even years) to see how productive a new worker will be. Then there is the possibility of having to pay severance wages if an employee has been on the job more than a few months and has not performed poorly (as opposed to not as well as others). Facing these issues, firms continue to be intensely interested in evaluating potential employees before they hire them.

Firms frequently use education as an important indicator, or signal, of a person's productivity when they make hiring decisions. This is understandable. More highly educated people tend to be more productive on many jobs because schooling imparts information and skills that help them work more effectively. But this is not the only reason. Schooling could still be a valuable signal even if it had no effect at all on a person's productivity. To see why, we turn now to Spence's model.

Spence assumed, in the spirit of the plight of our personnel director, that there were two types of workers. High-productivity workers had a productivity of 2 and low-productivity workers had a productivity of 1. A firm paying a wage w will therefore receive net profits of $2 - w$ or $1 - w$, depending on the type of worker it hires. Chapter 14 tells us that it would offer $w = 2$ to the high-productivity workers and $w = 1$ to the low-productivity workers—if only it could tell the difference.

[2] M. Spence, *Market Signaling* (Cambridge, Mass.: Harvard University Press, 1974).

Workers, before they enter the labor market, can work toward some sort of degree from some sort of educational institution. Let y represent the normal amount of time spent earning such a degree. Work toward a degree is expensive, though. Let the cost of this education for low-productivity workers equal y, but let the cost incurred by high-productivity workers be $y/2$. Spence, for the sake of emphasis, assumed that education had no effect on ultimate productivity. (Those of us who teach undergraduates object, but this assumption certainly adds strength to his conclusion.)

To make the model work, potential employers have to accept that the signal conveys some information. In particular, assume now that potential employers assume that any applicant with education y greater than some predetermined level y^* would signal a high-productivity candidate. That is, he or she would offer a wage of 2 to an applicant with $y > y^*$ and a wage of 1 to an applicant with $y < y^*$. An applicant with $y = y^*$ would be offered a wage of 2.

Given this structure, a potential applicant would offer the labor market either $y = 0$ or $y = y^*$ depending on which would maximize his or her surplus. So, potential applicants will appear for employment with either $y = 0$ or $y = y^*$. Employers will be content with this arrangement as long as it successfully separates applicants so that those with productivity 1 choose $y = 0$ while those with productivity 2 choose $y = y^*$. For low-productivity workers, therefore, the employers' condition requires that $1 - 0 > 2 - y^*$; only then would low-productivity workers choose $y = 0$. For high-productivity workers, however,

$$2 - \frac{y^*}{2} > 1 - 0$$

is required to pay for them to go to school. It follows that $1 < y^* < 2$ is sufficient to achieve the requisite separation. Moreover, the least-cost equilibrium is $y^* = 1$.

Can we put some realism into the Spence model? Suppose that gaining a college education would increase discounted lifetime earnings by $90,000 for high- and low-productivity workers, alike. This statistic could support a separating signal for employers who want to differentiate between the two types of workers, but only if a college education would cost high-productivity workers less than $90,000 and low-productivity workers more than $90,000. Tuition, room, and board would be the same for both, of course, but perhaps high-productivity workers could progress through college more quickly. Or perhaps they might receive more financial aid. It does not really matter. High-productivity workers would invest in a college education as long as firms used education signals to screen their applicants.

It is important to note that the Spence model made no claim that education would affect the productivity of prospective workers. The results were derived solely on the basis of the signaling character of education, and they relied only on a correlation between the attribute that the firms held to be important (productivity) and the cost of being able to make the proper signal (the cost of a college education). It made no difference, in other words, whether an applicant's college degree were in music, in physics, or in football. It was the education alone that was the signal.

In reality, of course, education does have an effect on productivity. Engineers who have graduated from MIT or Caltech are typically more productive than they would have been without a college education. But this does not deny that education also serves as a signal. Many employers insist on a college degree or an M.B.A. even though the specific training is much less important to them than the perseverance, intelligence, and drive of the job applicant. These employers recognize that achieving a college degree or an M.B.A. is a useful (if imperfect) indicator of a person's intelligence and willingness to work.

▢ Signaling Product Quality

We have now seen that education can be a signal in labor markets. What about product markets? Can the manufacturers of high-quality products signal consumers that their products are, indeed, of high quality? Sure. Issuing guarantees and warranties can be important signals for consumers. A TV manufacturer may, for example, issue a guarantee that it would pay for all repair costs within 2 years of the purchase. Why would such a warranty be an effective signal that this manufacturer's TV sets were of high quality? Because such a warranty would be very expensive to the manufacturer if they were not. The manufacturer could easily lose money by issuing such a warranty if its TV sets were not of high quality. Consumers would recognize this fact, and would see the manufacturer's willingness to accept the associated risk as an effective signal that its product was of high quality.

Example 17.3	Signaling in the Real World

We have suggested that signals can work in many contexts; and some are more contentious than others. A few small companies began to charge people with poor credit ratings higher rates for automobile insurance in the mid-1990s, for example. The idea has apparently caught on, because some big companies like Allstate, The Hartford, and Travelers followed suit in 2001. A bad credit history does not necessarily have anything to do with the quality of one's driving, but remember that the Spence model worked even if education had nothing to do with productivity. We simply need something that will separate one type of person from another, and it turns out that there is a very strong correlation between people who are prone to make claims on their auto insurance and people who have run into financial difficulty.

Is this something that should be applauded, since it brings insurance costs in line with risk? Or is this a practice that should be scrutinized? State Representative Art Feltman, a Democrat from Hartford, Connecticut, has argued that using such factors should be discouraged if they are discriminatory to a protected class even if they work to improve market efficiency. He has cited Freddie Mac data from 1999 that shows that 47 percent of African-Americans and 34 percent of Hispanic borrowers had poor credit ratings as compared with 31 percent of white borrowers. Why, he wonders, should these people pay as much as 25 percent to 40 percent more for car insurance, especially since nobody can describe why the correlation works? Following his lead, the Connecticut legislature is trying to end the practice, but not without a fight. The insurance industry argues that it has no intention of being discriminatory. Moreover, it argues that ending the practice would help a few consumers but hurt many more because it would redistribute premiums to force low-risk drivers to pay more while high-risk drivers pay less. The next section will explore the ramifications of this redistribution more carefully.

SOURCE: D. Levick, "Bad Credit Drives Up Insurance Costs," *Hartford Courant,* May 5, 2002.

ASYMMETRIC INFORMATION AND MARKET FAILURE

Figure 17.1 made it clear that asymmetric information can lead to complete market failure. If buyers do not have reliable information about the quality of products (or the prices, or any other economic variable that they deem to be relevant), then perfect competition may not lead to the sort of economic efficiency described in Chapters 8 and 9. If this problem were confined to the market for used cars, of course, it would not be a matter of great concern. But asymmetric information is present in many markets. Consider the case of credit cards—the staff of life for some people. Credit cards allow their holders to borrow up to several thousand dollars without putting up any collateral. The companies that issue the credit cards receive interest on the borrowed money, but they run the risk that cardholders will not pay what they owe. Like potential buyers of used cars, the card issuers have incomplete information. They find it difficult to tell whether an applicant for a credit card pays his or her bills in full or is a deadbeat, but the applicants themselves know. They are far more informed in this market than the credit card companies.

If the credit card companies must charge the same interest rate to all borrowers, then large numbers of deadbeats would find it worthwhile to obtain such cards. To offset their potential losses, the companies must raise their interest rates, but that would only increase the proportion of cardholders who are deadbeats. Why? Because people who pay their debts would be discouraged from applying for credit cards by the higher interest rates. But deadbeats, who are less likely to pay back what they owe, would be much less affected by higher rates; they're unlikely to pay anyway. In the extreme, in fact, only deadbeats would apply for such cards.

To prevent this, credit card companies sometimes obtain data concerning applicants' credit histories in an attempt to weed out deadbeats. The creation and dissemination of such histories has been criticized by some people as an invasion of privacy, but their existence unquestionably works to ameliorate the problem of asymmetric information so that credit markets can function.

ADVERSE SELECTION: A PROBLEM OF HIDDEN INFORMATION

Adverse selection

The problem faced by credit card companies is an example of **adverse selection**—the self-selection of the least desirable consumers. Joseph Stiglitz and Michael Rothschild produced one of the first models of this phenomenon in their early analysis of insurance markets.[3] We can use the apparatus developed in Chapter 5 to explore their model and examine the consequences of adverse selection.

Panel A of Figure 17.2 shows a low-risk individual (LR) who has fully insured against loss L given an initial level of wealth W_0. We know this because the expected utility-maximizing point (point E_{LR} lies along the 45° line, where

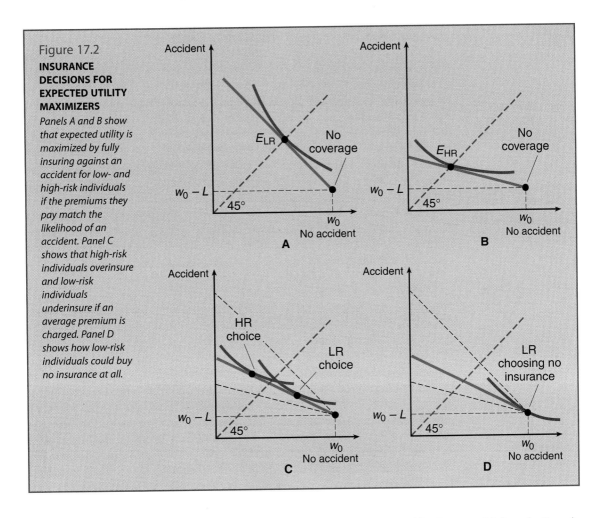

Figure 17.2

INSURANCE DECISIONS FOR EXPECTED UTILITY MAXIMIZERS

Panels A and B show that expected utility is maximized by fully insuring against an accident for low- and high-risk individuals if the premiums they pay match the likelihood of an accident. Panel C shows that high-risk individuals overinsure and low-risk individuals underinsure if an average premium is charged. Panel D shows how low-risk individuals could buy no insurance at all.

[3]M. Rothschild and J. Stiglitz, "Equilibrium in Competitive Insurance Markets: An Essay in the Economics of Imperfect Information," *Quarterly Journal of Economics,* vol. 90, no. 3, April 1976, pp. 629–650.

the outcome given an accident is equal to the outcome with no accident. If the probability of LR suffering a loss is Π_{LR}, then we know from Chapter 5 that the insurance company would be changing an actuarially fair premium $PR_{LR} = \Pi_{LR} \cdot \$100$ for every $100 of coverage. Recall, from Chapter 5 as well, that the slope of the budget constraint in panel A is $(1 - \Pi_{LR})/\Pi_{LR}$.

Panel B shows the same situation for a high-risk individual (HR) equipped with the same utility function facing the same potential loss L with a probability $\Pi_{HR} > \Pi_{LR}$. If the insurance company could tell HR from LR, then it would charge HR an actuarially fair premium equal to $PR_{HR} = \Pi_{HR} > \Pi_{LR}$ and HR would also fully insure; that is, HR's expected utility-maximizing point (point E_{HR}) would also lie along the 45° line. The slope of HR's budget constraint is smaller in magnitude, though, because $(1 - \Pi_{LR})/\Pi_{LR} < (1 - \Pi_{HR})/\Pi_{HR}$ under the differentiating assumption that $\Pi_{LR} < \Pi_{HR}$.

Suppose, now, that the insurance company could not tell the difference between HR and LR. It could charge a premium equal to

$$PR = \alpha\Pi_{LR} + (1 - \alpha)\Pi_{HR},$$

where α is the proportion of LR people in its client pool. This situation is depicted in panel C. Notice that LR individuals would now be overcharged for coverage, and so they would underinsure; and HR people would be undercharged, and so they would overinsure (this result is explained more fully in Example 5.7). As a result, the expected income of the insurance company would fall from the actuarially fair benchmark of zero. It would make money on the LR folks, but it would lose more than that on the HR people. The company could try to make up for this shortfall by increasing its premium, but that would only encourage the LR people to reduce their insurance coverages. In fact, panel D depicts the plausible circumstance in which the company has increased its premiums so much that LR people choose not to purchase any insurance. This is another case where asymmetric information can drive certain types of (desirable) participants out of a market.

CONSEQUENCES OF ADVERSE SELECTION

Who cares whether adverse selection occurs? Lots of people do. Larger-than-expected numbers of high-risk customers buying insurance would mean that insurance companies would have to pay claims on larger-than-expected numbers of policies. To remain solvent, they would have to raise the price of their insurance, but we have seen that this would discourage even more low-risk customers from buying insurance. The proportion of insurance buyers who were high-risk customers would become even higher, and insurance companies would have to raise their prices even further. It is not difficult to understand that the end result could be that only high-risk customers would be willing to buy this insurance, even though low-risk customers would be happy to buy coverage if its price were in keeping with their low-risk status. This should, by now, be a familiar result. It was, indeed, the point of Figure 17.1, and it was the moral of the analysis of the problems of credit card companies.

The news is not necessarily all bad, though. To see why, notice that the insurance company could deal with this situation by simply charging a higher price to high-risk customers than it does to low-risk customers. All it needs is some way of distinguishing between the two. And companies have developed methods for trying to elicit the relevant information. Applications for insurance coverage include a wide range of questions that are designed to distinguish high-risk customers from low-risk ones. Does anyone in the house smoke? How far away is the nearest fire hydrant? How far away is the nearest fire station? Is it volunteer or professional fire coverage? Does the house have smoke detectors? What is the house made of? And so on. Companies use the answers to these questions to adjust their prices from one house to the next.

This problem of adverse selection occurs in many insurance markets, not just in the market for fire insurance. In the health insurance market, for example, some customers may be much more likely than others to have serious illnesses, but it can be very difficult for the insurance company to determine whether this is the case. Here, as in the case of fire insurance, low-risk customers may be driven from the market because of increases in the price of health insurance due to the disproportionately large percentage of insurance buyers who are high-risk customers. Insurance companies have again devised a number of strategies to try to cope with the problem. Just like their fire insurance colleagues, health insurers often seek extra information. They frequently require physical examinations to obtain better information as to whether a person is high-risk or low-risk. They also often offer lower prices for health insurance to members of group plans, such as all employees of a large firm, than to individuals. Insurance is mandatory for all employees in these plans, and so there is little or no problem of adverse selection. Finally, insurance companies often set insurance rates that differ from one segment of the population to another. Expanding our coverage just a bit, it should come as no surprise that car insurance companies charge less to cover young women than young men, and less to cover drivers who are more than 25 years old. Why? Because their statisticians tell them that young women tend to be better drivers than young men and that people under the age of 25 tend to have more accidents.

Some people have, in recent years, argued that this gender-based or age-based discrimination is unfair. Others have responded that banning gender- or age-based insurance rates would discriminate against young women and older drivers (in the case of auto insurance) because it would ignore the actuarial facts. Whatever your position on this question, it is easy to see why insurance companies have responded as they have to the problem of adverse selection.

| Example 17.4 | **Responding to Adverse Selection: State Comparisons of Insurance Expenditures** |

We have seen that individuals will tend to fully insure if coverage premiums are set properly and that they will underinsure or overinsure if premiums are set too high or too low—that is, higher than the probability of loss or lower than the probability of loss. We have also seen that setting one premium for all customers can lead to adverse selection, not to mention profitability problems. It follows that insurance companies, not to mention

Table 17.1

HIGHEST AND
LOWEST
INSURANCE COSTS
ACROSS THE
UNITED STATES

A RENTERS INSURANCE

State	Annual expenditure	Rank
California	$257	1
Louisiana	$246	2
Nevada	$238	3
Texas	$237	4
Florida	$225	5
South Dakota	$100	49
Wisconsin	$99	50
North Dakota	$98	51

B HOMEOWNERS INSURANCE

State	Annual expenditure	Rank
Texas	$879	1
Louisiana	$692	2
Florida	$650	3
District of Columbia	$633	4
Alaska	$595	5
Delaware	$312	49
Ohio	$301	50
Wisconsin	$258	51

C AUTOMOBILE INSURANCE

State	Annual expenditure	Rank
New Jersey	$1,134	1
District of Columbia	$958	2
New York	$943	3
Massachusetts	$889	4
Delaware	$863	5
South Dakota	$484	49
North Dakota	$469	50
Iowa	$466	51

SOURCE: The Insurance Information Institute at www.iii.org/media/financials and the
National Association of Independent Insurers.

economists who want to promote economic efficiency, will want to match
the premiums with actual probabilities of risk as closely as possible. Do they?
Perhaps not exactly in all cases, but differences in premiums charged for similar coverage in different regions of the country certainly suggest that they
do not simply charge "one-size-fits-all" premiums to all possible customers.

   Table 17.1 records some evidence of these differences for the year 1999—
it displays the highest and lowest average annual expenditures by state for

renters insurance, homeowners insurance, and automobile insurance. Automobile insurance is most expensive in the Northeastern megalopolis, where traffic is heavy and theft is a relatively common occurrence; and it is least expensive (by more than 50 percent) in rural states with light traffic and little crime. Correspondingly, renters and homeowners insurance seem to be highest in states where the threat of large coastal storms or other natural disasters is high, and lowest (again by more than 50 percent) in states with relatively benign environments.

MORAL HAZARD: A PROBLEM OF HIDDEN ACTION

We mentioned, only in passing earlier in this chapter, that the holder of an insurance policy could alter his or her behavior in ways that would increase the probability that the carrier would have to pay a claim and without the carrier's knowledge. We also demonstrated, in Chapter 5, that individuals who are risk-averse and who act to maximize their expected utility in the face of uncertainty would fully insure against potential losses if the premiums charged by insurance companies were actuarially fair. Feeling that they had nothing to lose, they might stop taking prudent precautions and thereby increase the chance of theft, for example. Or they might be less careful with candles or fires in the fireplace.

Moral hazard   This is the **moral hazard** problem. It occurs whenever the insurance company cannot know what actions people take that may influence the likelihood of the unfavorable event for which it has sold coverage. The problem exists for various kinds of insurance. People who buy lots of accident insurance may drive less carefully because they are well insured, and they might therefore become higher risks—more likely to have an accident than if they had less insurance. Similarly, people with lots of medical insurance may spend less on preventive health care, and so they might make more visits to the physician and incur more expensive treatments when they do get sick than if they had less insurance.

To make these issues as clear as possible, consider the extreme case in which a health insurance policy reimburses the policyholder for all medical costs. In this case, a patient would pay nothing for extra treatment. Clearly, then, the patient would be more likely to consume medical services in excess of what he or she would consume if the extra services were not free. Any drug or treatment, whatever its price, could be prescribed by physicians who knew that the insurance company and not the patient would pay for it. Medical costs would increase (with demand), and the price of insurance would climb commensurately.

Insurance companies have responded to this problem by imposing limits on the amount of medical services that an insurance policy will cover. A particular policy may, for example, pay for no more than 4 days in the hospital for a person undergoing a gallbladder operation, and a new mother may be able to stay only one day after giving birth. In addition, many insurance policies

Co-insurance   have a feature called **co-insurance.** This feature means that the insurance company pays for less than 100 percent of the total bill, so that the policy-holder is obliged to pay the balance. Health insurance policies often have a 20 percent co-insurance rate, which implies that the insurance company pays 80 percent and the policyholder pays 20 percent of any bill. Someone with a $500 medical bill would then pay 0.20 × $500, or $100. Other plans have fixed co-payment schedules—$20 for a prescription, $10 for an office visit with a primary care physician, $20 for a consultation with a specialist, and so on. In any case, the point of co-insurance is to give the policyholder more incentive to hold down medical bills and to take preventive care.

Deductibles

Insurance companies have also responded to the moral hazard problem by inserting **deductibles** into the policies that they write. With a deductible, the policyholder has to bear part of the insured loss up to some limit. For example, a medical-insurance policy may stipulate that the patient must pay the first $200 of medical expenses that he or she incurs per year. If you had such a policy and if you ran up $1,000 in medical bills in 2003, then you would have to pay $200 of them before any of the other provisions of the policy came into force. This, too, provides patients with an incentive to consider the full costs in the case of minor treatments or injuries.

It is important to recognize that moral hazard can also impair the efficiency of other competitive markets. To take an extreme case, suppose that the owner of a dilapidated apartment building bought a great deal of fire insurance—so much that he could get more money from the insurance company if his building burned down than if he were to sell it. He would therefore have an incentive to stage an "accidental fire" that destroyed the building. Unfortunately, it is not unusual for mysterious accidents of this sort to occur. Savvy police officers and insurance agents check carefully to see whether or not burned-out buildings returned insurance payments that were larger than the buildings' worth on the open market. And they look for cases in which businesses in a burned-out commercial building were having problems, so that their value might be less than the insurance coverage. Intentional fires are illegal, of course, but they are also wasteful. The need to maintain this sort of vigilance adds to the costs borne by the insurance industry and moves the industry away from the competitive optimum.

Note, finally, the difference between moral hazard and adverse selection. Adverse selection is the result of not being able to observe some characteristic of a person *before* the parties have engaged in some trade or contractual relationship. Moral hazard, on the other hand, is the result of not being able to observe a person's action *after* they have entered into a contractual relationship.

| **Example 17.5** | **Deductibles and the Cost of Automobile Insurance** |

Try an experiment with your insurance company. Give them a call and ask them how much they would charge for collision coverage on your car if you changed your deductible. If you don't have a car, think of one that you might want to buy, and go on-line to investigate insurance costs. Insurance is, of course, a major expense, and many people do just that as they try to figure out exactly what type of car they can afford. In any case, most companies offer at least three choices ($500, $250, and $100), so you will be

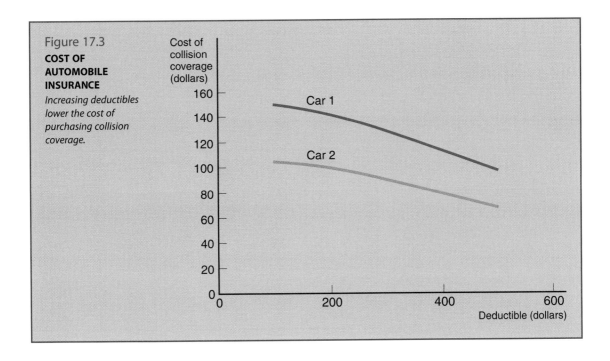

Figure 17.3

COST OF AUTOMOBILE INSURANCE

Increasing deductibles lower the cost of purchasing collision coverage.

able to see how premiums change with deductibles. Since we have suggested that deductibles are one way to reduce moral hazard problems, the cost of coverage should fall more than proportionately as the deductible increased. Why? Your willingness to accept a higher deductible should reduce the company's concerns about moral hazard because careful drivers should be willing, on average, to assume more of the risk of paying for an accident.

I tried the experiment and found that my company did reduce its price quotation for both cars; Figure 17.3 displays the results. For the record, car 1 is a 1994 Grand Cherokee and car 2 is a 1994 Toyota Camry. They cost about the same to buy, but either a Jeep costs more to fix or Jeep owners are more prone to having accidents. Notice that both lines do in fact become more steeply sloped for higher deductibles; that is, the cost of coverage did fall more than proportionately.

AUCTIONS

The take-home message from this chapter so far is that information matters. Differences in access to quality information can disrupt equilibrium and generate inefficiencies to the point where a market might actually collapse (or never form), but understanding how can help us see how to design structures that minimize those inefficiencies. The take-home message from Part Four of the text was that market structure matters. Differences in access to market power and information about competitors can also disrupt equilibrium and generate inefficiencies, but understanding how can again help us to intervene effectively to minimize these inefficiencies. What about market rules? Can different protocols that determine who gets to do what and who gets to buy how much for what price create different equilibria and generate inefficiency? And if so, can we learn how to avoid mistakes in this arena, as well? The answer to the first question is "It depends"—the same as the answer to nearly every question in economics; but an understanding of how it depends on what can help us avoid costly mistakes.

A growing literature explores these questions by examining the implications of creating different types of auctions.[4] Some researchers have conducted experiments to see how, whether, and perhaps why different types of auctions might support different market outcomes. Others have devised fairly elaborate models and crafted descriptions of Nash equilibria for a variety of auctions conducted under different rules. This section will report some of the fundamental findings from the latter tactic, but it will also offer an experiment that you could try on your own. You should understand, however, that focusing attention on auctions is more than an academic interest. Auctions have been around for more than 2,500 years. Auctions for flowers, used computers, used cars, the contents of estates, and many other commodities can be found in every corner of the United States on a daily basis—if not physically, certainly by virtue of Internet access to ebay.com. Governments conduct auctions, as well. The U.S. Department of the Interior has held auctions to sell the rights to drill for oil along the U.S. coast, and perhaps it will again for rights to drill in the Alaskan wilderness. Understanding how they work so that we can design auctions that produce desirable outcomes is serious business.

| Example 17.6 | The FCC and the "Biggest Auction in the Known Universe" |

Reed Hundt, chair of the Federal Communications Commission (the FCC), was ecstatic on March 13, 1995, after his agency had completed an auction that determined who would hold licenses for broadband personal communication services (PCS). Indeed, he exulted, "I am very pleased with how smoothly this auction—the biggest in the known universe—ran."

The idea of auctioning off rights to the radio spectrum was not new in the mid-1990s. The Nobel laureate Ronald Coase had proposed the idea as early as 1959.[5] For many years, though, spectrum licenses had been assigned by the FCC after hearings to decide which of a number of applicants was most suitable. These hearings tended to be long and costly to the applicants, the government, and the general public. Moreover, some observers charged that political favoritism played a role in the awarding of licenses. We now know, as well, that these sorts of rigid allocations do not necessarily lead to

---

[4]A "Symposia" section of the *Journal of Economic Perspectives* published in the summer of 1989 contains a short collection of papers that provide some of the basics; we will draw heavily on papers published there by Paul Milgrom ("Auctions and Bidding: A Primer") and Orley Ashenfelter ("How Auctions Work for Wine and Art").

[5]R. Coase, "The Federal Communications Commission," *Journal of Law and Economics,* October 1959.

efficient allocations—allocations for which the marginal values to the holders of each license are equal. The ability to buy and sell licenses after their allocation would help alleviate inefficiency, of course, but the transfers of wealth associated with each transaction could be enormous.

Wary of the inefficiencies of the original hearing process, Congress in 1992 gave the FCC the authority to award licenses by lottery. Subsequent experience indicated that this method of awarding licenses had its own set of problems. It quickly became clear, for example, that the requirements for entering the lottery were so low that the FCC was flooded with applications. In low-power television service alone, for example, there were 20,000 applications. It was cheap to apply and the licenses to be awarded were valuable, so it was not surprising that the number of applications was very large.[6]

As a result of this and other issues, the FCC was finally given the authority to auction licenses in 1993. Congress listed a variety of objectives for the auction of spectrum rights: to promote an efficient use of the spectrum, to encourage the development and utilization of new technologies, to limit the concentration of licenses, and to ensure that at least a minimal number of licenses went to minority-owned and female-owned firms, small companies, and rural telephone companies. Clearly, Congress hoped to improve both static and intertemporal efficiency and to promote equity in the final allocation.

What exactly happened in the FCC case? Beginning on December 5, 1994, the FCC auctioned off a variety of wavelengths, formerly reserved for the military, which were to be devoted to PCSs such as cellular telephones, portable fax machines, and wireless computer networks. Ninety-nine licenses to provide such services across the United States were auctioned off. The total amount bid for them was almost $8 billion. The bidders included telephone companies (long-distance, local, and cellular) and cable television firms. The biggest winner was Wireless Co., LP—a partnership among Sprint; TeleCommunications, Inc.; Cox Cable; and Comcast Technology—which placed winning bids in 29 markets; in all, its bids totaled about $2.1 billion. The second biggest winner was AT&T Corporation, which was the winning bidder in 21 markets, with bids totaling about $1.7 billion. The 10 highest bids per person in the market are recorded in Table 17.2. Please note that some of these companies have since merged, but that is, as they say, a different story.

▣ Auction Organization and Protocol

English auction

Auctions have been organized in many different ways. You are probably most familiar with the **English auction,** where items are put up for sale and prospective buyers offer higher and higher bids until only one bidder remains. At that point, the remaining bidder is declared the "winner" and pays whatever he or she has bid for the item in question. A **Dutch auction** runs

Dutch auction

[6]E. Kwerel and A. Felkner, "Using Auctions to Select FCC Licensees," Federal Communications Commission, May 1985.

Table 17.2

HIGHEST BIDS (PER PERSON IN THE MARKET) FOR U.S. LICENSES FOR BROADBAND PERSONAL COMMUNICATION SERVICES

Market	Winning bidder	Winning bid (in millions)	Price per person (dollars)
1. Chicago	PCS Primeco, LP[a]	$385	32
2. Chicago	AT&T Wireless PCS, Inc.	373	31
3. Atlanta	AT&T Wireless PCS, Inc.	198	29
4. Seattle	GTE Macro Communications	106	28
5. Seattle	Wireless Co., LP[b]	105	27
6. Washington/ Baltimore	AT&T Wireless PCS, Inc.	212	27
7. Atlanta	GTE Macro Communications	185	27
8. Los Angeles/ San Diego	Pacific Telesis	494	27
9. Miami/Fort Lauderdale	Wireless Co., LP[b]	132	27
10. St. Louis	AT&T Wireless PCS, Inc.	119	26

[a] A partnership among Bell Atlantic, Nynex, U.S. West, Air Touch Communications.
[b] A partnership among Sprint, Comcast, TeleCommunications, Inc., Cox Cable.
SOURCE: *Philadelphia Inquirer*, March 17, 1995.

in reverse. Starting with an unacceptably high price, the auctioneer lowers the price by fixed increments or at a fixed pace until somebody indicates a desire to make the purchase. That person is the "winner" and pays the then current (the last quoted) price. **Sealed-bid** auctions are also common. Under these rules, prospective buyers submit written bids before some specified time and date. The bids are then opened to determine the winner. Under **first-price sealed-bid rules,** the highest bidder "wins" a purchasing auction and pays the price he or she quoted. Under **second-price sealed-bid rules,** the highest bidder still "wins," but now pays the price quoted by the second highest bidder.

Sealed-bid

First-price sealed-bid rules
Second-price sealed-bid rules

◻ Private-Value Auctions

Before we contemplate how these different rules might support a market equilibrium, it is equally important to set context. **Private-value** auctions are conducted across participants who have their own private value of the item being auctioned. Think about an old barn in the country where somebody is auctioning off an antique lamp. Some of the prospective buyers might place a high value on the lamp because they know that they like it and there is a perfect place for it in their living room. Others might place a low value on the same lamp because they know that it really doesn't catch their fancy even though the antique book tells them that they should like it. Still others

Private-value auctions

are somewhere in between. The key point, here, is that a room full of potential buyers will present the seller with a distribution of values and bids for the lamp, but each individual buyer knows his or her own (and only his or her own) private and personal valuation.

What would an equilibrium outcome look like for a private-value auction? It would be an estimate of the winning bid; and so you can determine equilibrium by hypothesizing your own behavior under the assumption that your private value for some item like the antique lamp was higher than anyone else's. To make things simple, assume that a clairvoyant observer could deduce every bidder's private valuation and order the valuations from high to low. Let these values be V_1 through V_n, where n is the number of bidders. These values are often called **order statistics,** and our assumption about your behavior means that you think that yours is V_1. Of course, your valuation is V_i, which may or may not be V_1, but that does not matter in determining the winning bid. To see why, return to the hypothetical auction. If you were participating in an English auction, your dominant strategy would be to bid slightly more than the current bid until nobody was left *as long as the current bid was less than V_i.* This would keep you in the game but still guarantee that you never bid more than V_i. Your V_i may not match V_1, of course, but somebody at the auction will have V_1. The same dominant bidding strategy will lead him or her to keep bidding until the offer rose slightly above V_2, the second highest valuation. The bidding would stop, at that point, and the winning bid would be *very* close to V_2.

Order statistics

What if you were participating in a second-price sealed-bid auction? What should you bid? Bidding your private valuation V_i is again a dominant strategy—no more and no less. Why? To bid more than V_i would run the risk, even in a second-price protocol, of paying more for something than it is worth to you. But to bid less than V_i would run the risk of losing to somebody who actually paid less than V_i, and so you would miss out on the chance to buy something for a price that was less than your V_i. What is the equilibrium price in this case? The private valuation of the person with the second highest V (i.e., V_2) would be the winning price because that would be the bid of the person with the second highest valuation.

Now think about your bid in a Dutch auction. The offered price falls at a specified pace, and you have to decide when to step in and make the purchase. Again, assume your private valuation is V_i. If $V_i = V_1$, then you would be the first person at the auction who was tempted to stop the declining offers. Do you accept the price as soon as it reaches V_i? Probably not. To do so would miss the chance of making the purchase at a price lower than V_i. So at what price do you "pull the trigger"? Just before your best guess at the next highest valuation—the price at which someone else might snatch victory away from you. It follows that the one person in the auction with V_1 will win the auction, and the winning equilibrium bid will be the expected value of V_2.

Finally, think about your bid under a first-price sealed protocol. Do you bid V_i? No. You bid as far below V_i as you think you can get away with.

Again, you bid your best guess at the next highest valuation; again, the equilibrium price would be the expected value of V_2, because that will be the bid of the person with V_1.

You may have detected a theme, here. In each of these cases, the equilibrium bid has been anchored to some degree on the second highest valuation. Indeed, there is an equivalence theorem at work: if all bidders are identical and draw their values independently from identical ranges of possible valuations and if bidders are risk-neutral so that they care only about expected monetary reward, then the form of the auction has no effect on the outcome. There are lots of conditions in this theorem, of course, and each one suggests a way in which demonstrated equivalence can break down. As a result, each condition suggests circumstances under which the design of an auction could matter.

▣ Common-Value Auctions

Common-value auctions operate in a second context. They also present a seller with a distribution of values and bids, but not because each prospective buyer has a different value. In this case, there is one true value for the item up for sale, but prospective buyers don't know what it is. The FCC case in Example 17.6 provides a perfect illustration. Any specific license offered for sale by the FCC would turn out to be worth something (from as low as nothing, perhaps, to as high as you might imagine); but nobody could know in the mid-1990s what that would be. Not the seller (the government) and certainly not the bidders. Some bidders may have thought about making high bids because they came to the auction with optimistic and high estimates of the value of a license. Others might have considered making only low bids because their analysts were pessimistic and could not see how a license would make its new owner any money. The rest, of course, would be somewhere in between. A room full of potential buyers in this case will also present the seller with a distribution of values and bids for any license, but this time because each individual buyer has a different estimate of its actual value.

Does context makes a difference? Absolutely. People who offer the winning bid in a common-value auction can actually end up worse off than they would have been if they had missed the auction entirely. Why? Because their winning bid could have been the result of an overly optimistic estimate of the actual value of the good being sold. This is called the **winner's curse.**

To see that this is a likely result unless bids were carefully crafted, suppose that each participant in a common-value auction of some good came equipped with an estimate of V, and denote the individual estimates by E_i. Some of the estimates might be pessimistic; those E_i would be less than V. Others might be too optimistic; for them, $E_i > V$. Indeed, as an impartial observer, you might even expect that the average across all of the E_i would be a reasonable approximation of V because some estimates would err on the high side while others err on the low side. You would then understand that a bidding strategy that ignores this observation could easily produce a winning bid in excess of V.

You can experiment with the winner's curse by holding sealed-bid auctions for a jar of pennies. Fill the jar roughly halfway and solicit bids in a winner-takes-the-pennies auction. Widespread trials of this auction have shown that it almost always produces a profit for the person who collected the pennies, conducted the auction, and collects the winning bid. This is especially true if lots of people submit bids. Why? Because most bidders will carefully inspect the jar and come up with some crude way of converting volume into pennies and because the result will be a distribution of estimates that span a range that includes the actual number. People will then bid on the basis of their estimates, and it stands to reason that the winning bid will be from someone whose estimate was on the high side.

What sort of strategy would produce a bid in a common-value auction that appropriately matched the desire to win the auction against a desire to avoid a winner's curse? The answer to this question depends on many things and many assumptions about how others' estimates might be distributed over a range of possibilities. We offer only one simple illustration to provide a flavor of what might go on and to provide insight into the underlying complexity. To that end, suppose that you were planning to bid on the penny jar in Example 17.7, but now add the complication that the jar was opaque so that you could not see inside. You cannot even pick it up and shake it; but neither can anybody else. The jar may even be empty. You cannot know. All that you can reasonably assume is that your competitors have estimates of the value of the jar that range from E_1 down to E_n. How should you bid?

You know your estimate, E_i. If your estimate E_i happened to match the highest estimate E_1, then you would have the best chance to win the auction. You will want to contemplate how to bid under that assumption, but you will also want to minimize your chance of suffering the winner's curse. As you think about what to do, you will quickly come to realize that even the highest estimate could have been higher. Why? Because it was a random draw from a range of possible estimates and only represents the expected value of the highest of n estimates delivered to you and your $n - 1$ competitors. Let $E_{i, max} > E_i$ represent your perspective of this upper bound. Should you bid E_i? Or $E_{i, max}$, if you could make a guess? No. To do either would almost guarantee a winner's curse. You will want to bid something lower, but how much lower?

The first step in answering this final question is to compute your best guess at $E_{i, max}$. This can be difficult to do, in general, but assuming that the estimates of you and your $n - 1$ competitors were drawn randomly from an even distribution of possible values between 0 and I can help enormously. It turns out that the expected value of the highest estimate would be $[n/(n + 1)]I$ in that case. If you think that your estimate is the highest, it follows that you must think that

$$E_i = \frac{n}{n + 1} I.$$

More to the point, your best guess for I and thus your best guess for $E_{i,\,max}$ (under the assumption that your E_i matches E_1) would be

$$E_{i,\,max} = I = \frac{n+1}{n}E_i.$$

So what? Remember that the expected value of all possible estimates is a good approximation to the actual value—for a uniform distribution, this is the midpoint of the range of estimates. If this range were bounded on the high side by $E_{i,\,max}$, then you would think that the midpoint was

$$\frac{E_{i,\,max}}{2} = \frac{n+1}{2n}E_i.$$

Armed with this calculation, it would be wise for you to modify your evaluation of the likely value of the good being offered for sale. The resulting "private" revaluation, specifically, $[(n+1)/2n]E_i$, would be your best bid.

   Would others make different bids? Yes, if they adopted the same strategy, since their bids would be based on their own preliminary estimates of value and their own assumptions that they had E_1. Who would win the auction? The person who actually came to the auction with the highest estimate. And would he or she avoid the winner's curse? Maybe, but maybe not. There is no real guarantee that the range of value estimates would perfectly straddle the actual value, so there is no guarantee that $E_{max}/2$ or the true E_{max} would be smaller than V.

◻ Auction Design

Economists have long understood that auctions can reduce costs and delays in allocating scarce resources. Table 17.3 shows, for example, cost and revenue estimates incurred in selecting cellular licenses in a typical market under a hearing, a lottery, and an auction—the mechanisms that were under consideration prior to the 1994–1995 FCC auction described in Example 17.6. Notice that the costs incurred by applicants (excluding the winning bid under

Table 17.3	Costs or revenues	Hearing	Lottery	Auction
COSTS OF REVENUES OF SELECTING CELLULAR LICENSEES IN A TYPICAL MARKET BY HEARING, LOTTERY, AND AUCTION	*Costs*			
	Private application costs	$520,000	$595,000	$ 80,000
	Delay costs	91,205	62,304	16,162
	FCC costs	20,000	5,000	1,000
	Total costs	$631,205	$662,304	$ 97,162
	Revenues			
	Government revenue	0	0	$561,142

SOURCE: E. Kwerel and A. Felker, "Using Auctions to Select FCC Licensees," Federal Communications Commission, May 1985.

the auction, because that is a transfer from the winner to the government and thus not a social cost) were lowest under an auction. Furthermore, the costs to the FCC and to society due to the delay in assigning licenses were smallest under an auction. These are the sorts of transaction costs that are seldom reflected in economic analyses of markets, but inefficient allocation mechanisms can clearly be very expensive and significantly erode social welfare.

Economists also understand that auctions can backfire. A recent experience was particularly sobering for the designers of the FCC auction, for example. In April 1993, two licenses for satellite television service were auctioned in Australia. When the sealed bids were received, the winners were Hi Vision Ltd. and Ucom Pty. Ltd; their winning bids were about $140 million and $120 million, respectively. These bids were larger than expected, and neither firm was a major player in the Australian television industry. The government hailed a new era in the domestic communications industry—at least, until both companies defaulted on their bids. As a result, the licenses had to be awarded to the next highest bidders, but both bids had also been submitted by Hi Vision and Ucom. It soon became clear that both companies had made a series of bids that were about $5 million apart, and they finally paid $80 million for one license and $50 million for the other after a series of defaults. Australia's politicians called it a fiasco, and the communications minister was fired.[7]

The fundamental flaw in Australia's auction was the lack of a penalty for default, which implied that bids were really not meaningful. To help avoid such problems, the FCC stipulated that firms had to make down payments to the FCC based on how many people were in the geographical areas where they wanted to bid. For example, Wireless Co., LP, made down payments of about $120 million. In addition, according to the FCC's rules, if a high bidder were to withdraw its bid during the auction, it would be liable for the difference between its bid and the price ultimately obtained for the license. For bids withdrawn after the auction, there would be a supplementary penalty of 3 percent.

Following the recommendation of economic theorists, the FCC decided to hold an open auction rather than a sealed-bid auction. In an open auction, buyers raise their bids until only one (the winner) is left. In a sealed-bid auction, each bidder submits a sealed bid; the highest bidder wins. Open auctions are more subject to manipulation by bidders than a sealed-bid auction. In extreme cases, for example, bidders get together before the auction and agree on who the winner will be—an arrangement that is more difficult to create in the sealed-bid alternative. But bidders hear what other applicants are bidding in an open auction. As a result, they can be more confident in their valuations and less concerned about the "winner's curse." As a result, bids tend to be higher.

Prior to the "biggest auction in the known universe," a much smaller auction of 11 narrowband PCS licenses was carried out by the FCC in July 1994. This auction resulted in about $600 million in government revenue

[7]J. McMillan, "Selling Spectrum Rights," *Journal of Economic Perspectives,* vol. 8, no. 3, Summer 1994.

and was regarded as a big success. Table 17.4 shows the bids in each of the 46 rounds of this auction by seven of the major participants for one of the licenses. In each round, each of the bidders (and several others) had the opportunity to bid on each of the 11 licenses, not just on the one in Table 17.4. The length of each round was about 1 hour. The auction ended when a single round passed in which no new bids were submitted on any license. Page Net won the license in Table 17.4 with a winning bid of $80 million.

According to the FCC's auction rules, a new bid had to exceed the existing high bid by at least a certain minimum amount ($250,000 in the case of the license in Table 17.4). In most cases, a new high bid exceeded the existing high bid by more than this minimum amount. And in almost one-quarter of the cases, the "jump bids"—bids exceeding the existing high bid by more than the minimal amount—were offered by firms that had already made the then-highest bid! Why? As pointed out by P. Cramton of the University of Maryland, "This behavior seems to fly in the face of common bidding wisdom and perhaps even common sense. However, there are good reasons for jump bidding. . . . The basic idea is that the jump bid conveys information about a bidder's valuations. It is a measure of strength, conveying that the bidder has a high value for the particular license. Moreover, it conveys this message in a credible way. Jump bidding has a cost; it exposes the bidder to the possibility of leaving money on the table. It is precisely this cost that makes the communication credible."[8] J. McMillan of the University of California at San Diego has said, "The FCC's spectrum auction is unprecedented in its use of economic theory in the design of the auction.[9] Clearly, the FCC's auctions were a milestone in the application of economic theory, and also a notable experiment that generated interesting and useful data.

Example 17.8	Auction Fiascos and the Design of a Good Auction

Paul Klemperer has recently published a brief review of why some auctions succeed and others fail.[10] This example draws heavily on this work. His advice, quite simply, is to discourage collusion, to discourage anything that might deter entry, and to discourage predatory behavior. This is sound advice that should seem familiar. These are the same structural issues that economists worry about when they look for potential sources of inefficiency in any market. What difference can it make? How much of a difference is there between success and failure? Klemperer reports that six European countries auctioned spectrum licenses for "third-generation" mobile phones in 2000. The licenses sold for 600 euros per person in Germany and the United Kingdom ($80 billion overall); but they sold for 100, 170, 240, and *20* euros per person in Austria, the Netherlands, Italy, and Switzerland, respectively. Investors were growing skeptical of the winner's curse as the year went on, to be sure, but that was not the entire story. The auction in the Netherlands was conducted between

---

[8]P. Cramton, "Money Out of Thin Air: The Nationwide Narrowband PCS Auction," unpublished paper, September 1994, p. 43.

[9]McMillan, "Selling Spectrum Rights," p. 160.

[10]P. Klemperer, "What Really Matters in Auction Design," *Journal of Economic Perspectives,* vol. 16, no. 4, Winter 2002, pp. 169–90.

Table 17.4	Round	McCaw	Mtel	Page Net	Pmart	American Paging	U.S. Mobile	U.S. West
BIDS OF SEVEN MAJOR PARTICIPANTS IN EACH OF THE 46 ROUNDS OF THE FCC AUCTION OF A NARROWBAND PCS LICENSE, JULY 1994 (THOUSANDS OF DOLLARS)	1	10,000	500		20,000	511	5,422	1,050
	2				20,000			
	3				20,000			
	4				20,000			
	5				20,000			
	6			30,000	25,000	21,378		
	7			30,000	31,875			
	8			42,000				
	9			42,000				
	10			42,000				
	11			42,000	45,000			
	12			50,000	45,000			
	13			50,000				
	14			50,000				
	15			60,000				
	16			60,000				
	17			60,000				
	18			70,000				
	19			70,000				
	20			70,000				
	21			70,000				
	22			70,000				
	23			70,000				
	24			70,000				
	25			70,000				
	26			70,000				
	27			70,000				
	28			70,000				
	29			70,000				
	30			75,000				
	31			75,000				
	32			75,000				
	33			78,000				
	34			78,000				
	35			78,000				
	36			78,000	79,000			
	37			80,000	79,000			
	38			80,000				
	39			80,000				
	40			80,000				
	41			80,000				
	42			80,000				
	43			80,000				
	44			80,000				
	45			80,000				
	46			80,000				

SOURCE: P. Cramton, "Money Out of Thin Air: The Nationwide Narrowband PCS Auction," unpublished paper, September 1994.

the auctions in Germany and the UK, and analysts for the governments predicted revenues in excess of 400 euros per person just prior to the Italian and Swiss auctions. Clearly, poor design can make a real difference.

But how can participants collude in an auction? By using the early stages of simultaneous English auctions to send signals to each other. In 1999, for example, Germany sold 10 blocks of spectrum licenses at the same time with the rule that each bid must be at least 10 percent higher than the previous bid. Mannesman bid 20 million deutsche marks per megahertz on blocks 6 through 10, and 18.18 million on blocks 1 through 5. T-Mobil, the only other credible bidder, bid even less. There was no agreement between the companies, but T-Mobil took the Mannesman bids as an offer: stay away from blocks 6 through 10 and you can have 1 through 5 at 20 million marks. And how did T-Mobil pick up that signal? By noticing that 18.18 million was a strangely precise bid which, if raised by 10 percent, would climb to exactly 20 million marks. In fact, peculiarly priced bids are frequently used in English auctions to send signals.

And how can barriers to entry appear? From almost anywhere. Television franchises were, for example, auctioned regionally across the United Kingdom in 1991. Many sold for in excess of 10 pounds per head of population, but the only and thus winning bid in the sealed auction in the Midlands was one-twentieth of a penny per head of population. And the winning bid in Scotland was one-seventh of a penny. Why? Because bidders were required to submit very detailed programming plans for their regions, and the winners in the Midlands and Scotland figured out that they were the only ones capable of constructing such a plan.

The threat of a winner's curse can also produce a less dramatic barrier to entry because strong incumbent firms (1) can be more confident of their estimates in a common-value auction and (2) can sustain more of a loss should the curse arise. It follows that small, weaker firms make lower bids, but stronger incumbent firms know this. The 1995 auction for mobile-phone licenses in California and Chicago provides an example of this effect. Pacific Telephone had experience in California and came to the English auction armed with an estimate that was informed by an elaborate database of potential customers and name recognition. The bidding for Los Angeles stopped at $26 per capita. In Chicago, though, where the mainline existing company was not eligible to participate in the auction, the winning bid was more than $31 per capita.

PRINCIPAL-AGENT PROBLEM: FIRM OWNERS AND MANAGERS

We noted in Chapter 7 that economists regard the assumptions of profit maximization as only a first approximation of what motivates firm behavior.[11]

[11]For modern discussions of firm behavior based on assumptions other than profit maximization, see the symposium on "The Firm and Its Boundaries," *Journal of Economic Perspectives*, vol. 12, no. 4, Fall 1998. Note, in particular, papers published there by B. Holmstrom and J. Roberts ("The Boundaries of the Firm Revisited"), and P. Bolton and D. S. Scharfstein ("Corporate Finance, the Theory of the Firm, and Organizations").

It may be a very good approximation if the owners of the firm actually run the firm. It may, however, be less accurate if owners hire managers to run their business; and this is the dominant mode of organization in modern economies. The owners of firms—the stockholders—usually have little detailed information about how the firm is being operated. Even boards of directors of large corporations are not involved in day-to-day management decisions. Indeed, top management usually has a great deal of freedom to do what it wants, as long as it seems to be performing reasonably well. One might suspect, therefore, that firm behavior could be dictated in part by the interests of the management group and that those interests might not exactly match the interests of the owners. Large salaries, more perquisites, and large staffs all come to mind.

*Principal-agent
problem*

This is a so-called **principal-agent problem.** An agency relationship exists between the firm's owners and its managers because the managers are agents who work for the owners; the owners are the principals.[12] To see the issues that arise in this context, consider the hypothetical case of a businesswoman who is a manager and part owner of a firm. Assume that she gets satisfaction both from the profits that the firm earns and from the benefits (large staff, company-paid travel, and so on) that she receives from this firm. If she were the sole owner of her firm, then any extra benefits that she received would reduce her profits dollar-for-dollar. The cost of these benefits would, in other words, come entirely out of her own pocket. If she were only a one-quarter owner, though, then an extra dollar of benefits would reduce her share of the profits by only 25 cents—i.e., only one-quarter of the cost of these benefits would come out of her pocket.

Our hypothetical owner-manager would clearly be more likely to increase the amount of benefits she receives if it cost only 25 cents on the dollar. Since the other owners pick up three-quarters of the tab, why not take an extra "business" trip to Paris? If she had to pay the full cost, perhaps she would forgo the Paris trip; but since she would pay only 25 percent of the full cost, she could easily come up with a reason why it is worthwhile to go to Paris. And it would be difficult for the other owners to tell whether or not the trip was necessary (beforehand) or even profitable (after the fact).

This incentive problem can be even more severe when firm managers are not partial owners. The cost of the benefits would then be borne entirely by the owners, and so the managers could have an undiluted incentive to see benefits set as high as possible. Owners frequently find it difficult to distinguish between benefits that promote profits and benefits that do not. Managers therefore frequently have a lot of leeway in setting their own rewards. Owners are unlikely to put up with managers' awarding themselves excessive benefits of this kind, but how are they to know? What are they to do?

[12]See O. Williamson, *The Economics of Discretionary Behavior* (Englewood Cliffs, N.J.: Prentice-Hall, 1964), *Markets and Hierarchies: Analysis and Antitrust Implications* (New York: Free Press, 1975), and *The Economic Institutions of Capitalism* (New York: Free Press, 1985), for some early discussion of these issues. See, as well, R. Gibbons, "Incentives in Organizations," and A. Shleifer, "State versus Private Ownership," in the *Journal of Economic Perspectives,* vol. 12, no. 4, Fall 1998.

Owners can, to begin with, avoid investing in firms where the managers behave in this way. We need only look at how the market responded to management scandals like Enron in 2001 and 2002 to see that this might happen. Owners could, alternatively, formulate contracts that would limit managers' abilities to award benefits and thereby attract potential owners. The contracts might make the managers responsible, but they are very difficult if not impossible to enforce.

It might be more feasible for owners to establish a contract that gives the managers an incentive to reduce benefits and to pursue objectives that are reasonably close to profit maximization. Owners might, for example, give managers a financial stake in the success of the firm. Many corporations have stock-purchase plans through which managers are encouraged to purchase shares of common stock at below-market prices. These plans provide managers with an incentive to promote the firm's profits and to act in accord with the interests of the firm's owners, but only if they cannot sell their shares before bad news hits the market.

Firms that are poorly managed may also be taken over by owners who are tougher and more adept in handling the principal-agent problem. Some takeovers are relatively cut-and-dried: old owners are happy to sell to the new owners, and old management can be dismissed. In other cases, though, the old management may go to great lengths to avoid being taken over by new owners. Firms that are targets of hostile takeovers tend to be poorly performing companies, and their performance frequently improves after they are taken over.[13]

| **Example 17.9** | **Is a CEO Really Worth the Price?** |

Over the past decade or so, considerable controversy has erupted over how much major corporations in the United States pay their chief executive officers (CEOs). Panel A of Table 17.5 provides a glimpse at the source of this controversy by listing the salaries and other long-term compensations paid to the 10 highest-paid CEOs in 1998. According to many critics, these numbers are way too big, especially since their counterparts in developed countries like France, Britain, Germany, and Japan are paid much less. Why do U.S. executives get paid so much? Because that is what the market will bear. U.S. executives are highly paid, just like professional athletes, because they are perceived to be in short supply. But is this an accurate perception? There is only one Barry Bonds, but maybe there are 10 or 20 or 100 people who could run Disney as well as Michael Eisner.

That remains to be seen, and so we see one source of the controversy. There is, though, another reason that attracts even more attention. When a member of the "common" workforce gets fired, he or she might get two weeks' salary as severance pay. If he or she is laid off by a compassionate firm,

[13]R. Morck, A. Shleifer, and R. Vishny, "Characteristics of Hostile and Friendly Takeover Targets," in A. Auerbach, ed., *Takeovers: Causes and Consequences* (Chicago: University of Chicago Press, 1988).

Table 17.5 COMPENSATION FOR CEOs

A ANNUAL COMPENSATION FOR THE TOP 10

Name	Company	1998 salary and bonus (thousands of dollars)	Long-term compensation (thousands of dollars)	Total pay (thousands of dollars)
Michael Eisner	Walt Disney	$5,764	$569,828	$575,592
Mel Karmazin[a]	CBS	4,000	197,934	201,934
Sanford Weill	Citigroup	7,430	159,663	167,093
Stephen Case	America Online	1,177	158,057	159,233
Craig Barrett	Intel	2,280	114,232	116,511
John Welch	General Electric	10,105	73,559	83,664
Henry Schacht[b]	Lucent Technologies	2,020	65,016	67,037
L. Dennis Kozlowski	Tyco International	3,750	61,514	65,264
Henry Silverman	Cedant	2,818	61,063	63,882
M. Douglas Ivester	Coca-Cola	2,750	54,572	57,322

[a]Started January 1, 1999.
[b]Retired.

B SEVERANCE PACKAGES AFTER POOR PERFORMANCE

CEO	Corporation	Circumstances of departure	Severance package
John B. McCoy	Banc One Corp.	Resigned in December 1999 after a profit and stock price slump	$10.3 million plus $3 million annual pension
Doug Ivester[a]	Coca-Cola Co.	Resigned in February 2000 after slumping sales and stock prices	$17.8 million plus immediate vesting of $100 million in stock and options
Mark Willes	Times Mirror Co.	Resigned in late 2000 after a merger that he did not negotiate	$9.2 million
Jill Barad	Mattel, Inc.	Resigned in February 2000 amid slumping sales and losses from an acquisition	Almost $50 million
Eckhard Pfeiffer	Compaq Computer Corp.	Resigned in April 1999 with poor earnings and acquisition difficulties	$9.8 million plus extended options
Richard Huber	Aetna, Inc.	Resigned in February 2000 amid stock slump	$3.4 million

[a]Mr. Ivester was also one of the highest-paid CEOs identified in the first table.
SOURCE: D. Levick, "Huber's Parting Gift: $3.4 Million," *Hartford Courant,* March 23, 2000.

(continued)

Table 17.5 *(Continued)*

C BLOWS TO INVESTOR CONFIDENCE

Company	Purported misconduct	Stock price experience	CEO experience
Enron	Hid $1 billion in losses	Price fell from $44.07 in June 2001 to $0.09 in July 2002.	Kenneth Lay resigned.
WorldCom	Hid $3.9 billion in losses	Price fell from $14.20 in June 2001 to $0.25 in July 2002.	Chief Financial Officer Scott Sullivan is fired.
Merck	Reported $12 billion in uncollected revenue	Price fell from $72.55 in June 2001 to $48.86 in July 2002.	No fallout as of July 2002.
Xerox	Inflated revenue by $3 billion; paid $10 million fine	Price fell from $9.39 in June 2001 to $6.47 in July 2002.	Former CEO Paul Allaire is under investigation.
Qwest	Inflated revenue by $1 billion	Price fell from $31.87 in June 2001 to $1.82 in July 2002.	CEO Joseph Nacchio forced to resign.

a six-month package might be offered. When professional athletes do not perform, they may be traded or released or otherwise asked to fade into the sunset. It may take a while, and they may receive high salaries derived from long-term contracts even after their skills fade, but they will ultimately leave the field of action. And CEOs? They usually receive huge severance packages even if they walk out of the executive office suite after a bad performance. Panel B lists a few recent examples. They are compounded by the furor caused in the summer of 2002 by outright misreporting of profits. Panel C lists several of these examples and the ramifications for stock prices and CEOs. Is it any wonder that people question whether or not CEOs are worth the price?

OWNERS AND WORKERS: ANOTHER PRINCIPAL-AGENT PROBLEM

Similar principal-agent problems can arise among workers and employers. The worker can be viewed as an agent who works for the employer, who is the principal. The employer's welfare depends on the actions of the worker. But often it is not feasible for the employer to measure at all accurately how hard a particular employee is working and the extent to which this work is in accord with the employer's goals (as distinct from the worker's goals, which may be quite different). Therein lies the source of the asymmetric information: workers have much more complete information concerning these matters than do employers. This leads to the potential that workers might shirk—that is, not live up to their full potential in the best interest of their employers.

How can employers shape incentives to ensure that workers will work in accord with the employers' goals? Consider the case of a sales representative for a computer manufacturer. Suppose that he could generate $50,000 per month in profit for his employer if he worked hard and were lucky, but only $30,000 if he were unlucky. Also assume that he could generate $30,000 per month in profit if he were lucky but didn't work hard, and only $20,000 if he were unlucky and didn't work hard. Let these figures include the salesman's salary; to obtain the net profit to his employer, therefore, salary must be subtracted. If the salesman generated a $30,000 profit in a particular month, there would be no way that his employer could tell whether he had worked hard and was unlucky or whether he did not work hard and was lucky. Even if his employer took the trouble to monitor his behavior (which could be prohibitively expensive), there may be no accurate method of gauging how much effort he had really put forth—to judge how much was luck and how much was hard work.

Our salesman's employer would like to induce him to work hard because this would increase the firm's profit. It is instructive to compare how effective two alternative payment schemes might be in providing the correct incentives. In the first payment scheme, the salesman might receive a fixed monthly wage (say, $4,000) regardless of how much profit he generated for his employer. This payment scheme would clearly not induce him to work hard because he would receive the same compensation regardless of how hard he worked. Unless he liked work for its own sake, he would probably choose to shirk. If there were a 50 percent chance that he would be lucky in any month, then his employer could expect that he would generate, on the average, 0.5($20,000) + 0.5($30,000) = $25,000 in profit per month. Deducting his wage of $4,000 from this gross profit figure, his employer would therefore receive an average net profit of $21,000 per month (see Table 17.6).

Now consider a second payment scheme in which the salesman would receive a bonus if he generated high levels of profit. Specifically, suppose that he would get a low wage (say, $2,000) if he generated $20,000 or

Fixed wage

Bonus system

Table 17.6	Salesman's expected income				
A SALESMAN'S EXPECTED MONTHLY INCOME AND HIS EMPLOYER'S EXPECTED MONTHLY PROFIT: TWO ALTERNATIVE PAYMENT SCHEMES	Payment scheme	If he worked hard	If he did not work hard	Maximum expected income[a]	Employer's expected profit
	Fixed monthly wage of $4,000	$4,000	$4,000	$4,000	$25,000 − $4,000 = $21,000
	$10,000 wage if he generates $50,000 profit, $2,000 wage otherwise	$6,000	$2,000	$6,000	$40,000 − $6,000 = $34,000

[a]This is his expected income if he works hard or his expected income if he does not work hard, whichever is higher (if they differ).

$30,000 in profit in a particular month and a much higher wage (say, $10,000) if he generated a $50,000 profit in that month. If there were still a 50 percent chance that he would be lucky in any month, then the salesman could expect, on the average, to receive 0.5($2,000) + 0.5($10,000) = $6,000 per month if he worked hard. He would receive $2,000 during those months in which he happened to be unlucky and $10,000 in those months when his luck turned good. If, on the other hand, he did not work hard, then he would receive a certain income of $2,000 per month. Regardless of whether he were lucky or unlucky, he would fail to generate the $50,000 profit required to trigger the higher bonus.

The salesman would clearly have an incentive to work hard in the second scheme, since his monthly wage would be much higher if he worked hard than if he did not (unless he had a severe disinclination to work). His employer could expect that he would generate, on the average, 0.5($30,000) + 0.5($50,000) = $40,000 in profit per month. Subtracting his expected wage of $6,000 per month from this gross profit figure, his employer would expect to receive an average net profit of $34,000 per month. Notice in Table 17.6 that this figure is larger than under the first payment scheme. Clearly, both the salesman and his employer would be better off under the second payment scheme than under the first.

This example illustrates an important point. A bonus payment system can be used by firms to help induce workers to further the aims of the firm when there is no way to measure directly the amount of effort that a worker puts in. And the bonus scheme need not exploit the worker; both can be better off. Other incentive systems can be used as well. For example, the employer could have instituted a profit-sharing system in which the salesman earned a basic wage plus a certain percentage of the profits in excess of a particular amount. Properly designed, this type of system would provide an incentive for the salesman to work hard and to increase the firm's profit, and it could more easily accommodate situations in which there are more than two sales outcomes.[14]

Microlink 17.1 Perfect Information as a Benchmark

Perfect competition has, since its introduction in Chapter 8, been used as a benchmark of efficiency against which the potential costs of market distortions have been measured. The deadweight loss caused by exercising market power was, for example, computed by comparing a competitive equilibrium price and output against the higher price and lower output of a monopolist. Perfect information is used in much the same way throughout the literature on asymmetric information. Most analyses begin by characterizing what equilibrium would look like with perfect, or at least symmetric, information; and the potential harm of asymmetric information is then investigated by comparing that equilibrium with one that would emerge when some participants know more than others.

[14]The seminal work on this topic is S. Ross, "The Economic Theory of Agency: The Principal's Problem," *American Economic Review*, March 1973.

1. Buyers and sellers often do not have the same information. The seller of a used car, for example, generally knows far more about its performance and weaknesses than does the buyer. This asymmetry of information can have an important influence on how a market functions.

2. If a buyer learns whether a product (like an automobile) is defective only after buying it, then the price of the product in the market for used products may fall to the point where owners of nondefective units are unwilling to offer them for sale. "Lemons" would then dominate the used market.

3. Asymmetric information can lead to market failure. If the buyers of a product do not have reliable information about its quality, perfect competition may not lead to the sort of economic efficiency described in Chapter 8.

4. The makers of high-quality, high-priced goods could be run out of business by makers of low-quality, low-priced goods unless they can persuade potential customers that their products are in fact of high quality. To convey this sort of information, they engage in market signaling. They issue guarantees and warranties, and they have an incentive to maintain their reputations by actually producing high-quality goods. Signaling can also promote efficiency in labor markets if it costs less than benefits accruing to high-productivity workers and more than benefits accruing to low-productivity workers.

5. The "lemons" problem is essentially a problem of adverse selection. Insurance companies often obtain an adverse selection from the total group of their potential customers. Customers who are bad risks are more likely to want to purchase insurance against theft, fire, or other adverse events than customers who are good risks. Insurance companies may find it very difficult to tell whether a particular customer is high-risk or low-risk when they sell their policies.

6. Moral hazard problems arise when people or firms change their behavior after buying insurance and thereby increase the likelihood of a loss. Some people who buy lots of medical insurance may spend less on preventive medicine; if they get sick, they may make more visits to the physician and incur more expensive treatment than if they had less insurance.

7. Auctions come in many different styles; English (rising bids), Dutch (falling bids), and sealed-bid (either first- or second-price versions) are common examples. Participants come to private-value auctions with personal views of how much the item for sale is worth; the second highest valuation (or something close) should emerge as the winning bid in all four forms listed above. Participants come to common-value auctions with personal estimates of the actual value of the item for sale; the winner's curse refers to the chance that the winning bid will exceed that value.

8. A principal-agent problem often exists because workers' goals may be quite different from the firm's goals. To help induce workers to further the aims of the firm (when there is no way to measure directly the amount of effort that a worker puts forth), bonus payment systems are often used. The principal-agent problem can also exist if managers have goals that diverge from owners'.

QUESTIONS/ PROBLEMS

1. In fast-food companies like McDonald's, KFC, and Burger King, some restaurants are company-owned and some are operator-owned. Although they have the same menus, charge the same prices, and look the same, the operator-owned restaurants function under franchise agreements and are managed by their owners, who hire and fire workers, set wage levels, and

are the recipients of their restaurants' profits (or losses). Company-owned restaurants are, by way of contrast, managed by employees of the fast-food company who receive salaries and have no claim on their restaurants' profits. (a) In any fast-food restaurant, it is important for managers to monitor the performance of the workers who prepare and present the food. Do managers of company-owned restaurants have as much incentive as managers of operator-owned restaurants to monitor worker performance carefully? Why or why not? (b) Anne Krueger has reported that assistant managers at company-owned fast-food restaurants are paid about 9 percent more than assistant managers at operator-owned fast-food restaurants.[16] Why?

2. Rome Stifler, a Harley-Davidson employee, is reported to have suggested a new cutting-tool design that reduced the tool's cost by 60 percent. What sort of incentive systems could be adopted by a firm to encourage such performance? Is there a principal-agent problem with regard to inventive activity of this sort? If so, what is it? How could it be fixed?

3. Suppose that 20 percent of all new office safes were defective but that the defective ones could not be identified until they had been purchased. Assume that consumers value office safes without defects at $5,000 apiece. And assume, as well, that used office safes sell for $2,000. If consumers were risk-neutral and if office safes did not depreciate physically with use, what would be the price of a new office safe? If consumers were risk-averse, would the price be higher or lower?

4. *Consumer Reports* provides data to compare the quality of various cars based on repair records over time (usually for the first 6 or 7 years after purchase as new). Results of its annual compendium in 1979 and 1999 for cars produced in the United States and Japan are recorded in the accompanying table. (a) Do the results seem to suggest that the repair records of U.S. cars continue to be inferior to those of Japanese cars? (b) Do they suggest that Japanese manufacturers have, in moving many of their production facilities to foreign soil, lost some of their quality edge? (c) U.S. manufacturers have tried to improve quality and have issued warranties on parts and labor. Why? (d) Can warranties create moral hazard problems? How?

| | Percentage of models ranked in each repair-history category | | | |
| | 1979 | | 1999 | |
Rating	U.S.	Japanese	U.S.	Japanese
Much better than average	0	94	1	48
Better than average	15	6	12	34
Average	39	0	22	6
Worse than average	18	0	35	8
Much worse than average	28	0	30	4

5. There are 3,000 used personal computers in Monaco. Of these 3,000 units, 1,000 are worth $1,000 each, 1,000 are worth $2,000 each, and 1,000 are worth $3,000 each. Every owner of a personal computer is willing to sell

[16]A. Krueger, "Ownership, Agency, and Wages: An Examination of Franchising in the Fast Food Industry," *Quarterly Journal of Economics*, February 1991.

his or her computer for what it is worth. The demand for used personal computers is given by $Q = 2V - P$, where V is the average value of used personal computers offered in the market and P is the price of a personal computer (in dollars). (a) What would be the value of V if potential buyers based their estimates of V on the assumption that all used personal computers would be offered for sale? What would be the price of a used personal computer, and how many would be sold? Note that nobody will sell a computer for less than it is worth. (b) Now suppose that potential buyers based their estimate of V on the assumption that the used personal computers offered for sale would be like those offered for sale in the equilibrium of part (a). Would the demand curve shift? If so, would it shift to the left or to the right? (c) Characterize the final equilibrium for this market if the adjustment described in part (b) continued one more time.

6. Many firms use a single brand name for many of their products. For example, General Electric has used the GE brand name on its refrigerators, washing machines, light bulbs, and other products. On the basis of the theory of reputation presented in this chapter, can you explain why GE does this? Can you foresee any risks in doing that if, for example, the firm were better at making one product than another?

7. Bayer aspirin often commands a higher price than generic aspirin. Why?

8. Suppose that an entrepreneur's utility depends on the size of his or her firm (as measured by its output) and its profits; assume that these preferences are accurately portrayed by the indifference curves drawn in the next figure. (a) Will the entrepreneur maximize profit? (b) If not, will he or she produce more or less than the profit-maximizing output? (c) Draw a graph to indicate the point he or she will choose. (d) Would you expect output to rise or fall if the price of the entrepreneur's product were to rise? Would the utility-maximizing output rise or fall?

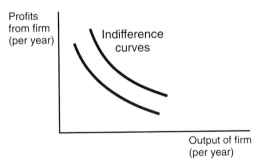

9. Suppose that State Farm Insurance Company were considering three different types of insurance against theft: (1) complete coverage of loss, (2) complete coverage above a $500 deductible, and (3) 80 percent coverage of loss. Which policy is most likely to result in problems of moral hazard? Why?

10. If Lucy Deering, a sales representative, works hard, she can generate $40,000 per month for her employer if she is lucky and $20,000 if she is unlucky. If she does not work hard, she can generate $20,000 if she is lucky and $10,000 if she is unlucky. In any month, there is a 50 percent chance that

she will be lucky. (a) Would she have any incentive to work hard if her employer paid her a fixed monthly wage of $5,000? What would be her employer's average net profit per month? (b) Would she have any incentive to work hard if her employer paid her $3,000 for every month that she generated a profit of $10,000 or $20,000 and $12,000 for every month that she generated $40,000 in profit? What would be her employer's average net profit per month in this case? (Note that Deering's salary has not been deducted from the above profit figures; salary must be deducted to get her employer's net profit figures.)

11. The table shows the percentage of pickup trucks requiring major engine maintenance; notice that new trucks are considered separately:

Year	Purchased used	Purchased new
1998	0.05	0.08
1999	0.13	0.11
2000	0.15	0.13

Turning to a seemingly unrelated topic, the next table shows the average number of days that baseball players spend on the disabled list before and after signing contracts at the end of 6 years of playing in the major leagues. Free agents are considered separately from those retained by their original teams.

	Before contract	After contract
Retained players	4.8	9.7
Free agents	4.7	17.2

(a) If potential buyers of used trucks could not determine before their purchases whether or not a truck was of high quality, would you expect to see trucks requiring major maintenance to be overrepresented in the market? Why or why not? Does the first table confirm your expectation? (b) Would you expect to see players with possible injury problems to be overrepresented in the free agent market for players with more than 6 years of major league experience? Why or why not? Does the second table confirm your expectation? (c) Describe the role of asymmetric information in both cases.

12. The United States witnessed the collapse of the savings and loan industry during the late 1980s and early 1990s. Savings and loan institutions lost hundreds of millions of dollars in investments that completely failed. As a result, nearly all savings and loans were unprofitable by the middle of the 1980s, but depositors persisted in putting their money into these institutions. (a) The big question is "Why?" Did federal insurance on deposits up to $100,000 have anything to do with their decisions? (b) Was there a moral hazard problem at work here? Recall that the owners of savings and loans felt that they had much to gain and little to lose as they invested in risky projects. (c) Why has the government continued to insure savings and loan institutions?

13. Tibor Scitovsky once suggested that the entrepreneur (that is, the owner-manager of the firm) maximizes utility—itself a function of the firm's profits and the amount of leisure that the entrepreneur enjoys. Suppose that a particular entrepreneur's indifference curves between profit and leisure were as shown in the accompanying graph. Suppose, as well, that the firm's output

was proportional to the amount of work supplied by the entrepreneur, so that the relationship between leisure and profit can be given by the curved line *ABCD*. (a) Why might the relationship between leisure and profit have the shape indicated by *ABCD*? (b) Will the utility-maximizing entrepreneur choose to maximize profit? (c) If the entrepreneur's indifference curves were horizontal lines, would he or she then choose to maximize profit? (d) What would horizontal indifference curves mean in terms of the entrepreneur's preferences between profits and leisure?

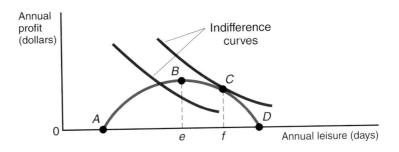

14. Chapters 12 and 13 offered a brief glimpse of how economists use game theory to gain insight into how people behave when the outcomes of their actions depend on the actions and reactions of others. This example will exploit some of the game-theoretic structure presented there to explore how asymmetric information might be employed as a barrier to entry.

Suppose, for the sake of argument, that there is some general uncertainty about a monopolist's cost of production. His costs may be high in any given year, depending on decisions that will have already been made, but they may be low, too. The monopolist has no direct power over whether they will be high or low, but he will know actual costs when he has to make his production decisions. This cost information, however, is hidden from everyone else until after the fact. It will, in particular, be hidden from a potential rival who must therefore decide whether or not to enter the monopolist's market without any idea of whether the monopolist's cost will be high or low. The payoffs for entry, depending on the monopolist's costs, are given by the following matrix.

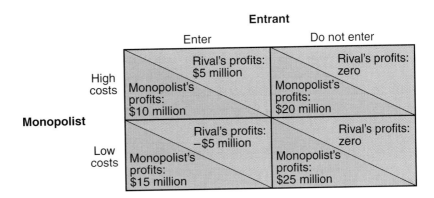

Notice that entry would be profitable only if the monopolist's costs were high. The monopolist would therefore certainly have an interest in maintaining at least the illusion that costs were low. How might he do that? And to what extent would it be necessary, given the fact that the monopolist has better information about costs than the potential entrant?

(a) Assuming that the potential entrant were "risk-neutral," she must decide to enter or not on the basis of expected profit (see Chapter 5). Would the potential rival actually enter if she thought that the probability that the monopolist's costs were high was 25 percent? 50 percent? 75 percent? (b) Is there a threshold probability for entry by the rival? If so, what is it? (c) Can you describe anything that the monopolist might do to manipulate his potential rival's subjective view of the likelihood that costs will be low? To explore this possibility, suppose that operating as if costs were low when they were in fact high would reduce the monopolist's profits from $20 million to $(20 - X)$ million, and let the probability that costs are high be 75 percent. X million is thus the cost of "faking" a low-cost environment when in a high-cost condition. Assume that the monopolist knows this cost with certainty and that the potential entrant can infer the likelihood of the high-cost environment only from the monopolist's behavior. Is there a value for the cost of "faking" the low-cost environment above which the monopolist will operate truthfully and allow the potential rival to enter? (d) Suppose, now, that an investment were available that would reduce the likelihood that costs are high from 75 percent to 25 percent. Assume that "faking" the low-cost environment reduces profits by $11.25 million. Is there a threshold cost for this investment above which the monopolist would not be at all interested?

15. Your estimate coming to a common-value English auction is $100; there are 19 other bidders. Under the assumption that the 20 bidders have estimates that were evenly distributed from $0, what would you bid if you thought that yours was the highest estimate? How would your bid change if your estimate had been $200? $50? How would your bids change under these circumstances if you suddenly discovered that there were 39 other bidders instead of 19? If there were only 9?

16. Explain how bids in a common-value auction might change if participants were risk-averse.

CHAPTER 18

Public Goods, Externalities, and the Role of Government

A perfectly competitive economy, despite its attractive features, cannot be expected to allocate resources efficiently into the production of public goods or into the production of goods that are responsible for important external economies and diseconomies. As a result, governments are charged with the responsibility of providing (but not necessarily producing) public goods. And they are asked to try to offset the distortions caused by externalities.

We will, in this final chapter, explore these roles. We begin with brief discussions of externalities and public goods. Exactly how much of a public good should be provided if the government's objective is to promote economic efficiency? We will then use environmental pollution as a case study within which we examine the effects of externalities on resource allocation and explore what the government can do to offset them. Can the same techniques be used to investigate exactly how much pollution would be the right amount? And when is government action necessary? We will discuss Coase's theorem—a theoretical result that identifies the circumstances under which a perfectly competitive economy can allocate resources efficiently even in the face of seemingly important external costs or benefits. Finally, we will offer some brief insight into microeconomic analyses of government activities. We will first discuss and illustrate the use of benefit-cost analysis—a technique frequently used by government agencies to help improve their decision-making. Second, we will discuss some of the limitations of government agencies as they try to allocate resources. To obtain a balanced picture, though, it is essential to recognize that both competitive markets and government agencies can be quite imperfect in this respect.

CHARACTERISTICS OF A PUBLIC GOOD

We learned in Chapter 16 that a perfectly competitive economy can sustain an efficient allocation of resources under some very specific conditions. It was always assumed, though, that none of the goods being produced were "public goods." What is a public good? How would we know one if we saw one? A **public good** has two characteristics. It is, first of all, "nonrival," in the sense that the marginal cost of providing the good to an additional consumer is zero. A (pure) public good can be enjoyed by an extra person without reducing the enjoyment that it gives to others. Consider the case of national defense. The interests of a newborn baby in the United States can be protected by the nation's military without reducing the protection that it affords to any other American citizen. National defense is perhaps the quintessential nonrival good.

A public good is also "nonexclusive," in the sense that people cannot easily or costlessly be excluded from consuming it. It is usually the case that people have to pay for a good to be able to consume it. But this is not always the case. Take the case of national defense, again. Once a country has created a military establishment, all of its citizens enjoy its protection *at the same time*. Since there is no practical way of excluding citizens from its protection, national defense is a nonexclusive good.

A public good can be defined as one that is both nonrival and nonexclusive. Not all nonrival goods are nonexclusive, and not all nonexclusive goods are nonrival. Some goods even change character over time, and some vary back and forth. Consider, for example, an uncrowded bridge. If you crossed an uncrowded bridge, it would not interfere with my crossing it, so the use of this bridge could be labeled "nonrival." It is, however, not a nonexclusive good because it is perfectly feasible to charge a fee for crossing the bridge and to prevent people who do not pay from crossing it. And at peak times during the day, it is not even nonrival, because your crossing during a congested time could easily interfere with my crossing.

Given all of this complication, it is perhaps not surprising to learn that the market mechanism is generally ill-equipped to provide public goods in the right amounts. Markets operate on the principle that those who do not pay for a good cannot consume it, but it is impossible to prevent people from consuming a public good if they do not pay for it. And so the market is in trouble.

Example 18.1	**A Schematic Portrait of Public Goods**

Pure public goods (for example, national defense) enter everyone's utility function at the same level. That is to say, consider a group of people whose utilities depend only upon their individual consumption of some private good X and some public good G. We could write the utility of any such individual as

$$U_i = U_i(X_i, G),$$

where X_i represents the consumption of good X specifically by individual i and G represents the level of public good provided to all. This does *not* mean that everyone derives the same utility from G. It means only that everyone sees the same level of provision. Public goods are therefore characterized by two conditions: the marginal cost allowing one more person to enjoy their provision is zero, and it is extremely difficult and costly to exclude anyone else from that enjoyment. Private goods are just the opposite. The marginal cost of a second person consuming a private good (consider sharing a hamburger) is equal to its price; and the cost of excluding a second consumer is quite small (consider offering a hamburger that you have already eaten).

There are, of course, a myriad of goods that display some public-goods characteristics even though they fall short of meeting the strict definition of a pure public good. Figure 18.1 portrays the range of possibilities schematically. The horizontal axis reflects the marginal cost of an additional consumer, and the vertical axis reflects the cost of exclusion. Various goods are placed in the scheme. Take, for example, a pure public good like national defense in the upper left-hand corner. The cost of adding one more citizen to the defense umbrella would be negligible, but the expense involved in excluding one citizen from protection would be quite high. Fire protection in the lower-left corner satisfies the low cost of servicing one more household, but it would be almost costless to designate a single property as "unprotected." An uncongested highway is somewhere in between, since erecting toll booths that would restrict access would be neither free nor exorbitant; but the cost of adding a marginal traveler could become high if the road were to become congested.

You can surely think of many more goods with some public character and place them according to the degree to which additional consumers can be excluded and the cost that they might impose on the existing user community.

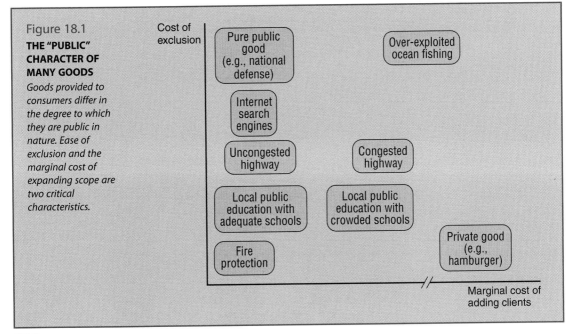

Figure 18.1

THE "PUBLIC" CHARACTER OF MANY GOODS

Goods provided to consumers differ in the degree to which they are public in nature. Ease of exclusion and the marginal cost of expanding scope are two critical characteristics.

EFFICIENT OUTPUT OF A PUBLIC GOOD

So how much production of a public good would be economically efficient? This is a complicated question whose answer is best explored initially in the context of partial equilibrium analysis. Suppose, to that end and for simplicity, that there were only two consumers, the Addams family and the Munster family. Let D_A in Figure 18.2 be the Addams family's demand curve for some good, and let D_M be the Munster family's demand curve for the same good. The supply curve, S, is also noted.

Panel A shows the efficient output of this good if it were a private good produced under perfect competition. We would then derive the market demand curve D by summing horizontally the demand curves of the two consumers. The efficient output would be Q, where this market demand curve intersects the market supply curve. Why would this be efficient? Because at this output, the marginal benefit each consumer would obtain from an extra unit of the good would equal its marginal cost. How do we know that? Assuming that the marginal benefit can be measured by the maximum amount that each family would pay for the extra unit, the marginal benefit of the last unit consumed by the Addams family would be CE and the marginal benefit for the Munster family would be FG. The marginal cost of the extra unit would meanwhile be QH at an output of Q. Recall from Chapter 8 that the supply curve shows the marginal cost at each level of output. Since $CE = FG = QH$, it follows that the marginal benefit to each consumer would equal the marginal cost at the equilibrium allocation.

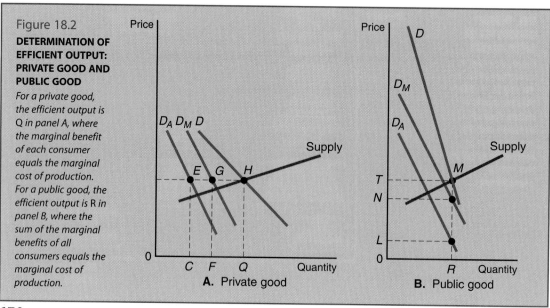

Figure 18.2

DETERMINATION OF EFFICIENT OUTPUT: PRIVATE GOOD AND PUBLIC GOOD

For a private good, the efficient output is Q in panel A, where the marginal benefit of each consumer equals the marginal cost of production. For a public good, the efficient output is R in panel B, where the sum of the marginal benefits of all consumers equals the marginal cost of production.

A. Private good

B. Public good

If, on the other hand, the good were a public good, then the efficient output would be as shown in panel B. In this case, the market demand curve would be obtained by summing the individual demand curves *vertically* and not horizontally. This fundamental difference stems from the fact that both consumers can consume the total amount of a public good *at the same time,* so the combined price willingly paid by the two consumers for the provision of the good should be the sum of the prices that each would pay individually. The efficient output of the good would therefore be *R*, and the total price (the sum of the prices paid by each consumer) would be *T*.

To see why *R* would be the efficient output, recall from Chapter 9 that the efficient output is the one where marginal social benefit equals marginal social cost. Next, note that the marginal social benefit from an extra unit of output of a public good is obtained by adding vertically the distances under every consumer's demand curve. This was reflected in the vertical summation of individual demand to generate market demand for a public good; it is appropriate because all consumers share equally in the consumption of whatever quantity of the good is made available. It follows, therefore, that the marginal social benefit must be the sum of the marginal benefits to each consumer. To see this point more precisely, recall as well that the marginal benefit to each consumer from any good is reflected by the individual demand curves. So, if output were *R*, then the marginal social benefit from an extra unit of output would be the vertical sum of *L* (the marginal benefit to the Addams family) and *N* (the marginal benefit to the Munster family); it would, in other words, equal $L + N = T$. Meanwhile, the marginal social cost of an extra unit of output is *RM* when output equals *R* (as was the case in panel A, when the good was a private good). It follows that *R* must be the efficient output, since marginal social benefits at *R* (the distance $0T$) equals the marginal social costs at *R* (the distance *RM*).

Panel B of Figure 18.2 therefore shows us that economic efficiency for a public good requires that the sum of the marginal benefits of all consumers equal marginal cost. But Figure 18.2 can only take the analysis so far. For one thing, the demand curves in panel B would not necessarily be revealed voluntarily by citizens who understood that the amount that they would pay for the provision of a public good would be related to the preferences that they revealed. This is especially true if these same people came to realize that the price of using the public good (after it is provided) would be equal to (or close to) zero. These consumers would, in short, find it worthwhile to

be **free riders.** They would act on the notion that the total output of the good would not be affected significantly by the action of any single person, and so they would disavow any interest in supporting the provision of the good even though they had every intention of using however much output happened to be forthcoming.[1]

---

[1] A partial equilibrium analysis of this problem has obvious limitations. For a general equilibrium analysis, see P. Samuelson, "Diagrammatic Exposition of a Theory of Public Expenditure," *Review of Economics and Statistics*, November 1955.

Example 18.2   **Meningitis Vaccine: A Free Rider Dilemma**

Free rider issues can arise whenever individuals' decisions impose negative (or positive) externalities on others. Consider one context with which you might have some experience. Meningitis is an extremely contagious and dangerous disease, and the close proximity of dormitory life can make college students particularly vulnerable if an outbreak occurs. There is, though, an effective vaccine, and some colleges and universities have made shots available to their students for a fee between $50 and $100. That is all well and good, but there are also risks associated with the vaccine.

The free rider problem can now be framed in terms of probabilities of the sort discussed in Chapter 5. Consider a college community of students. Let p_m and C_m represent the probability of any single student's contracting meningitis and the associated cost, respectively. What are the costs? The expense involved in hospital stays, quarantining entire dormitories, and the like—not to mention the possibility that somebody who has contracted meningitis could actually die. It is important to note that the probability p_m declines significantly as the number of students who are vaccinated climbs. This is the source of a positive externality.

Meanwhile, let p_v, C_v, and P represent the probability of having a bad reaction to the vaccine, the associated cost of treating the reaction, and the price of the vaccine, respectively. We know from Chapter 5 that any student who computes the expected cost of not being vaccinated and the expected cost of submitting to a vaccination would compare $p_m \times C_m$ with $p_v \times (C_v + P)$ and thereby ignore his or her possible contribution to reducing the chance of an outbreak of meningitis for the entire community. Indeed, he or she would be happiest if it were possible to "free ride" on others' being vaccinated—classmates whose actions would have lowered probability p_m to something close to zero so that the expected private cost of vaccination would surely be higher than the expected cost of skipping the shot.

You could, of course, object to the application of an expected cost-benefit calculation in this example. If the risk of meningitis can include death, then perhaps expected-value calculations are meaningless. Even if the probability p_m were very small, the expected cost could be undefined if death were not calibrated in terms of dollars; and who would want to do that? Perhaps, more to the point, the precautionary principle might be more appropriate because it would inspire individuals to become vaccinated as long as the probability of contracting the disease was above some critical threshold. Unless that threshold were zero, though, a free rider problem could still emerge. Why? Because the probability could fall below that threshold for a specific student if he or she lived within a population that was otherwise fully vaccinated.

Microlink 18.1   Efficiency Conditions: Private versus Public Goods

Chapter 4 demonstrated that the market demand curve for a private good is the horizontal sum of individual demand curves. We used this result to observe that an efficient allocation of resources to a private good can be characterized by equality between the marginal benefit of consuming the last unit of that good (regardless of who is doing the consuming) with the marginal cost of producing the last unit (regardless of which firm is doing the producing). It followed that the marginal benefit of the last unit consumed would be identical for every consuming individual. Chapter 16 allowed a more general characterization of efficiency for private goods—equality of the marginal rates of substitution between two private goods of all individuals and the marginal rate of transformation on the production side between the same goods (so the marginal rate of substitution for every individual would again be the same).

We now see analogous but different characterizations of efficiency for a pure public good. For one thing, total demand for a public good is the vertical sum of individuals' demands. For another, efficiency for a pure public good requires that the *sum* of the marginal benefits of the individual persons enjoying the good be set equal to the marginal cost of providing that good; it does *not* follow that the marginal benefit for each person is necessarily the same. More generally, efficiency also requires that the sum of the marginal rates of substitution between a public good and a private good across all individuals must equal the marginal rate of transformation.

PROVISION OF PUBLIC GOODS

It is not always the case that public goods will not be provided without government intervention. If the number of people in a society were quite small, for example, then it could be worthwhile for people acting individually to underwrite some level of public goods provision. To see why, consider an illustrative case in which there were two families on an island that was infested with poisonous snakes. Any reduction in the number of snakes would be a public good if there were no way of preventing the snakes from moving from one family's land to the other's; providing enhanced protection against the snakes for one family would then automatically provide it for the other family at no additional cost. Under these conditions, one of the families may well deem it worthwhile to engage in some activities to kill the snakes even though its actions would benefit the other family, as well. When numbers are small, therefore, it is a mistake to say that no public goods will be produced unless the government does so. This does not mean, however, that the proper amount of public goods would be produced.

There is a tendency for the provision of a public good to be too small if the decisions are left entirely up to people acting individually in their own self-interest, even if there are few people in the society. To see why, suppose that a family lived alone for some time on a snake infested island. It will have engaged in a certain amount of snake-protection activity. Now suppose that a family that formerly lived alone on another island moved in. The first family might well reduce its efforts to kill poisonous snakes because it would count on the other family to do some such work. Similarly, the other family would do less of this sort of work than when it lived alone on another island that was similarly infested. Both would, in summary, cut their activity so that even their combined efforts could easily fall short of the optimum, because each family would receive only part of the benefit even though each would pay the full cost. Ultimately, then, provision of this public good would fall short of the socially efficient level.

There is a tendency for those who have either the biggest interest in the outcome or the biggest share of the resources to provide a disproportionately large share of the burden of supplying a public good to a small society. To see why, suppose that the first family in the preceding paragraph owned 90 percent of the land (and other resources) on the island and that the second family owned 10 percent. Then the first family would recognize that whatever attempts were made to control the snake nuisance would rest largely on its shoulders, and it would act almost as if it were on the island by itself. The second family could, in addition, recognize that the first family had an incentive to do an effective job of snake control. If it did, then it would likely reduce its efforts to the minimum. So, the first family would probably be left to do more than 90 percent of the snake-control work while the second family did less than 10 percent.

The news is not any better when the society is larger. Large societies left to the individual devices of citizens pursuing their own self-interest generally fall well short of providing efficient levels of public goods. Indeed, the larger the number of people in the society, the farther short it will fall. In large societies like the United States, therefore, the government intervenes in an attempt to ensure the provision of the proper amount of public goods. There is general agreement that the government must provide public goods such as national defense, and the provision of such goods unquestionably accounts for a significant portion of the government's expenditure. In democratic societies, the ballot box is used to determine the amount spent on various public goods. Each person votes for candidates who represent (often imperfectly) the set of public expenditures and taxes that is closest to his or her own preferences.[2]

Example 18.3	**The Effect of Voting Rules**

Voting rules differ from situation to situation. Simple majority rule holds in many elections, of course. In other situations, like passing school bonds in a small town or impeaching a president, supermajorities may be required (i.e., two-thirds majorities or 60 percent—something much higher than 1 vote over 50 percent). Juries need to be unanimous to find a defendant guilty. Many economists, like the Nobel laureate James Buchanan, have studied the implications of various voting schemes. This example will offer a peek into the economic issues that voting rules can raise. Indeed, we will see that different voting schemes can produce entirely different outcomes.

Suppose that a small society were composed of five individuals who had to vote on a particular change in public policy. Table 18.1 records the benefits

---

[2]This section is based to a considerable extent on M. Olson, *The Logic of Collective Choice*, rev. ed. (New York: Shocken, 1971).

Table 18.1		John	Jane	Martin	Mary	Tom
COSTS AND BENEFITS OF A CHANGE IN POLICY	Cost	$50	$60	$80	$500	$70
	Benefit	$60	$80	$90	$10	$80

that each would receive as well as the costs that each would incur if the policy were changed. Would the people who benefited from the change gain more than it would cost those who lost out? No. Jane's net benefit would be $80 − $60 = $20. John, Martin, and Tom would each gain $10 so that the total would be $50. On the other hand, Mary's net loss would be $500 − $10 = $490. As a result, the change would clearly fail if unanimous consent were required. Indeed, requiring unanimous consent would be the same as imposing a Pareto criterion on the decision—that is, guaranteeing that nobody was made worse off. The proposed change in policy would, however, pass (by 4 votes to 1) if a majority rule were enforced unless, of course, Mary offered "side payments" to two voters to switch sides (paying John, Martin, or Tom as little as $10.01 could switch their votes).

POSITIVE AND NEGATIVE EXTERNALITIES

We have generally assumed up to this point, at least implicitly, that there is no difference between private and social benefits, or between private and social costs. Costs to producers have been assumed to be costs to society, and costs to society have been assumed to be costs to producers; meanwhile, benefits to consumers have been assumed to be benefits to society, and benefits to society have been assumed to be benefits to consumers. In many instances, though, these assumptions do not hold. Producers sometimes confer benefits on other members of the economy but are unable to obtain payment for these benefits. In other cases, producers act in ways that cause harm to others without paying the full cost of that damage. In these and other, similar cases, the pursuit of private gain will not necessarily promote the social welfare. The purpose of this section is to describe how differences between private and social returns are likely to arise and the ways in which these differences influence our results.

It is convenient and customary to classify divergences between private and social costs into two categories. On the one hand, the action of one economic actor could result in uncompensated benefit to others. This is called
Positive externality
a **positive externality**, and it can be either the result of a firm's production process or the result of an action take by a consumer. A firm might benefit others, for example, by training workers who eventually go to work for other firms that then do not have to pay the training costs. Or the firm's production may benefit other firms indirectly because its increased output makes it more economical for firms outside the industry to provide services. A great

675

expansion in an aircraft manufacturer, for example, may make it possible for aluminum producers to take advantage of economies of scale so that other metal fabricating firms also get the opportunity to buy cheaper aluminum. In either case, there is a difference between private and social returns—that is, the benefits accruing to society are greater than the benefits earned by the firm. Meanwhile, my neighbors could benefit if I maintain my house well or educate my children to make them more responsible citizens. The key in any case is that the beneficiaries do not pay for the ancillary benefit.

Negative externalitiy

All of the news is not good, however. **Negative externalities** can also be generated by either production or consumption when the actions of one economic actor could cause uncompensated harm for others. Firms may generate pollution that causes health and property damage downstream or downwind. People may covet SUVs that consume excessive amounts of fuel and cause excessive amounts of damage in a collision. Again, in either case, the key is still that the people who are harmed are not compensated.

Example 18.4	Basic Research as a Public Good

The theory of positive externalities can shed some light on issues surrounding policies designed to promote publicly sponsored basic research. The critical question can be simply expressed: Why should the government be involved instead of relying on private enterprise? To answer this question, it is important to realize that basic scientific research can generate substantial external economies. Important additions to fundamental knowledge can have significant impacts in many fields. It follows that a firm whose employees make a scientific breakthrough cannot generally hope to realize the full value of the new knowledge that it might create. It cannot fully engage in the range of activities that might be supported, and so it can seldom capture the full social value. Indeed, some discoveries into the laws of nature cannot even be patented.

All of these insights support a view that a divergence between the private and social benefits of basic research can exist and that we should therefore expect a competitive economy to devote fewer resources to such efforts than would be socially optimal. On pure economic grounds, as a result, a good case for government support can be made. Indeed, the 1987 report of the Council of Economic Advisers made just that case when it noted that "the Federal Government has an important role (to play) in funding basic scientific research. Such research can often contribute to technological advance in the longer term. However, its benefits are often too diffuse and difficult to profit from it to be undertaken by private business."

Similar considerations support a complementary argument that government support should extend to the technological underpinnings of broadly defined industrial areas. The National Advisory Committee on Aeronautics, for example, conducted research and development activities into wind tunnels, aircraft fuel, aircraft design, and other fundamental matters relevant to aviation. No individual firm would have had much incentive to do this work, because it could appropriate only a small share of the benefits. Nonetheless, social benefits to the economy as a whole were substantial; and the simple principles of microeconomics suggest that it was the right thing to do. The same argument applies today in the debate about the government's role, through the National Institutes of Health and the National Science Foundation, in sponsoring fundamental research in areas that help pharmaceutical companies develop new drugs for profit.

There is, however, a cautionary side to these arguments. Government-sponsored research can have private value, and private firms can occasionally be seen using public support to advance proprietary knowledge. The profit motive of private industry is therefore in direct opposition to the public-good motive that drives government involvement. This is why public support encourages and rewards the publication of research results and the rapid dissemination of data collected under its auspices.

See *Economic Report of the President* (Washington, D.C.: U.S. Government Printing Office, 1987), p. 49; and J. Hirshleifer, "The Private and Social Value of Information and the Reward to Inventive Activity," *American Economic Review,* September 1971.

ECONOMIC CONSEQUENCES OF EXTERNALITIES

How do externalities alter the efficiency of the allocation of resources under perfect competition? People who undertake actions that contribute to society's welfare without compensation are likely to undertake these actions less frequently than would be socially desirable. The same holds true for firms. If, say, the production of a certain good, such as beryllium, were responsible for creating external economies and if the producers were not compensated fully for those benefits, then they would likely produce less than the socially efficient quantity under perfect competition. Producers are not going to increase the output of their product simply because it reduces costs for other companies. By the same token, people who undertake actions that impose costs on others are likely to undertake these actions more frequently than is socially desirable if they are not held accountable for those external costs. The same holds true for firms. If the production of a certain good is responsible for creating external diseconomies, then more of this good is likely to be produced under perfect competition than is socially efficient.[3]

EXTERNALITIES: THE CASE OF
ENVIRONMENTAL POLLUTION

Having argued in general that there is a role for government when externalities distort the workings of competitive markets, we now turn to the most persuasive example—the problem of what to do in the face of environmental pollution.

[3]See W. Baumol, *Economic Theory and Operations Analysis,* 3d ed. (Englewood Cliffs, N.J.: Prentice-Hall, 1972), pp. 392–395 and 399–404.

Many of our streams and lakes have historically served as depositories of chemical waste generated by industrial plants and mines. Some are cleaner now, but many still suffer damage from earlier discharges of chemicals, like PCBs, whose "half-lives" are measured in hundreds of years. Many pesticides, fertilizers, and detergents used by farms and homes find their way into our lakes and waterways, where they have damaged commercial and recreational fishing. Automobiles are a primary source of many air pollutants. The residue of their emissions can foul both the air that we breathe and the land located close to the road that we drive on. Factories generate particles of various kinds, often through the combustion of fossil fuels; these pollute the air and fall onto the ground—both near and far. Some of our pollution has even been shown to cause damage on a global scale. The production and emission of chlorofluorocarbons has damaged the ozone layer and exposed much of the planet to increased ultraviolet (UV-B) radiation from the sun; the emission of carbon dioxide and other greenhouse gases has begun to warm the planet at rates that many find alarming.

Why does our economy tolerate any pollution of the environment? We now know that an externality occurs when one person's (or firm's) use or abuse of a resource damages other people who cannot obtain proper compensation. When this occurs, a competitive economy is unlikely to function properly. For market prices to produce an efficient allocation of resources, it is necessary that the full cost of using each resource be borne by the person or firm that uses it. If this is not the case, so that the user bears only part of the full costs, then the resource is not likely to be directed by the price system into the socially optimal use. And why do people use resources like the environment? Because pollution is a by-product of activities that add to their welfare. These activities bring economic gain to producers *and utility gain to consumers.* We do not pollute the planet just for fun; we do it as part of activities that improve our welfare. The economist's view of this is that pollution creates another trade-off of cost and benefit that must be weighed on a case-by-case basis.

Divergence of private and social costs

To explore this point a little further, recall from Chapter 16 that resources are used most efficiently in a perfectly competitive economy because they are allocated to the people and firms that find it worthwhile to bid the most for them. Underlying this scheme is the notion that the resulting prices of all resources would reflect their true social costs. Suppose, however, that the presence of external diseconomies made it possible that people and firms did not pay the true social cost for certain resources. Suppose, in particular, that some firms or people were using water or air for free even though other firms or people were incurring some cost from this use. Suppose, to be quite specific, that some firms were polluting the air or water and that others were suffering economic losses as a result. In this case, the private costs of using air and water would differ from the social costs. The prices paid by the user of water and air would be smaller than the true cost to society. But users of water and air would be guided in their decisions by the private costs of water and air—costs that would be reflected by the prices that they had to pay. Faced with this difference between private and social cost, these firms would "use" too much air and water from society's point of view, because the prices that they would pay for air and water would be too low.

Note that the divergence between private and social costs occurs if and only if the use of water or air by one firm or person imposes costs on other firms or other people. A paper mill that uses water and then restores it to its original quality would not be responsible for creating a divergence between private and social costs; it would be paying the full social cost of using the water in the (presumably minimum) cost of running the restoration process. But if the same mill dumped untreated wastes into a stream so that firms and towns downstream had to pay to restore the quality of the water, then it would be responsible for creating a divergence between private and social costs. The same is true of air pollution. If an electric-power plant used the atmosphere as a cheap and convenient place to dispose of wastes but people living and working nearby incurred some cost (including poorer health and the more frequent need to paint their houses) as a result, then there would be a divergence between private and social costs.

▣ Efficient Pollution Control

Any industry should, in general, be able to vary the amount of pollution that it generates at each level of output, especially in the long run. A representative firm may, for example, install pollution-control devices like scrubbers or electrostatic precipitators to reduce the amount of pollution that it generates at each level of output. What is the economically efficient level of pollution control for a specific level of industrywide output? This might appear at first blush to be a foolish question. Isn't it obvious that zero pollution is the best level? Strange as it may seem, the answer is no. Instead, the *economically efficient* solution for society generally involves tolerating a certain amount of pollution. This statement may not warm the hearts of some environmentalists, but it is true nonetheless.

To see why, consult Figure 18.3. It shows the total social cost of each level of discharge of an industry's wastes, holding constant the industry's output. Clearly, the more untreated waste the industry dumps into the environment, the greater the total costs. Figure 18.3 also shows the costs of pollution control at each level of discharge of the industry's wastes. Just as clearly, the more the industry cuts down on the amount of wastes it discharges, the higher are its costs of pollution control. In addition, Figure 18.3 shows the sum of these two costs—the cost of pollution and the cost of pollution control—at each level of discharge of the industry's wastes.

From the point of view of society as a whole, the industry should reduce its discharge of pollution to the point where the sum of these two costs is minimized. Specifically, the efficient level of pollution in the industry is R in Figure 18.3. Why? Because increasing pollution from a level lower than R would improve social welfare. Discharging one more unit of pollution would increase the cost of pollution, but it would reduce the cost of pollution control by more. Reducing pollution from a level higher than R would

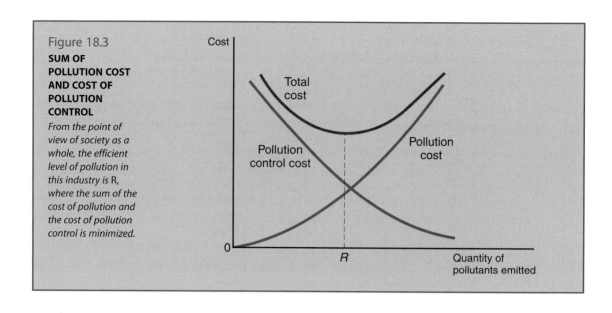

Figure 18.3

SUM OF POLLUTION COST AND COST OF POLLUTION CONTROL

From the point of view of society as a whole, the efficient level of pollution in this industry is R, where the sum of the cost of pollution and the cost of pollution control is minimized.

also improve welfare. In this case, discharging one fewer unit of pollution would increase the cost of pollution control, but it would reduce the cost of pollution by more.

To make this more evident, curve *AA′* in Figure 18.4 shows the marginal cost of an extra unit of discharge of waste at each level. Curve *BB′* in Figure 18.4 also shows the marginal cost of reducing the industry's discharge of waste by 1 unit. The economically efficient level of pollution for the industry occurs at the point where the two curves intersect. At this point, the

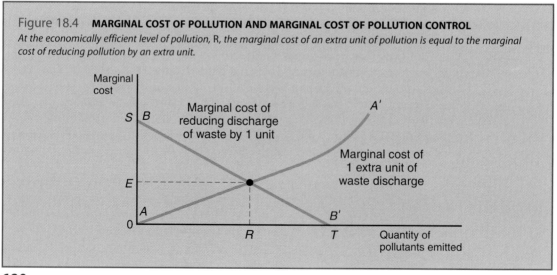

Figure 18.4   **MARGINAL COST OF POLLUTION AND MARGINAL COST OF POLLUTION CONTROL**

At the economically efficient level of pollution, R, the marginal cost of an extra unit of pollution is equal to the marginal cost of reducing pollution by an extra unit.

cost of an extra unit of pollution would just equal the extra cost of reducing pollution by an extra unit. Regardless of whether we look at Figure 18.3 or Figure 18.4, the answer is the same: R is the economically efficient level of pollution.

Earlier we observed that the efficient level of pollution is generally not zero. It should now be clear why this is true. The costs of reducing pollution can exceed the associated benefits if control is pushed beyond a certain point. In Figures 18.3 and 18.4, this point is reached when pollution is limited to R.[4] But could the efficient level of pollution be zero? Sure. Zero would be the right answer if the pollutant were so damaging that the marginal cost of even the first unit released into the environment exceeded the marginal cost of not allowing its release. Graphically, zero could be efficient in Figure 18.4 if marginal-cost curve AA' started from a point on the vertical axis that was higher than S (indicating that the cost of pollution would increase faster from zero than the cost of pollution control would fall).

▣ Direct Regulation, Effluent Fees, and Transferable Emission Permits

Left to its own devices, the industry in Figure 18.4 would not necessarily reduce its pollution level to R. Why? Because it would not necessarily pay all of the social costs of its pollution. Indeed, if the industry paid no private cost for its pollution, then it would emit T units—the quantity for which the marginal cost of control would equal zero. This, of course, is the heart of the problem. How can the government establish incentives that would lead industries to choose the efficient amount of pollution control in their own best interest, even if they do not face all of the social costs of residual emissions?

Direct regulation   **Direct regulation** of polluting activity (i.e., setting a legal limit for pollution) frequently comes to mind. The government could, for example, simply limit the industry's pollution to R units by decree. Direct regulation of this sort was popular in the United States shortly after the passage of the first Clean Air Act in the 1970s. The decrees were generally associated with definitions of the "best available technologies" for pollution control, but they were criticized frequently for being too rigid to accommodate efficiently the changing landscape of modern industry and the diversity of the suppliers of modern markets.

Effluent fees   **Effluent fees** offer governments a second approach to pollution control. An effluent fee is a unit price that a polluter must pay to the government for discharging waste. The idea behind their imposition is that they can bring the marginal private cost of polluting faced by firms closer to the true marginal social cost of their emissions. In Figure 18.4, for example, an effluent fee of E per unit of pollution discharge might be charged. If it were, then the (private) marginal cost of an additional unit of pollution

---

[4]For further discussion, see A. Freeman, R. Haveman, and A. Kneese, *The Economics of Environmental Policy* (New York: Wiley, 1973), or M. Cropper and W. Oates, "Environmental Economics: A Survey," *Journal of Economic Literature,* vol. 30, no. 2, June 1992, pp. 675–740.

discharge to the industry would be E, and so the industry would cut back its pollution to the efficient level, R. Why? Because it would be worth cutting back pollution so long as the marginal cost of reducing pollution by a unit were less than E. As you can see from Figure 18.4, marginal cost falls short of E as long as the pollution discharge exceeds R. To maximize their profits, therefore, the firms in the industry would reduce pollution to R units.

Effluent fees often have one major advantage over direct regulation. It is, of course, socially desirable to use the cheapest way to achieve any given reduction in pollution, and a system of effluent fees is more likely to accomplish this result than direct regulation. To see why, first consider a particular polluter facing an effluent charge. It would find it profitable to reduce its discharge of waste to the point where the (marginal) cost of reducing its emissions by 1 unit equaled the fee. The effluent fee would be the same for all polluters, so that imposing an effluent fee would guarantee that the marginal cost of reducing pollution by one extra unit would be the same for all polluters. And it is a simple matter to show that the total cost of achieving the corresponding reduction in total emissions across all of the polluters would thereby be minimized. To that end, suppose that the cost of reducing waste discharges by an additional unit were not the same for all polluters (as might be the case if they were given individual quantity limits). The cost of achieving the same amount of total pollution control could then be reduced by allowing polluters whose marginal control costs were high to increase their emissions (and lower their marginal control costs) while encouraging polluters whose marginal control costs were low to reduce theirs (by an equal amount).

Effluent fees do not, however, guarantee the same constant level of total emissions that could be expected if a set of individual quantity limits were issued. Why not? Because firms will pay for the right to more or less pollution as they increase or decrease their outputs. So, although direct regulation would restrict total emissions regardless of business conditions, an equivalent effluent fee could, at best, guarantee that the expected value of total emissions over a long period of time would correspond to the same total. Variation in the level of total pollution can be harmful in some cases, and not in others. The point here is that preference for effluent fees is not quite so clear-cut when the reality of uncertainty is brought to bear on the discussions.

Marketable emissions permits

Governments have recently learned that they can work the trade-off between the certainty of direct regulation and the efficiency of effluent charges by issuing a fixed number of transferable emissions permits—permits that allow the holder to generate a certain amount of pollution. The total number of permits can be limited, so that total pollution can be held below any targeted level. The economically efficient amount might be the pollution target, but there could be others (especially if it were difficult to collect the information necessary to identify the efficient level or if there were an emissions threshold beyond which damage would be severe). In any case, allowing permits to be bought and sold would mean that firms whose marginal control costs were high would probably try to buy some (so that they could increase their emissions) and firms whose marginal control costs were low would try to sell some (and make money even though they would have to reduce their emissions). In fact, the market would work to bring the marginal cost of pollution control at each firm equal to the market price of permits, and so it would bring the marginal cost of pollution control at every firm in line with the marginal cost at every other firm. Notice that this is exactly the condition for minimizing the cost of holding total emissions to a particular level.[5]

Example 18.5 | Alternative Pollution Policy Designs—Working a Problem

Consider a situation where an upstream farm pollutes a river with fertilizer runoff, and assume that a downstream town draws its drinking water from the same river. Figure 18.5 offers a generic portrait of the situation. Let line $0B$ represent either the marginal social cost to the town (or the marginal cost of cleansing the drinking water before it is distributed). Let line CD represent the marginal private benefit derived by the farm by applying fertilizer. The socially optimal level of pollution would be E units where the marginal benefit accruing to the farmer from his fertilizing would equal the marginal cost to the townsfolk of coping with the residual pollution from the associated runoff.

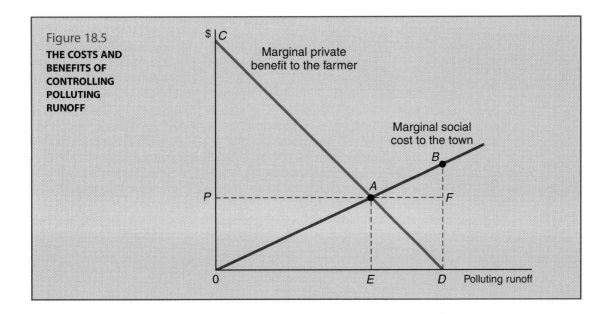

Figure 18.5

THE COSTS AND BENEFITS OF CONTROLLING POLLUTING RUNOFF

[5]See M. Weitzman, "Prices versus Quantities," *Review of Economic Studies,* October 1974; then G. Yohe, "Towards a General Comparison of Price Controls and Quantity Controls under Uncertainty," *Review of Economic Studies,* June 1978; and T. Tietenberg, "Economic Instruments for Environmental Regulation," reprinted as Chap. 16 in R. Stavins, *Economics of the Environment* (New York: W. W. Norton, 2000).

The government could intervene with a wide range of different sorts of policies. It could, for example, simply charge the farmer a tax equal to P for each unit of pollution that ran off into the river. The farmer would then decide how much to pollute by finding the level where his marginal private benefit equaled the tax; E units would be chosen.

The government could, alternatively, require that the farmer pollute no more that E units. If the penalty for violating this limit were sufficiently high, then the farmer could, indeed, fertilize up to the point where E units could be expected to run off into the river. What would be sufficiently high? If a fine were imposed for each unit in excess of the limit, then it would have to exceed the expected benefit of violation. Otherwise, the expected benefit of violating the limit would exceed the expected cost. So, if the probability of being caught and successfully prosecuted were given by PR, then the fine would have to be at least P/PR. The marginal private cost of pollution to the farmer would then have three segments. It would correspond to the horizontal axis at \$0 from the origin to point E; that is, the farmer would get the first E units of pollution for free. It would climb vertically at point E to at least point A, and it would then be horizontal again at a level at least as high as segment AF. The farmer would then again set marginal private benefit equal to this policy-driven marginal private cost to determine his level of pollution. The two curves would intersect at point A, and E units would run off into the river.

Microlink 18.2   Cost-Minimizing Conditions for an Externality

The example of a multifirm monopolist in Chapter 10 made it clear that the cost of producing any quantity of any good from multiple sources would be minimized if the marginal cost of producing the last unit were the same at each source. This condition was met automatically in the perfectly competitive models of Chapter 8 because each profit-maximizing firm would react to the same market price by setting marginal cost equal to that price. Cast in the context of a multiple-source pollution problem, this result states that the cost of reducing total emissions to any specific target would be minimized if the marginal cost of reducing the last unit from the effluent were the same for all sources. This condition can also be met automatically if the government intervened by imposing identical pollution charges on emissions from each source. Each polluter would then minimize the (now) private cost of pollution by setting the marginal cost of emissions reduction equal to the same "price."

PROPERTY RIGHTS AND THE SO-CALLED COASE THEOREM

A perfectly competitive economy can sometimes allocate resources efficiently even in the face of seemingly severe external costs or extraordinary external benefits. To see how, consider a firm that pollutes a stream. If downstream water users were entitled to water of a particular minimum quality (i.e., if these users were endowed with well-defined property rights to suitable water), then the upstream firm might be able to purchase the right to pollute the stream to a certain extent. Or, if the firm were endowed with property rights over the stream, downstream users might be able to purchase improved water quality from the polluter. In either case, the welfare calculations of both interested parties would now include the externality so that the divergence between social and private costs could actually disappear. At the very least, the divergence should be diminished. These stories are encouraging, but they do not lead to a very strong conclusion. They simply suggest that competitive markets *might* be able to handle external effects. Neither arrangement could work, though, if the costs of negotiating compensation were too large.

The Nobel laureate Ronald Coase was among the first to look at the externality problem in this context. Motivated by the stream example, he was able to argue that a competitive economy will allocate resources efficiently even in the face of significant external diseconomies if negotiations of this sort can be conducted with little or no cost. If downstream water users held the property rights to clean water, then an upstream firm that wanted to pollute would have to offer them compensation. How much pollution for what price? The firm, pursuing its own best interest, would not find it worthwhile to pollute more than the economically efficient level and would pay no more than the economically efficient price. Coase was also able to show that the efficient outcome could be obtained regardless of which party held the relevant property rights. Downstream water users would, more specifically, never find it in their best interest to negotiate water quality in excess of the economically efficient level; but they could never achieve that level without paying the economically efficient compensation.[6]

Coase theorem

The general result exhibited by the story of negotiating along a polluted stream is often referred to as the **Coase theorem.** It has attracted a lot of attention, and it is very important. We must, however, take special note of its applicability. It is essential to recognize that the Coase theorem assumes that the costs of negotiating and contracting by the interested parties are relatively small. It assumes, in the stream example, that the downstream water users can get together with the polluting firm and that they can negotiate effectively without prohibitive expense. When there are more than a relatively small number of interested parties, though, the costs of these sorts of negotiations may be so high that they are not feasible (especially when lawyers get involved). Indeed, negotiations of this sort may not be practical even with a relatively small number of interested parties. Unanimity might be impossible with a large number of interested parties, but the existence of mutually advantageous deals does not guarantee that they will be consummated even when only a few people are involved.

---

[6]See R. Coase, "The Problem of Social Cost," reprinted as Chap. 3 in R. Stavins, *Economics of the Environment* (New York: W. W. Norton, 2000), as well as N. Hanley, J. Shogren, and B. White, *Introduction to Environmental Economics* (New York: Oxford University Press, 2001), pp. 157–160.

The Coase theorem nonetheless suggests that the assignment of well-defined property rights might help to promote economic efficiency. To get around the difficulties caused by external diseconomies arising from waste disposal, society might find it useful to try to establish more un-ambiguous property rights for individuals and firms with respect to environmental quality. Assuming that the relevant negotiations are feasible, the interested parties in a particular area might then try to negotiate to determine how much pollution will occur. Note that these property rights must be exchangeable as well as unambiguous if these negotiations are to be effective. It must be possible for a person (or firm) to buy or sell his or her property rights.

DEMONSTRATING THE COASE THEOREM FROM A GAME-THEORETIC PERSPECTIVE

Return to the pollution problem of Example 18.5, but suppose now that the townspeople and the farmer were encouraged to negotiate a solution in lieu of government intervention. The first payoff matrix shown in panel A of Figure 18.6 depicts the outcomes (in terms of the points designated in Figure 18.5) of a negotiating game in which the farmer claims property rights to the river. The farmer could, in the absence of any negotiation, therefore fertilize his fields without regard to the resultant impact on water quality. Pollution in the amount D would run into the river with a total benefit equal to the area of triangle $0CD$ accruing to the farmer and a cost equal to area $0BD$ imposed on the town. If the town and the farmer both agreed to negotiate, however, they would discover that the town would be willing to pay up to P for each unit of pollution that the farmer *did not* allow into the river.

As shown in the payoff matrix, the farmer would receive compensation in an amount equal to the area of rectangle $EAFD$ (price P for each of ED units now *not* released into the river) in exchange for lost benefits equal to the area of triangle EAD for reducing pollution from D units to E units; total benefits would then equal area $0AEC$ in remaining private benefits from pollution, plus area $EAFD$ in revenue minus area EAD in forgone benefits. Meanwhile, the town would pay an amount equal to area $EAFD$ but see its costs of water purification fall by an amount equal to the area of trapezoid $EABD$. Since area $EAFD$ − area $EAD > 0$, the farmer's net benefit would climb above area $0CD$ by an amount equal to area AFD. In addition, area $EABD$ − area $EAFD > 0$, so the cost to the town would fall by area AFB. Negotiating would therefore be a dominant strategy for both players, and a Nash equilibrium would be discovered in the lower right-hand box of the payoff matrix. Notice that it would support an efficient level of pollution equal to E units.

If the town held the property rights, however, a second payoff matrix would apply; it is portrayed in panel B of Figure 18.6. Without negotiation

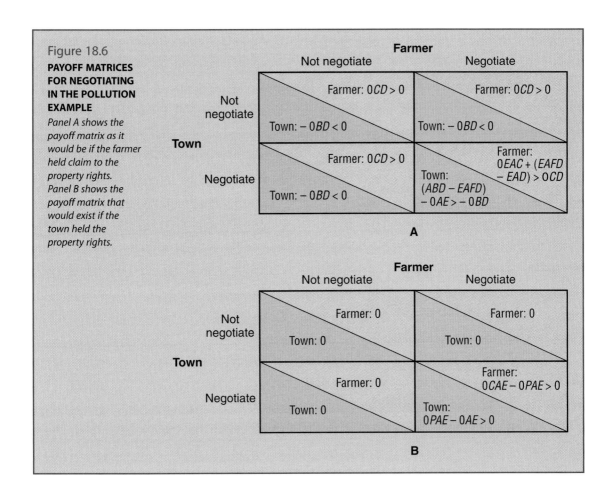

Figure 18.6

PAYOFF MATRICES FOR NEGOTIATING IN THE POLLUTION EXAMPLE

Panel A shows the payoff matrix as it would be if the farmer held claim to the property rights. Panel B shows the payoff matrix that would exist if the town held the property rights.

Farmer

	Not negotiate	Negotiate
Not negotiate	Farmer: $0CD > 0$ / Town: $-0BD < 0$	Farmer: $0CD > 0$ / Town: $-0BD < 0$
Negotiate	Farmer: $0CD > 0$ / Town: $-0BD < 0$	Farmer: $0EAC + (EAFD - EAD) > 0CD$ / Town: $(ABD - EAFD) - 0AE > -0BD$

Town

A

Farmer

	Not negotiate	Negotiate
Not negotiate	Farmer: 0 / Town: 0	Farmer: 0 / Town: 0
Negotiate	Farmer: 0 / Town: 0	Farmer: $0CAE - 0PAE > 0$ / Town: $0PAE - 0AE > 0$

Town

B

or intervention, pollution would be 0, and the farmer would now consider paying the town for the right to pollute up to E units (make sure that you can verify all of the entries by applying the same reasoning as before). Negotiating would still be a dominant strategy for both players, and *the same E units of pollution would be sustained.*

GOVERNMENT INTERVENTION AND BENEFIT-COST ANALYSIS

Government interventions into the workings of economies take many different forms. Governments provide public goods. They redistribute income. They regulate monopolies. They regulate polluters. Government officials (and more fundamentally, the general public) must continually decide whether it would be worthwhile for the government to carry out one

687

particular project or another. It is frequently difficult to make these sorts of decisions because it is so hard to measure the relevant social benefits and social costs. In some cases, though, benefits and costs can be measured well enough that benefit-cost analysis can be used to help guide these decisions. Benefit-cost analysis is no panacea, but it is a useful tool.

▣ The Basics of Benefit-Cost Analysis

We will begin with a simple constrained budget case to see how benefit-cost analysis operates. Consider a government agency that (1) has a fixed budget that limits the amount that it can spend, (2) faces a menu of alternative projects that it could choose to undertake, and (3) recognizes that these alternative projects are relatively indivisible. For example, suppose that the Department of Transportation had a fixed amount to spend on roads and that it was considering the construction of one or more of the roads described in Table 18.2. Its problem would be to decide which one or ones. Table 18.2 shows the benefits that would accrue to the people from each of these projects, and it shows that none of the roads would be free.

Assume that the government agency tried to maximize the difference between total benefits and total costs. Since we are assuming (for the moment) that its total costs are fixed, it follows that it would maximize benefits minus costs only if it maximized the total benefits obtained from this fixed expenditure. But how could it determine which projects would maximize total benefits? If the Department of Transportation in Table 18.2 had $1 billion to spend on roads, for example, which roads would maximize the total benefits? The answer is simple. It should calculate the ratio of benefits to costs for each project and accept those projects with the highest values of this ratio until it runs out of money. For the data in Table 18.2, then, the roads from A to B, D to E, G to R, and S to T should be built. These projects would have the highest benefit-cost ratios, and together their costs would

Table 18.2 BENEFIT-COST ANALYSIS, FIXED BUDGET	Possible roads	Benefits (billions of dollars)	Costs	Benefit-cost ratio
	A to B	0.30	0.20	1.50
	A to D	0.30	0.24	1.25
	B to C	0.10	0.08	1.25
	C to D	0.18	0.20	0.90
	D to E	0.70	0.40	1.75
	F to H	0.40	0.30	1.33
	G to R	0.40	0.20	2.00
	H to S	0.36	0.30	1.20
	S to T	0.35	0.20	1.75

sum to $1 billion.[7] Notice that the roads from A to D, B to C, F to H, and H to S all have benefit-cost ratios that exceed 1; benefits would exceed costs if these roads were built, as well. They would not be built, though, because the department could not afford to build all of them; they would not be chosen, because their contribution to the total benefit of the $1 billion budget would not be as high as it would be for the four roads selected.

What would the agency have done if its budget were not fixed? Undertake every project for which the benefit-cost ratio was greater than 1. If the Department of Transportation could spend as much as it wanted, then it would build all of the roads but the one from C to D. Why? Because this is the decision rule used in the private sector. Indeed, under perfect competition, spending in the private sector would proceed up to the point where the marginal benefit of an extra dollar of spending would equal one dollar. Ignoring the distortions of taxation, it follows, then, that a transfer of resources from the private sector to the public sector (to build roads, for example) would improve social welfare as long as a public project had a benefit-cost ratio that exceeded 1. Why? Because the marginal benefit of the transferred dollar would then be higher if it were spent by the public sector instead of by the private sector.[8]

▣ Measuring Benefits and Costs

The discussion so far may have left you with the impression that benefit-cost analysis involves little more than a straightforward calculation of the benefit-cost ratio for each project and a simple comparison of these ratios.[9] Things are not that simple. Application of benefit-cost analysis is often marked by great difficulties in measuring the benefits and costs of each project. Although it would be inappropriate for us to dwell at length on the ways in which benefits and costs should be measured, two important principles should be mentioned even in a brief review of the process. First, it is important to distinguish between **real benefits (and costs)** and pecuniary benefits (and costs). Real benefits augment society's welfare; they should be weighed against the

Real benefits and costs

---

[7]It is easy to see that this procedure will maximize the sum of the benefits received. Looking at the benefits and costs columns of Table 18.2, it is clear that the optimal choice would be the road from G to R if only $0.2 billion could be spent. If $0.4 billion could be spent, then the optimal choice would be the road from G to R and the road from S to T. And if $0.8 billion could be spent, then the optimal choice would be the road from G to R, the road from S to T, and the road from D to E. In each case, these same results could be obtained by picking the projects with the highest benefit-cost ratios. If you aren't convinced, try it in each case and see. Note, too, that we are assuming that the costs and benefits of each project do not depend on whether any of the other projects is carried out. Sometimes this assumption holds, but sometimes it doesn't. In the latter instance, more advanced techniques may be required.

[8]Government agencies should allocate funds among projects that are divisible so that the marginal benefit from an extra dollar of expenditure on each project is equal—and equal to the marginal benefit from an extra dollar of expenditure in the private sector of the economy if there is no budget.

[9]Although the basics are easy to master, the theory is not so straightforward once one gets beyond fundamentals. There are a number of theoretical problems that we have not taken up, since they would take us too far afield. In particular, a great deal of attention has been devoted in the literature to the question of what is the proper discount rate. For some relevant discussion, see J. Stiglitz, *Economics of the Public Sector,* 3d ed. (New York: W. W. Norton, 2000).

real costs of a project. **Pecuniary benefits and costs,** on the other hand, arise because of changes in relative prices that are the result of the economy's adjustment to the project. Pecuniary benefits and costs change the income distribution because some people gain from them while others lose. But the pecuniary gains of one individual are generally offset by the pecuniary losses of another, and so they are neither benefits nor costs to society as a whole.

To illustrate the distinction between real and pecuniary benefits (and costs), consider a dam that is being built by the government. The construction of the dam could cause wage rates paid for construction workers who live near the dam site to rise. This would be a benefit to them, but it would be offset by a reduction in relative wage rates paid to other people located elsewhere in the economy; these are the people who would see the effects of diminished demand from higher taxes. This would be a pecuniary and not a real benefit. The dam could also cause food prices in restaurants near the dam site to rise. But gains to the restaurant owners would be offset by the losses to the restaurant patrons; these too, would be pecuniary benefits.

Second, benefit-cost analyses rely on the estimation of all of the benefits and costs for each public project. This is much easier said than done. Some benefits and costs may accrue indirectly. For example, the dam may have indirect effects on consumers, laborers, investors, and firms in many parts of the country. Somebody would need to quantify them all if benefit-cost techniques were to be applied faithfully. And other benefits and costs are intangible. The dam may mar the scenery, an intangible effect that would not be valued in the marketplace; it, too, would have to be quantified. The situation has been described very well as follows:

> Needless to say, in reaching decisions, one should attempt to take into account all gains and all costs. Some people feel that there are two types of gain or cost, economic and noneconomic, and that economic analysis has nothing to do with the latter. This distinction is neither very sound nor very useful. People pay for—that is, they value—music as well as food, beauty or quiet as well as aluminum pans, a lower probability of death as well as garbage disposal. The significant categories are not economic and noneconomic items but (1) gains and costs that can be measured in monetary units (for example, the use of items like typewriters that have market prices reflecting the marginal evaluations of all users); (2) other commensurable effects (impacts of higher teacher salaries, on the one hand, and of teaching machines, on the other hand, on students' test scores); (3) incommensurable effects that can be quantified but not in terms of a common denominator (capability of improving science test scores and capability of reducing the incidence of ulcers among students); and (4) nonquantifiable effects. Examples of the last category are impacts of alternative policies on the morale and happiness of students, on the probability of racial conflicts, and on the probability of protecting individual rights. In taking a position on an issue, each of us implicitly quantifies such considerations. But there is no way to make quantifications that would necessarily be valid for other persons. This sort of distinction between types of effects does serve a useful purpose, especially in warning us of the limitations of cost-benefit analysis.[10]

[10]R. McKean, "The Nature of Cost-Benefit Analysis," reprinted in Mansfield, *Microeconomics: Selected Readings.*

Example 18.6

Anemia Reduction in Indonesia, Kenya, and Mexico

The developed world has created a large number of institutions whose major task is to try to alleviate disease and hunger around the world. On the health side, the World Health Organization has taken the lead, but UNICEF and the United Nations Development Programs both undertake health initiatives. Moreover, many nongovernmental organizations and government agencies in specific countries all contribute to the effort. But how do they decide what to do? The first principles of benefit-cost analysis are applied widely; this example applies the structure to evaluating the relative efficacy of measures designed to reduce anemia—a condition in which the concentration of hemoglobin in the blood is relatively low. It is generally caused by not consuming enough absorbable iron. Between one-third and two-thirds of the population in many developing countries is affected by anemia. Anemic people tend to be weak and listless, and their work capacity is thereby limited. The idea of the research project we will review was to see if international agencies should be trying to provide nutrients that would supply extra iron to the food supplies of various populations.

It was expected that one of the major benefits of such a program would be that people would be able to work harder and more effectively. Studies indicated that a 10 percent increase in the amount of hemoglobin in the blood could increase the productivity of the typical worker by between 10 to 20 percent. There was also some evidence that anemia affects a person's learning ability. Extra iron provided to children might therefore help them to learn more rapidly. H. Levin made rough estimates of the value of the extra output that would result if the amount of hemoglobin were increased by 10 percent through the provision of extra iron in Indonesia, Kenya, and Mexico. Table 18.3 displays a summary of his results; he estimated that the per capita annual benefit would be about $7 in Indonesia, $43 in Kenya, and $71 in Mexico.

And what would such a program cost? Iron supplements would cost about 20 cents per person annually. And workers would also have to eat

Table 18.3		Indonesia	Kenya	Mexico
ANNUAL PER CAPITA BENEFITS AND COSTS OF NUTRITIONAL PROGRAMS TO REDUCE ANEMIA IN INDONESIA, KENYA, AND MEXICO	Benefit	$7.32	$42.64	$71.10
	Cost			
	Iron	0.20	0.20	0.20
	Additional energy intake	0.82	0.82	0.82
	Total	$1.02	$1.02	$1.02
	Benefit-cost ratio	7	42	70

SOURCE: H. Levin, "A Benefit-Cost Analysis of Nutritional Programs for Anemia Reduction," *World Bank Research Observer*, July 1986.
NOTE: These figures pertain to iron fortification programs.

more food to take full advantage of the improved levels of hemoglobin in their blood. According to Levin, this cost would amount to about 82 cents per person per year. Table 18.3 displays these estimates, and it records benefit-cost ratios that initially seemed to be high—about 7 in Indonesia, 42 in Kenya, and 70 in Mexico. Levin pointed to a few limitations in his study, but the ratios were so large that he concluded that programs to reduce anemia would be highly productive investments in many developing countries.

LIMITATIONS OF GOVERNMENT EFFECTIVENESS

Before concluding this brief discussion of selected aspects of government activity, we should point out what many citizens take as fact—that government intervention need not always be beneficial. Although we cannot do more than scratch the surface of this topic in the space available, certain salient points should be recognized. For one thing, the political process is

Pressure groups

characterized by the existence of various **pressure groups,** and political action committees that band together to advocate certain policies to the people's representatives. These groups usually contain only a small proportion of the population, but they may be successful in convincing a majority of representatives to push through measures that benefit them at the expense of the general public. Industry groups lobby for and get special tax breaks and tariffs or subsidies, for example. The National Rifle Association has fought gun control for decades. And so on. Because these groups have a great deal to gain from such measures, they have the incentive to spend large amounts to influence legislation. And the free rider problem is really not an issue for them because they are generally small collections of citizens who are committed to the same objective. In addition, the general public, which frequently loses more than the pressure group gains through such measures, is often unaware of its losses. Why? Because the losses felt by each individual tend to be small and difficult to attribute. For these and other reasons, pressure groups are sometimes successful in persuading the people's representatives to adopt the policies that they support, even though these policies may be detrimental to the welfare of the public at large.

Bureaucracy

The efficiency of government action, even when it is directed at the public welfare, depends on the ability of government to design effective programs and of civil servants to make them work. Our understanding of the determinants of the behavior of civil servants is limited. According to some economists, though, two of their primary goals are tenure in office and agency growth. It is certainly not surprising that they should be interested in tenure of office. Without the sorts of civil service regulations that currently protect public sector jobs, it would be relatively easy for incoming administrations to replace hordes of civil servants with "deserving" cronies (and their equally "deserving" relatives and friends). And without these regulations, it would be very difficult for civil servants to withstand any serious pressure from elected officials or pressure groups.

Meanwhile, there are several reasons why civil servants may want their agencies to expand and not to contract. For one thing, the prestige (as well as pay and perquisites) of a bureau chief is related to the size of the bureau. Also, a bureaucrat's power tends to increase with the size and rate of growth of the bureau in which he or she works; this is especially true for bureau heads. Large and growing bureaus also have to keep lots of jobs filled, so their chiefs have power over the careers of many people. This is a fact that few job-seekers and ambitious junior bureaucrats are likely to ignore.

It is also alleged that civil servants have too little incentive to do away with activities and personnel that are not worth their costs. The Department of Defense in the United States has, for example, been charged repeatedly with "gold plating"—that is, with the development of increments of technical performance and other features of weapons systems that are not worth their cost. Since there are strong incentives for agency growth and weak ones for reduced scope and expenditure, some observers believe that there is a built-in tendency for government agencies to grow regardless of whether their responsibilities and workload expand at all. C. Northcote Parkinson claims that "there need be (in public administration) little or no relationship between the work to be done and the size of the staff to which it may be assigned."[11]

Although these allegations should be taken seriously, it is difficult to know how much truth they contain because it is difficult to construct reliable measures of the efficiency and value of public activities. Perhaps the most important lesson to be derived from this section is that one cannot justify government intervention in a particular area of the economy merely by showing that market forces work imperfectly. Why? Because it is necessary to show (or to have substantial reason to expect) that government intervention will do more good than harm. You must, in other words, be certain that the cure is not worse than the disease. Just as the private sector cannot be trusted to work for the public interest in all instances (because of monopoly, external diseconomies, and other factors we have discussed), so government agencies cannot always be trusted to do so either (because politicians may not represent the people's preferences and interests properly, civil servants may build empires and pursue their own interests, and so on). Further economic analysis of the behavior of government agencies is badly needed to indicate more clearly the circumstances under which government intervention of various sorts will be effective and worthwhile. Fortunately, economists in increasing numbers seem to be following the early thinkers in political economy and turning their attention to this topic.[12]

---

[11]C. N. Parkinson, "Parkinson's Law," reprinted in Edwin Mansfield, *Managerial Economics and Operations Research*, 5th ed. (New York: W. W. Norton, 1987), p. 20. International organizations are not free of these problems, either. According to a *New York Times* story, Parkinson's observations have applied remarkably well to the United Nations. They are reflected in the old saw, "How many people work at the United Nations?" Answer: "About half." See "Parkinson's Law at the U.N.," *New York Times Magazine*, November 23, 1980. An example:

[12]The early work on political processes by economists includes A. Downs, *An Economic Theory of Democracy* (New York: Harper and Brothers, 1956); A. Hirschman, *Exit, Voice, and Loyalty* (Cambridge, Mass.: Harvard University Press, 1970); Olson, *The Logic of Collective Choice;* and G. Tullock, *Towards a Mathematics of Politics* (Ann Arbor: University of Michigan Press, 1967).

SUMMARY

1. A public good is nonrival and nonexclusive. By nonrival, we mean that the marginal cost of providing the good to an additional consumer is zero. By nonexclusive, we mean that people cannot be excluded from consuming the good (whether or not they pay for it).

2. Economic efficiency requires that each consumer's marginal benefit equal marginal cost for a private good. Efficiency requires that the sum of the marginal benefits of all consumers equal marginal cost for a public good. It is difficult to get people to reveal their true preferences for a public good so that this condition can be met. People can avoid paying for the good if they underestimate their demand, and they can enjoy the benefits of a public good once it is provided because it would be nonexclusive. This behavior is called "free riding."

3. If the number of people in a society were quite small, then it might be worthwhile for people acting individually to provide some quantity of public goods. However, there is a tendency for the provision of a public good to be too small; the larger the number of people in the society, the more that society will fall short of providing an efficient amount of a public good. Governments therefore tend to intervene in an attempt to ensure the proper amount of such goods.

4. Besides providing public goods, governments sometimes intervene in an attempt to offset distortions caused by external diseconomies and economies. Environmental pollution is an important example of this sort of problem. To a large extent, undesirably high levels of pollution are due to external diseconomies in the disposal of environmental waste.

5. The efficient level of pollution (holding output constant) occurs at the point where the marginal cost of pollution equals the marginal cost of pollution control. In general, this point would sustain a nonzero level of pollution. To establish incentives that will lead to a more nearly efficient level of pollution, the government can establish effluent fees, enact direct regulations, and issue transferable emissions permits, among other things.

6. If the costs of negotiating are not too large, then the parties responsible for an external benefit or cost can negotiate with the parties affected by this externality. Under these circumstances, a perfectly competitive economy can allocate resources efficiently even in the face of seemingly important externalities. Moreover, regardless of which party is endowed with the relevant property rights, the outcome is the same. It is important, however, to recognize that the costs of negotiating and contracting by the interested parties may not be small and that negotiations of this sort may not be feasible in many situations.

7. Benefit-cost analysis is aimed at helping government agencies come to rational decisions concerning how much should be spent on various projects. If a government agency has a fixed amount to spend on projects of a certain kind (and the projects are indivisible), it should choose those projects with the highest benefit-cost ratios if it wants to maximize social benefits. If its total budget is variable, it should accept all projects where the benefit-cost ratio exceeds 1 if it wants to maximize net social benefits. Although the basic theory underlying benefit-cost analysis is relatively simple, the application of this theory is often by no means straightforward. Measuring the benefits and costs of any project can be enormously difficult.

8. Government intervention in a particular area of the economy cannot be justified merely by showing that market forces work imperfectly. It is

necessary to show (or have substantial reason to expect) that government intervention will do more good than harm. Just as the private sector cannot be trusted to work for the public welfare in all instances (because of such factors as monopoly and externalities), so government agencies cannot be trusted to do so either (because politicians may not represent the people's preferences and interests properly, civil servants may build empires and pursue their own interests, and so on).

QUESTIONS/ PROBLEMS

1. According to J. Pack, the estimated social benefits in 1989 from Philadelphia's commuter rail system included (1) $7 billion due to decreased automobile accidents, (2) $34 billion due to decreased car and truck commuting time, (3) $3 billion due to decreased noise and pollution, (4) $21 billion due to less congestion on other transit facilities, and (5) $72 billion in consumer surplus for commuter rail riders.[13] Should these social benefits have been included in the revenues of the Philadelphia transit system? If not, why not? Should derivative estimates of similar factors be included in a benefit-cost analysis of the advisability of expanding the commuter rail system?

2. The word "privatize" entered the dictionary in the 1980s. It means "to change from public to private control or ownership." In the 1980s there was considerable pressure for privatization both in the United States and in other countries, such as Great Britain. Why? Evidence surfaced that private firms have been more efficient at particular activities than government agencies. Refuse collection is one of the most thoroughly studied cases. The data in the accompanying table compare the inputs used to collect refuse (and the productivity of these inputs) in two cities of the same size in the New York metropolitan area. One used private firms to collect refuse while the other relied on the municipal government to perform this service.

	City with private refuse collection	City with municipal refuse collection
Truck shifts per week	39	63
Persons per truck	2	4
Person-days of labor per week	78	237
Tons collected per person-day of labor	9.67	3.40

(a) Do private firms seem to be more efficient at the performance of this service? (b) In 1975, about 21 percent of U.S. cities hired private firms to collect refuse; in 1982, about 35 percent did so. Is this growth in accord with the figures in the table? (c) According to many observers, the basic reason for the greater efficiency of private firms is competition. Why is competition important? (d) Some cities have fostered competition between municipal agencies and private firms and have allowed both to collect refuse. What are the advantages of this arrangement? (e) Does the fact that private firms often are more efficient than municipal agencies at refuse collection mean that the provision of most government services should be turned over to private firms?

[13]J. Pack, "You Ride, I'll Pay," *Brookings Review,* Summer 1992.

3. The Department of the Interior made a benefit-cost study of four alternative dam sites on the Middle Snake River in Idaho. The results are shown in the following table:

	Alternative sites			
	Appaloosa and low mountain sheep	High mountain sheep and china gardens	High mountain sheep only	Pleasant valley and low mountain sheep
Benefits (millions of dollars)				
Power	49.3	60.7	35.9	44.2
Fish and wildlife	6.6	None	None	None
Recreation	0.4	0.3	0.3	0.3
Flood control	0.2	0.2	0.2	0.1
TOTAL[a]	56.5	61.3	36.5	44.5
Costs (millions of dollars)	20.8	24.3	13.6	19.0
Benefit-cost ratio	2.72	2.53	2.69	2.35

[a]Individual figures may not sum to total because of rounding errors.

(a) Does it appear that a dam should be built at one of these sites? (b) Critics pointed out that this analysis took no account of fish and wildlife destruction. When these and other costs were included, the staff of the Federal Energy Regulatory Commission estimated that the benefit-cost ratio for none of these sites exceeded 1. Does it now appear that a dam should be built at one of these sites? (c) Could you imagine equity reasons why the benefit of more power might outweigh the destruction of fish and wildlife? (d) Would it matter if part of the wildlife destroyed was a species of rodent that lived nowhere else on earth?

4. Suppose that the Department of Transportation had a budget of $5 billion to spend on roads and that the costs and benefits from all roads under consideration were recorded in the following table:

Road	Benefits	Costs
	(billions of dollars)	
A	10	1
B	12	4
C	20	5

Which roads should the department finance, and why? If you were an adviser to the department, what questions would you ask concerning the derivation of these figures?

5. A. R. Prest and R. Turvey point out that the benefit-cost ratio for a cross-Florida barge canal was estimated to be 1.20 by the Army Corps of Engineers, whereas some consultants retained by the railroads put the ratio at 0.13. What

factors might account for the difference in these results? What can you learn from this example about when government intervention might be a good idea?

6. Education and health services can be provided by private enterprise on a fee basis. What is the rationale for government intervention in these areas? To what extent are education and health services public goods? In what ways can microeconomics help to shed light on proper public policy in these areas?

7. Suppose that there were only three citizens of a (very small) community and that the amount of police protection each would demand (at various prices) were as recorded in the following table:

Price of an hour of police protection (dollars)	Number of hours demanded per day		
	Citizen A	Citizen B	Citizen C
10	10	8	12
15	9	7	9
20	8	6	6
25	7	5	3
30	6	2	0

If the marginal cost of an hour of police protection were $70, what would be the efficient amount of police protection for this community?

8. Using the situation described in Question 7, suppose that the members of this small community agreed that if any citizen refuses to pay for police protection, then his or her property and person would not be protected. Under these circumstances, could a nongovernmental organization sell some of the services normally provided by the community's police force? If so, would ordinary market forces result in the efficient amount of police protection being provided?

9. Each owner of a well in any oil field is motivated to pump out the oil relatively fast because this makes it more likely that he or she will capture some oil under the others' land and prevent others from capturing oil under their land. Are there externalities present in this situation? Do you think that they lead to inefficiencies? If so, what sorts of inefficiencies result? Could negotiation solve the problem?

10. A paint plant is located upstream from plant A. Plant A's costs reflect the fact that it has to clean up the water that the paint plant pollutes. The firm that owns the paint plant decides to buy plant A. Why? Because it believes that the price of the product made by plant A will increase dramatically? Because it believes that markets will open dramatically? It does not matter. Is it likely that the paint plant will emit the same amount of pollutants as before the purchase of plant A? What factors would influence how emissions might change?

11. The Times Mirror Company wanted to complete the $120 million expansion of a papermaking plant near Portland, Oregon. State and federal officials were concerned about the effects on air quality. Eventually, the firm bought the right to emit about 150 tons of extra hydrocarbons into the air per year for $50,000 from a wood-coating plant that had gone out of business. According to the firm's manager of environmental and energy services, the firm would not have been able to get permission from the state and federal regulators to make this expansion if it had not bought this right.

Government agencies can reduce pollution by issuing transferable emissions permits. These permits can be bought and sold, much as the Times Mirror Company did, to accommodate growth. Suppose that you were an adviser to the Environmental Protection Agency and that you were asked to tell the agency's officials what determined the price of a permit. What's the answer? For simplicity, assume that there are many buyers and sellers of such permits, so the market for permits is competitive, and that each permit allows its owner to emit 1 ton of pollutants.

12. In choosing between taxes and standards to control the emissions of multiple polluters, taxes have the advantage of guaranteeing that the marginal costs of emissions abatement at each site are the same. Taxes, though, have the disadvantage that total emissions may vary from one period to the next as demand and cost conditions change; the expected damage caused by total emissions can therefore increase. Transferable permits pick up some of the advantage of taxes without increasing the expected cost of pollution because they fix total emissions even as they guarantee equal marginal costs of abatement at all sources. Explain how. Could taxes ever produce higher expected social welfare than a system of transferable permits? Why or why not?

13. Consider a lighthouse constructed to keep fishing boats away from treacherous rocks. The lighthouse can provide different levels of service at different cost. More powerful signals cost more but increase the probability that a boat would receive a timely warning. The figure shows the marginal cost of attaining various probabilities that a boat would be warned in time. Let there be three boats in the area, captained by Amos, Barnaby, and Columbus. The prices that each captain would pay for each level of service are also depicted on the graph. (a) Is the service provided by the lighthouse a nonrival good? (b) Is it nonexclusive? (c) What would be the efficient level of service, assuming that it is a public good? (d) Could the lighthouse be owned and operated privately?

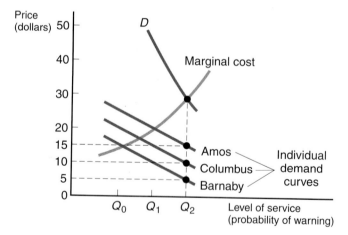

14. Recall that Chapters 12 and 13 presented some of the fundamentals of game theory. The point of those discussions was to demonstrate how economists use the theory of gaming to increase their understanding of how people behave when the outcomes of their actions depend on the actions and reactions of others. This example will exploit some fundamental game theory to examine how economic actors might overuse a common resource.

Suppose that two fishing companies, named Nantucket and Vineyard, worked the same fishery. Assume, as well, that daily profits are given by the payoff matrix shown in the figure (the units are thousands of dollars). Notice that the matrix reflects that each company has the option of sending one or two boats out to catch fish on any given day (assuming good weather).

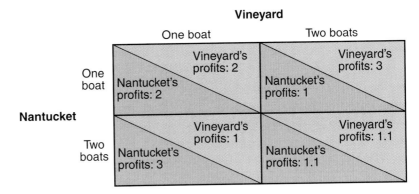

It is clear from the matrix that both firms are better off, collectively, if they refrain from overexploitation of the common resource—the fishery. Profits are higher if they share a modest catch than if they work to increase their short-term yields because the fishery has a fixed capacity. Overfishing can cause that capacity to decline in the long run, and overfishing quickly reaches the point of diminishing returns in the short run. The fishery represents the classic commons; and worrying about the fishing companies' physical realities is a classic issue of production externality.

(a) Is the game described in the payoff matrix a version of the prisoners' dilemma? What would the solution be if it were a one-shot game? How could the solution change over the long term if the game were played an indefinite number of times? (b) Suppose that the daily profits for both firms would be X (times $1,000) if both sent out two boats (instead of the $1,100 recorded in the matrix). Argue why the case in which $X > 1$ has been handled in part (a). (c) In contemplating the case in which $X < 1$, assume that the Vineyard Company incorporated its view of the likelihood that the Nantucket Company would send one boat out (instead of two) into its decision. Assume, in particular, that P (times 100 percent) represented Vineyard's view of the likelihood that Nantucket would send out one boat. Expected profits for the Vineyard Company would then be ($1,000)([2 times P] + [1 times $(1 - P)$]) = ($1,000)(1 + P) if it sent out one boat and ($1,000)([3 times P] + [X times $(1 - P)$]) = ($1,000)($X$ + [3 − X] times P) if it sent out two. Solve these two equations for a relationship that would define Vineyard's indifference between these two strategies. What would happen if Vineyard's perception of Nantucket's concern about overexploiting the fishery were expressed in terms of probabilities? What if, for example, Vineyard attached a higher probability to Nantucket's sending one boat out instead of two? Can you make any judgment about the correlation between the likelihood that one company would not excessively exploit the common fishery and its subjective view of whether or not its rival would do the same? If so, what would you conclude from this illustrative model?

Avoiding Dangerous Climate Change

As of January 2003, over 150 nations from six continents had signed the United Nations Framework Convention on Climate Change (the UNFCCC). The Climate Convention is a far-ranging document that commits its signatories to protecting the globe from "dangerous anthropogenic interference with the climate system" and to helping the most vulnerable nations on the planet improve their capacity to adapt to climate change.[1] The failed Kyoto Protocol was the first attempt at making the convention operational in anticipation that science would someday identify specific limits on the atmospheric concentrations of the so-called greenhouse gases that would accomplish the requisite protection. But its demise does not mean that limiting emissions of greenhouse gases through economically based climate policies is a dead issue. The Convention and its implicit call for reducing the emission of greenhouse gases are still taken seriously because the potential that climate change will cause significant harm is still hanging over us. This Applied Perspective will provide a brief introduction into both the why and the how of climate change. It will also show why a basic supply-and-demand model for fossil fuel can serve as a context within which we can examine the economic impacts of policies whose immediate objective is to reduce greenhouse gas emissions. Read it as if you were a decision-maker trying to understand the economics behind a global policy to reduce future emissions and concentrations of greenhouse gases. Or perhaps you are a representative of a developed or developing nation in climate negotiations. Or perhaps you are a concerned citizen trying to understand how the United States' position, as of June 2002, called for as many as 5 more years of scientific study to see what should be done.

In any case, of course, your first challenge is to understand the sources and consequences of climate change. The science is extraordinarily complicated, but the basic theory behind it is not. Stephen Schneider authored perhaps the most concise explanation of how the earth's atmosphere works to maintain a habitable temperature and how it might be altered by human activity.[2] He began by noting that clouds and particles in the atmosphere, together with the earth's surface, reflect roughly 30 percent of the incoming solar energy so that the remaining 70 percent of the energy is absorbed. This heats the surface of the earth and the atmosphere. An energy balance for the planet is achieved when some of this energy radiates into space, but only after energy trapped by clouds and greenhouse gases (GHGs) warms its surface. In fact, preindustrial concentrations of GHGs made the earth about 33°C warmer than it would have been otherwise, and increased concentrations can further warm the planet. Since it is now understood that concentrations are increasing from human activity, the fundamental questions

---

[1] Article 2 of the convention commits nations to stabilizing concentrations; Article 4 commits them to helping the most vulnerable to adapt. The full convention and support documents from at least seven meetings of the Conference of the Parties can be found on the UNFCCC Web site, www.unfccc.de.

[2] For a more complete description of the underlying science, see S. Schneider, "The Changing Climate," in *Managing the Planet—Readings from Scientific American,* (New York: W. H. Freeman, 1989), pp. 25–39.

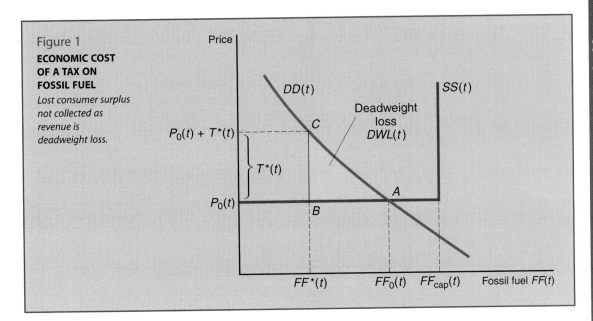

Figure 1

ECONOMIC COST OF A TAX ON FOSSIL FUEL

Lost consumer surplus not collected as revenue is deadweight loss.

are clear. How much higher will temperatures climb, and how fast? How will this warming be distributed across the globe? Will some regions warm more quickly than others? Will other regions actually grow colder? How will higher temperatures affect sea level? How might precipitation patterns change? Could warming change the frequencies and geographical distributions of extreme (weather) events? Might there be abrupt changes in climate? And for an economist like yourself, the issue is how much all of this might cost in adaptation expense and residual damage—this would be the benefit side of a global climate policy designed to reduce greenhouse gas emissions and concentrations.

If you take these questions seriously, then you must consider how policies might be designed to reduce the emission of greenhouse gases and thereby hold their atmospheric concentrations below yet-to-be-specified limits. This is the point of the Climate Convention, and it turns out that applying the foundations of supply and demand can provide some useful insight. To see how, consult Figure 1. A demand curve DD_t for fossil fuel is portrayed here for some future year t; so, too, is a perfectly elastic supply SS_t that would sustain equilibrium at $FF_0(t)$ if there were no policy interference. The policy problem will be interesting only if this "business as usual" quantity $FF_0(t)$ exceeds levels that would be consistent with achieving the goals of the Framework Convention. Adding an energy tax of $T^*(t)$ to the original equilibrium price $P_0(t)$ would work if $FF^*(t)$ were the targeted level for year t. So, too, would limiting total consumption to $FF^*(t)$ units, but only if the $FF^*(t)$ units were allocated efficiently across all sources of demand.

Now let's add some detail. Suppose, for example, that you wanted to gain some insight into how to minimize the economic cost of limiting concentrations of greenhouse gases in the atmosphere to the equivalent of 550 parts per million in volume (ppmv) of carbon by restricting fossil fuel consumption.

Figure 1 could help only if you understood its underlying structures so well that you could envision how they might change over time. Why would they change? Populations will grow over time. Economies will expand or contract. The relative prices of alternative energy sources will change. One or more distinct policy interventions will be imposed. And so on.

To add some specificity to your challenge, what would determine the position of the demand curve in Figure 1 for fossil fuel in year t? And how would demand change over time? What would determine the position of the supply curve? And how would supply change over time? How might a series of $FF^*(t)$ be determined if, as is the case, achieving a concentration target consistent with the Framework Convention were equivalent to limiting cumulative carbon emissions through, say, the year 2100 to a specific level? What would characterize an efficient allocation of the $FF^*(t)$ units of total consumption across the many sources of demand for fossil fuel, and how might a policy be designed to accomplish that allocation? And how could you estimate the economic cost of any policy intervention in any one year and over a period of up to 100 years? Each of these questions will be taken in turn, and answers based on fundamental microeconomic concepts will be offered along with references back to the relevant sections of the text. This discussion will not, however, be entirely academic. We will, at the end, integrate our new knowledge into a numerical exercise designed specifically to provide some insight into contemporary political and economic debate on climate policy.

A. POSITIONING THE DEMAND CURVE FOR ENERGY OVER TIME

Where would the demand curve for fossil fuel live at any point in time? Should it be elastic or inelastic? How would it move over time as economic activity expands in response to larger populations and/or larger capital stocks? These are the sorts of questions that can be answered only if we have a thorough understanding of the determinants of demand.

For the current context, it is sufficient to focus attention on industrial consumption of energy. Why? Because industrial emissions of carbon from the combustion of fossil fuel dominate the climate problem and are therefore the primary focus of much of climate policy. As a result, you can derive demand curve DD_t in Figure 1 directly from production processes. More to the point, you can conduct a useful analysis of prospective climate policy in the context of a function that relates the total value of goods and services (produced by a nation, a group of nations, or the globe as a whole) to the employment of a collection of inputs.[3] This may sound like a macroscale phenomenon, but it plants its roots in the same garden as the microscale production functions described in **Chapter 6.**

It turns out that four inputs provide sufficient texture to make the discussion interesting and informative. Labor comes to mind immediately because rates of population growth are important determinants of long-term sustainability and economic activity at any point in time. So does the stock of capital; it must be determined by intertemporal investment decisions that

---

[3]William Nordhaus and Joseph Boyer use this structure for nine regions that span the globe in their RICE-99 model; and they use a similar aggregate production function to explain global economic activity in DICE-99. See W. D. Nordhaus and J. Boyer, *Warming the World: Economics Models of Climate Change* (Cambridge, Mass.: MIT Press, 2000), pp. 232.

acknowledge the supply of labor and underlying rates of depreciation. Fossil fuel must be included, as well, because its combustion is the source of the climate problem; but fossil fuel cannot be the only source of energy. Some nonfossil sources of alternative energy and their associated price trajectories must be included to provide means other than simple conservation for reducing carbon emissions.

Climate modelers have adopted several conventions in conducting these sorts of analyses. First of all, they let the anticipated rate of growth of population be independent of economic activity. In the jargon of economics, therefore, they let the supply of labor be perfectly inelastic. Moreover, they adopt a long-run perspective by asserting that there is no unemployment. In addition, they take advantage of the notion that only relative prices matter so that we can make labor the numeraire; this is an approach that was first introduced in our discussions of general equilibrium in *Chapter 16.* They also assume that economic actors will try to minimize the economic cost of production; this brings the material of Part Three directly into play. *Chapter 7* taught you that cost-minimizing employment decisions at any point in time can be characterized by equality between the marginal-revenue products of all inputs, including fossil and nonfossil fuel, and their prices. But since marginal revenue product matches marginal product whenever output is measured in terms of total economic value, you quickly see that marginal-product schedules become derived demand curves for all four inputs.

So what determines the position and the elasticity of the demand curve for fossil fuel upon which we will build an analysis of climate policy? *Chapter 7* tells you that technology embodied in an aggregate production function, the stock of capital, price-sensitive consumption of nonfossil fuel, and population (labor through its contribution to output and thus investment) all play a role. The precise location of the derived demand for fossil fuel at any point in time depends on specific parameters, of course, but you can be certain that more population, more capital, and/or higher prices for nonfossil alternatives should cause the demand for fossil fuel to climb.

B. POSITIONING THE SUPPLY CURVE— EXTRACTION COST AND THE DETERMINANTS OF DEMAND OVER TIME

The same set of questions can be directed at the supply side of the market. Where would the supply curve for fossil fuel live at any point in time? Would it be elastic or inelastic? How would it adjust as an economy consumed larger and larger fractions of proven reserves? These are the sorts of questions that can be answered only if we have a thorough understanding of the determinants of supply.

As depicted in Figure 1, the supply side of the market for fossil fuel works best in the climate context when it is viewed as a series of perfectly elastic supply schedules that climb over time to reflect the economic implications of resource exhaustion. Why perfectly elastic (at least up to a capacity limit) for any given year, and why increasing over time? *Chapter 8* tells you to keep track of marginal cost when contemplating a supply curve; and Figure 2 displays one estimate of the long-term marginal cost of delivering fossil fuel to the market. Marginal cost increases at an increasing rate as cumulative extraction climbs, and the reason for this is quite simple. Suppliers exhaust

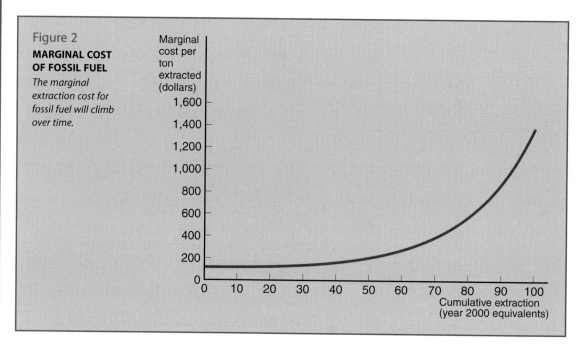

Figure 2

MARGINAL COST OF FOSSIL FUEL

The marginal extraction cost for fossil fuel will climb over time.

Marginal cost per ton extracted (dollars)

1,600
1,400
1,200
1,000
800
600
400
200
0

0 10 20 30 40 50 60 70 80 90 100

Cumulative extraction (year 2000 equivalents)

low-cost supplies of fossil fuel before moving to higher-cost sources. It follows immediately that the price of fossil fuel should climb over time at a rate determined by the rate of extraction. Use less fuel over an extended period of time, and the price should climb more slowly; but use more fuel over the same period of time, and the pace of rising energy prices should accelerate. In any one year, however, consumption should never be large enough to move very far along the cumulative marginal-cost curve. As a result, the supply curve should be horizontal (perhaps up to a capacity constraint like $FF_{cap}(t)$ in Figure 1) to reflect marginal cost that is constant over the short run.

C. SETTING CONSUMPTION TARGETS OVER TIME— ACHIEVING "WHEN" EFFICIENCY

The United Nations Framework Convention calls for limiting concentrations of greenhouse gases at a level that prevents "dangerous interference" with the climate system. We don't know what level that is, but scientists can tell us that achieving any concentration target is functionally equivalent to limiting cumulative carbon emissions over a long period of time (through, say, the year 2100). As a result, the challenge of meeting a concentration goal is the same as limiting the cumulative consumption of fossil fuel.[4] Armed with this insight, you can now see that the relevant policy question is one of efficiently allocating and pricing an (artificially) exhaustible resource over time.

[4]This is a bad assumption, of course, if we recognize that different types of fossil fuel—coal, oil, natural gas—have different carbon contents; but it makes the arithmetic a little easier for the moment.

Chapter 15 provided some direct insight into answering this question when it turned your attention to dynamic efficiency. You know from that discussion that, to a first-order approximation, we need only compute a scarcity price in excess of extraction cost that will

- Grow at the rate of interest,
- Be added into the price of fossil fuel along with marginal cost of extraction at any point in time, and
- Ultimately work through this growing wedge between the price paid by consumers and the price received by suppliers to limit cumulative consumption to the appropriate target.

This growing scarcity rent can function as the tax $T^*(t)$ in Figure 1, and the corresponding quantity target $FF^*(t)$ for any given year is simply the quantity associated with the sum of $T^*(t)$ and the contemporaneous marginal cost of extraction by the corresponding demand curve.

D. THE ECONOMIC COST OF CLIMATE POLICY

The notion of deadweight loss was employed repeatedly throughout the text as a metric of the economic cost caused by any market distortion or policy intervention that coerces a change in equilibrium. It should be no surprise that the economic cost of climate policy can be estimated by calculating the series of deadweight losses associated with systematic interventions in the evolving markets for fossil fuel. Referring again to Figure 1, more specifically, the deadweight loss caused by restricting consumption to $FF^*(t) < FF_0(t)$ in year t is the area of the usual triangle—area ABC. Who bears this loss? Consumers, who see the prices of goods and services climb with the cost of fossil fuel to a degree determined by producers' abilities to conserve energy and/or substitute into less expensive alternatives.

What about the long-term cost? How can we bring the economic cost of future policy interventions into the calculations when early reductions in consumption affect future extraction costs? By keeping track of the degree to which early interventions reduce pace of extraction and by anchoring deadweight loss calculations on lower future extraction costs. And how can the opportunity cost of a long-term climate policy be judged against the cost of other possible investments? *Chapter 15* makes it clear that computing the present discounted value of the series of annual deadweight losses would be appropriate.

E. ALLOCATING A CONSUMPTION TARGET ACROSS MULTIPLE SOURCES— ACHIEVING "WHERE" EFFICIENCY

Once the appropriate target has been defined for any given year, it must be allocated efficiently across multiple sources of demand for fossil fuel and carbon emissions. Setting a price by adding a tax equal to the scarcity rent to extraction cost would work. It would, by virtue of working through the horizontal addition of individual demand reflected in aggregate demand, cause all sources to set the marginal (revenue) product of fossil fuel consumption equal to the same after-tax price. You know from *Chapters 5 and 10* that such an allocation would minimize the economic cost of restricting total demand to $FF^*(t)$. It also follows that the cost-minimizing quantity allocation should mimic this cost-plus-tax outcome, and this can be achieved most effectively by allowing consumers to buy or sell permits to consume fossil fuel. The price of the permits would match the scarcity rent tax, and efficiency would be achieved.

F. SOME RESULTS FOR ALTERNATIVE CONCENTRATION TARGETS FROM A COMPUTABLE MODEL

We promised at the outset of this discussion that you would see more than a theoretical exercise, and so we now turn our attention to a specific economic/climate model built entirely from these fundamental constructions. Details of the model are provided in Section G. More complicated models rely on involved representations of production, particularly of the energy sector, and climate change; but our simple version works perfectly well in providing some reasonable insight into the cost of achieving specific concentration targets through the year 2100. We will, of course, try to convince you of its applicability by checking a few of our results against comparable calculations from the more elaborate constructions.

We begin, as a first experiment, by investigating how atmospheric concentrations might be limited to no more than 570 parts per million (ppmv)—a level equal to twice the concentration that characterized the planet before the start of the industrial revolution. Figure 3 shows how a least-cost intervention that achieves this goal would slow the consumption of fossil fuel over time. How was this regulated trajectory computed? As instructed by Section C, we searched for the smallest initial scarcity rent that would limit concentrations in 2100 to 570 ppmv if it were to grow at an annual rate equal to the rate of interest and if it were added to the marginal extraction cost of fossil fuel. How closely do these results match

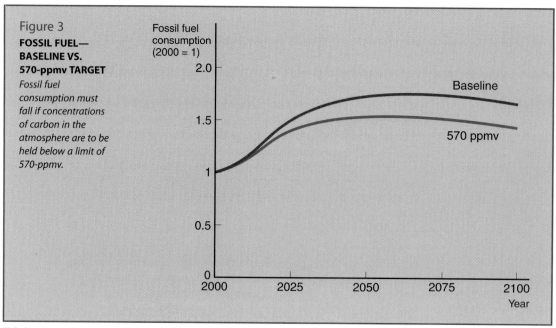

Figure 3

FOSSIL FUEL— BASELINE VS. 570-ppmv TARGET

Fossil fuel consumption must fall if concentrations of carbon in the atmosphere are to be held below a limit of 570-ppmv.

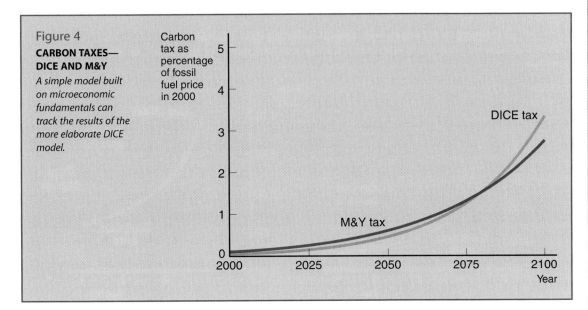

Figure 4

**CARBON TAXES—
DICE AND M&Y**

*A simple model built
on microeconomic
fundamentals can
track the results of the
more elaborate DICE
model.*

Carbon tax as percentage of fossil fuel price in 2000

DICE tax

M&Y tax

2000   2025   2050   2075   2100

Year

those reported from more elaborate models? Figure 4 tracks the requisite growing scarcity rent derived from this analysis and compares it with the comparable tax computed by Nordhaus and Boyer (2000) for a 570-ppmv target. Our "energy tax" is a little high early and a little low late, but it does not do too badly. Moreover, our estimated discounted cost, 2.8 percent of GDP in the year 2000, is only slightly larger than their published estimate of roughly 2.7 percent.

Returning to the geometric structure of Figure 1, we can also show how our model can be employed to depict how this intervention would influence both the supply and demand for fossil fuel over time. The various panels of Figure 5 do just that. Carefully notice that the vertical scales change as the future unfolds. This is required because demand shifts out and up over time—a reflection of how increased economic activity and changes in the relative price of nonfossil fuel would drive derived demand (recall Section A). Notice, as well, that the marginal extraction cost of fossil fuel climbs over time—a reflection of climbing extraction costs (recall Section B). Finally, the wedge between marginal extraction costs and the final price of fossil fuel (the expanding scarcity rent—the carbon tax) also expands with time—a reflection of the efficient scarcity rent described in Section C. The result is a series of deadweight losses that grow over time, represented by the shaded areas in three of the four panels. These areas are the source of our estimates of the present value of the long-term economic cost of achieving the 570-ppmv target (Section D).

Will climate negotiations eventually choose 570 ppmv as the concentration target that most appropriately reflects the mandate of the Climate Convention? (This is your problem to solve; remember.) Nobody knows, at this point, so it is important to explore how to accomplish efficient interventions

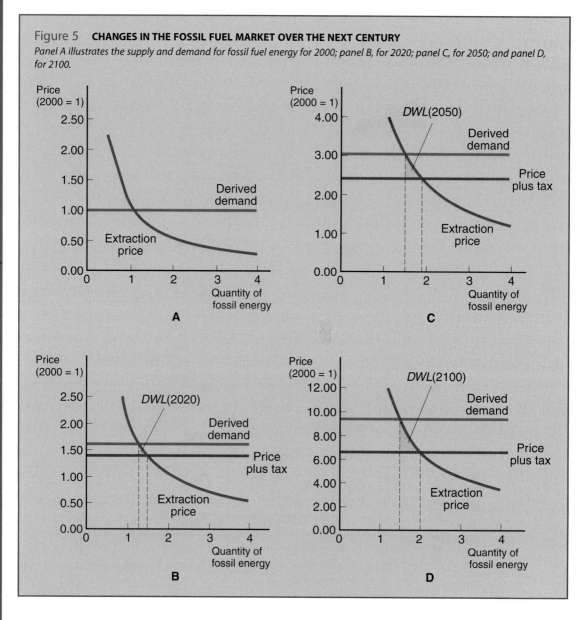

Figure 5 **CHANGES IN THE FOSSIL FUEL MARKET OVER THE NEXT CENTURY**

Panel A illustrates the supply and demand for fossil fuel energy for 2000; panel B, for 2020; panel C, for 2050; and panel D, for 2100.

to achieve different targets. Figure 6 displays trajectories of fossil fuel consumption and efficiency taxes for four alternative concentration targets running from 450 ppmv through 600 ppmv. Each target is feasible, but meeting the lower targets would be extraordinarily expensive. Our simple model suggests, for example, that the discounted cost of achieving a 450-ppmv target would be more than 50 percent of current world GDP. We cannot necessarily believe the number, but we can believe the qualitative result that the cost of meeting a 450-ppmv target would be *very* high; and so we have qualitative support for a very important conclusion. Limiting concentrations to levels

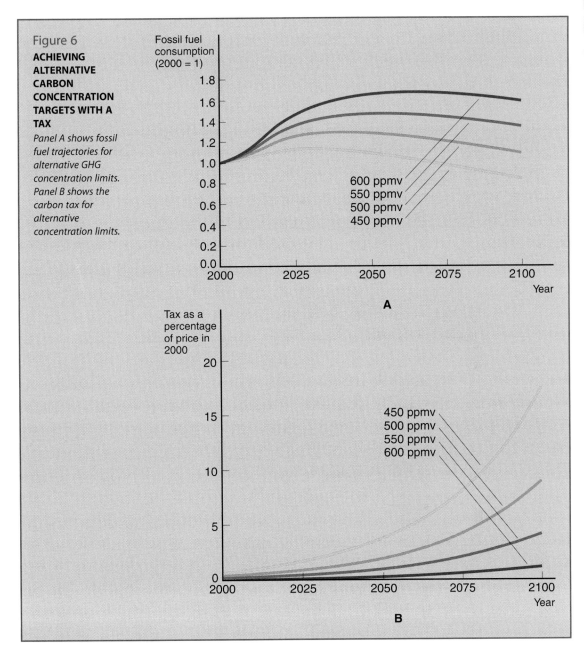

Figure 6

ACHIEVING ALTERNATIVE CARBON CONCENTRATION TARGETS WITH A TAX

Panel A shows fossil fuel trajectories for alternative GHG concentration limits. Panel B shows the carbon tax for alternative concentration limits.

that are very close to current levels (380 ppmv in 2000) would be a very expensive proposition regardless of when the decision was taken.

If your position favored doing nothing in the way of mitigating carbon emissions for a few decades, then deciding in 2030 to restrict concentrations to something like 550 ppmv could be comparably expensive even if current costs moderate. We can, in fact, run that experiment with our model. Suppose you turned the tax off until 2030. What would happen? The initial tax in 2030 would then be much higher than the one depicted in panel A of Figure 6, and the discounted cost of achieving the target would climb by roughly $250 billion (from 5.7 percent of current GDP to 6.7 percent).

G. A
COMPUTABLE
MODEL BASED
ON THE FIRST
PRINCIPLES OF
SUPPLY AND
DEMAND

1. The Demand Side of the Fossil Fuel Market

We begin construction of our model, as suggested in Section A, by postulating that the demand for fossil fuel can be derived from a production function with four inputs. More specifically, we adopt a Cobb-Douglas structure with constant returns to scale (recall **Chapter 6**) so that

$$Y(t) = F(L(t), K(t), FF(t), NF(t))$$
$$= A(t)L(t)^{\alpha}K(t)^{\beta}FF(t)^{\gamma}NF(t)^{1-\alpha-\beta-\gamma} \qquad [1]$$

where $A(t)$ reflects overall technological change through year t and $Y(t)$ represents the total value of economic output in year t produced by employing $L(t)$ units of labor, $K(t)$ units of capital, $FF(t)$ units of fossil fuel, and $NF(t)$ units of nonfossil fuel.[5] We let population grow exponentially at a rate denoted by g_L, so that

$$L(t) = L_0(1 + g_L)^t;$$

we let the productivity factor grow exponentially at a rate denoted by g_A so that

$$A(t) = A_0(1 + g_A)^t;$$

and we let the capital stock be determined by depreciation at some rate δ and investment $I(t)$ according to

$$K(t) = (1 - \delta)K(t - 1) + I(t). \qquad [2]$$

Microeconomic foundations described in **Chapter 15** would have us determine investment through an interaction of the supply and demand for loanable funds, but we simplify that structure by assuming that saving is always a constant fraction of output and that investment is always equal to saving; those of you who remember your macroeconomics will recall that this is a condition for macroeconomic equilibrium.

Turning now to the derived demand for energy, the marginal products of fossil and nonfossil fuels can be expressed in terms of output and employment. More to the point, the relevant marginal products for fossil and nonfossil fuel derived from the Cobb-Douglas technology of Equation 1 are simply given at any point in time by

$$MP_{FF}(t) = \frac{\gamma Y(t)}{FF(t)} \qquad [3a]$$

[5]Nordhaus and Boyer employ a Cobb-Douglas structure of this sort for each of the regions included in RICE-99 and for the globe in DICE-99.

and
$$MP_{NF}(t) = \frac{(1 - \alpha - \beta - \gamma)Y(t)}{NF(t)}, \qquad [3b]$$

respectively. Meanwhile, the output expansion path *(from Chapter 7)* in capital and fossil fuel can be defined in terms of the marginal rate of technical substitution between capital and fossil fuel, the price of capital (denoted by r), and the price of fossil fuel (denoted by $PF(t)$); that is, cost minimization guarantees that

$$MRTS(K(t); FF(t)) = \frac{r}{PF(t)}.$$

Since *Chapter 6* teaches us that this marginal rate of technical substitution is the ratio of marginal products, cost minimization also guarantees that

$$MRTS(K(t); FF(t)) = \frac{MP_K(t)}{MP_{FF}(t)}$$
$$= \frac{\beta FF(t)}{\gamma K(t)} = \frac{r}{PF(t)}. \qquad [4]$$

Equation 4 can finally be rearranged to produce the requisite derived demand for fossil fuel given $K(t)$ from Equation 3a:

$$FF(t) = \frac{r}{PF(t)} \frac{\gamma}{\beta} K(t). \qquad [5a]$$

Similarly, the output expansion path for the two types of energy shows that

$$NF(t) = \frac{PF(t)}{PN(t)} \frac{(1 - \alpha - \beta - \gamma)}{\gamma} FF(t). \qquad [5b]$$

Notice that both depend critically on the level of economic activity. This can be seen directly in the marginal-product representations displayed in Equation 3 and indirectly though $K(t)$ in the expansion path representations displayed in Equations 5.

2. The Supply Side of the Energy System

Turning now to the supply side of the fossil fuel market, let FF_{max} denote the level of proven reserves of fossil fuel. The long-run marginal cost of extraction can then be represented by an equation that sustains the shape depicted in Figure 2:

$$MC(F(t)) = PF_0 \frac{\text{cum}(F(t))}{FF_{max} - \text{cum}(F(t))} = PF(t) \qquad [6a]$$

where $\text{cum}(F(t))$ simply denotes cumulative consumption through year t; this is the baseline price of fossil fuel upon which policy intervention can be built. Meanwhile, let technological change in the supply of nonfossil fuel reduce its real price at some rate g_N so that the price of alternative energy can be

$$PN(t) = PN_0(1 - g_N)^t. \qquad [6b]$$

Notice that Equation 6b simply reflects the potential role of technological advance in alternative sources of energy through its price signal.

3. Links to the Atmosphere

All that remains is to calibrate the link between the consumption of fossil fuel and atmospheric concentrations. Following earlier modeling efforts from the climate community, we let σ(represent the carbon content of fossil fuel. Emissions in year t, denoted $E(t)$, are then given by

$$E(t) = \sigma FF(t). \qquad [7]$$

Concentrations in the atmosphere in any year t [denoted $M(t)$] can be linked to a first approximation to emissions by an "airborne fraction"; denoted ψ, this parameter represents the fraction of current emissions that remain airborne after one year's time. Since carbon "leaks" back out of the atmosphere slowly at some rate m, though,

$$M(t) = \psi E(t) - mM(t-1) = \psi\sigma FF(t) - mM(t-1). \qquad [8]$$

4. Calibrating the Model

Table 1 records values for the important parameters that calibrate our climate model. They were chosen (with one exception) to correspond

Table 1

CALIBRATING THE NUMERICAL MODEL

A. The production function

- $\alpha = 0.65$
- $\beta = 0.25$
- $\gamma = 0.03$

B. Driving parameters

- Productivity growth: 1.5% per year ($g_A = 0.015$)
- Population growth: 1.0% per year ($g_L = 0.01$)
- Depreciation: 10% per year ($\delta = 0.1$)
- Long-term interest rate: 2% per year ($r = 0.02$)
- Rate of change in the price of nonfossil fuel: 1% decline per year ($g_N = -0.01$)
- Fossil fuel reserves: 200 years ($FF_{max} = 2$)

C. Climate system

- Average carbon content of fossil fuel: 50% ($\sigma = 0.5$)
- Airborne fraction: 64% ($\psi = 0.64$)
- Atmospheric seepage factor: 1% per year ($m = 0.01$)
- Climate sensitivity to an effective doubling of carbon concentrations: 2.5°C
- Damage associated with 2.5° warming: 3% of gross world product

loosely with a leading model in the field—the DICE-99 model presented in Nordhaus and Boyer. The one exception? The production function sets global output in the year 2000 equal to 1 and indexes the prices of fossil and nonfossil fuel so that they also start at unity. One dollar is surely not a very close approximation of world economic product in 2000; that stood at something approximating $25 trillion plus or minus a few million. But starting at unity makes it easy to detect the overall pace of economic growth relative to the current benchmark. A value of 4 in the year 2050 would mean, for example, that output in 2050 was 4 times output in 2000.

ANALYTICAL QUESTIONS

1. Explain why the following six hypotheses make economic sense:
   (a) Higher population growth increases the taxes required to achieve any concentration target.
   (b) Slower rates of technological change in alternative energy sources increase the taxes required to achieve any concentration target.
   (c) Higher reserves of fossil fuels increase the taxes required to achieve any concentration target.
   (d) Higher carbon content of fossil fuel (i.e., increased reliance on coal versus oil or natural gas) increases the taxes required to achieve any concentration target.
   (e) Higher climate sensitivity (more temperature change for any increase in concentrations) or damage associated with any given climate change reduces the taxes required to achieve any concentration target.
   (f) Delay in mitigation increases the discounted cost of achieving any concentration target.

2. Now that you have seen that Figure 1 can be employed to portray how climate policy might work in the economic context, consider the following situation. International negotiations have thus far proceeded under the assumption that developing countries would not be subject to mitigation policy for the near to medium term. Use the general equilibrium constructions developed in *Chapter 16* to explore the implications of this presumption. In particular, start with two graphs of derived demand for fossil fuel—one for the developed world and one for the developing world. Pick a marginal extraction cost for some year t and depict equilibrium in the absence of policy intervention; for the sake of simplicity, assume that you are depicting a year where the quantity demanded in the developed world will be 3 times the quantity demanded by the developing world.

   Now pick an arbitrary carbon tax designed to restrain global emissions from reaching this equilibrium. This will be your benchmark. Assume that you must achieve the same reduction in total fossil fuel consumption without taxing fossil fuel in the developing world. Depict a new equilibrium. Finally, contemplate what would happen to marginal extraction cost and explain why the quantity demanded in the developing world might actually be larger than it would have been in the absence of any climate intervention.

3. Assume, for the sake of argument, that a price leader of the sort described in *Chapter 12* dominated the supply side of the global market for fossil fuel.

Assume, further, that this leader could and would adjust the price in response to climate policy so that its total revenue from the sale of fossil fuel could be maintained. Manipulate Figure 1 to show that this would reduce the tax required to sustain any demand target associated at any point in time with any concentration target.

4. We argued in *Chapter 15* that a monopolist would efficiently price an exhaustible resource because he or she would add an appropriate charge (inflated over time by the rate of interest) to the extraction cost. Why is monopolizing the supply side of the global fossil fuel market not a solution to the climate mitigation problem?

Glossary of Terms

Absolute advantage   A country has an absolute advantage over another country in the production of a particular good if it produces more of this good from a unit of resources than the other country does.

Adverse selection   Situation in which insurance companies find that a disproportionately large share of their customers come from high-risk groups.

Alternative cost   The value of the product that particular resources could have produced had they been used in the best alternative way; also called opportunity cost.

Arc elasticity of demand   If P_1 and Q_1 are the first values of price and quantity demanded, and P_2 and Q_2 are the second values, then arc elasticity equals $-[(Q_1 - Q_2)/(Q_1 + Q_2)]/[(P_1 - P_2)/(P_1 + P_2)]$.

Arc elasticity of supply   If P_1 and Q_1 are the first values of price and quantity supplied and if P_2 and Q_2 are the second values, then the arc elasticity of supply equals $[(Q_1 - Q_2)/(Q_1 + Q_2)]/[(P_1 - P_2)/(P_1 + P_2)]$.

Asymmetric information   The situation where two or more actors in an economic relationship have different information about each other and/or about their economic circumstance.

Auction   A market structure in which potential buyers make binding offers that indicate prices that they would be willing to pay for various items that have been put up for sale.

Average cost   Total cost divided by the quantity of output; also called average total cost.

Average fixed cost   Total fixed cost divided by the quantity of output.

Average product   Total output divided by the quantity of input.

Average variable cost   Total variable cost divided by the quantity of output.

Benefits   A cardinal measure of economic well-being expressed in currency units. Geometrically, benefits can be computed as the area under a demand curve in the absence of external economies or diseconomies of consumption.

Benefit-cost analysis   An economically based tool designed to inform decision makers who try to achieve the highest level (or at least higher levels) of total surplus. Calculating total benefits net of total costs is equivalent to calculating the sum of producer and consumer surplus. Benefits net of costs are maximized where marginal benefits equal marginal costs—a condition that is satisfied by equilibrium in a perfectly competitive market.

Budget line A line showing all combinations of quantities of good X and good Y the consumer can buy given a specific income. Its slope equals -1 times the price of good X divided by the price of good Y when X is measured along the horizontal axis and Y is measured along the vertical axis. The Y intercept in this case equals income divided by the price of Y.

Bundling A marketing technique whereby a firm that sells two products requires customers who buy one of them to buy the other as well.

Capital Equipment, buildings, inventories, and other non-human and producible resources that contribute to the production, marketing, and distribution of goods and services.

Cardinal utility Utility that is measurable in a cardinal sense, like a person's weight or height (which means that the difference between two utilities—i.e., marginal utility—is meaningful).

Cartel A form of market structure where there is an open and formal agreement among firms to collude in determining output, distribution, and/or price of a commodity.

Coase Theorem A result (attributed to Coase) that shows how, under a strict list of conditions, the efficient allocation of an economic good between two (types of) people would emerge from bilateral negotiations regardless of which person was originally granted ownership (property) rights to the good.

Cobb-Douglas production function A production function of the form $Q = AL^{a1}K^{a2}M^{a3}$, where Q is the output rate, L is the quantity of labor, K is the quantity of capital, M is the quantity of raw materials, and A, a_1, a_2, and a_3 are constants that are greater than 0 and less than 1.

Collusion Agreements by firms with others in their industry with regard to price, output, and other matters.

Common value auction An auction in which bidders come equipped with different estimates of the economic value of the item offered for sale.

Comparative advantage A country has a comparative advantage over another country in the production of a particular good if the cost of making this good, compared with the cost of making other goods, is lower in this country than in the other country.

Complements If goods X and Y are complements, the quantity demanded of X is inversely related to the price of Y.

Constant-cost industry An industry with a horizontal long-run supply curve and a linear cost function; its expansion does not result in an increase or decrease in input prices.

Constant returns to scale A condition in which output increases at the same rate as employment when the quantities of all inputs are increased or reduced at the same rate.

Consumer surplus The maximum amount that the consumer would pay for a particular good or service less the amount that he or she actually pays for it. Geometrically, it equals the area under the demand curve and above the price.

Contestable market A market in which entry is absolutely free and exit is absolutely costless. The essence of contestable markets is that they are vulnerable to hit-and-run entry.

Contract curve The locus of points where the marginal rates of substitution are the same for both consumers (in exchange between consumers) or the locus of points where the marginal rates of technical substitution are the same for both producers (in exchange between producers).

Cooperative game A game in which players can negotiate and enforce binding agreements with each other.

Corner solution Case in which the budget line reaches the highest achievable indifference curve at a point along an axis (analogous cases occur in the theory of production, too).

Cournot assumption Based on the Cournot model of oligopoly, the Cournot assumption refers to situations in which a player in a game expects that other players will not adjust their strategies in response to any action that he or she might undertake.

Cross elasticity of demand The percentage change in the quantity demanded of good X resulting from a 1 percent change in the price of some other good Y.

Deadweight loss A measure of welfare loss attributable to economic inefficiency; it is generally the sum of changes in producer plus consumer surplus.

Deadweight loss from monopoly If a perfectly competitive market is transformed into a monopoly, the deadweight loss is the reduction in total surplus resulting from this transformation.

Deadweight loss from monopsony If a perfectly competitive market is transformed into a monopsony, the deadweight loss is the reduction in total surplus resulting from this transformation.

Decreasing-cost industry An industry with a negatively sloped long-run supply curve; its expansion results in a decrease in average cost.

Decreasing returns to scale A situation in which output increases at a lower rate than inputs if the quantities of all inputs are increased at the same rate.

Deductible An amount of any loss that the insured must cover before his or her insurance policy kicks in with its coverage.

Demand curve A curve showing the quantity of a product demanded at each price.

Demand curve for loanable funds Relationship between the quantity of loanable funds demanded and the interest rate.

Discount rate When an interest rate is used to calculate the net present value of an investment, it is called the discount rate.

Dominant firm In an oligopolistic industry, a single large firm that sets the price but lets the small firms in the industry sell all they want at that price.

Dominant strategy A strategy that is best for a player regardless of the other players' strategy.

Duopoly A form of market structure in which there are two sellers. The Cournot model, among others, is concerned with duopoly.

Dutch auction An auction where the lower and lower prices are called until one bidder indicates that the downward sequence has finally reached a price at which he or she will agree to make the purchase.

Economic efficiency A situation in which all changes that harm no one and improve the well-being of some people have been accomplished. Such a situation is economically efficient (or Pareto efficient or Pareto optimal); no one can be made better off without hurting someone else.

Economic profit The difference between a firm's revenues and its costs, where the latter include the returns that could be gotten from the most lucrative alternative use of all of the firm's resources.

Economic resource A scarce resource that commands a nonzero price.

Economies of scope Economies resulting from the scope rather than the scale of the enterprise. They exist where it is less costly to combine two or more product lines in one firm than to produce them separately.

Efficiency wage The wage where no shirking takes place in a modeling context where an employee's productivity depends on how much he or she is paid.

Endowment position A consumer's initial allocation of income or bundles of goods.

Engel curve The relationship between the equilibrium quantity purchased of a good and the consumer's level of income.

English auction An auction where the higher and higher prices are called until the price is so high that only one bidder remains willing to make the purchase.

Equilibrium A situation in which there is no tendency for change. For example, an equilibrium price is a price that can be maintained.

Excess capacity The difference between the minimum-cost output and the actual output in a long-run equilibrium. A famous and controversial conclusion of the theory of monopolistic competition is that firms under this form of market structure will tend to operate with excess capacity.

Excise tax A per unit tax on the consumption of some good.

Exhaustible resource An economic resource whose total supply on the planet is limited.

Expansion path The locus of points where the isoquants corresponding to various outputs are tangent to the isocost curves (no inputs are fixed).

Expected monetary value To determine the expected monetary value of an uncertain situation, multiply the amount of money gained (or lost) with each outcome by the probability of its occurrence and add the resulting expected outcomes.

Expected profit The long-term average value of profit—that is, the (weighted) sum of the various possible levels of profit. The probabilities of occurrence are used as the weights.

Expected utility To determine the expected utility of an uncertain situation, multiply the utility associated with each possible outcome by the probability of its occurrence and add the resulting value.

Explicit costs The ordinary expenses of the firm that accountants include, such as payroll costs and payments for raw materials.

First-mover advantages   The advantages that accrue to the player who makes the first move in a game.

Fixed cost   The total cost per period of time of the fixed inputs.

Fixed input   A resource used in the production process (such as plant or equipment) whose quantity cannot be changed during the period under consideration.

Free rider   A person or group of people who earn benefits from the actions of others without paying compensation.

Game   A competitive situation in which two or more players pursue their own interests and no single player can necessarily dictate the outcome.

Game theory   A tool designed to facilitate our understanding of situations in which there is a mixture of conflict and cooperation between or among individuals.

Game tree   A schematic representation of how the outcomes of games depend on the strategic choices or players.

General equilibrium analysis   An analysis that (in contrast to a partial equilibrium analysis) takes account of the interrelationships among various markets and prices.

Giffen's paradox   A situation in which the quantity demanded of a good is directly related to its price. This occurs when the substitution effect of a price change is not strong enough to offset an inferior good's income effect.

Implicit costs   The alternative costs of using the resources owned by the firm's owner, such as his or her time and capital.

Income-compensated demand curve   A curve showing how much of a good the consumer demands at each price, when the consumer's income is adjusted so that, regardless of the price, the original market basket can be purchased.

Income-consumption curve   A curve connecting points representing equilibrium market baskets corresponding to all possible levels of the consumer's money income. Curves of this sort can be used to derive Engel curves.

Income effect   The change in the quantity demanded of good X due entirely to a change in the consumer's level of satisfaction, all prices being held constant.

Income elasticity of demand   The percentage change in quantity demanded resulting from a 1 percent change in consumer income when prices are held constant.

Increasing-cost industry   An industry with a positively sloped long-run supply curve; its expansion results in an increase in input prices.

Increasing returns to scale   A situation in which output increases faster than employment when all inputs are increased at the same rate.

Indifference curve   The locus of points representing market baskets among which the consumer is indifferent.

Inferior good   A good for which the income effect is negative, so that increases in real income result in decreases in the quantity demanded.

Input   Any resource used in the production process.

Insurance   An economic institution by which individuals can reduce their risk by purchasing some degree of coverage against various losses.

Interest rate   The premium received by the lender 1 year hence if he or she lends a dollar for a year. If the annual interest rate equals r, he or she receives $(1 + r)$ dollars a year hence.

Intermediate good   A good that is used to produce other goods and services.

Internal rate of return   The interest rate that equates the present value of the net cash inflows from an investment project to the project's investment outlay (i.e., to the present value of its cost).

Investment   The process of creating new capital assets.

Investment demand curve   The relationship between the total amount of investment and the rate of return from an extra dollar of investment.

Isocost curve   A curve showing the combinations of inputs that can be obtained for a fixed total outlay.

Isoprofit curve   A curve showing all input combinations that can produce a given level of profit.

Isoquant   A curve showing all possible (efficient) combinations of inputs that are capable of producing a certain quantity of output.

Isorevenue line   A line showing all combinations of outputs of two commodities that result in the same total revenue.

Labor   Human effort, physical or mental, used to produce goods and services.

Land   Natural resources, including both minerals and plots of ground, used to produce goods and services.

Law of diminishing marginal returns   According to this law, if equal increments of an input are added (and if the quantities of other inputs are held constant), the resulting increments of product will decrease beyond some point—that is, the marginal product of the input will eventually diminish.

Law of diminishing marginal utility   According to this law, as a person consumes more and more of a given commodity (the consumption of other commodities being held constant), the marginal utility of the commodity eventually will tend to decline.

Lerner index   A measure of the amount of monopoly power possessed by a firm. Specifically, it equals $(P - MC)/P$, where P is the firm's price and MC is its marginal cost.

Limit pricing   A form of pricing in which price is set so as to bar entry. A limit price is one that discourages or prevents entry.

Long run   The period of time in which all inputs are variable. The firm can change completely the resources it uses in the long run.

Marginal benefits   The change in benefits created as consumption increases by one unit.

Marginal cost   The addition to total cost resulting from the addition of the last unit of output.

Marginal cost pricing A pricing rule whereby firms or government-owned enterprises set price equal to marginal cost.

Marginal expenditure curve A curve showing the additional cost to the firm of increasing its utilization of input X by 1 unit.

Marginal product The addition to total output due to the addition of the last unit of an input (when the quantity of other inputs is held constant).

Marginal rate of product transformation The negative of the slope of the production possibilities curve. It represents the amount of one good that must be sacrificed to allow resources to be devoted to the production of one more unit of some other good.

Marginal Rate of Technical Substitution The number of units of come input I that must be added to a production process to exactly compensate for the loss of one unit of some other input J so that the output level is unchanged.

Marginal rate of substitution The number of units of good Y that must be given up if the consumer, after receiving an extra unit of good X, is to maintain a constant level of satisfaction.

Marginal revenue The addition to total revenue due to selling 1 more unit of the product.

Marginal revenue product The increase in total revenue due to the use of an additional unit of input X. It equals the marginal product of input X times the firm's marginal revenue.

Marginal utility The additional satisfaction (utility) derived from an additional unit of a commodity (when the levels of consumption of all other commodities are held constant).

Market A group of firms and individuals in touch with each other in order to buy or sell some good.

Market demand curve A curve that shows the relationship between a product's price and the quantity of it demanded in the entire market.

Market demand schedule A table that shows the relationship between a product's price and the quantity of it demanded in the entire market.

Market distortion Any economic condition that causes the market equilibrium to deviate from the efficient allocation.

Market period A period of time during which the quantity that is supplied of a good is fixed.

Market signaling A mechanism by which information about a product or input is conveyed to the market before a transaction occurs.

Market structure Four general types of market structure are perfect competition, monopoly, monopolistic competition, and oligopoly. The structure of a market depends on the number of buyers and sellers, as well as the extent of product differentiation and other factors.

Market supply curve A curve that shows the relationship between a product's price and the quantity willingly supplied across the entire market.

Market supply schedule A table showing the quantity of a good that would be supplied at various prices. Supply curves do not exist for all forms of market structure (e.g., monopolists do not have supply curves).

Markup A percentage (or absolute) amount added to a product's estimated average (or marginal) cost to obtain its price; this amount is meant to include costs that cannot be allocated to any specific product and to provide a return on the firm's investment.

Maximin strategy A strategy that strives to maximize the value of the worst possible outcome.

Microeconomics The part of economics dealing with the economic behavior of individual units such as consumers, firms, and resource owners (in contrast to macroeconomics, which deals with the behavior of economic aggregates like gross domestic product).

Model A theory based on assumptions that simplify and abstract from reality and from which predictions or conclusions about the real world are deduced.

Money income Income of the consumer measured in actual dollar amounts per period of time.

Monopolistic competition A market structure in which there are many sellers of differentiated products, entry is easy, and there is no collusion among sellers.

Monopoly A market structure in which there is only one seller of a product.

Monopsony A market structure in which there is only a single buyer.

Moral hazard Phenomenon by which a person's or firm's behavior may change after buying insurance so as to increase the probability of theft, fire, or other loss covered by the insurance.

Multinational firm A firm that invests in other countries and produces and markets its products abroad.

Multiplant monopoly A monopolist that owns and operates more than one plant and that must determine the output of each of its plants.

Multiproduct firm A firm that produces more than one product.

Nash equilibrium An equilibrium in game theory where, given every other player's chosen strategies, each player has no reason to change his or her own strategy.

Natural monopoly An industry in which the average cost of production reaches a minimum at an output rate large enough to satisfy the entire market, thus competition cannot be sustained and one firm becomes the monopolist.

Negative externality An uncompensated cost imposed on one person by the actions of another.

Net-present-value rule The rule that a firm should carry out any investment project with a positive net present value. An investment's net present value is the present value of its future cash flows minus its cost.

Non-cooperative game A game in which players cannot create or enforce agreements between or among themselves.

Nondiversifiable risk Risk that cannot be reduced by diversification.

Nonprice competition Rivalry among firms that use advertising and other marketing weapons, as well as variation in product characteristics due to research and development and style changes.

Normal goods Goods that experience increases in quantity demanded in response to increases in the consumer's real income.

Oligopoly A market structure in which there are only a few sellers of products that can be identical or differentiated.

Opportunity cost The value of the product that particular resources could have produced if they had been used in the best alternative way; also called alternative cost.

Optimal input combination The combination of inputs that is economically efficient or that maximizes profit (that is, is optimal from a profit-maximizing firm's point of view), or both.

Ordinal utility Utility that is measurable in an ordinal sense, which means that a consumer can only rank various market baskets with respect to the satisfaction they give him or her.

Pareto criterion A criterion to determine whether a particular change is an improvement; according to this criterion, a change that harms no one and improves the lot of some people (in their own eyes) is an improvement.

Partial equilibrium analysis An analysis assuming (in contrast to a general equilibrium analysis) that changes in price in a particular market can occur without causing significant changes in price in other markets.

Payoff matrix A matrix that indicates the payoffs received by every player in a game for every combination of player strategies.

Pecuniary benefits Benefits arising because of changes in relative prices that come about as the economy adjusts to a project (as distinguished from real benefits, which augment society's welfare).

Perfect competition A market structure in which there are many sellers of identical products, no one buyer or seller has control over price, entry is easy, and resources can switch readily from one use to another.

Perpetuity A bond that pays a fixed annual amount of interest forever.

Positive externality An uncompensated benefit received by one person as a result of the actions of another.

Precautionary principle A decision principle by which people choose to hold the risk of some event below some selected theshold.

Predatory pricing The practice of setting price at a low level in order to drive a rival firm out of business.

Present value The value today of a payment, or stream of payments, now and in the future (or in the past).

Price ceiling A government-imposed maximum for the price of a particular good.

Price-consumption curve A curve connecting the various equilibrium points corresponding to market baskets chosen by the consumer at various prices of a commodity.

Price discrimination The practice whereby one buyer is charged more than another buyer for the same product.

Price elastic Description of the demand for a product if its price elasticity of demand exceeds 1.

Price elasticity of demand The percentage change in quantity demanded resulting from a 1 percent change in price (by convention, always expressed as a positive number).

Price elasticity of supply The percentage change in quantity supplied resulting from a 1 percent change in price.

Price floor A government-imposed minimum for the price of a particular good.

Price inelastic Description of the demand for a product if its price elasticity of demand is less than 1.

Price leader A firm in an oligopolistic industry that sets a price that other firms are willing to follow.

Price system A system in which each good and service has a price and that, in a purely capitalistic economy, carries out the basic functions of an economic system (determining what will be produced, how it will be produced, how much of it each person will get, and what the country's growth of per capita output will be).

Principal-agent problem The problem that arises because managers or workers may pursue their own objectives, even though this reduces the profits of the owners of the firm. The managers or workers are agents who work for the owners, who are the principals.

Prisoners' dilemma A situation in which two persons (or firms) would both do better to cooperate than not to cooperate, but in which each feels it is in his or her interests not to do so; therefore each fares worse than if they cooperated.

Private cost The expense incurred by the individual user to obtain the use of a resource.

Private value auction An auction in which bidders come to the auction with known person valuations of the item offered for sale.

Probability The proportion of times that a particular outcome occurs over the long run.

Producer surplus The aggregate profits of firms making a good plus the amount that owners of inputs (used to make the good) are compensated above and beyond the minimum they would insist on. Geometrically, it equals the area above the supply curve and below the price.

Production function The relationship between the quantities of various inputs used per period of time and the maximum amount of output that can be produced per period of time.

Production possibility curve A curve showing the various combinations of quantities of two products that can be produced with a given amount of resources.

Profit The difference between a firm's revenue and its total economic costs; it is also called "economic profit."

Public good A good that is nonrival and nonexclusive. Nonrival means that the marginal cost of providing the good to an additional consumer is zero. Nonexclusive means that people cannot be excluded from consuming the good (whether or not they pay for it).

Pure rate of time preference A reflection of the rate at which an individual would trade a dollar's worth of consumption today for future consumption.

Quasi-rent   A payment to an input in temporarily fixed supply. For example, in the short run, a firm's plant cannot be altered, and the payments to this and other fixed inputs are quasi-rents.

Quota   a limit imposed on the amount of a commodity that can be imported annually.

Ray   A line that starts from some point and goes off into space. If capital is on one axis and labor is on the other, a ray from the origin describes all input combinations where the capital-labor ratio is constant.

Reaction curve   A curve showing how much one duopolist will produce and sell, depending on how much it thinks the other duopolist will produce and sell.

Real benefits   Benefits that augment society's welfare (as distinguished from pecuniary benefits, which arise because of changes in relative prices that come about as the economy adjusts to a project).

Rent   The return paid to an input that is fixed in supply.

Repeated game   A game that is repeated regularly over time.

Risk   A situation in which the outcome is not certain but the probability of each possible outcome is known or can be estimated.

Risk averters   When confronted with gambles with equal expected monetary values, rick averters prefer a gamble with a more-certain outcome to one with a less-certain outcome.

Risk lovers   When confronted with gambles with equal expected monetary values, risk lovers prefer a gamble with a less-certain outcome to one with a more-certain outcome.

Risk neutral   Risk-neutral individuals do not care whether a gamble has a less-certain or more-certain outcome. They choose among gambles on the basis of expected monetary value alone; specifically, they maximize expected monetary value.

Saving   A consumer's refraining from consuming part of the goods that he or she has.

Sealed-bid auction   An auction in which participants submit sealed for the item offered for sale within a specified time frame.

Second-degree price discrimination   Strategy by which a monopolist charges a different price depending on how much the consumer purchases, thus increasing the monopolist's revenues and profit.

Short run   A period of time in which some of the firm's inputs (generally its plant and equipment) are fixed in quantity.

Social cost   The cost to society of producing a given commodity or taking a particular action. This cost may not equal the private cost.

Static efficiency   Efficiency when technology and tastes are fixed. If departures from static efficiency result in a faster rate of technological change and productivity increase, they may lead to a higher level of consumer satisfaction than if the conditions for static efficiency are met.

Strategic move   A move that influences the other person's choice in a manner favorable to oneself by affecting the other person's expectations of how oneself will behave.

Substitutes   If goods X and Y are substitutes, the quantity demanded of X is directly related to the price of Y.

Substitution effect   The change in the quantity demanded of a good resulting from a price change when the level of satisfaction of the consumer is held constant.

Supply curve   A curve that shows how much of a product will be supplied at each level of the product's price.

Supply curve of loanable funds   The relationship between the quantity of loanable funds supplied and the interest rate.

Tariff   A tax imposed by the government on imported goods (designed to cut down on imports and thus protect domestic industry and workers from foreign competition).

Technological change   New ways of producing existing products, new designs enabling the production of new products, and new techniques of organization, marketing, and management.

Technology   Society's pool of knowledge regarding how goods and services can be produced from a given amount of resources.

Third-degree price discrimination   A situation in which a monopolist sells a good in more than one market, the good cannot be transferred from one market and resold in another, and the monopolist can set different prices in different markets.

Tit for tat   A strategy in game theory in which each player does on this round what the other player did on the previous round.

Total cost   The sum of a firm's total fixed cost and total variable cost.

Total cost function   Relationship between a firm's total cost and its output.

Total fixed cost   A firm's total expenditure on fixed inputs per period of time.

Total revenue   A firm's total dollar sales volume per period of time.

Total surplus   The sum of consumer and producer surpluses.

Total utility   A number representing the level of satisfaction that a consumer derives from a particular market basket.

Total variable cost   A firm's total expenditure on variable inputs per period of time.

Transaction cost   The cost of bringing buyers and sellers together, contracting, and obtaining information concerning the market.

Transferable emissions permits   Permits to generate a certain amount of pollution, limited in number, that are allocated among firms and that can be bought or sold.

Two-part tariff   A pricing technique whereby the consumer pays an initial fee for the right to buy the product as well as a usage fee for each unit of the product that he or she buys.

Tying   A marketing technique whereby a firm producing a product that will function only if used in conjunction with another product requires its customers to buy the latter product from it, rather than from alternative suppliers.

Unitary elasticity   An elasticity equal to 1.

Utility   A number that represents the level of satisfaction that the consumer derives from a particular market basket.

Utility possibilities curve   A curve showing the maximum utility that one person can achieve, given the utility achieved by another person.

Value of information   The increase in economic well being that can be achieved by taking advantage of new information that changes the degree of uncertainty (and perhaps eliminates uncertainty altogether). For risk-neutral decision makers, it is the difference in the expected monetary outcome that can be achieved with and without using the information. For risk-averse decision makers, it is the difference in the risk premiums that they would pay to eliminate uncertainty with and without using the information. In either case, it is the maximum amount that people would pay to obtain the new information.

Value of marginal product   The marginal product of an input (that is, the extra output resulting from an extra unit of the input) multiplied by the product's price.

Variable cost   The total cost per period of time of the variable inputs.

Variable input   A resource used in the production process whose quantity can be changed during the particular period under consideration.

von Neumann–Morgenstern utility function   A function showing the utility that a decision maker attaches to each possible outcome of a gamble; it shows the decision maker's preferences with regard to risk.

Winner's curse   If a number of bids are made for a particular piece of land (or other good or asset) and if the bidders' estimates of the land's value are approximately correct, on average, the highest bidder is likely to pay more for the land than it is worth if each bidder bids what he or she thinks the land is worth.

Brief Answers to Odd-Numbered Questions

1. The price of medical care will tend to rise if the quantity of medical care demanded goes up while the quantity supplied remains constant. Medicare and Medicaid would have been expected to increase the quantity demanded. An economic model of demand would allow you to explore how and why.

3. (a) The number of cigarettes bootlegged into a particular state depends on this state's tax rate relative to that of its neighboring states. If a state's tax rate is much higher than that of its neighbors, bootleggers can make money by bringing cigarettes into that state. Also, the number bootlegged into a particular state depends on the cost of transporting the cigarettes. The higher the cost per mile of transporting a truckload of cigarettes, the smaller the distance it is profitable to take them. (b) No. Florida's loss from tax evasion was over 15 percent of that in all states, which is disproportionately large. Its tax rate, therefore, would be expected to have been higher than that of neighboring states (which in fact was true). (c) Since its loss from tax evasion increased (while that in other states decreased) from 1975 to 1979, one would expect that the amount of tax levied increased relative to the amount levied in neighboring states. In fact, it increased its tax by 3 cents per pack. (d) Yes. The cost of transporting the cigarettes increased.

5. This is a complicated one, but the underlying fundamentals can be illustrated by supply and demand. There may be a supply effect—lots of people pursuing advanced degrees in history and sociology; indeed, history majors frequently outnumber all but English majors on liberal arts colleges. The stronger explanation lies on the demand side of these markets, though. Economists and computer scientists can work in business, government, and the academy; professionals from other disciplines frequently do not have alternatives. The basic theory therefore predicts that higher demand for economists and computer scientists should result in higher salaries.

7. Yes, because the latter statements reflect the value judgments of the economist.

9. (a) Supply fell. (b) Substitution is a reasonable response to higher relative prices. (c) It is hard to tell if producers were hurt. Their revenue could go up or down depending upon the price response. If prices rose faster than quantities fell (in percentage terms), then total revenue could actually climb.

11. The quantity demanded would equal the quantity supplied at 10 units with a price of $80, so expect the price to increase by $10 because there is excess demand at a $70 price.

13. Working with something like Figure 1.7 would do quite nicely. As the time for responding expands, more options become available. As a result, a short-run demand curve could be quite steeply sloped while a long-run demand curve, starting at the same price and quantity, could be far less sloped.

15. Supply is quite limited. Indeed, at the time of auction, there was one authentic copy of the Declaration available. Demand would climb with interest, but supply could not. The result was nothing but pressure on the price to climb.

CHAPTER 2

1. $1,000, since the budget line intersects the vertical axis at 20. $Q_A = 20 - 0.5Q_B$, where Q_A is the quantity consumed of good A and Q_B is the quantity consumed of good B. The slope is $-(20/40) = -0.5$. The price of good B must be $1,000/40, or $25. Her marginal rate of substitution in equilibrium is 0.5.

3. MRS reflects the rate of exchange; it is constant at 1 pound of meat for 1 pound of potatoes. It does not change. Realistic? Probably not, unless you consider small changes. The indifference curves would be linear with a slope of -1. Patricia would prefer meat or potatoes completely, but only if the price of meat were less than the price of potatoes, respectively. If the price of meat were higher, then she would want only potatoes. If the price were lower, then she would prefer meat.

5. The statement is a bit vague, but is okay. All that is required for consumer theory to work is that people have preferences that can be translated into rankings of over bundles of goods. Analytical techniques can provide numbers that reflect these rankings, and order is all that matters.

7. For the consumer, 2 pounds of steak is equivalent to 3 pounds of hamburger, but the market is willing to equate 2 pounds of steak to 4 pounds of hamburger, because the price of steak is twice the price of hamburger. Reducing the consumption (and purchase) of steak by 2 pounds would cost the consumer the utility equivalent of 3 pounds of hamburger, but it would allow her to increase consumption of hamburger by 4 pounds. Utility would therefore increase by the utility value of 1 pound of hamburger. If the price of steak were 50 percent higher than hamburger, then the consumer would be inequilibrium.

9. Draw A on the vertical axis and B on the horizontal axis. Spending $4,000 per month, Walcott could afford 20 units of A, and 5 units of B. These are the A- and B-axis intercepts. The slope of the budget line connecting these intercepts is $-(20/5) = -4$; it is also equal in magnitude to the ratio of the price of B over the price of A ($800/$200). If the price of A rose to $400 per unit, then Walcott could afford 10 units of A, and the slope would be equal to $-(10/5) = -($800/400) = -2$. The budget line would rotate around the fixed B-intercept (the maximum amount of B that could be purchased would not have changed, so that point would be the only original combination of A and B that Walcott could still afford). If both prices fell by 50 percent, the slope of the budget constraint would remain the same, but it would shift outward by 100 percent (with intercepts of 40 and 10 for the original prices). If both prices and income rose by 50 percent at the same time, then the budget constraint would not change at all.

11. If the threshold were real, then Coke and Pepsi are perfect substitutes as long as their relative prices are do not deviate far from unity.

CHAPTER 3

1. (a) The area under the curve from the 6th visit to the 10th is ($6 + $4 + $3 + $2 + $1) = $16. (b) The total area under the curve adds ($20 + $16 + $12 + $10 + $8) to $16 for a grand total of $82. Net of a $75 fee, benefits would be $7, so they would buy the permit. (c) Convex. (d) An $8 charge would support 5 trips. Total value is $66, but the total charge would be $40 = $8 · 5; consumer surplus would equal ($66 − $40) = $26. For a $4 charge, 7 visits would be enjoyed with total benefit of $66 + $6 + $4 = $76. These 7 visits would therefore produce $76 − $28 = $38 in consumer surplus.

3. (a) Yes. (b) If all consumers are maximizing utility (and if the optimal point is a tangency point, not a corner solution), then the marginal rate of substitution of telephone calls for newspapers must equal the price of a telephone call divided by the price of a newspaper. (c) No, the marginal rate of substitution for both consumers equals 25/50, or 0.5, regardless of where the tangency occurs.

5. Take, for example, off-premises food with an income elasticity of 0.28. Then plot consumption indexed to 100, 102.8, 128.0, and 184.0 for income indexed at 100, 110, 200, and 400, respectively. These are computed by adding the product of the elasticity and the percentage increase in income, so a 10 percent increase in income would increase consumption by 0.28 × 10 = 2.8 for an index number of 102.8. (a) The Engel curves would be nearly linear for goods with income elasticities close to 1: motor vehicles and parts, furniture and appliances (although this should show some discernible bend), and purchased meals. (b) A perfectly linear Engel curve means an income elasticity of 1. (c) 1 percent.

7. The Bureau of Labor Statistics would have difficulty keeping up with the new products and capturing the substitution in their surveys. That people spend lots of their money on these goods makes the issue significant.

9. (a) Adding the tax to the price of gasoline would change the slope all by itself. (b) The resulting change in price would be reflected by moving up along the existing demand curve. (c) Adding income to the individual in the form of the rebate would shift the demand curve, rotating it to something more inelastic around the original pre-tax price-quantity pair. (d) Referring to the graph in Example 4.2, note that the reduction in quantity demanded would be smaller with the rebate than without it.

CHAPTER 4

1. (a) A 1 percent increase in the price of electricity would cut electricity consumption by about 1.2 percent, because the price elasticity of demand is 1.2. A 6 percent increase in the price of natural gas would raise electricity consumption by about 1.2 percent, because the cross elasticity of demand is 0.2. Thus, if the price of natural gas were to increase by about 6 percent, this would offset the effect of the increase in the price of electricity. (b) On the basis of the data in the table, a 10 percent increase in income seems to result in about a 1 percent increase in electricity consumption. Thus, the income elasticity seems to be about 0.1, not 0.2. This discrepancy could be due to the fact that the inhabitants of this suburb regard electricity as more of a necessity than do most other Americans. (c) Both would be expected to be lower in the short run because consumers have less time to adapt to changes in income or price. In fact, Chapman, Tyrell, and Mount found both to be about 0.02 in the short run.

3. (a) There are a considerable number of important substitutes, notably plastics, aluminum, and concrete. For example, buildings and bridges formerly requiring structural steel can now use prestressed concrete. (b) No, because the demand curve for the output of a single firm (Bethlehem) is not the same as the demand curve for the output of the steel industry as a whole. In general, we would expect the demand curve for the output of a single firm to be more price elastic than the demand curve for the industry as a whole because the output of other firms in the industry can be substituted for the output of the firm in question. (c) If the demand for a firm's product is inelastic, its price elasticity of demand is less than 1. It follows from Equation 5.3 that the firm's marginal revenue must be negative. Since marginal revenue is the change in total revenue attributable to the increase of 1 unit to sales, it follows that a reduction in the amount produced and sold by the firm would increase total revenue (because price would be raised enough to more than offset the smaller number of units sold). In a case of this sort, the firm could increase its profit by reducing its output (and raising its price). Why? Because profit equals total revenue minus total cost, and a reduction in output would

increase total revenue and reduce total cost (since it would cost less to produce fewer units). Consequently, a reduction in output would increase profit; this means that the firm is not currently maximizing its profit. (d) The cross elasticity of demand is positive because Bethlehem steel and imported Japanese steel are substitutes.

5. Holding his income constant, the total amount he spends on Doritos is constant, too. That is, $PQ = I$, where P is the price of Doritos, Q is the quantity demanded by the consumer, and I is his income. As a result, $Q = I/P$. Since I is held constant, this demand curve is a rectangular hyperbola, and the price elasticity of demand equals 1. Since $Q = I/P$, it follows that a 1 percent increase in I will result in a 1 percent increase in Q when P is held constant. The income elasticity of demand equals 1. Since Q does not depend on the price of any other good, the cross elasticity of demand equals 0. When a consumer spends only 50 percent of her income on Doritos, then the demand curve can be derived from $PQ = I/2$, but all of the elasticity answers stay the same.

7. Substitutes have a positive cross elasticity of demand. Thus cases (b) and (e) are likely to have a positive cross elasticity of demand.

9. The price elasticity of demand would indicate the extent to which fare increases would decrease subway travel. For example, if demand were price inelastic, then fare increases would increase total revenue. Obviously, this is an important fact that might alter the mayor's view of the value of the "Big Dig" highway construction project. Income elasticity might also play a role.

11. Other factors—notably the general level of prices and incomes and the quality of the students—have not been held constant. Holding these factors—and the tuition rates at other universities—constant, it is almost surely false that large increases in tuition at this university would not reduce the number of students applying for admission to the university.

13. The Engel curve shows the relationship between money income and the amount of a particular commodity consumed. If this relationship is a straight line through the origin, it follows that the amount of this commodity consumed is proportional to the consumer's money income. Thus, a 1 percent increase in the consumer's money income results in a 1 percent increase in the amount consumed of this commodity. Consequently, the income elasticity of demand for this commodity equals 1.

15. No. Water cannot be transported from one geographic market to another, so there is no way a consumer in New England could buy California water.

17. (a) Let P_1 be the "bargain" price of $19.92, P_2 be the preconvention price of $29, Q_{D1} be the quantity of lunches demanded at the "bargain" price, and Q_{D2} be the quantity demanded at the preconvention price. Then the arc elasticity of demand equals

$$\eta = -\frac{\Delta Q_D}{(Q_{D1} + Q_{D2})/2} \div \frac{\Delta P}{(P_1 + P_2)/2}$$
$$= -\frac{150 - 40}{(150 + 40)/2} \div \frac{19.92 - 29}{19.92 + 29/2} = 3.1.$$

Thus, the price elasticity of demand equals 3.1. (b) Yes. Daily expenditure on lunches was $40 \times \$29 = \$1,160$ before the price reduction and $150 \times \$19.92 = \$2,988$ afterward. This is consistent with out finding in part (a) that the price elasticity of demand is 3.1. If the price elasticity of demand exceeds 1, a price reduction must lead to an increase in expenditure. (c) Yes. The first restaurant reduced its price by ($29 − $19.92)/$29 = 31 percent; the other restaurant reduced its price by ($24 − $19.92)/$24 = 17 percent, since its preconvention price was $29 − $5 = $24. Given that the price elasticity of demand is the same at both restaurants, the percentage increase in quantity demanded must be greater at the first than at the second because the first reduced its price by a greater percentage than the second. (d) The first restaurant increased its daily revenue from lunches by $2,988 − $1,160 = $1,828. If the extra cost of serving the $150 − 40 = 110$ extra lunches exceeded $1,828, it lost money.

19. The elasticity at any point is $\{P/X\}\{1/(\text{slope})\}$. Quantities for the three prices are $(a/4b)$, $(a/2b)$, and $(3a/4b)$, respectively; and the slope is b. So, just plug prices, quantities, and the slope into the formula. For price $\$(a/4)$ for example, the elasticity would be $\{(a/4)/(3a/4b)\}\{1/b\} = \{b/3\}\{1/b\} = (1/3)$.

CHAPTER 5

1. (a) No. If the prize for the winner is $1,000,000 and the prize for the runner-up is $0, then Tiger and David would be sure to receive $500,000 if they agreed to the split. If they did not, though, then both would be involved in a gamble where the probability of winning $1,000,000 would be .5 and the probability of winning $0 would be .5. The expected monetary value of this gamble is $500,000. But since a risk lover prefers a less certain outcome given an equal expected monetary value, then neither would prefer to split. (b) If the players split, then they would surely receive $500,000; thus the expected utility is 15. If they did not split, then the expected utility would be 0.5 times the utility of $1,000,000 plus 0.5 times the utility of $0; that is, it would equal $(.5 \times 20) + (.5 \times 0) = 10$. Since the expected utility of splitting exceeds that of not splitting, neither would want to pass up the opportunity to split. (c) If P were the top-seeded player's probability of winning, then his expected utility of not splitting would equal $(P \times 20) + [(1 − P) \times 0]$. If he were to prefer the split, the expected utility of not splitting would have to exceed the expected utility of splitting, which is 15 as we saw in the answer to part (b). So $(P \times 20) + [(1 − P) \times 0] > 15$, or $P > 3/4$. In other words, David must have regarded his probability of winning as being greater than $3/4$. By the way, he lost.

3. The expected monetary value of signing David Wells equals $P \times [(0.8 \times \$10,000,000) + (0.2 \times \$5,000,000)] + (1 − P) \times (−\$3,000,000)$, where P is the probability that Wells would not injure his arm. Steinbrenner's computation of the expected monetary value of signing Wells must have exceeded $6,000,000. If Steinbrenner signed Wells to that contract, then solving the equation, $P \times [(0.8 \times \$10,000,000) + (0.2 \times \$5,000,000)] + (1 − P) \times (−\$3,000,000) = \$6,000,000$, for P shows that Steinbrenner must have thought that $P > 0.5$ because $P = 0.5$ sets the expected monetary value of signing Wells equal to Wells' salary.

5. $.5(\$6,000) + .5(−\$12,000) = −\$3,000$. No, if she maximizes expected monetary value, she would not make the purchase because the expected monetary value of doing so would be negative. She would surely not buy the stock if she were risk averse. Expected utility would be 0 not buying this stock and $.5 (−20) + .5 (6) = −7$ when buying it. She would not buy it because expected utility would be higher if she didn't buy it. Perfect information would mean making $6,000 half the time and losing nothing the other half. Expected monetary value would climb to $.5(\$6,000) + .5(\$0) = \$3,000$. The value of this information would be $\$3,000 − (−\$3,000) = \$6,000$.

7. The utility function is linear in M, so Tyler is risk neutral; all dollar figures are in thousands. (a) Expected utility for investing is

$$0.5 \times (10 + 2 \times [\$32 − \$25]) + 0.5 \times (10 + 2 \times −\$25) = −28,$$

while not investing would leave $25,000 around with an expected utility of $1.0 \times (10 + 2 \times \$0) = 10$. (b) The investment would not increase expected utility. (c) With perfect information, there would be a 0.5 chance of making $(\$32,000 − \$25,000)$ and a 0.5 chance of earning 0 by not making the investment. Given risk neutrality, the value of perfect information would therefore be the difference between the expected monetary value of using the information efficiently, or $(0.5 \times \$7) + (0.5 \times \$0) = \$3.50$.

9. (a) No. (b) Yes. (c) Yes. It would be positive in the first case, and negative in the second because it would remove the risk, and the higher interval shows risk-loving behavior.

11. Virus protection reduces risk, but on a have it or not basis. Since people cannot really think they can estimate the likelihood of a virus attack or quantify the damage it would cause, the precautionary principle probably does a better job of explaining consumer activity in this market.

CHAPTER 6

1. (a) The complete table is:

Number of units of variable input	Total output	Marginal product	Average product
3	90	Unknown	30.00
4	110	20	27.50
5	130	20	26.00
6	135	5	22.50
7	136	1	19.44

(b) Yes, the marginal product falls throughout the range displayed in the table. You cannot tell where diminishing marginal returns set in.

3. Constant returns to scale result because doubling K and L doubles Q. If the exponents summed to 0.9, then the function would display decreasing returns (doubling input without doubling output); if they summed to 1.1, then the function would display increasing returns (doubling input while more than doubling output).

5. Yes. Consider a constant returns to scale function like $X = F\{K,L\}$. Multiply both K and L by $(1/L)$, and you multiply output by $(1/L)$. As a result, $(X/L) = F\{(K/L),(L/L)\} = F\{(K/L),1\}$. The last term is clearly a function of only the K–L ratio.

7. The isoquants are all straight lines with slopes equal to $-2/3$ when K is drawn on the vertical axis and L is measured on the horizontal axis. The MRS for any combination of K and L is therefore $2/3$.

9. Manager ownership would reduce, but not eliminate, the principal-agent problem. Risk from actions and returns to good decisions would still be shared. Since the managers would be motivated more by profits, equal opportunity lending would be less of a goal. The managers might be inspired to take more risk with business loans, however, depending on their risk aversion.

CHAPTER 7

1. The report suggests increasing returns to scale, so fewer companies can cover the market at lower cost if each produces more planes. Increased demand could undermine this trend if further expansion might increase costs.

3. The isocost curves drawn with grain on the vertical axis and hay on the horizontal axis all have slopes equal to $-\frac{1}{2} = -$(price of hay/price of grain) $= -\frac{1}{2} P/P$. The costs for the six combinations listed are: $8,654P$ [$= 6,154P + \frac{1}{2} 5,000P$], $8,204P$, $7,892P$, $7,673P$, $7,529P$, and $7,444P$ from top to bottom. Seventy-five hundred pounds of hay and 3,694 pounds of grain minimizes cost over these choices. The isoquant should still be steeper than the isocost curve drawn through this lowest combination.

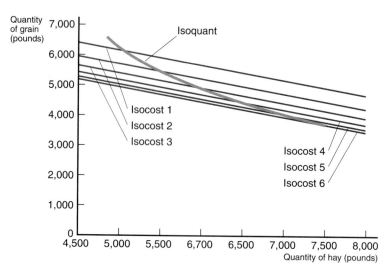

5. (a) No, since no information is given about the way in which cost varies with output when capacity is held constant. (b) The steam-reforming process using natural gas, since its cost is lowest. (c) Yes, because costs tend to fall as the scale of a plant increases. (d) Yes, the function shifted downward. In the early 1960s, it was not possible to produce ammonia for $16 a ton, as is evident from the graph.

7. The firm should hire K and L such that $MP_K/MP_L = \$2/\$1$. Note that $MP_K = 5L$ and $MP_L = 5K$, so that $K/L = 2$ means that twice as much labor should be hired as capital. So hire 2 units of K and 4 units of L and $Q = 5 \times 4 \times 2 = 40$.

9. (a) If you move the setup cost line up, then the minimum point for total cost moves to the right. (b) If you rotate the inventory cost line down, then the minimum point for total cost also moves to the right. (c) Five lots per year would mean total setup costs of $500,000. (d) The average inventory would be then 5,000 units. (e) Average inventory costs would be $10,000 for each setup period at $2 per unit; with 5 periods, total inventory costs would be $50,000, and total costs would be $550,000. (f) This graph summarizes the situation. Lot sizes of 10,000 do not minimize costs. In fact, one lot of 50,000 does the trick if planning must be done in one-year intervals. Otherwise, the minimum falls somewhere beyond one year. Extend the graph to see where.

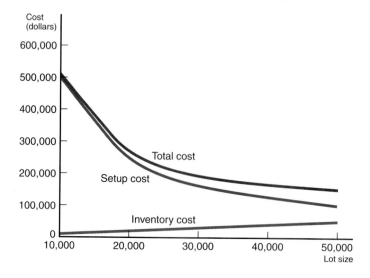

1. (a) No, because the demand curve for the product of a perfectly competitive firm is horizontal. (b) 13.3 cents. Under perfect competition, price equals marginal revenue, regardless of how much milk his farm produces. (c) No, because this price elasticity refers to the effect of changes in market price on the total amount of milk demanded. (d) Increases in consumer incomes are likely to have a very small effect on the market demand curve for milk. Thus, milk prices are not likely to rise appreciably for this reason.

3. Higher prices would result, increasing profits in the short run and attracting firms. If the government disallowed the higher prices, even in the short run, then the price signal would not materialize. Perhaps lines or shortages would appear, so the message would eventually be conveyed to new suppliers. Perhaps not. At the very least, the adjustment would be delayed.

5. A difference of about 3.24 percent. The coefficient of log P is 0.324 and indicates percent change in q associated with a 1 percent change in P. The forecasts differ by 10 percent.

7. (a) No. (b) Firms had to leave the textile industry during both periods, so that eventually the profit rate in cotton textiles would increase to the point where it approximated the profit rate in other industries. Also, the industry had to become more concentrated in the South, because the exit rate was higher in the North than in the South.

9. (a) It should be about 16 million barrels, because the cost of disposal must be added to the price required by suppliers, and the supply curve suggests that suppliers would supply nearly 16 million barrels even if the price that they received before having to cope with disposal fees were around $20 per barrel. (b) The Colorado restrictions might cost more than $20 per barrel in which case supplies would fall below 16 million barrels. (c) It could be, because it clearly reflects a capacity constraint at around 16 million barrels. (d) The investment would be risky because the future price of oil is uncertain and the historical price has been very volatile. Investment in the plant would be a fixed cost, though, so it would not affect supply, loosely interpreted as marginal cost. The risk might raise the expected price required to initiate the investment, however.

11. The average cost curve reaches a minimum at roughly $16.67 per unit at about 60 units; this would be the long-run equilibrium price. The upward sloping line on the graph below represents marginal cost summed horizontally for 10 identical firms; the downward sloping line is a demand curve that intersects this supply curve at $16.67, with 600 units being supplied.

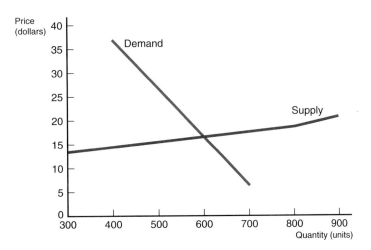

13. You can tell that the price is $3 (total revenue/quantity). It is below average cost. Marginal cost is rising, though, so profits are maximized even though they are negative. The firm is okay for the short run as long as there is hope that somebody will leave the industry.

15. You computed the equilibrium as $1 in Question 12. In Question 13, you know that the equilibrium price must be below $3.25 and above $3.00. It must be below $3.60 in Question 14.

CHAPTER 9

1. (a) Those consumers who are fortunate enough to occupy apartments under rent control will gain $700 − $600 = $100 per month. Since there are 100,000 such apartments, the gain in consumer surplus to these consumers will equal area A, which is 100,000 × $100, or $10 million per month. (b) The consumers who can no longer obtain apartments would have been willing to pay an amount equal to areas C + D + E for these 30,000 apartments. They would have had to pay only an amount equal to areas D + E. Thus, there was a consumer surplus equal to area C, which is ½($100 × $30,000) = $1.5 million per month. Because these consumers can no longer obtain this surplus, they will lose $1.5 million per month. (c) Without rent control, producer surplus would equal areas A + B + D, since this is the area above the supply curve and below $700, the rent (price) that would have prevailed. With rent control, producer surplus equals area B, since this is the area above the supply curve and below the new rent (price)—$600. Thus, producer surplus will go down by areas A + D, which is $11.5 million. (d) According to the answers to parts (a) through (c), consumer surplus will rise by $10 million − $1.5 million = $8.5 million, and producer surplus will fall by $11.5 million. Since the gain in consumer surplus is less than the fall in producer surplus, total surplus will go down by $11.5 million − $8.5 million = $3 million. This is significant because, if consumers are judged to be no more (or less) deserving than producers, it indicates that rent control will reduce total welfare. However, the limitations of this sort of analysis should be borne in mind; we will attend to some of them in Chapter 17. (e) The loss in total surplus is the deadweight loss; it equals areas C + D or $3 million.

3. (a) The demand and supply curves are as follows:

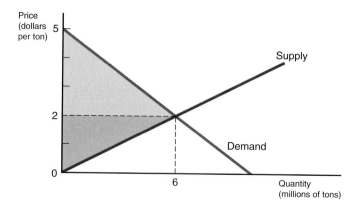

Producer surplus is the lower shaded area, which equals ½($2 × 6,000,000) = $6 million. (b) Consumer surplus is the upper shaded area, which equals ½[($5 − $2) × 6,000,000] = $9 million. (c) $15 million. (d) No.

5. No. In equilibrium, consumer surplus is ½($800 − $400) × 3,000,000 = $600 million, and producer surplus is ½($400 − $100) × 3,000,000 = $450 million. Thus, total surplus is $600 million + $450 million = $1.05 billion. If the cost of establishing and maintaining the market for this good exceeds this amount, buyers and sellers will not find it worthwhile to incur this cost.

7. No. Consumers still pay price plus the tax.

9. The deadweight loss, which is the shaded area in the graph below, equals ½($15 − $12.5) × 5,000,000 + ½($12.5 − $10) × 5,000,000 = $12.5 million.

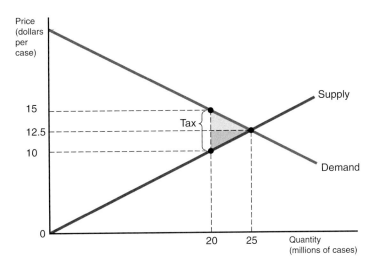

11. (a) No. (b) Yes. (c) No.

13. All consumers lose, but not for the same reasons. Some pay higher prices for reduced quantities; others lose because they cannot buy any steel for a price that they would be willing to pay. Employment changes are reflected in the increase in domestic production—an increase that presumably means more steelworkers can find work.

CHAPTER 10

1. (a) One cannot tell because the answer depends on the long-run (not the short-run) average cost curve. A firm is a natural monopolist if its long-run average cost reaches a minimum at an output rate that is big enough to satisfy the market at a price that is profitable. (b) Many natural monopolies—for example, electric power producers and cable providers—are privately owned, so it is by no means clear that government ownership is implied. (c) Four million pieces, since this is the point at which the average total cost curve intersects the demand curve. (d) First-class mail, because it earns a profit. With respect to parcels, there is already considerable competition (from United Parcel Service, Federal Express, etc.). (e) More competition might prod the post office to increase its own efficiency. Consumers could benefit. The U.S. Postal Service might fail, though, in which case only first-class mail would be carried.

3. For a profit maximizing monopolist, $MC = MR = P(1 − 1/\eta)$, where MC, MR, P and η are marginal cost, marginal revenue, price, and price elasticity of demand respectively. Since $P = 3\ MC$, it follows that $1/3 = 1 − 1/\eta$ so $−2/3 = −1/\eta$ and $\eta = 3/2$.

5. A monopolist maximizes profit where $MR = MC$. If $MC > 0$, then $MR > 0$, so that demand must be elastic, never unity. For a linear demand curve, $MC = MR > 0$ to the left of the midpoint in the elastic region. For a linear demand curve, draw the appropriate deadweight loss triangles at the midpoint (unitary elasticity) and above

the midpoint (elastic demand). The second is larger than the first as a percentage of total surplus.

7. Authors want to maximize revenue (a fixed proportion of price times quantity sold is the same fixed proportion of total revenue; it is maximized when total revenue is maximized). Authors want to go to a point of unitary elasticity. Publishers, with books that have some product differentiation, want to go to the point of maximum profit where $MC = MR > 0$, so they want to lower quantity into the region of elastic demand.

9. $MC = 6$ means $MR_1 = MC$ at 7 units while $MR_2 = MC$ at 3 units. The price in market 1 is \$13, since demand is $P = 20 - Q_1$; the price in market 2 is \$12.50.

11. The competitive outcome would have 3 units sold at \$6 where $MC =$ demand. The monopoly solution would see 2 units sold where $MC = MR$, with price $=$ \$8 and $MC =$ \$4. The area of the deadweight loss triangle is therefore equal to $\frac{1}{2}($\$8 $-$ \$4$) \times (3 - 2) =$ \$2.

13. (a) Yes. The area of rectangle C is $Q'(P' - P)$, which equals the amount of railroad services that would be bought after the merger (Q') times the increase in price ($P' - P$). (b) Yes. The extra amount paid by the shippers goes to the railroads. Thus, this is a transfer of income from one group (shippers) to another (railroads). (c) Yes. After the merger, the railroads would sell ($Q - Q'$) fewer units of output. On each of these units of output, they earned a profit of ($P - M$). Thus, the merger meant a loss to them of ($Q - Q'$) ($P - M$), which is the area of rectangle B. (d) Yes. The maximum amount that the shippers would pay for these extra ($Q - Q'$) units of output is the area under the demand curve from Q' to Q. The amount that they would have had to pay for them is ($Q - Q'$)P, so the consumer surplus equals the area of triangle A. (e) Yes. Shippers lose \$404 million $+$ \$22 million $=$ \$426 million, while the railroads gain \$404 million $-$ \$57 million $=$ \$347 million. (f) Yes.

15. To compute the single-price monopoly solution, note that the horizontal sum of the 100 individual demand curves is $10 - 0.002X$ up to 2,500 units and $5.4545 - .000182X$ from 2,500 units through 30,000 units. The single-price equilibrium then sets $MR = 5.4545 - .00364X$ equal to $MC = 2$ at roughly 9,500 units with a price of \$3.73. You could perhaps improve profits by mimicking third-degree price discrimination, i.e., charging the profit maximizing price to the two different customers. The idea works if they want different quantities at the resulting prices. For the first set of customers, $MR = MC$ at \$6, where 40 units would be demanded; for the second, $MR = MC$ at 150 units, with a price of \$3.50. So, second-order price discrimination could charge a price of \$6 for up to 40 units and \$3.50 for quantities of 41 or higher.

17. $MR = MC =$ \$2, so profits are maximized as long as MC is rising. Total cost is \$4,000 $+$ \$30,000 $=$ \$34,000 while revenue is \$25,000. So profits are negative. Demand is not high enough to sustain even a monopolist (absent some sort of two-part tariff).

19. This is a difficult problem, but the key is setting (expected) marginal revenue equal to marginal cost at the appropriate time. First, though, note that the profit maximizing capacity for either demand condition is given by $MR = MC$. Since marginal revenue has the same intercept and twice the slope, X^*_{capj} solves $a_j - 2b\,X^*_{capj} = c$ so $X^*_{capj} = (a_j - c)/2b$ in period j ($j = 1$ or 2).

(a) Solving for a common capacity X^*_{cap} that maximizes expected profits must set expected marginal revenue equal to marginal cost. So, X^*_{cap} solves

$$\pi\,(a_1 - 2b\,X^*_{cap}) + (1 - \pi)(a_2 - 2b\,X^*_{cap}) = c$$

so that
$$X^*_{cap} = \pi\,(a_1 - c)/2b + (1 - \pi)(a_2 - c)/2b$$
$$= \pi X^*_{cap1} + (1 - \pi)X^*_{cap2}.$$

(b) Plug X^*_{cap} into the two demand curves and remember that $a_2 > a_1$.

(c) The common price P^* will be determined by plugging the common capacity X_{cap} into the higher demand curve; so $P^* = a_2 - b X_{cap}$. Sales in period 1 will also solve $P^* = a_1 - bX_1$ so

$$X_1 = (a_1 - P^*)/b = (a_1 - [a_2 - b X_{cap}])/b = (a_1 - a_2)/b - X_{cap}.$$

As a result, marginal revenue in period 1 can be expressed as a function of X_{cap}:

$$MR_1 = (a_1 - 2(a_1 - a_2) - 2bX_{cap}.$$

Meanwhile, marginal revenue in period two is simply $MR_2 = a_2 - 2bX_{cap}$. Now, the solution can be found setting expected marginal revenue in terms of X_{cap} equal to marginal cost, i.e., setting:

$$\pi (a_1 - 2(a_1 - a_2) - 2b X_{cap}) + (1 - \pi)(a_2 - 2b X_{cap}) = c.$$

Solving for X_{cap} and plugging the result back into the demand curve for period 2 completes the process. The result is the same price that you computed for period 2 in part b.

(d) Regulation increase expected social welfare (and lower profits) in period 1. We know this because the firms could have chosen to charge the same price in both periods, but did not. Period 2 outcomes would be identical, so expected welfare must climb as long as the probability that the lower demand curve would appear is positive.

CHAPTER 11

1. Any could be an appropriate product group depending on focus. For example, fruit juices are a specific type of drink without caffeine.
3. Copper is too specific. Airlines along a specific route may be too specific, as well, unless it is very well traveled and therefore supports many different carriers. The rest are fine applications.
5. These firms are trying to expand their markets by getting people to think that they may need some new drug or another and by gaining name recognition. It is an application of trying to conduct an efficient advertising campaign in response to a perceived positive marginal revenue.
7. Yes. Exploiting economies of scale could produce positive pure economic profits, for a least a little while before other firms follow—just like advertising can.

CHAPTER 12

1. $MC = \$0$, so the competitive output is 10 units (demand is $P = 10 - Q$). (a) Colluding monopolists would share half of the competitive output (5 units) and charge $5; this would maximize profits by setting $MR = MC = \$0$. (b) The Bertrand model would collapse to the competitive solution with a zero price. (c) The Cournot duopoly solution sees the two firms sharing two-thirds of the competitive output ($6\frac{2}{3}$ units) and charging $3.33. (d) The one Stackelberg-leader solution has the leader selling one-half of the competitive output (5 units) with the other selling one-fourth (2.5 units); the price would be $2.50.
3. Simply confirm that the numbers in the text are located correctly in the payoff matrix.
5. (a) Marginal revenue equals marginal cost means that $100 - 8Q_A - 4Q_B = 4$. Collecting terms, therefore, $Q_A = 12 - 0.5Q_B$. (b) Since the firms are identical, $1.5Q_A = 12$ and so $Q_A = 8 = Q_B$. Plugging total output of 16 units into the demand curve, it is clear that the price is $36. (c) The only point on A's reaction curve that sustains a Nash equilibrium is the point where it intersects B's reaction curve; that is the only point where mutual expectations are achieved.
7. (a & b) Upper right and lower left are both Nash equilibria. (c) This is not a prisoner's dilemma game. (d) There is a clear first mover advantage—Zee would want to build on the east coast first; Ewe would want to do the same. (e) Actually starting construction, or hiring lawyers and architects, or buying land, or applying to a zoning board, etc. . . .

9. (a) The payoff matrix is given in the figure below.

Possible strategies for the Morgan Company

		Advertise	Do not advertise
Possible strategies for the Miller Company	Advertise	Morgan's profit: $2.5 million / Miller's profit: $4 million	Morgan's profit: $2 million / Miller's profit: $5 million
	Do not advertise	Morgan's profit: $2 million / Miller's profit: $2 million	Morgan's profit: $2.5 million / Miller's profit: $3 million

(b) Miller has a dominant strategy (advertise), but Morgan does not. (c) The Nash equilibrium will see both advertise. (d) This is not a prisoner's dilemma game.

11. (a) $MR = 12 - 4X$. (b) Cartel profits are maximized where $MR = MC = \$4$ at 2 million units with a price of $8. (c) Assuming that B holds firm at 1.5 million units, the effective demand curve facing A is $9 - 2X$; firm A therefore thinks that profits would be maximized at 1.25 million units. Total output would be 2.75 million units with a price of $6.50 per unit. Firm A would earn $3.75 million; B, $3.125 million. (d) Assuming that A would hold at 500,000 units, the effective demand curve for B would be $11 - 2X$. Firm B would therefore think that profits would be maximized at 1.75 million units. Total output would be 2.25 million with a price of $7.50 per unit. Firm A would earn $1.75 in profit; B, $6.125 million. (e) Assuming that A would produce 1.25 million units and B would produce 1.75 million units, total output would be 3 million units with a price of $6.00 per unit. Firm A would then earn $2.5 million in profit; B, $3.5 million. (e) The payoff matrix would look like:

Possible strategies for firm A

		Cheat	Do not cheat
Possible strategies for firm B	Cheat	A's profit: $2.5 million / B's profit: $3.5 million	A's profit: $1.75 million / B's profit: $6.125 million
	Do not cheat	A's profit: $3.125 million / B's profit: $3.75 million	A's profit: $2.0 million / B's profit: $6.0 million

(f) Cheating is a dominant strategy for firm A. The solution would be in the lower left-hand corner; it is a Nash equilibrium. This is not a prisoner's dilemma game.

13. (a) The payoff matrix is as follows:

(b) Providing prompt delivery is a dominant strategy for Duquesne. Duquesne would make more money if it provided prompt delivery than if it did not regardless of which strategy were chosen by Amherst. Amherst does not have a dominant strategy, since its optimal strategy depends on whether or not Duquesne provides prompt delivery. (c) Yes. The Nash equilibrium is for Amherst to buy all its steel from Duquesne and for Duquesne to provide prompt delivery; it appears in the upper-left corner of the matrix. Each firm would be doing the best it could, given the other firm's strategy. (d) Probably not. A Nash equilibrium assumes that all players are "rational" in the sense that they will adopt whatever strategy results in maximum profit. If Duquesne were not "rational" in this sense, it might not provide prompt delivery even though its failure to do so would reduce its profit. As a result, Amherst would lose $50 million if it bought all its steel from Duquesne. If Amherst had strong enough doubts about Duquesne's "rationality" (or were uncertain about what Duquesne's true payoffs are), it might buy only part of its steel from Duquesne and thereby cut its potential loss (if Duquesne did not provide prompt delivery) from $50 million to $1 million. In other words, it may adopt a maximin strategy. The solution would then appear in the lower-left corner of the matrix.

CHAPTER 13

1. (a) No, it is a temporary price war that pushed the price below average cost, so both firms were losing money. (b) No. Both firms are losing money.
3. (a) No. Entry does not seem to be free, and exit does not seem to be costless. (b) This shift in the long-run average cost curve occurred as a consequence of technological change. For example, on the closing line 900 cans could be moved per minute in 1965, whereas about 1,500 cans per minute could be moved in the late 1970s. (c) Certainly, this shift in the long-run average cost curve was one of the factors responsible for the decrease in the number of firms. Because breweries had to get so much bigger, fewer of them were required.
5. Since $Q = 300 - P$, and the demand for the firm's output is $Q - Q_r$ it follows that the firm's demand curve is

$$Q_b = Q - Q_r = (300 - P) - 49P$$
$$= 300 - 50P,$$

so that $$P = 6 - 0.02\,Q_b$$

Thus the firm's marginal revenue curve is $MR = 6 - 0.04\,Q_b$. And since its marginal cost curve is $2.96Q_b$,

$$6 - 0.04\,Q_b = 2.96\,Q_b$$
$$Q_b = 2.$$

7. Think of credible strategies of the sort outlined in the text. A history of fighting entry would help, too.
9. (a) Yes, because both firms would make an economic profit of $2.5 million (before deducting the attorneys' fees). Recall that an economic profit is profit above what could have been earned from alternative ways of investing the $10 million. (b) Without such a contract, each firm would have an incentive to not act in accord with its promises once both had invested in the joint venture. To see this, note that, whether or not Intel acts in accord with its promises, Microsoft would make more money by not acting in accord with its promises than by doing so. Similarly, whether or not Microsoft acts in accord with its promises, Intel would make more money by not acting in accord with its promises than by doing so. Violating the agreement is, in other words, a dominant strategy for both companies. Both would trust each other regardless of this observation, if the game were to be repeated an infinite or unknown number of times. Perhaps they would keep the agreement if the relevant managers of either firm were vulnerable to criticism and dismissal if they violated its spirit for short-term gain. (c) It is very difficult to foresee the full range of circumstances that may prevail in the future and to specify in a contract

completely and unambiguously what action each firm is to take under each possible set of circumstances. As a result, it is often impractical even to attempt to formulate such a contract. (d) No. In this case both firms have the option of not playing the game.

CHAPTER 14

1. If it is true that the quantity of nurses demanded currently exceeds the quantity supplied by 14 percent, then the current shortage equals $Q_D - Q_S = 1.14 Q_S - Q_S = .14 Q_S = H_g$, where Q_D is the quantity of nurses demanded and Q_S is the quantity supplied. Letting ΔH be the change in the size of the shortage due to the wage increase, it follows that $\Delta H = \Delta Q_D - \Delta Q_S$, where ΔQ_D is the change in the quantity of nurses demanded and ΔQ_S is the change in the quantity supplied. On the basis of the elasticities provided by the senator, a 1 percent increase in the wage for nurses would result in a 0.3 percent reduction in the quantity demanded and a 0.1 percent increase in the quantity supplied; this means that $\Delta Q_D = -0.003 Q_D$ and $\Delta Q_S = 0.001 Q_S$. Thus, $\Delta H = -0.003 Q_D - 0.001 Q_S$. Recalling that $Q_D = 1.14 Q_S$, $\Delta H = -0.003(1.14 Q_S) - 0.001 Q_S = -0.00442 Q_S$. Since the shortage currently equals $.14 Q_S$, the percentage change in the size of the shortage would be

$$\Delta H/H = -0.00442 Q_S /.14 Q_S = -3.2 \text{ percent.}$$

In other words, based on the senator's estimates, the answer is that a 1 percent increase in the wage for nurses would reduce the shortage by about 3.2 percent. However, before putting any confidence in this result, you would do well to check the senator's estimates against the results of studies carried out by economists and others.

3. The value of the marginal product is shown in the following table.

Number of days of labor	Output	Marginal product	Value of marginal product (dollars)
0	0		
		8	40
1	8		
		7	35
2	15		
		6	30
3	21		
		5	25
4	26		
		4	20
5	30		

Thus, if the daily wage of labor is $30, the firm should hire 2 or 3 days of labor.

5. Compute the marginal revenue product for labor by multiplying the marginal product of labor by the price associated with the corresponding level of production. For 2 units of labor, for example, the marginal product would be 10 and total output would be 23 units; the market will sustain a price of $5.00 for 23 units, so the marginal revenue product is $10 \times \$5 = \$50$. Marginal revenue product equals $6 for the sixth unit of labor.

7. $MRP = ME$ for the monopsony solution at 1.33 units. $MRP = P$ for the competitive solution at 2 units. $MRP = ME = 5.33$ at 1.33 units while $P = 2.67$. The area of the deadweight loss triangle is therefore equal to $\frac{1}{2}(2 - 1.33) \times (\$5.33 - \$2.67) = 0.33 \times \$2.67 = \$8/9$.

9. Equilibrium would occur at point A in the figure below if both the product and input markets were competitive. Equilibrium would appear at E_1 if the firm only exerted monopoly power in the product market; deadweight loss would be the area of triangle ABE_1. Equilibrium would appear at E_2 if the firm only exerted monopsony

power in the input market; deadweight loss would be the area of triangle ACE_2. Equilibrium would appear at E_3 if the firm exerted monopoly power in the product market and monopsony power in the input market; deadweight loss would be the area of triangle FDA. The loss would always be greatest in the last case; the other two cases could flip-flop depending upon the elasticities of the derived demand and supply of the input.

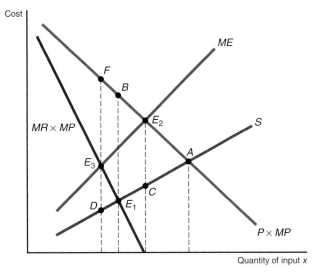

11. (a) The equilibrium wage absent union power would be $8. (b) Quantity demanded would fall from 40 million to 35 million; 5 million would be laid off. (c) Adding 5 million workers to the nonunion side would reduce the wage from $8 to $6. (d) The efficiency loss would equal the difference between the loss in the union sector (the area under the demand curve from 35 to 40 million workers) minus the gain in the nonunion market (the area under that demand curve from 60 to 65 million workers). It would be the area of a parallelogram with a height of 5 million workers and a base of $2; it would equal $10 million.

13. The wage P_L will equal the price P, of the product, times the marginal product of labor, which equals (the partial derivation of production with respect to labor):

$$\delta Q / \delta L = 0.8\, L^{-2}\, K^2 = 0.8\, Q/L.$$

Thus $P_L = 0.8Q/L \times P$, so

$$P_L L/PQ = 0.8.$$

Since $P_L L$ equals the total wages paid by the firm and PQ equals its revenues, this completes the proof.

CHAPTER 15

1. (a) The net present value (in millions of dollars) was

$$-10 + 2/1.1 + 2/1.1^2 + 2/1.1^3 + 2/1.1^4 + 2/1.1^5 + 2/1.1^6$$
$$+ 2/1.1^7 + 2/1.1^8 + 2/1.1^9.$$

This is equal to $-10 + 2(.9091 + .8264 + .7513 + .6830 + .6209 + .5645 + .5132 + .4665 + .4241) = -10 + 2(5.7590) = 1.518 million. (b) The net present value would be

$$-13 + 2/1.1 + 2/1.1^2 + 2/1.1^3 + 2/1.1^4 + 2/1.1^5 + 2/1.1^6$$
$$+ 2/1.1^7 + 2/1.1^8 + 2/1.1^9.$$

This is equal to $-13 + 2(.9091 + .8264 + .7513 + .6830 + .6209 + .5645 + .5132 + .4665 + .4241) = -13 + 2(5.7590) = -1.482$ millions of dollars. (c) The internal rates of return with and without cost overruns are approximately 13.71 percent and 7.06 percent, respectively; these are the values that set the present values to zero. (d) Let p be the probability of an overrun and solve $1.482\, p = 1.518\, (1 - p)$; so p is approximately .51. (e) No, the expected value would be negative, so this would not be a good investment even if the firm were risk neutral. (f) The investment would be marginally okay if the firm were risk neutral, but not if it were even a little risk averse (see Chapter 6).

3. The rate should equal $0.09 + 1.4(0.12 - 0.09) = 0.09 + 0.042 = 0.134$.

5. Compute ($\$10/r$) where $r = 0.05, 0.10, 0.20$, etc. . . . The curve you draw should be a rectangular hyperbola solving $Pr = \$10$ (where $P =$ price you would pay).

7. (a) The results are not promising; expansion does not look like a good idea. (b) Building a new plant is slightly better, but still not good enough. (c) Five years could be relevant if obsolescence would set in at that time. It may be too short, especially if low rates of interest were used. And if downstream returns would be positive, then the present values might be positive. Forecasting five years in advance of today is risky, however. (d) Not if the 15-percent figure includes a risk premium. (e) Rates that are too high bias present values down if future streams are positive and up if they are negative. Why? Because they make the denominators in the "out years" of the present value calculation larger. The risk of looking far into the future might make 15 percent okay.

9. People include taxes in these calculations of the price of a house. If they can afford $\$X$ and something lowers the tax component of the cost of a house, then they would be willing to pay the difference as part of the price of the house. So, a permanent tax savings of $\$1000$ would increase the price willingly paid by ($\$1000/r$). Different expectations of r mean different calculations.

11. Oil is a normal good. Higher consumption now means faster depletion and more rapidly rising prices in the future.

13. (a) Notice that Mason would earn $3 million per year if Newton entered (the solution to Figure 13.9) and $10 million if it made its threat credible by investing in excess capacity (the solution to Figure 13.10). The difference is $7 million per year. For a 10 percent interest rate, using Equation 15.6, the present value of an indefinite stream of $7 million per year would be $PV(10\%) = \$7$ million$/.10 = \$70$ million. Mason would be willing to pay up to $70 million on its investment in excess capacity. At 5 percent, Mason would pay up to $140 million, but at 15 percent, Mason would pay no more than $46.67 million. (b) The requisite present value calculation is determined by discounting $7 million by $[1/(1 + r)]^n$ up to $n = T$ years. A spreadsheet is the most efficient form of determining a T for which the present value of $7 million per year sums to $50 million, $70 million, and $30 million. The following table records the results:

Interest rate (percent)	Cost = $50 million	Cost = $70 million	Cost = $30 million
2.5	7 years	11 years	4 years
5.0	8 years	13 years	4 years
7.5	9 years	16 years	4 years
10.0	10 years	25 years	5 years
12.5	13 years	never	5 years
15.0	25 years	never	5 years

The investment in excess capacity would pay off quickly against low cost—a circumstance with little sensitivity to interest rates below 15 percent. The payoff period would be longer and more sensitive to the interest rate for a higher cost. And for some costs, the payoff would never happen and it would not be profitable for Mason to use excess capacity to deter Newton's entry.

CHAPTER 16

1. (a) No, because fuel must be used to produce and transport the corn required to produce the ethanol. (b) Yes. Although the cost of a gallon of ethanol was 35¢ higher (that is, $1.20 minus 85¢) than a gallon of gasoline, exemption from the federal gasoline tax was worth 40¢ per gallon and exemption from state taxes was often worth at least 40¢ more per gallon. Thus, the tax exemptions more than offset the higher cost of production of ethanol. However, some very optimistic forecasts in the late 1970s of gasohol sales were not achieved. Gasohol would never displace regular gasoline completely, because as more and more gasohol was produced, the price of corn would be bid up, and eventually, despite the tax exemptions, it would no longer be profitable to substitute more gasohol for regular gasoline. (c) Corn prices and the value of corn-producing land tend to rise. A general equilibrium analysis can handle these questions more adequately than a partial equilibrium analysis because the interconnections of multiple markets can be accommodated.

3. Simply move the demand curve down or the supply curve up by 1 dollar. With a close substitute, though, general equilibrium analysis would capture the interactions. The demand for margarine would increase. And if its price went up, then there would be a mild rebound in demand for butter.

5. The box would get taller, so the curves would shift up (the contract curve would still connect opposite corners). The production possibility frontier would shift out, but not necessarily symmetrically, since medicine and food might not be able to use the labor with equal productivity. You could expect everyone to be better off, but the relative prices of inputs could change and if people derive their incomes from supplying inputs, some might be worse off.

7. (a) Draw an Edgeworth box with 200 acres of land and 50 paintings defining its size. (b) The will would put Mary and John at the center of the box. (c) This initial endowment would not necessarily lie on the contract curve.

9. Movement from this point lowers the utility of all. It must, therefore, be Pareto efficient, and so it must lie on the contract curve.

11. These individuals should shift resources around so that they increase the production of the good that they find more valuable. The first such move would generate a surplus equal in value to one-half unit of their preferred good, so one or both could be made better off.

13. An important problem is that $50 may mean more to Mary than $100 does to Jean. This makes money, together with the existing distribution of income, a measure of the relative strength of feeling of individuals.

15. Rawls would like D: it maximizes Mary (the poorer). A point up and to the left with a slope of -1 on the utility frontier would maximize the sum of utilities.

CHAPTER 17

1. (a) No, because managers of company-owned restaurants do not receive profits but salaries that do not depend on how well run or profitable the restaurant is. (b) One of the principal jobs of the manager is to train and monitor assistant managers. Since the managers of company-owned restaurants have less incentive to do this carefully, the company may rely on efficiency wages to induce assistant managers to perform well.

3. There is a .8 probability that a new safe will not be defective (in which case it is worth $5,000) and a 0.2 probability that it will be defective (in which case it is worth $2,000, since all safes in the used market are defective). The price of a new safe is .8($5,000) + .2($2,000) = $4,400. The price would be lower if consumers were risk averse; they would not be willing to spend $4,400 for the same risk.

5. (a) $2,000. Q will equal $2(2,000) - P = 4,000 - P$. The quantity supplied will be as follows:

Price	Quantity supplied
$1,000	1,000
2,000	2,000
3,000	3,000

The price will be $2,000, since the quantity demanded (2,000 units) equals the quantity supplied at this price. (b) The average value of those offered in part (a) is $1,500; this means that $Q = 2(1,500) - P = 3,000 - P$. Thus, the demand curve has shifted to the left. (c) Ultimately, only the lowest quality computers will be supplied and sold for $1,000.

7. Because Bayer is a respected name. The reputation of the maker is responsible for the higher price.

9. Complete coverage of loss, because there is little or no incentive for a person with such an insurance policy to guard against theft.

11. (a) Yes, because the price offered to the sellers of better trucks would be too low; the table confirms this. (b) Yes, because the owners of players in questionable health would not pay salaries as large as other owners with less information; the table shows this, too. (c) Both examples show people exercising better information to their advantage: sellers who know that their trucks are poor and owners who know that their players are injury prone.

13. (a) Up to some point, increases in the firm's output result in increases in profit; beyond this point, they result in decreases in profit. Since the entrepreneur's days of work are assumed to be proportional to the firm's output up to some point, increases in the number of days he or she works, therefore, result in increases in profit; beyond this point, they result in decreases in profit. Finally, the entrepreneur's number of days of leisure equals the total time during the year minus his or her number of days of work. It follows that, up to some point, increases in his or her number of days of leisure are associated with increases in profit; beyond that point (indicated by e in the graph), they are associated with decreases in profit. (b) No. He or she maximizes utility by choosing point C, where there are f days of leisure and profit is below the maximum that could be achieved. (c) Yes. He or she would choose point B, where profits are maximized. (d) Horizontal curves would mean that the entrepreneur was concerned only with profits.

15. Bid $(n + 1)/(2n)$ times your estimate of the value where n is the total number of bidders.

CHAPTER 18

1. No. It would be very difficult, if not impossible, for the Philadelphia transit system to charge people (and collect) for all these benefits (which are frequently very hard to assign to particular individuals or to quantify very precisely). A cost-benefit analysis of expanding the commuter rail system should, however, take these derivative factors into account; they represent estimates of social benefits even if they cannot be captured in the revenue stream.

3. (a) Yes. Projects with benefit-cost ratios exceeding 1 seem worthwhile if the budget is variable. (b) No. (c) Increased supplies of power might lower the cost for less well-off customers. If equity is a primary objective, then the benefits that they receive might support claims that they be given higher weight. (d) The loss of a species could be extra weight on the cost side of the calculation.

5. The Corps of Engineers included many kinds of benefits that the railroad consultants did not include, such as enhancement of waterfront land values. Also, the Corps of Engineers made a lower estimate of the costs. To some extent, as Prest and Turvey point out, the difference may be "due to the facts that the Corps likes to build canals and that the consultants were retained by the railroads." The government might want to be involved when they can be the honest broker of impartial analysis so that decisions are not clouded by personal or private self-interest.

7. Six hours per day.

9. This is a perfect example of a common problem. Externalities surely exist, and they lead to overexploitation. Negotiation of enforceable quantity agreements could work.

11. If there is a sufficiently large number of firms and permits, a competitive market for the permits will develop. The price of a permit will tend to equal the marginal cost of reducing pollution by 1 ton, which will tend to be equalized among firms.

13. (a) It is a nonrival good; providing light to one boat provides it to all at no extra cost. (b) It is nonexclusive if all can see the light. (c) The efficient level of service is Q_2. (d) It could be private; the light could be withheld from a boat that had not paid in advance.

Index